# INTRODUCTION TO
# CRIMINAL JUSTICE

# FIFTH EDITION

# INTRODUCTION TO

# CRIMINAL JUSTICE

# Robert D. Pursley

**STATE UNIVERSITY OF NEW YORK**
**COLLEGE AT BUFFALO**

Macmillan Publishing Company
**NEW YORK**

Collier Macmillan Canada, Inc.
**TORONTO**

Editor: Christine Cardone
Production Supervisors: Eric Newman, Andrew Roney
Production Manager: Richard C. Fischer
Text Designer: Natasha Sylvester
Cover Designer: Natasha Sylvester
Cover illustration: Viqui Maggio
Photo Researcher: Chris Migdol
Illustrations: Wellington Studios, Ltd.

This book was set in Zapf Book by Waldman Graphics,
printed and bound by Von Hoffmann Press, Inc.
The cover was printed by Von Hoffmann Press, Inc.

Macmillan Publishing Company
866 Third Avenue, New York, New York 10022

Collier Macmillan Canada, Inc.
1200 Eglinton Avenue East, Suite 200
Don Mills, Ontario, M3C 3N1

**Library of Congress Cataloging-in-Publication Data**
Pursley, Robert D.
      Introduction to criminal justice / Robert D. Pursley.—5th ed.
          p.      cm. — (Macmillan criminal justice series)
      Includes bibliographical references and index.
      ISBN 0-02-396931-8
      1. Criminal justice, Administration of—United States.   I. Title.
      II. Series.
      KF9223.P86   1991
      364.973—dc20                                                    90-36635
                                                                              CIP

Printing: 1 2 3 4 5 6 7      Year: 1 2 3 4 5 6 7

# To the Instructor

It is a rare occurrence when an author has the opportunity to refine a textbook through an original and four subsequent editions. Oddly, the same concerns seem to be present in each subsequent edition of an introductory text. Such questions as what to delete, what needs to be added, and what requires greater or less emphasis are recurring concerns to the author. Although guidance is sought through colleagues, questioning other academics teaching in the field (especially those teaching an introductory course), obtaining feedback from students as consumers, and, yes, the analysis of successful competing texts, an author soon learns that viewpoints and predilections differ substantially about the question of what should be covered in an introductory text and how. Equally perplexing is that these important audiences often disagree quite strongly about how they view the need for change and what specifically should be changed, retained, or deleted.

Out of all this the author tries to make some sense and reach a happy medium—something that he or she can live with while at the same time considering those insights that are most thoughtful and relevant. A great deal of effort went into trying to accomplish that with this edition. More than any of its preceding editions, this text has been reworked substantially. Major changes include the deletion of the old Chapter 4, which dealt with victimless crimes. The consensus from our reviewers indicated that this topic is less salient today and no longer justifies a complete chapter devoted to a discussion of these types of crimes and the issues they raise. In its place, a new chapter on crime issues of the 1990s was added. Following suggestions by reviewers, certain chapters have been repositioned.

Another major change has been the adoption of marginal highlights as an aid to student learning and retention. Along with this was the organizational development of the text material into what are called by the consulted teaching experts "learning units." (This will be discussed later.) In addition to these organizational changes, all topics have been checked for the latest information available at the time of publication. Particularly incorporated were the most recent research findings and survey data from such sources as the periodic publications from the "Research in Action" monographs from the National Institute of Justice and the bulletins and special reports from the Bureau of Justice Statistics. The hope is that this adds a contemporary and useful scope to the related issues being discussed.

There has also been an attempt to incorporate new and relevant legal cases and issues to explain change and developments in legal-related areas and in the administration of the justice system itself. Also included are important new sidebars on issues of concern today. A special effort was made not to detract too much from the substance of the text by these sidebars, but to use this technique judiciously where it was thought their use would be of interest to the reader and "liven up" the text a bit.

# □ ORGANIZATION OF THE FIFTH EDITION

Several noted authorities in the discipline of education from the State University of New York system were consulted on the organizational arrangement of the fourth edition. The question was asked what might be done to improve its use by instructors while facilitating student learning. It was suggested that this new edition adopt a "learning unit" approach to the presentation of the material and the coverage of topical areas. These authorities felt that topical coverage should be more clearly delineated for the instructor's use and to aid students in understanding and assimilating the subject matter. It was also suggested that the new edition incorporate marginal highlights of the subject being discussed. This latter suggestion, if adopted, would serve as an aid to understanding and would assist in the learning and retention effort. Both of these techniques have found their way into this latest edition.

The next question became one of deciding how to organize the learning units. It was decided to divide the book up into four such units. This was a somewhat arbitrary division, but it tended to coincide with the general organization of the subject matter contained in previous editions. More troublesome was the question of the chapters which started out as "mini-learning units." The manuscript for the proposed revision was then sent to several reviewers in the discipline of criminal justice who routinely teach the introductory course. Generally, their consensus was that the learning units were beneficial and a welcome addition to the text. Less clear was the appropriate placement of the two chapters that constituted the mini–learning units. After careful review of their comments and in consultation with the editorial staff at Macmillan, it was decided that these two mini–learning units would each appear as a separate learning unit—i.e., as Chapter 16 (The Juvenile Justice System) and Chapter 17 (Crime Issues of the 1990s), respectively. This gives individual instructors who adopt this revised edition the choice of covering these chapters when and where they see fit. They could work them into their course by assigning them to be read by their students, or they could merely delete these as required reading by their students.

## About the Learning Units

The six learning units are divided along particular themes or topics of study. These are as follows:

Unit I is what is referred to as the General Foundations Section (chapters 1-3). This unit has been specifically devised to provide the student with a broad overview of the agencies which comprise the criminal justice system, the nature of the administration of justice, characteristics of the criminal law, and the nature of and complexities surrounding the issue of crime. It is the foundational springboard from which the specific agencies and operations can then be examined. In many ways it is the most important segment of the book and the course. For that reason it is called the "general foundations" unit.

Unit II (chapters 4-6) is the next section. This unit examines law enforcement and is the first unit specifically devoted to one of the major components of the criminal justice system. It has been written to provide the student with an appreciation of the history, organization, role, issues and concerns facing the police in America today.

Unit III (chapters 7-10) is the courts section. This unit takes the student into the somewhat arcane area of the criminal courts. This includes such topics as their composition, a step-by-step analysis of the adjudication of a major criminal case, including the roles of the actors in the courtroom and the court system, and issues and concerns which are focused on the actors and the process itself.

Unit IV (chapters 11-15) is entitled in its most broad sense, the corrections component. In addition to examining prisons, it also incorporates a look at the operations and issues surrounding our nation's jails and our system of probation and parole. Included in this section are such contemporary concerns as sentencing, prison and jail overcrowding, problems of prison and institutional control, the "privatization" of corrections and capital punishment.

Learning Unit V (chapter 16) consists of the juvenile justice system. This chapter, among other things, examines what we know about juvenile crime, particular aspects of criminality among youthful offenders, the origins and operation of the juvenile court, types of juvenile institutions, a brief examination of some types of delinquency diversion and prevention programs, and changes occurring in the system of juvenile justice.

Learning Unit VI (chapter 17) is a new addition to the book from past editions. It focuses on specific crime issues and concerns of the 1990s. Because these topics are of such significance to our nation and Americans, and since these topics could not be effectively integrated and covered in existing chapters of the text, they are included here. Four major crime issues are discussed: illegal narcotics, terrorism, environmental crime, and concern over the law's (and the criminal justice system's) ability to deal with the purposeful transmission of the AIDS virus. Although other important crime issues confront America in the years ahead, these four were chosen for particular examination.

There are three appendices to assist students and the instructor. The first of these is the United States Constitution in its entirety. There is also a glossary of legal and criminal justice-related terms provided for the reader. Finally, a list of major criminal justice journals and periodicals by subject area are listed. This can serve as a reference for further specialized or intensive reading on the subject matter.

## Acknowledgments

I am indebted to the thousands of students whom I have taught over the years in the introductory course at three universities. Serious and achievement-oriented students have provided both the insight and the motivation to continue to improve my teaching of the course and the text. Such students are often the best and most insightful critics. I thank them for their assistance.

I also want to thank the reviewers who examined the revised manuscript and made a number of suggestions for improvement. Where possible, I have tried to incorporate your recommendations.

I appreciate the assistance provided by my editor, Christine Cardone, and assistant editors, Diane Kraut and Mary Sharkey, as well as the Macmillan editorial and production staff. They listened patiently to my concerns and suggestions for improving the format of each successive edition. In this edition, particularly, they have incorporated many of these ideas and introduced some I had not considered.

A special word of acknowledgment and appreciation must be expressed to Professor Sam Chapman at the University of Oklahoma. Through the successive editions of this book he has provided the insight which has made each edition better than its predecessor. Now that Professor Chapman will soon be moving on to a well-deserved retirement, his wise counsel and sagacious insight will be missed. Sam, I thank you for your help and encouragement over the years. When any number of people wanted me to water the book down to make it more appealing to poorer students and weaker academic programs for the expediency of more adoptions, you encouraged me to stick to my original conception of this book as truly college-level material. Although there are any number of introductory criminal justice books in the market, I hope you are particularly pleased with this effort. I trust it reflects in large part what you stand for and what you insist upon from your students and from the academic discipline of criminal justice itself.

Robert D. Pursley

This semester you and your instructor will use this book to examine the American system of criminal justice. You will be exposed to this system's composition, its operations, its problems, and perhaps some small measures that might improve it. It is a system deeply troubled. Increasingly, it is recognized as a dangerously threatening failure—a major social institution that in our larger cities at least, is almost beyond comprehension in its failure: an edifice that too often neither provides justice nor deters, punishes, reforms, or protects.

The true meaning of this failure will not be found in the pages that follow. This can only be learned from closely observing and experiencing the justice system as it operates. *Failure* is a relevant term. Some parts of our criminal justice system fail more noticeably and with greater consequence than others. None do their jobs well. The apologists for the system will argue otherwise: This is to be expected. The professional groups who make up this aggregation—the police, prosecutors, attorneys, judges, probation and parole personnel, jailors, and prison personnel—will admit to various degrees that the system is not working. All have learned to be apologists for their individual contributions to this massive failure and to seek answers in the broader problems of society, which the justice system mirrors. Although there is some truth in their allegations, they cannot escape blame so easily.

A recent article written by an investigative journalist who followed the daily travail of a young prosecuting attorney in New York City illustrates the plight (Steven Brill, "Fighting Crime in a Crumbling System," *American Lawyer*, July/August 1989). All students interested in the criminal justice system should read this searing indictment. Although New York City may not be representative of what one finds in all of America's justice system today, there are still enough similarities to warrant deep concern. The author found judges who did not seem to care that criminal defendants and their lawyers failed seven, eight, and nine times to show up for the scheduled hearings; and police officers who had been pulled from their jobs or called from home to appear time and time again—often on overtime pay in a system seriously strapped for money—to wait for a hearing that doesn't take place that day . . . or the next . . . or several weeks later. He found criminal defendants whose acts of violence against innocent, unarmed working people were ineptly presented by prosecuting attorneys who couldn't keep up with the workload and defense lawyers who unscrupulously used the system to thwart justice; judges more interested in their social than their court calendars; witnesses who wouldn't appear in court to testify; jurors who were visibly fed up with the entire situation; and jailors who couldn't be counted on to get defendants to the courtroom when cases were scheduled for trial. The result was predictable: defendants who became openly contemptuous of them all and of the justice system itself. Brill sums it up this way:

What you have . . . is waiting. Delay, laziness. Resignation. Judges, court officers, lawyers reading paperbacks, doing crossword puzzles, scanning the sports pages, exchanging jokes, planning lunch, and generally shooting the [breeze]—there's no other way to describe it—while the criminal justice system, at least in this city, grinds to a halt.

If there is concern for crime in this country, then there should be concern for the almost criminal complicity of the system of justice itself and those who work in it. Their laziness, apathy, cynicism, and frustration is a testament to a system gone awry. Hard questions must be asked by the American people about why the system is the way it is. Nor can we count on the politicians to provide the answer. They are as much a part of the problem as those in the system itself—perhaps in some ways more so. If scandal is what tickles the American public and whips the media into a feeding frenzy, we need look no further than our nation's criminal justice system and many of our criminal courts.

# Contents

LEARNING
UNIT

**II**

# LAW ENFORCEMENT   119

## LEARNING UNIT III

# THE COURT — 265

# LEARNING UNIT IV

# CORRECTIONS

LEARNING
UNIT

# V

# JUVENILE JUSTICE                                                                      621

LEARNING
UNIT

# VI

# CRIME ISSUES OF THE 1990s   661

# GENERAL FOUNDATIONS

**CHAPTER 1**
An Introduction:
The Criminal Justice System

**CHAPTER 2**
Crime, Law, and Legal Terminology

**CHAPTER 3**
Crime in America: Issues, Trends,
Measurement, and Victimization

# An Introduction: The Criminal Justice System

## OBJECTIVES

**After reading this chapter, the student should be able to:**

Discuss the goals of the criminal justice system.

List the major and auxiliary components of the criminal justice system.

Generally understand the functions and goals of the major and auxiliary components.

Discuss the conflict over the role of the criminal justice system in terms of the crime control and due process models.

Discuss and understand the discretionary decision points in the administration of justice.

Discuss the operations of the administration of justice, including:

the discretionary aspects

low percentage of arrests made for serious crimes

the attrition "funnel effect" of the administration of justice

high percentage of charges dismissed or reduced

the victim's view of the administration of justice

high percentage of juvenile involvement

Discuss relative spending levels for our nation's justice activities.

Understand the fundamental principles underlying our system of criminal law.

## IMPORTANT TERMS

Components of the criminal justice system:
  law enforcement
  courts
  corrections

probation
parole
juvenile justice system
Criminal justice system
Due process model

Crime control model
Discretion
Case attrition ("funnel effect")
Principles of criminal law
Criminal justice spending
Justice activities by level of government

Criminal justice system
as a series of
interrelated parts

Our criminal justice system is composed of a series of interrelated parts. These parts constitute a social system; a system of cause, effect, and interaction. We can adopt from physics a model to explain this relationship. Imagine in your minds an atomlike structure. We have all seen drawings of an atom with its orbiting electrons. The atom consists of a nucleus surrounded by electrons, the arrangement and behavior of which determine the nature and interaction of the whole. Society is the nucleus, the center core, of the atom. And like society itself, the nucleus consists of many particles. Surrounding it are the electrons, the agencies of criminal justice. In this analogy, the nucleus exerts a controlling influence on the properties of the

City police, county sheriff, and state highway patrol are three components of the criminal justice system that often work closely together. (Clockwise from lower left: © Michael Newman/PhotoEdit; © Kent Reno/Jeroboam; © Vince Compagnone/Claremont Courier/Jeroboam, Inc.)

electrons. Likewise, a free society determines and defines the operations and performance standards that become the operating guidelines in the administration of criminal justice. Yet the relationship is not merely one-sided. The component parts of the criminal justice system are themselves highly interactive. In this way, the operational practices of one component, such as the police, affect other components, such as the courts. These practices also affect society in general.

What further complicates these relationships is the fact that for the most part our criminal justice system is administered at the state and, particularly, local levels of government. Just as these governments themselves differ somewhat throughout the country, so does the administration of justice. As a result, there is no *single* system of criminal justice in this country; rather, there are many systems that although similar are also individually unique. The complex interactions between the various components of the criminal justice system together with the somewhat unique characteristics existing in those locations where justice is administered make the study of criminal justice an extremely important new branch of the social sciences.

*Interrelationships and the localized nature of the administration of justice*

In fact, these relationships are so intricate that the student of criminal justice must be prepared to learn a great deal about society if he or she is to understand the criminal justice process. The beginning student should be cautioned that the criminal justice system can never be understood as an isolated entity; nor can it be understood merely by studying legal texts and court decisions, memorizing theories of crime causation, or examining factors associated with juvenile delinquency or the principles of police or correctional management. The challenge— and most certainly the reward—lies in applying our knowledge of human behavior, social development, political philosophy, and interrelated concerns—all of which have become mirrored in our criminal–legal system and the administration of justice itself.

*The role of a broad education*

## ▢ GOALS OF THE CRIMINAL JUSTICE SYSTEM

In a free society, the primary goal of a criminal justice system is to *protect the members of that society*. In this respect, it is a formal instrumentality authorized by the people of a nation to protect both their collective and individual well-being. Another major goal of any system of criminal justice is the *maintenance of order*. There is the need for political and institutional stability as a goal of an organized society. Because crime and disorder disrupt stability in society, we have given the criminal justice system the authority to act as society's representative and to serve as the instrument by which the existing order is maintained.

*Primary and secondary roles of the criminal justice system*

In addition, within these two major goals, there are a number of important subgoals:

- The prevention of crime
- The suppression of criminal conduct by apprehending offenders for whom prevention is ineffective
- The review of the legality of our preventive and suppressive measures
- The judicial determination of guilt or innocence of those apprehended
- The proper disposition of those who have been legally found guilty
- The correction by socially approved means of the behavior of those who violate the criminal law

## COMPONENTS OF THE CRIMINAL JUSTICE SYSTEM AND THEIR FUNCTIONS

To accomplish these primary goals and subgoals, a system of criminal justice has been established. This system generally consists of the police, courts, probation, corrections, parole, and the juvenile justice system (Figure 1.1). Many people might include other agencies such as the legislative branch of government as part of the criminal justice system because legislators pass the laws that define certain acts as crimes; however, such agencies are not part of the criminal justice system. Although they play a crucial role, they are not themselves considered agencies of criminal justice.

The criminal justice system can be broken down into *major* and *auxiliary* components. The major components consist of the so-called "big three": law enforcement, courts, and corrections. Assisting these major components are three specialized auxiliary services consisting of probation, parole, and the juvenile justice system. In reality, probation and parole services are generally grouped for classification purposes under the corrections component, because these services have a "corrective" responsibility. The juvenile justice system is a "system-within-a-system." It has been specially established to deal with offenders and problems involving youth below a prescribed legal age.

All of the components of the criminal justice system share certain common goals. For example, they collectively exist to protect society, to maintain order, and to prevent crime. But they also contribute individually to these goals in their own special way. In the discussion of the component functions that follow, you should pay careful attention to the system's overall goals as well as the individual contributions of each component.

### Law Enforcement

Law enforcement is the first component. It consists of all police agencies at the federal, state, county, and municipal levels. These agencies fulfill the following functions:

**General functions**

1. *To prevent criminal behavior.* Prevention involves all the efforts directed toward eliminating the causes of crimes. Among these efforts might be

FIGURE **1.1** Agencies of criminal justice in the United States.

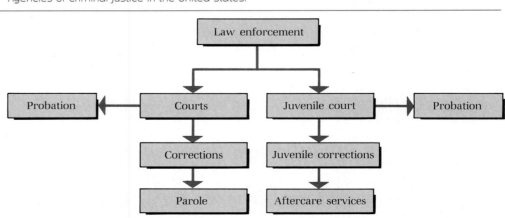

such activities as delinquency prevention programs and citizen education efforts. The purpose of the first is to reduce the likelihood of youths engaging in criminal activities. The second might counsel citizens on ways to avoid being victims of crime and what to do should they be victimized.

2. *To reduce crime.* Crime reduction essentially means eliminating and reducing opportunities for criminal behavior. Such police programs as preventive and conspicuous patrol activity; intelligence and information gathering on crime-producing situations and known criminals; and target-hardening strategies that attempt to make certain physical sites less vulnerable to criminals are examples of police crime reduction efforts.

3. *To apprehend and arrest offenders.* The police engage in criminal investigations; the gathering of evidence; presenting this evidence in the courtroom; and testifying before the courts against those who violate the criminal law.

4. *To protect life and property.* Protecting life and property includes the full range of police services in such areas as crime prevention, crime reduction, and investigation and apprehension strategies designed to protect society. It also includes the provision of specialized services designed to assure public safety.

5. *To regulate noncriminal conduct.* Every day the police are involved in efforts to ensure compliance by regulatory means with laws concerning public safety and security. This function includes activities such as traffic regulation and crowd control.

## Courts

The courts include those judicial agencies at all levels of government that perform the following functions in the administration of criminal justice:

1. *To protect the rights of the accused.* The courts are responsible for reviewing the actions of law enforcement agencies to ensure that the police have not violated the legal rights of the accused. Similarly, the courts are given the authority and responsibility to review the actions of other agencies of criminal justice to ensure that their actions do not violate the rights of the convicted offender. General functions

2. *To determine by all available legal means whether a person is guilty of a crime.* Review of all evidence presented by the police or private citizens to determine its relevance and admissibility according to established guidelines of acceptability. The court also examines the circumstances that surround the crime as it relates to the issues it must adjudicate.

3. *To dispose properly of those convicted of crimes.* The courts have the responsibility to examine the background of the accused and the circumstances of the crime. From this information, and according to existing and applicable laws, the court considers possible sentencing alternatives and then selects the most proper form of disposition for the convicted offender.

4. *To protect society.* After the accused has been found guilty and after consideration of all factors, the court must determine if the offender should be removed from society and incarcerated in order to protect the safety of life and property.

An important function of courts is to determine if the accused is guilty of a crime. (Billy E. Barnes)

5. *To prevent and reduce criminal behavior.* This is the task of imposing proper penalties and sanctions that will serve to deter future criminal acts by the offender and also serve as an example and a deterrent to others who would commit criminal acts or threaten public safety.

## Corrections

Corrections consist of those executive agencies at all levels of government that are responsible both directly and indirectly for the following functions:

*General functions*

1. *To maintain institutions.* The correctional component is responsible for maintaining prisons, jails, halfway houses, and other institutional facilities to receive convicted offenders sentenced to periods of incarceration by the courts.
2. *To protect law-abiding members of society.* Corrections is responsible for providing custody and security in order to keep sentenced offenders removed from the "free world" so that they cannot commit further crimes on society.
3. *To reform offenders.* During the incarceration of offenders in a correctional institution, corrections is given the function of developing and providing services to assist incarcerated offenders to reform. Additionally, corrections is responsible for developing programs that will assist the offender in returning to society and in leading a noncriminal life after his or her release.
4. *To deter crimes.* Corrections is responsible for encouraging incarcerated

and potential offenders to lead law-abiding lives through the experience of incarceration and the denial of freedom to live in society.

## Probation

Probation is a court-related component. It encompasses those services at all levels of government that supervise an offender who has been found guilty of a crime. It is responsible for the following:

1. *To provide a sentencing alternative other than commitment to a correctional institution.* Probation provides an alternative to the court other than having to sentence the convicted offender to a period of imprisonment. It accomplishes this by providing a system whereby the offender can remain in the community under the supervisory authority of probation officials and the sentencing court. General functions
2. *To deter and regulate potential criminal conduct.* Through direct community supervision and assistance, probation attempts to help the offender adjust to the strains of everyday life and to avoid situations that potentially might lead to further criminal behavior.
3. *To provide reports and guidance for judicial decision making.* Probation personnel often conduct court-directed investigations of the convicted offender's background and circumstances of the crime. Such information is then used by the court in determining the proper disposition of an offender. Probation officers also keep the court advised of the probationer's progress during the period of probation and of any failure of the probationer to live up to the conditions of the probation agreement.

## Parole

Parole is an executive agency function that is responsible for providing community supervision and assistance to an offender who has been conditionally released from a correctional facility before the statutory expiration of his or her sentence. The purposes of parole are as follows:

1. *To provide an alternative to maintaining an offender in custody.* Parole provides a means to release an offender to the community under the supervision of a parole agency at a time during the offender's period of incarceration when it is determined that the inmate is ready for release. General functions
2. *To provide needed services to an ex-offender.* Like probation, parole efforts are directed toward assisting the ex-offender to readjust to the strains of life in a free society. Such services might include obtaining employment and help in abstaining from drugs or alcohol, and providing general counseling.
3. *To deter and regulate potential criminal conduct.* Parole attempts to assist in the prevention of criminal conduct by regulating the parolee's behavior and conduct.
4. *To prepare reports and guidelines for decision making.* Parole personnel are often responsible for preparole investigations of the circumstances into which a potential parolee might be released. Such considerations would include the community and law enforcement attitudes toward having the individual released back to the community under parole supervision, the

attitude of the parolee's family, and the availability of a legitimate job. These factors are then transmitted to an independent parole board as an aid in determining whether the inmate should be paroled. Parole personnel are also responsible for advising the parole board of the satisfactory or unsatisfactory progress of parolees under their supervision and to initiate or request parole revocation if warranted.

### Juvenile Justice System

The juvenile justice system consists of a broad range of specialized juvenile agencies of an adjudicatory, treatment, and incarceraton nature. These agencies handle cases of delinquency and other matters involving minors and, in some cases, adults who have committed offenses against minors. This component of the criminal justice system also includes agencies and services that provide predelinquency (prevention), delinquency, and postdelinquency (treatment) services to youth. Its major functions are the following:

General functions

1. *To deter delinquent behavior.* By employing a wide range of programs that involve the juvenile court, the police, community agencies, and other sources, the juvenile justice system attempts to deter those youths who would commit delinquent acts. This is accomplished by both the provision of appropriate services and the use of specific sanctions.
2. *To provide needed care to the child.* The juvenile justice system is responsible for examining and determining the needs of youths who become involved with the system and providing appropriate services to deal with these needs.
3. *To determine if the child is to be adjudicated a delinquent.* The juvenile court as a component of the juvenile justice system is responsible for examining the facts that surround the offense and examining admissible evidence.
4. *To provide for the proper disposition of the adjudicated delinquent.* If available evidence and circumstances indicate that the child is delinquent, the juvenile court must determine the proper disposition of the youthful offender.
5. *To maintain institutions.* The juvenile justice system is typically responsible for maintaining a broad range of institutions for handling those children who come in contact with the system. These institutions can range from foster or group homes to more penal-like institutions for the dangerous or hardened youthful offender.
6. *To protect public safety.* The juvenile justice system is also responsible for institutionalizing the adjudicated delinquent if this is warranted by the need to protect society.

## CONFLICT OVER THE ROLE
## OF THE CRIMINAL JUSTICE SYSTEM

Although there is generally broad agreement over the goals of the criminal justice system, there is far less agreement over how best to attain these goals. Based on the American governmental principle of checks and balances, the enforcement, judicial, and correctional aspects of the system are not vested within the authority of one agency. For example, giving the police the authority to arrest, prosecute, and reform individuals would be an unacceptable practice. Such a system would obviously pose a dangerous threat to individual liberty in a free society.

However, although society provides the criminal justice system with certain guidelines as to how it is to operate, these guidelines are often expressed as contradictory values. For example, choices must be made among such competing values as the rights of the accused and the protection of society. This means that the administration of criminal justice must rest on some implicit idea of what justice is and what society requires. This is a difficult task, because people often interpret the meaning of justice and how it is to be accomplished very differently and inconsistently. As a consequence, the machinery of criminal justice has no all-encompassing consensual guidelines on how to operate in each case.

## ◻ CRIMINAL JUSTICE MODELS

Although no one would argue with the premise that the primary purpose of the system is to protect society, differing opinions on how to do this often subject individual agencies and the entire administrative process to criticism by one group or another. This problem has been placed in perspective by the late Herbert Packer, who suggests that the administration of criminal justice is complicated by the competition between two opposing value systems that underlie the process. He refers to these values as the *crime control* and *due process* models of criminal justice.[1]

### Crime Control Model

Packer's *crime control model* is based on the idea that the most important function of the criminal justice system is the repression of criminal conduct. This model is justified by pointing out that the failure of the police and other agencies of criminal justice to bring criminal conduct under control leads to the breakdown of public order and, as a result, the disappearance of social tranquility, which is an important condition of human freedom. To guarantee the maintenance of the existing social order, the administration of criminal justice must stress "efficiency"—that is, the increased capacity to apprehend, try, convict, and dispose of a high proportion of criminal offenders, with an emphasis placed on speed and finality in dealing with them. In many ways the crime control model reflects what may be called the conservative or "hard-line" approach to justice. In this model, procedural issues such as the rights of the accused, which some people feel lead to the offender's escaping justice, must be secondary to the need to protect society and control crime. The supporters of this position contend that the collective rights of society must take precedence over the rights of the individual; where there is conflict over this issue, collective public safety must be the first consideration.

The emphasis on public safety

Underlying the assumption of this model is the feeling that the offender is guilty—an assumption that contradicts the basic presumption of innocence that is supposed to surround the accused under our system of criminal jurisprudence. However, the crime control model sees this presumption of guilt as occurring only after extensive fact-finding procedures are employed by the police and prosecutors. In this way, all cases that probably would not result in a successful conviction are screened out at a preliminary stage, leaving only those in which the offender is almost certainly guilty. Thus, all fact finding is accomplished before the trial rather than through the trial process itself. Consequently, the trial and disposition process might resemble an assembly line.

Although such a system has a certain appeal to many Americans, it is also subject to criticism. For one thing, it is contended that such a viewpoint is overly simplistic and makes certain assumptions that do not exist. For example, the idea that the protective legal rights afforded those accused of crime lead to guilty persons escaping justice is questioned. It is said that there is little evidence of this occurring in the vast majority of criminal cases. In those few cases in which it does occur, the dangers of permitting the police to introduce illegally obtained evidence or to force confessions or admissions from a suspect far outweigh the ultimate costs of society of letting the individual off on a technicality.[2]

It is also argued that the reasons for the high crime rate in the United States

## FIGHTING CRIME BY THE RULES: WHY COPS LIKE MIRANDA

Like many reforms of the 1960s, the changes in police procedure mandated by the Supreme Court in that tumultuous era have been under bitter attack ever since. From the start, critics predicted that the exclusionary rule (barring the use in court of evidence seized in illegal searches) and the *Miranda* warnings (informing suspects of their right to remain silent or have a lawyer present during interrogations) would cripple law enforcement. "In some unknown number of cases," Justice Byron White warned in his dissent from *Miranda*, "[the] rule will return a killer, a rapist or other criminal to the streets."

But today a new consensus among scholars and police chiefs suggests that these due-process reforms have done little to hinder the cops. Not only have officers learned to live with the rules, says Prof. Yale Kamisar of the University of Michigan, but "most studies indicate that the prophecies of doom have not been fulfilled." Indeed, both rules are widely credited with improving professionalism among policemen—and as a result the

reforms enjoy growing support among even the most hard-bitten cops.

Columbia University law professor H. Richard Uviller spent eight months in a New York City precinct, observing compliance with the rules. A former assistant prosecutor, Uviller had some experience in the gritty world of cops and criminals. And after 14 years in the Ivy League, he wondered how well the Constitution he was teaching in his classroom was being observed on the beat. His experience with criminals had left him with some reservations about both reforms. But out on the street he found that they have become "part of the legal landscape," as much a part of police routine as using handcuffs, filling out forms and waiting around the station house for the next emergency call.

Uviller's new book, "Tempered Zeal,"* reports some griping on the beat about both reforms. He also observed occasional violations, particularly when officers casually questioned suspects in the back of the

*234 pages. Contemporary Books. $19.95.

squad car, saving the reading of their *Miranda* rights for the more formal setting of the station house. But on the whole, he found that the cops have "internalized" the rules and are sometimes even more scrupulous than the court requires in respecting suspects' rights. "To the extent that constitutional principles accord with what officers think is fair and decent," Uviller says, "they have no trouble applying the rules."

Others who have studied *Miranda* in a more systematic way say the warnings rarely stop people from confessing. Many suspects try to exonerate themselves in the eyes of the police and end up incriminating themselves instead; others simply don't grasp that they have a right to remain silent. "Besides," says former police lieutenant James Fyfe, now professor at American University, "hardly anybody walks": even when a suspect does not confess or his confession is thrown out in court because of a botched *Miranda* warning, there is usually enough evidence and other testimony to make a case against him. Peter Nardulli of the University of Illinois cannot be blamed on the administrative agencies of justice or the legal system, which operates to protect the rights of offenders. The causes of crime are much more complex: to think that "tightening up" procedural rights will have a meaningful effect on the crime rate is simply unwarranted. There is also concern that a "crime control" model poses dangers to fundamental liberties because it would dangerously shift the fact-finding responsibility from an independent source (the court and juries) to the police and prosecution elements of the system.

Ironically, both the supporters and opponents of a crime control model seek the same thing: the protection of society. Where they fundamentally disagree is in the method of accomplishing this goal. For the opponents of the crime control model, the ultimate protection of society is inseparable from assuring that individual rights are protected. If we lose these rights, they contend, the resulting inability to check the actions of government will pose a far more significant threat to the collective welfare of our society.

finds that less than 1 percent of all cases in his large statistical surveys were thrown out because of illegal confessions. Says Houston Police Chief Lee Brown, "I don't see any detrimental impact [from *Miranda*]."

[Ed. note: Lee Brown is currently serving as New York City's police commissioner.]

**NEW HABITS**

Experts have reached similar conclusions about the exclusionary rule. One 1982 survey by the government's National Institute of Justice warned that a large number of felonies were being thrown out of California courts because evidence was obtained in illegal searches. But later interpretations of the same data debunked this claim, proving that only a tiny percentage of cases were lost because of the rule. Says Fyfe, "There is not one study that shows it affects more than 1.5 percent of all cases." Even in narcotics cases, where the impact is greatest, Nardulli and others find that the rule has forced police to conduct searches more carefully. Says Uviller, "They have learned to stop and

think before they search—exactly what the fourth Amendment wants them to do."

By far the most striking findings suggest that cops are proud of the way the reforms have shaped up their departments. In 1987 law student Myron Orfield interviewed members of a Chicago narcotics squad and found that all opposed eliminating the exclusionary rule. "It makes the police department more professional" said one. Without it, said another, an investigating policeman "would be like a criminal released in the midst of society." Former Newark police director Hubert Williams reports a similar reaction to *Miranda*. "Officers want respect," he says. "We've gotten away from force and coercion. Nor do we want to be accused of that." And in his view, *Miranda* has made it much harder to level such charges.

**IDEOLOGICAL GAP**

Those who oppose the reforms are hardly convinced by these findings. Conservatives say history has more than borne out Justice White's grim

predictions for *Miranda*. And the Reagan administration is still campaigning hard to overturn both measures. "The issue is not whether the police have learned to live with the rules," says Assistant Attorney General Stephen Markman, "but whether society has learned to live with unprecedentedly high crime rates." Markman argues that no one really knows how many offenders decide not to confess after hearing their *Miranda* warnings. His own suspicion is that many take that route and go free as a result.

In the end, the debate boils down to ideology: a quarrel between those who favor battling crime with all available weapons and those who worry as much about the rights of the accused. Neither station-house stories nor academic studies are likely to change minds on either side of that divide. But surely it is welcome news that most police, far from finding their hands tied, have learned to reconcile due process with the fight against crime.

The famous "Miranda law" requires that arresting officers safeguard the rights of the suspect while apprehending him. (© Steve Starr/Picture Group)

### Due Process Model

Whereas the crime control model resembles an assembly line at the judicial stage, the *due process model* has the features of an obstacle course. Under this model, each stage of the criminal justice process from arrest through the court's disposition of the accused is designed to present formidable impediments to carrying the accused any further along in the process. It rejects the police and prosecutorial role under the crime control model and places the screening burden on the court.

The due process model, in addition to the criticisms it receives for overly protecting the rights of the accused, is often said to cause inordinate delays in the administration of justice. The old adage, justice delayed is justice denied, is often applied. There is some justification in faulting the due process model on its inability to dispense justice with swiftness and certainty. It can also be criticized for the fact that it lends itself to certain manipulations that may not be in the best interest of justice. For example, the truth or substance of an individual's guilt might become secondary to the legal maneuverings on a small point of law. In fact, this system may actually encourage these kinds of tactics by providing the opportunity for issues of this nature to be considered. Although it can be argued that these opportunities must exist, it can also be said that such actions bring criticism on our courts and legal system and undermine public safety.

Interestingly, some aspects of the crime control model are similar to the criminal justice process that exists in Great Britain and in some European countries, where the presumption of innocence must be demonstrated by the accused. The American ideal of criminal jurisprudence requires that the accused be considered innocent until proved guilty. Packer views both systems as striving for quality control but in very different ways. He suggests that the due process model emphasizes "reliability" (i.e., society must be willing to live with the fact that some guilty offenders will be found innocent in order to ensure that innocent persons are not unjustly convicted), whereas the crime control model emphasizes "efficiency" and "productivity" (i.e., society must be willing to accept the fact that some innocent people might well be incorrectly found guilty, but that the overall improvement in the administration of justice and, supposedly, the protection to society, would more than compensate for such mistakes).

The issues that these two models pose are fundamental ones for our society—issues we dare not take lightly or dismiss without very careful thought. Although we as Americans should be concerned about the problems of crime in our nation, we must not overlook the implications of disregarding issues concerning fundamental rights. This is particularly true today with the growing power of government and the threat of the intrusion of government into all aspects of our lives. In the final analysis it is this fundamental philosophical difference between these two models and the viewpoints they generate that injects the system of administering justice into the very social fabric of our nation.

## THE OPERATION OF THE CRIMINAL JUSTICE SYSTEM

Now that the goals, agencies, and value systems that underlie the administration of criminal justice in America have been discussed, let's examine an overview of the operation of the system itself.

The layperson usually perceives the system as operating in this manner: The police investigate a violation of the law, and, if sufficient evidence exists, arrest the violator and bring the accused before the courts. After a trial and the determination of the defendant's guilt, the court sentences the convicted offender to a form of community supervision, such as probation, or to an institution for incarceration. After serving a portion of the sentence, the offender might be released on parole or released completely without parole supervision upon completing the full sentence. In this way, the system of criminal justice can be thought of as a massive machine that proceeds in a linear manner as it moves the offender from arrest to final disposition. This linear flow is represented in Figure 1.2.

Although, in a sense, this procedure shown in Figure 1.2 is technically what occurs, there is a great deal of "slippage" within the system at various decision points in the process. A major characteristic of the administration of criminal justice is the discretion that exists at each critical decision stage in the system. Table 1.1 examines some of the most common discretionary decisions that can be made at each stage. Although there are those who would argue that such discretion is unwarranted and should be curtailed, this is difficult if not impossible to accomplish. The complexities of the law, the need for some degree of flexibility in handling individual cases, the involvement and contributions of each successive component of the criminal justice system, and the practical realities of the hundreds of thousands of offenders and situations that agents of the criminal justice system encounter each year require a high degree of flexibility and options. The administration of justice simply cannot operate as some impersonal and inflexible machine. As a result of the necessary characteristics of the system, circumstances are such that *relatively few of those charged with serious crimes are processed completely through all of the stages from arrest to a prison sentence.*

In part, the due process model of criminal justice to which we subscribe is responsible for this set of circumstances. This model, as we have said, is like an obstacle course for the state in its prosecution of criminal cases. However, due process procedures alone do not explain the "slippage" within the system. The

The criminal justice system as a giant funnel

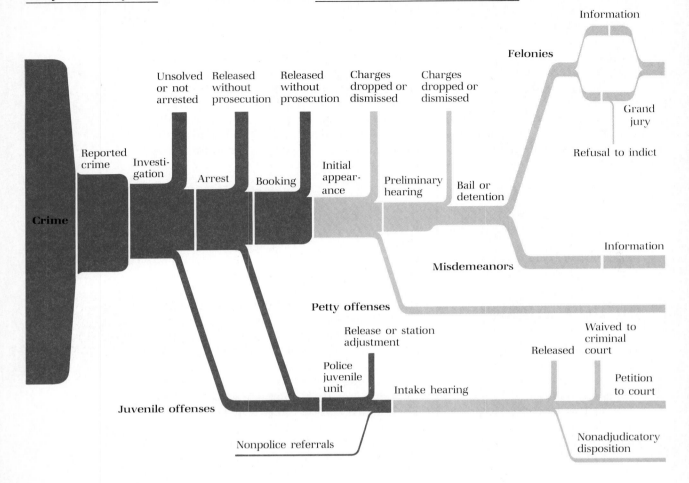

FIGURE **1.2**   What is the sequence of events in the criminal justice system? Note: This chart gives a simplified view of caseflow through the criminal justice system. Procedures vary among jurisdictions. The weights of the lines are not intended to show the actual size of caseloads. [*Source:* Adapted from *The challenge of crime in a free society.* President's Commission on Law Enforcement and Administration of Justice, 1967.]

criminal justice system operates like a complex filter, screening out offenders at various points. This is referred to as the case attrition, or "funnel effect," of justice.

Consider Figure 1.3 for a moment. This figure represents the findings of a two-year study supported by the U.S. Department of Justice that examined the processing of felony cases in fourteen different jurisdictions throughout the country. The results of this study generally confirm earlier studies of the same problem.

Several thought-provoking findings are shown. First, of all serious (felony) crimes committed, only one-half are reported to the police. Of the half that are

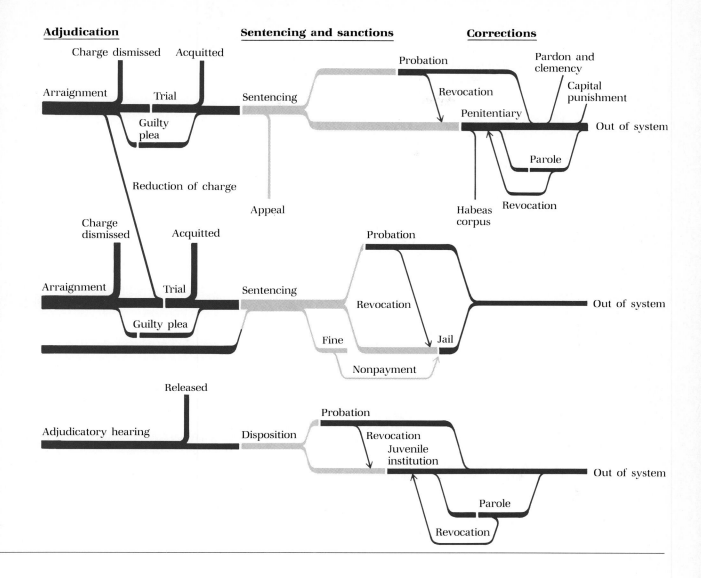

**Adjudication**  **Sentencing and sanctions**  **Corrections**

reported, the police make arrests in only about 20 percent of the cases. And there is an ominous trend here. Until the early 1970s, the police made arrests in about 25 percent of the serious crimes reported. Since then, the arrest rate has begun a slow downward spiral, stabilizing in the late 1980s at around 20 percent. This 5 percent difference is important when we realize that taken nationally, it represents thousands of serious crimes. In Figure 1.3, we see that of the 100 arrests made, 20 are rejected at the initial screening of the cases. Thirty more are later dismissed by the prosecutor or the court. Fully *one half* of the arrests end at this point. Those arrested do not go on to trial because either the prosecutor decides not to prosecute or the courts find some reason why the arrests can't be prosecuted.

At this point, our batting average gets a little better. Of the fifty arrests that

## TABLE **1.1**  Discretionary Decision Points in the Administration of Justice

| Component | Discretionary Decision to Be Made |
|---|---|
| Police | To enforce specific laws<br>To investigate<br>To conduct searches of people and buildings<br>To arrest<br>What charges to file |
| Prosecutor | What charges to file (e.g., reducing the charge to a "lesser and included offense")<br>To decline to prosecute the arrested party<br>To seek grand jury indictment<br>To go for the death penalty in capital cases<br>To plea bargain. This might include:<br>  Asking the court to sentence concurrently on two or more convictions<br>  Dropping one or more "counts" if arrested for several crimes<br>  Asking the court to suspend sentence or place the convicted offender on probation<br>  Asking the court to sentence the offender to a special institution or treatment program if available and permitted<br>In some jurisdictions to make the determination whether a youthful offender is to be tried as a juvenile or stand trial as an adult in an adult criminal court |
| Judge | For a juvenile court judge, to waive jurisdiction over the child so that he or she will stand trial as an adult (when permitted by state law)<br>To set bail or conditions for release<br>To entertain and rule on pretrial motions (e.g., change of venue, rule on evidence, hold hearings on mental capacity)<br>To rule on challenges to the suitability of potential jurors<br>To accept/reject negotiated pleas involving the court<br>To rule on procedural matters raised during the course of the trial<br>To order a presentence investigation report<br>To accept/reject the recommendation of the presentence report<br>To impose sentence<br>To revoke probation or suspended sentence<br>To convict or acquit in bench trials (i.e., a trial without a jury) |
| Jury | To convict or acquit<br>To return the death penalty in capital cases<br>In some jurisdictions to determine or recommend sentence |
| Probation | To conduct the presentence investigation and recommend disposition to the court<br>To suggest conditions of probation to the court<br>To bring the probationer back to the court for a probation violation |
| Corrections | To determine the prison institution where the offender will be imprisoned<br>To determine the types of programs to which the offender will be exposed<br>To determine the custody grade<br>To award privileges<br>To grant or deny "good time"<br>To punish for disciplinary infractions<br>To make recommendations to the parole board |
| Parole | To conduct preparole release investigation and make recommendation to the parole board<br>To grant or deny parole<br>To revoke parole |

have survived to this point, forty-nine are convicted of a felony or misdemeanor, and twenty-nine of these convictions end up being sentenced to jail or prison. How really bleak the overall picture is can be seen from the fact that of the initial one thousand *serious* crimes committed, only ten offenders are specifically sent to prison as opposed to receiving probation, a fine, or short-term jail incarceration. And you should remember that we are dealing with serious (felony) offenses.

One word of caution to the reader: At first glance it may appear that the rate of imprisonment is only 1 percent. That is, of every one hundred serious crimes committed only one defendant is sentenced. This may be an understatement. The individual who is sentenced to prison may have committed more than one crime—in fact it is likely that he or she has. This, of course, would improve the relative ''batting average'' of the criminal justice system, yet we don't know what effect this factor may have overall. Even if this were the case, however, the evidence still does not speak well for the operations of our justice system.

As increasing numbers of research projects have uncovered the existence of such circumstances, growing criticism has been leveled at the criminal justice system in recent years. This awareness of the facts has refueled the due process–crime control dispute. Figure 1.4, which depicts the so-called criminal injustice system, is a good portrayal of the types of criticism the criminal justice system is receiving. Here we see a possible sequence of events as they might occur for the individual charged with the crime and the victim. Although it may be a bit overdramatized in part, it unfortunately does contain a significant element of truth about what can and sometimes does happen.

However, as already stated—and it is worth repeating—our general insistence that due process rights must be afforded to a person charged wth a crime is *not* the major underlying reason for the "funnel effect." It is important to understand this.

What are the factors, then, that cause the funneling of cases as they are processed through the criminal justice system? This question and related issues will be briefly discussed here with greater attention coming in later chapters.

## Low Percentage of Arrests Made for Serious Crimes

Why are law enforcement agencies able to make arrests in only 20 percent of all reported crimes? Even if the arrest of one criminal results in his or her being convicted of two or more crimes, which makes the statistical comparison between **Police arrest success** crimes and arrests appear better than it really is, this is still a terribly low success rate. Although it is not known how much of a role such statistical differences actually play in the overall crime picture, the fact remains that the police arrest only a small percentage of offenders who commit serious crimes.

In part, the answer to this low crime/arrest ratio almost certainly lies in the traditional inefficiency of the police in solving crimes. However, this inefficiency cannot be considered simply as ineptness. Our criminal justice processes and the powers of the police are severely curtailed by society's concern for the rights of the individual and our unwillingness to permit the police a great deal of autonomous authority. Consequently, it would seem that a free society must be willing to forgo greater police efficiency for the assurance that police powers will not be used to curtail individual rights. A very precarious balance exists between police powers and a free society—one that requires constant vigilance, as history has repeatedly demonstrated.

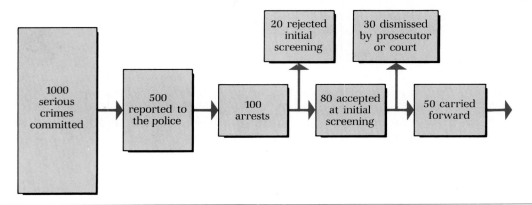

FIGURE **1.3**  The case attrition or the "funnel-effect" of the administration of justice. [*Source:* Adapted from *The Prosecution of Felony Arrests*, 1979 (Washington, D.C.: U.S. Department of Justice, Bureau of Justice Statistics, 1983), p. 2; FBI Uniform Crime Reports (various); Bureau of Justice Statistics Reports (various); and National Crime Survey Reports (various)].

FIGURE **1.4**  The criminal injustice system. [*Source:* Adapted from Marilyn Wagner Culp and Mary Lou Calvin, "Victim Services Programs," in *Justice and Older Americans*, Marlene A. Young Rifai, ed. (Lexington, Mass.: D. C. Heath, 1977), p. 127. Adapted with permission]

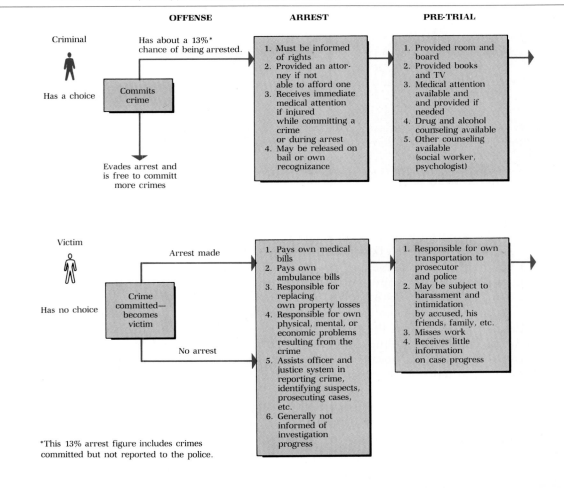

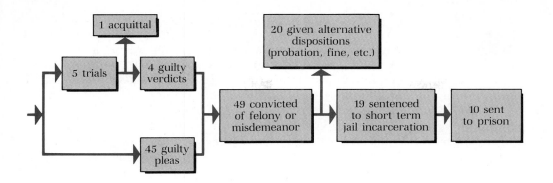

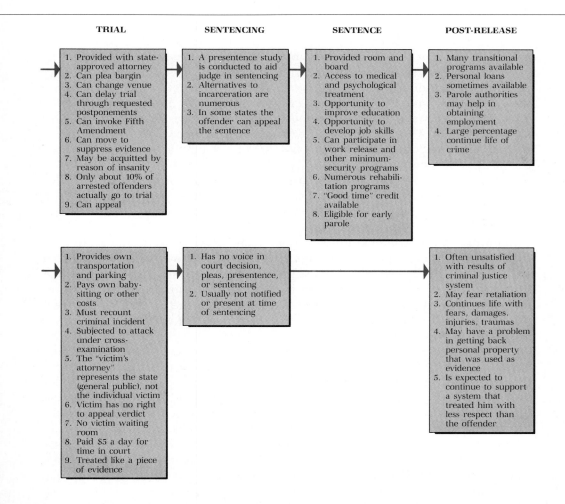

Another part of the answer lies in the very nature of most crimes. Much criminal behavior is covert, with the odds drastically in favor of the offender. The police, because of limitations in their resources, personnel, and operating strategies, play a defensive role in trying to curtail crime. The police usually must wait until a crime occurs before they can take action. This gives the criminal the tremendous advantage of choosing the time, place, and method of the crime. Even a police agency with the most qualified police personnel and the most sophisticated crime-solving technology would probably be only slightly more efficient than one that has only mediocre personnel and resources. Although many people place stock in the ability of "more qualified" police personnel to make an appreciable difference in crime levels, this relationship has never been demonstrated (and probably never will be).

## High Percentage of Juveniles Arrested

The statistics in Figure 1.3 conceal an important fact about arrest figures and the processing of offenders. In 1988, juveniles under the age of eighteen accounted for 30 percent of all arrests for serious crimes. Why is there such a high arrest rate of juveniles for serious offenses? One may simply assume that it is because juveniles commit such a high proportion of all serious crimes. However, several points could be raised to question such an assumption. First, the arrest in itself does not necessarily mean that the person arrested committed the crime. To make such an assumption conclusively, one would need to know the total number of crimes

Circumstances that hide
our knowledge of
juvenile crime

committed (including those not reported to the authorities), what percentage of these were committed by juveniles, and what percentage of the total population are juveniles. The total number of serious crimes committed will never be precisely known, and even if such information were available, in many cases it could not be determined whether the crime was committed by a juvenile or an adult because the offender will never be arrested.

Another problem is that states have set age limits within which an individual can be considered as a juvenile for the purpose of criminal prosecution. A person over these statutory ages (usually 17 or 18) is considered an adult.[3] Thus, the period of time when a child is perhaps psychologically and physically most capable of committing crimes is limited to four or five years. If the arrest statistics are interpreted literally, juveniles would have to be extremely active in their preadolescent and adolescent years in the commission of serious offenses. Although juveniles from the ages of twelve to seventeen may, in fact, be committing more serious crimes in proportion to their numbers than, say, those in the age bracket of twenty-five to thirty-two, we should not be willing on the basis of what little we know to say that they are committing nearly one-third of all serious crime!

Juveniles are probably so overrepresented in the crime statistics because of several factors. They probably do commit a higher percentage of traditional crimes than any other similar age segment of our society. Given the probability that they do commit a disproportionate number of crimes, they also tend to commit the types of "street crimes" with which police agencies are most capable of dealing. For example, arrest statistics show that juveniles have a high arrest rate for crimes of violence against the person. The police are more successful in making arrests for these types of crimes than they are for crimes against property. The common explanations for the differences in arrest rates for these two categories of crime are:

(1) violent crimes are more serious so the police devote more of their time and resources to solving them; (2) these crimes involve perpetrator–victim contact, which often provides an eyewitness who can identify the assailant; and (3) victims are more likely to report, or the police are more likely to be made aware of, the commission of these crimes, particularly when injury has occurred. It also may be assumed that juveniles commit crimes with a degree of ineptness that older, more cautious and experienced criminals are less likely to exhibit. It is also likely that more sophisticated criminal activities are generally not the province of youthful offenders. Many sophisticated property crimes such as fraud, embezzlement, hijacking, the increasing occurrence of electronic theft through the use of computer diversion, credit card counterfeiting, the wide-ranging area of white-collar crime, and highly structured forms of organized crime are beyond the resources of most juvenile offenders. Unfortunately, these types of crime (and offenders) are also beyond the control of most local police agencies to deal with effectively. Considering all of these possible factors, we may be able to partly explain why juveniles are so overrepresented in the arrest statistics.

One reason why the crime rate for juvenile offenders is so high is that they often commit the kinds of "street crimes" that police can easily deal with. (© Gale Zucker/Stock Boston)

## High Percentage of Charges Dismissed or Reduced

A third question raised by the data concerns the large percentage of arrests in which either no complaint is filed or the charges are dropped or reduced. Why is it that so many offenders do not complete the preliminary steps in the judicial process, are not prosecuted, and are not ultimately sent to prison for their crimes?

There are several reasons why so many arrestees do not go beyond the pretrial screening stage. The first obvious reason is that the police arrest suspects without obtaining enough evidence to warrant prosecution. Thus, the charges are dismissed. Another factor to be considered is that victims may refuse to file charges—for example, in crimes committed by one spouse against the other. Along this line,

**Factors that contribute to dismissal or reduction of charges**

### REPORT LINKS YOUTHS TO 40 PERCENT OF ARSON ARRESTS

A 1988 report by the National Fire Protection Service claims that juveniles accounted for 40 percent of all arson arrests in 1986. Nearly 7 percent of these arrests involved children under ten years old. There were 111,000 confirmed or suspected arson fires in the United States in 1986. The figures were compiled from information provided by fire departments nationwide. Although this figure was down slightly from the preceding year, it is a problem unprecedented among Western industrialized nations according to a spokesman for the Service.

The report said that arson caused 705 deaths and nearly $1.68 billion in property damage in 1986. This was an increase of nearly 5 percent in the arson death rate from the previous year and accounted for one of every seven lives lost in building fires. Arson was also singled out as the largest cause of property damage by fire, accounting for more than one of every four dollars lost in building fires, the report said.

**MORE VEHICLES SET AFIRE**
The number of vehicle fires attributed to arson in 1986, 57,000, was up 25 percent from 1985, causing more than $151 million in damage, the

highest figure since 1982. This particular category of arson showed the sharpest upswing in incendiary or suspicious fires in the 1980s. The report said 51 percent of all confirmed or suspected arson fires in 1986 were in residential properties. It linked arson to 71 percent of prison and jail fires, 60.3 percent of fires in vacant buildings, and nearly 56 percent of all fires in schools and other educational facilities.

The police arrested or identified suspects in 18 percent of the 1986 arson fires, the report said. It also pointed out that 86 percent of those arrested for arson were males.

the Vera Institute conducted a study of the reasons for various felony dispositions in New York City courts.[4] In these courts, judges, prosecutors, and defense attorneys cited the prior relationship of the defendant and the victim as one of the two most significant factors in determining the outcome of cases. For example, prior relationships existed in more than one-half of all felonies that involved victims. These relationships included husbands and wives, lovers, prostitutes and their pimps or customers, neighbors, in-laws, junkies and dealers, even landlords and tenants. These prior relationship factors often lead to dismissals, reduced charges, and light sentences in return for a plea of guilty. The most frequently cited reason for dismissal in these cases was lack of cooperation by the complaining victim.[5]

A related factor is that witnesses and even victims may be unwilling to testify for a variety of reasons—for example, the fear of retaliation by the accused, because of inconvenience, or because they have moved from the jurisdiction. Without the witnesses' testimony, the state often has no case and the charges must be dropped.

This raises the question of screening and the decision to charge by the prosecutor. The first decision a prosecutor makes about an arrest is what the charge will be or whether to charge at all. Typically, after the police take a suspect into custody, an assistant prosecutor will review the facts of the crime provided by the police, witnesses, and victim(s)—either directly or indirectly through the police. In large cities, the prosecutor's office may have a number of assistant prosecutors whose primary responsibility is to screen cases to decide whether or not to prosecute. These "screening assistants," in addition to screening the evidence, may gather information about the defendant, such as his or her criminal history, relationship to the victim, and possibly alcohol or drug use at the time of the incident. The prosecutor must then decide whether or not to charge the defendant and, if the decision to charge is made, whether to charge the defendant with the charge brought by the police, another related crime, or a lesser crime. After examining all the facts, the prosecutor may conclude that he or she cannot satisfy the legal requirements of proof required for conviction and reject the case.

Studies of case rejections in a number of courts show that the single most common reason for prosecutors to reject cases is because of "evidence problems." For example, in Los Angeles, of all the cases rejected, 70 percent were rejected because of this fact. The problem, however, is that this large research undertaking did not clearly define "evidence problems." It could have—in fact it undoubtedly did—include "prior relationships," "victim and witness problems," and similar situations all grouped into the category of "evidence problems."[6]

Plea bargaining is another probable reason why so many charges are reduced at this stage. The decision by the prosecutor even to consider this option may be determined from the facts uncovered in the screening and the reliability of the victim, witnesses, and other factors. In its most basic form, plea bargaining is a form of negotiation between the defendant (more likely the defendant's attorney), the prosecutor, and the court, whereby the accused agrees to plead guilty in exchange for a reduction in the original charge, probation, or a reduced sentence. A New York City study found that of the 101,748 felony cases that came before the city's courts in one year, more than 80 percent were settled by the plea-bargaining process.[7] A similar study conducted in New York three years later found the rate to be 74 percent.[8] The fact that 90 percent of those who go beyond the formal accusation and detention stage (as shown in Figure 1.3) entered guilty pleas suggests that many of these pleas were a result of plea bargaining when one considers how few of the offenders who pleaded guilty to serious crimes were then imprisoned. But because of the complexity of the criminal justice system itself, there are still other reasons that bear on the poor arrest–detention statistic.

## ◻ PRINCIPLES OF CRIMINAL LAW

Our system of justice operates on two key principles of criminal law. The first is the presumption of innocence. This means that those accused of crimes are considered innocent until proved guilty. This is a fundamental assumption of our legal system that at least in theory is supposed to exist. Thus, the accused is entitled to all the rights of any citizen until the accused's guilt has been determined by a court of law or by the accused's acknowledgment that he or she did indeed commit the crime. Although it might be difficult for one to imagine the so-called "innocence" of a manacled, tough-looking, and hostile suspect who stands before the bar of justice clad in a bright orange jail-issue jumpsuit, this is the way the law, at least, must look upon the accused. The second principle is the burden of proof, which in criminal cases means that the government must prove "beyond a reasonable doubt" that the suspect committed the crime. Because criminal prosecutions carry the penalty of imprisonment and even death in some cases, the state is given a difficult burden. Nonetheless, it is a bedrock of our social—and through it, our legal—system.

*Presumption of innocence and the burden of proof*

Theoretically, determining guilt is a process involving arguing the issues of fact or law in the particular case; in actual practice, however, this seldom happens. In many cases, the existence of guilt is supported by sufficient evidence; in others, where the issues of fact are such that the accused may or may not be found guilty beyond a reasonable doubt, concessions are worked out that may result in a reduced charge if the accused agrees to plead guilty.[9] In many criminal prosecutions, the main question becomes: Is there enough evidence to convict? Obviously, if there is ample evidence to convict, the prosecution is not interested in bargaining; by the same token, if there is not enough evidence to convict, there is no need for the accused to risk the prospects for a definite acquittal. It is in the gray area between certain guilt and probable innocence that plea bargaining takes place.

## ◻ CRIME AND THE CRIMINAL JUSTICE SYSTEM: RISING COSTS AND DIMINISHING PUBLIC CONFIDENCE

The cost to society of crime and the administration of justice cannot be accurately measured. There are simply too many hidden costs that escape any attempt to measure them. For example, in the case of crimes, many offenses are undetected. This is certainly a major limitation. There is also the immeasurable cost of pain and suffering and the anguish crime victims, their families and friends suffer. There are also the "hidden costs" associated with certain types of criminal activity. This would include organized crime's involvement in legitimate enterprises, unscrupulous business practices that gouge the consumer, and the higher prices that consumers must pay for goods and services as a result of employee theft. And what about such factors as lower property values because of high levels of neighborhood

*The "costs" of the administration of justice*

crime and the "cost" of having to alter one's life-style because of the fear of being a crime victim? These are just some of the more obvious costs, which at best, we can only roughly estimate.

Just as crime itself has many "hidden costs" so does the actual administration of justice. The cost of bringing an offender to justice varies a great deal and includes many different costs. Consider the occurrence of a typical serious crime and the arrest and processing of the accused through the system. What we are paying for includes such things as the police investigation of the criminal event, the arrest of the offender, and the appearance of the police in court (often on overtime) to testify as witnesses. There is also the cost of the prosecutor's office to investigate, prepare, and present the case in court. We must also pay for public defenders or court-appointed defense attorneys to represent defendants who are without financial resources and who have been charged with a crime. Judges and juries must be paid to hear the cases, consider the evidence, preside over trials, render verdicts, and sentence the convicted offender. State identification and information bureaus must exist and their staffs paid to check fingerprints and criminal histories of defendants. Probation departments must be staffed to prepare presentence investigation reports, conduct investigations, and assist the courts. There is also the need to maintain local jails to house defendants who are held in pretrial custody pending trial. Now imagine this occurring throughout all fifty states and at the level of the federal government.

Although there are many limitations on our ability to gather and pinpoint costs associated with crime and the administration of justice, research is beginning to give us a clearer picture of crime and the administrative costs of the justice system.[10] It should also be recognized that while the nation spends a great deal on crime problems and the administration of justice, it still is a relatively small percentage of overall government spending. In fact, the federal government's data show that in 1985 slightly less than 3 percent of all government spending—federal, state, and local—was for criminal and civil justice.[11] Justice expenditures, although estimated to be nearly $50 billion that year, ranked significantly behind government's insurance trust expenditures (e.g., social security, unemployment compensation, public employee retirement, etc.) and other areas such as defense spending, education, interest on government debt, welfare, and health services. And it is no different today. Although some slight adjustments can be made in the relative levels of spending among these various categories, it is safe to assume that today this relationship and ranking would generally still be the same.

Spending for justice activities also varies by level of government. Because the administration of justice has traditionally been a function of local governments, this is where we might expect spending levels for these activities to be the highest. This seems to be the case. County governments spend an average of 13 percent of their budgets for justice activities. They are closely followed by cities that spend 10 percent of their overall budgets for justice. States come in at 5 percent, and the federal government spends only about 1 percent of its budget on criminal and civil justice costs.[12] In recent years, the states and the counties have been taking over more of the expenditures from city governments as state and county governments expand their civil and criminal justice programs. Figure 1.5 shows some of these changes over time as a relative percentage of all justice expenditures by level of government. Particularly noteworthy is the decrease in spending by city governments and the corresponding increases by states and county governments.

**Justice spending by levels of government**

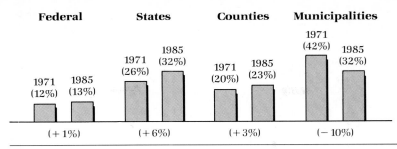

Federal    States    Counties    Municipalities

1971 (12%)    1985 (13%)    (+1%)
1971 (26%)    1985 (32%)    (+6%)
1971 (20%)    1985 (23%)    (+3%)
1971 (42%)    1985 (32%)    (−10%)

Relative percentage of criminal and civil justice expenditures by governments, 1971 to 1985. (*Source:* U.S. Department of Justice, Bureau of Justice Statistics, *Report to the Nation on Crime and Justice*, 2nd ed. (Washington, D.C.: U.S. Government Printing Office, March 1988), p. 116.)

FIGURE **1.5**

The levels of government also differ significantly in allocation of their justice monies. This reflects the types of traditional services provided by the various government levels. For instance, cities spend the bulk of their justice dollars for police protection, and this is particularly true given the size of the city. Per capita (per person) police expenditures increase drastically with city size. Cities of over 500,000 spend almost twice as much per resident of the city for police protection than do cities of less than 50,000.[13] States, on the other hand, spend more than half their justice dollars on corrections such as prisons. In fact, by the late 1980s the fifty state governments, on average, were spending about 4 percent of their total state budgets on corrections. It has been the "growth industry" of state governments in recent years; correctional institutions and programs have been the single fastest growing state government expenditure area in many states.

Counties, on the other hand, spend most of their justice budget on the courts. Although spending by the counties for courts, prosecution, legal services, and public defense is significant, these particular services do not dominate county justice spending to the extent that police protection dominates municipal spending or corrections dominates state spending. This is because the counties must also provide police services such as the sheriff's department as well as maintain some forms of correctional institutions such as county jails.

Looking at the national picture, police services account for nearly one-half of all justice expenditures. Figure 1.6 shows the breakdown by category and by level of government in each category. Regions and states also differ significantly in how much they spend on a per capita basis for justice expenditures. Areas such as the Northeast lead the country and are closely followed by the west. The South and the Midwest significantly trail the other two regions. There is no ready explanation for these differences. It may be because certain regions and states have a more serious crime problem or that they are more concerned about crime and are willing to spend more tax dollars to fight crime. In this way, a striking fact is found: States with the highest recorded levels of reported crime are also generally those with the highest expenditures for the justice system. Such states as New York, California, and Nevada, which have high recorded crime levels, spend about three times more per capita on criminal justice functions than do such states as Mississippi, Arkansas, or West Virginia. It may also include the fact that some states are more wealthy than others and can afford spending more tax dollars on the administration of

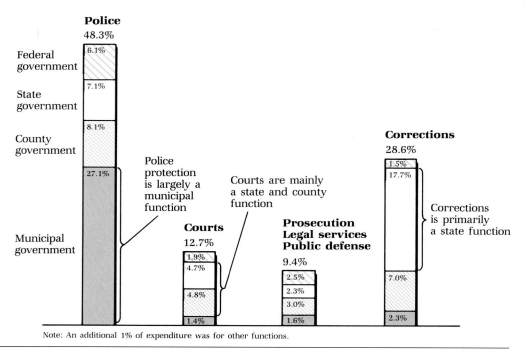

**Police**
48.3%

Federal government — 6.1%

State government — 7.1%

County government — 8.1%

Municipal government — 27.1%

Police protection is largely a municipal function

**Courts**
12.7%
- 1.9%
- 4.7%
- 4.8%
- 1.4%

Courts are mainly a state and county function

**Prosecution Legal services Public defense**
9.4%
- 2.5%
- 2.3%
- 3.0%
- 1.6%

**Corrections**
28.6%
- 1.5%
- 17.7%
- 7.0%
- 2.3%

Corrections is primarily a state function

Note: An additional 1% of expenditure was for other functions.

FIGURE **1.6** Criminal justice spending by category and level of government, 1985. [*Source:* Bureau of Justice Statistics, *Justice Expenditure and Employment, 1985* (Washington, D.C.: U.S. Department of Justice, March 1987).]

justice. Figure 1.7 shows state and local per capita criminal justice expenditures for the nation.

**Paying the people in the system**

Finally, criminal and civil justice is a highly "personnel-intensive" activity. For example, nearly three-fourths of state and local justice dollars go to pay salaries of those associated with the criminal and civil justice system.[14] Table 1.2 shows the average annual salary in the years indicated for the various actors within the system. It is obvious that should more recent data be available, the salaries would have improved since then. As might be expected, judges have the highest salaries of criminal and civil justice employees, while police and correctional officers have the lowest. Of course, such salaries are the "average" throughout the nation and will vary greatly among states. In the case of certain personnel such as local police officers and probation personnel, salary variations also will exist among local communities in the same state.

## THE STUDY OF CRIMINAL JUSTICE: A FASCINATING SUBJECT

By now we can see that the process of administering criminal justice is a very broad, complex area of study. More than that, it is a fascinating area of academic inquiry touched by the mystique of crime and criminals. It is also one of the most important social issues of our time or any time in history.

**The administration of justice as a critical social issue**

In fact, it may well be the most important mirror of society. With the possible exception of how a society chooses its leaders, no other human activity demon-

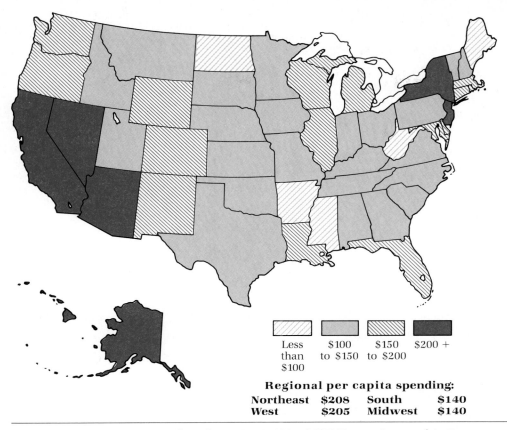

Regional per capita spending:

| Northeast | $208 | South | $140 |
|-----------|------|---------|------|
| West | $205 | Midwest | $140 |

State and local per capita expenditure for justice activities (1985) [*Source:* Bureau of Justice Statistics, *Justice Expenditure and Employment, 1985* (Washington, D.C.: U.S. Department of Justice, March 1987).] FIGURE **1.7.**

strates more clearly the values, attitudes, civility, and character of a nation than how it administers its criminal justice process. In recent years, this relationship has increasingly been recognized by a broad range of disciplines and scholars who have turned their attention to examining the criminal justice system of the United States and other nations. Many specialists have contributed and are continuing to contribute to a better understanding of crime and how we respond to it: Sociologists, political scientists, legal scholars, psychologists, anthropologists, and economists are busily engaged in examining the system. Their findings will add to the already growing and dynamic character of this field of inquiry.

## AN INTRODUCTION TO CRIMINAL JUSTICE

This introduction is intended to serve as a frame of reference for the chapters that follow. The material that follows will fill in this general overview in a series of gradual steps, each designed to build on the preceding step. We examine such basic concerns as the theory and development of law, the nature of crime, and the

## TABLE 1.2  Average Annual Salaries for Criminal and Civil Justice Employees

**Average Annual Salary (There are jurisdictions where the salaries are higher or lower than these averages)**

Law enforcement officers (1985 and 1986)

| | |
|---|---|
| City police officer (entry level) | $18,913 |
| City police officer (maximum) | $24,243 |
| City police chief | $33,158 |
| County sheriff patrol officer | Not available |
| State trooper (entry level) | $18,170 |
| State trooper (maximum) | $28,033 |
| Deputy U.S. marshal | $19,585 |
| U.S. border patrol agent | $23,058 |
| U.S. immigration inspector | $24,719 |
| U.S. immigration agent | $34,259 |
| Federal drug agent | $36,973 |
| FBI agent | $40,321 |

Prosecutors (1986)

| | |
|---|---|
| State and local prosecution personnel | Not available |
| Federal prosecutor | $53,027 |

Defenders (1986)

| | |
|---|---|
| State and local defense personnel | Not available |
| Federal defender | $43,582 |

Court personnel (1986 and 1987)

| | |
|---|---|
| State court administrator | $59,257 |
| State general jurisdiction trial court judge | $60,697 |
| State intermediate appellate court justice | $67,172 |
| State associate supreme court justice | $67,434 |
| State supreme court justice | $70,161 |
| U.S. Magistrate | $72,500 |
| U.S. Bankruptcy Court Judge | $72,500 |
| U.S. Court of Claims Judge | $82,500 |
| U.S. Court of International Trade Judge | $89,500 |
| U.S. District (trial) Court Judge | $89,500 |
| U.S. Circuit (appellate) Court Judge | $95,000 |
| U.S. Supreme Court Associate Justice | $110,000 |
| U.S. Supreme Court Chief Justice | $115,000 |

Correctional officers (adult facilities, 1986)

| | |
|---|---|
| Local jail officer (entry level) | $16,939 |
| State correctional officer (entry level) | $14,985 |
| State correctional officer (maximum) | $16,427 |
| State director of corrections | $59,947 |
| Federal correctional officer | $22,857 |

Probation and parole officers (adult clientele, 1986 and 1987)

| | |
|---|---|
| Local probation officer | Not available |
| State probation officer (entry level) | $19,402 |
| State parole officer (entry level) | $19,986 |
| State chief probation officer | $28,600 |
| State chief parole officer | $31,233 |
| State parole board member | $43,429 |
| State parole board chairman | $46,100 |
| Federal probation officer (entry level) | $22,458 |
| Federal parole case analyst | $22,458–42,341 |
| Federal parole hearing examiner | $38,727–59,488 |
| Federal regional probation/parole administrator | $53,830–69,976 |
| U.S. Parole Commissioner | $72,500 |

*Source:* U.S. Department of Justice, Bureau of Justice Statistics, *Report to the Nation on Crime and Justice,* 2nd ed. (Washington, D.C.: U.S. Government Printing Office, March 1988), p. 126.

## THE HIGH SCHOOL FOR
## LAW ENFORCEMENT AND CRIMINAL JUSTICE

Teenagers in Houston, Texas, are the first in the country to have a special Magnet high school that specializes in training students for criminal justice careers and prepares them for college-level training in the academic area of criminal justice. This is no vocational training program for academic underachievers. Since its inception in 1978, the school has been a leader among Houston's senior high schools in the results attained on academic achievement tests. The teachers in the school have also won awards for their students' scholastic achievements.

The program began in 1978 on three separate campuses as cooperative efforts between the Houston School District, the Mayor of the City of Houston, and the Houston Police Department. In 1980 the school was consolidated and expanded to include grades 9-12. The campus facility includes labs in microcomputers, chemistry, physics, and biology and a special science and mathematics resource center. Of special interest is a combined general purpose and law library, crime lab, mock courtroom, media center, criminal investigation facility, foreign language laboratory, gymnasium, exercise facilities, firearms range, and jogging trail.

The school provides students with the usual coursework supplemented with special courses for students who are interested in policework, court reporting, careers in the legal profession, and in such areas as corrections, probation and parole, criminology, private and industrial security, and social work. Many of the senior class students serve paid part-time internships with the Houston Police Department as police aides or in other criminal justice agencies in the metropolitan area.

An important component of the Houston educational program is career awareness preparation. Frequent appearances and discussions with criminal justice officials and seminar-type sessions acquaint students with the issues and problems faced by those who administer the criminal justice system. This blends the students' academic coursework with the views and insights of those in the field. Because of its success, the business and professional communities of Houston and the Harris County area have enthusiastically added their support to the school.

special problems in the administration of today's system of criminal justice. This leads to a detailed discussion of each individual component of the criminal justice process and how each developed, presently operates, and what changes are occurring in each—from the police, through the courts, into corrections, and concluding with the juvenile justice system.

## SUMMARY

The study of the administration of criminal justice borrows heavily from disciplines such as law, sociology, political science, psychology, anthropology, and history. The criminal justice system and its component agencies are guided by the standards imposed on them by a free society. Because of its interrelationship with other social institutions, both past and present, the criminal justice process cannot be studied as an isolated entity.

The primary purpose of the criminal justice system is to protect the collective and individual members of a society. The system also functions to maintain the existing order, which is crucial to the stability of an organized society. Within these two major goals are several subgoals such as the prevention and suppression of crime, the review of the legality of these efforts, the adjudicatory determination of those accused of crimes, and the correction by socially approved means of those who violate the criminal laws.

The criminal justice system consists of three major components—law enforcement, courts, and corrections—and the specialized auxiliary services of probation, parole, and the juvenile justice system. Each performs specific functions, yet all contribute in their own ways to the major goals of the overall system.

The criminal justice process is beset with growing conflict, particularly in the past several years, over philosophical differences in how best to attain the goals of the system. This conflict centers around the so-called arguments over the due process versus crime control models. This argument is of particular significance today as the specter of large government grows, which might raise concerns for the rights of the individual.

Those who criticize the due process model of criminal justice administration often point to the so-called funnel effect of the process as an example of justice denied. Although our insistence that due process rights be afforded those charged with crimes might be partially the reason for the effect, it is not the sole cause. The criminal justice system operates with a great deal of necessary discretion, and choices are made at critical decision points that result in those accused of crimes being filtered out at such critical stages. Yet the alternatives to the due process model may, in the long run, be even worse for society's well-being than the present system. This is one of the most vexatious problems that must be considered as we work to reform the overall process in the years ahead.

Finally, we saw how funding levels for the administration of justice are distributed among the various functions and among the various levels of government, regions, and states throughout the country. While some consistencies exist, such as municipalities among all levels of government devoting the largest percentage of their fiscal resources to the administration of justice, this seems to be changing. We also saw that various levels of government typically fund different aspects of the criminal justice system and that total public spending for justice activities varies greatly among the states.

## REVIEW QUESTIONS

1. What are the primary goals of the criminal justice system?
2. What are the secondary goals of the system?
3. Name the major components of the criminal justice system and briefly describe the function of each department.
4. Name the auxiliary functions of the criminal justice system and briefly describe their functions.
5. How do the two models of criminal justice— crime control and due process—differ? In what ways are they similar?

6. Trace the major steps of a criminal case through the criminal justice system.
7. Discuss the various points of discretion that exist in the administration of justice.
8. What are some of the possible reasons for the case-attrition or "funnel effect" of justice?
9. Discuss the issue of juvenile involvement in crime.
10. What principles of criminal law guide American jurisprudence?
11. What differences exist in spending for justice activities?

## DISCUSSION QUESTIONS

1. What obstables stand in the way of attaining the goals of the criminal justice system?
2. Is the criminal justice system a true system or a collection of unrelated parts?
3. Which of the two criminal justice models—crime control or due process—more accurately fits our system of criminal justice?

4. How might one go about making the criminal justice system more efficient?
5. What factors cause the so-called "funnel effect" of justice?
6. Discuss the issue of juvenile involvement in crime.
7. Should the federal government and the states devote more money to the administration of justice? If so, what are your specific recommendations?

## SUGGESTED ADDITIONAL READINGS

Bent, Allen E. *The Politics of Law Enforcement*. Lexington, Mass.: Lexington Books, 1974.

Boland, B., et al., *Prosecution of Felony Arrests—1982*.

Washington, D.C.: U.S. Department of Justice, Bureau of Justice Statistics, 1987.

Bureau of Justice Statistics. *U.S. Department of Justice,*

Report to the Nation on Crime and Justice, 2nd ed. Washington, D.C.: U.S. Government Printing Office, March 1988.

Chaiken, M., and J. Chaiken. *Who Gets Caught Doing Crime?* Washington, D.C.: U.S. Department of Justice— Bureau of Justice Statistics, 1985.

Committee for Economic Development. *Reducing Crime and Assuring Justice.* New York: CED, June 1972.

Culbertson, R., and R. Weisheit (eds.) *Order Under Law,* 3rd ed. Prospect Heights, Ill.: Waveland Press, 1988.

DeWolf, Lotan H. *Crime and Justice in America: A Paradox of Conscience.* New York: Harper & Row, 1975.

Feeley, Malcolm. *Court Reform on Trial: Why Simple Solutions Fail.* New York: Basic Books, 1983.

Forst, Brian. *What Happens After Arrest? A Court Perspective of Police Operations in the District of Columbia.* Washington, D. C.: Institute for Law and Social Research, 1977.

Hyman, Harold M., and William M. Wiecek. *Equal Justice Under Law.* New York: Harper & Row, 1982.

Misner, G. E., ed. *Criminal Justice Studies—Their Transdisciplinary Nature.* St. Louis, Mo.: C.V. Mosby Co., 1981.

Neubauer, David. *Criminal Justice in Middle America.* Morristown, N.J.: General Learning Press, 1974.

Petersilia, Joan. *The Influence of Criminal Justice Research.* Santa Monica, Calif.: Rand Corporation, 1987.

Quinney, Richard. *Class, State and Crime.* New York: David McKay, 1977.

Saunders, William B., and Howard C. Daudistel, eds. *The Criminal Justice Process.* New York: Praeger, 1976.

Silberman, Charles E. *Criminal Violence, Criminal Justice.* New York: Vintage Books, 1978.

Torbet, P. M. *Organization and Administration of Juvenile Services: Probation, Aftercare and State Delinquent Institutions.* Pittsburgh, Pa.: National Center for Juvenile Justice, 1987.

Viano, Emilio, and Alvin W. Cohn. *Social Problems and Criminal Justice.* Chicago: Nelson-Hall, 1977.

Wilson, James Q., ed. *Crime and Public Policy.* San Francisco: ICS Press, 1983.

Wilson, James Q. *Thinking About Crime.* New York: Basic Books, 1975.

## NOTES

1. Herbert L. Packer. *The Limits of the Criminal Sanctions* (Stanford, Calif.: Stanford University Press, 1968).

2. On these general issues, see: Thomas Y. Davies, "Do Criminal Due Process Principles Make a Difference? A Review of McBarnet's Conviction: Law, the State and the Construction of Justice," *American Bar Foundation Research Journal* 1 (Winter 1982): 247–268; and Hans Zeisel, "The Disposition of Felony Arrests," *American Bar Foundation Research Journal* 2 (Spring 1981): 407–462.

3. There are some exceptions. For example, some states have youthful offender statutes that may, in some cases, extend the jurisdiction of the juvenile court over a youth beyond the statutorily prescribed age of seventeen or eighteen.

4. Vera Institute of Justice, *Felony Arrests: Their Prosecution and Disposition in New York City's Courts* (New York: The Vera Institute, 1977).

5. Ibid., pp. 19–20; see also U.S. Department of Justice, *Offender-Based Transaction Statistics* (Washington, D.C.: U.S. Government Printing Office, 1975).

6. B. Boland, The Prosecution of Felony Arrests (Washington, D.C.: INSLAW, Inc., 1983), as reported in Bureau of Criminal Justice Statistics, *Report to the Nation on Crime and Justice* (Washington, D.C.: U.S. Department of Justice, October 1983).

7. Aryeh Neier, *Crime and Punishment: A Radical Solution* (New York: Stein and Day, 1976), p. 156.

8. Vera Institute, *Felony Arrests*, p. 134.

9. Frank W. Miller, *Prosecution: The Decision to Charge a Suspect with a Crime* (Boston: Little, Brown, 1969).

10. Bureau of Justice Statistics, *Report to the Nation on Crime and Justice*, 2nd ed. (Washington, D.C.: U.S. Department of Justice, March 1988), p. 115.

11. *Ibid.*

12. "City Police Expenditures: 1946–85" compiled from annual U.S. Census Bureau surveys of governmental finance available from the National Criminal Justice Archive, Inter-University Consortium for Political and Social Research, University of Michigan.

13. Bureau of Justice Statistics, *Report to the Nation, op. cit.*, p. 126.

14. *Ibid.*

CHAPTER **2**

# Crime, Law, and Legal Terminology

## O B J E C T I V E S

**After reading this chapter, the student should be able to:**

Explain the idea of elements of a crime.
Discuss intent.
Discuss theories of crime causation.
Explain inchoate offenses, identify some important crimes against the person and their characteristics,
and be familiar with the classification of crimes against property and their characteristics.
Explain the origins of criminal law.
Discuss the issue of criminal responsibility and the problems associated with the so-called insanity plea.
Define the following:
  arrest
  arrest warrant
  search warrant
  subpoena
  writ of habeas corpus

## I M P O R T A N T   T E R M S

Elements
Intent
Biological school
Psychological school
Sociological school
Economic theory of crime
Multifactor school
Felonies
Misdemeanors
Inchoate offenses
Attempt
Conspiracy

Crimes against the person (violent crimes)
  homicide
  rape
  robbery
  assault
Crimes against property (nonviolent crimes)
  burglary
  larceny
  motor vehicle theft
  arson

English common law
Federal and state constitutions
Statute
Stare decisis
Criminal responsibility
M'Naghten rule
Durham rule
Substantial capacity test
Arrest
Arrest warrant
Search warrant
Subpoena
Writ of habeas corpus
Venue
Bail
Extradition

This chapter looks at the definition of crime and the origins of criminal law. It then examines briefly some major theories that have attempted to explain the causes of crime. In the remainder of the chapter, specific crimes and their characteristics are discussed (Table 2.1) and a few of the major legal documents commonly used in the administration of justice are illustrated.

## ELEMENTS OF CRIME

A crime has been defined as a voluntary and intentional violation by a legally competent person of a legal duty that commands or prohibits an act for the protection of society. A crime is punishable by judicial proceedings in the name of the state.[1] From this legal definition, a number of things are apparent. First, the act must be voluntary. Thus, if the particular criminal act can be shown to be involuntary, such as when an individual is forced to commit a criminal act against his or her will, the person cannot be found guilty of the crime. The questions that must be answered in such circumstances are these: Did the offender actually act involuntarily, and what circumstances brought about this involuntary act? If, for example, a person was forced to participate in a crime at gunpoint, he or she committed the crime involuntarily and cannot be found guilty. In such cases, it must be demonstrated that the person's fear was justified and resulted in the individual committing the crime.

**What constitutes a crime**

For an act to be a crime, it must also be intentional. Thus, otherwise criminal acts that occur by accident generally are not considered crimes.

An act, in order to be considered a crime, must also be committed by a legally competent person. By law, certain categories of people are considered incompetent to commit crimes—for example, someone who was "insane" at the time of the act or someone very young; the law views the acts committed by such persons as not being voluntary and intentional because they are mentally incapable of comprehending the nature of their behavior.

The definition of a crime also indicates that behavior that constitutes a crime can be either an act of commission or an act of omission. One is guilty of committing a crime by doing something that the law says one should *not* do, as well as not doing what the law says one *must* do. In this latter case, not filing an income tax return as required by law would be a crime of omission. At this point, a fundamental requirement of criminal law should be explained. Any act of commission or omission, before it can constitute a crime, must be considered unlawful by statute *at the time that the act is committed.* For example, if you committed an act that at the time of its commission was not illegal, you could not be charged with a crime if the act was made a crime by law at a later date. Such laws are called *ex post facto* (after the fact) laws and are forbidden by the U.S. Constitution.[2] Thus, the criminal law cannot be applied retroactively to charge persons for criminal acts that at the time of commission were not prohibited by law.

**Ex post facto**

Finally, a crime is an act that threatens the welfare of society and is punishable by judicial proceedings in the name of the state. Crime is therefore considered to be an act against the collective well-being of society. In a theoretical and legal sense, a crime is more than merely the act of an offender directed against an innocent victim; the victim represents society itself. This is one of the major distinctions in the law between criminal law and civil law. In civil law, in which someone brings

**Criminal versus civil law**

## TABLE 2.1 What Are the Characteristics of the Most Common Serious Crimes?

| Crime | Definition | Facts |
|-------|------------|-------|
| **Homicide** | Causing the death of another person without legal justification or excuse | • Homicide is the least frequent violent crime.<br>• 93% of the victims were slain in single-victim situations.<br>• At least 55% of the murderers were relatives or acquaintances of the victim.<br>• 24% of all murders occurred or were suspected to have occurred as the result of some felonious activity. |
| **Rape** | Unlawful sexual intercourse with a female, by force or without legal or factual consent | • Most rapes involved a lone offender and a lone victim.<br>• About 36% of the rapes were committed in the victim's home.<br>• 58% of the rapes occurred at night, between 6 P.M. and 6 A.M. |
| **Robbery** | Unlawful taking or attempted taking of property that is in the immediate possession of another, by force or threat of force | • Robbery is the violent crime that typically involves more than one offender (in about half of all cases).<br>• Slightly less than half of all robberies involved the use of a weapon.<br>• Less than 2% of the robberies reported to the police were bank robberies. |
| **Assault** | Unlawful intentional inflicting, or attempted inflicting, of injury upon the person of another. *Aggravated assault* is the unlawful intentional inflicting of serious bodily injury or unlawful threat or attempt to inflict bodily injury or death by means of a deadly or dangerous weapon with or without actual infliction of injury. *Simple assault* is the unlawful intentional inflicting of less than serious bodily injury without a deadly or dangerous weapon or an attempt or threat to inflict bodily injury without a deadly or dangerous weapon. | • Simple assault occurs more frequently than aggravated assault.<br>• Assault is the most common type of violent crime. |

TABLE **2.1** (Continued)

| Crime | Definition | Facts |
|---|---|---|
| **Burglary** | Unlawful entry of any fixed structure, vehicle, or vessel used for regular residence, industry, or business, with or without force, with the intent to commit a felony or larceny. | • 42% of all household burglaries occurred without *forced* entry.<br>• In the burglary of more than 3 million American households, the offenders entered through an unlocked window or door or used a key (for example, a key "hidden" under a doormat).<br>• About 34% of the no-force household burglaries were known to have occurred between 6 A.M. and 6 P.M.<br>• Residential property was targeted in 67% of reported burglaries; nonresidential property accounted for the remaining 33%.<br>• Three-quarters of the nonresidential burglaries for which the time of occurrence was known took place at night. |
| **Larceny (theft)** | Unlawful taking or attempted taking of property other than a motor vehicle from the possession of another, by stealth, without force and without deceit, with intent to permanently deprive the owner of the property. | • Pocket picking and purse snatching most frequently occur inside nonresidential buildings or on street locations.<br>• Unlike most other crimes, pocket picking and purse snatching affect the elderly as much as other age groups.<br>• Most personal larcenies with contact occur during the daytime, but most household larcenies occur at night. |
| **Motor vehicle theft** | Unlawful taking or attempted taking of a self-propelled road vehicle owned by another, with the intent of depriving the owner of it permanently or temporarily. | • Motor vehicle theft is relatively well reported to the police because reporting is required for insurance claims and vehicles are more likely than other stolen property to be recovered.<br>• About three-fifths of all motor vehicle thefts occurred at night. |
| **Arson** | Intentional damaging or destruction or attempted damaging or destruction by means of fire or explosion of the property without the consent of the owner, or of one's own property or that of another by fire or explosives with or without the intent to defraud. | • Single-family residences were the most frequent targets of arson.<br>• More than 17% of all structures where arson occurred were not in use. |

*Sources:* Bureau of Justice Statistics, *Dictionary of Criminal Justice Data Terminology*, 1981; FBI, *Crime in America*, 1983; Bureau of Justice Statistics, *National Crime Survey*, 1981.

a lawsuit against another for damages, both parties in the case are viewed as private citizens. The party alleging damages and bringing suit is called the *plaintiff*, and the one from whom the damages are sought is called the *defendant*. The case is referred to by the names of the plaintiff and defendant, respectively, as in *Smith* v. *Brown*. In criminal cases, the government is referred to as the *prosecution* and the accused as the *defendant*. In criminal cases, the prosecution represents the people, and the case name reflects this, as in *United States* v. *Brown*, *People* v. *Smith*, or *Colorado* v. *Green*.

By law, every crime contains what are called *elements* of the offense. These elements are inherent in the specific legal definition of the crime. Before a person can be convicted of a crime, each of the following elements must be provided by the state:

1. The act
2. The intent
3. The concurrence of act and intent
4. The causation
5. The result[3]

For instance, looking at the legal definition of a crime given earlier, it is evident that before the government convicts someone of a crime, it must show (1) that an act was committed that, at the time of its commission, was prohibited, or that the accused failed to do something commanded by the law (the act); (2) that the accused did the act voluntarily and with full knowledge of what he or she was doing (the intent); (3) that the act resulted from the intent (the concurrence of act and intent); (4) that the act and the intent caused something to occur that was offensive to the law (causation); and (5) that it caused some harm to society (result).

A "coming together"

## ▢ CRIMINAL INTENT

Most of these elements of the law are fairly straightforward. For example, because every crime involves the commission or omission of an act, before the defendant in a criminal case can be found guilty of theft, there must be the actual taking of an object. In proving intent as an essential element of a crime, however, one enters into the gray area of criminal law. In criminal law, proving intent is more complicated because it demands an evaluation of the motive of the offender. The concept of intent is expressed in the Latin phrase *mens rea*, which means roughly that the law considers that the offender possessed the necessary intent as shown by his or her actions and by the common human experience.[4] For example, if a man commits a crime, it is assumed that he did so voluntarily, and because he did so voluntarily, he must also have intended to do so. The law then goes even one step further. Because it is presumed by the criminal's actions and our common experience that the crime was committed voluntarily, and thus intentionally and of free will, it is assumed that the act was committed *knowingly*.

Of course, the defendant in a criminal case can put into question this natural presumption of intent in various ways. The state may be able to show, for example, that the accused participated in a criminal act, but the accused may argue that by virtue of decreased mental reasoning capacity (e.g., insanity), he or she had impaired knowledge of the consequences of the act. Some states also permit the

Mens rea and its<br>underlying assumptions

consideration of "diminished capacity" as a partial defense. Although it does not have the significance of the insanity issue as it relates to the question of guilt, it is an issue the jury can consider as to the accused's state of mind at the time of the commission of the crime.

Two types of intent, *general intent* and *specific intent*, exist in our system of law.

## General Intent

General intent is considered to be present in the criminal's decision to commit an offense or deviate from standard conduct when that offense or deviation may expose members of the society at large to harm even without specific intent as to the object or consequences of such conduct.[5] In other words, behavior that does not conform to legal conduct is assumed to intend harmful consequences, whether the person actually intends harmful consequences or not. The most common example is drunk driving. Let us say that a woman operating an automobile while intoxicated strikes and kills a pedestrian or another motorist. Certainly, she did not "intend" the consequences of her act. However, under the principle of general intent, she would be charged with manslaughter or vehicular homicide. Her general criminal intent is based on the legal assumption that, first, she voluntarily became intoxicated and operated her car, which exposed others to harm. Second, there was foreseeable knowledge based on experience that the voluntary state of intoxication and the subsequent driving of an automobile in such a physical condition could conceivably result in injury or death to others. Thus, there exists general criminal intent, and the state does not have to prove that the individual had an actual intent to kill.

*Liability without specific intent*

## Specific Intent

Specific intent forms the basis for most crimes. Specific intent indicates that *before* the individual committed the act, he or she planned to carry out the offense. This specific intent exists as an element of all crimes except those that require only a showing of general intent. In rape, for example, the specific intent is to have carnal knowledge of a female who is not one's wife, against her will (this definition of rape has been rewritten in a number of states to delete the word *wife* and to include males as rape victims); in the case of theft, it is to take something of value from the true owner to permanently deprive the owner of his or her possession.

*The basis for most crimes*

 ## SEARCHING FOR THE CAUSES OF CRIME

Of course, there is no simple answer to the question of what causes crime. Attempts to explain the causative factors associated with crime, the characteristics of criminals, and society's response to crime and delinquency comprise the field of *criminology*.

Experts in criminology have studied the causes of crime from a number of different perspectives—sociology, law, psychology, psychiatry, anthropology, economics, political science, biology, and history. Traditionally, the study of crime causation focused on the fields of sociology, psychology, and psychiatry. During

*Criminology (definition)*

the past twenty years political scientists, political sociologists, and economists have become more active in this area. For instance the so-called *critical criminology* focuses on a Marxist perspective of society in which laws and the instruments of the administration of justice (the police, courts, corrections, etc.) are used by those in power for self-serving interests to maintain the status quo and to protect their interests from the have-nots.[6]

Although it is not possible for an introductory text to discuss all of the theories that have tried to explain crime, we can trace some of the major approaches and theories identified as milestones in the development of approaches to crime and criminological thought.

## ◻ HISTORICAL APPROACHES TO THE PROBLEM OF CRIME

In primitive societies, crime was attributed to the offender's "bad nature," and revenge was the motive in seeking redress. If someone was attacked, the victim, either alone or aided by family members or friends, would get even with the attacker.[7] Although this was a simple and expeditious solution, it led to lawlessness and blood-letting feuds.

Changing perceptions of crime, the criminal, and the legal system

The spread of religious ideas modified and extended the idea of revenge. In medieval times, criminal behavior was interpreted as an attack against the diety, which unless placated would bring great misfortunes such as flood, pestilence, and plague upon the individual and the community.[8] These feelings were further strengthened by beliefs that crime and the offender were manifestations of the devil. Thus, so "possessed," the individual not only had to pay a debt to society but also had to be reconciled with God. This, too, led to bloody examples of righteous retribution against the criminal.

By the Middle Ages, the state possessed established power. Crime then came to be viewed as an attack on the ruler, and severe punishments were imposed on those who would offend the "king's law."

In the eighteenth-century Age of Enlightenment, the bloody revenge that characterized earlier periods began to give way somewhat. By the end of the century, instead of severe physical punishment, more moderate means of correction were widely advocated. This was also accompanied by a legal shift in dealing with crime and offenders. By this time, crime was held to be an act against the public interest, and the administration of criminal justice had become a matter to be dealt with solely by the state.[9] Throughout Western Europe and the New World, reformers began calling for changes in the administration of criminal law. Of special concern was the protection of the rights of the individual against the arbitrary actions of the courts. Such reforms came to be widely implemented.

Although these reforms changed perceptions about the role of the state, procedural law, and the administration of justice, they had little impact on how the law viewed human behavior as it related to crime. Crime was conceived in purely legal terms: Punishment was regarded as a just response to guilt, not as a corrective or rehabilitative measure. The law (and the courts) operated entirely on the interpretation of the written law. The courts handed out punishment under the "free will" doctrine—that is, the assumption that the offender chooses to commit crime by his or her own free will.

The so-called "free will" doctrine has been hotly debated over the years. The argument against such a view says that criminal behavior, like all forms of behavior, is too complex to be merely ascribed to choice. Instead, criminal behavior is often the result of complex forces that are determined by the interrelationship of social factors and the characteristics of the individual. The "free will" doctrine

While it is true that viewing crime as the result of free will is perhaps too simple a view, rejecting free will as an explanation complicates the issue. When the idea of free will is rejected, the problem becomes one of explaining how these complex interactions result in crime and how society is then to deal with crime and its causes. Acknowledging that the criminal may not be totally responsible for his or her actions makes it more difficult to ascribe blame and punish the offender. It is far easier to view the criminal as someone who operates with free will; in this way it is much easier to punish the offender.

## The Origins of Modern Criminology

During the nineteenth century, the origins of modern criminological thought began. This was a period when certain notable figures attempted to discover specific causes of crime.

The first of these was a physician, Cesare Lombroso (1836–1909). During his service with the Italian army, he became interested in the anatomical characteristics of criminals. After examining hundreds of convicts, Lombroso concluded that particular biophysical characteristics were often found among criminals. He proposed that criminals bore certain atavistic physical characteristics—for example, low foreheads, receding chins, an abundance of wrinkles, and protruding ears—that suggested they were throwbacks to primitive humans.[10] Although Lombroso's ideas have no credibility today, they did mark a major attempt to study the factors associated with criminal behavior. The "holy three"

The next major contributor was Raffaele Garofalo (1852–1934). He contributed to the development of criminology through a discussion of many problems that are still applicable today, such as restitution to victims of crimes and the need for international efforts to combat crime. He rejected the idea that people commit crime by virtue of "free will"—at least as it was commonly defined by law. Criminals, he believed, lacked pity and probity, which he saw as a reflection of the moral sense of the community; they thus possessed a moral freedom to commit crime that, to Garofalo, denied the efficacy of the law in deterring potential offenders.

A disciple of Lombroso, Enrico Ferri (1856–1928) was the most modern of the three. Ferri saw crime as the product of geographical, anthropological, psychological, and economic forces. The core of Ferri's thought involved the replacement of moral responsibility with "social accountability."[11] His recommendations were consistent with his political belief in using the state as an instrument of social reform. Ferri maintained that free trade and abolition of monopolies would reduce food prices and therefore the crime of smuggling. Similarly, he felt that lowering taxes and building public works projects would do more to improve the quality of life and to reduce crime than harsh criminal penalties. He espoused a sociological criminology and recommended that judges be trained in psychology and psychiatry to enable them to recognize criminal types.

During the late eighteenth to early nineteenth centuries, other important developments took place. John Casper Lavater (1741–1801) proposed that biological factors *caused* individuals to behave differently. This was the so-called science of physiognomy, which purported to be able to judge a person's character solely by observing his or her outward appearance. Phrenology, the determination of one's characteristics by the shape of the skull and by the nature and location of "bumps" on the skull, also became popular as an explanation for behavior. During this period, the science of statistics also began. Several noted statisticians suggested that this science be used to measure and classify crimes in a way not unlike the use to which we put statistics and crime analysis today.

## ☐ MODERN THEORIES OF CRIME

Five major orientations have emerged in the last hundred years from attempts to explain crime. The *biological school* looks for the causes of crime in the criminal's physical characteristics. The *psychological school* seeks an answer to the problem of crime by studying the mental processes. The *sociological school* attempts to find the roots of criminality in the environment rather than in the individual. The relatively new *economic model* of crime sees the offender as someone who rationally commits crimes to satisfy certain personal economic needs. Finally, the *multifactor school* relates the causes of crime to a wide range of complex and multiple factors.

### The Biological School

The biological approach focuses on biological or anthropological explanations for crime. The idea underlying this approach is that the criminal is biologically different from normal human beings. Researchers for a number of years have been interested in the idea that certain biological characteristics make the criminal different from his noncriminal counterpart. The implication is then quite clear: This biological difference at least partly explains the reason for criminal behavior. Generally, the theories of the so-called biological explanation for crime fall into five areas: body types and physique; personality characteristics as determined by biological factors; abnormal chromosome makeup; genetic transmission; and IQ studies.[12]

Body types

The idea that physical characteristics in terms of body types and physique are related to criminal behavior is the oldest of the biological theories. Early research tried to establish the idea that individuals with certain physical characteristics were more predisposed to criminal behavior than persons with more "normal" physical attributes. Many such theories abound in this area. One of the favorite ways to "prove" such a theory was to compare the physical characteristics of criminals with noncriminals. It was claimed that certain characteristics—eye color, size of certain features, slope of the head, shape of the ears, and other physical attributes were more prevalent among criminals than noncriminals. For example, criminals were more likely to have a large-boned and muscular physique than their law-abiding counterparts.[13] These characteristics were also associated with personality characteristics, which implied a secondary reason for their behavior. For instance, the large-boned and muscular individual was seen as more aggressive, hedonistic, restless, adventuresome, and danger seeking.[14]

Personality theories

Personality theories recognize that personality traits are also heritable traits. These ideas are centered on the conclusion that the offender is more likely to exhibit such traits as impulsiveness, deficient emotional attachments and caring for others, indifference about the future, and aggressiveness. This can range from mild symptoms of these traits to seriously disturbed antisocial personalities or psychopathologies. Central to this idea is the belief—although it is not readily known to what degree—that these traits are genetically transmitted. Yet, the role of personality and the importance of genetic as opposed to environmental forming of personality characteristics is still unknown. Researchers have not been able to unravel all the aspects of personality let alone its relationship to criminal behavior.

One of the most popular biological explanations for crime has been the so-called XYY chromosome abnormality. While the sex-determining factor for females **Chromosomes and crime** is the XX pair of chromosomes, for the average man, it is an XY distribution. Certain

Among males who have been convicted of crimes, the XYY chromosome abnormality is disproportionately common. (Courtesy of Dr. Merlin Butler, Vanderbilt University)

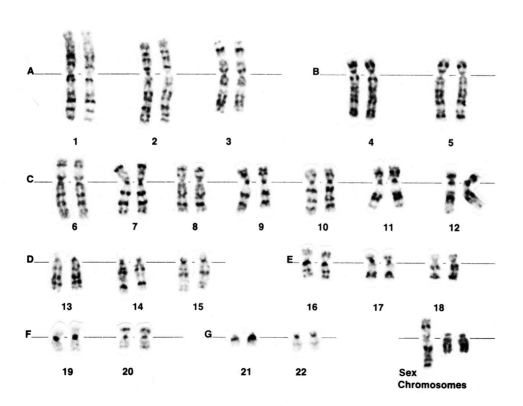

**CYTOGENETICS LABORATORY**
**Genetics Division/Pediatrics Department**
**Vanderbilt University**

PATIENT_____    DATE_____

LABORATORY NO._____    VUH NO. _____

SLIDE NO._____    PHOTO NO._____

INTERPRETATION____4 7, X Y Y_____

males, however, are found to possess an extra Y or male chromosome which gives them the XYY distribution. It is suggested that this particular phenomenon is especially prevalent among criminals.[15] It has been reported that men with this combination have a ten to twenty times greater tendency to break the law than do genetically normal men from comparable populations.[16] Such men also are taller than average and have other more male-pronounced characteristics. It is also suggested that such XYY men also evidence lower IQs. Although the XYY abnormality and its association with crime was particularly popular during the 1960s, and has enjoyed less attention today, it still is one of the more recent biological attempts to explain crime.

**Research involving twins**

Genetic transmission of criminal tendencies has in recent years focused on studies involving twins—both identical and fraternal. Identical twins are twins born of a single fertilized ovum, sharing identical genes. Fraternal twins are the result of two fertilized ova and have the same genetic overlap as ordinary sisters and brothers. Of course, identical twins are much more likely to share in similar attributes such as height, weight, and general appearance. They are also more likely to share in similar criminality.

An identical twin, as contrasted with a fraternal twin, with a criminal record implies approximately twice the likelihood of his or her twin having a criminal record. Identical twins are also more likely than fraternal twins to share in the frequency of criminal behavior. Genetic transmission of criminality has also been studied by looking at adoptions. European research among four thousand adopted boys also indicated that criminality among biological parents was more likely to be related to the subsequent criminal behavior of children than was the criminality of the adoptive parents.[17] The more serious an offender a biological parent was, the greater risk of criminality for his or her child, particularly for property crimes.[18] Children who had a criminal biological parent or parents and were placed at an early age in a noncriminal adopting home were more likely to be criminals than children from noncriminal biological parents who had criminal adopting parents. This raises fundamental questions about the age-old issue of biology versus environment as a major factor in what causes crime. Strikingly similar results also have been found in research among delinquent girls.[19]

**Crime and IQ**

Offender populations have also been studied in terms of their IQs. Generally, it has been found that while the normal average IQ for the general population is 100, the average IQ for offenders in institutions is between 91 and 93.[20] It is also suggested (although more evidence must still be gathered) that impulsive violent crimes and the opportunistic property crimes are most often committed by people in the low-normal and borderline retarded range.[21] A large body of evidence exists to suggest that biological parents have more to do with one's IQ than foster parents or where one is raised. Although intelligence can be affected by environment, biological factors seem to play an extraordinarily important role.

These undiscovered biological factors associated with crime may well become the single most fertile and interesting area of crime causation research. As scientists and geneticists begin understanding more about the biological factors and how these influence a host of human traits, a better picture of the elusive question of what may at least strongly contribute to crime will emerge. The biological factor can then be examined in conjunction with other theories—social, psychological, and even economic—to develop better explanations and to unravel many of the mysteries that are now only speculative.

## The Psychological School

To the adherents of the psychological or psychiatric school, the causes of crime are at least partly explained through the study of the psychological processes—the not yet understood complexities of human reasoning and motivation that underlie behavior. The sweep of this approach is very broad. Crime is viewed as another form of human behavior. The question then becomes the role of mental processes in contributing to this criminal behavior. Out of this grew the terms *psychopath* or *sociopath* to categorize certain type offenders. These terms are themselves determined by certain psychological characteristics of the individual. Great names such as Carl Jung and Sigmund Freud were the epoch-making theorists in this field.[22]

*The psychological aspects of behavior*

In recent years, studies that have examined defects in the nervous system, neurasthenia, and inadequate mental ability have further broadened this approach. As we saw in the discussion of the biological approach to crime, the relationship of certain biological determinants and their possible effect on what can be broadly called psychological processes have added to the scope of inquiry.

## The Sociological School

The sociological school, which contends that the criminal is a product of society, focuses on the interrelationships among people and calls attention to the fact that persistent deviance typically requires and receives group support and that most deviant behavior is culturally patterned. Advocates of the sociological approach to crime causation reject the idea that crime can be fully understood by the analysis of offenders as individuals. In this approach, the analysis is extended to include the community, social institutions, and group relationships that shape both criminal and noncriminal behavior. Instead of regarding offenders generally as biologically and psychologically abnormal, criminality is explained as a product of learned behavior in the course of social interaction. Sociologists regard criminals as "normal" in that their personalities were developed through the same processes by which noncriminal personalities were developed.[23]

*Social interaction and learning*

## The Economic Theory of Crime

In recent years economists have tried to explain the causes of crime based on the idea of the "rational man" concept and other factors associated with the ideas of economic choice. Economists assume that individuals have needs that they attempt to satisfy. Individuals then make a rational choice among alternatives that will permit them to satisfy these needs.[24] Economists do not deny that these choices may be socially conditioned, but they are not interested in explaining what causes or forms these choices. In the case of an offender, the individual is first confronted with the question of how might I improve my welfare? He or she first makes the choice that it is more likely he or she can improve his or her welfare through illegitimate (criminal) means than by working at a legitimate activity such as a regular job to obtain legally what is valued. The individual also calculates the "benefits and costs" of committing the crime and receiving something he or she values (the benefit) versus the cost of being caught and punished for the act. Of course, both considerations are taken together when one contemplates crime.

*Rational choice*

The offender then is seen as a rational and calculating individual who weighs the benefits and costs associated with his or her behavior. Economic theory of crime causation has had particular appeal to conservatives and those who feel that "increasing" the costs associated with crime will cause crime levels to fall. For example, if we can increase the chances that a potential offender will be caught and punished for his or her crime, we have tipped the balance to the "cost" side of the offender's calculation. The same can be said for increasing the punishment imposed for committing the crime.

All theories of crime causation have their critics. The economic theory of crime, for example, has been attacked on the grounds that such a rational, calculating choice does not exist. Many crimes are simply committed on impulse, while the offender is under the influence of alcohol or narcotics, or as a result of opportunity coinciding with need.[25] It is also questioned whether one who is thinking about committing a crime has a realistic idea of the probability of being caught and punished.[26] There is also the argument that harsher sentences and more police officers per population, which are supposed to act as "cost" deterrents, have not been shown to be associated with reduced crime levels.[27]

### The Multifactor School

The multifactor approach to explaining criminal behavior is a synthesis of the biological, psychological, and sociological schools. Adherents of this approach attempt to reconcile the differing disciplines with the goal of developing an integrated theoretical understanding of crime.[28]

Multiple causes

The pioneers of the modern multifactor approach were such notables as Adolphe Prins, Franz von Liszt, and G. A. von Hamel. Together they held to the idea of multiple causation and made efforts to rationalize the discrepancies among the three major groups of single-factor theories. This school recognizes the complexity of crime-producing factors and their interrelatedness. In addition, the multifactor school attempts to develop general theories that integrate the various efforts of other theorists who have tried to explain the causes for crime.

Although concern with the factors that produce crime is not new, a great deal more research is needed before we can fully understand the complex nature of crime. Such work in criminology is now being undertaken throughout the world.

## ▣ CLASSIFICATION OF CRIMES

Crimes are generally classified according to their seriousness in three broad categories: *treason*, *felonies*, and *misdemeanors*. This classification of crimes developed in early England and was brought to America by our nation's early colonists, where it remains relatively unchanged today.

*Treason* was the most serious crime in the common law. At one time it was more personal in its application: a crime that was directed toward the person of the sovereign. Later, it was viewed as an offense that threatened the institutions of government and the national security.[29] Today, some legal scholars eschew treason as a separate crime; it is merely the most serious felony.

For students of criminal justice, the distinction between felonies and misdemeanors is the most important in modern criminal law. Generally, the states have adopted the old common law distinction for these crimes, which turns on the question of the penalty that can be imposed for their commission. A *felony* is usually Felony vs. misdemeanor defined as a criminal act that may be punishable by death or by imprisonment for a year or more. A *misdemeanor* is a crime punishable by imprisonment for less than a year. Modern state laws also provide that the amount of fine that can be levied for the commission of a crime will vary according to whether it is a felony or misdemeanor.

## Specific Criminal Offenses

State criminal codes generally list crimes by specific categories—for example, inchoate offenses, crimes against the person, crimes against property, crimes against public morality and decency, and crimes against public order and administration of justice. In modern society, distinct general classifications of crimes have developed, such as organized and white-collar crimes. These two categories may consist of the more traditional offenses included in crimes against the person or property, but they are distinguished by how they are committed and by whom.

It is not possible to provide in this text a description and definition of all the various types of crimes found in these categories. If you are interested, examine the criminal code of your own state. Remember that the definitions of crimes and their specific elements vary among states.

## Inchoate Offenses

Inchoate offenses are crimes defined as *acts that are only partially completed*. Somehow, circumstances intervened, preventing these acts from being carried to their conclusion. They are considered crimes because their design and purpose are criminal in nature.

The first such inchoate offense is an *attempt*. An attempt consists of a sub- Attempt (definition) stantial step toward the commission of a specific crime but the completed criminal act is not carried through. Merely preparing to commit a criminal act is usually not enough to be charged with attempt—there must be a substantial step taken toward conclusion. Usually, an attempt is one step less serious in terms of the punishment that could be imposed than if the offender had completed the crime. For example, if a state arranges its criminal code into various categories of serious felony crimes such as A, B, C, etc., and robbery is a class A felony, attempted robbery would be a class B felony.

The other important inchoate offense is *conspiracy*. This is the crime of un- Conspiracy (definition) lawfully entering into an agreement with one or more persons to commit a specific offense. At the common law, the state had only to show that two or more persons merely entered into an agreement to commit a crime. Today, modern statutes require additional proof beyond the agreement—an overt act toward the completion of the crime itself.[30] Once an agreement is entered into, each member of the conspiracy is equally liable for the acts of all other conspirators whether or not the person was part of the subsequent acts. The members are all guilty as long as the acts were committed to further the agreed-upon illegal enterprise.[31]

## ☐ CRIMES AGAINST THE PERSON (VIOLENT CRIMES)

We can define crimes against the person as offenses that have direct physical harm or injury done to a victim. This category of crime includes such offenses as homicide, rape, and assault. It also includes the crime of robbery because this offense involves the use of force or threat against a person. Although property crimes are committed much more frequently than crimes against the person, incarceration is much more likely to occur after conviction for a violent crime than for a property crime.

*Homicide* often stems from other crimes such as assault, robbery, rape, or burglary. While some homicides may be committed that have no motive other than the murder itself, such as a paid or contract killing, such homicides are infrequent.

**General classifications** Homicides are sometimes classified as *premeditated, instrumental*, and *impulsive*. A *premeditated* homicide is an illegal killing of a human being that results from a well-planned action. These premeditated murders are considered very serious in the eyes of the law. Another type of homicide that is thought of in the law as very serious is *instrumental* murder. For example, a burglar kills a household member during the commission of a burglary. What makes it instrumental is the fact that this type of homicide results from the planned burglary, and the murder of the innocent party is instrumental in carrying out the purpose of the burglary. These are also sometimes referred to as *felony murders*. These are unlawful killings of someone during the commission of a specific felony-type crime.

An *impulsive* homicide is viewed less drastically by the law. In such killings, the offender may or may not intend to harm or kill the victim, but even when intended, the killing occurs without prior planning. An individual, for example, may get into a fight and kill his opponent. Although he was so angry that he wanted "to kill," the spontaneity of the situation is such that no actual preplanning (premeditation) occurred.

The media and law enforcement authorities often talk about other types of homicides: serial, spree, and mass murders. *Serial* murders are those that involve the killing of several people in several or more events over a period of time. They are also characterized by the fact that they generally involve a pattern. Ted R. Bundy, the killer and rapist who was executed by the state of Florida in 1989, is an example. Bundy confessed to sexually assaulting and killing a number of young women in various parts of the country over a period of several years. As such, he earned the epithet "serial killer."

A *spree* murder is a criminal event that involves killings at two or more locations during which there is little or no time to break between the killings. A man murders his wife and flees before the police arrive. A roadblock is established, and the killer murders a deputy sheriff at the roadblock. Police pursue the killer, who takes refuge in a farmhouse, and before he is himself killed by the police, he kills a hostage in the house.

*Mass* murders involve the killing of four or more victims at one location. In 1966, Charles Whitman climbed a tower at the University of Texas at Austin. Armed with a high-powered rifle, he opened fire on the campus below. Before he was himself killed by the police, he murdered sixteen people. Whitman's actions constituted an act of mass murder.

**Trends** Of all the serious crimes reported to the police, homicide is, of course, the most infrequent. Over the years, the level of homicides occurring in the United

States has fluctuated widely. Looking at national trends for the commission of this crime, a peak was reached in the early and mid-1930s. From there, the levels fell off drastically to a modern-day low in the late 1950s. Beginning in the early 1960s, however, the trends took on an ominous portent: Levels increased sharply and climbed nearly every year, reaching a century-high level in 1980.[32]

Since that peak year, the number of homicides has again begun a downhill trend. There are those, however, who are worried that we may be entering a new phase. A number of cities throughout the country are reporting that drug-related murders are increasing at alarming rates.[33] If present trends continue, we may be entering a period of the highest homicide rates in our nation's history. This is something worth closely watching in the years ahead.

The crime of homicide almost always involves the use of a weapon—particularly the use of a handgun. No other instrument of death is even close to handgun-related murders. Victims of homicides are most likely to be men and to be between the ages of twenty-five and thirty-four. Race of the victim seems to play an important role. Blacks, for example, are more than five times more likely to be murder victims than are whites.[34] As mentioned earlier in this chapter (Table 2.1), homicide is less likely to be committed by a stranger than any other violent crime. This is one of the factors that makes the solution of these crimes relatively easy for the police. Investigative attention initially focuses on friends, relatives, or acquaintances of the victim. These two factors—prior relationship and motive—explain a great deal about the focus of investigative efforts by law enforcement authorities in these crimes.

Just as most homicide victims are male, so are most homicide offenders.[35] And like sex offenders, the average age at time of arrest for the crime is relatively high. The average person arrested for murder is around thirty years of age.[36] This points out another distinct difference between violent crimes and property crimes: If one examines age-specific arrest rates in terms of these two broad categories of crimes, property offenses generally involve rather young arrestees as compared to those arrested for violent crimes.[37]

**Victims, offenders, and the criminal justice system response**

We hear a great deal about the influence of drugs and alcohol on crime. An interesting survey of their use and how it might have contributed to the commission of certain crimes was conducted in the late 1970s. Data were gathered through surveys of prison inmates. It was generally found that property crime offenders had the highest incidence of alcohol and narcotics abuse, with many of them claiming to be under the influence of drugs at the time of the crime. By contrast, smaller proportions of murderers and rapists claimed they were under the influence. Homicide offenders, particularly, denied they were under the influence of any substance when they committed their crimes.[38]

What about the issue of trial and imprisonment for those arrested for homicide? Although it is generally accepted that the more serious the charge the greater the likelihood of trial, is this always the case? In the case of homicide, at least, this seems to be the situation. In some interesting research into the prosecution of felony arrests in ten jurisdictions, those arrested for murder were most likely to stand trial for their crimes—much more so than the next category of likelihood, sexual assaults[39]—and were also most likely to be convicted and incarcerated and to serve the longest prison sentences.[40] Although conventional wisdom might expect this to be the situation, such conventional wisdom is not always substantiated upon closer examination and by research efforts. With this type of crime at least, it seems to be.

Until the mid-1970s, rape laws seemed to be geared toward protecting the alleged offender as much as the victim. The idea that a victim of rape might create a fantasy or lie about her victimization was a consideration that seemed to underlie the existing rape laws. At least it was the legal presumption that she would try just that. The prosecutor's job was to demonstrate that the victim did not consent. Then, in a wave of response to feminist arguments, nearly all states revised their rape statutes. Most dropped the requirement that the state prove nonconsent and limited testimony about the victim's sexual history. Appreciable changes followed in the way the police, prosecutors, and hospitals treat victims. But did changes bring more acquaintance rapes into the system?

Debbie Egan is a case in point. Ms. Egan, a twenty-one-year-old woman, had gone to her former boyfriend's apartment at his request to pick up some of her belongings. As the jury heard it later, he tied her wrists with telephone cord, raped her, and broke her nose. The jury convicted him of assault but he was acquitted on the rape charge.

Barbara Maislin, the Assistant District Attorney who tried the case, wasn't surprised. "Some of my colleagues in the D.A's office were even surprised I wanted to prosecute this case," she mused. "It's really very simple: She [Ms. Egan] should have known what she was getting into. Undoubtedly, this was what went through the minds of some of the jurors."

In spite of efforts by feminist groups, discussions on talk shows, articles in women's magazines, and most conspicuously, programs on college campuses, this problem persists. There is still a lingering resistance to complaints by women who knew their attackers. A great deal of skepticism still surrounds such allegations. There is evidence that such incidents are more common than rape by strangers. There is also evidence that today's victims of acquaintance rape are more willing to bring charges. Still, the system is not responding well. Change has been slow. The problem seems to be that rape is not defined so much by law as it is by social attitudes. "Couple these social attitudes, which center on the issue of greater sexual freedom—indeed sexual aggressiveness of women today—with the issue of voluntary or involuntary consent, and the issue gets murky to jurors," contends Joseph Harowitz of The Center for Family Violence, "particularly when the state must prove the question of involuntariness beyond a reasonable doubt as a sufficient element of the crime."

The statistics on the problem of acquaintance rape are sketchy even to the experts. In a Justice Department survey of rape, 45 percent of the victims said they knew their assailant or at least the assailants were "nonstrangers." A recent study of rapes reported to Massachusetts rape crisis centers found that only 28 percent were committed by strangers.[a] Nancy Hollomon, chief of the sex crimes unit in the Atlanta prosecutor's office, said that acquaintance rapes were about half of her office's rape caseload and had been for several years. She estimates that ten years ago the figure was no more than 30 percent.

Experts agree that at each step in the criminal justice system the attrition rate for these type rapes

[a] The New York Times, 19 February 1989, section E., p. 20.

is quite high. Often, a victim simply backs out. If a woman has a bad experience in the hospital, if the cops appear skeptical, the prosecutor seems generally disinterested, or the boyfriend apologizes and begs her not to prosecute, there is a high likelihood that the woman will think twice about pursuing the case.

Arguments also rage over the responsibilities of the state to prosecute the case. Susan Estrich of the Harvard Law School, who has written a book on the subject, argues that it is unjust not to prosecute such cases just because juries are discriminatory. Not so, contends Los Angeles County Assistant District Attorney Wilma Schmipf. "I don't consider it ethical to prosecute cases where we can't prove guilt beyond a reasonable doubt. If that was the case, we'd prosecute everything that comes to our office, which is ridiculous." Besides, she adds, "although I'm supposed to focus on the victim, what about the rights of the guy being accused of rape under some very questionable circumstances?"

Juries do indeed seem to be the clog in the system. Norman Wallermann of the prosecutor's office in Seattle says, "juries want the whole thing videotaped; if a woman is dragged off the street and raped in front of a TV camera, then we've got a case which will satisfy them. Still, we'll go forward with any case which is believable, out of our concern for the victim and the seriousness of this crime." He admits to one other problem. "Do you know there are still people out there who believe a woman can't be raped if she doesn't want to be." He goes off shaking his head as if what he is saying is as much a question as it is a comment.

*Rape* is another serious violent crime. What do we know about this offense Offender and arrest characteristics
beyond the general characteristics outlined at the beginning of this chapter? If
arrest rates are any indication, it is a crime in which the offender is a bit older than
those arrested for other crimes. While offenders arrested for such crimes as burglary
and motor vehicle theft average only twenty-two years of age at time of arrest, those
arrested for a forcible rape averaged twenty-eight years of age.[41] In fact, all forms
of sex offenses have an average arrest age of thirty. Only the crime of gambling has
age-specific arrest rates in which the average person arrested is over thirty years
of age.[42]

In addition, the arrest rates show that there is very little difference in the
arrest rates of black and white suspects for these crimes.[43] In the number of arrests,
forcible rape was near the bottom of all crime categories. In other words, of all the
arrests made in the United States, forcible rape as a crime is far overshadowed by
arrests for burglary, arson, robbery, forgery, counterfeiting, and other crimes.[44] Yet,
while this was occurring, the police were more successful in making arrests for the
forcible rapes that were reported to them than they were in these other crime
categories.

With the obvious exception of murder, it appears that forcible rape of all the **Victims**
violent crimes is most likely to seriously injure the victim or require medical attention. In compiling such data, however, the fact that the victim often seeks routine
postrape medical attention may give the impression that there was more serious
injury than actually occurred.

In looking at characteristics surrounding rape victims, we can generally make
several generalizations. Rape typically involves young women from the ages of sixteen to twenty-four. More likely than not, the victim is black and is divorced or
separated and is often in school or unemployed. Strangely enough, rape seems to
be a crime that equally victimizes women living in central city, suburban, or rural
areas.[45] Although it may be thought that living in the central city is more likely to
subject a woman to the possibility of being a victim of forcible rape, rates per one
thousand persons in these three areas are generally the same.

As mentioned in the characteristics of the most serious crimes at the beginning of this chapter, *assault* is the most frequently committed violent crime. Although official crime statistics (see Chapter 3) have tended to decline in recent
years, the crime of aggravated assault runs counter to this trend. It continues to
show disturbingly high levels.[46] Fortunately, the crime of assault generally does not
involve the use of a weapon.[47] Nonetheless, Americans are more likely to be a victim
of a criminal assault than they are to be injured in a motor vehicle accident.

The criminal assault victim is almost twice as likely to be a male as compared **Victims**
to a female and to be quite young. Youth between the ages of sixteen and twenty-
four are most likely to be its victims. Both blacks and Hispanics have high rates of
victimization, and unlike rape, rates of assault are much higher in central cities
than in other areas. Because of these characteristics, we might expect that most of
its victims have never been married (followed closely by divorced/separated) status,
enjoy relatively low levels of income, and are unemployed or in school. This is
exactly the picture that unfolds.[48] Most of the recorded assaults occur between
strangers, although many also occur between acquaintances.

Turning to those convicted of this crime for a moment, we see that of those **Offenders**
convicted of assault, alcohol use was very pervasive among this group, and many
reported they had used alcohol before they committed the crime. Almost nine out
of ten of those arrested for this crime were men; arrest rates for women, although

Assaults happen most often among young men who are Hispanic or black. (© Greg Foster/Stock South)

growing in recent years for this offense, are still proportionally small. Of all the so-called violent crimes, someone arrested and convicted for a criminal assault was the least likely to be incarcerated for this crime.[49] And of the major violent crime categories, if the offender was sent to prison, he or she served the briefest period of confinement.[50] One foreboding sign, however, was that such convicted and imprisoned offenders were more likely than those convicted of other serious crimes against the person, to be re-arrested, reconvicted, and sent back to prison after they had served their time for this offense.[51] Finally, of all the serious crimes of violence reported to the police, only murder enjoyed a higher arrest rate for the commission of the crime. The police seem to be fairly successful in making arrests for crimes of assault.

A last category of violent crime we want to examine is *robbery*. Sometimes a robbery is referred to as a stickup, holdup, or mugging. The crime is feared for both its actual and potential violence. Robbery offenders are more likely than any other category of violent offenders to use weapons.[52] In fact, studies of robberies show that guns were actually discharged in a fifth of all robberies.[53]

**General facts**

Of notable importance in examining the offense of robbery is that it is likely to be a stranger-to-stranger crime, and more than half of all robberies are committed by two or more robbers. Perhaps this largely explains why, of all violent crimes, robbery is least likely to result in an arrest. Robberies are most likely to occur on the street, followed in frequency by robberies occurring at or near the victim's house. Factors associated with the reporting of robberies to the police include crime-related factors such as whether anything was stolen and its value; whether the victim was injured and how badly; and the presence of a weapon during the crime's commission.

Firearms seem to be the weapon of choice for robberies followed closely by the use of a knife. Although victims of robberies are less likely to require medical attention for their injuries than those who have been victims of rape or aggravated assault, injury does occur with enough frequency to be of concern.

Men, again, are more than twice as likely as women to be victims of robbery— particularly young men in their early twenties. Many of the victims are unemployed or, if employed, have relatively low levels of income. Like victims of homicide and assault, victims of robberies tend to be residents of central cities and are predominantly black.[54]

What do we know about the types of persons who are arrested for this crime? First, they are very young. It appears that among the major crime categories, only the crimes of motor vehicle theft and burglary involve suspects of a younger average age at time of arrest. Studies of robbery offenders indicate that about one-half of those convicted for this crime committed fewer than five robberies per year. On the other hand, the most active 10 percent of convicted robbers committed more than eighty-five per year.[55] **Offenders**

A definite racial pattern seems to exist for this offense. For example, official arrest records and victim surveys indicate that blacks accounted for more than 60 percent of all robberies, according to arrests and victim accounts.[56] In self-reports of drug or alcohol use, robbers were more likely than any other category of violent crime offender to report they were under the influence of drugs at the time of the crime.

How does the criminal justice system respond to someone arrested for robbery? After those arrested for homicide and sexual assault, persons arrested for this crime are most likely to stand trial for their offense.[57] And in the case of conviction, robbers are second only to murderers in the likelihood that they will be imprisoned for the crime.[58] The time that they serve in prison is fairly long. Only convicted murderers and rapists have, on the average, longer sentences imposed by the courts. Interestingly, when the nation's prison population is examined, only those convicted of burglary make up a larger percentage of our inmate populations.[59] **Criminal justice system response**

We are not the only country that deals harshly with those accused of robbery or convicted for that crime. Studies of the criminal justice systems of Canada, England, Wales, and the Federal Republic of Germany show similarly high rates of conviction and incarceration for those accused and convicted of this offense.[60] Apparently, there is a broad general consensus that robbery is a particularly serious crime and deserving of punishment.

## □ CRIMES AGAINST PROPERTY (NONVIOLENT CRIME)

Crimes against property do not involve the violence or threat of violence associated with crimes against the person. Our English heritage and the English Common Law system recognized that the criminal law is a vehicle for economic and social planning as much as it is a code depicting current standards of morality. It is also an index to the division of power in a community. Throughout England's history, the **The law and protecting property rights** common law of England sought to protect property rights—some would say to protect the property and chattels of the "haves" (who were naturally most instrumental in the law's formation and enforcement) against the threat posed by the "have-nots."[61] This was carried over into colonial America, where such "economic" crimes were widely adopted to protect private property and to further the community's economic business.[62] In this section, we want to examine four such property crimes: burglary, larceny, motor vehicle theft, and arson.

The crime of *burglary* is unlawful entry, usually but not necessarily, attended by theft.[63] Many of the violent crimes that occur in the home are committed during an illegal entry. This includes the offenses of murder, rape, robbery, and assault. Fortunately, most burglaries occur to buildings or homes when nobody is present. Interestingly, a survey conducted by the National Crime Survey found no evidence that the increasing use of burglar alarms, sophisticated locks, and other security devices has had any effect on the rate of forcible entry.[64] In spite of growing precautions, about one in thirteen households in the nation are burglarized annually. Over a span of twenty years, most households will, on average, be victimized by burglary or larceny. Even this is an improvement, however. Of the crimes against households, residential burglaries show the largest drop in occurrence through the years 1976 to 1985. Like household larcenies, burglaries are more frequent in the summer months.

Like patterns in so many crimes, members of minority races are much more likely to suffer a household burglary than whites. Rates for Hispanic or black households are much higher. Correspondingly, they are likely to be households headed by a young person and to have low income. Furthermore, household burglaries occur predominantly among central city residents as compared with suburban or rural residents.[65]

Those arrested for burglaries (and auto theft) are the youngest of all persons arrested for major crimes. Serious California juvenile offenders were studied to see how many crimes they committed. Excluding larcenies, burglaries were by far the most frequent crime committed by this group.[66]

Looking at the characteristics of those arrested and charged with burglary, we find that although blacks still show a disproportionate arrest rate for this crime, it is far less than their arrest rate for violent crimes. In fact, the arrest rate of blacks for violent crimes overall is decidedly higher than their arrest rates for the property crime categories. It has long been said that narcotics addiction and abuse is associated with the crime of burglary. Perhaps this is partly demonstrated by the fact that convicted burglars of all major crime-category offenders were most likely to claim to have been using drugs at the time of the offense.[67]

Again, we turn our attention to how the criminal justice system deals with this type of crime and criminal. Fewer burglaries are cleared by an arrest than any other major crime category. Even larcenies have a proportionately higher commission-arrest rate than burglary.[68] Apparently, when such crimes are reported to the police, the police are not very successful in making an arrest.

When arrests are made, however, burglary ranks above other property crimes (including drug offenses) in the percentage of arrests that go to trial. And once convicted, offenders were sentenced to longer periods of imprisonment. As mentioned in our discussion of robbery, convicted burglars make up the largest percentage of offenders in our nation's prisons. Comparative data on similar sentencing patterns in other countries of Western Europe and Canada generally show that

*Victimization*

*Offenders*

*Criminal justice system response*

incarceration rates for convicted burglars in the United States are higher than those for similarly convicted offenders in these other countries.[69]

The next two major crimes, *larceny* and *motor vehicle theft*, are discussed together. *Larceny* is merely the legal term for theft. Motor vehicle theft is merely a particular type of larceny. The criminal law typically recognizes two general classes of larceny: petit and grand. The distinction between the two is generally arbitrarily established by law and reflects the value of the property stolen. For example, a state may set a cut-off point of $500.00 for the distinction. Anything stolen valued at $500.00 or more constitutes grand larceny; anything less is petit larceny. There is one other important distinction in the law. Petit larceny is a misdemeanor and grand larceny a felony.

Both crimes indicate that they are crimes in which the average arrestee is a young offender. This is particularly true with motor vehicle theft, which may reflect that kids or young adults are involved in "joyriding." About two-thirds of the persons arrested for these crimes are white. In the case of motor vehicle theft, it might be imagined that males are far more often arrested for this offense than females. This is indeed the case, in a ratio of about 9:1. With the crime of larceny, however, the ratio diminishes significantly. About one-third of all larceny arrests are female.[70]

Both crimes show rather low "clearance rates." That is, of all these crimes that are reported to the police, few are cleared by an arrest. This is particularly true in motor vehicle theft cases. Overall in the United States, property crimes make up about 90 percent of all serious crimes. And of this, larcenies constitute about two-thirds of all reported serious property crimes. Larceny also shows a wide distribution of offenses among all geographical areas: central cities, suburbs, and rural areas. A study of nine jurisdictions indicated that someone charged with either of these crimes and prosecuted and found guilty had about a 60 percent chance of being imprisoned or jailed for the offense.[71] Of all the crimes studied, the average length of sentence imposed upon conviction for larceny was shorter than for any other serious crime.[72]

*Arson* is the last specific crime category to be examined. Again, it follows patterns similar to many other serious crimes. Arrested offenders are typically young (early twenties) and predominantly male. Still, there is one significant departure. More than three-fourths of those arrested for this crime are white suspects.[73] Overall, in the nation's crime picture, there were relatively few arrests made for this offense. Whether this low arrest rate reflects the fact that few of these crimes are being committed or that the difficulties of proof associated with these types of offenses is unclear. Of all serious crime offenders in our prisons today, proportionately few inmates are serving time for the crime of arson.

## ▣ ORIGINS OF CRIMINAL LAW

In the United States, we can trace our criminal law to four basic sources: (1) the English common law; (2) federal and state constitutions; (3) laws passed by Congress and state legislatures; and (4) decisions of the courts in criminal prosecutions. Each of these sources has had an impact on our system of criminal law.

Our criminal law is founded in English common law. Records indicate that laws began to develop in England as far back as A.D. six hundred. These laws

*Clearance rates*

*Common law heritage*

Investigators after this Ohio bus company fire found evidence of arson, although a suspect was never apprehended. The profile of the typical arsonist implicates a young, white male.
(© Jim Christman)

reflected a strange and usually inconsistent mixture of Roman law and the tribal rules and customs of invaders from Scandinavia, northern France, and what was to become the modern state of Germany. After the Norman Conquest in 1066, William the Conqueror and his successors attempted to bring a uniformity to the applications of the criminal law. They were able to accomplish this by suggesting the development of a court system that would apply "equal" or "common" application of the law with some degree of uniformity throughout the land. However, the ruling monarchs were quick to sense that they should not interfere too much with the operations of the courts; they merely provided the means for more uniform application and development—the courts and the judges still enjoyed relative independence.

In the strictest sense, the common law developed by common understanding or by public consent. In deciding which acts should be classified as criminal, the judges drew from common experience and attitudes. Certain crimes were considered inherently and historically offensive, and in this way the common law crimes of treason, murder, battery, kidnapping, burglary, arson, rape, and robbery were established. Although the common law is normally considered "unwritten law," this is not necessarily so. A major part of the common law did develop without benefit of written statutes. But parliamentary legislation over the years has added numerous offenses that were not covered by the original common law. These, too, are considered part of England's common law tradition.

It was this common law tradition that the English colonists brought to America. As a practical matter, after independence, the states continued to use the basic English system. In parts of the United States, the new state governments automatically retained the common law. In others, the states confirmed this continuance with a statement of ratification. Some states did not adopt the common law as such, but rather, incorporated into writing, as new statutes of the state, practically all the basic principles of the common law.[74]

The federal and state constitutions are a second source of the criminal law. As fundamental laws of the nation and the respective states, these constitutions are sources of criminal law in that they provide the skeletal framework for the entire system of law. In this respect, all other sources of law—the common law, laws passed by Congress and the state legislatures, and the decisions of the courts—must conform to the basic guidelines established by these sources. *Constitutional law*

The third source of law is laws passed by Congress or the state legislative bodies. This power is affirmed by the respective federal and state constitutions as well as by numerous court decisions. This type of legislative law is referred to as *statutes*. When Congress passes legislation that defines certain behavior as a "crime," it is referred to as a *federal statute;* when a state legislature passes such a law, it is called a *state statute*. A law passed by the city council or other legislative body of a municipality is called an *ordinance*. *Statutory (legislative) law*

These various criminal statutes and ordinances are compiled into *codes*. For example, the state of Ohio compiles its criminal laws into the Ohio Revised Code. The federal equivalent is known as the *Federal Criminal Code*, or the *United States Code*, usually abbreviated as USC.

The last source of our criminal law is found in the decisions of our courts. This is an increasingly important area of modern criminal law. Through both their express and implied powers, the courts can interpret common law doctrines, constitutional law, and statutory law. Much of the courts' work is in the interpretation of the federal and state constitutions and existing statutory law. For example, the U.S. Supreme Court has broad powers to modify or redefine existing law through its interpretation of the federal Constitution. *Judicially interpreted law*

However, the courts cannot indiscreetly set aside prior court decisions. A fundamental doctrine in judicial decision making is the concept of *stare decisis*, which states that once a court reaches a decision, that decision sets a precedent for all subsequent and similar cases. Without this important principle, there would be no existing legal stability in our judicial system. On the other hand, it does not rule out the need for flexibility in our laws. This relationship is well expressed by Gammage and Hemphill when they say:

> Still, the principle of stare decisis does not always mean blind adherence to a previously decided case. It prevents capricious change, but it does not forbid a review of a case in view of a clear showing of error or injustice at the time of a later case. Also, in some instances conditions on which the earlier decision was based may have changed, so that the precedent is no longer desirable or just. Therefore, the doctrine of stare decisis provides for stability, but it is not so binding as to forbid change in the law when this is desirable to keep pace with changing social and economic forces that are an outgrowth of the times.[75]

## CRIMINAL RESPONSIBILITY

A discussion of criminal law would not be complete without a brief look at the concept of criminal responsibility. When a crime is committed, certain conditions in the mental or legal state of the accused might exist that could relieve the accused of criminal responsibility. If these conditions do exist, they can diminish or completely negate criminal responsibility. These conditions are *insanity, intoxication, infancy, mistake of fact, duress, entrapment, self-defense*, and *the statute of limitations*.

**Insanity and responsibility in the law**

There isn't space to discuss each of these conditions, but because it is sometimes at issue in criminal cases, *criminal insanity* should be explained further. In the law, criminal insanity is a legal defense that applies in two instances: first, if the accused is insane at the time of the commission of the act; and second, if at the time of the trial the accused is found to be insane although he or she may have been sane at the time the act was committed, he or she cannot be compelled to stand trial. In the first case, insanity is said to have diminished the person's ability to form the necessary intent. In the latter case, the accused is considered incapable of understanding the charges against him or her and of assisting in the defense.

**Some established "tests" of insanity**

Over the years, the rules governing insanity as a defense have often changed. Today, there are five basic tests for criminal responsibility involving insanity permitted in American courts. These are (1) the M'Naghten rule; (2) the "irresistible impulse" test; (3) the Durham rule; (4) the "substantial capacity" test proposed by the American Law Institute; and (5) the new federal insanity test.

The *M'Naghten rule* is the oldest. It arose from a famous nineteenth-century case in England in which the rule was established that if "at the time of the committing of the act, the party accused was laboring under such a defect of reason, from disease of the mind, as not to know the nature and quality of the act he was doing, or if he did know, but did not know he was doing wrong," he was considered insane.[76] This rule is usually referred to as the "right–wrong test."

The M'Naghten rule led to many problems, because such terms as "disease of the mind" and "know" could not be precisely defined. Consequently, some jurisdictions supplemented the M'Naghten rule with the *irresistible impulse* test. Under this doctrine, the defendant alleges that he is insane by a disease of the mind that prevented him from controlling his conduct.

Seeking to clarify the legal insanity question further, the *Durham rule* was later adopted. This rule states that "an accused is not criminally responsible if his unlawful act was a product of mental disease or defect."[77] Although the M'Naghten

## FACTS ABOUT THE INSANITY DEFENSE

A defense of insanity is recognized by all but three states—Montana, Idaho, and Utah. These states have passed laws that abolish the insanity defense. However, psychiatric evidence is allowed on the issue of whether there is an intent to commit a crime in these three states. In most states, when the defense intends to introduce the insanity defense, it must file its intent with the court and notify the prosecutor.

The majority of the states use the American Law Institute's insanity defense definition as contained in the Institute's Model Penal Code. Still, sixteen states still use the M'Naghten Rule. Several states rely on the "irresistible impulse" standard, and New Hampshire still clings to its "Durham Rule," which was adopted by that state's Supreme Court in 1871.

The new federal rule is the so-called Appreciation Test, which has been endorsed by the American Bar Association. It resembles the M'Naghten Rule in its reliance on cognitive capacity (the ability to understand the wrongfulness of the act), but it differs from the American Law Institute's test in that the defendant is not required to establish a lack of control over his or her behavior.

rule is worded somewhat similarly, the inability to distinguish right from wrong is not included. Under the Durham rule the question is only whether mental disease or defect may be present.[78]

A more recent test—and one that is increasingly being adopted by states—is the *substantial capacity test* developed by the American Law Institute and contained in the Model Penal Code. The test states:

> A person is not responsible for criminal conduct if at the time of such conduct as a result of mental disease or defect he lacks substantial capacity whether to appreciate the criminality (wrongfulness) of his conduct or to conform his conduct to the requirements of the law.[79]

The rule is basically a broader statement of the M'Naghten/irresistible impulse test. It rejects the Durham rule because that rule lacks a standard for reference and because it does not define the term "product" (of mental disease). The test's most significant feature is that the accused has to show only a lack of "substantial capacity" in being able to distinguish right from wrong.[80]

The insanity defense as a legal weapon has been coming under increasing attack in recent years. It has always been one of the most troublesome and highly debated areas of the criminal law. Although only an extremely small number of criminal cases involve the attempted use of the insanity plea, and a very small number of defendants who allege insanity as a defense are in fact found insane, the public has developed an image of vicious offenders (particularly muderers), who, because of it, go "scot free."

**Insanity defense under attack**

In the early 1980s, it seemed that a major movement was underway to abolish the insanity defense outright. The impetus for such a movement was the attempted assassination of former President Reagan and the finding of not guilty by virtue of insanity of Reagan's assailant. After the decision, state legislative bodies and some

After John Hinckley's attempt to assassinate President Ronald Reagan, many lawmakers spoke out in favor of abolishing the insanity defense. (UPI/Bettman Newsphotos)

members of Congress were in a howl over the need to rewrite the insanity laws and to change crucial aspects of the insanity defense. Several states passed laws that now make it more difficult to employ the insanity defense. Twelve other states have adopted laws that provide that the judge can still sentence a person to prison who has been found to be insane. These are the controversial "guilty but insane" verdicts. It should be pointed out, however, that in those states where this verdict

## CRIME, THE MENTALLY ILL, AND THE CRIMINAL JUSTICE SYSTEM

"They gave him $21 and put him back out on the street. They didn't try to help him in any way . . . the bastards didn't even give him counseling or try to help. He came home and three days later he killed our mother."

These words of anguish and hostility were directed at the Maryland prison authorities who released twenty-three-year-old James Webster. They were spoken by his seventeen-year-old sister who watched him smash his mother's skull with a lug wrench when the mother argued with him about staying home and "keeping outta trouble." Webster's release had been objected to by the prison psychiatrist who diagnosed him as ". . . a violent pathological inmate who potentially might kill someone if released."

This tragedy is becoming more commonplace as mentally disturbed and violent people are being released from prisons, jails, and mental hospitals without adequate treatment or concern for the ramifications of their release. The critics of such policies are growing in numbers and strength and are beginning to make their presence felt among state legislative bodies throughout the country. Debates are also raging in courtrooms over policies to keep dangerous and deranged offenders locked away. The arguments are being fueled by such circumstances as these:

- Charles Meach, while on a work release program after being acquitted by reason of insanity in a homicide case, killed and molested four teenagers in an Anchorage, Alaska, park.
- Maththew Quintiliano, a former Connecticut police officer, was acquitted of killing his wife by virtue of insanity. After spending three months in a mental institution, he was released. He subsequently remarried, then murdered his second wife.
- Robert Pates was in and out of mental hospitals and jails most of his adult life. Obviously disturbed even to laymen, he was arrested by the Biloxi, Mississippi, police for drunkenness. Without adequate precautions, he was placed in a padded jail cell, which he set afire. Twenty-nine inmates were killed.

Although most of the attention has focused on the insanity plea—particularly in the aftermath of the John Hinckley, Jr., case in which he was acquitted on the ground of insanity after shooting President Reagan—it is only the tip of the iceberg. Experts are saying that the real problem is less well known. It is the problem of the mentally ill generally and the justice system.

Both sides in the controversy—law enforcement people and the mental health community—are each blaming the other. A New York commission that studied the problem in that state reports: "The mentally ill inmate has become a problem for both systems, corrections and mental health. . . . Each claims the major responsibility lies with the other. The only thing they seem to agree on is that they both are ill-equipped to deal with the special needs of mentally ill inmates." The result is that neither side does a responsible job in recognizing, treating, and dealing with the problem.

The argument raised by those in law enforcement and mental health is the old standby: We simply do not have the money to do what needs to be done. The police, jailors, and correctional people, for instance, cannot be expected to diagnose the problem when even "experts" can't. Sander Gilman, a psychiatrist at Cornell University, says: Most stereotypes of violent and antisocial people are simply wrong. Many of them are unrecognizable even to trained specialists in the field." He blames the news media for portraying these people as dangerous and wild-eyed lunatics when, in fact, they may appear more rational and sane than most of us.

One point is certain: The relationship between mental illness and crime is quite high. This is not to say that mental illness necessarily causes crime, but many offenders suffer from various degrees of mental illness. How many? No one knows for sure, but some researchers have found that former mental patients have unusually high arrest rates, and this trend seems to be particularly pronounced in violent crimes or crimes against the persons. A spokesman for the National Coalition for Jail Reform claims that each is available, it is an alternative verdict. It is still possible in these twelve states to render the traditional verdict of not guilty by reason of insanity.[81]

Although it is not possible to discuss the full range of issues that surround the controversy of the insanity plea, several of the most troublesome areas the reformers are attacking are such things as the requirement that the burden of proof is on the state. Many believe that the state should not be required to "prove" the

year while 20,000 persons charged with crimes or convicted of crimes enter mental institutions, an estimated 600,000 of the mentally ill or retarded pass through detention facilities.

The way in which most jails are presently operated provide no mental screening for new inmates. Even if the mentally ill inmates could be identified, jail officials could not even see to it that they received separate cells because of the overcrowding that plagues most of the nation's jails. The mentally ill in our jails may be so assaultive and aggressive that they are a danger to staff, other inmates, and themselves. On the other hand, the mentally ill inmates may be so passive that they are powerless and become victims of attacks by other inmates.

Law enforcement officials claim that when they have mentally ill inmates they have trouble getting the state hospitals to take them, particularly if they're assaultive and violent. "Hell, the hospitals don't want them because they're trouble-makers so they dump them back on us," contends Bill Davis with the National Sheriff's Association. Even worse, such people who are labeled "not amenable to treatment" are put back on the streets by the hospital authorities without even notifying the law enforcement community.

When the competence of an accused offender is in doubt, a judge sends the defendant to a government expert for evaluation. Often this is a member of the psy-chiatric staff of the state mental hospital. In a case several years ago, a California judge found Michael Miller, the twenty-year-old son of former President Reagan's attorney, to be schizophrenic and incompetent to stand trial. Miller was arrested for the murder-rape of his mother. About twenty-five thousand such examinations are conducted annually in the United States. By the same token, although the insanity plea receives a lot of attention in the media, less than two thousand people use it successfully every year, and not all of these are murder cases.

Often the prosecution and the defense agree on the plea, and the judge simply affirms that a defendant is not guilty by reason of insanity. When the issue of insanity is contested by the state, both the prosecution and the defense call experts to establish the issue of insanity at the time the crime was committed. What often results next is a parade of such witnesses contradicting the findings of the other side. This makes the verdict one of the toughest that a jury could possibly have to deal with.

The issue has also been gaining momentum as a result of growing lawsuits for improper release. This has forced officials to look at raising standards for the release of the mentally ill. The trend stems from a 1976 California case in which a student told a psychologist that he planned to kill a woman friend. The therapist notified campus police but not the potential victim, whom the man later shot and stabbed to death. The California Supreme Court held the psychologist liable to the deceased girl's parents. In 1982, an Alabama jury returned a $25 million dollar verdict against five officials of a state hospital who had released a man who four years earlier had killed another man in a fatal stabbing and had been acquitted by virtue of insanity. Upon his release, the former patient went out and killed another man in a nearly identical crime. To avoid an appeal, the case was ultimately settled with the murder victim's family in an out-of-court settlement for nearly $1 million.

There is a great deal of concern about the implications of such suits. For one thing, there is concern that psychiatrists will refuse to treat potentially dangerous offenders. There is also the concern that such legal actions will force states to return to the "dark ages" of mental commitments, when it wasn't unusual to keep mental patients hidden away in institutions for years and in some cases even lifetimes—patients who could have been released safely.

Many are convinced that we are backsliding in dealing with the issue of the mentally ill criminal, and it will get worse before it gets better. Judge Barrington Parker, who presided in the Hinckley case, summed up the issue when he maintained, "To imprison a mentally ill person for a criminal act which is the result . . . of mental illness is a clear retreat to the Middle Ages."

defendant was sane; they suggest that when the defendant raises the issue of insanity as a defense, the burden of proof should shift to the defendant, who would then be required to show by an acceptable level of proof that he or she was indeed insane. In 1984 the newly revised federal code was adopted. One of the significant provisions of the new law is that in federal trials the burden of proof in the insanity issue now falls on the defendant. Many states have subsequently also imposed the burden of proof of insanity on the accused.

**Expert testimony problems**

Another problem deals with the so-called expert testimony phase of the insanity hearing. Because of the complexities of what in fact insanity is, and whether or not the defendant was actually insane at the time of the crime, psychiatrists for the state and the defense are paraded to the witness stand to contradict each other. The expert testimony of the psychiatrists for the state contends that the accused was sane at the time, and that for the defense contends that he or she was not. As a consequence, such determination is thrown back on the laypeople in the jury to determine which psychiatric testimony to believe. Obviously, if the so-called experts cannot agree, what can be expected of the average person serving on a jury? A third problem is the difficulty inherent in the legal versus the clinical definition of what

**Legal and clinical differences**

constitutes insanity. Psychiatrists define insanity in terms of clinical definitions, whereas the courts are bound by the legal definition. In many instances, this creates problems of interpretation and application. Although we do not know a great deal about the functioning of the human mind, advances in psychiatric diagnosis and classification outstrip the ability of the law to change apace.

In 1984 Congress passed the Insanity Defense Reform Act to govern the insanity defense and the disposition of those defendants in federal trials who are found to be suffering from insanity according to the new federal definition. One of the provisions of this new act is designed to restrict the conflicting psychiatric testimony of expert witnesses for the government and the defense. Without burdening the reader with too much legal detail, the act restricts the type of testimony that can be elicited and the opinions these experts can express. In the past, psychiatric experts could give opinions as to whether the defendant was sane, whether the defendant could distinguish right from wrong, and other issues. Now the responsibility for making these kinds of determinations is given to the jury. The psychiatric witness appears to be limited to presenting and explaining diagnoses with the conclusions left to the jury.[82] Only time will tell what possible problems this may cause jurors in their determinations.

**Commitment laws**

Another problem is existing commitment laws. In a large number of states, a person found innocent because of insanity can still be committed to a special state hospital. However, the law often requires that the person committed cannot be kept confined in such an institution beyond a year or two unless he or she consents to further confinement or the person has been committed through civil proceedings. And those who have been treated successfully cannot be committed by civil process. In theory, then, a person could kill someone, be acquitted because of insanity, and be back on the streets within months. Even so, this is not likely to occur. The state would simply not consider the person to have been "successfully" treated in such a short time period.

**Variation in tests**

A final problem that is often discussed is the wide differences that exist from state to state in the particular test to be used. We have seen various tests that have been developed and that are used to determine insanity, ranging from the M'Naghten rule to the substantial capacity test. There are still several others that have not been discussed but are used in a few states.

Like other areas of the administration of criminal justice, the recent furor over the insanity plea is threatening. Again, it would seem, much of the American public and their elected representatives are responding in a typical knee-jerk fashion. There is no doubt that improvement in the insanity issue is needed; but again, quick-and-dirty solutions to complex and interrelated problems are not the answer. Like so many other issues that surround crime and the administration of justice, the so-called simple solutions present the possibility of a system where the cure is worse than the cause. For example, the idea that commitment to a state hospital for the criminally insane rather than imprisonment constitutes a form of leniency is simply absurd. In some cases, the individual committed to such an institution will end up being confined longer—and usually under conditions at least as appalling—than if he or she had been sentenced to prison. Simply to abolish the insanity plea—and thus ignore the effect of such pathology—is to say that it does not exist when, in fact, the whole theory of the law and crime itself is built on a foundation of requisite mental state. Finally, as is too often the case, we take *one* known (and typically unique situation) and somehow infer that this is the case in *all* situations. We then write laws around this one case and apply them with disastrous results on many other cases.

## ☐ BASIC LEGAL TERMINOLOGY

Criminal justice students and citizens in general should have some familiarity with basic legal terms and documents. The terms *arrest, arrest warrant, search warrant, subpoena, writ of habeas corpus, bail,* and *extradition* are commonly heard, but few people really know the legal definitions and requirements of each. The remainder of this chapter explains these common legal terms and shows the reader examples of these documents.

### Arrest

An arrest is taking a person into custody in the manner authorized by law. Just as a specific offense has elements, so does the act of arrest. First, there must be an intention to arrest; second, the intention to arrest must be communicated to the person arrested; third, the one arresting must have the one being arrested under his or her control; last, there must be an understanding by the person arrested that he or she is being arrested.[83] However, if one or more elements are missing, the arrest *may* not be *in*valid. For example, if an intoxicated person is arrested while unconscious, the arrest is not invalid.

*Elements of authorization*

In most states, a police officer can make an arrest without a warrant under the following conditions; (1) if a felony has been committed in the officer's presence; (2) if there is probable cause (reasonable grounds) to believe that a felony has been committed and the person being arrested committed the felony; or (3) if a misdemeanor has been committed in the officer's presence. An arrest by a citizen, normally called a "citizen's arrest," is restricted in most states to instances where felonies have been committed in the citizen's presence or where the citizen has probable cause to believe a felony has been committed and the person being arrested committed the felony. Citizens are normally not empowered to make arrests for misdemeanors.

## Arrest Warrants

An arrest warrant is an order signed by a magistrate or judge that commands the person addressed or anyone authorized to execute the warrant to take a named person into custody and to bring that person before the court to answer for the crime specified in the warrant.

There are several ways in which an arrest warrant is issued. The victim of the crime or complaining witness may go directly to the prosecutor (district attorney) with the information about the crime. The prosecutor then prepares a supporting affidavit (a form of a sworn statement), which the complainant swears to and signs. The prosecutor and the complainant then go before a magistrate who is authorized to issue an arrest warrant for the particular offense. (In some states, complaints for minor misdemeanors may be sworn to before the prosecutor or the clerk of courts.) The magistrate questions the complainant thoroughly to determine if there is probable cause to believe a crime has been committed and if the one named in the complaint is the probable offender.[84] If the magistrate is satisfied that the facts are correct, the warrant will be signed and turned over to the police to serve.

Police officers may also initiate complaints. The police officer goes before the magistrate, or in some cases the prosecutor, to file the complaint. In these circumstances, the police officer becomes the complainant and has to swear to the facts. Figure 2.1 is an arrest warrant issued by a federal magistrate.

## Search Warrant

Fourth Amendment

A search warrant, like an arrest warrant, is an order issued by a magistrate that commands and authorizes a law enforcement officer to search the premises described on the warrant for articles listed on the warrant. The procedure and substance of search warrants are defined by the Fourth Amendment of the U.S. Constitution, which reads:

> The right of the people to be secure in their persons, houses, papers and effects, against unreasonable searches and seizures, shall not be violated and no Warrants shall issue, but upon probable cause, supported by oath or affirmation, and particularly describing the place to be searched and the persons or things to be seized.

To obtain a search warrant, a police officer must go before a magistrate and file a sworn affidavit that indicates the *particular place* to be searched and the *particular things* to be seized (Figure 2.2). Police officers are forbidden from searching any place other than that described in the warrant. However, police officers can seize items that are not listed in the warrant, as long as they are offensive to the law and the search did not exceed the scope of the warrant.[85] The magistrate must examine the officer's affidavit to determine if probable cause exists to believe that illegal objects or persons are present on the premises. If the magistrate is satisfied and there is probable cause, the warrant will be issued (Figure 2.3).

When the search warrant is executed, the law enforcement officer must leave a copy of the warrant with the person who occupies the searched premises. If the premises are unoccupied at the time of the search, a copy of the warrant must still be left in plain view. In addition, the police must leave an itemized inventory of all property seized and return a copy of the inventory and notice that the warrant has been served to the authorizing magistrate. Figure 2.4 shows the return and inventory portion of a search warrant. Once the search warrant has been issued, it is

# United States District Court

__Northern__ _____ DISTRICT OF _____ California _____

UNITED STATES OF AMERICA

V.

James Iona Washington

## WARRANT FOR ARREST

CASE NUMBER: 23971-90

To: The United States Marshal
and any Authorized United States Officer

YOU ARE HEREBY COMMANDED to arrest __James Iona Washington (AKA "Doobie" Jones)__

Name

and bring him or her forthwith to the nearest magistrate to answer a(n)

[X] Indictment ☐ Information ☐ Complaint ☐ Order of court ☐ Violation Notice ☐ Probation Violation Petition

charging him or her with (brief description of offense)

Title 18 U.S.C. Section 12-A (D). Robbery of banking institution insured by the Federal Deposit Insurance Corporation.

in violation of Title ___18___ United States Code, Section(s)___12-A (D)___

| Carl A. Wilbanks | U.S. District Court Judge |
|---|---|
| Name of Issuing Officer | Title of Issuing Officer |
| _Carl A. Wilbanks_ (signature) | May 12, 1990  San Jose, California |
| Signature of Issuing Officer | Date and Location |

Bail fixed at $ __50,000.__ by___Carl A. Wilbanks___

Name of Judicial Officer

| RETURN | | |
|---|---|---|
| This warrant was received and executed with the arrest of the above-named defendant at 323 Larchmont St., Fresno, California | | |
| DATE RECEIVED 5/13/90 | NAME AND TITLE OF ARRESTING OFFICER Michael T. Burbank Special Agent, FBI | SIGNATURE OF ARRESTING OFFICER _Michael T. Burbank_ |
| DATE OF ARREST 8/8/90 | | |

Warrant for arrest of defendant.

FIGURE **2.1**

# United States District Court

Western _____ Tennessee
DISTRICT OF _____

In the Matter of the Search of
(Name, address or brief description of person, property or premises to be searched)

646 Crosby Street
Memphis, Tennessee

### APPLICATION AND AFFIDAVIT
### FOR SEARCH WARRANT

CASE NUMBER:    10789-90

I ___ Joanne T. Wilmott _____ being duly sworn depose and say:

I am a(n) Special Agent, Drug Enforcement Administration _____ and have reason to believe
                          Official Title

that ☐ on the person of or ☒ on the property or premises known as (name, description and/or location)

646 Crosby Street, Memphis, Tennessee which is a one-story, ranch style,
yellow brick house, with black shutters, and a detached garage.

in the _____ Western _____ District of ____ Tennessee _____
there is now concealed a certain person or property, namely (describe the person or property to be seized)

Two oblong red ceramic placques depicting a matador and bull.

which is (state one or more bases for search and seizure set forth under Rule 41(b) of the Federal Rules of Criminal Procedure)

in violation of

concerning a violation of Title ___21___ United States code, Section(s) __140-143 (B)__ .
The facts to support a finding of Probable Cause are as follows:

On April 18, 1990, Inspectors T. O. Bryan and R. Jones, U.S. Customs Service, while
routinely inspecting incoming merchandise from Mexico at Metro Airport, inspected two
plaques shipped from Mexico addressed to Jay Carano, 646 Crosby St., Memphis, Tennessee.
In the plaques a white powdered substance was discovered.  Inspector Bryan conducted a
field test which indicated the substance was cocaine.  With the cooperation of Emery Air
Freight, the plaques were delivered to the 646 Crosby Street address.  Upon delivery of
the plaques, the Drug Enforcement Administration established an around-the-clock surveillance of 646 Crosby St.  The NCIC and the Tennessee Bureau of Investigation criminal files
were checked.  These files reflect that Jay Carano was convicted on two prior occasions
for selling and distributing a controlled substance.  Surveillance of 646 Crosby Street
disclosed frequent visits to this address by two individuals known to this affiant to
have previous felony convictions for the sale and distribution of a controlled substance.

Continued on the attached sheet and made a part hereof.        ☐ Yes    ☒ No

Signature of Affiant

Sworn to before me, and subscribed in my presence

May 3, 1990
Date                                                            at        Memphis, Tennessee
                                                                         City and State

Robert J. Abrahms, U.S. Magistrate
Name and Title of Judicial Officer                              Signature of Judicial Officer

FIGURE **2.2** Affidavit for search warrant.

# United States District Court

Western _____ DISTRICT OF _____ Tennessee

In the Matter of the Search of
(Name, address or brief description of person or property to be searched)

646 Crosby Street
Memphis, Tennessee

## SEARCH WARRANT

CASE NUMBER:  10789-90 (A)

TO: _____United States Marshal_____ and any Authorized Officer of the United States

Affidavit(s) having been made before me by _____Joanne T. Wilmott_____ who has reason to
                                                        Affiant

believe that ☐ on the person of or ☒ on the premises known as (name, description and/or location)

646 Crosby Street, Memphis, Tennessee which is a one-story,
ranch style, yellow brick house, with black shutters, and
a detached garage.

in the_____ Western _____ District of _____ Tennessee _____ there is now
concealed a certain person or property, namely (describe the person or property)

Two oblong red ceramic placques depicting a matador and bull,
the contents of which are in violation of Title 21, United States
Code, Sections 140-143 (B).

I am satisfied that the affidavit(s) and any recorded testimony establish probable cause to believe that the person
or property so described is now concealed on the person or premises above-described and establish grounds for
the issuance of this warrant.

YOU ARE HEREBY COMMANDED to search on or before _____May 12, 1990_____
                                                                    Date

(not to exceed 10 days) the person or place named above for the person or property specified, serving this warrant
and making the search (XX XXX XXXXXXXX XXX XXXX XXXX XX XX XXXX XXX) (at any time in the day or night as I find
reasonable cause has been established) and if the person or property be found there to seize same, leaving a copy
of this warrant and receipt for the person or property taken, and prepare a written inventory of the person or property seized and promptly return this warrant to _Robert J. Abrahms_
as required by law.                                    U.S. Judge or Magistrate

May 3, 1990   (10:45 A.M.)_____   at   _Memphis, Tennessee_____
Date and Time Issued                                   City and State

___Robert J. Abrahms, U.S. Magistrate___   _Robert J. Abrahms_____
Name and Title of Judicial Officer                Signature of Judicial Officer

Search warrant.                                                                    FIGURE **2.3**

AO 93 (Rev. 5/85) Search Warrant

## RETURN

| DATE WARRANT RECEIVED | DATE AND TIME WARRANT EXECUTED | COPY OF WARRANT AND RECEIPT FOR ITEMS LEFT WITH |
|---|---|---|
| May 3, 1990 | May 5, 1990 (2:03 A.M.) | Mary (NMN) Berisko, 646 Crosby St., Memphis, TN |

INVENTORY MADE IN THE PRESENCE OF

Special Agent Petrowski - DEA, and Mary (NMN) Berisko

INVENTORY OF PERSON OR PROPERTY TAKEN PURSUANT TO THE WARRANT

Approximately three and one-half (3½) kilos of cocaine. Marked for evidence. (10789-90)

Approximately six (6) ounces of marihuana. Marked for evidence. (10789-90)

1 Steiger 9mm. automatic machine gun Serial No. 12899320. Marked for evidence. (10789-90)

123 rounds of 9mm. ammunition. Marked for evidence. (10789-90)

## CERTIFICATION

I swear that this inventory is a true and detailed account of the person or property taken by me on the warrant.

Peter A. Petrowski

Subscribed, sworn to, and returned before me this date.

Robert J. Abrahams — U.S. Judge or Magistrate

May 5, 1990 — Date

FIGURE **2.4** Search warrant return.

common for statutes or courts to require that it must be executed within a fixed period of time, such as ten days.[86]

## Subpoena

A subpoena is a court order that compels someone to appear and provide testimony concerning a particular matter of which he or she is supposed to have knowledge (Figure 2.5). One form of subpoena is a *subpoena deuces tecum*, which directs the person named to appear with certain specified documents. In this manner, the court can compel the subpoenaed person to produce certain records and documents. The federal and all state governments provide by law that anyone who is issued a subpoena and fails to appear or testify (in the absence of self-incrimination) will be charged with contempt of court.[87]

## Writ of Habeas Corpus

Another important legal document is the writ of habeas corpus, which may be used when a person is held in restraint by the state. It is a court order that directs the police or penal authorities who have a particular person in custody to "produce the body" at a time and place specified in the writ and to show why the person is held in custody or restraint.[88] After the court hears the facts, the person may be placed back into custody, released on bail, or discharged. This is accomplished by a written order of the court that must be obeyed. Figure 2.6 illustrates a federal habeas corpus writ.

The courts have called the writ of habeas corpus the "great writ of liberty."[89] "Great writ of liberty" The first Habeas Corpus Act was enacted in the reign of Henry VIII of England (1485–1509) and was regarded as a great constitutional guarantee of personal liberty. The writ of habeas corpus was provided for in the U.S. Constitution and in the constitutions of all the states. Among the powers denied Congress in Article I of the Constitution is the right to suspend the privilege of the writ except in cases of rebellion and invasion.[90]

## Other Writs

There are other writs with which students of criminal justice should be familiar. A *writ of mandamus* is an order from a higher court to an inferior court or other agency such as the police or prosecutor that compels the performance of a certain act as required by law. A *writ of injunction* is an order from a higher court to a lower court or to some other governmental agency or private citizen to "cease and desist" from performing a certain act. Finally, a *writ of coram nobis* is a writ of review directed to the trial court by the accused. This writ petitions the court to set aside its judgment against the accused because certain facts existed that, through no negligence on the part of the accused, were not brought out at the trial and that, if presented, would likely have changed the court's ruling in the case.

## Other Terms

*Venue* is the geographical location of the crime and the jurisdiction of the court to try a particular case.

*Bail* is a procedure for obtaining temporary liberty after arrest or conviction

# United States District Court

Northern _____ DISTRICT OF _____ California

United States of America

v.

James Iona Washington

## SUBPOENA

CASE NUMBER: 23971-90

| TYPE OF CASE | SUBPOENA FOR |
| --- | --- |
| ☐ CIVIL    ☒ CRIMINAL | ☒ PERSON    ☐ DOCUMENT(S) or OBJECT(S) |

TO:    Jane T. Seymour
c/o Great Western Bank
1100 Pacifico Ave.
San Jose, CA

**YOU ARE HEREBY COMMANDED** to appear in the United States District Court at the place, date, and time specified below to testify in the above case.

| PLACE | COURTROOM |
| --- | --- |
| U.S. Courthouse 3113 Mulhaven St. San Jose, CA | 327 |
| | DATE AND TIME 2/1/91    9:00 A.M. |

**YOU ARE ALSO COMMANDED** to bring with you the following document(s) or object(s): *

Not applicable

☐ *See additional information on reverse*

This subpoena shall remain in effect until you are granted leave to depart by the court or by an officer acting on behalf of the court.

| U.S. MAGISTRATE OR CLERK OF COURT | DATE |
| --- | --- |
| Mary Beth Williams – Dubuque, U.S. Magistrate | December 14, 1990 |
| (BY) DEPUTY CLERK | |

| This subpoena is issued upon application of the: | QUESTIONS MAY BE ADDRESSED TO: |
| --- | --- |
| ☐ Plaintiff    ☐ Defendant    ☒ U.S. Attorney | A. B. Richards Asst. U.S. Attorney 3113 Mulhaven St., Rm. B-110 San Jose, CA 73931    (408) 731-1121 ATTORNEY'S NAME, ADDRESS AND PHONE NUMBER |

*If not applicable, enter "none".

FIGURE **2.5**  Subpoena to testify.

```
UNITED STATES DISTRICT COURT
WESTERN DISTRICT OF NEW YORK
```

```
UNITED STATES OF AMERICA      :
                              :
                              :
        -v-                   :      CR NO. 903-90
                              :
                              :
James Earle Bledsoe           :
            Defendant         :
                              :
```

WRIT OF HABEAS CORPUS AD PROSEQUENDUM

THE PRESIDENT OF THE UNITED STATES

TO:   Daniel B. Wright, United States Marshal, Western District of New York,

      or his Deputies; and Sheriff William T. Hardesty or his Deputies

GREETINGS:

YOU ARE HEREBY COMMANDED to produce the body of James Earle Bledsoe now detained in the Erie County Detention Center before the United States District Court, Part I, in and for the Western District of New York at the United States Courthouse in the City of Buffalo, New York on the 14th day of February, 1990, at 9 o'clock in the noon of said day, to inquire and thereafter said examination is to be returned to the Erie County Detention Center to be retained in federal custody until termination of federal proceedings.

WITNESS, the Honorable T. R. Morgan, United States District Judge for the Western District of New York, at Buffalo, New York, this 12th day of February, 1990.

```
                        Michael J. Kaplan
                        MICHAEL J. KAPLAN
                        CLERK
                        UNITED STATES DISTRICT COURT
                        WESTERN DISTRICT OF NEW YORK
```

Writ of habeas corpus.                                    FIGURE **2.6** by means of a written promise to appear in court as required. To obtain bail, it may be necessary to deposit cash, a surety bond (to guarantee their return to court), or evidence of ownership or equity in real property. In recent years, the practice of releasing on one's *own recognizance* has developed. In these cases, the individual is released without having to post any form of financial security.

*Extradition* is the legal process of initiating and requesting another state (or nation) to surrender persons who have committed crimes and are fugitives from justice in the requesting jurisdiction. The procedure by which one sovereign state yields or returns the individual to the state initiating the request is called *rendition*.

## SUMMARY

What constitutes a crime has been carefully determined by the criminal law. For example, it must be a voluntary and intentional (in some cases a foreseeable) act committed by a legally competent person. It can either be an act of commission or omission that threatens the welfare of society and is punishable by judicial proceedings in the name of the state.

The law is divided into two major classifications: civil and criminal law. Criminal law is further broken down into two major offense categories: felonies and misdemeanors.

The theory of what causes crime is as varied as those who have studied it. Modern theories of crime are generally grouped into four areas for purposes of classification and simplification. These are the biological, psychological, sociological, and multifactor views. The multifactor view is the most readily accepted today. It recognizes that the causes of crime often are determined by more than one single explanation.

A way to classify crimes—and a method used by most legal classification systems—is a system based on the object or nature of the crime. Thus, we have inchoate offenses, crimes against the person and property, crimes against public morality and decency, and crimes against public order and administration of justice.

There are four basic sources of our American criminal law system. Each of these has defined the characteristics and nature of our criminal law. An interesting aspect of the criminal law is what is called criminal responsibility. One area of criminal responsibility—the insanity issue—has become of increasing concern and discussion in recent years. This is both a very technical and confusing aspect of our legal system.

In addition to a general knowledge of the theory of criminal law, the beginning student in criminal justice should be familiar with other commonly used terms and instruments of the administration of justice. These include what constitutes an arrest and an arrest warrant, search warrant, subpoena, and the writ of habeas corpus.

## REVIEW QUESTIONS

1. List and define the various elements of a crime and the various categories of intent.
2. List the four major modern schools of thought that attempt to explain the causes of crime and the characteristics of each.
3. Define the following types of criminal offenses:
   a. Felonies and misdemeanors
   b. Inchoate offenses
   c. Crimes against the person
   d. Crimes against property
4. What are some of the characteristics associated with specific crimes against the person? What about property crimes?
5. Describe the origin of our criminal law. What has contributed to its development?
6. How is criminal responsibility determined?
7. What are the issues surrounding the insanity plea?

8. What are the problems the criminal justice system has in dealing with mentally ill offenders?
9. Define the following:
   a. Arrest
   b. Search warrant
   c. Subpoena
   d. Writ of habeas corpus
   e. Venue
   f. Bail
   g. Extradition

## DISCUSSION QUESTIONS

1. In your opinion, which of the four schools of criminology—biological, psychological, sociological, or multifactor—comes closest to explaining correctly the causes of criminal behavior? Explain why you think so.
2. In the text's discussion of the characteristics associated with the major crimes against the person and property, what aspects associated with these crimes did you find particularly thought-provoking?
3. Should the insanity defense be abolished in criminal cases? Why or why not?
4. What is necessary if the criminal justice system is to deal more effectively with the mentally ill?

## SUGGESTED ADDITIONAL READINGS

Bassiouni, M. Cherif. *Substantive Criminal Law.* Springfield, Ill.: Charles C Thomas, 1978.

Bureau of National Affairs. *The Criminal Law Revolution and Its Aftermath, 1960–72.* Washington, D.C.: Bureau of National Affairs, 1973.

Chambliss, William J. *Criminal Law in Action.* New York: Wiley, 1984.

Forer, Lois J. *Criminals and Victims: A Trial Judge Reflects.* New York: Norton, 1984.

Goebel, Julius. *Felony and Misdemeanor—A Study in the History of Criminal Law.* Philadelphia: University of Pennsylvania Press, 1976.

Jenkins, Philip. *Crime and Justice—Issues and Ideas.* Monterey, Calif.: Brooks/Cole, 1984.

Leonard, V. A. *The Police, the Judiciary and the Criminal.* Springfield, Ill.: Charles C Thomas, 1969.

Nelson, William E. "Emergency Notions of Modern Criminal Law in the Revolutionary Era: A Historical Perspective." *New York University Law Review* 42 (May 1967): 453–468.

Rich, Vernon. *Law and the Administration of Justice.* New York: Wiley, 1975.

Waddington, Lawrence C. *Criminal Evidence.* Encino, Calif.: Glencoe, 1978.

Walker, S. *Sense and Nonsense About Crime,* 2nd ed. Pacific Grove, Calif.: Brooks/Cole, 1989.

Wells, Paul W. *Basic Law for the Law Enforcement Officer.* Philadelphia: Saunders, 1976.

U.S. Department of Justice, *Report to the Nation on Crime and Justice,* 2nd ed. Washington, D.C.: United States Government Printing Office, March 1988.

## NOTES

1. M. Cherif Bassiouni, *Criminal Law and Its Processes* (Springfield, Ill.: Charles C Thomas, 1969), p. 50.
2. U.S. Constitution, Art. 1, sec. 9.
3. Bassiouni, *Criminal Law and Its Processes*, p. 50.
4. See Arnold H. Loewy, *Criminal Law* (St. Paul, Minn.: West, 1975), pp. 115–118.
5. Bassiouni, *Criminal Law and Its Processes*, p. 66.
6. For example, see Gresham M. Sykes, "The Rise of Critical Criminology," *Journal of Criminal Law and Criminology* 65 (June 1974): 206–213; and Berry Krisberg, *Crime and Privilege: Toward a New Criminology* (Englewood Cliffs, N.J.: Prentice-Hall, 1975).
7. See Stephen Schafer, *Theories in Criminology: Past and Present Philosophies of the Crime Problem* (New York: Random House, 1969), especially pp. 97–110.
8. Stephen Schafer and Richard D. Knudten, *Criminological Theory* (Lexington, Mass.: Lexington Books, 1977), p. xiii.
9. Donald R. Taft, *Criminology*, 3rd ed. (New York: McGraw-Hill, 1956), p. 357.
10. Elmer H. Johnson, *Crime, Correction, and Society*, rev. ed. (Homewood, Ill.: Dorsey, 1968), p. 154.
11. Enrico Ferri, *Criminal Sociology*, trans. J. I. Kelly and John Lisle (Boston: Little, Brown, 1917), pp. 502–520.
12. This five-fold classification is adopted from: Richard Herrnstein, "Biology and Crime," *National Institute of Justice—Crime File* (Washington: U.S. Department of Justice, n.d.).
13. William H. Sheldon, *The Varieties of Human Physique* (New York: Harper, 1940).
14. William H. Sheldon, *The Varieties of Temperament* (New York: Harper, 1942).
15. S. A. Shah, *Report on the XYY Chromosomal Abnormality.* U.S. Public Health Service, publication no. 2130 (Washington, D.C.: U.S. Government Printing Office, 1970).
16. Herrnstein, op. cit., p. 3.
17. For a good summary of the adoption studies, see: Lee Ellis, "Genetics and Criminal Behavior: Evidence Through the End of the 1970s," in Frank H. Marsh and Janet Katz (eds.), *Biology, Crime and Ethics* (Cincinnati, Ohio: Anderson Publishing Co., 1985), esp. pp. 75–84.

18. Herrnstein, op. cit., p. 4.

19. Ibid.

20. Ibid.

21. Ibid.

22. Schafer and Knudten, *Criminological Theory*, p. xx.

23. Johnson, *Crime, Correction, and Society*, p. 188.

24. For general readings on research that purports to support the economic theory of crime, see: Gary S. Becker, "Crime and Punishment: An Economic Approach," *Journal of Political Economy* 2 (March–April 1968); Peter Schmidt and Ann D. Witte, *The Economics of Crime: Theory, Methods and Application* (New York: Academic Press, 1983); Isaac Ehrlich, "The Deterrent Effect of Criminal Law Enforcement," *Journal of Legal Studies* 1 (1972); and Phillip S. Cook, "Research on Criminal Deterrence: Laying the Groundwork for the Second Decade," in Norval Morris and M. Tonry (eds.), *Crime and Justice: An Annual Review of Research*, Vol. 2 (Chicago: University of Chicago Press, 1980), pp. 211–268.

25. Herbert Jacob, "Rationality and Criminality," *Social Science Quarterly* 59 (1979).

26. Cook, op. cit., pp. 211–268.

27. Colin Lofton and David McDowall, "The Police, Crime and Economic Theory: An Assessment," *American Sociological Review* 47 (June 1982).

28. Schafer and Knudten, *Criminological Theory*, p. 200.

29. R. T. Prudhoe, *England's Great Common Law* (London: Cambridge University Press, 1922), p. 49.

30. H. Sayre, "Criminal Attempts," *Harvard Law Review* 41 (1928).

31. *State* v. *Carbone*, 10 N.J., 329, 91 A. 2d 571 (1961).

32. From Bureau of Justice Statistics, *Report to the Nation on Crime and Justice*, 2nd ed. (Washington, D.C.: U.S. Department of Justice, March 1988), p. 15.

33. "Drug-Related Homicide Rates Soar in Several Cities," *New York Times*, 17 July 1988, p. 2 col. 1.

34. Bureau of Justice Statistics, *Report to the Nation*, p. 28.

35. Federal Bureau of Investigation, *Age-Specific Arrest Rates and Race-Specific Arrest Rates for Selected Offenses 1965–85* (Washington, D.C.: Uniform Crime Reporting Program, December 1986).

36. Federal Bureau of Investigation, *Uniform Crime Reporting Program* (Washington, D.C.: FBI, December 1986).

37. The one exception to this is robbery. Robbery (a violent crime) involves rather young arrestees, according to official arrest records.

38. Bureau of Justice Statistics, *Survey of State Prison Inmates*, (Washington, D.C.: U.S. Department of Justice, 1979).

39. Barbara Boland with Ronald Sones, *The Prosecution of Felony Arrests* (Washington, D.C.: INSLAW, Inc., 1981).

40. Ibid.

41. Federal Bureau of Investigation, *Age-Specific Arrest Rates.*

42. Bureau of Justice Statistics, *Report to the Nation*, p. 47.

43. Ibid., p. 67.

44. Bureau of Justice Statistics, *National Crime Survey 1973–82* (Washington, D.C.: U.S. Department of Justice, 1985), p. 27.

45. Bureau of Justice Statistics, *Report to the Nation*, p. 27.

46. Ibid., p. 14.

47. Ibid., p. 20.

48. Bureau of Justice Statistics, *Criminal Victimization in the U.S. 1984 and 1985* (Washington, D.C.: U.S. Department of Justice, 1987).

49. Boland with Sones, op. cit., p. 21.

50. Bureau of Justice Statistics, *Prison Admissions and Releases, BJS Special Report.* (Washington, D.C.: U.S. Department of Justice, March 1986).

51. Bureau of Justice Statistics, *Recidivism of Young Parolees, BJS Special Report.* (Washington, D.C.: U.S. Department of Justice, May 1987).

52. Bureau of Justice Statistics, *Report to the Nation*, p. 5.

53. Ibid., p. 5.

54. Bureau of Justice Statistics, *Criminal Victimization*, p. 12.

55. Jan M. Chaiken and Marcia R. Chaiken, *Varieties of Criminal Behavior* (Santa Monica, Calif.: Rand Corporation, 1982).

56. Bureau of Justice Statistics, *Report to the Nation*, p. 47.

57. Boland with Sones, op. cit., p. 28.

58. Ibid.

59. Bureau of Justice Statistics, *Report to the Nation*, p. 110.

60. Bureau of Justice Statistics, *Imprisonment in Four Countries, BJS Special Report.* (Washington, D.C.: U.S. Department of Justice, February 1987).

61. Lawrence M. Friedman, *History of American Law*, 2nd ed. (New York: Simon & Schuster, 1985), p. 293–294.

62. Ibid.

63. Bureau of Justice Statistics, *Report to the Nation*, p. 6.

64. Ibid.

65. Bureau of Justice Statistics, *Criminal Victimization*, p. 14.

66. Bureau of Justice Statistics, *Report to the Nation*, p. 44.

67. Ibid., p. 51.

68. Ibid., p. 68.

69. Bureau of Justice Statistics, *Imprisonment in Four Countries*, p. 3.

70. Bureau of Justice Statistics, *Report to the Nation*, p. 46.

71. Boland with Sones, op. cit.

72. Bureau of Justice Statistics, *Felony Sentencing in 18 Local Jurisdictions, BJS Special Report.* (Washington, D.C.: June 1985).

73. Bureau of Justice Statistics, *Report to the Nation*, p. 47.

74. Allen C. Gammage and Charles F. Hemphill, Jr., *Basic Criminal Law* (New York: McGraw-Hill, 1974), p. 14.

75. Ibid., p. 22.

76. M'Naghten Case, 8 Eng. Rep. 718 (H.L. 1843), p. 722.

77. *Durham* v. *United States*, 214 F.2d 862, 874–875 (D.C. Cir. 1954).

78. Loewy, *Criminal Law*, pp. 222–223.

79. American Law Institute, Model Penal Code, 401 (1962).

80. Joseph J. Senna and Larry J. Siegel, *Introduction to Criminal Justice* (St. Paul, Minn.: West, 1978), p. 83.

81. Loewy, *Criminal Law*, p. 228.

82. U.S. Department of Justice, *Handbook on the Comprehensive Crime Control Act of 1984 and Other Criminal Statutes Enacted by the 98th Congress* (Washington, D.C.: U.S. Government Printing Office, December 1984), p. 61.

83. Although it is commonly believed that certain words and actual physical contact with the arrestee are required, this is not the case.

84. See Lloyd L. Weinreb, *Criminal Process* (Mineola, N.Y.: Foundation Press, 1969), pp. 17–22.

85. See *Bostwick* v. *State*, 124 Ga. App. 113, 182 S.E.2d 925 (1971).

86. See *Federal Rules of Criminal Procedure* 41 (d); and Yale Kamisar, Wayne R. La Fave, and Jerold H. Israel, *Basic Criminal Procedure* (St. Paul, Minn.: West, 1974).

87. For example, see *Mich. Stats. Ann.* 8 279 23 C.L. (1948).

88. Hazel B. Kerper, *Introduction to the Criminal Justice System* (St. Paul, Minn.: West, 1972), p. 404.

89. *Ex Parte Kelly*, 123 N.J. EQ 489, 198 A. 203 (1938).

90. *Encyclopedia Brittanica*, Vol. 10, pp. 1088–1089.

# CHAPTER 3

# Crime in America: Issues, Trends, Measurement, and Victimization

## O B J E C T I V E S

**After reading this chapter, the student should be able to:**

Discuss crime as a "national problem."

Identify the factors associated with being a crime victim.

Discuss the "politics of crime."

Identify the Uniform Crime Reporting Program and the Part I (Index) offenses.

Discuss crime as a social problem, including:
    historical incidence of crime
    crime cycles
    geography of crime

Discuss and identify the characteristics associated with career criminals.

Discuss white-collar, "respectable" crime and "official lawlessness."

Understand the controversy over the Uniform Crime Reports (UCR) and the crime rates they purport to show.

Discuss the role and the importance of the National Crime Survey.

Identify factors associated with organized crime.

Discuss compensation programs to aid crime victims.

## I M P O R T A N T   T E R M S

Uniform Crime Reports (UCR)

"Politics" of crime

Reported crimes

Seasonal variations in crime

Geography of crime

Crime Index

National Crime Survey (NCS)

Baseline data

Victimization studies

White-collar and "respectable" crime

Organized crime

Victim compensation

This chapter examines the nature and extent of crime in the United States and the means we employ to measure its impact. It should raise more questions than it answers. Perhaps given the existing knowledge about crime, the raising of such questions is the most important contribution that can be made.

In this vein, a compelling article in an issue of the *Annals of the American Academy of Political and Social Science* makes the argument quite well.[1] The article reviews data on crimes and their interpretations and suggests that reporting of major crimes such as rape, robbery, burglary, and larceny masks considerable differences in the seriousness of crime events. It is argued that a substantial number of crimes that are attempted rather than completed result in little or no material harm to the victim and are compensated for satisfactorily. This casts some questions on the view that most crimes against persons are violent and that crimes against persons and property necessarily result in substantial physical harm and economic loss. It also further clouds the overall issue of crime.

*The cloudiness of the crime picture*

A fact that is quite clear and should be kept in mind is that *national crime statistics tend to serve national rather than local needs and are not particularly suited to the needs of ordinary citizens in telling them about their risks as potential victims.* As crime is currently reported, the statistics also draw attention away from organizations as victims and offenders. Instead, they concentrate disproportionately on a few selected crimes, which are portrayed as violent and serious. If anything, this tends to mask the fact that not all so-called serious crimes are extremely serious. Crimes that are *officially* less serious, which are yet to be reported systematically, may be far more damaging to the population as well as to individuals. The reader should also try to keep these thoughts in mind while reading this chapter.

## CRIME AS A NATIONAL PROBLEM

Crime, which has always been a problem, became a major public issue in the United States during the turbulent 1960s. By 1970, several public opinion polls indicated that crime was viewed as the most serious social problem—surpassing race conflicts, inflation, and even the Vietnam war.[2] The media have dramatized the problem with examples of criminal acts that confirm official statistics indicating rising crime rates. *Life* magazine described a six-story building in New York in which 17 of 24 apartments had been burglarized. One resident even purchased a German shepherd watchdog to protect himself, but it too was stolen.[3] *Life* followed up this story with a questionnaire exploring individual experiences with crime. The 43,000 responses, which were not necessarily representative of the general population of the United States, indicated that at least 70 percent of those responding were afraid to go out on the streets after dark, were occasionally afraid of crime even while at home, and were prepared to pay more for improved protection.[4]

During the early 1980s, the general concern over crime seemed to diminish somewhat as new national issues elbowed their way to the forefront. Major crime-related attention during these early years of the decade focused on such crimes as international terrorism and white-collar offenses. Little widespread attention focused on more conventional crime issues. Yet, a new harbinger of drug-related crime concerns began to stir in America. By the middle of the 1980s, the insidious menace of cocaine and "crack" began receiving increasing media coverage. As stories of associated drug-related violence swept the country, public attention and fear became riveted on this new problem. This produced an outpouring of national concern and increasingly strident declarations by politicians that an all-out "war" on drugs and related violence become a major issue of national policy.

To many Americans, however, the concern and fear of crime has existed unabated. Many citizens—particularly those in high crime areas—still felt the fear of crime in spite of the downplay of "street crime" issues during the early years of the 1980s. During that time, the federal government's Department of Housing and Urban Development conducted a national survey of citizens on the quality of community life. In this survey, they provided residents with a list of problems and asked which of these the residents considered to be severe problems in their own communities. The list included such things as crime, drugs, unemployment, traffic congestion, condition of housing, air pollution, lack of medical care, and things to do. More than 70 percent of city residents surveyed considered crime a severe problem. No other issue even approached this figure for these residents. In suburbs, crime was seen as second only to drugs as a serious problem. Only in smaller towns was crime seen as less important than several of the other problems.[5]

**Comparing America's "crime problem"**

Many of us hear reports that the United States is the world's most violent country and that it has the highest crime rate.[6] No facts justify this conclusion. Such statements are myths fostered by official crime reports and the media. Violent crime, like all crime, is difficult to measure, and official reports are not comparable from one country to another. Homicide may be one exception. A few years ago,

The fortifications surrounding this house in Sao Paulo, Brazil, are typical of the anticrime measures that are taken for granted in many foreign countries. (Marcelo Uchoa, Sao Paulo)

INTERPOL, the International Police Organization (see Chapter 4), listed twelve countries with homicide rates higher than the rate in the United States. In addition, countries such as Mexico are not listed by INTERPOL but also have substantially higher homicide rates than the United States.[7] Today, the crimes of terrorism and violence so typical of areas such as the Mideast, Africa, Central and South America, and even Europe significantly eclipse similar problems of violence in America.

Let's look at some other facts. Britain, West Germany, and other Western European countries have also experienced rising crime rates.[8] Even the Soviet Union, which tries to conceal such facts, admits that there have been significant crime increases in that country.

A Dutch national victimization survey recently published in English by the Netherlands Justice Ministry compares American surveys (which will be discussed later in this chapter) with its own. Contrary to what one might expect, the percentage of victims of violent behavior *was higher among the Dutch than among*

## CRIME COLOMBIA STYLE

Bogotá, the capital of Colombia, was once called the Athens of Latin America. Today, it has a new name: Lebanon West. Violence has reached epidemic proportions. It has become so predictable in this city and in the city of Medellín, the headquarters of the Medellín cocaine cartel, that you can practically set your watch by it. A combustible mixture of drug lords, death squads, Marxist rebels, and street thugs have made the name *Colombia* synonymous with criminal violence.

Colombia's criminal justice system is not only riddled with graft, it is riddled with bullets. At least 220 officers of the courts (including 41 judges) were murdered in the less than ten years from 1979 to mid-1989. More are sure to die as the government struggles to gain control in a nearly lawless environment. Judges have resigned en masse following threats by narcotics traffickers. Judges intimidated by threats are refusing to hear cases against drug traffickers and other criminal elements. Many have fled the country. Special security forces dispatched by the United States have been sent to Colombia to train the national police to protect themselves and judges from assassinations.

In 1989, the Justice Minister fled to the United States, seeking sanctuary from death threats. She was the sixth Justice Minister in only three years to hold the position and about the only person who would take the job. The law, the Minister said, "is under siege in Colombia."

Not only the criminal justice system is under attack. In Medellín, the very social and governmental structure of the city is crumbling. This city of two million averages over ten murders a day, giving it a per capita homicide rate nearly nine times that of New York City. Assassins can be hired for as little as $10. Visitors are warned not to take taxis from the airport to their hotels. The only sure way to avoid robbers is to take a helicopter. Hotel guests are also warned to remove their jewelry before venturing into the crime-ridden streets, and frightened cab-drivers lock their doors after picking up a fare to guard against *gamines,* roving bands of children as young as nine who cruise for mugging victims.

Violence didn't arrive with the narco-terrorists. It has been a way of life for as long as most Colombians can remember. It has simply

grown worse. The countryside is parceled up into independent fiefdoms ruled by neofascist death-squad leaders, Stanlinist guerilla chieftains, and Mafia-financed private armies. Six leftist guerrilla armies, 138 right-wing paramilitary groups, and thousands of young apolitical assassins known as *sicarios* all vie for power. Drug overlords even hire private mercenary forces from Britain and the United States to train their forces. Amid all this, a burgeoning security industry consisting of thugs and bodyguards has become a major growth occupation. The tentacles of violence reach worldwide. Government officials who thought they could escape death threats by going to Europe or the United States have been brutally murdered in these countries.

Ironically, this paroxysm of violence and crime has spawned a new Colombian homegrown subspecies of sociology called "violentology." Academics are studying this cultural violence and trying to unravel this phenomenon as closely as social scientists in other parts of the world study other more conventional forms of human and social behavior.

*Americans.* More important, the percentage of victims who sustained physical injury was also higher in the Netherlands.[9]

Finally, if the reader feels that our age is particularly criminal and violent in comparison with other historical periods, one should read books that describe crime and violence during such periods as the Middle Ages or the Renaissance.[10]

## ▢ THE NATIONAL PROBLEM BECOMES A POLITICAL ISSUE

Because of the expressed concern over crime, it has naturally become a political issue. Just as crime has been a historical fact of our existence, so, too, has it been used for political purposes. The history of humankind points out that the definitions of what was considered "crime" were established by certain interests. In England, for instance, the criminal code became a vehicle by which the propertied classes attempted to retain the age-old privileges of wealth and to control the masses. By invoking very punitive measures for property crimes, the dominant social and economic classes sought to protect their property rights and maintain the distinction between the haves and the have-nots. And what better method to maintain this difference than through the enactment and effect of the law?

*The "politics" of crime*

Crime has also had a political tinge in America. In many ways it has expressed something of a class consciousness. It also has been expressed by means of a broad division in philosophy in our society, which we today refer to as liberal and conservative. There is probably no subject on which liberals and conservatives split more sharply than the causes and cures of crime. Since the turn of the century, liberals have downplayed the importance of the criminal justice system as a means to deal with crime. To liberals, the problems stem from deep within a society; to them, the search for more effective law enforcement is seen as an attempt to treat merely the symptom rather than the cause. To deal effectively with crime, a society must make some fundamental alterations to attack the basic causes of crime. In dissenting from the 1931 report of the National Commission on Law Observance, Henry W. Anderson, chairman of the commission, wrote:

*Liberals versus conservatives*

> Like eruptions on the human body criminal acts are symptoms of more fundamental conditions of personal or social deficiency or imbalance. . . . If the crime problem is to be solved, the attack must be made at the sources of the trouble and the remedy must be found in the removal of the causes.[11]

Conservatives, on the other hand, are more inclined to believe that deliberation, not desperation, is the root of crime. The feeling is that a great many offenders commit crimes because they want to commit them. This disagreement is classic and deep. To conservatives, people have always had a propensity to commit crime, yet they have the ability to control these impulses. To help them control their desires, society must emphasize a strong moral order, a respect for law, and a confidence in punishment as a deterrent to crime.

The right–left split so permeates legal thinking that Walter B. Miller of Harvard Law School's Center for Criminal Justice maintains that "ideology is the permanent hidden agenda of criminal justice." But ideological differences have recently started to blur under the impact of America's unabated problems with crime, and there is a renewed interest on both sides in making sure that violent criminals get locked up. As former Philadelphia Mayor Frank Rizzo liked to put it: "A conservative is a liberal who was mugged the night before."

A major turning point in modern times occurred in the 1964 presidential race. Barry Goldwater, the conservative Republican, together with a coalition of conservative Southern democrats, attacked the policies of the incumbent Johnson administration and his predecessor John F. Kennedy. The criticisms were wide-ranging: the need for a return to more states' rights, a retreat from federal encroachment, a clamping down on those involved in the growing problem of civil disorders, and a reversal of what was seen as the moral decay of society. Johnson and the liberal Democrats were accused of being "soft on crime" and responsible for fostering the so-called "due process revolution" that handcuffed the police while favoring the criminal.

In spite of Goldwater's criticisms, Johnson won the election, but he was stung by the remarks. Although not particularly anxious to involve the federal government in major anticrime efforts—and being particularly sensitive to Goldwater's criticism about the growing encroachment of the federal government—Johnson, spurred on by strong anticrime elements in Congress, felt compelled to act. In a March 1965 speech, Johnson outlined the idea of a limited federal role in assisting state and local governments to deal with crime. In that year he created the first federal grant-in-aid program to deal with the crime problem. Soon afterward he convened a national crime commission and increased federal aid to state and local law enforcement agencies. The political issue of crime was taking on a gigantic new meaning.

The presidential election of 1968 saw crime as the major domestic political issue. The nation had just suffered through a horrible period of urban rioting, rising levels of reported crimes, and the assassinations of several notable public officials. Nixon's slogans centered on "law and order," "war on crime," and "safe streets." Public concern about crime had reached new heights, and the politicians were there to assure the people that if elected they would do something about it. Many political analysts feel that Nixon's success in the presidential election of 1968 was due in part to the wide appeal his get-tough "law and order" campaign generated among the electorate. During his years in office, Nixon was reported to have carefully digested the compiled crime statistics for Washington, D.C., and on several occasions summoned the District's chief of police to the White House to explain personally why more was not being done to stamp out crime in the nation's capital.

Such anticrime platforms continue to inspire political campaigns. As several researchers have pointed out, promises to reestablish law and order and to make streets safe are especially effective in mobilizing political support for a candidate, for crime arouses deep-seated fears for personal safety and for the preservation of social order.[12] The Reagan administration continued to make crime one of its major priorities. Shortly after assuming office, President Reagan, through the Attorney General's office, convened a special Task Force on Violent Crime. Reagan frequently made it known that he supported a tougher stance on crime. This included many controversial measures for changing existing laws and Supreme Court decisions that he felt had contributed to the crime problem in the nation.

Today these issues are being injected into the political mainstream at all levels: Washington, our state capitals, and local political circles. "Stamping out crime" has become the rallying cry of politicials—particularly drugs and drug-related offenses. The off-year gubernatorial and congressional elections saw politicians falling over themselves trying to outdo their opponents in convincing the public that if elected they would do something about crime. In Arkansas, for instance, the conservative Republican incumbent governor built much of his campaign around the theme,

"I'm gonna execute some of these people," in referring to inmates on death row in that state. So vociferously did he play up this campaign issue that the state's largest paper ran a series of political cartoons in which he was depicted as dragging his "port-a-kill" machine—an electric chair on wheels—from political speech to political speech as a child might drag a wagon behind him.

President Bush picked up where his predecessors left off. In 1989 he appointed the nation's first "drug czar" to coordinate federal antinarcotic efforts. Later that same year, he took an almost unprecedented step by calling to Washington every federal prosecutor in the nation. In his words, he wanted "to give them their marching orders." They were to get tough with crime—particularly those crimes involving drugs, violence, and the use of firearms. He called on the assembled U.S. Attorneys to ban plea bargaining in such cases and to prosecute to the maximum extent of the law. He also urged Congress to appropriate more monies for the construction of additional prisons to house convicted criminals and called on Congress to provide funds to hire additional federal judges, prosecutors, and law enforcement personnel.

The fear of becoming a victim of crime and the chances for actual victimization (Table 3.1) differ in American society. The groups of people who have the highest risk of becoming victims of crime are not the ones who express the greatest fear of crime. Females and the elderly, for instance, express the greatest fear, yet they are not in the population groups most victimized by crime. Perhaps their fear is a result of their greater feelings of vulnerability. The Reaction to Crime project found that such impressions can be explained by the content of communications about crime. Such communications emphasize stories about elderly and female victims. These stories may become reference points for women and the elderly to judge the seriousness of their own condition.[13]

What do we know about crime victimization rates in general? An analysis of national victimization rates for the American public shows the following facts:

- Men are much more likely to be crime victims than women.
- Younger people are much more likely than the elderly to be victims of crime.
- Blacks are much more likely to be crime victims than whites or other racial groups.
- The divorced and never-married are more likely than the married and widowed to be crime victims.
- Violent crime rates are higher for low-income people.
- Theft rates are highest for people with low incomes (less than $3,000 per year) than those with high incomes (more than $25,000 per year)
- Students and the unemployed are more likely than housewives, retirees, or the employed to be crime victims.
- People living in cities are more likely to be victimized than are rural residents.
- Young black males have the highest violent crime rates; elderly white females have the lowest.[14]

From this we can see certain common factors associated with increased chances for victimization. Those who are male, young, poor, and black have the greatest potential risk of victimization. Situational aspects also play a role. One's life-style and place of residence, for example, would seem to contribute to one's potential for being "at-risk." We might assume, for instance, that young males by virtue of their life-styles would be in situations in which they increase the probability of victimization.

To obtain a better idea of crime in this country, we must know what specific crimes the authorities rely on to determine the nature and extent of crime and how these crime figures are gathered. We also need to know what these crime figures show. According to the *Uniform Crime Reports,* nearly 14 million so-called serious

What really constitutes the crime picture?

TABLE **3.1**  How Do Crime Rates Compare with Rates of Other Life Events?

| Events | Rate per 1,000 Adults per Year[a] |
|---|---|
| Accidental injury, all circumstances | 290 |
| Accidental injury at home | 105 |
| Personal theft | 82 |
| Accidental injury at work | 68 |
| Violent victimization | 33 |
| Assault (aggravated and simple) | 25 |
| Injury in motor vehicle accident | 23 |
| Divorce | 23 |
| Death, all causes | 11 |
| Serious (aggravated) assault | 9 |
| Death of spouse | 9 |
| Robbery | 7 |
| Heart disease death | 4 |
| Cancer death | 2 |
| Rape (women only) | 2 |
| Accidental death, all circumstances | 0.5 |
| Motor vehicle accident death | 0.3 |
| Pneumonia/influenza death | 0.3 |
| Suicide | 0.2 |
| Injury from fire | 0.1 |
| Homicide/legal intervention death | 0.1 |
| Death from fire | 0.03 |

These rates are an approximate assessment of your chances of becoming a victim of these events. More precise estimates can be derived by taking account of such factors as age, sex, race, place of residence, and life-style. Findings are based on 1979–1981 data, but there is little variation in rates from year to year.

[a]These rates have been standardized to exclude children (those under age 15 to 17, depending on the series). For injury/death, data are based on the total population, because no age-specific data are available in this series.

*Sources: Current Estimates From the National Health Interview Survey, United States, 1981, Vital and Health Statistics* (Series 10, no. 141, October 1982); "Advance Report of Final Divorce Statistics, 1979," *Monthly Vital Statistics Report* 30, no. 2, supplement (29 May 1981); "Advance Report of Final Mortality Statistics," *Monthly Vital Statistics Report* 31, no. 6, supplement (30 September 1982, National Center for Health Statistics, U.S. Public Health Service, Washington, D.C.). *Preliminary Estimates of the Population of the United States, by Age, Sex, and Race, 1970 to 1981,* Series P-25, no. 917 (U.S. Bureau of the Census, Washington, D.C., 1982). "Fire Loss in the United States During 1981," Michael J. Karter, Jr., *Fire Journal* 76, no. 5 (National Fire Protection Association, Quincy, Mass., September 1982); *Report to the Nation on Crime and Justice* (Washington, D.C.: U.S. Department of Justice, Bureau of Justice Statistics, October 1983), p. 18.

TABLE **3.2**  Eight Most Frequent Crimes for Which Arrests Were Made
by the Police (1987)

| Rank | Offense | No. of Arrests | Percent of All Crime Arrests |
|------|---------|----------------|------------------------------|
| 1 | Driving under the influence (DWI) | 1,410,397 | 13.7 |
| 2 | Larceny/theft | 1,256,552 | 11.6 |
| 3 | Drug abuse violation | 811,078 | 7.5 |
| 4 | Drunkenness | 700,662 | 6.5 |
| 5 | Simple assault | 671,938 | 6.2 |
| 6 | Disorderly conduct | 599,622 | 5.6 |
| 7 | Liquor law violation | 505,021 | 4.7 |
| 8 | Burglary | 374,963 | 3.5 |
| | TOTAL | | 59.3 |

*Source:* Federal Bureau of Investigation, *Crime in the United States* (Washington, D.C.: U.S. Government Printing Office, 1988), p. 174.

crimes were reported to the police during 1988. However, this represents only a small percentage of crimes committed and an equally small percentage of crimes for which arrests were made. The majority of crimes committed and handled by the criminal justice system are much less serious offenses. Crimes such as drunkenness, larceny (theft), driving under the influence, disorderly conduct, and crimes related to drug laws (particularly marijuana) are disproportionately represented in official crime statistics. Add to this the vast number of traffic cases and other misdemeanors that are processed by the police, courts, and jails, and a different picture of crime emerges. For example, Table 3.2 summarizes the most frequent types of crimes for which arrests were made in 1987.

This is not to say that the United States does not have a serious crime problem; however, a closer look would tend to call into question certain popular assumptions about crime and the ability of the criminal justice system to deal with it. Although the typical image of crime centers on the more serious offenses of murder, forcible rape, and robbery, these particular offenses actually constitute slightly more than 4 percent of the crimes *reported* to the police. If we considered just the crimes of homicide and forcible rape, this figure would diminish to a little less than eight-tenths of one percent. If, in fact, we knew the true total extent of crime in America (reported and unreported crimes), the relative percentage of these crimes would shrink even further.

The remainder of this chapter examines the question of crime and how very misleading crime statistics can be. As will be seen, we need to analyze crime and crime data much more rationally if we are to understand this particular social problem.

## ☐ THE UNIFORM CRIME REPORTING PROGRAM

The UCR

During the 1920s, the International Association of Chiefs of Police (IACP) saw the need to develop a national system for gathering and publishing crime statistics. In 1930 Congress authorized a national and uniform system of compiling crime sta-

TABLE **3.3**   Uniform Crime Report Offenses

| Part I | Part II (Other Offenses) | |
|---|---|---|
| 1. Criminal homicide | 9. Other assaults | 19. Gambling |
| 2. Forcible rape | 10. Forgery and counterfeiting | 20. Offenses against the family and children |
| 3. Robbery | 11. Fraud | |
| 4. Aggravated assault | 12. Embezzlement | 21. Driving under the influence |
| 5. Burglary | 13. Buying, receiving, or possessing stolen property | 22. Violation of liquor laws |
| 6. Larceny-theft | | 23. Drunkenness |
| 7. Auto theft | 14. Vandalism | 24. Disorderly conduct |
| 8. Arson[a] | 15. Weapons (carrying, possession, etc.) | 25. Vagrancy |
| | 16. Prostitution and commercialized vice | 26. All other offenses (excluding traffic) |
| | 17. Other sex offenses | 27. Suspicion |
| | 18. Drug abuse violations | 28. Curfew and loitering |
| | | 29. Runaway (juveniles) |

[a]*Arson was changed from a Part II to a Part I offense in 1979.*

tistics known as the Uniform Crime Reporting Program. Congress vested the Federal Bureau of Investigation (FBI) with responsibility for developing the program and authorized that agency to be the national clearinghouse for statistical information on crime. Under this program, crime reports were to be voluntarily submitted to the FBI by city, county, and state law enforcement agencies throughout the country. To provide for uniformity in reporting crimes by various jurisdictions, national standardized definitions of crimes and the method of reporting them were adopted. Although there still remain a few police agencies that do not routinely report crimes to the FBI, by 1988 nearly 16,000 law enforcement agencies voluntarily supplied crime data to the FBI. From these data, the FBI publishes annual *Uniform Crime Reports* (UCRs), which are statistical summaries of all reported crimes. States have developed central agencies that collect the data from all local governmental jurisdictions and then forward the statistics for the state to the FBI.

Offenses in the Uniform Crime Reporting Program are broken down into two categories. Part I of the UCR consists of eight major crimes that the FBI views as indicators of national and regional crime trends. These crimes are known collectively as the *Crime Index*. The data on these offenses are further broken down into specific areas such as age and sex, population groups, suburban and nonsuburban counties, arrest rates, and clearances. Part II consists of twenty-one other offense categories for which data are not as complete. Table 3.3 indicates the twenty-nine offenses covered in the UCR.

*Part I crimes and the Crime Index*

## CRIME AS A SOCIAL PROBLEM

Because of the nature of the factors that seem to be associated with crime, many authorities doubt that crime can ever be brought under control. James Q. Wilson, for example, sees crime as the result of three social factors: (1) the numbers of youth in society at a given time; (2) the disruptive effects of our society on the family unit; (3) the opportunities for crime in our urbanized society.[15] Whether or not we fully accept his ideas, these forces probably do, in important ways, influence the potential for crime. What is certain is that crime is not a problem that can be left entirely to the criminal justice system to solve. Clearly, the issues that underlie crime transcend the ability of the police and the courts to deal with this complex problem in any meaningful way.

## Historical Background

Crime is not only a recent experience in America. Every generation has been threatened by crime and violence. In San Francisco in the 1860s, accounts told of extensive areas of the city where "no decent man was in safety to walk the street after dark; while at all hours, both night and day, his property was jeopardized by incendiarism and burglary."[16] In New York, roving teenage street gangs who "preyed upon innocent victims" gave rise to the word "hoodlum" in 1877.[17] Even before the American Revolution, increases in robbery and violent crimes reported in New York, Boston, and Philadelphia led some citizens to complain that municipal governance was a failure and that citizens should revert to self-action if individual safety were to be preserved.[18]

Many instances of crime and violence occurred in our early history. During the great railway strike of 1877, hundreds were killed in outbreaks of violence and terrorism that swept the country and culminated in a massive confrontation between strikers and company police and militia; scores were killed or injured, and almost two miles of buildings and railway property were destroyed.[19] During the 1863 draft riots, the looting and takeover of New York for three days by mobs equaled the disorders that racked our cities in the 1960s. Racial disturbances have long plagued our major cities, as seen by the race riots in Atlanta in 1907, in Chicago, Washington, and East St. Louis in 1919, and Detroit in 1943.[20] Al Capone, "Pretty Boy" Floyd, and the Barkers are all examples of our heritage of crime.

Neither the specific variables that produce crime nor the interaction of those variables are fully understood. But some important factors are known. They are often broken down into three major categories:

SOCIAL CHARACTERISTICS
- Density and size of the community
- Social composition of the community in terms of age, sex, and race
- Existing cultural mores that control social behavior
- Economic conditions
- Relative stability of the population
- Educational and religious characteristics of the population

INDIVIDUAL CHARACTERISTICS
- Attitudes conducive to criminal behavior
- Perceived value and meaningfulness of legitimate behavior
- Self-esteem; perceived abilities to compete in the legitimate world

SPECIFIC CHARACTERISTICS OF THE CRIMINAL JUSTICE SYSTEM
- Effective strength of the police force
- Quality of police personnel and efficiency of the police
- Policies of the prosecuting officials and courts
- Attitude of the public toward the police and other criminal justice agencies

How accurately crime and its effects on society can be measured depends on the quality of the tools used to make the analysis. We are handicapped in understanding crime because we do not have adequate measuring instruments, nor do we have the knowledge to account properly for the multitude of factors that might have some relationship to criminal behavior. As a result of these limitations, any analysis of our existing crime statistics, and therefore any conclusions that might be drawn from them, must always be suspect. These limitations also present significant problems in measuring the impact and results of many of the programs that have been designed to reduce crime in this country.

## ▣ CRIME TRENDS AND CHARACTERISTICS

At this point, let us examine some of the data provided by the UCR. Although the UCR is not an accurate reflection of crime in America, as we shall see later, we can still analyze the trends and characteristics of crime that it purports to show.

Figure 3.1 shows the index of violent crime for the years 1978 to 1988. Figure 3.2 shows the property crime index for these years. Notice that both violent and property crime indexes follow the same general trends over the years, and they seem to rise and fall nearly proportionally. For a few years after 1981, the crime index began dropping. Many thought this signaled a turning point in America's struggle with rising crime rates—a struggle that began in the early 1960s and ran unabated through the late 1970s. This was to prove to be wishful thinking. By the mid-1980s, crime, as represented by the UCR, was again turning upward at an alarming level. Particularly thought-provoking was the sharp upswing in violent crimes. Many observers were of the opinion that the continued high levels of violent crime were particularly instructive: such crime levels served as a malaise for the fundamental and deep-seated problems that today underlie American society.[21] Figure 3.3 is a composite crime index that incorporates both the violent and property crime indexes for the years 1978 to 1988.

*Comparing UCR crime trends over time*

### Crime Cycles

Statistics indicate that there are seasonal, weekly, and even daily cycles both in the rate of crime and in the types of crime committed.

**SEASONAL VARIATIONS IN CRIME.** The relationship between the seasons of the year and the occurrence of crime has fascinated criminologists for many years. A number of nineteenth-century studies concluded that sexual crimes occurred more frequently in the summer months and that crimes against property were more likely to be committed in winter.[22] In 1912, Cesare Lombroso wrote the first important study of seasonal crime rates.[23] By examining statistical data on sexual crimes, murders, and political crimes of rebellion, he concluded that these types of crimes are most frequent during the hottest months.[24] Von Mayr arrived at a similar conclusion. From an analysis of criminal statistics in Germany from 1883 to 1892, he concluded that a correlation existed between the seasons of the year and certain types of crime; that is, offenses against the person reached their maximum in August and their minimum in December, whereas offenses against property reached their maximum in December and their minimum in April.[25]

*Historical explanations*

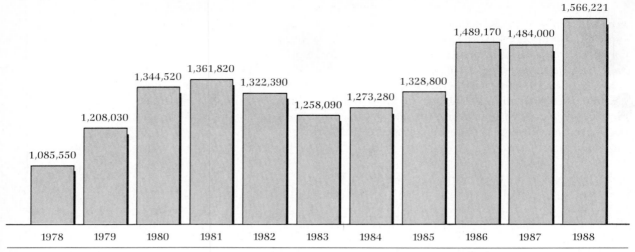

FIGURE **3.1** Index of violent crime in the United States, 1978 to 1987: number of violent index crimes (in millions). [*Source:* FBI, *Crime in the United States, 1987*, p. 41; and *Crime in the United States, 1988*, p. 49 (Washington, D.C.: Government Printing Office).]

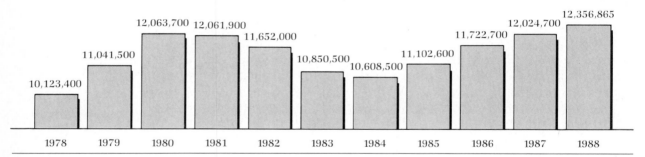

FIGURE **3.2** Index of property crime in the United States, 1978 to 1987: number of property index crimes (in millions). [*Source:* FBI, *Crime in the United States, 1987*, p. 41; and *Crime in the United States, 1988*, p. 49 (Washington, D.C.: Government Printing Office).]

FIGURE **3.3** Composite index of both violent and property crime in the United States, 1978 to 1987: number of index crimes (in millions). [*Source:* FBI, *Crime in the United States, 1987*, p. 41; and *Crime in the United States, 1988*, p. 49 (Washington, D.C.: Government Printing Office).]

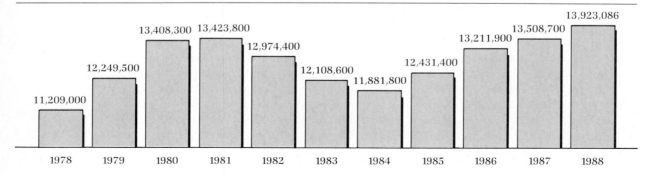

Some recent research has tried to examine more systematically the relationship between seasons and crime rates. The Bureau of Justice Statistics examined data from the UCRs and the National Crime Survey (this latter form of measurement to be explained later) for the period 1973 to 1984. In this analysis, some fluctuations in crime rates were found to exist during certain months of the year.[26] It was hypothesized that individual behavior patterns change with the seasons and with them the opportunity for crime to occur. People, for instance, spend more time outside in the warmer weather, increasing the number of potential targets for street crime. Doors and windows in homes are more likely to be left open or unlocked at these times, which provides easier access to intruders. More household articles are likely to be left outside, serving as invitations to theft. Patterns of economic activity also show seasonal changes that may affect crime rates. Weather could play a role by increasing the possibility that hot summer weather would result in heightened aggression coupled with the fact that there would be greater interaction among people. Summer was also a period when more kids were out of school and able to capitalize on targets of criminal opportunity. Winter on the other hand, might bring increases in crimes of stealth during periods of longer darkness.

The researchers found some variations in criminal acts on a seasonal basis. Seasonality was most pronounced with the crimes of larceny, rape, and unlawful entry. Rape, for example, was most likely to occur in the summer—particularly the early summer months—and reach its maximum decline in January. The usual pattern is for the high crime months to occur in the summer and the low crime months in the winter. There were two exceptions to this pattern, however. Crimes such as robbery and personal larceny with contact both peaked in December.[27] Other specific crimes examined showed no appreciable seasonal differences.

*Some seasonal variations*

It was impossible to try to explain these few differences from the data. Except for a few categories of crime, the lack of seasonal variations made further analysis unwarranted. As for those crimes that showed some seasonal variations, the possible reasons are murky at best and may be largely explained by the seasonal factors already discussed.

**DAILY VARIATIONS IN CRIME.** Most data indicate that major crimes are most likely to be committed on weekends, with the trend peaking on Saturday and then declining from Sunday through Tuesday, after which crime begins to climb again toward the Saturday peak.[28] There are also hourly variations in crimes. Many police agencies report that the incidence of crime is highest during the hours between 8:00 P.M. and midnight. The Kansas City Police Department in analyzing its crime occurrence trends found that a little over 28 percent of the crimes committed during any twenty-four-hour period occur during those four hours. Similar conclusions have been reached by other police agencies that have studied the hourly distribution of crimes.[29]

## The Geography of Crime

In addition to some seasonal and chronological differences in crime, there are other ways to examine the crime picture in the United States. Two such interesting ways are to look at the incidence of crime and its differences according to geographical areas of the country and by the type of community. Whether we use the UCRs or the newer National Crime Survey (NCS), differences according to regions and community characteristics seem to exist.

**CRIME BY REGIONS.** Dividing the nation into geographical areas for the analysis of crime produces some interesting variations. Generally, official crime statistics will divide the country into four regions: the South, the Western states, the Midwest, and the Northeast. Using the UCR classification as an example, these four areas will be examined as to the absolute and relative number of index crimes occurring in each. We say absolute and relative numbers of crimes because both are calculated. The South, for instance, may be examined according to how many total index crimes—or a specific crime (e.g., robbery)—occur annually in this region. This is an absolute measure. We may find, for example, that the states that comprise the South account for 30 percent of all index crimes recorded in the nation that year. To see how this compares, we may then want to use relative measures. One way we do this is to compare crime rates per 100,000 population. This standardizes the measure and takes into consideration population differences. One can then compare the rates more precisely. We may also want to compare the rate in the South with its percentage of the nation's population. Since the states that make up the southern region for the UCR contained 34.5 percent of the nation's population in 1987, the overall 30 percent figure for that region would show it to be below average when examined in terms of relative population.

*Absolute and relative measures*

As mentioned, regional differences are shown both in total crime and the relative frequency of certain index crimes. What this says is unclear. It may represent the fact that certain areas of the country have a higher proportion of young people as part of their overall population. This could be a factor. Likewise, the weather could play a role. Warmer year-round areas of the country might be expected to have higher overall crime rates. Regions also show some differences (although this is not as great as it was in the past) in other possible sociodemographic correlates of crime: age distribution, sex distribution, racial composition, life-style attitudes, urban versus rural, educational attainment, religious participation, occupational distribution, economic conditions, residential mobility, and other factors. These characteristics surely play some role in determining what types of crimes are likely to be committed, with what frequency, and probably, the likelihood that they will be reported or otherwise come to the attention of the authorities.

*Regional differences*

Tables 3.4 to 3.6 look at regional differences in crime as measured by the UCR for the year 1987. Several interesting facts are apparent. The South leads by a healthy

---

TABLE **3.4**   Percentage of Index Crimes Reported in the Four Regions of the United States (1987)

| Region | Percent of Nation's Population | Crimes (Percent) | | | | | | |
|---|---|---|---|---|---|---|---|---|
| | | Murder | Forcible Rape | Robbery | Aggravated Assault | Burglary | Larceny | Motor Vehicle Theft |
| South | 34.5 | 42 | 36 | 31 | 36 | 41 | 36 | 31 |
| West | 20.4 | 21 | 23 | 21 | 26 | 23 | 24 | 24 |
| Midwest | 24.5 | 20 | 24 | 20 | 20 | 20 | 23 | 20 |
| Northeast | 20.7 | 17 | 16 | 28 | 18 | 16 | 17 | 25 |

Note: May not add up to 100% because of rounding.
*Source:* FBI, *Crime in the United States, 1987* (Washington, D.C.: Federal Bureau of Investigation, 1988).

TABLE **3.5**   Percentage of Index Crimes in Violent and Property Crime Categories Reported by Region (1987)

| Region | Percent of Nation's Population | Crime (Percent) | |
| --- | --- | --- | --- |
| | | Violent Crime | Property Crime |
| South | 34.5 | 34.3 | 36.9 |
| West | 20.4 | 23.9 | 23.7 |
| Midwest | 24.5 | 20.2 | 21.8 |
| Northeast | 20.7 | 21.5 | 17.6 |

Note: May not add up to 100% because of rounding.
*Source:* FBI, *Crime in the United States, 1987* (Washington, D.C.: Federal Bureau of Investigation, 1988).

margin in the percentage and number of homicides. This is a phenomenon that has existed as long as official crime statistics have been compiled. Criminologists suggest its cause might be found in the greater tradition of violence that exists because of the cultural and social stratification that has historically been a part of this region. Still, nobody seems to have a supportable theory for the intermix of factors that might explain this long-puzzling situation.[30]

The Northeast shows unusually high (considering its percentage of the nation's population) levels of robberies and auto thefts and low levels of forcible rape when compared to other parts of the country. Yet, from Table 3.6 we can see this region of the country has the lowest overall index crime rate per 100,000 population. The West significantly outstrips the other three regions of the country in the index crime rates—particularly in the serious violent crime category. This too, is a long-standing phenomenon. Keith D. Harries, in examining national crime trends in 1968, and again in 1971, also showed the Western states to be the highest in overall crime rates.[31]

National crime victim surveys also tend to confirm the general distribution shown. In sampling crime victims throughout the country, it was found in 1986 that 30 percent of the households in the Western states were victimized by a serious crime. The lowest percentage of victimization for that year was the Northeast, where only 19 percent of the households surveyed reported a criminal victimization. In the South and Midwest, the figure was identical at 25 percent.[32]

TABLE **3.6**   Index Crime Rates per 100,000 Population by Region (1987)

| Region | Violent Crimes | Property Crimes | Total per 100,000 Population |
| --- | --- | --- | --- |
| United States (average) | 609.7 | 4,940.3 | 5,550 |
| South | 607.1 | 5,285.9 | 5,893 |
| West | 714.3 | 5,745.7 | 6,460 |
| Midwest | 504.3 | 4,403.3 | 4,907.6 |
| Northeast | 635.4 | 4,203.5 | 4,838.9 |

*Source:* FBI, *Crime in the United States, 1987* (Washington, D.C.: Federal Bureau of Investigation, 1988).

TABLE **3.7**  Victimization Rates for Persons Age 12 and Over (per 1,000 Population)

| Place of Residence and Population | Violent Crimes | Property Crimes |
|---|---|---|
| Total all areas | 31 | 77 |
| All central cities | 43 | 92 |
|     50,000–249,999 | 38 | 90 |
|     250,000–499,999 | 39 | 85 |
|     500,000–999,999 | 48 | 105 |
|     1,000,000 or more | 48 | 90 |
| All suburban areas | 29 | 82 |
|     50,000–249,999 | 25 | 72 |
|     250,000–499,999 | 30 | 79 |
|     500,000–999,999 | 30 | 88 |
|     1,000,000 or more | 33 | 93 |
| Nonmetropolitan areas | 22 | 58 |

*Source:* Bureau of Justice Statistics, *Locating City, Suburban and Rural Crime* (Washington, D.C.: U.S. Department of Justice, December 1985).

**CRIME BY TYPE OF COMMUNITY.**  Another established trend shows that cities have a much higher crime rate than rural areas. Table 3.7 shows crime victimization levels by type of community and size. However, some trends seem to be developing that indicate a possible narrowing of this gap. Since the early 1970s, the UCR has indicated that index crimes in towns of less than 50,000 and in suburban communities have been increasing rapidly. Although, since that time, increases in these crimes have slowed, the question still remains, what are the reasons for the drastic increases in reported crimes in areas that had previously been thought of as havens of security? Probably part of the answer is simply that more of these offenses are being committed in small towns and suburban communities than in the past. The movement of large shopping centers and commercial establishments to the suburbs has increased opportunities for crime and the vulnerability of these establishments to criminal attack. Suburban and rural banks are an excellent example. Minimum security and the proximity of arterial routes make them favorite targets for robbery. A study done by the DeKalb County Police Department (DeKalb County is adjacent to Atlanta, Georgia) indicated that a high percentage of crimes committed in that county were by individuals residing in Atlanta. Criminals in Atlanta selected sites to commit burglaries, robberies, larceny, and auto theft in the county and then, with the help of the freeway and interstate highway system, returned to Atlanta and disappeared.[33]

Another factor that may contribute to the increases of reported crimes in small towns and suburban communities is the actions of the local police. Police agencies in these areas are becoming more sophisticated in crime detection, recording techniques, and crime reporting. Just a few years ago, only a handful of the larger police departments employed advanced techniques in these areas. Now some of the smaller cities have even surpassed metropolitan police departments in levels of service and the use of advanced techniques, and, because of better reporting methods, send more complete data to the FBI.

**The gap is narrowing**

## THE CONTROVERSY OVER
## THE UNIFORM CRIME REPORTS AND CRIME RATES

Because most of the published information on crime in the United States is based on the UCR, it is appropriate at this point for us to analyze how meaningful an indicator of crime the report actually is. The Center for Studies of Crime and Delinquency of the National Institute of Mental Health has indicated that if criminal statistics are to be meaningful, they must fulfill the following requirements:

1. Provide information about the types of crimes commited.
2. Indicate something of the circumstances that surround the crime.
3. Provide some information about the kinds of persons involved.
4. Indicate the forms of disposal decided on by the courts or other authorities.
5. Separate first offenders (or first convictions) according to age, sex, and other social and psychological data.
6. Provide data on the cost of maintaining the services connected with the detection and prevention of crime and the treatment of offenders, and relate these to some measures of effectiveness.[34]

The fact that the UCR does not meet any of these requirements satisfactorily has led to its widespread repudiation by most knowledgeable people who have studied problems of crime in this country. Noted criminologist Lloyd Ohlin has said that the UCR index, which is often cited as the official summary of crime, is *almost worthless* (emphasis added).[35] Thorsten Sellin, another eminent scholar in the study of crime, has said that the United States "has the worst crime statistics of any major country in the western world."[36] Even former Attorneys General Edward H. Levi and Griffin B. Bell, whose agency was responsible for collecting and disseminating the statistics, stated that crime statistics shown in the UCR were of questionable validity.[37]

*Voiced criticisms of the UCR*

Faced with years of criticism about the UCR, the FBI and the Department of Justice are now considering efforts at improving and upgrading national crime statistics. The FBI wants to expand the scope of crime statistics to include information and details on such crimes as kidnapping and sexual abuse of children, because these have become of more interest to this agency in recent years. The FBI and Department of Justice hope this will provide them with a better statistical picture of these types of offenses.

*Thoughts for improvement*

To accomplish this, the FBI and the Justice Department in 1983 proposed a study draft that would significantly expand the Uniform Crime Reporting Program. This expansion effort would cost in the vicinity of $10 million annually. Supporters of the program claim that such an expansion would help improve the accuracy and utility of the crime statistics collected from the contributing police agencies throughout the country.

Among the proposals of the joint study would be to abolish the collection of summary data on matters such as the number of arrests and reports of crimes such as murder, rape, and larceny, and institute in its place a requirement that reports be filed on an incident-by-incident basis. This however, would entail significantly more time and attention and might cause problems of cooperation from the state and local police agencies that supply the data to the FBI. Such a system, however, would likely bring about increased accuracy and accountability. This incident data would include information such as the time and place of the crime, details about the suspects and the methods used, and facts about the victims of the crimes.

In addition to providing better data bases on crime, this system would significantly improve the study of crime, advise police departments how better to allocate their resources to deal with crime problems, and assist the police in detecting the changes in crime trends. It could also improve police efforts at preventing crime before it occurs according to those who advocate the new program. At this point we should examine the specific criticisms that have been leveled at the Uniform Crime Reporting Program.

### Reasons for Criticism of the UCR

The following ten points are the major criticisms generally given as reasons why the UCR cannot be considered a valid indicator of the extent of crime in the United States:

Major criticisms
of the UCR

1. *Unreported crimes are not included:* The UCR reflects only crimes reported to the police. This presents several problems: First, not all police agencies in America report crimes to the police. As of 1988, the police agencies' reporting covered 96 percent of the nation's population. Second, surveys indicate that many people do not report to the police[38] that they were victims of crimes and, therefore, these crimes remain unknown.[39]

2. *Reliance on voluntary submission of data:* Because the UCR relies on the reporting police agencies to submit data voluntarily, opportunities for the police to falsify crime records are always present. There have been several notorious instances of police departments underreporting crime to the FBI for political reasons.[40] However, when federal monies became available to local police agencies, there may have been an incentive to overreport crimes to obtain more federal funds.[41]

3. *Number of reported crimes influenced by numerous factors:* It is a demonstrated fact that police agencies with more sophisticated and accurate records systems may contribute to "paper" increases in crime.[42] Also, the fact that theft insurance is widely available may increase the number of crimes reported to the police. Because insurance companies require a police report for any claims payments, the insured must report the crime. Similarly, theft insurance may induce fraud. The insured may report nonexisting crimes and losses to the police to obtain an insurance settlement.

An increasing willingness by minority group members to report crimes may be another factor. In the past, the police may have overlooked and failed to report crimes in certain areas of the city. Minority groups, in particular, are far less inhibited today about reporting crimes to the police.[43] New attitudes toward rape may be encouraging higher rates of victim reporting for this crime. In fact, this crime has risen drastically in the last few years in the UCR, a fact that is certainly in part explained by increased reporting of rape incidents.

Finally, changes in classification also affect reporting. Before 1973 only larceny over $50 was a Part I crime. Since then *all* larcenies, regardless of the value of the loss, are Part I crimes. In 1979, arson was added as a Part I crime. As a result, "serious" crime rates shot upward.

4. *Data not meaningful:* For the most part, the UCR is only a tabular summary of crime and, as such, does not provide crime analysts with much meaningful information. For instance, the police in particular could improve their efficiency if they had more data on which they could rely such as crime data related to age, sex, race, and economic status;[44] the rate of population mobility as a basis for the measurement of crime rates;[45] occurrence data that indicate the extent to which different kinds of neighborhoods are subjected to different kinds of index crimes;[46] data on unreported offenses; and victim surveys to supplement the UCR.[47] Although the UCR is incorporating more data based on such factors as sex, race, ethnic origin, age, and location (i.e., city, suburban, rural), it is still very incomplete for purposes of careful analysis.

5. *Data based on inconsistent definitions of crime:* Although the UCR and the FBI try to define crimes and classifications uniformly, the President's Commission on Law Enforcement and Administration of Justice found that jurisdictional differences in crime definitions exist and that even the best police departments make mistakes in classifying crimes.

6. *Poor classification:* The UCR does not properly classify "serious" offenses in its Part I index. For example, larceny and auto theft are included, but more serious crimes such as kidnapping and the sale of hard narcotics are not.

7. *The way crimes are counted:* The police are instructed to record only the most serious crime when they compile their UCR statistics. Less serious offenses in a single criminal event are not counted. For example, a person is robbed and the robber steals the victim's car to escape. Only the robbery would be counted; the auto theft is not included.

8. *Overemphasis on crime control as a measure of police effectiveness:* The UCR may force the police to place too great an emphasis on crime statistics as an effective measure of their accomplishments. Increases in reported crime rates seem to imply that the police are ineffective when in fact the opposite might be true. A police department may report a high crime rate because it is managed efficiently, has developed an accurate records system, is administered with integrity, and has the confidence of citizens who are then more likely to report crimes to the police.

Also, the use of published UCR data as an indicator of police effectiveness may force the police, for political reasons, to commit resources to crime-related activities that are out of proportion to the strictly crime-related activities in which they are engaged.

9. *Lack of baseline data:* There are no accurate baseline data for analysis. For example, if we want to compare crime rates of time A with crime rates of time C, we must know the exact extent of crime at time A. This then becomes the baseline against which all subsequent comparisons will be made.

Although the UCR does make comparisons with preceding years, the comparison is faulty because the year that is used as the baseline is itself inaccurate. For example, if we compare the crime rates in 1990 with those in 1960, we know from the preceding discussion the many factors that can affect the crime rate: How can we say, with any degree of validity, that crime is *really* increasing, decreasing, or remaining constant? To do so, we would need an accurate baseline period and an accurate subsequent period against which to measure.

10. *Total exclusion of certain crimes:* The last widely criticized failure of the UCR is the general omission of many forms of white-collar crime. For instance, the UCR does not include such criminal acts as a politician taking a bribe, a merchant

cheating a customer, a lawyer swindling a client, or a physician injuring a patient while intoxicated. The police simply do not learn about many white-collar crimes. It has been estimated, for example, that 90 percent of crimes that involve computer manipulation are never reported.[48]

By now, it should be apparent that the question of whether crime in the United States is increasing, decreasing, or remaining stable cannot be answered with any degree of certainty. The next section examines a major step that has been taken to better measure the incidence of crime in America today.

## ▣ NEW EFFORTS TO IMPROVE THE MEASUREMENT AND RECORDING OF CRIME

**The National Crime Survey (NCS)**

As mentioned earlier in this chapter, the UCR indicated that nearly 14 million index offenses were recorded by the police in 1988. However, as we have seen from our discussion of the UCR, this underrepresents the actual amount because many crimes are not reported, and because those that are reported are counted using misleading criteria. In an attempt to develop a more accurate picture of unreported crime in the nation, a newer crime analysis program has been created and has provided some useful data. The program, called the National Crime Survey (NCS, formerly known as the National Crime Panel), was begun in 1973. It is the second largest ongoing survey undertaken by the federal government. Twice each year, the Bureau of the Census, under contract to the Department of Justice, interviews approximately 100,000 persons in a nationally representative sample of roughly 50,000 American households. The households chosen to be included in the survey are a representative cross-sample of all households in the nation. This method tries to ensure that within acceptable statistical limits, the data gathered from the survey is representative of what the results would be if every household in America was surveyed. When the program was first inaugurated it was introduced as the following:

> [The National Crime Panel] is one of the most ambitious efforts yet undertaken for filling some of the gaps in crime data; victimization surveys are expected to supply criminal justice officials with new insights into crime and its victims, complementing data resources already on hand (i.e., the UCR) for purposes of planning, evaluation and analysis. The surveys subsume many of the so-called hidden crimes that, for a variety of reasons, are never brought to police attention. They also furnish a means for developing victim typologies and, for identifiable sectors of society, yield information necessary to compute the relative risk of being victimized.[49]

**Victimization studies**

Using scientific sampling procedures, the survey began to examine crime victimization among individuals, households, and commercial establishments, concentrating on the crimes of forcible rape, robbery, assault, larceny, burglary, and auto theft.[50] Such undertakings are referred to as *victimization studies*. The NCS has been modified over the years to collect and analyze new and different forms of data about the criminal event. For example, in addition to examining victimization rates, the survey attempts to find out information such as whether the crime was completed or attempted; whether it was reported to the police; the number of offenders and their characteristics, including their relationship to the victim; substance abuse by offenders; use of weapons; any injury or property loss suffered by the victim; and any actions taken by the victim to protect self or their property at the time of the incident.[51] As of 1989, the NCS was undergoing further modification in an effort to provide more reliable information on the data it collects and to examine more fully aspects of victimization and criminal events.[52]

From its inception, the NCS data showed a marked discrepancy with the crime data reflected in the UCR. It appeared that the problem was not only the failure of citizens to report their victimization to the police, but also the fact that many reported incidents were not listed by the police in their official statistics. It should be recognized, however, that in some instances the police do not record crimes when reported because the reports prove to be unfounded. In any event, the data from this survey of serious crime added fuel to the controversy surrounding the validity of the UCR.

Since these preliminary findings were made, subsequent surveys indicate that the UCR discrepancies are not quite as large as the preliminary comparisons indicated. Nevertheless, major discrepancies still exist between the numbers of crimes reported to the police and those discovered through the victimization surveys. In the early 1980s, for instance, the UCR indicated a greater fluctuation among levels of crime than did the crime surveys that indicated that crime (as measured by victimization levels) declined in many categories and in others remained generally constant. Evidence from these years tends to indicate that the UCR recorded changes in crime levels that weren't confirmed by the NCS. For example, the UCR showed less of a decrease, a stabilizing pattern, or increases in certain crimes that were inconsistent with what the National Crime Panel survey showed. This may indicate that crime victims were merely more likely to report crimes to the police than in the past. This would explain some of the apparent conclusions in the UCR that would not be confirmed by the NCS. This theory seems to be borne out by the survey results that showed that while only 32 percent of interviewed victims in 1973 had reported their victimization to the police, by 1986, this figure had increased to 37 percent.[53] Table 3.8 compares the UCR and NCS.

The early crime surveys indicated that different forms of criminal events influenced reporting rates more than the demographic characteristics (sex, age, race) of victims. This still seems to be the case. Reporting of crimes is highly associated with the type of crime committed. Excluding murder, crimes such as motor vehicle theft, aggravated assualt, and robbery have the highest reporting rates, while larceny has the lowest.[54] Still, on the average, less than 40 percent of all serious crime included in the NCS is reported to the police (Figure 3.4). Before such a program of survey data was undertaken, most criminologists and criminal justice officials thought that forcible rape or attempted rape were crimes that were particularly underreported. Surprisingly, a little more than one-half of these crime victims went to the police. Those that didn't most often gave the reason that the incident was too private or personal or that they felt that the police would be insensitive or ineffective.[55]

What are some of the important characteristics about our national "crime problem" that the NCS can put into perspective? By 1986, criminal victimization rates had reached the lowest level in the 13-year history of the NCS. Still, if present levels continue, it can be expected that about 25 percent of American homes can expect some family member to be a victim of robbery, burglary, rape, assault, motor vehicle theft, or larceny in any given year. While all crime categories showed declines over this time period, it was most pronounced for property crimes. Crimes of violence, while showing a slight decline, stubbornly resist the abrupt downward trends indicated by property offenses. In fact, unless significant changes occur in violent crime rates, it can be expected that a typical twelve-year-old today has an

**Conflicting findings by UCR and NCS**

**Factors that influence reporting**

**The NCS picture**

TABLE **3.8**   The Uniform Crime Reports (UCR) Versus National Crime Survey (NCS)

| | UCR | NCS |
|---|---|---|
| Sponsor | FBI<br>Department of Justice | Bureau of Justice Statistics<br>Department of Justice |
| Offenses measured | Homicide<br>Forcible rape<br>Robbery (personal and commercial)<br>Aggravated assault<br>Burglary (commercial and household)<br>Larceny (commercial and household)<br>Motor vehicle theft<br>Arson | Forcible rape<br>Robbery (personal)<br>Assault (aggravated and simple)<br>Household burglary<br>Larceny (personal and household)<br>Motor vehicle theft |
| Scope | Crimes reported to the police<br>Covers most jurisdictions in the United States | Crimes both reported and not reported to the police; all data gathered in a few large geographic areas |
| Collection method | Police department reports to FBI or to centralized state crime data collection agencies that then report to FBI | Survey interviews of a selected national sample of 49,000 households consisting of 101,000 persons age twelve and over about their experiences as victims of crime during a specified period |
| Kinds of information provided | Number of offenses, crime clearance rates, persons arrested, persons charged, police officers killed and assaulted, and characteristics of homicide victims | Provides greater detail about victims (e.g., age, race, sex, education, income, and whether the victim and offender were related to each other) |
| | | Provides greater detail about crimes (e.g., time and place of occurrence, whether or not reported to the police, use of weapons, occurrence of injury and economic consequences) |
| Differences in ways some crimes are counted | Counts crime committed against all people, businesses, organizations, governments, etc., *as long as they are reported to the police* | Counts only crimes against persons age twelve or older and against their households |
| | In multiple crime events, only the most serious crime is counted; e.g., if a criminal stabs his victim and steals his car to escape, only the aggravated assault (the stabbing) is counted | Would count both—the aggravated assault as a personal crime and the auto theft as a household crime |
| Major weaknesses | Only reported crimes are counted | Tends to undercount crimes committed by persons related to the victim |
| | Is strongly affected by willingness of victims to report their crimes to the police | Relies on being a representative sample of American households |
| | Must rely on veracity of reporting police agencies | "Bounding" and "telescoping" problems (e.g., victims inaccurately report when the crime occurred, etc.) |

*Source:* Adapted from Bureau of Justice Statistics, *Report to the Nation on Crime and Justice,* 2nd ed. (Washington, D.C.: U.S. Department of Justice, March 1988), p. 11.

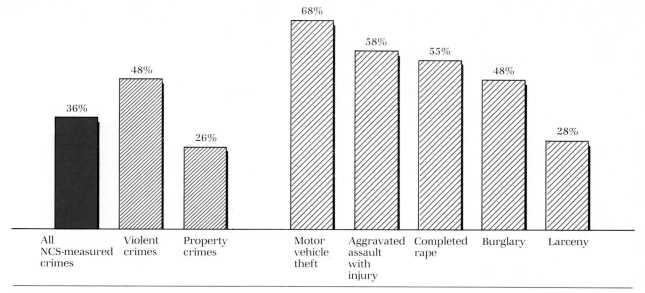

Percent of crimes measured by the National Crime Survey that were reported to the police. FIGURE **3.4**
(*Sources:* Bureau of Justice Statistics, *Criminal Victimization in the United States, 1973–85;*
*Reporting Crimes to the Police, Bureau of Justice Special Report,* December 1985. Bureau of Justice
Statistics, *Report to the Nation on Crime and Justice,* 2nd ed. March 1988.)

80 percent chance of being a violent crime victim sometime in his or her life. About half of all such twelve-year-olds can expect to be a victim two or more times.

There are also other disturbing aspects of this violent crime situation. The surveys also reported that in about six out of ten of the personal incidents involving violence or the threat of violence, the confrontation was between strangers—that is, between the victim or victims and one or more unknown assailants.[56] This conflicts with the often-expressed belief that a large percentage of such crime involves people who are in some way acquainted.[57] Although it is no less of a crime to be victimized by an acquaintance than it is a stranger, nor are injuries any less painful if administered by someone you know as compared to someone you don't, it does tend to inject a different element into the situation. Perhaps it is the greater fear of the unknown or the greater fear of personal invasion that seems to accompany stranger-to-stranger crimes.

You will recall from the analysis of national victimization rates on page 82 some of the characteristics associated with those who are most likely to experience violent crimes. What these don't show is the extent of the problem among certain classes of Americans. Consider for a moment the fact that black males in this country have about a 1 in 30 chance of being murdered. This is a higher rate of probable fatality than suffered by members of America's armed forces during World War II. This is a chilling statistic that points up only too clearly one manifestation of the significance of our nation's serious—and seemingly intractable—racial problem.

To shed some light on the question of why people do not report to the police that they have been victimized, Crime Panel researchers attempted to determine why those who indicated they had been the victims of crimes did not notify the

**Why people don't report their victimizations**

In the late 1970s and early 1980s, several major studies were released by the Rand Corporation.[59] Under a contract from the federal government, this nationally prestigious research institute had examined the career patterns of habitual criminals. In some ways the Rand findings disagreed with traditional criminological thought. In other ways, traditional assumptions about the career criminal were found to be accurate.

One of the most interesting findings of the Rand study was that career criminals—at least those who were studied in this research effort—did not follow traditional assumptions pertaining to criminal career development. That is, the systematic development pattern in which juvenile offenders graduate from peer-influenced and gang-related crimes to adult professional criminals is too simplistic a portrayal of how the process operates. Likewise, the common notion that adult professional criminals pursue crime as a preferred occupation and continually develop their skills in making their criminal occupation more specialized and financially rewarding is not necessarily the case. As a consequence, the study called for the reconsideration of many of the traditional assumptions about the development of habitual offenders.

A number of major findings resulted from the study. Some of the most important are the following:

Early Criminal Involvement: For the majority of those studied, early criminal involvement began at age thirteen to fourteen. Their first arrest occurred when they were 15. Many of the career criminals attributed their early involvement to peer-group influences. Although broken homes, lower economic status, and sibling criminal records were characteristic of many in the sample, they were not overwhelmingly so; nor did such factors explain differences in later criminal behavior. Following a conventional pattern, they progressed from auto theft and burglary as juveniles to a greater proportion of robberies and forgeries as adults. The majority of the criminals studied said they switched to robbery because it provided ample targets, required little preparation or tools, was easy to do, and seldom required hurting anyone. The primary influencing factor was what they could expect to "take"; the risks involved were only secondary considerations.

Rate and Types of Crimes: The offenders in the sample committed an average of twenty felony crimes per year for each year they were on the street. These were primarily property crimes. The level of criminal activity declined with age. Only the crime of robbery maintained relatively high levels of commission throughout the criminal careers of the offenders.

Asked how soon after their release from incarceration they began committing crimes again, the average was about four months. Slightly over one-half said they had serious intentions of not returning to crime after they had been incarcerated in the past. One-fourth of the offenders indicated that they intended to return to crime when they had previously been released from prison or jail. Most believed that their resumption to crime could not have been deterred.

Obviously, few of the offenses committed were followed by arrest. However, as the offenders got older in terms of their careers, they were arrested, convicted, and incarcerated more often for the commission of their crimes.[a] The sample pursued crime opportunistically. Rather than specializing on a particular type of crime or sticking with a particular method of committing the crime, they committed various types of crimes by various means as the opportunity presented itself. Whatever modus operandi or selectivity of targets an offender developed was usually a continuation of his most recent experience rather than the result of careful strategy.

Prison Experience: About half of the sample said they had participated in a formal prison rehabilitation program—mainly vocational training, education, or group counseling. Only a small minority had taken part in individual counseling or a drug or alcohol program. They found such programs more useful as they grew older. Vocational training was the program most favored.

When they were arrested for their crimes, they served the following average periods of incarceration: 2.4 years for the first prison term; 3.3 years for the second; 3.0 for the third; 3.7 years for the fourth; and 5.7 years for the fifth. Their five periods of imprisonment totaled over 18 years.

[a]This may reflect that they tended to commit more serious crimes against the person (e.g., robbery) as they progressed in their criminal careers.

Postrelease Experiences: Few felt that they were closely supervised when they were released on parole—particularly when they were released as a juvenile parolee. Few also felt that they were subject to more police surveillance after their release. Asked what they needed most when they were released from prison, the offenders interviewed said "someone who cared" for their juvenile period and "employment" as adults.

Criminal Sophistication: The majority of crimes committed by the sample were simple or even crude in execution. Only a small minority seemed to plan and execute their crimes with sophistication. For the typical offender, planning was limited to visiting the scene of the crime before the crime and, less often, staking out a target. Most of the sample remained in one geographical area to commit their crimes throughout their criminal careers. The idea that habitual offenders develop networks of persons to help them appears questionable. In fact, the more sophisticated criminals in the group preferred to operate alone to avoid the risk of betrayal or having to share the profits. These offenders—even in their later careers—averaged earning only a few thousand dollars a year from their crimes. There was little evidence that they grew more sophisticated in committing crimes as a result of their previous criminal career experience.

Motivation for Crime: Drugs and alcohol played a significant role in their criminal activities. Many of the sample contended that they were under the influence of drugs or alcohol at the time they committed their crimes. The most frequent reason (one-third of the sample) gave for committing crimes was to obtain money to purchase drugs and alcohol. Peer influence played a role only in the juvenile period of their criminal careers. About half depended on a legitimate job for their source of income when they weren't in prison. About 10 percent had little or no interest in a regular job throughout their careers. Fewer than 15 percent thought that the loss of employment had contributed to their criminal activity. They mentioned that they would have "crime-free intervals" at various times in their careers. These were taken as a "vacation" or as an obligation to a family member or girlfriend.

Among these career criminals, the researchers were able to identify two types: intensive offenders and intermittent offenders. The intensive offender was more likely to view himself as a "professional criminal." Their criminal activity seemed to be sustained over longer time periods and was consciously directed toward a specific purpose such as high-living, or to pay for a narcotics habit or to pay off debts. These type career criminals did not necessarily engage more in precrime planning, but they did, as a group, pay more attention to avoiding arrest than the intermittent career criminals in the group. Most striking is the fact that over his full career the average intensive career offender committed about ten times as many crimes as the intermittent career offender, yet was five times less likely to be arrested for any one crime and, if arrested, was less likely to be convicted and incarcerated.

The policy implications from the findings of this research on career criminals is not very optimistic. Rehabilitative techniques, for example, did not seem to influence these offenders to go straight upon their prior release from prison. It does, however, suggest that some attention might be focused on vocational training and programs to help with drug and alcohol abuse.

Similarly, the ideas of crime deterrence based on probability of arrest and imprisonment do not seem to deter this group. Only the certainty of arrest might have been a deterrent to them; longer prison sentences or closer parole supervision would not seem to have any deterrent effect on their criminal behavior.

Finally, the question of prevention. Making targets less vulnerable to these types of offenders, such as the use of burglar alarms and the private security patrol of property, would probably, in the views of researchers, only cause these career criminals to switch to unprotected property or to substitute different types of criminal activity such as street robberies for protected property targets.

The implications are obvious: For the habitual offender imprisonment may be the only means to ensure that these types of offenders do not continue to prey upon society. The need is to be able to identify these types of offenders—particularly the intensive habitual offender—and impose long-term imprisonment sanctions, particularly during the most active years of their criminal careers.

authorities. The most frequent reason given was that the victims felt "nothing could be done." About one-third of the victims felt that it "wasn't important enough."[58] There was no direct indication that they did not trust the police.

Although we cannot know why the victims felt so strongly that nothing could be done, we must wonder what is behind such an attitude. It may demonstrate a significant lack of confidence by victims in the ability of the police to bring the offender to justice. It may, in fact, be a general lack of confidence in the entire criminal justice system to perform its role in society.

## ☐ WHITE-COLLAR, "RESPECTABLE" CRIME AND "OFFICIAL LAWLESSNESS"

Criminal behavior seems to be endemic in every sector of American society, not merely in the decaying slums and ghettos of central cities. Although many of us have not been arrested, all of us have broken the criminal law without getting caught. Criminologists have done a number of studies in which they have asked people with and without arrest records to record any crimes they may have committed. Although the results vary and contain a certain amount of error, two major conclusions emerge.[60] An overwhelming majority of people have committed at least one serious crime without detection, and a substantial proportion have broken the law more than once. Second, criminal and delinquent behavior is distributed much more evenly among social classes than is indicated by police and court statistics.[61]

**Characteristics of white-collar crime**

A growing concern is with white-collar crime. Although this term is quite broad in its application, it is applied loosely to define a type of crime by the characteristics of those who commit it. Usually it refers to crimes committed by middle- and upper-middle-class segments of society. It is also characterized by how it is committed. Often, the violator has a position of trust, power, or influence that is used, often deceptively, to gain something illegal or to gain something legal through illegal methods. White-collar crimes include such offenses as embezzlement, bribery, fraud, theft of services, theft of trade secrets, forgery, smuggling, tax evasion, and obstruction of justice.

**Criminality among the "noncriminals"**

Although incarcerated adult and juvenile offenders typically commit a wider variety of offenses, many of which are more serious than the so-called undetected crimes of the middle and upper classes, the total volume of crime committed by "respectable" citizens is commonly estimated to exceed the total losses sustained through typical street crimes about which we hear so much. An article appearing in the *New York Times* points out how common is theft from hotels and motels. Industry security experts estimate that one guest in three takes some piece of hotel property upon departure—sheets, bedspreads, lamps, silverware, and even television sets, as well as the more familiar ashtrays and towels. "Believe me, I've paid for those things," a salesman who collects sheets and towels explains. "The places I've stayed at haven't lost anything because they jack their prices up so." "There's nothing wrong with taking little things from hotels," a suburban housewife remarks. "I think they expect you to at least take a towel." She and her husband have taken a great deal more—for example, a bedspread embroidered with a large "R," which they lifted from a Ramada Inn. "When I saw it in the motel room, I just knew I had to have it," the woman says, adding, "Anyway, if you have something marked with this crest, it's good publicity for them. After all, I show off these things to my friends."[62]

Cheating on income taxes is one of the most widespread forms of crime. (© David S. Strickler/ Jeroboam)

Such types of thefts, although widespread, do not begin to match the problem of employee theft. According to estimates by the U.S. Department of Commerce, what business firms euphemistically call "inventory shrinkage" came to more than $15 billion in 1988. Although shoplifting may account for 20 to 25 percent of retail outlet theft, the majority of this shrinkage is often simply the result of employee stealing. A Dallas department store chain in a period of two to three years lost nearly $500,000 in clothing items and television sets in a ring of fourteen employees.[63] Staggering losses are registered each year in all types of business enterprises— retail, wholesale, and manufacturing.

Numerous other examples could be cited. The widespread practice of cheating on expense accounts and on tax returns has become an American way of life. Some measure of the widespread efforts at tax evasion was provided in 1964, when the federal government first required banks and corporations to report all interest and dividend payments to individuals. As a result, the amount of interest and/or dividends reported on individual tax returns increased that year by 45 percent, and taxes on this kind of income increased by 28 percent.[64] Silberman points out that the *Wall Street Journal* has reported an interesting index of the number of people who seemingly commit securities fraud. When a Salt Lake City grand jury announced indictments of fifteen people for securities law violations but withheld their names pending arrests, nine persons surrendered to the U.S. attorney. Only one of the nine had been among those indicted.[65]

Corporate and privileged-class criminality is another menace that is not generally considered when we talk about the "crime problem" in the United States. Perhaps, as Balzac wrote, "Behind every great fortune there is crime." We can talk about the crimes perpetrated by such capitalistic financiers as the J. P. Morgans and others involved in the gigantic trusts that developed in America, but today the problem is perhaps more insidious and widespread because it seems to permeate the button-down collars of a large segment of our corporate structure. Here we can recount a too familiar litany of crimes. The larger pharmaceutical manufacturer, Richardson-Merrell, suppressed and falsified reports of laboratory tests on a drug it marketed, knowing that rats injected with the drug had died within weeks. As a result, hundreds of patients who took the drug suffered a wide range of serious toxic response. The Equity Corporation, one of the largest American insurance-finance institutions, went bankrupt after the fraudulent practices of its chief executives were revealed.

> Thousands of fake insurance policies were written up. They were then reinsured with other companies so that Equity Funding could generate an immediate cash flow. Fake death certificates for fictitious policyholders were forged. A leading CPA firm approved the Equity Funding financial statements.[66]

Another notable case is the Bunge Corporation, the third largest grain exporter in the world (annual sales about $2 billion), which pleaded no contest to two federal counts of conspiracy involving systematic thefts of grain from its customers over a ten-year period. Company officials manipulated the sales at the company's grain elevator in New Orleans to record more grain being put aboard ships than was actually loaded. To account for the shortages, "phantom" railroad cars, barges, and trucks appeared in the company's records. The stolen grain was then resold to other customers, and evidence indicated that the firm's corporate officials all over the country were involved in the systematic theft and "doctoring" of the firm's books.[67]

One outcome of the Watergate investigations has been a proliferation of evidence about the interactions of corporate crime and political bribery. Following the trail of funds raised by the White House and the Nixon campaign organization, the Special Prosecutor for the Watergate investigation, the Securities and Exchange Commission (SEC), and private investigators working for some of the litigants uncovered a deeply entrenched pattern of illegal and criminal corporate contributions to candidates of both parties. Between 1960 and 1972, Gulf Oil's chief Washington lobbyist distributed in excess of $4 million of corporate funds, mostly in cash, to a score of public officials, including Lyndon Johnson, Hubert Humphrey, Richard Nixon, Gerald Ford, and Senators Henry Jackson, Lloyd Bensten, and former Senate Republican leader Hugh Scott.[68] The practice was known to a number of Gulf's top corporate executives. In an effort to hide their actions, they devised a now-defunct Bahamian subsidiary. When confronted with the evidence and called before the SEC, the officials justified their behavior by claiming that because their competitors also engaged in such illegal activities, they were forced to do so to remain competitive and receive government favors.[69]

Although one of the major criticisms of our nation's response to white-collar crime is the infrequency of prosecutions for such offenses, there is some evidence that when these crimes are brought to the criminal justice system for handling, the system may not be as lenient as most people think. In a major study of white-collar crimes in eight states, it was concluded that prosecution rates for the crimes stud-

Paul Thayer and Billy Bob Harris are archetypical white-collar criminals—successful, wealthy, well-connected—and too often untouchable. Thayer, a former chairman of LTV, had connections all the way to the White House. In fact, he served in the Reagan administration as deputy secretary of Defense. Harris, a wheeler-dealer Dallas stockbroker, earned upward of $700,000 a year in fees.

Thayer and Harris were arrested by the federal authorities for obstructing justice—lying during a Securities Exchange Commission investigation of insider stock trading. As chairman of LTV and board member of several other companies, Thayer knew about various impending merger and takeover bids. He passed this information on to a former LTV employee who also happened to be his girlfriend. Harris and a small group of others were also provided with this inside information. This allowed the group to profit handsomely by buying stock before the deals were made known to the public. Although Thayer claimed not to have profited personally from his role—and it was never directly proved he had—the U.S. attorney argued that Thayer benefited from his girlfriend's gains because he probably would have otherwise given her the same amount out of his own pocket.

Thayer and Harris appeared at the Dallas Federal Courthouse expecting the usual slap on the wrist for their behavior. Their high-priced attorneys argued the old line: their clients had already suffered grievous harm by their arrests and the surrounding publicity and embarrassment that accompanied it. Furthermore, their careers and business interests had been irrevocably damaged. As a result justice had already been served. As an additional inducement to leniency, Thayer had arranged for an impressive list of character witnesses including Gerald Ford, Barry Goldwater, and General John Vessey, the then chairman of the Joint Chiefs of Staff.

Things seemed to be going their way. When Thayer and Harris had earlier pleaded guilty to the obstruction of justice charge, the prosecutor in return had agreed not to ask for a "substantial" jail term. And just a day before their sentencing, Thayer and Harris had agreed to pay $555,000 and $275,000, respectively, to settle the civil charges of insider trading. The expectation was that, at most, Thayer would receive a brief prison sentence in one of the federal government's minimum security institutions, or even probation. Harris had suggested to the Court that he be given community service—addressing other stockbrokers on the evils of insider trading—as an alternative to jail.

Whereas many judges might have leaned toward the traditional leniency associated with white-collar crimes, federal Judge Charles Richey was in no mood for it. Richey let it be known that equal justice includes treating criminals in the executive suite the same as any other criminal. "Yes, your defense attorneys are absolutely right in saying that the court should balance the scales of justice," Richey said. "This court has done that, and it is not going to pin a medal upon the lapel of your coats for breach of trust, for the false statements and the obstruction of justice you have engaged in." With that Richey pronounced sentence: Thayer and Harris were each sentenced to the maximum term of four years, and fined $5,000. Richey was also convinced from Harris' community service offer that Harris needed further instruction as to the seriousness of his crime. "I don't see where any good is going to come," said an obviously appalled Richey, "from Billy Bob Harris going around talking to other stockbrokers. That suggestion is wholly without merit and I was shocked and surprised to receive it."

In spite of the Reagan administration's downplaying of white-collar prosecutions by the Department of Justice, there is some evidence—particularly in securities cases—that more defendants are going to jail than have in the past. Yet, white-collar crimes still largely go unpunished. Perhaps this partly explains the growing incidence of illegal activities coming to light among defense contractors, financial institutions, and securities dealers in recent years. Perhaps messages such as the one Judge Richey gave Thayer and Harris will be heard in other corporate boardrooms and executive offices. It certainly seems to be a message that needs to be heard.

ied were similar to those for major violent crimes, property crimes, and public order crimes (drug and weapon offenses and commercial vice).[70]

The study also found the conviction rates for cases prosecuted to be about 74 percent, slightly higher than for violent crimes (66 percent) and public order crimes (67 percent) and about the same for property crimes (76 percent). About 60 percent of the defendants convicted for white-collar crime versus about 67 percent of those convicted for violent crimes were sentenced to prison. Eighteen percent of white-collar offenders sentenced to prison were sentenced to more than one year (about the same as persons convicted of public order offenses) versus 39 percent of volent offenders.[71]

"Official lawlessness"

Another growing concern of "crime" in this country, at least among some segments of the population, is what is called "official lawlessness." This type of illegal (and therefore criminal) activity involves many of the agencies of criminal justice themselves, at all levels of government.

Until recently, most of the writing in this area focused on the actions of police at the local level. Some writings also focused on the behavior of correctional officials and the behavior of certain members of the judiciary.[72] In the 1960s and 1970s, the interest began to shift, influenced by a series of revelations that made national headlines. (See Figure 3.5.) A significant portion of interest in official lawlessness by

FIGURE **3.5** The number of state and local officials indicted and the number convicted between 1970 and 1987 on federal charges involving abuse of public office. (*Source:* U.S. Department of Justice.)

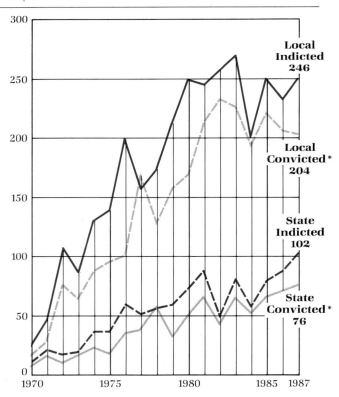

*Convictions include some persons indicted in previous years.

government became centered on the illegal acts of the presidency, members of Congress as uncovered by the Abscam scandals, and the FBI and CIA.

Most attention seems to be focused on illegal actions by the executive branch in the domestic area. In recent years, many people have come to believe that illegal activity on the part of the FBI and the CIA (which, at least in some instances, implied presidential backing) must be viewed as an important element in a movement toward a "new form of domestic tyranny" of a somewhat different kind.[73] These agencies, it is argued, have frequently gone beyond the limits of the law and concerned themselves not simply with crime or threats to national security, but with persons calling legitimately for changes in the status quo.[74] For example, Richard Rovere, a writer noted for his insightful essays on legal issues, has pointed out that

> investigations by Congress and the press have revealed that members of the FBI have, in the past, committed many crimes in the line of duty over a long period. Without any legal authorization, they have tapped telephones, they have opened and read private mail, they have planted electronic bugs in offices and bedrooms, they have written anonymous and false letters to the spouses and associates and employees of people they wanted to harm, they have committed burglaries and other break-ins, they have paid informants who later lied under oath, they have furnished funds and arms to paramilitary right-wing groups that have burned and bombed offices of left-wing groups and carried out assassination plots against left-wing leaders, they have used *agents provocateurs* to entrap others by planning and encouraging criminal conspiracies, they have incited police violence, they have blackmailed and slandered critics, and they have driven opposing radical militants to attack one another.[75]

It is these types of crimes that typically avoid inclusion in our officially tabulated crime statistics. Yet these forms of behavior are all crimes, and they may well be more significant in terms of both short-run dollar loss and their long-range effect on our nation than the more typical street crime with which we are more familiar. Perhaps in some ways it is just as well that they are not included in our crime index. Their inclusion would result in the total victimization of all members of our society. It would certainly point out how seemingly natural criminal behavior is to humankind.

---

 **CRIME WITHOUT PUNISHMENT**

To most Americans, the honesty of corporate executives is highly questionable. There is also widespread belief that those few who are prosecuted for committing white-collar crime receive comparatively light punishment. Those are the conclusions of a CBS–*New York Times* poll in which a sample of adults questioned said that most corporate executives were dishonest. Only 32 percent of those surveyed

felt that most executives were honest.

In some countries the problem of white-collar crime is dealt with a little differently. In Ghana recently, to deter white-collar crime, two bank officials and a confederate were shot by a firing squad for participating in a bank fraud involving $1.2 million—small potatoes, indeed, compared to the 2,000 counts of fraud to which the investment firm

of E. F. Hutton and Company pleaded guilty in 1985.

After cheating 400 banks out of $8 million, the brokerage firm was fined $2 million but not one of its employees was charged with a crime—not even a little one like check-kiting. The massive E. F. Hutton swindle, in the words of Lloyd Shearer, the noted columnist, is "a classic example of a crime without a criminal."

---

# ▣ ORGANIZED CRIME: DEFINING CHARACTERISTICS

An always-intriguing aspect of America's folklore about crime is its interest in "organized" crime. This rather loosely applied term has fascinated generations of Americans. We say loosely because the definition of organized crime is itself imprecise. Most of us have a limited understanding of this term. To many Americans, "organized crime" conjures up visions of Sicilian or Italian gangsters in baggy dark suits and off-color ties and shirts, as popularized in the *Godfather* movies. Organized crime has become symbolized by—if not exclusively identified with—La Cosa Nostra (Mafia).

This is a mistake. Although the Mafia is certainly a type of organized crime, "organized crime" fits many other forms of criminal organization and circumstances. It should also be recognized that organized crime efforts encompass a broad range of criminal events. Is it, for example, any less of a form of "organized crime" to be involved in a concerted and organized effort to defraud the taxpayer—something we saw a great deal of in our defense contractor scandals in the late 1980s? It might also be asked if it is any less of an "organized crime" for a group of car thieves and salvage yards to operate a multicity car theft ring. Or what about the operations of a large, illegal gambling enterprise where operations are financed, supported, and protected by locally prominent business interests and public authorities?

If organized crime runs the gamut from traditional crimes of murder and burglary through the range of illegal vice activities and into the realm of white-collar crime, what defining characteristics set it apart? The key of course, turns on the issue of "organized" and the incorporation of at least some or all of the supporting characteristics of this term.

**Characteristics of organized crime**

The first defining characteristic of organized crime is one of *structure*. In the most typical portrayal of organized crime, there is a hierarchical structure in which the activities are directed by a leader(s) through a system of subordinate ranks. This is best depicted by La Cosa Nostra, which is currently thought to include twenty-four individual "families," all under the general authority of a "National Commission" consisting of an estimated nine bosses. Yet, the structure of organized crime doesn't have to be this elaborate or clearly structured in some formal hierarchy. There will always be leaders and followers in any organized criminal activity. The leaders may lead by virtue of their particular expertise or contribution to the success of the enterprise or their willingness to use elements of fear and intimidation to keep other members of the criminal undertaking in line. It may be as much psychological fear (threatening to inform the authorities) as it is physical fear of injury that controls members and makes them support the organization's efforts. It could well be the simple ingredients of greed and opportunity that weld organized crime associates together in a cooperative undertaking.

Out of this common purpose and supportive undertaking, a form emerges: a contribution to the undertaking of the enterprise and one that helps the organized criminal activity accomplish its goals. It defines members' contributions and expectations. It establishes obligations, rewards, and punishments—all according to some established system. In this way, it shows a clear form of structure.

Organized crime, it is often said, is an undertaking that exhibits *organizational continuity*. In this way, organized crime groups have established operating policies that ensure they can survive the death or imprisonment of their leaders.[76] In cases

Reputed mafia boss John Gotti (left) has been detained by law enforcement authorities on various charges. Organized crime groups are structured to ensure continued functioning even if one of their leaders is imprisoned. (*The New York Post*)

of the Mafia and the organized criminal narcotic cartels, this is certainly so. Still, other forms of organized crime, while following most of the characteristics of organized criminal activity, may not necessarily provide for organizational continuity to the same degree. The loss, for example, of the kingpin of the group may cause the group's efforts to come to a standstill. Although provisions for organizational continuity are usually associated with organized crime, as long as other defining characteristics are present, it isn't absolutely necessary for this characteristic to exist to make a criminal enterprise an "organized" crime effort.

One way, however, by which organized crime is characterized is by its planning efforts and its willingness to take advantage of criminal opportunity—in fact, by its ability in many cases to actually establish the opportunity. This isn't to say that nonorganized criminal activities don't involve planning and opportunism; it merely points out that there is often a difference in degree between the two forms. Generally speaking, organized crime is likely to be much more thorough in its planning and much better suited to take successful advantage of criminal activity. They seem to go together: careful and thorough planning creates opportunity and the probability of success. Organized crime efforts recognize this fundamental relationship and make every effort to capitalize on it.

Another defining characteristic is that this type of criminal activity has a *restricted membership*. Participation may be restricted by any combination of factors:

loyalty, willingness to commit criminal acts, required expertise, and/or common background or ethnicity. Membership in organized crime efforts often require some form of acceptance beyond the mere loose associations that generally comprise many multiple-offender crimes or criminal events.

Established, long-term and sustained criminal activity of an organized nature also requires *the eventual use of violence*. Often, the mere threat of violence is not enough. Intimidation must be reinforced by the actual use of violence if the criminal enterprise is to continue operating successfully. A defining characteristic then of organized crime is the willingness and the ability to use force to ensure the continuation of the enterprise and its success.

Organized crime often involves the *use of legitimate business* as part of its criminal activity. A legitimate business front may provide the opportunity to launder illegally obtained monies. It may also provide an outlet for stolen goods. The appearance of a legitimate business may also provide respectability to organized crime figures, which serves to layer them from the suspicions and investigative efforts of law enforcement authorities.

A final characteristic of organized crime—one that provides it strength as well as being a possible element of weakness—is its *reliance on corrupt public officials, its need for private expertise, and its dependence on the general public*. The history of organized crime is replete with examples of corrupt politicians, judges, prosecutors, and cops who have been "bought out" by the criminal enterprise. Less well appreciated and understood by the general public is the fact that organized crime—particularly organized crime efforts today—must rely on "outside" sources of expertise to be successful. Lawyers and accountants have become particularly important to the success of ongoing operations; without their professional advice and assistance, corrupt organizations could not operate. The public, too, plays an important role. It is, after all, the public who knowingly or unwittingly buys the goods or services that organized crime has to offer. Without its customers and the source of income they provide, organized crime would not exist.

Some of the government's efforts to deal with organized crime will be discussed in later chapters. Although the federal authorities had some success in the 1980s in prosecuting Mafia figures and lessening the criminal tentacles of this organization, more insidious (and many would say dangerous) criminal organizations have come into prominence. Dealing, for example, with organized international narcotic cartels is proving even more challenging for antiorganized crime efforts.

## ⬚ CRIME AND VICTIM COMPENSATION

> The murderer of a family provider killed in a holdup, for example, had his basic needs of food, shelter and medical attention provided in prison. But the victim's family, suddenly deprived of all economic support, may be left destitute. Some form of public assistance is the only meaningful way to remedy this situation.[77]
>
> *Governor Edmund (Pat) Brown*

Rationale

With those words, California's Governor Brown signed into law the first state compensation program for victims of crime in 1965. Since that time, we have seen a growing interest in the development of victim-centered programs. The thrust for the development of these programs revolves around two issues: (1) the recognition that being a victim of crime often produces psychological trauma and economic loss; (2) the growing feeling that there is an imbalance in our system of criminal justice and law that tends to focus almost exclusively on the offender while ignoring the innocent victim.[78]

One way to assist victims of crimes is through victim compensation programs. Advocates of such programs sometimes argue that compensation is an "obligation of the state," because the state failed to protect the victim from harm. Legislators, however, have generally seen compensation as a "humanitarian duty," a responsibility as are public welfare programs, and "a matter of grace," not a legal right (as the statutes often say).[79] Some offer a third rationale, and one that may be the most appealing: that government should insure citizens against the "shared risk" that is part of life in society.[80] Whatever the ultimate justification for such programs, states have developed programs by which they compensate for losses that result from criminal attack.[81]

State victim compensation program characteristics

As of 1987, forty-four states and the District of Columbia have victim compensation programs (Table 3.9).[82] The majority of states finance their programs either solely or in part through revenues raised from fines and penalties. The inherent attractiveness of such an approach is clear in a period of fiscal cutbacks and strong competing claims on state treasuries; it is also politically popular. Advocates of this form of funding argue that such payments are a fitting way for criminals to pay back part of their debt for violating society's laws. Other states, however, rely on funds from their general revenues.

The states employ different types of fines and penalty assessments. Some use *fixed penalties:* for example, a set charge is imposed based upon the crime for which the offender is convicted. Other states use *proportional surcharges* such as an additional 10 percent of the fine imposed.

In defining persons who are eligible to receive compensation, all states include persons who were injured or killed as the direct result of a crime. The majority of states also compensate an individual who is injured or killed in the course of attempting to come to the aid of a crime victim, or to apprehend someone suspected of committing a crime. In all jurisdictions, dependents of a deceased victim are eligible for compensation.

States have had a few problems in defining who is ineligible to receive compensation under their programs. The most controversial class of individuals typically excluded from potential compensation are relatives of the offender, persons living in the same household as the offender, and/or persons engaged in a continuing (sexual) relationship with the offender.[83]

Victims' eligibility for compensation is also determined in part by the type of crime in which they are injured. Most states' compensation statutes include a general provision with a broad definition of conduct that includes a compensable crime. The other states set forth a list of specific crimes or classes of crimes that are compensable.

In addition to limiting the types of crimes for which coverage is available, all victim compensation programs also restrict the types of financial losses that are compensable. Typically, compensation can be given for (1) medical expenses, (2) lost wages, (3) funeral expenses, and (4) loss of support to the dependents of a deceased victim. These expenses, of course, must have been incurred as a direct result of a crime, and in most states the victim must have suffered bodily injury. Most of the states also make reparations for the costs of rehabilitation and coun-

TABLE **3.9**  State Victim Compensation Programs

| State | Victim Compensation Board Location[a] | Financial Award | To Qualify, Victim Must | | |
|---|---|---|---|---|---|
| | | | Show Financial Need | Report to Police Within | File Claim Within |
| Alabama | Alabama Crime Victim Compensation Commission | $0–10,000 | No | 3 days | 12 mos. |
| Alaska | Department of Public Safety | $0–40,000 | Yes | 5 | 24 |
| Arizona | Arizona Criminal Justice Commission | b | Yes | 3 | b |
| California | State Board of Control | $100–46,000 | Yes | c | 12 |
| Colorado | Judicial district boards | $25–10,000 | No | 3 | 6 |
| Connecticut | Criminal Injuries Compensation Board | $100–10,000 | No | 5 | 24 |
| Delaware | Violent Crimes Board | $25–20,000 | No | c | 12 |
| D.C. | Office of Crime Victim Compensation | $100–25,000 | Yes | 7 | 6 |
| Florida | Department of Labor and Employment Security, Workmen's Compensation Division | $0–10,000 | Yes | 3 | 12 |
| Hawaii | Department of Corrections | $0–10,000 | No | c | 18 |
| Idaho | Industrial Commission | $0–25,000 | No | 3 | 12 |
| Illinois | Court of Claims | $0–25,000 | No | 3 | 12 |
| Indiana | Industrial Board | $100–10,000 | No | 2 | 24 |
| Iowa | Department of Public Safety | $0–20,000 | No | 1 | 6 |
| Kansas | Executive Department | $100–10,000 | Yes | 3 | 12 |
| Kentucky | Victim Compensation Board | $0–25,000 | Yes | 2 | 12 |
| Louisiana | Commission on Law Enforcement | $100–10,000 | No | 3 | 12 |
| Maryland | Criminal Injuries Compensation Board | $0–45,000 | Yes | 2 | 6 |
| Massachusetts | District court system | $0–25,000 | No | 2 | 12 |
| Michigan | Department of Management and Budget | $200–15,000 | Yes | 2 | 12 |
| Minnesota | Crime Victims Reparation Board | $100–50,000 | No | 5 | 12 |
| Missouri | Division of Workmen's Compensation | $200–10,000 | No | 2 | 12 |
| Montana | Crime Control Division | $0–25,000 | No | 3 | 12 |
| Nebraska | Commission on Law Enforcement and Criminal Justice | $0–10,000 | Yes | 3 | 24 |
| Nevada | Board of Examiners and Department of Administration | $0–15,000 | Yes | 5 | 12 |
| New Jersey | Executive Branch | $0–25,000 | No | 90 | 24 |
| New Mexico | Executive Branch | $0–12,500 | No | 30 | 12 |
| New York | Executive Department | $0–30,000[d] | Yes | 7 | 12 |
| North Carolina[e] | Department of Crime Control and Public Safety | $100–20,000 | | 3 | 24 |
| North Dakota | Workmen's Compensation Bureau | $0–25,000 | No | 3 | 12 |
| Ohio | Court of Claims Commissioners | $0–25,000 | No | 3 | 12 |
| Oklahoma | Crime Victims Board | $0–10,000 | No | 3 | 12 |
| Oregon | Department of Justice/Workmen's Compensation Board | $250–23,000 | No | 3 | 6 |
| Pennsylvania | Crime Victims Board | $0–35,000 | No | 3 | 12 |
| Rhode Island | Superior court system | $0–25,000 | No | 10 | 24 |
| South Carolina | Crime Victims Advisory Board | $100–3,000 | No | 2 | 6 |
| Tennessee | Court of Claims Commission | $0–5,000 | No | 2 | 12 |
| Texas | Industrial Accident Board | $0–25,000 | No | 3 | 6 |
| Utah | Department of Administrative Services | $0–25,000 | b | 7 | 12 |
| Virgin Islands | Department of Social Welfare | Up to $25,000 | No | 1 | 24 |
| Virginia | Industrial Commission | $0–15,000 | No | 5 | 24 |
| Washington | Department of Labor and Industries | $0–15,000[d] | No | 3 | 12 |
| West Virginia | Court of Claims Commissioner | $0–35,000 | No | 3 | 24 |
| Wisconsin | Department of Justice | $0–40,000 | No | 5 | 12 |

[a] If location of the board is not indicated in the State statute, the board itself is noted.
[b] No reference in statute.
[c] Must report but no time limit specified.
[d] Plus unlimited medical expenses.
[e] North Carolina's program is administratively established but not funded.

*Source:* Bureau of Justice Statistics 1987 update of *Victim/witness legislation: An overview,* Bureau of Justice Statistics, July 1984 with assistance from National Organization for Victim Assistance.

seling services. Most of the states do not, however, provide compensation for pain and suffering. The majority of states with compensation programs also require a showing of financial need. How this is determined varies among the states.

Over half the programs also have a "contributory misconduct" provision in their statutes. This is the requirement of assessing whether and to what extent the victims' conduct contributed to their victimization. The idea is that the state should only make reparations to *innocent* victims of violent crime. The evidence indicates that states deny many claims for compensation on this basis.

All of the states require that to receive compensation, the victim must report the crime to the authorities and cooperate with law enforcement agencies in the investigation and prosecution of the case. Finally, states have enacted program filing deadlines in which a compensation claim must be filed within a specified period of time following the crime.

The policy of benefits differs widely among the states. The highest maximum allowed is $46,000 in California. The lowest is Tennessee, which has an established maximum of only $5,000. All victim compensation programs also reduce the level of benefits paid to victims by deducting any payments they may receive from other sources. This includes the offender, Social Security, Medicare, Medicaid, worker's compensation, and insurance compensation. Many of the states also provide for emergency awards to help victims meet pressing financial needs while their claims are being processed.

In 1984 Congress, following the lead of many states, passed the Victim Compensation and Assistance Act. The act has four provisions: (1) establishes an agency to administer a victim compensation program for victims of federal crimes; (2) establishes a Crime Victims Fund for the purpose of funding annual grants to the states for victim compensation and victim assistance programs; (3) imposes a penalty assessment upon all convicted federal defendants, which is to be deposited in the fund; and (4) authorizes the forfeiture of profits that convicted violent criminals receive from the sale of their stories of their crimes.[84] The interested reader is encouraged to examine the provisions of this legislation.

**Federal compensation program**

Like all governmental social programs, the costs of the victim compensation program are critical concerns. Several characteristics of crime victims' compensation programs have been particularly troublesome in comparison with more common social assistance programs. First, these programs have relatively large expenditures for the number of people served. This requires particularly detailed systems for screening cases and accounting for funds. Second, these programs experience particular difficulty in predicting how many claims will, in fact, be made for their funds. The level of crime and victims is difficult to predict. Third, as a result of the difficulties in predicting expenditures, legislatures have been very conservative in designing these programs and have specified numerous eligibility restrictions to ensure that costs do not become prohibitive. Finally, there is the argument of who should pay. Some contend that society at large should pay possibly in the form of an insurance policy paid by all citizens in the state. Others say criminals should pay—yet the issue is often one of who is a "criminal"—is a traffic violator a "criminal" and therefore automatically liable as many states assess fees from these types of offenses? Others simply deny that government is responsible for any type of compensation. [85]

There is, as might be expected, wide variation in program expenditures. Of the nearly $81 million paid by the states to crime victims in 1985, California clearly was the leader in compensation payments made.[86] Not only did states vary widely in the number of crime victims they compensated, but there was also great variation among the states in the average award given to a claimant.

Some recent research calls into question how successful these programs have been. One of the problems always associated with such programs is that they simply are not widely publicized and in that way made available to possible recipients.

Do they have any effect on the rates at which crimes are reported to the police? One study compares cities in states with compensation programs and cities in states without them. It was found that there was no difference in the rates of reporting serious crimes to the police between the two.[87] The same researcher also compared states before they established a compensation program and after such a program was established. There was no increase in conviction rates after these states established their programs.[88] There is also some evidence that those compensated were no more satisfied with the criminal justice system than those who were denied awards, nor did they express a greater willingness to cooperate with the criminal justice system in the future.[89]

## SUMMARY

Although it is often claimed that the United States has the highest crime rate in the world, there is really no way to prove or disprove this statement. What little facts are known about crime in America come mostly from official accounts published annually in the *Uniform Crime Reports*. The UCR indicates that certain characteristics appear to be associated with crime in this country; for example, some geographical areas have a higher relative incidence of certain types of offenses than other areas.

With more careful and thorough analyses in recent years, we have been able to isolate certain factors that are associated with the increased probability of being a crime victim. In many ways the characteristics of this "high-risk" group show interrelated factors.

The UCR is widely criticized for its inaccuracy in reflecting the types and numbers of crimes in the United States, and it is recognized as being woefully inadequate. In an effort to better measure the nature and extent of crime, the federal government has established the National Crime Panel (National Crime Survey [NCS]). This effort surveys citizens and commercial establishments to ascertain the amount of unreported crime that occurs. It appears that of the crimes surveyed, only about one-half of all crimes are reported to the police.

Another problem associated with our tabulation of crime and our knowledge of the true extent of crime in the United States is the virtual absence of certain offenses from our official reporting system. The fact that the vast majority of white-collar crimes never come to the attention of the police and that virtually no acts of "official lawlessness" are recorded seriously damages the credibility of our official statistics. These crimes that affect us all directly or indirectly and cost us billions of dollars a year are a serious menace facing this nation.

Organized crime is another type of crime that covers a broad range of criminal events. This type of crime—like white-collar crime—is defined by certain characteristics that are associated with how it is committed. This is often what distinguishes it from nonorganized criminal activity. Although the two have become synonymous over the years, organized crime consists of criminal activities and associations in addition to the Mafia.

A recent interest in the victim of the crime has led to the development of a number of victim compensation programs throughout the United States. A number of states now have such programs, and the federal government has established such a program for victims of federal crimes.

## REVIEW QUESTIONS

1. Name the eight Part I offenses in the FBI's Uniform Crime Report.
2. What regional area of the United States had the highest rate of robbery (in 1983)? Of aggravated assault? Of burglary? Of larceny? Of auto theft?
3. What are the general characteristics associated with crime victims in the United States?
4. The Center for Studies of Crime and Delinquency has identified six requirements that are necessary for an accurate criminal statistics report. What are these requirements?
5. What are the problems with trying to determine the extent of crime in the United States? Is there conflicting evidence?
6. Uniform Crime Reports have been criticized for several reasons. Select and describe the four that you think are most important.
7. What is the National Crime Survey? How does it work? Does it have any weaknesses?
8. What are the defining characteristics of organized crime?
9. What is victim compensation? In your opinion is the federal or state government obliged to compensate victims of crime?

## DISCUSSION QUESTIONS

1. Is there a crime problem in America? Discuss.
2. How can information-gathering methods on crime in the United States be improved?
3. What factors are likely to increase the chances to become a crime victim? Discuss how these might operate.
4. The weaknesses of the *Uniform Crime Reports* render them useless in giving an accurate picture of crime in the United States. Discuss.
5. What do you think of the National Crime Survey—is it useful? Explain your position.
6. Are so-called white-collar crimes and acts of "official lawlessness" serious crimes and threats to our society? Explain.
7. Does your state have a victim compensation program? If so, discuss it.

## SUGGESTED ADDITIONAL READINGS

Bureau of Justice Statistics. *New Directions for the National Crime Survey*, Washington, D.C.: U.S. Department of Justice, March 1989.

Bureau of Justice Statistics. *Report to the Nation on Crime and Justice*. 2nd ed. Washington, D.C.: U.S. Department of Justice, March 1988.

Bureau of Justice Statistics. *The Seasonality of Crime Victimization*. Washington. D.C.: U.S. Department of Justice, May 1988.

Churchill, Allen. *A Pictorial History of American Crime, 1849–1929*. New York: Holt, Rinehart and Winston, 1964.

Edelhertz, Herbert. *White-Collar Crime: An Agenda for Research*. Lexington, Mass.: Lexington Books, 1982.

Feinberg, Kenneth R. *Violent Crime in America*. Washington, D.C.: National Policy Exchange, 1983.

Friedman, Lee S. *Economics of Crime and Justice*. Morristown, N.J.: General Learning Press, 1976.

Graham, Fred P. "A Comtemporary History of American Crime." In H. D. Graham and Ted. R. Gurr, eds., *Violence in America*. New York: Bantam, 1970, pp. 485–504.

Kitsuse, John T., and Aaron V. Cicourel: "A Note on the Uses of Official Statistics." *Social Problems* 11 (Fall 1963): 131–139.

Lottier, Stuart: "Distribution of Criminal Offenses in Sectional Regions." *Journal of Criminal Law, Criminology and Police Science* 29 (1938): 1038–1045.

National Academy of Sciences. *Understanding Crime*, Washington, D.C.: U.S. Government Printing Office, 1977.

Nettler, Gwynn. *Explaining Crime*. 2nd ed. New York: McGraw-Hill, 1978.

Pepinsky, Harold E. *Crime Control Strategies: An Introduction to the Study of Crime*. New York: Oxford University Press, 1980.

President's Commission on Law Enforcement and Administration of Justice: *Task Force Report: Crime and Its Impact—An Assessment*. Washington, D.C.: U.S. Government Printing Office, 1967.

President's Commission on Organized Crime. *The Impact: Organized Crime Today*. Washington, D.C.: U.S. Government Printing Office, 1986.

Robison, Sophia M. "A Critical Review of the Uniform Crime Report." *Michigan Law Review* 64 (April 1966): 1031–1054.

Turk, Austin F. "The Mythology of Crime in America." *Criminology* 8 (February 1971): 397–411.

Wilson, James Q. *Crime and Public Policy*. San Francisco: ICS Press, 1983.

Winslow, Robert W. *Crime in a Free Society*. Belmont, Calif.: Dickenson, 1968.

Wolfgang, Marvin E. "Urban Crime." In James Q. Wilson, ed., *The Metropolitan Enigma*. Cambridge, Mass.: Harvard University Press, 1968, pp. 246–251.

# NOTES

1. See Albert J. Reiss, "Public Safety: Marshaling Crime Statistics," *Annals of the American Academy of Political and Social Sciences* 453 (1981): 222–236.

2. Frank F. Furstenberg, Jr., "Public Reaction to Crime in the Streets," *American Scholar* 40 (1971): 601.

3. "Fortress on 78th Street," *Life*, 19 November 1971, pp. 26–36.

4. "Are You Personally Afraid of Crime? *Life*, 14 January 1972, p. 28.

5. U.S. Department of Housing and Urban Development, *The 1978 HUD Survey on the Quality of Community Life* (Washington, D.C.: HUD, 1978), p. 217.

6. National Commission on the Causes and Prevention of Violence, *To Establish Justice, To Ensure Domestic Tranquility* (New York: Bantam, 1970), p. xxv.

7. National Council on Crime and Delinquency, *Criminal Justice Abstracts* 13, No. 3 (September 1981): 325.

8. David Lawrence, "Why Is Crime Now a Worldwide Epidemic?" *U.S. News and World Report*, 6 September 1971, p. 84.

9. Netherlands Justice Ministry, *The Burden of Crime on Dutch Society 1973–79*. The Hague, 1980.

10. For example, see Barbara A. Hanawalt, *Crime and Conflict in English Communities, 1300–1348* (Cambridge, Mass.: Harvard University Press, 1979): Guido Ruggiero, *Violence in Early Renaissance Venice* (New Brunswick, N.J.: Rutgers University Press, 1980).

11. Henry W. Anderson, "Separate Report of Henry W. Anderson," Report on the Causes of Crime, Vol 1., National Commission on Law Observance and Enforcement (Montclair, N.J.: Patterson Smith Reprint Series, 1968), pp. 66, 68.

12. For example, see John E. Conklin, *The Impact of Crime* (New York: Macmillan, 1975).

13. U.S. Department of Justice, "The Fear of Crime," from *Report to the Nation on Crime and Justice* (Washington, D.C.: Bureau of Justice Statistics, October 1983), p. 18.

14. Ibid., p. 19.

15. James Q. Wilson, "A Long Look at Crime," *FBI Law Enforcement Bulletin* 44 (1 February 1975): 1–6.

16. Daniel Bell, *The End of Ideology* (New York: Collier, 1962), p. 172.

17. Robert V. Bruce, *1877: The Year of Violence* (New York: Bobbs-Merrill, 1969), p. 13.

18. Bell, *The End of Ideology*, p. 165.

19. Bruce, *The Year of Violence*, pp. 138–158.

20. Robert M. Fogelson, "The 1960s Riots: Interpretations and Recommendations," A Report to the President's Commission on Law Enforcement and Administration of Justice, 1966 (mimeo).

21. For example, see Marvin E. Wolfgang, ed., *Annals of American Academy of Political and Social Science*, 364 (March 1966).

22. Hugo Herz, *Verbrechen and Verbrechertum in Osterreich* (Tubingen: Laupp, 1908).

23. Cesare Lombroso, *Crime, Its Causes and Remedies* (Boston: Little Brown, 1912).

24. Ibid., p. 7.

25. Georg Von Mayr, *Statistik and Gesellschaftslehere* (Tubingen: Mohr, 1917), p. 608.

26. U.S. Department of Justice, *Crime and Seasonality* (Washington, D.C.: U.S. Government Printing Office, May 1980).

27. Bureau of Justice Statistics, *The Seasonality of Crime Victimization* (Washington, D.C.: U.S. Department of Justice, May 1988).

28. Elmer H. Johnson, *Crime, Correction and Society* (Homewood, Ill.: Dorsey, 1968), p. 45.

29. See "Crime Distribution in Los Angeles," research report, Los Angeles Police Department, 1972.

30. For example, see Stuart Lottier, "Distribution of Criminal Offenses in Sectional Regions," *Journal of Criminal Law, Criminology and Police Science* 29 (1938): 336; Lyle W. Shannon, "The Spatial Distribution of Criminal Offenses by States," *Journal of Criminal Law, Criminology and Police Science* 45 (1954): 270; and Keith D. Harries. "The Geography of American Crime, 1968," *Journal of Geography* 70 (1971): 204–213.

31. Keith D. Harries, *The Geography of Crime and Justice* (New York: McGraw-Hill, 1974), pp. 16–36.

32. Bureau of Justice Statistics, *BJS Data Report— 1987* (Washington, D.C.: April 1988), p. 8.

33. Discussion with the chief of the DeKalb County Police Department, December 1972.

34. National Institute of Mental Health, *Criminal Statistics* (Washington, D.C.: U.S. Government Printing Office, 1972), p. 1.

35. "Crime Statistics Often Numbers Game," *New York Times*, 4 February 1968, p. 58.

36. National Commission on the Causes and Prevention of Violence, *Violence in America: Historical and Comparative Perspectives* (Washington, D.C.: U.S. Government Printing Office, 1969), p. 372.

37. See Richard Lyons, "Fuzzy Crime Statistics," *New York Times*, 18 September 1977, p. 14e., col. 3.

38. President's Commission on Law Enforcement and Administration of Justice, *Criminal Victimization in the United States: A Report of a National Survey* (Washington, D.C.: U.S. Government Printing Office, 1967), pp. 36–44.

39. President's Commission on Law Enforcement and Administration of Justice, *Report on a Pilot Study in the District of Columbia on Victimization and Attitudes Toward Law Enforcement* (Washington, D.C.: U.S. Government Printing Office, 1967).

40. For example, see Will Sparks, "Terror in the Streets," *Commonweal* 82 (11): 345–348; and U.S. National Commission on the Causes and Prevention of Violence, *To Establish Justice, to Ensure Domestic Tranquility* (Washington, D.C.: U.S. Government Printing Office, 1969).

41. See Michael E. Milakovich and Kurt Weis, "Politics and Measures of Success in the War on Crime," *Crime and Delinquency* 21 (January 1975): 1–10.

42. President's Commission, *Criminal Victimization in the United States*, p. 33.

43. Johnson, *Crime, Correction and Society*, p. 47.

44. David Pittman and William F. Handy, "Uniform Crime Reporting: Suggested Improvement," in Alvin Gouldner and S. M. Miller, eds., *Applied Sociology* (New York: Free Press, 1965), pp. 180–188.

45. Hugo O. Englemann and Kirby Throckmorton, "Interaction Frequency and Crime Rates," *Wisconsin Sociologist* 5 (1967): 33–36.

46. Sara Lee Boggs, "The Ecology of Crime Occurrence in St. Louis: A Reconceptualization of Crime Rates and Patterns," unpublished Ph.D. dissertation, Washington University, St. Louis, 1964.

47. Philip H. Ennis, "Crime, Victims and the Police," *Transaction* 4 (1967): 36–44.

48. Lyons, "Fuzzy Crime Statistics."

49. Law Enforcement Assistance Administration, *Criminal Victimization Surveys in the Nation's Five Largest Cities* (Washington, D.C.: U.S. Government Printing Office, April 1975), p. 1.

50. Author's note: Commercial establishments have been dropped from the survey.

51. Bureau of Justice Statistics Technical Report, *New Directions for the National Crime Survey* (Washington, D.C.: U.S. Department of Justice, March 1989), p. 2.

52. Ibid., p. 2.

53. Bureau of Justice Statistics, *BJS Data Report—1987*, p. 32.

54. Ibid., p. 32.

55. Ibid., p. 17.

56. Johnson, *Crime, Correction and Society*, pp. 31–32.

57. Bureau of Justice Statistics. *BJS Data Report*, p. 12.

58. Law Enforcement Assistance Administration, *Criminal Victimization Surveys*.

59. See: John Petersilia, *Criminal Careers of Habitual Felons: A Summary Report* (Santa Monica, Calif.: The Rand Corporation, 1977); U.S. Department of Justice, *Doing Crime: A Survey of California Prison Inmates* (Washington, D.C.: U.S. Government Printing Office, 1981); and Joan Petersilia and Paul Honig, *The Prison Experiences of Career Criminals* (Santa Monica, Calif.: The Rand Corporation, May 1980).

60. Charles E. Silberman, *Criminal Violence, Criminal Justice* (New York: Vintage Books, 1978), p. 55.

61. James F. Short, Jr., and F. Ivan Nye, "Extent of Unrecorded Delinquency: Tentative Conclusions," *Journal of Criminal Law and Criminology* 49, No. 4 (1958); Martin Gold, "Undetected Delinquent Behavior," *Journal of Research in Crime and Delinquency* 3, No. 1 (January 1966); Nils Christie et al., "A Study of Self-reported Crime," *Scandinavian Studies in Criminology*, Vol. I (London: Tavistock, 1965).

62. In Silberman. *Criminal Violence*, pp. 56–57; and Michael S. Lasky, "One in Three Hotel Guests Is a Towel Thief, Bible Pincher or Worse," *New York Times Travel Section*, January 27, 1974.

63. Silberman, *Criminal Violence*, p. 56.

64. The President's Commission on Law Enforcement and the Administration of Justice, *Task Force Report: Crime and Its Impact—An Assessment* (Washington, D.C.: U.S. Government Printing Office, 1967), p. 103.

65. Silberman, *Criminal Violence*, p. 57.

66. "This World," *San Francisco Examiner*, Sunday, 9 June 1974, p. 33.

67. Silberman, *Criminal Violence*, p. 58.

68. Ibid., p. 58.

69. Kenneth H. Bacon, "SEC Testimony Tells How Gulf Oil Gave $300,000 a Year to Politicians in the U.S.," *Wall Street Journal*, 17 November 1975, p. 30.

70. As reported in Bureau of Justice Statistics, *Report to the Nation on Crime and Justice*, 2nd ed. (Washington, D.C.: U.S. Department of Justice, March 1988), p. 9. Author's note: The white-collar offenses studied in this research effort consisted of the crimes of forgery, counterfeiting, fraud, and embezzlement.

71. Ibid., p. 9.

72. For example, see Rodney Stark, *Police Riots: Collective Violence and Law Enforcement* (Belmont, Calif.: Wadsworth, 1973); David Wise, *The American Police State* (New York: Random House, 1976): American Friends Committee, *Struggle for Justice* (New York: Hill and Wang, 1971); Robert Lefcourt, *Law Against the People* (New York: Random House, 1971).

73. See, for example, Morton H. Halperin et al., *The Lawless State: The Crimes of the U.S. Intelligence Agencies* (New York: Penguin Books, 1976); and I. F. Stone, "The Threat to The Republic," *New York Review*, 26 May 1976.

74. Gresham M. Sykes, *The Future of Crime* (Washington, D.C.: U.S. Government Printing Office, 1980), p. 56.

75. Richard Rovere, "Crime in the FBI," *New Yorker*, 8 August 1977.

76. Bureau of Justice Statistics, *Report to the Nation*, p. 8.

77. "California Aiding Victims of Crime," *New York Times*, 25 July 1965.

78. See Stephen Schafer, "Victim Compensation and Responsibility," *Southern California Law Review* 43. No. 1 (1970): 55–67; Joe Hudson, Bert Galaway, and Steve Chesney, "When Criminals Repay Their Victims," *Judicature* 60 (Feburary 1977): 312–321; Laura Nader and Elaine Combs-Schilling, "Restitution in Cross Cultural Perspective," in Joe Hudson, ed., *Restitution in Criminal Justice* (St. Paul, Minn.: Minnesota Department of Corrections, 1975), pp. 23–41; Gilbert Geis, "Compensation to Victims of Violent Crimes," in Rudolph J. Gerber, ed., *Contemporary Issues in Criminal Justice: Some Problems and Suggested Reforms* (Port Washington, N.Y.: Kennikat, 1976), pp. 94–115.

79. William E. Hoelzel, "A Survey of 27 Victim Compensation Programs," *Judicature* 63 (May 1980): 485–496.

80. National Institute of Justice, *Crime Victim Compensation* (Washington, D.C.: U.S. Government Printing Office, 1980).

81. Stephen Schafer, "Compensation to Victims of Criminal Offenses," *Criminal Law Bulletin* 10 (1977): 605–636.

82. Ibid., p. 37.

83. Ibid.

84. See: U.S. Department of Justice, *Handbook on the Comprehensive Crime Control Act of 1984 and Other Statutes Enacted by the 98th Congress* (Washington, D.C.: U.S. Government Printing Office, December 1984), Chapter 14.

85. McGillis and Smith, op. cit., p. 107.

86. Ibid., p. 36.

87. Rudolph Doener, "The Effect of Victim Compensation Programs upon Conviction Rates," *Sociological Symposium* 25 (Spring 1979): 40.

88. Rudolph Doener, "An Examination of the Alleged Latent Effects of Victim Compensation Programs upon Crime Reporting," *LAE Journal* 41 (Winter/Spring 1978): 71–76.

89. Hoelzel, "Survey of Victim Compensation Programs," p. 496.

# CHAPTER 4

# Local, State, and Federal Law Enforcement Agencies

## OBJECTIVES

**After reading this chapter, the student should be able to:**

Identify the two basic police roles.
Understand and identify important historical
  precedents in the development of law enforcement.
Discuss the development of:
  municipal police
  county law enforcement
  state police
Identify the responsibilities and authority of the
  following federal law enforcement agencies:
  Federal Bureau of Investigation
  Border Patrol
  Drug Enforcement Administration

Marshal Service
Organized Crime and Racketeering Section
Strike Force Operations
Secret Service
Customs Service
Bureau of Alcohol, Tobacco, and Firearms
Internal Revenue Service
Discuss the Law Enforcement Assistance Administration
  (LEAA). In particular, know:
  how it came into existence
  its purpose
  how it operated
  the contributions it made
  how and why it failed
  the National Institute of Justice and the Bureau of
    Justice Statistics
Discuss INTERPOL and how it is organized and
  operates.

## IMPORTANT TERMS

Maintain Order
Enforcement of the law
Henry Fielding
Bow Street Amateur Volunteer
  Forces
Patrick Colquhoun
Sir Robert Peel
Charles Rowan and Richard Moyne
Police fragmentation and
  decentralization

Sheriff
State police
Highway patrol
*Posse comitatus*
Federal Bureau of Investigation
Border Patrol
Drug Enforcement Administration
U.S. Marshal Service
Organized Crime and Racketeering
  Section

Strike Forces
Law Enforcement Assistance
  Administration (LEAA)
Racketeer Influenced Corrupt
  Organization Act (RICO)
National Institute of Justice
Secret Service
Customs Service
Bureau of Alcohol, Tobacco and
  Firearms
Internal Revenue Service
Postal Inspection Service
INTERPOL

In a free society, the police are both an anomaly and a necessity, because they are granted more power than other members of society—their right to search, to use deadly force, and to arrest is awesome to the degree that it can deprive individuals of their personal freedoms. The anomaly of this police power is that it is given under a system of government that grants authority reluctantly and, when granted, is sharply curtailed by a system of checks and balances. What is also thought provoking is the fact that this authority is delegated to individuals at the lowest level of the police bureaucracy.[1]

Yet, as Goldstein points out, a democracy depends heavily on its police, despite their anomalous position, to maintain the order that permits a free society to exist. The police, therefore, become *our agents* to prevent people from preying on one another; to provide a sense of security; to facilitate movement; to resolve conflicts; and to protect the very process and rights on which a free society exists. The strength of our democratic processes and the quality of life in America are determined to a large degree by the methods our police employ in discharging their functions.[2]

 **POLICE FUNCTIONS**

Within the framework of our Constitution and system of laws, the police play two important roles: They maintain order and enforce the law.[3] All of their activities, from directing traffic to conducting investigations and making arrests, are found in these two basic roles. The maintenance of social order is their prime responsibility, and only when they cannot accomplish this duty must they employ the more extreme measure of enforcement. Because the police require the authority to enforce compliance with the law, they have been given the powers of inquiry and arrest. Implicit, however, in our criminal justice system is the idea that the police through their efforts should be able to induce voluntary compliance, and only when this fails are they justified in using their arrest powers.

This relationship is apparent when examining police functions. The most obvious example is the basic level of police activity—the officer patrolling a beat. Such officers are concerned primarily with behavior that either disturbs or threatens the peace—from the neighbor who plays a stereo too loudly to a bank robbery. In each instance, the order of society is disturbed, obviously more so in the case of the bank robbery.

The order maintenance activities of the police involve far more time than the law enforcement aspects of their role. One study of a metropolitan police department indicated that more than half the calls the police received were for help or support in connection with personal and interpersonal problems that were not directly of a law enforcement nature.[4] In Detroit, one researcher found that only 16 percent of the calls to the police were crime related and called directly on their law enforcement powers.[5]

To understand how these roles developed, one must understand the historical relationship among society, law, and police powers, and how these factors became interrelated to produce the present conception of the role of the police. This chapter explores this historical relationship and also examines the growth, development, and organization of police agencies at all levels of government. Chapter 5 deals with how specific law enforcement functions such as arrest and investigation must meet these role criteria. Finally, in this section on law enforcement, there is a discussion of some of the reform efforts and concerns now being directed at the police to improve their ability to fulfill these roles.

## ◻ EARLY DEVELOPMENT OF LAW ENFORCEMENT

Historians have not provided us with much insight into the development of law enforcement. For the most part, early law enforcement duties in the ancient empires were performed by existing military forces. Around 500 B.C., Rome created the first specialized investigative unit, called *queastors* or "trackers of murder." Later, during the reign of Augustus Caesar (27 B.C. to A.D. 14), principles of police administration developed that were similar to some modern methods. For example, special detachments of quasi-military personnel operated out of designated districts in the city of Rome. They were responsible for maintaining patrols and searching out criminals. This same principle of organization was also established throughout the provinces conquered by Rome.

*Slow evolution of law enforcement and criminal justice*

With the fall of the Roman Empire, the kind of centralized government that was needed to maintain law and order came to an end. Western Europe then became enveloped in what historians often refer to as the "Dark Ages." Gradually, the feudal system evolved as a means to bring some social order out of the chaos that had followed the collapse of Rome. By the eleventh century, the feudal system had become established.

Under feudalism, a loose and decentralized social structure evolved; a social structure built on the idea of mutual responsibilities and obligations of the *vassalage* and *suzerain*. Generally, the feudal lords administered justice to those under their dominion as they saw fit. The church, too, had a role in determining what constituted criminal offenses and how the offender was to be dealt with. A major characteristic of the time was that the powerful feudal barons and the church did not answer to any central secular authority and that only a rudimentary and inconsistently interpreted and applied law guided justice. This period of history was characterized by a centuries-long struggle between the power of the crown to centralize control—including the administration of justice and law—and the determination of feudal lords and the church to retain their power independent of the monarchy.[6]

Nevertheless, inroads were beginning to be made. In England, Henry II (1133–1189) made an important effort to create a more systematic and uniform system for the administration of justice. During his reign, such features as the petit (trial) jury, the first rules of evidence to govern trials, the forerunner of the grand jury, the right to challenge jurors, and a superordinate system of courts began to develop. The office and duties of the shire-reeve (sheriff) became more prominent as Henry II, and some of his successors struggled to wrestle power from the feudal lords and the ecclesiastical authority. Although governed more by self-interest than the rectitude of justice, important changes were occurring.

##  DEVELOPMENT OF THE POLICE IN GREAT BRITAIN

America's model

It is important to understand the development of law enforcement in Great Britain for two reasons. First, it serves as the model for our own system of criminal justice. Many of the institutions, processes, and foundations of criminal justice developed in England and were adopted in America when the colonies were founded. Second, and perhaps more important, many of the attitudes now held by Americans about legal principles and the police are a result of the centuries of experience the English had under their existing system of criminal justice. For example, the distrust of strong centralized government and the fear of oppressive police systems under such governments have long been a historical fact and characteristic of the English experience. With such a historical perspective, it is easier to understand the foundation for such continuing concerns today.

## BEGINNINGS OF THE MODERN ERA OF LAW ENFORCEMENT

Five influential personalities

The British police system and the influence it has had in America were not because of the British people, but in spite of them. In the words of Reith, a noted historian on the development of the police, "It is almost solely the product of personalities: those of five individuals whose single-mindedness in vision, ideals and purposes was eventually brought by the last of them to practical adaptation in the shape of the police as we know them today."[7]

The first of the five creators of modern police concepts was the novelist Henry Fielding. Although he is most widely remembered for his novels, his achievements as a magistrate who worked to achieve social and police reform are certainly no less significant in terms of their lasting value to humanity. He conceived of the idea that police action should be directed at the *prevention* of crime instead of seeking to control it, as was the custom at the time, simply by waiting for its occurrence and then attempting to repress it by means of violence or brutal punishment.

Fielding

Fielding was a perceptive observer of the nature and causes of crime in London. He saw that crime and criminals had become so open in the city that the constables of the time were powerless to intervene and completely at the mercy of the criminal elements. The situation had become so bad that the constables would not dare to arrest the majority of the criminals. Fielding also observed that the law-abiding citizens of London did not grasp the possibilities of collective security against the criminal. Fielding conceived the idea that there was another method of dealing with crime and disorder besides that of waiting helplessly for its manifestations and then attempting to meet violence with violence. He proposed that people could collectively go into the streets, trace the criminals to their haunts, and arrest them. To test this theory, he selected six citizens of integrity and physical prowess, and under this leadership they swept the criminal elements from the Bow Street area of London. Many criminals were arrested; others fled. The work of these men and the simplicity of their methods caused a sensation. So astonishing were the results of his Bow Street Amateur Volunteer Force that the government provided Fielding with a salary and asked him to extend the idea into the other areas of

*View of the **PUBLIC OFFICE** Bow Street, with Sir John Fielding presiding & a Prisoner under examination*

Henry Fielding's Bow Street Raid and subsequent "Public Office" (shown here as perpetuated by his half-brother John Fielding) changed the way the British police functioned. (Culver Pictures)

London. Before he could accomplish this, he died in 1754, and for a few years his efforts were carried on by his brother. Soon, however, his original group degenerated into a motley band known as the Bow Street Runners, and it took another thirty years before Henry Fielding's values and ideas received the recognition they deserved.

The next reformer was Patrick Colquhoun, a prosperous Glasgow business- Colquhoun man who expressed a deep interest in social and criminal reform. He was appointed as a magistrate in London and began to study the significant social problems of the day and their relationship to crime. He worked diligently to help bring about needed social reforms for the poor. Intrigued by Fielding's earlier work, he crystalized the novelist's ideas into the "new science of preventive police."[8] He proposed that a large police force should be organized for London under the direction of a board of control. Although his plan was ultimately rejected, in 1789 he formed a special river police force patterned after Fielding's idea that proved to be a success and pointed to a solution to a citywide and nationwide problem. Unfortunately, his ideas were still too advanced for the times, for the English people still harbored a great deal of mistrust toward any form of organized police that could be entrusted with enforcement authority.

Peel

The next significant reformer was Sir Robert Peel, the home secretary of England. Although many writers give Peel credit as the most instrumental of police reformers, some historians who have thoroughly researched the history of the English police credit him only with the handling of the bill that created the Metropolitan Constabulary, and the foresight to choose wisely the first two commissioners of the new agency who actually planned, organized, and directed the establishment.[9]

Whatever Peel's contribution, the Metropolitan Constabulary for the city of London was created in 1829. In the creation of the Metropolitan Constabulary, certain principles of a police profession became embodied in its creation and operation. These principles are still relevant today. It was, for example, organized around such ideas that the police must be under government control; the police should be organized along military lines; police efficiency is to be determined by the absence of crime; deployment of police personnel by time and area is essential; police applicants should be appointed on their own merits; a command of temper is an indispensable trait; policemen should be hired on a probationary status; and police records and training assure greater efficiency.

Rowan and Moyne

Although these were the enunciated principles of the new London Metropolitan Constabulary, they were nothing more than ideas when the first two police commissioners, Charles Rowan and Richard Moyne, were appointed in 1829. The combined efforts of these two men established the concepts of modern policing and left an indelible mark on the functions of the British police to this day. The Metropolitan Constabulary, however, was almost disbanded before the principles could be tested. Parliament was being widely criticized by angry groups of citizens calling for the repeal of the act. Members of Parliament engaged in acrimonious argument, and the fate of the new department hung in the balance. While denunciations swirled about them and Parliament was locked in prolonged debate, these two dedicated and capable administrators began to assemble the agency. The first task was to screen personnel for positions in the new department. Rowan and Moyne realized that this was perhaps the most critical concern, for public approval would depend a great deal on the type of personnel they obtained. The applicants were offered a career for life if they satisfied the standards and could produce accordingly. Out of 12,000 initial applicants, 1,000 were chosen and placed into six divisions. They first concentrated their efforts in the high-crime areas of the city. During their probationary period, the new constables were supervised extensively. During the first three years of the department's operation, there were 5,000 dismissals and 6,000 required resignations. This use of the probationary period was a forceful indication of the commissioners' serious intentions.[10]

The success of the new department was almost phenomenal. Crime and disorder declined sharply, yet without the loss of individual freedom to the law-abiding. The commissioners were so successful in their efforts to organize, recruit, and train a professional police agency that within ten years the people considered Peel a sort of folk hero, and the constables of the London Metropolitan Constabulary became known as "Bobbies" out of respect for Sir Robert Peel. With this success, the idea of a centralized, trained, and well-organized permanent group of police constables soon spread throughout England.

## ◻ DEVELOPMENT OF LAW ENFORCEMENT IN AMERICA

If the history of law enforcement in England up to the nineteenth century can be considered shameful, the American experience must be considered a disgrace. America seems to be uniquely adept at ignoring the lessons of history. During the more than 200 years of our existence, we have overlooked the repeated lesson that laws are meaningless in the absence of the authority to secure the *observance* of those laws. During the early years of our nation's growth, the country was involved in the making of laws and the structuring of elaborate procedural machinery, while ignoring the need to provide effective means by which the laws could be enforced.

Although we patterned our police forces after the British model, we often **Adoption of weaknesses** adopted only those features that had already proved to be ineffective at best. We adopted the weak and defective constable system of rural England. The elected constables of England became the elected sheriffs and deputy sheriffs of the counties within our states and the elected marshals of our towns and cities. The lack of concern displayed by Americans for the necessity of law enforcement must, in part, be attributed to our heritage of disdain for strong central government and the Jeffersonian ideal of "little republics." Jefferson believed very strongly in the idea of local self-government, by which each citizen was afforded the opportunity to be actively involved in the conduct of government. It was Jefferson's belief, adopted from the writings of John Locke and later supported by Alexis de Tocqueville in his celebrated work, *Democracy in America*, that local government should have "preeminent authority over such responsibilities as the care of the poor, roads, police, administration of justice in minor cases, and elementary exercises for the militia.[11] These ideas received strong support from the American people and remain an ideological legacy today.

This traditionally held idea of the primacy of local government has had a significant impact on the development of police throughout the United States. No other country in the world has developed their police quite like America. What is so unique to our nation is the extreme fragmentation and decentralization of police authority. We are, for the most part, a nation consisting of a checkerboard of small police agencies who receive their jurisdiction and authority from the employing local or county unit of government. Table 4.1 shows the number of local and state police agencies and quasi-enforcement agencies operating. The vast majority of police services are provided by local units of government and by police agencies that are quite small. Although we might think of organized police services in terms of the New York City Police, the Los Angeles Police, or some similar large agency, such departments are very uncharacteristic of American law enforcement. In fact, more than one-half of all local police departments operating in this country employ less than ten full-time officers.[12]

Part of this is certainly attributable to the way we developed geographically as a nation. Yet, it is more likely a result of American philosophy and character. This issue of the primacy of local government carried with it another characteristic: Government services (including the police) were best provided and *controlled* by keeping them close to the people. Large government was viewed with deep suspicion and misgiving. This would prove to have an ironic twist. While it might theoretically be thought that local police could better be controlled by the local citizenry, it soon proved that the police were indeed controlled, but by certain

---

**TABLE 4.1** Profiling America's State and Local Law Enforcement Agencies (1987)

*Organization*

| | |
|---|---|
| Number of local police agencies (municipal, township, and general purpose police) | 13,562 (approx.) |
| Sheriffs' departments | 3,000 |
| County police | 79 |
| State police/highway patrols | 51 |
| State law enforcement agencies (includes various boards with limited law enforcement responsibilities, e.g., alcohol beverage control boards, state game and fish departments, state fire marshals, state marine patrols, etc.) | 355 |
| Special police agencies (e.g., park rangers, transit police, campus security, etc.) | 965 |

*Size of Agencies*

| | |
|---|---|
| Local police | Thirty-four local police agencies employed over one thousand sworn officers, but more than half had fewer than ten sworn officers and 987 employed just one full-time officer |
| Sheriff's departments | Twelve sheriffs' agencies employed over one thousand sworn officers each, and twenty-seven such agencies served populations of one million or more |
| State police | The main state police agency in each state had an average of 1,031 full-time sworn personnel (range, slightly over 100 to nearly 6,000) |

| | |
|---|---|
| *Number of employees* (local police agencies, sheriffs' departments and state police) | 758,000 |
| *Operating and capital expenditures* | More than $28 billion |
| *Racial and ethnic composition* (sworn personnel) | |
| Local police | 85.4% white, 9.3% black, 4.5% Hispanic |

elements of the local citizenry rather than the broader body politic. The local American police developed a legacy of serving special community interests and became the handmaiden of political factionalism. Whether it was the police in Northern cities employed to keep immigrant groups in line and later used against the emerging efforts of workers to form trade unions, or Southern police, who became tools of white oppression against blacks, the result was the same. This organizational arrangement would also prove to present almost insuperable problems for the development of responsible and effective policing in the United States—and for police professionalism generally. In no small way this would also contribute to the attitudes many Americans still have about the police. As historian Charles Reith says:

> The weakness of law enforcement machinery in the United States is because of the fact that, as the people's choice, the police were allowed to become corruptly the instruments and servants not of the law, but of policy and of local and corrupt controllers of policy. By her solution of the problem of the breakdown of the Constable

TABLE **4.1**   *(Cont.)*

|  |  |
|---|---|
| Sheriffs' departments | 86.6% white, 8.3% black, 4.3% Hispanic |
| State police | 88.7% white, 6.5% black, 3.8% Hispanic |

*Female sworn personnel*

|  |  |
|---|---|
| Local police | 7.6% |
| Sheriffs' departments | 12.5% |
| State police | 4.2% |

*Educational qualifications for sworn personnel*

All state police agencies and almost all local police (99.7%) and sheriffs' agencies (97.5%) with 135 or more sworn personnel required new officer recruits to have at least a high school diploma

About 10% of state and local police agencies and about 6% of sheriffs' departments required at least some college education

*Percentage of civilian (nonsworn) police employees*

|  |  |
|---|---|
| Local police | 24% |
| Sheriffs' departments | 22% |
| State police | 32% |

*Assignment*

Approximately 88% of sworn officers in large police agencies worked in field operations; 6% in technical support; and 5% in administration

*Collective bargaining*

Two-thirds of local police agencies authorized collective bargaining by employees

*Source: Bureau of Justice Statistics Bulletin, Profile of State and Local Law Enforcement Agencies, 1987* (Washington, D.C.: U.S. Department of Justice, March 1989); and The National Archive of Criminal Justice Data. Interuniversity Consortium for Political and Social Research (Ann Arbor, Mich.: Winter 1989).

system, England was able to abolish the old system entirely, and under the new system which she created in 1829, her police were made, entirely and exclusively, instruments of law and not of policy and servants of the public. By the fact of having secured independence, the United States lost the benefit of this conception, and the development of the American police has suffered ever since.[13]

The development of local law enforcement in the United States was often conditioned by predisposing factors and local conditions. For example, in the North the primary unit of local government was the town. At first, settlers in these areas banded together in small communities for mutual protection from Indian attacks. Later, as the Industrial Revolution made its impact, these towns grew, and so did the need for law enforcement. Because these were primarily urban settlements, the English urban police model of the town constable or watchman developed. As some of the cities grew larger, more elaborate systems were developed in which groups of night watchmen were given the responsibility to maintain law and order and to suppress crime.

The role of local conditions

In the South, the agrarian nature of this region led to the adoption of strong county government as the primary unit of local government. Just as the sheriff was the primary law enforcement official in rural areas in England, so did this office become one of the most influential in county government throughout the Southern states. Even today, although the authority has diminished somehwat over time, the office of the county sheriff is one of considerable importance in many areas of the South.

Law enforcement services in the West are an amalgam of organizational arrangements that predominated in the North and South. Settlers who migrated west tended to adopt police organizations like those in the areas from which they came. Many of the same factors that led to the creation of towns in the Northeast were also experienced in the westward movement. For example, the necessity to form protective communities against hostile Indian attacks resulted in the establishment of towns and adoption of constables or town marshals. At the same time, the vastness of the area encouraged an agrarian and livestock economy more suited to the adoption of the county sheriff form of law enforcement. As a result of these patterns, law enforcement services in the various regions of the country still have a somewhat distinctive difference today. In the Northern states, municipal police are more prevalent, whereas the South retains a great deal of authority in the county sheriff. In the Western states, more of a balance is struck between the jurisdictional authority of municipal police and the sheriff.

## Municipal Police

The development of city police in the United States is a part of the changing social, economic, and political forces that left their imprint on the history of municipal governance. In the early seventeenth century, major reliance was placed on the use of military forces, perhaps assisted by a constable or night watchman. Later, the constable system replaced the military in this role. Still later, a separate day watch was established, and finally the day and night watches were combined into a single police organization.

Night watch

The first night watch was established by Boston in 1636. In 1658, New York added a similar unit, followed by Philadelphia in 1700. New York's night watch was referred to at the time of its creation as the "Shiver and Shakers" or the rattle watch, because the night watchmen used rattles to announce their presence and to communicate with each other as they made their rounds. Like their counterparts in England at the time, these watchmen were often lazy, inept, and not entirely reputable. In a number of cases, minor offenders were sentenced to serve on the watch as punishment for their crimes. Just as in England, citizens called to serve on the watch could hire substitutes.

For the next hundred years, there were no major changes in providing law enforcement services. When cities grew large enough to warrant a form of law enforcement, they adopted the night watch system of Boston, New York, and Philadelphia and incorporated all their negative features.

In 1833, Philadelphia passed a city ordinance that was a major innovation. It established the first daytime police force consisting of salaried men who worked under the direction of a captain appointed by the mayor. In 1854, the day police were consolidated with the night watch into one department, under the leadership of a marshal who was elected for a two-year-term. During this period, the city of New York also developed a daytime police service, when the New York State legislature, in 1844, authorized communities to organize police forces and appropri-

CAPTAIN.     CAP-COVER FOR RAIN.     CHIEF.     RESERVE CORPS.     LIEUTENANT.     PRIVATE.

NEW REGULATION UNIFORM OF THE NEW YORK POLICE.

Police forces were first established in U.S. cities in the 1830s; however, the officers went about their work in street clothes. This 1854 newspaper illustration shows New York's newly adopted uniforms. (Culver Pictures)

ated special funds that could be given to cities to provide around-the-clock police protection. By the outbreak of the Civil War, a number of other cities, such as Chicago, New Orleans, Cincinnati, Baltimore, and Newark had adopted similar police organizations, and the foundation of today's municipal police departments had been established.

Politics and corruption

The following years were very difficult ones for the establishment of law enforcement, as the police were dominated by political interests and susceptible to corruption. Department reports of the time indicate instances of utter lawlessness on the part of the police themselves. For example, in 1852, documents of the New York Board of Aldermen reported such acts as assaulting superior officers, refusing to go on patrol, forcibly releasing prisoners from the custody of other policemen, drunkenness, theft, pimping, and extorting money from prisoners. These acts were daily occurrences that the police committed under the protection of their political overlords.[14] In Baltimore, Cincinnati, Boston, St. Louis, and other major cities, control of the police was vested in a patronage system controlled by the dominant political party. In many documented cases, such as in Baltimore, the police were employed as an instrument of the political faction in power to control elections.[15] Nowhere was the undisciplined attitude of the police more clearly shown than in their refusal to wear uniforms, which they considered to be a symbol of servitude. Gradually, they began to wear distinctive apparel, but this was brought about more by their identification with a particular precinct or group of politicians than by anything else. For example, in Philadelphia the police in one ward would wear felt hats to identify their source of patronage, whereas those in another ward would wear white duck suits as their badge of political identification.[16]

Reform efforts

Spurred by reform groups, a number of cities and states tried to bring about change. A few states tried to take the control of local police forces in certain large cities out of the hands of the local politicians by putting the departments under state control. This attempt met with great opposition and, except in a few cities, proved to be unworkable. In other cities, special supposedly nonpartisan police boards or commissions were established, and a few cities still retain this arrangement.

Today, for various reasons, significant reform has occurred among most municipal police departments. The major reason, however, is that municipal government itself has come under the influence of reform, and changes in police departments are part of an overall change. In the late nineteenth and early twentieth centuries, such reform groups as the National Municipal League began developing programs of municipal reform with the goal of eliminating corruption, increasing efficiency of city government, and making local government more responsive to the will of the public. Although it is not possible to examine all the features of municipal reform and their interrelationships, such characteristics as the adoption of civil service systems; nomination by petition; initiative, recall, and referendum; the short ballot; the council-manager form of government; nonpartisan elections; and certain sociological and demographic phenomena have brought significant changes to city governance and, as a direct consequence, to municipal police services.[17]

## County Law Enforcement

In most areas, the law enforcement services in rural and unincorporated portions of a county are handled by the sheriff's department.

The office of the sheriff dates back to eighth-century England. Under the tithing system, a reeve was given the responsibility for coordinating and directing the activities of the tithing members throughout the shire (county). Appointed by the local earl, the shire-reeve was the earl's chief ministerial representative in the shire. These shire-reeves were very powerful and influential local officials. Among their responsibilities were to protect and oversee the earl's property and the property of the king that the earl was obligated to protect. In addition, they were responsible for the collection of taxes, overseeing the conduct of local tribunals while serving as chief magistrate of these courts, the apprehension and prosecution of those who violated the king's law, and the other minor administrative tasks. Thus, unlike today's sheriffs, these early shire-reeves were not only responsible for the law enforcement or executive tasks of governance, but had judicial responsibilities as well—a combination of responsibilities that often resulted in a crude and perverse form of justice.[18] The early colonists adopted the idea of sheriff as an important county office, but by the time the Colonies were settled, the sheriff had become primarily a law enforcement and custodial officer with no direct judicial powers.

*Shire-reeve*

Because of a combination of historial and political reasons, the sheriffs in many states have broad authority and power. In thirty-three states, the sheriff is a constitutional officer and is regarded as the chief law enforcement officer in the county. This authority stems from early English law, which invested the sheriff with the power of *posse comitatus*—that is, authority to coordinate the activities of all other local police agencies. The sheriff's political power is derived from the fact

*Posse comitatus*

that the office is part of the county's executive branch. The sheriff's political status and the visibility of the police function make the sheriff a key political figure. Historically, the argument for retaining the sheriff's constitutional powers has been based on the need to protect the independence of the office. Politically, the office has retained this status because of its pivotal place in local party politics.

Today, the office of the sheriff has three primary responsibilities. The first is to provide law enforcement services in the county. Whether the sheriff provides law enforcement services to municipalities in the county is contingent on a number of factors. Some states, by virtue of home rule and other statutory provisions, have given cities the authority to provide their own police department. In some states, when this grant of authority is given, the city police department has primary jurisdiction over all offenses committed therein, and the sheriff's department has authority and jurisdiction only outside the municipality, except in a few instances. Often an agreement is reached between cities and the sheriff's department whereby the sheriff will not enforce the criminal laws within the city except to take specific action in cases such as when they are in "hot pursuit" of an offender, when they have been asked to assist the local police, in cases of civil strife, or other conditions that might warrant the sheriff's department's coming into the city to enforce the criminal code.

*Sheriff's responsibilities*

The other two responsibilities of this office are to maintain the county jail and to serve as an officer of the county courts. The sheriff often receives many of the prisoners who have been arrested in the county. In some cases, particularly where there are larger cities within the county, the city police retain arrestees in city jails, pending their trial. Even where cities have their own jail facilities, however, more serious offenders are often transferred to the county jail before trial because of the existence of greater security measures and other facilities that city jails do not provide. Even a serious felon who has been retained in city jail will usually be transferred to the county jail after the trial to await transportation to a state institution.

As an officer of the county courts, the sheriff has numerous responsibilities. Often, this office provides personnel to serve as court bailiffs, transports prisoners to and from the courts, transports juveniles who have been adjudicated as delinquents and sentenced to institutions, and transports mental patients who have been remanded to state mental health facilities. The sheriff's department is also responsible for certain civil process matters such as court-ordered liens, service of forfeiture and eviction notices, divorce papers, the sale of confiscated property, administration and sale of foreclosed property, and related civil judgments as directed by the courts. Figure 4.1 shows the typical organizational arrangement of a medium-sized sheriff's department.

In recent years, the enforcement responsibilities of the sheriff's department have come under attack from such prestigious groups as the Committee for Economic Development and the Advisory Commission on Intergovernmental Relations.[19] These and other groups argue that too many sheriff's departments are infused with self-serving political interests that detract from their professional law enforcement role. On balance, some of these criticisms are perhaps justified when one examines the characteristics of these agencies on a national scale. In too many documented cases, these agencies become patronage empires for the sheriff and other elected county officials, who use this office to reward their political followers. As a consequence, because the personnel are often not covered by civil service protection, there is a constant turnover in staff. Modern law enforcement requires

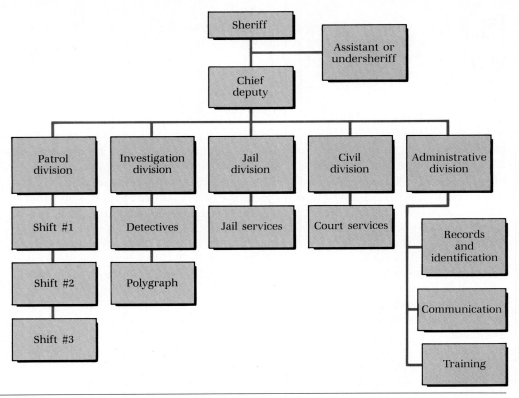

FIGURE **4.1** Administrative organization of a medium-sized sheriff's department.

extensive training and knowledge that personnel in these agencies do not have when hired and fail to acquire on the job. In many instances, the sheriff is more a politician than a professional in law enforcement.

Although sheriff's departments are often suceptible to criticism because of their selection standards, lack of training, and quality of service, there are certainly exceptions. In fact, a number of these departments, particularly in California, are among the finest law enforcement organizations in the United States. The Los Angeles County Sheriff's Department is one of the most professionally well-equipped and trained police agencies in the nation. The Multnomah County (Oregon) Sheriff's Department was one of the first nonfederal agencies to require a four-year college degree as a condition of employment. Unfortunately, such standards among police departments at other than the federal level of government are too often the exception rather than the rule.

**COUNTY AGENCIES TODAY.** In recent years, a number of recommendations

The idea of county police have been made to improve county law enforcement. One suggestion has been to abolish the constitutional authority of the sheriff and invest the office only with statutory powers. This idea is in line with county reform efforts designed to replace the plural executive organization of county government with a centralized county administration represented by a county chief executive or a county board of commissioners. County reorganizations along these lines would tend to increase the accountability of county agencies. As long as the sheriff retains constitutional status, however, it is nearly impossible for county officials to maintain meaningful control and accountability over the actions of the sheriff's department.

Another recommendation is that states, through appropriate legislation, provide the option of assigning the responsibility for countywide police services to an independent county police force under the control of the county chief executive or county board of commissioners. Today, there are about seventy-nine such county police departments throughout the United States. Many counties that have adopted the county police department have given this agency full authority and responsibility to perform all law enforcement functions. In some cases, the sheriff's department has been retained, but its responsibilities have been limited to operating the jail and providing the usual services to the county courts.

Unfortunately, for some communities, these reorganizations have created problems, many of which stem from the legal and political traditions inherent in the sheriff's office. Georgia, for example, recognizes the sheriff as a constitutional officer, yet permits counties to establish independent police agencies. As a consequence, a few counties in that state, to show their dissatisfaction with the quality of service provided by the sheriff, have created county police departments; however, they are forced to retain the sheriff, who still has the same full responsibilities. This duplication is costly, and people are confused as to whether to call the sheriff's department or the county police. A great deal of political acrimony has also been apparent between the heads of these two agencies as well as among political supporters and elected officials who side with either the sheriff or the county police. This results in charges and countercharges of incompetence, poor service, corruption, and a host of other claims being leveled at one agency by supporters of the other.

A number of reform-minded groups claim there is an immediate need to reappraise the office of the sheriff and its enforcement responsibilities. The Advisory Commission on Intergovernmental Relations recommended that states give metropolitan counties the option of assigning basic responsibility for countywide police services to an independent county police force under the control of the county chief executives or county board of commissioners. As part of this arrangement, the sheriff's department would turn over all court and jail duties to the appropriate court and correctional agencies.[20] Although this recommendation might have some merit, it is impractical. Perhaps a more workable solution is for the states to enact legislation to force sheriff's agencies to become more professional. Such legislation would place sheriff's department personnel under civil service, require them to be compensated solely on a salary basis, provide them with adquate retirement benefits, and require them to meet more rigorous levels of training.

## The State Police

In comparison with municipal police and county sheriff's departments, state police agencies are relatively new. The impetus for the development of state police agencies came from a number of circumstances. One was the realization that inefficient and corrupt municipal law enforcement agencies and sheriff's departments were unable to provide adequate law enforcement services in their respective jurisdictions. With the failure of state governments to impose state governing boards over the operations of local law enforcement services, some states chose to create special police agencies that would have the power to enforce all state laws.

Another factor was the introduction of the automobile, which provided crimi-

Reasons for creation

nal offenders with mobility. It became increasingly difficult for local and county police agencies to apprehend criminals, who could easily flee their jurisdiction. In addition, the automobile provided unique enforcement problems of its own. As the number of automobiles increased, so did state highway systems. As a consequence, increasing attention had to be devoted to traffic regulation on these highways— control that had to be multijurisdictional and that could not be handled satisfactorily by the local police and sheriff's departments.

Finally, state governments came to the realization that there was no agency that could enforce the criminal code of the state nor was there adequate regulatory legislation. If a particular law or regulation was not being enforced for whatever reason by the political subdivisions in the state, the state was powerless to compel local compliance or to force local police officials to take enforcement action.

**PROTOTYPES OF STATE AGENCIES.** The first state police-type agency was

Texas Rangers

the Texas Rangers. This agency was established by the Texas Provisional Government in 1836, when Texas was a republic.[21] It was originally established as a purely military unit for use on the Texas borders. Later, it began work in the area of criminal investigation and gradually developed into a state police force that effectively controlled sporadic outbreaks of anarchy resulting from the absence of any law enforcement machinery in the new state. Today it is concerned primarily with the conduct of criminal investigations and rendering technical assistance to other law enforcement agencies in Texas.

Massachusetts was the next state to recognize the need for a statewide enforcement agency. In 1865, responding to the problem of uncontrolled vice in certain communities, the state legislature gave the government authority to create a small group of state constables whose primary purpose was to investigate organized vice activities. In 1879, because of official corruption in this unit, it was reorganized into a new state investigative unit called the Massachusetts District Police, which became the Massachusetts State Police in 1920.

In 1903, Connecticut established a state investigative unit patterned after the Massachusetts District Police. Like the earlier Massachusetts constables, this unit was set up primarily to investigate vice, which had become rampant in certain communities and against which local police agencies were powerless to take enforcement action because of police corruption and political collusion. This unit also proved to be incapable of solving the problem and later was absorbed into a more effective organization known as the Connecticut State Police.

The credit for establishing the first truly professional and modern state police

Pennsylvania

organization belongs to Pennsylvania. In 1905, the Pennsylvania State Constabulary was formed. It is considered the first true state police organization, because the state law enforcement agencies that preceded it were created in response to limited needs, such as frontier problems or the enforcement of vice laws. This agency was established largely because local police forces were unable to control the riots that had become a feature of the coal mining regions. Armies of coal miners fought bloody labor disputes with mercenary forces hired by mine owners and management. It was also hoped that the new agency would improve law enforcement services in the rural areas of the state where county officials were unable to provide adequate protection. A last reason for the agency's creation, and one that is invariably cited by many who oppose the creation of state police forces today, was that Governor Pennypacker realized he needed some assistance in carrying out the responsibilities and mandates of his office. Pennypacker issued the following statement when he created the agency:

> In the year 1903 when I assumed the office of chief executive of the state, I found myself thereby invested with supreme executive authority. I found that no power existed to interfere with me in my duty to enforce the laws of the state, and that by the same token, no condition could release me from my duty to do so. I then looked about me to see what instruments I possessed wherewith to accomplish this bounded obligation—what instruments on whose loyalty and obedience I could truly rely. I perceived three such instruments—my private secretary, a very small man; my woman stenographer; and the janitor. So, I made the state police.[22]

Organizational and jurisdictional characteristics also entitle the Pennsylvania State Police to be considered the first such agency. In terms of organization, this agency was under the administrative control of a superintendent appointed by the governor. Troop detachments and posts were situated throughout the state so that even the most remote areas were protected.[23] This organizational arrangement and deployment of personnel served as the model for other state police agencies. In terms of jurisdiction, this agency was empowered to enforce all state laws throughout Pennsylvania.

**TODAY'S STATE AGENCIES.** Today, some states have bonafide state police departments and others have primarily traffic enforcement agencies, commonly referred to as *highway patrols*. There are some basic distinctions between the two. State police agencies have full jurisdiction and authority to enforce all state laws anywhere in the state. Their responsibilities are quite broad. For example, state police agencies in Pennsylvania, New York, and Arkansas provide a full range of police services and support activities. In addition to performing routine patrol and traffic enforcement activities, they have investigative units that investigate major crimes, intelligence units that investigate organized crime activities, juvenile units, crime lab services, statewide computer facilities that compile crime data for the state, and other related functions.

*State police and highway patrols*

Highway patrol organizations, on the other hand, such as those in Florida, Georgia, Ohio, and California, are mainly specialists in traffic regulation and enforcement. For the most part, their responsibilities are to enforce traffic laws on state and interstate highway systems. In some cases, they have the responsibility to investigate crimes that occur in specific locations or under specific circumstances, such as on state highways or state property or crimes that involve the use of public carriers. Generally, their investigative resources and functions are quite limited, and their support and technical services related specifically to traffic. States having such units usually have separate small investigative agencies that assist the highway patrol organizations and other local and county police agencies but operate under very limited jurisdictional authority.

Many state legislative bodies, faced with the growing volume of automobile traffic on state highways, recognized the need for a statewide regulatory police agency but were reluctant to create anything but a traffic control agency. As a consequence, the legislation that created highway patrol agencies was purposely designed to ensure that these bodies would be little more than traffic enforcement units. The reluctance to give these agencies full state police authority was the result of several factors. First, America has traditionally distrusted executive authority. Many legislators were afraid that a state police under the authority of the governor

*Politics and state police organizations*

would become an instrument of oppression led by the governor and easily used against his political opposition. The early use of organizations such as the Pennsylvania State Police in strike-breaking activities engendered a great deal of hostility among supporters of organized labor, who campaigned vigorously in a number of states against the establishment of state police forces. This opposition, combined with the legislature's traditional hostility toward increasing the power of the chief executive, proved to be decisive.

Probably more important, however, was the fact that the strong political connections of local law enforcement officials, particularly the county sheriffs, were brought to bear. These officials perceived the creation of a state police system as a direct threat to their own authority, Today, strong sheriff associations exist in almost every state and at the national level. Suggestions that highway patrol agencies be expanded into state police organizations meet strong opposition from these organizations, which have become quite adept and powerful in local political circles and in state capitals. The fact that these fears have never materialized in those states that have given their state police full police authority seems to be of no concern to those interests opposed to the concept of a state police.[24] Similarly, the fact that the state police have reached, in many states, a level of professionalism and detachment from control of political interests far beyond those of county and municipal police agencies seems also to have had little bearing. In many ways, the lack of a state police organization is an unfortunate and costly disservice to the citizenry of these states, who deserve and pay for better law enforcement than they often receive from their local departments.

## ☐ FEDERAL LAW ENFORCEMENT AGENCIES

**Enforcement powers**

Many people are confused about the authority of federal law enforcement agencies. These agencies can enforce only violations of federal laws as contained in the statutes passed by Congress or within the statutory authority of an agency's responsibilities. Federal agents cannot, for example, enforce state or local laws any more than state or local authorities have the jurisdictional authority to enforce federal laws. Sometimes, however, a crime is a violation of both state and federal law. In these cases, both governments can enforce their respective laws. A major drug dealer in Philadelphia is violating both the laws of the Commonwealth of Pennsylvania and the federal government. Under such circumstances, both jurisdictions could be involved in the investigation and arrest.

**Highly specialized**

Another distinctive characteristic of federal law enforcement agencies is their specialization. Most federal law enforcement agencies are highly specialized units that enforce a rather narrow range of federal crimes. Partly, this circumstance is a result of how federal laws and agencies to enforce these laws have developed over the years, and partly it is due to the reluctance of Congress to give to any particular agency the authority to enforce all federal crimes. Such a system would also likely be unworkable. There are simply too many federal crimes and too many specialized agencies that have enforcement or quasi-enforcement responsibilities. It is not practicable to entrust these broad enforcement responsibilities to any one "super agency." It is sometimes said that the reason Congress is reluctant to rewrite and adopt legislation that would give more power to enforce additional federal laws to a particular agency such as the FBI is the concern that such an all-powerful agency would in effect be a "national police"; a situation that would pose insuperable problems of control and threaten a democratic system of government. Undoubtedly, this could happen. It is also true that Congress doesn't seem to have the stomach to take on the vested interests that represent and support the existing fragmentation among the federal law enforcement community.

Over the years, the number of separate agencies scattered throughout the executive branch has proliferated. For example, the Departments of Agriculture, Labor, Justice, Defense, Treasury, Interior, and others have developed law enforcement or quasi-enforcement agencies to deal with criminal and regulatory functions within their jurisdictions. In addition, a number of independent regulatory bodies, such as the Interstate Commerce Commission, the Securities and Exchange Commission, and the Federal Trade Commission, perform certain regulatory and compliance functions that require enforcement and quasi-enforcement units.

In many instances, the enforcement problems of local and state governments are mirrored in the operations of federal law enforcement agencies. Jurisdictional disputes, lack of coordination among different agencies, agency rivalries, lack of interagency communication, and failure to share intelligence information and other resources have created some very serious problems in the effective enforcement of federal laws. And, given the nature of the federal bureaucracy, the problems seem even more difficult to solve than similar problems among the political subdivisions in our states. **Problems**

As a result, in 1977 President Carter instituted a plan to streamline and consolidate the approximately 141 federal agencies that now have law enforcement or quasi-enforcement powers. Prompted by his campaign promise to restructure the federal government along lines of greater efficiency and lower cost, he made the law enforcement agencies of the federal government a special target of what he and the Office of Management and Budget saw as examples of grossly inefficient and costly service duplication. As might be imagined, an immediate outcry was heard, particularly from some Treasury Department agencies, against such a proposal. As a result of entrenched opposition, the reorganization proposal was never carried out. Instead, greater efforts at informal cooperation and the creation of special joint task forces involving various agencies and the sharing of some jurisdictional responsibilities has been instituted. It is questionable how effective these "reforms" have been.

In 1789, when the Constitution was ratified, the police provisions of the federal government were quite specific and narrow. The framers of the Constitution wanted to form a stronger central government than had existed under the Articles of Confederation, but they were aware that the new states would not accept too strong a national government. As a consequence, they vested only certain powers in the national government and reserved the rest for the states.[25] Among the important specific police powers originally vested in the federal government were those given to Congress to "lay and collect taxes," "to regulate commerce," "to establish post offices and post roads," and "to provide for the punishment of counterfeiting." [26] These powers have played a very important role in the creation of federal police agencies, because much of the enforcement authority of federal agencies hinges on the power of taxation and the regulation of interstate commerce. With the growth of tax legislation and the expanded interpretation by Congress and the federal courts of what constitutes interstate commerce, the law enforcement authority of the federal government has grown substantially. Federal law enforcement authority has also derived from the power of Congress to enact all "necessary and proper" **Early limitations on federal police powers**

To most Americans, the war on drugs is taking place on our nation's streets. This is only part of the battleground. There exists a second "war zone" unfamiliar to most: the war being fought among federal (and state) law enforcement agencies who are given the Sisyphean task of stemming the flow of narcotics. This "war" may be as difficult to "win" as the more familiar one. In this second war many of the enforcement agencies involved see their counterparts almost as much the enemy as the drug traffickers.

Interagency rivalries among our nation's police is nothing new. There has always been more than a fair share of friction among many federal state and local law enforcement authorities. The local police, for example, often are critical of such agencies as the FBI, whom they feel take "the glory" after cases are successfully worked by local law enforcement agencies, when the FBI comes in for "the kill"—and the headlines that go along with major arrests. Although such criticism of the FBI has lessened in recent years,

it still exists among the law enforcement community. Jealousies and antagonisms are also often part of the jurisdictional disputes that arise between local and state police agencies. It may be the local cops who feel slighted by the actions of the "staties."

The drug problem has made the situation even worse. Nowhere is the problem more pronounced than at the federal level—especially between the two major agencies involved in the antinarcotics enforcement effort: the Drug Enforcement Administration and the Customs Service. Although fifty-eight federal offices have "responsibility" over drugs, it is these two lead agencies that jockey back and forth for the preeminent role. And it is not only the law enforcement agencies that are involved in the problem. The State Department got into the act. And the Coast Guard plays a role. With the discussed plans to involve the military—and with it, the Pentagon—in the antidrug efforts, the fray should really pick up.

Behind all this bureaucratic in-

fighting, headline seeking, and turf protection lies one factor that looms large: a bigger share of the $26 billion dollars the federal government has spent over the past nine years trying to stem the drug problem. As the bill for these efforts rises each year, so too, do the stakes. The Customs Service seems particularly adept at playing the bureaucratic game. Using their well-placed sources in Congress, their share of the pie has been growing faster than any other agency. They have learned to play the game as it is meant to be played: "you give me and I give you." For example, it is more than mere coincidence that major Customs installations for aircraft and a new center to coordinate their enforcement activities lie in Congressional districts that are home to their strongest supporters on Capitol Hill.

In a scene reminiscent of Vietnam, a new "body count" has become the way to tally "success": it's called the number of pounds, kilos, or tons seized. It makes little difference that the quantity of drugs on

laws and the federal judiciary's interpretation of the Fourteenth Amendment and from the immediate need of the federal government to enforce new laws and court rulings.

Although the beginning student of criminal justice should be aware that there are many law enforcement agencies of the federal government, only the major agencies can be examined in any meaningful way. Because a large share of enforcement activities of the federal government are centered in the Department of Justice and the Treasury Department, each of these is examined closely.

##  DEPARTMENT OF JUSTICE

The Department of Justice is responsible for the major enforcement functions of the federal government. To accomplish its broad enforcement responsibilities, it incorporates such agencies as the Federal Bureau of Investigation, the Immigration and Naturalization Service, the Drug Enforcement Administration, the U.S. Marshal

American streets is increasing and the price is dropping in spite of ever-growing seizures. The agencies jockey for federal bucks based on this elusive measure of "success." And Congress is only too glad to support such efforts. Without more meaningful measures—and given the public's growing clamor for action—Congress seems to be more than willing to shovel the money their way. Perhaps, to Congress, this is a way out. Our elected representatives can always claim to the hard-pressed American taxpayer that they did everything they could: they spent our money.

There is another insidious side to this destructive infighting. The agencies are locked in a posture of less than enthusiastic support for the efforts of other agencies and their antinarcotic efforts. This runs a broad gamut from refusing to provide or concealing intelligence information from their rivals or, as reported by *Newsweek,* actually refusing to assist or cooperate with other federal agencies. Even seizure assets are being used in the one-upmanship

game. In addition to providing a strong financial incentive to elbow other agencies out of the action (in 1988 Customs seized planes, automobiles, boats, and other items with a value twice that of their budget for that year), seizure is being put to use in other ways. Customs has been developing a policy of sharing some of the booty with local and state police. Obviously, the message is clear: cooperate with us and we'll cut you in.

In 1989 William J. Bennett was appointed by President George Bush as the director of the Office of National Drug Control Policy—the so-called "drug czar." As director, Bennett is responsible for the National Drug Control Program and for developing an annual plan called the National Drug Control Strategy, to be submitted to Congress by the president. It is Bennett's task to advise the President regarding necessary changes in the organization and management of the federal government's antinarcotics efforts. Although his role was seen by some as a means to coordinate the federal

agencies involved—especially those involved in enforcement activities—and to oversee their operations, there is evidence that his efforts have met with little success. The unwillingness of the involved federal agencies to cooperate and their unwillingness to be answerable to a "drug czar" have effectively thwarted any efforts at improvement.

Law enforcement agencies acting as independent fiefdoms with no centralized authority to control the growing bureaucracy of narcotics enforcement can only continue to thwart our country's efforts. America's penchant for fragmentation at all levels of law enforcement leads to serious problems of inefficiency and, yes, corruption and control by powerful special interests. On the other hand, centralized authority and control of the police might prove to be even more disastrous. If special interests ever gained control of a national police force, the consequences could well undermine our republic. It presents a quandary that appears to be incapable of solution.

Service, and the Organized Crime and Racketeering Section. It also includes the Law Enforcement Assistance Administration, which (although not an enforcement agency) has in recent years played a significant national role in the administration of criminal justice.

## The Federal Bureau of Investigation

The FBI is the chief investigative arm of the Department of Justice. Although the office of attorney general was established in 1789, the Department of Justice was not created until 1870, when the problems of post–Civil War reconstruction and the need to centralize and coordinate the federal government legal activities led to its formation. Before that time, the prosecution of federal violators was handled separately by the various governmental departments.

Chief investigative arm of Department of Justice

It soon became apparent that a special group of investigators would be needed to enforce the laws that would come under the jurisdiction of the newly created Department of Justice. However, opposition from Congress, private citizens, and the nation's leading newspapers was immediate. Again, the fear of a centralized police agency was expressed. Successive attempts to create a small law enforcement unit as a permanent subdivision of the Department of Justice were rebuffed by Congress at every turn. Without its own investigative personnel, the Department of Justice had to "borrow" investigators from other federal agencies.

At the incessant urging of President Theodore Roosevelt, Congress agreed to compromise. In 1909, Congress authorized the establishment of the Bureau of Investigation, but gave it very limited enforcement powers. In 1910, Congress passed the Mann Act, which prohibited the interstate transportation of females for purposes of prostitution and other crimes that involve interstate commerce. Enforcement of this law was turned over to the Bureau of Investigation. During World War I, espionage and selective service violations were added to its jurisdiction, and in 1919 Congress passed the National Motor Vehicle Theft Act, which increased the scope of its authority.

**Early defects**

Although the Bureau of Investigation can be credited with some noteworthy achievements during this time, especially with recovering large areas of public lands that had been illegally taken over by private citizens, these accomplishments were clouded over by serious defects. The agency was poorly managed and organized and was itself sometimes engaged in extralegal activities for corrupt politicians. Men with criminal records were sometimes appointed to positions of authority, and the bureau conducted brutal raids, illegal searches, and massive dragnet operations aimed at locating draft dodgers or aliens accused of sabotage. Innocent citizens were frequently arrested during these operations. As a result, there was serious talk about disbanding the bureau and transferring its jurisdiction to other federal agencies.[27]

**Reform efforts**

In 1924, a young government attorney by the name of J. Edgar Hoover was given the task of restructuring the agency and weeding out the corruption. Hoover agreed to accept the directorship only if the attorney general would assure him that the bureau would be free of politics and that all appointments and promotions would be based on merit. These conditions were accepted, and he was appointed director. He immediately set to work reorganizing the bureau, establishing new

J. Edgar Hoover directed the FBI from 1924 until 1972. (Culver Pictures)

J. EDGAR HOOVER

administrative procedures, and initiating a general clean-up campaign. He removed incompetent and unreliable personnel, and the character and ability of all applicants were thoroughly investigated before their appointment. In 1935, Congress changed the name of the Bureau of Investigation to the Federal Bureau of Investigation.[28]

The 1930s and the World War II years were important years for the Bureau's growth and public image. In the early to mid-1930s, the agency was instrumental in capturing some of the nation's major gangsters. Such notables as Lester Gillis ("Baby Face" Nelson), John Dillinger, Charles "Pretty Boy" Floyd, Alvin Karpis, and Kate "Ma" Barker fell to the efforts of Hoover's "G-Men." The war years saw the FBI expand its scope of investigative activity into such areas as espionage, sabotage, and subversion. Its domestic law enforcement activities against major criminal elements had expanded into domestic security and intelligence operations.[29]

After the war, with the loss of Eastern Europe and the ushering in of the Cold War, a period of "Red hysteria" gripped America. Hoover, taking advantage of the anti-communist paranoia sweeping the nation, catapulted the FBI into major investigations of subversive activities by the American Communist party and its sympathizers. Hoover relentlessly drove the Bureau with his obsession: "the Red Menace." As the 1950s faded, the 1960s presented new challenges for the Bureau. The adoption of the 1964 Civil Rights Act broadened the agency's jurisdiction. During the 1960s, the nation was wracked by civil discord. Visible civil dissident groups such as the Weather Underground, the Black Panther Party, and anti–Vietnam War protesters became targets of FBI investigative activities. It was also a period that saw Hoover's death in 1972. This brought an era of increasing accountability and concern about Bureau excesses in the area of domestic intelligence operations against protesters and so-called subversives. A great deal of criticism was being leveled at the FBI for its involvement in domestic intelligence activities and its methods—methods that themselves smacked of unconstitutional actions and violations of civil rights. The backlash ushered in a period of increasing oversight by Congress and the executive branch, a period culminating in the development of new guidelines for FBI domestic intelligence and domestic security activities.

It was also a period when Hoover himself came under attack. Perhaps afraid to attack him when he was still alive, his detractors now smelled blood. He was widely denounced for his feet-dragging in the area of bringing the Bureau into the area of organized crime activity. In fact, his famous denial that there even was such a thing as organized crime was widely ridiculed. So was his refusal to involve the FBI in narcotic investigations. Most damaging, however, were the revelations that he had used the resources and personnel of the FBI to spy on his enemies and public officials and that he used such information to blackmail these officials and to extort resources for the Bureau.

In recent years, without the visible menace of major gangsters or the communists to capture the attention of the public, the Bureau has been concentrating on more routine criminal matters. While the major headlines have shifted to narcotics law enforcement activities, the FBI has conducted some major investigations into such areas as the Abscam scandals, serial killers, and domestic terrorism.

**THE FBI TODAY.** Over the years, the legal jurisdiction of the FBI has been extended to cover all federal crimes that are not the specific responsibility of any other federal law enforcement agency. The FBI now has jurisdiction over more than 200 categories of federal violations. Generally, the FBI's investigative efforts fall into four main areas. The first of these are crime matters. The agency investigates specific federal laws that have been assigned to it. These include such crimes as bank robbery, kidnapping, assaulting or killing a federal officer, and interstate transportation of stolen motor vehicles. The investigation of domestic national security matters is another major and important role of the FBI. Such acts as sabotage, espionage, treason, insurrection, and rebellion, seditious conspiracy, and advocating the overthrow of the government are representative laws in this area. The Bureau is also involved in what are called applicant matters. In these cases, the FBI investigates applicants for various important government positions. In response to President Bush's controversial nomination of John Tower to be his Secretary of Defense, Democrats in Congress raised serious concerns about Tower's suitability because of his alleged drinking problems and his moral character. Although the FBI conducts background investigations on all such nominees, the Bureau was given additional responsibility to investigate the validity of such charges. Finally, the FBI conducts investigations into civil matters in which the federal government is a party in interest such as when claims are filed by or against the government.

**SERVICES AND OPERATIONS.** Most people are familiar with the FBI's Ten Most Wanted Fugitives Program, which began in 1950. Probably less familiar are other important services and programs operated by the FBI. One significant undertaking has been the development and operation of the National Crime Information Center (NCIC). The NCIC is a major computer network that operates out of Bureau headquarters in Washington. All states, many metropolitan areas, and a number of federal law enforcement agencies have access to the NCIC through the interfacing of their criminal justice computers or terminals to the master NCIC computer. The system can handle thousands of inquiries a day.

The NCIC stores information concerning wanted persons, computerized criminal histories of major and persistent offenders, missing persons, stolen vehicles and vehicle parts, descriptions of vehicles involved in felonies, stolen license plates, stolen and recovered guns, stolen boats, stolen and embezzled securities (including currency), and stolen articles that can be identified by serial numbers such as television sets, video cassette recorders, and similar items. (See Figure 4.2.) These are reported by local, state, and federal law enforcement agencies throughout the country and go into the master computer. The system is used extensively by the nation's police. A Detroit police officer on patrol might spot a suspicious car and radio the dispatcher to conduct an NCIC inquiry on the automobile, or the Idaho Highway Patrol might run a "records check" through NCIC on an arrestee to see if he or she is wanted elsewhere.

The FBI has one of the most sophisticated crime labs in the world staffed by leading scientific examiners of evidence. First established in 1932, it has grown to where its facilities are now available to police officers in the smallest town in America. Not only will these experts examine evidence and report the results to the police agency submitting the evidence, but they will testify at no cost to the requesting police department in any court of law concerning their findings. The laboratory services include such things as blood examinations, bombs and explosives identification, chemical analysis, copyright files, questioned document examinations, fraudulent check and gambling paraphernalia files, cryptoanalysis, hairs and fibers analysis, ballistics and gun powder residue analysis, paint comparisons, and voice-print analysis—just to name some of the forensic services available.

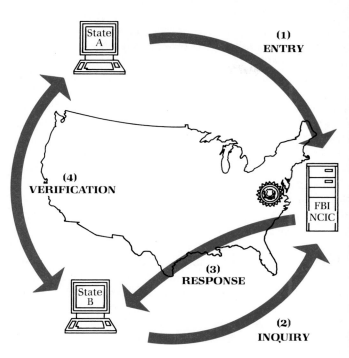

| COST/BENEFITS | |
|---|---|
| **Average Cost Per Transaction** | |
| **$.03** | |
| 1988 VEHICLE AND WANTED PERSON FILES BENEFIT SURVEY RESULTS FOR 12 MONTHS | |
| Vehicles Recovered | 169,435 |
| Value of Vehicles Recovered | $1,110,841,399 |
| Wanted Persons In File Located | 81,474 |
| Persons Arrested | 136,360 |
| Additional Charges | 71,030 |
| Missing Juveniles Found | 36,362 |
| Missing Adults Found | 9,244 |

The National Crime Information Center shares data with law enforcement agencies throughout the country. Shown here is a cost/benefit analysis of recent activities. (Courtesy of the National Crime Information Center) FIGURE **4.2**

The FBI also operates its Identification Division. It began in 1924 with twenty- **ID division** five employees and a little more than 800,000 fingerprint cards, which were obtained from the criminal records at Leavenworth Penitentiary and the files of the International Association of Chiefs of Police. By the early 1980s, it had amassed almost 175 million prints, with about 70 million people having their prints on file. The fingerprint files are broken down into two categories: criminal and civil files, with the two divided about equally.

The Bureau also has an extensive training program for police personnel **Training programs** throughout the nation using what it calls Special Agent Instructors who are assigned to each field office and to the National Academy at the U.S. Marine base at Quantico, Virginia. These agents instruct in such areas as firearms, defensive tactics, crime scene searches, collecting and preserving evidence, conducting interviews, and report writing. Specialists are also available on such topics as police management, legal matters, mob and riot control, and police–community relations.

One of the most noted of the FBI's training programs is the so-called National Academy at Quantico. Open to career police officers from the United States and some foreign countries, it selects officers nominated by their respective agencies for the eleven-week program. Here they are taught a wide range of subjects important to modern law enforcement. The National Academy also provides specialized coursework for police supervisory and administrative personnel from agencies throughout the free world. In recent years, the Academy program has been further expanded to examine even more esoteric areas such as the psychology of violent or repetitive serious offenders, research applications in law enforcement, and other topics involving highly respected professionals and scholars who are specialists in various areas. One such program is the highly touted National Symposia Program, which draws leading experts together for discussion of major national law enforcement and crime issues.

In the past fifteen years, other important investigative responsibilities have been assigned to the FBI. For example, new statutory enforcement authority has come about as a result of the Ethics in Government Act of 1978. Under this act, the much publicized Abscam cases arose. In addition, the FBI under this legislative authority has been extensively involved in the investigation of corruption involving government officials at the federal, state, and local levels.[30]

The FBI has also been given additional responsibilities under the Foreign Corrupt Practices Act of 1977 and the Foreign Intelligence Surveillance Act of 1978. One new and widely publicized area of responsibility is the Parental Kidnapping Prevention Act of 1980. Under this statute the FBI's traditional jurisdiction over crimes involving unlawful flight to avoid prosecution has been extended to cover parental kidnappers.

The most important new development, however, occurred in 1982. The attorney general assigned the FBI jurisdiction to investigate federal drug offenses. What had been the primary responsibility of the Drug Enforcement Administration (DEA) was transferred to the FBI. Although the DEA will continue to exist, it will report directly to the director of the FBI. This will significantly increase the involvement of the FBI in major narcotic investigations and provide a much more massive effort to deal with the serious drug enforcement problems the country faces.

This transfer of authority and supervisory responsibility is a direct outgrowth of problems that beset the DEA and severely hampered federal investigative efforts in the area of narcotics violations.[31] The DEA, like its predecessor agencies, seemed incapable of dealing effectively with the situation.[32] As a result, a special narcotics task force was created, which recommended FBI involvement in this area. And as a consequence of this recommendation, the FBI was assigned to supervise, coordinate, and become extensively involved in federal narcotics investigations.

## Immigration and Naturalization Service

The Immigration and Naturalization Service (INS), created in 1891, is responsible for administering the immigration and naturalization laws, which relate to the admission, exclusion, deportation, and naturalization of aliens. Under the Immigration and Nationality Act, the INS screens applicants for admission to this country in an effort to exclude categories of persons deemed to be "undesirable aliens" because of criminal histories, moral turpitude, or other related reasons. The agency also investigates aliens to identify those engaged in various types of criminal activity and is responsible for the detention and deportation of those who enter the United States illegally. The service maintains records of all persons granted or denied admission. With the adoption of the Immigration Reform and Control Act of 1986, the Service is given additional responsibilities to investigate and assist in the prosecution of cases involving employers who hire illegal aliens.

Border patrol

One of the most publicized units of the INS is the Border Patrol. The Patrol was created in 1924, when Congress allocated funds for the establishment of a border patrol unit within the then-existing Bureau of Immigration. The Border Patrol works to prevent the illegal entry of aliens and their smuggling of illegal goods or contraband. In addition to the Border Patrol, the enforcement efforts of the INS are also vested in an Investigations Unit, whose agents work mostly in major cities and inland agricultural areas.[33]

The Border Patrol seems always to have been the subject of congressional criticism for its failure to stop the illegal flow of aliens into the United States.[34] This criticism has become especially sharp in recent years as the flood of illegal alien immigration now seems to be reaching an epidemic in many of our states bordering Mexico. In addition to illegal aliens merely crossing our borders, the Border Patrol is confronting serious problems with massive illegal alien smuggling operations. Such operations often begin deep within the United States, when farmers, ranchers, or factory foremen contract through "labor brokers" for cheap labor from Mexico. Word is passed on down the line, and recruiters visit villages and promise unemployed Mexicans high wages in the United States. The workers then sign on, either paying on the spot or, more likely, promising to pay out of their wages when they arrive. They then become a *polloero's* property, and are passed from one to another. They are bought and sold like slaves.[35]

The federal government is increasing the number of Border Patrol officers and investigators and is providing increased funding for aircraft and a sophisticated computer system for keeping track of legal and illegal aliens. The Border Patrol is also involved with the U.S. Customs Service and other federal agencies in trying to stem the tide of narcotics brought into the United States by illegal aliens.

## Drug Enforcement Administration

The Drug Enforcement Administration (DEA) was created in 1973, when Congress approved the consolidation of the former Bureau of Narcotics and Dangerous Drugs, the Office of National Narcotics Intelligence, the Office for Drug Abuse Law Enforcement, and the drug investigation and drug intelligence operation of the U.S. Customs Service into one major federal agency with overall responsibility to enforce the federal narcotics and dangerous drug laws. This major reorganization occurred after previous attempts to stem the problem of narcotics had failed, owing partly to the fragmentation among various federal agencies of jurisdictional authority relating to illegal narcotics.[36] Ever since the Hoover Commission's Report on Governmental Reorganization in 1949, various commissions had recommended the consolidation of federal enforcement agencies. Finally, the seriousness of the narcotics problem forced Congress to act and create a consolidated federal agency to deal with this specific problem.

*Lead antinarcotics enforcement agency*

The basic responsibility of the DEA is the control of the distribution and use of narcotics and dangerous drugs. Its major targets are organized groups that deal in the growth, distribution, and marketing of these drugs. In this way its enforcement efforts are directed at national and international cartels that control the manufacturing and distribution networks. It operates its own network of enforcement personnel and regional laboratories throughout the United States and in several dozen foreign countries. Often, this agency conducts investigations in cooperation with local and state police in which major drug traffickers are involved.

To assist state and local governments throughout the country to combat illicit drugs, it has developed specialized training programs. It also conducts specialized narcotics training programs for police personnel of foreign countries in such diverse places as Mexico, Peru, Australia, and the Philippines. As does the FBI, the DEA makes available to other police agencies the scientific expertise of its crime laboratories and provides expert scientific testimony on evidence these labs receive and analyze for local and state police agencies. This agency is also authorized to regulate and inspect nearly 5,000 licensed drug manufacturing and distribution firms to prevent possible diversion of legally manufactured drugs to illicit sources.

For a period of time after the DEA–FBI merger in 1982, there was talk about phasing out the DEA except for its regulatory and compliance activities involving legal sources of drug distribution, such as pharmaceutical manufacturers. One recommendation was to transfer all of the criminal investigative efforts of the agency to the FBI or to a special drug enforcement division within the FBI. Rumor had it, however, that the FBI was strongly opposed to any total FBI–DEA merger. It was also said that the FBI did not relish the task of being the nation's lead drug enforcement agency.[37]

While the rumors of full merger floated around Washington and the federal law enforcement community, steps were being taken behind the scenes to ensure that this would not happen. In 1987 the Attorney General went public with the announcement that he was against a full merger. Although a formal study had begun in 1985 directed at ways consolidation could occur, both the FBI and DEA were not convinced. It was the Attorney General's contention that his decision was based on what he perceived as "fundamental differences in mission, structure, tradition and personnel practices" between the two agencies.[38] It was, however, decided that although the two would operate as separate entities in the Department of Justice, they would continue under the combined leadership of the director of the FBI.

The Attorney General stressed that steps were being taken to better coordinate the efforts of the two. This was to include joint training programs at the FBI Academy in Quantico, Virginia, the development of compatible communication systems, the possibility of combining in several cities the localities of their offices into single locations, and the possibility of consolidating all FBI and DEA lab functions. The Attorney General also mentioned in his announcement that the FBI since 1982 had been more actively involved in drug-related efforts, and this would increase as the Bureau's expertise in organized crime and money laundering lend themselves to a greater role in drug-trafficking investigations and prosecutions.[39]

### U.S. Marshal Service

The office of marshal appeared in England shortly after the Norman conquest. As this office developed, the marshal became the court officer who escorted into the courts the offender, the victim, and the witnesses to the crime. Today, there are two types of marshals in the United States. Some small communities not large enough to require a municipal police department have town marshals who are the equivalent of chiefs of police. In some instances, the town marshal may hire deputies to assist in providing law enforcement services in these communities, but usually the position is a part-time one. Town marshals are also usually responsible for serving the local municipal or mayor's court. In this capacity, they may be called upon to serve subpoenas and arrest warrants and escort prisoners to trial.

History

The other type of marshal is the U.S. marshal, a federal law enforcement officer who serves the federal courts under the jurisdiction of the U.S. attorney general. Although the Colonies had marshals who performed law enforcement services, it was not until the passage of the Judiciary Act of 1789 that this office became a federal one. This act prescribed the judicial structure of the federal government and authorized the appointment of a U.S. marshal for each state and territory to serve these newly created federal courts.

The first U.S. marshals were appointed by President Washington for four-year terms. In 1801, this appointive power of the President was recognized by law. These early U.S. marshals performed a wide variety of assignments for the federal government. They were directed by Congress to take the census, hire and supervise jails for federal prisoners, take into custody all vessels and goods seized by revenue officers, sell lands possessed by the United States, serve as fiscal agents of the courts, and perform other miscellaneous tasks as directed.[40]

The role played by U.S. marshals in the enforcement of the laws in the Old West has been well publicized. In many instances, they were the only federal law enforcement personnel in the Western states and territories.[41] Although the federal government had Post Office inspectors and later, Secret Service agents in these areas, these groups were too small and had too limited a jurisdiction to be very effective in maintaining law and order. As a result, the responsibility of enforcing most federal laws fell to the U.S. marshals.[42]

The modern office of the U.S. marshal has undergone several reorganizations in an effort to better carry out its broad functions. The service now operates under the authority of a director who reports directly to the associate attorney general in the U.S. Department of Justice. The director supervises 94 U.S. marshals in the 50 states, the District of Columbia, the Canal Zone, Guam, and the Federal District of Northern Marianas, the Virgin Islands, and Puerto Rico. All U.S. marshals (except the U.S. marshal for the Virgin Islands) are appointed by the President with the consent of the Senate for four-year terms.

The authority of the U.S. marshals and their deputies is fairly broad. In many cases their authority at the federal level is very similar to the authority of the sheriff at the state level. Generally, a U.S. marshal has the power to enforce all federal laws except those that have been specifically delegated to other federal agencies; the marshal is also responsible for serving legal documents issued by the federal courts, congressional committees, and governmental agencies.

In the last few years, the enforcement and protective activities of this agency **Responsibilities** have been broadened substantially through new authorization and the assumption of some responsibilities formerly carried out by other federal law enforcement agencies, such as federal fugitives, which used to be a responsibility of the FBI. Today, its activities are generally centered in six areas.

The Enforcement Operations Division of the U.S. Marshal Service is engaged primarily in locating and arresting individuals for whom federal fugitive warrants have been issued for prison escapes and bond violations. They are also responsible for assisting the U.S. Probation Service in locating and arresting persons charged with parole and probation violations. At the request of INTERPOL, the service has also assumed responsibility for the investigation and apprehension of most foreign fugitives believed to be in this country.

Since the 1980s, the service has increasingly concentrated its attention on apprehension of fugitives. Since the FBI relinquished this responsibility in 1979 at the Carter administration's insistence that the FBI concentrate on organized and white-collar crime, the Marshal Service has made this a major priority. In the highly competitive world of infighting among federal law enforcement agencies, authority and responsibility for fugitive apprehension gave the Marshal Service a unique expansion of its jurisdiction—an additional responsibility the service was only too glad to accept.

In the past seven years the Marshal Service claims to have captured thousands of wanted criminals. Its most stunning victory was the role it played in locating Dr. Joseph Mengele, the Nazi death camp overseer. Chosen to spearhead the United States efforts in this international undertaking, the service played a crucial role in providing the West German government with the intelligence information that led directly to the discovery of Mengele's grave.

The efforts at fugitive apprehension are coordinated through a number of Fugitive Investigative Strike Teams (FIST). In recent years such teams have led several coordinated efforts by international authorities in making arrests of known fugitives in the Miami area and throughout the Caribbean.

This agency is also involved in important ways in providing security for the federal courts—particularly in cases in which there is a threat of violence or witness intimidation such as the Hell's Angels motorcycle gang trials held in several federal courts throughout the country. These security provisions also include investigating threats against federal court personnel and conducting physical security analyses and developing comprehensive plans for protecting buildings that house federal courts.

In the 1970s and 1980s, much of the attention the Marshal Service received revolved around its witness security efforts. In the past this agency has come under

Federal Marshals are charged with providing security for federal courts and participants in trials. Here they escort a reputed drug kingpin into the U.S. Penitentiary in Atlanta. (David Murray, Jr./ Stock South)

a great deal of criticism for its slipshod handling of this program. Authorized under the Organized Crime Control Act of 1970, this program is responsible for the protection of individuals whose safety is jeopardized as a result of their testimony on behalf of the government. The service provides security protection, relocation, and new identities for such witnesses. As of fiscal year 1987, the service was providing protection and/or funding for more than 1,700 witnesses.[43]

This agency also oversees the negotiation of contracts with local governments for the confinement of federal prisoners in local detention facilities and is responsible for the scheduling and transportation of all federal prisoners who are sentenced to federal institutions or being transferred.

Finally, the service also has a special operations group capable of being dispatched in emergency situations requiring federal law enforcement personnel, such as the civil disturbances that struck in Miami in 1980. This group also provides security personnel at refugee holding camps.

Although its protective and law enforcement responsibilities have increased in recent years, the Marshal Service also continues to serve process and warrants for the federal courts. Today, U.S. marshals annually serve more than 900,000 civil and criminal subpoenas, summonses, and various other writs on behalf of the federal government.[44] They also maintain custody and control of property seized by the U.S. government.

## Organized Crime and Racketeering Section

In 1951, the Kefauver Committee, a congressional committee investigating organized crime, concluded after an exhaustive study: "There is a sinister criminal organization known as the Mafia operating throughout the country."[45] In the intervening years, the existence of organized crime has become generally acknowledged.[46] Numerous congressional committees have examined the problem, but organized crime continues to thrive.[47]

One of the major problems of dealing with organized crime is that the activities of large criminal cartels encompass geographically and statutorily the entire spectrum of enforcement and prosecutorial jurisdictions.[48] American law enforcement is too decentralized to handle the problem at the local and state level. The Organized Crime and Racketeering Section (OCR) of the Department of Justice was established in 1954 to spearhead and coordinate investigations of organized crime. Its specified functions were to:

Function

> Coordinate, generally, enforcement activities directed against organized crime and racketeering and to accumulate and correlate data related to organized crime and racketeering, . . . initiate and supervise investigations, formulate general prosecutive policies and assist U.S. Attorneys in preparing indictments and conducting trials in the field.[49]

By 1957, there were only ten attorneys in OCR. Its inability to grow and become effective during this period has been attributed to a "lack of coordination and interest by some Federal investigative agencies."[50] In 1958, following the famous meeting of leading organized crime figures in Apalachin, New York, the Special Group on Organized Crime was established within the Justice Department. The function of this office was to establish regional offices from which intelligence could be gathered and federal grand jury proceedings conducted regarding the activities of the organized crime figures who had met at Apalachin. Spurred on by congressional investigations of organized crime moving into labor unions, the FBI and Treasury enforcement agencies began supplying OCR with regular intelligence reports on leading Cosa Nostra figures. However, efforts were still on a small scale, and only minimal criminal intelligence information from other law enforcement agencies was available.

In 1961, Attorney General Robert Kennedy took an active interest in the Department of Justice's investigations and prosecution of organized crime figures. Under his leadership, the number of attorneys and federal investigators assigned to OCR grew dramatically, as did efforts to coordinate intelligence activities. Whereas in 1961 only 49 organized crime figures were convicted, by the time Kennedy left the Department of Justice in 1965, convictions had increased to 468.[51]

Attorney General Kennedy also set up a special group of Department of Justice attorneys to investigate the Teamsters' union. Through the efforts of this special group, Teamster President James R. Hoffa was convicted of jury tampering. The OCR also concentrated its efforts on police corruption and ties of the police to organized crime. The tactics that the OCR people typically use even today consist of special investigative grand juries, immunity for witnesses involved in organized crime activities, the use of search and arrest warrants, and the careful and painstaking construction of documentary ("paper chase") cases.

In 1967, President Lyndon Johnson's Commission on Law Enforcement and the Administration of Justice recommended the establishment of investigative teams such as the 1958 Special Group on Organized Crime. The first such group was established in Buffalo, New York, that same year, and it was called a "strike force." It consisted of five attorneys (including two veterans of the Teamsters investigating group), and supervisory agents from the federal investigative agencies, plus a Royal Canadian Mounted Police representative. So successful were its initial efforts that in 1968 similar strike forces were created in Philadelphia, Miami, Detroit, and Brooklyn. In 1969 new units were established in Boston, Cleveland, Chicago, and Newark. In 1970 offices were set up in Buffalo (again) and Los Angeles. In 1971, Baltimore, Kansas City, New Orleans, St. Louis, and San Francisco were added. The strike forces in Baltimore and St. Louis have been discontinued while Las Vegas has been added to the list.

With the passage of the Wire Tap Act in 1969 and the Organized Crime Control Act of 1970, the strike forces made important strides in terms of the numbers of indictments and convictions against organized crime figures. In 1977, the Department of Justice established "target priorities" consisting of involvement in labor racketeering, violent crime activity, the corruption of public officials, drug sales, and infiltration of legitimate business by organized crime as special priority areas on which the Organized Crime and Racketeering Section and the strike forces should concentrate their attention.

## Strike Force Operations

By the late 1980s, strike forces were operating in fourteen cities.[52] The OCR coordinates its strike force efforts through three groups: (1) the Administrative Unit; (2) the Intelligence and Special Service Unit; and (3) the Special Operations Unit.[53]

The Administrative Unit consists of the chief of the OCR and four deputy chiefs. This group manages the efforts of OCR, coordinating field activities and investigations among the various federal agencies involved. Each deputy chief is responsible for the operation of strike forces in a particular geographical area. There is almost daily contact between each local strike force and the OCR in Washington with respect to the status of pending investigations.

Before the strike force takes any prosecutive action, it submits to the OCR a prosecution memorandum setting forth the evidence obtained as a result of field investigation. The memorandum contains the strike force attorney's recommendations on whether or not a prosecution should be initiated. Unless the OCR approves, no criminal prosecution is begun.

The Intelligence and Special Services Unit provides a comprehensive, centralized intelligence file devoted exclusively to organized crime. Over the years, this unit has compiled a computer-based index with the names of thousands of individuals who have some association with organized crime. It also maintains a special "racketeer profile" on about thirty thousand individuals who are in some way importantly involved in organized crime. The bulk of the intelligence contained in this special file has been supplied by federal investigative agencies and includes such items as the names of known racketeers, their criminal activities, associates, place of employment or legitimate business activities, residence, telephone numbers, and automobile license numbers.[54]

*Targeting organized crime*

The files are utilized in a number of ways. The unit handles an average of fifty information requests daily from strike force personnel, federal investigative and regulatory agencies, and local and state law enforcement agencies.[55] An additional function of the system is to provide a data source for the preparation of comprehensive surveys of particular problems. One such use is to determine if a strike force should be established in a given area. The files are constantly reviewed to ascertain the activities of organized crime figures around the country. In addition, to keep the files as current as possible, a list of 3,700 principal organized crime leaders is periodically circulated to various federal agencies for updating.[56]

The Special Operations Unit performs four major functions: (1) the review of applications for electronic surveillance under federal statutes;[57] (2) the preparation of recommendations with regard to granting immunity from prosecution for witnesses; (3) the analysis of correspondence; and (4) legal research in the conduct of investigations and case preparation.

In recent years, there have generally been four to twenty strike forces operating throughout the country, usually in metropolitan areas where there are particular organized crime problems. In addition to these strike force cities, ten smaller field offices operate in areas in which organized crime is particularly active. The OCR designates the areas in which these strike forces will operate. In addition, strike force teams can be pulled in or out of a geographical area, depending on the need. Each strike force has an attorney-in-charge who is directly responsible for the work of other U.S. Department of Justice attorneys assigned to the strike force. The attorney-in-charge supervises the work of the strike force attorneys and investigators; he or she coordinates the efforts of the team with the U.S. attorney in the jurisdiction where the strike force is working and with the OCR in Washington.

A strike force usually consists of seven to fourteen attorneys and investigative personnel from various federal agencies. In recent years a local law enforcement representative has been added to each strike force. The Organized Crime and Racketeering Section is also developing a system of cross-using prosecutorial assistants. For example, a local prosecutor might be designated a special assistant to the federal government to assist in the federal prosecution and handling of the government's case. Likewise, a federal strike force attorney might assist local prosecutors in their case presentation in a state court.

*Composition*

During the 1980s, special investigative and prosecutorial efforts focused on the Racketeer Influenced Corrupt Organization Act (RICO). This statute, which was incorporated as an amendment to the Omnibus Crime Control Act, has received increasing emphasis by the Department of Justice as a tool for combatting organized crime. Much of the efforts of the strike forces are centered on violations of this act and its companion, the Continuing Criminal Enterprise Statute. Both of these laws will be discussed in greater detail later.

An important component of the strike force concept is the use of special federal grand juries. In jurisdictions in which strike forces operate, a special federal grand jury is empaneled to deal with organized crime activities in that area. The grand jury deliberates on the evidence gathered by the strike force to determine whether prosecution is warranted.

### Organized Crime Drug Enforcement Task Force Program

In 1982, President Reagan announced an unprecedented federal effort to attack the connection between organized crime and drug trafficking. The tool was to be a coordinated federal strike force; a strike force patterned after other organized crime strike forces that had been successfully used in other areas of organized crime activity.

After an analysis of the problem, the Task Force Program was divided into twelve Regions,[58] each of which encompasses a number of federal judicial districts. Participating federal agencies were to include the U.S. Attorneys' offices, the Drug Enforcement Administration (DEA), the Federal Bureau of Investigation (FBI), the U.S. Customs Service, the Bureau of Alcohol, Tobacco and Firearms (ATF), the Internal Revenue Service (IRS), the U.S. Coast Guard, and the U.S. Marshal Service. In each task force, the U.S. attorney at the regional headquarters, known as the core city, is responsible for overall task force performance. Task force attorneys and agents remain under the direct supervision of their respective agencies, but they conduct investigations jointly with other Task Force agents and attorneys.

**Major antidrug efforts**

Although the overall goal is to destroy the operations of organizations engaged in drug trafficking, the program has specifically incorporated the following as a means to attack the organized flow of narcotics. A first priority is to target, investigate, and prosecute individuals who organize, direct, finance, or are otherwise engaged in high-level illegal drug trafficking enterprises, including large-scale money-laundering organizations.

Another consideration is to make full use of financial investigative techniques, including tax law enforcement and forfeiture actions, to identify and convict high-level drug traffickers and recover profits derived from high-level drug trafficking. Along with this strategy is the attempt to promote a coordinated drug enforcement effort in each Task Force area and to encourage maximum cooperation among all drug enforcement agencies, including state and local narcotic enforcement units.

The program has identified four major target groups that are heavily involved in drug trafficking: (1) cartels of international exporters and importers of narcotics into the United States; (2) traditional organized crime families such as La Cosa Nostra or organizations involved in felony crime whose members also engage in drug trafficking; (3) outlaw motorcycle gangs consisting of the "big-four," the Pagans, Hell's Angels, Bandidos, and Outlaws who significantly control the manufacture and distribution of PCP, methamphetamine, and methaqualone channels in the

United States; and (4) prison-spawned gangs that developed in the California prison system in the 1960s including the Mexican Mafia, La Nuestra Familia, the Aryan Brotherhood, and the Black Guerrilla Family.

To combat the drug menace, the various Task Forces have put together quite an array of legal weapons. These include a number of currency transaction laws that among other things require banks and certain other financial institutions to notify the authorities whenever a customer engages in a cash transaction of more than $10,000. Similar methods are used to analyze reporting requirements when large amounts of money (over $5,000) are taken out of the country, and Foreign Bank Account Reporting laws, which are required for anyone with a foreign bank accounting exceeding $1,000.

The program relies heavily on Title III wiretap laws. This refers to Title III of the Omnibus Crime Control and Safe Streets Act of 1968, which gives the federal government the authority to engage in wiretapping and electronic surveillance of private communications.[59]

CCE and RICO laws

The real "kingpin" statutes, however, are the Continuing Criminal Enterprise statute, commonly called CCE, which was enacted as part of the Comprehensive Drug Abuse Prevention and Control Act of 1970, and the RICO statute, which is part of the Organized Crime Control Act, also adopted in 1970.[60] The CCE statute provides for the most strict sanctions of any federal criminal statute directed at drug-related activities. It carries a maximum penalty of life imprisonment and a minimum of ten years—with no parole in either case—and fines up to $100,000. It also provides for forfeiture of any and all proceeds of the specified criminal activity, or of any assets purchased with such proceeds. This means that the government has the right to take ownerhip of any real estate, automobiles, aircraft, boats, business equity, bank accounts, securities, or any kind of goods or entitlements that were used in criminal activity or purchased with money generated from it.

Because the penalties are so severe, the statute requires five stringent elements of proof for conviction of defendants charged with CCE: the defendant's conduct must constitute a felony violation of federal narcotics law; the conduct must take place as part of a continuing series of violations; the defendant must undertake his or her activity in concert with five or more persons; the defendant must act as the organizer, supervisor, or manager ("kingpin") of this criminal enterprise; and the defendant must obtain substantial income or resources from the enterprise.

The RICO statute also provides strong sanctions that deal with criminal organizations and their pernicious infiltration into legitimate businesses. Under RICO the defendant can receive up to 20 years' imprisonent, $25,000 in fines, and civil and criminal forfeitures. RICO focuses on the "enterprise" defined as "the association of a group of individuals," where that enterprise utilizes income from an illegal activity, acquires or exercises control through illegal activity, commits illegal acts, or conspires to do any of these things. The enterprise may or may not relate to drug dealing, but a prosecutor must show that each defendant is guilty of a pattern of racketeering. That is, within a ten-year period the defendant must have committed at least two acts of racketeering. These acts must be connected by a common scheme in order to demonstrate that they are not merely unrelated offenses. The RICO statute has been used extensively in those cases in which the CCE statute could not be applied.

The following actual case history from the Task Force Program called "moneybags" illustrates one of the many efforts of this program.

The "Moneybags" case began before the Task Force Program was initiated, but it was reinforced by Task Force resources and the Task Force mandate. It illustrates:

- The use of financial investigations to identify unknown traffickers
- Involvement with numerous foreign jurisdictions
- Potent and effective use of seizures and forfeitures
- Task force ability to pursue an investigation over a long period of time

In February 1982, a Southeastern Task Force district established a team of Federal agents from several agencies to use a financial approach to identify and prosecute the kingpin financiers and organizers of drug smuggling activities in the area. By May, the team was in place. (At its height, with the infusion of Task Force personnel, it included seventeen agents, from IRS, FBI, DEA, the Bureau of Alcohol, Tobacco and Firearms (ATF), and the State's Law Enforcement Division, plus seven Assistant U.S. Attorneys.) A special grand jury was empaneled to hear all testimony in the investigation and to issue subpoenas for records from banks, businesses, real estate offices, and law offices and other documents relating to the flow of money.

There was no list of suspects to question, no files to develop, and no leads, other than the names of many low-level people. No one knew who was at the top.

Initially, a pair of agents went to a resort area, where many "high-rolling" smugglers were said to visit.

They questioned realtors and developers to discover who had been buying expensive resort property; they searched court records to learn of mortgages and in whose name titles were registered; they interviewed car dealers to find out who was buying expensive imports; they questioned house and dock builders to see who was building on waterfront property. By late summer, they had interviewed hundreds and were beginning to uncover two separate drug organizations that had been operating without detection since 1974, importing many millions of dollars worth of marijuana and hashish. *None* of the financier/organizer suspects had ever been known to *any* law enforcement officials before.

In September, seizures began— $344,000 from an attorney's account, a $100,000 piece of resort real estate, and a fashionable $450,000 restaurant and nightclub. Seizures amounted to over $2 million by the end of the year, including resort property in Nantucket and a $160,000 certificate of deposit from a bank in the Bahamas. By mid-1983, seizures totaled over $5 million.

The investigators determined that the two rings had imported about **three-quarters of a billion dollars** worth of drugs over the previous ten years, from the Bahamas, South America, and Lebanon.

An indictment against the first ring, in May 1983, charged two men with CCE violations, and another twenty-two with various drug, currency, and tax violations. Before indictment, eleven men, including two attorneys, pled guilty. Three more pled guilty before trial, five

others were found guilty, and three were acquitted.

An indictment against the second ring charged four defendants with CCE violations, and nineteen others on related offenses. Of the major figures, one pled guilty to CCE and other charges under a plea agreement. Another pled guilty to tax, drug, and currency violations; four pled guilty to a variety of charges; four were found guilty by a jury on all counts; two others were found guilty on drug and currency charges; and one was acquitted.

In cooperation with Antiguan authorities, a fugitive kingpin defendant was located and extradited, and his $900,000 boat seized. Information from defendants who were now cooperating with the investigation made it possible to obtain a superseding indictment against this man, now including CCE violations and multiple counts of conspiracy and drug violations, plus forfeiture of all drug profits and interests.

Other international judicial assistance was sought from several foreign jurisdictions, including the Island of Jersey, the Bahamas, and Hong Kong. Materials from these proceedings contributed to the convictions.

As of the end of 1983, the investigation was continuing, with more indictments anticipated, and still other organizations being discovered. It is expected that over one hundred traffickers will be prosecuted as a result of this operation.

*Source: Annual Report of the Organized Crime Drug Enforcement Task Force Program* (Washington: U.S. Government Printing Office (March 1984), p. 66.

## Law Enforcement Assistance Administration

Although the Law Enforcement Assistance Administration (LEAA) was never a federal law enforcement agency, it deserves special attention because it may well have brought about the most important developments in the annals of American criminal justice. During its relatively brief period of existence, no other American crime control agency appears to have produced the far-ranging improvements that LEAA brought to American criminal justice.

The LEAA grew out of the Office of Law Enforcement Assistance (OLEA), which was created in 1965 to make federal funds available to states, localities, and private organizations to improve methods of law enforcement, court administration, and prison operation.[61] The act creating this agency was the first federal law that made money available to local government for the purpose of improving their administration of criminal justice.

In 1968, the Omnibus Crime Control and Safe Streets Act became effective. This act repealed the Law Enforcement Act of 1965 and replaced the Office of Law Enforcement Assistance with the LEAA. The Safe Streets Act was a milestone in that it expressed a fundamental philosophy about crime in the United States—namely, that although it is a problem of national dimensions, it is most appropriately addressed at the state and local levels through the support of federal monies. This was a drastic departure from the past. Traditionally, state and local law enforcement and other criminal justice activities did not seek federal involvement. Like public assistance activities in general, this area had not been regarded as belonging to the federal government's natural sphere of interest, but rather was seen as the responsibility of state and local governments.[62]

*1968 Omnibus Crime Control Act*

**BLOCK GRANTS.** Under the provisions of the act, as administered by LEAA, block grants based on population were made available to all fifty states, Guam, Puerto Rico, American Samoa, the Virgin Islands, and the District of Columbia. The grants were to be used to develop crime-related programs and to assist and improve local and state agencies in their enforcement of criminal justice. In addition, LEAA awarded action and discretionary grants to foster the development of state and local planning capabilities that would further improve the administration of justice.

LEAA required states to develop centralized state planning agencies (SPAs) as well as local planning units. These SPAs were responsible for allocating to local units of government much of the money that the states received from LEAA. Overseeing the operations of these SPAs, as well as the local planning units in the states, were supervisory boards whose members represented state and local criminal justice agencies, other public agencies, and citizen groups.[63] Legislation was written in 1973 requiring states to develop comprehensive master plans that were multiyear in nature to be eligible for federal funds from LEAA. Thus, each SPA was required to coordinate the activities of local planning agencies into a single master plan of how the problem of crime was to be handled in the particular state.

*State planning agencies (SPAs)*

In its early years, the programs LEAA funded as well as its priorities were heavily criticized by members of Congress and many large city mayors. Much of the money earmarked for local governments and distributed to the states went to regional planning councils instead of the major cities where the problems of crime were most acute.[64] As a consequence, the act was amended in 1971 to provide for direct assistance to local units of government consisting of a population of 250,000

*Criticisms and weaknesses*

In 1970 Congress passed a strong antiracketeering law. The law was ostensibly aimed at organized crime—especially Mafia mobsters who controlled the tentacles of organized crime in America. The prevailing Congressional attitude, which was supported by the Justice Department and the federal prosecutors of the time, was the need to bring broader powers against organized mobsters who had proved difficult to prosecute under then-existing federal law. The anti-organized crime elements carried the day. By an overwhelming majority, Congress adopted the Racketeer Influenced and Corrupt Organizations Act. Today, it is simply known in legal circles as RICO.

There is no doubt the Act must be considered a success. A number of major as well as less prominent convictions of organized crime figures have occurred because of the government's authority under RICO. Under zealous and skillful adoption by the Justice Department, major crime figures and their organizations have felt its lash in the hands of federal prosecutors. The law has become the most formidable arsenal in the federal government's long struggle with organized crime. In recent years, however, there has been a backlash against RICO. What has caused such criticism of a tool so widely acknowledged as a stunning success?

To answer this question it must be recognized that the law has two provisions: a criminal and a civil side. For years federal prosecutors used only the criminal provisions of RICO—and used these only on what might be called more conventional organized crime figures and their organizations. In fact, the civil provisions of RICO were virtually ignored. So much so in fact, that some legal scholars were critical of the federal government's failure to consider the value of using the civil provisions of the Act. It was argued, for example, that federal prosecutors were too used to thinking in terms of criminal prosecutions; a situation that resulted in them ignoring—or worse hampering them—in fully understanding and appreciating the value of civil actions.

In the early 1980s, this began to change. Federal prosecutors started applying the civil aspects of the law against defendants and started moving against unconventional targets in the use of both the civil and criminal elements of RICO. This was accomplished through the provisions of the law, which permit criminal prosecution of those in an "enterprise" that has engaged in "a pattern of racketeering activities." In addition to the stiff sentences imposed by conviction under the criminal doctrine of the law, the civil aspects called for the imposing of civil penalties triple the amount of damages.

As it has grown to be used, the legal issues turn on the question of what constitutes an "enterprise" and did there exist "a pattern of racketeering activities?"

The federal government has moved on several fronts in its use of RICO in recent years. They have, for example, used its criminal provisions against what they consider corrupt labor unions. The most controversial use, however, has been in the use (or threatened use) of its civil sanctions against businesses, accountants, and particularly, securities firms. The most highly publicized effort to use RICO occurred in 1988 when its use singled out the investment banking firm of Drexel Burnham Lambert for securities violations.

This was a strange case that brought civil libertarians and elements of the defense bar into Drexel's corner. The government is allowed under the act to seize a defendant's assets before trial. The government threatened to do this. It was contended that this was a misapplication of the provisions of the act. It was argued that an overzealous and politically aspiring U.S. attorney was using the statute improperly by threatening to use RICO to seize the firm's assets before any misconduct had been proved in court. The propriety of this became a major issue in the case.

Defenders of RICO's seizure pro-

or more.[65] Other criticisms were leveled at LEAA's past emphasis on funding law enforcement agencies at the expense of other components of the criminal justice system, and its funding of "hardware" items such as riot equipment, radios, and automobiles.

And the criticisms did not end there. In 1976, the Twentieth Century Fund, which is a private research foundation engaged in policy-oriented studies of economic, political, and social issues, published a report on the first seven years of LEAA's operations entitled *Law Enforcement: The Federal Role*.[66] Much of the report was very critical of the federal grant assistance programs to state and local governments.

visions contend that this is a crucial part of the legislation. It is argued that the government needs that right in racketeering cases to ensure that the defendant will not dispose of the ill-gotten gains before the government can seize them by a judgment after a lengthy court battle in which the defendant is finally proved guilty. It is also justified on the grounds that to cripple organized illegal activity, their economic assets must be forfeited to the government.

This is just one part of the controversy surrounding RICO. The other is that private parties are using RICO to bring civil suits against commercial interests who, among other things, perpetrate fraud and constitute an "enterprise" engaged in "racketeering activities." So far these private-initiated suits have been brought against such diverse interests as an import firm, a retirement village in Kansas City, and an abortion clinic.

Business and supporting interests are crying foul. They complain that this was never the purpose of Congress when it adopted RICO. It was not envisioned that it should be applied to these kinds of cases. It is claimed that because of the triple damages provision of the law, and the payment of attorneys' fees, it has become "open season" to use RICO to settle cases that could be better handled in state courts under conventional civil law practice or by administrative regulatory agencies using their resolution devices. It is said that attorneys and their clients are going after "deep pockets" and pressing frivolous charges hoping to be awarded the triple damages as provided by the act. It is also being murmured that it is causing a backlog of cases in the federal courts.

There is no evidence, however, that RICO is causing the so-called case backload in the federal courts. The lines have become drawn. On the one side are the consumer advocates such as Ralph Nader and the United Public Interest Research Group who say it is appropriate to use the criminal and civil aspects of the law against white-collar crime and unscrupulous business interests—be it government or private citizens who initiate its use. They point to increasing problems involving insider trading, government corruption, and the massive savings and loan scandals as appropriate targets. It is, in the final analysis they say, one of the only few effective tools against economic crime.

As long as the law focused on traditional organized crime activity, it was an acceptable, if not welcomed, piece of legislation. But by crossing over into white-collar crime and the prosecution or bringing of private suits against corporate and economic interests, it may have gone too far. At least, certain members of Congress seem to think so. Joint bills have been introduced both in the Senate and the House to rewrite significant portions of the original act to exclude its use from applying in many types of commercial activities. Not surprisingly, such efforts are supported by familiar probusiness groups such as the U.S. Chamber of Commerce, the National Association of Manufacturers, the Securities Industry Association, and in the case of its use against unions, the AFL-CIO.

The lines are drawn between consumer-protection interests and economic interests. Siding on behalf of the economic interests is the American Civil Liberties Union (ACLU), which contends that its seizure provisions illegally violate defendants' rights, the definition of a "pattern" of crimes is too broad, and it may be used as a club in labor–management disputes. Some of the consumer-protection interests admit that the act may need "tightening up" and that the term *racketeers* should be removed from the law. The fact that such a controversy has arisen, if nothing else, attests to the uniqueness of white-collar crime and the ascendancy of certain interests to be able to define "nontraditional" crime and to influence efforts directed at the enforcement of such criminal activities.

In the first place, the legislation that created the agency was passed in an atmosphere of fear and retribution. When Congress passed the Omnibus Crime Control and Safe Streets Act in 1968, it did so in the wake of the successive assassinations of John F. Kennedy, Malcolm X, Martin Luther King, Jr., and Robert F. Kennedy. The legislation was enacted against the background of the rise of black power, an increasingly militant anti–Vietnam war movement and a growing national polarization epitomized in the presidential election of 1968, when Richard Nixon ran as a law-and-order candidate.[67] The broad mandate to "stop crime" without giving any thought to the limited capacity of federal dollars to accomplish this goal plagued the agency ever after.

The operations of the agency and its grant programs have also been accused of being overpoliticized. There are documented cases, for instance, when the Nixon administration overruled the agency and awarded sizable grants to jurisdictions based on what must be understood as purely political considerations.[68] Then later, in 1972, LEAA established its most expensive and ambitious effort—the high-impact anticrime program. The goal of the program was to reduce the incidence of certain street crimes in eight selected cities at an overall cost of $160 million. It soon became apparent that almost all the cities involved viewed the massive federal aid as a "windfall." Rather than developing overall programs, cities such as Atlanta, Baltimore, and Newark used their first monies—before any planning or analysis—to put hundreds of new police officers on the payroll. In Newark, the Impact Cities director was active in the mayor's election campaign. Thus an aura of politics and patronage began early.[69]

Although the high-impact anticrime program was originally scheduled to run for five years, its failure became so obvious that LEAA finally terminated the plan in just over three years at a cost in excess of $100 million.

**NATIONAL INSTITUTE OF LAW ENFORCEMENT AND CRIMINAL JUSTICE.**
Nevertheless, it is hard to judge the relative success of LEAA. Some of the over $9 billion it has cost the American taxpayers has had a positive effect. For instance, it created the National Institute of Law Enforcement and Criminal Justice (now called the National Institute of Justice), which continues to serve as a research and evaluation agency for a now-limited number of criminal justice projects.* During the heyday of LEAA in the 1970s, this agency served as the research and evaluation arm of LEAA. Its purpose was to monitor the major grant programs that LEAA funded and to develop applied and empirical research capabilities that could then be used to improve the functioning of the criminal justice system. Most of the research conducted by the National Institute was of a contractual nature. This agency contracted with individual researchers, universities, and private consulting and research firms to study criminal justice operations, make recommendations for improvement, try new programs and alternatives, evaluate them, and, in general, improve our state of knowledge concerning systemwide operations and means of improvement. The National Institute then served as a clearinghouse to disseminate these findings to interested criminal justice agencies, practitioners, and academics.

As an example, one of the most significant undertakings of this unit was its Exemplary Projects Program. This program was designed to implement, evaluate, and identify outstanding criminal justice programs throughout the country, verifying their achievements and publicizing them so that other communities and agencies of criminal justice could adopt similar programs.[70]

*Marginal note:* National Institute of Justice (NIJ)

---

*Author's note:* Students who are majoring or planning to major in criminal justice/criminology should familiarize themselves with the services of the National Institute of Justice (NIJ). This is the principle federal agency for research, development, evaluation, and dissemination of programs to improve and strengthen the criminal justice system. The Justice Assistance Act of 1984 specifically mandates the Institute to (1) provide more accurate information on the causes and correlates of crime and juvenile delinquency; (2) develop new methods for the prevention and reduction of crime; (3) evaluate the effectiveness of criminal justice programs; (4) make recommendations for action to federal, state, and local governments for the improvement of their systems of criminal justice; and (5) serve as a national and international clearinghouse for the exchange of information on crime and criminal justice–related matters. Contact National Institute of Justice, U.S. Department of Justice, Washington, DC 20531.

The National Institute of Law Enforcement and Criminal Justice also developed the National Criminal Justice Reference Service and the National Criminal Justice Statistics Center. The reference service compiles and disseminates information on current research and publications in the field of criminal justice. Persons engaged in activities related to criminal justice are provided annotated bibliographies of publications that may be of interest to them. In addition, the service maintains a reference library of selected publications available to all its users through a document interlibrary loan program, as well as a microfiche distribution source in which certain materials not readily available through other sources are distributed free of charge to users of the service. A few years ago, a loan and referral program for films and other media materials was developed. In 1989 the National Institute of Justice established an electronic bulletin board for researchers and users interested in obtaining NIJ materials. Individuals with personal computers and modems can now use this valuable service.

The National Criminal Justice Statistics Center (now called the Bureau of Justice Statistics) gathers criminal justice statistics to promote a better understanding of the processes of justice and renders technical assistance to states that are also engaged in developing statistical centers. The center publishes and distributes a number of reference sources and monographs dealing with national statistics, such as the *Annual Expenditure and Employment Data for the Criminal Justice System*, *Directory of Criminal Justice Agencies*, *National Prisoner Statistics*, and *National Jail Census*. The primary interest of the systems analysis unit of the center is to identify the application of systems analysis techniques that might be useful in improving the administration of criminal justice. The center also maintained various information systems at the national level used to support the administration of LEAA programs and extend technical assistance to state and local governments in applying computer technology to automated records systems.

Bureau of Justice Statistics

**THE DEMISE OF LEAA.** As has been mentioned, LEAA received a great deal of criticism in certain areas. LEAA was criticized primarily for the excessive red tape involved in compliance with its guidelines, poor targeting of grant funds, insufficient local control over expenditures, and ineffective research and evaluation efforts.

Although the concept and the goals of LEAA and the legislation that created the agency were laudable, the history of this agency and its efforts serve as a vivid example of how broad social goals fare badly when transmitted from legislation to actual application. Like so many other social programs initiated at the federal level, federal crime policy under the Safe Streets Act met ideological and structural barriers that limited its effectiveness. It was also severely hampered by lack of understanding of the crime problem and a simple naiveté about how to deal with it.

In an interesting analysis of the Safe Streets Act and the LEAA, Malcom M. Feeley and Austin D. Sarat analyzed many of the operational characteristics of the program and its failures.[71] For example, the states were required to develop state planning agencies (SPAs) who were given the responsibility to develop comprehensive plans for statewide efforts at dealing with crime and improving the criminal justice system within their states. It was visualized that these SPAs would be important planning agencies that would coordinate state efforts. Instead, they were often undercut by local political interests serving on the boards established to supervise and give policy guidance to the SPAs. As a result, many SPAs did little more than divide the federal funds according to fixed formulas in rough proportion to the power of those agencies represented on their supervisory boards. Compre-

Some reasons for its failure

hensive statewide planning became nothing more than a compliance document, prepared to satisfy the requirements of the Safe Streets Act and LEAA rather than containing a real vision of the state of affairs and needs of the state's criminal justice system.[72] Rather than being a superimposed comprehensive planning agency, the SPAs became little more than a pipeline for federal funds.

The SPAs were also conceived as agencies that would encourage the development of innovative programs and strategies at the local and state levels to deal with crime and improve the operations of criminal justice agencies. In this way, they were to encourage an "applied laboratory" approach to existing problems. This soon proved to be a futile and idealistic viewpoint for several obvious reasons. First, the supervisory boards, who represented the police, corrections, courts, and other criminal justice agencies, simply were not interested in "pie-in-the-sky" innovation. They simply wanted the funds to provide more personnel, buy more cars and communications equipment, and renovate or build new jails and correctional facilities. The SPA staffs were not viewed as helpful "experts" by the agencies and could accomplish little without credibility. And the SPAs had little to offer in the way of incentives. In spite of the billions that were spent by the federal government during the existence of LEAA on state and local criminal justice programs, these annual LEAA funds constituted on the average only 3 to 5 percent of the state's annual criminal justice expenditures.[73] Such sums did not provide the SPAs with much leverage.

When President Carter assumed office, it was obvious that something had to be done to improve the operations of LEAA. Carter felt that there was a continuing need for a federal role in the area of intergovernmental crime control efforts and approved the passage by Congress of the Justice System Improvement Act. This act was targeted specifically at some of the areas of weakness and criticism and called for a major reorganization of LEAA and a rethinking of the federal role.

The Justice System Improvement Act was never really implemented. A short time after its passage, Ronald Reagan was elected President. His austerity efforts, backed by a supportive Congress, sounded the death knell for LEAA and the majority of state and local criminal justice programs funded and assisted by the federal government. The history of this agency also serves as a window on changing national priorities and viewpoints about the role of government—particularly the role of the federal government. In 1970, LEAA was viewed by then President Richard Nixon as the prototype of his "new federalism," which would be a shared partnership between the federal government and state and local governments. Priorities and spending would rest for the most part with state and local units of government; the federal role would be to share revenue and return federal tax monies to the state. Under "Reagan federalism," the role would be quite different: Federal presence in such areas as crime control would be withdrawn and criminal justice expenditures would again revert to their traditional source of funding and priority setting—state and local governments.

### ☐ TREASURY DEPARTMENT

Revenue-producing functions

Another very important department with law enforcement responsibilities at the federal level is the Treasury Department. The law enforcement agencies of this department are specialists in certain types of federal crimes that fall under the authority of the Secretary of the Treasury. For the most part Treasury enforcement agencies investigate crimes related to the revenue-producing functions of the federal government. Such crimes as income tax evasion, the failure to pay import taxes and duties, and the failure to pay special privilege taxes are enforced by the investigative agencies of the Treasury Department. Although such "revenue crimes" are the major jurisdictional authority of law enforcement efforts of these agencies, some agencies such as the U.S. Secret Service have been given additional enforcement responsibilities outside this traditional concern.

The primary law enforcement agencies of the Treasury Department are the Secret Service, the U.S. Customs Service, the Bureau of Alcohol, Tobacco and Firearms, and the Criminal Investigation Division of the Internal Revenue Service (IRS). The Treasury Department enforcement agencies have also played a major role in developing and maintaining liaison with the International Police Organization (INTERPOL).

## Secret Service

The counterfeiting of currency has been a problem in the United States since the country's inception. During the Revolutionary War, Britain tried to destroy the economic base of the Colonies by printing vast quantities of currency that appeared to be issued by the Continental Congress. The English felt that if it could destroy the Colonies' economic foundation, it could destroy their ability to wage war. The effort nearly succeeded. Owing to the presence of vast quantities of spurious currency, the country was hard-pressed to purchase needed war materials from European nations, and because of this came closer to losing the War of Independence than most people realize.[74]

*History and counterfeiting*

After the Revolutionary War, the problem of dealing with counterfeiting continued. This was a period when the greater part of American currency was issued by private banks that were licensed by the states to print money. Operating without adequate regulation, they designed their own currency and validated it with the signatures of their own officials.[75] "Wildcat banks," having little more than a charter and a printing shop, became common in many states. The tactic of these banks was to print and sell a huge amount of currency as quickly as possible and then leave town. A book published in 1839 maintained that there were 97 such banks whose currency, though legal, was worthless. It also listed 254 more banks whose currency had become the object of successful and widespread counterfeiting.[76]

In response to this situation, and because it became necessary to raise large sums of money during the Civil War, Congress passed the National Currency Act of 1863, which established a national banking system and a uniform national currency, called "greenbacks." The market value of these greenbacks, which were not backed by gold reserves, began to depreciate almost as soon as they were issued, and a sharp inflation affected the entire economy. Counterfeiters had a heyday circulating imitation greenbacks. The local police were the only enforcement authority against counterfeiters, and they were practically helpless. The Secretary of the Treasury set up a system of rewards for the detection of counterfeit currency, but the situation was so bad that the counterfeiters themselves were collecting the rewards. Finally, in 1865, the Secret Service was created as a federal investigative agency with authority to enforce the laws against counterfeiting.

When this agency was created, it was estimated that nearly one-third of all paper money in circulation was counterfeit. The agency immediately began the task of curtailing the problem. In its first year of existence alone, it arrested more than 200 counterfeiters.[77] Today, annual seizures of counterfeit bills approach $100 million a year.[78]

In addition to its investigative responsibilities in the area of counterfeiting, the Secret Service has another major investigative responsibility—suppression of the forgery and fraudulent negotiation of government checks and bonds. The area of check forgery is particularly troublesome to the Secret Service. Of all its major investigative activities including protective intelligence, check forgery cases are by far the most numerous.[79]

The Secret Service is best known for protecting the President and his family. Originally, there had been little concern for the safety of U.S. Presidents. The attempted assassination of President Andrew Jackson and the assassination of Presidents Abraham Lincoln in 1865 and James A. Garfield in 1881 failed to prompt Congress to pass legislation to assign special bodyguards for Presidents of the United States. In 1901, President William McKinley was assassinated in spite of the security provided by local police and soldiers. Informed of the assassination, the Secretary of the Treasury promptly assigned the Secret Service the duty of protecting Presidents, and in 1906, Congress appropriated the funds and officially assigned the Secret Service its protective role.

After the assassination of President John F. Kennedy in 1963, Congress increased the scope and responsibilities of the Secret Service as a result of recommendations by the Warren Commission, which investigated all of the circumstances surrounding the shooting of Kennedy. Among the recommendations implemented were an increase in the amount of training and number of Secret Service agents assigned to presidential protection, enlargement of the protective intelligence function, increased liaison with other law enforcement agencies, and acquisition of

The Secret Service is best known for protecting the President and his family. (© Ira Wyman/ Sygma)

sophisticated technical security equipment, computer systems, and communications.

Following President Kennedy's assassination, Congress passed legislation that authorized the Secret Service to protect the widow and minor children of a former President; it also made the assassination of the President a federal crime. In 1965, the Secret Service was authorized to protect a former President and his wife during his lifetime, and minor children of a former President. This responsibility was extended in 1968 to provide protection for the widow of a former President until her death or remarriage, and protection of minor children of a former President until the age of sixteen.

After the assassination of Senator Robert F. Kennedy in 1968, Congress authorized the Secret Service to protect major presidential and vice-presidential candidates and nominees. Since that time, the Secret Service has also been given the responsibility of protecting foreign dignitaries visiting the United States.

The Secret Service is organized into five main offices. The Office of Inspection **Organization** plans, directs, and coordinates the inspection and internal audit of all Secret Service field, protective, and headquarters offices in order to evaluate their operational effectiveness and procedures. This office also supervises and/or conducts special investigations and surveys involving major criminal cases, protective functions, and other activities.

The Office of Protective Operations plans and coordinates all protective policies, programs, and operations of the Secret Service. It also evaluates existing protective policies, standards, techniques, equipment, and operations. It also operates the Secret Service Uniformed Division, which is responsible for the security of the Executive Mansion, patroling the White House grounds, and providing security at several other buildings.

The Office of Protective Operations has several operating divisions, the most noted of which is the Presidential Protective Division. This unit is given primary responsibility to protect the President and all members of his immediate family at all times. There is also a vice-presidential protective division, which protects the Vice-President and members of his immediate family. There are also divisions assigned to each former President, his spouse, and any children under sixteen. For example, there are the Carter, Ford, Nixon, and Reagan Protective Divisions, which guard these former Presidents, their spouses, and their residences; they would also guard any minor children. There is also the Protective Vehicle Division, which provides security and maintains and equips all special vehicles used by the Secret Service in its protective responsibilities.

The Secret Service also maintains an Office of Protective Research. This office collects, evaluates, and disseminates information that is vital to the protective responsibilities of the Secret Service. It is also involved in technical support programs such as the installation of special equipment used by the Secret Service in performing its protective function. It extensively employs such equipment as computers, sophisticated communications equipment, and special weapons. This office also conducts extensive intelligence analysis of individuals and groups who pose a threat to the security of anyone protected by the Secret Service.

Another major office is that of Investigations. It, too, has several major divisions. Its Counterfeit Division analyzes counterfeiting techniques, provides assistance to field offices in their counterfeiting investigations, and provides intelligence information on these activities. The Forgery Division analyzes government check and bond forgery activity through such means as handwriting analysis and the use of scientific equipment used in forgery analysis. It also assists the field offices in the examinations and presentation of evidence for prosecution. In 1986, the Service was given authority to investigate certain types of computer frauds or unauthorized access to certain "federal interest" computers or computer systems.

In 1984 Congress passed new laws that increase the investigative responsibilities of this agency. The Secret Service is now authorized to investigate violations of federal law relating to electronic fund transfer frauds, credit and debit cards fraud, and false identification documents or devices.

## Customs Service

Responsibilities

The U.S. Customs Service is the oldest federal law enforcement agency. The primary mission of Customs is to combat smuggling along U.S. borders and to apply customs laws and regulations and collect revenue on imported merchandise. The law enforcement efforts of the Customs Service are carried out by several groups.

Customs patrol officers are stationed at almost all land, sea, and air ports of entry to the United States. Their efforts are directed at interdiction of smuggling. Using airplanes, helicopters, and boats, they concentrate much of their activity on the smuggling of narcotics into the United States. Although the service's nearly 4,500 inspectors, who check incoming merchandise, are the first line of defense against drugs and other contraband, patrol officers and investigative personnel play a major law enforcement function. In recent years, Customs has developed special enforcement teams consisting of specially trained dogs and officer teams, Customs patrol officers, special agents, and import specialists to search out narcotics in commercial cargo and passenger baggage at major points of entry.

The service also has a small group of special agents who are primarily responsible for ongoing investigations in such areas as revenue fraud, all types of smuggling violations, neutrality, and violations of the Currency and Foreign Transactions Reporting Act, which usually involve the movement of large amounts of unreported drug money into and out of U.S. ports, and major cargo thefts.

The special agents also work with other federal law enforcement agencies such as the DEA, the Border Patrol of the Immigration and Naturalization Service, the IRS, and others in joint organized crime efforts. In the area of narcotics alone, the Customs Service has seized billions of dollars worth of illicit drugs over the past decade. The smuggling of drugs has become a major investigative undertaking of this agency.

## Bureau of Alcohol, Tobacco and Firearms

Prohibition era

The basis for what is today the Bureau of Alcohol, Tobacco and Firearms (ATF) began with the adoption of the Eighteenth Amendment to the Constitution, which ushered in the Prohibition Era. With the ratification of this amendment came the Volstead Prohibition Enforcement Act, which gave the commissioner of Internal Revenue jurisdiction over the illicit manufacture, sale, or transportation of intoxicating liquors. During the years before the amendment was finally repealed in 1933, major efforts of the Bureau of Prohibition were concentrated on "bootlegging" and "moonshine" activities. The birth of the so-called "revenooers" had begun.

Since these beginnings, the Bureau of Alcohol, Tobacco and Firearms has been given additional enforcement responsibilities that it exercises to this day. In 1934 the National Firearms Act was passed during a period of unprecedented criminal violence in which gangs formed during Prohibition made war on each other and the public. ATF was given the responsibility to control and enforce laws against machine guns and sawed-off shotguns. Later legislation made it a federal crime for felons and fugitives to receive firearms in interstate commerce.

In 1951 tobacco tax duties were also delegated to the forerunner of the bureau. **Newer functions** Against the background of rising crime rates and the assassination of John Kennedy, Robert Kennedy, and Martin Luther King, Jr., the Gun Control Act of 1968 was passed by Congress. Bombs and other destructive devices were added to items controlled by the federal government. This was the first direct federal jurisdiction directed at the criminal use of explosives.

In 1970, the Organized Crime Control Act was passed. This law included sections known as the Explosives Control Act, which provided for both strict industry regulation and established certain bombings and arsons as federal crimes. In later years the Contraband Cigarette Tax would be passed to curtail the smuggling of cigarettes from low to high tax states. In the late 1970s ATF began to concentrate more of its attention to the use of explosives in criminal activities and the incidence of arson.

Today, ATF's activities are mainly centered on the criminal use of explosives and arson. In this effort it works closely with state and local police and fire officials in the solution of arson crimes. Of particular interest during the past several years has been ATF's efforts to arrest and prosecute outlaw motorcycle gangs. These gangs—notably the big four, Hell's Angels, Outlaws, Pagans, and Bandidos—have long been involved in narcotics trafficking. They have also violated federal firearms and explosives laws that confer investigative jurisdiction to the ATF. Working with other federal investigative agencies as part of the Organized Crime Drug Enforcement Task Force Program, several notably successful prosecutions have been made in recent years.

The bureau has also formed a National Response Team to investigate serious arson cases. The team, consisting of highly trained special agents, a team supervisor, a forensic chemist, and an explosives technician, is available to respond to any major arson incident in the United States. ATF also operates the National Firearms Tracing Center. This center keeps track of firearms as they are imported, manufactured, or sold. Through such tracing activities, invaluable assistance can be provided to law enforcement agencies at all levels of government.

## Internal Revenue Service

The Internal Revenue Service (IRS) performs a number of law enforcement functions primarily through its Criminal Investigation Division.

**Criminal Investigation Division**

The dramatic and colorful history of the Criminal Investigation Division began shortly after the passage of the Revenue Act of 1913, which was the first income tax law enacted by Congress after the Sixteenth Amendment was ratified. Immediately, problems of tax evasion became commonplace, as did complaints about dishonest employees of Internal Revenue. The first commissioner of the then Bureau of Internal Revenue was familiar with the work of the Post Office inspectors, whose jobs involved investigating frauds in the use of the mails and occasional cases of dishonesty among Post Office workers. The commissioner decided to establish a group to make similar investigations in the Bureau of Internal Revenue. With the cooperation of the postmaster general, six experienced Post Office inspectors were transferred to the Bureau of Internal Revenue; these inspectors became the first special agents in the new Special Intelligence Unit.

Today, with responsibility for investigations of dishonest employees transferred to a separate Internal Security Division, special agents of the Criminal Investigation Division spend the majority of their time conducting investigations of alleged criminal violations of federal tax laws, particularly those relating to income, excise, and employment taxes; making recommendations with respect to criminal prosecution; preparing comprehensive documented technical reports; and assisting the U.S. attorney in the preparation of cases for trial.

The enforcement activities of the Criminal Investigation Division fall into two general criminal tax enforcement programs; the Special Enforcement Program (SEP) and the General Enforcement Program (GEP). The SEP program is designed to identify and investigate those individuals who derive substantial income from illegal activities such as organized crime and who violate the tax laws through nondisclosure of illegal income. Over the years, the forerunner of the present-day Criminal Investigation Division has felled some of the giants of organized crime. Such notorious figures as Al Capone, Frank Nitti, Jake and Sam Guzik, Terry Druggan, Frank Lake, "Dutch" Schultz, Johnny Torrio, Albert Anastasia, Frank Costello, and Mickey Cohen are among the underworld leaders who have gone to prison on federal tax charges.

Today, special agents of this division continue to participate in the federal government's fight against organized crime by participating with other Treasury and Justice Department law enforcement agencies in federal organized crime strike forces. Of particular importance is a joint agreement between the DEA and the IRS to develop a tax enforcement program aimed at high-level drug traffickers and financiers. While the DEA concentrates on substantive narcotic offenses, it identifies individuals who seem to derive substantial income from narcotics activities and notifies the Criminal Investigation Division (CID). During the past few years more than one-half of the special enforcement efforts of the CID are concentrated on such major organized narcotic efforts.

Whereas the SEP is directed at individuals who receive income from illegal sources, the GEP targets for investigation those individuals who either receive income from a legal source and fail to report it or who attempt to circumvent the tax laws by fraudulent means.

Recently, two areas have come under special attention. These are illegal tax protesters and fraudulent tax shelters. The illegal tax protester program concentrates on the investigation of leaders and promoters of major protest groups and schemes with significant numbers of participants. The CID has also been directed to step up its criminal investigation effort against fraudulent tax shelters, particularly those involving nationwide promotions.

Although not a Treasury Department agency, an investigative service operating out of the U.S. Postal Service should be mentioned. This is the Postal Inspection Service. The protection of the U.S. Mail and the mail system is the primary function of this agency. It performs investigative, law enforcement, security, and audit functions. Among the crimes it investigates are such offenses as robbing the mail, burglary of any postal facility, assaults on Postal Service employees, theft of mail, the use of the mails to transport bombs, explosives or controlled substances, and the use of the mails to distribute obscene materials or commercial transactions involving child pornography.

## INTERPOL

The International Police Organization (INTERPOL), although not an agency of the United States, nonetheless has a very close working relationship with federal law enforcement agencies. The idea of achieving international cooperation among police agencies of different countries became a reality with the creation of INTERPOL in 1923. Initially conceived as a means for a small number of European countries to provide mutual assistance in law enforcement matters, it has now grown to a worldwide consortium of 130 countries.

In 1938, Congress provided legislative authority for the attorney general to accept membership in INTERPOL on behalf of the United States. The FBI was initially designated to act as the American representative to this agency. During World War II, INTERPOL ceased to function because of Nazi domination of Europe.

In 1946, INTERPOL was reconstituted under a new constitution, which provided for elected directors and other safeguards to prevent usurpation by any member country. The United States resumed participation in 1947, with the FBI again designated to operate the INTERPOL function for the United States. In 1950, however, the FBI withdrew from participation, claiming that the costs of membership outweighed the benefits INTERPOL provided. The U.S. Treasury Department, anxious to maintain international contacts to help with its enforcement responsibilities in narcotics, currency, and customs violations, continued an informal liaison with INTERPOL. In 1958, the attorney general officially designated the Treasury Department to be our INTERPOL representative. In the late 1970s an arrangement was made between the Treasury Department and the Justice Department to share responsibilities and to operate jointly as U.S. representatives.

In each member country, a point of contact and coordination is established for the INTERPOL function. Generally, this activity is undertaken by some component of the national police in the capital city of each country. This designated component is known as the National Central Bureau (NCB). Although staffing patterns and size vary, each member country operates its own NCB within the framework of its own national laws and policies, and within the framework of the INTERPOL constitution.

In the United States our NCB is located in Washington, D.C., in the main Department of Justice building. In addition to a full-time staff of Justice Department representatives, personnel are assigned from the Secret Service, the DEA, the Customs Service, the Immigration and Naturalization Service, the IRS, and the Postal Inspection Service. In this way, all the major federal law enforcement agencies are represented.

The headquarters of INTERPOL and the site of its General Secretariat is in Functions St. Cloud, a suburb of Paris, France. Contrary to the popular misconception, INTERPOL is not an international police force. Its sole purpose is to coordinate investigative efforts among its 130 member nations by requesting assistance and to serve as a clearinghouse and depository for criminal intelligence information. In this way its computer base can store and exchange information on international criminals. It also stores information on such items as wanted criminals, stolen items, and other related information supplied by user nations. Other INTERPOL services include transferring requests from one nation to another to conduct investigations leading to arrest or extradition, conducting criminal history and license plate or operator's license checks, issuing an international wanted circular and all-points bulletin in any or all of the member nations, and tracing weapons and motor vehicles.[80]

Essentially, the facilities of the INTERPOL-Washington NCB is the only means, unless federal jurisdiction is involved, that state and local police agencies have for obtaining the assistance of a foreign police agency. Should the Chicago police department want the assistance of the Tokyo police department, they would have to go through the Washington NCB, whose staff would handle, transmit, and disseminate the request through INTERPOL headquarters to the Tokyo police. All information would go through the Washington NCB rather than directly from Tokyo to Chicago.[81]

## SUMMARY

The police are the overseers of the criminal justice system. Although they are usually thought of in their role as law enforcers, the police spend more of their time in providing nonenforcement-related services than in enforcing laws.

The organization of police service as we know it today is less than 150 years old. During the history of Western civilization, various organizational arrangements were devised to enforce laws. As society became more complex, methods for providing police services were modified and improved. There has been a historical fear that a centralized and full-time police service could be employed to restrict individual liberties. This fear was particularly pronounced as a result of England's experience, which was carried over into the American Colonies.

The history of law enforcement in America, particularly in our cities, is not a proud one. Early city police departments were often corrupt organizations that served the interests of political factions more than they did the community. Gradually, as municipal reform became a reality in the late nineteenth and early twentieth centuries, law enforcement improvement began and continues to this day.

Federal law enforcement is generally a very specialized form of investigative authority. Unlike local and some state law enforcement agencies, the jurisdictional authority of most federal law enforcement units is quite narrow. In addition, federal law enforcement agencies tend to be investigative units, rather than providing more broad-based police services.

The major criminal investigative units within the federal government are found in the Department of Justice and the Treasury Department. In recent years, with the passage of additional crime-related legislation by Congress and the development of a larger federal role in law enforcement, important federal crime-related agencies such as the Law Enforcement Assistance Administration and the National Institute of Justice (NIJ) came into being. We are now seeing some problems of cooperation and coordination developing among some of the federal law enforcement agencies, which mirrors similar balkanization and decentralization problems among local and state law enforcement efforts. The years of the Reagan administration saw most of the law enforcement activities except for drug offenses turned back to the states and local units of government. A smaller federal presence became the order of the day. In its first years in office, the Bush administration seemed to be following a similar role. It will be interesting to note whether the federal government begins to assume a more enlarged role in our nation's law enforcement needs and what direction this role takes if it should occur.

## REVIEW QUESTIONS

1. What are the two functions of the police? Give two examples of each of these functions.
2. What are the responsibilities of the following levels of law enforcement?
   a. Municipal police
   b. State police
   c. County sheriff
3. What specific police powers were vested in the federal government by the Constitution? In what ways have these powers been expanded by Congress and other sources?
4. Which department is responsible for the major law enforcement functions of the federal government? What are the major subdivisions of this department?

5. What is the present mandate of the FBI? What crimes does the FBI investigate?
6. Briefly describe the law enforcement responsibilities or functions of the following federal agencies:
   a. Immigration and Naturalization Service
   b. Drug Enforcement Administration
   c. U.S. Marshal Service
   d. Organized Crime and Racketeering Section
   e. Law Enforcement Assistance Administration (LEAA)
7. What are the law enforcement duties of the following Treasury Department agencies?
   a. Secret Service
   b. Customs Service
   c. Bureau of Alcohol, Tobacco, and Firearms
   d. Internal Revenue Service
8. What is INTERPOL, and how does it operate?

## DISCUSSION QUESTIONS

1. How has the history of law enforcement had an impact on the American police today?
2. Discuss the operations and significance of the Law Enforcement Assistance Administration (LEAA).
3. What should be the role of federal law enforcement agencies in dealing with problems of crime that cut across all levels of government?

4. In 1989, a "drug czar" was appointed by President Bush. What should be his role with the many federal agencies involved in the antidrug efforts?
5. Can the federal government pull back its assistance to state and local levels of government in dealing with problems of crime and the administration of justice? Explain your position.
6. What do you see as the future of law enforcement in the United States? Explain the basis for your feelings.

## SUGGESTED ADDITIONAL READINGS

Ahern, James R. *Police in Trouble.* New York: Hawthorn, 1972.

Bayley, David E., ed. *Police and Society.* Beverly Hills, Calif.: Sage, 1977.

Broderick, John J. *Police in a Time of Change.* Morristown, N.J.: General Learning Press, 1977.

Chapman, Brian. *Police State.* New York: Praeger, 1970.

Dorman, Michael. *The Secret Service Story.* New York: Dekarte Press, 1967.

Goldstein, Herman. *Policing a Free Society.* Cambridge, Mass.: Ballinger, 1977.

Kelling, George L., and Mark H. Moore. *The Evolving Strategy of Policing.* Washington, D.C.: National Institute of Justice, November 1988.

Monkkonen, Eric H. *Police in Urban America, 1860–1920.* Cambridge, Great Britain: Cambridge University Press, 1981.

Moore, Harry W., ed. *The American Police.* St. Paul, Minn.: West, 1976.

Niederhoffer, Arthur. *Behind the Shield: The Police in Urban Society.* Garden City, N.Y.: Doubleday, 1967.

Ottenberg, Miriam. *The Federal Investigator.* Englewood Cliffs, N.J.: Prentice-Hall, 1962.

Reiss, Albert J. *The Police and the Public.* New Haven, Conn.: Yale University Press, 1971.

Skolnick, Jerome. *Justice Without Trial: Law Enforcement in a Democratic Society.* New York: Wiley, 1966.

Tobias, John J. *Crime and Police in England, 1700–1900.* New York: St. Martin's Press, 1979.

Turner, William W. *Hoover's FBI—The Men and the Myth.* Los Angeles: Sherbourne, 1970.

Walker, Samuel. *A Critical History of Police Reform: The Emergence of Professionalism.* Lexington, Mass.: Lexington Books, 1977.

Westley, William A. *Violence and the Police.* Cambridge, Mass.: M.I.T. Press, 1971.

Wilson, James Q. *The Investigators: Managing FBI and Narcotics Agents.* New York: Basic Books, 1978.

## NOTES

1. Herman Goldstein, *Policing a Free Society* (Cambridge, Mass.: Ballinger, 1977), p. 1.

2. Ibid.

3. James Q. Wilson, *Varieties of Police Behavior* (Cambridge, Mass.: Harvard University Press, 1968), p. 16.

4. Elaine Cumming, Ian M. Cumming, and Laura Edell, "Policeman as Philosopher, Guide and Friend," *Social Problems* 12 (1965):267–286.

5. Thomas E. Bercal, "Calls for Police Assistance: Consumer Demands for Governmental Service," *American Behavioral Scientist* 13 (1970):681–691.

6. James P. Gilchrist, *A History of the Middle Ages* (London: Oxford University Press, 1948), p. 179.

7. Charles Reith, *The Blind Eye of History: A Study of the Origins of the Present Police Era* (London: Faber, 1912), p. 31.

8. Ibid., p. 137.

9. For example, see Patrick Pringle, *Hue and Cry: The Birth of the British Police* (London: Museum Press, 1955); Charles Reith, *The Blind Eye of History*, pp. 148–149; and Albert Lieck, *Justice and Police in England* (London: Butterworth, 1936).

10. A. C. Germann, Frank Day, and Robert Gallati, *Introduction to Law Enforcement and Criminal Justice* (Springfield, Ill.: Charles C Thomas, 1973), pp. 61–62.

11. Anwar Syed, *The Political Theory of American Local Government* (New York: Random House, 1966), p. 38.

12. Bureau of Justice Statistics, *Profile of State and Local Law Enforcement Agencies, 1987* (Washington, D.C.: U.S. Department of Justice, 1989).

13. Reith, *The Blind Eye of History*, pp. 82–83.

14. Documents of the New York Board of Aldermen, Document No. 53, pp. 1047ff.

15. Raymond B. Fosdick, *American Police Systems* (New York: Century, 1920), p. 68.

16. James T. Allison and Robert T. Penrose, *Philadelphia, 1681–1887. A History of Municipal Development* (Baltimore: Johns Hopkins Studies in Historical and Political Science, vol. II, 1887), pp. 37–41.

17. For an excellent analysis of the reform movement in municipal government, see Edward C. Banfield and James Q. Wilson, *City Politics* (New York: Random House, 1966); Richard Hofstadter, *The Age of Reform* (New York: Knopf, 1955), especially chap. IV; Lorin Petersen, *The Day of the Mugwump* (New York: Random House, 1961); Frank M. Steward, *A Half Century of Municipal Reform: The History of the National Municipal League* (Berkeley: University of California Press, 1950); and T. R. Mason, "Reform Politics in Boston," unpublished dissertation, Department of Government, Harvard University, 1963.

18. T. A. Tobias, *The History of English Law* (London: Westholver and Westholver, 1920), pp. 109–110.

19. See Advisory Commission on Intergovernmental Relations, *State-Local Relations in the Criminal Justice System* (Washington, D.C.: U.S. Government Printing Office, 1971); and Committee for Economic Development, *Reducing Crime and Assuring Justice*.

20. Advisory Commission on Intergovernmental Relations, *State–Local Relations in the Criminal Justice System*, p. 27.

21. Vern L. Folley, *American Law Enforcement* (Boston: Holbrook, 1973), p. 64.

22. Katherine Mayo, *Justice to All: The Story of the Pennsylvania State Police* (New York: Putnam, 1917), pp. 5–6.

23. Folley, *American Law Enforcement*, p. 67.

24. Committee for Economic Development, *Reducing Crime and Assuring Justice* (New York: Committee for Economic Development, 1972), p. 31.

25. James M. Burns and J. W. Peltason, *Government by the People* (Englewood Cliffs, N.J.: Prentice-Hall, 1966), p. 63.

26. Art. 1, sec. 8.

27. Donald F. Whitehead, *The FBI Story* (New York: Random House, 1956), pp. 66–68.

28. Bela Rektor, *Federal Law Enforcement Agencies* (Astor, Fla.: Danubian, 1975), p. 36.

29. *Abridged History of the Federal Bureau of Investigation* (Washington, D.C.: Federal Bureau of Investigation, Office of Congressional and Public Affairs, n.d.)

30. Federal Bureau of Investigation, *Appropriation Request—1982* (Washington, D.C.: House Subcommittee on Appropriations, 1982), p. 36.

31. The history of federal enforcement efforts and the frequent reorganization of agencies and assigned jurisdiction in an attempt to deal with narcotics violations is as follows: 1915, Bureau of Internal Revenue (U.S. Treasury Department); 1927, Bureau of Prohibition (U.S. Treasury); 1930, Bureau of Narcotics (U.S. Treasury); 1966, Bureau of Drug Abuse Control (BDAC), Department of Health, Education and Welfare; 1968, Bureau of Narcotics and Dangerous Drugs (BNDD), Department of Justice; 1972, Office for Drug Abuse Law Enforcement, Department of Justice; 1973, Drug Enforcement Administration, Department of Justice; 1982, FBI.

32. For an interesting analysis of the problems DEA had in investigating narcotic crimes, see James Q. Wilson, *The Investigators: Managing FBI and Narcotics Agents* (New York: Basic Books, 1978).

33. "Hide and Seek at the Border: U.S. Agents Are Losing," *Police Magazine* 2 (September 1979): 6–17.

34. Ibid., p. 10.

35. Ibid., p. 12.

36. Vernon D. Acree, "This Is Customs," *Drug Enforcement* 1, no. 3 (Spring 1974): 10.

37. "Opposition to FBI–DEA Merger Heating Up," *Law Enforcement News* 8 (January 1987): 4.

38. "Attorney General Maps Out Combined Roles for FBI–DEA," *Washington Post*, 17 September 1987, p. 3.

39. Ibid.

40. Thomas F. Adams, *Law Enforcement* (Englewood Cliffs, N.J.: Prentice-Hall, 1968), p. 88.

41. Rektor, *Federal Law Enforcement Agencies*, p. 103.

42. Department of Justice, "Outline of the Office of the United States Marshal" (Washington, D.C.: Executive Office for United States Marshal, 1973), p. 2.

43. U.S. Marshal Service, *The Director's Report: A Review of the United States Marshal Service in FY 1987* (Washington, D.C.: U.S. Department of Justice, no date), p. 41.

44. U.S. Marshall Service, *Then . . . and Now* (Washington, D.C.: U.S. Department of Justice, no date), p. 13.

45. *Senate Special Committee to Investigate Organized Crime in Interstate Commerce, 3d Interim Report*, S. Rept. 307, 82d Cong., 1st Sess. 2 (1951).

46. See, for example, *Senate Select Committee on Improper Activities in the Labor or Management Field, 1st Interim Report*, S. Rept. 1417, 85th Cong., 2d Sess. (1958); *Permanent Subcommittee on Investigations of the Senate Committee on Government Operations, Organized Crime and Illicit Traffic in Narcotics*, S. Rept. 72, 87th Cong., 1st Sess. (1965); *House Committee on Government Operations, Federal Effort Against Organized Crime*, House Rept., 1574, 90th Cong., 2d Sess. (1968).

47. Former Attorney General John Mitchell stated that $50 billion per year is a conservative estimate of gross profits of organized crime. *New York Times*, 9 March 1969, p. 1, col. 2.

48. P. Johnson, "Organized Crime: Challenge to the American Legal System," part 1, *Journal of Criminal Law, Criminology and Police Science* 53 (1962): 418.

49. "The Strike Force: Organized Law Enforcement v. Organized Crime," *Columbia Journal of Law and Social Problems* 496 (1970): 502.

50. President's Commission on Law Enforcement and Administration of Justice: *Organized Crime* (Washington, D.C.: U.S. Government Printing Office, 1967), p. 11.

51. Ibid.

52. Discussion with David Margolis, Organized Crime and Racketeering Section, June 25, 1985.

53. Interview with Edward T. Joyce, deputy chief, Organized Crime and Racketeering Section, July 17, 1975.

54. Ibid.

55. "The Strike Force."

56. Ibid.

57. Specifically, Title III of the Omnibus Crime Control and Safe Streets Act (1968).

58. A thirteenth has now been added called the Florida/Caribbean Task Force.

59. These wiretaps or electronic surveillance activities are supposed to be tightly controlled and the law provides stiff penalties for those that are not sanctioned. When an investigative team is convinced of the propriety and necessity of a Title III operation, it is necessary first to obtain the approval of the U.S. attorney general to request a court-ordered warrant for the operation. The application for this authorization must be quite detailed and specific. The application is followed by a comparably detailed affidavit. Each court-approved intercept is then authorized for only a brief period, usually ten to fifteen days, and never more than thirty days. Any request for renewal requires a detailed review of the recordings or transcripts collected to date.

60. U.S.C. Title 21, Sec. 848.

61. Folley, *American Law Enforcement*, p. 83.

62. Eleanor Chelinsky, "A Primary-Source Examination of the Law Enforcement Assistance Administration (LEAA), and Some Reflections on Crime Control Policy," *Journal of Police Science and Administration* 3 (June 1975): 203–221.

63. National Advisory Commission on Criminal Justice Standards and Goals, *Criminal Justice System* (Washington, D.C.: U.S. Government Printing Office, 1973), p. 7.

64. National League of Cities and United States Conference of Mayors, *Criminal Justice Coordinating Council* (Washington, D.C.: National League of Cities, 1971), p. 3.

65. Pub. L. 91–644, Title I-4(2), Jan. 2, 1971.

66. Twentieth Century Fund, *Law Enforcement: The Federal Role* (New York: McGraw-Hill, 1976).

67. Ibid., p. 40.

68. Ibid., esp. chap. 3.

69. Ibid., pp. 54–57.

70. National Institute of Law Enforcement and Criminal Justice, *Exemplary Program* (monograph), April 1975, p. 3.

71. See Malcolm M. Feeley and Austin D. Sarat, *The Policy Dilemma: Federal Crime Policy and the Law Enforcement Assistance Administration 1968–1978* (Minneapolis: University of Minnesota Press, 1980).

72. Ibid., p. 69.

73. Ibid., p. 96.

74. James M. Thoreabeau, *The History of the American Revolution* (New York: Crittendon, 1912), p. 69.

75. Rektor, *Federal Law Enforcement Agencies*, p. 178.

76. Miriam Ottenburg, *The Federal Investigator* (Englewood Cliffs, N.J.: Prentice-Hall, 1962), p. 228.

77. Walter S. Bowen and Harry F. Neal, *The United States Secret Service* (Philadelphia: Clifton, 1960), p. 20.

78. Letter from the Director's Office, May 14, 1985.

79. Ibid.

80. David R. MacDonald, "Treasury Department Assistance Programs to State and Local Law Enforcement Agencies," *Police Chief* 42, No. 7 (July 1975): 30.

81. Adopted from U.S. House of Representatives, *Appropriation Committee Hearings, Fiscal Year—1982, Department of the Treasury, United States Secret Service*, mimeo, n.d., pp. 374–376.

CHAPTER **5**

# The Role of the Police

This chapter begins by examining some of the specific enforcement activities in which the police are engaged. These responsibilities are viewed in relation to established constitutional issues and cases that have affected these activities. This discussion is followed by an examination of the development of police roles and their attitudes toward those roles. Finally, the internal organization of police agencies is analyzed.

## □ ROLE OF THE POLICE

Any discussion of the role of the police must take into consideration the police operational process, because it establishes the framework for police behavior. In recent years, police operations have come under increasing scrutiny by the courts through their interpretations of police behavior in some major cases. This section examines some of the more typical enforcement processes engaged in by the police and highlights significant court cases that bear on the conduct of the police in their enforcement role.

### Crime Detection

The police are typically the first component of the criminal justice system to deal with the commission of a crime. This detection of the commission of crime usually occurs in one of several ways. The most typical way that crimes come to the attention of the authorities is for the victim to report its occurrence to the police. A less typical way for the police to be advised of a crime is through the reporting of a crime by someone who has witnessed its commission or has come upon evidence indicating that a crime has been committed. A third way is for the police themselves, through their routine operations, to discover that a crime has been committed or to witness its commission. For example, while patrolling his beat, a police officer might discover a building with a broken lock on a door, indicating that a burglary may have occurred or may be occurring.

Methods of crime detection

An important part of crime detection may be the result of aggressive police work. Experienced police officers and detectives sometimes concentrate their surveillance and investigative efforts on persons, situations, or places in which past experience has taught them that criminal behavior is likely. For example, investigators may receive a "tip" that a particular individual is dealing in narcotics. They will then try to arrange a "buy" or at least keep the individual under surveillance in the hope that they can gather enough evidence and satisfy the particular elements required for an arrest and a successful prosecution.

Situations also lead to many instances of crime detection. The police may be having problems with "car stripping" in a particular locale. They may then detail a group of detectives or plainclothes officers to watch a certain parking lot in the crime vicinity in the hope that they will be able to arrest the thieves in the act. Sometimes the police even contrive the situation. This is called a *decoy operation*. For example, in the past few years a number of jurisdictions have set up "sting operations." The police posing as "fences" or outlets for stolen goods would go into business. When the word got around of this "outlet," burglars, thieves, and real "fences" would come to these undercover police officers to sell or buy stolen goods. Such operations have led to a large number of arrests and the recovery of stolen property. In this type of case, police provided an opportunity for the commission of a crime. Sometimes such police behavior invokes the defendant to claim that the situation is in effect entrapment. *Entrapment* is a defense to a criminal charge when an individual is enticed by an officer of the law (or the officer's agent) to commit a crime that otherwise would not have been committed. Typically, the court will refute this argument on the grounds that the action of the police "merely by affording opportunities or facilities for the commission of the crime does not constitute entrapment."[1]

**Nonpolice examples of crime detection**

The police are not always the first and only criminal justice agency to initiate the crime detection process. The prosecutor's office, for instance, is sometimes involved in certain types of criminal investigations such as fraud, organized crime, or forms of political corruption. The investigatory grand jury is another method of crime detection that is used by some communities under certain circumstances. Yet another means is the investigative powers vested in the Congress through its legislative committees. Following congressional hearings and investigations, such facts can be turned over to law enforcement officials and the courts for appropriate action. Examples of this authority can be seen in the operations of the Senate Watergate Committee and the House Judiciary Committee in their investigation into the political operations of the Nixon administration or the more recent Iran–Contra affair.

## PROFILING VIOLENT OFFENDERS: A NEW INVESTIGATIVE TOOL

The police had hit a stone wall. Nearly eight months earlier, a twenty-three-year-old graduate student had been found in her apartment beaten and strangled to death. Even veteran homicide detectives were taken back by the grisly scene. The victim's genitals had been mutilated, her nipples cut off, and scrawled across her stomach in the victim's own blood were the words: "Fuck you cops."

The police in this large Midwestern city had heard about a new program developed by the FBI—The National Center for the Analysis of Violent Crime (NCAVC). Operating out of the Behavioral Science Unit of the FBI Academy in Quantico, Virginia, this unique assistance program was contacted. The local police were instructed to send copies of the autopsy report and pictures of the murder scene. The reply came back:

the probable killer would be a white male, possibly twenty-five to thirty-five years old, of low to moderate intelligence, who knew the victim and either lived or worked nearby, possibly in her apartment building, lived by himself or with a single parent, and owned an extensive collection of pornography. In all likelihood the murderer would have already been interviewed by the police.

Based on this profile, attention refocused on Fred Horvath, an early suspect in the case. Remarkably, Horvath fit the description. Earlier the police had all but dismissed his involvement. Now, armed with this new information, they continued to intensify their investigation. Slowly, the evidence was painstakingly gathered, and the pieces began to fit. After obtaining a warrant, the police arrested Horvath at home, where he lived with his invalid

mother. A search of the apartment uncovered a large collection of pornography and some undergarments later identified as belonging to the victim. Confronted with evidence, Horvath confessed to the crime. He is now serving a term of life imprisonment without parole.

This latest weapon in police investigation—psychological profiling—has been developed by the FBI's NCAVC. Basically, the center is a law enforcement-oriented Behavioral Science and Data Processing Center to consolidate research, training, and support for any police agency that finds itself confronted with unusual, bizarre, and/or particularly vicious or repetitive violent crime.

The center grew out of the recognition for the need to provide a national clearinghouse for unsolved crimes of violence, especially when these crimes are of an exceptional

## Criminal Investigation

Once a crime has been detected, the police may conduct an investigation depending on such factors as the seriousness of the offense, the availability of resources, and the probability of a successful investigation (which means an arrest and a successful prosecution). Often the victim may view the crime as having major importance, but the police will conduct nothing more than a preliminary investigation. For instance, if you live in a city in which motor vehicle theft is quite prevalent, you could have your car stolen, only to be notified by the police a few hours later that it has been found abandoned and slightly damaged. The police will often conduct nothing more than an initial investigation, which consists of taking a report of the incident. Given the situation and the lack of available evidence for an arrest and prosecution, the police often feel that such crimes are simply beyond their capability to solve.

Generally, the police investigative process revolves around certain objectives.[2] The first objective is simply to determine if a crime has been committed, and if so, what type of crime. This is usually accomplished by analyzing the available facts and evidence to see if the elements of a crime are present and, perhaps, whether the nature of the act is civil or criminal in order to determine if the police have jurisdiction over the matter. Second, the process attempts to identify the offender through the available evidence. The third objective is to apprehend the offender.

*Objectives of the investigative process*

nature or are part of a series of crimes that have come to be called "serial crimes." Through data gathering and analysis, computers can establish patterns and link characteristics associated with a particular crime to similar crimes. It can then link up various state and local police agencies who may be experiencing the same types and characteristics associated with say, a "serial murder"—one who commits in the same manner, a number of homicides throughout the country. Initially, the NCAVC is developing this capability for the crime of homicide. Steps are now underway to develop the same capability for the crimes of rape, child molestation, and arson.

Of particular interest is the Research and Development Program. In this effort, the program's behavioral scientists and law enforcement personnel study violent criminals,

their victims, and crime scenes in an effort to gain insight into violent offenders' personalities, to understand the motivations for their behavior, and to examine how they have been able to evade police efforts to identify, locate, apprehend, prosecute, and incarcerate them. The program personnel interview serial and exceptional violent offenders such as murderers, rapists, child molesters, and arsonists. Where necessary, the program performs ongoing research into specific questions on violent crime and recommends innovative investigative techniques and potential solutions.

The NCAVC provides to the criminal justice system the consultation and opinions of experienced criminal personality-profiling investigators and behavioral scientists. It conducts careful and detailed analyses of violent crimes on a case-by-case

basis to construct profiles of unknown offenders so that the scope of the investigation can be narrowed, such as in the Horvath case. Consultation is also furnished on serial and exceptional cases and also includes planning case strategies, furnishing information for search warrant preparation, providing personality assessments and interviewing techniques to use with suspects, coaching prosecutors on techniques of violent criminals, and offering on-site assistance to police departments in their investigative efforts.

Although not every effort has been as successful as the Horvath case, the program's potential has generated widespread enthusiasm both by the law enforcement community and among researchers who believe they are now closing in on understanding the characteristics of certain violent offenders.

In addition to these objectives, the police are responsible for gathering and preserving evidence that will both justify their enforcement action in the particular case as well as enable the fact-finding process of the courts to prosecute the case successfully and obtain a conviction. In this way, the police investigative process becomes a crucial aid to the prosecution and conviction of the perpetrator.

**Court-imposed "rules of the game"**

The police investigative process can be quite extensive or rather simple and routine. This will depend on factors such as the circumstances of the crime, the difficulty in obtaining evidence, and the characteristics of suspects or offenders. Whether the investigative process is complex or relatively simple, the police are still bound by certain "rules of the game." Procedures have been established by the courts to govern how the police can conduct the investigative process. These "rules of the game" are the result of case law interpretations—particularly the interpretations of the United States Supreme Court in light of the Constitution—as to what the police can or cannot do in conducting investigations. Such investigative efforts as electronic surveillance, conducting searches and seizing evidence, making arrests, obtaining confessions or admissions from a suspect, and using such techniques as "lineups" or "showups" are all governed by court decisions that apply to the police. Some discussion of these and appropriate court decisions will be used to explain this relationship.

Assume that the police want to employ some form of electronic surveillance to gather evidence against an accused. The police may, for example, receive information that a certain individual is dealing drugs out of his home. In addition to the standard surveillance of the suspect's residence, the police may want to employ some type of electronic surveillance such as a phone tap. The police can't merely decide to tap the suspect's phone. The Supreme Court has ruled that such police practices constitute an unwarranted invasion of privacy under the provisions of the Fourth Amendment. Yet the Court also realizes that in certain situations the police may have to use such a technique to obtain evidence. In such circumstances the police are authorized to tap the suspect's phone only if they receive the permission of a court that is authorized to approve such a practice. The police must go before the court and show cause for their request. If the court is satisfied of the necessity for such a phone tap, it can then authorize it. In most instances, however, such approval is itself controlled. Modern laws and court decisions in this area authorize such practices only in certain types of cases and for limited periods of time. The police, for instance, might be given permission to run the phone tap for only thirty days. After that period, the investigators would have to return to the authorizing court for additional permission to continue the phone tap.

**Police search and seizure in criminal investigations**

Other procedural guidelines govern the circumstances under which the police can legally search for and seize evidence that can then be used to prosecute the accused for a crime. This area of police search and seizure is also governed by the Fourth Amendment. Basically, the police can conduct a search of a suspect or constitutionally protected property only under certain circumstances such as when the police have a search warrant, incident to a lawful arrest, with the suspect's permission, and under limited circumstances when sufficient probable cause exists.[3]

If the police, in the course of their investigation, conduct a search and, as a result, seize evidence that they later intend to introduce at the trial, they cannot violate these rules. To do so runs the risk of the trial court ruling that the police violated the constitutional rights of the defendant. The consequences are damaging:

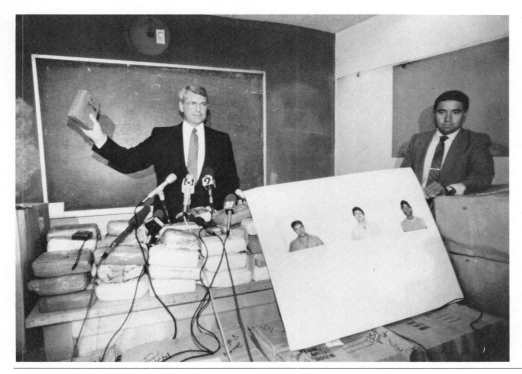

When police undertake a search for and seizure of illegal goods, they must follow prescribed procedures in order to use the seized goods as evidence in the prosecution of the suspect(s). (© M. Richards/PhotoEdit)

the evidence is not admissible. Without such crucial evidence, the government may well find that it cannot successfully prosecute the case and will have to drop the charges.

It is particularly in the area of drug offenses that challenges to police searches are most likely to occur. If the challenge to the police search in such cases is successful, it is impossible to convict the accused when the drug evidence is thrown out by the court. One of the favorite tactics of defense lawyers is to attack the legality of the police search. If the search falls, so does the right to seize the evidence and to use it.

This area of constitutionally permissible search and seizure has changed over the years through a series of Supreme Court decisions. During the 1980s the Court became more permissive in its interpretation of when and under what circumstances evidence seized by the police can be used to convict a defendant. To the consternation of civil rights advocates, the Court has seemed to tilt more toward the state and away from the rights of the accused in these areas. In a series of major cases beginning in 1914 and culminating in the famous *Mapp* v. *Ohio* decision of 1961, the Supreme Court restricted the circumstances under which the police could legally search and seize evidence. In the last few years in such notable decisions as the *Leon* and *Garrison* cases, the Court seems to be moving away from its earlier decisions and loosening police powers in this area.

The evolving nature of court decisions in search and seizure

# Search and Seizure

## MAPP v. OHIO (1961)

### Application of the Exclusionary Rule
### Against Illegal Searches and Seizures to the States

### FACTS

On May 23, 1957, three Cleveland, Ohio, police officers arrived at the home of Mrs. Mapp. They had received information that a person was allegedly hiding out in the home who was wanted for questioning in relation to a recent bombing, and that there was a large amount of policy paraphernalia being hidden in the home. Mapp and her daughter lived on the top floor of the two-family dwelling. The officers knocked on the door and demanded entrance to the house, but Mrs. Mapp, after telephoning her attorney, refused to admit them without a search warrant. The officers then advised their headquarters of the situation and undertook a surveillance of the house.

Three hours later, four additional officers arrived and again sought entrance. When Mrs. Mapp did not immediately come to the door, at least one of the several doors was forcibly opened and the police gained admittance. Meanwhile Mapp's attorney arrived, but the officers would neither permit him to enter the house nor to see Mapp. It appears that Mrs. Mapp was halfway down the stairs when the officers broke into the hall. Mrs. Mapp demanded to see the search warrant, and a paper, claimed to be a warrant, was held up by one of the officers. She grabbed the "warrant" and placed it in her bosom. A rough struggle ensued in which the officers recovered the papers. As a result, Mrs. Mapp was handcuffed because she had been "belligerent" in resisting their attempts to retrieve the "warrant" from her bosom. While handcuffed, she was forcibly taken upstairs, where the dressers and closets throughout the house were thoroughly searched. The police then searched the basement and found some obscene materials in a trunk. Mrs. Mapp was arrested for having such materials in her possession.

At the trial, no search warrant was produced by the prosecution, nor was the failure to produce one explained or accounted for. The facts tended to support the belief that a search warrant never existed. Mrs. Mapp was convicted of the crime and sentenced to prison.

### DECISION

The U.S. Supreme Court decided that the police exercised wanton disregard for the constitutional rights of the accused.

### SIGNIFICANCE OF THE CASE

The Supreme Court indicated that the Fourth Amendment is contained by inference in the Fourteenth Amendment, and that from this date, any evidence that was illegally obtained by the police would be inadmissible in any courtroom in the country.

## UNITED STATES v. LEON (1984)

**Insufficient Probable Cause
to Issue a Search Warrant**

### FACTS

A confidential informant of unproven reliability informed a Burbank police officer that two persons known to him as "Armando" and "Patsy" were selling large quantities of drugs from a particular address. The informant added that he had witnessed a sale of drugs by "Patsy" at that residence about five months earlier. He also knew of a shoebox that "Patsy" had, which contained a large amount of cash. He additionally stated that only small quantities of drugs were stored at that residence; the remaining drugs were kept at another Burbank location.

The tip initiated an extensive investigation. Surveillance was undertaken of both residences, which disclosed parked vehicles that belonged to individuals having records for drug violations. A suspect was seen leaving one of the premises with a small paper sack. A check of this suspect showed him to be employed by Leon. Leon had a prior record for drug charges. Leon's house was then also placed under surveillance, and relevant activity was also observed at this address.

An experienced and well-trained narcotics investigator from the Burbank Police Department prepared an application for a warrant to search all three addresses and automobiles involved. A facially valid search warrant was issued by a state superior court judge. Drugs were found in all three residences and in automobiles registered to the occupants. The parties were indicted and charged with conspiracy to possess and distribute cocaine and a variety of other counts.

All defendants filed motions to suppress the evidence pursuant to the warrant. The trial court agreed, citing that the affidavit was insufficient to establish probable cause. The government disagreed with the court's action and argued that the Burbank narcotics investigator who filed the application for the warrant acted in good faith. The court rejected this argument as a valid exception to the Exclusionary Rule.

The trial court denied the government's motion for reconsideration. A divided Court of Appeals upheld the trial court ruling. This court said that the affidavit for the search warrant was fatally stale and there was a failure to establish the informant's credibility. The government appealed this decision to the U.S. Supreme Court.

### DECISION

Inherently trustworthy tangible evidence obtained in reliance on a search warrant by a police officer acting in good faith, and which is issued by a detached and neutral magistrate, and such warrant is ultimately found to be defective, may nevertheless allow evidence to be introduced. A good-faith exception to the Exclusionary Rule exists with respect to the Fourth Amendment proscriptions. The decision of the Court of Appeals to exclude the search warrant and the evidence seized pursuant to the warrant is reversed.

### SIGNIFICANCE OF THE CASE

The case modifies substantially the Exclusionary Doctrine. It permits the police to search for and seize evidence where the police acting in good faith believe the warrant to be valid even when the warrant is later found to be defective.

## MARYLAND v. GARRISON (1987)

### Searching a Premise Other Than the One Authorized by Warrant Facts

FACTS

Police officers in Baltimore obtained a search warrant to search the person of a suspect and also "the premises known as 2036 Park Avenue, third-floor apartment." When the police applied for the warrant and when they later conducted a search after obtaining the warrant, they believed from their earlier inquiries that there was only one apartment on the third floor. The third floor however, was in fact divided into two apartments; one occupied by the suspect named in the warrant and one by another person.

The police searched the wrong apartment and, before they became aware of their mistake, discovered and seized drugs and money. The occupant of the apartment was charged with violation of Maryland's Controlled Substances Act. He was tried and argued that the search was illegal and asked the trial court to exclude the evidence, as a violation of the Fourth Amendment. The trial court refused his request, and he was convicted. On appeal, the highest court in Maryland upheld the defendant's appeal and reversed the decision of the trial court and ordered a new trial. The state then appealed this decision to the U.S. Supreme Court.

DECISION

The U.S. Supreme Court ruled in favor of the trial court and the state. The Court held that the search warrant was valid under the Fourth Amendment because when it was issued, the search warrant met all necessary requirements. The police also believed that there was only one apartment on the third floor when they applied for the warrant. It was only after they found the contraband and the warrant had been executed in a reasonable manner that the police realized that two apartments existed. The police then discontinued their search as soon as they discovered their mistake.

SIGNIFICANCE OF THE CASE

There is no Fourth Amendment violation where the officers' mistake is reasonable even though there is some ambiguity in the description of the place to be searched. This decision is a logical extention of the "good-faith" belief (the police are excused if acting in "good faith"), as held in the earlier decision of *United States* v. *Leon* (1984).

---

Lineups and suspect identification procedures

The police investigative process also involves two other frequent devices: the police showup or lineup (or the use of photographs) to identify a suspect and custodial interrogation. These too, are governed by certain procedures that have been established by the courts that govern police operations in these areas. And, like the area of police searches and seizures, they have been changing in recent years.

The first area examined by the Supreme Court was the use by the police of the showup or lineup. In 1967 in a series of cases, the Court ruled that a postindictment lineup might be conducted in a manner that would be suggestive, and therefore, prejudicial to an accused. As such, any lineups of a suspect after he has been indicted was "a critical stage of the prosecution," which entitled the suspect to the same rights of having an attorney present as he would have at the trial itself.[4]

At this point, it appeared that the Supreme Court was set on a path that would circumscribe the ability of the police to use this investigative technique and to use it effectively. This was not to be the case. The Supreme Court backed away from what appeared to be a logical extension of curtailing the use of the lineup. A few years later, the Court ruled that the police could legally conduct identification proceedings *before* the filing of formal charges.[5] Still, in later cases, the Court approved the right of the police to use photographic identification (e.g., the use of a "mug book") without defense counsel's participation whether conducted before or after the filing of formal charges.[6]

The final blow fell a short time later. The Court ruled that a "suggestive identification" was not in and of itself enough to warrant such identification techniques suspect.[7] What this shows is the impact of certain Supreme Court decisions on the investigative process. The Court in its rulings provided the guidelines by which the investigative process is conducted—or as mentioned, the rules of the game.

In-custody interrogations in an effort to obtain a confession are a frequent tactic of the police. They are also an area of the investigative process that has come under a great deal of scrutiny by the courts. The issue of in-custody questioning and interrogations by the police turn on two issues: the "voluntary" nature of such confessions and the Fifth Amendment right against self-incrimination.

*Police interrogation and confessions in the investigative process*

The voluntary issue is self-evident. The courts have been concerned that in-custody interrogations by the police can be coercive. In the famous 1936 case *Brown v. Mississippi*, where black defendants had been accused of raping a white woman and had made incriminatory statements, the deputy sheriff who had conducted the beatings of the defendants, which led to the incriminating statements, conceded that at least one had been whipped, "but not too much for a Negro."[8] The coercive nature of such confessions calls into question their reliability.

It isn't only physical coercion that becomes an issue. Psychological coercion can also play a role. In one famous case, a suspect was arrested by the police on suspicion that he murdered his wife. The accused was questioned in relays under a powerful light from 7:00 Saturday evening until 9:30 Monday morning without letup or the chance to rest. It wasn't clear whether he ever confessed to the crime, but the police claimed he implicated another individual in the murder. In overturning the admissibility of the confession, the Supreme Court called the thirty-six-hour relay questioning "inherently coercive."[9]

In the 1960s, the Supreme Court turned away from the so-called "voluntariness" test of the admissibility of confessions toward the "right to counsel" standard. It was felt that suspects had to be advised of their right to counsel and to have counsel present should they request this right. Implicit in the Court's reasoning was the idea that knowledge of this right would tend to better ensure that the police did not physically or psychologically coerce confessions or incriminating admissions from an accused.

The famous *Escobedo* and *Miranda* cases addressed this issue and established clear guidelines for the police as to the requirements that must be met before a confession or admission could be used against a suspect in a later trial. The outcry from the police was immediate. It was claimed, among other things, that advising the suspect of his right to counsel and his rights against self-incrimination would result in handcuffing the police. Criminals would go free because the cops wouldn't be able to get them to confess. The implication was obvious: such a restriction on the investigative process would ultimately lead to decreased police efficiency and higher crime rates.

Although there is some disagreement over whether these court-imposed rules have really "handcuffed" the police, the general conclusion from much of the research that has looked at restrictions on police in such areas as search and seizure and obtaining confessions from suspects is that such rules have not impeded the police.[10] In many instances, the police themselves admit that such rules have helped make the police more professional. It has certainly brought about better trained police personnel than was the case before the rules were imposed on police practices in these areas.

On the other hand, some claim the police have not so much complied with these court requirements as much as they've learned to get around them. As one public defender has noted, the police even gain an advantage from these supposed controls over the police.

> Police love the Miranda decision [requiring that a suspect be advised of his rights]. They speed-read the suspect his rights and tell him to fill in and sign a printed waiver form. He's frightened; he doesn't understand what was read to him; he's afraid he'll look guilty if he doesn't sign; he signs and school's out. The signed waiver is almost impossible for the defense to overcome.[11]

---

## ESCOBEDO v. ILLINOIS (1966)

### In-custody Police Interrogation as a "Critical Stage" and the Right to Counsel

FACTS

On the night of January 19, 1960, Danny Escobedo's brother-in-law was fatally shot. At 2:30 the next morning, Escobedo was arrested without a warrant and interrogated for approximately fifteen hours. During that time, he made no statement, and he was released at 5 P.M., after his attorney had obtained a writ of habeas corpus from the state courts.

On January 30, 1960, 11 days after the fatal shooting, Escobedo was arrested a second time at about 8 A.M., and taken to the police station for interrogation. Shortly after he arrived at police headquarters, his lawyer arrived, but the police did not permit the attorney to see his client. The attorney repeatedly requested to see his client and, at the same time, Escobedo requested to see his lawyer. The police told Escobedo that his lawyer didn't want to see him and that they would not allow him to see his attorney until they were finished interrogating him. It was during this second interrogation that Escobedo made certain incriminating statements that were used against him when he was convicted in the state courts for his involvement in his brother-in-law's murder.

The defense raised the issue at trial and before the Supreme Court that the interrogation stage was a "critical stage" in Escobedo's case and that he had been denied the right to counsel under the Sixth Amendment. The defense argued further that because Escobedo was denied the right to counsel under the Sixth Amendment, his incriminating statements should have been suppressed and should not have been used against him.

DECISION

The Supreme Court agreed that Escobedo's right to counsel under the Sixth Amendment had been denied, and consequently it suppressed his incriminating statements.

SIGNIFICANCE OF THE CASE

The Supreme Court held that the interrogation was in fact the most "critical stage" of his criminal proceedings. Because Escobedo was in police custody, he should have been notified of his right of counsel and afforded this right if he had so requested by virtue of the Sixth Amendment. If the right to counsel is withheld, incriminating statements cannot be used against the accused.

## MIRANDA v. ARIZONA (1966)

### Confessions and Police Interrogations

FACTS

On the evening of March 3, 1963, an eighteen-year-old girl was abducted and forcibly raped in Phoenix. Ten days later, Ernesto Miranda was arrested at his home by Phoenix police and taken to police headquarters, where he was put into a police lineup. There he was immediately identified by the victim and within a two-hour-period signed a confession, admitting that he had seized the girl and raped her.

At his trial, it was brought out in cross-examination by the defense counsel that Miranda had not been advised before his interrogation of his right to counsel and to have counsel present during the interrogation.

DECISION

The U.S. Supreme Court reversed the conviction and the introduction of his confession on the grounds that Miranda's rights against self-incrimination were not protected.

SIGNIFICANCE OF THE CASE

The Court ruled that the prosecution may not use statements that stem from custodial interrogation unless it demonstrates the use of certain procedural safeguards against self-incrimination by the accused. These safeguards include: (1) warning the accused of the right to remain silent; (2) explaining that all statements may be used in evidence against the accused; and (3) explaining that the accused has the right to the presence of an attorney, either retained or appointed, unless he or she voluntarily, knowingly, and intelligently waives these rights. If at any time the accused indicates that he or she wants to exercise these rights, the opportunity to do so must be made available; similarly, if the accused indicates that he or she does not want to be interrogated, the police cannot proceed with the questioning.

---

## MORAN v. BURBINE (1986)

### Refinement of the Miranda Case

FACTS

Michael K. Burbine was given his Miranda warnings by Providence, Rhode Island, police but waived them and signed written statements admitting a murder. Burbine's sister had called an attorney, and the attorney called police offering to represent Burbine if he was to be questioned that evening. Police lied to the attorney, saying they were not planning to question Burbine. Burbine subsequently appealed to have his conviction and confession set aside, contending that the police had denied him his right

to be represented by an attorney as provided in the Miranda decision.

DECISION

Justice Sandra Day O'Connor writing for the 6–3 majority said . . . "The Constitutional right to request the presence of an attorney belongs solely to the defendant. Because the evidence is clear that [Burbine] never asked for the services of an attorney, the telephone call from the lawyer had no relevance to the validity of the waiver or the admissibility of the statements."

SIGNIFICANCE OF THE CASE

This case refined the 1966 Miranda warning requirements as they pertain to the admissibility of incriminating statements by an accused. The police are not required to keep the suspect abreast of the status of his legal representation, and the right to demand legal counsel present belongs only to the accused. Police are not required to permit an attorney to see a suspect unless the suspect demands that right.

---

## NEW YORK v. QUARLES (1984)

### The Miranda Warnings and the Requirement to Advise an Arrestee of His Rights

FACTS

A young woman approached two officers and told them she had just been raped. Having given a good description of the suspect, she added that he might be found in a local supermarket and he was carrying a handgun. Upon arriving at the supermarket, the suspect, Quarles, was seen. He matched the victim's description. Upon seeing the police, the respondent ran toward the rear of the store. The police lost sight of him but quickly found him and ordered him to place his hands over his head. While frisking the suspect, the police discovered that he was wearing a shoulder holster that was empty. After handcuffing him, one officer asked the respondent about the location of the gun. He nodded in the direction of some empty cartons and stated, "the gun is over there." Finding a loaded .38 caliber revolver, the police placed the respondent under arrest and read his Miranda warnings. Respondent indicated his willingness to answer some questions without his attorney present. Quarles answered that he owned the gun and that he bought it in Miami.

Subsequently, he was charged with criminal possession of a weapon. The Court notes that he was originally charged with rape, but the record fails to indicate why this charge was not pursued. The trial court suppressed the gun, and the statement of "the gun is over there," because no Miranda warnings were given. The trial court also suppressed the other statements tainted by the violation of Miranda. The trial court decision was affirmed by the Appellate Division of the Supreme Court of New York. The Court of Appeals in a 4 to 3 decision affirmed the decision of the trial court. It found the respondent "in custody" within the meaning of Miranda. The state's argument of the exigency of the situation was rejected, based upon the officer's testimony lacking an indication of his subjective motive to protect his own safety or the safety of the public.

DECISION

There is a public safety exception to the requirement that Miranda warnings be given before a suspect's answers may be admitted into evidence, and that the availability of that exception does not depend upon the motivation of the individual officers involved. The U.S. Supreme Court finds that the gun and the statement "the gun is over there" should not have been excluded. The decision of the Court of Appeals is reversed.

SIGNIFICANCE OF THE CASE

This case establishes the "Public Safety" exception. In situations where there is an immediate need to protect the public safety, the threat to the public safety takes precedence over the Fifth Amendment's privilege against self-incrimination. The police officer can ask the necessary questions to protect himself or the public.

Another procedural area that is governed by law is the right of the police to arrest. The legality of the arrest also determines the legality of what subsequently occurs. For example, if the police make an improper arrest, any admission or confession of the accused is also tainted—as is the possibility that other considerations such as a search and seizure might crumble, given the circumstances of the original improper arrest.

In effect, an arrest is the beginning of imprisonment, when an individual is first taken by government and restrained of his or her liberty.[12] The law of arrest, which is generally uniform in all states as well as in the federal code of criminal procedure, has not changed significantly in nearly four hundred years. Our arrest laws have evolved from laws planted firmly in English common law. *The arrest as part of the investigative process*

Let us briefly review the basic law of arrest (see Chapter 2), which states that a police officer can arrest without a warrant on the following conditions: (1) if a felony has been committed in the officer's presence; (2) if there is probable cause to believe that a felony has been committed and that the person being arrested committed the felony; or (3) if a misdemeanor has been committed in the officer's presence. The authority for these arrest powers is contained in the various state and federal statutes, which, in turn, have been affirmed by various court decisions.

Although the police confront individuals in various circumstances each day, the mere stopping and questioning does not necessarily constitute an arrest. As Chapter 2 detailed, certain elements must be present for a valid arrest to occur. If these elements are questioned, the courts have the sole responsibility to determine whether a legal arrest has taken place.[13]

When making a *legal* arrest, the police officer has the authority to use whatever *reasonable* force is necessary. The key issues are the legality of the arrest and the reasonableness of the force used. If the arrest is not legal, the officer has no right to use force, and criminal and civil charges can be brought against the officer for the arrest and the subsequent use of force. Reasonableness is also an issue. Suppose that a police officer stops a motorist for a minor misdemeanor. While the officer's back is turned, the motorist starts to run away. The police officer cannot then shoot the fleeing misdemeanant; use of such force would be entirely inappropriate and unreasonable under the circumstances.

From this review of police investigative procedures, it is clearly seen how legal guidelines, particularly through court interpretations, provide the framework for police enforcement actions. The next section examines how the police themselves define their role and how this role definition is expressed.

## Concerns Over the Police Role

To say that the police role involves order maintenance and law enforcement tells us everything and, at the same time, nothing. In the first place, such statements without additional explanation do not really provide a meaningful picture of how the police interact with the overall administration of criminal justice. Second, they do not explain how these objectives are achieved. Criticisms of the police do not center on the goals of law enforcement and order maintenance, but rather on the ways in which the police attain these goals. It is the methods the police use to achieve these goals and the ways these programs and techniques interact with the criminal justice system that need further examination. The interrelated nature of the police function began to arouse curiosity at the beginning of the 1950s; before this period, studies of crime and the criminal justice system tended to be highly *The interactive nature of the police role* specific in nature. Because of this approach, the police, the courts, and corrections were treated almost as discrete and isolated entities. Examinations of the interrelationships among these component units were generally limited to statistical summaries of raw data. For example, reviews were made of statistical summaries of police arrests and successful prosecutions as indicated by guilty pleas or judgements of guilt. Such data were used to show that there was a high attrition rate between the numbers of arrests and the cases prosecuted successfully. However, no meaningful attempt was made to examine *why* this occurred. For instance, no attempt was made to relate the relative contribution that police actions and arrest policies had on this relationship.

In 1951, William Westley, a young sociologist, completed an interesting doctoral thesis that explored the complexities and interactions of a police department. Although his pioneering research into the actual operations of a medium-sized Midwestern police department was not to be recognized for its value until some years later, it did provide the most significant scholarly research into this hidden area of police behavior up until that time. In this way, it established a significant focus for the scholarly research that would come later.[14]

A few years later, the interactional policies of the police as they were related to the administration of justice became the subject of a significant research project undertaken by the American Bar Foundation. This effort became the first major attempt to record and report actual observations of the daily activities of police officers, prosecutors, judges, and correctional personnel.[15]

The Westley study, and the summaries and observations from the American Bar Foundation study, offered a sharp contrast to the general image of how the police functioned and how the criminal justice system operated. Most notably, the studies pointed out that the operations of these agencies differed from public perceptions and from formal police policies. In fact, the studies showed that the pressures of workload, citizen demands and expectations, and the interests and personal values of those working in the system were often more instrumental in how the system operated on the day-to-day basis than were such guidelines as established policies and procedures, the Constitution, laws, statutes, and ordinances.[16] It also pointed out that the police were both affected by and affected the administration of justice in ways that were not anticipated before the research had begun. Among the most important conclusions of the American Bar Foundation's survey were the following:

1. The functioning of the criminal justice system was heavily dependent on the police, who in turn were very affected by the other components. Police policies and practices affected the operations of the entire system.
2. The police used their arrest powers to achieve a whole range of objectives in addition to that of prosecuting wrongdoers. For instance, they used this authority to harass, to investigate, to punish, and to provide safekeeping.
3. The volume of business handled by the police was much more than the volume processed through the rest of the criminal justice system.
4. The police often used informal methods to fulfill their formal responsibilities and to dispose of the endless array of situations they encountered.
5. The police felt that they are in a "no-win" situation in which public expectations exceed the police's capacity to fulfill these expectations.
6. Individual officers were found routinely to exercise a great deal of discre-

tion in how to handle the many diverse situations they encountered. Specifically, the police exercised a great deal of discretion in deciding when to arrest for a wide variety of offenses.[17]

Looking back at these pioneering efforts, it is obvious that they had significant impact on subsequent studies of the criminal justice system. For example, when it was discovered that the police do not generally operate according to popular conceptions, the following key questions arose: How do they operate? Why do they operate in this manner? What are the implications of this behavior? These questions not only opened up new areas for researchers to examine but also provided a basis for viewing the administration of criminal justice in an interrelated way. Accepting the premise that the police both affect and are, in turn, affected by the other agencies of criminal justice, provides a more realistic and integrative approach.

Such a viewpoint was given additional credibility a few years later when the President's Commission on Law Enforcement and Administration of Justice released its various reports in 1967. The commission urged the development of a systemwide approach to the study of criminal justice. It was no longer considered feasible to study the police in isolation or to hold on to misconceptions about the actual functioning of the police. As a reflection of this new mode of thinking, college programs dropped such labels as "police science" or "police administration" programs and adopted the more inclusive title of "criminal justice studies." Similarly, textbooks that had been formerly devoted solely to the police broadened their focus to include other components of the criminal justice system. This integrated approach forms the basis for today's study of the administration of criminal justice.

## ◻ POLICE OPERATIONAL STYLES

Because the police do not always share a common perception of their role—and, in fact, because their role does vary depending on the circumstances and the individual characteristics of the police officers themselves—it is extremely difficult to define the full range of possible police roles. One way to deal with this problem of definition is to examine certain role categories into which police officers can be grouped. Using this approach, it is possible to divide most police behavior into four general operational styles: the *enforcer*, the *social service agent*, the *zealot*, and the *watchman*.[18] Although these are not "pure" categories in that none of these is strictly inclusive—that is, no police officer totally conforms to one role style to the exclusion of the others—it does provide a useful and convenient way of examining a very complex area of police role behavior.

**THE ENFORCER.** The *enforcer* is a police officer who places a relatively high value on social order and "keeping society safe" and a relatively low value on individual rights and legal due process. The popular media conception of this police officer is the "Dirty Harry" model. This type of officer is vehemently critical of such institutions as the Supreme Court, particularly as the Court expressed itself in its decisions during the 1960s. This type of officer is also very cynical toward society and critical of politicians, police administrators, minority groups, and others whom he or she views as corrupt, deviant, incompetent, weak, criminal by nature, or simple naive. Overall, this individual is likely to view these groups as dangerous and threatening to the established order. These officers may rationalize their nega-

*Characteristics of the enforcer*

tive attitudes toward such individuals and groups by convincing themselves that their "street experience" has provided them with a grasp of reality that eludes others. The enforcer is often guilty of stereotyping. For example, this type of officer might contend that most blacks are criminal, amoral, or a drain on the resources of white society and that politicians are corrupt, untrustworthy and potentially dangerous because of the sanctions they are willing to impose on the police for "political purposes." With such attitudes, enforcers are likely to harbor deep hostility toward these groups and feel that such groups likewise harbor deep-seated resentment toward them as police officers.[19]

This officer's primary preoccupation and interest lie in dealing with more serious crimes. This is not to imply that he or she doesn't consider less serious crimes unimportant—they are simply less important. As a member of "the thin blue line," the enforcer's first obligation is to come down hard on those engaged in such crimes as homicide, rape, robbery, and serious burglaries. Even in these instances, however, he or she selectively classifies crimes almost as much by the race and character of the perpetrator and victim as by the crime category itself. For example, if a black, Puerto Rican, or Hispanic kills another, the enforcer's reaction is initially, "it's just another 'nigger' [or whatever pejorative term applies in this case] just cuttin' on another nigger."

Because this type of police officer is most concerned with serious offenses, he or she may feel that intervening in such enforcement activities as domestic disputes and minor traffic violations is undeserving use of police time. If the enforcer does intervene in such situations, it is usually done with the preconceived idea that a domestic dispute constitutes an actual or potential felonious assault or that an erratic driver is, in fact, intoxicated and should be arrested. As the noted sociologists W. L. and Dorothy Thomas point out: "if men define situations as real, they are real in their consequences."[20] Such might also be said of the enforcer style of police officer.

THE SOCIAL SERVICE AGENT. The *social service agent* is another category. In many instances, social service agents may be more typical of the young, college educated, and more idealistic police officers who have in recent years been entering police service. It is not unusual to find these individuals working in middle- and

Role perceptions

upper-middle-class suburban cities. They have a diversity of perceptions about their role. They tacitly accept the idea that the police should be involved in a wide variety of activities. Furthermore, these activities do not have to be related directly to crime or police enforcement strategies. For example, social service agents might go out of their way to assist a stranded motorist or to counsel youth. They perceive this role as an important function of their job. In this way, they define their overall role quite broadly. They often have perceptions of themselves similar to those of the enforcer category. That is, they feel somewhat superior and capable of making appropriate decisions but for different reasons. Whereas the enforcers are convinced of their superiority by virtue of their "street experience" and their exposure to the pathologies of human behavior, the social service agents feel superior because of their education and the "rightness" (if not righteousness) of their perceptions. These types of police officers are also generally more accepting of our society's values on individual rights and due process. This helps them deal better—at least abstractly—with certain aspects of the administration of justice. For example, if a case is lost because of police error in collecting evidence or gathering the necessary facts, they can better understand under these circumstances the court's position in dismissing the case. They understand the legal necessity for proof. Often they are likely to commit themselves to learning to play the "game" better in future situations so that defense attorneys can't trip them up again. They are also less likely to externalize blame for such situations on "soft" or "corrupt" judges or defense counsels.

However, their idealism can be a two-edged sword. It can make them particularly vulnerable to cynicism. They may quickly find that the system doesn't operate as they thought, or it doesn't operate as they think it appropriately should. They find that their high-blown notions of public service are not appreciated by the general public; instead of being cooperative, much of the public is antagonistic or apathetic. While the enforcer can deal better with these kinds of realities since he or she expects this, the social service agent becomes frustrated and runs the risk of becoming over time deeply cynical.

Like the enforcer, the social service officer also places high value on social order and protecting society. Whereas the social service agent may be able to behave and think like an enforcer in certain situations, that behavior is usually situationally induced. When the situation changes, the social service officer has the flexibility to adjust his or her behavior accordingly. On the other hand, the enforcer typically remains inflexible in both outlook and behavior, regardless of the circumstances.

**THE ZEALOT.** The third category or style that can be used to define various police roles is that of the *zealot*. This type of role characteristic is a combination of the enforcer and the social service agent styles. The correctness of the zealot's actions is based on the belief in the righteousness of the cause. Zealots tend to categorize their perceptions of behavior into black and white, or right and wrong. They see their role as one of enforcing all the laws and dealing with all offenders equally. Like the enforcer, the zealot emphasizes the detection and apprehension aspects of police work, although the zealot is less likely to distinguish as much between major and minor crimes. A police officer of this type recognizes that serious crimes are more important and that their successful solution will provide the officer with greater prestige and status in the police organization. However, the zealot also recognizes that the solution of such crimes generally escapes the average police officer. Because of this, zealots often become advocates for the full-service range of police activities and particularly those that are related directly to the criminal enforcement activities of the job. This type of officer typically defines his or her role as a general law enforcement agent and is generally less critical than the enforcer. In fact, zealots tend to accept the diverse groups of society for what they are.[21]

Zealots are also ambivalent about the enforcer type. Although they agree with some of the enforcer's attitudes and values, particularly as they relate to concerns about enforcement, they disagree with the narrow concerns expressed by the enforcer in the types of crimes on which he or she concentrates. The zealots may feel that as police officers they are required to deal with a full range of both serious and minor criminal infractions. This being the case, the zealot-type officer may resent the narrow viewpoints of the enforcer, who tends to restrict the scope of enforcement activities.[22]

Although the zealots recognize concerns about individual rights and due process, they are not above bending them if they feel the situation warrants it and they can get away with it.

Finally, although they take a larger perspective of the police role than do the

Combining characteristics

enforcer types, zealots also tend to criticize the wide scope taken by the social service agent. They view the social worker role as unsuited to police work both because of its use of nonpunitive techniques and because of its demands on police time and resources, which detract from the basic role of general law enforcement.

THE WATCHMAN. The fourth major role style of law enforcement is that of the *watchman.* This term is derived from James Q. Wilson's study of the styles of policing practiced by several cities.[23] In the cities that Wilson studied, he developed a typology of various police styles. He categorized one style as the *legalistic,* combining features of the enforcer and zealot. A second typology was that of the *service style,* which is somewhat analogous to the social service agent style. A third orientation he referred to as the *watchman style.* This style is characterized by a set of values

*Maintaining public order*

and attitudes that emphasizes that maintenance of public order as the primary police goal rather than law enforcement or the broader-ranging public service model. In this type of role, the police officer ignores many common minor violations and general service situations. Wilson describes this model in this way:

> The police ignore many common minor violations, especially traffic and juvenile offenses, to tolerate, though gradually less so, a certain amount of vice and gambling, to use the law more as a means of maintaining order than of regulating conduct, and to judge the requirements of order differently *depending on the character of the group in which the infraction occurs* [emphasis added]. Juveniles are "expected" to misbehave, and thus infractions among this group—unless they are serious or committed by a "wise guy"—are best ignored or treated informally. Negroes are thought to want, and to deserve, less law enforcement because to the police their conduct suggests a low level of public and private morality, an unwillingness to cooperate with the police or offer information, and widespread criminality. Serious crimes, or course, should be dealt with seriously. . . .[24]

Although it is difficult and somewhat risky to generalize this role model to specific classes of police officers and situations, there are certain factors that might bear on its relevancy to the workaday police occupation. Through some years of observation, this author has seen the adoption of this role model and the values and attitudes it conveys become somewhat characteristic of certain types of police personnel. Most often it seems to be found among older police officers nearing retirement who find themselves working general patrol operations. These officers generally take a nonchalant view of their role. Their guiding policy is "take it easy," "don't get involved," and "do what you have to do and no more." Their focus becomes one of keeping things as easy as possible, which means overlooking certain forms of behavior that would more typically involve the zealot or the social service agent. Although they will take action in the case of major crimes, they differ from the enforcer in that they do not actively and aggressively seek to enforce these crimes or to become involved in their investigation. Because their attitude is one of "if it happens, I'll do what is necessary," they are guided by the situation rather than by any preconceived plan.

*Situational aspects*

This watchman role may also be situational in nature. The particular assignment of the police officer to a minority neighborhood, particularly if it is a walking beat, might induce this form of role behavior. For example, during the late 1960s, when there were inflamed feelings between the police and ghetto residents in many of our major cities, the suggested role for police personnel assigned to these neighborhoods was to "play it cool," "don't get the residents upset by busting up sidewalk crap games or giving out parking tickets." Police assigned to these neighborhoods, particularly if they were permanently assigned to these areas, would operate by overlooking many of the minor infractions in order not to bring about a confrontation or a possible riot. To some extent these same role models still exist in these neighborhoods today.

## ▣ THE POLICE AND CRIME

Although it is changing, the public's perception of the police often does not correspond with the realities of law enforcement. The public is aware of the drama involved in police work through popular depictions on TV and in movies. Such dramatic depictions show the police as a relatively efficient, organized force of crime fighters that keeps society from falling into chaos. Many police officers also view themselves as the "thin blue line," engaged in a dangerous and heroic battle with the criminal element and those who would subvert our established political and social order or prey on society. Although many police officers after several years of experience might candidly admit among themselves that they are not "super crime fighters," sometimes they are more than a little reluctant to admit this to the general public. They see it as in their best interest to try to perpetuate the myth of effective law enforcement.

Such actions are understandable. The problem is that such efforts mutually reinforce the myth. The police fall into the trap of giving the impression that they are more effective in dealing with crime than they actually are. The public in turn then expects higher levels of performance. In this way mutual reinforcement sets in. The police can only eventually lose in such a situation. As one researcher on

The primary function of police is to maintain general order in the community. (© Laura Sikes/Stock South)

police activities says, "although the police do engage in gunfights, in sleuthing, in dangerous chases, these are rare events. Most police work resembles any other kind of work: it is boring, tiresome, sometimes dirty, sometimes technically demanding, but it is rarely dangerous."[25] To some extent this, too, is an overstatement; yet the realities of police work typically fall between these two opposing views.

The scope of police activities

Playing "cops and robbers" is only a small part—in some ways the least important part—of what the police do. Like lawyers, judges, and—yes, social workers (this latter occupation police are loathe to use as a comparison)—the police are primarily involved in settling disputes or maintaining general order in the community. In particular they are engaged primarily with activities that threaten to breach the peace and disturb public order. An analysis of the activities of police personnel, with the possible exception of the relatively small functions of the detective unit, point out that the crime-related functions of the police consume a very small percentage of their time and resources.[26]

Because the idea that the police are basically a crime-fighting agency has never been challenged in the past, the police have never bothered to sort out their remaining priorities.[27] Instead, the police have always been forced to justify activities that did not involve law enforcement in the direct sense by either somehow linking them to law enforcement or by defining them as nuisance demands on their time.[28]

Negative aspects of the "crime-fighting" image

According to Egon Bittner, the dominance of this crime-fighting image as held by police personnel has created two very bad situations. First, it leads to a tendency to view all sorts of problems as if they involved culpable offenses and to an excessive reliance on quasi-legal methods for handling them. Confronted with situations that are not criminal but that they feel compelled to handle, they must maneuver the situation into one in which a crime has been committed so that they can use their enforcement power or at least its threat. For example, police officers might be called to the scene of a family argument. They arrive and find the husband intoxicated and in a heated argument with his wife. The police under such circumstances cannot arrest a man for being drunk in his own home, but perhaps fearing potential violence between the two, they induce the man to step outside to "talk." Once outside the house, they arrest him for public intoxication and take him to jail.

Second, the view that crime control is the only serious, important, and necessary part of police work has a negative effect on the morale of those police officers on uniformed patrol who spend most of their time on other matters. Because crime fighting is considered the only "important" and "real" part of police work—and because this attitude is pervasive among police personnel, there is strong peer group pressure to emphasize the law enforcement function of policing. Yet many police personnel have very limited opportunities to be involved other than indirectly in investigations and arrests of "heavy crimes." This is frustrating to many uniformed police personnel—and because non-crime-related services are considered unimportant by the rewards system in police agencies—such police personnel rapidly grow very cynical.

Impact on crime

If the only important and real part of police work is crime fighting, how well do the police perform this role? The evidence seems to suggest that the police have a very limited impact on crime. Furthermore, the police simply do not seem to know what to do to reduce crime.[29] Some outspoken police officials are not even certain that there is *anything* they can do to produce a significant and lasting reduction in crime. Robert diGrazia, the controversial former head of such police departments as Boston, St. Louis County, and Montgomery County, Maryland, upset his fellow chiefs when he made the public statement: "We are not letting the public in on our era's dirty little secret," namely, "that there is little the police can do" about crime.[30] Although this may be something of an overstatement, there is little doubt that the police are very ineffective in their crime-fighting role—and more disturbing, there seems to be very little that can be reasonably done to improve this situation.

During the 1970s, a number of efforts were undertaken to examine police effectiveness in controlling crime. These efforts set out to examine two important questions: What effect did traditional police practices have on crime rates; and what effects, if any, did some new methods of police organization and operation have?[31] Generally, the results were disappointing. Traditional police procedures seemed to have very little effect, and certain suggested reform programs didn't seem to provide much improvement. Nor does the increase in numbers of police personnel seem to make much difference. Although police chiefs and others during the late 1960s and 1970s called for more money to put more cops on the streets, there seems to be no evidence that this overly simplistic solution makes much, if any, difference. It certainly is no longer a realistic consideration today, given the financial situation faced by governments at all levels.

For all the research on police operations and effectiveness during the 1970s, there still is little that we can conclusively say. Maybe, as some experts are saying about the conclusion of these research efforts, "we generally know what doesn't work, we have yet to find out what does work."[32]

In spite of this, we might point out some conclusions and observations that, on the surface at least, need to be pointed out and studied further. We have come to the realization that the police cannot be held solely responsible or criticized for their seeming inability to deal with crime. The police simply cannot do the job alone. If, for instance, the deterrent effect of the police is to be realized, they must rely on the deterrent operations inherent in the judicial process. The courts must fulfill their role of deterrence. As one observer has said:

> whatever may be the value of the police presence as a deterrent to crime, the value of the police as apprehenders of criminals is not something that the police alone are capable of improving. The value of an arrest for incapacitating a criminal or for deterring would-be criminals from following his example depends crucially on what the courts elect to do with the arrestee, and here there has been virtually no careful experimentation at all. A few police departments in this country have shown themselves to be remarkably innovative, experimental, and open to evaluative research. There are not as yet many prosecutors or courts about which one can say the same thing.[33]

We have also learned that the police are highly dependent on citizens to help them in their law enforcement role. In the past the police often purposely isolated themselves from involvement with citizens. Now some police agencies at least are recognizing this mistake and are trying to become more involved with citizens and crime-prevention groups. We are also learning how crucial victim and witness assistance can be to the police (and the courts) and how much the police must rely on their help.[34]

Whether the police in coming years can improve their "batting average" is highly problematic; perhaps we shall see some improvement, but it is unlikely that there will be significant improvement in their abilities as crook catchers.

*Police require assistance in their crime-fighting efforts*

Trying to deal with the crime problem that has plagued the nation during the 1970s and 1980s is just the first problem the police face. This "crime-fighting" image is more make-believe than reality. Most of America's urban and rural police agencies find themselves involved in tasks that are far removed from criminal activity—and these tasks consume a lot more of their time than do police tasks dealing with crime and criminals. In many ways the police have become society's do-everything people. One consequence of this is the fact that the police are often criticized for not really doing anything well.

This situation may be getting worse before it gets better. Shrinking tax revenues for the support of local police, coupled with the cutback in federal funds as new priorities are established in Washington have certainly contributed to making the police officer's job more difficult. "Police work used to be a comfortable world in which we did pretty much as we pleased," says Anthony Bouza, a twenty-nine-year-veteran of the Minneapolis Police Department, where he served as chief until his recent retirement. But as he says, ". . . pressure of street crime has changed all that and created heavy demands for improved performance."

Although there is talk of a "new breed" of police officer who is as familiar with computers, racial issues, and psychology as his or her predecessors were with their .38 special, this "supercop" has not arrived on the scene in many departments. "Policing is so fragmented at the local level of government that such small police agencies cannot expect to attract the best and the brightest much less retain them," contends criminal justice professor Sam Chapman of the University of Oklahoma.

The United States has probably the most decentralized law enforcement system in the world. This compounds any already existing problems. Since the first full-time professional foot patrolman was assigned his beat in Manhattan in 1845, the various levels of law enforcement have proliferated. These include the municipal police forces, which range from New York City's nearly 32,000 officers to countless little hamlets and villages served by a single constable or village marshal. In addition, at the local level are the county sheriff's office, and our largest cities are served by special police forces such as transit authority cops and housing authority police. The states have all created state police or highway patrol systems. These are sometimes augmented by special state bureaus of criminal investigation or special highway police who deal primarily with over-the-road trucks. The federal law enforcement levels include investigative agencies such as the Federal Bureau of Investigation plus a multitude of special police such as park rangers and GAO guards for federal buildings. All together there are more than one hundred law enforcement or quasi-enforcement agencies at the federal level.

This often leads to a chaotic overlapping of jurisdictions. Imagine a situation in which a foreign student studying in Massachusetts picks up a hitchhiker in New York and brings him back to the state university campus in Massachusetts, where the hitchhiker is murdered. The investigation could involve the campus police, the state police since the murder occurred on state property, the FBI because the crime involved the crossing of state lines, the immigration authorities because the suspect is a foreigner, the Bureau of Alcohol, Tobacco and Firearms of the Treasury Department if a certain type of weapon was used; and if drugs were somehow involved, the investigation could also involve the federal government's Drug Enforcement Agency.

Still, the vast majority of police services are provided primarily at the local level, where the overwhelming majority of the estimated 490,000 sworn full-time police officers are found. Police work still remains for the most part the bastion of white males. Although male minority group members have made some significant inroads in police forces in the past twenty years, women have just begun appearing on the streets in uniform in the 1980s. However, currently less than 5 percent of all police officers are women.

Many police view their jobs as very dangerous. Each year about one hundred police officers are murdered, but this has dropped sharply from a peak in the 1970s. The death rate among law enforcement officers is about half that among construction workers, miners, farm laborers, and firefighters. Yet police personnel still continue to think of themselves as a special occupational category when it comes to death on the job.

Part of the problem, according to many critics, is the fact that police management is often so poor that inefficiency runs the department. The Washington-based Police Executive Research Forum, which was established by a group of progressively oriented police chiefs, found on a national average in towns with populations of fifty thousand and larger that only 45 percent of police officers available at any time for patrol duty were actually on the streets.

This is partially explained by the need to staff certain specialty assignments such as the detectives, communications, jail facilities, records, and other support services. But this is only part of the problem. "Police chiefs without management skills and training have over the years not paid enough attention to the negative consequences of over-specialization," contends police management consultant Kevin Parsons. Consequently, he says "we have a lot of headquarters people and nobody on the streets dealing with the crime problem and answering calls for service."

Although there has been recurring talk about creating a "West Point" for young men and women who aspire to careers in law enforcement and who will ultimately become the police leaders of the future, the hurdles to such an institution are insurmountable. Decentralized, small police agencies, a closed career system in which everyone starts at the bottom regardless of experience or credentials, and the opposition by police unions effectively kill any serious discussion of establishing an institution of this type.

An ominous trend is becoming apparent. Over the past decade, the arrest and clearance rates for serious crimes against persons and property have been declining nationally. The police have never had a "good batting average" in this area, but the situation seems to be getting worse. Now less than 20 percent of the most serious crimes are even cleared by an arrest. In the less serious crime categories, particularly in major urban high-crime areas, the police merely take reports of these types of crime, which are then filed away and forgotten. There simply aren't enough police available to investigate all of these crimes.

The relations between prosecutors and the police can be strained. Although they must rely on each other and they are both members of the same team, they often make critical statements of each other. The police get upset when prosecutors plea bargain a case. The police also often accuse the prosecutor's office of not preparing properly for trial but instead of going into court and trying to "wing it." Prosecutors

can be as equally testy toward the police. "They conduct a sloppy investigation and screw up some legal points on the evidence and they expect us to win the case" is a commonly heard complaint around prosecutors' offices. "Cops just don't seem to realize that because they made an arrest the court is not going to consider the accused guilty." A spokesman for the prosecutor's office in Seattle says, "It's amazing, no matter how much time some of these guys have on the [police] department, you would think they would learn that the court operates by different rules than they do on the streets."

Issues of police brutality or excessive use of force will not go away. In fact, there is some concern that many of the abuses curbed during the late 1960s and 1970s may be on the rise among the nation's police. Martha Hanover, a spokesperson for the American Civil Liberties Union, indicates that this legal watchdog agency is receiving an increasing number of complaints about abusive police actions toward suspects. Some are saying that the conservatism that is creeping back into America's social and political mainstream is making the police think they can get away with more as long as they couch their actions in terms of "getting tough with criminals."

But the police seem to be getting more wary at least in some parts of the country. Issues of civil suits against individual police officers, their supervisors, and their employers is causing some departments to examine their fundamental policies of operation. In the Northeast the police have begun countersuits against those who have accused them of committing wrongful acts.

Despite the many problems facing the police today, some police leaders are optimistic about the positive nature of change that they

see. One reason for this optimism, says former chief Kenneth Madeiros of Bismarck, North Dakota, a twenty-four-year police veteran, is that "the level of intelligence, education and professionalism has risen in the police community. And the screening process has improved. Gone is the day when you'd line up the applicants, look for the biggest, meanest one and give the badge and gun to him."

The training of police has also improved. In 1969, only ten states required even minimum training for police recruits. Today all states require minimum training with at least 120 hours required, and many states mandate far in excess of this. The courses in these programs emphasize more than the use of the revolver, defensive physical tactics, and the law.

Police work is also slowly adopting the available modern technology. This includes the use of computers and other work-saving aids that increase their efficiency. There is also some indication that communities are looking more favorably on cooperative efforts between their police agencies to lower the costs of law enforcement services.

One sure sign of change is the increasing importance of joint police–community efforts at crime-prevention activities. The police have acknowledged that they cannot do the job alone and are relying more on help from citizens in the community. Whether this cooperation is enough remains to be seen. Many say the police have fundamentally changed very little in the way they operate in the past 150 years. One thing is certain: whatever the police have been doing does not seem to be getting the job done. Perhaps the years ahead will see some fundamental and far-reaching breakthroughs in the provision of police services. It couldn't come at a better time.

## ☐ THE ORGANIZATION OF POLICE DEPARTMENTS

Police departments are generally organized in similar ways. What variations do exist depend on the size of the department, which itself depends on the size of the jurisdiction it serves and the type of law enforcement agency it is. In larger cities and counties, for example, there is a much greater demand for all types of police services. As a result of the need for such a broad range of services, police agencies in these communities provide many specialized and full-time services that a small-city police department does not. The type of law enforcement agency also determines organizational structure. A state police agency may have a large percentage of its personnel involved in traffic enforcement and related responsibilities. In this type of agency, then, such traffic functions will comprise the largest bulk of expenditures, and the agency will be organized around that particular function.

### Patrol

The backbone of police service

All state, county, and municipal police agencies have patrol units. Among city police departments, the patrol force is the largest operating unit. Typically, about 50 percent of all sworn personnel are assigned to this unit. Most of the marked police units we see on the streets twenty-four hours a day are manned by the uniformed men and women in our police department's patrol division.

How do officers on patrol operate and spend their time? To a large extent the answer to this question depends on department and personal priorities and on the kinds of public problems that come to the attention of the police during that shift. And yet, studies of police patrol activities show in many ways a striking similarity in terms of the general types of activities in which patrol officers engage and the time devoted to them.[35]

For example, although there is a great variation in the amount of time that police officers on patrol spend in answering assigned calls, in most jurisdictions this function takes up less than half of the officers' work time. Field-initiated activities in which police patrol officers initiate contacts with citizens averages about 10 percent of an officer's unassigned time. Such activities include making traffic stops, providing unassigned backup to other officers, and stopping and questioning suspicious-looking persons. Administrative activities, report writing, and police assignments other than calls for service averaged slightly over one hour's time on an eight-hour shift.

What this leaves is a sizable block of time that is available to the officer to use at his or her discretion. The major part of this time is spent "on patrol." This usually consists of driving about the beat, looking for problems that may require police action, or demonstrating police presence and availability. These activities are usually not directed either by supervisors or by conscious planning of the patrol officers themselves. Making security checks on the night shift of commercial buildings and issuing parking tickets are activities some officers engage in during their unassigned time. Yet it was found by observers who have studied patrol activites that the officers they observed spent very little time in checking buildings. More time, for example, was likely to be spent on "personal business" than on aggressive crime prevention efforts such as building checks and interviewing suspicious persons.

The police officers who provide these patrol services are usually the most important component of the police service. Although the media would give us the impression that such glamorized functions as those performed by the detectives are the most meaningful, the truth of the matter is that their overall role and contribution is generally far less important. It is the uniformed patrol officers who provide us with the full range of police activities on which we have come to rely. They answer the complaints of barking dogs that keep us awake at night; they respond to attempt to locate the lost child; they enforce traffic laws, help the injured, and deliver babies; and yes, they make arrests—from the obnoxious drunk to the most dangerous killer.

As was mentioned earlier, one of the major responsibilities of the police is the *maintenance of social order*. We saw in our discussion of the history of law enforcement that the desire for an orderly and peaceful society contributed greatly to the recognized need for the creation of police agencies. In fact, the term *peace officer* has become synonymous with *police officer*.

This peace-keeping function is a large and important responsibility of the men and women who operate our police patrol units. The following is a typical example of police activity in this area.

> Item (from report of a night on patrol): My overwhelming impression that night was of the helplessness of the people who called for assistance and their tendency to rely on the police to resolve problems middle-class people usually handle themselves and for which they turn to other professionals. A girl had overdosed on barbiturates; her family called the police, called an ambulance, and then sat helplessly in the dark, watching TV, until we arrived. On another call, a pair of neighbors wanted to invoke our authority to settle a longstanding and pointless dispute over a car in a driveway. Another woman called to give official notice that she would be justified in taking revenge on someone else in a dispute that had started out as a fight between two little children in a playground. The night before, M. told me, he had answered several family fight calls where the couple wanted him to decide which television programs they should watch![36]

Concepts of how best to provide patrol services to citizens have been changing in recent years. Years ago, the officer walking the beat was the visible symbol of police authority. In more recent years and particularly since World War II, police officers have been pulled off walking beats and assigned to multifrequency radio-equipped cars. The idea behind this change was that the police would be able to cover more territory and react to crimes a lot more quickly—and do so at far less cost. Police management thinking also underwent changes after the war. Departments were organized much more like the military. Police administrators emphasized centralized control, close supervision, instant communications, and motorization. Individual officers were not allowed to stay very long in one neighborhood. The emphasis was on internal mobility under the dual theories that a mobile department is a "clean" department and that the mobile police officer becomes a "well-rounded" officer. The whole concept was called "professionalism."[37]

*Changing concepts of patrol activity*

Today, the trend is reversing itself. Cincinnati, Oakland, Flint, Michigan, Los Angeles, and many other cities are bringing back the idea of the beat cop. Community-based policing is the new "buzz-word" in professional police circles. These programs can take various forms such as the team policing concept that enjoyed a great deal of discussion in the 1960s and 1970s. In this system, teams of police personnel were assigned to geographic areas or neighborhoods and given a great deal of flexibility and discretion in how they were organized and what specific police activities—patrol, plainclothes undercover operations, traffic enforcement, anti-vice activities—they engaged in.

Community policing programs reach out to the general public and involve individual citizens in crime prevention. (© Sally Myers/Tom Myers Photography)

Today, community policing is as much an attitude as it is a technique. It's an attempt to bring policing back to the close contact it once had with citizens. Those police departments that have in recent years emphasized this approach are trying to enlist the support of the police officers themselves to encourage them to work more closely with the communities they serve and to form joint police–citizen efforts to deal with problems of crime or public order in the community. It is this teamwork approach between the police and the citizens that characterizes this new wave of community policing efforts.

### Crime-Specific Enforcement Units

**Types of enforcement units**

Police agencies employ several general kinds of crime-specific enforcement units. One is a specialist tactical unit, whose responsibility it is to deal with special situations. Usually, such situations are those which routine police actions and police personnel are neither equipped nor trained to handle. Specially trained and equipped police personnel must then be brought in. Examples would be armed terrorist activity or armed and dangerous offenders who have to be subdued. The most common term for such units is *SWAT* (special weapons and tactics) units.

Some police agencies have also used special units to provide certain responses to critical situations. This might be a special anticrime unit whose responsibility it is to provide high-intensity patrol or undercover activities in high-crime areas. There have been occasional problems with the use of such units over the years. The aggressive nature of these units has led to a number of shootings in some cities. For example, the police might be having a series of armed robberies of liquor stores. In response to this, they assign police personnel armed with shotguns to the back rooms of such establishments. This has led to a number of shootouts and expressed fears from some citizens that the police are making the situation even more dangerous with such tactics. Such activities have produced particular concern among minority groups.

Another frequent use of such special units is on decoy operations. A city may be having a series of sexual assaults in certain areas at night. Female police officers or male police officers dressed as women are then assigned to these areas to entice, attack, and arrest.

A number of jurisdictions have also developed special metropolitan squads. Typically, this is a special group of investigative personnel from several jurisdictions. They concentrate on specific types of criminal activity that is usually organized and multijurisdictional. This might include major drug-related trafficking in a metropolitan area, or certain types of "organized crime" such as organized burglary or auto-theft operations.

## Traffic

Many larger communities have created special traffic units to deal with traffic-related problems. These traffic units are involved in such activities as enforcement, citizen education, investigation of traffic accidents and fatalities, parking, and providing police assistance and insight into problems involving traffic engineering.

Most of us think of police efforts in this area as primarily enforcement of existing traffic laws, which brings about such interesting exchanges as the following:

> Policeman to motorist stopped for speeding: "May I see your driver's license please?"
>
> Motorist: "Why the hell are you picking on me and not somewhere else looking for real criminals?"
>
> Policeman: "Cause you're an asshole, that's why . . . but I didn't know that until you opened your mouth."[38]

Although enforcement activities are an important part of the police traffic function—and yes, such exchanges do occasionally take place—a great deal of police effort is devoted to general traffic safety such as gathering statistical facts about accidents so that preventive action can be taken; offering public education and awareness programs dealing with the safe operation of motor vehicles and inspecting vehicles to ensure compliance with established safety standards; assisting the traffic engineer and traffic safety education agencies by providing them with Services provided information useful in their accident-prevention work; serving as the city government's inspection, investigative, and reporting unit to uncover problems and suggest improvements to expedite vehicular and pedestrian movement and parking; and determining facts about accident occurrence as a basis for both accident prevention and service to involved citizens to obtain justice in civil settlements of accident losses.[39]

## Criminal Investigation

The criminal investigator (detective) is a police specialist who concentrates on the apprehension and conviction of adult criminal offenders. Unlike most other police units, this specialist group has as its primary goal the apprehension of the offender rather than the prevention of crime. The primary responsibilities of this unit are (1) identification, location, and arrest of criminal offenders; (2) collection and preservation of physical evidence; (3) location of witnesses; (4) recovery and return of stolen property; and (5) case preparation and testifying in court.[40]

The criminal investigative unit is necessary because long-term continuing investigations cannot be accomplished by the patrol force without seriously depleting that unit's personnel. Often, the patrol unit conducts preliminary investigations and even complete investigations when feasible. However, given the present operating characteristics of most municipal police departments, the detectives must take over most sustained investigations.

Organization

In smaller departments a single investigative generalist handles most of the investigations; in larger departments the detective unit is subdivided into specialized subunits. The administrative recommendation in recent years has been to divide the detective unit into three specialist groups; (1) the crimes-against-persons unit; (2) the crimes-against-property unit; and (3) the general-assignment section.[41]

The crimes-against-persons unit conducts investigations when a person is the victim of a crime—for example, murder, forcible rape, robbery, or assault. The crimes-against-property unit conducts investigations that involve the loss of property. Such crimes as burglaries, larcenies, and motor vehicle theft fall into this category. The general-assignment section conducts all other investigations, such as fraud cases or general "con" games, embezzlement, and bad checks. Although this is a recommended organization for many of the medium-to-large city police departments in the United States, the very largest cities may need a greater degree of specialization. For example, New York City has special units that handle nothing but burglaries, homicides, and similar crimes. Even burglaries may be further broken down into business/commercial and residential.

There is a lot of misunderstanding on the part of the public as to the functions that police investigators perform. To examine this question the Rand Corporation has examined the operations of detective units.[42] Although Rand concentrated on the activities of the Kansas City, Missouri, Police Department, similar findings have resulted from the study of the detective function in other police agencies.

What police
investigators do

On the average, detectives in Kansas City spent about 56 percent of their time on "case work"—activities that could be related to specific reported crimes. Another 14 percent of their time was devoted to general administrative work that did not relate to specific cases. Only about 2 percent of their time was spent on general surveillance, crime prevention, and other services not related to specific cases.

Interviewing witnesses was the most time-consuming of the case-related activities conducted by Kansas City detectives. In fact, about one-third of all "case-work" time was spent interviewing witnesses—particularly in cases of property crimes.

Report writing was the second most time-consuming activity. About 25 percent of Kansas City detectives' case-related time was spent in writing reports. Report writing was a major use of time for all investigative units. Interrogation of suspects and attempts to locate suspects and witnesses were also major case-related activities in terms of the proportion of investigators' time they entailed. Interrogation of suspects took a higher percentage of the case-related time of detectives in units investigating property crimes. Attempts to locate suspects and witnesses were especially time-consuming for investigators of sex crimes. Such activities as surveillance and crime-scene searches, arrest, arraignment, time spent with prosecutors, and time spent in court took relatively small amounts of the investigators' cases-related functions.[43]

The amount of time that detectives spend on various types of crimes depends on three factors: the frequency with which the type of crime is reported; the difficulty detectives have in "clearing" cases of that type; and the priority that police attach to crimes of that type. Reports of crimes against property are much more numerous than reports of crimes against persons. Generally, however, crimes against persons receive more attention from detectives because these crimes are considered more serious and are easier to clear. They are generally easier to clear because the victim is an eye witness and the police are more likely to obtain information about the identify of the offender.

---

 **GIVING THE DETECTIVE FUNCTION A SECOND LOOK**

The media have presented an image of the detective as that of a clever, persistent, street-wise, and experienced police officer who may spend weeks on a case tracking down the offender through a Sherlock Holmesian combination of experience, contacts, and deductive reasoning. All in the best mold of the fictional whodunit.

Research conducted since 1970 on the investigative function rejects this picture. Instead, what emerges is the portrayal of a group of police specialists who among other things are often not particularly well selected for the job of criminal investigation; who contribute less to the solution of crimes than their numbers in police departments would warrant; who "solve" very few crimes in their case loads; and who make scant use of indirect evidence such as fingerprints, toolmarks, and the like.

For example, the most extensive study of police investigative practices ever conducted was undertaken by the Rand Corporation supported by the U.S. Department of Justice. The results of this two-year study were published in the late 1970s. Their analyses of investigative units in police departments throughout the country can be summarized in the following conclusions:

- Arrest and clearance rates by police departments are unreliable measures of the effectiveness of the detective function. The vast majority of clearances are produced by activities of patrol officers, by the availability of or identification of the perpetrator at the scene of the crime, or by routine police procedures rather than by skilled detective work.
- Although serious crimes are invariably investigated, many reported felonies receive no more than superficial attention from investigators. Most minor crimes are not investigated.
- Many police departments collect more physical evidence than can be productively processed. Allocating more resources to increasing the processing capabilities of the department is likely to lead to more identifications than some other investigative functions.
- In many large departments, detectives do not consistently and thoroughly document the key evidentiary facts that reasonably assure that the prosecutor can obtain a conviction on the most serious applicable changes.

Such findings should not come as a surprise to many experienced police personnel. The same criticisms were voiced by Raymond Fosdick's study of police departments, which was published as far back as 1921. For whatever reasons, these earlier findings were for the most part ignored. Today, however, at least among some of the more progressive police departments, the detective function is being looked at more closely. Although resisted by police detectives and supported in their resistance by some police unions, a few police administrators are making important changes. These include assigning more of the investigative responsibilities to uniformed officers at the scene, the paring back of large numbers of police personnel assigned to the detective bureau, and instituting new methods of accountability by which investigators can be judged and held responsible for their time and efforts.

As a result of these changes, the days of glory for the detective may be waning. We could be approaching a day when the uniformed officer on patrol is increasingly rewarded and recognized as the true backbone of the police department.

---

Not all case work is directed toward the identification of offenders. In fact, for cases that are cleared (that is, cases for which the police identify a suspect they believe to have been responsible for the crime), the total amount of time spent on the case work *after* clearance generally exceeds the time spent in clearing the case. This is the result of the work that investigators must perform in arrest, arraignment (preliminary hearing) investigations, and reports for prosecution and court testimony.[44]

The Rand researchers examined "special action" investigative techniques employed by the Kansas City detectives. These were defined as any activity involving investigator initiative or insight beyond the routine use of initial identification or identification through unsolicited tips, use of mug shots and line ups, matching of *modus operandi* (characteristics) of unsolved cases with cases already cleared, inadvertent discovery of stolen goods, or volunteered confessions. They concluded that no more than 3 percent of the Kansas City clearances involved more than routine investigative work.[45] A review of similar situations in other cities found similar low percentages of cases cleared through nonroutine methods.[46] It seems that most of the investigative efforts and methods of solving cases that detectives use are standard and routine.

In recent years, many police departments have undertaken organizational changes that have somewhat modified the traditional operations of the criminal investigation unit. In the first place, detectives are more often generalists who no longer are assigned to investigate only certain offenses but are required to be proficient investigators in a wider range of crimes. Second, patrol personnel are performing more and more the investigative functions formerly assigned to the detective unit.[47]

### Juvenile or Youth Bureau

Broadening involvement

Because a large percentage of police encounters involve juveniles, many police departments have created specialized juvenile units or youth bureaus to deal specifically with youth activities that directly affect the police.[48]

The specific responsibilities of such a unit are many. Not only do they deal with police-related problems involving juveniles, a well-run unit of this type also acts as liaison between the police and such other agencies as the juvenile court and youth and welfare service agencies.

In recent years, police juvenile units have begun to adopt policies that place them more in line with the broader philosophy of the juvenile justice system. In this way they are becoming more broadly involved with *all* aspects of juvenile problems rather than merely their traditional enforcement function. For example, they are working more actively with the juvenile courts and other agencies on programs to deter juveniles from committing crimes. Many such police agencies are also taking a larger role in situations involving neglected, dependent, or abused children. In many cases children who have been victimized and abused by their parents first come to the attention of the police. The police in many communities are taking an active role in identifying such children, bringing these problems to the attention of the juvenile court, and investigating and assisting in the prosecution of parents or adults who abuse such children.

The police are also becoming more involved in other areas as well. For instance, the revised juvenile code for the state of Washington was in large part developed by the police.[49] Because many of the crime problems the police must face involve juvenile offenders, the importance of the police role in this area cannot be overlooked.

## Community Relations and Crime Prevention

The issue of police–community relations (PCR) has assumed particular importance for the police in recent years. Until the 1950s, the concept of a formal community relations unit was virtually unknown in police departments, but by the late 1960s some far-reaching changes had been made. During the tumultuous 1960s, social unrest attracted the attention of four presidential and numerous local commissions; it was the subject of countless studies, articles, books, and speeches. As a result of this pressure, police departments began to adopt community relations programs.[50]

These initial PCR programs were concerned basically with police–minority relations. The police took two approaches to dealing with problems in this area, neither of which proved to be very successful. The first approach was to try to establish better relations with urban minority citizens. Police representatives might meet with such citizen groups to discuss problems and let minority groups explain their hostility and frustration with the police. Often, the police were defensive and uncomfortable in such situations. Sometimes militant and radical elements attended such meetings and purposely created an atmosphere of confrontation with the police in attendance.

It also made little difference what the PCR unit said and did; continued tactics of harassment, abuse, and lack of civility by other members of the police department in their daily contact with minority groups usually destroyed the efforts of this special unit. In too many instances, PCR efforts were denigrated by police personnel themselves. Police often viewed such efforts as worthless at best and as pandering to special interests at worst. Many police officers did not view such activities as part of what they thought real police work should be.

The second approach that PCR programs took was a public relations effort. The purpose of such efforts was to make the police department look good to the citizens. It was simply a "look at all we do for you" approach. Of course, such efforts did nothing to change the attitudes of those in the community who were already alienated from the police.

It is really questionable how sincere many police departments and police officials were about these programs. Because many of these programs and units were created in an atmosphere of crisis, token commitment seemed to be maintained only as long as the crisis was remembered and "pressures" were put on the police by city officials to "do something." All the while, low budgets, a large proportion of token black officers assigned to such programs, PCR training programs and issues divorced from the rest of the police training curriculum, the employment of civilians, and other characteristics openly communicated to police personnel that community relations programs were simply "window dressing."

Looking back at these programs today, most observers feel that, as used by most police agencies, PCR programs were more than a form of "public relations" gimmickry. As one such observer says:

> [A] good many of these divisions [police–community relations units] have been poorly organized, lack real constructive programs and guidelines for constructive improvement of police–community relations, and are merely "eye wash" to impress city officials and the public in general. ... Many have jumped on the bandwagon of police–community relations without knowing or preparing to handle the problems

*History*

*Weaknesses*

and obstacles that must be resolved in order to realize any of the potential benefits. This then seems to be the state of police–community relations at the present time.[51]

In recent years police–community relations programs have been remade into police crime-prevention programs. Perhaps this has occurred as a natural evolution: The police, being very uncomfortable with the concept of PCR, wanted something to use as a public relations effort that satisfied their concept of what they were all about and what they think they understand—crime. After all, it is much easier to focus on crime-prevention efforts—particularly if such efforts are directed at those segments of society such as the businessman and the middle-class homeowner, who are much more positively disposed toward the police to begin with—than it

## HOUSTON TAKES ANTI-FEAR TACK TO HELP POLICE BE EFFECTIVE

HOUSTON—Two years ago, Northline Park was in big trouble. Its residents were disturbed by hoodlums in the local park and speeders on the streets.

Burglaries, car thefts and petty crimes were common. Littered lots and junked cars gave the northern Houston community—a flat, lower middle class area of one-story homes and modest apartment buildings—a look of steady deterioration.

Homeowners felt the Houston police either couldn't do anything—or didn't want to. The fear of crime, both real and imagined, had begun to affect everyone—white, black and Hispanic alike.

That is why the Houston Police Department selected Northline Park as one of five target areas for its Fear of Crime Reduction Program in 1983. The purpose of this year-long experiment, directed by the Police Foundation in Washington, D.C., was to devise ways to reduce the fear of crime. It seems to have succeeded.

Houston began by consulting with crime-fighting officials in other cities. Houston police then decided to test five Fear Reduction strategies: a crime newsletter, door-to-door surveys, a police mini-station, community group organizing

and a victims follow-up program.

The goal in Northline Park was to establish a police community service station and to organize citizen cleanup and crime-prevention efforts. By becoming more visible and eliminating "signs of crime"—vandalism, abandoned vehicles, rowdy juveniles—the department hoped to make residents feel safer.

Houston police had a reputation for knocking heads, not shaking hands, however, so no one wanted to be the first to walk into the store-front station that opened in a strip mall on Nording Street in October 1983.

Officer Robin Kirk, a crusty, street-smart cop assigned to head the station, still remembers the initial encounter between the police and 150 citizens at Northline Park's first community meeting in February 1984.

"All the people were silent. They were scared, and a lot of officers were, too. So we set out to break down the barriers."

It took a year to do it, but Kirk, a community organizer and several patrol officers, working closely with residents, succeeded in turning Northline around.

The park was cleared of trouble-markers through the efforts of undercover officers and a vigorous

school truancy program. Now offduty patrolmen join residents for weekend baseball games. Speeders were ticketed, vacant lots were cleaned up by the city and abandoned cars were towed away. A monthly newsletter with crime prevention tips and information was circulated to raise awareness of actual crime levels. Gradually, Northline residents, encouraged by the police, began to take a renewed interest in revitalizing their area.

Homeowners have now formed Neighborhood Watch organizations, helped make their houses and businesses burglar-proof and started giving police tips that have led to the arrest of criminals.

The monthly community meetings, which attract standing-room-only crowds, have turned into back-slapping handshaking affairs where citizens and cops can talk about local concerns and how to deal with them. Officers also do voluntary fingerprinting of schoolchildren, and elderly citizens can attend free weekly blood pressure-testing clinics.

The people who live in Northline Park say they can see the marked change that has saved their community from thugs.

"We were a rough neighborhood, but now we've gotten pretty quiet," is to deal through PCR with the causes of hostility toward the police as expressed by urban poor and minority groups.

Even, however, with the move into crime-prevention programs, problems have developed. Although many police crime-prevention units have been established, their effectiveness, too, has been limited. Going to businesses and conducting security audits of the premises or etching serial numbers on TV sets or other expensive items of personal property owned by suburban homeowners is easy enough. The police can be quite "successful" in these kinds of efforts. On the other hand, more meaningful efforts at crime prevention—particularly when it involves police–citizen activities such as neighborhood patrols, especially in minority neighborhoods—present a different set of problems. In these situations, the mutual hos-

Earl Greenshield says.

"Our crime has dropped down tremendously. (Burglaries over a six-month period fell from 84 in August 1984 to 21 in February 1985.) We can get work done a lot quicker in the neighborhood with the community station. We'd never been close to our policemen, but now we can talk to them like friends."

The police involved in the Fear Reduction Program say their attitudes have changed, too.

"Our officers feel a lot better about themselves," Kirk explains. "They have more of a sense of caring for the citizens in the community, and they know there are people who are concerned about them and support them."

The community station in Northline Park proved so popular that the police department has been flooded by more than 150 requests for storefront stations. Plans are now being made to open others throughout the city.

One of the most effective strategies for reducing fear of crime, according to police, was the Direct Citizen Contact program, or "Avon Strategy," where patrol officers went knocking on doors to ask residents about their concerns and what the police could do to help. Community Organizing Response Teams were also used by the department to encourage citizens to meet with officers in their homes and discuss problems over a cup of coffee. Later citizens committees were set up to find ways to solve those problems using city, police and community resources.

Although the results of the Fear Reduction study are still being analyzed by the Police Foundation, Houston is firmly committed to combatting the fear of crime through close police–citizen teamwork.

"I see our role as one that's broader than the traditional role of police," explains Houston Police Chief Lee P. Brown, who brought the concept of community-oriented policing to Houston when he took over the troubled department three years ago.

"We are a service agency existing to improve the quality of life, so we have to address all community problems not just the traditional crime-fighting problems. We want to be part of the community. We want our officers to be problem-solvers rather than incident-responders."

Encouraged, the city's business community has thrown its support behind the police department.

"We look at it as an investment of the company," explains Ed Lively, a vice-president at Conoco, which printed 100,000 Operation Identification brochures for citywide distribution. "We feel a certain responsibility as a corporate citizen to do what we can to improve conditions in the community."

The city's crime rate has gone down in the past two years, and although it is too early to establish a clear link, Chief Brown says he believes that increased community involvement has contributed to that.

More important, Houston residents say they feel better about living in their city. Three years ago, 27 percent of the Houstonians questioned in a Rice University poll conducted by Dr. Stephen L. Klineberg said that crime was the city's biggest problem, and only 32 percent said they felt the police were doing a good job in protecting citizens.

Last month, a similar poll revealed what Klineberg terms a "tremendous change." Only 15 percent of those questioned said they still felt crime was their major concern, and 50 percent gave the police high marks for performance.

—by Claudia Capos

tilities and antagonisms are present. The police have always operated with a high concern for secrecy and, as a result, they have tended to try and insulate themselves from "outsiders." Now they are being asked to cooperate and work closely with citizen groups in a mutually shared effort. Because crime problems are very serious in minority neighborhods, prevention activities would seem to be naturally targeted for these areas. Yet the bottom line is that *these are minority neighborhoods.* Although many police administrators grudgingly acknowledge that citizen involvement is crucial in dealing with the problems of crime, they often have problems convincing themselves and almost always have problems convincing the police personnel under their command of the importance of this two-way relationship. And as in the case with earlier PCR programs, many police personnel in our large cities are now denigrating the value of police crime-prevention programs as "useless," "just another attempt at PR," or something "dreamed up by the chief to satisfy city hall and certain elements and do-gooders in the community."

### Vice, Organized Crime, and Intelligence

In some larger agencies, the problems and responsibilities of enforcing vice laws, dealing with organized crime, and gathering intelligence in these areas are handled by specialized units. Vice is often the responsibility of a small group of investigative specialists, with organized crime and intelligence gathering the responsibility of another group. However, many police agencies now recognize that there is often a direct relationship between vice activities in a community and organized crime, so that these formerly separate functions are typically made the responsibility of a single unit.

Ineffectiveness

The effectiveness of any police department, particularly a small specialist subunit, in these areas is questionable. Local police must overcome formidable problems in dealing with these types of crime. The first problem is that local police departments simply do not have the trained personnel, investigative equipment, or jurisdictional authority to counteract organized crime efforts. The federal agencies have demonstrated that successful organized crime investigations require extensive personnel commitments, the availability and use of technical and legal investigative resources, and a sizable operating budget.[52] In addition, organized crime efforts transcend local jurisdictional boundaries; therefore local law enforcement is hampered in conducting the necessary multijurisdictional investigations.[53]

Another major problem area that must be addressed when considering the problems of local efforts against organized crime is corruption among police and other local public officials. This has long hampered effective local investigations and prosecutions of organized crimes.[54] A final impediment is the traditional organization of local police departments and a general police reluctance to exchange intelligence between departments or even to share it among members of the same police agency. The President's Commission points this out when it says:

> The apparent versatility exhibited by professional criminals suggests that the traditional organization of police agencies into specialized squads such as robbery, burglary, auto theft, and bunco requires reconsideration. It suggests also the need for a much greater degree of communication between law enforcement agents with information on professional criminals. Detectives tend to be too reluctant to share their information sources with other detectives or to supply information to any centralized intelligence unit which may exist. Also the traditional complaint orientation of police

departments is not appropriate for dealing with persons who are engaged continuously, rather than episodically in criminal activities.[55]

As a consequence, most vice, organized crime, and intelligence units in local police departments are relegated to making isolated and unimportant arrests of small-time narcotics dealers, prostitutes, and other low-level criminal operatives.

## Internal Investigations

Since the 1960s, many persons outside law enforcement have urged the establishment of civilian review boards that would investigate complaints against police personnel. Undoubtedly, this demand has been prompted by feelings that the police have avoided making fair and vigorous investigations of wrongdoing within their ranks.

The function of an internal investigations unit is to investigate complaints against police personnel or other actions that may bring disrepute to the agency. This includes interviewing the complainant, any witnesses, and the police officer(s) involved, and presenting all the evidence to the police internal trial board or the prosecutor if the investigation reveals that the allegation of police misconduct is justified and criminal in nature. Specifically, the responsibilities of such a unit include making appropriate inquiry of the following:

*Function*

1. Any allegation or complaint of misconduct made by a citizen or other person against the department or any of its members.
2. Any alleged or suspected breach of integrity or case of moral turpitude from whatever source it may be reported or developed.
3. Any situation in which an officer has been killed or injured by the deliberate or willful act of another person.
4. Any situation in which a person has been injured or killed by an officer either on or off duty.
5. Any situation involving the discharge of firearms by an officer.
6. In addition, other delegated responsibilities might include: (a) assisting in any disciplinary case when requested by police management personnel; (b) assisting any member of the department by investigating cases of harassment, threats, or false accusations against the officer; and (c) fully advising citizen complainants of the decisions and actions taken following receipt of complaints.[56]

In larger agencies, the internal investigations unit should consist of a small group of carefully chosen and experienced personnel—police officers who possess the highest principles of professionalism and personal integrity. In smaller departments, the task of inquiry may be turned over to a trusted investigator; in some small agencies, the chief of police personally conducts such inquiries.

The police in recent years are lashing back at internal affairs units. Police complain that they have fewer rights when they are called before internal affairs investigators than do criminals who are brought before judges. Police unions throughout the country, as representatives of the rank-and-file of police personnel, are pressing for safeguards against what they regard as violations of officers' rights.[57] Yet many police administrators feel that such operations are the only means they have to deal effectively with the ever-present danger of police corruption.[58] In a

*Surrounding controversy*

## INTERNAL AFFAIRS: WHEN THEY WORK THE POLICE FEAR AND HATE THEM

When Officer Joe Estes reported for roll call, his sergeant handed him a terse note. "Report to Sergeant Williamson in the Internal Affairs Division at 9:00 A.M. tomorrow." Oh shit, Estes thought, what do they want? For the rest of the night's shift, Estes nervously replayed everything that he could possibly have done the past six months; things that could possibly get him in trouble with "those damn IAD types."

"Internal Affairs." To cops these words can be ominous. To many police officers the "headhunters" are fellow cops to be avoided at all costs either officially on the job and even socially during off-duty. Begun in the 1950s and early 1960s in response to growing citizen complaints, many police departments of any size now have them. Contrast this to a survey that was conducted in 1967 among police departments serving communities of over one hundred thousand people. At the time of the survey only twenty-seven such local police departments nationwide had an Internal Affairs unit.[a]

Internal Affairs Units have three main investigative functions—investigating citizen complaints, examining alleged violations of internal regulations, and investigating corruption. The first responsibility takes up most of their time; the last the least amount. It is also that last area in which IAD units perform least efficiently.

In many departments Internal Affairs [personnel] sit in no-man's land. On the one hand, they might be pressured by the chief and the mayor to control police abuses. On the other hand, they are seen as pariahs by their fellow police officers. The word in some departments is: "Don't cooperate with the IAD unless you absolutely have to." Although the police fight these internal tugs of war, they are often not respected or trusted by the community to do their job. Many citizens—particularly among minority groups—have absolutely no faith in their integrity or role. The fact that cops might investigate other cops and substantiate wrongdoing is widely dismissed by citizens.

The problems don't end here. The police unions and associations have been fighting IAD units for years. Such efforts as forcing officers to take lie detector tests, to appear before hearing boards, and to be forced to cooperate with investigating personnel in the giving of statements and other evidence have been widely attacked by these labor groups. Many unions, as part of their labor agreement with a city, have gotten the provision that no citizen complaint will be acted on unless there is a formal written charge or affidavit filed by the citizen. Some police observers note that such policies are designed solely to discourage citizen complaints. No one convincingly argues that this doesn't occur.

One of the biggest problems IAD people have is proving the citizen's allegation. Many times it is only the word of the citizen against the officer(s). Without additional unbiased corroborative evidence, the word of the police officer will be believed. Although this may not be acceptable practice to many citizens, there is simply no other way such allegations can be handled.

[a]Mentioned in Kevin Krajick, "Police Versus Police," *Police Magazine* (May 1980): 7.

number of cities, such as Detroit, the issue of internal affairs has become a political football. Such groups as minority citizens and certain elected officials come out strongly in favor of aggressive actions by police internal affairs investigators, whereas police personnel bitterly oppose the policies. Such polarization is then carried over into support or nonsupport of mayoral candidates and other elected officials. As police unions and associations gain in strength, the issues surrounding this controversial police function are certain to create widespread attention in the years ahead.

 ## POLICE TRAINING

The training of police personnel has made significant strides in recent years. Helped in large part by federal grants, states now require that police personnel obtain a minimum level of mandatory training. To accomplish this, states have established certified police training programs and facilities for training police officers. Although in most states police training programs and efforts are still not nearly as extensive as licensing requirements for barbers, beauticians, and undertakers, they are far more extensive than what existed twenty years ago. Although training requirements and programs still vary drastically from small city police departments and rural sheriff's agencies to major big city and state police organizations, at least efforts have been made to ensure that all police personnel receive a minimum exposure to basic training. The practice of giving a new police officer a gun, badge, nightstick, and ticketbook and telling him to go out and enforce the law (while carefully admonishing him to "stay out of trouble until you get some experience") is for the most part of a thing of the past.

Changes in police training

A comprehensive basic police training program covers a wide range of subjects, from the study of statutes and criminal law to how to deal with disturbed persons. Some of the more typical subjects police officers study are firearms training; accident investigation; defensive tactics; emergency first aid; note taking and report writing; court organization, procedure, and effective testifying; basic investigative techniques; laws of evidence; and collection, care, identification, and preservation of evidence.[59]

In the past, police training programs emphasized four major areas—law and related issues, firearms proficiency; physical training, and defense tactics—but modern police training school curricula places increased emphasis on sociopsychological areas. Such topics as police–community relations, racial and minority groups, effective techniques of crisis intervention, police–citizen encounters, and police ethics are now important parts of many training school programs.

## POLICE LABORATORIES

Only a few very large police departments maintain crime laboratory facilities. Both staffing requirements and the need for expensive equipment for evidence analysis preclude smaller police departments from conducting forensic examinations as an aid in criminal investigations. Many medium-size police departments use evidence technicians, who are usually specially trained police personnel, to conduct rudimentary examinations of crime scenes. Their equipment and skills are usually limited to the use of various types of cameras, the development of a police photographic darkroom, latent (invisible) fingerprint analysis capabilities, and perhaps some infrared equipment, such as night vision devices.

The FBI maintains an excellent crime laboratory in Washington, to which local, state, and federal police agencies can submit evidence for analysis. In recent years, states have been developing state crime labs to assist state and local police personnel. Some states, such as California and Ohio, maintain a system of regionalized crime labs in which evidence can be examined and forensic scientists who examined the evidence are available to testify as expert witnesses in local criminal cases.

Forensic science is playing a larger role in police investigative techniques and case prosecution today than ever before. For example, a few years ago in the Atlanta murder trial of Wayne Williams, who was convicted of the murders of the last two victims in a string of twenty-eight killings of young blacks in that city, the prosecution relied heavily on the Georgia state crime lab's work in fiber analysis. In this case, the laboratory experts matched fibers found on the two victims to fibers obtained from the defendant's bedroom.

During the past twenty years, perhaps a quarter of a million police officers have received some sort of college training. Much of this was made available through the now defunct Law Enforcement Education Program (LEEP), a federal program that provided grants and loans to in-service and preservice students who were either in a criminal justice occupation or sought a career in this area.

It was the police who particularly benefited from this program. Yet our local and state police are relatively ill trained and poorly educated compared to many of their counterparts in Western Europe and Japan. In most U.S. police departments, with but a few exceptions, the high school diploma or its equivalent is the basic requirement.

College education for police personnel has always been a sensitive issue. There are those—many of whom don't have a college degree among the police ranks, but some who do—who are openly critical of the value of a college education. The adage "It's common sense on the streets that's important; not someone with a college degree" is often their argument. Perhaps to some extent they are right. Research has never been able to conclusively demonstrate that a college degree makes someone a "better police officer" in spite of the numerous attempts to show a relationship between the two.

A college education has often been a divisive issue in many departments. Police officers with college degrees typically find that most departments don't recognize their degrees when it comes to promotional opportunities or choice of assignment. Personnel decisions often revolve around three factors: seniority, test scores on police exams, and internal politics. This is particularly frustrating to ambitious and well-educated officers. As a result, many of these officers grow bitter and cynical or leave law enforcement for more challenging careers. The issue often creates friction in the departments between those who are college-educated and those who are not. As one college-educated officer in a Midwestern city said: "The whole system's bullshit. It's geared for the average nonachiever who can make it on 'points' in a questionable exam process that rewards seniority, being one of the good ol' boys, and brownnosing. Those are the kind that generally get promoted."

In examining the question of police education, *Police Magazine* may have been right on target when it stated:

> Privately, many observers think that the greatest resistance to college education for police may come from the police themselves. While chiefs and other officials pay lip service to the concept of higher education, many of them fear that well-educated critically thinking officers may upset the status quo.[a]

There are also questions about the type of education that many of the nation's police officers received. When the federal funds became available, many two- and four-year colleges scrambled to create "police science" or "criminal justice" degree programs. Ill-conceived and hastily established with retired police or FBI members as instructors, these programs—particularly those at some community and junior colleges and some undistinguished lower-level four-year private colleges—became "diploma mills." In many instances these programs catered to police officers and other in-service criminal justice employees and lacked intellectual substance. In the classroom the more controversial and pressing social issues of the day were avoided in order not to offend the conservative nature and views of many police officers in attendance. Instruction was of the training school variety with little that would approach the academic rigor of other degree programs or at other colleges and universities. Today, many of these problems are behind us, yet an uneasy alliance still exists between higher education and the police, who are still often suspicious of the value of college training. Many officers with college educations still find that they must downplay their education to be acceptable to their peers and supervisory and management personnel. Yet cracks have been made. Captain Chris Wilkerson of the Denver, Colorado, Police Department, though not devaluing common sense as an important police attribute, believes that "All things being equal, the officer with the best education should have the advantage. . . . If I had to choose I'd select the one with the liberal arts degree." Likewise, San Jose, California, Police Chief Joseph McNamara, who holds a doctorate in public administration, agrees with Wilkerson. "All things being equal, it makes sense to have [a college-educated] police officer in today's society," he says. "There's no panacea about a college degree, but police officers should be up to the community's educational standards."[b]

[a]Philip B. Taft, Jr., "College Education for Police: The Dream and the Reality," *Police Magazine* 4 (November 1981): 9–20.

[b]Ibid., p. 17.

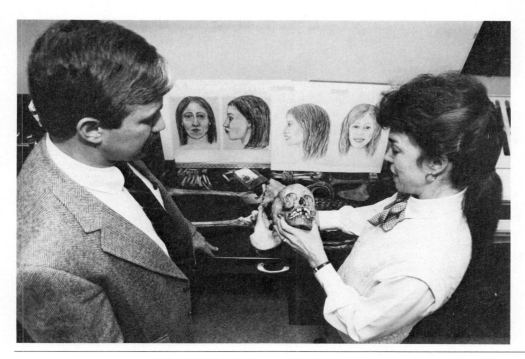

Law enforcement agencies engage forensic specialists, like this Georgia forensic anthropologist (right), to aid in evaluation of evidence. (© Walter Stricklin/Stock South)

In police work the forensic specialty area of criminalistics is used most often. Criminalistics is the examination of bloodstains, clothing, glass, hair, bullets, and **Criminalistics** other "trace evidence" obtained from crime scenes. The police also often use a second forensic specialty area in their work, document examination. Even the other five forensic specialties—forensic toxicology (analysis of poisons and other toxic substances introduced into the human system), forensic pathology (the examination of the bodies of people who have died under questionable circumstances), forensic psychiatry, forensic physical anthropology (the examination of skeletal remains of persons whose identity or cause of death is questioned), and forensic odontology (the identification of a corpse through dental examination), have been receiving more attention by the police in recent years.[60] This seems to be an expanding area in which well-trained young men and women with scientific backgrounds might find important career opportunities in the years ahead.

As we have seen in this chapter, the police role is both very broad and very important to our society. It has been only in recent years that we have begun to examine systematically the broad functions of the police and how they operate. There are some changes occurring both in the definition of this role and how the police accomplish their many responsibilities. It has been said that too many police agencies still operate in many important ways as they did fifty years ago. One must pause and wonder how this must certainly change during the next half-century. Perhaps the accelerating changes are already visible. Chapter 6 will examine some of these developing possibilities.

In 1911 Caesar Cella, alias Charles Crispi, was convicted of burglary. What was a commonplace conviction rested on an uncommon application of a new technology. Crispi's conviction was based on a new type of evidence: The ridges of his fingers formed an impression that matched prints found at the scene of the crime. This was the first instance of the use of fingerprints as evidence at a trial.

Today, fingerprints are but a small and inconspicuous part of the new technology that law enforcement and the courts are employing to combat crime. Forensic science now employs a wide array of technology and scientific applications, including the use of electron microscopes to examine minute traces of evidence, X-ray diffraction, uncovering latent (invisible) fingerprints with lasers, and matching voices with computers programmed to recognize speech patterns. In the 1970s, a new technique known as neutron activation analysis (NAA) burst on the scene. This permits the analysis of organic substances by the atomic particles they give off, which makes the matching of evidence practically foolproof.

In arson cases, a new polymer called Tenax can be used to detect as much as one millionth of a liter of gasoline. Even footprints are becoming accepted as a means of identification. In handwriting analysis, a new machine can distinguish between near-perfect matches.

The most recent and most publicized technology is DNA profiling.

DNA itself is an organic substance found primarily in the nucleus of living cells. It comprises the chromosomes within the nucleus and provides the genetic code that determines a person's individual characteristics. Scientists can examine body fluids and tissue specimens and make comparisons. The analyst can identify a particular individual based on a drop of blood or semen or a single hair. Although the technique has not yet been perfected, it holds great promise for the police if a system is developed to classify DNA test results, catalog them, and later conduct a search comparing them with other test results. Scientists working on DNA analysis claim that the chance for a mismatch is a billion to one.

The legal system requires that any new such technology be "reliable and trustworthy" by the scientific community before it is accepted as evidence. It is too soon for DNA "prints" to have satisfied this standard throughout the nation. Even though many American courts are still reluctant to use this type of evidence, it has been used in Britain to convict offenders. Interest is growing in the United States, as seen by a recent Florida case in which a jury convicted a twenty-four-year-old rape suspect whose DNA matched the genetic material of a semen sample taken from the rape victim.

The growing interest in scientific analysis and the use of technology in police work and in the courtroom is documented by a 1986 study by the National Center for State Courts.[61] In this survey of state criminal courts, about one-third of the cases the courts processed involved the use of scientific evidence—almost no such evidence was used twenty years ago.

Two things seem to be causing this increased interest. The first is the fact that technology has exploded in the past twenty years, and this has been carried over to law enforcement and the courts. Associated with this is a greater familiarization and ease with technology and science in our society. A second reason for its increased use in police work is that imposed restrictions on traditional forms of evidence gathered through searches and seizures or confessions and admissions has forced the police and prosecutors to rely more on technology-produced evidence.

Still, such technology is merely an aid rather than an end in itself. Investigative personnel still will have to conduct most investigations in routine and familiar ways. Such technological applications will revolutionize many aspects of the administration of justice, however. The police, prosecutors, defense counsels, and courts will have to familiarize themselves with new techniques and a new language of science. Special care will have to be taken to ensure the continued reliability of those who rely on and use such evidence. This may be the most difficult problem.

## SUMMARY

The law enforcement role of the police involves such activities as crime detection, criminal investigation, search and seizure, arrests, and in-custody interrogations. These functions are not left up to police personnel to determine on their own. The courts have played an important role in providing operating guidelines to which the police are required to conform. If nothing else, these guidelines provide an important as well as a controlling framework for the operational strategies of the police.

How complicated the police role is has come under increasing examination in recent years. What has been discovered is that these guidelines do not always assure that the police will comply with them. This causes many observers of the police to realize how limiting such controls can be. Because the police have so much discretion, they have the latitude to define how they will conform and under what circumstances.

The police have only limited ability to control crime. Although most police personnel identify themselves as primarily "law enforcement" officers, recent research seriously questions the ability of the police to perform effectively in dealing with this problem. The police must be aided by citizens and other components of the criminal justice system if they are to improve their rate of success in this area.

Finally, the major functions and responsibilities of the operating units of a police agency were examined. The units and functions discussed were patrol; crime-specific enforcement units; traffic; criminal investigation; juvenile (youth) bureau; community relations and crime prevention; vice, organized crime, and intelligence; internal investigations; training; and police laboratories.

## REVIEW QUESTIONS

1. What are the three ways in which the police learn of the commission of a crime?
2. In their investigative process the police have three objectives. What are these objectives?
3. Under what circumstances can the police conduct a search without a warrant?
4. What have the following cases signified in police investigative procedures?
   a. *Mapp* v. *Ohio*
   b. *United States* v. *Leon*
   c. *Maryland* v. *Garrison*
   d. *New York* v. *Quarles*
5. What has been the significance of the following cases in police interrogation?
   a. *Escobedo* v. *Illinois*
   b. *Miranda* v. *Arizona*
6. Briefly describe the following police operational styles.

   a. The enforcer
   b. The social service agent
   c. The zealot
   d. The watchman
7. Discuss the implications of the emphasis on "crime fighters" as the role for police agencies.
8. How effective are the police in their crime-fighting role? Discuss.
9. What is the importance of the patrol unit in police departments?
10. An analysis of the detective function has provided some interesting insights. Discuss.
11. What courses might be offered in a typical recruit training program for police officers?
12. What are the responsibilities of an internal investigations unit in looking into a complaint against police personnel?

## DISCUSSION QUESTIONS

1. Do the operational styles described in this chapter seem valid to you? Why or why not?
2. Have court rulings such as *Miranda* v. *Arizona* and *Escobedo* v. *Illinois* made police investigation procedures impossible? Explain.

3. Discuss the organizational arrangement of municipal police departments and the operations of these units.

## SUGGESTED ADDITIONAL READINGS

American Bar Association. *Standards Relating to the Urban Police Function* (Chicago: American Bar Association, 1972).

Bittner, Egon. *The Functions of the Police in Modern Society* (New York: Jason Aronson, 1975).

Bopp, William J. *Police Personnel Administration* (Boston: Holbrook Press, 1972).

Butler, Alan J. *The Law Enforcement Process* (Port Washington, N.Y.: Alfred, 1976).

Cohn, Alvin W., and Emilio C. Viano, eds. *Police–Community Relations: Images, Roles, Realities* (Philadelphia: Lippincott, 1976).

Horne, Peter. *Women in Law Enforcement* (Springfield, Ill.: Charles C. Thomas, 1980).

Klockars, Carl B. *Thinking About Police—Contemporary Readings* (New York: McGraw-Hill, 1983.)

Lundman, R. J. *Police and Policing: An Introduction* (New York: Holt, Rinehart, and Winston, 1980).

Manning, P. K., and J. Van Mannen, *Policing: A View from the Street* (Santa Monica, Calif.: Goodyear, 1978).

Meyer, F. A., and Ralph Baker. *Determination of Law Enforcement Policies* (Lexington, Mass.: Lexington Books, 1979).

Saunders, Charles B. *Upgrading the American Police* (Washington, D.C.: Brookings Institution, 1970).

Shanahan, Donald T. *Patrol Administration—Management by Objectives* (Boston: Holbrook Press, 1975).

Stahl, O. Glenn, and Richard A. Staufenberger, eds. *Police Personnel Administration* (North Scituate, Mass.: Duxbury Press, 1974).

Sykes, Richard E. *Policing: A Social Behavioralist Perspective* (New Brunswick, N.J.: Rutgers University Press, 1983).

Walker, Samuel. *The Police in America* (New York: McGraw-Hill, 1983).

Weston, Paul B. *Police Organization and Management* (Pacific Palisades, Calif.: Goodyear, 1976).

Whisenand, Paul M., and Fred R. Ferguson. *The Managing of Police Organizations*, 2nd ed. (Englewood Cliffs, N.J.: Prentice-Hall, 1978).

———, and Roy C. McLaren. *Police Administration*, 3rd ed. (New York: McGraw-Hall, 1972).

## NOTES

1. *Sorrels* v. *United States*, 287 U.S. 435.

2. This list of objectives is generally taken from John J. Horgan, *Criminal Investigation* (New York: McGraw-Hill, 1974), especially pp. 6–8.

3. Author's note: There are some exceptions and qualifying circumstances in several of these general rules that cannot be discussed in detail here.

4. *United States* v. *Wade*, 388 U.S. 218 (1967) and *United States* v. *Gilbert* 447 F2nd 883 (1971).

5. *Kirby* v. *Illinois*, 406 U.S. 682 (1972).

6. *United States* v. *Ash*, 413 U.S. 300 (1973).

7. *Manson* v. *Brathwaite*, 432 U.S. 98 (1977).

8. Cited in Jerold H. Israel, Yale Kamisar and Wayne R. LaFave, *Criminal Procedure and the Constitution* (St. Paul, MN: West Publishing, 1989), p. 240.

9. *Ashcraft* v. *Tennessee*, 322 U.S. 143 (1944).

10. For example, see Neal Milner, *The Court and Local Law Enforcement: The Impact of Miranda* (Beverly Hills, Calif.: Sage, 1971); Stephen Wasby, *Small-Town Police and the Supreme Court: Hearing the Word* (Lexington, Mass.: Lexington Books, 1976)

11. James S. Kuner, *How Can You Defend Those People? The Making of a Criminal Lawyer* (New York: Random House, 1983), p. 132.

12. J. Shane Creamer, *The Law of Arrest, Search and Seizure* (Philadelphia: Saunders, 1968), p. 48.

13. Ibid., p. 49.

14. See William A. Westley, *Violence and the Police* (Cambridge, Mass.: M.I.T. Press, 1970).

15. Herman Goldstein, *Policing a Free Society* (Cambridge, Mass.: Ballinger, 1977)

16. Ibid., p. 23.

17. See Kenneth Culp Davis, *Discretionary Justice: A Preliminary Inquiry* (Baton Rouge: Louisiana State University Press, 1969), and *Police Discretion* (St. Paul, Minn.: West, 1975); Donald M. McIntyre, Jr., ed., *Law Enforcement in the Metropolis* (Chicago: American Bar Foundation, 1967).

18. A similar typology has been developed by other observers of the police role. See John J. Broderick, *Police in a Time of Change* (Morristown, N.J.: General Learning Press, 1977).

19. See Seymour Martin Lipset, "Why Cops Hate Liberals and Vice-Versa," *The Atlantic* 223 (March 1969): 76–83.

20. W. I. Thomas and Dorothy S. Thomas, *The Child in America* (New York: Knopf, 1928), p. 51.

21. Broderick, *Police in a Time of Change*, p. 57.

22. Also see Joseph J. Senna and Larry J. Seigel, *Introduction to Criminal Justice* (St. Paul, Minn.: West, 1978), especially pp. 176–179.

23. James Q. Wilson, *Varieties of Police Behavior* (Cambridge, Mass.: Harvard University Press, 1968).

24. Ibid., pp. 140–141.

25. Peter K. Manning, "The Police: Mandate Strategies and Appearances," in P. Manning and J. Van Mannen, eds., *Policing: A View from the Street* (Santa Monica, Calif.: Goodyear, 1978), pp. 7–31.

26. For example, see John A. Webster, "Police Task and Time Study," *Journal of Criminal Law, Criminology and Police Science* 61 (1970): 94–100.

27. Egon Bittner, *The Function of the Police in Modern Society* (New York: Jason Aronson, 1976), p. 42.

28. Ibid.

29. Charles E. Sibberman, *Criminal Violence, Criminal Justice* (New York: Vantage Press, 1978), p. 270.

30. Robert J. diGrazia, "Police Leadership:

Challenging Old Assumptions," *Washington Post*, 10 November, 1976, p. 4.

31.  For example, see George L. Kelling, Tony Pate, Duane Dieckman, and Charles E. Brown, *The Kansas City Preventive Patrol Experiment: A Summary Report* (Washington, D.C.: Police Foundation, 1974); Lawrence W. Sherman et al., *Team Policing* (Washington, D.C.: Police Foundation, 1973). For an excellent overall review of the research and issues in police patrol and investigative efficiency, see Kevin Krajick, "Does Patrol Prevent Crime?" *Police Magazine*, September 1978, pp. 3–12; David C. Anderson, "Management Moves in on the Detective," *Police Magazine*, March 1978, pp. 13–19.

32.  These were the general comments of Gerald Caplan and Herman Goldstein when interviewed for an article by Richard S. Allinson, "The Uncertain Future of Police Research," *Police Magazine* 4 (July 1981): 55–56.

33.  James Q. Wilson, *Thinking About Crime* (New York: Basic Books, 1975), p. 111.

34.  For example, see *Felony Arrests: Their Prosecution and Disposition in New York City's Courts* (New York: Vera Institute of Justice, 1977); Brian E. Forst, Judith Lucianovic, and Sarah J. Cox, *What Happens After Arrest?* (Washington, D.C.: Institute for Law and Social Research, 1977).

35.  For general research into patrol activities see the following: William G. Gay, Theodore H. Schell, and Stephen Schack, *Improving Patrol Productivity*, Vol. I: *Routine Patrol* (Washington, D.C.: U.S. Government Printing Office, 1977); James M. Tien, J. W. Simon, and R. C. Larson, *An Alternative Approach in Police Patrol: The Wilmington Split-Force Experiment* (Washington, D.C.: U.S. Government Printing Office, 1978); John A. Webster, "Police Task and Time Study," *The Journal of Criminal Law, Criminology and Police Science* 61 (1970): 94–100; John E. Boydstun, M. E. Sherry, and N. P. Moelter, *Patrol Staffing in San Diego* (Washington, D.C.: Police Foundation, 1977); and George L. Kelling, Tony Pate, Duane Dieckman, and Charles E. Brown, *The Kansas City Preventive Patrol Experiment: A Technical Report* (Washington, D.C.: Police Foundation; 1974).

36.  Charles E. Silberman, *Criminal Violence, Criminal Justice* (New York: Vintage Books, 1978), pp. 321–322.

37.  Richard Baker, "Remember Your Friendly Neighborhood Cop?" *Sky Magazine* 3, No. 7 (July 1974): 21.

38.  Reported in John Van Mannen, "The Asshole," in Manning and Van Mannen, eds., *Policing: A View from the Street*, p. 228.

39.  George D. Eastman, ed., *Municipal Police Administration* (Washington, D.C.: International City Management Association, 1969), p. 106.

40.  N. C. Chamelin, Vernon B. Fox, and Paul M. Whisenand, *Introduction to Criminal Justice* (Englewood Cliffs, N.J.: Prentice-Hall, 1975), p. 120.

41.  For example, see International City Management Association, *Local Government Police Management*, pp. 130–133; and O. W. Wilson and Roy C. McLaren, *Police Administration*, 3rd ed. (New York: McGraw-Hill, 1972), p. 21.

42.  See: Peter W. Greenwood, Jan M. Chaiken, Joan Petersilia, and Linda Prusoff, *The Criminal Investigation Process*, Vol. 3: *Observations and Analysis* (Santa Monica, Calif.: Rand Corporation, 1975); and same authors, *The Criminal Investigation Process* (Lexington, Mass.: D.C. Heath, 1977).

43.  Ibid., p. 51.

44.  As reported in Gordon P. Whitaker et al., *Basic Issues in Police Performance* (Washington, D.C.: National Institute of Justice, July 1982), p. 76.

45.  Ibid., p. 76.

46.  Greenwood, op. cit., pp. 68–77.

47.  See Peter B. Bloch and Donald R. Weidman, *Managing Criminal Investigations* (Washington, D.C.: National Institute of Law Enforcement and Criminal Justice, June 1975).

48.  For a good insight into the role of the police in problems involving juveniles, see Robert C. Trojanowicz, *Juvenile Delinquency: Concepts and Control* (Englewood Cliffs, N.J.: Prentice-Hall, 1973), especially Chap. 7.

49.  See Michael S. Servill, "Police Write a New Law on Juvenile Crime," *Police Magazine* 2 (September 1979): 47–52.

50.  Robert Wasserman, Michael P. Gardner, and Alana S. Cohen, *Improving Police Community Relations* (Washington, D.C.: U.S. Government Printing Office, June 1973), p. 1.

51.  Bernard J. Clark, "Police–Community Relations," in Alvin W. Cohn and Emilo C. Viano, eds., *Police–Community Relations: Images, Roles, Realities* (Philadephia: Lippincott, 1976), pp. 70–76.

52.  Hank Messick, *The Silent Syndicate* (New York: Macmillan, 1967), p. 43.

53.  Gus Tyler, ed., "Combating Organized Crime," *The Annals of the American Academy of Political and Social Science* 347 (May 1963).

54.  For example, see Donald R. Cressey, "Corruption of the Law Enforcement and Political Systems," in John E. Conklin, ed. *The Crime Establishment* (Englewood Cliffs, N.J.: Prentice-Hall, 1973), pp. 131–145.

55.  President's Commission on Law Enforcement and Administration of Justice, *Crime and Its Impact—An Assessment* (Washington, D.C.: U.S. Government Printing Office, 1967), p. 101.

56.  Eastman, *Municipal Police Administration*, pp. 203–204.

57.  Kevin Krajick, "Police vs. Police," *Police Magazine* 3 (May 1980): 7.

58.  Ibid., p. 13.

59.  V. A. Leonard and Harry W. More, *Police Organization and Management*, 6th ed. (Mineola, N.Y.: Foundation Press, 1982), pp. 259–262.

60.  For a good summary of the issues and responsibilities of police laboratories, see Michael S. Serrill, "Forensic Sciences: Overburdened, Underutilized," *Police Magazine* 2 (January 1979): 21–29; and Marc Levinson, "Forensic Fiber Evidence: Is It Enough to Convict?" *Police Magazine* 4 (November 1981): 42–47.

61.  National Center for State Courts, *A Survey of the Use of Forensic Evidence* (Williamsburg, Va.: National Center for State Courts, 1986).

# CHAPTER 6

# Current Issues and Trends

## O B J E C T I V E S

**After reading this chapter, the student should be able to:**

Discuss "change" among police agencies generally.

Identify and discuss some of the organizational changes that are taking place.

Understand the issue of job enlargement as it pertains to organizational health.

Discuss how the police have practiced discrimination in the past in terms of employment and promotional opportunities and how this is now changing.

Identify the issues and concerns over increasing police productivity.

Discuss the problem of police corruption and its various forms.

Be able to discuss developing operational strategies such as directed deterrent patrol, differential police response, and new techniques of intervention in domestic disputes.

Indicate the issues and concerns underlying police decentralization problems.

Identify strategies designed to avoid fragmentation among police departments.

Discuss the growing concern and issues surrounding the use of deadly force by the police.

Discuss issues and trends in liability issues arising out of police misconduct.

Generally answer the questions "How effective are the police?" and "What is police accreditation?"

Discuss the growing field of private security.

## I M P O R T A N T   T E R M S

President's Commission Report, *The Police*

Job enlargement

Affirmative action

Discrimination in personnel practices

Directed patrol strategies

Crime prevention

Police productivity

Differential police response strategies

Police corruption

Conflict management strategies

Crisis intervention

Spousal abuse

Police consolidation

Consolidation of support services

Contract law enforcement

Special squads

Deadly force

Police civil liability

Police accreditation

Private security

The decade from the late 1960s to the late 1970s probably brought more funda- The police and change
mental and far-reaching changes to the police service in America than the entire
preceding century. Much of the impetus for change was a result of the release of
the President's Commission Report, *The Police*, which was published in 1967. This
was the most comprehensive study of law enforcement ever undertaken in the
United States. Its findings and conclusions became a blueprint for change that is
still contemporary. What has been so astounding about the change has been both
its magnitude and the brief span of time in which it has taken place.

Traditionally, change in law enforcement operations and philosophy was very Externally induced change
slow, so slow in fact that it was almost imperceptible, even to close observers. In
the past the police would point to such examples of innovation and change as the
adoption of the automobile or two-way communications systems. These, however,
were merely technological advances superimposed on old traditions, practices, and
philosophies. Today it is these traditions, practices, and philosophies that are the
immediate targets of change, or at least discussion.

When change in law enforcement has occurred, it has usually been brought
about by such *external* sources as the courts or reform groups rather than by the
police themselves. Although these outside influences have brought about many
needed reforms in the police service, such changes, because they are externally
rather than internally induced, have too often been temporary in nature. Once
external pressures relaxed, change had a tendency to decelerate rapidly.

One area of change has been in the organizational structure of police departments. Another was the result of the demand during the 1960s for more effective
police–community relations. A secondary effect of this demand was that affirmative
action programs were begun—often by federal court order in an effort to bring
about better representation of minorities and women in police work. Concern over
the apparent inability of the police to cope with crime has resulted in more attention to crime-prevention programs. Likewise, as the cost of law enforcement has
increased, communities have demanded more cost-effective police operations. In
this chapter, current issues such as police organization, affirmative action, crime
prevention, police corruption, and police liability for improper behavior are reviewed. Trends such as conflict management strategies, consolidation and decentralization, police use of deadly force, and the growth of the private security industry are also examined.

Generally, an observer of the American police service would be pleased with
the changes that have occurred in the past twenty years. Perhaps more than any
other component of the criminal justice system, the police have demonstrated the
capacity to change and to improve. Although this is certainly not true of all police
operations or departments, great strides have generally been made in upgrading
police services and police personnel. In no small way, this is also due to the slow
but steady improvement in police management. New advances are being made in
the use of police resources, and as a result, a better understanding of the police
role in a democratic society is occurring.

There is one danger, however. To sustain change and improvement, demands
for reform must continue. So too must the support for experimentation and strategies that have the potential for improvement. There is the concern that such efforts
significantly slowed during the 1980s. With the dismantling of the Law Enforcement
Assistance Administration (LEAA) and the reduction of federal funds for studies
and experimentation, the police at the local levels may backslide. The one hope is

that the impetus for reform that characterized the late 1960s through the 1970s has built the necessary foundation among police leaders so that the search for better and improved police efforts will continue as a new century dawns.

## ▢ ORGANIZATIONAL CHANGES

**The police and the semimilitary model**

Traditionally, the police have relied on a semimilitary model of organization. The military model, with its emphasis on superior–subordinate relationships, rank structure, discipline, and defined areas of accountability, was supposed to provide the necessary control and supervision over police practices. It was felt that this organizational model was most appropriate for several reasons: (1) The police, like the military, have a practical monopoly on the legal use of force in our society; (2) our English heritage and the perennial fear that if the police were not closely controlled, they might threaten civil liberties; and (3) our experiences during the nineteenth century, when in too many cases, police personnel operated with impunity in their relations with society and toward the commands of their superiors.

Whatever advantages the military model may have had in bringing some form of order and control to the police service, recent years and a growing body of evidence have increasingly demonstrated that the model has some major drawbacks. In the first place, it encouraged rigid bureaucratic behavior. It has been criticized for creating a rigidity in police agencies that is perhaps dysfunctional given the changing role of police today.[1] Rather than encouraging closer community–police interaction, the militaristic model has perpetuated a distance between the police and the public by the wearing of militaristic uniforms, visible rank and insignia of authority, and the use of technology (e.g., motorized patrol). It has certainly encouraged citizens to treat the police officer more as a symbol than as an individual.[2]

It also seems that new officers are often "depersonalized" by being required to suppress individual opinion in favor of assuming what is essentially a uniform personality molded by the department. It does not end here. In fact, in many police agencies, new recruits soon learn that they are rewarded for conformity and for nonthinking compliance with departmental directives and may be reprimanded or punished for minor infractions.

In this environment, the "go along to get along" people are rewarded. This blind adherence to traditional police dogma is becoming more irritating to the growing numbers of college-educated police officers. Although police agencies have been getting an increasing proportion of better-educated young people into their ranks, they still tend to demand the same conformance. As a result, policing as an occupation runs the risk of losing to other careers many young, well-educated officers through their frustration with the operations of the department and the attitudes of police supervisory and managerial personnel. If they are not lost to alternative careers, such officers may remain in police work but become cynical and unmotivated.

Today, some police agencies are attempting to correct these organizational problems by making three basic changes: (1) reorganizing the department so that police officers are more involved with the community; (2) involving police personnel more with the policymaking process of the department; and (3) involving police officers in expanded areas of personal responsibility in an effort to increase their job satisfaction.[3]

## Job Enlargement

The emphasis on increasing job satisfaction has often led to some interesting experiments in organizational change. Under job-enlargement opportunities in such cities as Baltimore, Cincinnati, and Kansas City, police officers in the patrol unit are given the chance to conduct criminal investigations and participate in the

## RECRUITING POLICE FROM COLLEGE

In the spring of 1988, approximately 130 young men and women who had spent two years as police cadets in the New York City Police Department graduated from college. It was the first moment of truth for an ambitious attempt by the department to recruit college graduates into police service.

The program is called the Police Cadet Corps. It is based on the idea that if the city assists young people in paying for their education and gives them a closeup look at police operations, many of them will choose a police career after graduation. It is willing to bet $1 million a year that the program will work out. The cadets are given loans totaling $3,000 toward the expenses of their last two years in college. If they serve at least two years after graduation, the loans are forgiven; if not, they must repay the loans at 3 percent interest.

As cadets, they are paid seven dollars an hour for two summers of full-time work and three days a month during their college years. Most of their service is done as observers with the Community Patrol Officer Program (CPOP) in forty-five of the city's seventy-five precincts. Precinct CPOP units are comprised of seven to ten officers, under the command of a sergeant, who patrol neighborhoods and try to improve the quality of life, as well as arrest criminals. The cadets wear uniforms that are quite similar to patrolmen's, but they carry no weapons and have no law enforcement powers. Like the regular officers, they are issued bulletproof vests.

George Adoff is a typical cadet. He is a senior at City College of New York who is assigned to the 79th precinct in the Bedford-Stuyvesant section of Brooklyn. He is very enthusiastic about the work. "CPOP is a fabulous program. We attended community board meetings, tenant association meetings, block parties. Sometimes we talk to crime victims and tell them about compensation that's available to them. And people would come up to us and tell us about the problems they have with drug dealers or parking. We also escorted senior citizens to the bank because if they went by themselves, it's very likely they would be robbed."

The police department's belief is that college graduates may bring greater sensitivity to the officer's job. The Cadet Corps commander commented, "The feeling is that people who have been exposed to a broad education will be able to handle more things, more confidently, and to understand the things that might be unfolding before his eyes, like the poverty we see, the homelessness."

Some research indicates that in addition to having such intangibles as greater sensitivity, college graduates also perform better than their less-educated colleagues in measures that can be quantified. For example, in a study that compared the first ten years of service by officers who joined the Los Angeles Police Department in 1965, it was found that college graduates did significantly better in the police academy, had fewer sick days and

injured-on-duty days off, were less likely to be disciplined, and were much more likely to be promoted.

The director of the Vera Institute of Justice, who is the chairman of the Police Cadet Advisory Council, which helped to set up the program, noted, "It's an open question, in part because as you might expect, whatever correlations are found between college education and performance measures like promotions, absences, or disciplinary actions, you're stuck with not being able to determine whether it's the college education that makes the difference or whether it's the mix of personality, ambition, and talent that leads people to get a college education."

In addition to all the cadets receiving similar training and having the opportunity to work with the CPOP units on the street, some cadets are given additional opportunities to work in specialized areas according to their education. A computer science major was transferred to police headquarters to work in the department's computer unit for his second summer as a cadet. In that assignment, he helped develop programming packages for the microcomputers slated to be in every precinct. "I had a great time down there," he said, "because the people were excellent and really knew their stuff." Another cadet, a senior majoring in public administration, spent his second summer working at headquarters in the budget unit.

organization and development of community crime-prevention and other programs that under traditional police organization would be the province of specialist units. Baltimore, for example, has experimented with a police agent program in which college-educated police personnel could expect to become police agents after a few years on routine patrol. The police agent is sort of a "supercop," who is expected to handle difficult investigations, perform operations research and planning, and be involved in the development of community programs and other more demanding (and rewarding) aspects of police work.

Increased involvement

In many departments, specialization among police personnel is being deemphasized. Instead, better training is encouraging the growth of the so-called police generalist. Patrol officers, for example, are having their responsibilities enlarged to include more emphasis on conducting preliminary investigations, working with citizen and neighborhood groups in joint crime-prevention activities, and participating with the agency's supervisory and managerial officers in devising better police strategies.

## The Affirmative Action Issue

The issue of discrimination in the personnel policies of police departments and the affirmative action programs that have been used to attract minorities have created a great deal of concern since the early 1970s. Increasingly, police agencies have found themselves involved in litigation over their traditional hiring, promotion, and dismissal policies. The basic issue is whether police agencies have practiced discrimination in their personnel policies of the past and are continuing to do so.

Legal history

**BACKGROUND INFORMATION.** A logical starting point in understanding the history of the affirmative action programs is the Civil Rights Act of 1964.[4] Title VII of this act prohibits discriminatory employment practices. On March 8, 1971, the U.S. Supreme Court issued a landmark decision in *Griggs* v. *Duke Power Company.*[5] This was a suit brought by a group of minority employees of Duke Power Company, who alleged that the firm was in violation of the Civil Rights Act of 1964 because the company, by requiring high school diplomas and the passing of a standard intelligence test for employment and promotion, was discriminating against minorities. The court held that intelligence tests and requirements were discriminatory *unless they could be shown to measure the attributes needed to perform the specific job.*

The Equal Employment Opportunity Act of 1972 extends the 1964 Civil Rights Act, and this legislation has been applied to state and local governments.[6] The federal Equal Employment Opportunity Commission (EEOC) was created to oversee the enforcement of the act, and various states have created their own fair employment practices commissions.

In recent years, suits and countersuits involving the police have sprung up all over the country. In a number of court cases, minority groups have been successful in having police employment examinations ruled discriminatory. In addition, such long-standing police requirements for employment as age, height, weight, sex, arrest record, and other factors have also been successfully challenged in the courts.[7] Unfortunately, the effects of personnel selection have sometimes been negative. For example, the EEOC ruled that the preemployment requirement of a college education by the Arlington, Virginia, police department was discriminatory.[8] Fortunately, the EEOC ruling was later struck down by a lower federal court. In 1989,

Affirmative action has led to the increased hiring of women police officers. (Jim West Photography)

the Supreme Court issued several important decisions dealing with affirmative action issues. Proponents of affirmative action contend that these rulings are chipping away at the gains made in affirmative action over the years.[9]

## Discrimination and Performance

Few would argue that police departments in the past discriminated in their hiring and promotional policies for both minority males and all females. This has been changing. Although change has occurred, it has been much more rapid for minority males than for women in general. Although it is not unusual to find increased numbers of minority males in many police departments and among the command and supervisory structure, women have been much slower to be accepted. Yet change has been forced on police agencies. In a study conducted in the early 1970s, minority males and women *combined* totaled about 4 percent of all sworn personnel in the departments studied.[10] A later study, released in 1981, indicated that among municipal police agencies, women *alone* constituted almost 4 percent of all sworn officers.[11]

*Affirmative action begins to take hold*

Still, there are those who, while admitting that some progress has been made, contend that the integration of minority police officers into the ranks of many departments continues to lag. One recent study compared the minority population of the nation's fifty largest cities with the percentage of minority police personnel employed in these cities. Based on the idea that a city's police force should reflect "proportional representation," it was concluded that overall these cities had police departments with less than their share of minorities on the force as determined by the corresponding percentage of minorities in the city's population.[12]

Some of the problem is based on forced layoffs in certain of these cities. Faced with fiscal problems, some cities such as Detroit and Philadelphia have had to lay off police personnel. Because minority officers (including women) are often those with the least seniority, they are the ones who felt the brunt of the necessary cutbacks.

Although attention was focused on minorities generally in police work, the bulk of attention in recent years has been on women in law enforcement. This includes not only their relative numbers in police departments but perhaps the more interesting question of how well women perform in police roles. This has spawned several notable research efforts to answer this question.

**Female police officers on the street**

Generally, the research has tried to examine how well policewomen perform when compared with men. For purposes of comparison, the laboratory becomes the street. Specifically, how well do women perform in police patrol operations that bring them into contact with a wide variety of persons and situations that require police action? Related to this is a secondary question: Does the traditional role and socialization process of women help or hinder them in the performance of police duties? There is also the question of how the different attributes and characteristics of women are expressed and accepted in what has always been a male-dominated occupation. As might be expected, there are gender-based differences. There are also instances when male and female police officers perform in strikingly similar ways. Studies conducted of female police officers in Washington, D.C., and in New York City discovered some interesting facts. Generally, women performed as well as men even when dealing with citizens who are dangerous, angry, upset, drunk, or violent. Male officers were likely to be slightly more aggressive in initiating police contacts, arrests, and traffic citations. In the Washington, D.C., study policewomen were less likely to be involved in behavior that necessitated departmental disciplinary action. In New York, the public tended to feel that women officers were more competent, pleasant, and respectful than their male counterparts. In most of the other measures used to judge police performance, male and female officers performed similarly.[13]

**Example of female role adaptation**

Yet, there are those who believe that the nature of law enforcement work and the organizational composition of police departments place women under unique forms of personal strain. An interesting piece of research examined two responses among policewomen.[14] One type of female police officer felt the need to overcompensate for being a female. Her role was to outmacho and outperform male police officers to be accepted by the men. Such women, to be accepted as police officers, strongly embrace the prevailing enforcement-oriented view of policing held by the men. Their coping mechanisms do not end here. They adopt a strong emphasis on assertiveness, occupational achievement, and loyalty to the department and other officers. Their loyalty to other department members ends, however, when it comes to other women in the department who do not meet "acceptable" standards. For example, if another policewoman has the reputation among her male colleagues of not being assertive enough or not being a "good police officer," she will find absolutely no sympathy from this type of female officer. In fact, this type of female officer personality strongly resents such a sister officer because her actions are harmful to all female officers.

At the other end of the spectrum is another type of female officer who falls into a group that includes both apathetic officers who are disinterested in their work except as a source of income, and who behave in a traditionally feminine manner, and women who are involved in their work, but struggling with discrimination.[15] These women lack assertiveness and desire to remain "ladies on the job as well as off." As officers, they are uncomfortable with aspects of their occupational roles that require them to control citizens' behavior. Most adopt a service-oriented perspective that is more compatible with their female sex role and that calls for behavior with which they are more familiar and comfortable.

These policewomen are not comfortable on the street. They often acquiesce to the stereotypic roles into which they are cast by men. They gain acceptance by being "pets" or "mascots" or "mother confessors" to the men. They do not socialize with the men off the job and are isolated from the informal activity of the department. Unlike the other type of female officer, they are much less career-oriented and less interested in promotion or assignment to special units such as the detective bureau.

While these two categories of female police officers might be extreme variations, they do point out the various problems and role conflicts that women face in law enforcement work. Although similar conflicts in role characteristics exist among men in police departments, they are less visible and less emphasized because of the gender similarity. The uniqueness of women in law enforcement often singles them out for special attention.

An interesting attempt to deal with the problems that women encounter in police work is being conducted at the Southeast Florida Institute of Criminal Justice. The institute recognized that women were exposed to developmental conflicts in their training to be police officers that were different in important ways from those confronting men.[16] As the women struggled for acceptance, they often perceived a rejection of their female qualities—qualities that could make positive contributions to police work.

**Female officers and role conflict**

It was found, for example, that women entering police training were generally self-confident and idealistic about their roles and interactions with male co-workers. However, their feeling about peer relations seriously worsened after just eight weeks in training. The more traditionally "feminine" they were, the worse they felt about themselves. Disillusionment and sex-role conflict occurred rapidly and were accompanied by denial, self-doubt, repressed anger, confusion, and attempts at resolution that sometimes ended in counterproductive behavior, either in training or at home.[17]

It was realized that policewomen are often placed in a no-win situation. Those who are too competent are threatening and considered to be unwoman-like; those who are less competent and more feminine in their roles are better liked by the males but less respected as police officers.

The institute began a counseling program using experienced and respected policewomen who developed a support program to assist the female trainees. These seasoned women police officers provided appropriate role models and provided advice on how to deal with certain organizational and street situations that women in police work must face.

Are males suited to police patrol work? This is the question Katherine van Wormer, a professor of Criminal Justice at Kent State University, asks in a very provocative article apearing in *Police Studies* magazine. Ms. van Wormer asks this question after reviewing all the available evidence of general male and female performance as patrol officers.

First, she cites the supposed advantages of using men on patrol. Looming above the other advantages mentioned is the physical strength of the male police officer combined with his greater stamina to subdue a suspect. This has been demonstrated in actual field tests of comparative strength. A survey of police chiefs throughout the country revealed that they were of the opinion that male police officers had proven themselves more physically rugged than women. Second, it is easier for men to handle night work, rotating shifts, and long hours. The male has a wife at home cooking for him and caring for his children. For the female, especially a mother, adjustment to police work is sometimes difficult.

Another important advantage that men have over women is their natural aggressiveness. If a woman is hired for police work, resocialization and assertiveness training are required. Men are also more likely to be persistent when they encounter obstacles and to emerge as the dominant partners in mixed situations while also making more arrests than women and participating more often in strenuous physical activity. Finally, males are more likely to have related job experience, such as service in the military police, or have worked in security, whereas most female recruits rarely have had such related background or experience.

Now for the disadvantages of males. Professor van Wormer points out the fact that male police officers are more likely than female officers to generate complaints or to provoke violence is frequently mentioned in the literature. In a dangerous situation, the presence of policemen is often provocative, whereas the female presence is said to have a disarming effect, inasmuch as women do not carry a threatening, violent image. Related to this is a second disadvantage. Studies show that male police officers are more likely to become involved in serious unbecoming conduct that can damage public and community relations efforts. They are also more likely to destroy or damage police property such as automobiles, they do not relate as well to the general public, and it is harder for them to get essential cooperation. Moreover, male officers are much more likely to resort to physical brutality, particularly among minority groups and the poor, than are policewomen. This is related to the macho image of two-fisted aggressive masculinity to which male police officers are supposed to conform.

The disadvantages don't end here. Male officers are too concerned with fears about their image to accept women into their ranks. Should a woman prove superior to them, this can be particularly damaging to their egos and their reputation among their male peers. Male officers also tend to overprotect female partners and then complain that women are a handicap. In failing to relate to policewomen on an equal basis, policemen "put them down." Joint decision making between a male and a female partner is a rarity. Educational differences are reported between male and female officers, with the latter often being better educated. Education is seen as a significant factor because of the relationship between low education and social class and authoritarian attitudes. Policemen are so absorbed with the use of physical coercive force that they are probably the worst people to intervene in domestic violence or deal with the problem of battered wives. Finally, women just perform some police tasks better. Male officers, for example, don't communicate as well with rape victims and are not as observant as women.

The question these findings pose for Ms. van Wormer is that after looking at the advantages and disadvantages, males have a role in police work, but it is a qualified one. As she says: "In short, many of the males presently employed by police departments are not suited to police work. But all is not lost.... [M]ore careful hiring practices and the positioning of females in positions of leadership as well as on patrol duty would do much to alleviate the overmasculinized police image that currently exists."[a]

[a]From: Katherine van Wormer, "Are Males Suited to Police Patrol Work?" *Police Studies* (Winter 1981). Quoted with permission.

In the years ahead we will probably see less of this role conflict problem. As women begin to seek acceptance and, are in fact, accepted into police agencies, their uniqueness will diminish. Along with this acceptance, the problems of role conflict will lessen somewhat. Although women in law enforcement will always be viewed somewhat suspiciously and differently by their male colleagues who feel "men still make the best cops," the "Beatles Phenomenon" will take over. In the early 1960s, the English singing group the Beatles were widely criticized for their long hair. Yet in a few years nobody noticed; most young men had even longer hair. We seem to accommodate quickly.

The same is true for minorities in general. The challenge in the area of affirmative action in the future is not one of merely making police departments more representative of our society. The challenge is to accomplish this goal while at the same time improving our selection, training, evaluation, and retention of qualified law enforcement professionals. They may require some fundamental changes in how police departments are organized. It will mean devising strategies to improve job satisfaction and commitment among the ranks of police personnel. It will also mean an effort to raise the image of police work so that our best and brightest young men and women seek careers in what can be a very self-satisfying area of public service.

And who knows? In the police departments of the future it may be the male officers who are in the minority. The following is a very thought-provoking view.

## ☐ CRIME PREVENTION

In Chapter 5 it was noted that more and more police agencies are stressing general crime-prevention programs in place of police–community relations efforts. The two are not necessarily at odds, however. Crime-prevention programs are, in fact, a form of police–community relations. But problems often arise when the police view their crime-prevention efforts as all that is required of them in police–community relations.

Today, crime-prevention efforts and programs are quite popular in the criminal justice literature. Yet crime prevention is nothing new; what is new is the recognition that for crime-prevention programs to be effective, they must involve the police and the community in a cooperative venture.

One of the positive by-products of the emphasis on crime-prevention programs is the restructuring of police organizations so that there is greater interaction with the public. In turn, this interaction seems to foster better understanding by the police of the community and vice versa.[18]

### Understanding the Concept of Crime Prevention

Both as a concept and as active programs, crime prevention rests on certain established premises. First, as discussed previously, there is no single explanation for the causes of crime. Social scientists have cited such factors as economic instability, a history of family problems, limited opportunities for legitimate access to economic goods and services, deviant peer group influences, and personal susceptibility to narcotics addiction as a few of the factors that underlie crime in this country. Such factors demonstrate a few key points: It has not been possible to isolate and identify the specific factor(s) responsible for crime. Second, even if they could be identified, the correction of these "social ills" is far beyond the present ability of society to remedy. Third, the police themselves have very little impact on the broad social problems that may underlie crime.

The police role in crime prevention

What this suggests is that society is faced with certain conditions that are so broad and encompassing that they reject any meaningful solution short of drastic measures and repression that are intolerable to a free society. Instead, what must be done is for society to assume a larger role, which, through collective action, can remedy some of the crime-producing problems; this expanded responsibility should also serve to control the behaviors of those who without certain externally imposed controls would continue to prey on society. This latter idea is based on the concept that in many instances the act of committing a crime results from two things: (1) the *desire* to commit the crime; and (2) the *opportunity* to do so. Because it is often very difficult to remove the desire, through collective action it should be possible to limit the opportunity. Although it is not possible to list all the existing crime-prevention programs, a few of the more popular and widespread programs are listed here:[19]

Typical police crime-prevention programs

- Operation identification: the inscribing of items of personal property with identifiable markings.
- Residential, commercial, and industrial security inspection: the inspection of these structures with the goal of improving security devices (locks, lights, etc.).
- Neighborhood alert: the involvement of neighborhood groups in conducting security inspections, watching for suspicious persons and activities, etc.
- Block clubs and block groups. These are similar to the neighborhood alert program except that they are usually more organized and have regular activities—for example, the formation and use of members to patrol the neighborhood on a regular basis.
- Physical planning programs: the design or redesign of structures and architectural arrangements to provide better security.
- Various senior citizen-related programs: special programs to reduce victimization among these groups (e.g., escort services, programs on how to avoid fraud and confidence game activities, etc.).

Gruff the Crime Hound serves as an appealing mascot for children participating in school crime prevention programs. (© Sally Myers/Tom Myers Photography)

Police administrators who were forced to reexamine their patrol operations after studies concluded that traditional random patrol is not effective in preventing crime, are looking at new alternatives. The idea is not to abandon patrol, but to make it less random and to better manage and control it.

Critics of traditional police patrol operations point out that although the patrol unit is the largest operating component of any police department, it is also the part over which police managers have the least control. Between calls for service, officers have traditionally been free to go where they want and do what they want as long as they remained in their patrol district. The justification for such freedom is that the officer knows his or her beat and can be trusted to know when and where to fight street crime.

This may be changing. In some cities police managers and supervisors are making efforts to better control the randomness of police activity. The use of computers is aiding this effort. Both automatic vehicle locator (AVL) and computer-assisted crime analyses are making inroads. AVL systems monitor mobile police units on the street so that police personnel at headquarters can keep track of their activities. More common, however, is the use of computers to analyze crime and then to assign patrol personnel accordingly.

The use of computer analyses and assignment of patrol officers in a particular way and in a particular area are often resented by patrol officers. The officers feel they are not trusted to make decisions. The truth of the matter is that they are probably right. Ample evidence suggests that police officers on patrol spend a great deal of unassigned time in nonpolice-related activities such as drinking coffee, running personal errands, and girl watching.

Such directed patrol activities involve management and supervision much more closely with day-to-day patrol activities. Police first-level supervisors, for example, are engaged in analyzing the computer printouts, assigning personnel, and monitoring them to assure they are patrolling as directed. In the past, too many of these supervisors merely gathered the reports from the various field units near the end of the shift and randomly checked on the patrol units during the tour of duty. Other than that, patrol supervisory officers had little to do other than to respond to the scene should a patrol unit request supervisory assistance.

One of the most publicized directed patrol strategies is the "split-force" concept that was adopted in Wilmington, Delaware. About three-quarters of the department's officers are assigned to a "basic" patrol unit. Their primary responsibility is answering calls. Calls are "prioritized," and shifts have been restructured accordingly. The rest of the patrol officers are assigned to the "structured" unit and do not normally answer calls except in extreme emergencies. The structured unit is deployed in high-crime areas, usually in plain clothes, to perform surveillance work, stakeouts, and other tactical assignments that normally might be handled by detectives. Their shifts and working hours are determined by crime trends.

In addition to creating a special group of officers who have the flexibility to handle situations as the need arises and to be assigned accordingly, Wilmington has tried to control the activities of its basic unit more closely. They have instituted fixed posts within each sector from which the patrol officers are supposed to operate. Still, the officers resented this approach, and gradually more discretion as to where to patrol and how has been turned back to the individual officer.

In spite of the reluctance on the part of patrol officers to be controlled in their patrol activity, more police administrators will likely increase their efforts to limit individual discretion and be more systematic in patrol assignments. Among professional associations of police managers, talk increasingly centers on the idea of directed patrol.

##  THE RISING CONCERN OVER POLICE PRODUCTIVITY

Increasingly, police departments are being held accountable for the costs of their services. The public is no longer willing to accept police excuses for not being more effective in controlling crime nor for demands for increased personnel and other resources as long as police are unable to demonstrate that the increase in the cost of police services has had a substantial impact on the well-being of the community. Although the years 1971 to 1985 saw only a 5 percent increase in per capita costs

The costs of police service

for police services in the United States (compared to 67 and 40 percent increases, respectively, for corrections and judicial services), police services are still extremely costly. For example, of every dollar spent in America for the justice system, 48 cents of that dollar goes for police protection.[20] It is city governments—particularly large cities, where the per capita cost for police services is the highest—that are feeling the pinch. During some major police-labor disputes in the mid- to late 1970s, the *Washington Post*, in a series of articles on police unionism and labor demands, called the situation "a major skirmish in the nationwide struggle by cities for financial survival."[21] Now, although things have generally improved somewhat, governments still struggle with ways to lower costs and to do so without jeopardizing public safety.

The problem is not whether there is a need to develop ways to measure police productivity, but how to measure police service in any meaningful and quantifiable way. Traditionally, the police have relied on official crime statistics as an indicator of their efficiency. Such statistics are unreliable and do not reflect other, more time-consuming tasks that the police perform.

Special research institutes such as the Police Foundation and the Urban Institute are now studying methods that might be used to measure police productivity. They have identified certain "levels of concern," among which are the following:

- The productivity of an individual police officer.
- The productivity of police units (e.g., shifts, police districts, neighborhood team policing units, or precincts).
- The productivity of particular kinds of units, such as motorized police, foot patrols, investigative units, tactical forces, canine corps, etc.
- The productivity of the police department as a whole.
- The productivity of the crime control system, including both police activities and private activities to reduce crime.
- The productivity of the total community criminal justice system, including the police, the courts, the prosecutor's office, corrections and social service agencies, and private-sector crime-prevention activities (such as use of locks, watchdogs, etc.)[22]

Although it is not possible to examine all the measures developed to gauge police productivity, Table 6.1 indicates some that might be applied. The effective measurement of police services, however, will not occur overnight. Like other public service agencies, police departments perform functions that almost defy quantitative measurement. This problem is compounded by the fact that where public safety is an issue, tolerances for misjudgments are very limited and the case for an insurance margin most compelling.

## □ POLICE CORRUPTION

"Nothing undermines public confidence in the police and in the process of criminal justice more than the illegal acts of [police] officers." Such was the opinion of the President's Commission on Law Enforcement and Administration of Justice in its report on the police.[23] In spite of law enforcement's improvements in the past several decades, the police establishment in America is still troubled. Particularly

**TABLE 6.1   Some Recommended Measures of Police Productivity**

| Police Function Being Measured | Measure Employed |
|---|---|
| Police patrol operations | 1. Number of patrol officers assigned to street patrol in terms of total patrol officers<br>2. Work-hours of patrol time spent on activities contributing to patrol objectives in terms of total patrol work-hours<br>3. Number of calls of a given type and response time for answering these calls<br>4. Arrests resulting from patrol that survive the first judicial screening<br>5. Felony arrests from patrol surviving the first judicial screening<br>6. Arrests (felonies and misdemeanors) that result in convictions |
| Provision of noncrime services | 1. Number of noncrime calls for service that are satisfactorily responded to in terms of work-hours devoted to noncrime service calls<br>2. Medical emergency calls that emergency room personnel evaluate as having received appropriate first aid |
| Human resource management | 1. Number of disciplinary charges filed and number substantiated in terms of total departmental personnel<br>2. Number of work-hours lost during the year due to illness, injury, or disciplinary action |
| Miscellaneous considerations | 1. Population served per police employee and per dollar<br>2. Crime rates and changes in crime rates for reported crimes (relative to dollars or employees per capita)<br>3. Clearance rates of reported crimes (relative to dollars or employees per capita)<br>4. Arrests per police department employee and per dollar<br>5. Crime rates, including estimates of unreported crimes based on victimization studies<br>6. Clearance rates, including estimates of unreported crimes based on victimization studies<br>7. Percentage of crimes solved in less than $x$ days<br>8. Percentage of population indicating a lack of feeling of security<br>9. Percentage of population expressing dissatisfaction with police service |

*Sources:* The National Commission on Productivity, *Opportunities for Improving Productivity in Police Services* (Washington, D.C.: National Commission on Productivity, 1973), pp. 14–28, 49–52: and the Urban Institute, *The Challenge of Productivity Diversity: Improving Local Government Productivity Measurement and Evaluation, Part III, Measuring Police–Crime Control Productivity* (Washington, D.C.: The Urban Institute, June 1972), p. 11.

since the urban disorders of the mid-1960s and recent police involvements in drug scandals, fundamental doubts concerning the credibility of police have arisen through a series of social, political, and judicial challenges.[24] Although they were only occasional subjects of concern in the past, police policy and practice are now under more intense scrutiny. In fact, problems of police corruption and malfeasance are just now being studied seriously.[25]

Authorities who have studied police corruption generally conclude that two

The myth for the need of rapid police response has been with us for a long time. Traditionally, police administrators have emphasized the ability to respond quickly to calls for service. The idea was simple. Rapid response to the scene of the crime will among other things: (1) increase apprehensions, (2) protect the scene, and (3) increase citizen satisfaction with police service.

Beginning in the 1970s, a number of studies began to question the need for rapid response to all police calls. It was found, for example, that the vast majority of calls for service are not of an emergency nature. Second, rapid response by the police may have little effect on arrests. Too much time is simply lost in most cases between the occurrence of the crime and when it is reported to the police. Finally, citizen dissatisfaction was more likely to occur when citizens were led to believe that the police would respond in a certain time and didn't. If citizens were told that the police could not respond immediately, they generally accepted the delay.

Police departments faced with budget cuts and demands for service are seeking ways to deal with their call loads for service. Rather than sending patrol units off in all directions to handle calls, some systematic procedures had to be established. A way to prioritize calls that permitted the police to be more flexible in their responses was needed. In this way calls that demanded immediate attention could be handled while other calls could wait. It was a case of the police trying to regain some control over their field units.

In 1980 the National Institute of Justice began research to see if effective alternative strategies could be developed. This was an attempt to experiment with alternative strategies, measure their consequences, and gauge citizen satisfaction.

The overall strategy was called the Differential Police Response (DPR) Field Test Program. Three cities—Garden Grove, California; Greensboro, North Carolina; and Toledo, Ohio; were selected as test sites. The cities differed in several ways. Garden Grove and Greensboro had civilians working in the police dispatch center and both had computer-aided dispatch (CAD) systems. Toledo used sworn police personnel in their dispatch center and operated without a CAD system. Toledo and Greensboro already took some crime reports of a minor nature over the phone, whereas Garden Grove did not.

The key to the new DPR system was to develop a new call classification scheme. When calls were received, they were classified according to certain elements: presence of injuries, time of occurrence, likelihood of apprehension, suspicious circumstances, and availability of witnesses. From this information, calltakers were able to select the most appropriate response, whether it was immediate police unit response, delayed mobile response, routine response by nonsworn personnel, or telephone response.

All the sites sizably reduced the number of nonemergency calls handled by the immediate dispatch of mobile units. Many calls such as larceny reports were taken by tele-

phone report units. There was also an increased use of telephone reports for burglary incidents and public nuisance complaints. The departments felt that sizable savings in patrol hours were realized that could be applied toward better investigations, preventive patrol, directed patrol efforts, and enforcement activities.

Findings revealed that citizens expressed an overall high degree of willingness to accept alternatives to the immediate dispatch of a patrol unit for nonemergency calls. Citizens were asked about their willingness to accept specific alternatives: telephone reports, appointments, mail-in reports, or reports filed in person at the police department. Overall, nearly one-half of the citizens reported that at least one alternative was acceptable. The most acceptable alternative was setting an appointment and the least acceptable was mailing in a report. Citizens accepted alternatives for nonpersonal crime-related calls, such as burglary or larceny, more than for "personal" events, such as assaults or domestic calls.

Police dispatchers, calltakers, and the officers in their field expressed high levels of satisfaction with the program. The communications personnel felt that the project increased the detail and complexity of their work and gave them more responsibility and guidelines for their efforts. Officers believed that there had been significant improvements in the level of detailed information on in-progress Part I crime calls, suspicious activity calls, and domestic disputes.

factors seem to be associated with corrupt police practices: a willingness to engage in such practices and associated opportunity. Police work by its very nature provides the opportunity. It is almost impossible for anticorruption efforts to eliminate the many and varied ways the police could engage in corrupt activities. The crucial factor seems to be an attitude favorable to corruption. It is when the police develop an outlook that says it's okay to engage in these practices or, perhaps even worse, when fellow officers look the other way when members of the department are involved in such activities, that real problems are likely to result.

Factors associated with police corruption

How does one become a "corrupt cop"? The answer to this is elusive. In some instances, police hiring practices are such that men and women who have moral standards easily bent by opportunity are hired. If placed in a situation where corruption among the force already exists or where supervision and sanctions are lax, it is likely that such individuals may soon begin practicing some form of corruption, improper behavior, or illegal activity. There may be one important corrupting aspect of police work most dangerous to anticorruption efforts: It is not only an attitude favorable to corruptive behavior, it is also the perceived opportunity to do so and the perceived likelihood of being able to get away it. Police officers may engage in some form of illegal behavior merely because a police officer feels "protected" by virtue of his or her job. In this way, behavior is not held in check by inhibition. An officer on patrol alone or with a cooperative partner in the early hours of the morning steals building materials from a construction site in the patrol district. What are their chances of getting caught? Unfortunately, too often their chances are slim. The corrupt officers are often likely to be successful, unless they are seen by a watchman hired by the construction firm or by a passing citizen, and assuming that the watchman or the citizen have enough "respectability" to be believable—a respectability, by the way, that will be thoroughly put to the test by the department if a complaint is made and by the officers' defense lawyer if criminal charges and a trial result.

But it is unlikely that it will get to such a point. The police officers thinking about stealing the building materials will have thoroughly checked out the construction site for any watchman under the pretext that they are merely making their presence known to the watchman should police help be needed. The police have a right—even a responsibility—to check such a construction site as part of their routine patrol activity in the district. And a visibly marked patrol car prowling a construction site area seen by a passing motorist or citizen is not unusual.

The "socialization process" involved in police work is another critical factor. It begins with the folklore that surrounds police work itself. The young police officer is told by the old veteran that he or she can't be an effective police officer by "going by the book." The implication is obvious: Rules must be bent to do the job. The question is how far and in what ways can the bending of the rules be acceptable behavior? A department may have a policy that prohibits all forms of gratuities being accepted by police officers. While this certainly means that the police can't take payoffs from narcotics dealers, does it mean that they can't accept free coffee and donuts from a local donut shop or discounts on their meals at certain restaurants?

Police "socialization"

Another problem of the police socialization process is what Sherman calls "mapping out their environment." As police personnel begin to gain experience on the job and encounter situations, they may develop attitudes that help them rationalize and to excuse—to them, at least—their deviant behavior. For instance,

Loyalty and camaraderie within the police department are important factors when an officer needs to call for backup. (© Laura Sikes/Stock South)

"The public is our enemy and they don't want the law enforced," "Politicians are crooked and aren't to be trusted," "Minorities are amoral, a drain on society's resources, and cop-haters who are not to be believed or shown respect," "Everybody's on a hustle," "Judges are too lenient," and "Police administrators are the enemy."[26] When such attitudes and views become part of the officer's perception of police work—indeed, become his or her view toward society itself—a situation conducive to illegal or at least improper behavior is established. Associated with the development of such attitudes is the pervasive notion that loyalty to fellow officers is essential if one is to survive and be accepted among one's fellow police peers. This loyalty may well extend to, if not actually participating in improper or illegal behavior, at least covering up for fellow officers who do.

Although this loyalty may be found in various degrees in all work organizations, it seems to be particularly strong among those in the police occupation. Among police this loyalty develops into a subculture of behavior and mutual expectations. Those who do not conform to these generally held expectations may expect (at minimum) to be ostracized by their fellow officers. In more extreme cases they may even be driven from the department. In the most extreme circumstances they may even be "set up" to be injured or caught in a serious infraction. The "unacceptable officer" might, for instance, find himself or herself in a situation requiring assistance. The officer radios for backup help, and other members of the department are purposely slow in responding. In this way is conveyed a message that says "The game is played our way and by our rules." Such practices convey the message not only to the individual officer but to other members of the force as well. It also serves to reinforce the expectations.

This loyalty as part of the police subculture is especially troublesome because, as mentioned, the police have greater opportunity to engage in questionable activities. In fact, in many cases this "opportunity" may actually be thrust upon them.

By virtue of their authority they are targets for those who would corrupt the police to obtain a valued outcome. This can be the motorist offering the traffic cop a bribe to avoid a ticket or a gambling operation paying off the local beat cop, district car, members of the vice detail, or police supervisory personnel to ignore illegal gambling. Opportunity is also present by the fact that police officers by the nature of their jobs are less likely to be closely supervised in ways that prevent inappropriate or illegal behavior. Being alone on patrol, away from the eyes of supervisors, and possessing the discretionary authority they have provide certain opportunities not available to members of most occupations.

Finally, there is the implicit issue of public trust that accompanies the job of police officer. Simply, law enforcement officers are expected to live up to higher standards of professional and personal conduct than most other occupational groups. When loyalty to fellow officers transcends this element of public trust, it is particularly damaging.

Much of the findings about corruption among the police in those jurisdictions where police corruption has been uncovered point to the fact that for sustained and widespread police corruption to exist, it must be sanctioned, or at least tacitly approved, by the department or at least a significant number of the members of the department. It could not exist otherwise. This destroys the idea that police corruption—at least where it is widespread—is the work of a few so-called "rotten apples in the barrel." This was pointed out some years ago in the Knapp Commission's investigation of police corruption in New York City. Although New York City cannot be compared to, say, Stillwell, Oklahoma, the same dynamics of corruption exist, regardless of the size of the city or the police department. Only the scale of corruption and the number of police officers involved are different. Along this line, it may be more serious that 75 of Stillwell's 125 police officers are corrupt than if 1,000 of New York City's 32,000 cops are similarly disposed. In discussing the "rotten apple" idea and the role of the department in fostering police corruption, pay close attention to what the Knapp Commission said after its investigation of corruption among certain elements of the New York City Police.

*Open or tacit approval of corruption*

> A fundamental conclusion at which the Commission has arrived is that the problem of police corruption cannot—as it is usually asserted—be met by seeking out the few "rotten apples" whose supposedly atypical conduct is claimed to sully the reputation of an otherwise innocent Department. The Commission is persuaded that the climate of the Department is inhospitable to attempts to uncover acts of corruption, and protective of those who are corrupt. The consequence is that the rookie who comes into the Department is faced with the situation where it is easier for him to become corrupt than to remain honest.[27]

Broadly, police corruption can be broken down into two types: the *corruption of authority* and *opportunistic corruption.* Much of what has been discussed about police corruption can be used to explain why and how both of these forms of corruption occur.

## Corruption of Authority

One noted observer of police corruption has defined corruption of authority as that corruption that comes from the broad discretion police have in much of their work and the tension between efficiency standards versus the activities that must ensure due process.[28] More simply put this means that the police either employ or might

*Efficiency and the misuse of police authority*

be tempted to employ certain corrupt practices—in this case violation of civil rights or rights of due process in an effort to be more efficient. And they can do this because of the discretion they have in certain situations. For example, the police may be under a lot of pressure to solve a serious crime that has occurred in the community, or they may be trying to solve a particular series of burglaries; in still another situation they may be out to get a certain individual or individuals and send them to prison.

The police are then corruptive of their authority by engaging in illegal practices such as abusing constitutional prohibitions against illegal searches and seizures, interrogations, and conducting unapproved and illegal wiretaps to gain leads—all of which violate established rights of due process. It doesn't end here. The police may also purposely "plant" contraband on a suspect and then deny it, perjure themselves on the witness stand in court to convict the defendant, use physical force unnecessarily and unreasonably, or employ deadly force when they may have the legal right for its use but not the moral justification.

There are less insidious ways the police use their authority corruptly. It may

## THE EVER-PRESENT DANGER: POLICE ABUSE OF AUTHORITY

The police in the small town of Brandon, Vermont, have received wide-ranging criticism for their behavior. According to the *New York Times,* it began when the publisher of the town's local newspaper published two letters written by town citizens that were critical of the department and its officers. Adding to the bad feelings by the police was a survey the newspaper published of town residents' attitudes about disbanding the department and contracting with the local sheriff's department for police services. The citizens supported the idea of contracting with the sheriff's department. The police allegedly then began an investigation of the newspaper's publisher. This, however, wasn't enough. They also developed a contrived plot to discredit him.

At the department's instigation, a wide-ranging background investigation of the publisher was undertaken. The investigative file indicated that twenty-seven different inquiries were made of police departments in several Western states where the publisher had lived before moving to Vermont. No police record or negative information was found to exist. In addition, the IRS was contacted for an inquiry. The publisher also claimed that the town's police began a program of harassment. His car was frequently ticketed, he was followed by police personnel, and his home and newspaper office were placed under surveillance.

The most serious charge leveled at the police was their instigation of a pedophile (child molester) file on the publisher. According to official police documents, later examined by the court looking into this matter, the publisher was thought by the police to be a pedophile. An investigative file was begun when a detective on the department returned from a Vermont Police Academy seminar on child molesters. This seminar pointed out that the typical profile for a child molester is an unmarried male over the age of twenty-five who has moved often, takes "family-type" photographs, and has "limited dating relationships." The police were convinced that the publisher fit this so-called profile.

Based on this, a detective from Brandon contacted an investigator from a neighboring police department. It was arranged that this out-of-town investigator would submit an ad to the newspaper posing as a photographer who wanted to take "discreet family pictures." The strategy was to lure the publisher into what appeared to be an opportunity to become involved in a pedophile ring. The publisher never responded to the ad.

The judge who heard the publisher's later civil suit against the police department forced the police to turn over their confidential investigative file to the publisher and his attorney. It was from this file that the extent and nature of police efforts to "get" the publisher became a public record. During the course of the ensuing lawsuit, a new police chief was appointed in the town. Although the new chief was not familiar with the contents of the investigative file or the total circumstances surrounding the case, he openly supported the use of such investigative techniques in these types of cases.

be the use of their position and authority to obtain unearned gratuities. Here the list is virtually endless: free meals, liquor, police discounts on merchandise, free admission to entertainment, and sexual services. Although such practices are not as serious as certain violations of the due process and civil rights of citizens—many of which are also illegal acts that make the police themselves criminal—they are a serious form of corruption that if tolerated could conceivably produce a climate of acceptability that could foster even more serious acts of corruption.

## Opportunistic Corruption

Opportunistic police corruption combines the aspect of police corruption of authority with specific opportunities to engage in corrupt and illegal practices. More important in this type of corruption is the presented opportunity to engage in these forms of conduct rather than a concerted or formulated plan of corruption. As one convicted ex-officer said: "I just took advantage of the situation when I got the chance; I didn't plan it as such, I'd just do it when I had the opportunity and thought I could get away with it."[29] This type of police corruption includes accepting a bribe offered by someone to avoid arrest or to obtain release if under arrest; taking care of traffic or parking tickets; stealing from drunks or victims; "looting" a crime scene after discovering a burglary; stealing unprotected property; confiscating narcotics from an arrestee for personal use or to supply an informer; taking money in the form of kickbacks from lawyers or bailbondsmen for referrals; and "leaking" police or prosecutorial information to unscrupulous defense attorneys.

## Developing Strategies to Combat Police Corruption

What can be done about police corruption and misbehavior, and what are some of the recommended strategies to counteract this problem? This subject has been widely discussed in recent years. Government study commissions, professional police associations, and special citizen and other groups have all examined the problem. Out of this have come certain insights into such factors as poor personnel selection and retention practices, poor administration and supervision, peer group influences, police attitudes of "us-against-them," inadequate salaries and poor working conditions, the vulnerability of the police to corruption, and importantly, apathy on the part of citizens and public officials to the problem.

Effective anticorruption strategies usually combine three elements: (1) developing more effective internal administrative policies; (2) identifying and dealing with situations that cause police corruption; and (3) instituting investigative policies designed to detect and apprehend corrupt officers.

Internal administrative policies typically consist of certain programs and procedures. One such policy holds not only police officers responsible for their actions but the actions of other officers as well: for example, imposing disciplinary actions on police personnel who do not report instances involving police misconduct of which they are aware. Other common strategies include closer supervision of field operations and the disbanding of precincts or operations that by their very nature are too decentralized and/or unsupervised to be effectively controlled or monitored. Other anticorruption efforts include random follow-up surveys of citizens receiving police services, adopting new procedures for accounting for prisoners' property, and requiring daily report logs and activity summaries. Also included in this cate-

*Elements of anticorruption strategies*

gory would be the closer inventory and control of confiscated property and evidence, particularly narcotics.

Along with such internal administrative efforts, the police administrator who is serious about police corruption must take certain other steps. Since vice-type crimes such as narcotics, gambling, and prostitution have the potential to be particularly corruptive, there must be a crackdown on such activities if they exist in the community. Police officials have also learned from some sad experiences that they must break up the enforcement monopoly of certain units and frequently rotate police personnel in and out of these units. The narcotics detail, for instance, should not have sole responsibility for dealing with narcotics. Nor should police investigators be assigned permanently to such units. There must also be an effort to encourage citizens to report instances of police corruption, "shakedowns," or improper behavior. Campaigns need to be mounted telling merchants not to give Christmas presents and other gratuities to members of the force. Tavern owners should be contacted about supplying free drinks to cops whether on or off duty. A strict policy of arrest needs to be publicized and followed, making arrest mandatory in cases of attempted bribery of a police officer. Some reform chiefs of police have dealt with the problem of politicians trying to influence or bribe police personnel by personally investigating and arresting public officials under existing laws that prohibit attempts to influence law enforcement officers in the performance of their duties.

The last element of an effective anticorruption strategy is an ongoing program of trying to uncover instances of police corruption and the investigation of circumstances or allegations of corruption. Corruption complaints usually come from several sources. They may come from citizens. Professionally run departments encourage such citizen complaints and are receptive to citizens who feel strongly enough about such situations to report them to the department. At the same time, certain rights must exist to protect the officer(s) from unfounded accusations. Another good source of information might be from members of the department itself. A professional and honest department does not want its reputation sullied, and it is much more difficult for any type of corruption to exist in such an agency. Fellow police officers themselves—the greatest assurance of lack of corruption—simply will not tolerate corruption or officers who are involved in such activities. Still another source comes from periodic probing of persons and situations where corruptive practices are a real possibility such as attorneys, bailbondsmen, towing companies, and so on.

Some departments that have suffered widespread and persistent problems with corruption employ periodic "integrity checks" on police personnel. For example, an internal investigations investigator (see Chapter 5) may pose as a drunk who lets it be known to the police that he has a lot of money on him and then pretends to pass out. Cars with expensive personal property in view on the back seat are left unattended and apparently abandoned. Surveillance is then undertaken, and the police are called to investigate. Of course, in both instances the internal investigations people are testing the police to see if they steal any property in these situations. As one might assume, police personnel are usually not very supportive of such anticorruption strategies.

Just as police corruption seemed to be losing headway, serious new challenges appeared in the late 1980s. This is especially true in those areas of the country where narcotics flourish, such as the police scandals that recently occurred in Miami. This points out the constant need for vigilance. Unfortunately, the corruptibility of a small percentage of police officers affects all men and women in law enforcement and discourages many from careers in a very rewarding and interesting occupation.

 ## CONFLICT-MANAGEMENT STRATEGIES

By the very nature of their occupation, police personnel are called on to intervene in situations of actual or potential violence. In examining police killings from 1965 to 1984, Samuel G. Chapman found that over 16 percent of all police officers killed in the line of duty died while responding to such disturbance calls as family quarrels, individuals with guns, or the handling of mentally deranged persons. These same types of circumstances led to even higher rates of assaults on police officers.[30]

*Police techniques to defuse potential violence*

 ### INTERVENING IN DOMESTIC DISTURBANCE CALLS: IS IT REALLY THAT DANGEROUS FOR THE POLICE?

A lot of traditional myth surrounds the question of police intervention in domestic disturbance calls. Many police personnel are taught that this type of call is potentially the most dangerous call they can receive. This idea of "dangerousness" pervades police thinking. This is seen by the type of training police receive in how to answer such "domestic" calls.

A new look at this issue has recently been released by a research project sponsored by the National Institute of Justice, an agency of the U.S. Department of Justice. Although the Institute and the researchers are not attempting to downplay the potential for injury—or worse—to police officers handling such calls, their findings raise some provocative questions.

Apparently, the myth of "dangerousness" is due in large part to how the FBI, which computes annual data on police officers killed in the United States, defines *disturbance*. This agency for many years used the general category of disturbance to record police officer deaths. Yet, this category included any number of disturbance incidents such as bar fights, gang calls, general disturbances (including domestic),

man with gun, and so on. The assumption for many years was that the FBI's disturbance category was in great part composed of *domestic* (emphasis added) disturbance incidents. The researchers, with the cooperation of the FBI (who in 1982 reclassified disturbance calls into specific categories, e.g., man with gun, family quarrels, etc.), said simply, after closer examination of the findings under the new classification, "the assumption is wrong."

In looking more closely at nationwide figures compiled over several years concerning "felonious deaths" of police officers, "domestic disturbances" ranked significantly behind any number of factors as incidents causing felonious police deaths. For example, in order of rank were "all others" (a broad miscellaneous category), then came robbery, traffic, other disturbances, and burglaries. After these came domestic disturbances. And there were important differences. From 1973 to 1984, of the seven categories, "domestic disturbances" accounted for only 5.5 percent of the felonious police deaths. Robbery situations and calls accounted for about 17 percent, traffic for 13 percent. The miscella-

neous category "all others" (which excludes domestic disturbances) accounted for a whopping 46 percent.

The data clearly pointed out that of the specific categories they could identify, robbery ranks as the most serious assignment. Unknown, however, is the seriousness of domestic disturbances in terms of generating disproportionately higher rates of assault or injury (as compared to deaths) than some other types of police assignments. The researchers also pointed out quite correctly that one of the reasons for perhaps the lower felonious death rates for police officers handling "domestic disturbance" calls was that the training as to the supposed inherent dangers associated with these type calls was paying off. Officers then went into these situations exercising more precaution. Yet, police are also trained to be very cautious and careful when answering robbery calls.

*Source:* Adapted from Joel Garner and Elizabeth Clemmer, "Danger to Police in Domestic Disturbances— A New Look." *Research in Brief* (Washington: U.S. Department of Justice, National Institute of Justice, November, 1986).

The management of interpersonal conflict is not only one of the most hazardous assignments but also probably the most time-consuming aspect of the police function. For example, one study monitored telephone calls to the Syracuse, New York, Police Department and found that almost 20 percent of them concerned disputes in public and private places and among family members, neighbors, and total strangers.[31] The police departments of Kansas City, Missouri; Dallas, Texas; Cambridge, Massachusetts; and New York City report similarly high percentages of time allocated to situations involving interpersonal conflict.

Beginning with efforts in the 1970s, a number of police agencies have sought ways to alleviate this problem by training their personnel in techniques of *crisis intervention* to protect themselves and to prevent injury to others. Social scientists trained in techniques of behavior analysis and control have been conducting intensive programs for police personnel to help them handle potentially violent situations.[32]

Crisis management services usually take two forms: (1) the *generalist–specialist* model; and (2) the *generalist* model.[33] In the generalist–specialist model, used by a number of very large municipal police agencies, a selected group of general patrol officers handles all family or mental disturbance and related calls in a specified area. These officers operate in uniform and on all tours of duty on a twenty-four basis. When not engaged in the management of disturbances, they provide general patrol services in an assigned area. This model has some noted advantages. The special group of police officers who handle crisis calls can be trained extensively in conflict management techniques, a practice that would not be feasible for all personnel in the department. The special group also can develop greater awareness of existing social agencies and their programs and thus can properly refer people

Crisis intervention techniques can make the difference between lives lost and lives saved, as with these rescued hostages. (© Jim Mahoney/The Image Works)

Roxanne Gay, widow of Philadelphia Eagles defensive lineman Blenda Gay, was charged with stabbing her 6-foot-5, 255-pound husband to death. Records show she repeatedly called the police for protection from beatings by him. The officers merely told him to walk around the block to cool off—and on one occasion they ended up talking football with him.

The police euphemism is "domestic disputes." Those outside the criminal justice system refer to it as "wife battering" or the more legalistic term "spousal abuse." Whatever it is called, it is a problem of widespread proportion—a problem that until recently was hidden in the closet with other almost taboo-like subjects such as incest.

There is no way to gauge the problem. Experts do agree, however, that it is widespread. One survey projected that annually 1.8 million wives are beaten by their husbands. They also agree that it affects all social strata; from the poorest families to the upper crust of the social hierarchy. Spurred on in recent years by women's groups, associations of battered former spouses, victim advocate groups, and increased public attention, the problem is demanding increased attention from the authorities.

Spousal abuse is a bit of misnomer. By extension, some groups use the term "family violence." This takes into consideration cohabiting sexual partners who are not married. Experts see the problem as attributed in large part to the way men and women are socialized to behave. Persons involved in such behavior are often themselves victims of brutality as children and/or have alcohol abuse problems. There is also the problem of the gender-based stereotypes of the aggressive, dominant male and the submissive, passive female.

The police are generally reluctant to take action in such cases and when an arrest is made, the prosecution is often reluctant to prosecute. The problem is the view these authorities have of the complaining victim. "Why bother?" is the attitude of the police. After the woman has had a chance to think it over, she won't want to prosecute. Police often feel that all the woman generally wants is for the police to get the man out of the house for the time being until he sobers up or "cools off." The police are also reluctant to take action because they know the prosecutor doesn't want to handle such "crap cases."

Yet such abuse is rarely an isolated violent episode. More often such attacks increase in both severity and frequency if they go unchecked. In Minneapolis the police decided to do something about it. Tired of repeated visits to the same families and armed with changes in the law that permitted the Minneapolis police to more effectively intervene in cases of domestic violence, they began locking up men for spousal abuse. As a result, an analysis of the program found that the repeated incidence of such problems—or at least the repeat calls to these situations—dropped drastically.

Recently, the National District Attorneys Association has taken an interest in this problem. Since the prosecutor's role is a crucial one, this association has tried to acquaint its members with the dimensions of the problem and how they might deal with it. Like so many familial crimes, however, the criminal justice system seems reluctant and ill equipped to deal with it.

---

in need of help to such agencies. Lastly, these specialists can be chosen because of their demonstrated abilities and willingness to handle conflict situations.

The generalist model is better suited to small police agencies that cannot support specialists in this area. In this model, all patrol personnel are given at least limited training in handling potentially dangerous encounters, and they all handle these situations along with their other responsibilities.

## THE POLICE CONSOLIDATION/DECENTRALIZATION ISSUE

Since World War II, certain developments have occurred among local governments throughout the United States, particularly in metropolitan areas. First, urbanization has occurred at a phenomenal rate, creating unusual problems in governmental management, increased demand for urban services, and problems in social adjustment. Second, numerous communities have incorporated to avoid annexation to central cities, provide tax relief, or achieve other ends, thus creating significant problems such as overlapping and fragmented jurisdictions. Third, many cities have found themselves unable to provide adequate urban services because of financial limitations. Finally, the antiquated governmental framework found in most counties does not allow effective responses by counties to urban problems. For example, large metropolitan areas in the Midwest and the Far West often contain more then 100 separate governments; in some of our largest metropolitan areas, the picture is even worse. The metropolitan area of Chicago has 1,113 governments, Philadelphia has 876, Pittsburgh has 704, and New York has 551.[34]

Urban fragmentation

Many of these local units of government in metropolitan areas maintain their own police departments. For example, in metropolitan Detroit there are eighty-five police departments. More than two-thirds of these departments have less than fifty members, and nearly one-third have less than thirty members. The Detroit Police Department has more police personnel than all the rest of the 84 surrounding jurisdictions combined.

This fragmentation of police services has caused many study commissions, consultant groups, and scholars to recommend that police services in metropolitan areas be combined.[35] The President's Commission on Law Enforcement and the Administration of Justice states: "Each metropolitan area and each county should take action directed toward the pooling, or consolidation, of police services through the particular technique that will provide the most satisfactory law enforcement service and protection at the lowest cost."[36] Those who support consolidated police services in metropolitan areas point out that a large police department could provide better police service at a far lower cost than is required to maintain many small independent departments.

Because local governments are facing problems of financing police services, consolidation of police services will be a major proposed reform in the years ahead. But is total consolidation of police services the answer? There is evidence that it has not always lived up to the promises of the reformers. For example, research of consolidated government in Nashville-Davidson County, Tennessee, indicates that consolidation of Nashville with its contiguous suburbs actually increased drastically the costs of providing local governmental services.[37] When residents of the suburbs were also asked if they perceived any difference in police services after the consolidation, 58 percent said services were the same and 8 percent thought services were worse.[38] Others who have studied this question have concluded similarly. Citizens living in the suburbs of Cleveland and Detroit were very satisfied with the services of their small, suburban police departments.[39]

Over the past twenty years, many community attempts to consolidate suburban police departments have been soundly defeated by voters. A proposal to make the Erie County (Pennsylvania) Police Department the single law enforcement agency in the county was defeated by suburban residents in twenty-four of twenty-five suburbs and all sixteen villages in the surrounding area.[40] Several years ago, suburban voters in Dade County, Florida, voted against further consolidation of the police departments that serve the area. Suburban residents in Marion County, Indiana, strongly opposed merging their smaller police forces with the Indianapolis Police Department.[41]

Given these facts, it would seem that the consolidation of local police departments (and governments) in the forseeable future is not as likely to occur as some of its advocates indicate. As some researchers, such as Ostrom and Canfield, have shown, many communities want to maintain their own individual police departments regardless of some definite advantages of consolidation.[42] Still, in certain regions of the country—particularly the South and West—"regionalizing" the local police is still discussed. What, then, are the issues and some of the proposed strategies for consolidating local law enforcement?

## Consolidation of Support Services

A community's desire to maintain its own police agency probably will not preclude some forms of consolidation, such as the consolidation of staff and auxiliary services on a metropolitan or regional basis. For example, such services as centralized communication operations in a metropolitan area will continue to grow. In these types of operations, a central dispatcher receives all calls for police assistance in a particular geographical area and dispatches units from the various participating cities. This system has been demonstrated to be very effective in Genessee County, Michigan, where Flint and twenty surrounding cities participate in a centralized communication network.

Similarly, records, laboratories, training, and jail services lend themselves to consolidation efforts. For example, areawide records centers and communications centers are needed for effective and coordinated police operations in metropolitan areas where many police agencies serve essentially a common area. If certain basic police information is collected on an areawide basis according to common standards and forms and then integrated into an areawide records center, several advantages will result. First, inquiring jurisdictions need check only one source rather than several; this should eliminate duplication of effort and of physical facilities and greatly increase the speed with which an inquiry or search may be handled. Second, detailed crime analysis and planning studies could be conducted that may suggest, for example, more effective deployment of personnel in high-crime areas.[43]

Laboratory, training, and jail facilities might also be more approximately handled on an areawide basis because of the prohibitive costs to individual units of government of providing and maintaining these services. Now that the states have enacted legislation requiring certain hours of training for police officers and have established legislation dealing with the maintenance and custody of jail facilities and prisoners, small cities must in many cases pool their resources to comply with these new standards.

## Contract Law Enforcement

Another form of consolidation that has received a great deal of attention in recent years is contract law enforcement. Under this arrangement, small communities contract with the county or an adjacent city for police services. The most notable example of this kind of arrangement is the Lakewood Plan, in which the Los Angeles County Sheriff's Department provides police services to a number of incorporated cites within the county.[44] Under the Lakewood Plan, each city pays the Los Angeles Sheriff's Department an annual fee based on the police services wanted. Connecticut has also experimented with this idea through its Resident State Trooper Program. Under this arrangement, small towns can contract with the state police for a resident trooper to carry out all of the functions of police service.[45] However, like consolidation attempts in general, contract law enforcement has still not been widely adopted.

### Special Squads

Another agreement that is becoming more common is one that provides for so-called metropolitan squads, major case squads, or metropolitan strike forces. Such agreements are made between police departments and, in many instances, are just informal agreements among police administrators to participate in a joint cooperative venture dealing with certain types of offenses. Because efforts to combat organized crime recognize no jurisdictional boundaries, many communities in a metropolitan area participate in an areawide investigative and ingelligence-gathering group. Usually, this special group is made up of representatives from each of the cooperating departments, and it concentrates on certain crimes and offenders. In some cases, the county prosecutor's office is responsible for supervising and coordinating the activities of the group; in other cases, a command officer from one of the participating police departments is placed in charge. In many instances, this arrangement has worked quite well; in other areas, political problems concerning the designation of control over the group and accountability of its members have limited the effectiveness of such joint efforts.

 **POLICE USE OF DEADLY FORCE**

 **TENNESSEE v. GARNER (1985)**

**Supreme Court Establishes Guidelines for Police Use of Deadly Force**

FACTS

Late one evening, Memphis police officers responded to a "prowler inside call." Upon arriving at the scene, one officer heard a door slam and saw someone run across the backyard. The decedent, Edward Garner, stopped at a six-feet-high chainlink fence on the edge of the yard. Using a flashlight, the officer could see the suspect's face and hands. According to the record, no weapon was seen. The officer stated that he was "reasonably sure" that the suspect was unarmed. The officer ordered the suspect to halt, but Garner began to climb the fence. Convinced that if the suspect made it over the fence he would escape, the officer shot him. The bullet struck Garner in the back of the head,

killing him. It was determined later that ten dollars and a purse were taken from the house. It was also later revealed that the suspect was fifteen years old and not seventeen or eighteen, as believed by the officer.

The officer acted pursuant to Tennessee law and department policy. The statute provides that "if, after notice of the intention to arrest, the defendant either flees or forcibly resists, the officer may use all the necessary means to effect the arrest."

A police review board and a grand jury refused to take action against the officer. The suspect's father brought suit in the federal district court for the Western District of Tennessee under 42 U.S.C. Sec. 1983, alleging violations of the fourth, fifth, sixth, eighth, and fourteenth amendments of the Constitution against the officer, the Memphis Police Department, its Director, the mayor, and the City of Memphis. The district court held for these defendants stating that the officer's actions were authorized by state statute, which, in turn, is constitutional.

The case was appealed to the U.S. 6th Circuit Court of Appeals. This court upheld in part and reversed in part the trial court's decision. The court acknowledged the officer's good-faith reliance on the Tennessee statute, thus acting within the scope of the qualified immunity it provided him. However, the court remanded back to the trial court three points for further consideration: the possible liability of the city; whether the use of deadly force and the use by the police of hollow-point bullets in these circumstances was constitutional; and whether any unconstitutional municipal conduct flowed from a policy or custom as required for liability. The district court on remand held that some doubt was possible concerning the city's liability. It upheld the statute and the officer's actions. The issue of police use of hollow point bullets was not considered.

The 6th Circuit then reversed and remanded reasoning that the killing of a fleeing suspect was a seizure under the fourth amendment and is constitutional only if reasonable. It added that the state statute failed because it did not distin-guish between felonies of different magnitudes. The case was appealed to the U.S. Supreme Court.

## DECISION

The Tennessee statute is unconstitutional insofar as it authorizes the use of deadly force against fleeing suspects who are unarmed and pose no threat to the officer or third parties.

## SIGNIFICANCE OF THE CASE

The Court rejected the application of the common law doctrine that was used to justify the use of deadly force in Tennessee. The common law allowed the use of deadly force in all felonies. Legal and technological changes have made the common law doctrine unjustified. Because taking a life is a seizure subject to Fourth Amendment protections, any use of deadly force must be reasonable under the circumstances. The Court, like the 6th Circuit, seemed to prefer the guidelines of the Model Penal Code, which restricts the use of deadly force by the police to more serious felonies and situations. As a result, jurisdictions across the country that have a more permissive deadly force policy for police will have to adopt more restrictive policies as to when police may use deadly force.

---

An issue that has grown in importance in recent years has been the use of deadly force by the police. This issue is usually tied inextricably to the broader issues of police–minority relations and the supporting issues of police violence and/or police brutality. Many of the cities that have seen problems occur as a result of a police officer's use of deadly force, by which a minority group citizen was killed, find on analysis that the public outcry over the killing was the culmination of deep-seated animosity between the police and the minority community that has existed for many years. Such shootings are then viewed by minorities in these communities as a culmination of long-standing instances of police brutality or improper use of force.

The Police Foundation conducted an extensive analysis of the issue of police use of deadly force. Its research findings have been summarized as follows.[46]

Some research findings on police use of deadly force

1. Police departments differ widely in their policies and review procedures relating to the use of deadly force. There is no universally accepted standard dictating when an officer should use a firearm.

Occasionally police find it necessary to use force to maintain order. These officers were prepared for a potential riot between white supremacists staging a rally and black counterdemonstrators. (© Walt Stricklin/Stock South)

2. There is a clear national trend in police departments toward the enactment of written policies governing the use of firearms. Often, however, these policies are not set forth in any single document but are scattered among several department orders or bulletins. Many of these policy statements are poorly organized and confusing.

3. Many departments appear to shy away from adopting firearms policies that are much more restrictive than state law, for fear of increasing their vulnerability to civil suits. In addition, police administrators have to cope with increasing police union opposition to the adoption of more restrictive standards.

4. The rates of shootings by police officers vary widely among jurisdictions, and it is impossible (within the limits of their study) to say what specific factors are responsible for these differences.

5. Many departments are beginning to develop record-keeping procedures designed to identify and monitor officer conduct involving the use of excessive force and repeated involvement in shooting incidents.

6. It is difficult, after the fact, to categorize certain shootings as "justified" or "unjustified." Some shootings are clearly and unequivocally acts of self-defense. Some manifestly fail to meet the requirements of law and local policy or appear to have served no compelling purpose, in that no lives were saved and no dangerous felons apprehended. Many incidents, however, fall into a middle ground where the officer's word may be pitted against that of a friend or friends of the victim, or where one or two facts appear to be inconsistent with the officer's version of events.

7. Most shootings are called "justified" by departments and very few are referred to criminal charges. For example, of the 1,500 killings of civilians by police from 1960 to 1970, very few cases were referred for prosecution and only three resulted in criminal punishment.[47] When an officer is formally charged in connection with an incident occurring in the line of duty, juries generally do not convict, perhaps because most witnesses are themselves participants and not impartial observers. Department discipline in such cases rarely goes beyond a verbal or written reprimand to the officer involved.

8. The formal review of shooting incidents by a civilian or part-time civilian body does not in itself guarantee a fairer or more systematic resolution.

9. The number of blacks and other minorities shot by police is substantially greater than the proportion in the general population but is not inconsistent with the number of blacks arrested for serious (Part I) crimes. Shootings of minority juveniles, in particular, have been responsible for increased tensions and occasionally violent disturbances in ghetto neighborhoods.

10. The review of shooting incidents in the cities surveyed for this study indicates that a sizable percentage involved out-of-uniform officers (both on duty in plainclothes and off duty), perhaps because out-of-uniform officers are less conspicuous and thus more able to intervene in situations in which criminal or suspicious activity is still going on.

The history of the legal right of the police to use deadly force is interesting. The doctrine was first established under the common law of England, which was adopted in the American colonies. It has become known as the "fleeing felon" law. Broadly, it provided that a police officer could employ deadly force in several situations: to protect his life or that of an innocent third party; to overcome resistance to arrest; and to prevent the escape of any felony suspect.[48] It was this last instance that gave the rule its name as the "fleeing felon" law.

At one time, the fleeing aspect of the rule was probably appropriate. Organized police forces were nonexistent, as was any rapid means of communication. Under such circumstances, escape of felons was more likely. Also considered was the fact that felonies were defined as serious crimes of the time—many calling for the death sentence. Since that time, organizational and technological changes have occurred as well as legal changes in what constitute felonies and the penalties that can be imposed for their commission. For example, many more crimes today are felonies than was the case under the common law. Under a literal interpretation of the fleeing felony rule, anyone committing any type of felony and trying to escape by fleeing from the police would justify law enforcement officers in employing deadly force to stop the fleeing suspect.

The common law and the "fleeing felon" doctrine

TABLE **6.2** State laws define the circumstances in which citizens may be justified in using deadly force

| State | Even If Life Is Not Threatened. Deadly Force May Be Justified to Protect | | Specific Crime Against Which Deadly Force May Be Justified |
|---|---|---|---|
| | Dwelling | Property | |
| Alabama | Yes | No | Arson, burglary, rape, kidnaping, or robbery in "any degree" |
| Alaska | Yes | No | Actual commission of felony |
| Arizona | Yes | No | Arson, burglary, kidnaping, aggravated assaults |
| Arkansas | Yes | No | Felonies as defined by statute |
| California | Yes | No | Unlawful or forcible entry |
| Colorado | Yes | No | Felonies, including assault, robbery, rape, arson, kidnaping |
| Connecticut | Yes | No | Any violent crime |
| Delaware | Yes | No | Felonious activity |
| DC | Yes | No | Felony |
| Florida | Yes | No | Forcible felony |
| Georgia | Yes | Yes | Actual commission of a forcible felony |
| Hawaii | Yes | Yes | Felonious property damage, burglary, robbery, etc. |
| Idaho | Yes | Yes | Felonious breaking and entering |
| Illinois | Yes | Yes | Forcible felony |
| Indiana | Yes | No | Unlawful entry |
| Iowa | Yes | Yes | Breaking and entering |
| Kansas | Yes | No | Breaking and entering including attempts |
| Kentucky | No | No | — |
| Louisiana | Yes | No | Unlawful entry including attempts |
| Maine | Yes | No | Criminal trespass, kidnaping, rape, arson |
| Maryland | No | No | — |
| Massachusetts | No | No | — |
| Michigan | Yes | No | Circumstances on a case by case basis |
| Minnesota | Yes | No | Felony |
| Mississippi | Yes | — | Felony including attempts |
| Missouri | No | No | — |
| Montana | Yes | Yes | Any forcible felony |
| Nebraska | Yes | No | Unlawful entry, kidnaping, and rape |
| Nevada | Yes | — | Actual commission of felony |

As changes occurred, so did some states change the old common law "fleeing felony" doctrine. For example, the most common change was to add the term *dangerous* to a fleeing felon. Police officers in these states could use deadly force only if the suspect had committed a "dangerous" felony (which implied that the offender was "dangerous"). And this was often defined. For instance, the law might prescribe the types of offenses—homicide, kidnapping, forcible rape or armed robbery as constituting the "dangerous" felonies for which the police could then employ deadly force. Not all states, however, adopted the more restrictive "dangerous" qualification. In the absence of this, some progressive police agencies and police managers adopted the "dangerous" qualification through their operating directives to the officers under their command. Other police agencies did not, and since the state had not restricted the common law doctrine itself, police in these areas were free to employ deadly force broadly so long as a felony had been committed and certain circumstances such as the suspect's flight or resisting arrest was present.

TABLE **6.2** *(Cont.)*

| State | Even If Life Is Not Threatened. Deadly Force May Be Justified to Protect | | Specific Crime Against Which Deadly Force May Be Justified |
|---|---|---|---|
| | Dwelling | Property | |
| New Hampshire | Yes | — | Felony |
| New Jersey | Yes | No | Burglary, arson, and robbery |
| New Mexico | Yes | Yes | Any felony |
| New York | Yes | No | Burglary, arson, kidnaping, and robbery including attempts |
| North Carolina | Yes | No | Intending to commit a felony |
| North Dakota | Yes | No | Any violent felony |
| Ohio | — | — | |
| Oklahoma | Yes | No | Felony within a dwelling |
| Oregon | Yes | — | Burglary in a dwelling including attempts |
| Pennsylvania | Yes | — | Burglary or criminal trespass |
| Rhode Island | Yes | — | Breaking or entering |
| South Carolina | No | No | — |
| South Dakota | Yes | — | Burglary including attempts |
| Tennessee | Yes | No | Felony |
| Texas | Yes | No | Burglary, robbery, or theft during the night |
| Utah | Yes | — | Felony |
| Vermont | Yes | — | Forcible felony |
| Virginia | No | No | — |
| Washington | No | No | — |
| West Virginia | Yes | No | Any felony |
| Wisconsin | No | No | — |
| Wyoming | No | No | — |

*Note:* This table provides a summary of State statutes and should not be used by citizens in planning their protection. Legal advice that considers the specific situation and the State statute is advised.

*Source:* Bureau of Justice Statistics, *Report to the Nation on Crime and Justice* (Washington, D.C.: U.S. Government Printing Office, March 1988), p. 31.

For a variety of reasons, state legislatures are reluctant to examine this problem and the existing moral issues of police use of deadly force. Instead, they typically give the police the broadest possible discretion and leave it up to the officer in the field or the administrator of the police agency to determine under what specific guidelines the police are justified in taking a life. This is understandable. No state legislator today wants to anger the rank-and-file of police officers in the state for obvious political reasons, or to be labeled "soft" on "criminals" when, as today, such a label is unfashionable at best, and political suicide at worst.

In this legislative vacuum, the Model Penal Code now adopted by a number of states tries to provide a more sensible statutory basis for the use of deadly force. In this way, the technical classification of a crime as a felony or misdemeanor is ignored for purposes of deadly force usage. When you think about it, such a classification under these circumstances is meaningless. Instead, it focuses on more important considerations: The need to apprehend suspects versus the safety of the arresting officer versus the value of human life. In this way the model penal code approach is based on the danger to the suspect, the officer, and to society on the whole.[49]

In recent years many, but not all, police administrators and police departments have tended to become more professional. With this growing professionalism have come efforts to deal with the issue of deadly force use. These departments have sought ways to protect their personnel, to ensure the safety of the public, and to give guidance to their officers as to when they may employ deadly force. Still, the problem lingers. Frank Horvath and Michael Donahue, in their study of police use of deadly force in Michigan, found some general deficiencies in the departments they examined in that state. They concluded by pointing out that there is a

## POLICE USE OF EXCESSIVE FORCE: THE GROWING CONCERN

Not since the 1960s has there been such growing alarm over increasing instances of police use of excessive force and its corollary, police brutality. Whereas the 1970s were relatively quiet, the 1980s saw a dramatic upsurge in not only the issue of police use of deadly force but also a broad range of concern over police-initiated actions of excessive force and brutality.

Although the media have pointed up the problems in such cities as New York, Indianapolis, and Houston, many people believe that the problem is not only one of police forces in our larger cities; it has spread threateningly to communities of all sizes.

Police Chief Joseph McNamara of San Jose, California, attributes the apparent increase in the police use of excessive force to larger numbers of young police officers in many departments and the failure of police management and supervision to control such behavior. Also cited is the rampant cover-up of such practices by police personnel who refuse to expose such actions by other police officers. Many police officials agree. A discussion, for instance, at the 1985 Annual Meeting of the Academy of Criminal Justice Sciences pointed to the apparent high correlation between the age distri-

bution of police personnel and instances of citizen complaints about excessive police force and brutality. The younger the distribution of police officers on a force, the more likely were such occurrences.

Other observers, though generally agreeing that these might be factors, also see other associated reasons. The police, they reason, feel less constrained today in their actions. The public's reaction to crime and the media's portrayal of the folk-hero characteristics of the tough "Dirty Harry"–type, no-nonsense cop is widely applauded by the public. So too is the any means vigilantism expressed by such movies as *The Star Chamber*. In this atmosphere police officers may feel more free to use force and less likely to be held accountable for their actions.

Public apathy probably plays an important role. Since police encounters and the use of excessive force are much more likely to occur among minority groups, the economically disadvantaged, and younger members of society, there is little voiced concern or demand from the elements of society whose voices would be heard by public and police officials. Voices that could be instrumental in demanding change and not tolerating coverups are simply not speaking out.

There is also the issue of police unions and associations. Increasingly protected by labor agreements and militant opposition by the police rank-and-file against reform efforts, police managers who might otherwise take action against the use of excessive force are reluctant to institute change. Disciplinary action, for example, has become such an obstacle course in many departments that police leaders back off. The police, noted for their conservative attitudes, suspicion, and organizing solidarity, present a formidable obstacle to change.

Also cited is a growing reluctance on the part of the federal government to vigorously investigate allegations of police brutality and civil rights violations. The responsibility for such investigations falls to the FBI. This has always been an unpalatable role for this agency because of its need to receive cooperation from the local police. The deemphasis on individual and civil rights issues by the Reagan administration was carried over to the attitudes of the Department of Justice. The growing conservative nature of the investigative and prosecutorial arm of the federal government has not encouraged the review of police behavior.

critical need for more and better training of police officers on the proper use of firearms and on decisions to use deadly force. Subsequent research could then focus on the relationship between such training and its effect on police deadly force use.[50] On the other hand, some police personnel, encouraged by a "get tough" attitude on the part of some segments of American Society, are pushing to thwart their superiors' efforts to limit their right to use their weapons. Police often see such efforts as a clear danger to their safety and as an effort to limit their "field discretion." Such attitudes are often abetted by police administrators themselves. A few years ago, the publicity-seeking sheriff of Pulaski County (Little Rock), Arkansas, now an elected member of Congress, called a press conference in which he waved a sawed-off shotgun at the cameras and announced that his department would "blow away" any would-be robbers in his jurisdiction. Although some people might be sympathetic with the former sheriff's intentions to deter such crimes, this kind of sensationalistic behavior creates further problems and detracts, for most thinking people, the image of professionalism and reason in law enforcement.

It will be interesting to watch over the next several years, in light of the Supreme Court's ruling in *Tennessee* v. *Garner*, what direction this issue takes. Like so many other concerns surrounding crime and criminals, discussion of such issues tends to be more emotional than logical. To minorities it is simply a means to further oppress and show disregard for blacks or Hispanics; for many white Americans it is simply giving the robbers, the rapists, and the murderers what they deserve—after all, they say, it's not our problem that a disproportionate number of them are black or Hispanic. For the police themselves, it's an issue of perceived safety, and they naturally feel at "greater risk" when confronting the more perceived prevalence of violence among minorities.

## □ POLICE CIVIL LIABILITY

Students are often inquisitive about police behavior and possible police abuse of authority. Questions such as "Can the cops search my trunk if they stop me?" are commonly asked of instructors teaching an introductory course in criminal justice. But questions about abusive and improper or negligent police behavior are not confined merely to college students and young people. In recent years, the issue of police misconduct has everyday citizens, civil rights advocates, minority citizen interests, and some members of the organized bar asking how can this problem be controlled?

One commonly prescribed remedy for improper police behavior is to be able to seek effective remedies through court actions against offending officers and the jurisdictions that employ them. Just as other professions such as medicine are coming under increasing legal scrutiny, so too do advocates for reform of abusive police practices seek similar opportunities. They have been pushing for the courts to agree to serve as a mechanism for redress by issuing judgments awarding monetary compensation for improper police behavior.

The issue of police civil liability is a complicated one. Although a great deal of case law governing police misconduct is taking shape, the subject cannot be approached understandably by the uninitiated or answered simply. Even such seemingly simple questions as "Do the police have the right to destroy my property

Complicated issue

in conducting a search?" or "Who is responsible when the police during a high-speed chase of a traffic violator kill or injure an innocent third party?" need to be approached cautiously. In pursuing such a question, one soon enters a legal thicket as to existing state law, possible avenues of redress through the federal civil rights laws, and other highly technical legal questions.[51]

Both federal and state laws provide substantive protections against various forms of police misconduct. In court, the plaintiff can make both civil rights violation claims (e.g., depriving someone of their constitutional rights) and negligence claims against the police. Traditionally, litigation against the police has been pressed in the federal courts rather than the state courts. The federal courts have been more receptive and sensitive to civil rights claims than their state counterparts. Several noted authorities in the field of litigating police misconduct say this may be changing, however. A conservative Supreme Court is closing off access to the federal courts for civil rights suits. By the same token, state courts—at least in some areas of the country—seem more willing than they have been in the past to call cops to task for misconduct.[52]

Although the courts have been slow to comply, the trend has been slowly and inexorably in favor of such opportunities. This has not come without a fight, however. Police unions and local governments have resisted any attempts to establish accountability through court-ordered judgments. Police unions, for example, often retain legal counsel to defend members being sued by aggrieved citizens. Individual police officers have also adopted the tactic of filing countersuits against the citizen complainant. Government jurisdictions are concerned that if liability for the actions of officers is extended to them, they will be seen as "deep pockets" by attorneys and potential litigants, which will encourage lawsuits. In this atmosphere, concern over increasing legal liability has been growing.

Areas of litigation  While many forms of improper police action can result in civil (and to some extent criminal) actions against offending officers, most of what has been happening in recent years can be conveniently grouped into five classes of suits. First, there are the areas of arrest and detention. This is made up of suits against the police alleging that there has been a false arrest and imprisonment. Often, the citizen will contend that there was insufficient probable cause to justify the arrest. The police also have been sued when arrests have been made under a statute or ordinance, which is unconstitutional.[53]

Another major area of police misconduct litigation have been cases against the police alleging excessive force and physical brutality. Associated with this issue is the use of deadly force by the police. These are both difficult areas for the courts to deal with—particularly the excessive force or brutality issue. Invariably, the police are going to claim that unusual force was necessary because the plaintiff "resisted arrest" and greater than usual force was then required to subdue him. Or, as it is often the case, there are no witnesses to the incident other than the arresting officer(s) and the complainant. And, of course, there is that old police argument that the plaintiff accidently "fell down some stairs."

Police also sometimes find themselves in court as defendants in civil cases in which they are accused of conducting illegal searches and seizures or they have violated someone's right to privacy. The issue of illegal searches and seizures is getting less play today, again, because of Supreme Court rulings such as *United States* v. *Leon* (see Chapter 5). The illegal search issue, together with the right to privacy, has been successfully used in several recent actions against police departments for unwarranted strip searches of arrestees.[54]

## BERGQUIST v. COUNTY OF COCHISE (1986)

### A Questionable Search and Police Civil Liability

FACTS

A confidential informant told agents of the Drug Enforcement Administration (DEA) that marijuana plants were growing in a greenhouse on a particular farm. Aerial surveillance failed to confirm this. The DEA contacted the Cochise County, Arizona, Sheriff's Department, and a joint raid was planned. A deputy sheriff obtained a search warrant from a local magistrate for the Burwell Hatch farm based on the informant's information. The next day, thirteen officers— members of the Cochise County Sheriff's Department's Special Response Team, dressed in military-style uniforms and armed with military-style weapons—arrived at the Bergquist farm to execute a search, which was actually authorized for the Burwell Hatch farm. The two minor children of the Bergquist family were at home alone. The officers threatened to shoot the children's pet dogs. The deputies searched a greenhouse and other buildings on the property. In the process of the wide-ranging search, they damaged or destroyed photographic equipment and ceramic art works in the Bergquists' studio.

The Bergquists filed a civil action in the federal District Court, complaining, among other things that the search warrant was issued without appropriate probable cause; that it was then mistakenly executed at their residence and carried out in an unreasonable and excessive manner; and that Cochise County was negligent in not properly training and instructing the local magistrate who issued the warrant and the police in their duties.

This trial court dismissed the Bergquist's

contentions, saying that as plaintiffs in this action, they had no validity to challenge the search warrant, because it was directed at a third party. The court also said that the sheriff's men were shielded from liability by the magistrate's decision to issue the warrant. The court ruled that the officers reasonably relied on the warrant in conducting the search, and their mistaken execution on the wrong residence was not a constitutional violation.

The Bergquists then appealed the court's ruling to the 9th Circuit Court of Appeals.

DECISION

The Court of Appeals remanded the case back to the trial court, holding among other things that the Bergquists have standing to challenge the execution of a warrant on their property because they have a "legitimate expectation of privacy in [their] premises." The officers' conduct in executing the warrant may be subject to judicial review into its reasonableness. The trial court is to re-consider the degree of negligence involved by the officers, and if it is found to be "gross negligence" in training or supervision, this gives rise to liability. This court has no right to impose training requirements on state officers such as County Magistrates.

SIGNIFICANCE OF THE CASE

This case points out the difficulty in getting judgment against police personnel even in the most egregious cases.

---

Given the difficulty of getting judgments against individual police officers, it has been suggested that the best recourse to controlling improper police behavior is to make the employing jurisdictions liable for police misconduct.[55] If governments could be held financially accountable for improper police actions, they would begin to provide better training, policy development under which the police operate, and closer supervision. It is well established legal doctrine that employers can be held liable by means of civil damages for injuries caused by employees who are acting within the scope of their employment. Gradually, this doctrine has been applied to governments. Governments can, for example, be held liable for wrongful actions committed by police personnel when it can be shown that the employer failed to train police officers appropriately, which directly resulted in some form of injury occurring from the improper action taken by law enforcement personnel. In spite of this rule, however, successful suits against employing governments have been rare.

Supreme Court makes it more difficult

This may become even more the situation, given an important 1989 ruling by the U.S. Supreme Court. The Court, relying on its earlier doctrine that a city can be held liable in a civil court for failing to properly train its police officers, extended this doctrine to allowing civil suits against governments if this failure demonstrates that the employer was *deliberately indifferent* to the deprivation of an individual's constitutional rights. But, by adopting this standard and the burden of proof associated with it, the door to civil actions against cities whose officers violate the constitutional rights of citizens may have swung closed even further.

In 1978, Geraldine Harris was arrested by the Canton, Ohio, police. She was driven to the police station in the back of a police wagon. When the officers arrived at the station, Harris was slumped in the back of the wagon. Although the officers asked Harris is she needed medical attention, no assistance was ever summoned. Instead, the police held Harris in the police station for over an hour. While there, Harris fell down several times and was finally left by the police slumped on the floor. After being released from custody, she was taken to a hospital in an ambulance provided by her family. Harris was diagnosed as suffering from several emotional ailments and spent a week in the hospital. She continued to receive outpatient treatment for the next year.

Some time later, Harris brought a civil suit against the City of Canton, alleging that she had a right to seek medical treatment while in police custody. Furthermore, she charged, the failure of the police in providing an opportunity for such treatment violated her due process rights under the Fourteenth Amendment. In the case, Canton's municipal regulations became an issue. Under these regulations, shift commanders were authorized to determine, in their sole discretion, whether a detainee required medical care. Although the shift commanders were granted such authority, they were not required to seek such care, nor were they provided with any special instruction beyond standard first-aid training to determine when to summon care for injured persons.

The thrust of Harris's argument was that the city of Canton "had a custom or policy of vesting complete authority with the police supervisor of when medical treatment would be administered to prisoners." Because these supervisors received no education with regard to their duties, Harris claimed that the city was grossly negligent or reckless by vesting "carte blanche authority" in these officers "without adequate training to recognize when medical treatment is needed."

The Court in its holding circumscribed the use of the ruling to those "limited circumstances" in which municipalities may be held liable "... when the failure to train its employees in a relevant respect evidences a *deliberate indifference* to the rights of persons with whom the police come into contact."[56] This "deliberate indifference" standard by the Court would seem to insulate governments from liability by setting a high standard of culpability. This ruling obviously stems from the concern that every time a police officer makes a mistake, the government's training program would be called into question. This was pointed out by Justice White, who wrote the majority opinion when he said, "The fact that [adequately trained officers occasionally make mistakes] says little about the training program or the legal basis for holding the city liable. To hold municipalities liable for mere neglect in their failure to train police officers would expose them to unprecedented liability. In virtually every instance where an individual's constitutional rights were violated by a police officer, the person will be able to point to something the city 'could have done' to prevent the incident."[57]

To avoid this type of judicial scrutiny, the Supreme Court has required proof that the municipality's policy or custom is "so obvious, and the inadequacy so likely to result in the violation of constitutional rights, that the policymakers of the city can reasonably be said to have been indifferent to the need." In addition, as Justice O'Connor said in a concurring opinion, when "policymakers were aware of, and acquiesced in, a pattern of constitutional violations involving the exercise of police discretion," liability should also be imposed.[58] The Court remanded the case back to the Court of Appeals to determine whether the Canton police policy constituted deliberate indifference to Harris's constitutional rights.

Many legal scholars looking at the Court's holding in this case conclude that although the Court stated unequivocally that municipalities may be held liable under certain circumstances, it is questionable whether someone whose constitutional rights have been violated will ever meet the standard set by the Court.[59] Accountability of the police may now have been further removed from scrutiny. Already, such provisions as protective job security through civil service regulations, militant police union activities, and the police subculture of mutual protection have all served to insulate the police from public accountability. By the same token, other mechanisms such as civilian review boards don't seem to have worked or to have improved the situation.

A tug-of-war seems to be raging between the need to control improper and illegal police behavior toward citizens and legitimate concerns over the authority the police need to deal with the problems they contend with today, and the dangerous situations more commonly faced by officers on the street. The police must have the resources and support they need, yet they cannot be held unaccountable for their actions. So far, no acceptable mechanism has been found that permits these two seemingly opposed goals to co-exist. Neither mechanisms internal to the police organization such as internal affairs units or external means such as civilian review board oversight seem to be doing the job. Now the courts have also backed away from any meaningful supervisory role except under egregious circumstances. It is possible that a dangerous void has been created, which along with other associated police problems, may warrant careful attention and concern by thoughtful Americans. Somehow a balance must be reached between public safety needs and the requirement that police remain accountable for their actions.

How to make the police more accountable?

## POLICE RESEARCH AND EFFECTIVENESS OF OPERATIONS

During the 1970s, the function and operations of the police were the subject of more analysis and research than had ever been accomplished in the past. The recognition of crime as a major social concern beginning in the mid-1960s, together with the recognition that the police play such a critical role and the availability of federal funding, has spawned many efforts at research.

This has brought about the establishment of a research capability unknown

**Growing research
capability**

in police circles just a few short years ago. Today, law enforcement research skills have been established and institutionalized in major police departments, among universities, and in private research institutes. Many progressive police administrators have themselves become knowledgeable in social science research techniques and foster their use in planning and analyzing police operations under their command. In 1976, for example, the Police Executive Research Forum (PERF) was founded; it consists of sixty chiefs of police from the nation's largest departments. The purpose of PERF is to provide a forum for these administrators to promote, exchange information, and discuss police research efforts.

Generally, the police research has focused on two broad areas: the complex role and behavior of the police in our society and basic operations research on police policies and procedures. Typically, academics have been involved in the former, and public and private institutions and police agencies themselves in the latter.

The results of the many research efforts have been a mixed bag. In the area of the police role and behavior, no comprehensive theory has emerged. Police roles, styles, and behavior seem to be as varied as the number of police agencies themselves and the men and women who constitute our nation's police forces.

**Impact of police
research**

It is also questionable what impact police operations research has had. Much of the research in these areas has tended to indicate what police techniques and procedures don't work but has contributed little insight into what does work and under what conditions. For example, police operations seem to have very little effect on deterring and controlling crime.[60] Police investigative work does not usually solve a crime. Its solution comes about through factors other than investigation.[61] Also, most patrol and investigative functions were consumed by nonpolice functions (e.g., running personal errands) or by spending investigative time in reviewing reports, documenting files, and attempting to locate and interview victims on cases that experience showed could not be solved.

**What needs to be done
and obstacles**

At this point, the operational research on the police needs to be continued. Promising strategies need to be tested in different jurisdictions and results examined. Such a program, however, faces two major obstacles: (1) the often-expressed disclaimer that characteristics of jurisdictions and police departments differ too much for testing programs through replication and (2) the unwillingness and lack of resources among jurisdictions to continue to do applied research and examine "what works."

The danger of such attitudes is that the police will retrench and fall back on conventional and time-tested means to provide services. Curiosity and innovation will be lost. In its place, the traditional conservative nature of police operations will take over, and attempts to improve on what the police do (or what they should be doing) will receive little attention. The question is Will the momentum and interest generated during the 1960s and 1970s be sustained? Already, there are dangerous signs that innovation is slowing down.

## □ POLICE ACCREDITATION

In the last few years, an effort has been underway to establish standards and an accreditation program for state and local law enforcement agencies that would be similar to an accreditation program that has been established for corrections.[62]

Begun initially with Law Enforcement Assistance Administration funds and the support of four major law enforcement associations, a Commission on Accreditation for Law Enforcement Agencies was formed in 1979.

The commission has developed 944 standards. About 60 percent of these are Developing standards "mandatory" standards that all police departments seeking accreditation must comply with if they are applicable to the particular agency. In developing the standards, the commission identified what it considered to be examples of the best professional practices in each area of law enforcement management: administration, operations, and support services.[63] For example, the agency must have a procedure for reviewing incidents in which there is an application of force through the use of a weapon by agency personnel. The department, depending on its size, must also have a planning and research component. There are many more similar requirements.

The accreditation process goes through five stages from the initial application by the police agency to the award of accreditation itself. This includes an on-site assessment by the commission staff and a final review and decision by the commission. Every five years an accredited department is required to undergo reaccreditation complete with a review of its continuing compliance with applicable standards.[64]

Although the program is a major step toward professionalism for the police, it is unfortunately not being considered by the vast majority of state and local police agencies. By 1988 only a small handful of police departments were accredited, although a larger number were in the process of self-assessment. This means that they have signed a contract with the commission and are working their way toward compliance with all the applicable standards. Illinois leads all the states in terms of agencies seeking accreditation followed by Florida, Texas, Georgia, and Ohio, in that order.[65]

The reasons for this apparent lack of interest are unknown. Yet, one can speculate that the lack of professional management standards existing in many of the agencies and the unwillingness to be scrutinized and examined by an independent outside source is threatening. It must also be understood that some police administrators and public officials want to unilaterally establish operating policies for their police departments and will not share their authority in this area with others—particularly with outside interests.

This points up many of the problems that seem to face American law enforcement today. The tremendous fragmentation and balkanization of authority and the lack of common standards among police departments themselves leads in many instances to wide differences in the standards of services that communities and citizens receive. It is unlikely that this will change much in the near future. As far as policing in America goes—particularly at the local level—police professionalization will continue to be of a very spotty nature indeed.

## THE GROWING ROLE OF PRIVATE SECURITY

Society's efforts to prevent and control crime have traditionally relied almost exclusively on the police and the other agencies of criminal justice. Today, this is changing in some dramatic ways.

A major American growth industry in the past decade has been the private

TABLE **6.3** Estimates of the Private Security Business

| | |
|---|---|
| Proprietary security | 448,979 |
|     Guards | 346,326 |
|     Store detectives | 20,106 |
|     Investigators | 10,000 |
|     Other workers | 12,215 |
|     Manager and staff | 60,332 |
| Contract security | 640,640 |
|     Guards and investigators | 541,600 |
|     Central alarm station | 24,000 |
|     Local alarm | 25,740 |
|     Armored car/courier | 26,300 |
|     Security equipment | 15,000 |
|     Specialized services | 5,000 |
|     Security consultants | 3,000 |
| Total | 1,100,000 |

*Source:* Cunningham and Taylor, *Private Security and Police in America: The Hallcrest Report* (Portland, Ore.: Chancellor Press, 1985)

security resources of business, industry, and institutions. Today, private security plays a major protective role in the life of the nation.[66] It is estimated that private security organizations employ 1.1 million persons, and the total expenditures in 1988 for its products and services are estimated at over $25 billion (Table 6.3). This is significantly more than our total expenditures for federal, state, and local law enforcement services.

*Two general types*

Private security is broken down into two general types of programs—*proprietary* security measures undertaken when an organization employs its own security personnel and *contractual* services such as guards, investigations, alarm services, and armored car services. In these latter programs an organization contracts for these services with a provider security firm. To these must be added the manufacture and sale of security products such as safes, electronic access control, and closed circuit television.

Within the two general types of security programs, there are three major components: physical security, information security, and personnel security. The use of guards for physical security is probably the component most people recognize. In recent years information security is becoming extremely important to many private (and public) organizations. This includes provisions to protect customer lists, marketing plans, research and development data—particularly in high-technology industries—and the growing concern to protect unauthorized access to computer systems and records. Personnel security includes day-to-day protection of workers, as well as executive protection and protection against terrorism for many if not most multinational businesses.

This shift in protection resources seems to parallel cutbacks in public expenditures for law enforcement. In recent years, while police agencies showed a slowing increase, private security gained momentum. This was also a period when growing numbers of Americans undertook self-help measures against crime, increasing the use of locks, lighting, guns, burglar alarms, citizen patrols, and security guards. One federally funded study found that 40 percent of respondents in ten major U.S. cities had installed some form of security device in their homes.[67] Similar findings have come from other studies.

The problems of regulation

This growth has not been without its drawbacks. A major problem—especially among contractual security firms—is the need to regulate them. States are finding that such firms must be carefully regulated and their employees screened and trained. About one-half of the states have passed licensing laws aimed at accomplishing these goals. Some states require, for example, that security personnel receive specified training. This is particularly true if the employee is armed. Likewise, background and criminal history checks must be run on security firm employees. Some states require that security firms indemnify their responsibility by posting bond with licensing authorities, but in other states no requirements or only the most minimal are imposed on private security firms.

This lack of training, screening, and general competency is reflected in the attitudes many police personnel have about private security services. In the federal government's study, law enforcement gave private security low ratings in ten areas, including quality of personnel, training received, and familiarity with legal authority.[68] The study also pointed out that there is little formal interaction or cooperation between the police and private security. A few security managers reported some sharing of information, personnel equipment, and other resources with law enforcement, but most cooperative efforts appear to be initiated by the private sector.

Faced with mounting cost-containment problems, the police in future years may find that they must turn to private security providers to concentrate on crime-prevention efforts while the police turn their attention to violent crimes and crime response. Economic realities are forcing law enforcement to look at ways to reduce workloads. In the federal study the 384 police administrators surveyed indicated a willingness to discuss such a transfer of responsibilities to private security. Among those they cited were public building security, parking enforcement, and court security.[69]

The hiring and training of private security personnel is usually done on an informal basis. (© Donald Dietz/Stock Boston)

The growth in private security-provided services shows no leveling off. Even though problems abound, there are also some important areas of opportunity in this growth field. The years ahead will almost certainly see efforts to regulate this industry still further. With the required regulation will likely come greater reliance by the police on the use and acceptability of such services to supplement their own.

## SUMMARY

Until recently, police change has been quite slow. Under unremitting pressure, changes are not occurring in American law enforcement that will have meaningful future implications. Some of the more important changes are occurring in the traditional nature of the police organization itself. The old quasi-military model of police operations seems to be breaking down a bit. Faced with such changes as better-educated young officers seeking careers in law enforcement and the need to create more opportunities for job satisfaction, alternative police models are being considered. One of the most highly touted approaches is the team policing concept.

Another issue of current importance is affirmative action. Police personnel policies that have traditionally excluded females and minority group members are being changed. Increased opportunities for careers in the police service should open up for these groups in the future.

The police are also beginning to somewhat redefine their role. More and more emphasis is being placed on the preventive aspects of police work. This can be seen by the growing awareness of crime prevention strategies as an important aspect of police work.

Because of the financial problems that face many communities today, police productivity has also become an important issue. Increased emphasis is being placed on techniques to improve police productivity and to measure the effects of alternative police strategies.

The issue of police use of deadly force and civil liability is creating a great deal of controversy in some cities that have experienced police shootings of suspects, especially if they are members of a minority. Such issues tend to polarize the police and minority residents and threaten to cause major confrontations.

The issue of police research and effectiveness was also discussed. Police research has tended to call into question the effectiveness of traditional methods of police operations. Through such research efforts, the police have been seen as even more limited in their ability to deal with crime than was previously imagined. Unfortunately, police research, while pointing out the shortcomings of police operations, has not been very successful in providing answers to what could serve as more effective techniques.

Finally, the chapter concluded with a discussion of the growth of private security and the potential and promise this rapidly expanding area provides.

## REVIEW QUESTIONS

1. What is the purpose of such programs as job enlargement and neighborhood team policing?
2. What is affirmative action? How are police agencies responding to it?
3. In attempting to improve the effectiveness of crime prevention, various programs have been initiated. Name six of these programs and explain their purpose.
4. What are two types of police corruption? Why is police corruption a continuing problem?
5. What is conflict management? What models are used in handling conflict situations?
6. What are the arguments for and against consolidation of metropolitan police services?
7. What is the issue of police use of deadly force? Who are the "actors" involved in the determination of such policies? What roles do they play? What seem to be their general feelings?

8. What is the issue of police liability? What are your general impressions of its effectiveness in reducing police misconduct?
9. What is the status of police research? What have such efforts demonstrated?

10. What is the potential for private security to supplant some functions of the police?
11. What are directed patrol strategies and differential police response programs?

## DISCUSSION QUESTIONS

1. It is said in this chapter that police corruption will most likely never be totally eradicated. Do you agree with this statement?
2. Is consolidation of police services on a metropolitan or regional basis a good idea? Discuss the advantages and disadvantages.

3. Are there any implications for using women more extensively in police work? Discuss these.
4. How do the issues of deadly force and police liability relate to each other?
5. Which of the issues discussed in this chapter is most important for the improvement of the police in the future? Why?

## SUGGESTED ADDITIONAL READINGS

Abrecht, M. E., and B. L. Stern. *Making of a Woman Cop.* New York: Morrow, 1976.

Allinson, Richard S., "The Uncertain Future of Police Research." *Police Magazine* 4 (No. 4, July 1981): 55–56.

Bittner, Egon. *The Functions of the Police in Modern Society.* Washington, D.C.: U.S. Government Printing Office, 1970.

Chaiken, Marcia, and Jan Chaiken. *Public Policing—Privately Provided.* Washington, D.C.: National Institute of Justice, 1987.

Eastman, George D., and Samuel G. Chapman. *Short of Merger: Countywide Police Resource Pooling.* Lexington, Mass.: Lexington Books, 1976.

Finn, Peter. *Police Response to Special Populations.* Washington, D.C.: U.S. Department of Justice, 1987.

Fyfe, James J. *Readings on Police Use of Deadly Force.* Washington, D.C.: Police Foundation, 1982.

Hartmann, Francis X. (ed). *Debating the Evolution of American Policing.* Washington, D.C.: U.S. Department of Justice, November 1988.

International City Management Association, *Local Government Police Management* (Washington, D.C.: ICMA, 1977).

Juris, Hervey A., and Peter Feville. *Police Unionism.* Lexington, Mass.: Lexington Books, 1973.

Kelling, George L., and Mark Moore. *The Evolving Strategy of Policing.* Washington, D.C.: U.S. Department of Justice, November 1988.

Krajick, Kevin, "Does Patrol Prevent Crime?" *Police Magazine* 1 (No. 6, September 1978): 8–13.

*Measuring Police-Crime Control Productivity.* Part III of *The Challenge of Productivity Diversity—Improving Local Government Productivity Measurement and Evaluation,* prepared for the National Commission on Productivity by the Urban Institute. Washington, D.C.: National Technical Information Service, U.S. Department of Commerce (Document no. PB223117), 1972.

Moore, Mark H., and Robert C. Trojanowicz. *Corporate Strategies for Policing.* Washington, D.C.: U.S. Department of Justice, November 1988.

Ostrom, Elinor, and Roger B. Parks. "Suburban Police Departments: Too Many, Too Small?" *Urban Affairs Annual Reviews,* Vol. 7. Beverly Hills, Calif.: Sage, 1973.

Police Executive Research Forum. Investigative Consultant Team, *A New Approach for Law Enforcement Cooperation* (Washington, D.C.: PERF, 1982).

Washington, Brenda E. *Deployment of Female Police Officers in the United States.* Gaithersburg, Md.: International Association of Chiefs of Police, 1974.

Weisbord, Marvin R., Howard Lamb, and Allan Drexler. *Improving Police Department Management Through Problem-Solving Task Forces.* Reading, Mass.: Addison-Wesley, 1974.

## NOTES

1. For example, see Robert D. Pursley, "Traditional Police Organization: A Portent of Failure?" in William Bopp, ed., *Police Administration* (Boston: Holbrook, 1974), pp. 83–86; and Egon Bittner, *The Functions of the Police in Modern Society* (Washington, D.C.: U.S. Government Printing Office, 1970), especially chap. VIII.

2. See Herman Goldstein, *Policing A Free Society* (Cambridge, Mass.: Ballinger, 1977), especially chap. 10.

3. For example, see Tony Pate, Jack W. McCullough, Robert A. Bowers, and Amy Ferrara, *Kansas City Peer Review Panel: An Evaluation Report* (Washington, D.C.: Police Foundation, 1976).

4. 42. U.S.C.A. 2000 et seq.

5.   *Griggs* v. *Duke Power Company*, 915 Sup. Ct. 849 (1971).

6.   Pub. L. No. 92–261.

7.   For example, see *Morrow* v. *Crisler*, Civil Action No. 4716, U.S. District Ct., S. Miss. (1971); *Smith* v. *East Cleveland*, 363 F. Supp. (1973); *Wilson* v. *City of Torrance*, Civil Action No. 74–963. U.S. District Ct., E. Ca. (1974).

8.   Memo from the *Washington Post*, January 27, 1975.

9.   James Becker, "Court's Affirmative Action Stance Threatens Gains," *Washington Post*, 25 June 1989, p. 3.

10.   Terry Eisenberg, Deborah Ann Kent, and Charles R. Wall, *Police Personnel Practices in State and Local Government* (Washington, D.C.: Police Foundation, 1973), p. 17.

11.   Cynthia F. Sulton and Roi D. Townsey, *Executive Summary: A Progress Report on Women in Policing* (Washington, D.C.: Police Foundation, 1981), p. 4.

12.   Sam Walker, "Employment of Black and Hispanic Police Officers: Trends in the 50 Largest Cities," *ACJS Today* (November 1983): 3–7.

13.   See Peter B. Bloch and Deborah Anderson, *Policewomen on Patrol: Final Report* (Washington, D.C.: Police Foundation, 1974); and Joyce L. Sicheletal, *Women on Patrol* (Washington, D.C.: U.S. Government Printing Office, January 1978).

14.   See Susan E. Martin, "Policewomen and Policewomen: Occupational Role Dilemmas and Choices of Female Officers," *Journal of Police Science and Administration* 7 (September 1979): 314–323.

15.   Ibid., p. 320.

16.   Sally Gross, "Women Becoming Cops: Developmental Issues and Solutions," *The Police Chief* (January 1984): 32–35.

17.   Ibid., p. 33.

18.   See National League of Cities, *Community Crime Prevention and the Local Official* (Washington, D.C.: National League of Cities, 1974).

19.   See California Council on Criminal Justice, *Selected Crime Prevention Programs in California* (Sacramento, Calif.: 1973).

20.   See: Bureau of Justice Statistics, *Report to the Nation on Crime and Justice*, 2nd ed. (Washington: U.S. Department of Justice, March 1988), pp. 116–123.

21.   Leroy F. Aarons, "Police-Fire Strike Unnerves Other Cities," (*Washington Post* syndicated column), *The State Journal*, Lansing, Mich., 26 August 1976, p. A11.

22.   Harry P. Hatry, "Wrestling with Police Crime Control Productivity Measurement," in ibid., p. 90.

23.   The President's Commission on Law Enforcement and Administration of Justice, *Task Force Report: The Police* (Washington, D.C.: U.S. Government Printing Office, 1967), p. 208.

24.   Allan N. Kornblum, *The Moral Hazards* (Lexington, Mass.: Lexington Books, 1976), p. 1.

25.   See, for example, Douglas S. Drummond, *Police Culture* (Beverly Hills, Calif.: Sage, 1976); Herbert Biegel, *The Closed Fraternity of Police and the Development of the Corrupt Attitude* (New York: John Jay Press, 1978);

Thomas Barker and Julian Roebuck, *An Empirical Typology of Police Corruption: A Study in Organizational Deviance* (Springfield, Ill.: Charles C. Thomas, 1973); and Antony Simpson, *The Literature of Police Corruption*, vol. I (New York: John Jay Press, 1977).

26.   Lawrence Sherman, "Learning Police Ethics," *Criminal Justice Ethics* (Spring–Winter, 1982), pp. 10–19.

27.   *The Knapp Commission Report on Police Corruption* (New York: Braziller, 1972).

28.   Kornblum, op. cit., p. 2.

29.   "More Indictments Handed Down in Miami Cop Probe," *Miami Herald*, 17 September 1987, p. 3.

30.   Samuel G. Chapman, *Cops, Killers and Staying Alive—The Murder of Police Officers in America* (Springfield, Ill.: Charles C Thomas, 1986). Also see Federal Bureau of Investigation, *Uniform Crime Reports—1986* (Washington, D.C.: U.S. Government Printing Office), pp. 280–289.

31.   E. Cummings, *Systems of Social Regulation* (New York: Atherton, 1968).

32.   See Morton Bard, *Family Crisis Intervention: From Concept to Implementation* (Washington, D.C.: LEAA, December 1973).

33.   Ibid., p. 9.

34.   Advisory Commission on Intergovernmental Relations, *Urban America and the Federal System* (Washington, D.C.: U.S. Government Printing Office, 1969), pp. 75 and 117.

35.   For example, see David L. Noorgard, *Regional Law Enforcement* (Chicago: Public Administration Service, 1969); Advisory Commission on Intergovernmental Relations, *State–Local Relations in the Criminal Justice System* (Washington, D.C.: U.S. Government Printing Office, 1971); Committee for Economic Development, *Reducing Crime and Assuring Justice* (New York: Committee for Economic Development, June 1972).

36.   President's Commission, *Task Force Report: The Police*, p. 308.

37.   Elinor Ostrom and Roger B. Parks, "Suburban Police Departments: Too Many and Too Small?" in Louis H. Masotti and Jeffrey K. Hadden, eds., *The Urbanization of the Suburbs* (Beverly Hills, Calif.: Sage, 1973), chap. XIV. An increase in the per capita costs of municipal services also occurred after the Ontario legislature created Toronto Metro; see K. Kaplan, *Urban Political Systems; A Functional Analysis of Metro Toronto* (New York: Columbia University Press, 1967).

38.   Robert E. McArthur, *Impact of City–County Consolidation of the Rural–Urban Fringe: Nashville–Davidson County Tennessee* (Washington, D.C.: U.S. Government Printing Office, 1971), pp. 19–22.

39.   See Adam Campbell and H. Schuman, "A Comparison of Black and White Attitudes and Experiences in the City," in C. H. Harr, ed., *The End of Innocence: A Suburban Reader* (Glenview, Ill.: Scott, Foresman, 1972), p. 109.

40.   David L. Skoler and J. M. Hetler, "Government Restructuring and Criminal Administration: The Challenge of Consolidation," in *Crisis in Urban*

Government: A Symposium on Restructuring Metropolitan Urban Government (Silver Spring, Md.: Thomas Jefferson Publishing, 1970), pp. 53–75.

41. Elinor R. Ostrom, Roger B. Parks, and Gordon P. Whitaker, "Do We Really Want to Consolidate Urban Police Forces? A Reappraisal of Some Old Assertions," Public Administration Review (October/November 1974): 423–432.

42. For example, see Elinor R. Ostrom, "Community Public Services and Responsiveness: On the Design of Institutional Arrangements for the Provision of Police Services," paper presented at the American Political Science Association annual meeting, Chicago, 29 August to 2 September 1974; and Roger B. Canfield, "Citizen Satisfaction and Police Effectiveness: Perspectives Beyond Productivity and Social Equity," paper presented at the 1974 National Conference of the American Society for Public Administration, Syracuse, N.Y., 17–24 March 1974.

43. Noorgard, Regional Law Enforcement, p. 24.

44. Letter from Gilbert E. Schollen, Los Angeles County Sheriff's Department, 17 December 1975.

45. James H. Ellis, "The Connecticut Resident State Police System," Police 5 (September–October 1960): 69–72.

46. See Catherine H. Milton, Jeanne Wahl Halleck, James Lardner, and Gary L. Abrecht, Police Use of Deadly Force (Washington, D.C.: Police Foundation, 1977), pp. 10–11.

47. Arthur L. Kobler, "Figures (and Perhaps Some Facts) on Police Killings of Civilians in the United States, 1965–69," Journal of Social Issues 3, No. 1 (1975): 185; and J. G. Safer, "Deadly Weapons in the Hands of Police On Duty and Off Duty," Journal of Urban Law, Fall 1972, p. 566.

48. John C. Hall, "Police Use of Deadly Force to Arrest—A Constitutional Standard," (Part I) FBI Law Enforcement Bulletin (June 1988), pp. 23–30.

49. Ozell Sutton, "Police Use of Excessive Force: A Community Relations Concern," in National Institute of Law Enforcement and Criminal Justice, A Community Concern: Police Use of Deadly Force (Washington, D.C.: U.S. Government Printing Office, January 1979), p. 37.

50. Frank Horvath and Michael Donahue, Deadly Force: An Analysis of Shootings by Police in Michigan, 1976–1981 (East Lansing, Mich.: Michigan State University, School of Criminal Justice, 3 November 1982), p. 215. George L. Kelling, Tony Pate, Duane Dieckman, and Charles E. Brown, The Kansas City Preventive Patrol Experiment (Washington, D.C.: The Police Foundation, 1974).

51. Author's Note: Typically, the police will not be held responsible for the destruction of property while lawfully performing their responsibilities. The issue often turns on the question of "reasonableness of conduct," which has been interpreted rather broadly (and protectively for the police) by the courts. The generally established rule is that pursuing a suspect at high speeds does not constitute a civil rights violation. See Galas v. McKee, 801 F. 2d 200 (6th Cir. 1986). The police might, however, be held liable if their conduct was shown to be "grossly negligent."

52. Michael Avery and David Rudovsky, Police Misconduct—Law and Litigation (New York: Clark Boardman Co., 1988), p. 1.

53. Fields v. City of Omaha, 801 F. 2d 850 (8th Cir. 1987).

54. Logan v. Shealey, 660 F. 2d 1007 (4th Cir. 1981).

55. James D. Lochmeyer, "Controlling Police Brutality" New York Times (2 September 1988), p. 7.

56. Canton v. Harris, 57 LW 4270 (1989).

57. Ibid., 4273.

58. Ibid., 4274.

59. For example, see Joseph Welter, "Training Failure and the Threat of Liability," Law Enforcement News 15 (30 April 1989): 5, 15.

60. Joan Petersilia, An Inquiry into the Relationship Between the Thoroughness of Police Investigation and Case Disposition (Santa Monica, Calif.: Rand Corporation, 1976); and Peter W. Greenwood, An Analysis of the Apprehension Activities of the New York Police Department (Santa Monica, Calif.: Rand Corporation, 1970).

61. Kelling, The Kansas City Preventive Patrol Experiment; and David C. Anderson, "Management Moves in on the Detective," Police Magazine 5 (March 1978): 14–24.

62. This is the Commission on Accreditation for Corrections.

63. Commission on Accreditation for Law Enforcement Agencies, Inc., Accreditation Program Book (Fairfax, Va.: Commission on Accreditation, October 1983).

64. Ibid., pp. 1–5.

65. Letter from Frank J. Leahy, Jr., Assistant Director, Commission on Accreditation for Law Enforcement Agencies, Inc., 26 November 1985.

66. Much of this section is adopted from W. C. Cunningham and T. H. Taylor, The Growing Role of Private Security (Washington, D.C.: National Institute of Justice, October 1984).

67. Ibid., p. 3.

68. Ibid., p. 3.

69. Ibid., p. 4.

# THE COURT

# CHAPTER 7

# The Role of the Court

## OBJECTIVES

**After reading this chapter, the student should be able to:**

Discuss problems with "change" in our judicial system.

Identify and discuss the features of court organization in the United States.

Discuss the problems associated with how our courts are organized.

Discuss the historical development of state and local court systems and important changes and developments.

Identify the composition of state court systems today, including the types of courts, their respective jurisdictions, and their specific characteristics.

Discuss the federal courts, including the types of courts, their respective jurisdictions, and their specific characteristics.

Discuss the operations of the U.S. Supreme Court and the issues and controversies that surround it.

Discuss the implications of a dual system of courts for the administration of justice.

## IMPORTANT TERMS

Dual system of courts
Federal exclusionary rule
Absence of supervisory control
Court specialization
Geographical organization of courts
Colonial court development
Postrevolutionary court development

Judicial review
*Marbury* v. *Madison*
Appellate courts
Intermediate appellate courts
Courts of general jurisdiction
Courts of limited or special jurisdiction

Original and appellate jurisdiction
Justice of the peace
Magistrate's courts
Municipal courts
U.S. magistrate's courts
U.S. district courts
U.S. attorney
Appellate court proceedings
U.S. courts of appeal
U.S. Supreme Court

Situated between the police and the corrections component of the criminal justice system, the American system of courts plays perhaps the most important role in the administration of American justice—a role that has often been criticized for not being effectively fulfilled. Americans seem to have become increasingly disenchanted with the courts. For example, a survey a few years ago indicated that citizens expressed varying levels of discontent in describing their confidence in our courts. This was particularly true in their feelings for state and local courts. Nearly 40 percent of the respondents interviewed in this survey were only slightly or not at all confident in the performance or operations of this branch of government.[1]

An examination of the progress made in recent years by all the agencies of criminal justice would probably show that the courts have demonstrated the least progress and the least willingness to improve the ways in which they discharge their responsibilities. Part of the reason for this lack of change is due to the unique structural and procedural characteristics of our courts. The fact that our courts are bureaucratic entities certainly impedes any attempt to introduce greater flexibility and bring about change, but the additional fact that they are *unique* bureaucracies makes them even more rigid. Their uniqueness derives from the fact that the legal process by which they operate requires in many instances a procedural similarity and routinization to a degree unknown to most other government institutions. As interpreters and appliers of the law, the courts are often bound by legal rigidity to an extent unshared by other criminal justice components. This, in turn, solidifies the characteristics under which they operate.

There is yet another reason for their lack of change. The criminal court operates to a large extent as a closed community, which, in the view of one noted scholar and observer of the legal process, brings about an "almost pathological distrust of outsiders."[2] This is perhaps a bit of an overstatement. More correctly, it might be argued that courts, as a collective group of legal specialists, resent attempts by nonprofessional (defined as not law-trained) groups to exert any influence over their operations. This is not to say that the courts resist any attempt to influence the process of adjudication and justice; rather, they are too often less than receptive to ideas and strategies that actually might improve these two objectives. Like some other professions, such as medicine, the system is defined by and operates primarily for the benefit of those in the profession. Any lengthy observation of our criminal courts should provide the insightful observer with the realization that they too often operate primarily to serve the interests of the judges and lawyers who operate and practice within them. In such a situation, "outsiders" or those who are not members of the "inner circle" will have little, if any, direct impact on the functioning of the court. Any attempt to change such a situation will quickly result in the legal profession closing ranks to protect "their system." Along this line James Eisenstein and Herbert Jacob, in their study of the courtroom as an organizational entity that expresses the interests of the courtroom elite (prosecutor, defense attorney, and judge), say:

> Thinking of (courts) as organizations directs our attention to courtroom work as a group activity. Most persons in the courtroom perform quite specialized functions, and their activity fits into a broader pattern and is constrained by it. Incentives and shared goals motivate the persons in a courtroom workgroup. Workgroup members develop relationships that are cemented by exchanges of inducements as well as by shared goals. They operate in a common task environment, which provides common resources and imposes common restraints on their actions.[3]

Surveys have also shown that many citizens have had no direct experience in courts, particularly in criminal courts. In the same survey quoted previously, it was found that the American people exhibit a disturbing lack of knowledge and familiarity with, and understanding of, court processes. As the survey concluded: "The public is misinformed about many topics related to court jurisdiction, operation, and procedure."[4]

Public ignorance of the courts

This section first examines certain characteristics of the court system, its development, and present structure. Then the functioning and responsibilities of court personnel, institutional arrangements, and the trial process are discussed. Finally, an examination is made of the particular changes that courts are undergoing and of recommendations being made to improve the handling and disposition of criminal cases by our courts.

##  JUDICIAL ORGANIZATION

The organization of the American judicial system is characterized by the following features: (1) a dual system of courts; (2) an absence of supervisory control; (3) specialization; and (4) geographical organization.[5]

### A Dual System of Courts

The court system in the United States is organized on the principle of political federalism. Although the first Congress, acting under the authority of the Constitution, established the federal court system, the states were permitted to establish their own court structures. In fact, most legal matters were left to the state courts. Only in later years did the federal government and the federal courts begin to exercise increasing jurisdiction over crimes and civil matters. In this context, jurisdiction means simply the authority to enforce the laws and to try those who violate these laws. As a result of new federal legislation and broad interpretation of the power to regulate interstate commerce, the federal courts now have authority for literally thousands of federal crimes.

Federal and state courts

Thus, a dual system of state and federal courts exists. In many instances, the state and federal courts have *concurrent jurisdiction* over specific crimes. For example, someone who robs a bank in California is in violation of the State of California Criminal Code as well as the U.S. Criminal Code, and theoretically, could be brought to trial in either a state or a federal court, or both.

Some consequences of a dual court structure

Although being tried in both systems for the same crime can occur legally, it seldom does in reality. The local U.S. attorney, following policies established by the U.S. Department of Justice, generally works out an agreement with local police and judicial authorities to decide whether the federal government or the state will prosecute the case. In recent years, the Department of Justice has encouraged U.S. Attorneys to let the state try the accused and to imprison the offender in a state prison if found guilty. If there is any confusion or disagreement over where the trial should be held, the determining factor is usually which jurisdiction made the arrest and maintains custody of the offender.

Although in theory an individual could be tried in a state court, serve a sentence in a state institution, and then, as mentioned, be subjected to the same process by federal authorities, this situation rarely occurs. Normally, where concurrent jurisdiction exists, federal authorities simply decline to prosecute. However, there have been notable exceptions. If the federal authorities feel that the state courts have rendered a serious miscarriage of justice (e.g., a major drug dealer receives a 6-month sentence), the federal authorities may, with the approval of the U.S. Department of Justice, pursue an "independent interest" and prosecute the individual in federal court on his or her release from the state authorities.

The implications of this dual legal system and court structure have had other significant implications for the administration of justice. For example, in a 1914 case, *Weeks* v. *United States*,[6] the U.S. Supreme Court established the Federal Exclusionary Rule. Weeks was charged by federal agents with conducting a lottery in interstate commerce by use of the mails. He was arrested at his place of employment, and his residence was searched without the authority of a search warrant. During this search, incriminating evidence was found and was later introduced at his federal trial. On appeal to the U.S. Supreme Court, he alleged that this search was unlawful under the provisions of the Fourth Amendment. The Supreme Court agreed and established the Federal Exclusionary Rule, which held that evidence unlawfully obtained by federal agents in violation of an individual's constitutional rights could no longer be introduced into federal prosecutions. The Supreme Court, however, made it quite clear that this decision applied only to federal agents and federal courts and not to police officers or courts at the state level. This led to the famous "silver platter doctrine." Because the Federal Exclusionary Rule prohibited only federal officers from illegally seizing evidence and introducing it into federal trials, nothing prevented federal police officers from illegally searching for and seizing evidence and turning it over to the state authorities on a "silver platter" for introduction into the state courts. It was not until 1961, in the now famous *Mapp* v. *Ohio* case,[7] that the U.S. Supreme Court finally imposed the Federal Exclusionary Rule on state courts.

The jurisdiction of federal courts and the laws that guide their actions are often shaped by different political interests than are the laws and court actions of the states. For example, minority groups that have received no consideration from their state courts have frequently sought help from Congress in having the jurisdiction of the federal courts enlarged so that they may obtain redress for their grievances through the federal judiciary. A good example is the Civil Rights Act of 1964. This legislation and subsequent laws empowered federal law enforcement officials to investigate and bring to trial individuals who interfere with the exercise of civil rights. This legislation has frequently been used in cases in which state agents such as law enforcement personnel have violated the civil rights of citizens within their states.

## Absence of Supervisory Control

The second most notable characteristic of American courts is that they perform their function with little or no supervisory control. The U.S. Supreme Court and the state supreme courts are usually supreme courts only in the sense that they serve as appellate courts from the lower judiciary, and they establish certain procedures for the lower courts.

For instance, many people believe that there is an automatic right to appeal to the U.S. Supreme Court and that in this way the Supreme Court exercises authority over the lower federal courts and the state courts. In fact, the Supreme

The relative
independence of courts

Court only hears an extremely small portion of cases disposed of by the lower courts. There are a number of reasons for this: First, before someone who is tried for a crime on a state level can appeal to the Supreme Court, that person must have exhausted every appellate process available in the particular state (see Figure 7.3). Second, the case must involve a substantial federal question and/or constitutional issue. Third, the issue must be of significant social/legal importance to warrant a Supreme Court hearing. And last, the process is extremely costly and time-consuming, which, in itself, is often a major inhibiting factor.

This absence of supervisory control over the courts is also manifest in other ways. Often, no single authority has the power to control the assignment of court personnel, the formulation of the budget, or the distribution of supplies and facilities among the courts or the flow of cases through each court. Although some states are moving in the direction of giving supervisory authority over lower state courts to the state supreme court, this movement is not uniform throughout the nation. At the federal level, this situation is somewhat remedied by the Administrative Office of the United States Courts and by the assistance now being provided this office by the Federal Judicial Center. In many states, however, the legislature is required by state constitutions or statutes to ensure the necessary operating budget for the judiciary. Because most state judges are elected, they are theoretically responsible only to the people, which makes it nearly impossible to supervise them or remove them from office except through the ballot box.

This absence of supervisory control is even extended to court support personnel. Court bailiffs, probation officers, clerks, and other functionaries in many instances are appointed by the court; these positions are often patronage appointments for faithful political support in the state or local political arena.

## Specialization

Another important feature of the court system, particularly at the state and local levels, is its arrangement according to specialized areas. For example, the lower courts at the local and municipal levels are often courts of limited jurisdiction that can try only misdemeanors. In felony cases, the trial is conducted by a court of general jurisdiction at the county, district, regional, or state level. In a similar vein, specialized juvenile courts have been established to handle crimes committed by youths, and in some larger municipalities, specialized branches of local courts handle traffic offenses or minor crimes. This same procedure is also carried over into civil law, where different courts have been established to handle claims, wills and estates, and civil suits, based on the amount of money sought for damages.

Jurisdictional authority

## Geographical Organization

Our courts are also organized by geographical boundaries. The states and the federal government are divided into judicial districts, with various levels of courts situated in each area.

Possible consequences of the geographical organization of our nation's courts

This arrangement has important implications for the administration of criminal justice. The particular location of a court influences its responsiveness to political interests. Rural courts are often less tolerant of certain forms of criminal behavior than urban courts might be under the same circumstances. For instance, judges in rural areas often perceive that their constituents are less likely to sanction offenses against blue laws, which prohibit certain businesses from operating on Sundays, liquor and drug offenses, gambling, and other normative vice offenses.

Numerous studies have been made of how courts and individual judges differ in terms of the sentences they impose in different locales. In one study of the federal system, the average prison sentence for narcotics violations was 83 months in the Tenth Circuit, but only forty-four months in the Third Circuit.[8] Another study some years ago found that the average sentence for forgery ranged from a high of 68 months in the Northern District of Mississippi to a low of 7 months in the Southern District of that state; the highest average sentence for motor vehicle theft was 47 months in the Southern District of Iowa, and the lowest was 14 months in the Northern District of New York.[9]

This is not to imply that differences in sentences imposed by courts in different areas necessarily reflect different social values and attitudes. No research has ever conclusively established such a relationship, though the constituency of each local community clearly must have some effect on the operation of the courts in that region. After all, elected judges are responsible to the electorate in their districts, and it is safe to assume that judges—particularly in criminal cases—will generally respond to what they think the community expects.

## HISTORY AND DEVELOPMENT OF STATE COURT SYSTEMS

In their three-hundred-year history, the state court systems have undergone a remarkable evolution. This section examines notable changes from the colonial period to the present.

### The Colonial Period

Generally speaking, court organization in the early American colonies followed a pattern of social evolution not unlike the struggling young colonies themselves. The colonies began with simple court structures. Indeed, it is almost a mistake to call them *courts* as we use that term today. It would take years for the courts to evolve into more complex entities—a judicial system composed of courts with specialized jurisdiction over cases and specific forms of legal dispute. The situation was not a result of our heritage. The rudimentary court structure of the colonies was in sharp contrast to what existed in the mother country. England in the seventeenth century boasted an amazing, cumbersome collection of courts that were already highly specialized and widely overlapping in authority.[10]

Simple, unspecialized court structure

Life in the colonies was precarious. The complexity of social interaction and the growth in commerce and trade that was a characteristic of England at the time—a system that required a more extensive court system in that country—was conspicuously absent in the colonies. The colonies needed simple mechanisms of government to regulate lives that were also simple. The company charters issued by the crown in such colonies as Massachusetts, Maryland, and Virginia primarily provided for a system of administrative organization of the colonies that would ensure their development and commercial advantage to England. Many of the subtle niceties, such as the structure of courts, were at most secondary concerns to an administrative structure devised to develop the colonies—and to ensure England's hegemony over her bitter rivals France and Spain—for the advantages promised by the New World.

The early courts in this environment became at least as much administrative in their operations as they were judicial. They became all-purpose extensions of civil authority and management. They handled taxes, and they dealt with probate and matters of administration, apportionment for the repair of bridges, punishment of heretics, settlement of the poor, licensing of new meeting houses, and punishment of vendors seeking excessive prices.[11] Almost as an afterthought, they also became instruments for enforcing the criminal law.

Yet another characteristic of these early courts would appear perverse to Americans today. Although local courts began to develop to handle crimes and civil matters, rights of appeal from these decisions went not to higher courts as such but to the appointed and later elected ruling bodies of the colonies. At first, these were the colonial governors. Later, their appointed advisors took over this function. Finally, the mantle of appellate authority from the lower courts came to rest with elected or appointed legislative or representative bodies. Thus, with a strange blending, the executive, legislative, and judicial branches of government became one and the same. The separation of powers so familiar to Americans today was largely nonexistent in these early "judicial systems."

The courts of colonial America were as diverse as the colonies and the people themselves. It was, indeed, an eclectic nation: The Dutch settlers in New York, the Calvinist planters in South Carolina, the Quakers in Pennsylvania, the Catholics in Maryland, and the Puritans in Massachusetts. Each brought with them attitudes about the laws that would govern their colonies and their citizens and how such laws would be applied and through what mechanisms. As the colonies grew and social and economic relations became more complex, county and town courts were established to administer local justice. County seats developed, patterned after similar arrangements in English shires. These county seats became logical sites for the establishment of courts having jurisdiction and administrative authority over laws and county functions. The town courts also developed after a model that itself could be traced back to medieval England, when the settlement of local, minor squabbles or offenses demanded a mode of judicial administration unhampered by the inconveniences of a highly centralized system. To meet this problem, the office of *justice of the peace* was developed: an appointed official with authority to settle petty civil cases and try minor criminal offenses. The justice usually was a respected townsman without legal training but blessed with common sense. The system of local justices became a permanent part of the English system and was transported virtually unchanged to American soil, where it has remained in use in some states for more than three hundred years.[12]

**INFLUENCES ON THE COURT'S DEVELOPMENT.** As mentioned, the early colonies were often settled by different groups—Maryland by Roman Catholics, Pennsylvania by Quakers—and thus the judicial and legal systems developed differently in each colony, depending on local beliefs and customs. With only a few exceptions, the English common law tradition and English court structures were adopted. However, the individual colonies soon modified these somewhat to suit the requirements of local demands. The commercial development in each colony also contributed to different rulings and court arrangements.[13] In a number of ways, these early variations among the colonies are still reflected in the variety of court systems in the states.

H. R. Glick and K. N. Vines consider that the lack of legal experts in the colonies was an important feature in the early development of the colonial court systems.[14]

*Diversity of court arrangements*

*Religious, social, and economic influences*

There are a number of reasons why legal and judicial talent was not available to assist in the creation of colonial courts. In the first place, the king's law and those who administered it were held in disrepute by many of the colonists. As a result, very few professionally trained lawyers and jurists were attracted to the colonies from England and Europe. In addition, lawyers and judges were not welcomed by the colonial merchant class and wealthy landowners, who were concerned that the development of a professional class of attorneys would renew the persecution by the law they had experienced in the past as well as create competition for the general social, economic, and political control they enjoyed in the colonies.[15]

As a consequence, these early courts came under the domain of prestigious laymen in the towns and counties. The judges were usually wealthy merchants, planters, or landowners, who, without benefit of legal training, settled the local disputes that arose. As might be imagined, these courts often served the interests of the wealthy, and in terms of political control, judicial, economic, and financial interests became interlocked.

As the population grew, courts were added to the judicial system to respond to increased litigation. The major impetus behind the expansion of colonial courts, however, was the economic growth of the colonies. As commerce increased, so did the need for courts to settle differences between economic interests. As early as the late seventeenth century, the colonies of Massachusetts, Pennsylvania, and Connecticut began to divide cases among existing courts. In this way, specialized jurisdictions of courts began to be established, and the early development of a higher court for appeal began to appear. In 1698, Connecticut established a few special courts to deal with wills and estates, which until this time had been handled by the county courts. These new courts were called probate courts, and the idea of this type of specialized court spread to other colonies.[16] The spread of these specialized courts encouraged the development of legal experts and judges to service these courts. This, in turn, fostered the growth of rules and procedures to process the growing litigation.

## State Court Development in the Post-Revolutionary Period

After America gained its independence, the powers of the governors of the new states were drastically reduced, and the state legislatures became the focus of government power. The courts that existed in the states at this time were purposely kept very weak. The legislative bodies, and indeed the citizens of the new nation, were quite content with this arrangement. The citizens still remembered the courts as extensions of the authority of the colonial governors, and they did not relish the possibility that the courts might serve the same function for the governors of the new states. This fear that the executive branch and the judiciary might wield too much power at the expense of the states' legislative bodies prevented the development of an independent state judiciary. The state legislatures scrutinized quite closely the actions of the state courts, and they freely appointed and removed judges and even abolished courts that did not agree with their policies.[17]

The development of the nation's courts after the American Revolution cannot be separated from the development of the criminal law during this period. Like all revolutions, it was a struggle for the reins of power. The criminal law is a mighty instrument through which government brings power to bear on the individual citizen. The Revolutionary leaders recognized this fundamental fact. They rightfully identified oppression with the abuse of criminal law and identified the rights of

Post-revolutionary political philosophy

The role of legal reform in developing court systems

man with basic rights to a fair criminal trial. The Bill of Rights is itself a minicode of criminal procedure. Particularly disturbing to many colonists had been the harshness of the English law and the early pre-Revolutionary laws in the colonies. Yet penal reform is never easy to accomplish. Nonetheless, some states made important strides. In 1794 Pennsylvania enacted a law that included "degrees" of murder. It has changed little to this day. First-degree murder, for example, was murder "perpetrated by means of poison, or by lying in wait, or by any other kind of willful, deliberate or premeditated killing, or which shall be committed in the perpetration, or attempt to perpetrate any arson, rape, robbery or burglary."[18] All other murder was murder in the second degree. In many states, the death penalty was abolished excluding certain few offenses.

The power of juries was important to the reform of this period. Initially, the eminent legal historian Lawrence Friedman points out that juries in the immediate post-Revolutionary period enjoyed tremendous power. It was the American characteristic to believe that justice could best be served by the deliberations of one's peers. The jury system was also seen as a check on the arbitrary powers of judges and the criminal law itself.[19] This was not to last long, however. By the mid-1800s, the unfettered power of juries gave way to at least an equal sharing of power with their major antagonist for courtroom power—the judge. Through their growing political power and convincing rhetoric, judges had persuaded state legislatures to change existing laws. Judges had convincingly argued that too much uncontrolled

Until the mid-19th century, juries in England and America had almost unlimited power. Shown here is the 1843 trial of Daniel M'Naughten, who was acquitted by reason of insanity, setting a precedent that endures to the present day. (The Granger Collection)

CENTRAL CRIMINAL COURT, OLD BAILEY—M'NAUGHTEN'S TRIAL.

power in the hands of juries was what actually invited arbitrary application of the law. While this might be true, the fact of the matter is that it also threatened the power of judges.

Beginning in the early 1800s, distrust of the judiciary became even more pronounced as some courts began to rule that the actions of legislative bodies were unconstitutional. This power of the courts to declare the actions of the legislative or executive branch to be in violation of constitutional provisions is known as the power of *judicial review*. In 1803, in the famous case of *Marbury* v. *Madison*,[20] the U.S. Supreme Court established this power for the nation's highest tribunal. This power of judicial review of legislative action is largely an American creation. Before the Revolution, it had been used on a few occasions to justify opposition to the crown's edicts, but it did not become an important instrument of authority until the early nineteenth century. Exercise of the power of judicial review often led to a struggle for political power between the judiciary and the legislative branches of the states. Despite the efforts of the state legislatures to curtail the power of the courts by removing judges and eliminating certain courts, the state courts became more assertive and openly declared, in a number of instances, that state legislative action, particularly in the area of economic interests, violated state constitutions.

**Judicial review and muscle flexing**

These struggles were instrumental in developing state court organization because they nurtured the idea that an independent judiciary was necessary to maintain an equal and meaningful separation of powers between the branches of state government. Although certain state legislatures continued to perform an appellate function for a number of years, by the beginning of the Civil War the power of state legislatures to serve as appellate bodies from judicial decisions had been abolished in all states.

## The Development of the State Courts from 1850 to the Present

**Growing social and economic complexity**

The rapid growth of our nation from 1850 to 1900 had pronounced effects on the growth of the state court systems. This was a period of rapid industrial expansion and massive immigrations from Southern and Eastern Europe. As America moved into its "golden age" of industrialization, the courts, like all institutions of that period, were affected by the fundamental changes that society was undergoing.

The growth of industry and commerce led to new conflicts that had to be resolved; rules had to be imposed, and legislative bodies had to enact new laws to regulate the changing character of American society. The advent of the automobile alone contributed enormously to the workload of the courts. As people clustered together in large cities, the incidence of crime increased, and the courts were called on to adjudicate more and more criminal matters. While this was occurring at the state level, similar problems and developments were happening at the federal level. Congress, through its express powers to regulate commerce between the states, coin money, lay and collect taxes, and make all laws "which shall be necessary and proper," was passing more legislation and enacting criminal penalties for noncompliance. Thus, the criminal (and civil) workloads of the federal courts increased drastically as the need to enforce these laws grew apace.

As the existing courts found themselves inundated with litigation, specialized branches began to appear. For a time, existing city courts, primarily justices of the peace, dealt with much of the new litigation, but because most of these justices and lower-level magistrates had little or no training in the law, they were unable to deal with the complex legal questions involved in many of the cases that came

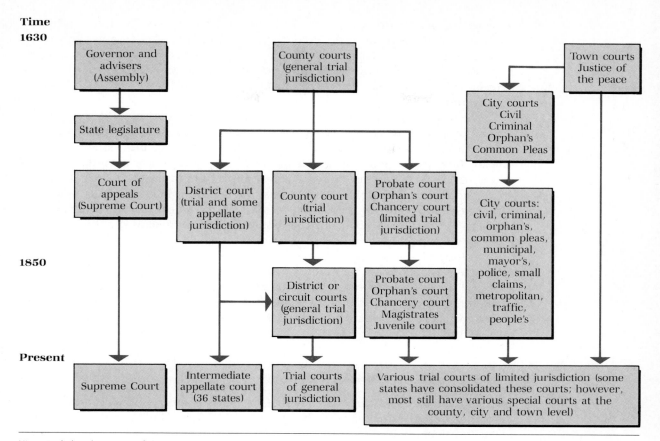

Historical development of the court system. (*Source:* Henry Robert Glick and Kenneth N. Vines, *State Court Systems.* © 1973, p. 20. Reproduced by permission of Prentice-Hall Inc., Englewood Cliffs, N.J.), as amended.)

FIGURE **7.1**

before them. As a result, new court systems were created. Small claims courts were added in a number of states to simplify legal procedures and to collect small debts at minimal cost. Juvenile and family relations courts were also developed to handle cases involving juvenile offenders and troubled families. Many communities created special courts to handle motor vehicle offenses. As these courts developed, so did the need for specialists such as social workers, psychiatrists, and other treatment personnel assigned to juvenile courts. The adult criminal courts expanded their staffs and added probation officers to supervise the offender after adjudication of guilt. Figure 7.1 depicts the growth of state court systems in America.

## The Effects of Change on the Courts

This rapid growth of state court systems did not occur without cost. The sheer numbers of these courts and the complexity of the judicial system have had significant effects on the administration of justice. In a 1930s study, Albert Lepawsky found that Chicago had 556 independent courts, 505 of which were justice of the peace courts.[21] The remaining courts were divided among various state and local

Unsystematic growth

courts and included municipal courts, circuit courts, a superior court, a county court, a probate court, a juvenile court, and a criminal court. The jurisdiction of these courts was not exclusive. A single case could be brought before any number of courts, depending on the legal and political advantages each one offered. As a consequence, "courtroom shopping" prevailed, and the alternatives open to attorneys were vast.[22]

For example, depending on the value of the particular criminal case to the state, a prosecutor would consider the reputation of the judge for handing down lenient or stiff sentences, how difficult it was to get evidence introduced, and how quickly the particular courts could dispose of a case, and choose accordingly. Often attorneys would "shop" for a court whose procedures were such that the sheer confusion, red tape, and delay would frustrate the opposition or where the particular magistrate, who was paid on a fee basis, might be eager to trade a favorable decision for a lawyer's client for the assurance that he would get the particular attorney's business in the future.[23]

Unfortunately, the proliferation of state courts and the complexity of their jurisdiction is still confusing in too many states. Although a number of states have tried to "streamline" their courts through court-consolidation efforts and in some cases the outright abolishment of some existing courts, the problems of multiple courts with concurrent jurisdiction in the same geographical area still exist in many parts of the country.

## Problems with the Present System

Despite their numbers, there are not enough courts to go around. Because of a lack of administrative resources and a host of other problems, the lower courts in many states, particularly in densely populated areas, must cope with enormous caseloads. The President's Task Force on the Courts estimated in 1965 that more than 4.5 million misdemeanor cases were brought before the lower courts of the United States. We can safely assume that the number is now much higher.

Caseload growth and effects

Data from various cities illustrate the seriousness of this problem. In the early 1970s, Washington, D.C., had eight judges in the District of Columbia Court of General Sessions to process the preliminary stages of more than 2,400 felony cases and to hear and determine 9,300 serious misdemeanor cases, 41,000 petty offenses, and nearly 44,000 traffic offenses.[24] In 1969, the courts that handled the criminal cases in Milwaukee disposed of 11,078 cases; thirty judges handled most of these cases in addition to 95,000 civil cases. Jacob reports that if each judge in Milwaukee shared this workload equally and worked 255 days a year, he or she would have to dispose of 13 cases every day.[25] In Detroit, more than 20,000 misdemeanor and nontraffic petty offenses must be handled each year by one judge in a particular division.[26] And the situation has not improved. Our trial courts today, particularly in major urban areas, continue to struggle under enormous caseloads.

Unsystematic growth and poor administration have left the courts facing a critical situation. As litigation has increased, the problems have been compounded. One of the major problems is the delay in processing cases. In analyzing Manhattan's criminal courts, J. B. Jennings says:

> Congestion and delays in courts throughout the country threaten to strangle our system of justice. For, as delays increase, the innocent who cannot afford to make bail suffer longer in jail, the guilty who are released pose greater threats to society,

and the deterrent value of speedy justice is lost. The resulting pressures to dispose of cases more and more quickly lead to still other wrongs: less and less attention is given to each case, greater reliance is placed on the disposition of cases through "plea bargaining" and the likelihood of injustice increases.[27]

The National Center for State Courts analyzed state court structures throughout the country and concluded that the existing organizational methods of many state court systems resulted in a host of problems that worsened case delay. Court structure was only part of the problem. Other factors were inadequate court resources, workload differences, and the lack of systematic and uniform procedures.[28]

The Center identified several major consequences of delay in processing cases. Each of these has costs both to society and to the individual. The first is the *cost to the litigant*. In criminal cases the effect of delay on the defendant varied in direct relation to pretrial custody status. For the defendant awaiting trial in jail, whatever good that delay might have produced was outweighed by the cost to the defendant in terms of confinement with all manner of criminals and disillusionment with the judicial process.

A national study of bail practices indicated major differences among jurisdictions in pretrial release rates for felony defendants. Among the twenty cities studied, the percentage of defendants incarcerated varied from 16 percent in Minneapolis to 66 percent in Boston. The median for all the cities in the study was 36 percent.[29] Although jailed defendants are almost always brought to disposition more quickly than defendants who are released on bail, the average time spent in jail before disposition ranged from 13 days in Boston to 134 days in Denver, with a median of 56 days.[30]

Lengthy case-processing time has an impact on the outcome of the case. One such effect is the "deterioration of the evidence" problem. As time passes, witnesses forget what happened, move away, or die. Thus, the state's case weakens over time. The defense is therefore more likely to receive a favorable verdict or dismissal of the charges.[31]

Another cost of case delays is the *social cost*. Excessive time to dispose of criminal cases is said to hinder all purposes of the penal law: deterrence, societal protection, and even rehabilitation. In the case of deterrence, delays reduce the so-called deterrent effect of "swift and sure" punishment.[32] Societal costs are obvious when defendants who are out of jail and awaiting trial commit new crimes during their period of release. One study in Washington, D.C., concluded that the "crime cost" of delay is linked directly to the length of time released defendants await disposition.[33]

## ☐ THE COMPOSITION OF THE STATE COURT SYSTEMS TODAY

All 50 states have at least three levels of courts. The highest level consists of the appellate courts. At this level is the state court of last resort as well as intermediate appellate courts, which exist in the more populated states. The main function of these appellate courts is to review the decisions of the lower courts. The middle level is made up of those courts of general jurisdiction that usually handle felony criminal trials and major civil cases. The lowest level consists of courts of limited and special jurisdiction that have original jurisdiction to try misdemeanor cases, conduct preliminary hearings for felony offenses, try traffic cases, adjudicate civil

**Three levels of courts**

TABLE **7.1**   Structure of State Court Systems

**Supreme Court**

All states have one supreme court. In Maryland and New York it is called the court of appeals.

**Intermediate Appellate Courts**

Thirty-six states have intermediate courts of appeal. Oklahoma and Texas have separate courts for criminal and civil appeals. These courts have various names: court of appeals, appellate division of supreme court, and superior court.

**Trial Court of General Jurisdiction**

Forty states have one type of trial court of general jurisdiction; eight states have two; Indiana has three; and Tennessee has four. The names of these courts vary widely: circuit court, district court, court of common pleas, supreme court (New York), and superior court.

**Trial Courts of Limited or Special Jurisdiction**

Eighteen states have only one or two of these kinds of trial courts; eleven states have five or more; New York has nine and Texas has ten such different courts. The names and functions of these courts vary widely. They include probate courts, police courts, small claims courts, justice of the peace courts, city courts, municipal courts, juvenile courts, and magistrate courts.

*Source:* Adopted from the Council of State Governments, *State Court Systems* (Lexington, Ky.: The Council of State Governments, 1978); American Judicature Society, *State Intermediate Appellate Courts* (Chicago: American Judicature Society, 1980); and Bureau of Justice Statistics, The Growth of Appeals (Washington, D.C.: U.S. Department of Justice, February, 1985).

matters that involve small amounts of money, and in some states, handle wills and estates.

Although the basic structure of state court systems is similar, the specific number, names, and functions of state courts vary widely. Normally, court systems are divided into four levels, as shown in Table 7.1, with the supreme courts and the intermediate appellate courts grouped into one level. The major differences among the states are in the presence or absence of intermediate appellate courts and the great variation in the number of trial courts of limited or special jurisdiction. Most states have only one or two types of trial courts of general jurisdiction. State court systems vary from very simple, with clearly defined jurisdictions, to highly complex systems that have numerous trial courts of limited jurisdiction whose functions frequently may overlap.[34]

**JUSTICE OF THE PEACE.**   The office of justice of the peace represents the

*The lowest rung on the judicial ladder*

lowest rung in the judicial organization in a number of states. Although it boasts an honorable tradition dating back to the fourteenth century, today this office is often the object of scorn. In the early days of our nation's history, this was an appointive office, but since the days of Andrew Jackson, this post has usually been elective. With few exceptions, legal training is not required. A survey conducted in the late 1960s in Oregon and Pennsylvania indicated that fewer than 2 percent of the justices of the peace in those two states possessed a law degree.[35]

Another study showed the following educational backgrounds among 411 past and then-existing members of the Association of Justices of the Peace of Virginia: four were lawyers, 71 percent had never gone to college, and 18 percent were not even high school graduates.[36] Compensation is usually in the form of fees collected from litigants, a system that has led to a great deal of abuse. The term of office is

One of the best-known functions of a justice of the peace is to perform marriage ceremonies. (© Joel Gordon)

short, usually two years. Although the office was at one time found in virtually all localities, it has all but disappeared in urban areas.

The jurisdiction of justice of the peace varies among the states, but in all instances it is very limited. Typically, the jurisdiction of this court extends only to minor misdemeanors and traffic offenses. In a few states that retain crimes that constitute high misdemeanors, this court is empowered in some instances to hold preliminary hearings on these offenses. The justice sometimes has authority to settle civil disputes that involve very small sums of money—usually not more than a few hundred dollars. Other duties might include providing notary services, performing marriage ceremonies, and issuing minor warrants. Decisions of the justice are commonly appealable to higher courts, where the case may be tried *de novo*—that is, a completely new trial is held. In most instances, there are no provisions for jury trials in these courts.

Years ago, when travel was difficult and communications were slow, justices **Problems with the** of the peace served a useful purpose. They were able to handle petty cases without **system** the expense and loss of time involved in carrying grievances to higher courts. In modern society, these same conditions do not exist, and many states have eliminated these particular courts. The major criticism of justice of the peace courts is that because legal training is generally not required, this office is frequently occupied by individuals who are totally unfit to administer the law. There have been instances when illiterates were elected to this post, and often the office is filled by small-time politicians more interested in the political opportunities of the office than in its legal responsibilities. In most instances, the justices also operate without a courtroom, with the result that proceedings may be, and usually are, conducted in any kind of setting. Justices are forced to keep their own records, because no clerical assistance is provided, and thus frequently no permanent records are maintained. Another major criticism is that this court generally operates entirely unsupervised by any other judicial or court regulatory authority. In the words of one state's attorney general, "They are a form of justice unto themselves."

Because of these weaknesses, a number of states have adopted drastic reforms or abolished the office outright. States that have purposely set about to unify the structure of their courts usually absorb the functions of these courts by transferring their jurisdiction to local courts of record. In other instances, their jurisdiction has been sharply curtailed. A few states have provided for their gradual elimination, and still others have undertaken various reforms, such as requiring the maintenance of records, abolishing the fee system, and requiring that justices have law degrees and be licensed to practice in that particular state or that they be certified and licensed by completing formal training programs. There are, of course, many justices of the peace who execute their duties honestly and efficiently, but there are still too many who contribute to an already bad system of justice at this level and who continue to perpetuate the fact that this particular court, overall, is the weakest link in the judicial chain.

**MAGISTRATE'S COURTS.**  Magistrate's courts are the urban counterpart of rural justices of the peace. These courts are sometimes referred to as police, mayor's, city and in some states, recorder's courts. Usually, their jurisdiction is similar to that of the justice of the peace. The major difference between the two is the settings in which they are found. For example, a state might permit smaller cities to operate this type of court to deal with minor misdemeanor, traffic, and city ordinance violations that occur within their corporate limits. These courts may also have minor civil authority and responsibilities. Whereas larger cities have just about abandoned the use of these courts, they do still exist in a few major cities in certain parts of the country. In such areas, these courts will often handle many minor misdemeanor and traffic cases.

The urban counterpart

Magistrate's courts are often criticized as having the same weaknesses as the justice of the peace courts. In fact, the situation may be even worse in these urban tribunals because of the pressures and influences exerted on them by unscrupulous politicians and lawyers. In a notable public statement, former Philadelphia District Attorney Arlen Specter, now a U.S. senator and a long-time foe of the magistrate system that existed in that city when he was the district attorney, declared that "the only difference between Chief Magistrate Walsh and his 27 cohorts and Ali Baba and the 40 Thieves is that one group is somewhat larger."[37] The history of judicial corruption in such large city courts is not an attractive legacy. For these and other practical reasons, many of these courts have been abolished and their functions taken over by municipal courts.

**MUNICIPAL COURTS.**  Because of the volume of cases, many large cities have established municipal courts. The first municipal court was established in Chicago in 1906. The jurisdictions of these courts are sufficiently broad to include many cases that might be heard by magistrates or the general trial courts of the state. These courts are usually authorized to try misdemeanor cases and civil cases that involve amounts up to a few thousand dollars, to serve as initial-appearance and preliminary hearing tribunals in cases of felony offenses, and to hear appeals from magistrate's courts if such courts are retained after the creation of the municipal courts.

A major lower court reform effort

The municipal court is typically much better equipped and staffed than are the magistrate's and justice of the peace courts, and the decorum is more typical of what one expects to see in a courtroom. The judges usually must be trained in the law, are usually elected to longer terms of office, and are provided with clerical assistance.

Municipal courts are often part of a unified state court structure and must adhere to certain uniform policies and procedures imposed on them by law. Still, in spite of the recommendations of many judicial reform groups, a number of states have retained a nonunified state judiciary and have imposed only minimal requirements on these courts. In large cities, the municipal court is often divided into specialized sections assigned to hear certain types of cases—for example, one section may hear traffic cases, another criminal cases, and a third civil matters. In this type of arrangement, a chief judge, either appointed or elected, has responsibility for the overall administration of the court, which usually includes the authority to assign or transfer judges within the court as case dockets require or depending on the particular talents or predilections of the judges.

**MISCELLANEOUS LOCAL COURTS.** Some cities have created special courts to handle specific types of cases. Michigan, for example, has created special local courts on the county level in each of that state's eighty-three counties to handle probate matters and all juvenile delinquency cases as well as cases that involve neglected or dependent children.

Many states also have county courts, which serve as the tribunals between justices of the peace and the general trial courts. The jurisdiction of these county courts varies widely from state to state. In some states, they exercise a great deal of authority, and in others they play a very limited role in the judicial process. Often, their jurisdiction overlaps with that of the justice of the peace courts and the general trial courts. Usually, these county courts are presided over by judges trained in the law, and they have many of the features of the municipal courts that are their urban counterparts.

**GENERAL TRIAL COURTS.** All fifty states are divided into judicial districts, with each district usually composed of one or more counties, depending on population. In each district, there is a general trial court. States use a variety of titles to identify this court—for example, in New York, general trial courts are called supreme courts; in California, superior courts; in Minnesota, district courts; and in Ohio, common pleas courts. General trial courts are usually presided over by a single judge or, in more populated districts, a number of judges. The judge, who must be a member of the bar, presides over scheduled sessions held in courtrooms usually located in the county courthouses.

Persons accused of felonies are prosecuted in these general trial courts. The attorney who prosecutes in the name of the state is the locally elected prosecutor, district attorney, state's attorney, or county attorney. Trials, which are conducted before juries, are heard only after formal accusation is brought either by grand jury indictment or the filing of an information. Violations of state criminal laws are as a rule tried in these courts unless some other court is specifically directed or empowered to hear these cases.

General trial courts usually have what is referred to as *original jurisdiction* over felony cases—that is, felony trials are initiated and held in these courts. Most states specify that their lower courts of limited jurisdiction have original jurisdiction in misdemeanor cases (crimes punishable by sentences of up to one year in jail). Many states also authorize general trial courts to exercise *appellate jurisdiction* as

Major trial courts at the state level

well. Under these provisions, a misdemeanor tried under the original jurisdiction of the lower courts can be appealed to the general trial court in instances where there is some dissatisfaction with the legal rulings of a lower court. When an appeal is made to a general trial court, there will be a trial *de novo*, or completely new trial. This procedure differs significantly from that in intermediate courts of appeal or the state supreme court, where only the particular legal points in question are reviewed.

INTERMEDIATE STATE APPELLATE COURTS. Just as backlogs in cases are being felt by the trial courts in many of our states, so too is the problem of congestion and delay being felt at the appellate court level. For example, a study by the Bureau of Justice Statistics that examined the growth in the workload of state appellate courts found that between 1973 and 1983, our nation's state appellate courts had an increase of 107 percent in criminal cases filed and an increase of 114 percent in civil filings.[38] This is a staggering increase in only ten years' time. Whereas case congestion can be relieved at the trial court level by establishing more trial court judgeships and support personnel, it is not feasible for states to increase drastically the number of judges on state supreme courts to handle the increased number of appeals.[39]

A court between

To handle the explosion in appeals cases, thirty-six states have created intermediate courts of appeal. The years 1976 to 1984, for example, saw no less than twelve states create such courts. The primary purpose of intermediate appellate state courts is to provide an appellate court between the general trial courts and the state supreme court. In this way, this court can reduce the caseload of the state supreme court while increasing the capacity of the court system to accommodate more litigants. An American Judicature Society study demonstrated that justices of the supreme court in states with intermediate appellate courts believed that the intermediate court had aided in reducing the caseload of the high court. The survey indicated that 80 percent of the supreme court judges and 83 percent of the intermediate court judges credited the establishment of an intermediate appellate court with "very significantly" reducing the workload of their state supreme court.[40]

There are also those in legal circles who oppose the creation of such intermediate appellate courts. They argue that the creation of such a court can cause problems in case distribution between the supreme court and the intermediate court so that confusion will result as to which appellate court has jurisdiction over a particular case. They also argue that failure to make the intermediate appellate court a court of last resort for at least some classes of cases will lead to double appeals, thus adding to the problem of delay.[41]

Characteristics

Intermediate appellate courts share some important similarities with state supreme courts and some important differences from general trial courts. The justices who sit on these courts typically serve for a longer term than trial court judges. These terms of office vary from four years in Kansas to a lifetime appointment in Massachusetts. Many of the more populous states also have their justices sitting in various court districts throughout the state. For example, California has five intermediate appellate court districts, as does Florida. Louisiana has four and Georgia has three. States such as Idaho, Alabama, Alaska, and Iowa have a single centralized court with statewide rather than merely district jurisdiction.

In many states that have these courts, the judges of the intermediate appellate courts are authorized to sit in panels or *en banc* to hear cases. In this way, for

In some appellate courts, three or more judges may sit to hear a case en banc. (© Jim Harrison/Stock Boston)

example, three judges of the court will sit to decide a case. The jurisdiction of these courts differs significantly throughout the nation. An example of the broadest jurisdictional grant is provided by the Arizona Court of Appeals. The court has appellate jurisdiction in all actions and proceedings originating in the general trial court, except criminal actions for which the sentence of death or life imprisonment has been imposed, which go directly to that state's supreme court.[42] In this way the intermediate court of Arizona is the appellate court of first resort in almost all cases that are appealed from the trial courts of Arizona.[43]

In contrast to the broad jurisdiction of the intermediate court of Arizona is the newly created intermediate appellate court in Idaho. The jurisdiction of the Idaho court is limited to cases assigned to it by the state supreme court. The remaining states with intermediate courts have established courts with jurisdictional grants that fall between these two extremes.[44]

Like state supreme courts and the federal courts of appeal, these courts typically have *appellate jurisdiction* only, although they may have some very limited *original jurisdiction*. In both civil and criminal appeals, the usual procedure is for the attorneys for both sides to submit briefs to the court and present oral arguments before the judges. The judges examine these briefs, hear the arguments, and review the record of the case in the lower court. The judges then, in consultation with each other, reach a decision by means of a majority vote. Ordinarily, an intermediate appeals court does not concern itself with the facts of a particular case, but bases its decisions on whether the law has been correctly interpreted and applied by the trial court.

Because the jurisdiction and procedures surrounding the operation of these courts vary so much from state to state, interested readers may want to compare the preceding discussion of how these courts often operate with the actual operations of the appellate court in their state (where one exists).

State court of last resort **STATE SUPREME COURTS.** As is the case in the federal judiciary, every state court system has an appellate court of last resort, usually called the state supreme court. These courts are established by the respective constitutions of the states. In almost all states, judges are elected to this court. Usually, they are elected for longer terms of office than those of judges in the lesser courts in the state. In most states, a candidate for the supreme court bench must have had a required number of years in the practice of law to become eligible to run for this position. Typically, the chief justice of this court is either the senior member, is chosen by the other justices, or is elected by the voters. A few states still follow the practice of having the chief justice appointed by the governor or the legislature.

The primary purpose of this court is to receive and adjudicate appeals on major questions that arise in the lower courts. Where a state has an intermediate court of appeals, the supreme court will receive most of its caseload from appeals from this court. The main purpose of the state supreme court is to interpret the law and apply it in the particular case. This court normally has the final word in the state on all issues that pertain to the state constitution. Its decisions are final and authoritative on state and local laws.[45]

Just as with the U.S. Supreme Court, decisions are written and published in an official series of volumes called a *reporter*. In most cases, decisions by a state supreme court mark the end of litigation. Review by the U.S. Supreme Court is restricted to those cases that involve a federal question—that is, an issue of federal law. When review is sought on the grounds that state action has resulted in a denial of due process of law as guaranteed by the Fourteenth Amendment, it becomes the U.S. Supreme Court's responsibility to decide if the federal question is important enough to warrant a review of the case.

A special agreement or judicial courtesy known as *comity* has developed between the federal and state courts. This is an understanding that federal courts will accept and apply the interpretations of state law as it pertains to state statutes and state constitutions. If no significant federal question is involved or if there is no conflict between state and federal law, the decisions of the state courts will not be reviewed by the federal courts.

**COMPARATIVE STATE COURT SYSTEMS.** All the courts discussed so far might typically be found at the state level. The number of courts, their names, and their respective jurisdictions vary considerably from state to state. Table 7.2 indicates how the court organizations of three states differ. Although it is the most populous state in the nation, California has streamlined its system so that there are only five types of courts in the state. California has been one of the leaders in centralizing the state judiciary and making it more efficient. Delaware provides an example of a state that has an intermediate form of court consolidation, which although not ideal is still far better than the fragmented structure that exists in Georgia. The courts of Georgia are extremely decentralized, as can be seen by that state's multitude of courts of limited and special jurisdiction. In spite of periodic efforts to abolish this system, Georgia has, for various political reasons, been unable

TABLE **7.2** **A Comparison of the Judicial Structure in Three States**

| California | Delaware | Georgia |
|---|---|---|
| | *Appellate Courts* | |
| Supreme court | Supreme court | Supreme court |
| Court of appeals (5) | | Court of appeals |
| | *Courts of General Jurisdiction* | |
| Supreme court (58) | Court of chancery (3) | Superior court (42) |
| | Superior court (3) | |
| | *Courts of Limited and Special Jurisdiction* | |
| Municipal court (83) | Court of common pleas (3) | Juvenile court (55) |
| Justice court (100) | Family court (3) | Civil court (2) |
| | Justice of the peace court (16) | Municipal court (2) |
| | Alderman's court (14) | State court (62) |
| | Municipal court of Wilmington | County court (3) |
| | | Justice of the peace court |
| | | Magistrate's court (4) |
| | | Small claims court (97) |
| | | Probate court (159) |
| | | Recorder's court, |
| | | Mayor's court, |
| | | Criminal court, |
| | | Municipal court, |
| | | City council court, |
| | | Police court (383) |

*Source:* Mary E. Elsner, National Center for State Courts, letter, March 2, 1982.

to restructure these lower courts and bring its judiciary in line with some of the more progressive court systems.

## ☐ THE FEDERAL JUDICIARY

In many respects, the federal court system is far less diversified than the various state systems. Even in the federal system, however, there are more courts than most people realize. There are two major types of courts at the federal level in terms of both their creation and their functions: the *legislative* courts and the *constitutional* courts. The power to establish legislative courts is vested in Congress by Article I of the Constitution, which gives Congress "the power to create tribunals inferior to the Supreme Court" and the power to make all laws "necessary and proper" for executing its powers.

Legislative and constitutional courts

  These legislative courts are courts of special jurisdiction, such as the tax court, which has jurisdiction over controversies that involve taxpayers and the Internal Revenue Service. Also included are some territorial courts. Finally, there are district and appellate courts in the District of Columbia, which were created by Congress through its constitutional power to govern the nation's capital. Because legislative courts have only a limited relationship to the administration of criminal justice, they will not be examined here.

## The Constitutional Courts

Although Article III of the Constitution provided for a Supreme Court, the creation of the entire organization of the lower federal judiciary has been left to Congress to create. With the exception of the specialized District of Columbia courts, four constitutional courts handle federal criminal cases and, in some instances, state criminal cases on appeal. These are the U.S. magistrate's courts, U.S. district courts, courts of appeal, and, of course, the U.S. Supreme Court. Table 7.3 shows the appellate and original jurisdiction of the federal courts.

The lower federal court

**U.S. MAGISTRATE'S COURTS.** U.S. Magistrate's courts are the lowest courts in the federal judicial structure. Presided over by U.S. magistrates (formerly called

TABLE **7.3** Appellate and Original Jurisdiction of the Federal Courts

| Court | Original Jurisdiction | Appellate Jurisdiction |
|---|---|---|
| U.S. Supreme Court (1) | Cases between the United States and a state<br>Cases between two or more states<br>Cases involving foreign ambassadors, ministers, and consuls<br>Cases between a state and a citizen of another state or country | All lower federal constitutional courts and some legislative and territorial courts<br>The highest state court in cases of a substantial federal question |
| U.S. courts of appeals (13) | | U.S. district court<br>U.S. territorial courts, Tax Courts, and some District of Columbia courts<br>U.S. regulatory commissions and certain administrative agencies |
| U.S. district courts (94)[a] | All federal crimes<br>All civil actions under the constitution, laws, and treaties of the United States<br>Cases involving citizens of different states or aliens if the matter in controversy exceeds $50,000[b]<br>Review and enforcement of orders and actions of certain administrative agencies and departments | Limited appellate jurisdiction involving certain actions tried before U.S. magistrate's courts<br>Bankruptcy, social security, and other administrative tribunals, commissions, and boards. |
| U.S. magistrate's courts | Misdemeanors<br>Preliminary hearings<br>Setting bond<br>Issuance of warrants | |

[a]Actually, there are 90 district courts in the 50 states and the District of Columbia and four territorial courts, which are also considered district courts.
[b]Effective May 1989.

U.S. Commissioners), they used to occupy a place in the federal system similar to that of the justice of the peace in the state judicial system. Since the passage of the Federal Magistrate's Act of 1968 and subsequent 1976 and 1979 legislation, their authority has changed somewhat. They now have authority in four broad areas. First is the power to conduct initial proceedings in criminal cases. This includes such powers as the issuance of search warrants, arrest warrants, and summonses; the conduct of initial appearance proceedings for criminal defendants, informing them of the charges against them and of their rights, and setting bail or other conditions of release; and preliminary examinations or "probable cause" hearings in criminal cases.

Second, a magistrate who has been specially designated by the district court to try criminal misdemeanor cases can conduct these types of trials upon the written consent of the defendant. The magistrate can hold such trials only after informing the defendant of his or her right to trial; judgment and sentencing by a district judge and receiving a consent waiver from the accused to be tried by a magistrate. The magistrate may try the case with or without a jury as determined by the particular law. The majority of cases handled by magistrates consist of traffic; immigration violations; hunting, fishing, or camping violations on federal lands; drunk and disorderly conduct; and theft offenses.[46]

An increasingly important area of duties performed by magistrates consists of referrals by U.S. district court judges of pretrial matters and other proceedings. These include hearing and determining noncase dispositive pretrial matters, such as procedural and discovery motions (see Chapter 9); motions for suppression of evidence, the review of cases involving prisoner litigation, and the conduct of pretrial conferences and settlement conferences.

Finally, magistrates also have the power to try civil suits when authorized by a district court. The same provisions apply as their authority to try misdemeanor cases, that is, the parties must agree to trial before the magistrate and must consent to having this official order the entry of final judgment in the case. A civil case tried before a magistrate can be a jury or nonjury trial.

Until the 1968 legislation that created the office of U.S. Magistrate, the former U.S. Commissioners were part-time judicial personnel who were paid on a fee basis and were not required to be attorneys. Since the 1968 act, magistrates now must be attorneys with considerable legal experience. Many of the full-time appointees are former state and county judges, assistant U.S. attorneys, public defenders, or trial lawyers with many years of criminal and civil experience. Federal magistrates are chosen from a five-person list submitted to the active judges on a particular federal district court. The judges then choose one of the candidates, and he or she is appointed for an eight-year term.

**U.S. DISTRICT COURTS.**   At the present time, there are ninety-four federal judicial districts courts, with at least one in each state. The more populous states, such as California, New York, and Illinois, are divided into two or more districts with a U.S. district court in each. For example, Illinois has a northern, southern, and central district. A district may be divided into divisions and may have several locales where the court hears cases. Each district has from one to twenty-seven judges, depending on the caseload. By law, a fixed number of district judgeships are authorized. These judges are appointed for life by the President with the advice and consent of the Senate. In districts with two or more judges, the judge who is senior in service and who has not reached seventy years of age is the chief judge.

The federal government's major trial court

These courts are the workhorses of the federal judiciary. By the late 1980s, these courts were handling over 300,000 filings of criminal and civil cases annually.[47] District courts in the Northern Mariana Islands, Guam, and the Virgin Islands have jurisdiction over local cases as well as those that arise under federal laws. Because the courts in these three places are not limited to the types of cases defined in the Constitution as part of the federal judicial power, they are legislative rather than constitutional courts.

Federal district courts have original jurisdiction over almost all criminal cases that arise under federal criminal law. These courts are similar to the courts of general jurisdiction in the state systems. Although the district courts, for the most part, have original jurisdiction only, when necessary, they do have the obligation and authority to review actions and orders tried before U.S. magistrates. The felony criminal workload of these district courts during the 1988 fiscal year was more than 27,000 cases. The most frequently prosecuted federal crime was fraud, followed by prosecutions for drug laws, burglary and larceny, immigration violations, forgery and counterfeiting, assault, robbery and homicide.[48]

Court officials in each district court

Each district has a number of important officers for the court. The first of these is the U.S. marshal's office. A federal marshal is appointed by the President with the advice and consent of the Senate and assigned to each district. The U.S. marshal in each district has deputy federal marshals to assist in the responsibilities of the office. A district will also have U.S. magistrates, probation officers, a clerk's office, court reporters, and one or more bankruptcy referees. Each district court also has a system under which lawyers are provided for indigent defendants in criminal cases. To assure adequate legal service to indigent defendants, full-time public defenders are appointed in districts where criminal cases are especially numerous.

One of the most important officials found at the district court is the United States Attorney, an officer comparable to the local prosecutor or district attorney in the state court. Like the U.S. marshal, the President, with the advice and consent of the Senate, appoints a U.S. attorney for each judicial district. This official then appoints assistant U.S. attorneys to assist him or her in the prosecution of crimes and in the handling of the federal government's cases. The U.S. attorney and his or her assistants are not supervised by the court. They are members of the executive branch of government and are under the direct supervision and authority of the United States Attorney General and the Department of Justice. Typically, U.S. attorneys are members of the President's political party and are often removed when an opposition party candidate is elected to the White House.

Of growing importance in recent years is the so-called federal habeas corpus jurisdiction of the federal district courts. A great deal of litigation in this area has lately been the subject of media attention. Under this provision, many inmates who have been tried and sentenced by state courts and are now confined in state penal institutions or jails are challenging their incarceration by state authorities. This type of postconviction remedy is filed on behalf of the prisoner contending that a factor leading to his or her confinement violates some aspect of the federal Constitution, federal law, or treaty of the United States. In most cases, however, the petition for the writ of habeas corpus is made on the grounds of violation of some provision of the U.S. Constitution. The requirement for asking the federal district court to intervene is that the petitioner must have exhausted all other appeal rights through the courts and that a "federal issue" is involved, such as the alleged violation of the provisions of the U.S. Constitution.

This is a complex but increasingly important and now frequently used legal tactic. It provides for a whole series of additional appeals. Say that an individual has been sentenced by a trial court for a crime in Indiana. He then appeals his case through the entire appellate process in that state and even to the U.S. Supreme Court. Not satisfied with the decision of any of these courts, he can then file in the federal district court for this habeas hearing.[49] If he is not satisfied with the outcome of the hearing at that level, he can then appeal to the Seventh federal Circuit Court of Appeals, which includes the state of Indiana, and then on to the U.S. Supreme Court itself. In this way, the same petitioner can have two hearings before the U.S. Supreme Court: the original appeal, which would go through the various appeals levels of state courts in Indiana, and, once these are exhausted, on to the U.S. Supreme Court. Once this has been done, the petitioner could file for a habeas hearing in the local U.S. district court and then appeal any adverse ruling from this tribunal to the Seventh Circuit Court of Appeals and on to the U.S. Supreme Court again.

This situation explains why so many individuals convicted of a capital crime and sentenced to be executed take so long before their sentences are carried out. They are filing habeas appeals and receiving "stays of execution" until the entire appeals process has run its course. Interestingly, although the state is typically not permitted to appeal a decision made in favor of the defendant by the lower courts in a criminal case, the state can appeal the decisions of the lower courts in these habeas hearings.*

**COURTS OF APPEALS.** Standing immediately above the U.S. district courts in the federal court system are the federal courts of appeals. They consist of thirteen circuits including twelve with regional jurisdiction and the Court of Appeals for the Federal Circuit with national jurisdiction. Each circuit includes three or more states, except the District of Columbia Circuit and the Federal Circuit. Figure 7.2 is a map of the U.S. Courts of Appeal and District Courts. U.S. Courts of Appeals are essentially what the name implies—appellate courts only. Criminal appeals may be taken from a federal district court to the court of appeals of the circuit where the trial court is situated. For example, someone tried in Miami for a federal crime would have his or her case heard in the U.S. District Court for Miami (Southern Florida U.S. Judicial District). If the individual appealed, the case would go to the Court of Appeals for the Eleventh Circuit, which is located in Atlanta, because the Eleventh Circuit includes Florida.

The federal government's intermediate appellate court

The courts of appeals hear cases that are appealed from the district courts. In only three instances can a case that has been tried in the lower federal courts

*Author's note: In 1990, the U.S. Supreme Court significantly modified the habeas corpus rule which permits the federal courts to review the constitutionality and convictions or sentences of state prisoners. Its major impact will be felt among those appealing their death sentences. Generally, federal court scrutiny through habeas corpus ensured that the Supreme Court's evolving constitutional interpretations found direct application in the states.

As the habeas corpus interpretation was applied prior to this decision, any subsequent ruling by the Court after the sentence was imposed was grounds for appeal. For example, if an offender was convicted for a crime in 1986 and if in 1989 the Supreme Court expanded a constitutional protection that was applicable to the circumstances in the offender's conviction, he or she could appeal through the habeas process to have this ruling applied retroactively to his or her case. In this way, the subsequent "liberalizing" interpretations acted like a ratchet. No more. The Court ruled that habeas corpus will not be available in the federal courts to state prisoners seeking either to establish a "new rule" of law or to benefit from any "new rules" in decisions handed down since the date their convictions became final.

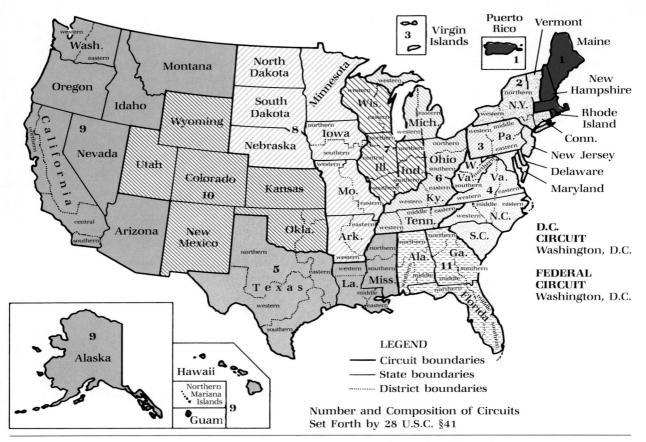

FIGURE **7.2** Geographical Boundaries of United States Courts of Appeals and United States District Courts
[*Source:* Administrative Office of the U.S. Courts—1985.]

bypass the particular court of appeals and go straight to the Supreme Court: (1) If the case has been decided by a special three-judge district court; (2) if it is a case where a federal statute has been held unconstitutional by a U.S. district court and the United States is a litigant in the case; or (3) it can be shown that the case is "of such imperative public importance . . . as to require immediate settlement."

**Proceedings**

Proceedings in the U.S. Courts of Appeal vary somewhat from circuit to circuit, and like the Supreme Court, the individual personalities of the judges play a role. Sometimes the judges on the courts of appeal are assisted by U.S. district judges in the circuit who sit temporarily on the courts of appeal to hear cases. This is done when there is a significant backlog of cases to be disposed of or to familiarize federal district court judges with the operations and procedures of the court of appeals.

All appellate court proceedings, whether at the state or federal level, share certain features yet differ in important ways from the trial courts. Trial court judges, for instance, are often less active during the trial process than are appellate court judges hearing a case before them. Appellate court judges are usually very actively involved with the attorneys representing both parties and in questioning the issues. They often engage in sharp cross-examination of the attorneys when a brief is rendered or an oral argument advanced. The primary responsibility of the appellate court is a fact-finding exercise in the application of the law. They are not examining, for example, whether the individual committed the crime as the trial court might do; they are concerned, rather, with whether or not the law has been properly applied by the lower court. They are thus concerned more with the procedural application of the law rather than the issue of the substantive offense itself. Juries are not used in appellate courts. Cases are decided on their merits after hearing or submission.[50]

The thirteen circuits of the U.S. Courts of Appeal currently receive about 32,000 cases every year. Usually, they hear cases in a *panel* consisting of three judges. In some special cases, or for a particular reason, the case might be argued before the court *en banc*. Generally, one judge of the panel writes the opinion on behalf of the court. Even in these rare instances when the entire court meets *en banc*, one judge writes the opinion, but opinions in such instances can also be rendered *en banc* by the entire court speaking as one.

The appeals court may affirm the decision of the district court or may reverse it and send it back for further proceedings before the district court. Criminal appeals to the U.S. Supreme Court from the courts of appeal may be taken in certain cases that involve federal constitutional questions or where the constitutionality of a statute is being called into question. Cases appealed from state supreme courts are not heard by the federal courts of appeal except for habeas hearings that have been transferred to the federal district court and then appealed.

**U.S. SUPREME COURT.** The U.S. Supreme Court stands at the apex of the federal judiciary. It consists of nine justices, appointed for life by the President with the advice and consent of the Senate. One justice is designated as the Chief Justice.

*The nation's highest court*

The Supreme Court, with (clockwise from top left) Justices Scalia, Stevens, O'Connor, Kennedy, Blackmun, White, Rehnquist, Brennan, and Marshall. (© 1988 Supreme Court Historical Society)

As the U.S. Supreme Court enters its third century, it faces a caseload unparalleled in the Court's two hundred years. This avalanche of cases from state courts and lower federal courts is made worse by the broad philosophical differences among its members and the frequent special interest attacks it must endure. In this light, the growing importance of the Supreme Court as an instrument of public policy has not been lost on special interest groups. The unsuccessful attempt to confirm Robert Bork's nomination demonstrates not only the Court's importance but also the growing emphasis on special interest groups and their ability to influence, at least, the appointment of the Court's members.

The nine members of our most prestigious court are finding it more and more difficult to perform their historical and constitutional role—to protect the rights of individual Americans while at the same time guiding the nation in the meaning and application of the law. In some ways, perhaps as certain legal scholars suggest, the two goals may be becoming too divergent to deal with effectively in our increasingly complex society.

The volume of appeals of an increasingly litigious nation has reached the flood stage. Today, a citizen who claims that he or she "is going to take it to the Supreme Court" has a very slim chance of ever making it that far. In the past several years the Supreme Court has received in excess of five thousand appeals each year. Of these, the Court can review in detail only about two hundred cases annually. Each October, when the Court begins its new session, it finds its docket already two-thirds full. Consequently, many meritorious cases are bypassed or scheduled to be heard the following year. In 1789, when the six-member bench was established, almost every case filed on appeal was heard. As former U.S.

Solicitor General Erwin Griswold says, "All you can do is knock at the door and ask to be let in."

Three of the Justices are over eighty years of age. Although it was thought that the Reagan administration would have a rare opportunity to pack the court by being able to appoint new members of obvious conservative leaning, this did not occur. Liberal Court members such as Justice Brennan simply refused to retire, thus thwarting Reagan's carefully conceived plan to rework the Supreme Court. Still, as recent events show, the Reagan appointees have been able to tilt the Court in a more conservative direction.

Since the famed 1803 case of *Marbury* v. *Madison,* the Supreme Court has exercised its power to review the acts of the other two branches—the executive and Congress—as well as to interpret the Constitution. Initially in our young nation's history this power was questionable; today, except for some disgruntled few, this power is accepted.

About one-third of the Supreme Court's caseload is determined by law. This includes such actions as lower federal courts interpreting or striking down federal laws, state supreme court rulings on issues affecting foreign ambassadors, and controversies between states.

The rest of the cases rely on the votes of four Justices who feel the case warrants the Court's consideration before it will get a full hearing. Beyond that the rules are for the most part nonexistent, contends University of Georgia law professor Norman Matlock. "Each Justice votes to grant review of cases that he or she thinks are important enough to be addressed by the Court. Of course, individual predilections will play a role."

Partly because of the caseload and the attitudes of the Justices themselves, socially sensitive issues such as abortions, due process rights in criminal cases, responsibili-

ties of state and local governments, and matters of governmental regulation can remain unresolved for years. This might exist even though there are conflicting rulings on such questions by different federal appeals courts.

A fundamental conflict over the role of the Supreme Court is the extent to which the Court can broaden its own past interpretations of constitutional rights. Critics such as former U.S. Attorney General Edwin Meese have gone one step further. Instead of being concerned about the broadening tendencies of the Court, he and similar strict constructionist supporters are calling for the Court to roll back several major criminal due process issues to the state of the law in the 1950s. This "judicial activism" of the Court has increasingly alienated conservative and fundamentalist groups during the past few years. Although such groups have not gone to the extremes of the John Birch Society in the late 1960s, with billboard ads calling for the impeachment of the then Chief Justice, the criticisms are unremitting.

In many major decisions of the Court since the 1960s, narrow split opinions have been the difference between success and failure over many important and controversial social issues. For example, the Court has split over such areas as the right of women to have abortions, prayer in schools, rights of suspects to be free from coercive police interrogations and searches of residences, school desegregation, and the power of the federal government and its courts to set minimum standards in prisons and mental hospitals. In the 1981 to 1982 term of the Court, nearly one-fifth of the opinions issued were settled by a one-vote majority. Although such narrow one-vote majorities have in recent years been less common, such voting patterns are still far more frequent than they were during much of the Court's history.

Particularly during the early 1960s and 1970s, the Supreme Court was active in voiding federal, state, and local statutes that it found to be violative of some aspect of the U.S. Constitution. This trend, which began in the 1930s, continued up into the late 1970s. During this time, many more such laws were overturned by the Court than in the one hundred forty-odd years preceding. This was especially true during the tenure of Chief Justice Earl Warren, who was appointed in 1953.

Today, the Court represents a spectrum of philosophies among its membership. Two holdovers from the Warren Court days, William Brennan, Jr., the senior member of the Court, and Thurgood Marshall, have continued to be supporters of an activist, most would say liberal, viewpoint. On the other end are more constructionist or conservative members, such as Chief Justice Rehnquist, and Justices O'Connor and Scalia, who are more likely to defer to the executive and legislative branches of government. The real power then, the so-called "swing vote," rests in the hands of the other members of the Court. These members are more likely to change from one camp to the other, depending on the issue. In this way, coalition-building by either of the two groups is necessary for success.

One way the Court husbands its valuable time and power is its refusal to accept for consideration hypothetical or theoretical issues in the law. The Justices do this no matter how interesting or intriguing they might find the question. Unless it is a real case involving actual litigants, the Court steers clear of the issue. In this way it more than follows the traditional view of the role of the courts: to wait until a litigative matter comes before it.

In spite of the well-publicized differences in philosophies on the Court, there is at least the formalized ritual of collegiality. Each week the

Justices gather together as a group, shake hands, and exchange traditional courtesies. Discussion on the cases and their issues then ensues. A preliminary vote is taken on the decisions. Should the Chief Justice be in the majority, he can write the opinion or assign it to another majority member. If the Chief Justice is not in the majority, this responsibility falls to the senior Justice voting with the majority.

The writing of the opinions—both majority and dissenting—may take months. The responsible writer of the majority opinion will circulate it among his or her like-minded colleagues. Several things are likely to happen. The Justice may sign the opinion as written, try to persuade the drafter to alter it, or write his or her own version. This may be the most time-consuming aspect of the process as the Justices quibble about the language. Sometimes an alternative version of the preliminary draft written by another Justice is so good, it becomes the basis for the written majority opinion. Columbia University's Supreme Court scholar Daniel Friedbaum says of this process: "There is a lot of ego at stake in the wording of these opinions, but they do sharpen the issues in most cases and the end-result is generally better law."

Yet some legal scholars are concerned about the nature of the law coming out of our Supreme Court. Constitutional law professor Arthur English at the University of Texas at Austin says, "Sharp and shifting divisions among the Justices which are becoming more commonplace as evidenced by the narrow 5 to 4 splits and abstruse language often produce murky decisions that confuse lawyers and judges alike and inspire even more lawsuits."

Although it is important that ideological disagreements never end on the Court, reformers have at least suggested several ways in which the increasing case load can be better handled.

One idea championed by former Chief Justice Burger and several of his colleagues is for the creation of a "National Court of Appeals" to which the Supreme Court could refer cases that require attention but are not of critical national importance. Those of critical national importance could then get more time and attention by the Supreme Court.

The Justices have also suggested that Congress eliminate the requirement that the Court must hear certain types of cases. Others have recommended that the traditional hour-long oral argument sessions in which the Justices pepper opposing attorneys with questions about the case be curbed or even abolished in certain instances. Another suggestion is that the Justices be given more help—particularly more law clerks to help them with their workloads and in researching and drafting opinions. Others argue that too much law is in reality already being written by the law clerks.

Many critics of the Court see reform as more basic. For example, conservatives are calling for efforts to curb the Court's power by removing from all federal courts the authority to hear certain types of cases such as those dealing with prayer in the schools, abortions, and desegregation. They are also calling for the periodic popular election of all federal judges rather than the lifetime appointment they now receive. The Supreme Court members themselves refuse to comment on these efforts in the event that sometime in the future they might have to rule on the constitutionality of such efforts.

There is little evidence that a philosophical majority will be a reality on the Court in the years immediately ahead. Like America and Americans, the Supreme Court mirrors the deep ideological cleavages that have become so much a part of our society but that in strange ways may also prove ultimately to be its greatest strength.

The officers appointed by the Court include a clerk to keep the records, a marshal to maintain order and supervise the administrative affairs of the Court, a reporter to publish its opinions, and a librarian to serve the Justices and the lawyers of the Supreme Court bar. The Chief Justice is also authorized to appoint an administrative assistant.

The Court meets annually on the first Monday of October of each year. It usually continues in session until June and receives and disposes of more than 5,000 cases each year. Most of these cases are disposed of by the brief decision that the subject matter is either not proper or not of sufficient importance to warrant full court review. But each year between 200 and 250 cases of great importance and interest are decided on the merits; about one-half of these decisions are announced in full published opinions.

**Certiorari**

The Constitution does not spell out the Supreme Court's appellate jurisdiction but leaves this question to Congress. In an effort to relieve the Court from an intolerable burden of cases, Congress passed a law in 1925 that permits the Court to exercise its own discretion in deciding what cases it will hear. This is called its *certiorari power* and comes from a special *writ of certiorari*, which is a writ of review issued by the Court. The writ of certiorari commands a lower court to "forward up the record" of a case that it has tried so that the Supreme Court can review it. For example, a defendant who has been found guilty in a criminal trial in a state court and who has exhausted all judicial appellate remedies available in the particular state may petition the Supreme Court for a writ of certiorari. The Supreme Court may grant or deny the petition. If the Court decides to hear the case, it will request that the highest state court (or, when applicable, the particular federal court of appeals) send the records in that case to the Supreme Court for review. The Supreme Court will not try the case *de novo* but will decide on the particular point of law involved and render its decision.

**The Fourteenth Amendment and the "incorporation doctrine"**

In a state trial for a criminal offense, before the defendant can have the case reviewed by the U.S. Supreme Court, he or she must invoke the rights to due process and dual citizenship under the Fourteenth Amendment as well as the particular constitutional right that has been violated. This amendment prohibits the states from depriving citizens of the due process of law and grants dual citizenship as citizens of both their respective state and the United States. These two clauses allow a defendant to raise an appeal to the Supreme Court based on a violation of a constitutional right. The Fourteenth Amendment reads in part:

> All persons born or naturalized in the United States, and subject to the jurisdiction thereof, are citizens of the United States and of the State wherein they reside. No State shall make or enforce any law which shall abridge the privileges or immunities of citizens of the United States: nor shall any State deprive any person of life, liberty or property, without due process of law; nor deny to any person within its jurisdiction the equal protection of the laws. . . .

Getting back to our example, let us assume that an individual who was convicted in a state court alleges that his or her Fourth Amendment rights regarding search and seizure have been violated. The defendant cannot merely petition the Supreme Court to grant certiorari based on the violation of the Fourth Amendment. Instead, the appeal would have to be framed in a manner similar to this: Because my Fourth Amendment rights have been violated, and because this is a violation of my right to due process, and because I am also a citizen of the United States (Fourteenth Amendment), I am petitioning the Supreme Court for review of my case. Thus, the Fourteenth Amendment acts as the "carrier" or incorporation amendment—that is, it must accompany the particular constitutional violation (in this case, the Fourth Amendment) before it can come before the Supreme Court. The defendant on trial in a federal court for a federal crime would need merely to show that his or her Fourth Amendment rights were violated and would not have to invoke the Fourteenth Amendment to appeal the case.

Because of its vested constitutional power, the only federal court whose decisions are binding on state courts is the U.S. Supreme Court. This means that in criminal cases, the Supreme Court decides if the accused in a case before it has been accorded all his or her due process rights. When the Supreme Court decides a case, the ruling is usually not retroactive. For example, if the Court overturns the conviction of a defendant on a legal technicality, all other persons convicted under the same set of circumstances before the decision in this particular case would not have their convictions set aside because of the present ruling. In most situations, the new rule would be applied only from the date of decision forward. Whether a decision will have a retroactive effect is determined by the Supreme Court, based on the nature of the right, the extent to which the previous rule has been relied on, the possible consequences that such a change in the rule would have on the administration of justice, and other considerations.[51]

Over the years, the U.S. Supreme Court has been extending its supervisory authority over state courts by applying the due process clause of the Fourteenth Amendment to constitutional issues in state criminal trials. Table 7.4 depicts the

TABLE **7.4** **Twelve Major Provisions in the Bill of Rights Applicable to the Criminal Process**

| Amendment | Provision | Applicable to States | Case |
|---|---|---|---|
| IV | Unreasonable searches and seizures | Yes | *Wolf* v. *Colorado,* 338 U.S. 25 (1949); *Mapp* v. *Ohio,* 367 U.S. 643 (1961) |
| V | Grand Jury presentment/ indictment | No | *Hurtado* v. *California,* 110 U.S. 516 (1884) |
| | Double jeopardy | Yes | *Benton* v. *Maryland,* 395 U.S. 784 (1969) |
| | Privilege against self-incrimination | Yes | *Malloy* v. *Hogan,* 378 U.S. 1 (1964) |
| VI | Speedy trial | Yes | *Klopfer* v. *North Carolina,* 386 U.S. 213 (1967) |
| | Public trial | Yes | *In re Oliver,* 330 U.S. 257 (1948) |
| | Jury trial | Yes | *Duncan* v. *Louisiana,* 391 U.S. 145 (1968) |
| | Confrontation of witnesses | Yes | *Pointer* v. *Texas,* 380 U.S. 400 (1965) |
| | Compulsory process | Yes | *Washington* v. *Texas,* 338 U.S. 14 (1967) |
| | Right to counsel | Yes | *Gideon* v. *Wainwright,* 372 U.S. 335 (1963): *Argersinger* v. *Hamlin,* 407 U.S. 25 (1972) |
| VII | Excessive bail and fines | No | None |
| | Cruel and unusual punishment | Yes | *Robinson* v. *California,* 370 U.S. 660 (1962) |

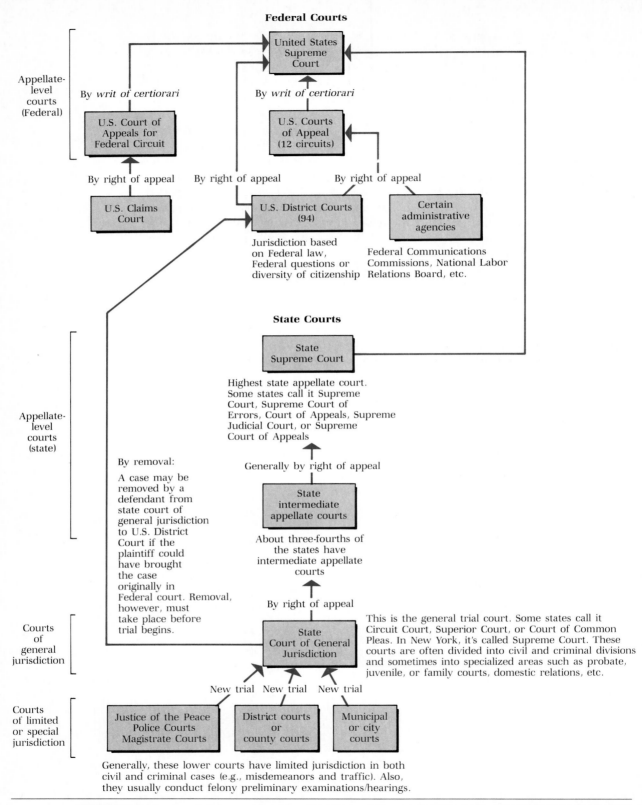

**Federal Courts**

United States Supreme Court

Appellate-level courts (Federal)

By *writ of certiorari*

U.S. Court of Appeals for Federal Circuit

By *writ of certiorari*

U.S. Courts of Appeal (12 circuits)

By right of appeal

U.S. Claims Court

By right of appeal

U.S. District Courts (94)

Jurisdiction based on Federal law, Federal questions or diversity of citizenship

By right of appeal

Certain administrative agencies

Federal Communications Commissions, National Labor Relations Board, etc.

**State Courts**

State Supreme Court

Highest state appellate court. Some states call it Supreme Court, Supreme Court of Errors, Court of Appeals, Supreme Judicial Court, or Supreme Court of Appeals

Appellate-level courts (state)

By removal:

A case may be removed by a defendant from state court of general jurisdiction to U.S. District Court if the plaintiff could have brought the case originally in Federal court. Removal, however, must take place before trial begins.

Generally by right of appeal

State intermediate appellate courts

About three-fourths of the states have intermediate appellate courts

By right of appeal

Courts of general jurisdiction

State Court of General Jurisdiction

This is the general trial court. Some states call it Circuit Court, Superior Court, or Court of Common Pleas. In New York, it's called Supreme Court. These courts are often divided into civil and criminal divisions and sometimes into specialized areas such as probate, juvenile, or family courts, domestic relations, etc.

New trial    New trial    New trial

Courts of limited or special jurisdiction

Justice of the Peace Police Courts Magistrate Courts

District courts or county courts

Municipal or city courts

Generally, these lower courts have limited jurisdiction in both civil and criminal cases (e.g., misdemeanors and traffic). Also, they usually conduct felony preliminary examinations/hearings.

FIGURE **7.3** Federal and state courts and how they interact. [*Source:* Reprinted with modifications from *Report to the Nation on Crime and Justice* (Washington, D.C.: U.S. Department of Justice, October 1983), p. 63.]

major amendments that pertain to the administration of criminal justice and the particular cases that imposed these safeguards. It should be remembered, however, that not even the U.S. Supreme Court has absolute authority and jurisdiction over all litigative matters (Figure 7.3).

## The Federal Judicial Center

In an effort to help the federal courts improve their efforts, in 1968 Congress created the Federal Judicial Center to carry on research and to conduct training programs for judges and other court personnel. The Judicial Center serves as the research and development arm for the federal judiciary. An independent board made up of the Chief Justice of the United States, a chairman, two Courts of Appeal judges, three District Court judges, a bankruptcy judge, and the director of the Administrative Office of the United States Courts, guides the work of the center and appoints its director. The appeals, district, and bankruptcy judges who are members of the board are elected by the Judicial Conference of the United States and serve for staggered terms.

*An effort to improve the operations of the federal courts*

The Judicial Center is concerned with solving problems of court congestion by developing new methods and procedures for improving efficiency in the management of court affairs. Its education and training activities include orientation programs or seminars for newly appointed judges, United States magistrates, bankruptcy judges, and other court officials, as well as training sessions for clerks and deputy clerks.

## SUMMARY

The American judicial system has a dual system of courts—one system that operates at the state level and the other at the federal level. Both systems are organized geographically. Because external supervision is not imposed, the courts can, in many instances, operate more autonomously than the executive or legislative branches of government. Our courts are highly specialized. This specialization is usually determined by their limited jurisdiction.

The historical development of court systems reflects the general cultural, demographic, and political trends that have been a part of our history as a nation. As American society became more complex, the need increased for laws to regulate behavior and for courts to enforce these laws. The state court systems reflect the particular social forces within each state. In recent years, a number of states have attempted to streamline their judiciary and to consolidate the random prolif-

eration of courts. Although some states have been able to accomplish this, many others have not.

State and federal courts have similar organizational characteristics. Both systems maintain courts of special and limited jurisdiction at the lowest level in the judicial hierarchy. Next are the courts of general jurisdiction, which handle major criminal and civil cases, and above them are the appellate courts. About three-fourths of the states have created intermediate courts of appeal to handle the growing litigation and caseload that is resulting in ever-increasing appeals. The primary function of such intermediate appellate courts, whether at the federal or state level, is to remove the crush of appeals from the U.S. Supreme Court or the state court of last resort. Each state also has a court of last resort, which is commonly known as the state's Supreme Court. The court of highest authority and last resort is the U.S. Supreme Court.

## REVIEW QUESTIONS

1. Name and briefly describe the main features of the American judicial system.
2. What is the Federal Exclusionary Rule?
3. Explain the role of each of the following components of the state court system.
   a. justice of the peace
   b. magistrate's court
   c. municipal court
   d. general trial court
   e. intermediate state appellate court
   f. state supreme court
4. What are the two major types of courts at the federal level? How do they differ?
5. Under what conditions will a case bypass the court of appeals and go directly to the U.S. Supreme Court?
6. Identify the following: U.S. Magistrate's Courts, District Courts, Courts of Appeal, U.S. Supreme Court.
7. Name twelve major provisions of the Bill of Rights that have been applied to the criminal process. To which constitutional amendments do these provisions apply?
8. How does the U.S. Supreme Court operate? What problems and pressures does it face today?
9. What is the role of the Federal Judicial Center?

## DISCUSSION QUESTIONS

1. What are the features of judicial organization? How do these features influence the operations of our courts?
2. Discuss the structural characteristics of state court systems.
3. Discuss the structural characteristics of the federal court system.
4. Name some of the important officers found at the various state and federal court levels.
5. What are some of the weaknesses of America's court system? What might be done to rectify these problems?
6. Explain how the federal and state courts interact.

## SUGGESTED ADDITIONAL READINGS

Abraham, Henry J. *The Judicial Process.* London: Oxford University Press, 1968.

American Bar Association. *Law and the Courts: A Handbook About United States Law and Court Procedures.* Chicago: American Bar Association, 1987.

Aumann, Francis R. *The Changing American Legal System.* Columbus: Ohio State University Press, 1940.

Becker, Theodore L. *Political Behavioralism and Modern Jurisprudence.* Chicago: Rand McNally, 1961.

Church, Thomas. *Justice Delayed: The Pace of Litigation in Urban Trial Courts.* Williamsburg, Va.: National Center for State Courts, 1978.

Council of State Governments. *State Court Systems.* Lexington, Ky.: The Council of State Governments, 1978.

Hays, Steven W. *Court Reform: Ideal or Illusion?* Lexington, Mass.: Lexington Books, 1978.

Jacob, Herbert. *Justice in America: Courts, Lawyers and the Judicial Process,* 3d ed. Boston: Little, Brown, 1978.

Klein, Fannie J. *Federal and State Court Systems.* Cambridge, Mass.: Ballinger Pub. Co., 1977.

Knob, Karen M. *Courts of Limited Jurisdiction: A National Survey.* Washington, D.C.: U.S. Government Printing Office, 1977.

President's Commission on Law Enforcement and Administration of Justice. *Task Force Report: The Courts.* Washington, D.C.: U.S. Government Printing Office, 1967.

Vanderbilt, Arthur T. *The Challenge of Law Reform,* Princeton, N.J.: Princeton University Press, 1956.

## NOTES

1. National Center for State Courts, *State Courts: A Blueprint for the Future* (Williamsburg, Va.: National Center for State Courts, 1978).

2. Abraham Blumberg, *Criminal Justice* (Chicago: Quadrangle Books, 1970). p. 17.

3. James Eisenstein and Herbert Jacob, *Felony Justice: An Organizational Analysis of Criminal Courts* (Boston: Little, Brown, and Company, 1977), p. 10.

4. National Center, op. cit., p. 6.

5. Herbert Jacob, *Urban Justice: Law and Order in American Cities* (Englewood Cliffs, N.J.: Prentice-Hall, 1973), pp. 80–91.

6. 232 U.S. 383 (1914).

7. See *Mapp* v. *Ohio*, 367 U.S. 643 (1961).

8. Federal Bureau of Prisons, *Statistical Tables* (Washington, D.C.: Government Printing Office, 1965), pp. 26–27. At the time of the study, the Tenth Circuit consisted of Colorado, Kansas, New Mexico, Utah,

Oklahoma, and Wyoming; the Third Circuit was made up of Delaware, New Jersey, Pennsylvania, and the Virgin Islands.

9. A. Youngdahl, "Sentencing Disparities in U.S. District Courts," *Report of the Institute for Judicial Administration* (Washington, D.C.: U.S. Government Printing Office, 1965), pp. 33–41.

10. Lawrence M. Friedman. *A History of American Law*, 2nd ed. (New York: Simon & Schuster, 1985), p. 37.

11. See: David T. Konig, "Law and Society in Puritan Massachusetts: Essex County, 1692–1692," *The New England Historical Review* 75 (1979); Douglas Greenberg, "Crime, Law Enforcement and Social Control in Colonial America," and Louis B. Wright, *The Cultural Life of the American Colonies, 1607–1763* (Chapel Hill, N.C.: University of North Carolina Press, 1957).

12. Russell W. Maddox and Robert F. Fuquay, *State and Local Government* (Princeton, N.J.: Van Nostrand, 1962), p. 208.

13. Francis R. Aumann, *The Changing American Legal System* (Columbus: Ohio State University Press, 1940), p. 6.

14. H. R. Glick and K. N. Vines, *State Court Systems* (Englewood Cliffs, N.J.: Prentice-Hall, 1973), p. 19.

15. Charles Warren, *A History of The American Bar* (Boston: Little, Brown, 1911), p. 8.

16. David Mars and Fred Kort, *Administration of Justice in Connecticut* (Storrs: Institute of Public Service, University of Connecticut, 1963), p. 22.

17. Herbert Jacob, "The Courts as Political Agencies," in Herbert Jacob and Kenneth N. Vines, eds., *Studies in Judicial Politics* (New Orleans: Tulane University Press, 1962), p. 17.

18. Edwin R. Keedy, "History of the Pennsylvania Statute Creating Degrees of Murder," *University of Pennsylvania Law Review* 97 (1949): 759.

19. Friedman, op cit.

20. U.S. (1 Cranch) 137 (1803).

21. Albert Lepawsky, *The Judicial System of Metropolitan Chicago* (Chicago: University of Chicago Press, 1932), pp. 19–23.

22. Ibid., pp. 43–62.

23. Ibid., p. 61.

24. *Report on the District of Columbia Courts* (Washington, D.C.: U.S. Government Printing Office, 1973), p. 2.

25. Jacob, *Urban Justice*, p. 105.

26. President's Commission on Law Enforcement and Administration of Justice, *Task Force Report: The Courts* (Washington, D.C.: U.S. Government Printing Office, 1967), p. 31.

27. J. B. Jennings, *Evaluation of the Manhattan Criminal Court's Master Calendar Report, Phase I* (New York: Rand, 1972), p. iii.

28. Lee Thomas W. Church, Jr., *Pretrial Delay: A Review and Bibliography* (Williamsburg, Va.: National Center for State Courts, 1978).

29. W. H. Thomas, Jr., *Bail Reform in America* (Berkeley: University of California Press, 1976), p. 54.

30. Ibid., p. iii.

31. L. R. Katz, L. P. Litwin, and R. H. Bamberger, *Justice Is the Crime: Pretrial Delay in Felony Cases.* (Cleveland: Case Western Reserve University Press, 1972), pp. 52–53; L. Banfield and C. D. Anderson, "Continuances in Cook County Criminal Courts," *University of Chicago Law Review* 35 (1968): 262; M. A. Levin, *Urban Politics and the Criminal Courts* (Chicago: University of Chicago Press, 1977), p. 198; and T. C. Clark, "The Omnibus Hearing in State and Federal Courts," *Cornell Law Review* 59 (1974): 118–119.

32. President's Commission on Law Enforcement and Administration of Justice, *Task Force Report*, pp. 80–82.

33. National Bureau of Standards, *Compilation and Use of Criminal Court Data in Relation to Pretrial Release of Defendants: Pilot Study* (Washington, D.C.: U.S. Government Printing Office, 1970), p. 160.

34. Glick and Vines, *State Court Systems*, pp. 28–29.

35. *The Christian Science Monitor*, May 9, 1967, p. 5. Note: Pennsylvania now requires its justices of the peace either to be licensed attorneys or to complete a course of training and instruction in the duties of that office.

36. Weldon Cooper, "Justice of the Peace in Virginia: A Neglected Aspect of the Judiciary," *Virginia Law Review* 52, no. 151 (January 1966): 33–40.

37. Public statement, 1 December 1966.

38. Bureau of Justice Statistics, *The Growth of Appeals* (Washington, D.C.: U.S. Department of Justice, February 1985), p. 2.

39. Marlin O. Osthus, *State Intermediate Appellate Courts* (Chicago: American Judicature Society, 1980), p. 1.

40. Robert A. Shapiro and Marlin O. Osthus, *Congestion and Delay in State Appellate Courts* (Chicago: American Judicature Society, 1974), pp. 42–43.

41. Osthus, *State Intermediate Appellate Courts*, pp. 2–3.

42. *Arizona Rev. Stat. Ann.* sec. 12-120.21 (1956).

43. Osthus, *State Intermediate Appellate Courts*, p. 5.

44. Ibid.

45. Henry J. Abraham, *The Judicial Process*, 3rd ed. (New York: Oxford University Press, 1975), p. 143.

46. The Federal Magistrates System, *Report to the Congress by the Judicial Conference of the United States* (Washington, D.C.: U.S. Government Printing Office, December 1981), p. 12.

47. Data supplied by Administrative Office of the United States Courts, May, 1985.

48. *Federal Court Management Statistics—1988* (Washington, D.C.: U.S. Government Printing Office, 1988), p. 19.

49. Note: U.S. magistrates in noncapital habeas appeals will often be the first level of the federal judiciary to hold this habeas hearing. I have bypassed mention of this to simplify the example.

50. Stephen T. Early, Jr., *Constitutional Courts of the U.S.* (Totowa, N.J.: Littlefield, Adams, 1977), p. 103.

51. Hazel B. Kerper, *Introduction to the Criminal Justice System* (St. Paul, Minn.: West, 1972), p. 226.

# CHAPTER 8

# Court Personnel

## OBJECTIVES

**After reading this chapter, the student should be able to:**

Discuss the role of the judge, including constraints placed on his or her role.

Discuss the function of the prosecutor, including the plea-bargaining role, the "gamesmanship" that sometimes occurs, his or her role in the grand jury process, as supervisor, and as investigator.

Tell how prosecutors are selected and characteristics of this office generally.

Discuss the role of the criminal defense attorney and some of the associated characteristics of this type of legal work.

Tell how the system of indigent defense came about and the types of indigent defense systems operating.

Understand the function and responsibilities of the public defender's office.

Discuss juries, including composition and deliberations.

Identify two types of witnesses.

Explain the functions and responsibilities of the bailiff, court clerk, court reporter, and coroner.

## IMPORTANT TERMS

Judge
Plea bargaining
Prosecutor
Reduction in the charges
Charge dismissal
Sentence recommendation

U.S. attorney
Criminal defense attorney
Indigent defense
*Gideon* v. *Wainwright*
Assigned counsel system
"Preference assignment process"

Contract defense system
Public defender
Jury
Deliberations
Lay (ordinary) witness
Expert witness
Bailiff
Court clerk
Court reporter
Coroner

By now the reader recognizes that the administration of justice and the system we have devised to administer justice affects all of those involved—the police, attorneys for the prosecution and defense, offenders, victims, witnesses, judges, juries, probation officers, jailers, and correctional personnel. Modern humans are truly organizational creatures. Our attitudes and behavior are shaped by our work and our careers. The system of criminal justice and its agencies are, after all, organizations. This, however, is but one side of the coin. Those who make up these organizations also, in turn, affect the organization. In our case, they determine how justice is administered, which in turn determines how the entire system operates.

One aspect of this relationship has been an increased emphasis on the aspect of decision making in criminal justice. In recent years, this has become a subject of wide-ranging and intense examination: from such decision making research as to why people commit crimes (which implies a conscious decision) to an analysis of police behavior or discretionary actions by prosecutors. All involve decisions in which our two primary factors—the criminal justice system and the individual—come together.

In this chapter we will look at the role of court personnel as major "actors" in the system, as indeed, they are. They all share roles that are determined by the system in which they operate. Yet they also bring their own values and outlooks to bear. Keep that in mind as we examine both the obvious and the hidden nature of this fascinating and complex interaction.

## ▣ THE JUDGE

To most people, the judge is the final and most visible symbol of criminal justice. Although the police may, in fact, be more conspicuous agents of criminal justice, the police serve as the initiators in the process rather than as the final arbiters of justice. Because of this final decision-making responsibility, judges (other than those at the lowest level of the judiciary) are generally accorded the highest status among all the personnel involved in the criminal justice process.

*As a visible symbol of justice*

The role (and usually the prestige) of judges is often *institutional in nature*—that is, the status of the court in the judicial hierarchy as well as the level of government in which the court is located are important. For example, justices of the peace and judges in local courts are usually accorded less prestige than judges who preside over state courts of general jurisdiction. By the same token, federal judges are accorded greater prestige than state judges on comparable judicial levels.

What does the workday world of a judge consist of? A survey among judges showed them to be involved in reading case files; calendaring cases for trial; presiding at trials; discussing case-related matters with attorneys; discussing settlements and plea negotiations; researching the law; preparing and writing decisions, judgments, and orders; and supervising court employees.[1]

*A judge's day*

In this overall context, the role that judges directly play in the administration of justice is very broad and meaningful. The judges of our criminal courts are advisers and guardians of the accused's legal rights. Every person arrested is brought before a judge to be advised of his or her rights. The judge inquires into the circumstances of the arrest to ensure that the police have not infringed upon the individual's rights. Judges also have discretion over whether the individual may

*Responsibilities*

As the arbiter of justice, the judge interprets the law, rules on motions, grants or refuses bail, supervises the courtroom, advises the jury, and sentences the guilty. (© Shelley Gazin/ The Image Works)

be released, either by posting bail or on his or her own recognizance. The judge hears and rules on pretrial motions of the accused and the state. At the arraignment, a judge hears the defendant's plea, and if the accused pleads guilty, the judge is responsible for examining the understanding and basis for the plea. In a jury trial, the judge interprets the law and determines the admissibility of evidence. In a non-jury trial, the judge rules not only on issues of law, but on issues of fact, and determines the defendant's guilt or innocence. When guilt has been determined after the trial or when the defendant voluntarily enters a guilty plea, the judge is responsible for deciding the proper sentence.

Another important but less visible role that judges perform is that of a manager. The judge is often responsible for the management of the court and courtroom. Among these managerial duties might be the selection and employment of court stenographers, the compiling of initial court records, and the recruitment and supervision of probation officers. The scheduling of cases is often at least indirectly the responsibility of the judge, as is the appointment and supervision of the court bailiff in many jurisdictions. In larger jurisdictions, these administrative tasks are the responsibility of the senior presiding judge. In recent years, professionally trained court administrators have been employed by a growing number of the larger state court systems so that judges can concentrate strictly on their judicial responsibilities.

## Constraints on Judges

Bail laws and lack of knowledge

Although judges apparently have a great many opportunities to exert a decisive influence on the administration of justice, they are, in fact, constrained by a number of factors. The process of setting bail, for example, is governed by the criminal code of the state; both state law and the Eighth Amendment prohibit excessive bail. The criminal codes also limit the discretion of the judge in rendering sentence for an offense by prescribing the statutory maximum and minimum sentence that can be imposed. Judges are also constrained by their relationship with other actors in the administration of criminal justice. Because the judiciary must rely on the police and the prosecutor to bring cases before them, these individuals can significantly determine the workload of the court. Judges may also be hampered by a lack of knowledge of the facts that have been developed through prearrest and pretrial investigation. In many instances, the judge is completely unfamiliar with the case until the testimony begins to unfold during the trial.

PLEA BARGAINING. The absence of independent and complete information is probably most visible in the area of plea bargaining. This practice, sometimes referred to as plea negotiation or "copping a plea," is quite common in the administration of justice. Although a prosecutor plays a more significant role than the judge in these negotiations, the judge does become involved in a number of ways. The judge must decide if the court will accept the recommendation of the prosecutor. This recommendation itself is often the result of a negotiation between the prosecutor and the defendant (or, more likely, the defendant's counsel) in the judge's absence. In many instances, the judge accepts the recommendation, which, in effect, is a vote of confidence in the prosecutor's judgment. In plea bargaining, the judge's only responsibility is to ensure that the defendant *voluntarily* and *intelligently* entered into the negotiated plea according to the guidelines imposed by the U.S. Supreme Court.[2] For instance, if the defendant agrees to plead "guilty" for some negotiated consideration, the defendant waives certain fundamental rights such as the right to jury trial, the right to confront witnesses, and the privilege against self-incrimination. The judge must then determine if such justice by guilty plea is voluntarily and intelligently given by the accused.

The extent of plea-bargaining inducements, together with the tendency of some judges to accept almost unquestionably the recommendation of the prosecutor, can significantly reduce the importance of the role of the judge in criminal proceedings. In this way, judicial behavior is significantly constrained.

But it is not only in the area of plea bargaining that the absence of independent and complete information might determine what a judge may do. Often, judges defer to the judgment of other members of the courtroom work group—prosecutors, witnesses, defense attorneys, psychiatrists, clerks, jail wardens, sheriff's deputies—who may have a better knowledge of the case. It is, for example, typical for judges to defer to bail recommendations offered by prosecutors.

PROBATION OFFICER'S RECOMMENDATIONS. The judge may also be constrained by the suggestions made by probation officers in their presentence investigation reports.[3] Usually, the judge requests that these reports contain the dispositional recommendations of the officer who investigated the accused's background. If the judge trusts the probation officer's wisdom, these recommendations will probably be adopted. How much this approach constrains the judge we do not know, for a second set of factors may be operating. The probation officer may often accommodate his or her recommendation to the judge, rather than vice versa. For example, through experience with a particular judge, the probation officer may recommend a disposition that he or she thinks the judge wants or will accept.

Presentence investigation

**BACKLOG OF CASES.** The backlog of cases in the lower criminal courts in many urban areas severely limits the role of judges. Although the judge is supposed to serve as an adviser and guardian of the legal rights of the accused, this important function often cannot receive the attention it should because of time restrictions. Preliminary and bail hearings and hearings on motions and arraignments are typically conducted on an assembly-line basis, often lasting no more than a few minutes per case in these trial courts.[4] In bail hearings, for instance, judges typically do not consider the facts that surround the commission of the crime or the characteristics of the accused. They must concentrate instead on the particular offense charged and the prior record of the defendant. Using these factors as guidelines, the judges often rely on a bail bond schedule or, as mentioned, accept the suggestion of the prosecutor or even the arresting police officers.

These constraints on judges and the gulf that separates the ideal from the actual vary from city to city and court to court. In courts that have lighter workloads, the judge may have adequate time to exercise the proper judicial role. In smaller communities, the judge may develop closer relationships with the local prosecutor and defense attorneys that will provide better insight into the cases that come before the bench. In larger cities, where the judge must deal with hundreds of attorneys from the prosecutor's office, private law firms, and public defender's offices, the situation is typically much different.

There are not only important differences between levels among our nation's court system, there are also some important differences between civil and criminal courts that have an impact on the judge's role and performance. Along this line, David W. Neubauer makes some interesting distinctions between courts that try civil cases exclusively as compared with criminal courts. He points out that the frustrations and the working environment for judges working the civil courts typically differ from their criminal court counterparts'. Civil courtrooms are relatively more peaceful: dockets are less crowded, courtrooms quieter, legal issues more intriguing, and witnesses more honest than in the criminal court atmosphere.[5] Judges in criminal courts deal with a different class of people and an operating ethos between lawyers, clients, and the bench. In such a situation, a different atmosphere prevails, which even carries over into some rather unique social and professional relationships between the key criminal courtroom players: the judge, the attorneys, and police personnel.

## ▫ THE PROSECUTOR

The office of the prosecutor is known by various names in different states. In some states, the office is referred to as the district attorney, the county solicitor, or the state's attorney. At the federal level, the prosecutor is known as the U.S. attorney. The prosecutor plays perhaps the most crucial role in the administration of criminal justice because the office occupies a central and very important position between the police and the courts. In fact, the prosecutor is the "traffic cop" of the

criminal justice process. The decisions that the prosecutor makes determine how cases that are brought by the police will be disposed of. For example, the prosecutor may decide to "nolle pros" (*nolle prosequi*) a case—that is, to decline prosecution, or he or she may decide to reduce the charge through plea bargaining or for some other consideration. In a number of jurisdictions, warrants of arrest must some-

It is suggested that the real-world criminal process is far different from that portrayed by the media or perceived by someone who is not intimately involved in the operation of the courts. It is even different from that outlined in textbooks on the subject. To the outsider, the perception of the judicial process is that it exists as an adversarial forum. The court then plays an important fulcrumlike role: balancing the interests of society and the accused's rights through a carefully established system of laws, rights, and obligations.

In fact, this is not always the case. When viewed through the eyes of the courtroom actors—the judge, prosecutor, defense counsel, defendant, and court personnel—the process is far more administrative and managerial in nature than it is adjudicative, adversarial, or protective. For instance, research has indicated the following:

- The apparent separateness of the police, prosecution, judge, probation officer, defense counsel, and the defendant is more an illusion than reality. The bureaucratic nature of the court and the need to be expeditious create pressures for compromise that may not always be in the best interest of justice.

- Judges do not always inform defendants of their legal rights.

- Judges are less likely to apprise accused persons individually or at all in legally nonserious cases in which the defendants were less likely to protest their dispositions.

- Because the vast majority of defendants, especially those in minor cases, plead guilty, the court is more of a sentencing than a fact-finding enterprise.

- If the accused should demand his or her right to trial and be later found guilty, many judges will, by means of the sentence imposed, penalize the offender more harshly for not admitting guilt.

- Reduced charges often net the defendant approximately the same type of punishment as would be typical for a more serious charge. In these cases, defendants are punished for what they seem to have done rather than for what they were convicted of doing.

- The criminal court has become an agency of rehabilitation, aside from its function of detecting the truth. Thus, it has compromised itself as a judicial truth-seeking forum. Under the guise of psychological and social services, an accused and his or her family together with the prosecution, judge, defense counsel, and probation personnel enter into an arrangement whereby the court does little more than publicly affirm the informal arrangements that have been previously concluded in private.

times be approved by the prosecutor before the court issues the warrant. In many of these instances, the screening by the prosecutor results in the court's merely "rubber stamping" the petition for a warrant that the prosecutor brings before the court.

Although the American prosecutor is a very important and powerful actor in the administration of justice, his or her European counterpart often has even more extensive powers in certain areas. Some European prosecutors can levy fines without judicial approval (as can the police in some European countries), some can convict defendants without trials, and some can initiate convictions and punishments by written orders instead of trials.[6]

## Role in the Plea-Bargaining Process

As mentioned in the preceding section, although the judge is involved in varying degrees, it is the prosecutor who plays the most direct role in the plea-bargaining process. The prosecutor is in a position to offer a number of important inducements to the defendant to plead guilty, although the ultimate acceptability of these in-

About 18,000 lawyers in the United States are employed as prosecuting attorneys. They aren't as visible as the police or judges, but they may be the most powerful players in the justice system. As James Vorenberg of Harvard Law School puts it: "The fate of most of those accused of crime is determined by prosecutors, but typically this takes place out of public view."

What the public is most aware of are the arrests the police make and the sentences that judges impose. Yet it is the prosecutor who decides which cases go to court and what violations will be charged. "Most people not familiar with our system of justice do not realize this," says William E. Ferrier of UCLA.

Sometimes known as district attorneys, these officials are the most political of all those involved in law enforcement. Many times the office of prosecutor is a springboard to a higher political calling. This makes it very attractive to political parties and factions who want their candidate ensconced, or worse, who want to use the office to protect their own interests against prosecution. Dean John Jay Douglas of the National College of District Attorneys says: "The biggest myth about prosecutors is that they charge people for malicious reasons. I'm more concerned about what they don't do—by failing to investigate or dismissing cases—than what they do."

About two million serious criminal cases are filed in our nation's courts each year. Of these less than one case in five actually goes to trial. Whereas the majority of the cases are disposed of by guilty pleas, others must be dismissed. Critics charge that prosecutors are successful in getting so many guilty pleas because they will often settle for pleas to lesser charges than the offense actually warrants.

This practice is called plea bargaining. Case in point: James Elrod was arrested by the Cleveland, Ohio, police for robbery and assault in which the victim was seriously injured. An assistant county prosecutor following standard acceptable policy agreed to drop the assault charge if the suspect agreed to plead guilty to a robbery charge. Elrod quickly agreed. Whereas this procedure avoids the need and expense of a trial, it also reduces the maximum penalty that the court can impose—a practice that often angers crime victims and critics of the criminal justice system.

Many district attorneys say that the large volume of cases they must handle and the lack of resources and staff make it necessary for them to engage in plea bargaining. Bronx District Attorney Michael Scanlon does not like the process any better than do the critics. "If these so-called critics want to do something meaningful let them get out and get some more money for running this office and we'll prosecute the cases," Scanlon says. "The public has the notion that prosecutors are giving away the store, but it's not true," says District Attorney Edwin Miller of San Diego. "And if anyone goes too far, he must answer to the voters."

Whereas they are called prosecutors or DAs at the state and local levels, their counterparts at the

ducements usually rests with the judge. If the prosecutor has a good "track record" of influencing the court to accept these plea-bargained recommendations, additional pressure is imposed on the defendant to accept some form of negotiated plea, particularly if the state has a good case against the accused.

The inducements to plea bargain that the prosecutor can use are numerous.[7] For example, the "benefit" most frequently offered a defendant by the prosecutor is a *reduction in the charges*, which in most cases automatically reduces the possible maximum sentence. The prosecutor, for instance, might offer the accused who is charged with the offense of robbery or burglary a reduction to the less serious crime of larceny in return for a guilty plea to a larceny charge. Aggravated assault might likewise be reduced to a simple assault.

**Prosecutor's inducements**

The *charge dismissal* is the second most commonly offered inducement. By obtaining dismissal of one or more related charges, the accused avoids the possibility of multiple convictions and longer sentences. Sometimes the prosecutor will agree not to press additional criminal charges that could subject the defendant to more severe punishment under a habitual offender statute.

Another common proposal is a specific sentence recommendation—such as federal level are known as U.S. attorneys. Unlike their state and local counterparts, who are almost always elected, federal prosecutors are appointed by the President. Yet politics also plays a big role in who will receive these appointments. There are ninety-four federal prosecutors around the country who have the power to appoint nearly 1,900 assistant U.S. attorneys. These ninety-four U.S. attorneys and their assistants prosecute all federal cases ranging from kidnapping, narcotics trafficking, fraud, and bank embezzlement, to racketeering and tax fraud.

Stung by charges that they bargain justice away, many prosecutors are taking steps to crack down on criminals. Much of this work goes on behind the scenes. While the public image of prosecutors as shaped by the media portrays DAs as doing battle with defense lawyers in court, this is only a small part of their roles; a good deal of their time is spent working with the police and overseeing the gathering of evidence.

In the past prosecutors would wait until the police brought them evidence of wrongdoing and from this evidence they would decide whether the case had merit, but some DAs' offices are now changing this procedure. Prosecutors now work with the police in determining what evidence is needed before an arrest can be made. Particularly in major or complex cases prosecutors are working more closely with police detectives or, in some of the larger jurisdictions, supplementing police with their own investigators.

Supported by research findings that a small percentage of criminals commit a large percentage of offenses, prosecution efforts are being directed at these so-called "major career criminals." Working with the police, prosecutors target such offenders for investigation. If these suspects are arrested, the case is turned over to their best trial prosecutors for preparation and prompt prosecution. "We're getting these cases to trial within two months," says District Attorney Harry Connick of New Orleans, who adds that his

aggressive pursuit of such offenders is prompting judges to impose stiffer sentences when these criminals are convicted. Local prosecutors are also working more closely with federal prosecutors in these cases. "We have a common interest in getting these type of people off the streets and in prisons—and whether it's a federal or a state prison doesn't really matter," says U.S. Attorney Sam Rosenthal in Miami.

The long-neglected problem of victims and witnesses is also being addressed by many prosecutors. Ignored by the criminal justice system and subject to delays and postponements in their cases, many victims and witnesses become frustrated and uncooperative. To counteract this, some prosecutors have formed special victim and witness assistance units to familiarize such persons with court proceedings and to keep victims and witnesses on top of case developments as they occur. This also serves to improve the image of the prosecutor's office and the entire system of justice.

probation or a fine—to the sentencing judge. Again, although judges are not required to accept a prosecutor's recommendation following plea negotiations, they often will acquiesce to the prosecutor's proposals.

Other prosecutorial plea-bargaining inducements include (1) a promise not to oppose probation or a suspended sentence; (2) a promise not to prosecute the defendant's accomplices; (3) a stipulation that the defendant enlist in the armed forces; (4) a promise to recommend that the defendant serve his or her sentence in a particular rehabilitation program; and (5) a promise that a youthful defendant will be adjudicated in a juvenile court.[8]

In exchange for this, the defendant may also be required to promise, for example, that he or she will cooperate with the police, supply additional information to the prosecutor, or testify as a witness in a subsequent trial.

Plea bargaining seems to be an important ingredient of the criminal process to both the prosecution and the defense. It is an important "tool" for the prosecutor because it helps to reduce the system's workload so that every arrest and prosecution can be handled without having to resort to a full trial on the issues. Prosecutors are also aware that they are often judged by the number of successful convictions they obtain, and getting the accused to plead "guilty" to a reduced charge through plea bargaining does result in this objective.

For the defendant there is some benefit in plea bargaining in that it is generally known that defendants who plead guilty receive lighter sentences than they would have had they exercised their constitutional rights to a trial and had been convicted.[9]

On the basis of research into the plea-bargaining process in the Connecticut courts, Milton Heumann paints a very interesting picture in the following observation:

> Typically, in the circuit court a line forms outside the prosecutor's office the morning before court is convened. Defense attorneys shuffle into the prosecutor's office and in a matter of two or three minutes, dispose of the one or more cases "set down" that day. Generally, only a few words have to be exchanged before agreement is reached.[10]

The need for the prosecutor to prepare his or her case thoroughly is well represented in an article written by a prosecutor that was published in a newsletter subsequently sent to all the prosecutors in the state. It provides us with an insight into the thinking of most prosecutors about the relative merits of plea bargaining:

> The obvious reason for thoroughly preparing for the trial of a criminal case, of course, is to insure a conviction should the case go to trial. There are, however, several other reasons that complete and early trial preparation is important. If a case is thoroughly prepared long before trial time, the prosecutor, in his dealings with the defense attorney, is able to show in a concise manner that he is able to obtain a conviction should the subject case go to trial. *That, in turn, will aid the prosecuting attorney in persuading the defense to accept a negotiated plea* [emphasis added].[11]

Workload role and "gamesmanship"

Extensive plea bargaining reflects the heavy workload of the prosecutor's office and of the court itself. But there is a certain amount of "gamesmanship" involved as well. If the prosecutor feels that the evidence is sufficient to convict the accused for the crime charged, there is little incentive for the prosecutor to negotiate. If, on the other hand, there is a probable chance that the accused will be acquitted, the situation changes. The prosecutor, to obtain a conviction, may be predisposed to bargain with the defendant. Defense attorneys can often use this set of circumstances to their advantage.

Also, experienced criminal defense lawyers and defendants often feel that a defendant who is found guilty will receive a harsher sentence than one who has plea bargained. Many defendants with records of arrest and conviction ask their defense lawyers to try to "cop a plea." They know there is a good chance that the prosecution will win if the case goes to trial and that their past record will have an important influence in the sentence they receive.

Another form of "gamesmanship" may take place between the police and the prosecutor. In some situations the police may overcharge because of their feeling that the prosecutor and the courts are too lenient, and the prosecutor may reduce the charges because he or she feels the police often overreact and overcharge. Blumberg's study of the New York courts points out how this occurs.

> Judge Sobel of the court who collected the data, did so largely to demonstrate that relatively few persons who are initially charged with a crime are indeed found to have committed the original version of the crime charged. It is not an uncommon administrative device of the police to couch the original version of the charge in the most

extreme form possible within the given confines of a set of facts. Thus, very often, an original charge of a felonious assault (with a weapon) is reduced at the initial hearing to a more realistic one of simple assault, or even to disorderly conduct.[12]

How prevalent is plea bargaining in our criminal courts? Nobody really knows. We might, however, get some idea of its extent from the number of criminal court cases that are settled by pleas of guilty and, therefore, never go to trial. This is not to say that all guilty pleas are the result of plea-bargaining considerations, but they are many times interrelated. Donald J. Newman, in his examination of criminal court cases in Wisconsin, found that over 90 percent of all cases in that state during the period studied were disposed of by a guilty plea without trial.[13] The President's Commission on Law Enforcement and Administration of Justice examined the number of criminal cases that were disposed by guilty pleas in the federal courts and the courts of eight states and the District of Columbia and found that an average of 87 percent of all defendants in those areas entered pleas of guilty. We can conclude that many of these guilty pleas resulted from plea bargains.

The extent of plea bargaining

Of course, the extent that plea bargaining is engaged in depends in part on the willingness of the prosecutor and the judges to employ this tactic. Locale also seems to be a factor. One researcher points out that the courts of the primarily rural state of Maine, without the backlog of cases of our major metropolitan areas, infrequently engage in plea bargaining.[14] Yet, community size and caseload do not always explain its occurrence. He also claims that major metropolitan cities such as Philadelphia and Pittsburgh use the negotiated settlement in less than one-third of the cases.[15] In these cities, a system of expedited trials has reduced the administrative pressures for bargaining, and, as a result, the police and prosecutor screen the cases more carefully.[16]

It would seem that plea bargaining has become institutionalized in some of our major urban areas. Heumann found such a system existing in Connecticut's urban courts in his recent study.[17] Detroit at one time had a highly developed system in that city's Recorder's Court. In that city there was a special "bargaining prosecutor" available to consult with the defense attorneys, who would queue up for consultation and plea negotiation. Near the prosecutor's office, there was a "bullpen" where prisoners awaited trial or arraignment. A steady stream of lawyers flowed back and forth between these holding cells and the prosecutor's office, trying to negotiate a plea when the defendant appeared for trial.[18]

Table 8.1 shows the results of a major study of guilty pleas in selected jurisdictions throughout the United States. What percentage of this is due to plea bargaining, of course, is unknown. The data may reflect other factors as well. It might be that Los Angeles "screens out" cases so that a higher percentage of cases in which there is probable evidence of guilt survive the initial screening. In this way, with fewer cases surviving—and with more of these evidencing guilt and probable conviction—a higher percentage of defendants seek to negotiate with the District Attorney's office, which results in a high percentage of guilty pleas.

In cities where guilty pleas are not so prevalent, any number of factors could be operating. For example, the prosecutors' offices in these cities might follow a practice of less initial case screening. In such jurisdictions, there is less inducement for the defendant to plea bargain. We could expect fewer guilty pleas under such circumstances. It may also be a circumstance in which there is less pressure on prosecutors in these cities to plea bargain. Perhaps greater resources or the adoption of expedited trials (which itself would require greater resources) diminishes

TABLE **8.1**  Percentage of Cases Resulting in a Guilty Plea in Select Jurisdictions

| Jurisdiction | Percentage of Cases Resulting in a Plea of Guilty | Number of Cases Filed |
|---|---|---|
| Los Angeles, Calif. | 82 | 49,483 |
| San Diego, Calif. | 73 | 11,534 |
| New Orleans, La. | 73 | 3,659 |
| Dallas, Tex. | 72 | 14,784 |
| Miami, Fla. | 70 | 21,413 |
| Seattle, Wash. | 68 | 3,126 |
| Lansing, Mich. | 68 | 1,358 |
| Denver, Colo. | 68 | 3,772 |
| Greeley, Colo. | 66 | 630 |
| Minneapolis, Minn. | 66 | 2,364 |
| Des Moines, Iowa | 64 | 1,401 |
| Manhattan, N.Y. | 63 | 30,810 |
| St. Louis, Mo. | 63 | 3,649 |
| Ft. Collins, Colo. | 63 | 776 |
| Portland, Ore. | 62 | 3,892 |
| Salt Lake City, Utah | 61 | 2,745 |
| Davenport, Iowa | 60 | 1,312 |
| Golden, Colo. | 58 | 1,838 |
| Geneva, Ill. | 58 | 1,263 |
| Brighton, Colo. | 57 | 1,142 |
| Pueblo, Colo. | 56 | 339 |
| Rhode Island | 55 | 5,485 |
| Colorado Springs, Colo. | 50 | 1,484 |
| Tallahassee, Fla. | 50 | 2,879 |
| Washington, D.C. | 47 | 8,442 |
| Chicago, Ill. | 41 | 35,528 |
| Cobb County, Ga. | 38 | 4,427 |
| Philadelphia, Pa. | 26 | 13,796 |

*Source:* Barbara Boland with Ronald Sones, INSLAW, Inc., *Prosecution of Felony Arrests, 1981* (Washington, D.C.: Bureau of Justice Statistics, September, 1986).

the need to plea bargain—and without the inducement of a plea-bargained arrangement by the state, fewer guilty pleas result. These kinds of unknown factors confuse the often assumed relationship between plea bargaining and guilty pleas.

### Role in the Grand Jury Process

In almost all states, it is the general practice for the prosecutor or an assistant to attend the grand jury. The primary duties of the prosecutor in this role are to advise the members of the grand jury on their rights and powers and to counsel them on points of law. In many instances the prosecutor plays a crucial role in determining if an indictment will be returned. Although the prosecutor is barred from being present during deliberations of the grand jury or when they vote on a matter under consideration, his or her influence is still enormous.

Prosecutor's influence

The influence of prosecutors stems from two important sources: They provide the evidence to the grand jury, and they advise the grand jury on legal matters. Because most grand jurors are laypeople with no experience in the law, the prosecutor's powers to guide and persuade are magnified. Their powers of persuasion are also increased by virtue of the fact that in almost all states the grand jury is an *ex parte* proceeding, where opposing testimony or evidence by the defendant is not permitted. (This will be explained more thoroughly in Chapter 9.)

Even in the few states such as North Carolina and Connecticut where prosecutors do not attend the grand jury at any stage of its proceedings, they still can influence the process and the outcome. They prepare the forms for the bills of indictment, provide the grand jury with bills of particulars and affidavits, and advise by written communication on points of the law. In this way they still importantly control the flow of information, which is so crucial in obtaining the decision the prosecution wants.

The grand jury and its relationship to the prosecutor's role is also obvious in other areas. Its existence provides prosecutors with a means to reject sensitive cases or makes it possible for them to use the grand jury to make decisions they do not want to make publicly. Prosecutors can also escape their responsibility for the screening and review of cases and shift this responsibility to the grand jurors. Finally, it enables prosecutors to take as much time as necessary in presenting complicated or sensitive cases—cases that would be too time-consuming for a routine preliminary hearing, too complicated for an untrained magistrate, or too expensive if formal court testimony had to be taken instead of hearsay or depositions.[19]

*Use of grand juries by prosecutors*

## Role as Supervisor and Investigator

Prosecutors are also investigators and initiators of the criminal process in other ways. As the chief law enforcement official in many jurisdictions, the prosecutor often works closely with the police on important investigations; in many cases that deal with complex and technical matters such as fraud, organized crime, homicide, and the corruption of public officials, the prosecutor may even supervise the police investigation. In larger cities, the office is usually assigned a special staff of investigators; in many instances, the investigators are police detectives temporarily detailed to this office, but in some instances they may be an independent group of investigative personnel working for the prosecutor's office.

*Relationship to the police*

Of course, because the prosecutor has the responsibility of presenting the government's case in court, he or she needs to fulfill the role of a skillful trial attorney. In fact, the role of the prosecutor is a very broad one that is sometimes very difficult to grasp. For example, one noted legal expert offers this observation about the role of the prosecutor:

> Appraisal of the role of the prosecutor is made difficult because that role is inevitably more ambiguous than that of the police or the trial court. It is clear that the police are concerned with the detection of crime and the identification and apprehension of offenders; it is likewise apparent that courts must decide the issue of guilt or innocence. A prosecutor, however, may conceive of his principal responsibility in a number of different ways. He may serve primarily as trial counsel for the police department, reflecting the views of the department in his court representation. Or, he may serve as a sort of "house-counsel" for the police, giving legal advice to the department on how to develop enforcement practices which will withstand challenge in court. On the other hand, the prosecutor may consider himself primarily a representative of the court, with the responsibility of enforcing rules designed to control police practices and perhaps otherwise acting for the benefit of persons who are proceeded against. Another possibility is that the prosecutor, as an elected official . . .

will try primarily to reflect community opinion in the making of decisions as to whether to prosecute. The uncertainty as to whether the prosecutor is responsible for all these tasks and as to which is his primary responsibility creates difficult problems in current administration.[20]

## Selection and Jurisdiction

The "political context" of the prosecutor

Because of the immense power prosecutors have, the position is very attractive to some attorneys who have political ambitions. With the possible exception of the mayor's office, no one local official has such opportunities for public exposure through the media. The important trials they prosecute, the investigations they conduct, and their public statements are often given widespread publicity. The important political value of this publicity can be seen in the fact that, with the exception of the tiny states of Delaware and Rhode Island, in which the attorney general handles criminal prosecutions for the state, the prosecutor is a local official. In forty-five states, the office is an *elective* one, with all but one state using a partisan ballot. In the remaining five states, the prosecutor is an appointed official. The prosecutor is elected on a county basis in twenty-nine states, by judicial district in twelve states, and from both county and judicial districts in four states.[21] In thirty-eight states, the prosecutor has both criminal and civil responsibilities; in only twelve states does the prosecutor handle criminal cases solely.[22] The Advisory Commission on Intergovernmental Relations classified the prosecutor systems of the states into the following nine categories:

1. State prosecutor systems: Alaska, Delaware, and Rhode Island
2. State-appointed local prosecutors: Connecticut and New Jersey
3. Local (judicial district) prosecutors with criminal and appeals responsibilities: Georgia and Massachusetts
4. Local (judicial district) prosecutors with solely criminal responsibilities: Arkansas, Colorado, Indiana, New Mexico, North Carolina, and Tennessee
5. Local (judicial district) prosecutors with civil and criminal responsibilities, but no appeals duties: Alabama, Louisiana, Oklahoma, and South Carolina
6. Local (county) prosecutor with criminal and appellate responsibilities: Hawaii, Illinois, Kansas, Michigan, Minnesota, New York, North Dakota, Ohio, Oregon, Pennsylvania, Vermont, and Washington
7. Local (county) prosecutors with solely criminal responsibilities: Missouri and Texas
8. Local (county) prosecutors with criminal and civil but not appellate responsibilities: Arizona, California, Idaho, Iowa, Maine, Maryland, Montana, Nevada, New Hampshire, South Dakota, Virginia, West Virginia, Wisconsin, and Wyoming
9. Overlapping county–judicial district prosecutors: Florida, Kentucky, Mississippi, and Utah[23]

Most of the more than 1,800 state prosecutors serve in very small offices with just one or two assistants. Although in the largest cities this office may consist of several hundred people, including assistant prosecutors and various staff assistants, most prosecutors lack the assistance and facilities they need. Many prosecutors serve only part-time and rely on their outside private law practices to support them. In 1966, the National District Attorneys Association conducted a survey of all state and local prosecutors in the nation and found that the median annual salary for a prosecutor was less than $4,000.[24] By 1986 this figure had increased to a median salary of slightly over $37,000, but the post still remains a less than lucrative one.[25]

**CHARACTERISTICS.** The prosecutor's office generally attracts two kinds of individuals. In smaller communities, where the salary of the prosecutor is low, young attorneys who are struggling financially and who are relatively inexperienced are most likely to be attracted to the office. They often seek the position of prosecutor or assistant prosecutor because the public exposure of the office will provide them with the opportunity to build up a clientele for their private practice and to acquire trial experience. The second type often comes from the lower or middle ranks of the legal profession and is someone who has become interested in politics to further his or her career. Such individuals are most likely to be found in larger cities and are often more experienced attorneys of middle age who hope that the office and the publicity that surrounds it can propel them into a judgeship or some higher political office. They are aware that the office of the prosecuting attorney is an excellent stepping-stone for such political ambitions.

Consequently, the turnover in most prosecutor's offices is quite high, with the average tenure rarely exceeding two four-year terms.[26] Some studies have put the turnover rate even higher. W. Gelber, for instance, contends that the turnover rate in prosecutor's offices across the country runs as high as 33 percent annually.[27] In many cities, prosecutors also select a high proportion of their assistants primarily on the basis of party affiliation and the recommendations of ward leaders and elected officials.[28] These factors create foreseeable conflicts of interest. As the attorney for the state, the prosecutor is supposed to vigorously and impartially prosecute the crimes that come to the attention of the office. Yet, because the prosecutor is usually very politically sensitive and must rely on informal accommodations with other attorneys and with private clients, it is very questionable whether he or she can, in fact, be impartial in some cases.

This lack of impartiality may be expressed in other ways that endanger the proper administration of justice. One such concern is that prosecutors, as legal representatives of the people, do not zealously prosecute corrupt or illegal actions by the police or members of the judiciary. For example, because prosecutors must work closely with law enforcement authorities, they may not find it in their best interests to bring charges against the police. In certain localities throughout the country, there have been a number of very questionable killings of citizens during encounters with the police. It is almost unheard of for prosecutors to bring criminal charges against the police in these situations. Many people contend that in these cases there is a "rush to judgment," in which after a perfunctory investigation, the prosecutor's office issues the standard ruling: "justifiable homicide." In those very rare instances when a police officer is prosecuted for a wrongful killing—or even for excess brutality—a "special prosecutor" must be appointed to prosecute the case or oversee the operation of a specially convened investigative grand jury. Most prosecutors simply want no part of such a situation. Any action in these matters must then be referred to the federal courts for action under the relatively limited jurisdiction and penalties of federal civil rights law.

Another major characteristic of state prosecutors is the absence of supervision by the states. The prosecutor is virtually unrestrained in his or her conduct or in the management of the office and the cases handled. Even the state attorney gen-

*Career attractiveness*

*The prosecutor and police abuses*

eral's office has virtually no control over prosecutors. A few states have attempted to remedy this by giving the attorney general's office the right to inquire into the operations of local prosecutors, but this legislation has had little supervisory effect.

The U.S. Attorney

**U.S. PROSECUTORS.** This set of circumstances does not exist at the federal level. The term of office for U.S. attorneys is four years. Although U.S. attorneys are politically appointed by the President, the Department of Justice screens nominees for the position and maintains continuous contact and supervision over the U.S. attorneys situated throughout the country. All U.S. attorneys are provided with specific guidelines from the Department of Justice, which they are expected to follow. If a U.S. attorney is dealing with a particularly important or sensitive criminal case, the case must often be referred to Washington for review and instructions on how it should be handled. In recent years, the Department of Justice has taken a special interest in the handling of organized crime investigations and prosecutorial action by the U.S. attorneys in the field. In many of these cases, Washington delegates a special strike force of attorneys and investigators to assist, coordinate, and supervise the efforts of the particular U.S. attorney in the field.

## Training

Many attorneys become prosecutors without any meaningful experience in the criminal justice process and only a rudimentary knowledge of criminal law. Part of this problem stems from the lack of preparation law schools provide in the area of criminal law. Most law schools require only one course in criminal law during the entire three-year course of study. The National District Attorneys Association survey mentioned earlier found that the typical assistant prosecutor is hired after very limited experience in practice and that most of that experience is in civil law. Even the prosecutor who is elected to office often lacks substantial criminal law experience.[29]

Limited criminal law education or experience

This lack of experience and knowledge of criminal law has some strange consequences. More often than is generally known, the fledgling prosecutor relies on veteran police detectives for assistance in coping with the intricate nature of criminal law and the criminal law process. Because almost no jurisdictions provide any form of training for new prosecutors, they have to learn through experience. In larger offices that employ assistant prosecutors, a young assistant is often assigned to the traffic court or the complaint bureau. The idea is to give him or her experience in handling minor cases so that if errors are made they will not be important ones. After gaining experience and demonstrating ability, the assistant can progress to handling more important cases. Although there certainly may be advantages to such on-the-job training, there are some less visible problems as well. Many times, young and inexperienced prosecutors who are assigned to the complaint bureau become advocates of the police. They may tend to become overly reliant on the police officer's judgment in determining what complaints should be filed rather than acting as impartial legal experts who screen complaints based on their merit.[30]

Even our largest cities sometimes offer no formal training. In some cases, the new assistant is provided with a written manual of policy guidelines, but these directives do not explain *how* to handle the many situations that confront a prosecutor. Occasionally, the new assistant is exposed to staff meetings and discussions about certain policies or cases with which the office must deal, but for the most part, staff meetings deal with office procedures and details. Recognizing this serious deficiency, the National District Attorneys Association is pressing states to develop programs for certifying attorneys and aspiring prosecutors in the specialties of criminal trial advocacy.[31]

## ▣ THE CRIMINAL DEFENSE ATTORNEY

Most people have a very distorted view of the practice of criminal law, most of which can be attributed to the media. Several morally repugnant themes emerge. **Media images** One is the character of a wealthy and sophisticated lawyer who has obviously enjoyed life's advantages; a man who uses his important and cultivated connections and his well-honed legal skills to defend major organized crime figures. Such a character is inevitably pitted against the honest, hard-working and rough-around-the edges detective. The other lawyer type is a sleazy "mouthpiece" who is without any moral scruples; a man who would use without compunction any existing or contrived legal advantage to get his client's release, regardless of the heinousness of the crime. Both are viewed with derision. They become instruments of venality who readily use an already corrupt system to thwart justice.

There is a third and less popularly depicted view of the criminal defense lawyer. This type of an account would have us believe that the private practice of criminal law is a stimulating challenge in which the skillful art of criminal trial advocacy is pitted against the legal adversary of the state in the cause of triumphant justice. The defense counsel is depicted as a tireless and thorough investigator, a skillful legal adversary, and the champion of justice for the "little man."

The fact is that the practice of criminal law rarely fits into such a neat stereotyping. The average criminal defense lawyer is neither the sleaze nor the saint these images portray. Nor is the practice of criminal law so stimulating or intellectually challenging. Unfortunately, for Hollywood and the television industry, the life and practice of criminal law and trial advocacy—as it is really practiced—would have little appeal.

The defense counsel plays an important role in our system of law and justice. Theoretically at least, our legal system is an adversarial one—that is, circumstances, **Advocacy and the** and indeed the truth or falsity of legal issues, can be made known by submitting **adversarial nature** them to the test of advocacy in which one side is pitted against the other. Because **of the legal process** the law is complex and the accused is unskilled in its intricacies, the individual needs assistance in preparing a defense. Thus, the defendant almost by necessity must obtain legal counsel in cases in which the penalty could be severe.

The primary responsibility of the defense attorney is to *represent* the client. The defense attorney is responsible for preparing the case and for selecting the strategy of defense. To do this, mutual confidence and cooperation must exist between attorney and client. Without a good relationship, the lawyer (and indeed the client) cannot function effectively under our system of trial advocacy.

Many people wonder why a defense lawyer consents to defend a guilty client. They feel that this is a perversion of justice and that under the circumstances the accused should not be entitled to legal assistance. Similarly, many law-abiding citizens are upset when they hear of a defendant who by the lawyer's skillful maneuverings is able to "beat a rap" on a legal technicality.

Admittedly, this is very difficult for many of us to accept. However, you must understand the theory of law in America and the responsibilities the adversary system of criminal justice entails. Because it is an adversary system, our laws recognize that those accused of crime have every right to use the skill and resources at their disposal to gain the ultimate goal of winning. In fact, the code of the legal profession demands that the attorney represent the client with all the resources and legal skills at his or her command. This is true without regard to the defendant's guilt or innocence. To do otherwise would violate the principles of American jurisprudence. The doctrine of fairness also plays a role. The resources of the state are quite formidable, and defendants must be entitled to use whatever resources they have at their disposal. If this means that a case is dismissed because of a technical error on the part of the police, this is the price that we must pay to ensure the scales of justice remain in balance between the power of the state on the one hand and the rights of the individual on the other. In this way, we also maintain that delicate system of governmental checks and balances between the executive branch (in this case the police) and the judiciary. Without such checks and balances we could not enjoy those fundamental liberties that are uniquely ours in the United States.

## Characteristics

How then does the practice of criminal law square with the popular image, and how far does it depart from the ideal? First, the practice of criminal law and the professional competence of many of its practitioners leave a great deal to be desired. Many criminal attorneys who practice regularly in our criminal courts are members of what has been called "the courthouse gang." In the District of Columbia, they are called the "Fifth Streeters," and in Detroit they are referred to as the "Clinton Street Bar Group." In most large cities, certain criminal attorneys have their offices conveniently situated near the building that houses the criminal courts and are often found prowling the courts searching for clients who can pay a modest fee.[32] As Blumberg so well describes them, these criminal defense lawyers, whom he refers to as "regulars," are

> highly visible in the major urban centers of the nation; their offices—at times shared with bail bondsmen—line the back streets near courthouses. They are also visible politically with clubhouse ties reaching into judicial chambers and the prosecutor's office. The regulars make no effort to conceal their dependence upon the police, bondsmen, jail personnel, as well as bailiffs, stenographers, prosecutors and judges.[33]

The average criminal law trial lawyer is certainly no F. Lee Bailey or Melvin Belli, both of whom enjoy national reputations as criminal defense lawyers. These individuals are at the pinnacle of their profession and usually accept only the most sensational and dramatic cases or those that assure them sizable fees. Many criminal legal specialists just manage to eke out a modest living. Defending criminals, except in a few celebrated cases, is certainly not a financially rewarding undertaking. Many defendants are not well off, and they can scarcely afford to pay high fees to their legal counsel. Attorneys who practice this type of law soon realize that fact. Sometimes, criminal trial attorneys have contacts with pawnbrokers, used car and used furniture outlets, or similar places of business that will dispose of the property of the defendant so the attorney can be assured of receiving something in the way of a fee. In other cases, the attorney makes every effort to either obtain money in

The "sleaze factor" of criminal defense practice

advance or somehow work out a financial obligation that will bind the family of the accused to paying the fee.

> "The lawyer goes out and tries to squeeze money from the defendant's mother or an aunt," explains Judge Charles W. Halleck, of the local trial court in Washington, D.C. "Sometimes, he asks a jailed defendant, 'You got $15 or $25? Here let me hold it for you,' and, later, that becomes part of the fee."[34]

This situation is very different from that found in civil trial practice, where the attorney may take part of the settlement as the legal fee or may work on a contingency basis. As a consequence, criminal trial attorneys are most likely to be the strongest advocates of plea bargaining. They thus avoid the expense and work of a trial for a client who cannot pay.

Social skills and "contacts"

Much of their success depends on their sociability and contacts rather than their legal skills. For example, many criminal attorneys spend a great deal of their time trying to develop contacts with the police and bail bondsmen for possible referral of clients and with the prosecutor's office and the judges for plea-bargaining considerations. If they get the reputation for defending their clients too zealously, particularly in more serious crimes, they run the risk of alienating the judges, prosecutors, and police. This is especially true if the attorney is able to gain acquittals based on legal technicalities. Judges, prosecutors, and the police do not like to look foolish when their cases are overturned by the higher courts or when their investigative and arrest procedures are brought into question or receive publicity.

Because of these characteristics of criminal trial practice, the legal profession holds the average criminal trial lawyer in lower regard than most other specialists in the profession. Cole describes the status of the criminal trial attorney within the legal profession as follows:

> The membership of the urban bar appears to be divided into three parts. First, there is an inner circle which handles the work of banks, utilities and commercial concerns; another circle includes lawyers representing interests opposed to those of the inner circle; and finally, an outer group scrapes out an existence by "haunting" the courts in the hope of picking up crumbs from the judicial table. With the exception of a highly proficient few who have made a reputation by winning acquittals in difficult, highly publicized cases, most of the lawyers dealing with criminal justice belong to this periphery.[35]

Inadequate defense counsel

Consequently, many attorneys either avoid the practice of criminal law altogether or, even worse, do not prepare themselves adequately for the cases they do defend. In a study of the criminal courts of Virginia, more than 40 percent of the criminal appeals heard by the Virginia Supreme Court of appeals during a particular term affirmed the decision of the lower court without consideration of the constitutional issues involved, because during the trial the defense attorneys failed to make proper and timely objections.[36]

This picture of criminal trial practice is more typical of large urban areas; in smaller cities and communities, the practice of criminal law is usually more respectable, and there are, of course, conscientious, dedicated, and honest criminal trial lawyers who practice their specialties throughout the criminal courts of our nation. For example, Malcolm M. Feeley, in his study of the criminal courts in New Haven, Connecticut, gives us a different picture of the criminal case specialists practicing in that city's courts. He says:

Another distinctive feature of criminal law practice in New Haven is the relatively high number of criminal law specialists with Ivy League educations and degrees from prestigious law schools. . . . Whatever the reason, there apparently has never been a cadre of full-time criminal attorneys who obtained clients by haunting the corridors of the courtroom and splitting fees with jailers, bondsmen, and the like. The private attorneys who most frequently appeared in the cases included in my sample were reasonably well-regarded by other defense attorneys, prosecutors and judges. Those held in the least regard were not "court regulars," but a handful of lawyers who only occasionally handled criminal cases. They frequently came into court inexperienced, forgetful, and confused, then blundered their way through the complicated and unfamiliar processes in a way that often did their clients great disservice.[37]

**The potential challenge**

However, it does remain an unfortunate fact of our society that criminal law practice is generally held in low esteem. The tragedy of this situation is that the practice of criminal law has the potential for being one of the most challenging undertakings of the entire legal system. However, until there is a significant overhaul of the machinery of criminal justice, the practice of criminal law will often be relegated to the making of deals in the back rooms of police stations, the recesses of the criminal court corridors, or the prosecutor's office.

## Defense of Indigents

Studies have shown that in some of our major cities as many as 75 percent of all defendants in criminal cases are unable to afford the cost of having an attorney to defend them.[38] Perhaps this explains why between the years 1979 and 1985 per capita public defense expenditures grew by nearly 25 percent. During this period, only the corrections component of the administration of justice increased by a larger percentage.[39]

**Legal basis**

The U.S. Supreme Court has consistently broadened the scope of the right to counsel for indigent defendants as applied through the Sixth Amendment's right to the assistance of counsel in one's defense and the due process rights of the Fourteenth Amendment. In a long series of cases beginning in 1932[40] and climaxing in *Argersinger* v. *Hamlin* in 1972, the right to counsel has been extended from a narrow federal court requirement to many state and local misdemeanor prosecutions.

**Gideon and Argersinger cases**

The true landmark decision in the area of an indigent's right to counsel was made in 1963, when the Court held in *Gideon* v. *Wainwright* that the defendant has a right to counsel in all felony cases, including state crimes. Although many states had preceded *Gideon* by providing counsel to those defendants who could not afford private counsel, the *Gideon* decision guaranteed the participation of counsel as a right of all citizens accused of serious crimes who could not afford their own attorney. (See *Gideon* v. *Wainwright*, page 326.)

The extension of the coverage from the *Gideon* decision for felony prosecutions to misdemeanor prosecutions occurred in the Court's decision in *Argersinger* v. *Hamlin*, which held: "absent a knowing and intelligent waiver, no person may be imprisoned for any offense, whether classified as petty, misdemeanor or felony, unless he was represented by counsel at his trial."[41] With this ruling, the right to counsel was extended to all cases punishable by imprisonment. In the course of implementation, the generally accepted criterion for determining the right to counsel became whether the defendant was placed in jeopardy of imprisonment for a period of six months or more.[42]

Whereas the Supreme Court from *Gideon* through *Argersinger* defined the rights of indigent defendants to legal representation during the trial, it also afforded this right to other "critical stages" of the trial process such as the preliminary hearing, arraignment, and sentencing. It also examined other aspects of the various pretrial and posttrial phases. Again, the Court considered these "critical stages" as ones that warranted the presence and assistance of counsel. For example, counsel was guaranteed at such stages as police investigation,[43] during police questioning,[44] at postindictment police lineups,[45] on appeal,[46] and at probation revocation hearings.[47] Counsel was also guaranteed for juvenile defendants in certain types of cases and situations.[48]

The holding of the Supreme Court that indigents had a right to representation in all cases and at the various "critical stages" did not, however, immediately ensure that all defendants would receive aggressive or even adequate defense representation. A survey conducted during the period of the passage of these requirements by the court indicated that of the 313,000 licensed lawyers of the time, only 2,500 to 5,000 could be considered criminal lawyers.[49] Yet at the time 2,750 counties in the United States were appointing lawyers from the private bar to provide indigent defense services. Obviously, the supply of experienced criminal defense attorneys was inadequate, and this raised serious doubts as to the quality and uniformity of publicly provided defense systems.[50] A second problem that arose concerned the types of defense systems that were created or modified to respond to the Court's ruling. Different jurisdictions developed their own distinctive variations, which to this day still exist. As a result of this, Joan E. Jacoby says of the nature of public defense systems: "No ideal system has been identified. A diversity of operational and structural types pervade the defense function, making it as disparate as the prosecution [function]."[51]

Three basic types of programs throughout the country provide defense **Three major forms** services to the poor: assigned counsel systems; public defender programs; and contract defense services. Of these, the public defender system is probably the best known. The contract defense service is relatively new. Under this arrangement, the funding source such as the county enters into a contractual agreement with a particular lawyer, legal firm, the local bar association, or a nonprofit legal organization to represent indigent defendants. The most common way payment under a contractual agreement is made is through a block grant. For example, the attorney or the law firm is paid a fixed sum annually to represent indigents within the jurisdiction.[52]

National surveys taken during the 1980s have shown some changes occurring **Changes occurring** in indigent defense services throughout the country.[53] One change is a growing shift in the funding of these programs. Increasingly, states are taking over the responsibility of providing the operating funds for indigent defense. Although counties still are the major funding source in most states, other states are shifting the responsibility away from the county and to the state. Another change that is worth watching in the years ahead is the growing adoption of contract defense services throughout the country. It seems the assigned counsel system is becoming less popular. The total number of indigent defense cases is also rising rapidly and so are the associated costs of providing defense counsel for the poor. This may partly explain why the states with their greater resources are taking over the support and in some cases the operations of these programs from local levels of government. Figure 8.1 shows the states and the type of indigent defense services most prevalent in each state.

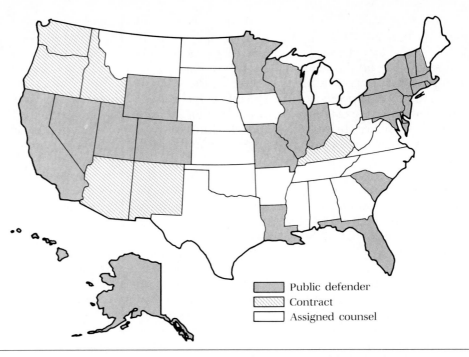

Public defender
Contract
Assigned counsel

FIGURE **8.1** State defense systems, by type in majority of counties, 1986. [*Source:* Bureau of Justice Statistics, *Criminal Defense for the Poor* (Washington, D.C.: U.S. Department of Justice, September 1988, p. 1]

**ASSIGNED COUNSEL SYSTEM.** The assigned counsel system exists in about 60 percent of the counties in the United States,[54] particularly in smaller counties in which there are not enough cases to justify the cost of a salaried public defender program. The largest percentage of funds for the operation of such services comes from local (generally county) units of government.

**Smaller jurisdictions**

It should come as no surprise that funds for indigent defense services— whether it be assigned counsel, public defender, or contract-provided services— are not a priority item among local units of government. It is also not a particularly popular expenditure of public funds. Many taxpayers are disturbed by the thought that "criminals" should have the assistance of legal defense paid for out of tax dollars. Too often it does little good to explain to these people such issues as the presumption of innocence that surrounds a defendant under the American legal system, nor does it do much good to try to explain to them that our legal system is very technical in nature and is based on the adversarial principle, which requires the services of a lawyer.

**Forms**

Under most assigned counsel systems, a list of eligible and willing attorneys is maintained by the court, and lawyers indicate to the court that they want to be placed on the list. In some jurisdictions, attorneys who want to be placed on the list must qualify by experience and/or training before they can be assigned. This is more the exception, however, than the rule. Generally, the judge is responsible for the actual appointment of a defense counsel to a particular case.

The differences in assigned counsel systems can be attributed largely to the different methods used to select the attorneys. In some jurisdictions, the trial judge

chooses the attorney from a list of all private attorneys within the jurisdiction. A Rotational assignment
rotational system of assignment is set up so that all attorneys participate. The idea
for this type of assignment procedure is the court's belief that it is in the general
public interest to engage all members of the local bar in the process of providing
indigent defense services. By this procedure, a more equitable distribution of legal
resources is realized. This also minimizes the need to use only younger and less
experienced members of the bar to provide criminal defense for the poor while the
older, more experienced busy themselves with private practice.[55] Yet, even with this
system many general members of the bar are not experienced or proficient in
criminal defense work.

Another form of assigned counsel used by the court is to select attorneys from **Criminal trial experience assignment**
a list of lawyers with criminal trial experience. Although in some ways this might
be a more preferable way to assign indigent criminal cases, it runs the real risk of
having a small group of attorneys trying to handle a large number of indigent cases.
Of course, under such pressures and given the likelihood of earning only relatively
small fees for their services, adequate investigation and case preparation may not
be undertaken. This then further encourages "working out" pleas rather than taking
the required time to prepare and try a case in court.

Another method is the so-called preference assignment process. In this type **Preference assignment**
of system, attorneys from the local bar who are interested in indigent defense work
sign up with the court. The court then assigns cases to these attorneys only. Such
a system has been criticized because only the least experienced or least successful
members of the bar will sign up. On the other hand, as Jacoby points out, in many
areas, this procedure is viewed as a strong incentive for bringing young lawyers
into rural or less populated areas. Without the financial base provided by indigent
defense work while they establish their private practice, many could not afford to
move into these areas.[56]

One recommendation that seems to be popular among reform groups is the **Coordinated assigned counsel system**
coordinated assigned counsel system. Under this form, the power to assign attor-
neys is taken away from the trial court judge and given to an administrator who
assigns cases to capable criminal law practitioners from the local bar. The administrator, if he or she so chooses, does not have to limit case assignments merely to
criminal law practitioners or only to those with extensive experience. In this way,
the administrator can strike a balance between providing good legal defense and
encouraging young attorneys to participate in the process. By distributing cases
based on their degree of seriousness and complexity, the younger attorneys may
be included in the pool of legal talent available and gain experience over time.

As Jacoby goes on to say about such a system:

> Although these same options are open to the judge of the trial court, there are more
> advantages if an administrator performs them. First, an administrator has more time
> to monitor the flow of cases and to schedule the attorneys. Second, any possible
> conflicts that might arise when the judge who assigns counsel must hear the subse-
> quent litigation are avoided. Third, by funding all assignments through one adminis-
> trator, the caseloads of all attorneys can be viewed as a totality. This last advantage
> supports the development of standards for criminal defense and creates a mechanism
> for evaluating defense attorney performance.[57]

In spite of its advantages, the coordinated assigned counsel system does not
succeed in small jurisdictions. The cost of hiring an administrator is simply too
high. Given low demand for defense representation because of lower crime rates

---

and fewer attorneys skilled in criminal practice, small jurisdictions must rely on other forms of court-assigned counsel. All in all, the most prevalent method of providing the indigent with assigned counsel legal services rests with the court-assigned system. Most jurisdictions use this type of approach.

Compensation patterns

Attorneys are compensated for indigent defense work according to a variety of fee schedules. This is usually broken down into a separate hourly basis depending on whether it is out-of-court or in-court work. Other methods of payment include the use of a flat fee per case or payment according to the type of appearance. In many states the law provides that assigned attorneys receive "reasonable compensation" for their work. This gives judges some discretion in what to pay the assigned attorneys. A few states have established by legislation a fee-payment schedule that the courts are then required to pay. A survey conducted in the early 1980s of assigned counsel systems throughout the country indicated that the average defense counsel's fee was $20 to $30 per hour for out-of-court work, $50 for in-court misdemeanor work, and $65 for felonies.[58] Many states also set a maximum fee limit on any particular case, which in many instances is quite low considering the time and effort it may take to develop the defense case. There are wide differences among the states in the amount of money they spend for indigent defense on a per capita taxpayer basis. States such as Alaska, California, and Oregon pay ten to twelve times as much on a per capita basis as does Arkansas, which ranks last.[59] The same is true of regions. The West pays significantly more on a per case basis than do states in the South.

In addition to compensation for assigned counsel, a few states, in a recognition of broader defense needs, make provisions for compensating investigators, expert witnesses, and other special defense services. The most recent data available show that the most common maximum limit for such services is $300 per case. Some states that compensate for these services restrict them to capital cases, and almost all states require prior approval of the court.[60]

In recent years a number of states have enacted legislation or adopted court administrative rules requiring indigent defendants to repay some portion of the cost of defense services, according to their abilities. Although such recoupment requirements exist, collections are obtained in only a small number of cases.

**THE PUBLIC DEFENDER'S ORGANIZATION.** The office of the public defender is usually found only in more populous jurisdictions. Since its beginnings in Los Angeles County in 1914, it has become the most typical method of handling indigent defense cases in our urban court systems. Since it is found in primarily urban areas, this form of defense service serves 68 percent of the nation's population.[61] The public defender's office, like its counterpart, the prosecutor's office, functions as a public law firm with only one purpose—to provide legal services to indigents within that jurisdiction who are accused of crimes. The public defender's office is headed by a public defender, who may be an elected official in some jurisdictions but in other jurisdictions is typically appointed by the judges of the court having jurisdiction over criminal cases. Still other states that want to minimize local control and the problems that might cause have created statewide public defender's offices supervised by a central office and authority. Some jurisdictions have defender organizations that are not public agencies. These operate as private, nonprofit corporations and are often financed through a local community fund.

Urban indigent defense

A survey of public defender programs throughout the country shows that an important change in service-delivery patterns is occurring in some public defenders' offices. A growing number of cases are no longer being handled by public Some recent problems defenders, primarily because of the increasingly strict definition of what constitutes a conflict of interest.

The problem is that the code of professional legal ethics historically has prohibited one attorney from representing co-defendants when a conflict of interest has been found. The U.S. Supreme Court and other appellate courts have been applying a more strict interpretation of what constitutes a conflict. Because all attorneys employed in a public defender's office are considered to be members of the same firm, if a conflict exists between co-defendants, the public defender's office cannot represent both defendants. Under these circumstances, the court must appoint a private member of the bar, thus essentially creating a second indigent defense program in the jurisdiction.

There is yet another change taking place. Individual judges have been authorized to appoint the public defender to a case unless there is an obvious conflict. Judges have often done this without regard for the existing caseload or resources of the public defender's office. Faced with staggering caseloads, some public defender programs have been able to negotiate a fixed caseload level with their funding sources; others have been relieved of assignments through informal agreements with local judges; and others have been successful in limiting caseloads through litigation. Whatever method is adopted, the result is to add substantially to the volume of cases in public defender jurisdictions handled by private attorneys.

There are those who believe that when all factors are considered, the public defender system is probably the best method for providing legal assistance to indigent defendants. The arguments for this position are several: Because it operates on public funds, the office has a relatively stable base of financial support. Because it is generally a full-time position, it can provide extensive criminal trial experience for members of the office, which may not be the case for attorneys appointed by the court under the assigned counsel system. Moreover, defender offices, particularly in larger communities, often have funds available for investigative purposes, and some even have their own investigative staff. Finally, since the income of the public defender continues regardless of whether or not a case goes to trial, there is less likelihood that the public defender will plea bargain away an otherwise meritorious case or engage in delaying tactics so as to frustrate the prosecution into a bargaining position.

## How Do the Systems Stack Up?

There has been a great deal of research into the functioning of the assigned counsel and the public defender's systems. Although it is impossible to discuss more than a small number of such studies, some of the findings are important and interesting.

What about differences in the quality of defense? Much of the research in this area has examined the differences between indigent defense systems and private retained counsel. Overall, the conclusions are mixed. A *Harvard Law Review* study Inconclusive findings of various U.S. district courts showed that substantially more guilty pleas were entered for indigent defendants than were entered for defendants who retained their own counsel.[62] Similar conclusions were reached in a series of studies conducted in Indiana.[63] Another study, however, underwritten by the U.S. Department of Justice and conducted by Ohio State University showed that the dispositions for public defenders were not significantly different from those for privately retained counsel in Los Angeles courts.[64]

The problem in such studies is, of course, how one can effectively compare the differences. There are so many factors—economic, organizational, and legal—that effective comparisons are difficult to make. In addition, can one say that because the focus of study in a particular jurisdiction shows a certain result, this can then be used to generalize conclusions about other courts and other jurisdictions? Obviously, the answer is no.

Another question that has been examined is the difference in the experience of attorneys who handled court-assigned cases as compared to the public defender's office. A national survey of defender systems produced some concern for the quality of assigned counsel systems as they were operating. The survey found that very few of those assigned considered themselves criminal lawyers or had criminal trial experience or training. Only 1 percent of all assigned counsel identified themselves as criminal lawyers; 20 percent had never attended a single criminal jury trial; 75 percent had never attended a training session or seminar in criminal defense.[65] As one noted expert says: "In fact there is strong evidence to suggest that judges tend to appoint those lawyers with the least experience to handle indigent cases rather than experienced counsel."[66]

**Inexperience under the assigned counsel system**

Such circumstances are explained by a simple fact. In many areas the indigent defense caseload, as mentioned earlier, is seen as the province of young, inexperienced attorneys who need trial experience. An Oregon study showed that the lawyers who were most often privately retained were the least often assigned, and those with the fewest private clients were assigned most often. The "indigent bar" had almost 10 years less experience than the general bar average. Those lawyers rated most competent by the local judges were the same lawyers who were least often appointed to indigent cases; those rated least competent were most often appointed.[67]

In discussing such circumstances, one noted researcher on the American legal system concludes:

> In general, these statistics and studies place in doubt the assumptions that assigned counsel are more experienced or perform a watchdog function, or are more independent than the public defender. Nor do they substantiate claims for lower caseloads or more individual attention to cases. In fact it appears that the overriding reasons for utilizing assigned counsel systems are economic rather than qualitative concerns about the better delivery of services.[68]

---

### GIDEON v. WAINWRIGHT (1963)

**Whether the Indigent Defendant in a
Criminal Felony Has the Right to Court-Appointed Counsel**

FACTS

Clarence Gideon was tried and convicted in a Florida state court of the felony of breaking and entering with intent to commit a misdemeanor. Gideon was too poor to hire his own defense attorney, so he requested that the trial court appoint counsel to represent him. The request was denied because, under Florida law, appointed counsel was available to indigents only in capital cases. Gideon represented himself but was convicted by a jury and sentenced to five years' imprisonment. The Florida Supreme Court upheld the trial court. He then appealed to the U.S. Supreme Court.

Clarence Gideon
devoted his years in
prison to proving that
he, as an indigent
defendant, should have
been entitled to a court
appointed lawyer.
(© Flip Schulke/
Black Star)

## DECISION

In its decision the Supreme Court cited the
Sixth Amendment, which says, "In all criminal
prosecutions, the accused shall enjoy the right
. . . to have the assistance of counsel for his
defense." The Court ruled that access to counsel
was a fundamental right of an accused person.
This right was to be observed by the states
through the equal protection guaranty of the
Fourteenth Amendment. The judgment of the
trial court and the Florida Supreme Court was
overturned.

## SIGNIFICANCE OF THE CASE

Indigent defendants have the right to court-
appointed attorneys in felony criminal cases.
(Note: This was later clarified and extended to
indigent defendants in misdemeanor cases. See
*Argersinger* v. *Hamlin*, 1972).

Historical basis

The role that juries serve today is far different from their originally intended purpose. The original jury system, which developed in England during the Middle Ages, was designed to compel testimony in trials. Early jurors were not unbiased members of the community or representative samples of peers, they were witnesses who were brought before the courts of the crown and commanded to relate what they knew about the crime and the accused. The present use of the jury originated from a major concession forced on King John in the Magna Carta that henceforth noblemen were granted the right to a trial by their peers.[69]

Although juries play an important role in the administration of the criminal justice system, the truth of the matter is that their infrequency of use limits their

Rarely used

importance. In most criminal cases, including felonies, they are rarely used. We

---

TABLE **8.2**  Jury Trials as a Percentage of Criminal Cases Filed in Select Jurisdictions

| Jurisdiction | Percentage of Cases Filed Resulting in Jury Trial | Number of Cases Filed |
|---|---|---|
| Seattle, Wash. | 15 | 3,126 |
| New Orleans, La. | 10 | 3,659 |
| Washington, D.C. | 9 | 8,442 |
| Des Moines, Iowa | 8 | 1,401 |
| Lansing, Mich. | 7 | 1,358 |
| Portland, Ore. | 7 | 3,892 |
| Denver, Colo. | 6 | 3,772 |
| Minneapolis, Minn. | 6 | 2,364 |
| St. Louis, Mo. | 6 | 3,649 |
| Dallas, Tex. | 5 | 14,784 |
| Salt Lake City, Utah | 5 | 2,745 |
| Brighton, Colo. | 4 | 1,142 |
| Colorado Springs, Colo. | 4 | 1,484 |
| Philadelphia, Pa. | 4 | 13,796 |
| Tallahassee, Fla. | 4 | 2,879 |
| Davenport, Iowa | 3 | 1,312 |
| Fort Collins, Colo. | 3 | 776 |
| Geneva, Ill. | 3 | 1,263 |
| Manhattan, N.Y. | 3 | 30,810 |
| Rhode Island | 3 | 5,485 |
| San Diego, Calif. | 3 | 11,534 |
| Chicago, Ill. | 2 | 35,528 |
| Cobb County, Ga. | 2 | 4,427 |
| Golden, Colo. | 2 | 1,838 |
| Greeley, Colo. | 2 | 630 |
| Miami, Fla. | 2 | 21,413 |
| Pueblo, Colo. | 1 | 339 |
| Jurisdiction median | 5 | |

*Source:* Barbara Boland with Ronald Sones, INSLAW, Inc., *Prosecution of Felony Arrests, 1981* (Bureau of Justice Statistics, September, 1986).

saw earlier in our discussion of the prosecutor and plea bargaining that most criminal cases result in guilty pleas. In this way no juries are used. This same national survey shows us the infrequency of jury use in criminal case filings. Table 8.2 reflects this fact.

Although juries are infrequently used, their importance still stems from those criminal cases in which they are employed. As an instrument of justice, the decision rendered by a jury usually terminates the trial process in criminal cases. A jury-rendered verdict of not guilty cannot be overturned on subsequent appeal by the state. Along the same line, a verdict of guilty is rarely overturned through the appellate process. Research has also indicated that the more serious the case, the greater the likelihood of both a trial (as compared to a negotiated plea of guilty)—and a trial that involves the use of a jury.[70] The reader should also recall from our discussion of case attrition in Chapter 1 that most cases that go to trial in our felony courts result in conviction.

*Importance*

## Composition

It is well recognized that the decision a jury renders depends at least to some extent on the makeup of the jury and how the jurors were chosen. It is true that most juries are composed of ordinary citizens, but they are often not representative of a true cross-section of the community. For the most part, they also operate without any guidelines from their fellow citizens. In fact, the entire deliberative process of the jury is so designed by its secretiveness and its seclusion to eliminate the impact of community attitudes on the members' judgment. As Jacob puts it: "They are selected by chance to *serve* their community rather than *represent* it."[71]

*The issue of "representativeness"*

Let us explore this question of community representation further. Although in theory every citizen should have an equal chance to be selected for jury duty, this does not occur. Statutes usually prescribe that jurors be chosen from voter registration lists, which is discriminatory. Citizens who are not qualified to vote and citizens who have not been in the community long enough to satisfy residency requirements are automatically excluded. In studying voting behavior, political scientists have often found that the poor and members of minority groups, which are often synonymous, are not registered voters and, therefore, are automatically excluded.

In many states, certain occupations such as attorneys, physicians, dentists, elected officials, police officers, firefighters, teachers, and sole proprietors of businesses are exempted from jury service. Also exempted are working people who can show a substantial financial hardship by having to serve on a jury. Although these are the usual categories of exemptions, many states have been eliminating or reducing many automatic class or occupation exemptions. The bar to jury service based on financial hardship is also disappearing in areas where union contracts or employers automatically provide that employees are reimbursed for the difference between what they are paid for jury service and what they earn.[72]

Studies conducted in Baltimore, Los Angeles, and Milwaukee indicated that housewives, retirees, professionals, managers, and proprietors are overrepresented on juries, whereas working-class citizens are underrepresented.[73] In Baltimore, for example, people in the occupational classifications of manager, professional, or proprietor made up 40.2 percent of the jurors but constituted only 18.7 percent of the general population. On the other hand, although 41.3 percent of the population

The composition of juries tends to differ from the general population; blue-collar workers are underrepresented, while housewives, retirees, and professionals are overrepresented. (© Billy E. Barnes)

consisted of working-class people, only 13.4 percent of blue-collar workers were found on the juries studied.[74]

Similarly, studies have documented the fact that discrimination seems to run along racial lines. A study in Virginia indicated that adult blacks, although constituting an average of 14 percent of the population of the jurisdictions studied, constituted only slightly less than 2 percent of the jurors empaneled in those particular districts.[75]

The Center for Jury Studies estimates that only 15 percent of American adults have ever been called for jury service. This is probably due to several factors: the age limits on prospective jurors set by many states; the use of voter registration lists to select potential jurors, which represent only a portion of eligible voters; the replacement of jurors into the jury pool at too-frequent intervals; and the number of exemptions permitted by the law or granted by the court.

Regarding the issue of representative juries, 1986 was an interesting year for U.S. Supreme Court decisions on this subject. In addition to the attention given the so-called death-qualified jury issue (discussed in Chapter 9), the Court also addressed other representative issues. In a Kentucky case the Court held that prosecutor's must justify racially suspect peremptory challenges.[76] (See *Batson* v. *Kentucky* in Chapter 9.) This decision was aimed at the prevalent practice among prosecutors to remove members of minority races from criminal juries because prosecutor's feel such jurors are too likely to vote for the defense—particularly when a member of a minority race is on trial. The Court also ruled that in an interracial capital case the defendant is entitled to the right to probe potential jurors for racial bias.[77]

## Deliberations

Research conducted using simulated and real juries has provided some interesting insights into this normally secret process. The research suggests that juries are far less deliberative in criminal cases than might be imagined. A University of Chicago research group, after conducting extensive interviews of criminal trial jurors in New York and Chicago, found that almost all juries voted as soon as they retired to their chambers. In 30 percent of the cases, it took only one vote to return a unanimous verdict. In those cases in which subsequent votes were taken, the eventual vote was unanimous 90 percent of the time. The striking fact was that in this 90 percent, if the original vote was a majority one, that was the way the final vote ended up. It would seem that peer pressure was enough to change the minds of the dissenters. The instance of an individual holding out and not voting in accord with the majority and causing a hung jury is very rare indeed.[78]

In a later study by this same research group, additional interesting facts were uncovered. As might be imagined, the juror's occupation and biases seemed to play an important role. Jurors let the defendant's vocation influence their estimate of his or her worth. In criminal cases racial prejudice by jurors from a variety of occupational backgrounds seemed to influence their decisions concerning defendants who were members of minority groups.[79]

*The role of juror's occupation, biases, and other factors*

Videotape simulations of jury deliberations have indicated that there are some obvious decision-making dynamics that occur in jury deliberations. Women played a far more passive role than men in these deliberations.[80] The more formal education a juror had, the more likely that individual was to participate openly and frequently in the discussions and deliberations.[81] Most of the discussion in the jury room centered on how to conduct the deliberations and on an exchange of personal experiences that the jurors felt would aid them in making an appropriate decision. There was far less discussion of the testimony offered during the trial or the instructions that they had received from the judge than might be imagined.[82]

The national origin of the jury members seemed to play an important role in determining if the accused would be found guilty. Jurors of German, Scandinavian, and English ancestry were much more likely to vote for the state, whereas jurors of African or East European background were much more likely to side with the defense.[83]

An extensive study of juries by Harry Kalvern, Jr., and Hans Zeisel found that judges agreed with the decision of juries in about 80 percent of all cases. In those cases in which the judge disagreed with the jury, it was usually because the jury was perceived as being too lenient. Many of the disagreements between the judge and the jury also centered on such factors as the jury's belief that the punishment for the crime was too severe since the defendant had already suffered as a result of having committed the crime and need not be punished further. Juries were also more sensitive to improper police methods and to defendants who were charged with crimes that occurred among subcultures where norms differed from those of the jury members themselves. Finally, juries tended to weigh more heavily than judges the contributory fault of the victim in rape and assault cases.[84]

Although there are certain reform groups who would abolish the jury system, history and the lack of an acceptable substitute seem to indicate that juries will continue to play an important role in the administration of criminal justice. If the future should indicate any changes in the traditional jury system, it is likely to occur only in the manner of selection and composition and the number of jurors used.

**VIVIAN GORNICK**

Had the young black been caught with a loaded revolver? Or was the gun planted by the white policeman who made the arrest? The judge asked jurors to reason from the evidence; no one counted on the implacable weight of racial hostility.

The case before the court was a criminal one: illegal possession of a loaded gun. The elements in the case were the testimony of two undercover policemen, the testimony of the accused, and the presence of a gun on the prosecutor's table. The policemen—both white, in their middle thirties—said the defendant had the gun in his hand when they arrested him. The defendant—black, eighteen—said it was all a lie, he'd never seen the gun until the moment the cops were pushing him up against a wall and handcuffing him. The gun—silver-plated, .32 caliber— lay there mute, an indifferent prop to be seized upon alternatively by prosecuting and the defending lawyers.

It took a day and a half for all the principals in the case to say what they had to say. At the end of that time, the judge turned to the jury box. He reminded the jurors, twelve good and true, that the burden of proof lay with the People; that unless, in their judgment, the People had proved beyond a reasonable doubt the guilt of the accused, it was incumbent upon them to bring in a verdict of not guilty. He enjoined the jurors to reason out of the evidence. He further enjoined them to search and make up their own minds, but at the same time to be open to the thought and feeling of their fellows, as the essence of deliberation was the interaction of open minds.

The judge spoke these profound words easily and carefully, yet mechanically and rhetorically: somewhat like a stewardess on a plane rehearsing her passengers in the lifesaving steps they were to take in case of an emergency whose po-

tential reality no one believed in.

The policemen (whom I will call Galella and Kowalski) told substantially the same story: At approximately 7:30 P.M. one night last July, while on a regular tour of duty (wearing street clothes, driving an unmarked car), they spotted two boys, one of whom was the defendant, sitting at the edge of an alley on West 37th Street, a few feet in from 10th Avenue. As this was a neighborhood that Galella and Kowalski knew well—densely commercial during the day, equally dense with prostitution after dark—they automatically registered the presence of strangers. They drove on by and continued their tour. An hour later they heard over their car radio a report that someone had been seen with a gun in or around those same streets. They drove back and found a marked patrol car parked at the corner of 10th and 37th. The uniformed police said they too had had the gun report and had seen two boys they thought suspicious, had questioned and searched them, found nothing, and sent them on their way. The uniformed police described the two boys Galella and Kowalski had seen earlier. The four policemen parted and went back to their respective cars.

Galella and Kowalski drove up 10th Avenue, turning east on 38th Street. Halfway to 9th Avenue, they spotted the two boys in question walking back toward 10th Avenue. Why, they wondered, when the boys had been told to leave the neighborhood? They decided to swing through a bus lot in the middle of the block and return to 37th Street. They parked their car a third of the way up the block, beside a parking lot enclosed by a chainlink fence. In a few minutes they saw the boys standing on the corner, looking around. Then, the cops said, the boys walked into 37th Street, one of them ducked for a moment in and out of the alley, and they continued at a quick pace, half walking, half loping up the street toward Galella

and Kowalski. When the two boys were within thirty feet or so of the unmarked car, both Galella and Kowalski said, they saw a gun in the left hand of one of the two. They leaped from their car, their own guns drawn, and said to the two: "Don't move. Police." The boys froze in their tracks. Kowalski said, "Drop the gun." The boy with the gun stood motionless. A second time Kowalski said, "Drop the gun." Then, Kowalski said, in one swift motion the boy raised his arm and threw the gun back and up over the chain link fence. The cops pushed the boys up against the building beside the fence, their faces turned toward the wall. Galella stood watch over them. Kowalski climbed the fence, retrieved the gun (with four bullets in it), and arrested the two. The one with the gun was the defendant.

The defendant (whom I will call David Moore) told an entirely different story. He said he and a friend from his neighborhood in Queens had decided to go that evening to a disco at 39th Street and 9th Avenue. They took the train into Manhattan, arriving at Times Square at 8:30 P.M. When they got to the disco, it was just opening for the evening. They decided to take a walk and return later, when their friends would have arrived. They walked down 9th Avenue, looking for a place to buy a beer. Couldn't find one. Walked over to 10th Avenue. Found a grocery store, bought the beers, and returning along 10th, found the alley on 37th Street with steel drums in front of it. They sat down on the drums and began to drink their beers. Suddenly, a police car appeared at the corner. One of the cops came over and began questioning them: Who were they? What were they doing here? Did they have any weapons? They told them who they were, said no, they didn't have any weapons. The cop looked around, pushed his feet through the trash around the steel drums, frisked them, then told them to get going.

The boys got up and began

walking up 37th Street toward 9th. As they walked, David Moore's friend said to him: "Come on. They're gonna be back. They ain't gonna leave us alone." And they began to walk quickly. Halfway up the block, as they came alongside a chain link fence, two men with guns in their hands appeared from out of nowhere. They said they were police, and they wanted to know where the gun was. "We know you got a gun," they said. "Where is it?" The boys said: "We got no gun." The police pushed them up against the wall, made them kneel facing the wall. David Moore said: "We asked them, 'Why you doin' this?' One of them began to climb the fence. The other one said, 'It's all right. If he don't find a gun, we'll let you go.' And then the other one, he came back with a gun."

We were six women, six men, five blacks, seven whites on that jury. Our occupations were postal worker, nurse's aid, clerk-typist, school secretary, community center worker, engineer, actor, writer, carpenter, investment analyst, housewife. It was impossible, sitting on the jury box during the trial, to know much more about any one of us, so well concealed did the people behind these surface identifications remain during the voir dire (jury selection process).

I had become irritated with the questions about possible police prejudice, and had said I thought these questions were designed to elicit stereotypic responses rather than to encourage thinking about individuals; after all, a policeman was only one human being, not the entire police force. Afterward, the postal worker (a bull-necked black man with steady eyes behind thick glasses, who had been chosen as a juror during the same round in which I was chosen) shook his head at me and said, "Didn't think you'd make it. Nosir. Not after all that lip you give 'em."

I looked around at the ten people then occupying jurors' seats: Mary

Davis, the clerk-typist; Loren Levine, the investment analyst; Todd Graham, the engineer; Shirley Silvers and Laura O'Connell, the housewives; Oscar Williams, the community center worker; Anna James, the nurse's aid; David Barnes, the postal worker; Claire Moran, the school secretary; Richard Garcia, the carpenter. I thought back to the moment when the judge and the lawyers had asked each of us to assure them that we could and would be impartial listeners, that we would reason out of the evidence given, that a policeman's testimony would "give us no trouble" (what a euphemism!). Each of us had without hesitation simply said yes or no, and I remember thinking then, We lie. Every last one of us.

But we were all surprised when Gerald Anderson, the actor, was chosen as the last juror. The judge asked him if he was married and Anderson replied, "I live in sin, judge, but no children." All heads in the courtroom jerked in his direction, but Anderson's face bore an unflappable expression, and his smile of resignation said plainly: "I've seen it all; nothing you can say or do would unbalance me; being off balance is my natural condition." Then, when Anderson revealed that one of his many odd jobs as an often unemployed actor had been that of a worker in the New York courts, Richard Garcia laughed merrily and poked Claire Moran in an open, friendly manner, saying, "that's it."

Suddenly, we all knew why Anderson was accepted as the twelfth juror: it was six o'clock in the evening; we had been jury-picking for a full day and a half; if Anderson was rejected, the court would have to call for a fresh batch of prospective jurors. Neither lawyer was willing to sustain such a delay on "a simple gun possession case."

The jury room was a gray-green, institutional rectangle: coat hooks on the wall, two small bathrooms off to one side, a long, scarred table surrounded by wooden armchairs,

wastebaskets, and a floor superficially clean, deeply filthy. We entered this room on a Friday at noon, most of us expecting to be gone from it by four or five that same day. We did not see the last of it until a full twelve hours had elapsed, by which time the grimy oppressiveness of the place had become, for me at least, inextricably bound up with psychological defeat.

We ate the sandwiches brought up from the coffee shop, drank the atrocious coffee, carefully put the wrappings and the remains of our lunches into a large paper carton, wiped off the table. Then the guard took out the garbage, locked us into the room, and we began with a vote around the table. It took exactly two minutes for each of those voices to be heard pronouncing the words *guilty, not guilty*. The vote was eight *not guilty*, four *guilty*. I was one of the four who voted guilty; the other three were Loren Levine, Gerald Anderson, and Shirley Silvers.

A wave of surprise. Most of the jurors voting *not guilty* had seemed vigorously conservative as they sat in the box, the ones voting *guilty*, predictably liberal. Then—perhaps appropriately—the *guilty*s had been spoken in hesitant, musing, this-is-open-for-discussion voices, while the *not guilty*s had been announced in flat, closed, nothing-to-discuss voices.

"Well," said I, the novice juror, to myself, "it's just like the movies. Now we begin. Now we will talk, we *will* listen to one another, we will see how we have arrived at these opinions. Because that, surely, is all they are now: opinions, not settled convictions."

But I was wrong. The twelve hours that followed would in no essential way alter the attitudes made clear during those first two minutes. What did happen, though, is that, one by one, all four *guilty*s were "persuaded" to change their votes to *not guilty*. That persuasion came about not through the irresistible uses of reason but through the disintegrating power of emotional cave-in.

Nearly everyone seemed to speak at once: over, under, and through each other. No one heard anything anyone else said, and no one actually *said* anything new, just repeated, in even louder tones, *guilty, not guilty*. Richard Garcia said: "I just *feel* he's innocent. Don't ask me why, I just feel it." Anna James—whose voice bore an uncanny resemblance to that of Butterfly McQueen—said, "I can't *believe* that boy ain't innocent." Claire Moran and Laura O'Connell stated flatly: "I don't believe the cops." Todd Graham, a solid man whose rimless glasses made his large afro look conservative, simply smiled and shook his head repeatedly, "No way, no way." Mary Davis, a large black woman endowed with a maternal appearance, compressed her lips, crossed her arms on her huge bosom, and shook her head, *loudly*. Shirley Silvers, middle-aged, well-dressed, brimming with nervous sweetness, turned agitatedly from one to another, chattering: "I don't know, maybe I'm wrong, I *think* he's guilty, I don't know."

In the midst of all this, a sudden flare-up between Richard Garcia and Loren Levine: yelling, foot-stamping, slamming of bathroom doors, Garcia's voice shrill, crying, "Let me talk! Dammit, *will* you let me talk?" Levine retorting hotly, "That's all you've *been* doing. And not saying a single thing of substance. If we let *you* go on, we'll be here for a week!"

What was this? Levine—thin, remote, with a voice trapped between nasal drip and lockjaw, always reading the *Times* when the others were talking, and polishing his glasses, thoughtfully—why was he standing there with a faceful of twitching irritation as though he were exploding inside? And Garcia—black-haired, wide-faced, mustachioed, manner expansive, above all jolly—why was he on his feet, his voice screeching, his hands on his hips, as though to say, "I can't take this

another minute"? Were we going to have juror "revelations" so soon? We had only just begun.

Order. Order. Let's have some order here. Now—*calmly*—let each one of us tell the others exactly why we think *guilty, not guilty*.

We went around the table again, Richard Garcia, Mary Davis, and Anna James repeated that they couldn't believe that boy wasn't innocent.

Loren Levine, under tight control again, said quietly that he felt the police story hung together; it was logical in all its parts and it made sense to him.

Todd Graham said he felt the police story *didn't* hang together; why, he couldn't or wouldn't say.

Laura O'Connell—born, raised, married, and still living in the same working-class neighborhood—said in an uninflected, tenement-pitched voice: "I don't believe the cops. I know cops. Some of my best friends are cops. I know what they do. I just don't believe them."

Claire Moran, a small, thin, birdlike woman in her forties, nodded her head and said, "That's right. I can't help feeling the same. I just don't believe that police story."

It was my turn. I said, "In order for me to vote *not guilty,* I would have to believe that these two policemen deliberately framed this boy. I would have to believe they planted that gun on him. I find that almost impossible to believe."

"Oh, for God's sake," said Mary Davis.

"They do it all the time," protested Todd Graham.

"Everybody knows *that,*" cried Laura O'Connell.

"That's true, you know," said Claire Moran.

"Yes," said Gerald Anderson, speaking for the first time, "they *do* do it all the time. But only for a reason. In this case there was no reason." Everyone turned to Gerald, the street-smart actor who proved to be the best juror in the room, the man who most loved reason, and the only one to return again and

again to the question of the evidence before us.

"I probably know more about cops than anyone else in this room," Gerald said, "and I certainly know they are capable of planting a weapon on somebody. But, in my experience, it's almost always because they know or they think they know a person they're after is guilty of a crime they can't prove. Usually it's narcotics. Sometimes it's some hard-nosed kid in a neighborhood they've worked in who's given them trouble, they hate the kid, they want to put him away. But to plant a gun on a perfectly strange kid? Just to bring a charge of gun possession? When there are a thousand such arrests a day in New York, all perfectly legit? That doesn't make any sense to me at all."

"Besides, where would the gun have come from?" asked Shirley Silvers.

"Oh, cops have two guns on them quite often," said Todd Graham. "The one you see, and the one you don't."

"Oh, for Chrissake," said Gerald Anderson. "Do you realize what you're saying? You know if a cop walks out of the station house with a gun secreted on his person, and he's discovered, it's his job? Right then and there. He's finished. You think a cop does a thing like that so lightly?"

Todd Graham shrugged his shoulders, closed his mouth, and looked down at the table. Clearly, Gerald's words had only silenced him.

"Well, that may be true, Mr. Anderson," said David Barnes softly, his voice all self-conscious dignity, "although we only have your word for it, you'll pardon my pointing out, that some of us here may have had experiences that contradict that statement, but I don't believe the police story either. I can't exactly say why. It just don't sit right with me. And if it don't sit right, I gotta vote *not guilty.*"

Six people turned to the right and to the left and mouthed, "That's right. That's the way *I* see it, too. If you don't believe the cops . . ."

Oscar Williams, the community center worker—tall, thin, middle-aged, very black-skinned, a face and manner suffused with a quiet that passed for calm—had not said one word during this entire time. I turned to him: "Mr. Williams, what do *you* think?" He looked at me for a long moment before he spoke. There was silence in the room. And then, in a low, steady voice, making extraordinary use of the rhetorical device of dividing a sentence into its phrases, Oscar Williams said: "I cannot believe. That boy raised his arm. With a gun in it. When a policeman had told him to freeze. And that boy ain't a dead boy. I simply cannot believe that."

One instant of utter stillness, and then a jam of voices in the already thickening air: "Amen!" "That's right, that's right." "I'm with *him*." "I can't believe that either." "No-sir. I don't believe that either."

Gerald Anderson and I stared at each other. We were shaken by Williams's eloquence and its effect on the room. "But *still*," I could almost see me and Gerald thinking at the same moment.

"Mr. Williams, does that mean you think the cops framed the boy?" I asked.

"I didn't say that." He closed his eyes and spread the fingers of his thin, fine hand in the air. "I don't know whether they framed the boy or not. And I'm not sayin' they *did*. I'm only sayin' I cannot *see* that thing happening."

Williams took off his glasses; the skin just below his eyes and on the bridge of his nose glistened. He wiped his face with a soft white handkerchief. He carefully lifted one pressed pants leg over the other. Then he said: "I'm no social worker. I'm no bleeding heart. I know how rotten kids are. They *stink*. And there is absolutely nothing worse than a teenager with a gun in his hand. Don't you think I *know* that? But," his voice dropped one husky octave, "I

cannot see that thing happening. And I keep thinking: If I blow this, if I give that kid a record . . . well, I just wouldn't be able to live with myself."

Mary Davis removed her arms from across her capacious chest and said, "Well, as far as I'm concerned, the man just said it all. Now we either all vote *not guilty* or we go in and tell the judge we are stuck." She was sitting directly opposite me. She leaned across the table toward me and said, "Sweetheart, cops, they shoot first, ask questions later. All of 'em."

"You said in the courtroom you weren't prejudiced against the police," I said faintly.

"I *ain't* prejudiced!" she replied angrily. "I'm just telling you what they *do*."

"It doesn't matter what *they* do," I said. "You've got to look at what *these* two did. Or what you *think* they did. And *why* you think they did it."

"Oh, there's no talking to this girl," Mary Davis said, twisting her face and body into a tortured profile position. (She really was a very large woman.)

"Yes," said Gerald Anderson drily. "Well, I *do* think the question of whether we think the police framed the boy is the crucial one, and it isn't enough to say you can't or won't think about that one. Now, no one's experience here is sacred. It carries no more authority than anyone else's. Our experience is all supposed to be in the service of the evidence before us. Not the other way around."

Everyone nodded, but Gerald's words meant nothing. On and on it went. For hours. It was not merely that the same words and phrases were repeated endlessly; it was that our "positions" seemed to have become congealed; minds and eyes glazed over; we didn't even hear ourselves speaking after a while.

Two curiosities emerged during these hours. One was that Anna James—the nurse's aid who just couldn't believe that boy wasn't

innocent—proved to be a near mental incompetent. She could not keep in her mind the details of the story told by the police and the one told by the boy. At one point she mused out loud, "How that boy get over from Lexington Avenue so quick? They must be crazy to think we swallow that." We all stared at her. Lexington Avenue? What on earth was she talking about? Worse yet, what had been transpiring in her mind all this time?

I discovered afterward that Anna James was the most professional juror among us. She had over the years been chosen to serve in innumerable criminal and civil cases; and before my own term as juror was over, I saw her chosen to serve on a complex case of embezzlement. I knew why, too. Her manner was one of middle-class reserve, indicating (to one who asked no vital questions) a quiet but firm capacity to think, slowly but responsibly. During the twelve hours I was locked up with her, I discovered that that manner masked a slow-witted stubbornness functioning in the service of two profound disabilities: she was at all times oblivious to evidence, and she hated the cops. Hated them.

The second curiosity was that each of the others who had voted *not guilty* also hated the police. Hated, distrusted, disbelieved, did not want to think about anything said or done by anyone who was a policeman. "Cops shoot first, ask questions later." Young, old, black, white, blue-collar, white-collar: they all drew a pugnacious blank on police testimony.

At six o'clock, Gerald Anderson, who had been staring morosely at a diagrammatic chart of the streets in which "the incident" had taken place, said, "Hey, wait a minute. I just realized something." Everyone perked up. Anything to break this deadly boring tension. "The kid may or may not be innocent," Gerald went on, "but one thing is certain. He lied on that stand. Look, everyone agrees that four policemen questioned him. I mean, the cops said that, and he said that, too. There's no argument there. Now, *he* says he was questioned at the corner by the uniformed police. And then questioned again *halfway down the block* by the undercover cops. If that's true, then the undercover cops must have been sitting in their car when he was questioned by the uniformed police. Because it only takes half a minute to get down the block. They'd have *seen* it. Why would they have grabbed the kids a minute later if they'd just seen them questioned and searched? That certainly doesn't make sense. He *must* be lying about that."

Excitement generated quickly. Confused, disturbed, everyone was glad to have something new to think about. Eager attention was turned to Gerald's "discovery." None but one thought of where this attention could lead. Oscar Williams sat still and silent, hands folded on knobby knees, glasses glistening in the dull yellow light. He looked up into the noise and very softly said, "Just because he's lyin' don' mean he's guilty as charged." It was as though a schoolmaster had rapped the children for rowdiness. Todd Graham said very soberly, "Yeah, that's right." So did Mary Davis. So did Claire Moran. So did Richard Garcia.

Shortly after this we were taken to dinner, herded together at two or three tables in a chop house, given a selective menu that did not permit so much as a glass of beer, watched over by the guards. It was a depressed and depressing meal.

No sooner had we returned to the jury room, hung up our coats, and taken our seats, than David Barnes stood up, approached the diagram, cleared his throat, and said, "I've been thinking." We all

looked at him, supposing him about to carry Gerald's point further. Barnes then, after a fashion, repeated the original point as though he were introducing it for the first time, and then proceeded to garble the details so that the point was utterly lost and the exercise at the diagram without meaning.

It seemed impossible that everyone in the room would not instantly see that Barnes had just caricatured not only the point but the point of the point. But no. Garcia said, "Now there's an idea." Claire Moran said, "Would you mind going over that again, Mr. Barnes?" Laura O'Connell, straining nearsightedly at the diagram, said, "I kinda see what you're getting at." Todd Graham looked down at the sheet of doodle drawings under his right hand. Oscar Williams inspected his fingernails. Loren Levine nearly took out the *Times*.

I swung in my seat to look at Gerald. He was staring into space. I thought I saw something close over his eyes, some invisible shutter come down, and I think in that moment his switched vote was being born. As I looked at his face I knew we were lost. I remembered a moment a few hours earlier when Williams had said something, and Gerald had replied curtly: "You *know* you're putting pressure on us," and Williams had demurred, and I had thought: "No, the pressure is being applied from within."

I did not know if my conviction that the police did not frame David Moore constituted evidence any more than Oscar Williams's conviction that the boy could not have raised his arm with a gun in it and not be shot dead constituted a reasonable doubt. And I did not really care if the boy was guilty or not guilty, if he was punished or set

free, if the police were supported or attacked. But the abdication of thought frightened me. That *did* matter. In fact it seemed to be the only thing that mattered, and it mattered that it was we—Gerald and I and all the rest—who wouldn't do the thinking.

I realized that I had become strangely attached to the people in the room. In these hours together, unwilling and most peculiar bonds had been forged. It was not that we had revealed ourselves to each other, although to some extent we had. It was certainly not that we were sealed by shared understandings of the mind or heart. No, it was rather, I began to see, that we had been locked up here randomly, thrown together willy-nilly like a family, and like a family had inflicted our emotional prejudices on each other. This act cast long shadows. Certainly it touched something in me, made me responsive to mysterious claims I could not at that moment identify. The situation began to seem metaphoric. Civilization seemed to hang on the willingness here in this room to think. In the emotional grandiosity of that moment was born *my* switched vote.

For an instant I saw things clearly. "Hang the jury," I said to myself, "there is no way out of this." But the next moment I said to myself, "No. They must see. I must *make* them see." And from that moment on I was, essentially, pleading with everyone "to see" what was happening here. I knew I should hang the jury but I simply could not do what I knew should be done. It was then a given that I would let myself be overcome. Clearly, I needed them more than they needed me.

At nine o'clock Shirley Silvers cried out, "I change my vote! I vote *not guilty*." Half an hour later, Gerald

Anderson, still staring into space, looking absolutely bleak, said, "I vote *not guilty.*" Directly afterward, Loren Levine, who had retreated into near total silence since his altercation with Richard Garcia, said crisply, "Me, too. *Not guilty.*" Why had none of them hung the jury? What personal mystery struggled up in each of them? To what were they "attached" that they had caved in, one by one?

I was the last holdout. All around me pressed voices, faces, shadows, that said, "Explain yourself. Justify yourself. We know who *we* are. Can you say as much? What is all this nonsense about? Never mind the others. What are *you* doing here?"

I looked at Oscar Williams now sitting silent, watching me. I begged him with my eyes to understand and support me. He looked at me. His face said, "I do understand, but you're in this alone." The memory of his voice saying, "That boy would be a dead boy" entered into me, made me quail somewhere inside myself. Conveniently, I lost my nerve against that haughty pain of his; conveniently, couldn't hold on to what I knew, began to get fogged up, didn't quite know anymore what was evidence, what a reasonable doubt . . .

"For God's sake," I cried as though I were going under. "What *reason* would these two cops have had for framing this kid? Cynically, recklessly, cold-bloodedly, framing a boy they'd never seen before? Now you know goddamn well it's not these two people whose testimony you've been listening to. It's *cops.* All cops. So what have we got here? Where does that leave us? With two stereotypes: on the one hand" (I raised my left arm at the elbow, hand palm out), "we have 'the cops.' On the other hand" (I raised my right arm), "we

have a 'young black boy' . . ."

The word black was a match struck to a can of gasoline: conflagration blazed in less than thirty seconds.

"Color, color, who said anything about color?" David Barnes thundered. "What chu bringing in color for? I don't like that. Nosiree, I don't like that one bit."

"I *knew* she had that in her mind all the time!" Anna James shrieked, "I knew it."

"I don' wanna hear a word about black or white," Mary Davis boomed. "Now you hear me? That boy's mama raised him up just like everybody else's. Didn't do it no different from yours."

Shirley Silvers got hysterical and began to scream: "She didn't mean it. She didn't mean it."

Todd Graham smiled mockingly at me and said, "I know. You're not prejudiced."

Oscar Williams's eyes met mine in amazement for a single second. Then he buried his face in his hands.

Gerald Anderson and Loren Levine stared, openmouthed, but remained silent.

It was just easier for everyone to let happen what was happening.

As for me, I felt relief. The charge of racism—painful and frightening at first—was, in fact, a smokescreen behind which everyone, myself included, was only too glad to hide. "You win," I said. "*Not guilty.*" Everyone looked down, or away.

At midnight the verdict was announced in the courtroom. The jurors fell all over themselves fleeing the building. Claire Moran turned in the doorway and said, "Please don't misunderstand this, but I hope I never see any of you again!"

Only Gerald Anderson and I stayed behind. Ours was the sick feeling of cowards that compels

hanging around. The lawyers, both of whom were young and eager for details as to what had happened in the jury room, also hung around. We talked a long while together.

We told them many things, and then we told them how persuasive had been Oscar Williams's assertion that he couldn't imagine the boy making a motion with a gun in his hand while facing a cop and not being shot, and how Williams had agonized that this was the boy's first arrest and Williams would be ruining his life with a conviction. The young assistant district attorney listened silently, nodding his head forlornly at every word I spoke as though he knew *this* litany by heart. I looked at him, puzzled.

"It *was* Moore's first arrest, wasn't it?" I asked.

"No," he shook his head. "He was arrested in 1974 at the age of fourteen."

"What was the charge?" asked Gerald.

"Pointing a loaded .22 caliber gun at a policeman."

On Monday morning I returned, as directed, to the large jurors' room in the Criminal Courts Building. Almost everyone from the jury was there. Mary Davis, Richard Garcia, and Anna James sat together, but everyone else sat alone in widely separated seats. I walked directly over to Oscar Williams. He rose as I approached him. We looked at each other. I told him what the district attorney had told me about David Moore's previous arrest. Williams's black skin turned the color of cigarette ash. It exactly matched the taste in my mouth.

## ☐ WITNESSES

Witnesses in criminal trials are classified into two categories: (1) the lay, or ordinary, witness; and (2) the expert witness.

Lay and expert

The lay, or ordinary, witness is a person who has some personal knowledge of the facts of the case and who has been called on to relate this information in court. Police officers usually fall within this category. The lay witness is permitted to testify only about facts and generally may not state an opinion unless this is permitted by the judge.[85] Lay witnesses are allowed to testify only to what they perceived through their five senses that is relevant to the case.

With the great advance of science and with the wide variety of skilled occupations, juries are often called on to pass judgment on many matters about which the jurors have no personal knowledge. The services of the expert witness have been developed to assist them. The function of the expert witness is to give the jury the benefit of his or her knowledge of a particular science or skill. Expert witnesses are permitted to express their opinions concerning a particular set of facts or circumstances or about some examination of evidence made by them. Of course, the jury may or may not accept their opinions.

An expert witness must satisfy two fundamental rules: (1) The subject to which the expert witness will testify must be a field in which the average person has little or no knowledge; and (2) the witness must have the qualifications that are necessary to make him or her an expert in the field. A voir dire examination is conducted by both the prosecutor and defense counsel to establish the expertise of the witness. However, the final decision as to whether or not someone qualifies as an expert witness is made by the trial judge. Even though the trial judge rules that the individual is indeed an expert witness, the opposing counsel can cross-examine the expert in an effort to destroy his or her credibility to the jury.

## ☐ THE BAILIFF

Responsibility

The bailiff is an officer of the court. This office evolved from the Statute of Winchester in 1285, by which King Edward I tried to establish a uniform system of law enforcement in England. The original responsibilities of this official were to keep persons under surveillance who were traveling about town streets after dark and to check periodically on all known and observed strangers. Today the bailiff is responsible for keeping order in the court and protecting the security of jury deliberations and court property. At the county level, the bailiff is often a member of the sheriff's department, who, as a uniformed officer, is assigned to the court. Many municipal courts rely on a form of political patronage to fill this position, and the bailiff is appointed by the judge to serve in a particular court.

## ☐ THE COURT CLERK

The office of court clerk is normally attached to the main trial court of the county or municipality. In most states, the court clerk is a popularly elected official. In some states, this position is considered a patronage appointment for the party represented by the senior judge on the bench or by the party that is represented by the majority of judges in the court. The court clerk collects fines, forfeitures, penalties, and court costs in criminal cases, is usually responsible for keeping records of the court proceedings and actions, and may be empowered to prepare formal writs and process papers issued by the court. Court clerks usually are salaried officials, but in some states they are still paid on a fee basis. In several states, the position of court clerk is combined with that of the elected county clerk, who records legal papers in the county as well as handles the administrative and clerical responsibilities of the court.

## THE COURT REPORTER

Court reporters are employed to record and transcribe trial or other court proceedings. In the past, the court reporter normally used shorthand, but most now use stenotype machines. In the last few years, courts, in an effort to become more cost-effective, are increasingly turning to tape recorders. One of the problems of using tape recorders is the difficulty of editing the tape to remove objectionable comments. In most cases, the court reporter is salaried and is also paid an additional sum, usually by the page, for transcribing and preparing the court record in cases of appeal. In some instances, the court reporter is responsible for the care and security of the physical evidence introduced during the trial if it is not the express responsibility of the bailiff to do so. However, this responsibility extends only to the time that the evidence is in the courtroom; permanent responsibility for the maintenance of the evidence during the trial is usually the task of the court clerk or, in the case of the state's evidence, the police in certain circumstances.

Court reporters are better able to accurately record every word that is said with newer, more sophisticated shorthand machines. (Comstock)

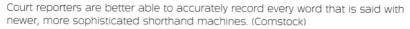

## THE CAMERAS ARE ROLLING IN KENTUCKY COURTS

The tiny television cameras mounted high on the walls of the courtroom are as unobtrusive as their advocates claim. Only the judge pays any attention to them, checking a monitor now and then to make sure they're operating. The judge is also making handwritten notes on such matters as the names of the witnesses and when their testimony started and ended, because there is no court stenographer to do it. The cameras, and the microphones that are connected to them, are making a record of the trial—the only record.

There are twenty-five such "video courtrooms" in the state of Kentucky. The system, now in its fourth year of operation, is designed to create a more accurate trial record, one that will be available at a lower cost to litigants than the typical transcribed testimony compiled by court stenographers. Needless to say, court reporters are not happy, because their jobs are being abolished, although turnover is high in these jobs, and Kentucky has not yet actually had to lay off any reporters. The savings in court reporters' salaries and in the expense of providing transcripts for litigants who are paupers have already almost paid for the system.

The system does have its critics. It was initially feared that attorneys would "grandstand" or that the camera would intimidate witnesses. Neither has happened. Another criticism has been that using court reporters made it easier than the videotape to find the particular piece of testimony that the jury asked for. Although this has been the case, new technology is even solving that problem through faster scanning techniques.

The visual record has been taken into account by an appellate court in at least one case. A defendant appealed on the ground that he had been insane at the time he entered his guilty plea. The appeals court said the tape showed he was "cogent and responsible," thus failing in his attempt to convince the higher court.

## THE CORONER

The office of coroner, although not a judicial office in the strictest sense, does perform quasi-judicial functions. The first mention of this official is recorded in 1194 during the reign of King Richard I of England. Unfortunately, little is known of his specific responsibilities other than that he was a representative of the crown assigned to perform ministerial tasks at the county level.

The present-day function of the coroner seems to date from 1275, when under Edward I his responsibilities were expanded to include the specific task of conducting investigations into unnatural and sudden deaths. He was also charged with the duties of overseeing criminal prosecutions that involved the forfeiture of the accused's property to the crown, the collection of taxes, and the levying and collection of fines.

Today, the coroner in the majority of states is an elected county official whose chief function is to investigate the cause of death that occurs in the absence of witnesses, under suspicious circumstances, or where there is evidence of possible violence. The coroner is authorized to conduct *inquests* concerning suspicious deaths. These are quasi-judicial hearings that have some of the same characteristics as a trial. The coroner usually has the authority to subpoena witnesses and documents, cross-examine witnesses under oath, introduce evidence, and receive testimony. Most states do not require that the inquest follow the exacting rules of criminal procedure that govern trials. If the hearing suggests just cause, the coroner is authorized to issue warrants of arrest or at least require the prosecutor to initiate the obtaining of such a warrant.

Inquests

One of the major criticisms of this office has been the lack of qualifications required to be coroner. Because, in many cases, coroners have no background in medicine or law, they cannot perform their obligations satisfactorily. As a result of this, a number of states have abolished the office of coroner and created the office of *medical examiner* in its place. The medical examiner must be a licensed physician and in some instances must also be a qualified specialist in pathology. Many states, such as Massachusetts, which was the first to adopt this idea in 1877, have vested the legal responsibilities in the office of the county prosecutor and the medical responsibilities in the appointed medical examiner. A few states have appointed medical examiners who operate out of a central state agency.

**Medical examiner**

## SUMMARY

The judge, prosecuting attorney, defense counsel, and jury play extremely important roles in the administration of justice—roles that are often very different from those commonly portrayed through the media. For example, judges are much more constrained in their actions by other members of the court and criminal justice system than most people imagine.

By the same token, the power and discretion of the prosecuting attorney is much broader than most people realize. In fact, the prosecutor is probably the most important actor in the judicial process—and perhaps in the entire criminal justice system. This official's power to decline to prosecute a case, to play a central role in plea bargaining, and to exert authority over grand jury inquiries and police investigations

make the prosecutor a very formidable instrument of justice.

The role of the defense attorney is also often perceived far differently than the role that he or she actually plays. The "Perry Mason" image of the defense lawyer as a crusading searcher for justice and trial advocacy is more than a little farfetched. In fact, the defense attorney's role is more likely to be one of accommodation and expediency in many criminal cases.

Finally, the role of the jury was examined. In addition to these major roles, this chapter explored the characteristics of indigent defense arrangements, and various secondary officials such as witnesses, court bailiff, the court clerk, the court reporter, and the coroner's office.

## REVIEW QUESTIONS

1. Name the principle actors involved in a criminal court proceeding.
2. What is the role of the judge in court?
3. Briefly describe common constraints placed on judges in the hearing of a case.
4. Why is the prosecutor called the "traffic cop" of the criminal justice system?
5. What are three inducements that a prosecutor might use in plea bargaining?
6. What are the extraordinary powers the prosecutor has over the proceedings of a grand jury?
7. Is the office of prosecutor politically important? Why?

8. What is the primary responsibility of the defense attorney? Explain your answer.
9. In the text, the role of the defense attorney is described as adversarial. What does that mean in relation to the other actors in the judicial process?
10. Discuss defense systems for indigent defendants and the three types.
11. What purpose does the jury serve in the criminal justice system?
12. What are the two general categories of witnesses? How do they differ?
13. Identify the role and responsibilities of the bailiff, court clerk, court reporter, and the coroner (medical examiner).

## DISCUSSION QUESTIONS

1. Plea bargaining undermines and destroys the purpose of the judicial process. Is this statement true? Discuss.
2. Politics play too important a role in the selection of prosecutors and district attorneys. Thus prosecutors should be appointed, not elected to their office. Discuss.
3. A defense attorney should do everything possible to win a favorable verdict for his or her client. Discuss.
4. There are many who say that those accused of crimes should not have taxpayer-supported legal counsel. Do you agree or disagree? Why?
5. Should unanimous jury verdicts be required in criminal cases? Explain your position.
6. What role should the jury play in a criminal case? Explain your position.

## SUGGESTED ADDITIONAL READINGS

Eisenstein, James, and Herbert Jacob. *Felony Justice: An Organizational Analysis of Criminal Courts.* Boston: Little, Brown, 1977.

Feeley, Malcolm M. *The Process Is the Punishment: Handling Cases in a Lower Criminal Court.* New York: Russell Sage Foundation, 1979.

Hans, Valerie, and Neil Vidmar. *Judging the Jury.* New York: Plenum, 1986.

Jacoby, Joan E. *The American Prosecutor: A Search for Identity.* Lexington, Mass.: Lexington Books, 1980.

Letman, Sloan. *Legal Issues in Criminal Justice: The Courts.* Cincinnati: Pilgrimage, 1984.

Levin, A. Leo and Russell Wheeler (eds.). *The American Judiciary: Critical Issues.* Beverly Hills, CA: Sage Publications, 1984.

McDonald, William F. (ed.). *The Prosecutor.* Beverly Hills, Calif.: Sage, 1979.

Nagel, Stuart. *Improving the Legal Process: Effects of Alternatives.* Lexington, Mass.: Lexington Books, 1975.

Nagel, Stuart, and M. Neff. "The Impact of Plea Bargaining on Judicial Process Changes." *American Bar Association Journal* 62 (1976): 1020–1023.

Nardulli, Peter F. (ed.). *The Study of Criminal Courts: Political Perspective.* Cambridge, Mass.: Ballinger, 1979.

Neeley, Richard. *Why Courts Don't Work.* New York: McGraw-Hill, 1982.

Neubauer, David W. *America's Courts and the Criminal Justice System,* 3rd ed. Pacific Grove, Calif.: Brooks/ Cole, 1988.

Nimmer, Raymond T. *The Nature of System Change: Reform Impact in the Criminal Courts.* Chicago: American Bar Foundation, 1978.

Rovner-Pieczenik, Roberta. *The Criminal Court: How It Works.* Lexington, Mass.: Lexington Books, 1978.

Vera Institute of Justice. *Felony Arrests, Their Prosecution and Disposition in New York City's Courts.* New York: Vera Institute of Justice, 1977.

## NOTES

1. J. P. Ryan, A. Ashman, B. D. Sales, and S. Sane-Debow. *American Trial Judges* (New York: Free Press, 1980).
2. *Boykin* v. *Alabama,* 395 U.S. 238, 89 S. Ct. (1969).
3. For example, see Marvin E. Frankel, *Criminal Sentences: Law Without Order* (New York: Hill & Wang, 1973).
4. Maureen Mileski, "Courtroom Encounters: An Observation Study of a Lower Criminal Court," *Law and Society Review* 5 (1971): 473–538.
5. David W. Neubauer. *America's Courts and the Criminal Justice System,* 3rd ed. (Pacific Grove, Calif.: Brooks/Cole, 1988), p. 159.
6. William L. F. Felsteiner and Ann Barthelmes Drew, *European Alternatives to Criminal Trials and Their Applicability to the United States* (Washington, D.C.: National Institute of Law Enforcement and Criminal Justice, 1978), p. 7.
7. This section was adopted from Peter W. Lewis and Kenneth D. Peoples, *The Supreme Court and the Criminal Process* (Philadelphia: Saunders, 1978), pp. 974–975.
8. Ibid., p. 975.
9. For example, see Milton Heumann, *Plea Bargaining—The Experiences of Prosecutors, Judges and Defense Attorneys* (Chicago: University of Chicago Press, 1978); J. Ferguson, "The Role of the Judge in Plea Bargaining," *Criminal Law Quarterly* 15 (1972): 50–51; and *Dewey* v. *United States,* 268 F. 2d 124, 128 (8th Cir. 1959).
10. Heumann, *Plea Bargaining,* p. 35.
11. Henry A. Allen, "Trial Preparation," *Informant* 3 (March 1978): 6.
12. Abraham Blumberg, *Criminal Justice* (Chicago: Quadrangle Press, 1970), p. 53.
13. Donald J. Newman, "Pleading Guilty for Considerations: A Study of Bargain Justice," *Journal of Criminal Law, Criminology and Police Science* 46 (March–April 1956): 780–790.
14. George F. Cole, *The American System of Criminal Justice* (North Scituate, Mass.: Duxbury Press, 1975), p. 297.
15. Albert N. Alschuler, "The Prosecutor's Role in

Plea Bargaining," *University of Chicago Law Review* 61 (1968), pp. 212–234.

16. Cole, *The American System of Criminal Justice*, p. 297.

17. Heumann, *Plea Bargaining*, p. 35.

18. Ibid.

19. Joan E. Jacoby, *The American Prosecutor: A Search for Identity* (Lexington, Mass.: Lexington Books, 1980), p. 195.

20. Wayne R. LaFave, *Arrest: The Decision to Take a Suspect into Custody* (Boston: Little, Brown, 1965), p. 515.

21. Advisory Commission on Intergovernmental Relations, *State–Local Relations in the Criminal Justice System* (Washington, D.C.: U.S. Government Printing Office, 1971), pp. 113–114.

22. Yong Hyo Cho, *Public Policy and Urban Crime* (Cambridge, Mass.: Ballinger, 1974), p. 57.

23. Advisory Commission, *State Local Relations*, p. 113.

24. National District Attorneys Association, *The Prosecuting Attorneys of the United States* (Chicago: NDAA, 1966), pp. 193–195.

25. National District Attorneys Association, *National Prosecution Standards* (Chicago: NDAA, 1980), p. 9.

26. Richard L. Enstrom, "Political Ambitions and the Prosecutorial Office," *Journal of Politics* 33 (1971): 190–194.

27. W. Gelber, "Who Defends the Prosecutor?" *Crime and Delinquency* 14 (1968): 315–323.

28. President's Commission on Law Enforcement and Administration of Justice, Task Force Report: The Courts (Washington, D.C.: U.S. Government Printing Office, 1967), p. 73.

29. National District Attorneys Association, *The Prosecuting Attorneys of the United States*, p. 194.

30. H. R. Wildermann, "The Process of Socialization in the Role of the Prosecutor," *Journal of Social Interaction* 2 (Spring 1965): 26–35.

31. National District Attorneys Association, *National Prosecution Standards*, p. 51.

32. Cole, *The American System of Criminal Justice*, p. 257.

33. Abraham S. Blumberg, "Lawyers with Convictions," *Transaction* 4 (July 1967): 18.

34. As quoted in Leonard Downie, Jr., *Justice Denied* (New York: Praeger, 1971), p. 173; and Cole, *The American System of Criminal Justice*, p. 263.

35. Cole, *The American System of Criminal Justice*, p. 260.

36. Board of Governors, Criminal Law Section, Virginia State Bar, *Report to the Governor and the General Assembly of Virginia: A Study of the Defense of Indigents in Virginia* (Annapolis, Va., 1971).

37. Malcolm M. Feeley, *The Process Is the Punishment: Handling Cases in a Lower Criminal Court* (New York: Russell Sage Foundation, 1979), pp. 78–79.

38. J. Edward Lumbard, "Better Lawyers for Our Criminal Courts," *Atlantic Monthly* (June 1964): 86.

39. Bureau of Justice Statistics. *Report to the Nation on Crime and Justice*, 2nd ed. (Washington: U.S. Department of Justice, March 1988), p. 121.

40. *Powell* v. *Alabama*, 287 U.S. 45 (1932).

41. *Argersinger* v. *Hamlin*, 407 U.S. 25 (1972). In 1979, in the Case of *Scott* v. *Illinois*, the Supreme Court limited the right to counsel where imprisonment was actually imposed rather than merely authorized by statute.

42. Jacoby, *The American Prosecutor*, p. 82.

43. *Escobedo* v. *Illinois*, 378 U.S. 478 (1964).

44. *Miranda* v. *Arizona*, 384 U.S. 436 (1966).

45. *United States* v. *Wade*, 388 U.S. 218 (1967).

46. *Douglas* v. *California*, 372 U.S. 353 (1963).

47. *Mempa* v. *Ray*, 389 U.S. 128 (1967).

48. *In re Gault*, 387 U.S. 1 (1967).

49. Research note, "Dollars and Sense of the Right to Counsel," *Iowa Law Review* 55 (1970): 1249–1259.

50. Jacoby, *The American Prosecutor*, p. 82.

51. Ibid.

52. Bureau of Justice Statistics, *Criminal Defense Systems* (Washington, D.C.: U.S. Department of Justice, August 1984), pp. 5–6.

53. Bureau of Justice Statistics Bulletin, *Criminal Defense for the Poor* (Washington, D.C.: U.S. Department of Justice, September 1988). p. 1.

54. Bureau of Justice Statistics, *Criminal Defense Systems*, p. 6.

55. Jacoby, *The American Prosecutor*, p. 85.

56. Ibid.

57. Ibid., pp. 85–86.

58. Bureau of Justice Statistics, *Criminal Defense Systems*, p. 5.

59. Ibid., p. 7.

60. Jacoby, op. cit., p. 89.

61. Bureau of Justice Statistics, *Report to the Nation*, p. 74.

62. "The Representation of Indigent Criminal Defendants in the Federal District Courts," *Harvard Law Review* 76 (1963): 579–586.

63. Norman G. Kittel, "Defense of the Poor: A Study in Public Parsimony and Private Poverty," *Indiana Law Review* 45 (1970): 89–94.

64. Marlene Lehtman and Gerald Smith, "The Relative Effectiveness of Public Defenders and Private Attorneys," *NLADA Briefcase* 13 (1974).

65. Lawrence Benner, "The Other Face of Justice: A Summary," *NLDA Briefcase* 12 (1974); and "Tokenism and the American Indigent: Some Perspectives on Defense Systems," *American Criminal Law Review* 12 (1975); Paul B. Wice and Mark Pilgrim, "Meeting the Gideon Mandate: A Survey of Public Defender Programs," *Judicature* 58 (1975).

66. Jacoby, *The American Prosecutor*, p. 92.

67. Michael Moore, "The Right to Counsel for Indigents in Oregon," *Oregon Law Review* 44 (1965): 118–133.

68. Jacoby, *The American Prosecutor*, p. 93.

69. Herbert Jacob, *Justice in America* (Boston: Little, Brown, 1972), p. 121.

70. Barbara Boland with Ronald Sones, INSLAW Inc.

*Prosecution of Felony Arrests.* (Washington, D.C.: Bureau of Justice Statistics, 1981).

71. Jacob, *Justice in America*, p. 122.

72. Ibid., p. 123.

73. Edwin S. Mills, "Statistical Study of Occupation of Jurors in a U.S. District Court," *Maryland Law Review* 22 (1962): 205–216; W. S. Robinson, "Bias, Probability and Trial by Jury," *American Sociological Review* 15 (1950): 73–78; and Marvin R. Summer, "Comparative Study of Qualifications of State and Federal Jurors," *Wisconsin Bar Bulletin* 34 (1961): 35–39.

74. Mills, "Statistical Study," p. 208.

75. S. W. Tucker, "Racial Discrimination in Jury Selection in Virginia," Virginia Law Review 52 (1966): 749.

76. *Batson* v. *Kentucky* as reported in *The Criminal Law Reporter* 39 (7 May 1986): 1021.

77. *Turner* v. *Murray* as reported in *The Criminal Law Reporter* 39 (16 April 1986): 1013.

78. Dale W. Broeder, "University of Chicago Jury Project," *Nebraska Law Review* 38 (1959): 746–747.

79. Dale W. Broeder, "Occupational Expertise and Bias as Affecting Juror Behavior: A Preliminary Look," *New York University Review* 40 (1964): 1079–1100.

80. Fred L. Strodtbeck et al., "Social Status in Jury Deliberations," *American Sociological Review* 22 (1957): 713–719.

81. Rita M. James, "Status and Competence of Jurors," *American Journal of Sociology* 64 (1959): 563–570.

82. Ibid.

83. Broeder, "University of Chicago Jury Project," pp. 748–749.

84. Harry Kalvern, Jr., and Hans Zeisel, *The American Jury* (Boston: Little, Brown, 1966).

85. Gilbert B. Stuckey, *Evidence for the Law Enforcement Officer* (New York: McGraw-Hill, 1968), p. 61.

# CHAPTER 9

# The Criminal Pretrial, Trial, and Posttrial Process

## O B J E C T I V E S

**After reading this chapter, the student should be able to:**

Identify the differences in the processing of felony and misdemeanor cases.

Discuss the steps and procedures in the accusatory process, including the initial appearance, the preliminary hearing, the grand jury, the setting of bail, and the arraignment.

Identify the differences in the conduct of the preliminary hearing.

Discuss the function of discovery and inspection.

Compare and contrast the hearing and the investigative grand juries.

Discuss the arraignment and the various types of pleas and their consequences.

Identify some pretrial motions.

Discuss the jury selection process and its examination of prospective jurors.

Understand the various steps in the conduct of a criminal trial.

Explain the purpose and use of the presentence investigation.

Identify and define the new victims' rights laws and what seems to be happening.

Explain applications/types of postconviction reviews.

## I M P O R T A N T   T E R M S

Complaint
Accusatory process
Initial appearance
Indigency hearing
"Critical stage"
"Probable cause"
Bail
Preliminary hearing
Delay
*Prima facie* case
"Heard enough" approach
Eighth Amendment
Discovery and inspection
Grand jury
Hearing/Investigative grand jury
"True bill"
Indictment

Presentment
Original indictment
Pleas
*Nolo contendere*
Standing mute
Motion for a bill of particulars
Motion to suppress or quash evidence
Motion for change of venue
Motion for continuance
Venire
Voir dire examination
"Death-qualified" Juries
Challenge for cause
Peremptory challenge
Opening statements
State's case

Direct examination
Cross-examination
Redirect examination
Recross-examination
Defense case
Closing arguments
Jury instructions/deliberations
Verdict
Posttrial motions
Presentence investigation
Victims' rights laws (sentencing)
Definite sentence
Habitual offender statutes
Indeterminate sentence
Mandatory sentencing acts
Concurrent/Consecutive
Appeals/Appellant/Appellee
Writ of certiorari
Pardon/Commutation/Reprieve

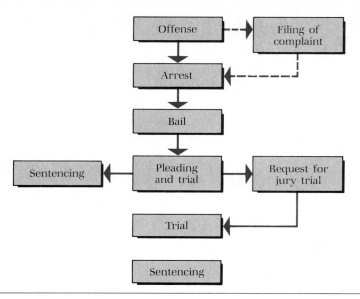

FIGURE **9.1** Basic criminal process for a misdemeanor.

This chapter examines in detail the various steps in the accusatory process and the conduct of a criminal trial. Before beginning this chapter, the student should become familiar with the basic criminal processes for a misdemeanor and a felony, as shown in Figures 9.1 and 9.2. It is also advisable to read the provisions of the Fifth and Sixth Amendments of the Constitution (see Appendix A).

### □ PRELIMINARY TRIAL PROCEEDINGS

The preliminary trial proceedings begin with the arrest of someone for a crime. In most cases the arrest process is initiated by the police. An arrest is generally defined as the taking of a person into custody for the purpose of charging him or her with a crime. This ordinarily involves the officer's exercise of physical control over the suspect for the purpose of first transporting the arrestee to a police facility and then requesting that charges be filed against the suspect.

There are other less common ways someone can be arrested. One such method is to file a complaint before a magistrate or judge, usually in a court of limited jurisdiction. The purpose of filing a complaint is to determine if an arrest warrant should be issued. The existing evidence and, in some cases, the testimony of the complainant is presented to demonstrate that there is probable cause to believe that the accused has committed a crime. If the judge or magistrate determines that probable cause exists, he or she issues the arrest warrant. If the accused is in custody, the warrant authorizes that individual's detention pending an initial appearance; if the accused is not in custody, the warrant directs the police to arrest the individual and bring him or her before the court issuing the warrant.

In some jurisdictions the prosecutor is authorized to issue an arrest warrant for certain offenses. In these circumstances the prosecutor's office is permitted to issue the warrant, but the accused must be brought promptly before a judge to determine the sufficiency of the charges and the attendant warrant. This hearing

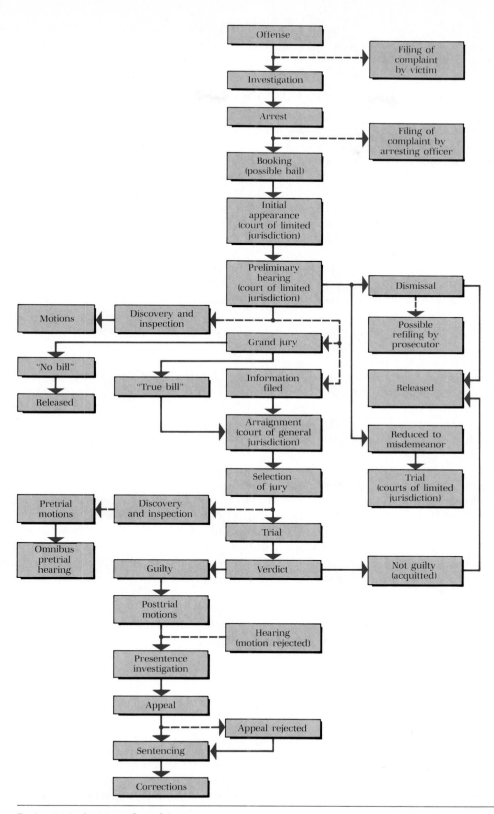

Basic criminal process for a felony.

FIGURE **9.2**

before a judge is often referred to as the initial appearance and will be discussed later.

 ## CONDUCT OF MISDEMEANOR CASES

The conduct of a misdemeanor trial and the steps in the process are much less elaborate than those for a felony. An accused arrested for a misdemeanor is brought before the particular court of limited jurisdiction that has the authority to try such cases. When the defendant appears before the court, the offense complaint is read and explained. Before the court can proceed, the defendant must attest that the charges are understood. Depending on the particular nature of the case, the judge may ask whether the defendant wants court-appointed counsel if he or she cannot afford to retain private counsel.

If the defendant pleads guilty, the magistrate, after a limited inquiry that may include the testimony of the accused and others concerning the circumstances of the case and the characteristics of the offender, will impose a fine, a limited jail sentence, or both as prescribed by the particular statute or ordinance, or the judge may place the offender on probation.

If the defendant pleads not guilty, the judge has several alternatives. The judge may immediately conduct the trial, which is sometimes what occurs when the defendant is charged with a minor traffic infraction or a minor misdemeanor. If the defendant indicates a desire to postpone the trial until a later date so that he or she can obtain an attorney, if the defendant wants a jury trial in those jurisdictions in which is it permissible,[1] or if the defendant needs time to prepare the case and obtain witnesses, the judge sets a date for a later trial and establishes bail or releases the individual in his or her own recognizance without requiring the posting of a cash bond.

Most misdemeanor cases of a minor nature are disposed of by guilty pleas. In some jurisdictions the state is not represented by a prosecuting attorney in the lower courts. In these cases, the only parties usually present are the defendant, the arresting officer, and the judge. In these bottom-rung misdemeanor courts, it is only in cases in which the defendant pleads not guilty and a subsequent trial is arranged or where the defendant retains counsel or requests a jury trial that a prosecutor appears to represent the state or the trial is transferred to a higher court. However, even in jurisdictions that normally assign an assistant prosecutor to such cases, there are usually some significant differences in the conduct of misdemeanor trials. The proceedings are often less adversarial in nature and are conducted with greater courtroom and legal informality than are the more serious felony cases in the courts of general jurisdiction.

 ## CONDUCT OF FELONY CASES

### The Accusatory Process

The steps following arrest and before the actual trial are often referred to as the accusatory process. The reader must realize that certain aspects of the accusatory process will vary from state to state. States differ in their accusatory process in two

Variations among states

ways: in the order of the steps and what these steps are called. This often creates some confusion. One state may refer to the initial appearance as an *initial arraignment* or simply an *arraignment*; another state will have the arraignment take place after the filing of an *information* or the return of an indictment by a grand jury. Still another state will not even routinely use a grand jury.

For the purpose of illustration in this chapter, a model of the accusatory process used in federal proceedings has been adopted with some slight modifications. This has been done in an effort to include all possible alternatives and steps in the process. By familiarizing yourself with the steps—and more importantly what occurs at each step—you should have a good understanding of the overall process. Once you have mastered this, examine how the process works in your own state for a comparison.

A final and important point about the accusatory process needs to be noted. **The role of courts of limited and special jurisdiction** Each step in this process up to the arraignment in our example either occurs before a court of limited or special jurisdiction or before a special tribunal such as a grand jury. Although a person arrested for a felony crime will normally be tried in a court of general jurisdiction, most of the steps in the accusatory process are conducted in a state's inferior courts, which we called courts of limited and special jurisdiction in Chapter 7.

The accusatory process in a felony case covers such steps as the initial appearance, the preliminary hearing, the grand jury, and the arraignment. In addition, other important happenings occur at these various stages, such as the setting of bail, the filing of an information (in some instances), and the application for discovery and inspection. Remember that this process might differ somewhat in your own state, but the functions of each stage generally are somewhat similar in all jurisdictions.

**INITIAL (FIRST) APPEARANCE.** As mentioned, some states use what is called **Purpose** an *initial appearance*. In some jurisdictions it is called *an initial presentment* or *the arraignment on the complaint* (or arrest warrant). The primary use of this step is to assure that the accused will have a first appearance before the court as quickly as possible, to ensure that the arrest is justified and that the accused is made aware of his or her rights. For example, the American Law Institute's Model Code requires that this first appearance occur within twenty-four hours of arrest. This initial appearance is usually conducted before a lower-level court of limited jurisdiction such as a magistrate's or municipal court. At this stage, the accused is provided with the notice of such rights as the right to counsel, the right to remain silent, and the right to a preliminary examination. The accused will also be informed of the charges.

Typically, this is not a fact-finding or probable cause hearing as such. Although some fact finding will occur, as in a case in which the prosecutor has issued an arrest warrant and the sufficiency of the justification for the warrant needs to be examined, the more probing fact finding will occur later, when probable cause is examined at the preliminary hearing. Because the U.S. Supreme Court has established the necessity that counsel be present during any "critical stage" of the criminal process, or when the criminal investigation has narrowed down from a general search to the investigation of a single individual,[2] the court will note whether the accused is represented by counsel. If not, the court will indicate the advisability of obtaining counsel before the accusatory process moves on to the preliminary hearing. If the individual indicates that he or she wants counsel but cannot afford one,

**Indigency hearing**

an inquiry will be made into the defendant's financial status; this is often referred to as an "indigency hearing." If the accused claims indigency, the court requires that an indigency affidavit be signed in which the accused swears to financial impoverishment. Once this is done, the court appoints counsel or assigns the case to the public defender's office.

**BAIL.** The judge usually determines bail at this stage. Some states permit the arrested person to make bail at the time that he or she is booked for certain crimes. If the defendant has already done this and is not incarcerated at the time of the initial appearance, the judge can still modify the amount of bail bond required as long as it conforms to the maximum limit prescribed by statute. Likewise, the judge has the discretion in a number of crimes to release the individual on his or her own recognizance without requiring the posting of a form of cash bond. In more serious crimes and in some jurisdictions, the accused cannot be released on bail until he or she has undergone the initial appearance.

**Requirement that a bail hearing be held promptly**

Under existing rules, the accused must be brought before the magistrate at this stage "without unnecessary delay." This emphasis on conducting a prompt inquiry arose from two U.S. Supreme Court rulings in which the Court held that an unjustified delay is unreasonable and sufficient to presume that all statements made by the arrestee between the arrest and the delayed hearing are inadmissible in evidence as the product of an unlawful detention.[3] As a result of these rulings and to ensure that there is no delay, the federal government and many states require that trial courts hold a bail hearing to be conducted by a judge within a

## POSTING OF BAIL

The Bureau of Justice Statistics of the federal government has recently released a research summary of bail practices among the federal courts. A summary of its findings includes:

- The amount of bail is particularly determined by three things: (1) the seriousness of the charged offense; (2) the particular court in which bail is imposed; and (3) the offender's criminal record.
- The bail that was required was somewhat lower for defendants who had lived at the same address for several years as compared to more transient arrestees; somewhat lower for women than for men; and lower for defendants with college

and high school educations than for defendants with no high school education.
- Holding other factors constant, there was no relationship between the amount of bail imposed and such factors as race, age, drug use, income, employment history, number of dependents supported by the defendant, and past history of jumping bail.
- As one would expect, the probability of posting bail decreases as the amount of bail increases.
- Certain factors were found to be correlated with pretrial misconduct (i.e., arrest for a new crime while out on bail, willful failure to appear for a court date, and violations of the

technical conditions of release). These were (1) the longer the person was out on bail before the trial, the greater was the likelihood of some kind of pretrial misconduct; (2) the more extensive the prior criminal record the greater was the likelihood of misconduct; (3) drug use increased the likelihood of misconduct; (4) those who were economically and socially "unstable" have higher misconduct rates; and (5) the probability of misconduct was higher for males, noncaucasians, and younger defendants.[a]

[a]*Source:* Bureau of Justice Statistics, *Pretrial Release and Misconduct* (Washington, D.C.: U.S. Department of Justice, January 1985).

prescribed time period, such as twenty-four hours. The federal government pursued this one step further when Congress adopted a "Speedy Trial Act," which requires that the defendant be processed through the various trial stages within certain stipulated times.[4] Failure by the federal courts to comply with these times can result in a motion for a dismissal of the charges.[5]

Although many states have similar provisions that call for an initial appearance without unnecessary delay, some states (unless they, too, have adopted specific time frames under a "speedy trial act") consider delays simply to be a part of the overall judicial process. In reality, the problems of delay in processing the defendant through the initial appearance are usually not that serious. The more serious delays usually occur later, in bringing the accused up for a preliminary hearing, arraignment, or the actual trial.

**PRELIMINARY EXAMINATION (HEARING).** During the initial appearance, the accused is scheduled for a preliminary hearing. Many states require that the preliminary hearing be held within a specific time after the initial appearance, such as within ten days or two weeks.[6] The U.S. Supreme Court has ruled that a probable cause hearing is required where the defendant is likely to have his or her liberty restrained.[7] The preliminary hearing serves as this required probable cause hearing, as does the grand jury.

The purpose of the preliminary hearing is to allow a judge or magistrate to Purpose determine if there is enough evidence for a reasonable person to believe that a crime has been committed and that the accused may have committed it. This is the essence of the so-called probable cause. The preliminary hearing also serves to determine if there is probable cause to detain the suspect in view of the constitutional prohibitions against restraint of liberty.

The accused has the right to waive a preliminary hearing if he or she chooses. Where, for example, a grand jury exists, the accused may waive the preliminary hearing and the case then goes immediately to the grand jury stage. In those states that employ both the preliminary hearing and the grand jury, the accused's attorney is more likely to recommend to his or her client that the grand jury step be waived. This is because they are duplicative probable cause steps, and the grand jury serves little purpose in such instances.

In more and more states, particularly in the West, the prosecutor is given the discretion of using the grand jury or going the preliminary hearing route. This indicates the changing nature of the accusatory process and how unsettled and nonuniform the procedures are from state to state. Yet, concerns of due process and equal protection are raised when a prosecutor has the option of using the grand jury rather than filing an information and employing a preliminary hearing to determine the sufficiency of the evidence to bind the accused over for trial. For example, the California Supreme Court ruled in a case that a defendant charged in an indictment issued by a grand jury is "seriously disadvantaged in contrast to a defendant charged by an information."[8] Specifically, the fundamental rights of counsel, confrontation of adverse witnesses, and a hearing before a judicial officer were cited as unavailable to a defendant charged by grand jury indictment as compared to an information filed after a preliminary hearing has been held. The California Supreme Court solved this problem by requiring a postindictment preliminary hearing in those cases where the prosecutor has selected the grand jury route as a screening device. The following year Wisconsin enacted the same requirement by the adoption of a statute that reads:

[u]pon indictment by a grand jury a complaint shall be issued [and] . . . the person named in the indictment . . . shall be entitled to a preliminary hearing . . . and all proceedings thereafter shall be the same as if the person . . . had not been indicted by a grand jury.[9]

**State's burden of proof**

The preliminary hearing has only some characteristics that we associate with a trial. In many important ways it is far different. For one thing, it does not attempt to prove the defendant's guilt beyond a reasonable doubt, which is the burden of proof the state has during the trial. It is a *hearing*, not a trial. The prosecution need only develop a *prima facie* case; that is, the reasonable belief that a crime has been committed and the accused committed it. This reasonable belief constitutes only "probable cause"—it does not show the defendant's guilt "beyond a reasonable doubt," which is a far different and more exacting measure of proof.

**Characteristics**

Since a preliminary hearing is a hearing rather than a trial, it also is a bit less formal and procedural in nature. For example, hearsay evidence that would not be permitted to be used by the trial court is admissible under certain circumstances. For example, a police officer might testify at the preliminary hearing: "Lab analysis showed the drug to be marijuana," or "A medical doctor told me that the victim's injuries were consistent with the knife that was recovered." Although such hearsay evidence would be permitted at the preliminary hearing, the lab expert would have to testify at the trial as to the analysis he or she made and the conclusions reached as would the medical doctor upon whom the police officer is relying.

As at trial, the defendant in a preliminary hearing may cross-examine witnesses and introduce evidence in his or her own behalf. However, many states limit the extent of cross-examination that the accused can conduct at the preliminary hearing. There are two reasons for this: First, this procedure is not meant to be a trial; the preliminary hearing is only a mechanism for binding the defendant over and preventing possible abuse of power by the police and prosecutorial officials, not for the ultimate adjudication of guilt or innocence. Second, with the expanded right to pretrial discovery and inspection (to be explained later), there is no need for the defense to try to use the preliminary hearing as a "fishing expedition" to obtain more insight into the state's case. The accused who is determined to be unable to afford counsel—the so-called indigent defendant—is also entitled to have appointed counsel available at this stage.

As mentioned, the primary purpose of the preliminary hearing is to provide an independent evaluation by a judge of the police and prosecutor's decision to arrest and charge. Since, unlike for the burden of proof required at the later trial, the judge at the preliminary hearing is not interested in whether the defendant is guilty beyond a reasonable doubt; the judge is only ruling on the probability of guilt. In this way the burden of proof is only minimal. But how "minimal" is often a point of disagreement in the law. A few states require that the prosecution present enough evidence at the preliminary hearing to justify a trial judge submitting the case to the jury. On the other hand, most states (and most judges) seem to follow the so-called "heard-enough" approach as sufficient. Unfortunately, such minimal requirements dilute this important step in the formal screening process.

The preliminary hearing also has some secondary functions. When a state has restrictive discovery and inspection rights for the defense, the defense attorney can use this stage to gain more insight into the state's case. The opportunity to cross-examine by the defense may permit the testing of the credibility of witnesses on the stand and the identification of possible defense strategies. It may also provide a means to preserve testimony of those witnesses who later cannot testify at the trial because of death, illness, or relocation. The recorded transcript of the testimony taken at the preliminary hearing may be used to refresh the memory of certain witnesses such as young children who may later have to testify at the trial. The recorded transcript can also be used to impeach the credibility of witnesses who might testify to one thing at the preliminary hearing and change their testimony at the trial. Opposing counsel can point out the discrepancy between the two. Finally, the preliminary hearing can serve as a mechanism for determining the legality of detention, reviewing the conditions of release, inducing a negotiated plea to the charge(s), thereby avoiding the expense and necessity of a trial, and serving as a consideration for a sentencing decision when the accused later pleads guilty to the charge(s) and a transcript of the preliminary hearing is available to the sentencing judge for review of the facts before imposing sentence.

      Deborah D. Emerson and Nancy L. Ames's examination of the conduct of preliminary hearings in the Phoenix and Tucson metropolitan areas found, in these jurisdictions at least, that the normal preliminary hearing was conducted in about 30 minutes.[10] These hearings were rather abbreviated affairs. This probably is in line with what one would find in the majority of jurisdictions throughout the country. *Their characteristic brevity* The study also found that police officers, investigators, and the victims were most likely to be the ones who testified at these hearings. In very few cases was testimony taken from the accused.[11] There were very few dismissals for lack of "probable cause" at the preliminary hearings studied. Although this might cause one to think that the preliminary hearing was not effectively operating to screen out cases, this was not necessarily the case in this study. Under Arizona law, the defendant at the preliminary hearing is permitted to plead guilty to the charge(s) after being advised of his right to trial, and other considerations. Many of the preliminary hearings ended in this way.[12]

**RELEASE AFTER PRELIMINARY HEARING.** If the state fails to show probable cause, the defendant is dismissed by the judge. The preliminary hearing assures only that the defendant will not be incarcerated without the existence of valid probable cause and gives the accused the opportunity to be released on bail. A release by a judge on a preliminary hearing or a dismissal of the charges is not, however, binding on the state. Because the defendant has not stood trial and has not been placed in jeopardy, the prosecutor in most states can file another complaint on the same offense, having the individual arrested and brought again before the courts for another preliminary hearing. In recent years, some states have required that the prosecutor provide additional evidence that was not known to the state at the time of the first preliminary examination before the accused can be rearrested and brought back before the court for another preliminary hearing on the same charge.

**BINDING OVER AND REVIEW OF BAIL.** If the state satisfies the court that it has met its burden of proof, the judge issues an order binding the defendant over to the next step in the judicial process. The judge is also required to certify that a preliminary examination has been held and that the evidence presented has established probable cause to believe that a crime has been committed and that the accused committed it. *When a prima facie case has been established* This certification confers jurisdiction upon the grand jury or the trial court and authorizes the prosecutor to continue to the next step in the judicial process.

      The defendant, at this time, is advised of the right to waive grand jury examination. This right exists only in federal courts and those states that still use the grand jury. If the defendant waives these rights, the court will bypass the grand jury and transfer the case to the court that has jurisdiction over the conduct of felony cases. In some states, such as New York, if the crime charged is a serious felony, the accused is not permitted to waive an examination of the case by the grand jury.

Lastly, the court again reviews the bail that may have been set at the initial appearance. The bail may be raised or lowered depending on the authority vested in the judge by virtue of existing statue, and the judge's discretion to exercise that authority. This practice of requiring a bond to obtain the release of an accused gives some assurance to the court that the accused will return for trial. During the period of release on bail, the accused is under the authority of the court and must comply with any conditions established by the judge who authorizes the bail. The terms *bail* and *bond* are often used interchangeably, but there is a distinction. *Bail* is the process of releasing an accused before trial. *Bond* is the means used to guarantee that the accused will return for the trial. It typically requires the posting of a surety bond by a bail bond company or the deposit of money or some other valuable consideration by the accused. If the accused fails to appear, the surety is forfeited to the court. In some instances, a bond may be merely the accused's word that he or she will appear at the trial. This is referred to as a *recognizance bond*.

Generally, the court is required to permit bail in all but the most serious capital cases. The amount of bond that the court can demand for a specific crime is usually determined by statute. Some jurisdictions permit the denial of bail if the release of the accused poses a "significant threat to society." However, because of the significant constitutional question involved in the denial of bail to an accused, states have been reluctant to pass legislation that would give additional powers to judges to deny bail. During the 1980s, however, there was increasing clamor for legislation that would permit courts to deny bail in such cases as trafficking in narcotics.

**DISCOVERY AND INSPECTION.** Once the preliminary hearing has been conducted and the accused has been bound over to the next stage in the judicial process, many jurisdictions provide that discovery and inspection procedures be instituted. Over the last twenty years, expanded rights of discovery and inspection have developed, particularly in the federal court system. States have now adopted similar procedures to guide the conduct of criminal trials in their courts. The idea behind discovery and inspection is to ensure that each party has the opportunity to test the evidence submitted by the other side. It is contended that advance knowledge of the evidence to be used is essential to prepare for the cross-examination of a witness or to gather evidence to refute testimony.[13]

The most commonly expressed opposition to discovery is based on the prosecutor's fear that exposing his or her case to defense scrutiny will jeopardize the prosecution's chances of winning.[14] With the increasing use of preliminary hearing in recent years, and the availability of defense counsel representation at these hearings, the opportunity for the accused to gain more insight into the state's case has increased. Although the state does not have to introduce all of its evidence in the preliminary hearing—only enough to establish a *prima facie* case—skillful and persistent defense counsel can obtain a great deal of information on the state's case at the preliminary hearing. Under such circumstances, prosecutors may feel that they have little of importance that still remains unknown to the accused and

Bail and bond

Some issues about the use of bail

Purpose

will be less reluctant to offer full discovery and inspection rights. On the other hand, they may want to guard any undisclosed evidence as much as possible and be even more reluctant to provide additional information to the accused. Unfortunately, little research has been done in this area to provide insight into the dynamics of such situations.

Although pretrial discovery exists both for the prosecution and the defense, it is the defense that generally has the most extensive rights to obtain information from the prosecutor. An example of what could be called very "liberal" defense rights to pretrial discovery exist in New York State. In that state the defense has the general right to request among other things the following from the state: any written, recorded, or oral statement made to law enforcement officials by the defendant or co-defendant; any written report or document concerning a physical or mental examination or scientific test or experiment relating to the criminal action made by or at the request of the police or of whomever the prosecutor intends to call as a witness at the trial; any photograph, photocopy, or drawing that is intended for use at the trial; any property, tapes, or electronic recordings to be introduced at the trial; any written or recorded statement including any testimony before a grand jury by a witness; any record of conviction of any witness; the existence of any pending criminal action against a witness; and all specific instances of a defendant's prior uncharged criminal, vicious, or immoral conduct of which the prosecutor has knowledge and which the prosecutor intends to use at trial for purposes of impeaching the credibility of the defendant.[15] **Defense rights to pretrial discovery**

The defense also has some responsibilities under modern discovery statutes. The standards of the American Bar Association prescribe that certain types of evidence also be made available to the prosecutor.[16] This includes such facts as the defendant's intent to rely on an alibi or an insanity defense; any reports, results, or testimony that support such defenses; physical or mental examinations or scientific tests, experiments, or comparisons; or any other reports or statements of experts that defense counsel intends to use at a hearing or trial.[17] **Defense responsibilities to disclose**

Of course, these standards exclude such information as statements made by the witness (which might be incriminating) or whether the defendant will testify at the trial.[18] Those who advocate the liberalization of discovery and inspection do so on the grounds that it will maximize the early resolution of issues regarding the admissibility of evidence and will encourage administrative disposition of cases with no significant increased danger of conviction of innocent defendants and no unjustifiable infringements on the right of guilty defendants to be treated with dignity.[19]

## ▣ THE GRAND JURY

As discussed earlier, the case may be bound over to the grand jury after the preliminary hearing. The beginnings of the grand jury can be traced back to 1166, when the Assize of Clarendon was established. An assize was a court session that had developed earlier in France and was brought to England by the Norman conquerors. The assize was to consist of twelve individuals who personally knew the accused. These jurors would then question witnesses to determine if the accused appeared to be guilty of the alleged crime. Because they knew the accused and often the **Historical development** accusor as well, these "grand jurors" were supposed to be in a good position to screen out unfounded accusation and, theoretically at least, afford certain protections to the accused.

Legal historians, however, point out that this was not what usually happened.[20] Some historians indicate that this "grand jury" was not created to shield the citizen from false accusations or the powers of the state. In fact, it was created expressly by King Henry II to enable the king to wrest the administration of justice from the Church and the feudal barons. The grand jury thus served primarily as a weapon for the monarch, enforcing his law, whether or not it was legal and proper. Because of its misuse, the grand jury was often cited in a condemnation of the monarch.[21] Some five hundred years later, during the religious strife in England in 1681, the grand jury finally threw off the yoke of the king and asserted its role as a shield for the innocent against malicious and oppressive prosecution.

The idea of the grand jury was incorporated into the U.S. Constitution and the constitutions of most states. The Fifth Amendment to the U.S. Constitution

English monarchs prior to the 1680's used the grand jury to help administer justice on their own terms. Shown here is the Court of the King's Bench at the time of Henry VI (1422–61, 1470–71), with prisoners awaiting sentencing in the foreground. (The Bettmann Archive)

provides that "no person shall be held to answer for a capital, or otherwise infamous crime, unless on presentment or indictment of a grand jury." From this it would appear that the Constitution clearly requires that persons accused of major crimes be accused by a grand jury, yet less than half the states use the grand jury today. The reason is that the U.S. Supreme Court has not seen fit to require that the grand jury requirement be made applicable to the states through the due process clause of the Fourteenth Amendment.

Today, the grand jury is supposed to serve three important functions: **Functions**

1. Determine if an accused should stand trial by virtue of the fact that there is probable cause to believe that a felony has been committed; and
2. Protect the innocent from false accusations and harassment by the state where there is no reason to believe a felony has been committed.
3. Conduct specific investigations into such areas as criminal or alleged criminal activities or wrongdoings, and inquire into the operations of certain public agencies.

In recent years, the grand jury has been widely criticized for failing to accomplish the first two tasks. Because of its inadequacies, it has come to be viewed by some observers as actually inhibiting justice and the rights of due process.

## Filing an Information

In states that do not routinely use the grand jury, an individual is usually brought to trial after the preliminary hearing by the filing of an *information* by the prose- **Prosecutor's information** cutor. This information must state the charges, the statute that was violated, and the approximate time and place of the occurrence of the crime; subsequently, the accused must be served with notice of these facts and specifications. In recent years, even states that still have the grand jury are increasingly bypassing it by using the information. In many other instances, the accused waives this right to grand jury and thereby also bypasses it.

Although the grand jury is an extension of the court, it has the authority to **Powers** act independently of the court. Neither the court nor the state may limit the scope of grand jury investigations. It has the power to subpoena witnesses and documents, to seek a grant of immunity to witnesses who testify before it, and, in the case of a special grand jury, to proceed in independent criminal investigations. These investigations may be of public officials as well as of private citizens. The grand jury is charged by statute to inquire into matters relating to crime and corruption within its jurisdiction and to bring to trial those whom it feels the state has been derelict in not prosecuting. In addition, many jurisdictions require that the grand jury periodically investigate certain functions or governmental operations within the jurisdiction, such as jail facilities or law enforcement agencies, and publicly report its findings and recommendations. These particular functions are called its *investigatory responsibilities;* however, in routine criminal cases most of the work of the grand jury falls under its *hearing responsibilities.*

The prosecutor's decision to use the grand jury or to file an information and proceed by means of the preliminary hearing route will often be determined by a number of factors. Emerson and Ames found in the jurisdictions they examined that prosecutors, when given the choice between the grand jury and the preliminary hearing, were more likely to choose the former when the case involved multiple defendants, complex documentary evidence, or large numbers of witnesses (particularly if they are undercover agents from out-of-state, or professionals such as doctors or scientific experts). The grand jury was also favored by prosecutors for cases involving crimes covering more than one lower court district since a separate preliminary hearing would otherwise have to be held in each district.[22]

## Hearing Responsibilities (The Hearing Grand Jury)

Composition and selection

The grand jury is usually composed of twelve to twenty-three citizens of the judicial district who are chosen by a statutorily prescribed selection process and summoned by a court with general jurisdiction over criminal cases.[23] After the grand jurors are selected and before they commence their activities, the court selects a foreperson from among them. The responsibility of the foreperson is to verify that a quorum of grand jurors is always available when evidence is being presented and that there are a sufficient number of votes to return an indictment. In a few jurisdictions, the foreperson also administers the oath to witnesses who testify before this body and performs related administrative tasks required to handle the grand jury proceedings.

Unanimity not required

The decisions of the grand jury need not be unanimous. Most state statutes prescribe that a two-thirds or three-fourths majority is all that is necessary to return or refuse to return an indictment. An indictment is a formal accusation by the grand jury that is arrived at after consideration of the evidence against the accused.

"True bill"

To indict someone, the foreperson writes on the indictment "A True Bill" and attests to this with his or her signature. For example, let us assume that in a particular state there are eighteen jurors, of whom twelve must concur for an indictment. After hearing all the evidence, thirteen grand jurors conclude there is sufficient evidence to believe that a crime has been committed and that the accused committed it. Thus, the thirteen would vote for indictment, and a true bill would be signed. The accused would then be bound over for trial. If the required two-thirds

"No bill"

majority could not be reached, the foreperson would write "No Bill" on the indictment, and the accused would be released.[24]

## Grand Jury Proceedings

Ex parte characteristics

Grand jury proceedings have some important characteristics. First, they are referred to in the law as *ex parte* (one-party) proceedings. This means that the accused and his or her attorney are not permitted to be present during the conduct of the grand jury hearing. The accused and his attorney cannot sit in on the testimony and cross-examine adverse witnesses to object to their testimony or to the introduction of evidence. While the accused can't sit in on the grand jury hearings, some states do permit the defendant to appear and give testimony before the grand jury or to request that the grand jury call specific witnesses. For the most part, however, those witnesses who are called by the prosecution (and we can assume these are often witnesses for the state) are the only ones to testify in grand jury proceedings.

Role of the prosecutor

It is the prosecutor who largely controls the grand jury. He or she generally runs the show and controls the introduction of witnesses and evidence and sets the general framework for the questioning during the grand jury proceedings. Although individual grand jurors are free to conduct questioning of witnesses, the prosecutor plays the key role.

This can be seen in those studies of the grand jury in which this has been examined. In the Emerson and Ames study mentioned previously, police officers alone testified in about 95 percent of the grand jury deliberations studied. It was very unlikely for civilians to be called to testify before the grand jury. Obviously, police officers are witnesses for the state. Interestingly, in the cases examined, the police officers who testified often recited no more than the facts already contained in the police report.[25]

Emerson and Ames also give us some insight into how much the prosecutor actually controls the grand jury proceedings. In studying the transcripts of grand jury proceedings, it was found that the grand jurors themselves would ask no more than one or two questions from a witness—all the other questioning was done by the prosecutor.[26] It was also pointed out that any evidence that might tend to show that the accused was innocent—even though the prosecutor knew of the existence of such evidence—was rarely brought to the attention of the grand jurors by the prosecutor.[27] The typical procedure in the grand juries studied was for the prosecutor to frame the questions and explain the law to the grand jurors. After the witness testified and perhaps one or two questions were asked by the grand jury, the witness was then excused. The grand jurors were then permitted to ask questions of the prosecutor.[28]

**Grand juror questioning**

Witnesses are usually not permitted to be represented by counsel during the grand jury hearing. The conduct of these hearings is very informal in comparison to that of a trial. Usually, the witness is brought in, the oath is administered, and the witness relates what he or she knows in response to questions from the prosecutor or grand jurors. As an example, hearsay evidence is admissible. In a trial, a witness, except under a few limited circumstances, could not testify to what he or she heard someone say because the witness does not have direct knowledge of the facts and the truth of the matter; no such prohibition applies to witnesses before the grand jury.

**Right to counsel**

The grand jury has the right to compel witnesses to testify except in cases in which the witness is subject to the right against self-incrimination. However, at the federal level and in many states, the prosecuting attorney or the grand jury can request that the court grant immunity to a grand jury witness. This is a guarantee that even though the testimony is self-incriminating, the witness will be immune from later prosecution for testifying.[29] In some states, such as New York, any witness before the grand jury is automatically given immunity unless the witness waives that right. Because immunity can be granted, the grand jury has the authority to cite witnesses for contempt and to seek through the court of general jurisdiction empaneling it a contempt citation that could result in the uncooperative witness being jailed.

**Grand jury immunity**

The proceedings of grand juries are secret. When testimony is being given, the only persons usually present are the witness, the prosecutor, the grand jury members, and a stenographer to transcribe the proceedings. There are several exceptions to this general policy. In some rare instances a witness may be permitted the presence of his attorney in the room during testimony. An interpreter might be permitted if the witness does not speak or understand the English language. A police officer, jailer, or prison guard who is holding a witness in custody is permitted to be present. In cases of sexual offenses against a minor, states now permit the presence of a social worker, rape crisis counselor, or psychologist to provide emotional support for the child during the child's testimony. Since the proceedings are secret, all such persons are sworn to secrecy by the grand jury. During the actual voting only the grand jurors are present. Even the prosecutor is excluded from the actual deliberations and vote by the grand jury. Grand jurors themselves

**Secrecy**

are sworn to secrecy and told that under penalty of law, they are not to divulge any matter discussed before them. They are also informed that all legal advice is to come from the prosecutor or the court, and they are to disregard all information they hear outside of the grand jury room that may be related to the case and to report immediately any attempt to influence them by any outside source.

**THE INVESTIGATIVE GRAND JURY.**   Although hearing grand juries also conduct investigations of cases, there is another type of grand jury called an *investigative grand jury*. In its purest form, an investigative grand jury is empaneled to investigate particular circumstances for which it is authorized by the laws of a particular jurisdiction. The state may authorize such a special grand jury to conduct investigations of political corruption, the operations of state and local government, organized crime, a specific case, or other matters.

Conducts special
investigations

Because there are so many situations and variations under which an investigative grand jury can operate, perhaps an example of a typical use of this process will serve to explain. Assume that in a particular community there is evidence suggesting that a certain political figure is involved with local organized crime. The prosecutor may feel, however, that there is not enough evidence to warrant an arrest. The prosecutor may then ask the court with the proper authority to empanel a special investigative grand jury. The court grants this request, and the grand jury is empaneled and begins its investigation by examining the evidence, issuing subpoenas, and hearing testimony of witnesses. After its fact-finding efforts are concluded, it finds sufficient evidence to initiate a prosecution. This could be done by issuing a *presentment* to the court having jurisdiction over the crime(s) being considered. Because it was not empaneled by the initial use of an indictment, the presentment must be used. In this way the grand jury "presents" its findings and calls for prosecution. The court then issues an arrest warrant for the defendant who may then be brought to trial to answer the charges. In some jurisdictions the issuance of the presentment calls for the issuance of an *original indictment* (it did not originate elsewhere), which is then served on the accused so that he or she can be brought before a competent court to answer the charges at an arraignment.

Presentment

## ▣  PRELIMINARY PROCEEDINGS IN THE TRIAL COURT

### Arraignment

After an indictment has been returned as a "true bill" by the grand jury or an information has been filed by the prosecutor, the accused is arraigned before a court of general jurisdiction that has the authority to try the case. The arraignment is the procedure whereby the accused is called into court to answer the charge. It is not a trial, and the court does not at this time examine any matters that pertain to the accused's guilt or innocence. If the defendant has not previously been given a copy of the indictment or information, he or she is now given one. The contents of the indictment or information are also read to the defendant. In this way, the state informs the defendant that it is ready to proceed with the charges.

Appears before a court
of general jurisdiction

If the defendant still does not have counsel, the court must assure him or her of this right, and if indigent, the defendant will be given court-appointed legal assistance. The court will point out that counsel is advisable so the accused knows and understands the nature of the charges and the implications of the plea that the accused might make. In the event that the accused does not have counsel, many courts will automatically enter a not guilty plea.

## Pleas

During the arraignment, the accused is asked to enter a plea to the charge. Basically,    Types
depending on the statutory provisions of the particular jurisdiction, the defendant may enter a plea of *not guilty, nolo contendere,* or *guilty* or may merely stand mute.

If the defendant pleads not guilty, he or she denies each allegation in the accusation, and in so doing requires the state to establish these allegations beyond a reasonable doubt. In states that permit the practice, the accused, after entering a plea of not guilty, will be advised of the right to trial by jury or before a judge without a jury.* Once the defendant indicates this choice, the case is placed on the court calendar or docket and scheduled for future trial.

The plea of *nolo contendere* literally means "I will not contest it." This plea technically means that the individual does not wish to contest or argue the issue of guilt or innocence. Such a plea, in a number of jurisdictions, must be approved by the prosecutor and the judge. In essence, it is a guilty plea and has the same effect. It authorizes the court to enter judgment and sentence on the plea. This plea has some legal significance in that in subsequent criminal or civil proceedings, the admission of guilt is not present, as it would be if the accused had entered a plea of guilty to the charge. Under these circumstances, the acknowledgment of guilt could not be introduced into a later trial. Because it serves no purpose other than to protect the individual from the consequences of his or her conviction, some states do not feel it serves the purpose of justice and have abolished it.

If the defendant remains mute when asked how he or she pleads to the charge, an automatic plea of not guilty will be entered by the court. The major advantage of standing mute is that in some jurisdictions a plea is the same as saying that the defendant accepts the jurisdiction of the trial court and, as a result, waives the right to protest any irregularities or defects that may have occurred in the preliminary examination or grand jury.[30]

If the defendant pleads guilty, the judge immediately inquires whether the plea is made with the full understanding of its ramifications and whether it is made voluntarily. The courts have held that a guilty plea must be free from coercion or promises and must not be otherwise unfairly obtained or the result of ignorance or fear.[31] If the court is not thoroughly convinced that these requirements have been met, it cannot accept the plea. Nor should the court assume that these requirements are fully met simply because the defendant is represented by an attorney. Because a guilty plea is the same as a waiver of the defendant's right to require the prosecution to prove his or her guilt beyond a reasonable doubt, the judge is under strict responsibility to be certain that such a plea is voluntarily and knowingly given. If it should later be proved that this is not the case, grounds will exist for reversal of the conviction.

If the plea is guilty, the court may immediately sentence the defendant. Today, however, most states require that a presentence investigation be conducted of the defendant's background so that the judge can be guided in determining the appropriate sentence to impose.

*In states that have retained the death penalty and when the prosecutor notifies the defendant of his or her intent to seek the death penalty, trial must be by jury.

## Pretrial Motions

After the indictment or information has been filed, the defendant may, before the trial, employ a number of motions in an effort to have the case dismissed or to gain a particular legal advantage in the preparation of the case or the introduction of evidence at the trial. A motion is a request that the court examine a particular legal point that the defense contends is an error in the state's case. In filing the motion, the defense hopes that the ruling will be in behalf of the accused. Although it is not possible to review all the motions the defense might raise, some of the more frequently encountered and important motions are (1) motion for discharge or dismissal of the case; (2) motion for a bill of particulars; (3) motion to suppress evidence; (4) motion for change in venue; and (5) motion for continuance.

Most common pretrial defense motions

Probably the most important of the pretrial motions is the *motion to discharge or dismiss* the case. It is initiated on written request of the defendant before the trial but usually after the arraignment. The defendant, in filing this motion, asks the court to dismiss the indictment or information for any number of reasons. He or she may contend, for example, that if a grand jury returned an indictment, the grand jury was illegally selected or empaneled. It may be argued in this motion that the grand jury permitted the presence of unauthorized individuals during their deliberations. Most typically, the defense will claim under this motion that there has been a fundamental denial of the defendant's constitutional rights. This could range from contending that the defense counsel did not have an appropriate opportunity to cross-examine witnesses at the preliminary hearing or that there was a failure to advise the defendant of his or her rights against self-incrimination. The defense may also contend that the indictment or information is not technically correct in that it fails to clearly specify the offense or that the statute of limitations (a period of time in which prosecution must begin) has expired.[32]

How valuable such tactics are is questionable. In the case of an attack by the defense on a minor procedural error, the court will direct that the error be corrected such as a deficiency in a particular charging instrument. More often than not, the major consequence of such motions is merely to delay the start of the trial as the defense counsel files the required motion and supporting documentation that is then considered by the court.

The *motion for a bill of particulars* is a motion filed by the defense that asks the court to order the state to provide additional facts in the indictment or information. The defense argues in such instances that without this additional information, it cannot adequately prepare or conduct its defense. An example might be a case of an adult bookstore owner having been charged with the sale of pornography. The defense would say it needs to know specifically what items among those confiscated the state is relying on as evidence. The prosecutor, on the other hand, can refuse to comply with the request, arguing that the item of factual information requested is not authorized to be included in a bill of particulars or that such information is not necessary to prepare or conduct a defense. In such cases, the court, after holding a hearing, can either uphold the defense request and order the prosecutor to supply the information or rule in favor of the state's argument.

The *motion to suppress evidence* is used most often in cases in which the defense argues that certain evidence is tainted in that it was illegally obtained by means of a violation of the defendant's rights and is, therefore, not admissible. Like other pretrial motions, it must be made on a timely basis or it cannot be made at all. The reason is quite simple: These issues must be disposed of before the trial

Timely requirement for motions

begins in order that the ongoing trial is not interrupted and delayed while the lawyers argue whether such evidence is to be admitted or excluded.

The most common items of evidence that the defense might seek to have suppressed are such things as confessions or admissions obtained by the police from the defendant. It is also not unusual in cases involving search and seizures, wiretap, or other electronic eavesdropping cases to have the evidence challenged through a suppression hearing request. The burden of proof is on the defense generally in these suppression hearings. There are some exceptions, however. If the police, for example, relied on a search warrant or made a search without a warrant incident to an arrest, the state must show that it complied with the law governing the obtaining of search warrants or conducting searches following a lawful arrest.

Most laypersons probably are most familiar with one type of pretrial motion: *the motion for a change of venue.* This is simply a motion introduced by the defense asking that the trial be moved to another jurisdiction. This motion is based on the defendant's argument that because of existing circumstances a fair trial cannot be held in the particular jurisdiction having authority to try the case. It is most likely to be an issue in cases about which there has been a great deal of pretrial publicity—publicity that makes it difficult to find potential jurors who have not in some way been influenced by the set of pretrial circumstances. Some states provide that as an alternative to moving the trial to a different location, it is permissible for the court to bring in jurors from contiguous jurisdictions who ostensibly have not been exposed to the publicity and can then be considered unbiased.

A last frequently employed motion is one that seeks a *continuance.* With the "speedy trial" provisions enacted in many states, this right to request a continuance

Defense attorneys often cite pretrial publicity as a reason to move for a change of venue. (Rob Crandall/Stock Boston)

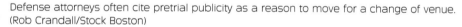

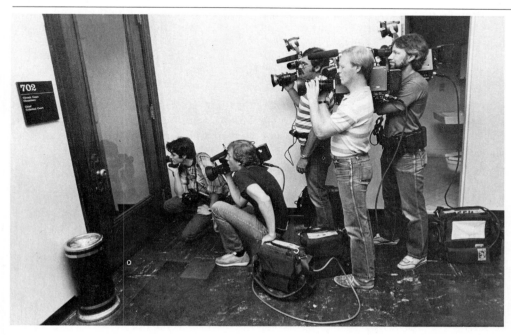

often rests only with the defense. The defense asks that the established date for the trial be postponed. States in recent years have tried to control this all too often occurrence by specifying conditions that must be met before trial judges can grant such continuances. For instance, if it can be shown that the counsel for the defense or the prosecution is ill, has died, or is engaged in the trial of another earlier scheduled case, either side can apply for a continuance. Other circumstances might be that a material witness is unavailable at the time, or that the bill of particulars that amended the original indictment or information has introduced new facts or allegations that require additional time to prepare an adequate defense.

There are other less frequently used pretrial motions that occur from time to time. These include a motion for joinder of related prosecutions, motion for severance of joint prosecutions, and motion for a change of judge.

### The Omnibus Pretrial Hearing

The omnibus pretrial hearing is among the recent innovations designed to enhance the efficiency of the criminal justice system. It may be defined as a procedural device in which a single hearing with a minimum of formalities and filings is conducted "to ensure that discovery has been properly conducted and that issues are simply and efficiently raised."[33]

Purpose

Essentially, it is a hearing in which a judge (hearing the case) entertains any motions by either side and rules on them (e.g., challenges to the voluntariness of admissions or confessions, challenge to suppress evidence, motion for continuance, etc.) In addition, the hearing is used to satisfy the court that such things as standards regarding the provision of counsel have been complied with and to inquire whether the parties have completed the discovery process, and if not, to issue orders appropriate to expedite completion. The idea behind this process is to complete these matters in one comprehensive hearing before the trial. In this way, the omnibus pretrial hearing results in a sharpening and narrowing of issues for trial, an economizing of cost and time, and a reduced likelihood of appeal—all of which are particularly important in light of the ever-increasing litigation before our federal and state courts.[34]

### Selection of the Jury

After hearing any motions, the judge rules on them. If the accused pleads not guilty or stands mute, the court asks if the defendant wants a jury trial. If the accused indicates he or she does, the case is placed on the general trial court's criminal docket, and the next step in the trial process is the selection of jurors.

History and constitutional basis

The right to trial by jury has historically existed in the common law. In 1215, when the Magna Carta was signed, it contained a special provision that no freeholder would be deprived of life or property except by judgment of his or her peers. This right was incorporated into the U.S. Constitution, where Article III, Section 2, states: "The trial of all crimes, except in cases of impeachment, shall be by jury." Likewise, the Sixth Amendment provides that "in all criminal prosecutions, the accused shall enjoy the right to a speedy and public trial by an impartial jury of the State and district wherein the crime shall have been committed."

Although the right to a jury trial is a fundamental constitutional guarantee, until 1968 the U.S. Supreme Court did not guarantee this right to defendants in state courts.[35] In that year, the Supreme Court overruled one of its earlier decisions

The right to a trial by jury was guaranteed in the Magna Carta and the U.S. Constitution. Shown here is the courtroom in Pottsville, Schuylkill County, Pennsylvania, in 1891. (© Brown Brothers)

and applied the right to jury trial to defendants in state courts by virtue of the Fourteenth Amendment.

The trial jury in a felony case usually consists of twelve jurors. Why the courts have settled on the number twelve is not known for certain, although some believe it is based on the fact that Christ had twelve disciples. The Constitution does not specify the number of jurors required, and generally, states use fewer than twelve jurors in misdemeanor cases. Under the early common law, jurors were witnesses who were summoned to testify for the state or the defense. Today, jurors are impartial persons who render a decision based on the facts presented them during the trial.

The prospective jurors are chosen by means specified in the particular legislation of the state. Usually, names of prospective jurors are compiled by the designated official (jury commissioner, clerk of the court, sheriff, etc.) from voter registration lists, motor vehicle registration records, or some appropriate source. The names are placed on slips of paper and drawn at random by some means. These prospective jurors constitute what is known as the jury panel or *venire*. The number of individuals ultimately selected at the beginning of each term of court depends on the number and nature of the cases pending. If cases have received notoriety, more individuals may need to be selected to find unbiased jurors.

How chosen

From one to four alternate jurors are also chosen, depending on the particular state. These alternate jurors substitute for primary jurors who become ill during the trial or the jury deliberations. These alternate jurors sit in on the trial but do not vote unless they have replaced one of the original jurors.

Representative nature

The selection of jurors must satisfy minimum standards of due process in that the jury must be a representative sample of the community, and there can be no discrimination based on race, religion, or national origin. All states prescribe that certain characteristics will exclude an individual from jury service. Some of the more common are the inability to read, write, or understand the English language; mental deficiency or some disabling physical defect such as deafness or blindness; blood relationship to the defendant, the victim, a prospective witness at the trial, the defense attorney, or the prosecutor; and service on the grand jury that returned the indictment. Certain individuals are exempt from jury by virtue of their occupation or particular status. Some examples are physicians, dentists, attorneys, and, in some jurisdictions, military personnel on active service and mothers whose absence from the home would create a particular hardship.

---

## WILLIAMS v. FLORIDA (1970)

### Whether the Use of Trial Juries of Less than Twelve Persons Violates a Defendant's Constitutional Right to a Trial by Jury

FACTS

Johnny Williams was tried and convicted of robbery by a six-member jury in a Florida state court. During the proceedings, Williams objected to being tried by a six-member jury, which, under Florida law, was permitted in all cases involving noncapital offenses. He asserted that a jury of less than twelve members violated his constitutional rights under the Sixth Amendment, as made applicable to the states by the Fourteenth Amendment. His argument was denied, and he was sentenced to life imprisonment. The Florida Court of Appeals upheld the conviction, and the case was appealed to the Supreme Court.

DECISION

The Sixth Amendment, as applied to the states through the Fourteenth Amendment, does not specifically require that a twelve-member jury be used in criminal cases. As long as a criminal jury is a representative body, fewer than twelve jurors is permitted. The decision of the trial court and the Florida Court of Appeals was upheld.

SIGNIFICANCE OF THE CASE

The Supreme Court left the respective states to decide how many jurors should hear a criminal trial as long as the number is large enough to assure a cross section of the community.

---

Defined

**VOIR DIRE EXAMINATION.** After these exclusions, the prospective jurors are drawn, and the process known as the *voir dire examination* begins. This is the process of examining and questioning each prospective juror under oath to see if he or she is acceptable to both the prosecution and the defense. In some states, the examination is conducted by the attorneys for the prosecution and defense; in other states, the judge does the questioning, with the counsel for the state and the accused indicating specific questions they want the judge to ask. Both sides may challenge prospective jurors they want removed from the jury. When it can be shown that the juror is prejudiced or is otherwise unable to perform the duties of

Cause challenge

a juror fairly and impartially, the challenge is called a *challenge for cause.* Both the prosecution and defense can exclude an unlimited number of jurors for cause, and

## EXCLUDING JURORS FOR CAUSE: THE DEATH-QUALIFIED ISSUE

A particular issue in the jury selection process caused a great deal of discussion in certain legal circles in the early 1980s. This was the issue of the so-called "death-qualified" jury. In a death-qualified jury, the judge for cause removes a prospective juror from sitting on the jury in a capital case when the prospective juror says he or she has a moral objection to the death penalty. Underlying this removal is the idea that such a juror cannot "uphold the law" by imposing the maximum penalty in a capital case.

This controversial issue was first addressed by the Supreme Court in 1968 when the Court ruled in a capital murder case, *Witherspoon* v. *Illinois* that general, conscientious, or religious opposition to the death penalty *was not* grounds for exclusion unless the prospective juror said he or she could never impose the death penalty or vote for conviction if death were a possible sentence.

As a result, "Witherspoon excludables" are people taken off jury panels who say they would not impose the death penalty under *any* circumstances.

Removing "Witherspoon excludables" from a jury does not make for a "death-qualified" jury if they are removed with a peremptory strike. But removing for *cause* prospective jurors who say they would vote against the death penalty regardless of circumstances, or removing those who say their values are so ingrained it would affect their ability to judge guilt or innocence knowing that guilt would mean a death penalty, or removing those whose views would affect their ability to judge guilt or innocence because death would be automatic upon conviction *does* constitute a "death-qualified" jury.

Two issues are associated with the removal of such potential jurors: First, because those having objections to the imposition of the death penalty are a significant group in our society, their exclusion from jury service would constitute a jury that is not representative of the community. It would particularly seem that women and minorities would be more likely to be excluded. It has been argued that this violates those provisions of the Sixth Amendment and the due process and equal protection clauses of the Fourteenth Amendment. It is also argued that to exclude such citizens from service on a jury results in a jury that is more "conviction prone"; a jury that is more likely to favor the prosecution, to be more hostile to defendants, and to regard too lightly significant constitutional rights.

The state, of course, argues against these contentions. The social science research that purports to support the idea that "conviction-prone" juries are likely to be the result of such a practice and, once the decision to convict is made, are more likely to impose the death penalty is subject to attack by those groups who find nothing wrong with excluding such jurors in a capital case.

In 1986, such an issue reached the U.S. Supreme Court. A federal Court of Appeals had overturned the convictions of five state inmates who had been convicted of murder in trials during which objectors to the death penalty had been purposely excluded by the trial courts from serving on these juries. The issues were drawn. Arguments were presented on both sides of the controversy. The Supreme Court, in a sharply divided opinion between its conservative and liberal factions, overturned the Court of Appeals ruling and upheld the constitutionality of states to remove such jurors. In this way the so-called "death-qualified" jury is constitutionally permissible.

---

the voir dire examination continues until a full panel of qualified jurors is found. In heavily publicized cases, this can be a very time-consuming process. For example, in December 1970, when Black Panthers Bobby Seale and Ericka Huggins were put on trial in New Haven in connection with the murder of another Black Panther, it took more than four months to conduct the voir dire, and more than 1,000 prospective jurors were excluded for cause.

**PEREMPTORY CHALLENGE.** Jurors can also be excluded through a *peremptory challenge*. A peremptory challenge, as its name implies, is a challenge that requires no reasons or explanation, and its use is wholly discretionary.[36] The number of peremptory challenges is strictly limited by statute and varies from state to state and according to the seriousness of the crime. More such challenges are available to both parties if the trial involves a felony than if a misdemeanor crime

*Defined*

*Number of peremptory challenges*

is being tried. In those states having capital punishment, there are provisions for even additional peremptory challenges beyond what would normally be available in other felony accusations. Some states also allow the defense in felony cases to have more such challenges than the prosecution. A peremptory challenge is used when either side feels that it would not be in their best interest to have this person on the jury but there is no justification for removing the potential juror for cause.

A third but rarely used challenge is a challenge to the array. Here, the entire jury panel is challenged. Generally, such a challenge is available only to the defense. It must occur before the selection of the jury begins. Such a challenge contends that the selection of the jury panel was in some way improper or that the manner in which potential jurors were called is prejudicial to the interests of the defense.

---

## BATSON v. KENTUCKY (1986)

**Whether Prosecutor's Use of Peremptory Challenges to Exclude Blacks from Jury Trying Black Defendant Violated Defendant's Constitutional Rights (Jury Selection)**

### FACTS

During the criminal trial of a black man, the judge conducted a voir dire examination of prospective jurors and excused certain jurors for cause. The prosecutor then used his peremptory challenges to strike all four black persons on the venire, and a jury composed only of white persons was selected. Defense counsel moved to discharge the jury on the ground that the prosecutor's removal of the blacks violated the defendant's Sixth Amendment rights to a jury drawn from a representative cross section of the community and also violated the accused's Fourteenth Amendment right to equal protection under the law. The trial judge denied the defense motion, and the jury ultimately convicted the defendant. Defense then appealed the decision to the U.S. Supreme Court.

### DECISION

Such a use of peremptory challenges to remove jurors because of their race violated the idea that juries are to be a representative cross section of the community and violates an accused's right to equal protection of the law.

### SIGNIFICANCE OF THE CASE

Prosecutors cannot use a peremptory challenge against jurors because of their race or on the assumption that black jurors as a group will be unable to impartially consider the state's case against a black defendant. A defendant in a criminal case may establish a *prima facie* case of purposeful racial discrimination based solely on the evidence concerning the prosecutor's use of peremptory challenges at the trial. Once the defendant makes such a *prima facie* showing, the burden shifts to the state to show a neutral explanation for such exclusion by use of a peremptory challenge.

---

 **THE TRIAL**

The opening statement

Once the jury has been selected and sworn in, the trial process begins. The indictment or information is read, and the state makes its *opening statement*. In its opening statement, the prosecutor usually explains how the state plans to introduce witnesses and physical evidence that will show beyond a reasonable doubt that the defendant committed the crime for which he or she is being tried. In the opening statement, the prosecutor is required to stick to the facts of the charges and the manner in which the state plans to prove its case.

Next, the defense is permitted to make its opening statement, although it may waive this right if it desires. If the defense elects to make an opening statement, it will also explain to the jury how it plans to introduce and develop its own evidence to show that the defendant did not commit the alleged crime.

Once the opening statements have been concluded, the state's *case* is pre- sented. At this point, the state calls its first witness, who usually establishes the elements of the crime; subsequent witnesses then introduce any physical evidence the state may have. The prosecutor begins with a *direct examination* of the witness. Usually, this direct examination consists only of eliciting facts in some chronological order from the witness. After this direct examination, the prosecution rests, and the defense is permitted to *cross-examine* the witness. `State's case`

In this defense cross-examination, most states apply what is referred to as *the restrictive rule*. Under the rule, the defense counsel must restrict questions to those facts brought out by the prosecutor in the direct examination. After the cross-examination, the defense rests, and the prosecutor is given the opportunity to conduct a *redirect examination* of the witness. Often, the prosecutor may question the witness on only those new facts brought out in the defense cross-examination. After the redirect examination, the defense is then given the opportunity to conduct a *recross-examination* of new facts that were brought out in the redirect examination. After the state had concluded its case, it rests.

The *defense case* is the next stage of the trial. Sometimes the defense at this stage will make a motion for dismissal on the grounds that the state did not prove the defendant guilty "beyond a reasonable doubt." If the judge concurs, the case is dismissed, and the accused is released. If the judge does not accept the motion, the defense then begins its case, following the steps outlined previously. After the defense has concluded its case, it rests. `Defense case`

The next phase of the trial is called the *prosecutor's rebuttal*. The prosecutor may elect to introduce new witnesses or evidence in an effort to rebut the defendant's evidence. The same format of direct examination, cross-examination, redirect, and recross-examination is followed. At the conclusion of the prosecutor's rebuttal, the defense can again make a motion for dismissal of charges, which is usually referred to as requesting a directed verdict or verdict of acquittal. If the motion is denied, the defense is entitled to the *defense surrebuttal*, and alternating examinations by both sides are again conducted.

Finally, both sides present their *closing arguments* to the jury. The prosecutor always makes the final summation and closing arguments to the jury since the state has the burden of proof in the case. Both the state and defense usually have broad latitude in their range of discussion, the use of illustration, and the employment of persuasions, so long as they confine themselves to the discussion of evidence presented and to normal deductions that might be made from the evidence.[37] `Closing arguments`

## Instructions to the Jury

At the conclusion of the closing arguments to the jury, the judge charges the jury to return to the jury room and consider the facts of the case and the testimony presented and from their deliberations to return a just verdict. In some jurisdictions the judge will read a statement of instructions to the jury immediately before the `Judge's charge` beginning of the closing arguments. The judge's charge to the jury includes instructions as to the possible verdicts. The jurors are given a written form for each verdict. The foreperson is instructed to sign the appropriate verdict and return it to the court after the jury has reached agreement. The typical forms of verdict in a criminal case are "guilty" or "not guilty." The jury in certain types of cases, however, may have the option of determining the particular degree of the offense, for example, murder in the first degree, murder in the second degree, and manslaughter. In certain cases, the verdict of "not guilty by reason of insanity" may also be a possible verdict. In some states the jury must return the death verdict in capital cases before the accused can be sentenced to death.

**Sequestering and the court bailiff**

After the jurors have been charged by the judge, they are placed in the custody of the court bailiff, who sees that they are sequestered (isolated from nonmembers of the jury) during their period of deliberation. Normally, they retire to a jury room to deliberate the verdict. The jurors take with them the pleadings in the case, the judge's instructions, and sometimes any evidence that has been introduced at the trial. Some states, however, do not permit the jurors to take anything with them to the jury room. No jury is permitted to leave the jury room until a verdict has been returned or unless the jurors have to be accommodated for the night, if the jury's deliberation lasts that long. The bailiff, who has the responsibility of maintaining complete security over the jury deliberations, must ensure that the jurors are not approached by any person who is not a juror and that they do not receive any communications that might influence their vote.

If, during the course of their deliberations, the jurors want to refresh their memories about the testimony of a witness or want further explanation of the instructions given by the court, they contact the bailiff. If necessary, the court clerk provides them with the transcript of the testimony, and the judge and the attorneys send new instructions to them by way of the bailiff. However, a great deal of caution

---

## JURY INSTRUCTIONS

### CALIFORNIA

Ladies and Gentlemen of the Jury.

It becomes my duty as judge to instruct you concerning the law applicable to this case, and it is your duty as jurors to follow the law as I shall state it to you.

The function of the jury is to try the issues of fact that are presented by the allegations in the information filed in this court and the defendant's plea of "not guilty." This duty you shall perform uninfluenced by pity for the defendant or by passion or prejudice against him. . . .

You are governed solely by the evidence introduced in this trial and the law as stated to you by me. The law forbids you to be governed by mere sentiment, conjecture, sympathy, passion, public opinion, or public feeling. Both the People and the defendant have a right to demand, and they do demand and expect, that you will conscientiously and dispassionately consider and weigh the evidence and apply the law of the case, and that you will reach a just verdict, regardless of what the consequences may be. . . .

### MARYLAND

Members of the jury: This is a criminal case, and under the Constitution and the laws of the state of Maryland in a criminal case, the jury [members] are the judges of the law as well as of the facts in the case. So whatever I tell you about the law, while it is intended to be helpful to you in reaching a just and proper verdict in this case, it is not binding upon you as members of the jury, and you may accept the law as you comprehend it to be in the case.

*Source:* Excerpts from California and Maryland jury instructions in criminal cases.

---

exists in some jurisdictions over this practice. In some states, the court may not emphasize any testimony or instruction by rereading it. In other states, any additional instruction by the judge requires that the jury be returned to the courtroom and the instructions given with both the defense attorney and prosecutor present.

## Jury Deliberations and Return of the Verdict

The foreperson of the jury often begins the deliberations by taking a vote of the jury. Although the first vote can result in a unanimous verdict, usually, the first vote indicates a divided jury. The jurors then discuss the case further in an attempt to resolve their differences and reach unanimity.

If after a prolonged period the jurors cannot reach a unanimous verdict, they report this fact to the court. A jury that cannot reach a verdict is called a "hung jury" and is dismissed by the judge in open court. A hung jury does not automatically result in the acquittal of the defendant. The accused can be retried with a new jury. But the fact that a jury cannot reach a unanimous verdict sometimes results in the state deciding not to conduct another trial. The state may reason that if it could not convict the defendant in the first trial, there is little reason to believe that it could do so in a second trial.

**"Hung jury"**

In recent years, some states have passed laws that permit defendants in criminal cases to be convicted with less than unanimous verdicts. Oregon, for example, requires a minimum requisite vote of ten to two. When this law was challenged by a convicted defendant, the U.S. Supreme Court upheld it. The Court ruled that a verdict that is less than unanimous does not violate the Sixth Amendment right to a trial by jury.[38]

**Nonunanimous verdicts**

Once the jury has reached a verdict, the jury is brought back into the courtroom, where the defendant, the judge, and the attorneys for the prosecution and defense are present. The judge inquires if the jurors have reached a verdict. When they reply that they have, the bailiff takes the written verdict that the foreperson has signed and attested to and hands it to the judge. The judge then reads it and hands it back to the bailiff or to the jury foreperson to read aloud in court. The verdict is usually phrased in the following language: "We, the jury, duly empaneled and sworn, find the defendant guilty [or not guilty] as charged."

The prosecutor or defense counsel may request that the jurors be *polled*. When a jury is polled, the judge or perhaps the bailiff asks each juror individually if the verdict announced is his or her individual verdict. This is done to determine that each juror is in accord with the verdict rendered and has not been pressured into voting a particular way by the other jurors.

**Polling the jury**

## ▣ POSTTRIAL MOTIONS

If the verdict is not guilty, the defendant is immediately released from custody. If a guilty verdict is returned by the jury, most jurisdictions permit the accused the right to file for a motion for a new trial or to set the judgment of the jury aside. Usually, the defense has a limited time in which to file this motion. The grounds are usually one of the following: (1) The state failed to charge an offense in the indictment or the court lacked proper jurisdiction in the case;[39] (2) the jury was guilty of misconduct in its deliberation (e.g., a juror was in contact with an outsider

Against mounting criticism, the jury system hangs on. Perhaps the reason for its longevity in the United States is the widespread feeling that for all its problems and faults, it still does a pretty good job of dispensing justice.

The use of the jury system, although not unique to this nation, is used far more often in America than anywhere else in the world. Even Great Britain, which popularized the use of the jury over the centuries, uses juries in only a relatively small number of trials. This is not so in the United States. When a case goes to trial—whether it be civil or criminal—most of the time it will involve a jury.

The authority for jury trials is contained primarily in the Sixth Amendment to the Constitution. This fundamental right is a cherished one. Some reformers think the right has impeded the development and experimentation with better means to determine truth and administer justice. The majority of Americans would probably disagree.

Jury duty is for many not a pleasant task. Although jury duty is one of the foundations of citizen responsibility, many people try to shirk their duty to serve. But more than apathy is at the root of the problem. The general treatment afforded jurors by the justice system, the tedious and intrusive selection examination, and the antics of lawyers and judges who often confuse more than they clarify are often disturbing to jurors. Out of this legal hocus pocus, jurors must then sift through the facts and return a verdict.

More than three million citizens are summoned for jury service each year. Although some of them are on duty for several months, the trend that has begun in some jurisdictions is toward the so-called one-day, one-trial system: Jurors who are not selected go home after one day; those who are chosen serve for just one trial.

There are some other promising changes. The old key-man system of calling only community leaders has been largely abandoned in favor of more representative ways to select jurors. Today the choice is made through the use of voter lists, tax rolls, telephone books, and car registrations. Many jurisdictions are also computerizing juror lists for selection.

The magical number of twelve is no longer inviolate in civil and some criminal cases. As few as six jurors are now used in many trials, and thirty-one states allow less-than-unanimous verdicts in civil cases.

Once potential jurors are notified to report to the courthouse, they initially find that they are on trial. They are examined for their attitudes and prejudices by both sides in the case. Any number of jurors can be excused for cause—for example, some may have heard so much pretrial publicity about the case that they are biased toward the prosecution or the defendant and cannot be impartial fact finders.

It is also becoming a concern that jury selection can now take almost as long as the trial itself. In one California murder trial involving three defendants, it took five months to question more than 250 potential jurors in a screening that filled more than 10,000 pages of transcript. The trial itself took seven months.

For years, attorneys have been guided by experience and hunches in selecting or excusing potential jurors. Today this is becoming more sophisticated, particularly in major civil suits. The use of "mock juries" to hear the case and report their impressions to the trial attorneys for one side or the other have been used. So too, is the adoption of "microcommentaries," fleeting changes of expression that indicate whether a potential juror is telling the truth. Also being adopted are "alpha factors," which indicate juror assertiveness, and trick questions to spot hidden juror biases.

When MCI Communications Company brought suit against AT&T, the attorneys for MCI used simulated opening statements and oral arguments before a surrogate jury. They also watched these "jurors" deliberate through at two-way mirror so they could better sharpen their tactics during the trial. Something paid off. MCI won a $1.8 billion antitrust judgment in the case that was the largest antitrust verdict in U.S. history.

Whereas lawyers see jury research as an aid in winning cases, critics see such psychological screening as at least an invasion of privacy and perhaps even unconstitutional. Minnesota judge Thomas Sasz admits, "it raises fundamental questions which must be addressed before it goes much further." Judge Sasz is also concerned that the costliness of such a process will slant the dispute to the advantage of the richer side.

Jurors' ability to understand the issues in complicated cases is being called into question. This has an important bearing on their ability to render a fair and intelligent decision. This fact, more than anything, explains England's moving away from the jury system. Former Chief Justice Warren Burger of the U.S. Supreme Court has commented that "it borders on cruelty to draft people to sit for long periods trying to cope with issues largely beyond their grasp."

Other experts are not so convinced. Richard Lempert of the University of Michigan says: "We currently know little about the capacity of juries to evaluate rationally the evidence in complex cases or about the capacity of judges to do the same."

Although unpopular jury decisions fuel the fires of the debate, nothing is conclusive. Even though the supporters of the jury system admit that the process could be improved, nobody has any acceptable ideas of how this might be done.

who influenced him or her); (3) the court made a mistake in judgment in permitting some evidence to be introduced or in overruling an objection, etc.; or (4) the instructions the judge gave to the jury were improper.

The trial judge may grant or deny any of these posttrial motions. Again, a hearing on the motion is held, and the judge, after listening to the arguments, issues a ruling. Most motions are denied. In some instances, these motions permit the judge to review the case before the accused files for an appeal by the appellate courts. In this way, an error can often be corrected at this level without having to go to the higher courts.

## ◻ THE PRESENTENCE INVESTIGATION

After the conclusion of any hearing on posttrial motions that do not change the guilty verdict of the jury, the judge in most jurisdictions has a presentence investigation conducted. As mentioned, states generally require a presentence report in $\quad$ *Purpose* all felony cases. These reports are usually conducted by the probation officers assigned to the court. The presentence report often serves more than merely a background on the accused that aids the judge in imposing sentence. It can serve such other purposes as assisting the probation officer in the rehabilitative efforts during probation; aiding the department of corrections in its classification and treatment efforts and program planning; assisting the parole board in its determination when the individual applies for parole consideration; and providing some insights into the offender that can help the parole officer in his or her supervisory efforts.[40]

A new wrinkle has been added to sentencing. In 1982 the Report of the President's Task Force on Victims of Crime encouraged states to pass laws permitting $\quad$ *Victim participation in* victim participation and input into the sentencing decision. A number of states $\quad$ *the sentencing decision* have done just that. California is a good example. Voters in that state enacted a special proposition called the Victims' Bill of Rights. Under the California law, the

### THE HIGH COURT SEES DANGER IN "VICTIM IMPACT" STATEMENTS

While many court reform and so-called victims' rights groups are urging greater concern for victims by permitting courts to take into account a crime's impact on the victim and his or her family, the Supreme Court is not convinced of the value of such an opportunity.

In 1987 and again in 1989, the High Court struck down the use of "victim impact" statements—at least as these statements are conveyed during the trial. In the 1989 case, the liberal wing of the Court in a 5 to 4 decision ruled that a jury choosing between the death penalty and a life prison term for a convicted murderer generally may not be told about the victim's personal characteristics. The majority of the Court considered such information prejudicial to the interests of the convicted defendant.

The justices ruled that Demetrious Gathers of Charleston, South Carolina, was unfairly sentenced to death after a prosecutor told jurors that the victim was a religious, community-minded person. Writing for the Court majority, Justice William J. Brennan said a defendant's sentence, whether the death penalty or not, cannot be based on factors of which the defendant was unaware. This is the second major setback for those who would like to see trial courts take victim-related factors into greater consideration.

### OFFENSE:

On October 28, 1988, a one-count information was filed in the Central District of Virginia at Richmond charging the defendant with a violation of Title 18 U.S.C. 1343, Wire Fraud.

On that same date, the defendant appeared before the Honorable Barbara E. Sirvis and pled guilty to the information. A written plea agreement was offered to the Court wherein the defendant waived his right to prosecution by indictment. The Government agreed not to prosecute the defendant for any other offenses arising from his conduct as an agent of the Holidays Travel Service. The defendant agreed to cooperate with the Government by providing complete and truthful information regarding his knowledge of all facts relating to the events from which this criminal prosecution arose.

The plea agreement does not preclude the prosecution of the defendant for perjury or making false statements to the Government. If the defendant remains in compliance with the agreement, any information he provides will not be used against him. If for any reason the agreement is declared null and void through the defendant's failure to satisfy its terms or conditions, all statements, information, and testimony given by the defendant may be used against him.

The court accepted the plea agreement and adjourned sentencing to December 18, 1988, pending the receipt of a presentence report. The defendant was released after signing a $5,000.00 signature bond.

### PROSECUTOR'S VERSION

The following information was obtained by review of file material contained in the U.S. Attorney's Office.

The defendant was employed from January 1983 until the date of the offense as the Richmond Branch Manager for Holidays Travel Service. This firm is engaged in the business of booking travel accommodations for its clients.

In January 1985, the defendant opened a business checking account at the Henrico Branch of Sovran Bank located at 10 East Drive, Hinckley, Virginia. The account, which was to be for business purposes only, was in the name of Holidays Travel Service, and Mr. Vaccara had signature authority over it. In September of 1985, the defendant, without the knowledge or approval of Holidays Travel Service, converted the checking account to the name of James P. Vaccara in care of Holidays Travel Service.

Following this conversion of the account, the defendant wrote checks against the account for goods and services that he knew were not related to the business of Holidays Travel. Checks were drawn and negotiated for such items as a hot tub, extensive remodeling at the defendant's home, two new automobiles, real estate purchases, extensive travel expenses, expensive jewelry costing more than $85,000 and other goods and services of a personal nature. From September 1985 until his arrest, checks wrongfully written on the account exceeded over $300,000.

The largest client of Holidays Travel Service was NATCO Industries. In 1986 the travel agency was awarded the contract for handling the travel arrangements for NATCO employees. In conjunction with this award, a leased Delta Airlines computer was installed in the Richmond office of Holidays Travel Service. The defendant knew that NATCO routinely used Delta Airlines and Delta billed NATCO directly for travel reservations. The information contained in the Delta terminal included "profile" information of NATCO employees authorized to charge airlines travel. When a NATCO employee had to make an airlines reservation, the employee would contact the defendant, who would then make the travel reservations. The defendant would use information in the computer to fraudulently overcharge NATCO for employees' business trips.

By using the office computer, the defendant would display the NATCO employee profile information on the screen. This information, together with the requests for air travel reservations, was transmitted via telephone wires to the Delta master computer in Atlanta, Georgia. As a result of this process, Delta billed NATCO directly, and a copy of the billing was received by the Richmond office of the Holidays Travel Service. NATCO authorized the travel agency to pay these billings. The defendant knowingly took these billing copies and transposed them over to fraudulent Holidays Travel Service invoices and, in effect, charged NATCO twice for the same reservation. The amount of money involved in the double billing exceeded $300,000.

### VICTIM IMPACT STATEMENT

As the result of this scheme, Holidays Travel Service and NATCO Industries suffered a loss of no less than $325,000. The total loss could be as high as $450,000. The exact amount is undeterminable because of the mixing of business expenses in these accounts.

### DEFENDANT'S VERSION

On October 27, 1988, during the course of the initial interview, the defendant was advised of his right to submit his version of the instant offense and of his right to submit any mitigating information to be considered in sentencing. As of the date of the dictation of this report, Mr. Vaccara has not submitted his written version.

### PRIOR RECORD

Investigative checks with federal, state, and local law enforcement agencies failed to reveal a criminal arrest/conviction record for the defendant.

## PERSONAL AND FAMILY DATA

### The Defendant

The defendant was born on August 23, 1950, in Baltimore, Maryland, to the lawful union of George Vaccara and Mary (nee: Ferrier) Vaccara. He was one of two children and was raised in the Baltimore area. The defendant indicates a normal childhood.

In 1975 he was married to Nancy M. Holloway, and they have two children by this union. In 1980 he was divorced from his wife and has not remarried. The defendant's divorce was largely brought about by his sexual orientation. He is an acknowledged homosexual. He contends that he is a responsible gay man, very aware of gay issues, and practices safe sex. He has not been tested for AIDS. Currently, he is living at 1232 Sycamore St., Richmond, Virginia, with a friend, William Wimberly.

Before accepting his position with Holidays Travel, the defendant was the treasurer of a volunteer community organization, Our Way Inc., a not-for-profit charitable agency that assists homeless children. An investigation disclosed that after the defendant left this position monies were found to be missing from the agency's accounts. It is suspected by William Haver, chairman of this organization, that the defendant took these funds without the agency's authorization.

### Parents and Siblings

The defendant's parents, Mr. and Mrs. George Vaccara, were interviewed by a probation officer in the Eastern District of Maryland. Both parents indicated that the defendant was welcome in their home. Their home life appears to be normal, and they appear to be an industrious working-class family.

The defendant has a sister, Mary Joe Shaver, who lives in Chevy Chase, Maryland. The defendant indicates that she knows of the

prosecution and remains supportive of him.

### Marital

This officer conducted an extensive interview with the defendant's ex-wife, who has resumed her maiden name. Ms. Holloway is very embittered toward the defendant. They were married after a brief engagement. She accuses him of manipulating her and the children and causing a great deal of trauma and grief in the family. Several times during their marriage she had to call the police to report instances of domestic violence directed toward her. No arrests were made. In each instance the police recommended that she contact the local prosecutor's office to file a complaint. After several years of marriage, his sexual preferences became known to his ex-wife, and she sought a divorce and custody of the two children. This was awarded on February 12, 1980, by the Domestic Relations Court of Henrico County, Virginia.

On December 20, 1982, Ms. Holloway received an Order of Protection in Henrico County. In this order the defendant was ordered to stay away from the residence of Ms. Holloway and the two children, Anne, age 12, and Henry, age 11. The Order further states that the defendant must keep no less than 100 yards away from Ms. Holloway and he must refrain from harassing, threatening, intimidating or offensive conduct toward them. Ms. Holloway reports that she has had some trouble in obtaining the court-awarded child support payments from the defendant but has not had to take legal action to secure payments. Ms. Holloway reported that he has not seen the children in over three years. The defendant corroborated this.

Ms. Holloway reports that the defendant used marijuana and cocaine frequently during their marriage. She indicated that she does not know of his use of other drugs.

She also reported that the defendant spent a great deal of money on liquor and drank excessively.

The defendant advises that he has a deep love for his children and enjoyed an excellent relationship with them. Interviews with people knowledgeable about this relationship confirmed this fact.

### Education

The defendant advises that he graduated from McNeese State College in 1973 with a Bachelor's degree in sociology. This was verified.

### Employment

September 11, 1988, to present: The defendant advises that he is currently working as a waiter at Denny's Restaurant in the Central District of Virginia.

June 1988 to September 30, 1988: During this time period, the defendant was employed as a Commercial Travel Operations Supervisor at Liteco Travel Agency in Williamsburg, Virginia. He earned $28,000 per year. In this position he supervised about 30 people and had access to ticket and baggage vouchers, as well as payments received. He was asked to resign on September 30, 1988, when he admitted embezzling company funds. He used blank airlines vouchers to receive payment from United Airlines for refunds, which he ordered. Approximately $7,300 were [sic] obtained and placed into the Liteco account, which he then withdrew for his personal use. No restitution has been made. To date, the defendant has not been prosecuted for these acts.

January 1983 to May 1988: During this time the defendant was employed as the Richmond Branch Manager of Holidays Travel Service. It is a result of this employment that he stands before the Court for the instant offense.

July 1978 to January 1983: During this period the defendant was employed by Tidewater Travel Agency,

Norfolk, Virginia. This officer conducted an extensive interview with the owner of this firm. The owner advises that the defendant began as a sales representative and eventually became the operations manager. Mr. Vaccara was described as an excellent agent with a bright future. However, this firm requested his resignation when several accounts complained of overbilling by the defendant. Mr. Vaccara received approximately $1,200 in overbilling fees. In lieu of prosecution, he agreed to make restitution, which he did.

### HEALTH

#### Physical

The defendant is a male Caucasian who describes his health as excellent. He claims to have no problem with alcohol abuse and admits to the periodic use of marijuana and cocaine. He claims to have no substance abuse problem and has not sought help for this.

### FINANCIAL CONDITION

At the time of the initial interview, the defendant advised that his salary was approximately $1,500 per month. He claimed several thousand dollars in a bank account. He pays approximately $300 a month in child support payments and about $600 a month in living expenses. He claims no other debts or liabilities.

### EVALUATION

The penalty for violation of Title 18, U.S.C. Section 1343, Wire Fraud, is custody of the Attorney General for five years, and/or a $1000 fine. There is a $50 Mandatory Monetary Assessment fee.

The defendant impressed this officer as an individual who likes to portray a life of drama and intrigue. He is an extremely engaging and articulate man who possesses effective communication skills. It is not difficult to understand how easy it is to be manipulated by the defendant because of his seeming ability to develop interpersonal relationships.

This officer feels that the defendant engaged in his criminal activity for two reasons: personal gain and for the ego-involved "thrill" of his crimes. His continued record of involvement in embezzlement shows a total disregard for the law and the unwillingness to control his conduct. His history of these offenses have been documented in this report and show a clear pattern of lack of remorse.

The defendant received enormous cash benefit as a result of the instant offense. As a deterrence to himself and others and as a safeguard to the community and as a punishment for his greed and wrongdoings, it is respectfully recommended that the Court impose the maximum incarceration penalty of five years. Given the defendant's estimated parole guidelines, the reality of a five-year incarceration sentence is that he will serve approximately twenty four months.

Respectfully submitted,

Richard A. Hall
U.S. Probation Officer

Approved by:

William B. Seitz
Supervising U.S. Probation Officer

victim or the victim's surviving kin are permitted to address the court before any felony sentencing.

The National Institute of Justice supported research to examine the effects of the new law.[41] The results are not particularly encouraging. In California at least, victim appearances had little effect on the criminal justice system or on sentencing. The researchers surveyed crime victims in that state after the adoption of the law and found that the victim appeared in less than 3 percent of the cases examined. It was concluded that several factors contributed to such little change in the system and the poor exercise of the right by citizens. One factor is plea bargaining. Since so many cases were plea bargained, the decision of the courts to agree to the plea bargaining curtailed any consideration the court might have given the victim. Two other important factors were identified. One is California's determinate sentencing law, which doesn't give the sentencing judge a great deal of discretion so the sentence can be adjusted according to the wishes of the victim. It was also determined that many victims simply don't know about their right.

Of those who knew about their right and didn't exercise it, the most common explanation was that they were satisfied with the criminal justice system's response or that they thought their appearance before the judge wouldn't make a difference anyway. Of those victims who spoke at sentencing, less than half thought their appearance and participation affected sentencing. Most of these victims felt that the judge was too lenient and didn't really consider their opinion. Interestingly, when the judges themselves were surveyed for the study, two-thirds thought the right wasn't needed, while two-thirds of the prosecutors thought it was.

The box on pages 374–376, "Re: James P. Vaccara," is an example of a presentence report as it might appear in a federal court.

## ◻ THE SENTENCE

Once the presentence investigation is completed and reviewed by the trial court judge, the accused is brought back into court for the imposition of sentence. The state legislatures and the U.S. Congress provide by statute the sentences that state and federal judges can impose for various crimes. However, as mentioned earlier, many state legislatures prescribe that in capital cases the determination of the sentence rests with the jury rather than the judge. This practice is widely disavowed by reformers, who would abolish the authority of the jury to render sentence. Several years ago, there was a trend in a few states to turn the sentencing authority over to an administrative body. One such former administrative body was the California Adult Authority. Under this system, a defendant was merely sentenced by the court to be imprisoned in a state penitentiary. The individual was then turned over to the director of corrections, and the department of corrections fixed the particular term of imprisonment. This proved to be very controversial and was abandoned.

One form of sentence is the *definite sentence*, which is for a stated number **Types of sentence** of years. An *indeterminate sentence*, which most states employ, has a minimum and a maximum length. Thus, an individual may be sentenced to imprisonment for two to five years or for a set period that falls within that range.[42] A *truly indeterminate sentence* is one that theoretically has no maximum and no minimum. Thus, the individual could be incarcerated from one day to life.

Many states also have *habitual offender statutes*. These statutes call for an increased period of incarceration for someone who has previously been convicted of two or more felonies or two or more felonies of a certain type. Under certain circumstances, then, someone could be sentenced to life imprisonment upon the conviction of a third felony. However, habitual offender statutes are rarely invoked by the courts.

In the last few years, almost all states have passed *mandatory sentencing acts*. These acts impose an *additional* mandatory penalty for certain circumstances that pertain to the crime. For example, if the convicted offender used a dangerous weapon in the commission of the crime, he or she would be sentenced to a period of incarceration in excess of that received for committing the crime itself.

## THE APPEAL PROCESS: AN OVERVIEW

An appeal occurs when the defendant in a criminal case (or either party in a civil case) requests that a court with appellate jurisdiction rule on a decision that has been made by a trial court or administrative agency.

Appellate courts receive two basic categories of cases, appeals and writs. By far the most time-consuming and important matters considered by appellate courts are appeals. These occur when a litigant's case receives a full-scale review after losing at the trial level, or in some cases, after losing in certain administrative proceedings.

The appeal process begins when the party losing the case at the trial court level (the appellant) files a note of appeal within a prescribed period of time. The appellant is then required to file with the appellate court the record of the trial court in the case. This record, which is often quite extensive, consists of the papers filed in the trial court together with a transcript of the trial testimony. Next the appellant and the opposing party (the appellee) file briefs that are written arguments for their respective positions. The briefs are usually followed by short oral arguments by both sides before the appellate court. The judges then decide the case and issue a written opinion. In recent years, because of the number of appeals that are filed and heard, appellate courts find themselves having to decide some appeals without written opinions.

Supreme Court decisions at both the federal and state levels are usually issued by the full Court; intermediate appellate court decisions are generally issued by three-judge panels. Often the appeals process can be resolved within a year or so. Yet in many states that have a large backlog of appeals, the decision process may take several years.

There are a number of ways in which the appellate court can decide the case. Special terms are applied. For example, the court may do the following:

- Affirm the lower court ruling which means uphold it.
- Modify the lower court ruling by changing it in part, but not totally reversing it.
- Reverse or set aside the lower court ruling and not require any further court action.
- Reverse and remand the case. This overturns the lower court ruling and requires further proceedings at the lower court level in accordance with the findings and instructions of the appellate court.
- Remand all or part of the case. This does not overturn the lower court's finding but it does send the case back to the lower court for further proceedings in accordance with the appellate court's findings and instructions.

Accordingly, the termination of an appeal case may or may not be the end of the case. Depending upon the appellate court's ruling, the case may have to go back for further proceedings. If federal law is involved, the party can petition the U.S. Supreme Court for review. In criminal cases, defendants have different routes of appeal in which they can file petitions in a federal or state court.

---

Another characteristic of sentencing is that when a defendant has been found guilty of more than one crime, the sentences imposed may be served on a *concurrent* or *consecutive* basis. An offender may be tried for more than one offense at the same time or may be tried on more than one count. For example, an individual who is apprehended and charged with the commission of three robberies could be tried separately for each offense or charged in one trial on three counts. If the accused is found guilty, most states permit the judge to run the sentences concurrently or consecutively. If the sentences run concurrently, they run simultaneously; if they run consecutively, the individual must serve one after the other.

 **APPEALS AND POSTCONVICTION REVIEWS**

The right of appeal, as prescribed by modern American statutes, is not found in the common law.[43] The early English courts began to permit very limited rights of appeal around the fifteenth century. Most of the rights of appeal, as we know them today, began to develop in the nineteenth century. Since then, extensive procedural rights have been developed for an accused to obtain a review of his or her case.

Rights of review from the decisions of state trial courts of general jurisdiction are made to either the state supreme court or the state court of appeals if the state has adopted an intermediate-level appellate court. In an appeal, the defendant alleges that the trial court erred in some manner when interpreting or applying the law in the specific case.

Appeals are based on the written record of what transpired in the trial at the lower court level. Thus, the appellate court concerns itself only with the particular errors alleged by the defendant. The appellate court does not conduct a new trial but merely examines the transcript of the case and any supporting briefs by the attorneys for both sides, hears oral arguments that are presented, and rules accordingly. However, if a defendant is appealing a case from a court of limited or special jurisdiction (e.g., magistrate's or municipal court) to a general trial court for review, the general trial court usually holds a completely new trial.

Before the higher courts accept an appeal from a lower court ruling, they usually require the party who is appealing to show that the particular point on which the appeal is based was appropriately objected to during the course of the trial. The higher court must be convinced that the rights of the defendant were so violated as to adversely affect the course of the trial and its results.

In most cases, appeal is not automatic—that is, the aggrieved party must apply for appellate review. However, states provide for an automatic appellate review of a trial court's decision if the defendant has been sentenced to death and in some cases where the defendant has received life imprisonment. The individual who appeals the case must show the higher court that he or she has exhausted all remedies such as writs and motions in the lower trial court.

In most cases, the rights of appeal of the state are very limited, and therefore the prosecutor can rarely appeal an adverse ruling. Such a practice would constitute a form of double jeopardy and would also put a burden on the defendant in having to defend himself or herself again.

Most appeals from state trial courts of general jurisdiction never get past the state intermediate court of appeals or the state supreme court. The number of cases heard in state trial courts that eventually get to the U.S. Supreme Court is almost infinitesimal. In most cases, the state appellate courts refuse to grant a review. In a few instances, if the defendant alleges that his or her constitutional rights have been violated, the defendant may file a petition for a writ of certiorari with the U.S. Supreme Court for review.

The petition for a writ of certiorari indicates the particular nature of the case, **Writ of certiorari** the errors alleged, and the previous court dispositions of the case.[44] The writ is granted by the Supreme Court when four justices feel that the issues raised are of sufficient public importance to merit consideration. Petitions for writs of certiorari are filed in accordance with prescribed forms, the petitioner stating why the Court should grant the writ. The opposing party also may file a brief, outlining why the case should not be reviewed by the Court on certiorari. According to the revised rules of the Supreme Court, "a review on writ of certiorari is not a matter of right, but of sound judicial discretion, and will be granted only where there are special important reasons therefor."

If the writ of certiorari is not granted, the defendant may resort to a collateral attack on the judgment. Although various post-appeal remedies are available in different states, the most universal method of collateral attack is by petition for a writ of habeas corpus.[45] This writ, which has its origin in the ancient common law, has been incorporated as a right in state constitutions and in Article I, Section 9, of the U.S. Constitution. A petition for a writ of habeas corpus questions the legality of the detention of the petitioner and requests that the court issue an order that directs the state or the person who has custody of the petitioner to bring the individual before the court to see whether the person is being held illegally.

If, upon hearing, the court determines that there is no legal authority to detain the petitioner, the court must order his or her discharge, and the individual holding the petitioner must release him. The petition for habeas corpus can be granted even after the final judgment by the highest court of competent jurisdiction.[46] Generally, the petition may be filed with the trial court, but in some states the state supreme court has original jurisdiction in such matters. These petitions may also be filed in a federal court and in the U.S. Supreme Court from an individual incarcerated in a state. Federal judges may grant writs of habeas corpus whenever it appears that a petitioner is being detained in violation of his or her constitutional rights by either federal or state authorities.

### Review by the Chief Executive

The President of the United States and the governors of each state have the power to pardon individuals convicted of crimes, to commute the sentence to a less severe one, or to grant a reprieve in some cases. A *pardon* is a forgiveness for the crime committed and bars subsequent prosecution for the crime. It has the effect of legally

The most famous example of a president exercising his constitutionally granted power to pardon a criminal was Gerald Ford's pardon of Richard Nixon in 1974. (UPI/ Bettmann Newsphotos)

erasing the conviction. A *commutation* does not remove the defendant's guilt but mitigates the punishment imposed. It has usually been used to reduce the penalty from death to life imprisonment without requiring any demonstration or condition of future behavior. A *reprieve* is a delay in the execution of a sentence and has no effect on the defendant's guilt or punishment. It is most likely to be used in postponing execution of the death sentence so that the accused may have additional time to file a motion for relief in judgment.

Most of these powers are usually vested exclusively in the chief executive and may be exercised at his or her discretion. A few states, however, require that petitions for executive clemency be first filed with a clemency board or committee for review. This board or committee reviews the petition, in some cases holds public hearings on the matter, and makes its recommendations to the governor accordingly. In a couple of states, the clemency board may only have to agree in the affirmative before the governor can exercise executive prerogative in this area.

## SUMMARY

The judicial process in misdemeanor cases is very simple compared with the procedure in felony cases. In a felony case, the arrestee is first brought before a court of limited or special jurisdiction for an initial appearance or a preliminary hearing. If there are reasonable grounds to believe that a felony has been committed and that the accused committed it, the defendant's case may be bound over to a grand jury, which issues an indictment if it believes a trial is warranted. More commonly, the case is brought to trial by the prosecutor's filing an information.

Once the accused is bound over to a court of general jurisdiction for trial, the next step is an arraignment. At this stage of the judicial process, the accused is asked to enter a plea to the charge(s). If he or she pleads not guilty and wishes a jury trial, selection of the jury takes place. Once the jury has been chosen and empaneled, the trial begins. Evidence is presented in a very formalized manner.

After receiving its instructions from the judge, the jury retires and deliberates. If the jury returns a verdict of guilty, most jurisdictions require that a presentence investigation be conducted before the judge imposes sentence. Following the imposition of sentence, the offender can employ a number of postconviction remedies and appeals.

## REVIEW QUESTIONS

1. What are the steps in the judicial process in a misdemeanor case?
2. What are the steps in the judicial process in a felony case?
3. Is the use of the grand jury mentioned in the Constitution? In what way?
4. Name two important functions of the grand jury.
5. What is an *information*? What purpose does it serve?
6. What is a "true bill" of indictment? What must the indictment state?
7. What pleas can a defendant enter at the arraign-

ment? How will the court react to each of these pleas?
8. List and briefly explain the pretrial motions that a defendant can file before arraignment or the trial.
9. What is the difference between a hearing and an investigative grand jury? What is a presentment?
10. Define the following:
    a. Jury panel or venire
    b. Voire dire examination
    c. Challenge for cause
    d. Peremptory challenge
    e. Prosecutor's rebuttal
    f. Defense surrebuttal
    g. Closing arguments

h. Presentence investigation
i. Victims' rights in sentencing
11. Define the following:
   a. Definite sentence
   b. Indeterminate sentence
   c. Truly indeterminate sentence
   d. Habitual offender statutes

e. Mandatory sentencing acts
f. Concurrent sentence
g. Consecutive sentence
h. Appellant
i. Appellee
j. Writ of certiorari

## DISCUSSION QUESTIONS

1. Are there too many due process procedures in processing a felony case? Discuss.
2. Do you think the accusatory process needs to be streamlined? Defend your position.
3. Do you agree with the Supreme Court's ruling in *Williams* v. *Florida* that a twelve-member jury is not specifically required in trying a criminal case? Why or why not?
4. What might be done to encourage greater victim participation in the sentencing decision? Should judges give more weight to the victim's feelings in sentencing than they now do? What about the victim's feelings about plea bargaining? Should victims be consulted?

## SUGGESTED ADDITIONAL READINGS

Church, T. *Justice Delayed: The Pace of Litigation in Urban Trial Courts.* Williamsburg, Va.: National Center for State Courts, 1978.

Israel, Jerold H., Yale Kamisar, and Wayne R. LaFave. *Criminal Procedure and the Constitution.* St. Paul, Minn.: West, 1989.

Israel, Jerold H., and Wayne R. LaFave. *Criminal Procedure in a Nutshell*, 4th ed. St. Paul, Minn.: West, 1988.

Rembar, Charles. *The Law of the Land: The Evolution of Our Legal System.* New York: Simon & Schuster, 1980.

Schantz, William T. *The American Legal Environment.* St. Paul, Minn.: West, 1976.

Strick, Ann. *Injustice for All.* New York: Penguin Books, 1977.

Zerman, Melvyn B. *Beyond a Reasonable Doubt: Inside the American Jury System.* New York: Crowell, 1981.

## NOTES

1. Some minor courts have no provision for a jury trial. In these instances, if the accused demands a jury trial, the case will usually be transferred to another court that is set up to routinely empanel juries for cases.

2. See *Gideon* v. *Wainwright*, 372 U.S. 335 (1963), and *Argersinger* v. *Hamlin*, 407 U.S. 25 (1972).

3. See *McNabb* v. *United States*, 318 U.S. 332, 63 Ct. 608 (1943); *Mallory* v. *United States*, 354 U.S. 499, 77 S. Ct. 1356 (1957); *Upshaw* v. *United States*, 335 U.S. 410, 69 S. Ct. 170 (1948).

4. Pub. L. 93–619, (1975).

5. See U.S.C. Chap. 28, 3161–3174.

6. See Lewis R. Katz, *Justice Is the Crime: Pretrial Delay in Felony Cases* (Cleveland, Ohio: Case Western Reserve University Press, 1972), app.

7. *Gerstein* v. *Pugh*, 420 U.S. 103 (1975).

8. *Hawkins* v. *Superior Court*, 22 Cal. 3d 584, 586, p. 2d 916 (1978).

9. Chapter 291 of the Laws of 1979. Sec. 968.06

10. Deborah D. Emerson and Nancy L. Ames, *The Role of the Grand Jury and the Preliminary Hearing in Pretrial Screening* (Washington: National Institute of Justice, May 1984).

11. Ibid., p. 54.

12. p. 71.

13. President's Commission on Law Enforcement and Administration of Justice. *Task Force Report: The Courts* (Washington, D.C.: U.S. Government Printing Office, 1967), pp. 43–44.

14. Joan E. Jacoby, *The American Prosecutor: A Search for Identity* (Lexington, Mass.: Lexington Books, 1980), p. 209.

15. See Article 240, Criminal Procedure Law of the State of New York.

16. American Bar Association Project on Minimum Standards for Criminal Justice. *Standards Relating to Discovery and Procedure Before Trial*, approved draft (Chicago: American Bar Association, 1970).

17. National Advisory Commission, *Courts*, pp. 89–91.

18. In criminal cases, the accused cannot be compelled to take the stand and testify.

19. National Advisory Commission, *Courts*, p. 91.

20. See Marvin E. Frankel and Gary P. Naftalis, *The Grand Jury—An Institution on Trial* (New York: Hill and Wang, 1977).

21. Ibid., pp. 6–7.

22. Emerson and Ames, op. cit., p. 77.

23. James L. LeGrande, *The Basic Process of Criminal Justice* (Encino, Calif.: Glencoe, 1973), p. 98.

24. M. Cherif Bassiouni, *Criminal Law and Its Processes* (Springfield, Ill.: Charles C Thomas, 1969), p. 454.

25. Emerson and Ames, pp. 95–96.

26. Ibid., p. 100.

27. Ibid., p. 99.

28. Ibid., p. 101.

29. This immunity is often granted by the court and bars the use against the witness of any statements or evidence derived from these statements in any legal proceedings against him.

30. LeGrande, *The Basic Processes of Criminal Justice*, p. 102.

31. *Kercheval* v. *United States*, 274 U.S. 220, S. Ct. 348 (1927).

32. The statute of limitations normally begins when the crime is committed, not when it is discovered. The statute of limitations can be "tolled," or stopped from running, when a formal complaint is issued, an indictment returned, or an arrest warrant issued.

33. R. Van Sickle, "The Omnibus Pretrial Conference." *North Dakota Law Review* 50 (1976): 178–189.

34. National District Attorneys Association, *National Prosecution Standards* (Chicago: National District Attorneys Association, 1977), p. 162.

35. *Duncan* v. *Louisiana*, 390 U.S. 145, 88 S. Ct. 1444 (1968).

36. See Paul B. Weston and Kenneth M. Wells, *The Administration of Justice* (Englewood Cliffs, N.J.: Prentice-Hall, 1967), pp. 193–196.

37. LeGrande, *The Basic Processes of Criminal Justice*, p. 132.

38. *Apodaca* v. *Oregon*, 406 U.S. 404, 92 S. Ct. 1628, 32 L. Ed. 2d 184 (1972).

39. These grounds may serve the same purpose as a pretrial motion to dismiss the indictment. However, there are some distinguishing differences. A reason sufficient to sustain dismissal of an indictment may be insufficient to sustain a motion in arrest of judgment. It must be shown that the defect in the indictment or information was such that it affected the legal basis of the offense charged and the proof of guilt. See Bassiouni, *Criminal Law and Its Process*, pp. 506–507.

40. Administrative Office of the United States Courts, "The Selective Presentence Investigation Report," *Federal Probation* 38 (December 1974): 48.

41. See: E. Villmoare and V. V. Neto, "Victim Appearances at Sentencing Under California's Victims' 'Bill of Rights,' " *National Institute of Justice—Research in Brief* (August 1987).

42. Although this example seems to imply that the individual must serve a minimum of two years, this is often not what happens. For example, states and the federal government employ "good time" to reduce the period of imprisonment. This "good time" might be computed on the basis of three months for every year served. Thus, the inmate serving a two- to five-year sentence could be released on parole after only eighteen months. The time might even be less than eighteen months if the state credits the inmate with the time served in jail before trial.

43. J. O'Halloran. "Development of the Right of Appeal in England in Criminal Cases," *Canadian Bar Review* 27 (1949): 153.

44. LeGrande, *The Basic Processes of Criminal Justice*, p. 152.

45. Ibid.

46. See Hazel B. Kerper and Janeen Kerper, *Legal Rights of the Convicted* (St. Paul, Minn.: West, 1974), pp. 207–238.

# CHAPTER 10

# Current Issues and Trends

## O B J E C T I V E S

**After reading this chapter, the student should be able to:**

Discuss the major historical milestones in court reform.
Identify and discuss some recommended reforms of
  the judicial process, including:
    changes in the pretrial process
    relief of case processing by lower courts
    abolition of plea bargaining

abolition of grand jury
    timely processing of criminal cases
    jury size and unanimity
Discuss the issue of judicial selection, discipline, and removal.
Discuss the reforms that have been suggested to improve the prosecutor's role and performance.
Identify the problems associated with witness cooperation.
Discuss the issue of bail reform.
Discuss the concerns over court security.
Identify some strategies to improve the management and operations of the courts.

## I M P O R T A N T   T E R M S

Judicial process
Pretrial process
Timely processing of criminal cases
Jury unanimity and size

Commission plan of judicial selection
Judicial discipline and removal
California Commission on Judicial Performance

Witness intimidation
Bail reform
Federal Bail Reform Act
Computerized court assistance
Court security
Court administration

**MAJOR HISTORICAL MILESTONES IN COURT REFORM**

As mentioned in Chapter 7, the courts in recent years seem to be suffering from a lack of public confidence. A *New York Times* poll indicated that the public felt that the courts were in need of more drastic reform than any other component of the criminal justice system.[1] There is probably a great deal of justification for the general feeling that some aspects of our courts need reform. While law enforcement and correction agencies have adopted some important reform efforts, the courts continue to lag behind. It should be recognized, however, that the courts, because of their unique role in the administration of justice, have many built-in constraints that make reform more difficult than other criminal justice components.

*Public confidence in the courts*

For example, a wide variety of mechanisms are required to institute the reforms that the courts need. Some changes can be made simply by changing procedural rules under the control of the presiding judge or chief administrator. One change of this nature would be to provide an improved method of calendaring cases. Other changes would require more extensive modifications in rules that can only be accomplished by legislation, decisions of the state supreme courts, or state constitutional changes. Changes in the use of a grand jury would constitute an example of this process. Additional modifications to the courts could involve the development of service agencies (e.g., diversion programs and bail agencies), which would require procedural changes as well as special funding.[2]

*Impediments to court reforms*

The problem does not end here. In addition to procedural, legislative, or fiscal actions, the adoption of many recommended court reforms would require a strong organizational commitment to the changes proposed. But, as mentioned in Chapter 7, courts operate in highly decentralized systems that tend to maximize the autonomy of individual courts. In such an environment, large-scale changes cannot be mandated by a central authority; although recommendations might be made, the relative existing autonomy of most state court systems are a significant obstacle to improvement. This is the major reason many reform groups call for a unification of state court structures, or at a minimum, for a vesting of the state supreme court with additional powers to supervise not only the procedures but also the operation of lower courts.

Most Americans are critical of the courts because they feel the courts are failing to prosecute, convict, and incarcerate those offenders who appear before the bar of justice. The fact is that there is little concrete evidence that the courts today are performing worse than they have in the past. On the contrary, there seems to be evidence that our judicial system today does prosecute, convict, and incarcerate a higher proportion of offenders than our criminal courts have in the past. For example, in 1926 only 19.5 percent of people arrested for a felony in Chicago were convicted, and three-quarters of these were convicted on a lesser charge than that for which they were arrested. During that year, charges were dropped in about 70 percent of the cases coming before the Chicago criminal courts. Studies of criminal case processing in Kansas City and St. Louis in 1924 show the same dismal results. Charges were dropped in 70 percent of the cases, and convictions were obtained in 27 percent. The incarceration rate of 19 percent was divided almost equally between prison and jail sentences.[3]

*Improvements in case dispositions*

Contrast this with more recent evidence. Studies conducted in several jurisdictions in New York State and by a major research center in twenty-six jurisdictions throughout the United States showed improved results. In examining all felony arrests in these jurisdictions, charges were dropped in about 27 percent of the cases. Of those cases that remained, the accused entered a plea of guilty in over 60 percent of the cases. Of the cases in which the accused did not plead guilty and went to trial, the median conviction rate was 73 percent. Of those convicted, over one-half were sentenced to jail or prison.[4]

In spite of what appears to be a growing ability of our courts to deal better with their responsibilities, the clamor for improvement continues.

Historical efforts at court reform

Recognition of the need for court reform is not new. In 1906, Roscoe Pound, who later became dean of the Harvard Law School, delivered a famous plea to the American Bar Association in which he claimed that the judicial system was archaic in three respects.[5] First, he maintained that there were simply too many courts, which created duplication, waste, and inefficiency. Second, he argued that concurrent jurisdiction (more than one court having jurisdiction in the case) was unnecessary and out of place in modern society. Finally, he pointed out that because of jurisdictional boundaries, unequal workloads existed, which often resulted in considerable judicial waste; some jurisdictions had too much work and others too little. Pound's comments led to the creation of an American Bar Association committee given the responsibility to propose reform legislation for the judiciary. In 1913, the now-famous American Judicature Society was founded to promote the efficient administration of justice.

During the 1930s, another important figure in the history of court reform emerged. While president of the American Bar Association, Arthur T. Vanderbilt emphasized the need to reform state courts. Of particular concern were such issues as improving pretrial procedure, methods of selecting juries, improving trial practice, improving the law of evidence, simplifying appellate procedure, controlling state administrative agencies, and improving judicial organization and administration.[6] Reform efforts were curtailed during the war years. In 1952, the Institute of Judicial Administration was founded under the leadership of Vanderbilt. Associated closely with the New York University School of Law, it conducted numerous studies of state court systems.[7]

In 1963, the National College of the State Judiciary was established through the efforts of former Supreme Court Justice Tom C. Clark and the American Bar Association. During the 1960s and 1970s, reform efforts were continued through the efforts of former Chief Justice Earl Warren, the recent Chief Justice, Warren Burger, and such associations as the American Judicature Society, the American Bar Association, and other interest groups.[8] Through these efforts, such notable court reform institutions as the Institute for Court Management, the National Center for State Courts, and the Federal Judicial Center were established to improve the overall judicial process. These efforts continue today, and such institutions continue to study, offer technical assistance, and make recommendations to our nation's judiciary on means to improve their operations. It is not possible to review and discuss all the current suggestions for court reform. Nonetheless, some of the more frequently (and passionately) discussed reform efforts are the subject of the remainder of this chapter.

## ◻ RECOMMENDED REFORMS OF THE JUDICIAL PROCESS

Many recommendations have been made in the past fifteen years to reform the court system and the judicial process itself.[9] One of the most popular of these among reformers and the most widely discussed seems to be the creation of a centrally administered state court system and the consolidation of existing courts of general and limited and special jurisdiction. For example, why have ten different courts of limited and special jurisdiction when only two to three are necessary? The merit selection of judges and the creation of judicial discipline and removal commissions are other frequently made recommendations. It is also frequently suggested that the states adopt unitary state financing and budgeting for all courts within the state. In this way states, rather than local governments, assume the responsibility for paying for the costs of judicial services. This will supposedly bring greater statewide uniformity to the judicial process and remove funding considerations from local governments. It is also recommended that along with this the states need to establish central rule-making authority. The state supreme court, for instance, should be given the authority to impose standardized rules and procedures to which all courts must comply. It is also proposed that the states develop unified merit personnel systems for all court employees and that the courts adopt modern technology and professional court administrators.

*Centrally administered state court systems*

The list of proposed modifications to the state court system does not end here. In terms of the judicial process itself it is suggested that written standards and guidelines be prepared for the screening, diversion, plea-bargaining, and sentencing stages of the process. Monitoring programs, according to one view, must be established to ensure that cases are disposed of properly and in a timely manner. Other recommendations include the consideration of jury selection and deliberation, the treatment of witnesses and victims, the issue of bail reform, and the reform or abolition of the grand jury.

Obviously, we cannot touch on all of these issues in this chapter; instead several have been chosen for closer examination. The serious student is encouraged to read the literature on court reform for a better and more thorough understanding of the issues (see Suggested Additional Readings at the end of this chapter).

### Changes in the Pretrial Process

In the pretrial process, it is often recommended that more emphasis be placed on screening and diversion. If more attention were placed on these alternatives, fewer cases would come to trial.

The rationale behind screening and diversion from the judicial process is twofold: (1) The number of cases that burden the courts must be reduced; and (2) there may be more appropriate ways to deal with some offenders than through the trial process. This is not a call for leniency. Rather, it recognizes that in terms of both financial and less tangible costs to society, it may be more practicable to consider alternatives. The purpose of pretrial screening is to reduce the number of cases so the criminal courts can concentrate on those cases that deserve the time and expense of adjudication.

*Screening and diversion strategies*

The pivotal figure in the pretrial screening and diversion process is the prosecutor. In a pretrial process, prosecutors would examine the case much more closely than they now routinely do. They would create certain decisional guidelines on whether a trial is in the best interests of society, the courts, and the accused. Some considerations might be the nature of the crime and the sufficiency of the evidence against the defendant, which would indicate if a conviction was likely and if the conviction, once obtained, could be sustained on appeal. The more difficult questions that the prosecutor would have to consider if the trial process is invoked concern the potential of preventing future criminal behavior by the accused (and by others). Furthermore, the prosecutor would have to weigh whether the safety of society would be endangered if a diversionary method were used in dealing with the accused. The prosecutor would also have to consider the possibility that a trial and incarceration might seriously disrupt family ties, create severe financial hardship, and expose the accused to an experience that would produce an individual who was even more embittered and less likely to mend his or her way than when he or she entered the criminal justice system.

Although such proposals have a great deal to recommend them, many prosecutors are reluctant to openly and publicly explore the possibilities of a diversion program. The political implications are too obvious. Although diversionary programs operate informally in all prosecutors' offices, it is far different from announcing them as established policy.

Such a policy would also require another consideration: a forum would have to be established to deal with such defendants and circumstances. Otherwise, the impression would be given that the individual can commit an offense and get off "scot-free" without the possibility of some form of punishment imposed. This would be, in the interest of justice, unacceptable to the public and to the nation's prosecutors. What is going to be discussed next is perhaps a model of such an alternative.

### Relieving the Lower Courts of Certain Misdemeanor Cases

Alternative mechanisms

In 1976, the National Conference on the Causes of Popular Dissatisfaction with the Administration of Justice was held. One of the conference's main recommendations was to find alternatives to the lower courts to process the many minor matters that now glut these courts and detract from their more important judicial role. The conference supported establishing alternative dispute resolution mechanisms other than our lower courts. It was felt that in addition to unburdening the lower courts, such arrangements might expedite justice by avoiding the encumbrances of the legal system.

Generally it was recognized that formal litigation was not necessarily the best way to resolve differences. For example, mediation and fact-finding procedures and hearings could be used as informal methods whereby parties could voluntarily work toward their own resolution of the dispute, and community members could be employed as hearing officers. Instead of the limited options of the court to settle problems through the imposition of fines, probation, or incarceration, disputants could be referred to social service agencies or to small claims courts, or they could engage in community service or victim restitution programs.[10]

Such informal hearings could also serve as a screening device. If it became apparent that the circumstances warranted the intervention of more formal trial court proceedings, the case could be referred to the proper criminal or civil court.[11]

Such a system is known as a Neighborhood Justice Center. As a result of the recommendations of the 1976 conference, the federal government sponsored the

Neighborhood Justice of Chicago uses mediation and fact-finding procedures to resolve criminal and civil cases. (Chicago Tribune)

development of several of these models throughout the United States.[12] There is no recommended model on how they should be established, what specific jurisdiction they should have, or how cases should be adjudicated. Because the concept is still novel, the idea and its application are still in the developmental stage. In some localities, these justice centers have been established by the prosecutor's office; others have placed the center under court sponsorship.[13] Neighborhood Justice of Chicago began as a project of the Chicago Bar Association and operates as an independent, private, nonprofit agency. This agency mediates disputes referred not only from misdemeanor branch courts, but also from legal assistance agencies, social service agencies, and a variety of other sources, including self-referral by the parties in a dispute.

A great many problems still need to be ironed out in the concept. For instance, there are questions of jurisdiction and authority, about the format for resolving differences, and about what types of personnel are needed to operate such a system and whether it would be best to operate by court, police, or prosecutor referral or some combination of these. Also, a policy remains to be set regarding self-initiated referral by a crime victim or civil disputant.

In 1987 a survey was made of members of the Conference of State Court Administrators. The survey reported that there were 458 dispute-resolution centers operating in the states surveyed.[14] The bulk of the criminal cases mediated by these centers involved misdemeanor and juvenile crimes. Most of the workload of these centers, however, was comprised of civil matters such as domestic relations, small claims, creditor suits, and similar legal issues. The apparent willingness or usefulness of these centers to handle criminal matters seems to be far less prevalent. Perhaps this is to be expected. Criminal cases raise certain issues not present in

**Cases handled by alternative dispute resolution centers**

dealing with civil matters such as the authority to invoke punishment, the rights of defendants in criminal matters, and other concerns. For these reasons, the courts and the legal system are less receptive to giving up their authority over such matters. Although such alternative dispute-resolution centers would seem to offer some promise to relieve the courts of limited and special jurisdiction of the crush of misdemeanor cases, we will probably see limited use of these alternatives.

## Abolition of Plea Bargaining

As mentioned earlier, the majority of criminal convictions are obtained in many courts because the defendant enters a guilty plea, often as a result of plea-bargaining arrangements between the prosecutor and the defense counsel. To many people, this is a particularly pernicious practice that destroys the basic concept of justice.[15] Some see it as harmful to society because it reduces the deterrent impact of the law. It can also be harmful to the accused, who by engaging in plea bargaining, forfeits those rights that have been incorporated into the trial process for his or her protection. Invariably, in any discussion of court reform, one of the major recommendations that arises is to abolish plea bargaining. Prosecutors and judges justify its existence on the grounds that if it did not exist, the entire judicial system would break under the strain of the workload.

Perhaps we need to look at this problem more carefully. There is no question that such practices lead to injustices. Perhaps, however, the alternative of abolishing such practices might be just as bad. In the United States today there is an attempt by legislative bodies to eliminate, or at least drastically curtail, discretionary decision making in imposing punishment for the commission of crimes. Discretionary decision making includes the practice of plea bargaining. Although there seems to be a quest for "efficiency," this approach may well overlook the fact that mechanical law enforcement is both undesirable and impossible.[16] The problem with trying to eliminate discretion by abolishing plea bargaining also presents the danger of not being able to consider the mitigating circumstances in individual cases. This may be the real crux of the illusive concept of justice. If prosecutors and judges must treat every case of burglary the same without consideration for these factors, is it any better than the so-called nonjustice system brought about by bargaining and negotiation? In attempting to bring about uniformity, we might in fact be creating a system that results in greater injustice. Such changes and their possible effects must be considered thoroughly before changes are implemented.

There is also some question of whether plea bargaining is really a form of leniency. Most lay people seem to feel that plea bargaining results in the offender receiving less than a deserved punishment. Research does not seem to substantiate this. Utilizing extensive computer data of what happens in the courthouse, some recent research found no support for the image of plea bargaining as a tool for leniency.[17] Indeed, the study found evidence to the contrary. After a careful and thorough examination of the data, plea bargaining appears to be a more effective instrument for crime control than trials.

The study examined the four most frequently committed serious crimes: robbery, burglary, larceny, and assault. For all of these crimes except robbery, defendants who pled guilty received substantially the same penalties as they would have received if convicted at trial. Statistical analyses also suggested that a significant proportion of the plea-bargained cases would have resulted in acquittals had they

*Discretionary decision making*

*As a form of leniency*

gone to trial. In this instance at least, it seems that prosecutors are achieving more by plea bargaining than they could achieve by going to trial.

The one exception was robbery. Concessions were routinely awarded for robbery pleas, and these sentencing concessions were accompanied by higher rearrest rates for robbers who pled guilty compared with robbers who were found guilty. Statistical estimates, however, indicated that a significant proportion of the robbery plea bargains would have resulted in acquittals if taken to trial. When this fact is taken into account, the concessions do not appear to be very significant.[18]

For these and other reasons, it probably is neither practical nor advisable to attempt to abolish plea bargaining. There seems to be little indication that abolishing plea bargaining, as Alaska and several local and county jurisdictions throughout the country have experimented with, will necessarily improve all the many considerations that go into having "better justice." However, if plea bargaining is to remain with us—which is certainly likely—there are those who point out the need to reform plea bargaining as a process itself. One of the concerns in this area is that judges do not assume a large enough role in the process. It is felt that judges too often merely acquiesce in the bargain arrived at by the prosecutor and the defense counsel without making the necessary *independent* assessment of the circumstances surrounding the charge, the justification for plea bargaining under these circumstances, and how the process was conducted. Although state statutes typically require that judges make a full, open-court inquiry of the accused as to whether he or she fully understands the consequences of the bargain and that he or she thereby forfeits the constitutional right to a trial, this needs to be done more carefully than is the practice in many courts. Otherwise, we run the always-present risk of having the defense counsel unduly influence a defendant in what may be the lawyer's best interest but may not necessarily be in the best interest of the client.

*Role of the judge*

It is not only the behavior of the defense attorney that needs to be carefully considered. Prosecutors also are known to "play games" that affect—or at least have the potential to affect—the plea-bargaining process. What this may mean for justice I leave to the imagination of the reader. For instance, in William F. McDonald's exhaustive study of plea bargaining in six jurisdictions, he uncovered evidence that, although blatant coercion to plea bargain has pretty well been done away with in recent years, less obvious prosecutor-induced techniques of coercion still exist.[19] The favorite tactic is to play a "bluff" with the defendant's counsel— particularly if the defense counsel isn't experienced with criminal defense work, doesn't interact frequently with the particular bargaining prosecutor, or is lazy and unwilling to call the bluff. What we're saying is that the prosecutor might be tempted to present the case and the evidence against the accused as stronger than it really is or to not mention some facts that the prosecutor has that are exculpatory and the defense counsel isn't aware of. This leads to a form of psychological coercion that might induce a plea. This is a dangerous tactic. The prosecutor in such cases walks a thin line between extralegal and unethical behavior in doing this— and McDonald admits that most of the prosecutors he studied wouldn't (or claimed they wouldn't) do this.

*Questionable prosecution tactics*

Perhaps so, but the possibility for such abuses exist, and without some control can be poisonous to the concept of justice if we accept the idea that "justice" should be determined by the facts as they exist and the pitting of the state against the defendant in an open and fair examination of the evidence. There is little to prevent this kind of thing happening other than relying on the integrity of the prosecutor and the skills and experience of the defense counsel as a check. What compounds this problem—and calls for the need for more careful supervision of the plea-bargaining process by the judge—is what McDonald also found in his study: Except in very unusual plea agreements, judges are not in a position of second guessing the agreements worked out by prosecutors. To do so would require the judge to assess the evidentiary strength of the case as well as other tactical matters.[20] In most cases, judges simply do not have the time or the inclination to do this.

## Abolition or Reform of the Grand Jury

A number of reform groups are saying that the grand jury has by and large outlived its usefulness in the majority of criminal proceedings. Table 10.1 shows which states use grand juries and for what types of crimes. The issue of abolishing grand juries rests only with the states who employ this device. For the federal government to abolish federal grand juries, a Constitutional amendment would be required. This would be a very difficult, if not impossible task, which makes any discussion of doing away with grand juries at the federal level unrealistic. A major argument for its elimination among states is that since the U.S. Supreme Court has required states to adopt "probable cause" (preliminary examinations), the functions of the two duplicate each other.

*An anachronism?*

Great Britain abolished the use of grand juries in 1933, although the right to be indicted by a grand jury had existed in that country since the fourteenth century. Willoughby puts the entire issue of the grand jury into perspective when he says:

> A grand jury is in the nature of a fifth wheel; that real responsibility for the bringing of criminal charges is, in fact, exercised by the prosecuting attorney, the grand jury doing little or nothing more than following his suggestions, that it entails delay . . .; that it renders prosecution more difficult through important witnesses getting beyond the jurisdiction . . . or through memory of facts becoming weakened by lapse of time; that it entails unnecessary expense to the government; and that it imposes a great burden on the citizen called upon to render jury service.[21]

Grand juries are extremely costly to select, service, and maintain. Although the grand jury was originally conceived as a screening device to protect the accused from false accusations, it no longer serves this objective. For example, a study of the operations of the grand jury in Baltimore indicated that this grand jury returned indictments in 98.18 percent of those cases it heard, only to have 42 percent of these indictments later dismissed before trial because of insufficient evidence or some technicality that made prosecution impossible.[22]

The use of grand juries also has another dysfunctional consequence for the administration of justice. In some cases, their legal intricacies of empaneling, conduct, and deliberations have actually thwarted justice. Individuals who may have been guilty have had charges against them dismissed because of legal irregularities in the grand jury process that a skilled defense attorney has been able to use advantageously.

*Suggested reforms*

Even those who think that the grand jury should be retained often admit that the rules and procedures of the grand jury might need some reforming. This is particularly true in the need to implement a number of due process protections for witnesses or those who might be indicted by the grand jury. The best-known

## TABLE 10.1   Requirements for Grand Jury Indictment to Initiate Prosecutions

| Grand Jury Indictment Required[a] | Grand Jury Indictment Optional | Grand Jury Lacks Authority to Indict |
|---|---|---|
| *All Crimes* | Arizona | Pennsylvania[d] |
| New Jersey | Arkansas | |
| South Carolina | California | |
| Tennessee[b] | Colorado | |
| Virginia | Idaho | |
| | Illinois | |
| *All Felonies* | Indiana | |
| Alabama | Iowa | |
| Alaska | Kansas | |
| Delaware | Maryland | |
| District of Columbia | Michigan | |
| Georgia | Missouri | |
| Hawaii | Montana | |
| Kentucky | Nebraska | |
| Maine | Nevada | |
| Mississippi | New Mexico | |
| New Hampshire | North Dakota | |
| New York | Oklahoma | |
| North Carolina | Oregon | |
| Ohio | South Dakota | |
| Texas | Utah | |
| West Virginia | Vermont | |
| | Washington | |
| *Capital Crimes Only* | Wisconsin | |
| Connecticut | Wyoming | |
| Florida | | |
| Louisiana | | |
| Massachusetts[c] | | |
| Minnesota | | |
| Rhode Island | | |

[a]With the exception of capital cases a defendant can always waive his right to an indictment. Thus, the requirement for an indictment to initiate prosecution exists only in the absence of a waiver.

[b]The information on the laws of Tennessee derives exclusively from our statutory analysis. No survey instrument was returned from that state.

[c]In Massachusetts, felonies punishable by five years or less in state prisons may be prosecuted on the basis of a complaint in the District Court. However, if this option is selected instead of prosecuting the case in Superior Court following an indictment, the defendant may not be sentenced to state prison but only to 2½ years in the House of Correction. Capital offenses and felonies punishable by more than five years in prison must be prosecuted by indictment.

[d]The grand jury in Pennsylvania has investigative powers only and does not have the authority to issue indictments.

*Source:* National Institute of Justice, *Grand Jury Reform: A Review of Key Issues* (Washington, D.C.: U.S. Government Printing Office, January 1983), p. 12.

set of proposals for grand jury reform has been developed by the American Bar Association's Section on Criminal Justice Grand Jury Committee.[23] These principles, which were approved in 1982, suggest among other things: the rights of witnesses should be protected by including the right to counsel in the grand jury room, and the right against answering questions that might be self-incriminating (unless immunity is granted); target witnesses should be informed that they are possible targets of an indictment; prosecutors must also present any evidence that would negate guilt; the prosecutor should not be able to present any evidence for consideration that would be constitutionally inadmissible at trial; a target witness should be permitted to testify if he or she waives immunity; grand jurors should be made aware of the elements of the offense; and the period of confinement for a witness who refuses to testify and is found in contempt should not exceed one year.[24] Since the ABA's adoption of these principles, a 1983 survey of states shows no rush to adopt these recommendations and to incorporate them into operational standards for grand juries.[25] Only a few states have made efforts to comply. For example, only about fifteen states provide for the assistance of counsel to witnesses summoned before the grand jury to testify. And, even in these cases, this right is limited to particular witnesses or situations. Only a handful of states require the transcribing and maintaining of a permanent record of grand jury hearings and more exacting and explicit standards on the introduction of evidence.

**Secrecy**

Another area of concern to grand jury reformers is the issue of grand jury secrecy. The idea for the need to keep the grand jury process secret is argued along several lines. It is said that secrecy is required to prevent those individuals who know they are being investigated from fleeing the jurisdiction if they learn or think an indictment is forthcoming. Secrecy, it is also argued, assures freedom in grand jury deliberations. In addition, it encourages testimony that might not occur if the witness thought his identity might be made known, it protects witnesses from intimidation, and it protects the reputation of those who are under investigation by the grand jury and are later exonerated.[26]

To this there is an important counterargument. It is said that such secrecy poses the real risk of violating the due process rights of those being investigated and closes the grand jury room door to proper scrutiny for legal and procedural fairness. This need for secrecy versus the more openness argument both present some compelling issues. Both positions raise valid concerns.

While imposing secrecy certainly does run a risk, so does opening up the grand jury process to outside sources. And does the grand jury really operate in secrecy? A study by the General Accounting Office (GAO) of the secrecy aspect of federal grand juries found that in spite of the so-called secret conduct and deliberations of grand juries, the fact of the matter is that in many cases, information was leaked to outside sources for a number of reasons. The GAO was also able to identify in a number of cases how these leaks affected cases or participants in the process. Witnesses were identified, reputations were damaged even though no indictments were handed down, and grand jury investigations had to be dropped or delayed because of these leaks. As a result of the loss of secrecy, witnesses also were intimidated, disappeared, or were murdered.[27]

**Investigative grand jury**

The continued use of the investigative grand jury is, however, recommended by most legal reform groups. The grand jury that is routinely used in the processing of criminal cases, as you will recall, is the hearing grand jury. The investigative grand jury is a special type of grand jury convened to inquire into particular areas such as organized crime or official corruption in the community. In some politically sensitive areas, where the police or the prosecutor are reluctant to conduct the necessary investigations or file charges, these special grand juries can perform an important role in the investigation and accusation that leads to the prosecution of crime.[28]

Many times these investigative grand juries have extraordinary powers beyond that of a hearing grand jury. For example, under federal law a "special" federal grand jury can be convened for a period of 18 months. If it has not completed its investigative work during that time, it can be extended even further. These special grand juries can be convened when the attorney general, the deputy attorney general, or any designated assistant attorney general certifies in writing to the chief judge of the district that such a grand jury is necessary because of criminal activity in the district. A state will often vest similar authority to convene an investigative grand jury with its attorney general, the chief judge of the particular criminal court district, or the prosecutor.

Whereas the hearing grand jury can consider only cases presented to it by the federal prosecutor, these special federal grand juries can commence and conduct investigations on their own. This is typically also true of the states. In this way they are not limited to those cases brought to them by the prosecutor. They also have the power to issue subpoenas, seek immunity, and then compel testimony, as well as to indict. In most jurisdictions they are required to make a public *present-ment* of their findings upon completion of their investigation.

It should be pointed out, however, that investigative grand juries also pose some serious problems for the administration of justice. History is replete with examples of the unscrupulous use of such an instrument for personal and political interests. For example, during Lincoln's administration they were used against those who did not support the Union's cause. During Roosevelt's and Truman's administrations they were used to silence Bolshevik and Nazi sympathizers. Later they were used by Senator Joseph McCarthy and Representative Richard Nixon during the red-baiting scare of the 1950s.[29]

Civil rights abuses

Although the investigative grand jury can be used effectively to weed out local corruption and organized crime, it must be controlled very carefully, if it is to serve as an effective instrument of justice and not a tool of government or prosecutorial oppression against certain interests. In fact, this concern for the almost tyrannical power of both hearing and investigatory grand juries is coming under a great deal more scrutiny today.

The accompanying is verbatim testimony of a former district attorney for Los Angeles County during a hearing before the Senate Judiciary Committee. It points up well the weaknesses and problems associated with the grand jury system.

## Timely Processing of Criminal Cases

Concern about court delay is also old hat. In 1818 the Massachusetts legislature adopted a system to ease court congestion and delay.[30] The problem is still with us today. One of the immediate goals of court reform is to shorten the time between arrest and the beginning of trial. It has been suggested that every state should require that an arrestee be brought before a magistrate within a few hours of arrest for initial appearance. This initial appearance would be for the purpose of advising the individual of his or her constitutional rights and to examine the facts and circumstances of the arrest. Similar steps should be spelled out through all the pretrial stages to avoid case-processing delay. What constitutes "delay" is a bit unclear; the U.S. Supreme Court has not clearly specified what is meant by a delay that violates the provisions of the Sixth Amendment that gives the accused the right to a "speedy trial." In 1972 the U.S. Supreme Court set down four factors to be weighed in determining whether a defendant had been denied his right to a speedy trial.[31] These factors dealt with the length and reason for the delay and whether the delay prejudiced the case of the defendant.

TESTIMONY OF HON. JOHN K. VAN DE KAMP, DISTRICT ATTORNEY,
LOS ANGELES COUNTY, CALIF.; ACCOMPANIED BY CAROL WELCH,
DISTRICT ATTORNEY'S OFFICE, LOS ANGELES COUNTY, CALIF.

Mr. Van de Kamp. Thank you, Mr. Chairman.

With me this morning is Carol Welch, from the District Attorney's Office in Los Angeles.

Senator Mathias. We are glad to have her here today.

Mr. Van de Kamp. You have already given me a very ample introduction. The question still remains as to why I am here.

I am serving as the District Attorney of Los Angeles County; but up until last year most of my criminal justice experience comes from within the federal system where I served as Federal Public Defender from 1971 to 1975, and as an assistant U.S. attorney and U.S. attorney in Los Angeles from 1960 to 1976.

During the time I was in the U.S. Attorney's Office, I took more than a thousand cases to Federal grand juries starting in the early sixties; as the Federal Public Defender I represented nearly 500 defendants, most of them charged by way of grand jury indictment.

So I have seen the workings of the Federal grand jury system both as a prosecutor and as a defender.

From that experience I have drawn several conclusions which I would like to summarize.

First, in my view, the constitutional right to indictment by grand jury should be abolished. In lieu thereof, I believe that a defendant should have the right to a preliminary hearing.

Second, short of constitutional amendment, which will be very difficult, I believe that this committee can produce substantial reforms in the grand jury system to promote the integrity of the grand jury, to promote the rights of witnesses appearing pursuant to its process, and to protect the rights of defendants charged with violations of Federal Law.

To that end, the chief recommendations that I have made are as follows:

First, that all grand jury proceedings should be recorded and, when necessary, transcribed.

Second, that an indicted defendant should, as a general rule, obtain full disclosure of all testimony before the grand jury relating to the indictment.

Third, a witness should be entitled to the presence of his counsel, either retained or appointed, when he testifies before the grand jury.

Federal rule changes should also be sought which would give to a defendant the sole power to determine whether an indictment should be waived; if waived he would be entitled to a preliminary hearing, followed by the filing of an information rather than an indictment.

If the case were initiated by indictment, as is sometimes the case, the defendant would be unable to file such a waiver. When this occurs the Federal rules should provide for complete disclosure to the defendant of all evidence presented to the grand jury.

These recommendations are based on several conclusions that I have drawn based on my own experience.

First, the grand jury today is little more than a rubber stamp for assistant U.S. attorneys.

I do not say that in derogation of assistant U.S. attorneys or to disparage them; as a matter of fact, Federal cases are screened carefully at an early stage. I know. I ran the complaint unit in Los Angeles for over 2 years, where cases were thrown out if they did not pass evidentiary muster. The result was that very few cases were lost either at trial or by way of dismissal.

In the 7 years I served as an assistant U.S. attorney in Los Angeles, I can recall only one or two cases where the grand jury returned what is known as a "no bill," and a small handful of cases where the grand jury actively solicited the U.S. attorney's office to take another look at the case, to reinvestigate, or to call in additional witnesses.

Second, the grand jury, which was introduced into our Constitution to act as a charging body, that is as the sword, and to act as a shield, a shield for the accused against unjust prosecution, no longer performs that second function.

I say that because it is commonplace for a case agent to go before a grand jury and, in the typical run-of-the-mill case, make a 5-minute summary narrative presentation to the grand jury and then leave the room with the prosecutor, leaving

---

**"Speedy trial" provisions** As mentioned in Chapter 9, the federal government and many states have adopted "speedy trial laws," which ostensibly attempt to give some guarantee of a speedy trial. Often these laws are modeled on the federal law which provides that 30 days are allowed from arrest to filing of an indictment or information; seventy days are then allowed between information or indictment and trial. Certain time periods such as requests by the defense are not counted. If case processing time exceeds the limit, the case may be dismissed.

the grand jury to deliberate for all of a minute before voting for an indictment.

In Los Angeles, it is not unusual for a grand jury to indict somewhere between 25 to 30 cases in a morning's sitting.

Now, this kind of procedure is not apt to protect anybody. It is clear that the Federal grand jury system today does not act as the so-called shield that it was originally intended to provide.

Third, since most grand jury hearings are unreported, there is no opportunity presented to the defense for discovery of the Government's case as presented there. As a result, the relationship between prosecutor and grand jury is often free and easy; it is easy for the prosecutor to provide irrelevant prejudicial information about the accused to the grand jury to sway their deliberations. Since there is no reporting, no one finds out about it.

Fourth, use of the grand jury today, in fact, shields the prosecutor from defense discovery since there is no reporting. Ironically it also shields him from better discovery of his own case because of the common practice of calling the case agent to present the case in summary form rather than percipient witnesses whose credibility he—and the grand jury—might do well to evaluate.

So the conclusions which I have drawn today are relatively simple. They are presented more fully in the form of a long written statement, which I understand will go into the record.

There is real irony in the fact that this institution which had a real purpose years ago no longer serves that purpose today; that has gone relatively unnoticed.

The public criticism of the grand jury as an institution in recent years has been primarily aimed at its use to go after political dissidents in such a way as to chill and inhibit First Amendment rights.

I suggest today that there may be a stronger and less controversial basis upon which to levy criticism; primarily that in its mundane day-to-day operations the grand jury no longer serves the purpose for which it was established.

So I support the thrust of this committee; but I would also respectfully suggest that the Abourezk bill, one of the bills which brings us here today, should be broadened extensively to include the provisions I just mentioned.

I would add this: Even though I support elimination of the grand jury indictment as a constitutional right, the grand jury should continue to exist and serve to perform important functions.

There are certain types of investigations which can be investigated thoroughly and properly through the grand jury mechanism—for example, organized crime investigations, governmental misconduct, investigations, and white-collar crime investigations of a complex nature.

In my view, a prosecutor should have the opportunity to take these cases to the grand jury. Overzealousness would be guarded against by requiring complete recordation and full disclosure to the defense.

I base these recommendations not only on my own experience in the federal system, but on the California experience with grand juries.

Our California constitutional system does not require indictment by grand jury as a constitutional right. During this last year we had somewhere near 20,000 felony prosecutions initiated in Los Angeles County. All but 81 defendants had their cases initiated by complaint and went the preliminary hearing route. We indicted 81 defendants. So, by and large, we've done away with the grand jury as the principal charging body. We have a system which has worked well.

Our experience indicates that we can make the kind of reforms I suggest without unduly interfering with the criminal justice process.

Senator Mathias. Thank you very much, Mr. Van de Kamp.

Let me direct that the full text of your prepared statement be included in the record after your oral testimony.

Mr. Van de Kamp. Thank you.

*Source:* Senate Judiciary Committee, Subcommittee Hearing on Constitutional Rights, *Reform of the Grand Jury System* (Washington, D.C.: U.S. Government Printing Office, 1976), pp. 29–31.

Still, the states differ substantially in what they consider "speedy" trial provisions. The major difference among the states who have such laws is the amount of time they allow between arrest and trial, which varies from 75 days in California to 365 days in Massachusetts. Many states set shorter time limits for the disposition of the case if the defendant is being detained in jail than if he or she was out on some form of bail awaiting trial. Laws also generally require that criminal prosecutions take precedence over civil trials. Since the states differ so much in their

Because of the need to physically detain criminal defendants, court reform efforts have often focused on shortening the interval between arrest and trial. (UPI/Bettmann Newsphotos)

laws in these areas, the interested reader is encouraged to check the specific law in his or her own state and, as a point of reference, compare the law to the federal model.

Reform efforts in recent years have been even more specific in their recommendations about timely processing of criminal cases. For example, the individual should be brought before a court for his or her initial appearance within three days of the arrest, the preliminary hearing within one week of arrest, and so on. Although laudable efforts, breaking down of the frames into discreet steps and times may not be practical or workable. It may be better to have states provide—as many do—general timeframes, such as seventy-five days between arrest and the start of the trial, which requires only that all the intermediate steps before the trial must take place during that seventy-five-day time period rather than trying to specify specific times for each step.

**The problem with "continuances"**

Reforms in scheduling court trials must also deal with the problems associated with continuances. In many jurisdictions, the granting of continuances often unnecessarily prolongs the time required to get the case to trial. Defense counsels are particularly notorious for using delaying tactics. Many times, they ask a judge for a continuance on the grounds that they need additional time to prepare the defense. In some cases, this may be a meritorious request; other times it is used to frustrate the prosecution, the state's witnesses, or the complaining victim, or to cover up the fact that they have as yet made no effort to prepare the defense case. There are many who are saying that judges should be more careful in granting such continuances and insist on a definite showing of need.

Fortunately, many states have tightened up provisions for defense counsels to obtain continuances. Judges are admonished by law to grant continuances only if the court is satisfied that postponement is in the interest of justice, taking into account the public interest in the prompt dispositions of criminal charges.[32]

## Jury Size and Unanimity

During the past two decades a number of states have enacted laws that permit the use of six jurors in courts of limited jurisdiction that try misdemeanor cases. In a 1970 case (*Williams* v. *Florida*), the U.S. Supreme Court held that Florida's use of a six-person jury did not violate defendants' Sixth and Fourteenth Amendment rights to a trial by jury. The Court's opinion in this case held that the important factor was not the size of the jury but whether the group of jurors was "large enough to promote group deliberation, free from outside attempts at intimidation and to provide a fair possibility for obtaining a representative cross section of the community."[33]

In light of the Court's ruling, reform groups have recommended that in all but capital cases, juries of less than twelve but at least six in number be used in criminal cases.[34] The argument is that a jury composed of less than twelve members can still provide the required group deliberation and resistance to improper outside influences while representing an appropriate cross section of the community. It is also argued that a smaller jury would be far less costly to empanel and maintain. This is particularly true in cases that involve sensational crimes that have had a lot of pretrial publicity, which makes it very difficult to select and empanel a jury composed of people acceptable to both the defense and the prosecution. Researchers have jumped into the argument. Some, using elaborate statistical models, contend that a six-person jury is much more likely to convict an innocent person or to acquit the guilty than a larger jury.[35] Still other researchers contend that a smaller jury is less likely to be a hung jury (a jury that cannot reach a decision) than a twelve-member body. Although at first glance this may appear to be an advantage of the smaller jury, it is said that this is simply not the case. The smaller jury is less likely to be a hung jury because such juries reduce the chances that minority positions among jurors will be maintained.[36]

*Issues surrounding jury size*

Although given the green light to use less than twelve jurors in criminal cases, the states have been less than enthusiastic to change. Most states still require them even in misdemeanor cases, although a number of states operate with six-member juries for misdemeanor violations. In felony proceedings, only six states permit juries of less than twelve in number, and all states require a twelve-person jury in capital cases. It should be noted, however, that some of the states, while requiring twelve jurors for felony cases, will permit a smaller jury to be empaneled to hear the case if both the prosecution and defense agree to the smaller jury. Figure 10.1 shows a breakdown on jury size by type of cases and number of jurors required.

Another question relevant to juries concerns the fact that a unanimous verdict of guilty beyond a reasonable doubt must generally be found before a jury can convict. It has been argued, for example, that "the unanimity of a verdict in a criminal case is inextricably interwoven with the required measure of proof."[37]

*Issue of jury unanimity*

Although about 60 percent of the states do not require unanimity in civil cases, most state constitutions require that there can be no conviction in criminal cases except by unanimous verdict; only five states permit conviction by less than a unanimous verdict for crimes. The proportion of jury votes needed to convict varies among these five nonunanimous states, ranging from two-thirds in Montana to five-sixths in Oregon.[38]

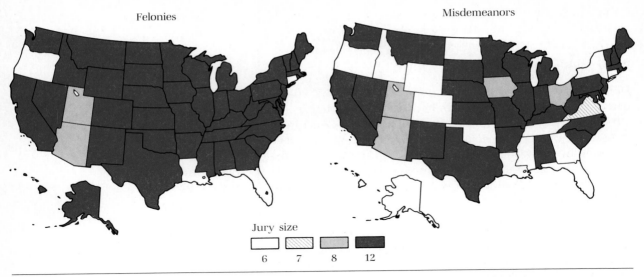

Felonies

Misdemeanors

Jury size

| 6 | 7 | 8 | 12 |

FIGURE **10.1** Jury size by type of case. All states require twelve-member juries in capital cases; six states permit fewer than twelve-member juries in felony trials. (*Source:* National Center for State Courts, Center for Jury Studies, December 1986.)

As in the case of jury size, arguments rage on both sides of the unanimity issue. Many legal scholars adamantly maintain that unanimity must be retained in criminal cases. One of the most succinct arguments for the retention of the unanimous requirement has been expressed by R. Holtzoff, who says:

> Unanimity is important and vital for two reasons: first, it leads to a more thorough consideration of the questions at issue and a more careful deliberation in the jury room than might otherwise be the case, since debate and discussion must continue until a unanimous verdict is reached; and second, the fact that the verdict is unanimous is in itself strong assurance of its fairness and justice. The only possible drawback to the requirement of unanimity is that occasionally it leads to a deadlock and, thereby, requires re-trial before another jury. The percentage of cases in which this happens in jurisdictions in which the common law system still prevails is, however, not sufficiently large to constitute an important factor.[39]

In spite of this, the American Bar Association, in examining the research on the question of jury deliberations as well as the legal considerations involved, concluded that the requirement for unanimity serves no useful purpose. Its Advisory Committee stated that "the minimum standards should recognize the propriety of less than unanimous verdicts as now permitted in five states."[40]

## JUDICIAL SELECTION AND REMOVAL

Many students of the American judiciary have been concerned about the methods used to select judges because selection processes can impede the appointment of the most qualified to judgeships. These concerned groups, which include the American Bar Association, the American Judicature Society, state and local bar associations, and numerous civic organizations, have been instrumental in producing needed reforms in a number of states.

States employ a variety of methods to select state court judges. Nearly half of the states still rely on partisan elections. In these states, a disproportionate number of which are in the South, individuals are popularly elected after receiving their party's nomination at a political convention or after winning a primary election. The next most frequent method is the nonpartisan election, in which the individual is popularly elected on a ballot that does not specify any affiliation with a political party. In fourteen states, mostly in the Northeast, some judges are selected by the chief executive of the jurisdiction. This method is similar to the procedure used in the federal system, where judges are appointed by the President with the advice and consent of the Senate. A few states still retain the system that was popular in the early years of our nation's history, in which the legislative body selects judges. For the most part, however, this form of selection is only for judgeships in courts of limited and special jurisdiction.

Methods of judicial selection

Over the past several decades, there have been increasing efforts to reform the traditional methods of selecting judges. The best-known reform idea has been the commission, or as it has sometimes been called, the Missouri plan of merit selection. Since it was first adopted for certain courts in that state in 1940, thirty-one other states have adopted variations of the commission plan.[41] Under the commission plan, a nonpartisan nominating commission consisting of lawyers and nonlawyers (appointed by a variety of public and private officials) actively recruit and screen prospective candidates. The commission then forwards a list of three to five qualified individuals to the governor, who must make an appointment from the list. The newly appointed judge serves for a one-year probationary period and then must win approval of the voters by running unopposed on a separate nonpartisan judicial ballot. The only question appearing on the ballot is: "Shall —— be elected to the office for the term prescribed by law?" If there is a majority of affirmative votes, the individual is elected to the full term of office. Some states use these nominating commissions only for particular judgeships. Indiana, for example, uses the commission appointment for its Supreme Court and Intermediate Appeals court bench but uses a partisan election procedure for most of its courts of general and limited and special jurisdiction.[42] A few other states have adopted the idea of separate nominating commissions or, as they are sometimes called, merit commissions or judicial qualifications commissions. For the most part, however, they nominate judges only for certain state or city courts.[43]

Merit selection

At least one major study of the nation's criminal justice system has expressed concern over the fact that politics plays such an important role in the selection of judges in most states and that political selection in no way ensures that top-notch people will be elected or even consent to run. Regarding the role of politics in the selection of judges, the study says:

The role of "politics" in judicial selection

> In our largely urban society where only a small portion of the electorate knows anything about the operation of the courts, it is usually impossible to make an intelligent choice among relatively unknown candidates for the bench. The inevitable result is that in partisan elections the voters tend to follow their party's nominations without any serious attempt to evaluate the relative merits of the candidates. In normally Democratic or Republican districts, designation as the majority party's nominee ordinarily assumes election.[44]

Under this system, the leaders of the dominant party select the judges. This selection process takes place in closed meetings in which compromises and bargaining strategies are carried on in an effort to reward party supporters; under these circumstances, too little attention is given to the abilities of the party's nominees. In an effort to avoid such situations, many people advocate nonpartisan elections for judges. Although this method may appeal to those who would like to diminish the impact of partisan politics, it is also argued that it has some evils associated with it. Glenn R. Winters and Raymond Allard question this method on the following grounds:

> It nullifies whatever responsibility political parties feel to the voters to provide competent candidates and thereby closes one of the avenues which may be open to voter pressure for good judicial candidates. Indeed, experience indicates that where appeal to the voters on political grounds is made impossible . . . other considerations equally irrelevant to a candidate's qualifications for judicial office are injected into the election. . . .[45]

The President's Commission on Law Enforcement and Administration of Justice is a strong advocate of the merit selection plan. The commission recommends that nonpartisan nominating boards be supplied with professional staffs and be made permanent agencies. It further recommends that the states direct intensive efforts toward developing standards that the nonpartisan nominating committee can employ in the selection of qualified potential jurists. Yet, any movement in this direction has been very slow.

**Removal or discipline of judges**

Another issue of proposed reform is to develop effective means to remove incompetent or corrupt judges. In most states the removal of an unsuitable jurist is almost an impossibility. Of course, because most state judges are elected, they can be voted out of office by the voters of the district, but other procedural means to remove them present very formidable obstacles. For instance, looking at means that can be employed by states to remove judges, we see that it can be done in only one of three ways, depending on the laws of the particular state. In many states there must be an impeachment and a conviction, which typically requires a two-thirds vote of the combined state legislature or at least the upper house. The use of citizen-initiated recall is also available, but this method usually requires a substantial number of qualified voters to sign the recall petition. Some states permit removal only by the governor and then only after a majority vote and address by both houses of the legislature. All of these methods have the effect of almost guaranteeing that judges will not be removed unless they lose an election.

The issue of judicial discipline and removal is a very sensitive one. Unquestionably, judges must be able to decide cases before them without fear of retribution or the influence of favor. The idea of such an independent judiciary is a cornerstone of our form of government. On the other hand, there is the need to make the judiciary (along with all government servants) more accountable to the public. This is not an easy question to resolve. Today, for example, we see many instances of judges becoming involved in deciding "public law litigation," which involves the courts in the economic and social life of a community as cases are brought involving complex and controversial questions formerly left to other public and private institutions to resolve.[46] By the same token, as judges have expanded the scope of constitutional protections, often acting to protect rights where other branches of government have declined to act, there has been renewed emphasis on the value of judicial independence.[47]

In the first part of the nineteenth century, a trend developed to limit judges to fixed terms,[48] and, around midcentury, to require them to be elected to office.[49] These trends reflected a desire to curb judges' disregard for popular opinion in the decisions they handed down. It wasn't until the 1940s and 1950s, however, that judicial discipline and removal became a concern of some reform efforts.

## CALLS FOR COURT REFORM IN CHICAGO . . . AGAIN

A new scandal-driven effort to reform Chicago's courts is under way. To a criminal justice system long sullied with periodic scandals, this appears to be but another in a long list of recurring efforts. Advocates of judicial reform in Illinois are again trying to bring some fundamental changes to the state judiciary. Despite a reversal at the polls, reform advocates have vowed not to give up their efforts to convert the state to appointment, rather than election of judges. This is the most significant of the many reforms recommended by a citizens' commission after a federal investigation disclosed massive corruption in the circuit courts of Chicago and the rest of Cook County.

The decade-long investigation, dubbed Operation Greylord, has led to the conviction of dozens of attorneys and law enforcement officers, as well as thirteen judges. Many have gone to prison for their role in a network of bribes in which verdicts were bought and sold for cash, with judges and police officers often acting as bagmen.

The investigation also led to the creation of a Special Commission on the Administration of Justice in Cook County, which was convened in 1984 by Circuit Court Chief Judge Harry G. Comerford to examine the structural and procedural problems that permitted such pervasive corruption. Its final report contained 195 recommendations from the sweeping to the specific, from how judges are selected to the need to have keys to court libraries—and what hours these libraries should be open.

Some recommendations have already been implemented. A strong new financial disclosure rule for judges is in place, and Cook County courts have adopted a new rule barring private conversations with a judge concerning a dispute before him or her. Judges are no longer permitted to dismiss parking tickets in their chambers; such dismissals must be requested and granted in open court.

But the push to appoint state judges continues to be an uphill fight. The General Assembly has steadfastly refused to make this change, which would require a con-stitutional amendment. And in November 1988, the state's voters refused by a margin of 3 to 1 to call a constitutional convention to consider it.

Nevertheless, advocates remain convinced that appointing judges is, in the long run, the only way to go "if we're really serious about preventing something like Greylord from happening again," says Peter Manikas, executive director of the citizens' commission.[a] Shifting to an appointive system, they maintain, would insulate judges from the system of political favors that underlies Chicago's local government.

The General Assembly will face the issue again, promises John R. Schmidt, a Chicago attorney who is a longtime proponent of appointing judges. But it will probably be 1990 before the proposal comes to a vote, he says. If approved by the General Assembly, the change then goes to the voters.

[a]"Court Reform Called for in Chicago" *Governing* 2, No. 11 (Washington, D.C.: Congressional Quarterly, Inc.) August 1989, p. 7.

---

In the 1940s and 1950s, such states as New York and New Jersey adopted constitutional amendments to provide for mechanisms to adjudicate complaints of judicial misconduct. These two efforts gave rise to the idea that judicial discipline should reside in the judiciary and not in some nonjudicial commission or board. This is still the general feeling today.

This principle was particularly bolstered by California when, by constitutional amendment, that state established a Commission on Judicial Qualifications, now called the Commission on Judicial Performance. In many ways, the California commission is a model that reformers are encouraging other states to adopt. The commission is composed of five judges selected by the California Supreme Court, two lawyers selected by that state's bar association, and two nonlawyers appointed by the governor. The function of the commission is to receive and investigate complaints on five specific grounds: (1) willful misconduct in office; (2) willful and persistent failure to perform judicial duties; (3) habitual intemperance; (4) conduct prejudicial to the administration of justice that brings the judicial office into disrepute; and (5) disability that interferes with the performance of duty.[50]

California's Commission on Judicial Performance

## JUDGES: WHERE POLITICS AND LAW MEET

Judges, who define the application of the law and establish its ground rules, find their way to the bench on the well-traveled if not always well-principled road of politics. The helping hand of politicians guides many a judicial career. Once they have made it, however, many judges enjoy a relatively safe harbor from the vicissitudes of the political arena.

The federal judges sit at the summit of the judiciary. The 138 appeals and 575 district court judges are nominated by the President and must be confirmed by the Senate. Most federal judges are nominated by the senators from the state. A home-state senator who happens to be a member of the President's party has what amounts to a veto over any nomination.

Under the Reagan administration, the ire of a number of senators was raised. Breaking with established tradition, the White House instituted a highly developed screening process to make sure that all federal judicial appointees were "correct thinkers" in that administration's mold. Although such screening has always existed, it was raised to a new level by President Reagan and

his staff. This upset even Republican senators.

Once such a nominee survives these hurdles, a federal judge has a lifetime appointment. Only impeachment and conviction by Congress can remove him—the last such removal until 1986 was over fifty years earlier. In 1980 Congress passed a law that gave the federal judiciary more power to discipline its own members including the authority to suspend a judge's right to hear cases. Many questioned whether the new law would make much difference. In the ten years since its adoption, there has been little effort by the federal judiciary to discipline its members.

The duties and selection of the nearly 27,000 judges at the state and local units of government vary widely. All states have supreme courts and thirty-six states have intermediate courts of appeal. All states also have trial courts, and many cities also have courts to deal with infractions of city laws such as traffic cases.

When the nation was founded, most state judges were chosen by

governors or legislatures. "But by the 1830s, people resented the control that property owners had on judicial appointments and began the process of popular election for judges," claims Larry Berkson of the American Judicature Society.

In the decades that followed, judges generally were elected to office in most states. This led to some notorious instances of political corruption and "political machine" politics. As a consequence, some states shifted to nonpartisan ballots for judgeships. This was refined even further in a few states that adopted merit systems in which screened candidates are chosen and appointed by the governor but must periodically go before the voters for a yes-or-no vote.

One of the major problems facing many states is to find an effective means to discipline judges and to remove them if necessary. Although most states have laws by which this can be accomplished, some of these laws are so cumbersome as to be for all practical purposes useless, except perhaps in very extreme cases.

The commission receives complaints from any interested source. If the information contained in the complaint appears to merit further consideration, an informal inquiry is made to see if there is any substance to the complaint. The next stage is the conduct of a preliminary hearing in which the judge is asked to respond to the complaint. If the commission still is not satisfied, it arranges for a formal hearing in which the judge has the right to counsel, the right to introduce evidence in his or her own behalf, and to examine and cross-examine witnesses.

Following the hearing, the commission either dismisses the complaint or recommends censure, removal, or retirement of the delinquent judge to the Supreme Court, which enters its order. Those who advocate the plan feel it has made a substantial improvement in the California judiciary. In its first six years of operation, forty-four judges became motivated to leave the bench voluntarily during commission investigation. It is also said that the commission serves an educational function; practices that have developed through carelessness or as a result of lack of insight can be discreetly brought to the judge's attention. Finally, the commission serves as a deterrent to judicial misconduct simply by being "visible and viable."[51]

As a result of growing concern about judicial fitness to hold and retain office, a number of states are now making some important changes. Although improvements in methods of selecting, disciplining, and removing judges have been made, there are still too many states in which such concerns are not addressed effectively or sometimes not addressed at all.

 ## UPGRADING THE PROSECUTOR

Among those who desire to improve the judicial process, changes in the present methods of selecting, retaining, and training of prosecutors and their legal assistants are absolutely essential. There is a recognized need to improve the caliber of persons attracted to this office and to retain them as careerists. It has been suggested that selection of prosecutors be based on their qualifications similar to the selection of judges under the Missouri plan. In addition, there is a need to increase their salaries and those of their assistants to retain them in this very important position. The National Advisory Commission, in its study of our nation's criminal courts, recommends that prosecutors receive the same remuneration as the presiding judge of the trial court of general jurisdiction.[52] Once this has been accomplished, it would be possible to prohibit them from engaging in the private practice of law, which could lead to conflicts of interest.

*Career, salary and resource considerations*

Likewise, the salaries for assistant prosecutors should be commensurate with salaries paid to attorney associates in private law firms in the area. In addition, there is a real need to provide prosecutors and assistant prosecutors with extensive training in criminal law and trial practice and with an adequate legal research capability. In medium-sized cities, the prosecutor's staff should have at least one researcher to help research the necessary case and statutory laws. In smaller jurisdictions where this may be practicable, the prosecutor should at least have access to an adequate legal library.

 ## ASSURING DEFENSE SERVICES FOR THE INDIGENT DEFENDANT

As we have seen from the discussion of indigent defense services in the preceding chapter, much still remains to be accomplished in this area. Reformers concerned with the way indigent defense services now operate are not asking for the ridiculous—they are merely recommending, given our adversarial process and the resources of the state, that the accused indigent defendant be given adequate legal representation. It is only in this way, many feel, that the system as designed can possibly work.

One of the most frequently heard suggestions for reform is to abolish the assigned counsel system in all but the smaller jurisdictions and to institute in its place a full-time public defender's office. Although this might be a step in the right direction, such a system is often itself fraught with problems. For instance, public defenders are torn between their legal responsibility to their client and their responsibility to the court. When judges have the power to hire and fire the public

*Doing away with the assigned counsel system*

defender, some very real strains can develop over respective obligations. It is also an observed fact that public defenders soon become part of the "system," with some negative consequences. Jonathan D. Casper expresses it quite well when he says:

> For the bulk of defendants—represented by Public Defenders—their attorney is at best a middleman and at worst an enemy agent. Not only is the process of criminal justice—with its bargaining, politics, charades—an assembly line dedicated to turning over cases and based upon a production ethic, but the defendant's own attorney is thought often to be himself a production worker on the line. He is not "their" representative, but in league with those who would determine the defendants' fates.[53]

It is not clear what can be done to improve defense services, or if, indeed, in this time of cutbacks in local government services and funds, anything can or will be done. Likely as not, any improvement in this area is a long way off. Given existing attitudes among many Americans who have no real understanding of the meaning and operations of our criminal justice system, we may do well merely not to regress in this area.

## WITNESS COOPERATION

**The crucial nature of witnesses**

Increasing concern is developing over problems with witnesses. An article in the *Los Angeles Times* reports that criminal justice personnel throughout the nation are growing uneasy about increased reluctance by witnesses to cooperate with investigators and to testify in court.[54] Two recent comprehensive studies of the prosecution of criminal cases in Washington, D.C., and New York City indicate that the most frequent reasons cases are rejected at the initial screening or lost in court are due to problems with witnesses.[55] For example, prosecutors in the Washington study gave "witness problems" as the most significant factor in dismissing robbery and other violent crimes and second only to "insufficiency of evidence" as a reason for rejection in nonviolent property crime cases.[56]

Another recent study in our nation's capital indicated that witnesses in criminal cases in that city voiced several complaints that directly or indirectly resulted in less than effective or no cooperation on their part. The most significant complaint was that there was a need for better protection against reprisals by the accused. The next most frequently mentioned complaint was that the courts needed to speed up trials and to display better attitudes toward the witnesses themselves. Finally, they recommended better pay for witnesses, and lastly, better facilities and other conveniences.[57]

**Problems of witness intimidation**

A study of witness intimidation gives us some insight into the problem.[58] The types of witnesses who were most likely to be threatened were those who had a prior acquaintance with the defendant, those who had been involved in more serious cases, and those who appeared especially vulnerable because they were female, elderly, or young.[59] Studies conducted in both Washington, D.C., and New York City tended to show that witnesses often feared that the defendants would seek revenge.[60]

The threats received by witnesses range from ominous looks or gestures, to rumors circulated around the neighborhood, to direct verbal and physical confrontations. Many witnesses reported being threatened by the defendant or by the defendant's family or friends or that they received anonymous threats. One of the most surprising and disturbing findings of the New York City study was that the largest number of witnesses were threatened in their homes, neighborhoods, schools, or workplaces—areas where criminal justice officials can exert little control.[61]

Those witnesses who reported their intimidation found that officials usually did little more than warn defendants not to harass the witnesses. The defendant was arrested for his or her intimidation or had his or her bail raised or revoked in only a very few cases. This may have occurred because of the difficulty of proving such intimidations with sufficient evidence.[62]

Officials infrequently responded to intimidation by protecting the witness. Only 4 percent of those witnesses who reported threats said that they had received some form of protection. Witness protection that was provided included being escorted by the police to school or to court and increased police surveillance in witnesses' neighborhoods.[63]

In the New York study, many intimidated witnesses said that the officials did nothing beyond making a note of the threat, telling them to call back if it happened again, counseling them, in some cases telling them that nothing could be done, or reassuring them that they needn't worry about the threats.[64] In the face of mounting criticism, many states have at least passed harsher penalties for attempting or accomplishing an act of witness bribery, tampering, or intimidation. Yet, such laws, without proper attention or resources directed toward enforcement, are meaningless gestures.

**Problems of witness cooperation**

It would seem that the problem of witness cooperation in the courtroom is just one aspect of the overall problem in this area. Lack of witness cooperation spills over into such other areas as not reporting crimes to the police or not cooperating with the police in their investigation. Concerning this problem, a law enforcement spokesman in Detroit quips, "With a shooting in the bar, you'll have thirty people tell you they were in the john at the same time and didn't see anything."[65] So the problem is not simply one that can be attributed to the criminal justice system. In too many cases it is one of poor public attitudes toward the responsibilities of citizenship. In those instances when the major blame must rest with the criminal justice system's treatment of witnesses, it is not always an easy problem to resolve. Some witness problems are more difficult to deal with than others. For example, the concern about reprisals is more properly a function of police protection. However, it should come as no surprise that police personnel resources are so limited that little can be expected in this area. Even the federal government, with its special Witness Security Protection Program, is extremely limited in the types of cases and resources it has to deal with the problem. However, because these are concerns outside the immediate discussion of judicial improvements, they will not be dealt with here.

**Possible methods of improving the situation**

What can be done? One of the major problems seems to be that the police do not obtain the correct names and addresses of witnesses. Later, subpoenas are returned as "addressee unknown." Another study in Washington, D.C., indicated that the police did not verify witnesses' names and addresses from identification documents such as driver's licenses. Some of the police were observed asking for the name and address of the witness in the presence of the arrestee.[66] Many of the witnesses indicated that they were confused about the entire process, what specifically they were supposed to do, and what they could expect. A major complaint of many witnesses is the delay in getting their property back from the authorities. As one article cited, "Seldom is a victim of a burglary more annoyed than when his stolen property is recovered only to be lodged in a police property room as evidence for a trial."[67] Another witness remarked, "I had my tools taken which I need in my business. Consequently, I had to buy new ones when they said it could be four to five months before they are returned."[68] Some jurisdictions have worked out co-operative arrangements between the police and the prosecutor's office to return a witness's property promptly. Still other jurisdictions permit a photograph of the property to be used for evidentiary and identification purposes.[69] This points out a very serious problem in failing to communicate with the witness by the prosecutor's office. Some cities now have the police provide witnesses with a pamphlet that explains the process to them. Washington, D.C., is also considering the development of a program to protect witnesses from possible reprisals. Under this program, as soon as the prosecutor receives the names of witnesses, he or she contacts them to inform the witnesses that any threats or acts of intimidation should be reported and that protection will be provided. Suggestions are being made that communities with such problems establish and widely publicize a special investigative unit that would conduct the necessary investigation and, if threats have been made, would notify the prosecutor to seek bail revocation or have the police provide protection.

Among some of the other suggestions relative to solving the witness problems are better management of court schedules so that trial delays would be prevented, and the development of special career-criminal case reporting systems in which witnesses would be provided with closer monitoring and protection if necessary. Another suggestion is to use paralegals to assist in the interviewing of witnesses, obtaining statements, coordinating witness conferences, staffing a witness-notification unit, coordinating requests for continuances, answering inquiries, monitoring cases for witness problems, and supervising issuance and processing of subpoenas. Although the problem with witnesses is not new to the administration of criminal justice, it seems to be only since the mid-1970s that it has received the attention it deserves.

## □ BAIL REFORM

Arguments

The issue of bail reform always centers around the three traditional arguments in this area: (1) Bail is discriminatory because it works against the poor defendant; (2) bail is a form of assuring the court that the accused will appear for trial; and (3) bail is a way of ensuring that certain dangerous offenders will not be put back on the streets before trial. In this latter instance, it is assumed that by keeping the required bail as high as possible, the accused will be kept incarcerated until his or her trial and disposition.

Those who advocate bail reform usually point to the first argument; those who feel that traditional bail measures should be employed justify their position by citing the last two arguments. Although it is not possible to discuss all of the issues that surround bail and bail reform in any depth, certain facts about bail, its administration, and suggested reforms should be understood.

Pretrial release methods

There are several methods of obtaining pretrial release. The first method is cash bond. This is the most widely used form. The defendant raises the required bond either through direct payment of the full amount to the court or with the help of a bondsman. The amount of the bail is set in one of three ways: (1) by reference to a fixed bail schedule that lists the amount according to a specific crime; (2) by the judge who may have complete discretion to set bail at any amount he or she desires as long as it is not "excessive or unreasonable"; (3) by a judge who may use the bail schedule as a guideline although he or she maintains the authority to select the exact amount within these limits.[70]

If the defendant obtains the bond from a bondsman, the defendant is normally required to pay as a deposit 10 percent of the bond's value. The bondsman is a private businessman and does not have to post bond for the accused if for some reason he doesn't want to. Many states and the federal government also employ a *deposit bond.* In this procedure the defendant posts a portion of the bail bond, typically 10 percent with the court, and is responsible for the rest if he or she fails to appear for court.

Another form of obtaining pretrial release is the *collateral bond,* in which the defendant posts collateral such as real or personal property instead of a cash bond. There is also release on *unsecured bond,* in which the accused posts no bail bond but risks forfeiting a prescribed amount for failure to appear. Finally, there is the *release on personal recognizance,* by which the defendant posts no bail bond but may be prosecuted for failure to appear for a scheduled court date.

The subject of bail reform has been hotly debated in recent years. There are those who advocate a "get-tough" with bail position. Such an attitude was reflected in the passage of the District of Columbia Court Reform and Criminal Procedure Act of 1970. Under the provisions of this act, the courts were directed not only to set bail at an amount that would assure that the defendant would appear for the court date, but they were also instructed to determine and obtain without bail any defendant who would endanger "the safety of any other person in the community."[71]

Critics contend that one of the major problems is that traditional bail practices too often permit the release of a person who is dangerous, who might pose a threat to witnesses, or who will continue committing more crimes while out on bail. There is also a problem in some major drug-related cases. Major narcotics traffickers pose a serious risk of fleeing; it is also almost certain that such individuals will continue their narcotics operation while they are out on bail and awaiting trial. Because of the vast sums of money involved in drug trafficking, imposing very high bond is no assurance that the individual will not be able to make bond and will have to remain in jail. It is also no assurance that such individuals will return to trial. Several years ago a federal judge in the Miami area required a $1 million dollar cash bond. The suspect immediately posted the million dollars in cash and has not been heard from since.

In an attempt to deal with some of these problem areas in bail, Congress in **Federal Bail Reform Act** 1984 passed the Bail Reform Act.[72] Before this statute was adopted, defendants in **(1984)** federal noncapital cases generally could be jailed without bail only when a federal judge found a high risk that the accused would not appear in court. This is the same standard that is applied in most state laws. This important piece of legislation provides several needed changes. First, it permits the judge to detain for ten working days any arrestee who is already on some form of conditional release, such as probation or parole for another federal or state offense. This gives the government ample time to notify the authorities from the jurisdiction granting probation or parole of the arrest and incarceration of the suspect so that they can take appropriate steps.

The new act also requires that on the motion of the government a pretrial detention hearing must be held for cases that involve one of the following category of offenses: a crime of actual or threatened use of force (e.g., robbery, assault, and loansharking); other felonies that involve a substantial risk that physical force against the person or property might be used (e.g., burglary); an offense for which the maximum penalty is life imprisonment or death; and narcotics offenses which under federal law can lead to imprisonment for ten years or more after conviction.[73] The act also provides for a hearing if the person arrested has been convicted of prior violent or nonviolent felonies or a ten-year drug conviction. Finally, such a hearing can be held on the government's motion where there is a serious risk that the person will flee or where the arrestee if released will obstruct or attempt to obstruct justice, or threaten, injure, or intimidate a prospective witness or juror.

The accused has no right to be released pending the hearing, but the hearing must be held immediately on the defendant's first appearance before the judicial officer unless the defendant or the government seeks a continuance. Such a continuance is limited to five days by the defendant and three days by the government. At the hearing the defendant has the right to be represented by counsel—court appointed if he or she cannot afford to pay—and has the right to testify, to present witnesses and other evidence on his behalf, and to cross-examine witnesses for the government.

At these hearings the new law sets forth certain presumptions that aid the government. For example, it provides that when the accused is charged with a crime of violence, a capital offense, or a one-year drug felony, there is a rebuttable presumption that releasing the individual will jeopardize the safety of another person or the community. Should these presumptions not be rebutted by the accused at the hearing, the judge is authorized to issue a detention order, which denies bail and remands the accused to confinement until his or her appearance.[74]

Several final points of the 1984 Bail Reform Act are worth mentioning. Should the judge after the hearing decide to release the accused on bail and the accused is convicted of a new felony while on release, an additional penalty of two to ten years' imprisonment will be imposed. Should the accused commit a misdemeanor while on release, a mandatory additional period of ninety days to one year will be imposed. Likewise, if someone is released on bail either for a felony or misdemeanor and "jumps bail" (does not show up for trial), significant additional imprisonment penalties can be imposed.[75]

In 1987 the Supreme Court, in a 6 to 3 vote written by Chief Justice Rehnquist, upheld the constitutionality of the pretrial preventive detention feature of the Act. The defendants in the case were organized crime figures who had been arrested by federal agents for Racketeer Influenced Corrupt Organization (RICO) violations. The government's evidence showed that they were leaders of the Genovese crime family and had participated "in wide-ranging conspiracies" involving violence and in two murder conspiracies. The government contended that the safety of the community was threatened and the defendants should be detained before trial. The defendants argued that the preventive detention provision violated due process. Chief Justice Rehnquist held that due process would be relevant if the issue was *punishment* before trial. Rehnquist, however, held that pretrial detention under the Bail Reform Act is "regulatory, not penal."[76]

**Other bail reform efforts**
This "get-tough" approach is one aspect of bail reform. Another change in bail practices is the creation of bail reform projects. These programs systematically

investigate arrested defendants using standardized fact-finding mechanisms to determine the defendant's reliability for release on a personal recognizance bond. Such a system attempts to predict the defendant's likelihood for appearing in court by examining the defendant's community ties, past criminal record, and the seriousness of the current charge.[77] Such programs are often conducted by law and graduate students, VISTA volunteers, or sometimes by programs employing former police officers or probation officers. Upon completion of the investigation, a written report is submitted to the judge that suggests whether the defendant should be released on his or her own recognizance.

In the years ahead, there will probably be increased adoptions of variations of both systems. Attention will be focused on the career or dangerous criminal, who will then face preventive detention guidelines. On the other hand, increasing use will likely be made of investigative examinations and recognizance programs for those who qualify. Perhaps in this way society can be better assured that the career criminal or dangerous offender is not released on bail and, on the other hand, that those who present little danger will not be penalized by their inability to raise the required bail or to purchase the services of a bail bondsman.

Despite security measures, the judiciary is sometimes the target of terrorism. Here a police officer disarms a bomb that had been planted in a courthouse. (Diane Laakso/ Sygma)

## COURT SECURITY

**Growing concern**

A growing concern in recent years has been over courthouse and courtroom security. This problem has been brought about by the concern that courtrooms and those who routinely practice law in our nation's court's are being subjected to increasing threats and acts of violence. It is not only violence that is finding its way into some of our courtrooms; other crimes are becoming too frequent an experience in some of our large and crowded urban courts and in the buildings that house these courts. What lies behind this is unclear. Perhaps it is a growing willingness on the part of violent offenders to use violence and to use it against those judicial figures who they feel have wronged them. It may partly be attributable to a lack of faith in the justice system.

**New efforts**

Whatever the cause, attention is being focused on methods to better protect the safety of judicial officials, court personnel, juries, and spectators in many of our urban and federal courts. The U.S. Marshal's Service, for example, has developed special training programs to assist their personnel in providing court security for federal courthouses and for federal court employees and litigants. A number of larger cities have also developed special training programs for law enforcement security officers assigned to the courts.

Today's security provisions at some of our courts employ electronic security systems to monitor all persons coming into the building or courtroom. It is not unusual in such efforts to find individuals carrying concealed guns or other dangerous weapons into the courthouse. Courtrooms increasingly are implementing a "controlled access" form of security control. Persons are permitted to enter and leave court buildings by only one or a few entrance or exit points. At each of these points, they are "screened" with electronic detection scanners and all packages are searched.

New courthouses in some areas of the country are also being designed with security precautions as a primary architectural consideration. Existing courthouses are being remodeled to better provide security and to minimize the vulnerability of the building's occupants. Judges who receive threats are also being provided with round-the-clock security personnel and bodyguards for their safety.

## ☐ SYSTEMS ANALYSIS IN THE MANAGEMENT OF CRIMINAL CASES

Computer technology applications

In the 1980s some courts successfully adopted new technology to improve their operations. Notable among these efforts is the introduction of computer technology in such areas as case scheduling, jury service lists, and case management. One of the most promising of these is the development of computerized systems to aid prosecutors. Such systems share common features. They make available to the prosecutor's office a wealth of information on each case, as well as reports and analyses of all case data. This is accomplished by computerizing a great deal of information about persons who have been arrested and are scheduled to appear for trial. Along with this, relevant information is gathered on the circumstances of the arrest, the nature of the crime, facts about evidence seized by the police, and witness information.

Computer systems permit the prosecutor's office to identify priority cases and individuals, identify strengths and weaknesses in the cases, and plan prosecution strategy accordingly, providing better management of the overall caseload of the office. Prosecutors can, for example, concentrate their attention on more serious cases and defendants and identify and handle potential problem areas in advance of the trial date. They can also track cases to ensure that mandatory "speedy trial" provision time frames are being followed. The most publicized computer system is the Prosecutor's Management Information System (PROMIS), which was first developed in the early 1970s and has been refined and used in a number of larger court systems in the country. PROMIS, for instance, provides the prosecutor's office with the following kinds of information:

> Information about the defendant, including name, alias, sex, race, date of birth, address, facts about prior arrests and convictions, employment status, and alcohol or drug abuse.
>
> Information about the crime, including the date, time, and place of the crime, the number of persons involved, and information about the gravity of the crime in terms of the amount and degree of personal injury, property loss, or damage.
>
> Information about the time, date, and place of arrest; the type of arrest; and the identity of the arresting officer.
>
> Information about criminal charges including the charges originally placed by the police, and the charges actually filed in court, and the reasons for changes in the charges by the prosecutor.
>
> The dates of every court event in a case from preliminary hearing through arraignment, motion hearing, continuance hearing, and final disposition to sentencing; the names of the principals involved in each event, including the defense and prosecution attorneys and the judge; the outcomes of the events; and the reasons for these outcomes.
>
> The names and addresses of all witnesses and victims, the prosecutor's assessment of whether each witness is essential to the case or not, any indications or reluctance to testify on the part of the witness, and other witness characteristics, such as whether he or she is related to the victim or defendant.[78]

## ▣ THE COURT ADMINISTRATOR

States are realizing that the responsibility for the management of the courts can no longer properly rest with the judiciary. If the court process is to be speeded up and judges are to devote their time to adjudicating cases, reviewing plea-bargaining agreements, and generally improving the legal process, they must be relieved of the responsibilities of court management.

"Managing" the courts

Although Connecticut is credited with the first state use of a court administrator in 1932, the model that has served as an impetus to develop the concept at the state level has been the Federal Judicial Center. This center, created in 1967, has been given the responsibility to develop and apply relevant management techniques to the administration of the federal courts. Among its important accomplishments are the application of systems analysis and design to reorder the case-calendaring systems in metropolitan district courts, a feasibility study of the use of circuit law clerks, an examination of the impact of specific types of litigation on the resources and workload of the courts, the use of computers for case scheduling, and the conduct of training sessions for judges and other court personnel.[79]

At the state level, the court administrator is often appointed by the chief justice or presiding judge of the state's highest appellate court. The responsibilities of this office are to establish across-the-board policies and guidelines for the management and operations of all state courts. This includes (1) the development of a general budget for the operation of all state courts for submission to the state legislature; (2) the establishing of uniform personnel practices in recruitment, hiring, removal, compensation, and training of all nonjudicial employees of the courts; (3) the compilation of statistical summaries on court operations; (4) complete fiscal management responsibilities such as purchasing, disbursement, accounting, and auditing for the entire state court system; (5) training programs for judicial and nonjudicial personnel assigned to the courts; and (6) judicial assignment under the auspices of the presiding or chief justice to ensure that judges will be assigned to those jurisdictions where they are needed.[80]

Statewide adoptions

Because of this recent interest in court administration, career opportunities and programs have been developed for individuals interested in court management as a vocation. One such program, the Institute for Court Management at the University of Denver, has been duplicated by other universities that have developed special graduate degree programs in court management. Usually, these programs apply public and business management to court operations and include courses in the legal process, budgeting and fiscal management, personnel, and computer applications. From all indications, this career field will continue to grow in the years ahead.

## SUMMARY

Court reform continues to be a major issue. Yet efforts at court reform measures and concerns about court improvement are nothing new. Much of the existing criticism centers around issues of how court systems are structured and how they process cases. It is particularly difficult to bring improvement to this segment of the criminal justice process. For one thing, courts operate under some unique constraints. Another inhibiting factor is the unreceptiveness of judges to change and the decentralized nature and operations of the judicial system in most states.

One of the issues discussed to improve court operations is the development of both a system and a workable mechanism for relieving the criminal courts of their heavy workloads. In this sense it is suggested that alternative programs and the development of such things as dispute resolution centers might pose a partial answer. It has also been suggested that such things as reform in plea-bargaining practices and the use of the grand jury are warranted.

The issues of judicial selection, discipline, and removal are frequently mentioned as in need of change. Various models have been adopted in some states to address this concern, and reformers argue that such systems should be more commonplace in an effort to improve the judiciary.

Other recurring complaints and efforts at reform center on the issue of jury size and unanimity, upgrading the office of the prosecutor, providing a better system of indigent defense service, and providing needed improvements in the handling of witnesses and witness problems. In recent years another concern has arrived on the scene. Courts are increasingly experiencing problems associated with threats, violence, and disruption in our nation's courtrooms. This has increased the emphasis on providing adequate courtroom and personal security for judges, witnesses, juries, and courtroom spectators.

Finally, the need for better overall management of the workload of the courts is being considered. Two of the most widespread recommendations is for the greater adoption of technology such as computer-based information systems and the creation of the position of the court administrator. Both of these have seen fairly widespread adoption in some locales in recent years. Still, many courts have not done much to improve their operations. For these courts, their operation has changed little in the past century.

## REVIEW QUESTIONS

1. How would screening and diversion reduce the court's burdensome caseload?
2. If misdemeanor cases were taken out of hands of the lower courts, who would hear and settle these cases?
3. What advantages might be realized by abolishing plea bargaining? What disadvantages?
4. Has the grand jury outlived its usefulness? Why or why not?
5. Why is it important to shorten the time between the arrest of a defendant and the beginning of the trial?
6. Are a defendant's rights placed in jeopardy by reducing the number of jurors that hear a case?
7. Must a jury deliver a unanimous opinion to convict someone of a crime?
8. Should judges be elected or appointed to office? What safeguards are needed in either method of selection?
9. How can witness cooperation be improved?
10. What are the arguments for and against bail reform? Which do you agree with and why?

## DISCUSSION QUESTIONS

1. Of the court-related issues and trends discussed in this chapter, which do you feel are the most important? Why?
2. Discuss some of the reasons why the courts as a component of the criminal justice system have been so slow to adopt change.
3. Explain the importance of and the problems related to witness cooperation. What might be done by the criminal courts in your community to improve such situations?
4. Discuss bail reform and its implications. Do you approve or disapprove of the way bail is handled today by most courts? What alternatives and implications do reform measures pose?

## SUGGESTED ADDITIONAL READINGS

Aaronson, David et al. *The New Justice: Alternatives to Conventional Criminal Adjudication.* Washington, D.C.: U.S. Government Printing Office, 1977.

Advisory Commission on Intergovernmental Relations, *Court Reform.* Washington, D.C.: U.S. Government Printing Office, 1971.

Carlson, Kenneth, *One Day/One Trial Jury System.* Washington, D.C.: National Institute of Law Enforcement and Criminal Justice, July 1977.

Eisenstein, James, et al. *The Contours of Justice: Communities and Their Courts.* Glenview, Ill.: Scott, Foresman, 1988.

Feeley, Malcolm. *Court Reforms on Trial: Why Simple Solutions Fail.* New York: Basic Books, 1983.

Friesen, Ernest, Edward C. Gallas, and Nesta M. Gallas. *Managing the Courts.* Indianapolis, Ind.: Bobbs-Merrill, 1971.

Hays, Steven W. *Court Reform.* Lexington, Mass.: Heath, 1978.

Jacoby, Joan E. *Pretrial Screening in Perspective.* Washington, D.C.: U.S. Government Printing Office, 1976.

James, Howard. *Crisis in the Courts.* New York: McKay, 1971.

Mileski, Maureen. "Courtroom Encounters: An Observation Study of a Lower Criminal Court." *Law and Society Review* 5 (1971):473–538.

Rosett, Arthur, and Donald B. Cressey. *Justice by Consent.* Philadelphia: Lippincott, 1976.

Saari, David J. *American Court Management.* Westport, Conn. Quorum Books, 1982.

Vera Institute of Justice. *Programs in Criminal Justice Reform.* New York: Vera Institute of Justice, 1972.

Watson, Richard A., and Rondal G. Downing. *The Politics of the Bench and Bar: Judicial Selection Under the Missouri Nonpartisan Court Plan,* New York: Wiley, 1969.

## NOTES

1. "A Growing Dissatisfaction with Our Courts," *New York Times*, August 17, 1977, p. 14.

2. "The Plague of Violent Crime," *Newsweek*, 23 March 1981, p. 47.

3. C. E. Gehlke, "Recorded Felonies: An Analysis and General Survey," Illinois Association for Criminal Justice, *Illinois Crime Survey* (Montclair, N.J.: Patterson, Smith Reprint Series, 1968), chap. 1; Gehlke, "A Statistical Interpretation of the Criminal Process," *Missouri Crime Survey* (Montclair, N.J.: Patterson, Smith Reprint Series, 1968), part VII.

4. Vera Institute of Justice, *Felony Arrests: Their Prosecution and Disposition in New York City's Courts* (New York: Vera Institute of Justice, 1977), pp. 1–22; Barbara Boland with Ronald Stones, *Prosecution of Felony Arrests, 1981* (Washington, D.C., INSLAW, Inc., 1986).

5. Roscoe Pound, "The Causes of Popular Dissatisfaction with the Administration of Justice," *Journal of the American Judicature Society* 20 (February 1937): 178–187.

6. See Arthur Vanderbilt, "Section of Judicial Administration Launches Program on Wide Front," *American Bar Association Journal* 24 (January 1939): 5–6.

7. Larry C. Berkson, Steven W. Hays, and Susan J. Carbon, *Managing the State Courts* (St. Paul, Minn.: West, 1977), p. 11.

8. For example, see William F. Swindler, ed., *Addresses and Papers on the National Conference of the Judiciary, Williamsburg, Virginia, 11–14 March 1971* (Washington, D.C.: U.S. Government Printing Office, 1971).

9. For example, see: Geoff Gallas, "Court Reform: Has It Been Built on an Adequate Foundation?" *Judicature* 63 (June–July 1979): 28–38.

10. American Bar Association, *Report on the Pound Conference Follow-up Task Force* (Chicago: American Bar Association, August 1976), p. 1.

11. See Daniel McGillis and Joan Mullen, *Neighborhood Justice Centers: An Analysis of Potential Models* (Washington, D.C.: U.S. Government Printing Office, October 1977), p. 30.

12. Ibid.

13. See: E. Johnson, V. Cantor, and E. Schwartz, *Outside the Courts: A Survey of Diversion Alternatives in Civil Cases* (Denver: National Center for the State Courts, 1977); and R. Shonholtz, *Proposal for Neighborhood Justice Centers* (San Francisco Community Board Program, unpublished manuscript, 1977).

14. John M. Demerest, "State Adoption of Alternative Dispute Resolution," *State Court Journal*, 12, no. 2 (Spring 1988): 14–18.

15. It should be pointed out that some observers feel that plea bargaining is absolutely indispensable to true justice. See Arthur Rosett and Donald R. Cressey, *Justice by Consent* (Philadelphia: Lippincott, 1976).

16. Donald R. Cressey, "Doing Justice," *The Center Magazine* 10 (January–February 1977): 21–28.

17. W. M. Rhodes, *Plea Bargaining: Who Gains? Who Loses?* (Washington, D.C.: Institute for Law and Social Research, 1978).

18. William A. Hamilton, "Highlights of PROMIS Research," in William F. McDonald, ed., *The Prosecutor* (Beverly Hills, Calif.: Sage, 1979), pp. 125–136.

19. William F. McDonald, *Plea Bargaining: Critical Issues and Common Practices* (Washington, D.C.: U.S. Department of Justice, July 1985).

20. Ibid.

21. W. F. Willoughby, "Principles of Judicial Administration, in James M. Burns and Jack W. Peltason, eds., *Government by the People* (Englewood Cliffs, N.J.: Prentice-Hall, 1963), p. 202.

22. National Advisory Commission on Intergovernmental Relations, *State-Local Relations in the Criminal Justice System* (Washington, D.C.: U.S. Government Printing Office, 1971), p. 75.

23. American Bar Association, Section on Criminal Justice, *Grand Jury Committee Principles* (Chicago: ABA, 1981), p. 31.

24. National Institute of Justice, *Grand Jury Reform: A Review of Key Issues* (Washington, D.C.: U.S. Government Printing Office, December 1983), p. 14.

25. Ibid. pp. 15–16.

26. *United States* v. *Proctor and Gamble Co.*, 35 U.S. 677, (1958).

27. *General Accounting Office Report to the Congress: More Guidance and Supervision Needed Over Federal Grand Jury Proceedings* (Washington, D.C.: U.S. Government Printing Office, 1980).

28. For example, see the recommendations in

Committee for Economic Development, *Reducing Crime and Assuring Justice* (New York: CED, June 1972), chap. 3.

29. See Richard Harris, "Annals of Law, Taking the Fifth—Part III," *New Yorker*, 19 April 1976, pp. 42–97.

30. John Eckler, "Lagging Justice," *Annals of the American Academy of Political and Social Science* 328 (March 1960).

31. *Barker* v. *Wingo*, 407 U.S. 514 (1972).

32. For example, see: *Criminal Procedure Law of the State of New York*, Sec. 30.30.

33. 399 U.S. 78, 100 (1970).

34. National Advisory Commission, *State–Local Relations in the Criminal Justice Systems*, p. 101.

35. See Alan E. Glefand, "A Statistical Case for the 12-Member Jury," *Trial* 13 (February 1977): 41–42.

36. See Hans Zeisel, "And Then There Were None: The Diminution of the Federal Jury," *Chicago Law Review* 38 (1971): 710–724.

37. *Hidbon* v. *United States*, 204 F. 2d 834 (6th Cir. 1953).

38. Bureau of Justice Statistics, *Report to the Nation on Crime and Justice*, 2nd ed. (Washington, D.C.: U.S. Department of Justice, March 1988), p. 84.

39. R. Holtzoff, "Modern Trends in Trial by Jury," *Washington and Lee Review* 27 (1959): 27–28.

40. American Bar Association Project on Standards for Criminal Justice, *Standards Relating to Trial by Jury* (New York: Institute of Judicial Administration, 1968), p. 28.

41. Twenty states use commission plans to aid the governor in selecting judges; eleven other states use them only for vacancies.

42. See: Larry C. Berkson, "Judicial Selection in the United States: A Special Report," *Judicature* 64 (October 1980): 176–193.

43. For example, see Glenn R. Winters, "The Merit Plan for Judicial Selection and Tenure: Its Historical Development," in Glenn Winters, ed., *Judicial Selection and Tenure*, pp. 29–44.

44. President's Commission on Law Enforcement and Administration of Justice, *Task Force Report: The Courts* (Washington, D.C.: U.S. Government Printing Office, 1967), p. 66.

45. Glenn R. Winters and Raymond Allard, "Judicial Selection and Tenure in the United States in American Assembly," *The Courts, the Public and the Law Explosion* (Englewood Cliffs, N.J.: Prentice-Hall, 1965), pp. 142–144.

46. Russell R. Wheeler and A. Leo Levin, *Judicial Discipline and Removal in the United States* (Washington, D.C.: Federal Judicial Center, 179), p. 4.

47. Ibid.

48. See H. Jacob, "The Courts as Political Agencies: An Historical Analysis," *Tulane Studies in Political Science* 7 (1962): 19–20.

49. Ibid.

50. Richard S. Buckley, "The Commission on Judicial Qualifications: An Attempt to Deal with Judicial Misconduct," in Glenn Winters, ed., *Selected Readings: Judicial Discipline and Removal* (Chicago: American Judicature Society, 1973), pp. 60–74.

51. Jack E. Frankel, "Judicial Discipline and Removal," *Texas Law Review* 44 (1966): 1117–1131.

52. National Advisory Commission, *State–Local Relations in the Criminal Justice System*, p. 229.

53. Jonathan D. Casper, *American Criminal Justice: The Defendant's Perspective* (Englewood Cliffs, N.J.: Prentice-Hall, 1972), p. 18.

54. Phillip Hager, "Justice Sought for Witnesses, Victims of Crime," *Los Angeles Times*, December 2, 1984.

55. Brian Forst et al., *What Happens After Arrest?* (Washington, D.C.: Institute of Law and Social Research, August 1977); and Vera Institute of Justice, *Processing Felony Cases Through New York City Courts* (New York: Vera Institute of Justice, 1976).

56. Forst, *What Happens After Arrest?*, p. 67.

57. Frank J. Cannavale and William D. Falcon, *Witness Cooperation* (Lexington, Mass.: Heath, 1976), especially chap. 5.

58. These findings are adopted from Elizabeth Connick and Robert C. Davis, "Examining the Problem of Witness Intimidation," *Judicature* 66 (May 1983): 439–477.

59. Ibid., p. 442.

60. Cannavale and Falcon, op. cit., and R. C. Davis, "Role of the Complaining Witness in an Urban Criminal Court," *Report of the Victim Services Agency and the Vera Institute of Justice*, 1980.

61. Connick and Davis, op. cit., p. 443.

62. Ibid., p. 444.

63. Ibid., p. 444.

64. Ibid., p. 444.

65. William M. Bulkeley, "Head Homicide Sleuth in Detroit Is a Man With Endless Work," *Wall Street Journal* (January 16, 1975), p. 80.

66. Cannavale and Falcon, op. cit., p. 28.

67. "Returning to the Loot" *Newsweek*, January 6, 1975, p. 35.

68. As quoted in Frank J. Cannavale, Jr., *Improving Witness Cooperation: Summary Report of the District of Columbia Witness Survey* (Washington, D.C.: National Institute of Law Enforcement and Criminal Justice, August 1976), p. 29.

69. Ibid., p. 29.

70. Paul B. Wice, *Freedom for Sale* (Lexington, Mass.: Heath, 1974), p. 8.

71. District of Columbia Court Reform Act of 1970, Public Law 91–358, sec. 23–1321.

72. 18 U.S.C. 3142(f).

73. 18 U.S.C. 3142(e).

74. 18 U.S.C. 3142(i).

75. See: 18 U.S.C. 3146–3148.

76. *United States* v. *Salerno*, 103 U.S. 421, (1987).

77. Wice, *Freedom for Sale*, p. 99.

78. Ibid., p. 97.

79. Joseph D. Tydings, "The Courts and Congress," *Public Administration Review* 31 (March–April 1971): 116–117.

80. See National Advisory Commission, *State Local Relations in the Criminal Justice System*, chap. 9.

# CORRECTIONS

# CHAPTER 11

# Corrections: Historical Perspective

## O B J E C T I V E S

**After reading this chapter, the student should be able to:**

Understand the broad concept of "corrections."

Discuss the historical purposes of correction and identify each social response.

Identify major British reforms and reformers of penology.

Discuss the features of the Pennsylvania system.

Discuss the Auburn plan.

Identify important milestones in America's correctional efforts.

Discuss the importance of the reformatory movement.

Discuss the development and operations of the U.S. Bureau of Prisons.

## I M P O R T A N T   T E R M S

The Period of Enlightenment
Punishment
Deterrence
Isolation
Rehabilitation
Reintegration
Quakers

Pennsylvania system
Walnut Street Jail
Solitary existence
Auburn Plan
John Howard
Robert Peel
Alexander Maconochie

Walter Crofton
Tickets of leave
Benjamin Rush
Open-congregate system
Congregate inmate labor
National Prison Association
Elmira Reformatory
Industrial prison model
U.S. Bureau of Prisons

Today, imprisonment and corrections are practically synonymous. Yet the evolution of imprisonment as a form of modern correctional effort mirrors many things. Mostly, it reflects the changing attitudes of a more enlightened society. A vestige of this enlightenment arose in the question How is the legal system to deal with a person who violates the criminal law? It must be initially recognized, however, that changes in the law necessarily preceded changes in the law's correctional effort. In a historical sweep, it was the criminal law that itself became the first target of reform. Closely associated with the reform of the criminal law was the question of the appropriate punishment for specific crimes. It was only when these two questions had been dealt with that consideration was given to the use of the penitentiary and long-term incarceration as an appropriate sanction—one more suited to the new purpose of the criminal law and the search for a more appropriate form of punishment. In the final analysis, although murder, robbery, rape, and theft have always been forms of punishable conduct, we have at least, over the centuries, changed the way we punish those who commit such acts.

To see this interrelationship, we need to roll back the clock several centuries. To understand the use of imprisonment and the modern penitentiary as our major form of "correctional" effort, we need to know how this came about. Realize initially that prisons are relatively recent in origin. In fact, it wasn't until the nineteenth century that imprisonment became widely adopted. When this occurred, it was the culmination of many years of dissatisfaction with both the criminal law and how it was administered. It also reflects the efforts at reform that accompanied this dissatisfaction. In England and throughout Western Europe, the criminal law and the punishment it imposed was, by today's standards, harsh and unforgiving. Not only were acts such as disrespect to one's parents, blasphemy, witchcraft, fornication, and adultery serious offenses, but the punishments that could be imposed for these and other crimes were exceedingly harsh. Parental disrespect and adultery, for example, were both capital offenses under the English criminal code of the seventeenth century. And these attitudes and their expressions found root in the American colonies.

A typical account of the day tells of one poor miscreant named Burton, who had been found guilty in 1647 of the crime of libel. He was sentenced to the pillory, where his punishment was to be carried out:

> When the executioner had cut off one ear which he had cut deep and close to the head in an extraordinarily cruel manner, [Burton] never once moved and stirred for it. The other ear being cut no less deep, he was freed from the pillory and came down, where the surgeon waiting for him presently applied a remedy for stopping the blood after the large effusion thereof.[1]

The harshness of the criminal code and the offenses that were punishable were just part of the problem. The law was also arbitrary in its application. Judges of the day, for example, had wide-ranging discretion in the punishment they could impose. Punishment and "corrections" also consisted of another characteristic we would find peculiar today: It was purposely designed and expressed as open punishment in an era of punishment-as-spectacle. Not only did punishment largely consist of such methods of punishment as execution, torture, whipping, maiming, disfigurement, and the use of the pillory and stocks—it was publicly imposed punishment. Punishments were carried out in a carnival-like atmosphere as the crowd joined in the festivities associated with the public spectacle it provided. Historians contend that the harshness of the punishment and the public nature of the way it

Until the present century, hangings and other forms of criminal punishment were public events with many spectators. (Culver Pictures)

was imposed were no mere accident. They were the result of three factors: the spectacle of punishment re-affirmed the propriety of lawful behavior; they provided an outlet for society's sense of opprobrium and need for retribution; and they were a visible public symbol of the power and majesty of the state or monarch—a symbol that needed to be reinforced and nurtured from time-to-time.[2]

So the criminal law and its "correctional" efforts of the time were characterized by four general circumstances: It was extremely harsh; it was arbitrary and capricious in its application; the law provided in many instances for measures of corporal cruelty; and it was publicly administered.[3] In time of course, this would change—but change would come slowly and tentatively. It would come only because of the broad currents of social and political dissent that were sweeping Europe by the mid–eighteenth century. Social dissent would focus on, among other things, the existing system and methods of criminal jurisprudence. Of course, it was inevitable that these swirling eddies would also touch upon America's shore. And these changes would affect America more than any nation and would have an important influence on the young country.

Most historians of penology and the law describe the so-called Period of Enlightenment in the eighteenth century as the important point of departure for reform efforts. During this time notable thinkers, scholars, and intellectuals challenged traditional assumptions about government, society, and the individual. It was a period of rationalism: the notion that reason and not emotion should govern society's response to crime and the treatment of the criminal. It was a logical step by such thinkers as the English philosopher John Locke and such notable French political and social philosophers as Rousseau, Montesquieu, the satirist and humanist Voltaire, and Diderot the essayist. Together they called for a fundamental

The Period of Enlightenment

reevaluation of the nature of the state, the rights of the individual, and the system of equality before the law—the very antithesis of the privileges and the privileged that had so long governed Europe and found expression in its criminal laws.

If these noted personages established the philosophical framework for social change, four thinkers, in particular, contributed to the reform of corrections. The first of these was Cesare Beccaria (1738–1794). His influential essay *On Crimes and Punishment* raised important philosophical questions about the purpose of the criminal law and punishment. Jeremy Bentham (1748–1832) argued that punishment was only justified in proportion to the crime committed. Sir Samuel Romilly (1757–1818), a noted English lawyer and legal reformer, campaigned for the abolition of the harsh capital statutes contained in the Elizabethan Code, which called for the imposition of death for over two hundred different crimes. John Howard (1726–1790), as the sheriff of Bedfordshire, England, wrote *The State of the Prisons in England and Wales*, which called attention to deep-seated problems and offered suggestions for improvement.

The stage was then set. Swirling currents of social, philosophical, and political change had occurred. America had established its independence from England, and in 1789 France had overthrown the *ancien régime* and ushered in the French Revolution. The age of industrialization was dawning; the age of colonization was already beginning to wither. Profound social changes were afoot. The western world was ready for change. Table 11.1 shows the general transformation of punishment, social relationships, and sanctions throughout Western history.

TABLE **11-1.** Historical Development of Law and Punishment

| Period | 500,000–2000,000 B.C.: Appearance of genus homo | 200,000–25,000 B.C.: Appearance of early modern man | 25,000–3500 B.C.: Development of rudimentary religion | 3500–400 B.C.: Development of first criminal codes | 400 B.C.–500 A.D.: Development of Roman law | 500–1750: Medieval and feudal justice | 1750 to present |
|---|---|---|---|---|---|---|---|
| **Nature of Social Relationship** | Pretribal | Incipient group and tribal | Intermediate group and tribal | Intermediate group and tribal | Advanced group and tribal; incipient state | Feudal and intermediate organized state | Advanced organized state |
| **Sanctions** | ? | Incipient customs and mores | Intermediate customs and mores | Customs and mores; incipient laws | Customs and rudimentary laws | Customs and common law | Statutory laws |
| **Form of Punishment** | Personal retribution | Personal retribution; group and tribal retribution | Personal retribution; group and tribal retribution | Personal retribution; group and tribal retribution; state retribution | State retribution; group and tribal retribution; personal retribution | State and ecclesiastical retribution | State retribution, reformation, rehabilitation and reintegration |
| | | Injury, torture, death | | Torture, injury, death, banishment, forfeiture | | Torture, forfeiture, injury, death, excommunication, banishment | Fine, supervision, incarceration, death |

##  SOCIETY AND CORRECTIONS

It must be recognized that, as in all aspects of the administration of justice, corrections and the instrumentalities of corrections—our nation's correctional systems—do not exist apart from the influence of society. It is society that ultimately Society and consensus determines how the correctional process is to be defined. In other words, What forms of of "correction" are appropriate, and under what circumstances are these appropriate? In the increasingly heterogeneous and pluralistic society the United States is becoming, the task is growing increasingly difficult. Consensus is becoming ever more elusive. In the first instance, strong disagreement exists among segments of our society as to the overall seriousness of many forms of criminal conduct. Although we can agree on the "wrongfulness" of certain crimes, others pose more serious problems for agreement. If we can't agree on the seriousness of certain crimes, we certainly can't agree on appropriate ways to deal with those who commit these acts we try to define as criminal.

The problem, it would seem, is far less pronounced for those societies that are more homogeneous in their heritage and culture. One of the most obvious manifestations is the issue of capital punishment. Unlike for some other offenses, we can all agree that criminal homicide is wrong. Yet Americans cannot begin to resolve their deep and divisive disagreement over what should be done with those who commit such crimes. And this disagreement seems to be increasingly patterned along racial, economic, gender, and even geographical lines. For example, public opinion polls show that disagreement over capital punishment can be broadly broken down along any number of dimensions: whites versus blacks, men versus women, and citizens living in the East versus Westerners.[4]

## PURPOSES OF CORRECTIONS

Throughout history corrections has served such purposes as punishment, deterrence, isolation and incapacitation of the criminal, rehabilitation, and reintegration.

### Punishment

Over the centuries, corrections and punishment have been synonymous. This attitude was well expressed by an early nineteenth-century advocate of the value of punishment, the Reverend Sydney Smith, who said that a prison should be "a place The oldest purpose of punishment from which men recoil with horror—a place of real suffering painful to the memory, terrible to the imagination . . . a place of sorrow and wailing, which should be entered with horror and quitted with earnest resolution never to return to such misery. . . ."[5] Even today, this attitude is held by a sizable segment of the American public, particularly in cases that involve serious crimes. Although basic attitudes toward punishment have not changed significantly, at least the means of exacting the punishment have. Today, through more "humane" techniques, society acts as the agent of punishment on behalf of the victim rather than permitting the private settling of feuds. In some views, punishment has been defended as permitting the offender the feeling of having atoned for his or her antisocial actions while reaffirming the appropriateness of noncriminal behavior among the law-abiding members of society.

## Deterrence

Next in importance as a meaningful principle of corrections is deterrence—the concept that punishing the criminal will reduce the incidence of criminal behavior in a society. The concept of deterrence as an aspect of punishment received serious attention during the Enlightenment. In fact, it might be said that those who sought to reform the criminal law of the time and its imposition paid primary attention to deterrence as the appropriate goal of the law and punishment. Rather than the harsh penalties that could be imposed, the primary purpose of the law and punishment (or corrective effort) was to deter. Crimes should be examined as to their severity and different penalties attached. These penalties should only be such that they served as a deterrent. In this way, deterrence remains a cornerstone of our corrective efforts.

General and special deterrence

Criminologists usually discuss deterrence in terms of two major applications. The first of these is the concept of *general deterrence*. This can be thought of as the power of the criminal law and the agencies of criminal justice to deter potential offenders from committing crimes. In this way the criminal law and the agencies of justice are perceived as having the power to impose sanctions and punishment on those who violate our laws. The threat of arrest, conviction, and imprisonment then prevents us from committing a crime, which in the absence of these sanctions we might otherwise commit.

The second type is called *special deterrence*. Unlike general deterence, which acts before the fact to prevent the commission of crime, special deterrence is an after-the-fact form of prevention. This form of deterrence theoretically is designed to prevent further crimes by someone who has already experienced the sanctions imposed by the criminal law through the mechanisms of the courts and imprisonment. Thus, some convicted criminals, having failed the test of general deterrence, can yet be persuaded to avoid future crimes by experiencing some form of punishment.

## Isolation/Incapacitation

Removal and protection of society

The idea of incapacitation rests on the idea that convicted criminals should be rendered physically unable to continue their criminal acts—whether this is accomplished by imprisonment and thereby the removal of the individual from society or by the imposition of the death penalty in capital cases. The principle of isolation was the major impetus behind the exile and transportation method of dealing with the offender. Even after the curtailment of exile and transportation, this purpose of corrections remained and was expressed in the fortress-like structure and security precautions characteristic of many early prisons. Although isolation has been increasingly deemphasized in recent years as an appropriate response for the majority of convicted offenders, it still exists.

The reluctance of some communities to the building of a prison or correctional institution or to the housing of offenders in a community-based program are modern examples of society's desire to isolate convicted criminals—i.e., to remove them from the population at large. While isolation may be growing less popular in theory, incapacitation seems to be enjoying a resurgence of popularity. The increased emphasis on the use of prisons and lengthened periods of incarceration for offenders is an example of the ideal of incapacitation.

## Rehabilitation

Yet another philosophical goal of corrections that has received major emphasis is rehabilitation. This goal links criminal behavior with abnormality or some form of deficiency in the criminal. It assumes that human behavior is the product of antecedent causes and that to deal effectively with any deviant behavior, these various causes must be identified—be they physical, moral, mental, social, vocational, or academic. Once the offender's problems are diagnosed and classified for treatment, the offender can be corrected by the right psychological therapy, counseling, education, or vocational training. Unfortunately, it is now being recognized that regardless of how laudable it may sound and how it appeals to our more humane instincts, the goal of rehabilitation suffers from a number of weaknesses that make it very elusive.

First, in many cases, it is impossible to identify these antecedent conditions and how they interact in causing criminal behavior. For example, how can it be said with any assurance that poverty and the lack of education are the causes for criminal behavior when there are many wealthy, well-educated people who commit crimes? Furthermore, the vast majority of poor people with little formal education are not criminals. How, then, can treatment programs be measured in any meaningful way in determining their effectiveness in correcting a problem? Second, the rehabilitative philosophy assumes the characteristic of a medical model, implying the offender is somehow "sick" because he or she cannot adjust to society. This is fallacious reasoning. Offenders may well be aware of their actions and completely rational in deciding that their involvement in crime has a higher personal payoff than legitimate behavior. The rehabilitative model also assumes that the one being treated must accept or learn to accept the values of those conducting the treatment even though their backgrounds, perceptions, and attitudes may be completely different. This is a particularly questionable assumption in prisons today, where increasingly larger percentages of inmates are expressing open hostility to the assumptions of the rehabilitative model. Career criminals, for example, are disdainful of any efforts to "rehabilitate" them. Other inmates who are usually racial minorities and members of militant sects sometimes see themselves as defacto political prisoners of a social system of laws and justice that is purposely designed to ensure that any threats to the established political, social, and economic order are dealt with through the administration of justice. Still other prisoners simply view themselves as victims of society's capricious system of laws and justice, which operates under a dual standard for the poor and well-to-do.[6] In these instances, rehabilitative efforts and rehabilitative personnel are seen as an extension of a social system and a set of values they find unacceptable. "Rehabilitation" under such circumstances is perceived as nothing more than an attempt to brainwash them into some form of compliance.[7]

Many critics of this model also claim that the rehabilitative ideal, which is supposedly therapeutic in nature, takes on a punitive harshness in application. They point to the rehabilitative ideals that underlie the founding of the juvenile courts and sexual psychopath laws as examples of rehabilitative ideals gone awry.[8] The report on the experiences of New York State's famous Attica prison riot pointed out that rehabilitation and reform are often no more than a facade. In the words of the official commission's report:

> Prison administrators throughout the country have continued pledging their dedication to the concept of rehabilitation while continuing to run prisons constructed in

*The medical model*

the style and operated in the manner of the 19th century walled fortresses. "Security" has continued to be the dominant theme: The fantasy of reform legitimized, but the functionalism of custody has perpetuated them.[9]

## Reintegration

The interlocking role of society (environment) and the offender

The newest philosophical basis for corrections is reintegration of the offender into the free community. This model is a more practical and realistic extension of the rehabilitative philosophy and tries to compensate for the weaknesses of that approach while adopting some more acceptable ideas. It sees the cause of crime and the functions of corrective efforts along two dimensions. Like the rehabilitative model, it views the offender as needing help—but at the same time it recognizes that criminal behavior is often a result of disjunction between the offender and society. It is this characteristic that separates it from the rehabilitative model. In the rehabilitation model, emphasis is focused on treating the offender as an isolated entity and looking for the cause of behavior as emanating from within the individual. The reintegrative model realizes that society and the individual are inseparable, and therefore the offender's environment is also emphasized. If offenders are to be helped, then they must be assisted in coping with the forces of the everyday environment to which they will return upon release from prison. This environment is a very different world from the highly controlled and artificial world of the penitentiary or similar institution.

In reintegration, contact and interaction with positive elements of the free society are an important part of the overall inmate assistance program. This appears to be the direction that corrections has been moving in the past few years and probably will continue to emphasize in the future.

## ▣ EARLY BRITISH REFORMERS AND REFORMS

The history of English penology is not a very enlightened one. Although by the late eighteenth century, the English were the acknowledged and unrivaled world leaders in such areas as colonialism, commerce, and maritime trade, they did little to advance penology. As a nation, they demonstrated surprisingly little in the way of leadership when it came to devising more enlightened ways to deal with crime and criminals. This role would pass to America. Yet, certain personalities and reform efforts made a lasting impression on America's own efforts at penal reform. While the political and social theorists and philosophers of the eighteenth century provided the framework for reform, certain Englishmen would provide the practical working model that became so useful to America's own reform efforts.

We saw that, like the colonies, England relied primarily on torture, branding, mutilation, and hanging as a means to deal with criminals. Events were occurring, however, that would bring changes. As Britain's colonial empire began to develop, so did the need to provide labor for settlement efforts. This was particularly true in the New World. The courts of England, under special laws passed by Parliament,

Transportation

issued orders of transport, which sent convicted offenders to the New World colonies, where they worked as penal labor. After losing the American colonies in the Revolution, Britain was forced to discontinue transportation. The immediate problem then became one of dealing with criminals found guilty by the courts. Because

One of the more extreme solutions ever tried for dealing with offenders was the transportation of English prisoners from overcrowded jails to the unsettled territory of Australia. (National Library of Australia, Rex Nan Kivell Collection)

transportation to America was no longer an option, there was increasing discussion by the government as to what should be done. Although some in parliament favored the building of prisons to house offenders, there was strong opposition to the cost of such a proposal.

A solution was found by using the old hulks that were moored on the Thames River as prisons. Later Gibraltar, off the coast of Spain, would become another major **Prison hulks** site for prison hulks. This expedient proved unsatisfactory. The squalid hulks became infested and disease ridden. Although the government and the English people weren't particularly concerned about the conditions aboard these prison hulks, they were concerned that the contagion might spread to the nonconvict populace. Parliament was again forced to consider the possibility of having to appropriate public funds to build prisons. As conditions aboard the hulks grew increasingly worse, and Londoners grew more insistent that something be done, Parliament gave in. A sharply divided House of Commons agreed in 1779 to build two permanent, long-term penitentiaries. Fortune, however, smiled on Parliament. In the end, the prisons didn't have to be built. With the discovery by Captain Cook of the vast land area of Australia, transportation was given another reprieve. Now the ships carrying supplies and settlers to Australia could carry another cargo—those sentenced to penal labor and servitude.

Mark Twain was fond of saying about history, "while it doesn't repeat itself, it rhymes." This seems to express the feelings of New York correctional officials today. In the eighteenth century, England used hulks moored on the Thames River as a place to house that country's increase in convicts. Now, two hundred years later, the State of New York is adopting the same strategy.

Although New York has no intention of turning its prisons into the notorious Thames River hulks, it has purchased at auction a large barge, which will be used to accommodate a seven-hundred-bed minimum security facility. It is planned that the barge will berth somewhere on the Hudson or East River to accommodate the state's dire need for more prison beds.

The so-called Floating Accommodation Barge stands five stories tall, is as long as a football field, and is 120 feet wide. It has been described as a "floating city," because it is virtually self-contained with its own sewerage system, salt/fresh water conversion ability, mess halls, kitchens, and recreation areas.

The barge was purchased by the state at auction from a British firm that built and then leased the barge and two others like it to the British Ministry of Defense. It was used to house Royal Marines during the Falklands War with Argentina. When permanent barracks were completed in the Falkland Islands, the Ministry of defense decided it no longer needed the barge. New York saw this as an opportunity to help relieve its prison overcrowding and bought it.

Earlier in this chapter, John Howard was mentioned as a major reformer—as indeed he was. His influential and famous *State of Prisons* was published in 1777. It was the climax of his firsthand experiences as an English jailor and of the terrible abuses of prisoners he had seen throughout England. Howard also traveled extensively across Europe, inspecting prisons and jails and learning from these observations and experiences. He not only documented the terrible conditions he found, he called for fundamental reform. He became the leading spokesman and prison and jail reform advocate in England. Howard realized that England would have to provide long-term imprisonment sooner or later. To this end, he proposed a number of "correct principles" for handling prisoners. Some of these principles were as follows:

1. Female offenders should be segregated from males and young offenders from old and hardened criminals.
2. Jailers should be honest, active, and humane . . . and should have salaries proportioned to the trust and trouble.
3. No prisoner should be subject to any demand for fees. The jailer should have a salary in lieu of having to rely on fees.
4. There should be provisions for an infirmary, a chaplain, and a proper diet of wholesome food.
5. Separate cells for each prisoner should be provided as well as linen and bedding and stoves to warm the day-room in winter.[10]

**Sir Robert Peel**

A second notable penal reformer was Sir Robert Peel. In 1821, Peel was appointed as home secretary and immediately set about reforming the criminal code and applying Howard's principles to local prisons. Through his efforts, capital offenses were reduced from two hundred to fourteen. He pushed through Parliament a law requiring prison facilities to meet certain minimum requirements for proper health and sanitation facilities.

**Maconochie and Norfolk Island**

Alexander Maconochie was the third reform figure. In his capacity as commander of the Norfolk Island Prison Colony off the coast of Australia, he learned that any prison system which debases prisoners could never expect to reform them. Thus, he developed an administrative system in the Colony with the following provisions:

1. Sentences should not be for a period of time, but for the performance of a specified and determined quantity of labor; in brief, time sentences should be abolished and task sentences substituted;
2. The quantity of labor a prisoner must perform should be expressed in a number of "marks," which he must earn by improvement of conduct, frugality of living, and habits of industry before he can be released;
3. While in prison, he should earn everything he receives; all sustenance and indulgences should be added to his debt of marks;
4. When qualified by discipline to do so, he should work in association with a small number of other prisoners, forming a group of six or seven, and the whole group should be answerable for the conduct and labor of each member of it;
5. In the final stage, a prisoner while still obligated to earn his daily tally of marks, should be financially compensated for his labor and be subject to a less rigorous discipline in order to prepare him for his release and return to society.[11]

Maconochie also abolished flogging and use of chains as disciplinary measures except in extreme cases. And he instituted the first form of inmate participation in running a penal colony.

Unfortunately, Maconochie's ideas were too revolutionary for his staff and the Board of Overseers to whom he reported. The guards particularly resented his curtailment of their use of corporal punishment on prisoners. In 1844 he was relieved of command under the charge that discipline had disappeared without any improvements in the moral character of the prisoners. The real reason was that his system had increased operational expenses.[12]

The last notable reformer was Sir Walter Crofton and his so-called Irish system. Like England, Ireland's prisons were not reforming prisoners. In 1854, Crofton was appointed chairman of the board of directors of the Irish prisons. He became convinced that reform did not come through corporal punishment and prisoners had to be treated as humans and not as convicts.

**Crofton and the Irish system**

When England passed legislation permitting the use of tickets of leave (see next section), Crofton developed a classification program that would be tied to the eventual rewarding of the prisoners with earned tickets of leave. When the prisoner entered prison he was placed under close discipline and supervision for four months. After this period of time, he was transferred to the second stage. In this stage he could work in his trades or in the maintenance of the prison. The inmates in this stage were given elementary schooling if they wanted it.

If the prisoner warranted consideration, he was transferred after eight months to another prison where he labored on military and penal fortifications in the area. The prisoner earned marks for satisfactory behavior, and each step required the accumulation of a certain number of marks. In addition, small wages were paid according to the conduct class the inmate was in.

Crofton employed a moral instructor who counseled the prisoners in the advantages of leading a law-abiding life, maintaining regular employment, and avoiding evil companions.[13] The moral instructor also worked with the inmates to obtain their tickets of leave and in seeking employment for those who were released.

He even continued to visit the released offender and supervise his conduct after he returned to free society.[14]

### Tickets of Leave

Forerunner of parole

In 1857, Parliament passed an act that ended the transportation of offenders. Now a way had to be found to handle offenders who in the past were shipped off to a penal colony and forgotten. Because Parliament still did not want to spend money to build prisons to house offenders for long periods of time, it passed legislation authorizing tickets of leave. Under this system, prisoners who had served a year of congregate labor could earn, by hard work and good conduct, a conditional release and thus be permitted to return to their homes before the completion of their sentences. Their freedom was on two conditions: They had to abstain from crime and be legitimately employed.

 ## CORRECTIONS IN COLONIAL AMERICA

Most of America's young colonies were a mixture of existing English law and practices mingled with a strong theocracy and religious fervor. In this way the early colonists often adapted the English Common law traditions to their own peculiar beliefs. In the Massachusetts colony, the Puritan tradition called for corporal punishment, banishment, the pillory, and death for crimes patterned after similar laws and punishments existing in England. To this they added a new wrinkle: Severe punishments were imposed for nonsecular (religous) crimes or immoral acts.

New England Calvinism

Throughout New England, the doctrine of Calvinism held sway. The Puritans of the region, as disciples of Calvin, subscribed to the Calvinist doctrine of predestination. Since men were pre-ordained to their particular fates, there was nothing that could be gained by trying to reform them in this world. The inherent imperfectibility of man was beyond human control. Retribution and punishment were warranted where reformation or rehabilitation was an impossibility.[15]

Pennsylvania and the Quaker

In Pennsylvania different ideas took root. Here, the Quakers rejected the harsh English law and substituted "The Great Law," which was based on a more humanitarian view of the law and punishment. In addition to the use of an extensive system of fines for crimes, all capital crimes except premeditated murder were abolished. In place of the death penalty and forms of mutilation and torture, hard labor in a house of correction was emphasized. Atonement and redemption became the order of the day. In accomplishing the writing of their new law, the Quakers went too far. This aroused the anger of the King of England, who saw this as an attempt to challenge the sovereignty of the mother country over the colony. The Quaker code was eventually abolished by the king, and the Anglican Code was restored. The Pennsylvania colony was forced to accept it. Capital punishment was reinstituted for felony crimes, and the Quakers became a force of opposition to the edicts of the crown and the existing English criminal law. One result of this was the increasing reluctance by the colony's courts and juries to find defendants guilty. This persisted until the colony was finally able to throw off the yoke of England after the Revolutionary War.

There were some initial efforts to develop correctional alternatives. Interestingly, in spite of the Puritan influence in Massachusetts, this colony was one of the first to experiment with a facility to house offenders for an extended period of incarceration. In 1632, Boston became the sight of a small wooden building that could be considered the first—or at least one of the first—prison-like institutions in the colonies. For six years it served as the only such institution in the Massachusetts Bay Colony. Several years later, another small facility was constructed in New Plymouth. In 1655 the general court of the Massachusetts Bay Colony issued a statement calling for the need to establish institutions in each county to house petty offenders, drunkards, and debtors. In this way, it recommended the forerunner of our county jails. Although it would be many years before such a system of facilities became a reality, it was a harbinger of the future.[16] Successive years also saw the development of small institutions in Connecticut and New York.

The years of the eighteenth century leading to the Revolutionary War were quiet ones for correctional innovation in America. It was a period, however, when less bloody forms of punishment came into more frequent use. Extensive use of fines, banishment from the community, and service in the pillory or stocks became a more frequent occurrence. Nonetheless, the historical record indicates that the law was still harshly imposed in many circumstances. There are records, for example, that indicate that the New York Supreme Court regularly sentenced more than 20 percent of convicted offenders who came before it to death. This included those convicted of murder, robbery, counterfeiting, and horsestealing as well as the lesser offenses of burglary, grand theft, and pickpocketing.[17]

## THE POSTREVOLUTIONARY PERIOD: AMERICA ASSUMES CORRECTIONAL LEADERSHIP

### The Pennsylvania System

America now stood free of English domination. As such, the new states were free to develop their own laws and methods for dealing with crime and criminals. The Quakers of Pennsylvania turned their attention to methods of prison reform. In 1787, a group of Quakers formed the Pennsylvania Society for Alleviating the Miseries of Public Prisons and set about immediately to redress the shocking conditions found in Philadelphia's Walnut Street Jail. The Society under the leadership of   Walnut Street Jail
Benjamin Rush consisted of many of the leading citizens of the city. This interest group sought legislative approval for transforming the Walnut Street Jail into a prison. Approval for the conversion was granted, and the Walnut Street Jail is recognized by penal historians as the first true prison in America.

The members of the Philadelphia Society were committed to the following ideas: First, prison should be controlled by a group of citizens who would serve voluntarily as members of an unpaid board of inspectors. This was viewed as a way in which more efficient, less costly, and more humane treatment could be given the prisoners. Second, public labor by prisoners would be abolished, and "more   Solitary isolation
private or even solitary labor" would be substituted.[18] Third, reformation would occur through an individual offender's being subject to solitude, where he or she could "reflect" on his past offenses and atone for his actions.

**PHYSICAL SETUP OF THE PRISON.**   The Pennsylvania legislature passed a law authorizing all county courts, at their discretion, to send to the Walnut Street

**BENJAMIN RUSH**

Benjamin Rush (1745–1813), American physician and signer of the Declaration of Independence, was born in Byberry, Pennsylvania, and educated at the College of New Jersey (now Princeton University) and at the University of Edinburgh. In 1769 he was appointed professor of chemistry at the College of Philadelphia. He served as a member of the Continental Congress (1776–77) and the following year became surgeon general of the Continental Army.

Rush was a noted humanitarian. He is known as the father of American psychiatry in recognition for his efforts to establish humane treatment for the mentally ill. He was also interested in the treatment of prisoners. His interest in methods then being used to punish criminals led him to protest laws assigning such punishments as whippings, the stock, shaved heads, and other public displays. In *An Inquiry into the Effects of Public Punishment Upon Criminals* (1787), he maintained that such excesses served only to harden criminals. Opposed to capital punishment, he wrote *On Punishing Murder by Death* (1792), condemning the practice as an offspring of monarchical divine right, a principle contrary to a republican form of government. He is probably best known for advocating the penitentiary as a replacement for capital and corporal punishment and for his efforts to encourage the development of the penitentiary.

Jail convicts sentenced to hard labor for terms of more than one year.[19] For the more hardened offenders, there were sixteen solitary cells in a specially constructed "penitentiary house" adjacent to the Walnut Street Jail. These cells each measured six feet wide, eight feet long, and nine feet high. In addition, six similar cells were constructed on the ground floor of one of the workshops where convicts could labor in total solitude.

Offenders convicted of more serious crimes were confined to the solitary cells. These prisoners were not permitted to have visitors or any contact with the outside world except for an occasional visit by a clergyman. They performed no labor and they were to spend their solitary existence contemplating their sins and atoning for their crimes. Each of the cells had double doors and a small hatch that covered the single tiny window, which was locked from the outside. In this way, the convict was exposed to almost total darkness even during the day. The prisoner was fed a daily diet of maize and molasses. For a primitive toilet, a large uncovered leaden pipe in the floor of each cell led to an outside sewer in the prison courtyard. The only heat was provided by a totally inadequate, small stove in the common corridor of the cell block.

Offenders who were considered more tractable or who had been sentenced for less serious crimes lived together in eight rooms where they worked together at carpentry, shoemaking, weaving, and nail making. The unskilled prisoners were given more menial tasks to perform. The few women sent to the Walnut Street Jail lived together in other quarters and were employed spinning cotton, carding wool, preparing flax and hemp, washing, and mending. Unlike the male prisoners, the women were permitted to engage in conversation in the shops and during meals. The men were forced to work in total silence, but some conversation was permitted prior to retiring at night. Each of the male prisoners was credited with roughly the prevailing wage for the particular work he performed. Out of this was deducted the cost of his maintenance, his trial, and his fine. If he still owed money for his maintenance when his sentence expired, he was held in confinement until the debt was fully paid. If, on the other hand, he was owed money for his labors, he was given it in full. During the period of confinement, special emphasis was placed on the value of religious services and the development of Christian ideals.[20]

Under such leadership and organization, the Walnut Street Jail became, in the words of its founders, "the happy reformation of the penal system. The prison is no longer a scene of debauchery, idleness and profanity; an epitome of human wretchedness; a seminary of crimes destructive to society; but a school of reformation and a place of public labor."[21] However, this success was short-lived. Increasingly, larger numbers of more serious offenders were sent to the Walnut Street Jail for longer sentences, and it soon was so crowded that it became a mere warehouse of humanity. The original unpaid supervisory board of citizen-inspectors was supplanted by Philadelphia politicians, who took over the operation and management of the institution. As a result, after 1800 the Philadelphia Society became a force of opposition and campaigned bitterly for the reenactment of its form of penal system.

**THE PRINCIPLES OF THE SYSTEM.** The principles governing the Pennsylvania system advocated by the Quakers were well expressed by Robert Vaux in his *Letter on the Penitentiary System of Pennsylvania* in 1827:

1. Prisoners should not be treated with revenge; but rather in a manner to convince them that the way of the transgressor is hard, and by selective forms of suffering they can be made to amend their lives.
2. To prevent the experience of imprisonment becoming a corrupting experience, prisoners should be kept in solitary confinement.
3. Solitary confinement and the seclusion it affords will give the offender the opportunity for deep reflection and moral guidelines so that he may repent for his transgressions.
4. Solitary confinement offers the same variety of discipline as any other mode affords. It is particularly punishing to man, who by his very nature is a social animal.
5. Solitary confinement is more economical since prisoners will: (a) not have to be sentenced for such long periods of time for the required penitential experience, (b) fewer keepers will be required, (c) expenditures for clothing will be diminished.[22]

Based on the principles of the Pennsylvania system, in 1818 the Commonwealth of Pennsylvania began construction of the Western Penitentiary at Pittsburgh. One hundred ninety solitary cells, measuring seven by nine feet each, were constructed in a semicircle around the central prison yard. However, this arrangement quickly proved unworkable. Solitary isolation was not provided, and the cells were too small to permit solitary labor. As a result, by 1833 the board of managers recommended the demolition of the prison because it was unsuitable for the purposes for which it was originally designed.[23]

**NEW YORK'S AUBURN PLAN.** The efforts of the Philadelphia Society and the transformation of the Walnut Street Jail into a prison was noticed by other states. Thomas Eddy, himself a New York Quaker, sought to duplicate the reformative efforts of the Walnut Street Jail. Although subscribing to the general ideals of the Philadelphia Society, he envisioned a prison with a different form of organization.

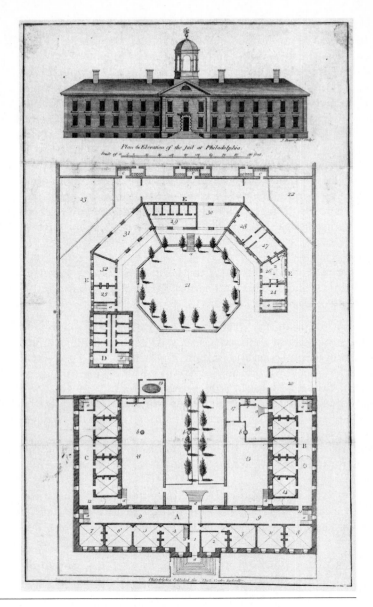

The Walnut Street Jail and the Auburn System attempted to reform inmates through the enforced contemplation inherent in solitary confinement. (Historical Society of Pennsylvania)

**The congregate system**

Under Eddy's guidance, Newgate Prison opened near New York City in 1797, and he became the first warden. Newgate consisted of fifty-four rooms and was constructed as a *congregate prison*—that is, convicts were lodged together in large rooms with eight prisoners to a room. The inmates were employed in a rather extensive system of prison industries, and as in the early days of the Walnut Street Jail, the prisoners were paid the prevailing wage for their work, less the cost of their maintenance and trial. Immediate problems arose with the system of congregate lodging, and politicians began to meddle in the operation of the institution and eventually took over the management and control of the prison itself. In a short time, overcrowding aggravated moral contamination and created disorder. Mass pardons favored nonobedient prisoners over penitent and reformed criminals, and as a result, Eddy resigned in 1803.[24]

This "failure" of the Newgate Prison led to what has been called the Auburn plan of prison program and design. It was recognized that there was a certain value to permitting prisoners to work together at congregate labor as Newgate had done and which the Pennsylvania system, with its emphasis on solitary confinement, did not effectively provide. However, the experiences at Newgate also indicate the disadvantages of congregate work and housing facilities in terms of the potential for disorder. Somehow, the best features of both Newgate and the Pennsylvania system would have to be incorporated.

In 1816, New York began the construction of a new prison at Auburn. In 1819, the prison opened with a master carpenter as the warden and a hatter as his assistant. Originally, the prison was to have been constructed after the model provided by the Pennsylvania system, with its emphasis on solitary confinement. However, it was felt that the cost of constructing separate solitary cells would be prohibitive, and so only a few such cells were built to meet the requirements of the law as to solitary confinement and to provide a solitary cellblock for disciplinary cases. As a result, most of the prisoners were housed in large, congregate night rooms.

**PHYSICAL SETUP OF THE PRISON.** In the first few years of operation, an experiment was conducted in which a classification or grading system was devised. The most incorrigible offenders were placed in solitary cells without labor in order to test the relative merits of the Pennsylvania system over the congregate system in terms of reformative effects. In the second category, less recalcitrant prisoners were also placed in solitary confinement with labor being provided as a form of recreation and reward. In the third category were the most tractable offenders and those who appeared to have the best chance of reforming. In this grade, the prisoners worked together as a group during the day and were secluded at night.[25] The experiment was abandoned in 1823 as a failure. Particularly obvious was the terrible impact of idleness and solitary confinement on the minds of inmates. Many of those confined to solitary went insane and horribly mutilated themselves or committed suicide. In addition, solitary confinement without labor had deleterious effects on the inmates' physical health, and most of them were severly impaired for life. As a result, the governor in 1823 pardoned most of the inmates who had been confined to solitary cells.

**THE PRINCIPLES OF THE SYSTEM.** However, in the open-congregate system, problems of control, discipline, contraband smuggling, and inmate corruption similar to the experience of Newgate began to develop. As a result, a compromise plan was adopted that became known as the Auburn system. Under this system, instead of mingling freely in the yard, workrooms, and congregate sleeping quarters, prisoners were permitted to associate with each other only during the day to permit maximum industrial production. This association, however, was conducted in strict silence, and the rule of total and perpetual silence was harshly enforced. Nor was the prisoner permitted to communicate with anyone on the outside except under the most unusual circumstances. At night, the prisoners were separated totally. This was felt to be necessary in order to eliminate the corruption of prisoners by their fellow inmates and to reduce the opportunity for inmates to develop plans that would be disruptive to the operation of the institution. Another characteristic of the Auburn system was the emphasis placed on hard manual labor as a reformative tool and as a means of economic self-sufficiency for the prison. Warden Elam Lynds believed that adult convicts were hopelessly incorrigible and that industrial efficiency was the overriding purpose of the prison.[26] Finally, a great deal of emphasis was placed on the use of corporal punishment to maintain absolute discipline and obedience. Warden Lynds is reported to have said:

> I consider the chastisement by the whip the most efficient and at the same time the most humane which exists; it never injures health and obliges the prisoners to lead a life essentially healthy. Solitary confinement, on the contrary, is often insufficient and always dangerous. I have seen many prisoners in my life whom it was impossible to subdue in this manner and who only left the solitary cell to go to the hospital. I consider it impossible to govern a large prison without a whip. Those who know human nature from books only may say the contrary.[27]

## THE CONTROVERSY OVER THE PENNSYLVANIA AND AUBURN SYSTEMS

A hot controversy arose over the relative merits of the Pennsylvania and Auburn plans. The Philadelphia Society pushed for the adoption of the Pensylvania system, while the Boston Society for the Improvement of Prison Discipline and the Reformation of Juvenile Offenders supported the Auburn plan.[28] Both societies were convinced of the merits of their plans, and both groups were zealous crusaders for reform as well as completely unscrupulous in their use of facts to prove their arguments. The controversy even spilled over into other nations that were developing prisons modeled after America's system. In addition, famous international figures became involved in the controversy. Charles Dickens, after a visit to America, extensively criticized the Pennsylvania system in his *American Notes*. However, Beaumont and de Tocqueville praised it quite highly.[29] In fact, most European countries were in favor of the Pennsylvania system and adopted it in a modified form.

Revenue-producing
factor

The single, most instrumental spokesman for the Auburn system was Reverend Louis Dwight, who, as secretary of the Boston Society, traveled extensively to proselytize the merits of the Auburn system. He became the best-known American prison expert during the first half of the nineteenth century and was particularly influential in convincing the states to adopt the Auburn system. His argument focused attention on the economics of each system. Under the Auburn system, prison construction costs were lower because of the reduced emphasis on total solitary confinement. The use of congregate inmate labor also had definite revenue-producing advantages. As a result, the Auburn system was adopted by all the states except Pennsylvania and New Jersey. In a short time, even these two states abandoned the Pennsylvania solitary system because overcrowding forced the placing of two inmates in a cell. All this controversy and the attention it focused on prisons was responsible, however, for the creation in America, by 1835, of the first genuine prison system in the world. The historical development of this system is shown in Table 11.2.

TABLE **11.2**   Early American Prisons, 1790–1835

| State | Name and Location of Prison | Year of Receiving First Prisoner |
|-------|------------------------------|----------------------------------|
| Pennsylvania | Walnut Street Jail, Philadelphia | 1790 |
| New York | Newgate Prison, New York City | 1797 |
| New Jersey | State Penitentiary, Lamberton | 1798 |
| Kentucky | State Penitentiary, Frankfort | 1800 |
| Virginia | State Penitentiary, Richmond | 1800 |
| Massachusetts | State Prison, Charlestown | 1805 |
| Vermont | State Prison, Windsor | 1809 |
| Maryland | State Penitentiary, Baltimore | 1812 |
| New Hampshire | State Prison, Cocord | 1812 |
| Ohio | State Penitentiary, Columbus | 1816 |
| Georgia | State Penitentiary, Milledgeville | 1817 |
| New York | Auburn Prison, Auburn | 1819 |
| Tennessee | State Prison, Nashville | 1831 |
| Illinois | State Penitentiary, Alton | 1833 |
| Louisiana | State Penitentiary, Baton Rouge | 1835 |

Source: Wayne Morse, ed., *The Attorney General's Survey of Release Procedures* (Washington, D.C.: U.S. Printing Office, 1940).

## THE CREATION OF THE NATIONAL PRISON ASSOCIATION

After the Civil War, attention again refocused on the nation's prisons. It was obvious that neither the Pennsylvania nor the Auburn systems were bringing about the sought-after reform among its prisoners. It was a time for rethinking the future of America's developing prison system.

The year was 1870, and gathered in Cincinnati, the Queen City of the Ohio, were many of America's most noted penologists. These were more than interested reformers; they were experienced prison administrators who knew firsthand the operations of prisons and the need to develop progressive and innovative policies for prison operation. Among the famous and soon-to-be famous prison administrators assembled that October were Enoch C. Wines, secretary of the New York Prison Association; Franklin Sanborn, secretary of the Massachusetts State Board of Charities; Zebulon Brockway, head of Detroit's Michigan House of Corrections; and Gaylord Hubbell, warden of Sing Sing, who a few years before, had visited and observed the Irish system and returned with a conviction that progressive reform was needed in America's developing prison system. Those in attendance were imbued with the same humanitarian concerns that were expressed years before by the Quakers. There was one noted difference however: They were practical men—men well versed in the difficult realities of reform and prison management.

Out of this meeting came the creation of the National Prison Association, which would serve as the forerunner of today's American Correctional Association. Also in attendance were the die-hard advocates of the Pennsylvania System, who continued to call for solitary confinement and loudly denounced the congregate system of confinement. Although vocal, they were outnumbered and silenced by the realities of prison operation experienced by those present. Papers written by Maconochie and Crofton were circulated and discussed. The keynote speaker was

**New design for American penology**

Zebulon Brockway, who in his address, "The Ideal for a True Prison System for a State," urged the adoption of the principles as espoused by Maconochie and Crofton. The association advocated a new design for penology. The goal of imprisonment should not be the "infliction of vindictive suffering," but a program of moral regeneration that would hold the only hope for the reformation of the criminal. This goal could be accomplished only if corrections would adopt certain reforms: the provision for progressive classification of prisoners, the indeterminate sentence, and the development of inmate's self-respect. Penitentiary practices that had evolved during the first half of the nineteenth century—the fixed sentence, the lockstep, enforced rules of silence, and isolation were debasing and destructive of initiative and inmate reformation.

A blueprint for reform was needed. This was provided by the association's famous Declaration of Principles. These principles embodied the most comprehensive and far ranging penal strategy ever devised to that time—some might say they still share that distinction. They covered a wide range of concerns and observations not only of prison management and operation but reformation of the criminal and observations on the nature of crime itself. The key thought contained in the principles was that prisons should operate to bring about reformation in the criminal; a system conducive to inmate self-initiated change. Fixed sentences should give way to indeterminate sentences that would reward an inmate by release when he was reformed rather than mere release upon serving the sentence. Incentives should be provided by a system of rewards based on demonstrated self-reformation which would be tied into a system of inmate classification.

Like the Quakers before them, the 1870 reformers saw the prison as a means to bring about change in the criminal. In this way it could serve as the vehicle for change but only if the experience of the prison was properly channeled to help the offender seek atonement; a system that would help the criminal adjust to the role of a law-abiding citizen after release. Like a clarion call, the challenge, as

---

## NATIONAL PRISON ASSOCIATION PRINCIPLES (1870)

- Reformation, not the vindictive infliction of suffering, should be the purpose of penal treatment.
- Prisoners should be classified on the basis of a mark system patterned after the Irish system.
- Rewards should be provided for good conduct.
- Prisoners should be made to realize that their futures rest in their own hands.
- Indeterminate sentences should be substituted for fixed sentences and disparities in sentences removed.

- Religion and education are the most important agencies of reformation.
- Discipline should be administered so that it gains the cooperation of the inmate and so that the inmate maintains his or her self-respect.
- The goal of the prison should be to make industrious free citizens not orderly and obedient prisoners.
- Industrial training should be fully provided.
- Prisons should be small. Separate institutions should be

provided for different types of offenders.
- The social training of prisoners should be facilitated; silence rules should be abolished.
- Society at large must realize that it is responsible for the conditions that breed crime.

*Source:* Adapted from Enoch C. Wines, ed., *Transactions of the National Congress on Penitentiary and Reformatory Discipline* (Albany, N.Y.: Argus, 1871).

---

embodied in the principles, became the road map for progressive penal reform in America. It also established American penology as the frontrunner of progressive reform—at least in principle and theory.

##  THE REFORMATORY MOVEMENT

The opportunity to first adopt the 1870 principles occurred with the so-called reformatory movement, which was the next major step in the history of American corrections. This period, which lasted until 1910, began with the opening of New York's Elmira Reformatory in 1877. Originally designed for adult felons, the Elmira Reformatory took, instead, offenders between the ages of 16 and 30 who were serving their first prison terms. The inmates were classified according to conduct grades and could earn higher classification through good conduct in the institution's education and shop programs.

The emphasis of the movement was on rehabilitation, and toward that end an extensive educational program was provided for the inmates. In addition, programs in plumbing, tailoring, telegraphy, and printing were established to provide the prisoners with trade skills. Those sentenced to Elmira were given indeterminant sentences that permitted their release at a time corresponding to their demonstrated rehabilitation. Parole services were also extended to those released under the indeterminate sentence.

*Indeterminate sentences and parole*

The reformatory and rehabilitation programs established at Elmira soon spread to other states, but the movement generally died out after 1910 because it failed to meet the high expectations of its advocates. Among the major reasons for its failure were that the "old guard" prison employees were too conditioned to a punitive ideology and did not support the new concepts; the educational staff was too overworked to develop the academic program; and hard-core offenders were sentenced to the reformatory, which turned the system into a junior prison.

Although it was not a success, the reformatory movement left an important legacy in some of its contributions—notably, the indeterminate sentence and parole; the idea of educational programs and vocational training; and efforts to develop rehabilitation programs. These reforms gained increasing emphasis in correctional systems in the years ahead.[30]

##  THE INDUSTRIAL PRISON MODEL AND BEYOND

The twentieth century ushered in the industrial prison. As inmate populations rose, many large Auburn-type institutions were built by the states as new facilities were required to handle the increasing prison population. Such massive institutions as the large maximum security prisons represented by the California State Prison at San Quentin, Illinois State Penitentiary at Stateville, and the State Prison of Southern Michigan were built very early in the twentieth century.

*Auburn fortress-like institutions*

These fortress-like structures operated on the principle of mass congregate incarceration. The use of inmate labor to produce industrial goods for sale in the open market, thereby creating a self-sustaining prison system, was widely encouraged. However, restrictions on the use of prison-made industries backed by orga-

Until recently, prisons typically earned income from selling goods made by inmates. These Maryland convicts manufactured brooms. (Culver Pictures)

nized labor's efforts soon made its impact felt, and the industrial production of prisons shifted to the production of items that could be used by the state such as the manufacture of license plates.

The years from 1935 to 1960 have been called the "period of transition" for American prisons.[31] These were the years when notable reformers and the Federal Bureau of Prisons began to introduce new reforms that focused more on the rehabilitation of the individual. For example, the Federal Bureau of Prisons introduced such procedures as diagnosis and classification of inmates and the use of psychiatrists and psychologists in their rehabilitative efforts. The state systems soon followed the reforms introduced in the federal prisons.[32]

Since the 1960s there has been something of a conflict in prison philosophy. On the one had, society continues to subscribe to the rehabilitative goals of prison ideology. This can be witnessed in the increased efforts to develop community-based programs that have rehabilitative potential. On the other hand, the past several years have seen a growing support for viewing prisons simply as places to incarcerate offenders. What the future holds for our penal efforts seems to be unclear at this time. One thing is certain from the study of the history of corrections— these same issues have been with us for as long as we have had organized corrections in the United States.

## THE FEDERAL PRISON SYSTEM

In addition to the corrections systems of the states, there is a federal prison system. Most people are familiar with at least two of its facilities—Alcatraz (now closed) and Leavenworth. In 1776, the Continental Congress provided that persons convicted of violating federal laws be confined in colonial and local institutions. These institutions would be paid a fee on the basis of the cost for housing each prisoner. During the late eighteenth and most of the nineteenth centuries, there were rela- Few federal prisoners tively few federal prisoners because the law enforcement authority of the federal government was limited to the offenses of smuggling, counterfeiting, piracy, and other felonies committed on the high seas. As Congress began to extend the enforcement powers of the federal government, federal prisoners began to populate local and state prisons. The states did not object to boarding federal prisoners as long as they were permitted to sell their labor to private individuals. Many abuses resulted from this practice, and in 1887 Congress prohibited the employment of federal prisoners by contract or lease. As a result, the states began to charge the federal government the then exorbitant rate of 25 to 35 cents a day per prisoner for board. Some states refused to accept any federal prisoners because they could no longer sell their services for profit.

As the numbers of federal offenders increased, the problem of their custody became more acute. In 1891, federal commitments to penitentiaries numbered 1,600, and it was recognized that something had to be done.

## The First Federal Prisons

Because the history of the federal prison system is in a number of important ways an excellent chronology of American prison development in general, it needs to be discussed in some detail. Particularly important for our understanding is the changing philosophy of the purposes of imprisonment and the organizational reforms that resulted from these changes.

In 1889 Congress authorized the purchase of three sites for federal penitentiaries. It was decided to construct one in the South, one in the North, and one in the far West; however, no money was appropriated for their construction. In 1895, Congress transferred the military prison at Fort Leavenworth, Kansas, to the Department of Justice for the confinement of federal civilian prisoners. In a few short years, this facility proved to be much too small, and the Department of Justice finally convinced Congress that it was completely inadequate. Congress then appropriated funds for a federal penitentiary to be built on an eight-hundred-acre site adjacent to Fort Leavenworth. Using prison labor, the 1,200-capacity institution was first occupied in 1906, but it was not completely finished until 1927. After the prisoners were transferred to the new institution, the old Fort Leavenworth facility was returned to the War Department for the use of military prisoners.

The number of federal prisoners grew rapidly. In June 1895, there were 2,500 Growth in inmate numbers prisoners; a year later, 3,000. In 1899, Congress appropriated funds for a federal penitentiary at Atlanta, Georgia. Construction began in 1900, and in 1902 a group of 350 prisoners first occupied the institution.

The penitentiary slated for the West was eventually located at McNeil Island, Washington, a seven-mile stretch of territory lying in Puget Sound. The federal government first established a small territorial jail at this site in 1875. It offered to donate this jail to the new state of Washington in 1889, but the offer was declined. Although the Department of Justice urged that this territorial jail and its site be abandoned on a number of occasions, it remained federal property. In 1903, Congress voted funds to convert the jail into a penitentiary.

All three penitentiaries embraced the Auburn style of architecture character- Auburn victory ized by multitiered cellblocks and a fortress-like appearance. The Auburn philosophy of prison operation was also adopted. Although the lockstep was never implemented in federal institutions, it was another triumph for the Auburn plan.

A rudimentary classification system was established. Inmates were placed into one of three grades based on their institutional adjustment. Prisoners were kept busy in basic institutional industries and housekeeping activities. There was a conspicuous absence of any form of programming except for some limited educational training that was made available only to a few inmates.

This was a period of enforced hard labor by inmates. There was no consistency in programming because there was simply no central direction or consistency in running the prisons. Politics played a big role in operating the prisons. The warden was in reality chosen and appointed by the senior U.S. senator from the state in which the prison was located. Politics also determined who would be employed in the prisons.

By 1900 the penitentiary system in the United States had struck its stride. Although prisoners were supposedly sent to prison as a punishment for their crimes rather than for mere retribution, one would be hard pressed to demonstrate that idea. Punishment was severely imposed for the slightest rule violation, and few attempts were ever made to classify or segregate inmates. Work assignments were based on institutional need or opportunity, rather than on individual choice or vocational guidance. Between 1900 and 1935, American prisons, including federal prisons, were primarily custodial, punitive, and industrial. Overcrowding at federal institutions during this period left few resources for anything but custodial care.

The first U.S. reformatories for women opened in 1927. This 1935 newspaper photo shows convicts playing baseball at a California women's prison farm, "where over the fence is *not* out." (UPI/Bettmann Newsphotos)

During these early years of the twentieth century it was a few progressive states rather than the federal government that began to establish improved standards of prison administration and correctional theory. Yet there were a few important developments. In 1910, in an effort to relieve overcrowding, Congress passed parole and good-time laws patterned after similar correctional developments that were then operating in some states. The paroling mechanism was vested in a committee of three: the superintendent of prisons in the Department of Justice, the warden of the prison, and the institution's physician. Interestingly, all paroles were subject to the approval of the U.S. attorney general. Inmates who were paroled came under the supervisory authority of the U.S. Marshal Service.

In the 1920s Congress passed a number of major anticrime laws that quickly swelled the inmate population in the federal prisons. It was recognized that a reformatory had to be built to house young males between the ages of 17 and 30 who did not need to be incarcerated in one of the federal prisons. In 1926, the ground was broken for the federal reformatory near Chillicothe, Ohio. *Additional federal crimes*

Female prisoners were also becoming a problem. Until the 1920s federal female inmates were boarded in institutions operated by the states. By the 1920s, however, the number of female prisoners warranted building a special federal facility. It was proposed that such a facility be constructed at one of the existing male institutions, but Assistant Attorney General Mabel Walker Willebrandt, aided by a number of women's organizations, campaigned successfully for an independent reformatory for women. In 1927 a five-hundred-inmate institution for women opened at Alderson, West Virginia.

## The Establishment of the Bureau of Prisons

The problems were critical: severe overcrowding, inconsistent and often inept administration, and a decentralized organizational operation. All of these created pressures on the federal government to address the problems in federal prisons. A special committee of the House of Representatives was given the responsibility to study the problem and to make recommendations. In 1929, the committee released a very critical report. Adopting the correctional philosophy of those states that were then considered the leaders in penal reform, the committee called for a fundamental overhaul of the federal prisons. Attacking the problems of overcrowding, the committee called for immediate programs to improve housing, segregating, classifying, employing, and properly caring for federal prisoners. *Changes in the federal system*

The major recommendation of the committee was to call for the centralized administration of federal prisons. The committee also recommended increased expenditures for probation officers to be appointed by federal judges, the establishment of a full-time parole board, the expeditious establishment of two narcotic treatment farms, two new penitentiaries, a house for the criminally insane, and a system of federal jails and workhouses in more congested urban areas. The committee also stressed the need for greater attention to rehabilitation as a fundamental goal of corrections.

Urged on by the recommendations in the report, Congress passed and President Hoover signed into law an act creating the United States Bureau of Prisons within the Department of Justice. The new bureau was to provide centralized administration for all federal institutions. Instead of political appointments, all new wardens were to be appointed by the director on the basis of merit. Extensive upgrading of selection criteria and training were instituted for the employees of the bureau.

### The Early Growth of the Federal Bureau of Prisons, 1930 to 1955

When the Bureau of Prisons was established in 1930, it faced overcrowded conditions of emergency proportions in the federal prisons. The adoption of new federal criminal statutes, particularly the prohibition laws, was significantly increasing the number of inmates and creating havoc in the federal prisons. The states became increasingly reluctant to accept federal prisoners to ease prison overcrowding. Abandoned army camps were pressed into service. In 1930 alone, eight new prison camps were opened.

A growing number of federal prisoners were being sentenced to a year or less for the violation of prohibition and immigration laws. By law these inmates could not legally be confined in the penitentiaries, and many were unsuited physically or custodially for confinement in the open camps.

The bureau embarked on a program of adding additional facilities including a new reformatory, a network of regional jails, and a hospital for inmates who were mentally ill or who had chronic medical ailments. Still it was not enough. During the 1930s new anticrime legislation was enacted that brought more serious types of offenders into the federal prisons. The Federal Kidnapping Act and the Threatening Communications Act were passed in 1932; in 1933 it became a federal offense to assault or kill a federal officer; and in 1934 the National Bank Robbery, Anti-Racketeering, Fugitive Felon, National Firearms, and National Stolen Property Acts were passed. The "crime wave" of this period and the resulting increase in importance of the federal government in crime control, as indicated by these statutes, brought the old military prison of Alcatraz Island in California under the control of the Department of Justice in 1934.

Alcatraz

Intense criticism was leveled at the Bureau of Prisons when it acquired Alcatraz as a maximum security institution for intractable offenders. The criticism focused on the apparent contradiction between the bureau's correctional philosophy that stressed rehabilitation and the reality of Alcatraz.

Yet the bureau had little choice in the matter. The public, outraged by the wave of bank robberies, was calling for more punitive measures against criminals. These critics were ably aided in their efforts by J. Edgar Hoover, director of the Federal Bureau of Investigation, who called criminals "mad dogs" and convinced Congress of the value of the increased use of punitive sanctions as a means to reduce crime. While Hoover preached incarceration, penologists argued that a mere philosophy of punishment would not protect society.

While the public debate continued, the Bureau of Prisons was working to institute more individualized treatment of inmates and the use of various types of therapy and counseling to help inmates. It was also a time that saw the expansion of a federal industries program. Probation and parole was reorganized. Legislation was passed providing for an independent parole board within the Department of Justice. The supervision of parolees was transferred from the U.S. Marshal Service to the probation offices of the federal courts.

At the outbreak of World War II, the Bureau of Prisons for the first time in its history was not suffering from overcrowding. During the war years, the inmate population declined further. Bureau administrators convinced government officials to permit released offenders to elist in the armed forces. After the war, however, the population of the federal system again began to climb, and new facilities had to be built. By 1955 the federal prison system had grown to twenty-seven institutions—six of which were penitentiaries.

## The Intervening Years, 1955 to 1970

The 1950s and 1960s were characterized by two major developments: the diversification and growth of the rehabilitative model in corrections. Diversification meant the growing use of a broad range of correctional alternatives. For example, during the 1950s the Youth Corrections Act was passed, calling for the increased use of the indeterminate sentence and the creation of a Youth Division in the U.S. Board of Parole. In 1958, diagnostic services and the indeterminate sentence were made available for adults through legislation. The 1960s saw the adoption of the Prisoner Rehabilitation Act, which, among other things, provided for work release, emergency furloughs, and certain prerelease privileges for adult inmates.

The Bureau of Prisons played a major leadership role in developing the rehabilitative model. Program improvements were made, and training was developed to assist state and local correctional efforts in developing rehabilitative efforts. The bureau also extended its technical assistance role. Classification was modified and was accomplished by a functional team with increased inmate participation. Specialists and social workers were assigned the diagnostic and planning facets of the inmate's program, and attempts were made to match offender needs with specific treatment programs and institutional placement.

*Heyday of the rehabilitative model*

## The 1970s: Years of Change and Critical Self-Analysis

Public attitudes about criminals and corrections were influenced by many factors during the 1970s. Chief among these were the increasing crime rates and the growing problems of managing prisons as depicted by wide-scale inmate rioting. The aftermath has been a call for law and order that prompted a public debate about crime and criminals similar to that which occurred in the 1930s.

The Bureau of Prisons—like all American prison systems—has tried to respond to the public concerns. This has required the formulation of a new master plan. The specific activities in which the bureau engaged during this troubled decade include an increased emphasis on professional staff development; the development of correctional programs relevant to a changing society; the increased development use of research and evaluation capabilities; and the expansion of the Bureau's technical assistance to state and local correctional systems.

Programs to involve community resources and reintegration efforts spread. Treatment teams were increasingly used to plan and manage treatment programs that involved the inmates themselves. Studies were conducted to try to measure the effectiveness of these teams and the experiences of imprisonment. During the 1970s increased emphasis was placed on inmate education programs, both academic and vocational. These were increasingly supplemented by outside educational agencies such as local colleges and universities. The use of community treatment centers for inmates increased drastically during this time. Realizing that the debilitating effects of dependency and isolation exist even in newer facilities, the bureau expanded the use of these centers (Figure 11.1). Today, the bureau operates a system of community treatment centers through which nearly one-half of all

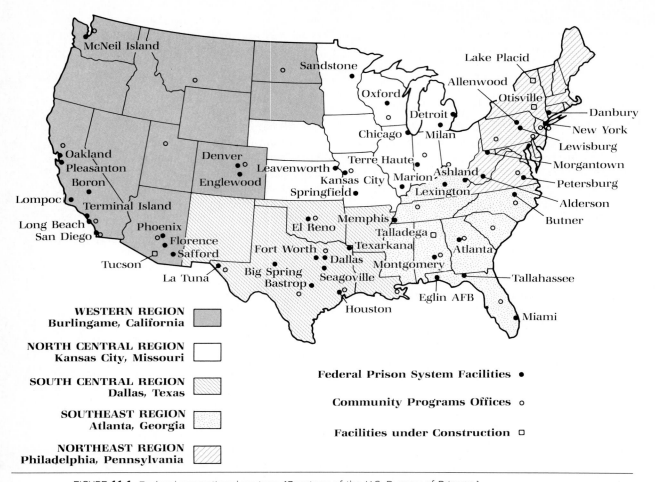

FIGURE **11.1** Federal correctional system. [Courtesy of the U.S. Bureau of Prisons.]

federal inmates are ultimately released. The primary purpose of the system still remains to successfully reintegrate the offender into society.

Beginning in the 1960s and continuing through the 1970s, the courts abandoned their traditional "hands off" attitudes toward inmate rights and granted to inmates such things as freer exercise of religion, greater access to courts and legal counsel, more liberal correspondence and visitation rules, due process standards for prison disciplinary proceedings, and procedures for the redress of grievances.

**Demise of the rehabilitative model**

Ominous clouds were developing, however. The Bureau of Prison's rehabilitative thrust was coming under increasing attack. Academics, researchers, and practitioners pointed out that traditional rehabilitation in prisons did not seem to be working.[33] Others challenged the rehabilitative model, saying that it was used unjustly to control inmates.[34] Prisons throughout the country were forced to give their programs another look. As a result, the medical model of prisons that had guided the rehabilitative ideas of the Bureau of Prisons was deemphasized in 1975. In its place, the bureau instituted a balanced philosophy of rehabilitation, retribution, deterrence, incapacitation, and reintegration. This change in philosophy was current with the developing idea that the prison exists for purposes other than treatment. Rather than requiring mandatory participation in rehabilitation programs, inmate participation in such programs is now voluntary.

With the demise of the medical model, the prison population count began to rise. From slightly over 20,000 in 1970, the number of inmates in federal prisons jumped to nearly 24,000 in 1975, and then to a dramatic increase of over 30,000 inmates at the end of the 1977 fiscal year. By 1989 this figure had nearly doubled.

During the mid-1970s another spurt in construction activities was undertaken by the bureau. Intense opposition to the expansion was raised by the National Council on Crime and Delinquency and other concerned groups. These groups are concerned that more penal institutions will encourage the idea of "you build em' we'll fill em'" in place of what is really needed—decarceration efforts and community-based programs.

One of the key developments in corrections in recent years has been accreditation. Sponsored by the American Correctional Association and first funded by the federal government, the Commission on Accreditation for Corrections was created. During the 1977 to 1979 period, the commission developed and issued ten sets of standards covering every aspect of corrections including community and juvenile programs. Accreditation creates a widely accepted set of standards for corrections that will help agencies obtain the resources necessary to upgrade corrections and meet the mandates of the courts. To maintain and improve conditions for staff, the federal prison system has begun the process of accreditation for its institutions. **Correctional accreditation**

The Federal Bureau of Prisons experienced as much change in the decade of the 1970s as in any other time in its history, yet many of the activities of the bureau have for the most part remained unchanged. This apparent contradiction can possibly be explained as the result of contradictory inputs from the Congress, the public, professional corrections personnel, and others who, on the one hand wish prisons to be secure and protective of the public and on the other wish in some way to reform or change the individual inmate.

During the 1970s American prisons were more closely examined than at any time since the early nineteenth century. Although the Bureau of Prisons has always been sensitive to the public's wishes for its prisons, the bureau's policies and programs were not immune from this examination, as not only the development of new bureau facilities but also the philosophical foundation upon which the bureau was operating came under intense scrutiny.

The bureau is still trying to deal with many of the problems facing state correctional systems. As in state prison systems, the number of inmates in federal prisons has been growing. In spite of this growth, the emphasis continues to be on smaller institutions. This requires additional facilities that are currently under construction. **Growth in numbers of federal prisoners**

Although in recent years the federal government has tried to lessen its prison population by permitting the states to prosecute and incarcerate offenders using the state laws as a sentencing device, this has not worked too well. Compensating for this effort has been the adoption of more criminal law violations by Congress such as the new "get-tough" policies of the 1984 Comprehensive Criminal Control Act, and the more strict sentencing practices being followed by federal judges. Of particular importance for the possibility of increases in the future prison population is the passage of the Sentencing Reform Act of 1984. This legislation, among other things, abolished parole after 1988 for federal prisoners. Although the act provides for the establishment of a sentencing commission to establish guidelines for sentencing, the overall impact may be to sharply increase federal prison commitments. This is an area that is worth watching closely. Whereas in many ways the bureau has served as a model for states to emulate, it now faces—as do all prison systems—some formidable problems.

Today the Bureau of Prisons operates a widespread network of different institutions. Forty community program offices also oversee the operation of three hundred halfway houses that operate under contract to the federal government. A relatively new classification system has been established. Rather than using the old correctional terms such as *maximum security*, *medium security*, and the like, federal institutions are classified into six security levels, the most secure of which is a level-six institution. Inmates are classified and sent to these various institutions according to such factors as the severity of their offense, their history of escapes or violence, the expected length of their incarceration, and the type of their prior commitments.[35]

## SUMMARY

The development of modern principles of corrections historically has relied on reforms in the legal system and in criminal law. The Period of Enlightenment, which swept Europe in the late eighteenth century, contributed to needed social and political reforms, which would have a bearing on America and her legal-correctional system. Over the years, the historical quest for philosophical goals in corrections has been elusive. We have subscribed to—and continue to subscribe to—such goals as punishment, deterrence, isolation, incapacitation, rehabilitation, and now reintegration as goals of correctional efforts.

In the nineteenth century, rather than adopting a European model to develop our prison system, the United States became a world leader in prison reform. The two models—the Pennsylvania system and the Auburn plan—were widely studied by European nations for adoption. The Pennsylvania system, developed by the Quakers, emphasized solitary confinement, while the Auburn plan operated on the principle of the congregate system.

America's leadership in reform efforts was in no small way indebted to a handful of farsighted reformers in Britain and Ireland. They included such notable figures in penal reform as John Howard, Alexander Maconochie, and Walter Crofton. These pioneers in prison management were truly the beacons of which our own efforts were reflections. Their leadership pointed the way.

In addition to the notable contributions of the Pennsylvania and Auburn models, the United States developed the famous 1870 principles, the reformatory plan, and ushered in the industrial prison system. Over the years, prison programming has changed significantly. With the demise of the rehabilitative model of prisons in the 1970s, the concept of reintegration as a goal has become a new and important concern. Although somewhat of an extension of the rehabilitative model, it rests on different assumptions about the offender, the purpose of imprisonment, and the relationship between the offender, his or her environment, and society. On the other hand, while reintegration enjoys wide favor among penologists, the tone of the times is becoming one that increasingly espouses punishment and incapacitation as primary correctional goals.

## REVIEW QUESTIONS

1. What role did the so-called European Period of Enlightenment play in the area of prison reform?
2. Corrections has served many purposes throughout history. Briefly describe the reason behind each of the following:

a. Punishment
b. Deterrence
c. Isolation
d. Rehabilitation
e. Reintegration

3. What correctional reforms did John Howard call

for in his book, *State of Prisons?* Why are these reforms noteworthy?

4. What were tickets of leave? Why were they important in the history of corrections?

5. List the principles that governed the Pennsylvania system.

6. What was the Auburn plan?

7. What role did the 1870 Cincinnati conference play in American prison reform?

8. The reformatory movement, though shortlived, had a lasting effect on corrections in the United States. What reforms grew out of this movement?

9. What was the industrial prison? Why did it fail as a correctional method?

10. Using the history of the U.S. Bureau of Prisons as a guide, what changes swept corrections during the past one hundred years?

## DISCUSSION QUESTIONS

1. In your opinion, what is the primary purpose of corrections? Why?

2. What were the differences between the Pennsylvania system and the Auburn plan? How did each system contribute to modern penology?

3. Should the federal government run its own prison facilities, or should it contract with state institutions to house prisoners in state institutions?

4. Is there a collaborative role for prison systems in the future? If so, what might it be?

## SUGGESTED ADDITIONAL READINGS

Allen, H., and C. Simonson. *Corrections in America,* 5th ed. New York: Macmillan, 1988.

Barnes, Harry Elmer. *The Story of Punishment.* Boston: Stratford, 1930.

Bartollas, C. *Correctional Treatment Theory and Practice.* Englewood Cliffs, N.J.: Prentice-Hall, 1985.

Burns, Henry Jr. *Corrections: Organization and Administration.* St. Paul, Minn.: West, 1975.

Clear, Todd R., and George F. Cole. *American Corrections.* Monterey, Calif.: Brooks/Cole, 1986.

Conrad, John. *Crime and Its Correction.* Berkeley: University of California Press, 1965.

Eriksson, Thorsten. *The Reformers: An Historical Survey of Pioneer Experiments in the Treatment of Criminals.* New York: Elsevier, 1976.

Heath, James. *Eighteenth-Century Penal Theory.* London: Oxford University Press, 1963.

Honderich, Ted. *Punishment: The Supposed Justifications.* Middlesex, England: Penguin, 1969.

Huff, C. R. *Contemporary Corrections—Social Control and Conflict.* Beverly Hills, Calif.: Sage, 1977.

Ives, George. *A History of Penal Methods.* London: Stanley Paul, 1914.

Jarvis, D. C. *Institutional Treatment of the Offender.* New York: McGraw-Hill, 1978.

Jones, Howard, "Punishment and Social Values." In Grygier Tadeusz, Howard Jones, and John C. Spencer, Eds., *Criminology in Transition.* London: Tavistock, 1965, pp. 1–23.

Lewis, Orlando F. *The Development of American Prisons and Prison Customs,* 1776–1845. Albany: Prison Association of New York, 1922.

Menninger, Karl. *The Crime of Punishment.* New York: Viking, 1968.

Rusche, George, and O. Kirchheimer. *Punishment and Social Structure.* New York: Columbia University Press, 1939.

Sellin, Thorsten. "A Look at Prison History." *Federal Probation* 18 (September 1967): 18–23.

Sutherland, Edwin. *Criminology.* Philadelphia: Lippincott, 1924.

Teeters, Negley K. *They Were in Prison.* Philadelphia; Winston, 1937.

Teeters, Negley K., and John D. Shearer. *The Prison at Philadelphia: Cherry Hill.* New York: Columbia University Press, 1957.

## NOTES

1. Robert C. Mackelvey, *The Coming of the Enlightenment* (London: Tavistock, 1958), p. 175.

2. Graeme Newman, *The Punishment Response* (Philadelphia: J. B. Lippincott, 1978), p. 116.

3. *Ibid.,* p. 117.

4. See: Bureau of Justice Statistics, *Sourcebook of Criminal Justice Statistics—1986* (Washington: U.S. Department of Justice, 1987), p. 104.

5. Sydney Smith, *On the Management of Prisons* (London: Warde Locke, 1822), pp. 226, 232.

6. James W. L. Park, "What Is a Political Prisoner?" *American Journal of Corrections* (November–December 1972): 22–23.

7. Notes from a discussion with inmates of Southern Michigan Prison, Jackson, Mich., during a series of meetings in 1975.

8. Francis A. Allen, "Criminal Justice, Legal Values and the Rehabilitative Ideal," *The Journal of Criminal Law, Criminology and Police Science* 50 (September–October 1959): 226–232.

9.   New York State Special Commission on Attica, *Attica* (New York: Bantam, 1972), p. 2.

10.   John Howard, *State of Prisons*, in George G. Killinger and Paul F. Cromwell, Jr., eds., *Penology* (St. Paul, Minn.: West, 1973), pp. 5–11.

11.   Quoted by John V. Barry in "Captain Alexander Maconochie," *The Victorian Historical Magazine* 27, no. 2 (June 1957): 5.

12.   Ibid., p. 147.

13.   Robert A. Terrell, *History of the Irish Prisons* (London: Trafalgar, 1929), p. 49.

14.   Ibid.

15.   Newman, *The Punishment Response*, p. 124.

16.   Ronald C. Wolcott, *Jails in History* (New York: Schribner, 1952), p. 34.

17.   David J. Rothman, *The Discovery of the Asylum* (Boston: Little, Brown, 1971), p. 51.

18.   Thorsten Sellin, "The Origin of the Pennsylvania System of Prison Discipline," *Prison Journal* 50 (Spring–Summer 1970): 14.

19.   Ibid.

20.   Orlando F. Lewis, *The Development of American Prisons and Prison Customs, 1776–1845* (Albany: Prison Association of New York, 1922) pp. 26–28.

21.   Francis C. Gray, *Prison Discipline in America* (London: Murray, 1848), p. 22.

22.   Sellin, "The Origin of the Pennsylvania System of Prison Discipline," pp. 15–17.

23.   Lewis, *The Development of American Prisons*, pp. 43–57.

24.   Elmer H. Johnson, *Crime, Correction and Society*, rev. ed. (Homewood, Ill.: Dorsey, 1968), p. 485.

25.   Lewis, *The Development of American Prisons*, p. 80.

26.   Ibid., pp. 86–95.

27.   Gustave de Beaumont and Alexis de Tocqueville, *On the Penitentiary System in the United States and Its Application in France* (Carbondale: Southern Illinois University Press, 1964), p. 201.

28.   See Steward H. Holbrook, *Dreamers of the American Dream* (New York: Doubleday, 1957), pp. 240–244.

29.   Beaumont and de Tocqueville, *On the Penitentiary System*, pp. 57–58.

30.   Harry E. Allen and Clifford Simonsen, *Corrections in America*, 2nd ed. (Encino, Calif.: Glencoe, 1978), p. 53.

31.   Ibid., p. 57.

32.   Ibid., p. 58.

33.   Robert Martinson, "What Works?—Questions and Answers About Prison Reform," *The Public Interest* 35 (1974): 22–54.

34.   Norval Morris, "The Future of Imprisonment: Toward a Punitive Philosophy," *Michigan Law Review* 72 (1974): 1161–1180.

35.   Letter from Kathryn L. Morse, public information specialist, Federal Prison System, 28 May 1985.

# CHAPTER 12

# The Jail and Other Temporary Detention Facilities

## O B J E C T I V E S

**After reading this chapter, the student should be able to:**

Discuss the history of jails and jail development.

Discuss the crucial role that jails play in the criminal justice system.

Identify major problems and areas of neglect with today's jail systems.

Explain some suggested reforms in dealing with misdemeanants and restructuring jails.

## I M P O R T A N T   T E R M S

Jail overcrowding
The shameful legacy of jails
Diversity of offenders
Local control and politics of jails

Jail physical facilities
Inadequate jail personnel
Jail administrative problems
Alternative programs and dispositions

Diversionary measures
Jail restitution programs
Citation in lieu of arrest
Jail regionalization
State supervision of local jails
Jail volunteers

In most states, jails are locally operated facilities. Jails are used to house a wide range of inmates at various stages of criminal justice processing. Those who cannot post bail either because they can't afford the required bond or the services of a bail bondsman or who have been denied bail by the courts, are housed in jails awaiting trial. Jails also house persons convicted of a crime (usually a misdemeanor) who have been sentenced to serve their time in a jail facility. A person found guilty of a felony is usually remanded by the court to the custody of the jail until the appropriate sentence is decided. Jails also hold individuals charged with or convicted of probation or parole violations. Many jails also hold convicted felons who have been sentenced to prison by the courts and are awaiting transfer to the state corrections department. Many jurisdictions authorize the courts to remand a material witness to a crime to jail if it appears that the individual's safety is jeopardized and he or she needs custodial protection or if there is reason to believe that the witness will flee the jurisdiction and therefore not be available to testify in court. In most cases, however, material witnesses are placed under protective custody in their own homes, with relatives in another city, or in a hotel rather than being confined in jail.

Jails are usually operated on a county basis under the authority of the county sheriff. In some larger cities, jails are operated at the municipal level and are under the administration of the local police. Although many smaller police departments have a few cells to hold arrested persons temporarily, strictly speaking, these are not jails but lockups. Those arrested for certain minor offenses, such as public drunkenness or driving under the influence, are detained in lockups until the next day or so, when they appear before the city magistrate to stand trial.

A survey taken a few years ago found that we have about 34,000 locally operated jails in the United States. This number would have been even higher if the survey had included such facilities as drunk tanks and lockups operated by local police departments and the state-operated local jail systems, which are found in some New England states.[1]

Many of these facilities are quite small. For instance, most of them housed fewer than fifty inmates when the survey was taken. What this points out is the fact that we have a national jail system that is highly fragmented and under the control of local authorities. Although there are some very practical reasons for the continued maintenance of jails at the local level, such an arrangement does not offer much promise for major reforms in our so-called jail system.

## Jail Conditions: Overcrowding and Other Factors

The jail is the most frequently experienced form of incarceration. Our nation's jails handle about 8½ million admissions a year.[2] On any day, they house about 300,000 inmates. And like prison inmates, jail inmates are disproportionately members of minority groups. They share still another characteristic with prisons: The number of jail inmates has shown a staggering increase in recent years. For example, between the 1978 and 1986 Jail Census surveys, our nation's jails experienced an overwhelming 60 percent increase in numbers of inmates.[3]

Nowhere is this more pronounced than in certain regions of the country. Eight of the ten states with the highest incarceration rates are in the South. It is also this region that has had to house the highest number of prisoners in jails because of the overcrowding in those states' correctional facilities.[4] Louisiana, the nation's leader in jail incarceration rates per 100,000 population, had nearly double the national inmate average in its jails. Interestingly, Louisiana also led all states in the percentage of jails under court order for overcrowding. Compounding Louisiana's problems was the fact that the jails in that state also held the largest number of prisoners of any state who were being held in jails awaiting transfer to prison; prisoners who couldn't be transferred because of existing prison overcrowding.

In the past fifteen years, the absolute growth in numbers of women in jails has nearly doubled. Still they constitute only about 8 percent of all jailed prisoners.[5] Here, California leads the nation. About one-fourth of all female inmates in American jails can be found in the Golden State.

One possible explanation for the relatively high proportion of females in California jails was the availability of a variety of alternative jail-based sentencing choices, such as work furloughs and counseling programs, that may have increased the likelihood of accused female lawbreakers in that state being assigned to jail custody and participation in such programs.[6]

The efforts in the past decade to remove juveniles from jails seems to have had some effect. Many states have moved to have juveniles placed in special detention facilities for juveniles or other placements in lieu of jails. Only 1 percent of the jail population is made up of juveniles. Yet, this figure too, varies widely.

Juveniles in jail

There is some evidence that states which have recently passed "get-tough" laws, which permit the authorities to lock up youthful offenders, are experiencing increasing numbers of juveniles incarcerated in local jails. It is likely that authorities in these states are doing just that. And without the necessary construction of additional juvenile detention facilities to handle the increase, jails are being used.

The inmates in American jails seem to be pretty evenly divided between those who are not convicted and are awaiting trial and those who have been found guilty and are serving their sentence in jail or awaiting transfer to prison. In fact, slightly more of the nation's jail inmates are unconvicted pretrial detainees.

There is an evident trend occurring among the nation's jails; the number of jails is diminishing. What we are ending up with is fewer but larger jails. This indicates that jail consolidation is slowly occurring. Local jurisdictions are cooperating more on jail consolidation efforts. Probably, this is partly attributable to court-ordered requirements that jails meet certain minimum standards with which some jurisdictions cannot comply. This forces consolidation efforts and the transfer of prisoners to jails that meet these standards.

Still, most of the nation's jails are small facilities. This reflects the fact that the jails are operated on a county basis and virtually all of these more than 3,100 jurisdictions operate local confinement facilities. Yet it is the medium-size and larger jails that hold the vast number of jailed inmates. These larger facilities account for only 6 percent of all the nation's jails yet house more than half of all jail inmates.[7]

Local nature of jails

Much of the overcrowding in American jails has been generally attributed to the backup in these institutions from prisons that are overcrowded. Convicted offenders who have been sentenced by the courts to prison are finding themselves confined in jail until bed space becomes available in our state prisons to which they can then be transferred.

The evidence does not, however, support this fact. Jail surveys taken during the 1980s show that only about 3 percent of the nation's jail population was being held for other authorities as a direct result of crowding in federal or state prisons. Of course, this problem is more acute in some states than in others. One of the reasons for the overcrowding in many jails is the simple fact that more people are

Overcrowding is a serious problem in most U.S. jails, including this county facility in Michigan. (Michael Hayman/Stock Boston)

being sentenced to jail. This, coupled with the fact that many jurisdictions are without alternative institutions or programs to which convicted offenders can be sent, largely explains the problems some communities are experiencing with jail overcrowding.

**Effects of overcrowding**

The problem of overcrowding in jails may in some important ways be worse than prison overcrowding. Jails are simply not set up to house inmates for long periods of time. As a result, few programs are available to jailed prisoners. Even such minimum considerations as recreational facilities are absent in many, if not most, jails. With the exception of a television viewing room and the availability of some reading materials, most jail inmates lead a life of enforced idleness and frequent "cell time" in which they are confined to their cells. Densely packed together with no recreational outlet, work programs, or other activities, pressures begin to mount, and the potential for problems increases. The only mitigating factor may be that inmates in jails are typically less dangerous in a relative overall sense than those who have been sentenced to prisons. Yet this appears to be changing. Increasingly, jails, like prisons, are being populated with more hardened and serious crime offenders.

**Operating costs**

Like prison, the cost of jail incarceration is high. It is estimated that the annual operating expense per inmate is about $13,000. There are wide variations in these costs. The Northeast, for example, spends on an average much more than the nation as a whole. The South spends much less. It costs five times as much to keep an inmate jailed in Alaska as it does in South Carolina. Like other aspects of the administration of criminal justice, the overall cost to the taxpayer is high: estimates are that jail operations cost the American taxpayer over $3 billion dollars in 1987.

The pages ahead will explore what little we seem to be getting for such an outlay. Table 12.1 presents a summary of facts about jail inmates.

##  HISTORY OF JAILS: A SHAMEFUL LEGACY

A great deal has been said about America's jail system—most of it bad. In 1931, the National Commission on Law Observance and Enforcement conferred on the nation's jail system the unsavory epithet: "Most notorious correctional institution in the world."[8] More than half a century later, that same institution—if no longer considered the *world's* most heinous penal establishment—was still characterized as "the worst blight in American corrections,"[9] "a major disaster area," "the yardstick of the inadequacies and breakdowns in a community's health and human service system,"[10] and a place where "anyone not a criminal when he goes in, will be one when he comes out."[11] Added to the ignominy of this institution is the

---

TABLE **12.1** Composite Facts About Inmates from the 1978, 1983 and 1986 Jail Census Surveys

Jail populations consist of approximately 92 percent males.

Single persons—those who have never married or are divorced or separated—made up three-fourths of the inmate total, as contrasted with only a third of the U.S. population as a whole.

The jail population is reversing earlier trends toward more youthful jail populations. This can probably be explained by two factors: the general aging of the American population itself and states' removing juveniles from adult jails.

Sixty percent of jail inmates lack a high school diploma, compared to only 25 percent in the general population.

Blacks are particularly overrepresented in jail populations.

Three of every one hundred jail inmates was being held in 1986 as the result of overcrowding in state, and to a lesser degree, in federal prisons. This figure is down significantly from the 1978 level.

People experiencing economic hardships contributed disproportionately to the jail population. This is particularly true for black female inmates.

Drug and alcohol abuse played a significant role in the lives of many inmates. About 40 percent had used some drug daily. Twenty-five percent of all women inmates had been heroin addicts—far more than the proportion for men. About a fifth of the convicted inmates were under the influence of drugs at the time of their offense. With respect to alcohol abuse, a fourth of the convicted inmates had been drinking heavily just before they committed their offense, and the proportion of whites who had was greater than twice that of blacks.

Inmates were incarcerated for the following offenses: property crimes, 42 percent; violent crimes, 30 percent; offenses against public order, 19 percent; drugs, 8 percent; other, 1 percent.

*Source:* U.S. Department of Justice, *Profile of Jail Inmates—Sociodemographic findings from the 1978 Survey of Inmates of Local Jails* (Washington, D.C.: U.S. Government Printing Office, October 1980), pp. 1–9; Bureau of Justice Statistics, *The 1983 Jail Census* (Washington, D.C.: U.S. Department of Justice, November 1984); and Bureau of Justice Statistics, *The 1986 Jail Census* (Washington, D.C.: U.S. Department of Justice, October 1987).

---

ruling in recent years by state and federal courts that many such facilities are operated in ways that deny inmates certain constitutional rights.[12]

Given the history of American jails, little more could be expected. The jail is the oldest institution for incarcerating offenders. American jails trace their ancestry to England, where jails developed in the tenth century.[13] At this time, the shire or county was a very important locus of government authority. County governments were independent and powerful, and jails became a part of that machinery. As towns and cities grew and formed their own governments, they created separate penal institutions. Thus, county and municipal jails developed side by side.

By the late sixteenth and the seventeenth centuries, two hundred "common jails" existed in England.[14] They were provided, owned, and administered by several different authorities. Responsibility for maintaining the county jail rested with the sheriff. Towns had their own jails under the jurisdiction of their own officials. Indeed, nearly every municipality during this time, however small, had its own jail.[15] Private jails were also established by various ecclesiastical orders, members of the church hierarchy, and high-ranking noblemen, who operated them on a profit basis.[16] In theory, each of these jails was the property of the crown, and those who operated them were responsible to the monarch as keepers of common jails.

As mentioned in the previous chapter, these early jails had little resemblance to today's jails. The sheriff was authorized to repair or rebuild with county funds any county jail that was "presented" by the grand jury to be insufficient or inconvenient.[17] (Even today, grand juries in a number of states are responsible for investigating conditions in county jails.) By law, the grand jury could levy a sum known as the "county bread" that was used to buy food for poor prisoners. Although the sheriff was considered the caretaker of the jail, he seldom exercised direct custodial control over its operations. His position was one of importance and influence, and he contracted a keeper to perform the actual duties of caring for the jail and its occupants.[18]

Usually, the keeper did not receive a salary. He was paid by a system of fees that made jail keeping a lucrative occupation. In fact, the job of keeper was sometimes sold by the sheriff to the highest bidder. Under the supervision of the keeper were turnkeys, who were paid from the fees collected by the keeper. He had no obligation to the prisoners themselves, other than to see that they did not escape.[19]

Inmates had to support themselves. To do so, they were allowed to beg. Sometimes relatives and friends helped them when they could, or charitable persons donated food and clothing. Some limited work was also available. In some jails, inmates were permitted to work at producing nets, laces, and purses, which were sold outside the jail. Frequently, the inmates were tied to a chain that was fixed to the front wall of the jail from which they pleaded with passersby to purchase their wares.[20]

Not until the beginning of the nineteenth century did England's jails begin to assume functions more characteristic of modern jail administration. Up to this time the jails were not special institutions designed to house prisoners for short-term periods of incarceration. Instead, they were temporary holding or security facilities to which convicted offenders were sent for very brief periods of incarceration before being placed in the stocks, executed, subjected to branding or some form of mutilation for their misdeeds; or, in the seventeenth and eighteenth centuries, transported to penal colonies. Only in the case of debtors, who were kept imprisoned until they paid their creditors, were these early jails used for any form of long-term imprisonment. By the nineteenth century, some parts of the criminal code had been modified, and jails began to house those who had been convicted of minor offenses. About this time jail imprisonment for debt began to disappear, and the jails began to receive both accused and convicted criminals on a regular basis.[21]

## Jail Development in the United States

The English jail tradition came with the colonists to the New World. The oldest jail system in America was established in Virginia at the time of the founding of the Jamestown colony. In 1626, Virginia prescribed that the marshal's fee for admission and discharge of prisoners was two pounds of tobacco.[22] Five years later, the Virginia general assembly raised and restructured the fee schedule so that the marshal would receive ten pounds of tobacco for arresting an individual, ten pounds for admitting him to jail, and another ten pounds for his discharge.[23]  

*Early colonial jails*

In 1634, the Virginia colony was divided into eight shires, each run by a sheriff. In 1642, the general assembly of that colony passed the first laws dealing with the erection and maintenance of jails. It stipulated that jails were to be built in each county by the county commissioners and were to house those arrested and awaiting trial. The sheriff was to maintain custody of the jail and its prisoners. Payment for food and lodging was to be provided by the prisoners themselves. The cost was to be determined by mutual agreement between the sheriff and the inmates.[24]

The counties were slow to comply with these laws and continued to use such facilities as the back rooms of taverns as jails. It was not until the general assembly enacted a penalty against the counties for noncompliance in the form of a fine of 5,000 pounds of tobacco and liability for the escape of any prisoners that the counties started to build the required jails.

During this time, Pennsylvania was also developing a jail system, a process that passed through three stages. The typical English jail system was established under the laws of the Duke of York in 1676.[25] By 1682 this system was replaced by the adoption of the Quaker workhouse or house of correction, which became the basis of the colony's jail system for about thirty years.[26] This idea was abolished in 1718. The Crown forced the Quakers to abandon their more humanitarian criminal code and their enlightened way of dealing with offenders. The harsh English law was reimposed on the colony, and corporal punishment became the approved method of dealing with offenders. There was little need for a workhouse as a place of confinement under these circumstances. Instead, whippings, branding, and other forms of physical punishment were meted out. In other cases, fines were established as substitutes for imprisonment. Still, the Quakers refused to accede.

The first law that created a county jail in Pennsylvania was passed on March 20, 1725.[27] This legislation later became a model for other states in establishing county jail systems. The law provided for the appointment of a board of five special county commissioners or trustees, who were authorized to purchase the land for the jail site and to estimate its cost. Each county was to follow this procedure and was required to establish a county jail. The administrative control of each county jail was to rest with the sheriff. The five commissioners were responsible for maintaining the facility and were authorized to assess taxes for its support. The sheriff had the authority to appoint an undersheriff or keeper to run the day-to-day operations of the facility.

The customary extortion and other forms of abuse associated with the English jail system were present in the early jails of Pennsylvania.[28] The sheriff was able to demand fees from those confined. Sometimes for a price prisoners were able to live  

*Fee system*

in taverns or even the sheriff's own house. Wealthy prisoners could escape altogether from the degradation of jail confinement by simply bribing the sheriff to permit them to live in private homes with little or no control or surveillance.[29] Normally, no attempt was made to feed or clothe the inmates, who were compelled to provide for their own needs. Whereas wealthy inmates might live quite comfortably, it was not unknown for prisoners who had no resources to die of starvation.[30] Most had to rely on public charity.

Beginning about 1730, attempts were made to eliminate some of these abuses. The sheriff was prohibited from selling intoxicating spirits to the prisoners. However, all this accomplished was to provide a middleman's profit to the sheriff, who now would merely send out for liquor or food at the request of the prisoner and charge him a "handling fee" for this service. Laws were also passed that prohibited a sheriff from holding office for more than three successive years, after which time he would not be able to hold the office again until three years had passed. This resulted in attempts to gouge the prisoners even more during the time that the sheriff was in office. In many instances, this law was circumvented by having the sheriff and the undersheriff "trade off" official positions. When the incumbent sheriff's three years were up, his undersheriff would be appointed as sheriff, and he in turn would be appointed as the undersheriff. In this manner, they traded the office back and forth.[31]

This then was the heritage that was passed on from Virginia and Pennsylvania to other colonies and later states. The idea of the jail was adopted by New Jersey in 1754, South Carolina in 1770, and Georgia in 1791.[32] As our country grew and expanded westward, jails became a feature of local government.

## ▣ THE JAIL IN THE CRIMINAL JUSTICE SYSTEM

**An important subsystem**

The jail is an integral part of the criminal justice system. Although it might be considered a subsystem of the corrections component, it plays a far more important role than this classification would suggest. Because it is a subsystem of a larger system, it must coordinate its efforts with other parts of the criminal justice process. Like the human body, the criminal justice system does not function well if any of its parts are operating below acceptable standards. As we shall see, the jail has traditionally operated below standard.

**The portal to the criminal justice system**

The jail serves as the portal to the criminal justice system. It is important as an indicator of the interest and concern with justice, punishment, and rehabilitation expressed by society and the local community. The person who is awaiting trial or serving a sentence experiences firsthand and with varying degrees of intensity what it is like to be exposed to the values of society as they relate to crime and punishment.

As mentioned, a stay in jail is the most widely experienced form of incarceration. Only the police and the lower criminal courts represent the criminal justice system more directly to the American public. The 8.5 million annual admissions to our nation's jails is a staggering number. This figure, however, should not be interpreted to mean that 8.5 million separate individuals are locked up in our jails each year. Many of these admissions often involve the same chronic misdemeanants such as street alcoholics who are arrested in jurisdictions that don't provide detoxification centers to house them when arrested. These people may be arrested several times during the course of a year. Still, the fact is inescapable: Many Americans are likely to experience jail time.

## The Jail and the Police

The jail is important not only in terms of the number of persons to come in contact with it and the influence it has on them, it also performs a service function for the other agencies within the system. The relationship of the jail to the police is one of accommodation and necessary cooperation. The jail has the responsibility to accept any prisoner who is legally arrested and can be legally received and detained by the jail. Not all persons arrested by the police can be legally received and detained. For example, in some jurisdictions juvenile arrestees have to be detained in special juvenile facilities.[33] Initially, the jail plays a passive role in the justice system, and to some extent the jail population reflects this. If the community, and therefore the police, are particularly concerned with enforcing laws against drunks or vagrants, the jail will probably contain a large number of such people. If it is the policy of police department personnel to "rough up" certain individuals they arrest, those arrested may become angry and aggressive and provide further problems for the jail personnel. The point is that community attitudes and police arrest policy affect the jail. By the same token, the way the jail operates will also certainly affect the criminal justice system.

*Necessary accommodation and cooperation*

Because the jail holds the accused until the formal machinery of criminal justice begins to move, jail personnel and the police have to work together. For example, if accomplices must be kept separated, the police will request jail personnel to do this. When a long-term investigation is required, the police and the jail may need to coordinate their efforts in scheduling investigative interviews or in making the accused available to the police, the prosecuting attorney, and defense counsel. This need for coordination and information exchange is also necessary and important if the jail is holding a material witness for the police or the prosecutor.

## The Jail and the Courts

The jail and the courts must also work in close cooperation. The court both influences the jail's activity and in turn is dependent on the jail's successful handling of the court-imposed workload. Unlike the passive role it plays in its relationship with the police, the jail takes a much more active and coordination-oriented role in its relationship with the court—so much so in fact that it almost seems that the jail in many instances is a department of the courts.

*Interdependence and coordination*

The extent of this interdependence between the court and the jail can be demonstrated by examining the sentencing decision rendered by the court. The courts can sentence an individual to jail, modify a sentence before completion, place an offender on probation, and in some instances sentence him or her to a work release program. These decisions affect the jail population, its composition, and the extent to which the jail must be involved in alternative programs. For example, the court in some jurisdictions may want to institute a system of work release for certain individuals sentenced to jail. To do this, the court must obtain the cooperation of the jail authorities. A number of communities are also using

Although some experts recommend that jails be located on the outskirts of cities, the advantages of proximity often outweigh other considerations. Shown here is the Manhattan Detention Complex (left), a short walk away from the court building (right). (Joan Meisel)

**Jail sites**

"weekend" jail programs in which offenders are free to live in the community during the week and serve their sentences on weekends. Again, the cooperation of the jail is necessary for such programs. If courts in certain jurisdictions have the option of sentencing individuals to local jails rather than other local facilities that may be available such as a county detention center or county workhouse, the sentencing decisions of the courts determine both the number and kinds of prisoners the jail receives. If the local courts have a policy of incarcerating in jail those convicted of driving under the influence, these offenders will have to be housed. By the same token, if the courts have a policy of setting aside public drunkenness arrests, fewer of these people will serve jail time because the court is not sentencing them. Under these circumstances the police will also deemphasize arrest practices for these crimes because they know the courts are setting aside such arrests. In both cases the jail will be affected.

The jail functions as the distributor in the criminal justice system. It serves as the transfer point for prisoners who have been sentenced to a county detention facility or a county workhouse or farm if such institutions exist. It also serves as the transfer point to the prison system after someone has been sentenced to the state department of corrections. Some jails also hold individuals who have been arrested by the federal authorities and are awaiting their trials in federal courts or persons sentenced by the federal courts and are awaiting transfer to a federal prison.

Until recently, the jail served a passive role in bail proceedings, which are court-supervised even though in some cases the matter is routine. The accused either made bail and was released or was unable to make it and was held for trial. Some new bail projects have now expanded the roles of the jail. In a few jurisdictions today, jail authorities are now involved in selecting persons for release on their own recognizance. In some cases this may be done by jail personnel themselves, although in most cases it is handled by the probation department or by joint agreement and consultation among the courts, probation personnel, and jail officials.

Because of the need for close coordination between the court and jail, jail facilities have been built in close proximity to the court. This has been done to make it easier to transport offenders to the court and limit the problems of security when prisoners are transferred. In recent years, jail consultants and progressive jail administrators have increasingly recommended that jails be built on the outskirts of cities, particularly in larger cities that must house a sizable number of prisoners.[34] Admittedly, this has created some problems, because the courts and police headquarters are situated downtown. However, the advantages of situating the jail on the outskirts of the city may outweigh the disadvantages. The use of downtown jails limits jail programming. With no facilities available for recreational and similar programs, prisoners are confined to the internal recesses of the jail and their activities are quite limited. In these situations, pent-up frustrations and crowding can lead to serious jail disruptions and rioting, as witnessed in jail facilities in a number of cities. It seems that the inconvenience of locating such facilities away from the central city is more than compensated for by the increased opportunities this presents for the development of a wider range of programs for prisoners. And strangely enough, except for the problems of security during the transfer of prisoners to and from the court, it may be easier to maintain institutional security in an area that is far less congested than having the jail in the crowded central city.

## The Jail and Corrections

Many view the jail as having primarily a law enforcement function because of the nature of many of its operations and because the chief administrator of the jail is usually a law enforcement officer. However, the jail does not have specific law enforcement functions. It does not serve as a base of operations for criminal detection or apprehension, although it may be part of a department where these activities go on. Jail personnel may be sheriff's deputies or police officers; however, their specific duties while working in the jail are not in the area of law enforcement.

Jails are part of the overall corrections program. They are, in fact, penal institutions. Like other correctional institutions, they hold many prisoners who are serving sentences, and they have a responsibility for their care. In the past, the emphasis of most jails was on detention. In recent years this traditional role has been redefined, and now the courts and the community in some locales are working to see that their jails develop at least some correctional and rehabilitative programs.

Part of corrections

The jail, in many cases, has a particular advantage over other correctional institutions in that it is located in the community and can coordinate community resources to develop effective programs. It also includes among its population a certain percentage of sentenced misdemeanants, who may be more tractable and amenable to various programs than are felons. It is particularly important that rehabilitative efforts be developed for the misdemeanant before the offender reaches the point at which his or her actions or attitudes require long-term incarceration.

Special situations, such as the arrest of a large number of demonstrators, call for innovative solutions. These antinuclear protestors are being held in an armory awaiting arraignment. (Timothy Carlson/Stock Boston)

One argument for the role of the jail in the overall correctional process has been well stated by the President's Commission on Law Enforcement and Administration of Justice:

> On the correctional continuum, jails are the beginning of the penal or institutional segment. They are, in fact, the reception units for a greater variety and number of offenders than will be found in any other segment of the correctional process, and it is at this point that the greatest opportunity is offered to make sound decisions on the offender's next step in the correctional process. Indeed, the availability of qualified services at this point could result in promptly removing many from the correctional process who have been swept in unnoticed and undetected and who are more in need of protective, medical and dental care from welfare and health agencies than they are in need of custodial care in penal and correctional institutions. In a broad sense, the jails and local institutions are reception centers for the major institutions.[35]

In addition to its own correctional function, the jail must develop close and effective coordination with the state correctional program so that both can learn from the experiences of the other. Because the jail typically has too few personnel and resources to develop a training program, the state department of corrections can be of important assistance in providing training opportunities. The state can also share its knowledge with jail personnel, particularly in terms of program implementation, rehabilitative techniques, and security systems that have proved to be of some benefit and can be adopted by local jails. The jail system is also important as a focus of research efforts and data gathering that can aid state correctional efforts in program evaluation, particularly as states move into the area of developing community-based treatment alternatives.

## THE JAIL TODAY: MAJOR PROBLEMS AND AREAS OF NEGLECT

The harsh reality is that most jails remain a serious problem in the system of American justice. For years, criminologists, study commissions, interested citizen groups, and some governmental officials have deplored the conditions of our nation's jails. The ill and the healthy, the old and the young, petty offenders and hardened criminals, the mentally defective, the psychotic and sociopathic, the vagrant and the alcoholic, the habitual offender who is serving a life sentence in short installments—all continue to populate our jails in an indiscriminate mass of human neglect. Because there are over three thousand local jails in the United States, they are shaped by characteristics as varied as the social fabric of the communities in which they are found.

Certain negative characteristics associated with our jails almost defy improvement. Often, one or more of these characteristics affect the other characteristics, so that any overall solution is that much more difficult to attain. Some of these negative characteristics are:

1. The diversity of the offenders in our jails
2. The problems of local control and politics
3. Demeaning physical facilities
4. Inadequate personnel
5. Inept administration
6. Failure to adopt alternative programs and dispositions

## Diversity of Offenders

The diverse nature of our jail population presents problems in terms of program development and rehabilitative strategies. At any time, our jails are likely to be populated by women, perhaps juveniles, the first offender, the habitual criminal, the dangerous and assaultive individual, and the down-and-out "wino." When jails must deal with such a broad range of offenders, their individual needs, and security considerations, it is not really possible to develop specific programs to deal with each situation. Lack of available resources further complicates the problem. As the Advisory Commission on Intergovernmental Relations (ACIR) says of the problem in its important 1984 report, *Jails: Intergovernmental Dimensions of a Local Problem:*

A broad mix

> Today, youths are still mixed with adults and unsentenced first offenders with hardened criminals; many jails are overcrowded while others are underutilized; little in the way of interjurisdictional consolidation has occurred; and although orphans and debtors are no longer jailed as such, the mentally ill and the inebriate are routinely locked behind steel bars. In many instances, the minimum in constitutional conditions remains doggedly unattainable.[36]

Jail inmates do, however, share certain socioeconomic characteristics. Inmates are typically poor, have low levels of educational attainment, and have histories of chronic unemployment. A relatively high percentage of them are members of minority races. Unfortunately, these characteristics are most likely the reasons they languish in jail to begin with. This is particularly true among pretrial detainees. Those who are employed or have the means to post bond escape incarceration.

Although inmates might be similar in financial status, race, and other characteristics, they are completely dissimilar in needs. The petty thief, the alcoholic, the juvenile or female prisoner, the narcotics user, the child beater, the assaultive armed robber, and the wife deserter are, to one degree or the other, all in need of different programs of treatment and require different security concerns.

### BOY CONTRACTS VD FROM INMATES IN JAIL

Washington, D.C., which has long been known for the problems associated with that city's detention facility, acquired another black mark on one of its detention centers. This time it involved the cell block at the District of Columbia Superior Court.

The *Washington Post* reported that an eleven-year-old boy charged with hitting a playmate on the head with a baseball bat was sexually assaulted by two other boys in the courthouse cell and later contracted syphilis. The two youths, one age fourteen and the other seventeen, pleaded guilty to two felony sodomy charges and were held in the city's juvenile detention facility in suburban Maryland.

The boy, according to the report of one social worker, hit his playmate with the baseball bat as the result of "playful antics," and not malice. The child, who had no prior criminal record, had suffered numerous emotional traumas before he was sexually assaulted and became suicidal after the incident, said psychiatrists who were treating him.

After suffering recurring bouts of depression, the child was admitted to Children's Hospital. During the examination doctors discovered that he had contracted syphilis of the mouth. He told a hospital social worker about the incident in the cell block, and she notified the police.

The boy previously had been hospitalized for depression when his stepfather had left home. One month before his arrest, a close friend of his had hanged himself, and four months after he was attacked in the courthouse cell block his mother died, the *Post* reported.

Relatives of the unidentified boy informed the Justice Department they planned to file a $1 million suit against the U.S. Marshal Service, which runs the cell block at the courthouse. Several local groups pledged their assistance in helping the boy.

## Local Control and Politics

Lack of resources

The fact that jails are local institutions is another of the major problems. Many communities are without the leadership, insight, or resources to bring about change. Having to rely primarily on property taxes for a financial base, local communities facing higher operating costs and demands for educational support, roads and streets, capital improvement, and a host of other considerations cannot give priority to jail services without foregoing needs in other areas. Because jail improvement has a low priority for most citizens, money to finance a jail or to provide the most rudimentary correctional program is usually absent.

Local politics have also played an important role. Of all the jails in the United States, three-fourths are administered by the sheriff.[37] In many states, the sheriff is an elected officer whose responsibilities for maintaining the local jail are clearly spelled out in the state constitution. Thus, the sheriff is free to operate with almost no control by the state. Even in fiscal appropriations, this officer is relatively unsupervised. Monies are usually appropriated by the county legislative authority in accordance with constitutional or statutory declarations that the county government must provide monies for the maintenance of the jail. In many cases where the states have tried to extend some supervisory control over the jail, individual sheriffs and their state political associations have been able to rebuff these attempts.

Another problem that makes it more difficult to wrestle controls of jail away from the county sheriff is the encroachment of municipal and separate county police forces into the enforcement responsibilities of the sheriff's departments. As these functions are reduced, the county jails become a larger share of each sheriff's vested interest and, thus, a function that sheriffs are less willing to relinquish.

Strangely enough, studies have shown that the population of a jail is not related directly to the size of the population in the jurisdiction it serves. The Nebraska Commission on Law Enforcement and Criminal Justice did a study of its jails and the counties they serve. It found that the jail populations, in this state at least, reflect the particular sentencing policies of the local courts and the policies of law enforcement practices more than the absolute population of the county itself.[38] Much of this, of course, results from the existence or nonexistence of alternative dispositions and institutions, such as detoxification centers and state misdemeanant institutions.

Although many inmates are in jail only temporarily until they come to trial, the "temporariness" of this period of incarceration can be quite lengthy. An Illinois survey found that pretrial detention, in some cases, can run into many months, depending on the legal maneuvers in the courts brought about by the prosecution and defense postponing or continuing cases, unavailability of witnesses, and so on.[39] Although such lengthy delays are very unusual, because court decisions and statutory pronouncements are designed to avoid such occurrences, this problem does exist to various degrees in some jurisdictions.

In fact, for different reasons the problem has grown worse in recent years. With state prisons filled to capacity, some jails are forced to take serious offenders who have been found guilty by the courts and are being held in jails because the prison system cannot admit them. This is bad for a number of reasons. For one thing, most jails do not separate offenders based on their particular characteristics or the crimes they commit. The only exception to this is in terms of segregating female and juvenile prisoners from adult males. Very little, if any, effort is made to separate those awaiting trial from those who have been convicted and sentenced.

This is a potentially serious problem. The risk is that more hardened and violent prisoners will exploit the weaker or less "jail-wise" inmate. There are many documented cases of this occurring in our nation's jails—particularly those in large urban areas.

## Deteriorated Physical Facilities

A 1973 study of the old District of Columbia jail points out the terrible state of affairs in many of America's jails today. One wonders if even the best programs available would make any difference in such squalor. The report provides an insight into the jail conditions that until recently existed in the capital of the nation that prides itself on its humanitarian concerns and position of leadership in the Western world. In the words of the report:

> The District of Columbia jail is a filthy example of man's inhumanity to man. It is a case study in cruel and unusual punishment, in the denial of due process, in the failure of justice.
>
> The jail is a century old and crumbling. It is overcrowded. It offers inferior medical attention to inmates, when it offers any at all. It chains sick men to beds. It allows—forces—men to live in crowded cells with rodents and roaches, vomit and excreta. It is the scene of arbitrary and capricious punishment and discipline. While there is little evidence of racial discrimination (the jail "serves" the male population of the District of Columbia and is, therefore, virtually an all-Black institution), there are some categories of prisoners who receive better treatment than others.
>
> The eating and living conditions would not be tolerated anywhere else. The staff seems, at best, indifferent to the horror over which it presides. This, they say, is the

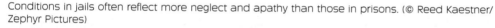

Conditions in jails often reflect more neglect and apathy than those in prisons. (© Reed Kaestner/ Zephyr Pictures)

job society wants them to do. The facilities and amounts of time available for recreation and exercise are limited, sometimes by a guard's whim. Except for a few privileged prisoners on various details, there are no means by which an inmate may combat idleness—certainly nothing that could be called education, counseling or self-help.[40]

In the 1960s, a special Presidential commission examined America's jails. It reported that 35 percent of the jail cells then in use across the country were at least fifty years old and that some of them were built in the nineteenth century.[41] The commission noted that one New England state had four jails with a total of 899 cells without any sanitary facilities. Because the construction of many of these institutions predates inside plumbing and electricity, the sanitary and safety conditions are often deplorable. Inmates are kept in large, unsegregated bullpens rather than in individual cells. One New England state was reported to have three jails that were more than 160 years old. A 1978 survey of jails in Arkansas disclosed that nearly two-thirds of the jails in the state did not meet even minimum sanitary and security standards.[42]

In the 1970s a second follow-up report was issued. It found little improvement. It concluded that jail facilities in use at the time still were being neglected. Jails that held few prisoners tended to be neglected and those that were constantly overcrowded were forced to push their physical facilities and their equipment beyond the breaking point.[43] Under either set of circumstances, the physical facility would soon deteriorate.

The ensuing years have seen some improvements. Still, even though some local units of government and certain states have made improvements, little real progress has been made. In the early 1980s a third survey of our nation's jails was undertaken. This time it wasn't the federal government or a special Presidential commission doing the survey. In this case it was done by the National Sheriff's Association—the professional organ of the operators of most of America's jails. Their findings differed little from the reports that preceded them. They found that many jails still remained hopelessly antiquated: they were without proper ventilation and failed to meet even minimum acceptable standards for fire protection, food services, health care, and sanitation.[44]

## Inadequate Personnel

The neglect of local jails is obvious in the absence of staff personnel and the caliber of operating personnel as it is in dismal physical facilities.[45] Jail employees—either professional staff or operating personnel—are invariably too few in number, untrained and underpaid. They, too, are victims of society's general disinterest in those housed in our jail system.[46]

Again, this is not a new revelation. Survey after survey has indicated that any professional staff are conspicuous by their absence. Even qualified social workers are unavailable to provide counseling services.[47] In those larger jail facilities where they can be found, they are hopelessly understaffed. In such situations they can accomplish little.[48] This situation exists in spite of the fact that the federal government during the 1970s provided significant financial assistance to help local units of government to upgrade the most deteriorated jail facilities and to encourage more professional staffing. Instead, the vast amount of money went into brick-and-mortar projects and little if any, into program activities. Professional staff services were, and largely remain, a nonpriority item in jail operating budgets.

The National Sheriff's Association survey mentioned earlier found that nothing has changed in this regard. Although this is one aspect of the personnel problem faced by local jails, the association found others. In fact, the association contends that the absence of professional staff may not be the most critical personnel problem faced by our local jails. It may be far more fundamental. The survey concludes that problems with jail operating staff is really the major personnel weakness faced by the nation's jail system:

Operating staff

> Today, many non-jail experts have suggested that overcrowding is the biggest problem. This survey makes it abundantly clear that the number one problem is personnel. . . . Many of the comments penned to the questionnaire explained that personnel difficulties span a range which touches on the lack of jail training, inadequate salaries, and heavy staff turnovers due to lack of career incentive programs.[49]

The nation's sheriffs—many of whom know firsthand the problems—are not the only ones who realize the seriousness of inadequate and ill-trained jail personnel. In commenting on problems in the nation's correctional institutions, former U.S. Supreme Court Chief Justice Warren Burger has said:

> One of the gravest weaknesses of our prisons has been the lack of training of guards and attendants who have hourly eyeball-to-eyeball contact with inmates—who by definition are abnormal people—prison disturbances, costly riots and often loss of life will result.[50]

The National Council on Crime and Delinquency has also examined the types of qualifications of the personnel who supervise local jail facilities. The majority of jail staff (78 percent) are custodial guards. Many jails have no minimum educational requirements for jail guards, nor is there much in the way of training required for jail custodial personnel. The Sheriff's Association states that "jail training today is where police training was twenty years ago."[51] For most recruits (47.9 percent), that means in-house, on-the-job training rather than academy training. Where in-service training is required, it usually consists of the handling of firearms, techniques of physical restraint, training in riots and disorders, and the supervision of correspondence.[52] Moreover, the survey found that training seems to be the most expendable item in budgets, and budget cuts are frequently given as the excuse for not conducting training.[53]

Whereas specialized academy training might be advisable, police-type academy training is of limited value. Again, the comments of the Sheriff's Association survey:

> If local academy training means police personnel are involved in the jail training then it is not acceptable. . . . Police officers usually are not trained correctional officers unless they work in departments where correctional and police work is rotated. Jail officers and administrators should be principally involved with the training of jail officers.[54]

In recent years a number of law enforcement agencies that provide both police and jail services have tried to develop separate career tracks for personnel assigned to these two areas. This arose out of the recognition that police-trained personnel did not make the best correctional officers; jail personnel needed to develop separate identities, skills, and career paths. Yet this has not been without its problems. It has been found that salary levels for jail personnel are often not comparable to the salaries paid to similarly experienced officers who provide law enforcement services in the same agency.

Separate career paths

Philadelphia prison officials had suspected for years that the city's overcrowded jails were riddled with graft and corruption. But like other jurisdictions with similar problems, prosecutors had trouble gathering evidence and making cases against jail officials and correctional guards. Few guards were willing to testify against other guards, and neither judges nor juries tend to believe the accusations of inmates.

Beginning in 1988, a series of arrests rocked the city's jails. Initially, more than sixty arrests of correctional officers were made when city police and members of the prosecutor's office following long months of undercover investigation marched into the warden's office with arrest warrants for members of his staff. It is expected that this is merely the tip of the iceberg: More arrests are pending, and long lists of disciplinary actions for violation of prison rules are expected.

The arrests were the result of a tip by a former inmate named Albert Harris. Harris had been arrested for burglary. Detectives thought he might be willing to trade information for leniency. He was—but instead of providing the cops with information about burglaries, he told a fantastic story of corruption inside the city's jails.

The ensuing months saw the investigation spread through the jail system like ripples in a pond. Undercover sales of narcotics and trafficking by guards and staff had become commonplace occurrences. In addition to being charged with smuggling drugs into jail, staff were accused of smuggling money and weapons to prisoners. Other guards were caught red-handed helping inmates escape. The alleged kingpin was an inmate named John Santiago. Testimony before the grand jury was that he supplied at least three hundred inmates in the facility with drugs, which had been supplied to him by guards and staff members he had bribed. Guards brazenly handed the drugs over to him in the prison or slipped drugs into his pocket as they pretended to frisk him. A network of inmate "runners" then distributed the drugs, weapons, and money obtained from Santiago throughout the jail.

As the months went by, a typical profile of the corrupt guards began to form. Most came from the same neighborhoods as the inmates; like the prisoners, guards were largely uneducated, and more than eighty percent were black or Hispanic. Many of the guards were heavy drug users themselves. There is no evidence that jail officials ever conducted proper preemployment background investigations of the guards or ever did any drug testing of the employees.

Most of the guards openly admitted that they participated either for the drugs they could obtain or the money that could be made. None seemed to show any remorse for the violation of their oaths of office; they were sorry only that they had been caught. Apologists for the jail system quickly blamed it on the lack of funds to do the proper screening of employees and on affirmative action requirements that prevented them from more carefully selecting guards.

The educational and training qualifications are similarly poor for those in jail administrative positions. Wardens, superintendents, and head jailers are often not trained, long-term career correctional professionals. Even training in prisons is not necessarily a prerequisite to success in working in and operating a jail. Many experts feel that the diversity of jail inmates and the frequent turnover in jail populations as compared to prisons imposes unique problems that traditional prisons do not face.

In spite of efforts to create separate career paths, most jails are still operated by law enforcement personnel. Even in states such as California, Minnesota, and Michigan, which have more professional and advanced jail systems, the county and city jail systems are operated by sheriff's departments and local police. These agencies, in turn, assign their sworn law enforcement personnel to jail duties. It is not unusual for many police agencies to assign personnel to the jail as a form of punishment. In other instances, police agencies send to the jail officers who have recurring problems with the public, have reputations for frequent use of excessive force, or have characteristics that make them less than effective as police officers on the street. The implications for such personnel practices is obvious. Assigning to the jail someone who cannot control himself or herself on the street seems to ask for problems—particularly given the civil liability that exists today for police agencies and communities.

Even if such police personnel are not assigned routinely to the jail, the use of sworn police officers in the role of jailers has some implications. The psychological role-set of a law enforcement officer is to arrest offenders and to see that they are jailed; the role of a correctional worker should be more rehabilitative in nature. Although correctional workers must be concerned about the broad role of security in the institution, they also have a responsibility to help prisoners who need assistance and can benefit from it. However, the use of low-paid custodians to relieve law enforcement personnel in jails is no solution to the problem. In many cases, such individuals are even less qualified and competent to perform the responsibilities than are the law enforcement officers they replace.

Nationally, there were 5.1 inmates for each custodial officer in our nation's jails in the early 1980s. This number varied from state to state and ranged from 1.4 to 13.9.[55] On the surface, this might appear adequate. However, this figure includes part-time custodial personnel, and the typical custodial person is also involved in administrative tasks, such as record keeping, booking, and other forms of paperwork. In addition, jails must be manned twenty-four hours a day, every day of the year. Thus, the effective ratio of jail personnel to inmates shrinks to 1:23. Given the conditions that exist in many jails, this does not even permit the custodial officer to effectively supervise the inmates in terms of security, let alone becoming a participating member in alternative programs that might be developed. The Nebraska study indicated that staff personnel could not observe all prisoners from their assigned stations.[56] In Idaho, research pointed out the seriousness of this problem, particularly at night. It noted that when its jail survey was taken, only 32 percent of the jails in that state had a full-time staff member present during the night.[57]

## Administrative Problems

One of the major impediments to change in our jails is the quality of administrative leadership. Many sheriffs and police chiefs are not well trained in aspects of administration. If they suffer from a lack of managerial skills and training in their primary service area of law enforcement, they are even less qualified to oversee the operations of a jail facility. Ironically, it is the office of sheriff that has both law enforcement and jail responsibilities in which managerial skills in the complex areas of law enforcement and jail operations is most noticeably absent. Too often, county sheriffs have limited law enforcement experience and even more limited expertise and experience in police and public administration. Their primary skills are in the political arena. Although they may compensate for their deficiencies by the appointment of qualified subordinates in key command and managerial positions, this is not always possible because of the lack of available resources to attract qualified personnel.

If they have to demonstrate any managerial competency, it is in the law enforcement function, because citizens are much more likely to demand high levels of police service than they are to concern themselves with jail operations. The only time most citizens are apt to question the managerial competence of the jail operation is when disorders or escapes occur.

Because most of the citizens who are politically powerful in a community are those least likely to find themselves in jail, they have no firsthand knowledge of the

*Lack of jail-management skills*

*Operational priorities*

conditions that exist. Even if arrested, they are most likely to make bond and thereby avoid an actual experience with the jail facility and its operations.

Given these circumstances, most sheriffs or police chiefs with responsibility for maintaining detention facilities are concerned first with security and next with ensuring that riots and disorders do not occur. They wish to avoid the negative publicity that is associated with escapes and disorders. Third, jail administrators want to appear to be servicing the courts properly. This generally means developing operating policies that ensure inmates will be present before the court on their trial date and that court orders are carried out. Finally, jail administrators are concerned with keeping operating costs for the jail at a minimum to avoid inquiries and citizen concern. This is not meant to imply that these should not be important concerns; however, in too many instances these are the *only* concerns.

All in all, the emphasis seems to be on maintaining a high degree of anonymity in terms of the operation of the jail. The objective appears to be to keep the entire operation removed as far as possible from contact with the public, and in those instances when public contact is unavoidable, to make that exposure as brief as possible, and to make it appear at least superficially that the agency and its chief administrator are competent.

The overriding concern for security has manifested itself in some strange accommodations in the operating policies of many jails. Given limited manpower, custodial personnel have often knowingly or unwittingly turned over the internal control of the jail to the inmates themselves. In this way, they rely on the inmates (or at least the inmate leaders) to maintain order. The ramifications of this policy are farreaching. Inmate leaders become exploiters, not only of other prisoners, but even of the jailers themselves. They begin to make innocent demands on the custodial staff for certain concessions. As they win concessions, they strengthen their power base and become more demanding.[58] As the power cliques develop, disastrous consequences can ensue. A study of the Philadelphia jail pointed out that development of certain leadership cliques in that facility led to "mass intimidation" and sexual assaults on other inmates. Even the jail administrators themselves were forced to acknowledge that virtually every young man of slight build committed by the courts is sexually approached within a day or so after he is admitted. Many of the young men were repeatedly raped by gangs of prisoners.[59]

*Inmate control*

## Lack of Alternative Programs and Dispositions

Because it has been mentioned that jails are without professional treatment or helping staff, it can be assumed they are without such program activities as well. This is the case. Very few jails have any type of educational program, few have any form of vocational training, and many have no rehabilitative programs whatsoever. Even such activities as group and substance abuse counseling are often not available to inmates.

*Absence of "helping" programs*

For example, the Sheriff's Association survey showed that slightly over a third of the jails responding to the survey claimed to offer substance abuse counseling; less than half offered any type of personal counseling.[60] And this probably doesn't tell the whole story. Whereas the respondents may indicate that they have such programs, there is no way of determining what types of programs these are, how available they are, what are their staffing and operational characteristics, and other factors that would help us analyze them.

It was also found that the nation's jails offer very little in the way of educational or vocational training—including educational release. Most smaller jails had no reading materials available to prisoners, and fully one-half of the jails made no recreation or entertainment available.[61] In the early 1980s, only sixty-seven jails nationwide had been accredited by the American Medical Association (AMA) for meeting its minimum health care standards.[62] It was also pointed out in the ACIR study that although a number of jails reported having work release programs, it is probably safe to assume that very few prisoners were affected by these programs.[63]

These, then, are just some of the negative features that have come to be associated with American jails. They are certainly not an all-encompassing list. Together they impose formidable obstacles to change. Can anything be done to improve the nation's jails? The next section looks at some of the more widely discussed possibilities for improvement. Again, the topics that follow are not an exhaustive list of recommended changes; they are merely some of the more commonly made suggestions.

## NEW MEANS OF DEALING WITH MISDEMEANANTS AND RESTRUCTURING JAILS

With the courts burdened by impossible case loads and many of our urban jails overpopulated, new means are being sought to alleviate these problems. In addition, several practical solutions have been voiced concerning reforms of the jail system.

### Diversionary Measures

One of the major recommendations for reform is to divert some of those accused of misdemeanor crimes and certain adjudicated offenders from the process of incarceration. The development of diversionary programs has been recommended by the President's Commission on Law Enforcement and Administration of Justice, the American Bar Association Commission on Correctional Facilities and Services, several federal agencies that have studied the problem, and a variety of individuals, including judges, legislators, correctional workers, police, prosecuting attorneys, and defense lawyers.[64]

One such increasingly common diversionary program is a citation or summons in lieu of arrest program now authorized by law in many jurisdictions. This strategy for minimizing the use of detention as an alternative is directed at the point of first contact with the criminal justice system—the arrest. Just as the police are authorized to issue summons or citations for traffic violations, they are authorized in some areas to issue citations for given types of offenses if certain other conditions are met. The citation directs the individual to appear at court for trial on a specified date. Many of the statutes that give the police permission to use this diversionary device spell out under what conditions such an alternative to jail can be employed. For example, the crime must usually be a misdemeanor in which there is no danger of physical harm to the individual or others if he is released; the accused is identified as a member of the local community; and there is no reason to believe that the accused would flee from the jurisdiction if he should be released. Many times the arrested person, to be able to be released on such a citation, must show proof of permanent residency in the jurisdiction and bona fide employment.

Often, the police will impose by administrative policy other conditions before

*Citation in lieu of arrest programs*

someone can be released under such a program. A check for outstanding warrants may be employed to determine if the arrestee has any other arrest warrants outstanding to which he or she must answer. Obviously, the presence of such a warrant(s) would normally make the individual ineligible for release under citation.

Police agencies usually follow one of two policies in authorizing release on citation. Some agencies give the arresting officers in the field clear guidelines and then leave it up to the arresting officer's discretion on the spot. In addition to diverting offenders from jail, such a policy makes it possible to keep arresting officers on the street rather than having to return to the jail with the arrestee and go through the process of transporting the prisoner. This keeps the arresting officer out in his or her district rather than having to leave to take the prisoner to jail.

Other jurisdictions follow what is called a *station house arrest procedure*. An individual is arrested and taken to the police agency, where he or she is booked and fingerprinted. Often, the decision to release on citation is then made by a supervisory officer following existing law and departmental policy. Many police

---

### RETHINKING THE DRUNK TANK

As the problem of overcrowded jails threatens to overwhelm facilities nationwide, some state and local officials have hit on their own solutions for easing the crunch. One tack: to separate out individuals convicted of drunk driving.

For example, an 18-month backlog of DUI offenders waiting to serve mandatory 48-hour sentences inspired Tennessee Governor Ned McWherter, a Democrat, to make his state the first to allow National Guard armories to be used as ad hoc county jails for DUIs. So far, a dozen of Tennessee's 95 counties have taken advantage of the program, which started last spring. Generally the more urban counties, where the competition for space is most acute, are participating, says McWherter press aide Ken Renner. Adding to the problem of tight space is the fact that, like 37 other states, Tennessee is under federal court order to ease crowding in state prisons, says Renner.

The program has been valuable, says Phillip L. Whittenberg, chief administrative officer for Shelby County. Three weekends a month, the county sends between 150 and

175 individuals to the armory, he says.

Under the guidelines, county officials simply work out with the commanders at the various armories what weekends the buildings will be free. The local sheriffs provide guards and food, and the armory provides the cots and toilet facilities, billing the county a minimal amount for the space. The cost of constructing and staffing a place to handle DUIs in the absence of the armories would be in the millions of dollars, Whittenberg estimates.

A slightly more involved program has recently started in Summit County, Ohio, where second- and third-offense DUIs can now serve their time at the Glenwood Jail, a community-based non-profit corrections facility. There they may serve shorter sentences in a less restrictive jail, but many have to pick up part of the tab for the counseling that's part of Glenwood's procedure. Judges are providing lots of incentive for going to Glenwood, routinely hitting second- and third-time offenders with harsh sentences and agreeing to suspend a portion of the time if the offender accepts

treatment there. In the first three months, Glenwood served more than 100 DUI offenders, charging them for the counseling based on their ability to pay.

Depending on the jurisdiction of the conviction, the county or the city of Akron picks up the balance, including the entire bill for those who have no money. The county provides the inmates' food and sheriff's deputies as guards, which this year [1989] will cost $59,630. That, says county information officer Karl Perdue, is a bargain.

According to Bernard Rochford, associate executive director of Glenwood, the program has even received the endorsement of such groups as Mothers Against Drunk Driving. "Initially MADD was critical, but I think that was out of ignorance," says Rochford. "Once we met with them and showed them these people were not only doing serious time but were being evaluated and counseled in the process, they had no problem with it at all."

*—Jonathan Walters*

*Source: Governing 2, No. 12 (Washington, D.C.: Congressional Quarterly, Inc.), September 1989, p. 10.*

---

agencies claim that their experience with such programs has been generally good. Very few of the people receiving the citations later failed to appear in court.[65]

Another form of diversion that has received a lot of attention in recent years is a "community-service" sentence. Rather than sentencing a convicted offender to a period of jail confinement, the judge places the individual on probation and sentences him or her to a period of community service performing a prescribed task. This could range from cleaning city parks to delivering meals to the community's elderly shut-ins. The assignments are as broad in scope as one's imagination and the needs of the community. Juvenile court judges have also employed this approach extensively in some jurisdictions with youths adjudicated for certain delinquent acts.

"Community service" sentence

The "weekend incarceration" program mentioned earlier is also a form of jail diversion. Although the individual will be confined to jail on the weekends, such programs at least relieve some pressure on the jail population during the week. Unfortunately, with some jails being so overcrowded—particularly in major cities, this approach is somewhat limited in its usefulness because large jails themselves are typically at peak populations during the weekend. One innovative idea is to confine such people in a public school over the weekend, when such a facility is vacant.

## Restitution

Along with community service, restitution programs are growing more popular as diversionary strategies in lieu of sentencing the accused to jail. In some cases a combination of both restitution and community service is imposed. Restitution is a court requirement that a convicted offender pay money or provide services to the victim of the crime. Typically, restitutive payment is made in cash or in kind (services).

Like other types of diversionary techniques, imaginative restitution programs have been developed in certain locales. Several jurisdictions, for instance, have adopted programs in which convicted offenders who are not employed are provided public service jobs at slightly above minimum wage. They are then required to take a percentage of their earnings and give this to the victim as restitution. The feelings of those involved in such programs is that everyone benefits: the offender benefits, in that he or she is given employment, while the victim receives restitution. Interestingly, such programs are opposed in certain areas. Its critics say that such a program imposes an illegal "condition of servitude" on offenders.

## Regional (Multijurisdiction) Jails

Another recommendation for improving America's jail system is to consolidate existing small jails on a regional basis. In one such arrangement, a major city or cities and the county could form a consolidated jail facility. In another, two adjacent rural counties could establish a regional jail serving both jurisdictions.

Jail consolidation

In terms of cost analysis, particularly when the "costs" of not being able to provide the necessary services to inmates housed in local detention facilities and not being able to comply with minimum jail standards are considered, the arguments are impressive. This latter point is becoming particularly troublesome. Some communities are finding that they cannot manage the costs of bringing their jail facility up to meet state- or court-mandated minimum standards. They may have to seek alternative arrangements. Sharing the cost of jail operations with other cooperating jurisdictions may be the only answer.

Various forms of financing are available. The cooperating jurisdictions can share the proportional costs of operating the jail, or a city might contract with the county on a per diem basis in which it agrees to pay so much per prisoner per day. Some states have encouraged such cooperative arrangements by making state funds available to local communities for jail consolidation.

The basic attraction of interlocal agreements for jail consolidation is the pooling of resources. Participating jurisdictions are able to increase economies of scale in constructing, maintaining, and operating physical facilities and in developing and conducting diversified programs. It is also argued that such arrangements can encourage the development of professional jail management and staffing. For example, the hiring of career jail correctional officers rather than the use of police personnel is possible. Such a system would also make possible a distribution of inmate population to avoid problems of overcrowding or underutilization that might well exist if individual communities continued to maintain their own jails.

Jail regionalization is not, however, without certain inherent drawbacks. It may not be practicable to house pretrial detainees in these facilities if the various courts the facility serves are widely dispersed. Such an arrangement makes it difficult to transport defendants to and from the courts and makes it difficult for attorneys to consult with their clients.

It has been argued that regional jails are less than satisfactory because they might remove an individual from his or her family in the event that public transportation is not available. The idea is that such family contact is positive and should be fostered. Of course, this may be a questionable assumption. Nonetheless, such an argument loses much of its validity today as personal transportation is generally available. It is also argued that developing a jail site that is available to sharing jurisdictions such as two rural counties may effectively remove the site of the jail from access to available community resources. Again, this argument loses much of its merit when it is realized that jails and community services have very little or no cooperative arrangements in most jurisdictions. Although it might be useful if these arrangements could exist, the fact of the matter is that they don't. Under such circumstances it is hard to defend this argument.

**Political impediments**     The biggest problem, however, is merely political in nature. As mentioned in Chapter 6, consolidating law enforcement efforts is complicated by political problems; the same stumbling blocks thwart jail consolidation efforts. Communities do not want to share decision-making with other communities. And since these cooperative efforts require a great deal of planning, cooperation, and compromise to establish and operate such a facility, this becomes a formidable obstacle to overcome.

Another proposal that combines the advantages of the regional jail but with better programming is for the state to enact legislation that would turn these facilities over to the state department of corrections. Because the states have more highly developed correctional systems, including more highly trained correctional and treatment specialists, and more sound fiscal bases, they could incorporate the existing jail systems into statewide systems of misdemeanant institutions. In this manner, reception and classification programs could be developed, alternative community-based programs implemented, and more effective research and evaluative data gathered.

Presently, six states have state-administered jail systems. According to the ACIR, these six states share some common features. They are generally small in area and/or population. County government, the most common unit with jail responsibility in the American system of local government, has been abolished or is weak. In these states the state government is clearly dominant in the sharing of state–local financing and spending responsibility. And the state's assumption of the jail function took place in several of these states (Delaware, Hawaii, and Vermont) in the context of a more comprehensive reform of correctional activities.[66]

Obviously, many states do not share these common characteristics. Opponents of state-administered jail systems argue that the jail function is a "natural" local function because of the local characteristics of law enforcement. They also do not agree with the idea that state control of jail systems will provide additional resources. On the contrary, they contend that jail operations will in such circumstances be forced to compete for funds with other state priorities in general and other segments of the total correctional system. Such an arrangement will also force increased power struggles that jail officials will face with the rest of the corrections bureaucracy. Finally, the inevitable movement away from ties with the community runs counter to the current trend toward greater emphasis on community-based programs.[67]

It is not likely that the states will fall over themselves in the near future to take over the operations of local jails. There are simply too many hurdles to overcome. On the other hand, jail regionalization holds a greater promise of adoption. Even in this case, however, progress toward consolidation will be slow and not very widespread.

**STATE SUPERVISION OF LOCAL JAIL FACILITIES.** About twenty years ago, the first-ever national survey of our nation's jail system was undertaken.[68] It was found that only about 40 percent of the states had established any standards for the operations of their local jails. And the standards that did exist were for the most part minimal. They were concerned only with construction issues—particularly those dealing with security—and basic health standards. Even the federal government's Bureau of Prisons (which for a number of years has operated a jail inspection system whose responsibility it is to inspect and certify local jails for use in holding federal prisoners) was concerned only with issues of jail construction, security, and health-related programs.

There have been some important changes since then. The states have taken a more meaningful role in supervising local jail facilities. A lot of this is attributable to the federal courts. Fearing the consequences of federal court action in condemning local jails, many of the states have moved to put their jail systems in better order. By the mid 1980s, about 80 percent of those states that have jails operated by local units of government have passed laws imposing some kind of mandatory jail standards. These, however, run from very strong standards and aggressive compliance inspections to very weak. A number of states, such as Michigan, have adopted both encompassing legislation and, at the same time, have created special agencies within the state department of corrections to enforce the provisions of the standards. A comprehensive statute in this area might seek to regulate through inspections such areas as adequate security; mail and visitation privileges; special programs for prisoners; separation of juveniles from adults and women from male prisoners; provisions for adequate food, health services, and clothing; the mainte-

A broad range

Volunteer programs, such as this one sponsored by the Salvation Army, provide counseling and instruction for jail inmates. (The Salvation Army Archives and Research Center)

nance of minimum exercise or recreation facilities, established security standards, fire protection, escape procedures, riot provisions, and training; and around-the-clock availability of jail supervision.[69]

Other states may have created broad standards but at the same time ended up by watering the process down by assigning the responsibility to an oversight board consisting of local jailers, judges, prosecutors, and citizens. This points up the pitfalls of such regulatory legislation. It is not only the scope of regulations in the law that is important, but what oversight authority is provided to ensure compliance and who is given the responsibility to ensure that the legislation is carried out. For this reason, many critics contend that the standards and the inspections are a sham.[70] One ready indicator of how effective such standards and their enforcement are is the number of jails in these states that, in spite of the standards, are under court order for improvement. This does not mean those instances in which the inspection agency was able to obtain a court order to correct the situation, but rather instances in which *external* sources (grand juries, prisoners' suits) and other means were employed. Unfortunately, such information is not readily available. Yet the fact that such externally induced court orders exist in states with purported standards and inspection services raises the issue of the *real* effectiveness of existing jail standards.

## The Use of Jail Volunteers

**Advantages**

Recently, there has been interest in using volunteers in assistance-directed programs in jails. However, few jails have tried to establish such programs. The use of volunteers inside the jail has several advantages, one being that it reduces the public's ignorance of how bad the situation is. Conditions considered to be tolerable by the jail administration may seem intolerable to the volunteer. For example, few if any volunteers would accept almost a total lack of medical service as a condition of incarceration in even the smallest jail. In addition to their usefulness as providers of supplementary services in the jail, volunteers are thus a source of public information and of public demands for improved jail conditions.[71]

One of the leading jail volunteer programs in the country has been established at the Ingham County Jail outside Lansing, Michigan. This institution has a broad rehabilitative program, offering services designed to meet the vocational, academic, social, and personal needs of inmates. An outstanding component of the assistance plan at the jail is its volunteer involvement. In the first two years of the program, volunteers were instrumental in establishing programs in auto mechanics, blueprint reading, math, physics, arts and crafts, and accounting.

**Drawbacks**

The use of jail volunteers is not without its pitfalls. For one thing such individuals and groups must be thoroughly screened before they can be used. This is a time-consuming and potentially costly undertaking. There is also the question of liability if something were to happen to a volunteer. A final problem is simply finding qualified people who would be willing to devote their time to working with prisoners. Many people are simply not interested in this type of public service activity when there are so many similar needs among other population groups such as kids and the elderly who could also benefit from citizen volunteer services.

The American jail seems to stand at the crossroads. Although significant improvements have occurred in many aspects of the administration of justice and in corrections itself over the past quarter of a century, the nation's jail system still lags behind. The road to jail reform has been a slow tortuous path of resistance and futility. Even today, the overall picture still remains dismal and unpromising. Under the circumstances, if we haven't been able to substantially and comprehensively improve our nation's jails in the past two hundred years, it is unlikely things will significantly change in our lifetimes. Perhaps in another one hundred years, we'll have begun to have shown some real improvement in our short-term incarceration facilities—on the other hand, perhaps we'll still be lamenting the same problems and failures.

## SUMMARY

The jail serves as the gateway to the criminal justice process. The history of jails in both England and later in America is a story of neglect, brutality, and debasement. Although jails have improved substantially in the twentieth century, they still are operated in a manner of which we as a nation cannot be proud.

The major problems that confront our jails are interrelated and complex. First, the sheer numbers and variety of offenders create difficult problems for devising meaningful rehabilitative programs. The problem is made more difficult by the fact that jails are under local control, and jail administrators are often local politicians with law enforcement interests. Many jails are totally inadequate in terms of physical facilities and personnel and are hampered by the lack of qualified professional jail administrators. As a

result of these factors, we have failed to adopt meaningful alternative programs to deal with the hundreds of thousands of individuals who each year serve some time in jail.

In the past few years, a number of changes have been proposed and adopted in some jurisdictions throughout the country. For example, increasing emphasis is being placed on diverting the offender through such programs as citations in lieu of arrest and reforms in the bail bond system. Other suggested reforms are jail regionalization, state supervisory authority over local jails, and the increased use of volunteers and support programs in jails. In spite of a few examples of success, jails still remain as the overall weakest link in our nation's correctional system.

## REVIEW QUESTIONS

1. What kinds of offenders are held in jails?
2. Why is the jail called the "portal" to the criminal justice system?
3. Approximately how many offenders are held in U.S. jails in any one year?
4. In what ways do jails serve the courts?
5. Is the purpose of the jail primarily to detain or to rehabilitate?
6. What is meant by the diversity of offenders?
7. What are six negative characteristics of most jails in the United States? Briefly state why each is a problem.
8. What have some states done to try and improve their jails? Have they been successful?
9. Name the prescribed conditions under which a police officer would issue a citation to someone for a noncriminal offense rather than arrest the person.
10. Is there regional control of your local jail system? How does the regional control work?

## DISCUSSION QUESTIONS

1. Do modern-day jails still reflect some of the characteristics of their predecessors? Discuss.
2. What should be the function of the jail in the criminal justice system?
3. How does the jail serve other components of the criminal justice system?
4. What are the major problems facing America's jails today?

5. Will the new proposals for handling misdemeanants, such as citations instead of jail sentences, be effective? Why or why not?

6. What needs to be done to improve our nation's jail system?

## SUGGESTED ADDITIONAL READINGS

Advisory Commission on Intergovernmental Relations, *Jails: Intergovernmental Dimensions of a Local Problem.* Washington, D.C.: ACIR, May 1984.

Alexander, Myrl. *Jail Administration.* Springfield, Ill.: Charles C Thomas, 1975.

Allen, Harry E., and Clifford E. Simonsen. *Corrections in America,* 2nd ed. Encino, Calif.: Glencoe, 1978.

Amir, Menachem. "Sociological Study of the House of Correction." *American Journal of Corrections* 29, no. 2 (March–April 1976): 36–41.

Fishman, Joseph F. *Crucibles of Crime: A Shocking Story of American Jails.* New York: Cosmopolitan Press, 1923.

Flynn, Edith E. *Prisoners in America.* Englewood Cliffs, N.J.: Prentice-Hall, 1973.

Glaser, Daniel. "Some Notes on Urban Jails." In Daniel Glaser, ed., *Crime in the City.* New York: Harper & Row, 1970.

Goldfarb, Ronald. *Jails: The Ultimate Ghetto.* Garden City N.Y.: Anchor, 1975.

Mattick, Hans. "The Contemporary Jails of the United States." In Daniel Glaser, ed., *Handbook on Criminology.* Chicago: Rand McNally, 1974.

McGee, Richard A. "Our Sick Jails." *Federal Probation* 35 (March 1971): 3–8.

National Institute of Justice. *The 1983 Jail Census.* Washington, D.C.: U.S. Department of Justice, November 1984.

National Sheriff's Association. *Manual of Jail Administration.* Washington, D.C.: National Sheriff's Association, 1970.

National Sheriff's Association, *The State of Our Nation's Jails.* Washington, D.C.: National Sheriff's Association, 1982.

Palmer, Ted. *Correctional Intervention and Research: Current Issues and Future Prospects.* Lexington, Mass.: Lexington Books, 1978.

Wayson, Billy L., et al. *Local Jails.* Lexington, Mass.: Lexington Books, 1977.

Webb, Sidney, and Beatrice Webb. *English Prisons Under Local Government.* Hamden, Conn.: Archon, 1963. (Originally published in 1906.)

## NOTES

1. U.S. Department of Justice, *Sourcebook of Criminal Justice Statistics—1980* (Washington, D.C.: U.S. Government Printing Office, 1981), p. 482.

2. Bureau of Justice Statistics, *National Jail Survey—1986* (Washington, D.C.: U.S. Department of Justice, 1987), p. 4.

3. Ibid.

4. Ibid.

5. Ibid.

6. Bureau of Justice Statistics, *1983 Jail Census* (Washington, D.C.: U.S. Department of Justice, 1984).

7. Bureau of Justice Statistics, *Report to the Nation on Crime and Justice,* 2nd ed. (Washington, D.C.: U.S. Department of Justice, March 1988), p. 34.

8. National Commission on Law Observance and Enforcement, *Report on Penal Institutions, Probation and Parole* (Washington, D.C.: U.S. Government Printing Office, 1931), p. 273.

9. Daniel Fogel, quoted in "The Scandalous U.S. Jails," *Newsweek,* 18 August 1980, p. 74.

10. Barry Krisberg, *Changing the Jails,* Manual prepared for the conference, Changing the Jails, University of San Francisco, April 1975, p. 1.

11. National Assembly on the Jail Crisis, *New Partnerships for Reform: Proceedings of the National Assembly on the Jail Crisis* (Kansas City, MO: May 22–25, 1977), p. VII.

12. Advisory Commission on Intergovernmental Relations (ACIR), *Jails: Intergovernmental Dimensions of a Local Problem—A Commission Report* (Washington, D.C.: ACIR, May 1984), p. 1.

13. Frederick Pollack and Frederick W. Maitland, *History of the English Law* (Cambridge, England: Cambridge University Press, 1952), p. 516.

14. Sidney Webb and Beatrice Webb, *English Prisons Under Local Government* (Hamden, Conn.: Shoe String, 1963), p. 3.

15. Henry Burns, Jr., *Origin and Development of Jails in America* (monograph) (Carbondale: Southern Illinois University Press), p. 2.

16. See John Howard, *The State of the Prisons* (London: Dent, 1929).

17. E. M. Leonard, *History of English Poor Relief* (Cambridge, England: Cambridge University Press, 1900), pp. 220–221.

18. H. E. Barnes and N. K. Teeters, *New Horizons in Criminology* (Englewood Cliffs, N.J.: Prentice-Hall, 1949), p. 389.

19. Burns, *Origin and Development of Jails in America,* p. 4.

20. Ibid.

21. Ibid., p. 6.

22. Ibid., p. 8.

23. Ibid.

24.   Oliver P. Chitwood, *Justice in Colonial Virginia*, vol. XXIII (Baltimore: Johns Hopkins, 1905), pp. 111–112.

25.   Louis N. Robinson, *Penology in the United States* (Philadelphia: Winston, 1922), p. 37.

26.   Burns, *Origin and Development of Jails in America*, p. 11.

27.   Harry E. Barnes, *The Evolution of Penology in Pennsylvania* (Indianapolis, Ind.: Bobbs-Merrill, 1927), pp. 58–63.

28.   Ibid., pp. 63–65.

29.   Burns, *Origin and Development of Jails in America*, p. 13.

30.   Harry E. Barnes, *The Story of Punishment* (Boston: Stratford, 1930), p. 192.

31.   Robert T. Treymine, *Early Colonial Jails* (New York: Meinster, 1899), pp. 111–113.

32.   Robinson, *Penology in the United States*, pp. 36–37.

33.   A number of federal courts are now ruling that the confinement of a juvenile in a county jail for adults is in violation of the provision against "cruel and unusual punishment" of the Eighth Amendment; see Bureau of National Affairs, Inc., *The Criminal Law Reporter* 16 (18 December 1974): 1045.

34.   Public Management Consultants, *Recommended Changes for Jail Management in Atlanta, Georgia* (Atlanta, Ga.: 1969).

35.   President's Commission on Law Enforcement and Administration of Justice, *Task Force Report: Corrections* (Washington, D.C.: U.S. Government Printing Office, 1967), pp. 162–163.

36.   ACIR, *In Jails*, p. 17.

37.   Richard A. McGee, "Our Sick Jails," *Federal Probation* 35 (March 1971): 5.

38.   Nebraska Commission on Law Enforcement and Criminal Justice, *For Better or for Worse? Nebraska's Misdemeanant Correctional System* (Lincoln: 1970), pp. 97–105.

39.   Hans W. Mattick and Ronald Sweet, *Illinois Jails: Challenge and Opportunity for the 1970s* (Washington, D.C.: U.S. Government Printing Office, 1970), p. 49.

40.   American Civil Liberties Union, *The Seeds of Anguish: An ACLU Study of the D.C. Jail* (Washington, D.C.: ACLU, 1973), pp. 3, 5.

41.   President's Commission, *Corrections*, p. 166.

42.   Ibid.

43.   National Advisory Commission on Criminal Justice Standards and Goals, *Corrections* (Washington, D.C.: U.S. Government Printing Office, 1973), p. 275.

44.   James Bencivenga, "U.S. Corrections Officials Seek Ways to Improve Local Jails," in John J. Sullivan and Joseph L. Victor, (eds.), *Criminal Justice 84/85* (Guilford, Conn.: Dushkin Publishing Group, 1984), p. 252.

45.   ACIR, *Jails*, p. 90.

46.   Mattick and Sweet, *Illinois Jails*, p. 368.

47.   Law Enforcement Assistance Administration, *The Nation's Jails*, p. 29.

48.   National Council on Crime and Delinquency, *Corrections in the United States* (New York: National Council on Crime and Delinquency, 1967).

49.   National Sheriff's Association, *The State of Our Nation's Jails* (Washington, D.C.: National Sheriff's Association, 1982), p. 3.

50.   As quoted in ACIR, *Jails*, p. 7.

51.   National Sheriff's Association, op. cit., p. 125.

52.   President's Commission, *Corrections*, p. 165.

53.   Ibid, p. 125.

54.   National Sheriff's Association, op. cit., p. 17.

55.   U.S. Department of Justice, 1982 *Survey of Inmates of Local Jails* (Washington, D.C.: U.S. Government Printing Office, 1983), p. 20.

56.   Nebraska Commission on Law Enforcement, *For Better or for Worse?* p. 27.

57.   Idaho Law Enforcement Planning Commission, *State of Idaho Jail Survey*, p. 9.

58.   For an excellent portrayal of how this occurs and the results of such power shifts, see Gresham M. Sykes, *A Society of Captives* (New Tork: Atheneum, 1970), especially Chap. 3.

59.   Allen J. Davis, "Sexual Assaults in the Philadelphia Prison Systems and Sheriff's Vans," *Trans-Action* 6 (1968): 9.

60.   National Sheriff's Association, op. cit., p. 199.

61.   See: E. Eugene Miller, *Jail Management: Problems, Programs, and Perspectives* (Lexington, Mass.: Lexington Books, 1978).

62.   As cited in ACIR, *Jails*, p. 16.

63.   Ibid., p. 18.

64.   Raymond T. Nimmer, *Diversion: The Search for Alternative Forms of Prosecution* (Chicago: American Bar Foundation, 1974), p. 3.

65.   Vera Institute of Justice, *The New York Community Service Sentencing Project: Development of the Bronx Pilot Project* (New York: Vera Institute of Justice, 1981), pp. 1–3.

66.   ACIR, op. cit., p. 121. Note: Vermont law provides for temporary lockups run by the city or county even though the state operates the former county jails.

67.   Ibid., p. 122.

68.   Law Enforcement Assistance Administration, *1970 National Jail Census* (Washington, D.C.: U.S. Government Printing Office, 1972).

69.   U.S. Bureau of Prisons, *Jail Management—Legal Problems* (Washington, D.C.: U.S. Government Printing Office, 1973).

70.   For example, see Ronald Goldfarb, *Jails: The Ultimate Ghetto* (Garden City, N.Y.: Anchor Press, 1975); William S. Edmonds, *Improving the Operations of Local Temporary Detention Facilities* (draft) (Washington, D.C.: Police Executive Research Forum, 1982); and Richard Allison, "Crisis in the Jails," *Corrections Magazine* (April 1982), 22.

71.   Tully L. McCrea and Don Gottfredson, *A Guide to Improved Handling of Misdemeanant Offenders* (Washington, D.C.: U.S. Government Printing Office, 1974), pp. 28–29.

# CHAPTER 13

# Prison Systems

## OBJECTIVES

**After reading this chapter, the student should be able to:**

Identify the major types of prison institutions and their particular characteristics.

Discuss the administration of state correctional systems.

Identify the roles and responsibilities of institutional staff members in prisons.

Identify the traditional programs found in prisons.

Discuss and differentiate between the traditional and the collaborative models of prison programming.

Identify characteristics of male prison inmates.

Identify characteristics of female prison inmates.

Discuss the problems associated with reforming our correctional efforts.

## IMPORTANT TERMS

Maximum security
Medium security
Minimum security
Prison camps
Prison warden
Correctional officer

Prison psychiatrist
Prison psychologist
Prison counselors
Classification
Vocational training
Prison industries

Traditional model
Collaborative model
Fragmentation of corrections
Overuse of corrections
Overemphasis on custody
Lack of financial resources and support
Attitude of the community
Direct expenditure per inmate

The correctional system in the United States is extremely diverse. It includes a broad range of institutions, theories, programs, and operating strategies. The problems associated with institutional and program diversity are compounded by the diversity of offenders with which the system must deal. A number of offenders are hardened recidivists who are irrevocably committed to criminal careers; others subscribe to more conventional values; still others are aimless individuals committed to neither socially appropriate nor socially inappropriate behavior. Each offender must be handled by appropriate techniques as determined by his or her needs as well as by appropriate security safeguards.

## ▣ OUR NATION'S PRISONS: SOME GENERAL CHARACTERISTICS AND FACTS

Before discussing the types of prisons that exist, a brief discussion of certain important facts about our nation's prison systems and those who inhabit and operate these institutions is in order. Most Americans have read accounts about how seriously overcrowded our prison systems have become in recent years. This, however, tells only part of the story. In the mid-1980s, data were released by the federal government's clearinghouse on criminal justice statistics that were shocking. One and one-half percent of all American adults that year were under some form of correctional control.[1] This does not mean this many adult offenders were in prison. In fact, the largest percentage of these offenders were under some other form of correctional supervision such as probation, parole, community-based institutions and programs, home confinement through electronic monitoring, or whatever other ingenious way we can devise to impose some form of correctional sanction. Still, a significant chunk of this 1.5 percent of all Americans were in some type of prison or institution for their crimes.

Many people might think that most prisons are run by the federal government and that the largest number of inmates in prison are in the federal system. This is not the case. In fact, states like California and Texas have more inmates in their prison systems than does the federal government in its entire system. It has been said that America has a "lock-em-up" mentality; we imprison more people than other countries of the Western world. The facts do not necessarily support such a conclusion, at least in some crime categories. Estimates of conviction and incarceration rates in the United States as compared to Canada, England, Wales, and the Federal Republic of Germany for the selected crimes of robbery, burglary, and theft show strikingly similar patterns.[2] Of course, caution must be exercised in making such comparisons because of differences in criminal justice systems, how crimes are classified, and how data are collected and reported. Nonetheless, it raises fundamental questions. Obviously, part of the reason we might have so many people in prison is simply because we have a large population. Associated with this may be the fact that we have such a high rate of these crimes being committed—if not in a relative sense, at least in an absolute one.

By the end of the 1980s, there were almost 700 state-operated prisons in the nation. Of this figure, the Southern states operated about 46 percent of these, which together held over 40 percent of the total number of prisoners in our nation's state prisons. The Southern states, in terms of their populations, have the largest prison systems and the largest number of prison inmates of any region in the country. In spite of the flurry of building activity in constructing new prisons to handle the

**State prisons**

spurt in prison populations during the 1980s, a third of the nation's prisons are still over fifty years old, and these prisons still house the majority of all prisoners. A sizable number of our nation's prisons still are over one hundred years old.

The nation's prison business is a mammoth operation, not only in terms of capital costs to build new prisons and to maintain those already existing, but in terms of personnel and operating costs as well. The national average of prison personnel to inmates is on the order of one to three. For every three inmates, there is one prison employee. Although this is the national average, this ratio varies from state to state, with the states of New England having the fewest prison employees per inmate and the Southern and Midwest states having the highest ratio. Although the growth in numbers of prison employees has risen in recent years, commensurate with the increase in prison populations themselves, the largest increase has been in the numbers of prison workers who provide security rather than in prison staff employees who are engaged in providing some form of service such as counseling, training, or education to prison inmates.[3]

## ▣ CLASSIFYING PRISONS

There are several basic types of institutions found in today's prison systems. They are usually classified according to the security they provide. This, in turn, is determined by the dangerousness and the security risk of the inmates who are housed in them. They are usually distinguishable not only by their appearance but by the way they are operated in terms of the security precautions that are taken.

### Maximum-Security Institutions

Characteristics

The more hardened and dangerous male offenders are found in maximum-security prisons. A typical maximum-security prison is usually enclosed by massive concrete or stone walls from eighteen to twenty-five feet high or by a series of double- or triple-perimeter fences topped with barbed or razor wire and spaced fifteen to twenty feet apart. Located on the outer perimeter walls are well-protected towers strategically placed so that guards have an open field of fire and can observe the external and internal sections of all the surrounding walls and the prison yard. Today, increasing numbers of institutions also use electronic sensing devices to monitor the prison's perimeters.

The internal security considerations are just as formidable. The inmates are housed in interior cell blocks, each of which has its own self-contained security enclosure. The cell blocks are partitioned off from each other by a series of enclosures that purposely limit internal movement. The idea behind this construction is to create a series of miniature prisons within a prison so that in the event of riots or escapes, each section can be sealed off from the others. Thus, any prisoners seeking to break out would first have to penetrate the internal security system before they could challenge the external wall and perimeter security devices.

In the past twenty years, the trend has been away from the construction of these types of institutions, particularly those surrounded by massive stone walls, because of their prohibitive cost. New maximum-security institutions often use technological intrusion and security devices, such as infrared sensors and closed-circuit TV, which permits the state to avoid the cost of building massive perimeter walls. Even so, America's prison confinement facilities are still predominantly of the maximum-security type. Over 40 percent of all state inmates for instance, are housed in what are classified as maximum-security prisons.[4]

## Medium-Security Institutions

More medium-security prisons exist in the nation's prison systems than any other type of prison. Medium-security institutions house inmates who, although not as dangerous to society and their fellow inmates as those confined in maximum-security prisons, do pose a threat of escape and often have served prior sentences. Normally, medium-security prisons are not fortresslike structures, although, in most instances, a series of fences or enclosures surround the perimeter. Many of these institutions are constructed on a block arrangement in which inmates live together in designated units. Less emphasis is placed on controlling the internal movement of prisoners. These facilities sometimes have dormitories, honor units, or some similar forms of housing for inmates who have earned the privilege of living in such quarters. There is often a special maximum-security unit for inmates who pose a threat to the security of the institution or to other inmates. Often, such inmates will be housed in the maximum-security unit only temporarily until they can be transferred to a more secure maximum-security prison.

Characteristics

## Minimum-Security Institutions

Minimum-security prisons do not use fixed observation posts for armed guards on the perimeter. In fact, depending on where they are situated and the type of offenders they contain, there may be no perimeter fence. Inmates in minimum-

Minimum security institutions, like this campus-style prison in New York state, house prisoners who have shown good conduct. (Alan Carey/The Image Works)

security institutions are generally housed in private or semiprivate rooms or in dormitories. Although housing inmates in individual rooms has certain advantages, such facilities are often too costly to construct, and thus most inmates live in small dormitories accommodating from ten to twenty inmates. Since the early 1970s we have seen a sizable growth in the number of minimum-security facilities. Even so, however, these minimum-security institutions are still few in number and house about 20 percent of all inmates in prison today.

The minimum-security institution, of course, houses less dangerous offenders. In many instances, offenders with relatively short sentences and without extensive criminal records are housed in these facilities. Because these institutions offer greater freedom to the inmate, many correctional departments transfer inmates to them from medium-security institutions when the inmates have demonstrated by their conduct that they have earned this privilege. Often, the minimum-security institution provides an adjustment stage before release. For example, inmates of more closely guarded institutions who have a year or less left to serve may be transferred to one of these facilities to help them adjust to less controlled discipline so that they will be better prepared for their ultimate release.

## Prison Camps

Prison camps are a form of minimum-security institution that started in the Midwest, the West, and the South. In the Midwest and the West, they usually were farming and forestry camps. In the past 25 years such camps have become less numerous, except in certain Southern and Western states, and their functions largely have been taken over by urban community-based programs. These institutions provide instructive work for inmates within a more favorable environment than can be created within traditional institutions. They also enable prisoners of various types to be separated, thus reducing the possibility of contamination of attitudes. Work camps relieve the problem of overcrowding in other correctional institutions and are less costly than maintaining traditional prisons.

Until the 1970s, Southern prison camps had a very poor reputation. First begun during the period of Reconstruction following the Civil War, they were operated under a lease system. Private bidders contracted with the state for the use of inmate labor; the bidders then leased the inmates to private individuals, who used them in lumbering, quarrying, and turpentine operations. When the federal courts began to prohibit the leasing of prisoners, this practice disappeared, and the Southern states turned to using their inmate labor on road crews and chain gangs, which labored under brutal conditions. In the last 25 years, however, the Southern states have all but abolished their road gangs, and several states in this region have developed various camp institutions devoted to farming and forestry. In many cases, these modern Southern prison camps are some of the best-operated prison programs in the country.

## Special Institutions

Some specialized institutions have been developed to handle certain categories of offenders. States, for example, may operate camps and special facilities under a Youth Authority agency for young offenders. Many such facilities have various programs to meet the needs of youthful offenders. In a few of the larger states, some of these institutions have become specialized in either vocational or academic programs. Such camps or special facilities permit the state to separate young offenders by age, crime, and individual needs so that younger, first-time offenders do not associate with more criminally sophisticated and intractable youths.

A few states and the federal government have developed special facilities for inmates who need intensive medical and psychiatric help that is not normally available in other institutions. Among these are the California Medical Facility at Vacaville and the United States Medical Center at Springfield, Missouri. States have also developed special institutions and programs for the criminally insane; Michigan constructed the first such facility in 1885. Special institutions and programs are also available for women offenders—for example, the state institute at Clinton, New Jersey, and the federal reformatory at Alderson, West Virginia. Today, the various types of social institutions and programs offer a choice of alternatives for meeting the particular needs of offenders.

## ADMINISTRATION OF STATE CORRECTIONAL SYSTEMS

Until the beginning of the twentieth century, prisons in the various states operated almost as independent fiefdoms. The wardens and superintendents of these institutions reported directly to the governor or the legislature. This was a period of political patronage, and prison administrators and custodial staff held their jobs by virtue of political connections. It was not unusual for newly appointed governors to engage in large-scale dismissal of prison personnel, replacing them with their own political followers. During this period, the governor or the legislature did the hiring, the purchasing, and the budget making for the prisons within the state. After the Civil War, some of the states attempted to bring their prisons under some sort of administrative control by appointing boards of charities or corrections, which were the forerunners of present state departments of correction.

Today, every state has a centralized department of corrections. It may be an autonomous agency or a unit within a department of human resources or similar body. The corrections department supervises all state-run correctional institutions and is also responsible for all state-sponsored community-based correctional institutions and programs. In many states, parole services, including all parole officers and, in a few instances, the parole board, are also part of the department of corrections. In recent years, additional responsibilities have been given to various state departments of correction. For example, some are now responsible for inspecting or in some cases, even operating local jails, lockups, and other misdemeanant institutions. Some states are also beginning to incorporate probation services within the department of correction.

*Modern features*

The head of the state department of corrections is usually referred to as the *director of corrections*. In most states, this officer is appointed by the governor with approval of the legislature. Many states have filled these directorships with qualified penologists and career correctional managers as political considerations become less important. In states in which the department of corrections is an autonomous state agency, the director is responsible for the administration of the entire state penal system, which includes presentation of the budget to the chief executive and its defense before the state legislature. Besides being a knowledgeable penologist and administrator, the director must often be skilled in the area of politics so as to represent the agency effectively before the legislature and obtain the required program authorizations and appropriations.

Some states have created Boards or Correctional Commissions whose responsibility it is to either oversee the operations and policies of the state's prison system or to advise the governor and the director of corrections of the need for policy changes. In some cases these special boards have been created in an effort to check the governor's authority in the operations and policies of the prison system. One way this is done is to make these boards answerable to the legislature rather than to the governor.

## ▣ PRISON ADMINISTRATION

*Custody and treatment divisions*

The head of the prison is known by various titles, usually *warden, superintendent, or director.* The responsibilities of this individual are to manage the institution and to present the institution's budget to the director of corrections or some fiscal agent of the executive department. In some instances, the warden may also be required to defend budget requests before the executive fiscal agency or even the state legislature or one of its committees.

In larger institutions, the warden is usually assisted by one or more associate wardens. Many states and the Federal Bureau of Prisons have adopted the organizational recommendations developed by the American Correctional Association, which call for two associate wardens in medium to large prisons. One associate warden is directly responsible for custody, which includes the custodial guard force, and the other is responsible for the classification and treatment maintained by the institution. *Custody* and *treatment* are the major operating units within most prisons. Directly under the associate warden for custody is the supervisor of the guard force, who is the commanding officer of the custodial line personnel. This custody section also consists of a number of watch lieutenants and sergeants and a large number of correctional officers or guards. Contrary to popular belief, the custodial officer's main job is not to prevent escape from the prison; perimeter security devices such as high walls and guard towers generally perform this function. The main responsibility of the custodial officer is to maintain control within the prison to assure the safety of both inmates and prison employees. The custodial line personnel are in daily contact with the inmates, and they set the general tone of the institution by their policies and practices.[5]

Depending on the institution, its budget, and the prevailing philosophy, the treatment unit may consist of such professional personnel as psychiatrists, psychologists, social workers, medical personnel, chaplains, counselors, and teachers of academic and vocational programs. In addition, there may be a prison industries manager responsible for the industrial production enterprises of the prison; a business manager responsible for accounting, procurement, payroll, and supplies; and a medical services manager responsible for the medical, dental, and other health-related facilities within the prison. Figure 13.1 shows an organizational chart for a medium-sized prison for men.

The management of a prison is no small task, rivaling that of many large industries in its complexity of administrative functions. The large inmate population with the special problems associated with the prison environment makes it even more difficult to manage. Under these circumstances, the management of

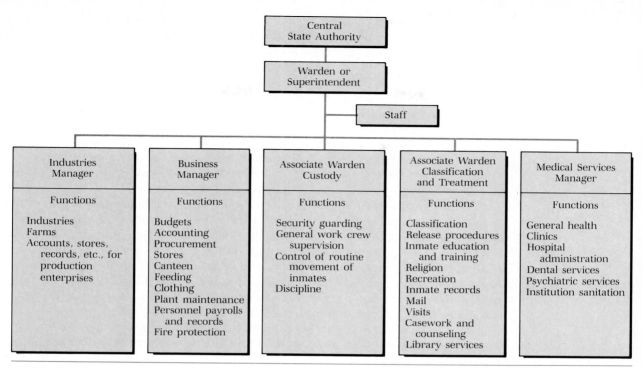

Organizational arrangement for an adult male institution of fewer than 2,000 inmates. (*Source:* Reprinted, with change in title, with permission of the American Correctional Association, from the *Manual of Correctional Standards*, 1966 ed., p. 319.)

FIGURE **13.1**

prisons may indeed be one of the most complex and demanding tasks facing any public administrator. It certainly requires managers as capable as those found in any area of public service today.

## ☐ THE INSTITUTIONAL STAFF

As mentioned, large prisons are typically divided into two major operating units: custody and treatment. Within each of these, there are certain key personnel. Some of the more common and important members of the prison staff are correctional officers, staff psychiatrists or psychologists, and prison counselors or social workers.

### Correctional Officer

The correctional officer or guard is responsible primarily for fulfilling the custody role of the prison. In this role, he or she is responsible for such diverse activities as maintaining discipline among the inmates, preventing the smuggling of contraband, controlling inmate movement within the institution, protecting inmates from other inmates, and preventing escapes.

In spite of the correctional officer's, or guard's, important responsibilities, little was known until recent years about the day-to-day complexity of his or her functions and the difficulties inherent in this crucial job. Research on critical role-related responsibilities and problems faced by correctional officers in today's prisons has shed some new light on this function.[6] For example, too many people tend to perceive correctional officers as brutish, authoritarian figures of only marginal intelligence—after all, it is assumed, who else would want such a job? Such stereotyping is simply wrong. Although such characteristics may be associated with some guards in today's prisons, they certainly are not characteristic of the majority of correctional officers. Such public misconceptions are fed by the average citizen's lack of understanding about prisons and prison life; the false impressions often given by the media about prisons; the history of corrections, when such traits were common; and probably, most of all, the fact that prisons and people who work in them have been veiled in secrecy. All of these factors are in large part responsible for these misconceptions and why they continue to persist.

An interesting insight into the secretiveness that tends to surround the role of the prison guard is afforded by correctional officers themselves. Their work isn't exactly the subject of cocktail party chatter. In an interesting study by Lucien X. Lombardo of a maximum-security institution in New York State, one guard was relating his reluctance to discuss his work even with his wife. He is reported to have said to the researcher, "What am I going to say? Gee, honey, I looked in three guys' assholes today for contraband; or boy, I wrote a guy up today for taking an extra pork chop. Hardly exciting stuff."[7]

It must be recognized that both the type of institution and the types of inmates in a particular institution will play a large role in the guards' job characteristics and responsibilities. These factors will also determine other job-related issues. Being a correctional officer at a small, minimum-security facility will differ from being a guard at a large, maximum-security institution. Perhaps, as a former warden and head of a state department of correction once said, "The problem with prisons today is that we need a better class of inmate." (personal communication).

What do correctional officers do? In a large, maximum-security institution (one patterned after the nonagricultural prison, which is more prevalent outside the South), a correctional guard will find himself (and in some cases herself) assigned to any number of responsibilities. Guards are block officers who are assigned to the cell blocks, work detail supervisors, industrial shop and school officers, and yard officers. Guards are assigned to the administration building and its functions and to wall posts, where they sit in towers to observe and prevent escapes.

In many of America's overcrowded prisons that house the more serious and hardened offender, interviews with correctional officers point out a similarity of feelings about their job and their roles. Many of these guards express a degree of fear for their own safety. Associated with this fear—and probably at least partially attributing to it—is the mental strain they undergo.[8] Most officers express the opinion that large-scale prison violence is a constant possibility and can be precipitated by seemingly random events. Yet it is more than the large-scale prison riot that worries them. They are also concerned about attacks on them by individual inmates and being injured or killed if they have to intervene in a fight between prisoners. As Lombardo points out, this perception of danger by the officers is not related to the high probability that it will occur, rather it is the unpredictability of prison violence they find so unnerving.[9] Correctional officers would seem to share this set of circumstances with police officers. The unpredictability of violence in police work is also a contributing factor to police stress. As one guard related to Lombardo in the study:

**Areas of responsibility**

**Job attitudes**

The knowledge that prison riots can and do occur is a contributor to job stress for corrections officers. (Calvin Cruce/Sygma)

> The most difficult thing is the mental strain. It's more mental than anything else. Your mind's working all the time. You can go in there for every day for 20 years and never break up a fight, never get assaulted. But the thought's there that it can always happen. This is more taxing than having to tussle with anybody.[10]

Officers who were interviewed also expressed job-related dissatisfaction with what they felt was the way inmates feel about guards in general and the difficulties correctional officers have with obtaining inmate compliance to orders. Guards were heard to grumble that inmates complain when they feel they are not being recognized as individuals by the guards but themselves see all guards as the same. Correctional officers also try to show complete impartiality to all the prisoners because it is crucial to avoid problems that are bound to occur when the inmates perceive partiality exists. Still, inmates will try to play "games" with the guard. It is difficult to maintain impartiality in such a setting—especially with inmates who purposely give a guard a "hard time."

The correctional officers also expressed feelings of powerlessness and lack of support from the prison administration. Again, they are much like cops, who also tend many times to feel that they are expected to do a job but are unsupported by the "higher-ups" in the department. In the Lombardo study, which may or may not be typical of other prisons and prison systems, even acts of discipline imposed by guards may be overturned by prison supervisors or administrators. This undercuts the guard's ability to deal with the inmates on a day-to-day basis. And, like

OUT OF BOUNDS

Women corrections officers may work in prisons for men; this woman is a guard at San Quentin. (© Kent Reno/Jeroboam)

**Women correctional officers**

many people in the lower echelons of organizations, the guards often expressed frustration with having so little input into the operations and policies of the prison. They felt unvalued for the contributions they could make.

As in the typology of police officers discussed in Chapter 5, correctional officers also fall into various classifications as to how they perceive their jobs and the attitudes they hold about their work. The easiest way to dichotomize the guard's role is in the convenient overall prison classifications of custody and treatment. Although, as pointed out, the primary purpose of correctional officers is a custodial (security and order maintenance) role, they also play an important and valuable role beyond more custody and security. In fact, how well they perform a counseling or assistance role in their relationships with the inmates may well determine how well they perform their security- and order-maintenace role. In fact, it is a crucial relationship, especially for those correctional guards such as block officers who are in close contact with the inmates on a daily basis.

This was pointed out in an extensive survey of correctional officers undertaken by *Corrections Magazine* a few years ago. In many cases the guards interviewed expressed the "worthwhile" aspects of their jobs as helping inmates unsnarl administrative problems or providing them with some form of help that contributed to the inmate's success on release from the prison.[11] Additional research on work attitudes of guards indicated that many guards—particularly those with more years of seniority on the job, felt that "compassion" was a very important ingredient of their jobs. It would seem from this (and other) research that guards develop more of a "human service" orientation as opposed to a mere custodial viewpoint as they gain more job experience.[12] According to F. T. Cullen and others, officers who emphasize human service and compassion are also better able to deal with job-related stress and have higher levels of job satisfaction than the more punitive custody-oriented corrections officer.[13]

Over the past ten years, a number of prison systems are employing women as correctional officers in male institutions. In some cases, however, this integration of the sexes has only been a token one, for example, having female guards work "safe" assignments such as the perimeter wall towers or in the administration building. In those prisons where women are assigned a broader range of responsibilities, which brings them into closer and more frequent contact with the inmate population, the question is How well are women performing in these roles? Those who have examined this situation say quite well. It is contended, for example, that female guards in men's prisons are more likely to take a human relations view of the correctional officer's job.[14] Although women guards don't necessarily have a more positive view of inmates, they exert a "softening" and calming influence on the prison environment, which is said to make prisons less violent and potentially explosive.[15] It is also pointed out that women guards are more likely to be ostracized by their more custody-oriented male peers.[16]

Is the work of prison guards changing? The answer to this seems to be both yes and no. The traditional functions of maintaining security, doing head counts, conducting searches for contraband, and manning access points are traditional responsibilities that will never change. Still, some prison institutions are trying to bring greater emphasis on job enlargement to the correctional guard force. This has taken two forms: involving correctional officers more in the helping role (providing inmates with advice, counseling inmates, etc.), while supporting this emphasis and involving officers more in the policy-making process by which the prison operates. Different needs of the institution, differences in the composition of the inmate population, the attitudes of the administration, and the overall quality of the guard force will determine the likelihood of these kinds of changes continuing to occur.

## Psychiatrist

The role psychiatry plays within the correctional system is burdened by some fundamental disagreements within the profession. Although psychiatrists have been long-time critics of the rigid controls and restrictions of prison life, they are often in disagreement among themselves concerning the role and need for psychotherapy in prisons. Psychiatrists also tend to be abstract in their diagnoses. This often makes it difficult for the action-oriented custodial staff to accept them into the treatment team as readily as, say, psychologists.

The few psychiatrists who are employed in prisons make diagnostic examinations, write reports for parole boards, and advise on the disposition of problem prisoners. They serve as referring agents when psychotic prisoners are transferred to mental hospitals. In most prisons, psychiatrists have little time or hospital space to conduct programs of individual or group therapy, which, ideally, should be their major function. Once a prisoner is diagnosed as requiring psychiatric treatment, the absence or shortage of therapeutic resources frequently requires the assignment of the psychiatrist to routine classification and counseling duties.[17] Under these conditions, psychiatry is reduced to lip-service support of a custodial regime. The psychiatrist can also be useful in training prison personnel, especially custodial staff, to recognize and handle mental disturbances and emotional reactions to confinement.[18]

## Psychologist

Like psychiatrists, the qualified psychologist with a doctorate in psychology is too infrequently found in correctional systems. The psychologist performs any number of responsibilities. Two of the most important are psychological testing and diagnosis, which serve as the foundation for any treatment program suggested for the prisoner. Psychologists are most typically used at the time of classification when an inmate first arrives at the institution. In addition to administering various psychological tests, the psychologist may conduct intensive interviews of inmates on a selected basis. These interviews are used to supplement personality and projective tests, intelligence scores, and other devices used in determining appropriate custody classification and treatment programs.

Psychologists also assist the counseling staff in its efforts and help to develop in-service training programs for custodial people who work as counselors. They also provide input for discipline and classification committee decisions.[19]

## Counselors

Counselors fill the major roles in the wide-ranging treatment programs in most prison systems. Today the most common forms of treatment can generally be referred to as group methods—for example, group therapy, group counseling, guided group interaction, and psychodrama. In recent years more attention has focused on drug and alcohol abuse programs. Prison counselors play an important role in developing and operating such programs on a daily basis. One of the more prom-

Counselors and other mental health professionals work with prisoners to resolve a wide range of conflicts and behavior problems. (Cathy Cheney/Stock Boston)

ising approaches is to make the inmates themselves part of the overall group process. The idea of using peer pressure to promote improvement is a product of the 1960s. In this process, the inmates themselves participate in groups and provide the leadership that helps individuals improve themselves.[20] The prison counselor plays an important role in the development, supervision, and maintenance of such efforts.

Some types of institutions have developed a therapeutic community approach. This is a system whereby the entire institutional program is geared toward treatment. In this setting, treatment-oriented staff and custodial personnel work as a team in the treatment effort. As members of the treatment team, prison counselors are often given the primary responsibility to develop a treatment approach and to maintain it among the custodial staff and the inmates.

## ▣ PRISON PROGRAMS

Penal institutions have varied programs, depending on the security needs, age, sex, prior criminal record, education, and medical and psychiatric needs of inmates. Because it is not possible to review all the specialized programs that exist, emphasis is placed on those programs that typically are found in most adult prisons today.

### Classification

**Assessing inmate needs**   Classification attempts to match the needs of the offender with the appropriate program. In the past, judges sometimes had the authority to sentence convicted offenders to any institution within the state. Usually, this provided no means to match the needs of the offender with the various treatment programs that existed in different institutions. Beginning in the 1930s, a few correctional systems in the United States began to adopt the classification concept, and other states have now followed their examples. Under this system, the department of corrections has the authority to assign inmates to institutions where they can participate in the types of programs they need. The only exception to this is that in some instances, in the case of less serious crimes, the judge can sentence someone on a short-term basis to a local facility or workhouse.

Out of the classification concept have arisen reception and diagnostic programs and facilities. The first of these was the diagnostic depot at the Joliet, Illinois, prison. Where such programs exist, all inmates sentenced to a state correctional system are first sent to a special centralized facility for extensive testing and evaluation. The objectives of these facilities are typically:

1. Diagnosis of case problems
2. Prescription of classification to specific programs to meet diagnosed problems
3. Induction and orientation of inmates to the correctional system
4. Medical examination, quarantine, and treatment of new inmates[21]

At the reception and diagnostic center, the new inmate is interviewed and examined by specialized clinical personnel such as psychologists, psychiatrists, physicians, dentists, and a chaplain. Often, a presentence report (see Chapter 9) gathered by probation authorities accompanies the individual to the center and provides background information to guide the clinical personnel in their evaluation. Sometimes, letters of inquiry are also sent to the inmate's immediate family and to previous employers and schools in an effort to obtain better information on the individual's background. Sometimes, the center personnel might contact social welfare agencies in the prisoner's former locale that may have had prior contact with him or her.

After all this information has been gathered, a social history is prepared. The staff of the center then classifies the inmate in terms of his or her particular needs and potential security risk. For example, the individual might be found to be in need of intensive psychiatric help, alcohol or drug-related rehabilitation, group therapy, educational programs, or some combination of these. Once these needs are determined, the inmate is sent to the particular institution that provides the necessary security and/or necessary assistance programs. Although these centers perform a very important function, knowledgeable observers point out that they tend to drain the institutions themselves of professional personnel, thus placing a premium on diagnosis rather than on treatment.[22]

In states without centralized reception and diagnostic facilities, individual **Classification committee** institutions have developed their own classification committees. The committees vary somewhat in composition but usually consist of the associate warden for classification and treatment or the associate warden's immediate subordinate, a high-ranking custodial officer, and the counselor, psychologist, or the social worker who prepared the social history. This classification committee meets with the inmate and makes an appropriate program assignment on the basis of the social history report, an interview with the inmate, and the security risk the inmate poses.

A more recent development in classification is the treatment-team concept developed at the federal correctional institution in Ashland, Kentucky, and the Air Force Retraining Facility at Amarillo, Texas. In the team approach, a counselor, a custodial officer, and a teacher from the institution's academic program are assigned jointly to individual inmates. The same team may be assigned all the prisoners in a particular dormitory or cell block. In addition to being responsible for the original classification, the team also handles all disciplinary problems among its assignees. This approach relieves the classification committee of its very time-consuming disciplinary function and provides some continuity in supervision. It also makes custodial and academic staff more treatment oriented by virtue of their involvement in the correctional treatment process.

## Health

Most prisons have health and medical programs. In states without centralized reception and diagnostic facilities, the prison medical facility quarantines all inmates for a week or ten days. The medical services unit is responsible for maintaining proper sanitary conditions in the physical plant and in the food service area. Medical infirmaries are usually maintained in most of the larger prisons and are staffed by physicans, nurses, and other health-services personnel. Prisons contract the services of an optician and dentist, who make periodic visits to the institution. In some of the largest institutions, there are prison hospitals that are reasonably well equipped, even for major surgery. When necessary, nearby hospitals are used. Psychiatric services are very limited. A survey of adult prisons in the mid-1970s indicated that only slightly more than 1 percent of them provided resident psychiatric services. It probably is not much better today.[23]

## Academic Programs

Academic programs in prisons range from courses for illiterates to college extension courses. Most prisons have some sort of prison school, administered by a director of education.

The quality of academic programs runs from very good to mediocre. In the past, some adult institutions used inmate teachers—almost all of whom lacked the basic professional credentials required to be a teacher. Today, correctional institutions routinely require that members of their teaching staff be certified teachers. Because of the poor educational backgrounds of many of the inmates, special emphasis is placed on teaching remedial subjects. It is not unusual, for example, to see classwork in a correctional institution being conducted at a sixth-grade level.

The teachers who make up the academic staff also range from very good to mediocre. Some are rejects from the public school system who take jobs as teachers in prisons because the requirements are less demanding. Others enjoy the challenge of teaching adult inmates, some of whom with a little encouragement, become excellent students who do quite well in their academic work.

## Vocational Training

Many American prisons have developed a variety of vocational training programs. With the passage of the amendments to the Vocational Rehabilitation Act, significant vocational training opportunities became available to inmates because correctional institutions were then able to acquire the necessary equipment and trained instructors. Shops such as automobile repair and maintenance, radio and television repair, welding, sheet metal work, and woodworking are now rather common. The well-organized shops have civilian vocational instructors, a place to do the shop work, and space in which to conduct the necessary instruction. This situation has greatly improved from the time, thirty to forty years ago, when the usual vocational activity consisted of making license plates, doing laundry, or producing brooms and twine.

One of the recurring problems that prisons face in developing meaningful vocational training programs is finding appropriate jobs for former offenders who have acquired a skill while in prison. It is often difficult for a released offender to acquire a job as a mason, carpenter, or other skilled worker because of the reluctance of unions to permit ex-offenders to join. Often, regardless of the person's skill, the ex-offender is relegated to an apprenticeship, because the unions do not consider prison-sponsored vocational training programs sufficient qualification for a journeyman's level. In recent years such problems have become even more serious because of high unemployment in many sectors of the economy.

## Libraries

Most prisons have some kind of library, but these usually range from bad to mediocre in terms of available reading materials. Cost is the major problem in trying to develop adequate libraries. Because very few institutions set money aside in their operating budget to purchase up-to-date library materials, they often must rely on books donated from outside sources, which are usually outdated and may not be of general interest to the inmates.

Of special concern to some inmates is access to legal books. Many inmates spend a great deal of time filing legal petitions with the courts for relief by way of habeas corpus writs. The courts have held that inmates must have access to legal documents.[24] As a result, many prisons have various court *reporters* available for

Academic programs provide prisoners with educational opportunities. (Alan Carey/ The Image Works)

the use of inmates. Some "jailhouse lawyers" become quite proficient in skills of legal research. Although the prisons do not have to have extensive legal research resources available, they must provide minimum legal holdings for use by inmates.

A number of good libraries are maintained by the Federal Bureau of Prisons. Some have professional librarians to operate the libraries and to supervise the prisoners who act as attendants or helpers in the library. An excellent example of an institutional library can be found in the federal government's Kennedy Youth Center in Morgantown, West Virginia. The library at this facility is impressively large, with an excellent collection as well as audiovisual and other learning aids. In this institution, a special committee with inmate representatives selects the materials that the library acquires.

### Prison Industries

The subject of prison industries has an interesting history. Prison industries have been based on the so-called sheltered and open-market systems. Today, prison industries are based on the state-use system and the public-works-and-ways system, both considered sheltered-market operations.[25] The state-use system produces goods and renders services for agencies of the state or its political subdivisions. Thus, prison industries manufacture goods that are not sold on the open market but only to other state or local governmental jurisdictions. Public-works-and-ways systems involve road construction and repair, reforestation, and soil-erosion control activities on public property.[26]

This was not always the case. During the nineteenth century, prison industries sold their goods and services in competition with private industry. Labor unions and manufacturing and merchant associations applied a great deal of pressure on Congress and state legislatures to prohibit the sale of inmate-produced goods or inmate services on the open market. They simply didn't want the competition. In 1929, Congress passed the Hawes-Cooper Act, which deprived prison-made goods of their interstate character and made them subject to state law. The Ashurst-Summers Act of 1953 prohibited transportation of prison-made goods into states forbidding their entry and required the labeling of prison-made goods shipped in interstate commerce.

In any institution usually only a small percentage of the prison's total inmate population is engaged in prison industries. Many inmates are assigned to kitchen or mess duties, the laundry, maintenance work, and unskilled tasks such as pushing a broom or cleaning windows.

Prison wages are very nominal in American prisons. In the mid-1960s, a married prisoner might earn 8 cents an hour for working a 40-hour week; half of this would be sent to his family and half would be deposited in his account (one-quarter for use in the prison commissary and one-quarter for going-home money).[27] Even today, the average prevailing pay in those state institutions who pay some of their inmate labor is generally still less than a few dollars per day. Some federal institutions pay their inmate labor more, based on the skill involved in performing the specified job.

Several renowned penologists have suggested that prisons pay their inmate labor the prevailing wage for the particular work they perform and then charge them for their maintenance and care after taking out an appropriate share of the individual's earnings for his family's support. In 1981, former Chief Justice Warren Burger of the U.S. Supreme Court, in a speech in which he addressed the problems of crime in the United States, suggested that prisons become industrialized. In this way prison inmates could be taught and involved in productive enterprise. However, such ideas have little chance of becoming a reality today, when unemployment exists and our productive capacity is already underutilized. Such ideas also run counter to the widely held attitude that demands that as part of the inmate's punishment, the prisoner be legally, socially, and economically disabled.[28]

## Recreation Programs

Almost all prisons have developed recreation and leisure-time programs. The major sports of basketball and baseball are often participated in by intramural teams, and some prisons even have extramural teams that compete with teams from the outside community. Some prisons that have adequate funds to hire a director of recreation and purchase equipment have developed fairly broad recreation programs. Some institutions even have gymnasiums, most have weight-training programs and a host of other athletic sports. For inmates who do not engage in the very active sports, most prisons provide alternative forms of recreation. Arts and crafts are often available, as are organized chess matches, debating teams, and music groups. Even dramatic groups have been formed in some places. Movies are provided on a routine basis, as are TV-viewing rooms, and some institutions permit radios in individual cells or dormitories. Still other institutions permit outside entertainers to perform in the institution periodically as well as permitting inmates with special entertainment skills to perform on the outside.

 **CLASSIFYING INSTITUTIONS BY PROGRAM EMPHASIS**

In addition to classifying penal institutions by the degree of security they offer or by the age and type of offenders they contain, they must be further defined according to their administrative characteristics. Administratively, prisons may follow either the *traditional* model or the *collaborative* model.

## The Traditional Model

The traditional institution is administered with the idea that security is of paramount importance to protect the community as well as the institutional staff. To accomplish this, high walls are constructed, mechanical security devices and armed guards are employed, and inmate searches and body counts are made frequently. It is not necessary however, that all the physical aspects of gun towers, fences, and other obvious displays of security be present for an institution to be traditional. Administratively contrived security precautions, such as frequent searches and "shake-downs," head counts, disciplinary segregation, and other forms of control less visible to the outside world can prevail even in institutions that are not bounded by high walls or fences.

> Control and regimentation

Traditional institutions adhere to the idea that deterrence requires strict discipline, regimentation, and punishment, all in an atmosphere of impersonality and quasi-military rigidity. Visitation privileges are closely controlled, privacy is virtually nonexistent, internal movement is limited and controlled, and inmates march in groups to work assignments and other activities.

Certain operational policies characterize such institutions. Particular emphasis is placed on maintaining staff and inmate "distance." Inmates are required to defer to the status of custodial and staff personnel by addressing them as "mister" or "ma'am" or by their appropriate rank. Disciplinary infractions are dealt with summarily—for example, guards are required to "write up" any offensive conduct by an inmate; failure to do so brings an immediate reprimand from the guard's superior.

This impersonality and social distance is maintained by mass handling of prisoners. Inmates, for example, may be marched in groups to meals, to work, and to recreation. As a consequence, inmates and staff have very little opportunity for personal interaction. This massive impersonality of the traditional institutions can be seen in Gresham M. Sykes's study of a maximum-security institution in New Jersey. Each inmate who came to the institution was issued a *Handbook for Inmates*, which stated, among other things, the following:

> Form by twos when passing through the Center. Keep your place in line unless you are ordered to step out.

> When walking in a line, maintain a good posture. Face forward and keep your hands out of your pockets.

> When the bell rings for meals, work, or other assignment, turn out your light, see that your water is turned off, and step out of your cell promptly.

> On returning to your Wing, go directly to your cell, open the door, step in, and close the door without slamming it.

> Gambling in any form is not allowed.

> Do not speak or make gestures to persons who are visiting the institution.[29]

Although prison systems typically no longer demand such tight regimentation, it still exists in less obvious and visible ways in some institutions.

A number of observers who have studied the patterns of interaction in a traditional prison have pointed out that this distance does break down. It is simply not possible for custodial personnel to maintain tight authority and control over inmates. For one thing, custodial guards are overwhelmingly outnumbered in most correctional institutions. In prisons in which overcrowding and other factors have increased tensions, attempts at rigid control over inmates heighten an already potentially explosive situation. Likewise, the use of sactions is not always that effective in maintaining tight discipline. Certain inmates and inmate groups are not intimidated by sanctions. In fact, punishment may afford them greater status among their fellow prisoners.

Another factor is that the courts and various administrative rules have imposed limitations on the actions that correctional officers can invoke for disciplinary infractions by inmates. Although correctional personnel might violate these rules, they do so with some degree of risk.

There is also the "dynamics" of the guard–inmate relationship. Correctional personnel must rely on the inmate population to help them operate. A correctional officer cannot be seen as one who must constantly assert his official authority to control an assigned area. If the correctional officer is constantly writing disciplinary infractions, the officer is going to draw attention to himself or herself from superiors who may feel the guard is unable to control the situation otherwise. The officer is also going to increase tensions within the unit. Consequently, many correctional staff personnel develop a go-along, get-along attitude in which many infractions by inmates are ignored.

Within most traditional prisons, the pressures that prison officials apply have been shown to increase the rapid growth and development of an inmate subculture. Such prison subcultures present an interesting view of human behavior under conditions of enforced control and confinement.

The most obvious manifestation of these subcultures is the formation of inmate groups. These groups are fostered by the stresses and deprivations associated

## HOLT v. SARVER (1971)

### Prison Conditions That Violate Prisoner's Constitutional Rights

FACTS

A group of prisoners in the Arkansas prison system brought suit in the U.S. District Court for the Eastern District of Arkansas alleging that their rights, privileges, and immunities secured to them by the due process and equal protection clauses of the Fourteenth Amendment were being violated by that state's prison system. They contended that they had the following rights: (1) not to be imprisoned without meaningful rehabilitative opportunities; (2) to be free from cruel and unusual punishment; (3) to be free from arbitrary and capricious denial of rehabilitation opportunities; (4) to have minimal due process safeguards in decisions that determined fundamental liberties; (5) to be fed, housed, and clothed so as not to be subjected to loss of health or life; (6) to have unhampered access to counsel and the courts; (7) to be free from the abuses of fellow prisoners in all aspects of daily life; (8) to be free from racial segregation; (9) to be free from forced labor; and (10) to be free from the brutality of being guarded by fellow "trusty" inmates.

The court upheld most of the prisoners' allegations and held that because of the existing conditions, confinement in the Arkansas penitentiary system amounted to cruel and unusual punishment, which is prohibited by the Eighth Amendment. Prison officials then appealed this decision to the U.S. Eighth Circuit Court of Appeals.

DECISION

The Eighth Circuit Court of Appeals upheld the lower court decision. This court found, among other things, that: (1) the prison was run largely by inmate trusty guards, who bred hatred and mistrust; (2) the open barracks within the prison invited widespread physical and sexual assaults; (3) the isolation cells were overcrowded, filthy, and unsanitary; and (4) there was a total absence of any rehabilitation or training program. Like the lower court, it then concluded that these conditions, as a whole, constituted cruel and unusual punishment. The court also upheld the lower court's order that these deficiencies must be corrected and also upheld the lower court order that placed the supervision of the Arkansas penitentiary system under the scrutiny of the federal courts to ensure compliance with these findings.

SIGNIFICANCE OF THE CASE

This landmark decision found that conditions within penal institutions could be such that they constitute cruel and unusual punishment. It also placed an entire state's prison system under the direction of the federal courts, which would supervise the required remedial action to bring the prison system up to an acceptable standard. It was the first time the federal courts found an entire state prison system in violation of the Constitution.

with imprisonment. Because inmates spend extensive time together under the circumscribed environment of regimentation and confinement, they are drawn together on the basis of similar experiences, which develop into common perceptions and interests. These prisoner groups provide meaningful rewards to their members because they offer protection from the actions of the prison officials and other inmates. The group, in turn, exerts influence over its members and restrains nonmembers. The leader's knowledge of prison life is used to manipulate official policies and custodial personnel so that they can be used for the benefit of the group. The "old con" instructs the new inmate. Through membership, the individual inmate gains access to special privileges and "grapevine" communication, which is particularly important when officials restrict communication. In return for conforming to the demands of the inmate group, inmates gain satisfaction from membership among persons who understand them, and they enjoy the greater physical security the group provides.

Certain mechanisms maintain the inmate groups. Newcomers are screened for membership qualifications and, once accepted, are taught certain values and attitudes that have been transmitted through generations of prisoners. In addition, a novice learns certain argot or slang expressions that are part of the inmate subculture. This argot permits inmates to classify their perceptions of others into some sort of role framework. In the free world, we speak of Mr. Smith, the attorney, or of Mr. White, the engineer. Thus, some role-sets develop according to the occupation of the individual. In prison, almost everybody is just another "con"; to differentiate and identify individuals by role-sets, such expressions as a "real man," "fag," "wolf," or "ball buster" are applied. Thus, newcomers learn that their fellow inmates are as varied as people in the outside world. Some are okay; others are dangerous and should be avoided. Group ties are supported by sanctions ranging from ostracism to violence. Inmate commitment to these groups is encouraged by the basic split between officials and inmates, the emphasis on custody, and the inmate's hostility against officials.[30]

For an individual to become a member of an inmate group, the novice must first be accepted for membership and then must be willing to accommodate himself or herself to the values and customs of the inmate group. Donald Clemmer calls this the process of "prisonization," which is the taking on by the inmate "in a greater or less degree, the folkways, mores, customs, and general culture of the penitentiary." The newcomer adapts to the life of the prison, accepting the role of prisoner, new habits of eating and sleeping, and a new language. The prisoner makes the values of the inmate group his or her own.[31]

Gresham Sykes and Sheldon I. Messinger have examined the values and general culture that prisoners within custodial-oriented institutions adopt as a part of the inmate society. They refer to these values as the "inmate social code," which is similar to Clemmer's idea of prisonization. This social code admonishes inmates:

1. Do not interfere with other inmate's interests
2. Never rat on another con to the prison officials
3. Don't be nosy; don't have a loose lip; keep off a man's back
4. Be loyal to your class—the cons
5. Don't exploit other inmates. This means breaking your word, selling favors, being a racketeer, or welshing on debts
6. Play it cool—do your own time

7. Don't be a sucker—guards are hacks or screws and aren't to be trusted
8. Be tough—don't suck around; don't whine or cop out.[32]

A number of researchers have examined how inmates become socialized to the values of the inmate subculture over time. Stanton Wheeler set about to see the degree to which prisoners identified with the values of the institutional staff as compared with the values of the inmate code. He found that the period of time a prisoner spends inside the institution affects the way he identifies with the values of the staff or the values of other inmates. For the first six months of incarceration, the attitudes and values of the inmates are more similar to those of the prison staff. After six months of imprisonment, the inmate begins to identify more and more with the other inmates and the prison social code. When it comes near the time for release from prison (less than six months to serve), the inmate becomes more accepting once again of staff values and influence.[33]

Another study of prisoners in a maximum-security institution, conducted by Peter G. Garabedian, confirmed Wheeler's findings and found that inmates in the early phases are twice as likely to conform to staff norms as inmates in the middle period. This trend suggests that there may be a steady absorption of the prison culture similar to the process of prisonization but that this process is reversed as inmates come to the end of their prison careers.[34]

## The Collaborative Model

In recent years, prison administration has undergone some significant changes. Increased emphasis is being placed on the development of a more collaborative model that offsets the negative consequences of the authoritarian programming in the traditional model. The collaborative model maintains that inmate reintegration can be better accomplished through closer interpersonal relationships between inmates and the institutional staff and through the use of any available community resources.

This model stresses the need to reduce mass treatment and depersonalization. A number of prisons have implemented certain policies in this regard. Under certain circumstances, inmates are allowed to express their individuality by wearing civilian attire rather than traditional prison garb. Some freedom is also permitted in hairstyles or the growth of a beard, sideburns, or mustache. The old policy of requiring inmates to march to the dining hall and to sit in silence on one side of long, narrow tables has given way to the use of small, scattered, informal dining rooms, where inmates sit around a conventional table and are able to converse with each other.

*Greater inmate freedom and responsibility*

Greater emphasis is placed on decreasing the size of residential units. In medium- and minimum-security institutions, some states want to be able to build institutions with small dormitories or individual rooms. In fact, in spite of the cost, some institutions are being so constructed as to make it physically impossible to house a second person in the room. Hygiene facilities, such as toilets, washrooms, and showers, are being partitioned for greater privacy.

One of the most important and imaginative features of the collaborative model is its emphasis on a coordinative endeavor to achieve inmate reform.[35] One such promising program is the integrated treatment team concept. This arrangement may prove to be the single most meaningful contribution of the collaborative approach. In the traditional model, custodial personnel were often suspicious of treat-

*Greater integration of treatment and custody*

ment pesonnel and vice versa; inmates were often distrustful of both and would play one off against the other. Although line personnel were in much more frequent contact with inmates than were members of the treatment staff, they were often downgraded by the treatment personnel for their preoccupation with security rather than treatment. By the same token, the treatment staff was often criticized by custodial people for not understanding the necessity for security and for being "bleeding hearts."

The integrated treatment team approach recognizes that, for purposes of rehabilitation, certain conditions and attitudes must prevail. It is based on the following beliefs:

1. Effective communication must exist between treatment and custodial personnel and between these groups and the inmates.
2. Custodial personnel have a very important role to play in treatment and rehabilitation because of their daily contact with inmates.
3. The experience of custodial people can be of importance to the rehabilitative objectives of the treatment staff.
4. Treatment personnel can be of assistance to the custodial force in helping them to recognize certain behavioral manifestations of inmates and to diagnose and deal with inmate problems.
5. Any program of meaningful change must involve the inmate in the program.

This development is in sharp contrast with the classification and counseling practices that usually prevail in traditional institutions. In these, a single classification committee, presided over by senior custodial personnel, is concerned primarily with security classification of inmates and work assignments. Caseworkers present information regarding an inmate to this committee and make recommendations for educational and vocational training and work assignments. Rarely are members of the custodial force consulted, nor is the inmate significantly involved. Consequently, the custodial staff feel no obligation to participate in the inmate's program or to oversee his or her progress. The prison social workers usually have so many prisoners to counsel that counseling sessions are nothing more than a few minutes' discussion with the inmate. The social workers have no idea of how well inmates are doing because they lack contact with the custodial personnel assigned to the cell block or work area. Only in serious disciplinary cases is the caseworker even aware of any problems the inmate might be having; by the time the case becomes serious, what might have been prevented has already occurred. By the same token, the inmate, who is unable to receive help from the infrequent counseling sessions with the caseworker and is ignored by custodial personnel, turns to fellow inmates for support.

**The collaborative model and communications**

It is said that the collaborative model has contributed to the growth of communication among treatment staff, custodial personnel, and the inmates themselves. Custodial personnel, in most instances, have found that inmate morale and cooperation are related more directly to the manner in which inmates are treated than to how strictly discipline, security, and other control measures are imposed. This should come as no surprise. Inmates who have provided some meaningful input into the decisions made about them are more likely to react favorably to their particular programs and to be more interested in proving that their ideas are correct than are inmates who are given little or no opportunity to express themselves.

Inmate expression is very important to the concept of the collaborative model, and therefore, group counseling is used extensively to foster communication. Group counseling sessions, involving treatment and custodial people and inmates, are held periodically. Although most of these sessions center on the concerns of the inmate, they provide the treatment and custodial personnel the opportunity to understand the range of problems and attitudes associated with prison life and to express themselves and explain their actions to the inmates as well.

In these counseling sessions, a primarily nondirective method is employed by both treatment and custodial staffs. The custodial staff is trained by counseling specialists in how best to develop their own counseling techniques. Many of these sessions are quite frank and open. Although some inmates often use these sessions to blame the police, the correctional personnel, or others for their problems, they do provide the custodial and treatment personnel some insight into who might be potential troublemakers, and they give inmates a chance to express their feelings. Without these sessions, the institutional personnel might never know who these individuals are and how to deal with their negative attitudes. Without opportunities for mutual discussion, an inmate is likely to express negative attitudes in disruptive behavior within the institution, which heightens tension and could conceivably lead to serious problems of disorder within the prison.

Another significant feature of the collaborative model is the use of inmate representatives in the institutional policymaking process. This inmate representation has two purposes:

*The collaborative model and participatory decision making*

1. To enable inmates to have some advisory input in the management policies and decisions of the institution
2. To assist the administration in the actual day-to-day management of the institution by offering alternative mechanisms to solve inmate grievances and to improve discipline[36]

The idea of inmate councils or a form of inmate self-government is not new. In the 1860s, the Detroit House of Correction, under the leadership of its director, Zebulon Brockway, established a policy whereby selected prisoners were assigned to custodial and monitorial duties. [37] In 1888, the warden of the Michigan State Prison in Jackson formed the Mutual Aid League of Michigan, to which he appointed nine prisoners to serve as an advisory board for the purpose of preserving "good order."[38] The individual most responsible for the development of inmate governance was Thomas M. Osborne, who, beginning in the first quarter of the present century, established inmate governments at the Auburn and Sing Sing prisons in New York and at the naval prison at Portsmouth, New Hampshire. Inmate governance councils based on the system developed by Osborne were then adopted by a number of other prisons in the eastern United States.

Inmate governance councils generally have certain features in common. Inmate representatives are chosen by the inmates themselves. These representatives then meet at periodic intervals with institutional representatives to discuss rules and regulations that guide the policies of the institutional staff in their handling of the prison population. This affords inmates some input into the regulatory process. In some cases, these inmate councils serve as adjudicatory boards to handle inmate grievances and discipline. For example, an inmate court can be established to determine appropriate disciplinary measures for the violation of certain regulations by inmates. Instead of the prison administration unilaterally deciding what disciplinary action to impose, the matter is turned over to the inmate council for disposition. There are problems with such a system, however, in that it may foster resentment and retribution on the part of the disciplined inmate toward members of the inmate court.

Inmate governance councils can also keep the prison administration aware of certain grievance areas that threaten the stability of the institution. The problems associated with racism are a particularly sensitive area within many prisons today. One of the major difficulties in combatting this situation is the absence of dialogue between prison staff and inmate groups. Without this dialogue, attitudes are often expressed in aggression and violence, inmate strikes, and a further polarization between inmate groups as well as between inmates and prison officials. The importance of opening up channels of communication through inmate participation in decision making can be seen by the following report of the South Carolina Department of Corrections:

> One way in which to head off confrontation is the use of the concept of maximum feasible participation. This term means little more than the notion that those who are allowed a voice in the rule-making process are more likely to obey such rules. It does not mean that the prisons would be run by a town meeting of the cell blocks or even that there would be any real power given to inmates to control the prisons. All that is implied by the notion is that at some point along the line, the inmate (either individually or through a representative) is allowed to make a meaningful input into the decision-making process that surrounds him with rules. One means of accomplishing this goal would be the establishment of an inmate council with elected representatives. Such a council should be able to present questions to the administration concerning various rules and practices of the institution and receive a straightforward answer. The inmate council would then be able to accept the explanation or suggest alternatives for the consideration of the administrators. Through a serious of long-range dialogues between inmates and administrators, many of the problems which plague our prisons could be worked out.[39]

It must be pointed out that shared decision making through the development of inmate councils has not enjoyed a great deal of success in the past. Typically, a number of problems have arisen. First, correctional officials have been very reluctant to share any of their prerogatives with inmates. This has led to situations in which inmate councils have little legitimacy with the prison officials and, as a result, even less legitimacy with the inmate population. Thus, rather than advising on problems that are meaningfully connected with the actual management of the institution, the inmates are often given less sensitive tasks, such as organizing inmate recreation and cultural activities, athletic contests, talent shows, and arts and crafts projects.

Much of the opposition prison officials have toward these shared decision-making programs stem from past negative experiences. Sometimes, inmate cliques have controlled elections to councils or have put pressure on those elected to reduce their orientation to staff objectives. Often these advisory groups are oriented primarily to articulating and exaggerating inmate complaints and presenting their demands to prison officials without addressing the merits of the complaints objectively. In some instances, inmate council members have used their position on the council to extort special considerations from other inmates. In a few institutions where these councils do function in any meaningful way, the trend in recent years has been to engage them actively in important areas of mutual concern such as food service, housekeeping, and safety, but to retain key management decision making by prison officials.

# MEN IN PRISON

What are the characteristics of the "typical" adult male in America's state prisons? This question has been answered in recent years through a series of surveys. It paints a portrait of a young man who is likely to be an ethnic minority—especially black or Hispanic—someone without the qualities our society associates with the promise of success. He is likely to be poorly educated, to have suffered an abusive and neglected childhood, to be an abuser of both drugs and alcohol, to have little or no record of gainful employment or a stable work history, and not to have been very successful in establishing and maintaining such social bonds as family or marriage.

As a group, their criminal careers and problems with the authorities are often symptoms of their own disorganization and estrangement from mainstream American society. Many of them began their criminal careers at an early age and progressed from juvenile courts and juvenile institutions into adult criminal courts and prisons. Their present period of imprisonment is more than likely the result of committing a violent crime. This category is followed by property crime and drug offenses. If recidivism is any sign of what the future holds for them on release, the picture is bleak. Once released for the crime for which they are now imprisoned, it is more than likely that they will again return to prison. How long it will take them to "break out" of this cycle, if ever, is anybody's guess. Figure 13.2 is a profile of this "typical" adult male inmate in our nation's state prisons.

**Age:** Young: 81 percent are between the ages of 20 and 39; 56 percent between the ages of 20 and 29.

**Ethnic:** 47 percent are white; 42 percent are black; 10 percent are Hispanic.

**Education:** Far below national average (45 percent have not completed high school).

**Marital Status:** Most are unmarried or divorced; 54 percent have dependent children.

**Offense:** 23 percent for robbery; 18 percent for homicide; 16 percent for burglary; 12 percent for drug offense; 6 percent for larceny; 5 percent for forcible rape; 4 percent for forgery, fraud, embezzlement; 3 percent for aggravated assault; 2 percent for motor vehicle theft.

**Personal Characteristics:** Nearly one-half have grown up in one-parent homes or with other relatives; many have been abused extensively as children; many have immediate family member (father, mother, brother, sister, spouse, or child) who had been incarcerated in the past; 78 percent have used drugs; a high percentage have alcohol abuse problems; most were unemployed immediately before their arrest; many have never worked or have held only short-term jobs.

A composite profile of the typical adult male offender in state prison. [*Sources: Statistical Abstract of the United States—1981;* FBI, *Crime in the United States, 1983;* Bureau of Justice Statistics, *Prisoners in State and Federal Institutions, Year end 1983;* Bureau of Justice Statistics, *Survey of Inmates of State Correctional Facilities, 1979;* U.S. Department of Justice, *National Prison Statistics, 1983, 1984, and 1985; Prisoners and Drugs,* March 1983; Bureau of Justice Statistics, *Report to the Nation on Crime and Justice* (2nd ed.), March 1988.]   FIGURE **13.2**

## □ WOMEN IN PRISON

Until recently, the problems of female offenders have been largely ignored because women comprised a very small percentage of the total adult offender population. In 1976, there were about 11,000 females in state and federal prisons. By 1988, this figure had grown to over 24,000—a rise of about 118 percent. During the same time the percentage of increase for men in prison was only about 83 percent. Along with this has come a significant surge, when compared to men, in arrest rates among women over the same time period. This is true for both property crimes and crimes of violence.[40] It is, however, violent crime arrest rates for women that have shown the most drastic increase in both an absolute sense and in comparison to males. Perhaps it is to be expected that with such an upsurge of arrests of women for violent crimes over this time period, we can expect a similar increase in the number of women being sent to prison.

With this sudden spurt in women being sentenced to prison, the housing and treatment of female adult offenders has assumed greater importance. The problem prompted the federal government in the late 1970s to launch a large-scale study of women's correctional programs throughout the country. Because like male prisoners, most female inmates in prisons are in state institutions, it was the first major attempt not only to examine aspects of programs provided by the nation's womens' prisons but also to develop a better understanding of the characteristics and prob-

**Age:** Young: two-thirds are under 30; the median age of sentenced felons is 26.

**Ethnic:** 50 percent are black; 9 percent are Hispanic. American Indians are also overrepresented.

**Education:** Far below national average for women. This is particularly true for black and Hispanic women in prison.

**Marital Status:** At the time of imprisonment, 27 percent were single, 19 percent were nonmarried but living with a man, 28 percent were separated or divorced, 20 percent were married.

**Children:** 74 percent have dependent children. The average number of children per inmate mother was 2.48.

**Offense:** 43 percent in prison for violent crimes (murder, armed robbery); 29 percent for property crimes (forgery, fraud, larceny); 22 percent for drug offenses.

**Offense History:** Over one-third have been arrested as juveniles and spent time in juvenile institutions. By age 24 two-thirds had been arrested. The women with the most extensive involvement with the criminal justice system are the habitual offenders—prostitutes, drug offenders, and petty thieves.

**Personal Characteristics:** More than one-half have grown up in one-parent homes or with relatives; many were sexually abused as children; like males, many have immediate-family members who had also served time in prison, and a high percentage of the female prison inmates have drug and alcohol abuse problems.

FIGURE **13.3** A composite profile of the typical adult female offender in state prison. [*Sources:* Law Enforcement Assistance Administration, National Study of Women's Correctional Programs (Washington, D.C.: U.S. Government Printing Office, June 1977); *National Prison Statistics, 1983, 1984, and 1985;* Bureau of Justice Statistics, *Report to the Nation on Crime and Justice* (2nd ed.), March 1988.]

lems of women in prison.[41] Much of the following discussion is based on that research effort.

Although women in prison have always presented special problems, such problems were generally ignored both in terms of the women inmates themselves and the institutions that housed them. Prison research invariably focused on the male inmate population and male institutions. In recent years a change has been noticeable, largely because of a growing public awareness of the changing role of women in society. The women's movement has helped to focus attention on the way women are treated by the criminal justice system, and most certainly by the correctional component of that system.[42]

The same problems that have traditionally plagued male inmates and prisons have been even more of a problem with the female offenders. Many of the problems of female offenders are a result of our traditional views of women and their roles in society. For example, women's programs showed an early shift from punishment to treatment when, in the late nineteenth century, social reformers urged the establishment of separate institutions for women. These new prisons were called reformatories and were intended to help women learn to accept appropriate female role behavior.[43]

Research into the characteristics of women prisoners indicates that severe pathological problems are often present (see Figure 13.3). In many cases, their lives have been based on rejection and exploitation by men and the inability to form lasting positive relationships. Unlike the male role of the exploiter, they are exploited.[44] Typically, female prisoners have a very negative self-image, which is often reinforced by incarceration and being labeled as an ex-con. If they are mothers, the problem of self-image is further compounded by the feeling of having failed in this role. Under such circumstances, the problems of rehabilitation are often much more difficult to deal with than for male prisoners.[45] Burkhardt claims that the life experiences of the female inmate population tend to produce so much hostile behavior that up to 80 percent of women in prisons receive Thorazine, Librium, or other drugs on a daily basis to keep them "manageable."[46]

One of the popular theories about women in prison is that many of them are in prison because they got romantically involved. Karl Rasmussen, Executive Director of the Women's Prison Association of New York, maintains that although no specific data on the subject exist, 85 percent of women were in a sense "victimized" by their relationship with a man. As he says: "They hook up with a thief, a drug dealer, a robber and get caught up in a crime out of misguided loyalty, for what they think is love. Or sometimes the men threaten them—or worse, their children—so the women end up being co-conspirators, participating as the passive ones in the crimes."[47]

But a passive role may not always be the case. Like many male offenders, women may also become more active participants once they are exposed to the quick and easy money that can be made by drug dealing or committing robberies. Persons who have examined the aspect of female criminality point out that the drive for material things so characteristic of our society also plays a role, but a somewhat different one for many women offenders. While the drive to be materially successful seems to affect men more than it does women, the motivation for the female offender is merely to survive in our increasingly materialistic society. Largely lacking in skills, self-esteem, and the experience of knowing women in their own lives who can function well and independently as wage earners, they react by

Women's prisons generally offer fewer and less effective rehabilitation programs than do men's prisons. (© Melanie Carr/Zephyr Pictures)

**Issues of female criminality**

turning to crime as their only means to provide anything above a public assistance or welfare-based existence.

If there has been one traditional characteristic that seems to have separated female from male prison offenders it was that women, much more than men, seemed to abhor the use of violence in committing their crimes. Only a relatively small percentage of women in prison at one time were there for violent crimes. This seems to be changing. Increasingly, our female prison population consists of women sentenced for crimes such as homicide, robbery, and aggravated assault. Although men are still far more likely to engage in these violent crimes than women, the idea—which is still popularly misperceived—that women sentenced to prison are still passive property offenders needs to be looked at more carefully. Apologists for this kind of thinking contend that much of this violent crime representation is for child abuse—as if to say that it really doesn't count.[48] Along with this is the feminist contention that many women classified as violent crime offenders in our prisons today are there because they acted out of "self-defense" against a history of being battered by their husbands or boyfriends. Acting out of fear or frustration, they kill or injure, which puts them in prison.[49] Although this is possible, the evidence still remains unclear.

What this points out is that we still know relatively little about the motivations of the female offender. One aspect of the violence issue that appears plausible is that women typically do not evidence the brutal wantonness more characteristic of males. Women, for example, rarely torture their victims. Yet the aspect of increasing violence among women, at least as shown by arrest rates and prison incarceration, has yet to be examined in any meaningful way. It is a research item needing attention.

Traditionally, effective rehabilitative programs in women's prisons have been nonexistent. If resources for such rehabilitation as vocational training, education, and related programs have been conspicuously absent in men's institutions, women's institutions have fared even worse. About one-third of the women in institutions are enrolled in some type of vocational or academic program. However, these vocational "rehabilitative' programs are often geared to stereotyped female tasks such as sewing, food service, and laundry. Burkhardt reports that only a handful of women prisoners throughout the country are trained in jobs such as dental assistants, and none received official credentials. Similarly, although a few learn cosmetology, as convicted felons, they cannot obtain licenses in many states.[50]

It is likely that improvements have been made in this situation today. Although problems still exist in providing effective rehabilitation programs for women prisoners and truly meaningful vocational training programs are certainly not available everywhere, we have and continue to make important and progressive strides. It is perhaps time to take another comprehensive nationwide look at women in prison and the institutions that house them.

In the federal survey, administrators of women's institutions were asked their views concerning the special needs of female prisoners. Their comments indicate the range and depth of the problem:

- The inmate's social role in society is homemaking; she needs a homelike setting, even in prison (this is why women inmates turn to homosexuality); she needs strong ties to family and better relationships with her children; she needs to learn how to care for her children.
- Being "head of a household" is a big problem for many women inmates.

- Women inmates are unmotivated; they need more counseling and positive social involvement; they need to acquire problem-solving skills; women inmates have low self-esteem because of societal stigmas.
- Women have difficulty dealing with institutionalization.
- Women inmates need to learn to be self-sufficient.
- They seek more medical help more often.
- The women have few skills; they have employability problems.[51]

 **CORRECTIONAL REFORM**

Reform has always been a burning issue in corrections, as mentioned in Chapter 12, in discussing the history and development of modern correctional efforts. Seen in this context, the subject of reform is nothing new. The issue is as relevant today as it was in the nineteenth and early twentieth centuries. Chapter 16 examines some of the more important issues and reforms that are today impacting on corrections in the United States. Although corrections has made some important and progressive strides over the years, true reform has been elusive. In 1973 a major national task force was convened to examine our nation's overall correctional efforts. One of the major conclusions of the study was that corrections suffered from some major impediments to change; circumstances that seriously hindered any truly meaningful reform efforts. Six major impediments to reform were identified:

1. The existing fragmentation of corrections
2. Overuse of corrections
3. Overemphasis on custody
4. Community ambivalence
5. Lack of adequate financial support and resources
6. The lack of a knowledge base for planning[52]

Unfortunately, we have made very little progress in correcting these problems, and in many ways they impede our efforts to this day.

### Fragmentation of Corrections

Corrections, like all other agencies of criminal justice, is structured and administered on the concept of political federalism in which the maintenance of correctional institutions and programs is divided among jurisdictions at the federal, state, county, and municipal levels of government. This fragmentation has produced semiautonomous responsibility for dealing with convicted offenders among a multiplicity of programs and jurisdictions. The result has been the poor utilization of resources, inequities in financial support for program improvement, lack of effective supervisory control, duplication and waste in institutional construction and program implementation, and the influence of local politics in the administration of these programs and facilities.

Multiplicity of independent facilities

In the past, there may have been a need to maintain local correctional facilities because of the problems associated with inadequate transportation and communication systems, but this is certainly no longer the case. Today, the trend in modern penological thinking is toward the consolidated administrative control of all correctional programs and institutions in the state.

The consolidation idea does, however, recognize some exceptions. It is not feasible or probably legal to even consider merging federal and state correctional institutions and programs. Offenders in these prisons have been sentenced for the commission of crimes against different governments—federal and state. It certainly would be extraordinarily difficult, if not impossible, for the states to assume the responsibility for housing convicted federal offenders in state prisons. Although there are situations for which the federal government, for instance, will agree to house a state prisoner in a federal facility, this occurs only in rare situations, such as when a state prisoner must be transferred out of the state system for his or her own protection. On the other hand, although it might be theoretically possible for the federal government to operate all prisons in the United States, this simply will not occur. The states are not going to relinquish this role to the federal government.

There are a number of sound arguments for consolidation within states. In the first place, the taxing resources of states have a number of advantages not available to local or county governments. Thus, program support for the purchase of required resources for a statewide correctional system would be better. Consolidation would also provide for a more equitable distribution of taxes required to support correctional institutions. Statewide systems could also develop standardized policies and procedures that would ensure higher standards of program performance and efficiency.

A centralized administrative authority would also have other positive benefits. For example, a large agency would have the political leverage to compete better for scarce appropriations. Career opportunities, training, salaries, and a host of other personnel considerations would conceivably also improve. It has been argued, however, that state control of correctional facilities invites massive bureaucratization and the inability of correctional programs to enjoy the flexibility and closer operating supervision afforded facilities that are locally operated.[53] This has never been demonstrated. Seen in the context of local jail operations and the problems associated with these type facilities, such an argument loses much of its support.

Last, with the movement of corrections toward community-based programs and specialized institutions tailored to the particular needs of offenders, it is almost mandatory that the states assume responsibility, because local and county governments are not capable of providing such facilities and programs. Yet in spite of the obvious need to deal with the problems of correctional fragmentation, it is not likely to occur. The reasons are the same as those prohibiting jail consolidation (discussed in Chapter 12)—entrenched political interests do not want to see change and the inertia of tradition. Both of these factors will thwart any efforts to improve the situation. Reformers will be no more successful in this area than they have been in other areas of the justice system.

## Overuse of Corrections (Traditional Institutionalization)

Society's response to criminal behavior has traditionally been that of punishment. In this way punishment has been seen as a means of deterrence and retribution. From the inception of American corrections, we have increasingly turned to the use of incarceration as our means of punishing offenders. For nearly two centuries, prison reformers have been trying to create an institution that could punish without brutalizing. The ball and chain and the rock pile are gone, along with enforced silence, lockstep marching, and other harsh disciplinary methods designed to keep

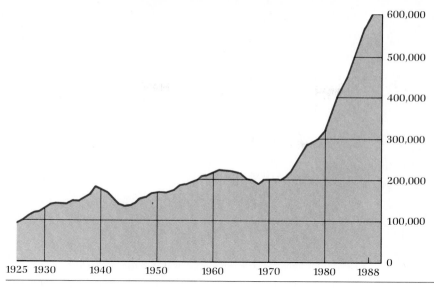

Number of sentenced adult inmates in state and federal prisons, 1925–1988. [*Source:* Bureau of Justice Statistics, *BJS Data Report,* 1988 (Washington, D.C.: April 1989).]

FIGURE **13.4**

prisoners docile and compliant.[54] If it is punishment we seek—and if incarceration is our vehicle—then it would seem that we are increasingly successful in our efforts to punish. Figure 13.4 shows the changes in prison populations in the United States since 1925. These figures do not reflect simply the effects of increased population in the United States. They do, in fact, reflect that we are incarcerating more offenders than at any time since such statistics have been kept. For example, in 1939 the incarceration rate was 122 per 100,000 population; by 1971 this had dropped to 96.4; by 1978 the figure had reached 195 and is now nearly 230 inmates per 100,000 population (see Figure 13.5).[55] Only the Soviet Union and South Africa have a higher percentage of their populations in prison. So much for the argument that our courts are not sentencing offenders to prison!

And what about the cost of such increasing incarceration rates? In 1985 the federal government reported that construction costs for new state prisons—maximum-, medium-, and minimum-security institutions together—averaged about $50,000 per bed. The breakdown can be seen in Table 13.1. Then there are the annual operating costs of custody, which run between $15,000 to $20,000 per inmate per year. Even if new facilities did not need to be built, the mere cost of housing an offender in prison plus additional social costs (e.g., lost tax revenues, welfare payments to prisoners' families, etc.) bring the price tag up to a national average of $25,000 per year for each offender in prison.[56] What have we gotten ourselves into? We seem to be on a perpetual treadmill of increased incarceration leading to overcrowding, which in turn leads to increased tension and violence in our prisons. This in turn reduces any chance for efforts to "correct" offenders and increases the costs of imprisonment drastically to the American taxpayers.

Yet we persist, in spite of overwhelming evidence, that traditional incarceration in no way serves as a deterrent. The criminal laws are still violated with im-

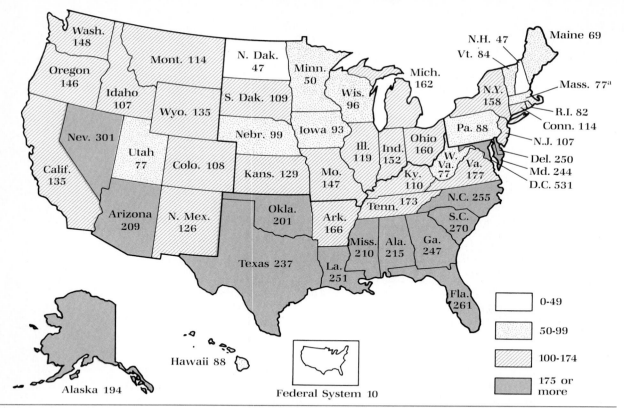

FIGURE **13.5** Rate of sentenced prisoners in state and federal institutions per 100,000 civilian population on January 1, 1983. Unpublished U.S. Bureau of the Census estimates for the resident population on July 1, 1982, were used to calculate sentenced prisoners per 100,000 persons for both the states and the nation as a whole. Sentenced prisoners are defined as persons serving sentences longer than a year.

[a]Massachusetts cannot distinguish inmates by sentence length; therefore, the incarceration rate is based on the total prisoner population. [*Source:* U.S. Department of Justice, Bureau of Justice Statistics, *Prisoners in 1982*, Bulletin NCJ-87933 (Washington, D.C.: U.S. Department of Justice, April 1983), p. 2. and U.S. Department of Justice, Bureau of Justice Statistics, *Sourcebook of Criminal Justice Statistics, 1983* (Washington, D.C.: U.S. Government Printing Office, 1984), p. 569.]

punity, and the institutionalization of offenders stands as a monumental failure to deterrence, as indicated by the high percentage of offenders who, upon release, commit new crimes and are returned to prison.

We must carefully and courageously rethink what we are trying to accomplish and how. If we as a society are interested merely in retribution as the sole goal of the administration of justice, then perhaps incarceration can be justified on these grounds. It seems that it can be justified in no other way.

If history has taught us anything, it is that the mere construction of more prisons and the "warehousing" of inmates in traditional prisons is bound to be a failure. Although some classes of offenders do pose a real threat to society if they are allowed their freedom, a great many inmates could be handled much more meaningfully outside the walls of traditional prisons in special facilities and community-based alternatives. Many prison administrators say that our prison systems

TABLE **13.1**  New Correctional Facility Costs
for State Institutions

| Type of Facility | Cost per Bed |
|---|---|
| Maximum security state prison (1985) | $70,768 |
| Medium security state prison (1985) | $53,360 |
| Minimum security state prison (1985) | $29,599 |
| "Constitutional" jail (1982)[a] | $43,000 |
| Juvenile facility (1985) | $26,470 |
| Average remodeling for additions to prisons (1985) | $19,944 |

[a]A "constitutional" jail is one that meets minimum acceptable standards of construction and operation.

*Source:* Bureau of Justice Statistics, *Report to the Nation on Crime and Justice,* 2nd ed. (Washington, D.C.: U.S. Department of Justice, March 1988), p. 124.

should exist primarily to deal with those offenders who can be helped only by intensive institutional supervision and care and with those individuals whose freedom is a clear threat to the safety of society.[57] This argument and its supporting logic calls for greater consideration of alternative methods of dealing with offenders.

In essence, society is victimized twice: first by the crime and then by the need to support the confined criminal at an exorbitant cost. Perhaps if, as many experts rightly contend, our prisons are not reforming criminals, we should find ways to at least minimize the costs of incarceration on the American taxpayer. This does not mean that we should neglect the welfare of inmates, it merely means that we should look at ways to reduce costs to society by enforcing programs in which inmates must offset these costs through some type of productive contribution. As long as we seek solutions by increasing our subsidy of what clearly has and continues to be a failure, we as a nation are fools in terms of our correctional efforts.

## Overemphasis on Custody

The security of any facility is determined by the most dangerous inmate in the prison population. Although an institution may have only a few such individuals, security precautions must be guided by the possible actions of these few. Because of the public concern with prison escapes, wardens and other administrators risk their careers if they manage institutions where such occurrences are frequent. Under these circumstances, the primary concern expressed by prison administrators for maintaining tight security is quite understandable.

However, this emphasis on security works against the development of effective treatment programs within institutions. For example, the massive structures that for years dominated prison design were completely unsuitable for vocational programs, recreational facilities, and more diversified prison industries programs. Security in an institution that has treatment programs is more difficult to maintain because of the movement of inmates within the institution as they attend classes, counseling sessions, and vocational training programs.

Security versus treatment

This overemphasis on custody can also be seen in the proliferation of jails, juvenile detention homes, and large institutions for adult and juvenile offenders. The National Advisory Commission commented on the results of years of emphasis on custody in prison design and programming:

The mega-institution, holding more than a thousand adult inmates, has been built in larger number and variety in this country than anywhere else in the world. Large institutions for young offenders have also proliferated here. In such surroundings, inmates become faceless people, living out routine and meaningless lives. And, where institutions are racially skewed and filled with a disproportionate number of ill-educated and vocationally inept persons, they magnify tensions already existing in our society.[58]

Prison administrators and penologists have suggested many times that smaller institutions would provide both the necessary security and at the same time a better situation for the development of programs and the environment more conducive to correctional efforts. It would certainly contribute to the "livability" of the prison institution. The trend in recent years has been to build only smaller prisons. Such gigantic institutions as Southern Michigan Penitentiary are not the way of the future. But as long as such institutions continue to exist, their massive size and prison populations numbering in the thousands require that custody and security considerations be paramount.

## Lack of Financial Support

Unpopular funding priority

Considering the number of inmates who must be supervised and the facilities that must be maintained, the corrections component, including jail services, probation, and parole, does not receive a large share of the revenues that support the operations of the criminal justice system. Although the picture has improved somewhat in recent years with corrections' share of criminal justice expenditures showing the largest relative increase in funding of all criminal justice components, resources still do not meet needs. When we stop and remember that on average 1.5 percent of all American adults in any one year are under some form of correctional supervision or program, we get some idea of the size of the problem.

Prison funding is particularly unpopular with state legislatures. While legislatures are less reluctant to fund parole or probation programs, they are especially reluctant to give money to the department of corrections to operate or build prisons. There are any number of reasons for this. There certainly is little if any direct or indirect payoff to legislators themselves for this activity. Legislators have no constituency among inmates, and they realize that having to fund prisons at the expense of roads, parks, or education actually causes them problems among those who vote and elect them; voters and taxpayers prefer that tax dollars be spent on these other activities. This points out that prison funding certainly is not popular among taxpayers either. It's safe to assume that if prison operations required the approval of the electorate by means of a referendum, such as a mileage increase so common for local school district operations, prison funding would probably never be approved.

Although no clear evidence exists on this fact, it may well be that legislatures (and the public) have become increasingly reluctant to fund something that simply does not seem to work. The author has heard legislators complain that funding prisons is "like throwing money down a sewer."

It isn't much better with jails. The one possible difference is that the jail is at least seen by the public as a local facility. Spending money on a jail may be slightly more acceptable than spending money to house murderers, rapists, and robbers in a remote area of the state several hundred miles away. As one county legislator said, "At least the people can see where their money is going; it's not like sending it off to the capitol, where those idiots can fight over who gets what and where—with the "big dogs" likely to end up ultimately getting it in their districts regardless if it [the prison] isn't needed more someplace else." (Personal communication.)

## Attitude of the Community

Because large correctional institutions often provide substantial numbers of jobs for local residents, nearby communities often tolerate the presence of penal institutions. In fact, some states have experienced a situation of economically depressed rural areas actually having competed to have a new correctional facility built in their area. Even in these cases, however, the acceptance of such a facility is often conditional. It exists as long as the inmates are locked up and out of sight; the surrounding communities feel reasonably safe, provided that the convicts are maintained behind massive walls and elaborate security precautions exist to prevent escapes. When these conditions do not exist, neighboring communities are far less likely to accept a penal institution on their doorstep. In recent years, as state correctional authorities have tried to start community-based programs or facilities in local areas, strong opposition has arisen from local neighborhood groups and property tax owners' associations. It is more than merely their fear of the offenders who are housed in these facilities or participating in programs; local residents also fear depreciation in property values as a result of the location of the community-based effort.

Part of the blame for such attitudes must rest with prison administrators of

The acceptance of a prison by the community may depend on the visibility of security structures like these. (© Bryce Flynn/Stock Boston)

the past, who were only too quick to isolate corrections from the general public by high walls and locked doors. This is the way the public wanted it, and locating an institution in a rural area provided better security against escape, kept the operations of the prison away from outside view, and tended to cut down on the ever-present problem of smuggling contraband into the prison. Yet this isolation has been recognized as having a bad side. It makes it very difficult to operate certain programs that rely on the resources and opportunities available in the community.

### Lack of Knowledge Base for Planning

One of the major obstacles to correctional reform lies in our failure to develop sound knowledge of the problem based on thorough research activities. Such data would give us the ability to determine which correctional practices are effective with which types of offenders.

We need to know more about crime, not only in the most obvious ways such as how to prevent it but also how to treat individuals who engage in criminal behavior and are sent to prison. Ideally, for example, do certain correctional efforts work better with violent crime offenders? With property crime offenders? Such a strategy would rest on knowing if the two (i.e., violent and property crime offenders) are truly distinct or are violent and property crime offenders generally the same, in that they commit both forms of criminal activity according to circumstances and opportunity.

As it is now, our correctional efforts fly by the seat of their pants. We know so little about the complexities of crime that we can neither prevent it before it occurs or after it's taken place by "reforming" those convicted and imprisoned. Should we abandon our efforts to "rehabilitate" certain offenders who have never been habilitated to begin with and impose a prison-based regimen of "aversive conditioning," as some people suggest, such as to ensure that the prison experience becomes truly something to avoid? Can we do that? Should we do it? Would it work, or is it simply counterproductive and overly simplistic?

### ▣ CURRENT STATUS OF CORRECTIONS

Although corrections have made definite progress in recent years, hard questions are being raised as to how meaningful this progress has really been. A great deal of concern is being expressed over whether prisons, even with the employment of innovative programs, will ever succeed in reforming a significant number of inmates. Many knowledgeable penologists feel that because of the very nature of the environment within prisons, even the best-devised programs can, at best, achieve only a limited success by almost any standard.

Today, the situation is somewhat paradoxical. On the one hand, we are developing more and better programs and personnel to operate them; on the other hand, problems within prisons are also accelerating. In the face of mounting fiscal problems, states are unable to allocate the necessary resources to operate correctional systems; at the same time, more and more offenders are being sentenced to institutions that are often unable to accommodate them. With greater use of probation and other diversionary measures, our prison populations are increasingly becoming populated with more hardened and intractable offenders. Racial problems, drugs, violence, and a multitude of other concerns face prison managers. Society continues to subsidize this failure in ever more costly ways.

As in all aspects of the administration of justice, there is also great diversity among the states in their efforts to commit resources to improving their correctional operations or to innovate with new, and hopefully, more effective prison programs. New Hampshire spends nearly seven times the amount of money per inmate than does Texas.[59] These two states are at the extremes on the high and low end of the scale among the states. Still, nobody would claim that New Hampshire is seven times more successful than Texas in what its correctional programs accomplish. This points up part of the quandry: Merely increasing resources alone is not the answer.

Along this line, it sometimes is falsely assumed that because a state or region of the country spends more money for its correctional efforts, it must be better than another state or region that spends less. This same argument can be raised about funding levels for all aspects of the administration of justice. The South, for example, as a region spends less for corrections on a per inmate basis than does New England. Yet, the South uses more community-based programs than any other area of the country. For example, in surveys taken in both 1979 and 1984, it was found that the Southern states accounted for about half of the state-operated, community-based halfway houses and for more than 60 percent of the residents of such houses.[60] Perhaps this partly explains the lower operating cost per inmate. It certainly shows a willingness to be more innovative, which seems to be conspicuously absent in the New England states, which are much more traditional in the construction and operation of their prison systems. The point is that caution is warranted in making certain assumptions without fully understanding the complexity of the issue.

One final comment should be made. This need for more meaningful alternatives is not meant to imply, as some may recommend, that we abolish prisons completely—such suggestions are ludicrous. A certain percentage of offenders pose a threat to the safety of society and must be imprisoned. However, there are many prisoners in our penal institutions today who could be dealt with more effectively by means other than imprisonment. Assuming that these prisoners can be identified, the question then becomes: Are we, as a society, more interested in punishment, or do we really want to improve the chances of an offender leading a noncriminal life in future? The next two chapters examine some new correctional programs that are attempting to accomplish that goal.

## SUMMARY

The corrections component of the criminal justice system in the United States is a checkerboard affair of various programs, philosophies, and institutions. Overall, it suffers from a number of weaknesses: It is overly fragmented; it has been overused; it has traditionally emphasized custody; and it suffers from citizen apathy, lack of financial support, and lack of an effective means to evaluate its work.

Prison programming generally includes vocational and academic training, health programs, libraries, recreational programs, prison industries, and some form of classification procedure. Prisons may be classified by the degree of security they provide and by their program emphasis. Whereas the traditional model emphasizes an authoritarian environment, the collaborative model emphasizes integrating treatment and custodial personnel in a team approach that includes inmates in the operations of the institution and in their own programs.

In recent years there has been a sharp increase in the number of female inmates. With the lack of resources, program efforts, and the particularly difficult task of dealing effectively with the unique problems of female offenders, corrections has another burden added to its already troublesome task.

## REVIEW QUESTIONS

1. What are the chief characteristics of the following types of institutions, and what kinds of inmates are housed in each?
   a. Maximum security
   b. Medium security
   c. Minimum security
   d. Prison camps
   e. Special institutions
2. What is the primary purpose of a state department of corrections?
3. Draw an organization chart for an adult male institution of fewer than 2,000 inmates.
4. Describe the duties of each of the following key prison personnel:
   a. Correctional officer
   b. Psychiatrist
   c. Psychologist
   d. Counselor
5. What is the purpose of a diagnostic center in a state correctional system?
6. Briefly explain the characteristics of the traditional model in administering a prison facility.
7. Briefly explain the characteristics of the collaborative model in administering an institution.
8. Describe the general characteristics of adult male and female prison inmates.
9. Identify and briefly describe six problem areas that are hindering correctional reform.

## DISCUSSION QUESTIONS

1. Are there valid reasons for having five separate categories of prison institutions? Why or why not?
2. What possible factors might explain the differences in rates of imprisonment in different areas of the country?
3. Compare and contrast the traditional and collaborative models of prison administration. Why is the collaborative model more appropriate from the viewpoint of rehabilitation?
4. What similarities and dissimilarities are evident in the composite profiles of male and female prisoners?
5. Can anything be done to address the problems facing correctional reforms today? Discuss what they might be.

## SUGGESTED ADDITIONAL READINGS

Allison, Richard S. "The Politics of Prison Standards." *Corrections Magazine* (March 1979).

Clark, Ramsey. "Prisons: Factories of Crime." In David M. Petersen and Charles W. Thomas, eds., *Corrections: Problems and Prospects*. Englewood Cliffs, N.J.: Prentice-Hall, 1975.

Glaser, Daniel. "Politicization of Prisoners: A New Challenge to American Penology." *American Journal of Correction* 33 (November–December, 1971): 6–9.

Goldfarb, Ronald, and Linda Singer. "Disaster Road: The American Prison System." *Intellectual Digest* 2 (December 1971).

Jarvis, D. C. *Institutional Treatment of the Offender*. New York: McGraw-Hill, 1978.

Kalinich, David B., and T. Pitcher. *Surviving in Corrections—A Guide for Corrections Professionals*. Springfield, Ill.: Charles C. Thomas, 1984.

Malloy, Edward A. *The Ethics of Law Enforcement and Criminal Punishment*. Lanham, Md.: University Press of America, 1983.

McGuigan, Patrick, and Jon S. Pascale. *Crime and Punishment in Modern America*. Lanham, Md.: University Press of America, 1987.

Megathlin, William L., and Sherman R. Day. "The Line Staff as Agents of Control and Change." *American Journal of Corrections* 34 (May–June, 1972).

Melossi, Dario, and Massimo Pavarini. *The Prison and the Factory: Origins of the Penitentiary System*. Totowa, N.J.: Rowman & Littlefield, 1981.

Sechrest, Dale K. "The Accreditation Movement in Corrections." *Federal Probation*. (December 1976).

Teeters, Negley K. "State of Prisons in the United States: 1870–1970." *Federal Probation* 33 (December 1969).

Toch, Hans. *Living in Prisons—The Ecology of Survival*. New York: Free Press, 1977.

U.S. Department of Justice. *Draft Federal Standards for Corrections*. Washington, D.C.: U.S. Government Printing Office, June 1978.

Zimmerman, Sherwood E., and Harold D. Miller. *Corrections at the Crossroads—Designing Policy*. Beverly Hills, Calif.: Sage Publications, 1987.

# NOTES

1. *Bureau of Justice Statistics Bulletin, Probation and Parole—1984* (Washington, D.C.: U.S. Department of Justice, February 1986).

2. *Bureau of Justice Statistics Special Report, Imprisonment in Four Countries* (Washington, D.C.: U.S. Department of Justice, February 1987).

3. Bureau of Justice Statistics, *Report to the Nation on Crime and Justice,* 2nd ed. (Washington, D.C.: U.S. Department of Justice, March 1988), p. 107.

4. Bureau of Justice Statistics, *Sourcebook of Criminal Justice Statistics—1983* (Washington, D.C.: U.S. Government Printing Office, 1984), p. 132.

5. Louis P. Carney, *Introduction to Correctional Science* (New York: McGraw-Hill, 1974), p. 128.

6. For example see: Lucien X. Lombardo, *Guards Imprisoned—Correctional Officers at Work* (New York: Elsevier, 1981); Dae H. Chang and Charles H. Zastrow, "Inmates and Security Guards' Perceptions of Themselves and Each Other: A Comparative Study," *International Journal of Criminology and Penology* 4, no. 1 (1976): 89–98; and J. R. Hepburn, "The Erosion of Authority and the Perceived Legitimacy of Inmate Social Protest: A Study of Prison Guards," *Journal of Criminal Justice* 12, no. 6 (1984): 579–590.

7. Lombardo, *Guards Imprisoned.*

8. Ibid., p. 115.

9. Ibid.

10. Ibid.

11. E. May, "Prison Guards in America—The Inside Story," In Robert Ross, (ed.) *Prison Guard/Correctional Officer* (Canada: Butterworth, 1981), pp. 37–38.

12. Hans Toch and J. D. Grant, *Reforming Human Services: Change Through Participation* (Beverly Hills, Calif.: Sage, 1982).

13. F. T. Cullen, B. G. Link, N. T. Wolfe, and J. Frank, "The Social Dimensions of Correctional Officer Stress," *Justice Quarterly* 2, no. 4 (1985): 505–533.

14. Robert Johnson, *Hard Time—Understanding and Reforming the Prison* (Monterey, Calif.: Brooks Cole, 1987), p. 138.

15. P. J. Kissel and P. L. Katsamples, "The Impact of Women Correctional Officers on the Functioning of Institutions Handling Male Inmates," *Journal of Offender Counseling, Services and Rehabilitation* 4, no. 3 (1980): 213–231; and B. A. Owen, "Race and Gender Relations Among Prison Workers," *Crime and Delinquency* 31, no. 1 (1985): 147–159.

16. B. M. Crouch, "Pandora's Box: Women Guards in Men's Prisons," *Journal of Criminal Justice* 13 (1985): 535–548; and N. C. Jurik, "Striking a Balance: Advancement Strategies for Women Working as Correctional Officers in Men's Prisons," *Feminist Studies* 6 (1986), p. 16.

17. Johnson, *Crime, Correction and Society,* 3rd ed. (Homewood, Ill.: Dorsey, 1974) p. 504.

18. Ibid.

19. Henry Burns, Jr., *Corrections: Organization and Administration* (St. Paul, Minn.: West, 1975), p. 417.

20. Vernon Fox, *Introduction to Corrections* (Englewood Cliffs, N.J.: Prentice-Hall, 1972), p. 188.

21. Michigan Governor's Committee on Corrections, *Committee on Corrections Report* (Lansing, Mich.: 1972), p. 12.

22. Fox, *Introduction to Corrections,* p. 174.

23. Law Enforcement Assistance Administration, *Health Related Services in Adult Institutions* (Washington, D.C.: U.S. Government Printing Office, June 1976), p. 3.

24. *Gilmore* v. *Lynch,* 400 F.2d 228 (9th Cir. 1968) aff'd *Younger* v. *Gilmore,* 404 U.S. 15, 92 S. Ct. 250, 30 L. Ed. 2d 142 (1971).

25. Johnson, *Crime, Correction and Society,* p. 560.

26. Ibid.

27. Walter C. Reckless, *The Crime Problem* (New York: Appleton-Century-Crofts, 1967), p. 705.

28. Ibid., p. 706.

29. Gresham M. Sykes, *A Society of Captives* (New York: Atheneum, 1970), p. 23.

30. George H. Grosser, "The Role of Informal Inmate Groups in Change of Values," *Children* 5 (January–February 1958): 26.

31. Donald Clemmer, *The Prison Community* (New York: Holt, Rinehart and Winston, 1958), pp. 298–300.

32. Gresham Sykes and Sheldon I. Messinger, "The Inmate Social Code," in Norman Johnston et al., eds., *The Sociology of Punishment and Correction* (New York: Wiley, 1970), pp. 401–408.

33. Stanton Wheeler, "Socialization in Correctional Communities," *American Sociological Review* 26 (October 1961): 699–700.

34. Peter G. Garabedian, "Social Roles and Processes of Socialization in the Prison Community," *Social Problems* 11 (Fall 1963): 145.

35. For example, see Robert B. Levinson and Ray E. Gerard, "Functional Units: A Different Correctional Approach," *Federal Probation* 37 (December 1970); 8–15.

36. Stanley Vroman, "Models of Inmate Governance," *Corrections Digest* 2 (June 1975): 12.

37. Zebulon R. Brockway, *Fifty Years of Prison Service* (New York: Charities Publication Committee, 1912), pp. 96–97.

38. Harold M. Helfman. "Antecedents of Thomas Mott Osborne's 'Mutual Welfare League' in Michigan." *Journal of Criminal Law, Criminology and Police Science* 40 (January–February 1950): 597–600.

39. South Carolina Department of Corrections, *The Emerging Rights of the Confined* (Columbia, S.C.: 1972), p. 94.

40. FBI, *Uniform Crime Reports* (various).

41. Law Enforcement Assistance Administration, *National Study of Women's Correctional Programs* (Washington, D.C.: U.S. Government Printing Office, June 1977).

42. Ibid., pp. xxi–xxii; and Ann Grogan, "Women Locked Up: Feminist Perspectives and Alternatives," text of keynote address of Conference of Women in Prison, Denver, Colo., 18 January 1975.

43. See Rose Giallombardo, "The Seasonless World: A Study of a Women's Prison." Doctoral dissertation, University Microfilms, Ann Arbor, Mich., 1965, p. 103.

44. See Kathryn W. Burkhardt, *Women in Prison* (New York: Doubleday, 1973).

45. For example, see Dorie Klien, "The Etiology of Female Crime: A Review of the Literature," *Issues in Criminology* 8, no. 2 (Fall 1973): 3–30; Margery Velimesis, "Report on the Survey of 41 Pennsylvania County Court and Correctional Services for Women and Girl Offenders," 1969; and Helen Gibson. "Women's Prisons: Laboratories for Penal Reform," *Wisconsin Law Review* (1973).

46. Burkhardt, *Women in Prison.*

47. Sherrye Henry, "Women in Prison" *Parade Magazine*, 10 April 1988, pp. 4–7.

48. Ibid., p. 6.

49. Ibid.

50. Burkhardt, op. cit.

51. Law Enforcement Assistance Administration, *National Study of Women's Correctional Programs*, pp. 38–39.

52. National Advisory Commission on Criminal Justice Standards and Goals, *Corrections* (Washington, D.C.: U.S. Government Printing Office, 1973), pp. 10–14.

53. Advisory Commission on Intergovernmental Relations, *Jail Consolidation: An Opportunity for the States* (Washington, D.C.: ACIR, 1978).

54. Charles E. Silberman, *Criminal Violence, Criminal Justice* (New York: Vintage Books, 1978), p. 503.

55. National Institute of Justice, *American Prisons and Jails, Volume II, Population Trends and Projections* (Washington, D.C.: U.S. Government Printing Office, October 1980), pp. 13–18.

56. Edwin W. Zedlewski, *National Institute of Justice—Research in Brief, Making Confinement Decisions* (Washington, D.C.: U.S. Department of Justice, July 1987).

57. For example, see Harry E. Allen and Clifford E. Simonsen, *Corrections in America*, 5th ed. (New York: Macmillan, 1989), esp. chapter 26.

58. National Advisory Commission, *Corrections*, p. 1.

59. *Report to the Nation*, p. 105.

60. Ibid.

# CHAPTER 14

# Parole and Probation

## OBJECTIVES

**After reading this chapter, the student should be able to:**

Discuss the historical antecedents of parole.

Identify how state parole authorities are organized.

Identify and discuss factors on which the parole decision is often based.

Explain the use of parole prediction models and how they are developed.

Understand arguments for and against the use of parole models.

Discuss "good-time."

Discuss the role functions of a parole officer.

Discuss developing trends in parole.

Discuss the abolition of the indeterminate sentence and parole.

Explain the origins of probation.

Discuss how probation is administered.

Discuss shock probation, probation subsidy programs, and use of indigenous paraprofessionals and volunteers.

Identify the function of interstate parole and probation compacts.

Discuss probation as a career.

Explain intensive parole and probation.

## IMPORTANT TERMS

Parole

Conditional pardon

Supervised ticket of leave

Indeterminate sentence and parole

Institutional model

Independent model

Consolidated model

Detainer

Parole plan

Prediction methods

Oregon's Parole Matrix

State parole boards

Parole success

Parole officer

Parolee's rights

"Good-time"

Institutional and field services

Parole teams

Parole contract plan

Abolition of indeterminate sentence and parole

Probation

John Augustus

Organization of state probation

Shock probation

Intensive parole and probation

Probation subsidy

Indigenous paraprofessionals and volunteers

Interstate parole and probation compacts

The figures are staggering. In late 1988, the federal government released a report from a 1987 survey of corrections indicating that nearly 1.5 percent of all Americans at the time the survey was conducted were on probation or parole.[1] Since 1983 alone, the figures had increased by 47 percent. If we just consider the adult population of the United States (those over age eighteen), imagine this for a moment: One out of every fifty-three American adults was under some form of correctional supervision in 1987.[2] If more current figures were available, it would even be higher today.

This is a disturbing commentary on our society. The answers are not as clear as the questions. Has American society become so involved in crime that we find this the explanation for such increases? Or is it better explained by a situation of an expanded net of criminal justice that has simply caught more people in the formal machinery of the justice system. Does this explain the ever-increasing spiral upward? Are we becoming a society in which basic social controls are breaking down—or have broken down—a situation of increasingly relying on the government in the person of the criminal justice system to deal with the problem of social control?

Such concerns and the questions they pose raise intriguing issues for speculation. The figures point out, if nothing else, the enormous workload shouldered by the parole and probation authorities throughout the country. It also points out the importance of these auxiliary functions of the criminal justice system and those who administer them. This chapter will look at key aspects of these two important components of our correctional system.

## ▢ PAROLE

Among the four correctional components—jails, prisons, probation, and parole—only probation has grown more rapidly than parole since the mid-1980s.[3] Parole is the conditional release of an individual from a correctional institution back to the community. About 80 percent of those released from prison receive some kind of parole supervision in the community. In most jurisdictions, the parole board has discretionary authority to release prisoners to conditional supervision. The offender must abide by rules of conduct that are specified by the paroling authority and enforced by a parole officer.

These rules of conduct are of two types: *general* conditions of parole and *special* conditions (see New Jersey Conditions of Parole, Figure 14.1). All released parolees must conform to the general conditions of parole. The special conditions of parole are those authorized by the parole board to impose on a particular parolee. A parolee may have a history of drug or alcohol abuse. In this case the parole board is likely to impose certain special conditions on this individual such as the requirement to submit to periodic urine tests to see if he or she is using drugs. This individual may also be required as a special condition of parole to participate in certain community-based antidrug programs. These rules are in effect until the expiration of the parolee's sentence or, if before expiration of sentence, when he or she is released from the authority of the parole agency. If the parolee breaks one of these conditions, parole may be revoked and the offender returned to a correctional facility.

It is important to note that parole operates *after* the offender has served a period of posttrial incarceration.

State of New Jersey
State Parole Board

CERTIFICATE OF PAROLE

GENERAL CONDITIONS OF PAROLE

From the date of your release on parole until the expiration of your maximum sentence(s) or until you are discharged from parole, you shall continue to be under the supervision of the Bureau of Parole. A warrant for your arrest may be filed, and this parole may be revoked for serious or persistent violations of the conditions of parole. You shall not be credited for time served on parole from the date a parole warrant is issued for your arrest if you are in violation of parole to the date that you are arrested and placed in confinement for violation of parole.

1. You are required to obey all laws and ordinances.

2. You are not to act as an informer for any agency that requires you to violate any conditions of your parole.

3. You are to report in person to your District Parole Supervisor or his or her designated representative immediately after you are released from the institution, unless you have been given other written instructions by the institutional parole office, and you are to report thereafter as instructed by the District Parole Supervisor or his or her designated authority.

4. You are to notify your parole officer immediately after any arrest and after accepting any pretrial release including bail.

5. You are to obtain approval of your Parole Officer:
   a. For any change in your residence or employment location.
   b. Before leaving the state of your approved residence for longer than 24 hours except as otherwise directed for good cause by the Parole Officer.

6. You are not to own or possess a firearm for any purpose.

7. You are required to make payment to the Bureau of Parole of any fine or penalty and any restitution imposed by the sentencing court and/or the New Jersey State Parole Board. Total Penalty: $40.00

SPECIAL CONDITION(S):

You will be paroled with the following Special Conditions:

You are to participate in random urine monitoring acceptable to the District Parole Supervisor until discharge is approved by said Supervisor.

You are to participate in outpatient drug counseling (Narcotics Anonymous) acceptable to the District Parole Supervisor until discharge is approved by said Supervisor.

You are to refrain from drug usage.

The District Parole Supervisor is authorized to impose any additional Special Conditions deemed supportive to your parole. You are to comply with any Special Conditions imposed until discharged by your District Parole Supervisor.

In consideration of the action of the State Parole Board in paroling me, I hereby accept this parole, and I hereby agree to be bound by the foregoing conditions, which shall constitute my parole contract with the State of New Jersey. Any serious or persistent violation of the conditions herein shall be suffcient cause for revocation of my parole.

Witness:                              Dated _____ 19 ___

_____          _____

State of New Jersey conditions of parole. (*Source:* Courtesy New Jersey State Parole Board.)

FIGURE **14.1**

## Historical Background

The history of parole, like the history of corrections, reflects the changing philosophy of how society deals with offenders. The reader will recall that in the late eighteenth and early nineteenth centuries, the philosophy that guided the development of corrections shifted from punishment to reform. The idea became that if prisons were to be institutions to reform offenders, then there had to be a continuation of the reform efforts of the prison in the lives of those released. In this way parole developed as a means to assist in the reform and rehabilitation efforts begun in the prison and to help the inmate adjust to the conditions of the "free world" on release.

**Conditional pardon**

There have been several precursors to modern parole. The first was called a *conditional pardon*. Under this system the English courts recommended to the king a list of prisoners who would be transported to the English colonies under stays of execution. A stay of execution was granted if the offender agreed to go to the colonies in the service of the king for a prescribed period of years. After completion of this service, the offender would be granted a conditional pardon.

**Indentured service**

Another forerunner of parole was the practice of *indentured service*. The Crown would give "property in the service" to the shipmaster who transported the prisoner to an English colony. On arriving at the colony, the shipmaster would then sell the prisoner's service to the highest bidder. At that moment the prisoner ceased technically to be a criminal and became an indentured servant to his or her new master for the period of the original sentence.

**Ticket-of-leave**

A third precursor was transportation to Australia and the *ticket-of-leave system*. Initially, prisoners transported to Australia were given conditional pardons by the Australian governor after satisfactorily serving their sentence. These pardons were at first granted quite freely, but problems arose. The Crown then authorized the governor to use tickets-of-leave with conditional pardons. In this situation the prisoner was given a conditional pardon and released on a ticket-of-leave license. The offender was required to refrain from further criminal acts, find legitimate employment, and avoid the company of notoriously bad characters. If he or she violated the conditions of the ticket-of-leave, the person was apprehended and recommitted to prison under the original sentence.[4]

**Crofton**

A later extension of the ticket-of-leave system was developed by Sir Walter Crofton in Ireland. Under Crofton's sytem, a *supervised ticket-of-leave program* developed. Crofton created the position of inspector of released prisoners. The inspector found employment for prisoners and saw that they lived up to the conditions of their release. In addition, he required that they report to him at regular intervals, he visited their homes every two weeks, and he verified their employment. Because of the success of this system, England later abandoned its unsupervised ticket-of-leave system and adopted Crofton's program. Crofton's program also influenced American corrections.

## Prison Reform in America and the Indeterminate Sentence

In addition to the direct influence of the Irish ticket-of-leave system, the development of parole in the United States was based on three basic concepts: (1) shortened imprisonment as a reward for good conduct; (2) the indeterminate sentence; and (3) supervision.[5] The idea of shortening the term of sentence gained statutory recognition in 1817 when New York passed the first good-time law. In 1869, Michigan adopted the first indeterminate-sentence law. However, it was in New York that the indeterminate sentence became a reality. Zebulon Brockway, first warden of New York's Elmira Reformatory, was familiar with ticket-of-leave policies (particularly Ireland's). He convinced New York officials that the length of an inmate's sentence should be flexible, depending on his conduct. He campaigned for the use of the indeterminate sentence for inmates sentenced to Elmira, and in 1876 New York passed the necessary authorizing legislation. Under the provisions of the indeterminate sentence, the offender was to be released at a time when his conduct demonstrated that he was ready to be returned to society. Because the offender was released before the expiration of his sentence, special provisions were made to provide him with community supervision, and parole became a reality. In this way, parole became an indispensable partner of the indeterminate sentence. Brockway's reforms, as practiced at Elmira, are credited with establishing the concept of parole in the United States.

New York's Elmira Reformatory

At first, responsibility for supervising the paroled offender was assumed primarily by private reform groups. Later, a few states appointed agents to help released offenders obtain employment. Only in the first two decades of the twentieth century did the states finally adopt the idea of professionally trained public employees—parole officers—to carry out the task of supervision.

## The Functions of Parole

Parole can be considered as an extension of the *rehabilitative* (and now, *reintegrative) program of the prison.* Although parole is often considered a form of leniency by its critics, it is an extension of the corrective efforts begun in the prison that seeks to release the inmate at a time when he or she is most able to benefit by release and return to society to lead a law-abiding life. If prisons are, in fact, to be concerned with modifying criminal behavior so that the offender can eventually be reintegrated as a law-abiding member of society, parole is supposed to provide the supervision and assistance that makes this successful reintegration possible. Finally, parole is a means to protect society. By careful selection and community supervision, parole should afford an element of protection not available if the offender were simply released at the expiration of his or her sentence.

Reintegrative function

## The Organization of State Paroling Authorities

The states vary somewhat in the way they organize their parole authority and in the responsibilities of the parole authority. States also separate adult and juvenile parole authorities. Although many people believe that the adult paroling authority is responsible only for reviewing applications and granting or denying parole, this is not necessarily the case. In addition to these typical responsibilities, parole authorities sometimes perform other functions as well. A survey conducted by the National Council on Crime and Delinquency of adult parole authorities throughout the country discovered that some state parole boards were involved in other responsibilities such as:

Responsibilities

- Conducting clemency hearings
- Commuting sentences
- Appointing parole supervisors
- Administration of parole services

- Granting parole from local institutions
- Granting or revoking "good-time"
- Supervising probation services
- Determining standards for "good-time"
- Recommending pardons[6]

In addition, many parole boards since the 1970s have expanded their reponsibilities and duties to include establishing policies regarding the need for further background investigations on inmates received by the state prison system; formulating written guidelines for use in making parole release decisions and fixing minimum periods of imprisonment; revoking the parole or conditional release of any person; issuing warrants for the retaking of delinquent parolees; the issuance of subpoenas to compel the attendance of witnesses and the production of books, papers, and other documents that are the subject of a board inquiry; the authorization of board members or hearing officers to administer oaths and to take testimony of persons under oath; and certifying parole jail time (i.e., crediting a parole applicant with the time he or she served in jail).[7]

**THREE TYPES OF ADULT PAROLE AUTHORITIES.** Although states employ a variety of organizational arrangements for their adult paroling authorities, there are basically three classifications into which most adult paroling authorities can be grouped—the institutional, independent, and consolidated models.[8]

Institutional model

The *institutional model* is based on the idea that parole should be carefully linked with the correctional institution in which the offender is incarcerated. Behind this model is the theory that institutional staff members are in the best position to judge the suitability of the inmate for parole and that the parole decision itself can be more appropriately coordinated with the overall institutional program devised for the particular offender.

Those who argue against this arrangement contend that institutional factors may play a major role in deciding whether or not an inmate should be paroled. For example, an institution faced with problems of overcrowding may tend to release individuals prematurely. Prison officials may also use the threat of not granting parole as a means of keeping inmates in line and enforcing strict rules and regulations. Because of such abuses, about fifty years ago reformers began efforts to remove decision-making authority from institutional officials. This reform movement was so effective that today the purely institutional model (for dealing with adult offenders) does not exist in any state.

Independent model

The *independent model* arose when reformers advocated that independent parole boards should make the ultimate decision on granting parole. Although it may be argued that this model is more objective than the institutional model, it too suffers from a number of weaknesses. First, independent parole boards may not thoroughly understand the programs carried on by the correctional institution and the role that parole plans play in the overall treatment plan once an individual is released. Independent boards are also criticized for relying too heavily on subjective and inappropriate considerations such as the feelings of the local police chief. Occasionally, these independent boards are tainted with scandals of political corruption, such as those that occurred some years ago in Georgia, where it was alleged that members of the parole board were paid to award parole to certain inmates. Another frequent criticism is that members of independent parole boards are often appointed for strictly political reasons and lack the necessary training or experience in corrections.

This lack of knowledge about the correctional process and correctional programming may be the single most important argument against this type of organizational arrangement. With the increased use of release programs, halfway houses, and other community-based alternatives, overall programs must be linked very closely with institutional efforts for parole considerations. This requires that parole board members have a broad knowledge of corrections and develop a close working relationship with correctional institutions.

The third type is the *consolidated model*, which most states have adopted. It combines the best features of the institutional and independent models while diminishing the negative features of both. This arrangement consolidates all state correctional programs within a state under a department of correctional services divided into institutional and field programs (parole services). Although the parole board is a separate entity, actual parole services and supervision are carried out by the parole division of the state's Department of Corrections.[9] To ensure a close working relationship with the Department of Corrections, an official of the Corrections Department might sit as a nonvoting member of the parole board. In other states special advisory panels or boards have been established to coordinate institutional and field services with parole board efforts.

*Consolidated model*

Advocates of the consolidated model maintain that because parole services is actually a part of the correctional services system, there is a greater understanding of the overall correctional process. They claim that sensitivity to institutional programs seems more pronounced in consolidated systems than in autonomous ones. It is also contended that the removal of parole decision making from the control of the correctional institution gives greater weight to a broader set of considerations, a number of which are outside direct institutional concerns.[10]

Advantages

The primary organizational concerns of parole require that states support close coordination between parole decision makers and the increasingly complex set of programs now being developed in many correctional systems, while at the same time preserving the autonomy that permits parole boards to serve as checks on the overall system. At present, the consolidated authority seems to be the best means to accomplish this task.

## The Functioning of Parole Boards

By now the reader is aware that all states have a parole authority and most states have adopted the so-called consolidated parole model, which places parole services under a state's department of corrections. Although parole services are consolidated, it must be remembered that the paroling authority—the parole board itself—is typically independent from the corrections department. While the provision of day-to-day services by parole officers might operate as a division of the state's corrections department, the parole board as a decision-making body retains independent authority and status.

State parole boards generally consist of from three to ten members appointed by the governor. One of the appointees serves as the board's chairperson, and the others serve as parole board members. In many states such members have no correctional experience. For that matter, it is not unusual to have parole board members appointed who are not even that experienced with the criminal justice system.

Composition

What then are the typical criteria or considerations that govern selecting an appointee for the parole board? Often, individuals are appointed because of their

Selection factors

political support for the governor or the governor's political party. Many times appointees might represent certain interests that the governor considers of "political importance." Choices might revolve around racial or ethnic background factors or to balance out certain needs for geographical representation in the state. Most governors try to carefully select board members who, even though they may be without professional experience, will exercise good judgment and not prove to be an embarrassment. This has become increasingly important in recent years as the political ramifications of improper parole board actions can have an impact on the governor's political fortunes.

Many states have adopted legislation that limits the parole board appointive authority of the governor. For example, the members are appointed for single terms to serve for a period of years that does not correspond to the term of office of the governor. Members might, in such cases, be appointed for six- to eight-year terms. Appointees are also likely to serve staggered terms so that no governor has the opportunity to appoint a majority of the board members. Sometimes, there are also provisions that limit the number of board members who can be from the governor's political party.

Most states have adopted full-time parole boards. Generally, only the less-populated states have a parole board consisting of members who serve only part-time. Even in states that retain the part-time status of parole board members, a number of such states have at least made the chairperson's position full-time.

The parole board usually travels to the various institutions on an established schedule to conduct parole application hearings or to hold revocation hearings involving inmates who have been arrested for some form of parole violation and returned to prison pending the hearing. In lieu of the board hearing all cases, the federal government and the State of Ohio employ hearing examiners. These hearing examiners actually conduct the parole application hearings at the various institutions and make their specific recommendations to the central parole authority.

A great deal of public confusion often surrounds parole eligibility hearings. Occasionally, the public will learn from the media that a particularly notorious offender is coming up for parole consideration. A case in point is the periodic announcement that someone such as the assassin Sirhan-Sirhan or Charles Manson, the mass murderer from California, is scheduled to appear before the parole board. The public is alarmed, thinking that these individuals are about to be released on parole.

Parole eligibility

This is not the case. What is happening is that these convicted offenders are merely appearing before the parole board in accordance with the mandatory hearing opportunities provided by law. States generally prescribe that after a certain period of imprisonment, the offender has an automatic parole eligibility date. For example, a state might prescribe that all inmates not sentenced for a capital offense that carries a term of imprisonment for life without parole are eligible for parole consideration after serving one-third of their sentence or five years, whichever comes first. Under such circumstances, an inmate has the automatic right to appear before the parole board on this eligibility date. It doesn't mean that the parole board is going to look favorably on releasing the offender to parole.

The inmate can waive the automatic right to appear if he or she wishes. Typically, such a waiver must be in writing and must be knowingly and intelligently given. Once the initial eligibility date arrives and the inmate has a hearing in which he or she is denied parole, states also provide for automatic reappearances for consideration every six months or annually thereafter.

Some changes in the laws in the past twenty years have provided the oppor- Changes in parole hearings tunity for the parole eligibility hearing to take on some new twists. This has been brought about by laws that permit the inmate to be represented by counsel at these hearings or to have persons appear in his or her behalf. Even newer legislation, which recognizes such concerns as victims' rights, provides for the victim to be notified of the impending hearing and the right to appear before the parole board in person or to submit his or her feelings about parole to the board for its consideration. Still other states require notification of authorities such as the sentencing judge, the prosecutor's office, or the local police chief or sheriff from the jurisdiction in which the crime was committed. These authorities are then given an opportunity to convey their feelings to the parole board.

At the conclusion of the hearing, the panel informs the prisoner of its decision and, if the decision is for denial of parole, the reasons for such a denial. Later these reasons are provided in writing. Conversely, if the decision of the parole board is such that it approves parole, it is generally the policy that the board will specify a particular date in the near future at which time the inmate will be released on parole. For example, the parole board might set a release date six months hence. This is to provide the correctional authorities the opportunity to transfer the soon-to-be-paroled inmate to a community release center or other special facility or program in anticipation of parole release.

Normally, a prisoner who has been granted parole remains under community supervision until the sentence has expired. For instance, if a parolee is released after serving four years of a ten-year sentence, the offender remains in parole status for six years of a ten-year sentence, the offender remains in parole status for six years. However, many states and the federal government have special provisions for early termination of parole. For example, the state parole authority can request that the parole board terminate parole supervision before the individual's maximum sentence has expired. If the parole board approved this request, the parolee is discharged from supervision.

**DETAINER.** In some cases, a *detainer* may be associated with an offender's parole picture. A detainer is a claim by another jurisdiction that it has charges pending against someone incarcerated in another state. Assume that a prisoner in Oregon is wanted in New Hampshire for a crime he committed before he was imprisoned for his present crime. New Hampshire officials could apply for a detainer writ and notify the Oregon officials. The prisoner could then be released on parole (or upon the expiration of the sentence) and be immediately turned over to New Hampshire to answer the charges in that state.

## Decisions on Which Parole Is Based

Most parole boards base their decisions on whether an inmate should be granted parole on a number of factors.

**PRIOR RECORD.** Because an extensive criminal record is one of the better predictors of further criminality, this factor weighs very heavily. First offenders have the best prospects for parole success, so most paroling authorities give special consideration to such offenders. Also often considered for early parole are situational offenders—that is, individuals who acted under impulse and the situation of the moment in committing the crime and do not have past histories of law violations.

The habitual offenders—particularly if they are chronic sex offenders or armed robbers, show a history of assaultive crimes, have a history of drug or alcohol abuse, or have previously demonstrated little or no response to incarceration and to institutional programs—must usually show significant change before parole boards consider their parole requests favorably. Parole boards consider professional criminals to be bad risks. Many such offenders consider the risk of imprisonment a cost of doing business and almost invariably return to their former life-styles on release.

**SERIOUSNESS AND NATURE OF CURRENT OFFENSE.** A second very important consideration is the offense for which the individual is currently incarcerated. Normally, the criminal code and the sentencing judge set the prison term so that it is relative to the seriousness of the offense. However, because the type of offense has some predictive value with respect to the commission of further crimes, parole boards may often consider this factor, especially when the current offense is part of an established behavior pattern that is likely to continue. Studies have shown that larceny, burglary, forgery, and motor vehicle theft seem to be the most likely to be repeated.[11] Similarly, persons who are serving sentences for escapes have proven to be poor parole risks.[12] Likewise, the younger an offender is at time of release, the less likely are his or her chances for success. Parole boards must also carefully consider paroling the individual whose offense, if repeated, would be a serious threat to the safety of the public.

**CIRCUMSTANCES OF THE OFFENSE.** The personal and social circumstances that the sentencing court took into consideration may also be relevant to the parole decision, because the board must consider the likelihood of recurrence of such circumstances or situations. For example, an individual whose crimes are related to alcoholism or drug abuse may be a higher risk for parole than an individual who committed the same offense but who does not have these aggravating factors. The knowledge of circumstances that either extenuate or aggravate the offense can be useful in predicting whether a repetition will occur.

**THE PAROLE PLAN.** The board also carefully reviews and considers the situation into which the individual will go if paroled. This includes where the offender will live, in what sort of housing and with whom; what employment is assured or expected and at what rate of pay; any special conditions of parole recommended by the prison staff (participation in an alcoholism clinic, staying away from former partners in crime); and any indications of possible adverse community reaction to the inmate's release. In some states, as mentioned, the victim and the prosecutor and judge who were responsible for the conviction and sentencing are given an opportunity to comment on the desirability of paroling this person.[13]

**INSTITUTIONAL RECORD.** The board reviews the individual's incarceration behavior record. Prisoners who do not behave responsibly in prison are usually poor risks for a successful return to the community. The individual who is assaultive, who cannot get along with people, or who cannot work responsibly will probably have similar problems on the outside. On the other hand, a prisoner who has made a sincere effort toward rehabilitation is more likely to be a prospect for reintegration into society. In attempting to determine the prisoner's efforts, the board reviews such matters as the type and quality of work; the prisoner's performance in any academic or vocational training courses; any disciplinary charges made against the prisoner and the subsequent action taken on each; the prisoner's socialization within the prison community; his or her health record; and reports by psychiatrists, caseworkers, instructors, and other staff members.[14]

There are, however, many critics of the parole board's reliance on the inmate's institutional record as a major factor in deciding to grant or deny parole. Yet the inmate's record remains a prime consideration, particularly in those states that operate a parole commission made up of part-time, political appointees who serve as parole board members. In these situations too much attention might be given to the institutional record, because these states may not have well-thought-out and developed parole policies and guidelines and, of course, the parole board members themselves are not full-time professional specialists. This situation can produce several problems: First, inmates learn to "play the game" to look good. This may involve such things as their becoming "born-again Christians," frequently attending church services so as to appear repentant, or becoming involved in Alcoholics Anonymous or Kiwanis programs in the institution, although, in reality, no fundamental changes have occurred in their lives. Inmates may participate in these programs merely for the record. These considerations by the parole board also have the possible effect of giving the institutional staff tremendous power over the inmates; power that they may use in an arbitrary way to control the prisoners. For example, unscrupulous institutional staff can use the threat of bad conduct reports to bring about servile conformance on the part of the inmates. Such forced compliance through threats engenders greater hostility and antiauthority attitudes among the inmate population. The possible consequences are obvious and thought provoking.

**Meaningfulness**

How successful are inmates in obtaining parole when they appear before the parole board? Although no comparative national data exist to answer this question, we can examine this issue in at least one state that publishes such information. From this we might draw some inferences to other states. We must be cautious, however, because different parole policies and laws exist in every state.

Recent data compiled by New York State indicate that the New York Division of Parole releases slightly more than 50 percent of the inmates who appear before the Board each year. This figure takes into consideration those released on their first appearance before the Board as well as those who have been turned down previously and reappear for consideration. This figure also includes those inmates who had previously been released, violated their parole, had parole revoked, and were returned to prison and reappeared for consideration. On the average, inmates in New York have a 40 percent chance of getting parole as a result of their first appearance before the Board.[15]

**THE DEVELOPMENT AND USE OF PREDICTION METHODS.**  In the last two decades, there has been a great deal of interest among researchers in developing prediction criteria that could aid parole boards in making their decisions.[16] The best known of these is the Salient-Factor Score used by the United States Parole Commission in determining parole release for federal prisoners. Researchers have gathered data on successful and unsuccessful parolees in an effort to identify the specific characteristics that are associated with success and failure. With the increasing adoption of better research designs and computer technology with its data-gathering and analysis capabilities, the future seems to hold some promise for more "scientifically" enlightened decisions by parole boards. However, current prediction methods still suffer from a number of weaknesses. First, researchers have not been able to identify all the factors that may lead an individual to commit a crime nor all the factors that may cause the commission of further offenses once the prisoner is released. The second problem is one of reliability. For example, a parole board may be provided with prediction tables suggesting that offenders with certain characteristics have a 75 percent chance of success on parole. Assume that the offender before them has these characteristics. The problem then becomes to determine whether the prisoner falls into the 75 percent who will be successful or the 25 percent who will fail. Although this may be an improvement over having no predictive statistics, it tells the board very little about the particular individual's chances for parole success.

## A State Develops a Parole Prediction Device: Oregon's Experience

The experience of the State of Oregon serves as an especially good illustration of why a state may decide to adopt a parole-prediction device. Oregon is one of a handful of states that have developed a parole-prediction model.[17] This discussion will also point out the types of factors that a parole-prediction device might generally consider in determining an appropriate parole eligibility date for an offender.

The factors that led up to Oregon's adoption of its so-called Parole Matrix are not unique. A number of states have experienced many of the same problems and frustrations with parole, sentencing, and prison overcrowding. In Oregon these problems came together to bring about a demand for change. What is perhaps unique is that the State of Oregon took the initiative to develop a more systematic and rational way to deal with these problems. Several years before Oregon had adopted its Parole Matrix, the Oregon Board of Parole began experiencing a great deal of criticism from such diverse groups as law enforcement officials, district

attorneys, judges, politicians and inmates. The criticism centered on what was seen as inappropriate, arbitrary, and disparate decisions by the parole board. These concerns focused on Parole Board determinations such as who was to be released on parole, when release was justified, and the reasons underlying the board's decisions to release or deny parole.

The lack of established standards combined with the absence of written reasons for the board's decisions contributed to this perception and the mounting criticism. The durational uncertainty of prison terms caused dissatisfaction among the state's inmates and prison administrators. Prisoners often did not know how long they actually had to serve until well into their terms of sentence. Prison administrators complained they could not effectively manage bed space and programs without the knowledge of when inmates might be released. These problems became more serious as the state's prison population began to grow.

Judges also got into the act. The judges argued that Parole Board policies made it impossible for them to exercise any meaningful control over the sentence served. Legislators were also upset because they felt that too much authority and discretion was vested in the parole board. Law enforcement authorities and District Attorneys throughout the state voiced frequent denunciations that the board lacked accountability to the public and was too lenient. The media was also quick to cover a sensational story about a parolee who had committed a new crime or the plight of an inmate not released by the board whom they felt deserving. As criticism mounted, the Board became increasingly defensive and cautious and, under unremitting pressure, less able to satisfactorily justify its decisions.

Finally, the situation came to a head. The public became incensed by incidents resulting from the release of two inmates, both of whom were convicted murderers. Both inmates murdered again shortly after their release. Only one was a parolee and the other was out on a furlough release, but this made no difference to the anti-parole board forces. The resulting outcry was loud and immediate. Stiffer penalties were demanded, petitions to reinstate the death penalty were circulated, and proposals for mandatory sentences began to surface.

The governor, reacting to these demands, appointed a Task Force on Corrections. A research team from the University of Oregon and a special commission appointed by the state legislature initiated studies of the state's entire correctional system including the Board of Parole. Interestingly, the conclusions of these groups differed significantly from those voiced by the general public and certain segments of the state's criminal justice system. Each of the groups concluded that constructing more prisons was not the answer. They felt this would be an expensive, short-lived, and unacceptable solution to the problem. Instead, they suggested the expansion of community corrections programs and the reform of policies and practices of the state's correctional institutions and the parole board. Specific recommendations aimed at the Board of Parole included proposed requirements that the basis for parole decision making be explicit, that the board develop guidelines articulating the weight to be given to specific factors considered, that these guidelines be made available to the public, and that the uncertainty of terms be reduced.

While this was happening, simultaneous changes were occurring among the composition of the Parole Board itself. New members were appointed as several members retired or resigned. This change in board membership stimulated an atmosphere for innovation. The new members of the Board felt uncomfortable having unguided discretion and far-reaching responsibility without rules and guidelines for decision making. As a result, the Board began examining its decision making process. They studied policies and practices of other state parole boards and consulted with experts and academics involved in the study of criminal justice. From this, the board began to develop a "guideline" model for decision making.

In the late 1970s, the Oregon legislature passed a comprehensive new parole act. Although some interests were calling for the total abolition of parole, the legislature refused to be swayed by such arguments. An important component of the new parole act was the Parole Matrix. The Matrix was in large part influenced by the Salient-Factor parole-prediction device then developed and used by the federal government.[18] The Matrix was to be a guideline that the Parole Board was to follow in granting parole. The idea underlying the development and use of the Parole Matrix was one of "just deserts." This simply means that committing a crime is wrong and deserves punishment. Although it does not deny the value or the idea of rehabilitation, it does reaffirm that punishment, incapacitation, and deterrence are also valued ends of the correctional experience. It also subscribed to the idea of proportionality: that is, the punishment should fit the crime. Also incorporated in the new Matrix was the idea of fundamental fairness—like crimes should be treated similarly, and different crimes should be treated differently. It also incorporated the idea that the public and the convicted offender should know what to expect through established guidelines and how and in what way deviations from these guidelines could operate in terms of aggravating or mitigating circumstances.

Underlying ideas of the Parole Matrix

Lastly, it should consider other important factors (e.g., prior convictions) in determining appropriate parole release dates.

A parole decision-making model such as Oregon's begins with the ranking of crimes according to their seriousness. We will call this our "Offense Seriousness Scale." In this way, crimes are arrayed or categorized from most serious to least serious. These crimes are taken directly from a state's criminal code. Forcible rape, for instance, is considered more serious than an assault. Developing such a scale requires that specific offenses themselves be broken down. As an example, the crime of assault might be broken down into four to five categories as determined by factors associated with the assault and the injury sustained. Thus, you might have Assault I, Assault II, and so on. Then these offenses must be assigned a numerical weighting according to their seriousness. Assault I might be given a weight of 3, and Assault II a weight of 2. Although this might sound pretty straightforward, such classifications are difficult to devise and open to the criticism that they are too arbitrary. This is also the case when you are ranking different crimes. Should Forgery I carry the same ranking as Assault II, or perhaps it should be ranked and weighed the same as Assault I. These are the kinds of decisions that must be made and consensus reached on the appropriate values assigned if the matrix itself is to be accepted.

After this first step is completed, a second set of decisions must be made. A history/risk scoring instrument must be devised. What factors are to be used in such an instrument? One such common factor is prior felony convictions. If a convicted offender has four or more prior felony convictions, a certain numerical score is assigned. If an offender has two to three prior felony convictions, another numerical score is used. If an offender has no prior felony convictions, still another (or no) numerical score is assigned that factor. Other suggested factors, and weighted accordingly, might be misdemeanor convictions, documented substance abuse problems, juvenile convictions, present age at time of conviction, status at time of commission of crime (e.g., was the offender on parole when he committed the present crime?), number of years since last conviction, and so on.

The numerical scores assigned from the "Offense Seriousness Scale" together with the individual's score on the history/risk scoring instrument are then totaled. This total is then placed into the matrix. The matrix itself is merely a list of the number of months that a convicted offender should serve in prison before being released on parole according to the total combined scores assigned by his or her points accumulated on the "Offense Seriousness Scale" and the history/risk scoring instrument.

Although this is an over-simplification of the complexities of the development and use of a parole-prediction instrument, it generally corresponds to how these instruments are developed and the factors employed in determining how long an offender can expect to serve in prison before being released on parole. In that regard, it does accomplish several things: it reasonably assures that individuals charged with the same crime and having similar backgrounds will serve the same approximate time before being eligible for parole; it gives the offender an immediate idea of when he or she can expect to be released on parole; and it gives correctional administrators a better idea of how long many prisoners will be incarcerated so that they can plan for resource needs accordingly.

Some of the limitations of the instrument have already been alluded to, but they need to be pointed out again. A major problem is the subjective nature of assigning specific weights to the factors and what factors should be considered. It also is criticized on the ground that it takes away the decision-making discretion of the parole board. But this latter criticism can be a two-edged sword. Although it may in fact, eliminate the traditional discretion of the parole board, it could also work in its favor. It might serve to blunt the criticism of a parole board that releases an individual who then goes out and commits another serious high-publicity crime. The parole board in such a case could claim the defense that they were merely following the guidelines adopted.

**RESISTANCE BY STATE PAROLE BOARDS.** Although the federal government and some states use prediction methods rather extensively, many states do not. Norman S. Hayner has examined why state parole boards are reluctant to use such devices, and he believes there are several reasons:[19] First, parole board members are extremely sensitive to public opinion and therefore are reluctant to parole individuals to whom the public would object, even though these individuals might possess all the predictive characteristics of being able to return successfully to society, as many murderers do. In the last few years, parole decisions have become highly politicized. Many actual or aspiring politicians have sensed the "get-tough" attitudes many Americans are expressing toward crime and criminals. Such "law-and-order" candidates are quick to blame the parole board for what they perceive as policies of leniency. In this type of political environment, boards are pressured to become increasingly conservative and, when there is any doubt, to refuse to grant parole. Under such situations, parole boards are not likely to open themselves up to further criticism by the use or encouraged development of some possibly misunderstood prediction device. Second, parole boards want to encourage constructive use of prison time. As progress is made in the administration of correctional institutions, increasing opportunities for self-improvement are available to inmates. Boards want to facilitate the work of prison staffs by rewarding prisoners who take advantage of their opportunities. The majority of prediction instruments give little weight to the institutional factors on which many parole boards rely in making their determinations. Researchers do not include institutional behavior and adjustment factors because these factors, as mentioned earlier, are recognized as having little validity. Third, parole board members share the conviction that each case is unique. Although they may act on the basis of hunches about uniformities in prisoner backgrounds, they hesitate to admit the hunches. The idea is strongly entrenched that there is no substitute for careful study of the individual case.

Another problem is that many states have imposed legal restrictions that make it impossible for a parole board to release a prisoner when it appears that the offender will be able to avoid involvement in further offenses. For example, a number of states have adopted deadly weapon statutes that make certain sentences mandatory when the offender has been convicted of using a firearm in the commission of the crime. These statutes usually prohibit parole until a fixed portion of the sentence has been served. Finally, there is the problem of overcoming traditional ways of thinking. Many parole board members simply refuse to accept that prediction studies have any merit and would rather rely on intuition and common sense to guide their decisions.

The few states that use parole prediction devices, such as Oregon, claim that such a system has certain political value. Although some judges want to have a greater say in the sentence imposed, other judges are glad to have difficult sentencing considerations removed from their responsibility. Judges can also avoid being criticized for not sentencing individuals to longer prison sentences with the

*Parole board reluctance*

public having the often misguided notion that length of sentence ensures that parole will be postponed. The judges can merely blame the sentence on the prediction device and the release time provided. Of course, the parole board can itself escape a great deal of criticism for its decisions by merely claiming that it was following the guidelines determined by the legislature as provided in the guidelines.

Such parole-prediction devices also give the legislature a great deal of control over the actual time served; this is what legislatures often contend they have too little control over. In Oregon, officials on the parole board also believe that the state's parole matrix has helped to avoid the traditional antagonism expressed by the police and the prosecutors toward the board.

## Characteristics Associated with Parole Success or Failure

Probably the most comprehensive research on the postrelease success of inmates is the encyclopedic work of Daniel Glaser.[20] In a five and a half-year study of the rehabilitative effects of parole and prison agencies of the Bureau of Prisons, Glaser followed the postrelease successes and failures of inmates and developed a number of important associations between certain characteristics and success or failure. Some of the conclusions he reached follow:

- The older a person is when released from prison, the less likely he or she is to return to crime.
- The younger a person is when first sentenced, convicted, or confined for any crime, the more likely he or she is to continue in crime.
- Drug offenders and individuals committed for economic-related offenses such as motor vehicle theft, burglary, larceny, and check forgery are most likely to recidivate. Those convicted of robbery, kidnapping, and violation of liquor laws have intermediate levels of recidivism. The best chances for parole success are for persons convicted of homicide, rape, embezzlement, and income tax fraud.
- Race is not related in any meaningful way to parole success or failure.
- The more prior felony sentences an individual has, the more likely he or she is to continue in crime.
- Most parolees seek noncriminal careers. When they fail, it is because of a complex set of social, economic, and personal relationships.

Although Glaser and other researchers have made some headway in examining factors related to success or failure on parole, these scholars would be the first to admit that, like other predictive criteria, much more extensive and intensive examination is needed. There is an immediate need for more extensive *cohort analysis*, in which a large selected group of offenders are tracked from the time they are arrested until perhaps five years after their release from prison or until they recidivate.

One study done by the U.S. Parole Commission tried to do exactly that.[21] It selected a sample of 50 percent of the prisoners who were released from federal prison during the first six months of 1970. Using FBI arrest records, the commission study looked at these individuals six years later. Although it can be argued that conviction records would be more appropriate than merely whether or not these individuals were subsequently arrested, the conviction records were not available. The research also suffered from the fact that the sample group did not contain merely parolees but also included prisoners who were given mandatory release and those who had been released when their prison sentence was completed.

The results were not favorable. By the end of the six-year follow-up period, Poor success record 62 percent of the sample had been arrested at least once or had violated parole. Of the arrested sample, 41 percent had more than one arrest. The research confirmed other similar studies by showing that the first year of release is the most likely period for rearrest. Each subsequent year showed a decline in arrest rates for the sample group.[22] Unfortunately, the researchers also did not examine the arrest rates for those who had been released on parole compared to those who were given mandatory release. Figure 14.2 shows parole failure data from a 1984 U.S. Department of Justice survey.

## "Good-Time"

An important aspect of parole eligibility is what is referred to as "good-time" allowances. Before the 1800s, when a person was imprisoned, he or she would remain in custody for a certain period of time regardless of behavior while in prison. As mentioned, New York in 1817 became the first state to design a system to encourage discipline by awarding time off from a sentence for good behavior while in prison. By 1900 forty-four states had passed similar legislation. Although such credits were initially given to encourage good behavior, over the years prison systems have come

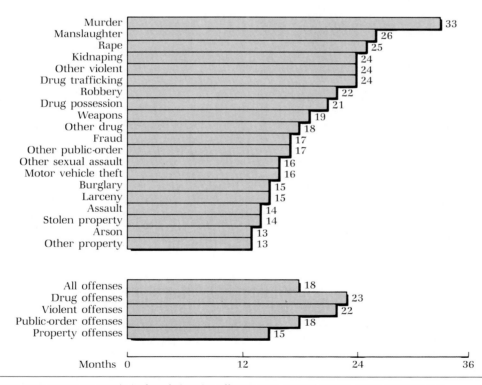

Average time spent on parole before failure by offense type, United States, 1984. [*Source:* U.S. Department of Justice, Bureau of Justice Statistics, *Time Served in Prison and on Parole 1984*, Special Report NCJ-108544 (Washington, D.C.: U.S. Department of Justice, January 1988), p. 8.]

FIGURE **14.2**

A recent and more thorough analysis of parole release success than the U.S. Parole Commission's, previously mentioned, appeared in 1987. A sample of young adults paroled in 1978 from twenty-two states was analyzed. Like the U.S. Parole Commission's work, the parolees were studied for a six-year period following their release. Although most of the sample was made up of males, females were also included. From what we know from similar studies, we could expect young adults to pose the most likely group to incur further difficulties once they are released. Success or failure among this group was measured by three factors: rearrest, reconviction, and reincarceration records. In this study the researchers used a subsequent arrest for any felony or serious misdemeanor as indicating rearrest. Reconviction meant a conviction for at least one felony or serious misdemeanor. Reincarceration was defined as any return to prison or any admission to jail with a new sentence.[a]

Like the U.S. Parole Commission's study, the results were disturbing. The findings are in many instances similar.

Within six years after their release from prison in 1978, more than two-thirds of the sample of nearly 4,000 young parolees had been rearrested; 53 percent had been reconvicted; and about one-half had been reincarcerated. Obviously, their prison experiences did little to deter them from further criminal acts.

Not counting violations of parole and probation, these parolees were rearrested for more than 36,000 new felonies or serious misdemeanors, including approximately 6,700 violent crimes and nearly 19,000 property crimes.

Evidence of systematic and highly active career criminality seems to exist for at least a small percentage of the parolees, as indicated by subsequent arrest records. In the sample, a small number of the parolees accounted for many of the arrests made. In this study 10 percent of the sample of parolees counted for 40 percent of all subsequent arrests.

Where did the arrests occur? It was found that about a fifth of the subsequent arrests occurred in states other than the state that granted the parole.

How many were rearrested while still on parole? It was estimated that 37 percent of the parolees were rearrested while still under parole supervision.

Failure rates as expected were highest in the first two years after the offender's release from prison with the first year being the most likely period. For instance, within the first year, nearly one-third of the sample had been rearrested. By the time two years had passed, the rate was approaching 50 percent of all parolees.

Failure rates were higher among men, blacks, and persons who had not completed high school than among women, whites, and high school graduates.

Approximately one-third of both property offenders and violent offenders were rearrested for a violent crime on release from prison.

Prior arrest record seems to be related to success or failure on release at least as measured by subsequent arrests. Ninety-seven percent of the parolees in the study who had six or more prior arrests at the time they were released experienced additional arrests. For those who were first-time offenders when released, only 57 percent were subsequently arrested.

As expected from similar studies, the earlier the parolee's first adult arrest, the more likely the chances for rearrest on release. For instance, if the offender was first arrested as an adult at age seventeen, he or she was half again more likely to be rearrested than if the first arrest had come when the parolee was age twenty or older.

Time served in prison had no consistent impact on failure rates. Those who had served six months or less in prison were about as likely to be arrested as those who had served more than two years.

Both those paroled for property offenses as well as those paroled for violent offenses were rearrested for a serious crime at high levels. Strangely, those in the sample who were paroled for property offenses were slightly more likely to be rearrested than were violent crime parolees.[b]

From these and similar studies, a better understanding of factors associated with parole, and indeed correctional success or failure, is occurring. Although evidence of certain trait characteristics associated with offenders' chances have been uncovered in recent years, a great deal remains unknown. For instance, an important component of parole-release analysis and predictability would include an examination of both prearrest and postarrest factors such as the individual's environment, his or her psychological characteristics, and more detailed offense examination—all of which seemingly would have some relationship to criminal behavior and postprison success or failure. Associated with this is the need to study the effects of different forms of imposed sanctions and punishments on behavior. Realistically, however, it is extremely unlikely that such factors can ever be studied and related with any degree of predictive validity to parole success or failure.

[a]Allen J. Beck, "Recidivism of Young Parolees" *The Criminal Justice Archive and Information Network Bulletin* (Fall 1987):1

[b]Ibid., pp. 1, 3.

to give them automatically. In this way they moved from a positive inducement to a negative form of punishment, where they could only be taken away for violations.[23]

Two basic types of good-time allowances have developed. The standard type is the awarding of good-time to all eligible inmates except those who violate certain institutional rules. This is called automatic good-time. The other type of allowance is called "special good-time" and can be awarded in addition to standard good-time credits. For example, some states give such credits for blood donation; many other states list "meritorious conduct," "exemplary work performance," or "participation in or completion of educational or rehabilitative programs." Automatic and special

The granting or denial of special good-time credits is almost entirely subject to the discretion of correctional officials, either at the state or institutional level. Most states have statutes specifying the maximum amount of good-time credits that can be earned, whereas a few leave the schedule of earnings more to the discretion of corrections officials.[24] Even in those states that specify a schedule, however, prison officials may have the flexibility to establish other categories for which credit may be awarded. Other than the statutory generalizations as to what constitutes sufficient good behavior to justify a reduction in a court-ordered sentence (and these generalizations are frequently concerned with what behavior is to be avoided rather than what positive traits an offender should exhibit), there are usually no detailed guidelines indicating policies to be followed in the decision of how much good-time to award in any given case. The denial or revocation of credit is equally discretionary, and many statutes specify that there is no legal right to good-time credits and foreclose inmate access to the courts in this area.[25]

In 1974 the U.S. Supreme Court established minimum due process requirements for prison disciplinary procedures, including the deprivation of good-time credits. Among other things the Court opinion requires advance written notices of the charges; a written statement by the fact finders indicating what evidence was relied on and the reasons for the action; and the right of the inmate to produce witnesses in his or her own behalf.[26]

In approximately half of the states, good-time deductions advance an inmate's parole eligibility date through reductions in the minimum and/or maximum term. In all the jurisdictions in which there is no effect on parole eligibility, good-time credits are deducted from the maximum term to hasten either conditional release or complete discharge from prison. In many jurisdictions, good-time credits affect both parole eligibility and discharge dates.[27]

The rate at which good time credits are earned varies widely from state to state. For example, in many states the rate of earned good time after ten years is ten or fifteen days a month. In a few other states, provisions are made for certain classes of inmates to earn one day of good time for each day served. This has the potential of cutting (or nearly cutting) the sentence in half. The highest ratio of reduction in some other jurisdictions is one to three or one to four, and it may take many years to reach this reduction.[28]

## Parole Officer

The functions of the parole officer normally entail several important responsibilities. The relative importance of each of these roles is often determined by the needs of the parolee and the parole officer's perception of his or her own role.

In a *helper* role, the parole officer may assist the parolee in finding and keeping a job, dealing with family or marital problems, budgeting money, or in assisting the Various roles parolee to contend with problems such as alcohol or drug abuse. In general, the officer provides assistance in helping the parolee adjust to free society and to avoid reverting to antisocial or criminal behavior. In this way the parole officer serves as a social caseworker and must be knowledgeable about the principles of casework.

The second role of the parole officer is that of an *investigator*. The officer investigates the situation of release and advises the parole board of conditions so that it can determine the likely success of paroling the individual. This investigation normally involves such factors as the attitude of the parolee's family about his or her release, attitudes in the community toward the prisoner, and the attitudes of local law enforcement officials toward the individual's return to the community. The parole officer also investigates whether the parolee is living up to the conditions of parole.

The third major role is that of a *police officer*. The parole officer uses the threat of coercive power through the ability to at least initiate the parole revocation process.

These various roles and responsibilities receive different emphasis according to the individual parole officer's style. For example, many parole officers subscribe more to their helping and investigative roles than they do to their roles as police. On the other hand, there are those parole officers who take the attitude that "my job is to keep them in line." Of course, the parolee's behavior to a great extent may also determine the role that the parole officer will assume in dealing with a particular client.

Parole agencies provide two types of parole services: institutional and field work. It is in these two areas that most states assign their parole officers. Institutional parole services operate within the state's penal institutions. Parole officers assigned to an institution are primarily responsible for helping inmates prepare for parole and for providing supervision summaries—usually called Parole Summaries—which are one of the major sources of information that parole boards use to consider whether to release an inmate to parole supervision. Although the compilation of information that goes into a parole summary may vary somewhat from state to state, it typically includes such things as information gained from a review of the inmate's case folder and institutional record, an interview with the inmate, and interviews with correctional staff.

Parole officers must be skillful interviewers. These preparole interviews, which will become part of the parole summary, are often conducted in special facilities or areas inside the institution. Although such interviews may cover a broad range of subjects, they include, as a minimum, such points as the offense for which the inmate is serving time, the social and personal lifetime history of the offender, work history, educational record, relatives and relationships in the community, drug/alcohol abuse, institutional record, and a discussion of the programs that the inmate was involved in during his or her period of incarceration.

These are often not the only topics discussed. Inmates are often very anxious about the probability of parole. They may pepper the institutional parole officer with questions about their chances to obtain a favorable consideration from the parole board, or they may sometimes complain that they weren't credited with enough jail time on their sentence. In these sessions, most inmates try to convince the parole officer that they are worthy of the parole officer's favorable recommendation in the parole summary if the particular parole board has a policy of having the institutional parole officer make a recommendation.

Institutional parole services

Most people think of a parole officer as someone who is responsible for supervising the parolee once they have been released on parole from prison. This is the job of the field parole officer. The major responsibility of the field parole officer Field parole services is to provide those services—which may range from counseling and various forms of assistance to arrest—to ensure community protection. In many ways, field parole work can be thought of as "casework in an authoritarian setting." The parole officer must know both the parolee and his or her environment. Office interviews are held on a regular basis, at which time the parole officer will question the parolees on such matters as where they are staying, their employment situation, whether they are experiencing any personal problems, or whether they are having any police-related problems.

The field parole officer uses other means to maintain community protection. These may include home visits, visits to the place of employment, contacts with law enforcement agencies in the area, and monitoring drug use and surveillance.

Institutional and field parole officers often share joint responsibilities for an inmate. Institutional officers, in developing the parole plan, require the offender to propose residence and employment programs for release considerations. Field officers are then notified of the proposed program and follow-up with an investigation to determine the adequacy of the proposed program. If the proposed program is unsatisfactory, the field officer notifies the institutional officer, who then asks the inmate to propose a new program. This process continues until a satisfactory program acceptable to the parole board has been developed.

Institutional parole work is more predictable than field work. Most parole officers at institutions spend their days interviewing inmates, reviewing inmate cases files, making contacts with correctional staff, and report writing. Yet, there are a number of problems that frustrate the efforts of institutional parole officers. Many officers complain that they don't have enough time to do the counseling they feel is needed. There is also the problem of getting the information to do the parole summaries. This might be particularly true in those more secure institutions in which security considerations make it difficult to arrange meetings with inmates, conduct interviews, and interview correctional staff.

For the field parole officer, the problems that arise in their caseloads determine their activities for the day. Such "field time" is juggled between supervising their caseloads and conducting the required prerelease investigations for institutional parole staff. In addition, the field officer will have to schedule office time and court time. Many area parole offices assign senior parole personnel to serve as the Duty Officer of the Day. One day each week is set aside to receive office visits from their parolees, handle the variety of problems that arise, and interview parolees for the parole officers who are unavailable.

In recent years, with overcrowding in many local jail facilities, field parole officers in some areas are reporting increased problems of getting local jails to accept parole violators without a parole violation warrant executed by the parole board. This entails additional paperwork and supervisory involvement in obtaining such warrants. Once the violator has been remanded to the custody of the jail, the parole officer faces the time-consuming nature of the parole revocation process.

Parole work can combine satisfaction, frustration, and danger. A rewarding experience is to see parolees succeed by turning their lives around and becoming law-abiding and productive members of society. The frustration is the inevitable failures. Experience soon teaches parole officers to emotionally detach themselves from the less than rewarding situations they encounter: The parolee who commits another serious crime while on parole and while under the parole officer's supervision.

Danger is also present in parole work. For this reason, parole officers are authorized to be armed and have limited arrest powers. Having to arrest a parolee with the possibility that the arrest will result in reconfinement in prison injects a real degree of risk into parole work. The parole officer can never be sure how the parolee will react when faced with the possibility of arrest and being sent back to prison. Many parole agencies downplay this role and caution their parole officers to seek assistance from the police when an arrest is contemplated and enough time is available to enlist the aid of the police in making the apprehension.

An examination of entry requirements for state and federal parole officers indicates that a bachelor's degree is typically required. The applicant must also have a heavy emphasis on coursework in the behavioral and social sciences.[29] It is important that students majoring in criminal justice or criminology who plan for a career as a parole officer take extensive coursework in these areas.

## Parolee's Rights

In the past fifty years, the states have developed certain procedures for returning a parole violator to prison. Because of Supreme Court decisions that pertain to parole revocation, states must provide a parole revocation hearing (unless this is waived by the parolee) before a parolee can have parole revoked. To understand this development, we must examine the parole process more closely.

How parole is actually revoked varies somewhat from state to state. Assume that there is a "technical violation" of a parolee's general or special conditions of parole. In some states on evidence that the parolee has violated the conditions of parole, the parole officer can arrest the alleged parole violator without warrant, pending a revocation hearing. In other states, the parole officer does not have the power to arrest, and instead must apply to the parole supervisor or the parole board to issue a holding warrant before the individual can be taken into custody for a parole violation.

Past abuses

Once an individual is arrested for parole violation, he or she must have a parole revocation hearing. Until the late 1960s, however, the "hearing" was often nothing more than a request by the parole agent or the parole supervisor that the parole board revoke an individual's parole, a request with which they usually complied automatically. In too many instances, parolees were sent back to prison for such ambiguous and undefined reasons as "poor attitude" or allegations of "failure to cooperate." It was generally felt that because the parolee was on parole by grant of his privilege, there was little need for parole boards to concern themselves with questions of the parolee's right of due process, the right to a hearing and review, and matters of proof.

A study of parole board revocations during the 1960s indicated that there was no hearing at all in at least seven states. Even in those states that did provide for a revocation hearing, the individual was immediately returned to prison, and often it would be weeks before any type of hearing was held.[30] When the parole board did get around to conducting a revocation hearing, it was usually so superficial and one-sided as to render it meaningless.

In only a few cases did the parole board conduct meaningful hearings, and in even fewer cases was the warrant canceled and the inmate again released to parole. Even if the warrant was withdrawn, the parolee had already suffered a disruptive experience, and family relationships and employment were already disturbed. During these revocation hearings, it was almost unheard of to permit the parolee to be represented by counsel, to cross-examine the witnesses against him, to demand proof, or to introduce witnesses in his own behalf. In those rare instances when counsel was permitted, the states would not assign an attorney to indigent parolees, which was the category into which many fell.

**COURT RULINGS.** Beginning in the late 1960s, the appellate courts became increasingly concerned with parole practices. Although the entire parole process has come under a great deal of scrutiny in recent years, parole revocation practices have come under the closest examination. The courts have developed a distinctive theme in the law that states if a privilege such as parole is to be denied, it can be done more readily before rather than after it is granted.

The courts have taken a rather zigzag approach in dealing with the legal questions that surround parole revocation. At first, the courts held that parole revocations were entirely within the discretion of parole boards and that, as a consequence, there was no justification for making the hearing an adversarial process in which the parolee had the right to counsel, to be confronted by his or her accusers, and to cross-examine witnesses. However, since the late 1960s and early 1970s the courts have been chipping away at the idea that the parolee has no right to invoke certain requirements from the parole board. In 1967, in *Mempa* v. *Rhay*, the Supreme Court addressed itself to this question in the case of a probationer who had his probation revoked and was sentenced to an institution.[31] The Supreme Court held that a state probationer had the right to a hearing and to counsel when it was alleged that a probationer had violated probation and was to be sentenced to an institution. As a result of this decision, many states began adopting this rule not only for probationers, but for parolees as well.[32]

*Extending certain rights*

In 1973, the Burger Court modified the Court's holding somewhat in the case of *Gagnon* v. *Scarpelli*. In this case, the Court held that providing counsel to indigent probationers in a revocation hearing was to be decided on a case-by-base basis. Nonetheless, the earlier holding of the *Mempa* case meant that drastic changes were called for, not only in longstanding legal positions, but also in the procedures required to revoke the parolee's or probationer's privilege. For example, the New York Court of Appeals, basing its decision on the *Mempa* case, reversed its former position and required the state parole board to permit parolees to be represented by counsel at revocation hearings. The changing philosophy of the courts in their concern for procedural due process is quite well expressed in *Murray* v. *Page* [429 F.2d 1359 (10th Cir. 1970)]:

> Therefore, while a prisoner does not have a constitutional right to parole, once paroled he cannot be deprived of his freedom to be informed of the charges and the nature of the evidence against him, and the right to appear and be heard at the revocation hearing is inviolate. Statutory deprivation of this right is manifestly inconsistent with due process and is unconstitutional: nor can such right be lost by the subjective determination of the executive that the case for revocation is "clear."[33]

Generally, parole boards have resisted these court orders, regarding them as an arbitrary encroachment by the courts into their area of authority. Many parole board members feel that the adoption of an adversarial format will cause the fact-finding mission of the hearing to be lost in legal argument and maneuvering.

On June 29, 1972, the U.S. Supreme Court rendered a landmark decision that has had a significant impact on parole boards throughout the nation. In this case of *Morrissey* v. *Brewer*,[34] two parolees petitioned the Supreme Court on the grounds that their paroles had been revoked without a hearing, which was in violation of their rights to due process. The Court stated that the question was not whether parole was a "right" or a "privilege" but whether, by the actions of a governmental agency (parole board), the individual can be made to suffer a "grievous loss." Although the Court admitted that the parolee is not entitled to the full range of rights due a defendant in a criminal proceeding, it did rule that due process requires that a parolee be given a two-stage hearing. First, a preliminary examination must be conducted promptly by a hearing officer after the arrest or alleged violation. The purpose of this hearing is to determine if there is probable cause to believe that the parolee has committed a parole violation. At this preliminary hearing, the parolee may appear and speak in his or her own behalf and may bring whatever documents and witnesses are necessary to support his case. The parolee is further entitled to receive advance notice of the hearing, its purpose, and the alleged violation.

Then, if the parolee desires a subsequent hearing before the final decision, he or she must be afforded this right. In this hearing, the parolee has certain fundamental rights, among which are (1) the right to receive written notice of the conditions of parole he allegedly violated; (2) the right to be informed of all evidence against him; (3) the opportunity to be heard in person and to present evidence in his behalf; (4) the right to confront and cross-examine adverse witnesses unless the hearing examiner or parole board considers it in the best interests of the witness not to have his identity disclosed; and (5) the right to receive a written statement by the board or the fact finders as to the specific evidence relied on to revoke parole.

## The Parole Revocation Process

To show how a parole revocation process operates, we illustrate the process using a hypothetical federal parolee. Although states may vary somewhat in their particular procedures, there is still enough similarity to give the reader a general idea of what actually transpires when parole is revoked.

Ensuring due process

If a parolee is alleged to have violated the conditions of his or her release, either by failing to comply with the general and special provisions of parole or by committing a crime while on parole, a summons or warrant will be issued. If a summons is issued, it requires the parolee to appear for a preliminary interview or local revocation hearing. If a warrant is issued, it authorizes the immediate apprehension and return of the offender to custody. In deciding to issue a summons or a warrant—the latter calls for immediate apprehension and incarceration—the U.S. Parole Commission considers such things as the frequency or seriousness of the alleged violation or violations, the likelihood that if a summons is issued the parolee is not likely to appear for a preliminary interview or local revocation hearing, and the possible danger the parolee poses to himself or herself or to others. If in the judgment of the authority empowered to issue the summons or warrant, any of these conditions likely exist, a warrant rather than a summons will probably be issued.

The warrant application serves two purposes: (1) it advises the parolee of the violation charged and the evidence for the violation; and (2) it provides allegations of violations and statements of facts that will be considered at the preliminary interview or revocation hearing. The application as a minimum must convey such information as when the violation occurred, the nature and location of the violation, and the particular evidence to support the alleged violation. If the parolee is having his or her parole revocation hearing scheduled because of the commission of a new crime for which he or she is now incarcerated in another jurisdiction, a parole violation warrant may be placed against the parolee as a detainer. Under these circumstances, when the individual is released from his or her present custody, he or she will immediately undergo a parole revocation hearing by the federal authorities.

If a summons is issued, it must indicate whether it commands the parolee's presence at a preliminary interview or whether it is to be a revocation hearing. If a preliminary interview is held and there is probable cause established to believe that a parole violation occurred, the parolee will then be issued with a summons or an arrest warrant to appear for a revocation hearing. If an arrest warrant is issued, the U.S. Marshal's office is instructed to arrest the alleged violator.

At the preliminary interview or revocation hearing, the parolee is afforded the right to counsel. If he or she cannot afford to retain counsel, the parolee can apply to the U.S. District Court for appointed legal assistance. The parolee can request that the commission use its subpoena powers to compel the presence of persons who have given information on which revocation may be based. Unless the interviewing officer finds good cause for their nonattendance, these individuals will be required to attend and the parolee has the right to cross-examine them. The parolee also has the right to examine all evidence on which the finding of violation might be based and to introduce evidence and testimony on his or her own behalf.

At the preliminary interview, the established burden of proof is one of "probable cause." If the interview examiner, after conducting the interview and affording the parolee his or her rights, determines that probable cause has been established, the commission can either (1) order the parolee reinstated to supervision, (2) direct that a revocation hearing be conducted in the locality of the charged violation(s) or place of arrest, or (3) direct that the prisoner be transferred to a federal institution for a revocation hearing.

The revocation hearing requires a more exacting burden of proof. Here the commission must establish a parole violation by "a preponderance of evidence." Again, the alleged parole violator is afforded the full range of procedural rights (statement of charges, cross-examination, and the like). If, after hearing the evidence, the examiner panel finds by a preponderance of the evidence that the charges are substantiated, parole may be revoked.

If parole is revoked for a *technical* violation of the parolee's conditions of parole, the time he or she was under supervision will be credited to the sentence.[35] For example, let us assume that the parolee had originally been sentenced to four years. After two years in prison, he or she is released on parole. The parolee has two years of parole remaining. One year later, parole is revoked by a technical violation. He or she would be credited with the one year of street time and have only one more year to serve in prison.

On the other hand, if the same original sentence existed and the parolee were released on parole and one year later committed a new crime for which a term of imprisonment could be imposed, the parolee would forfeit all street time. If parole were revoked in this case, the parolee would be sent back to prison for the full two years remaining on the original sentence.[36]

Although the Supreme Court has specified particular guidelines to be followed in parole revocation cases, many states have, in reality, a rather weak and perfunctory system of assuring due process rights to the parolee at the revocation hearing. Although this might be more understandable in cases in which the prisoner's violation is established by means of a subsequent conviction for a new crime while on parole, it is less acceptable in certain technical violation cases. Here again, the possibility for arbitrary and capricious behavior on the part of the parole officer or the parole office staff may warrant closer examination. These type situations, it would seem, were those the Supreme Court was particularly concerned about in its *Morrissey* decision. Yet the attitude still is prevalent that a parolee should have no rights other than those we choose to give him or her. Since in our minds the parolee is not entitled to any rights to begin with, the niceties of due process need not be of too much concern.

## Developing Trends in Parole

**DEVELOPMENT OF PAROLE TEAMS.** In most instances, a parolee is arbitrarily assigned to a parole officer who has a vacancy in his or her caseload. This traditional pairing up is being modified in a number of parole offices throughout the United States today. In its place, a team approach is being employed in which a team of parole officers assumes collective responsibility for a parolee group as large as their combined former caseloads. Under this system, parolees are assigned to parole officers who are best able to relate to and supervise them. For example, if certain parole officers seem to have better success with drug-related offenders, then parolees with this type of history are assigned to them.

This team approach seems to be a much more prudent use of human resources available in parole agencies. It also facilitates the use of paraprofessionals and volunteers, which is becoming more widely used as a means to assist parole officers and parolees. Often the use of carefully selected volunteers has proved to be very beneficial, as it provides a means to match parolees with individuals who can understand their particular problems of adjustment and, as a consequence, relate in more meaningful ways.

In some parts of the country, volunteer groups have developed to help prisoners even before their release. In the state of Washington, concerned citizens developed a volunteer sponsors group to visit men in prison, particularly those who had infrequent contacts from the outside. The group's goal was to establish a human contact in which there is real commitment and to follow it up with specific help when the inmate is paroled. This program at one time numbered more than five hundred volunteers.[37] In California, a program that uses volunteer parole aides, some of whom are ex-convicts, has begun. One of the most interesting developments is the National Parole Aid Program begun by the American Bar Association. This program was started as a result of the feeling that the citizen volunteer movement, although very popular in probation, was not being used to its fullest potential in parole. The program operates by enlisting attorney volunteers to act as parole officer for a single offender under the general supervision of an experienced parole officer.[38]

Matching

Use of volunteers and paraprofessionals

## Intensive Parole

In the past few years there has been increased interest in intensive parole supervision. Rather than operating with caseloads of 75 to 150 parolees, some people are suggesting that parole officers be assigned a smaller number of parolees. There are two basic ideas behind this. First, since the research seems to indicate that parolees are most likely to fail in their first year of release, this should be a period of intense concentration; that is, during the critical period, special attention should be focused on the parolees. Associated with this is the idea that large caseloads provide no time for the parole officer to effectively supervise or assist the parolees.

**Caseload reduction**

The research, however, on caseload size does not seem to indicate that reduced numbers of parolees (and probationers) and more intensive supervision are necessarily correlated with success on parole. In fact, there are some indications that such a situation leads to more revocations through technical violations.[39] Parole (and probation) officers who have more time to supervise their clients are likely to find parolees in violation more often.

The point may be academic. With the growing numbers of parolees and pro-

---

## NEW YORK'S "DIFFERENTIAL SUPERVISION"

New York State has instituted the idea of Differential Supervision as an improved method of structuring parole caseloads in that state. The idea is to improve the caseload structure in a way that is responsive to the different needs of parolees while recognizing that scarce resources limit what the parole authority can accomplish.

In establishing the program, New York's Division of Parole conducted recidivism studies over the past decade. The conclusion was that 80 percent of the parolees who violate their conditions of release will do so during their first fifteen months on release. To deal with this problem, all parolees during their first fifteen months are placed into caseloads requiring intensive contact standards. These caseloads average thirty-eight parolees. After fifteen months of intensive supervision, a parolee is moved to a regular supervision caseload which averages ninety-seven parolees.

The program is designed to pro-

vide the intensive supervision of parolees during this critical fifteen-month period. It began with a pilot project in the Bronx in 1985. Since that time, the Division has been actively working to complete the implementation of the program statewide in a series of phase-in stages. Implementation has been stalled in several areas as parole officers ran into problems trying to jail those who violated parole. The overcrowding in that state's jails resulted in additional workload demands required to process violators, which took away the time required for more intensive supervision. In 1987, the highest court in New York State handed down a decision that required all countries to accept parole violators in their jails. This is expected to free up jail-processing time for parole personnel enabling them to fully implement the intensive supervision program.

Along with this program, New York has stepped up its efforts to deal with parole absconders. It is

hoped that by reducing caseloads, evidence of absconding will be brought to the attention of the Parole Division's Absconder Search Unit (ASU) that much more quickly. Preliminary evidence indicates that this is occurring. This provides for earlier follow-up investigations and efforts at locating and arresting parole absconders.

In conjunction with these efforts, the Parole Division's ASU has entered into a joint cooperative program with the New York City police. Special Task forces are being formed, consisting of teams composed of one parole officer and one police investigator to conduct fugitive investigations. Such efforts are being assisted under the Parole/New York Police Department Information Exchange. It is hoped that this formalized relationship will provide for exchange and dissemination of information relating to parolees such as the locations of suspected illegal operations and unlawful activity of parolees.

---

bationers, the situation for most parole and probation officers is getting worse rather than better. It is ironic that we should be talking about increased services and surveillance while at the same time relative budgets for such services are dropping because of the increased number of clients.

The problem seems to be fundamentally this. In any given population of parolees and probationers, there are three groups: those who will probably certainly fail and recidivate regardless of what is done; those who will successfully complete supervision and lead law-abiding lives even if nothing is done; and those who might be able to make it if the proper help is provided at the right time. Of course, the target for our efforts should be this third group. Yet, who are these people? What kinds of help are most beneficial and under what circumstances? Until better answers are available to these fundamental questions, intensive parole or probation is a costly undertaking with only a hit-or-miss probability of success. As a public policy issue can we afford such a benefit/cost ratio? While the reader ponders this question, consider the other side of the coin. Can we ever really identify these people and the specific effects of intensive supervision unless we implement such policies and study them closely? Under the present circumstances, parole and probation practices seem to offer little or no assistance to the clients or answers to the questions we ask. What does it do then? Does it only delude the public that these people are being "supervised," which somehow makes us all feel "safer" and more secure? Yet by fostering this illusion—and given the present realities—we have tailored in the inevitable: failure, public frustration, and blame on parole and probation authorities and our system of criminal justice.

**PAROLE CONTRACT PLAN.** During the 1970s, several states developed what appeared to be a promising and unique idea: the parole contract plan. Underlying this idea was an interesting attempt to tailor prison rehabilitative programs to individual needs while at the same time involving the inmate in a planned program of self-help and motivation.

Matching needs to an agreement

Under the parole contract plan, an inmate met with counseling specialists when he or she first arrived at the prison. Together the counselors and the inmate devised a mutually satisfactory plan that the individual would engage in during the period of imprisonment. For example, the inmate may have been in need of further education and may have expressed a desire and willingness to finish high school and to complete a vocational trade program in electronics. The counseling staff would then draw up a contract agreement with the inmate. The contract would specify that the Department of Corrections agrees to provide the inmate with the opportunity to obtain a high school diploma and to participate in a vocational electronics training program. In turn, the inmate would agree to fulfill these goals by a certain date. The parole board was also brought into the planning process and would agree to parole the inmate on completion of the contractual obligation.

The idea of such a system is a simple one. It was a means to provide a more effective system for delivery of rehabilitative services within correctional institutions—one in which the inmate played a key participative role in determining his or her needs and what he or she would like to accomplish. This was a major departure from what traditionally occurred. In most prison systems, the inmate had far less input into the diagnosis and the decision-making process.

It was also thought that such goal-oriented planning would be a positive motivating force for many of the inmates who wanted to take advantage of the parole contract plan. Through a series of intermediate steps, a long-range sequence of specified objectives could be accomplished. This would have a definite carry over to the "free world," where such skills as planning, self-discipline, and self-supporting behavior would likely ensure better success on parole—indeed in life in general. For many inmates who had demonstrated a lack of self-discipline throughout their lives, this was an opportunity to help them deal with this problem and to do so under careful supervision and guidance.

The programs that were devised also built in some flexibility. If for some reason the inmate was having trouble reaching his or her goals, the contract could be renegotiated. Only the inmate, however, had the option to change the conditions of the parole contract. The agreement could not be changed unilaterally by the other two parties: the correctional authorities or the parole board.

Unfulfilled expectations

The promise of such an innovative idea fell far short of expectations. Like so many attempts to rehabilitate prison inmates, it seemed to enjoy little success. Michigan is a good example of a state that kicked off its parole contract plan with high expectations, only to be disappointed by the results. Eventually, this led to its abandonment in that state. Begun in 1973, it was terminated five years later.

Research into the operations of the Parole Contract Program in Michigan examined the success or failure on parole as measured by recidivism rates of inmates who had participated and completed their parole contracts against those inmates who had not but were later paroled. For further purposes of comparison, inmates participating in the plan were placed into three categories based on past experience with parole success or failure: high-risk, medium-risk, and low-risk offenders. Overall, there was no appreciable difference in recidivism among these groups as determined by whether or not they had completed their parole contracts.[40] The conclusion was that the parole contract program did not provide a test for later behavior on parole.

Another objective of the Michigan program was the hope that to avoid losing one's contract, institutional behavior by the participants in the program would improve. Many of the inmates who entered into the contract were involved in institutional misconduct during their imprisonment. This indicated that the contract itself was not a very strong influence toward staying out of trouble for the persons concerned.[41] This occurred even though the participating inmates realized that the contract could be cancelled for serious institutional infractions.

Michigan was not the only state experiencing problems with its parole contract plan. Other states such as Arizona and California had serious problems that led to the cancellation of their parole contract efforts.

Coming at a time when rehabilitative efforts in prisons were being widely denounced as a failure, the experience of states with the parole contract plan added additional fuel to the debate. The experience also was a harbinger of the growing criticism directed at parole itself as a process that had little to meaningfully offer. The parole contract was not so much a measure of the efficacy of parole as much as another clear sign of the problems underlying the rehabilitative model of corrections. It managed to drive another nail into the coffin of rehabilitation.

**THE NEED TO ATTRACT QUALIFIED PROFESSIONAL FULL-TIME PAROLE BOARD MEMBERS.**  A few states have begun to realize the need to attract qualified individuals to serve on parole boards. Very few states require any specific qualifications for appointment to the boards—nor does the federal government.

As mentioned, several problems exist in the composition of many state parole boards; very few states require any specific qualifications for those appointed to serve as parole board members. The same is true of the federal government's Parole Commission.* In some jurisdictions, highly qualified and competent individuals have been appointed and others have gained experience through their service on the board. Still, it was also pointed out that in most states, parole board members serve terms of six years or less. Experience has also shown that it is not unusual for new parole board members to be appointed whenever there is a change in the governor's office and when an incumbent board member's term expires. The politics of a patronage system become more important than the appointee's qualifications or experience. A final last problem is that some states still cling to a part-time parole board.[42] Any number of parole reform groups have argued against such a situation.[43]

**Innovative trends**

In an effort to curb this practice, states such as Michigan and Ohio have placed their parole board members under the state civil service system with indeterminate periods of tenure. Michigan and Wisconsin require appropriate college degrees and experience in corrections or closely related areas. Many parole board members in these states have extensive experience in responsible positions in corrections before joining the parole board. Florida requires that appointees pass a special examination in penology and criminal justice, administered by a special examining board of specialists in these areas. As more complex and diverse institutional programs develop, states must begin to realize that parole board members must be trained professionals in the field of corrections.

## Abolition of the Indeterminate Sentence and Parole

A topic of growing interest throughout the country has been for a reform in sentencing structures. The basis for this is a growing dissatisfaction with the indeterminate sentence.[44] Since 1869, when Michigan enacted the first indeterminate sentence law, it was widely believed that an indeterminate sentence was the best mechanism to rehabilitate inmates. By providing for some degree of indeterminancy in sentencing—for example, from two to ten years for a specific offense—an inmate would be motivated to take advantage of the rehabilitative aspects of prison in an effort to be paroled near the minimum sentence. The indeterminate sentence also shifted the responsibility from imposing the actual length of sentence from the judge to the parole board. The judge merely sentenced the individual according to the range provided for the particular crime. The parole board then decided when, within that range, the individual had been "rehabilitated" and could be released.

**Determinate sentencing**

Since the late 1970s indeterminate sentence has been under attack, and with it, parole. In the years from 1977 to 1982, for example, no less than thirty-seven states passed mandatory sentencing laws and eleven states enacted new legislation calling for determinate sentences. Because the justification for parole was to provide community supervision for someone who was released from an institution before serving the statutory maximum, the abolition of the indeterminate sentence is also bringing about the clamor that there is no need for parole. Indeed, at least seven states have technically abolished parole.

Maine was the first state to abolish parole. That state's decision in 1976 set off shock waves throughout the correctional and legal communities. The change of

*While the U.S. Parole Commission is scheduled to be phased out in 1991, there is a great deal of concern about what will take its place to accommodate the thousands of prisoners in federal institutions who were sentenced before the adoption of the new federal sentencing guidelines, which abolished, among other things, parole and with it the Parole Commission.

the parole law in Maine was prompted by a number of considerations. First, correctional administrators recognized that the use of the indeterminate sentence and parole forced many inmates to volunteer for rehabilitative programs in which they had no interest, in order to "look good" to the parole board. Under such a situation, rehabilitation was a sham. It was also felt that parole served no useful rehabilitative purpose and was not effective in preventing further crimes by present and former parolees. *Corrections Magazine* says the real reason for the abolition of parole in Maine was that the legislature in that state was reacting to what it saw as an overly lenient parole board.[45]

The result was a new criminal code incorporating determinate sentences and the abolition of parole. The new law provided for a sentencing range for the commission of a particular crime. The judge then sentenced the offender to a flat sentence within that range. The inmate then could accrue "good-time," which would be taken off his or her sentence. When the inmate's determinate sentence less the accrued good-time provided for his or her release, the inmate was turned loose without parole consideration or supervision. Although Maine called its sentencing system a determinate one, it was not truly "determinate" in the strictest definition of how determinate sentencing has subsequently developed in other states. For example, providing the sentencing judge with a wide range of sentencing discretion for the conviction of a particular crime violated the *true* determinative nature of the Maine law.

California quickly followed suit. In 1977 that state implemented its Uniform Determinate Sentence Law. After sixty years of existence, California's indeterminate sentence law had been repealed. The California law was the first to attempt a true determinate sentencing format. California judges under the new law gave out definite "flat" sentences for each class of crime. For aggravating or mitigating circumstances, they may add or subtract specific periods of time. The law was quite complex, and many of those involved in the sentencing decision—judges, prosecutors, and public defenders—had to be schooled in the computational intricacies of the new law.[46] Parole supervision after release and the possibility of recommitment for the original term as a penalty for parole violation was virtually abolished.

As other states abolished parole, the threat of widespread adoption of antiparole legislation grew. Although there was an initial rush to follow Maine and California's lead, there has been a rethinking of this issue in more recent years. Following the widespread talk of parole abolition in the late 1970s, by the mid-1980s we saw little in the way of further discussion of abolishing parole in the states. Still, shifts in sentencing and release policies seem to be occurring. For instance, the percentage of persons discharged from state prisons as a result of a parole board decision fell from nearly 72 percent in 1977 to 41 percent in 1987.[47] Even so, the parole abolition movement seems to have generally run its course.

The studies of the effects of parole abolition among some of the states passing such legislation is perhaps illustrative. With the exception of three abolition states—Maine, Connecticut, and Washington—other so-called "abolition states" still impose some type of postrelease supervision. It may be a practice of releasing the inmate ninety days before compiling enough good time credit to leave unconditionally, such as in North Carolina, or a form of "mandatory parole," which is a period automatically added to the original determinate sentence—a practice that has been imposed in some abolition states.

It has been also reported that states that have tried to abolish parole outright have been resisted in some strange ways. In Maine and Connecticut, the abolition of postrelease supervision has angered many judges in those states. To counter the effects of the new laws, judges are increasingly sentencing offenders to "split-sentences"—that is, terms of jail or imprisonment to be followed by probation—in an effort to ensure that inmates will not be released without some kind of supervision.[48] In Maine, the use of split sentences has doubled since the abolition of parole supervision.[49] Among some members of the criminal justice community, there is still the feeling that some form of supervision is necessary after release.

There is also a growing recognition that whereas the abolition of parole may have done away with inmates' "playing games" to look good for the parole board, there now exists no motivation for inmates to make any attempt to enter into programs in the institution. "Why bother?" is the answer given. As long as inmates marginally behave in order not to lose good time, no other motivation exists.

It was also felt that the abolition of parole and the indeterminate sentence would be better liked by the prisoners. Under the determinate sentence, the inmate would know exactly when he or she would be released and there would not be the uncertainty posed by the indeterminate sentence and the whims of the parole board. This is not always the case, especially for those serving long sentences. In the past such inmates were able to cling to the hope that the parole board might favorably consider them for release some time in the future. Now that this hope has been removed, inmates know they will not be released before the expiration of their determinate sentence.

The complexities of the parole and indeterminate sentence abolition movement point out the realities of change and reform in the administration of justice. It is, as was pointed out in the first chapter, a system. Change one aspect and changes—both beneficial and not so beneficial—occur in other components of the system. Indeed, these changes often result in unanticipated consequences. It is like puncturing a tube of toothpaste with many small holes: when you squeeze, you are not sure where the toothpaste is likely to come out.

## ◻ PROBATION

Defined

Whereas parole is the conditional release of an offender who has served a period of incarceration in prison, probation is the conditional release of an individual by the court after the offender has been found guilty of the crime charged. While parole is a function of a state executive branch agency (the parole board), probation is a function of the courts. At the judge's discretion—and if state law permits—an individual may be placed on probation by the sentencing judge. The offender is supervised by a probation officer, who typically is employed by the court. A violation of the conditions of probation, which are imposed by the court, may cause the judge to revoke probation, and the offender may be sentenced to a period of incarceration as prescribed for the crime committed.

Variations on probation

While probation usually occurs before the offender has been sentenced to prison, this is not always the case. In recent years, some states have adopted variations on the traditional way probation is handled. These variations permit a combination of prison and probation. This includes the so-called split-sentence alternative in which the court specifies a period of incarceration to be followed by a period of probation. The judge, where authorized, might sentence an individual to three to six months in prison, after which the offender will be released to probation

Oliver North is the most famous defendant sentenced to probation. (J.L. Atlan/Sygma)

supervision. This serves two purposes: It gives the sentencing judge an alternative, which is not usually available under more conventional forms of sentencing. In most cases, the judge has only two alternatives—send the offender to jail or prison or place him or her on probation. The judge may be uncomfortable with such an either–or situation; given the circumstances, a standard period of imprisonment is too harsh and probation is too lenient. With the split-sentence alternative, the judge can find that middle ground. Such a sentence also permits the court to give the offender a taste of what prison or jail is like. Perhaps this will better serve to deter future criminal behavior by the offender. This alternative is also called shock probation and will be discussed in more detail later in this chapter.

Still another variation of probation is what is called modification of sentence. Here, the sentencing court within a limited and prescribed time may reconsider an offender's prison sentence and modify it to probation. Another variation on traditional probation is intermittent incarceration. This has become popular in recent years. An offender on probation in such a program might be required to spend weekends or nights in a local jail.

Table 14.1 shows the newly adopted conditions of probation for federal offenders sentenced under the Sentencing Reform Act of 1984. State-imposed conditions of probation are often similar.

The decision to place an offender on probation is generally a combination of factors: the nature of the crime; the recommendation (if any) of the prosecuting attorney; the presentence investigation report prepared by the probation officer, which would include a host of considerations concerning the commission of the crime and the offender's characteristics; the attitudes of the community and per-

## TABLE **14.1** Conditions of Probation

(A) Mandatory Conditions. The court shall provide, as an explicit condition of a sentence of probation:
    (1) that the defendant not commit another federal, state, or local crime during the term of probation; and
    (2) if convicted of a felony, the defendant must abide by at least one condition set forth in subsection (B)(2), (B)(3), (B)(13) below;
    (3) if the court has imposed and ordered execution of a fine and placed the defendant on probation, payment of the fine or adherence to the court-established installment schedule of payment shall be a condition of the probation.

(B) Discretionary Conditions. In addition to the above mandatory conditions the court may also impose any of the following as determined by nature and circumstance of the offense and the history and characteristics of the offender:
    (1) support his dependents and meet other family responsibilities;
    (2) pay a fine as imposed by law;
    (3) make restitution as provided by law;
    (4) give to the victims of the offense the notice pursuant to the provisions of Sec. 3555;
    (5) work conscientiously at suitable employment or pursue conscientiously a course of study or vocational training that will equip him for suitable employment;
    (6) refrain, in the case of an individual, from engaging in a specified occupation, business, or profession bearing a reasonably direct relationship to the conduct constituting the offense, or engage in such a specified occupation, business, or profession only to a stated degree or under stated circumstances;
    (7) refrain from frequenting kinds of places or from associating unnecessarily with specified persons;
    (8) refrain from excessive use of alcohol, or any use of a narcotic drug or other controlled substance, without a prescription by a licensed medical practitioner;
    (9) refrain from possessing a firearm, destructive device, or other dangerous weapon;
    (10) undergo available medical, psychiatric, or psychological treatment, including treatment for alcohol or drug dependency as specified by the court, and remain in a specified institution if required for that purpose;
    (11) remain in the custody of the Bureau of Prisons during nights, weekends, or other intervals of time totaling no more than the lesser of one year or the term of imprisonment authorized for the offense in section 358(b), during the first year of the term of the probation;
    (12) reside at or participate in the program of a community corrections facility for all or part of the term of probation;
    (13) work in community service as directed by the court;
    (14) reside in a specified place or area, or refrain from residing in a specified place or area;
    (15) remain within the jurisdiction of the court unless granted permission to leave by the court or probation officer;
    (16) report to a probation officer as directed by the court or the probation officer;
    (17) permit a probation officer to visit him at his home or elsewhere as specified by the court;
    (18) answer inquiries by a probation officer and notify the probation officer promptly of any change in address or employment;
    (19) notify the probation officer promptly if arrested or questioned by a law enforcement officer; or
    (20) satisfy such other conditions as the court may impose.

---

haps the attendant publicity of the crime; and, in some cases, the attitude of the police. The judge normally considers many of these factors, including the complete criminal and social history of the accused, in trying to reach a decision whether the interests of justice would be served by probation and whether it would also be in the best inerests of the defendant.[50]

**As a sentence**

Like parole, many critics of probation consider it a form of leniency. Compared with the alternative of incarceration, it may be. Nonetheless, probation is, in fact, a sentence and not a dismissal of the charges. The court specifies the conditions of this form of sentence, which might be to obtain or remain in gainful employment, to make restitution to the victim, to abstain from the use of drugs or alcohol, to remain in the jurisdiction of the court, or other conditions. The probationer agrees to these conditions for the duration of the probationary period, after which he or she is discharged from the sentence.

A sentence of probation is imposed by a judge in one of two ways: The judge may impose a sentence as determined by the statute violated and then suspend its execution and place the offender on probation; or the judge may defer sentencing and place the individual directly on probation. If the offender should violate the conditions of probation in the first instance, the period of incarceration has already been determined. If in the second instance the conditions of probation are violated, the probationer is brought back to the court to have sentence imposed.

In most jurisdictions, the judge's discretion in granting the time an offender serves on probation is limited by the period of time that the sentence specifies. For example, if the statute calls for a possible period of incarceration of one to three years, the judge cannot sentence the offender to probation for more than the three-year maximum. However, in some states, the length of the probated term may exceed the term that the defendant would be required to serve if incarcerated.[51] Many states also specify that, in the case of more serious crimes, probation is not an alternative. In a few jurisdictions, a jury may recommend probation and the judge must follow the recommendation; in most jurisdictions, however, the decision rests solely with the judge.

## Origins of Probation

Modern probation stems from early common law practices that developed as methods of avoiding the severity of criminal laws. During the period of its widespread temporal power, the Roman Catholic Church demanded the right of immunity from secular law for clergy.[52] This immunity was known as *benefit of clergy*. Later, *rights of sanctuary* developed by which those accused of crimes were granted immunity from the civil authorities by seeking the protection of the Church.

Probation, as we know it today, is primarily an American development. In 1841, while a spectator in the Boston Police Court, John Augustus requested that the judge permit him to be the sponsor for an offender about to be sentenced. The court agreed to his request, and the convicted offender was sentenced to his custody. Augustus, who is considered the father of probation, continued his efforts and developed several features that often characterize probation today. First, he selected offenders who were charged with their first offense and appeared amenable. Second, he assumed responsibility for an offender only after a careful examination of the facts of the case and of the history and character of the defendant. Third, he agreed to send the offender to school or to see that he obtained employment and housing. Finally, he developed a system of making impartial reports to the court on the status of those committed to his supervision and of maintaining a careful register of his probationers.

John Augustus

In 1878, the Massachusetts legislature approved the idea that the mayor of Boston should appoint a probation officer as part of the police force. From Boston, the idea spread slowly across the United States. At first, most probation officers handled only juvenile cases, but as the years passed, courts were increasingly inclined to extend this service to adult offenders. The idea of using probation as an alternative to incarceration spread to other countries as well. The first countries to adopt it outside the United States were Australia and New Zealand. When England adopted the Probation of Offenders' Act in 1907, the idea soon spread to European countries, where it was eventually adopted.

## The Growth and Use of Probation

Probation is the most commonly used sanction in the United States. Nearly three times as many convicted offenders are placed on probation each year as are sentenced to prison and jail combined. In 1985, nearly 65 percent of the nearly three million adult offenders under correctional supervision were on probation.[53] While we hear a great deal about prison populations drastically increasing in recent years, the number of people on probation have increased even proportionally faster. There is no doubt it has become a serious problem. Some observers contend that "probation crowding" poses a more serious threat to the criminal justice process and to community protection than prison overcrowding.[54]

We really do not know, however, exactly how prevalent is the use of probation; this will vary from court to court (Table 14.2). A study of sentencing practices among Indiana's courts in the 1970s, for example, indicated that of those persons convicted of an offense for which imprisonment was an alternative, 56 percent received probation.[55] It is generally felt that the success of probation is fairly high. For instance, the Michigan Department of Corrections studied 2,411 cases of adults placed on probation. The success rates of these probationers were studied for three years, and it was found that 79.1 percent of the offenders were successful under probation. Of the 20.9 percent who failed, 15.3 percent had their probation revoked for technical violations, while only 5.6 percent committed new offenses.[56] Of course, one could argue that because only the "best risks" are placed on probation, it would be expected that they would have higher success rates.

The "success" of probation

But do these "best risks" really have higher success rates? There is increasing evidence that they are not as successful as many proponents of probation would have us believe. For instance, a major study by the federal government's General Accounting Office, entitled *State and County Probation: Systems in Crisis*, concludes:

> State and county probation systems are not adequately protecting the public; the majority of probationers do not successfully complete probation. Federal, state and local government must cooperate to improve the situation.[57]

Success alone is not the only issue that is causing some concerns about the efficacy of probation—or for that matter other types of community alternatives such as parole or community-based facilities for handling offenders. Advocates for probation and these community alternatives often argue that costs must be considered: These are simply cheaper alternatives than imprisonment or jail. But are they? A study of the costs of prosecuting repeat felony offenders in Salt Lake County, Utah,

---

TABLE **14.2**   Increases in Probation Use

**Probationers were one of every**

| | |
|---|---|
| 1983 | 109 adults |
| 1984 | 100 |
| 1985 | 94 |

Source: Bureau of Justice Statistics. Report to the Nation on Crime and Justice, 2nd ed. (Washington, D.C.: U.S. Department of Justice, March 1988), p. 104.

found that probationers who commit crimes while on probation and are prosecuted for it very quickly cost victims and the criminal justice system the amount of money "saved" by not incarcerating them for their earlier crime. Repeat offenders (some of whom commit hundreds of crimes a year) can cost society many times over the cost of incarceration if they recidivate while on probation or parole or in a community-based facility.[58]

## The Organization of State Probation Agencies

State probation departments are organized in diverse ways. They may be a part of the executive or the judicial branch, and they are administered by both state and local governments. For example, in some states, certain probation departments are administered by local courts, whereas others are under the control of the state department of corrections or another state agency that is part of the executive branch. In most states, juvenile probation is a local function of the courts that deal with juvenile matters.

There has been a great deal of argument over which administrative arrangement is best. Although the National Advisory Commission on Criminal Justice Standards and Goals advocates placing all state probation services under a unified state correctional system, many argue that this function should be retained by the local courts. The arguments for both sides have been summed up as follows:

*Local versus centralized administration*

### Arguments for Having Probation Services Administered by Local Courts

Under this arrangement, probation would be more responsive to court direction. Throughout the probation process, the court could provide guidance to probation workers and take corrective action when policies were not followed or proved ineffective.

This arrangement would provide the judiciary with an automatic feedback mechanism on effectiveness of dispositions through reports filed by probation staff. Judges would place more trust in reports from their own staff than in those compiled by an outside agency.

Courts have a greater awareness of needed resources and may become advocates for their staffs in obtaining better services.

Increased use of pretrial diversion may be furthered by placing probation services under the auspices of the courts. Since courts have not been inclined to delegate their authority to persons not connected with the judiciary or its staff, it is likely that probation services which are not under the court will have less discretion in employing diversionary measures.[59]

### Arguments for Having Probation Services Administered by a Central State Executive Agency

When probation services are attached to the courts, judges frequently become the administrators of probation in their jurisdiction—a role for which they are usually ill-equipped. Judges cannot effectively divide their time between administering probation services and yet perform their judicial functions.

When probation is within the judicial system, the probation staff is likely to give priority to services for the courts such as issuing summonses, serving subpoenas, etc., rather than providing services to probationers.

Since the criminal courts in particular are adjudicatory and regulatory rather than service-oriented organizations, probation services that are attached to courts will not develop a professional identity of [their] own.

The executive branch contains the allied human service agencies, including so-

In 1985 the Rand Corporation supported by the U.S. Department of Justice issued the findings of a significant research effort on the effects of probation for felony offenders. The report concluded that placing felony offenders on probation constitutes a threat to public safety since such offenders tend to persist in committing high rates of crime while under supervision.

The Rand researchers tracked, over a 40-month period, the histories of 1,672 men convicted of felonies and sentenced to probation in Los Angeles and Alameda counties. The findings were disturbing. Of these probationers, 65 percent were again arrested, 51 percent of them were convicted, and 34 percent ended up in jail or prison. Of those convicted, about one-third were placed back on probation.

The repeaters tended to commit burglary, theft, and robbery offenses; these three crimes alone accounted for 75 percent of the new charges filed against the probationers. Although property crimes accounted for the majority of arrests and convictions, 18 percent of the 1,672 were convicted of serious, violent crimes while on probation.

The study, which is the first systematic attempt to examine the effectiveness of probation as a punishment for adult felons, comes at a time when the nation's probation programs are under unprecedented strain. Because of prison overcrowding, probation is increasingly being used as an alternative to institutionalization. Convicted offenders who might at one time have gone to prison are now being given probation. In fact, as the report points out, probation has become "the predominant sentencing alternative to imprisonment." It is being used in 60 to 80 percent of all criminal convictions. Probation may be being used too indiscriminately. The study showed, for example, that the crimes and criminal records of about 25 percent of the offenders who were granted felony probation are indistinguishable from those of offenders who go to prison.

In the past five years, both the prison and probation populations have shot up alarmingly. In 1983, for example, while the growth in the number of prisoners slowed from 12 to 6 percent annually, the number of adults on probation increased 11 percent. In this way probation has become a "safety-valve" for overcrowded prisons. In 1984, in California, one out of every eighty-three persons between the ages of nine and sixty-five, or just over 1 percent of its population, was on probation. About one-third of these probationers are offenders who have been convicted of felonies as opposed to misdemeanors.

While probation caseloads have soared, the funding has not kept up. In fact, comparing expenditures to the number of probationers being supervised, budgets show a more drastic decline than any other component of the criminal justice system. We are spending far less per probation case than we ever have in recent history. Besides the problems of trying to supervise probationers in their caseloads, probation officers are finding themselves having to conduct more presentence reports and other functions.

Because of the growth in the number of felony offenders they must supervise, probation workers have less time to spend on more traditional probation subjects—first offenders, petty thieves, drug offenders. The authors of the report see a danger if these minor criminals interpret the criminal justice system's apparent indifference to them as encouragement for them to commit more crimes, believing they can "get away with it." Apparently, this is already occurring. The petty criminal in such cases is being ignored in an effort to deal with

cial and rehabilitative services, medical services, employment services, and housing, which can be used to develop more coordinated cooperative and comprehensive program efforts with probation agencies.[60]

### Shock Probation

One of the suggested methods of handling offenders is to incarcerate them for a brief part of the sentence, suspend the remainder, and place them on probation. This approach, called *shock probation*, attempts to avoid the long-term prison commitment and its effects on the offender. Those who advocate the use of shock probation contend that: (1) short-term institutionalization may be to the inmate's advantage, because the period of incarceration can provide probation agencies the

Brief imprisonment

the increasing number of felony probationers.

All of this does not mean that the only answer is to build more prisons, the report says. Although the public is obviously protected from criminals who are locked up, there is little evidence to suggest that imprisonment diminishes the likelihood that criminals who are incarcerated will commit serious crimes when they are eventually released.

What then can be done?

The report states that the criminal justice system needs alternative forms of punishment intermediate between prison and probation. One promising new approach being tried in some states is intensive surveillance coupled with substantial community service and restitution. Such programs must be restrictive enough to ensure public safety and punitive enough to satisfy the public's sense of justice.

The report discusses several programs that it states are moving in the right direction.

A New Jersey program, for example, enforces a strict curfew—participants must be home every night from 10 P.M. to 6 A.M. These individuals must also have contact with their probation officers four or five times a week, maintain employment, pro-

vide community service, and pay back their victims.

In addition, such programs can save money; they can maintain an offender for $5,000 a year—in contrast to maintaining a prisoner for an estimated cost of $15,000 a year.

The report contends that these programs force offenders to become employed, functioning members of the community. According to the authors, "Intensive surveillance holds the promise of rehabilitating criminals who might otherwise be hardened by the prison experience."

Although intensive surveillance programs would cost considerably less than building prisons, they would cost more than traditional probation, the report notes. To help pay for these programs, some states have begun to collect probation supervision fees from the felons themselves. A program in the State of Washington, for example, charges traditional probationers $15 per month, and those under intensive supervision are charged up to $30 per month.

The report maintains that rising felony crime rates and prison overcrowding have made risk prediction a central issue for criminal justice policy in the 1980s. If the criminal justice system is to establish sen-

tencing alternatives, then courts must be able to determine which criminals present the most danger to the public.

As an example, the authors cite research that has repeatedly shown a strong association between juvenile records and adult criminality. Early involvement in violent crime, age at first arrest, drug use, number of juvenile incarcerations, length of time between arrests, family arrangements—are all factors that courts should consider in passing sentence. Yet this information often fails to appear either in an offender's record or in presentence investigation reports.

The study includes only offenders who were convicted of felonies, and their poor probation performance should not be taken to mean that probation has failed as a sanction for juveniles or for the less dangerous adults for whom it was originally designed. Probation appears to work for these groups, particularly if the financial resources are adequate.

*Source:* Joan Petersilia, Susan Turner, James Kahan, and Joyce Peterson, *Granting Felons Probation: Public Risks and Alternatives* (Santa Monica, Calif.: Rand Corporation, 1985).

opportunity to evaluate the needs of the offender in more detail so that they are in a better position to help; (2) it will jolt the individual into a realization of the realities of prison life and thereby serve as a more meaningful deterrent to future criminal behavior than probation alone; and (3) it provides a way to combine probation with short jail terms as a compromise between immediate release and a regular prison sentence.[61]

Ohio was the first state to pass such an act. Since 1970, several other states have passed laws that give judges the option of applying shock probation as an alternative. Under the Ohio law as amended in 1967 and 1976, offenders can apply for shock probation between their thirtieth and sixtieth day in prison. Under the statute, the offender may be sentenced to prison and then released by a judge after serving between 90 and 130 days. In response to public complaints that serious offenders were being released too soon under the law, a 1976 amendment excluded from shock probation all "dangerous" offenders and all those convicted of violent crimes or crimes that involved a weapon.[62]

During its first year of operation, only eighty-five cases were released on shock probation. The numbers grew rapidly in the following years. Partly because of the Ohio Department of Rehabilitation and Correction's inadequate research facilities, and partly because of the difficulty in gathering data from all the courts in Ohio's eighty eight counties, statistics on the success or failure of the program are scarce. The only figures made available by the department are the number of shock cases per year and the number of recommitments to state prison. There are no figures on types of crimes committed by shock probationers or on those who committed new crimes out-of-state, committed new crimes without being incarcerated, or absconded from supervision.[63]

The department claims that only slightly more than 10 percent of shock probationers are recommitted. A research study of probationers under the program during its first four years of operation came up with a similar success rate.[64] However, these rates have been challenged by a five-year study of the program, completed by Harry R. Angelino of the Behavioral Sciences Laboratory of the Ohio State University. Angelino's study of 554 men and women released on shock probation between 1966 and 1970 showed that, over a five-year period, 31.3 percent were convicted of subsequent felonies. However, the study also showed that most of the crimes committed by shock probationers after release were nonassaultive and less serious than those for which they were originally imprisoned.[65]

## Probation Subsidy Programs

A few states, notably California and Michigan, have experimented with juvenile probation subsidy programs. Originally established to help counties develop probation services for juveniles—and to help states keep down the costs of institutionalization—these subsidy programs are now being considered as a means to deal with the adult offender. Under these programs the state subsidizes the jurisdiction providing probation services for each probation case retained.

Reduce overcrowding

The idea behind such subsidy programs is quite simple. States and local jurisdictions need to reduce their overcrowded institutional facilities. It is far less costly to provide probation services than it is to incarcerate an offender. Second, probation authorities need additional funds to keep up with increasing case loads and the need to provide more intensive probation programs to certain offenders. Additional funds are needed to hire probation officers for supervision as well as to complete the increased demands for presentence investigations.

Although probation subsidies have merit, they are not without certain drawbacks. The first criticism is that such subsidies may induce the court to place on probation offenders who should not receive probation. This might be particularly true when a court has increased its staff through such payments and in this way has grown dependent on this source of income.

Another consideration is a little more complex. It is not popular to place on probation offenders who have committed crimes that are serious enough to cause them to be sentenced to state institutions—which means prison. The state that has an interest in keeping the numbers of inmates down is seen as encouraging leniency by the courts. Although state correctional officials may encourage the increased use of probation, their encouragement of this practice is likely to be more covert. Announcing such a plan runs a political risk that they and state officials are not willing to take.

There is also little or no interest by local authorities to subsidize the courts for such a practice. Cities, for example, are not willing to subsidize a county criminal court for its increased use of probation—at least not through a probation subsidy arrangement.

## Intensive Probation

Like intensive parole, intensive probation seems to be gathering support. Intensive probation has been targeted at offenders who have committed property crimes and who otherwise would have gone to prison. At least one state has instituted intensive probation services for probation violators who, in the absence of this alternative, would have been sent to prison.

In addition to the substantial cost savings of such an approach over imprisonment, there is the feeling that intensive probation will serve the needs of those who require more than routine probation but do not warrant imprisonment. Many prison observers contend that many inmates in correctional institutions do not need to be incarcerated and would benefit from what this service could potentially provide. There is also the feeling that intensive supervision, if it is successful, will renew the efficacy of probation to the public as a sentencing mechanism. In this way it would blunt the widespread criticism that probation has suffered.

The handful of states that have adopted this procedure share several similar characteristics in the way they conduct their programs. First, they choose carefully the individuals they feel will benefit from this type of handling. This does not mean choosing only those prisoners who are good risks at probation success. Such individuals are, in fact, carefully screened out and placed in routine probation in which they will likely be successful. Instead, those individuals who otherwise would have gone to prison and who share characteristics of those in prison are chosen. In this way, the effects of intensive supervision can be better measured.

A necessary component of such a program is a significant reduction in caseload from perhaps one hundred to two hundred probationers per probation officer to caseloads of approximately twenty-five. Along with this reduction, probation officers are required to spend extensive time supervising their clients. Whereas in most routine probation activities the typical probation officer spends nearly all of his or her time preparing presentence investigation reports and doing the necessary paperwork generated by their huge caseloads, now they are free to make frequent checks on probationers and offer services that might help their clients. In reality there is more of a law enforcement aspect to this type of program than exists in routine probation. For example, strict curfew hours might be imposed as are frequent "house checks" at odd hours to ensure compliance with the more rigorously required conditions of probation.

Caseload reduction

Well-managed programs of this sort would also carefully select the probation officers assigned. Many probation officers operating under traditional probation practices might not have the counseling and one-on-one interactive skills required for such intensive supervision. Just as selection criteria are imposed for clients, it is also necessary to screen probation officers for the necessary skills and aptitudes.

How well are these programs working? The answer is not clear. We do know that they can divert offenders from prison and if they work, they are far more cost-effective to operate than incarceration. Whether or not these programs can rehabilitate offenders remains to be seen. The real danger is that under pressure judges and probation authorities will begin to assign more clients to intensive supervision and that this will cause individual caseloads to rise, thereby undercutting the purposes of these programs before they can be effectively evaluated. Already these pressures are occurring. There is also the fear that if pressure does not force intensive supervision caseloads to increase, probation officers who are handling intensive supervision will be required to help out in other areas, such as doing more presentence investigations for the court, which will have the same effect of diminishing the intensive nature of the supervision.

## Use of Indigenous Paraprofessionals or Volunteers

Identity problems

In the past ten years, there has been a growing trend among probation departments to recruit auxiliary personnel from the same social class as the probationers. Such persons are referred to as *indigenous paraprofessionals*. Many probation officers agree that their clientele are often alienated from the mainstream of society by virtue of their norms, values, and life-styles. Frequently, these probationers are referred to as hard to reach, unmotivated, mistrustful, and resentful of authority. As Donald W. Beless and others have said, "There exists a marked *social distance* between many middle-class professional corrections workers and a large segment of their lower-class clientele."[66]

As a consequence, a few probation departments are experimenting with the use of indigenous paraprofessionals to assist probation officers. C. F. Grosser sees the local resident worker as a bridge between the lower-class client and the middle-class professional worker.[67]

Use of former offenders

In addition to the indigenous paraprofessional, a number of probation agencies are now using former offenders in their assistance programs. This idea draws on the experience of such groups as Alcoholics Anonymous and Delancey Street, which operate on the idea that those who have experienced and overcome a problem have a unique capacity to help others with similar problems. F. Riesman characterized this phenomenon as the helper therapy principle and concluded:

> Perhaps, then, social work's strategy ought to be to devise ways of creating more helpers! Or, to be more exact, to find ways to transform recipients into dispensers of help, thus reversing their roles, and to structure the situation so that recipients of help will be placed in roles requiring the giving of assistance.[68]

One such program was the Chicago-based Probation Officer Case Aide (POCA). This program used indigenous paraprofessionals for federal probation and parole, with some being former offenders. Applicants for probation officer assistant (POA) were recruited primarily from neighborhoods that have a high proportion of offender clients. Applicants came to the project by way of recommendations of probation staff officers, referrals from local social service agencies, and self-referrals. In establishing the program, the crucial issue was the selection criteria. It was decided that applicants would be chosen by a selection committee of the project staff. Once selected, the POA attended orientation and training sessions and was then assigned to a probation officer who supervised ten POAs.

It has been found that these indigenous paraprofessionals are interested, available, and able to work well under professional supervision. It also has been demonstrated that they provide a productive and effective service to professional pro-

"Probation has a default identity," says Douglas Thompson of the University of Illinois, Chicago Circle. "It's seen in terms of avoiding something else."

It's no secret that, across the country, probation has a serious image problem. Two years ago, Judge Lois Forer of the Philadelphia Criminal Court said: "Probation is a meaningless rite; it is a sop to the conscience of the court." Thomas Callanan, director of probation in New York State, puts the problem in the vernacular: "People think that probation is soft on crime."

Making probation tough on crime is the goal of intensive probation programs. Two nationally known authors have been thinking about other ways to do the same thing lately. One, David Fogel, former director of the Minnesota prison system and author of *"We Are the Living Proof": The Justice Model for Corrections,* recently spent a year examining European correctional systems. He describes European probation programs as the most adaptable alternatives to incarceration. One form of probation he mentions is Sweden's intensive supervision,

which requires a probationer to report in person to the police several times a week. The fact that this is an unpleasant intrusion into the life of the probationer is essential, he says, quoting a government report: "The disagreeable content of the sanction becomes absolute, something which must be accepted."

"We have to create a much tougher form of probation, with public safety as its cardinal mission," Fogel said in an interview. "It's the only way we can save probation."

John Conrad, former head of research for the U.S. Bureau of Prisons and author of several books on corrections, goes even further in a paper prepared for the National Institute of Corrections. Conrad proposes taking the functions of surveillance and control away from probation officers entirely and turning them over to the police. "It is one thing to accept an occasional home call from a harassed and overworked probation officer, or to appear in his office on a Saturday morning," he writes. "It is quite another to make a regular trip to a police station for a report to a uniformed or juvenile officer, and

to be subject to periodic visitation and investigation by the police."

In an interview, Conrad said: "This is not a welcome idea to probation officers. But something really has to be done to solve the control problem. We have to beef up surveillance."

As Conrad foresaw, these proposals are not eagerly greeted by probation officials. Callanan, who is past president of the American Probation and Parole Association, called Conrad's call for turning surveillance over to the police "absolutely ridiculous. What's he's looking for is a guardian angel. I would hate a society where someone was looking over people's shoulders 24 hours a day. They don't do that even in China or Russia. That's ludicrous."

To these comments, Conrad replied: "I don't see anything ludicrous or police-state about it. The police do surveillance all the time anyway."

*Source:* Adapted with permission from Stephen Gettinger, "Intensive Supervision—Can It Rehabilitate Probation?" *Corrections Magazine* (April 1983).

bation officers. They are frequently able to intervene in cases where probation staff officers might encounter problems.[69]

In addition to the use of indigenous paraprofessionals or volunteers, many probation authorities across the country have established general volunteer programs. These programs have grown by virtue of the fiscal problems many probation agencies face in light of increased workloads. There are three major arguments in support of the use of volunteers in adult probation: (1) they are cost-effective ways to provide services without having to increase probation staffs; (2) such programs enhance the public relations of the probation agency; (3) they provide benefits to the probationer.[70]

Volunteers in these programs are screened by the probation agency for their suitability. Once accepted, the volunteer assists an assigned probation officer in his or her caseload management. This would include such typical responsibilities as interviewing, presentence investigation, counseling, and courtroom assistance. Patricia M. Shields and others make a well-reasoned argument for the increased

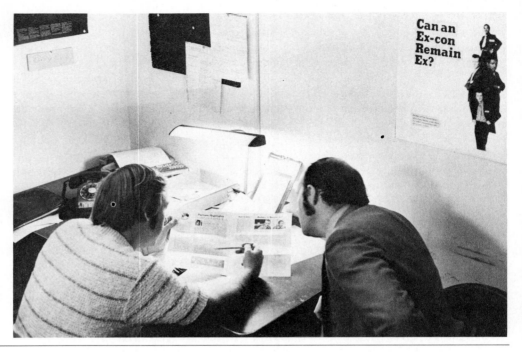

A variety of strategies, such as this volunteer counseling program, are employed to help parolees adjust to life in the community. (Bettye Lane/Photo Researchers)

## PUNISHMENT NOW INCLUDES
## HOUSE ARREST AND ELECTRONIC MONITORING

Offenders in a growing number of communities are being given a choice between jail and a new form of community supervision. Usually incorporated with a restitution or community service program, this new experiment requires that participants in the program confine themselves in their homes between 6 P.M. and 8 A.M. How do the authorities ensure that those in the program are really at home? By requiring that the arrestees wear an ankle bracelet that is really an electronic device that notifies a central monitor if the wearer moves more than 100 feet from his or her home or tries to remove the device.

Begun in Palm Beach, Florida, it is considered a successful alternative to jail and more effective than traditional probation. Fred Rasmus-

sen, who heads a private, nonprofit organization called PRIDE, Inc., which runs several prison programs including this one, says: "I thought we'd be chasing down monitors all over the planet. But so far we haven't lost one yet. We had one kid who was arrested for breaking and entering and he still had the device on his ankle. That's the worst episode we've had."

Offenders usually prefer the program to jail. A twenty-five-year-old man convicted of his second Driving While Intoxicated offense was given the choice between ten days in jail or thirty days on the monitor.

"The embarrassment factor is quite high," he said. "I have to tell friends why I can't go out. I have to ask people to go to the store for me. It's a real hassle."

Some arrestees benefit in unexpected ways. Rasmussen describes them as "people whose natural instinct is to hit the road, find a bar or a place to hang out. When someone is forced to spend time with his family every evening, it has a positive influence on his behavior."

The program has additional cost benefits. It certainly is a lot cheaper than to sentence these offenders to jail. It also helps to relieve the probation people who in many courts are staggering under the growth in probation caseloads in recent years. Harvey Goldstein, director of probation and parole services for the state of New Jersey, also believes that such programs greatly facilitate the ability of probation people to supervise their clients.

use of students who are planning a career in criminal justice or social work as volunteers in these programs. Upper-level and graduate students in such programs are often willing to exchange their time and efforts as volunteers for the practical experience that they gain in the criminal justice system.[71]

Programs of this sort must be aware of several potential problems, however. The most fundamental concern is one of recruiting and selecting volunteers. Not all applicants will be suitable as volunteers for any number of reasons. Some may not have the requisite maturity and motivation. Others may be well intentioned but ineffective. Still others may have questionable motives. There are also concerns that volunteers recognize and adhere to the strict provisions of confidentiality that must exist in probation activities. In addition, there are voiced concerns among probation professionals that volunteer activities might increase agency legal liability and require of the probation staff careful and close monitoring of volunteers.

Electronic monitoring devices like this one allow convicted offenders the opportunity to continue many of their usual activities, while saving the cost of housing them in jail. (B.I., Inc.)

## Interstate Compacts on Probation and Parole

Although most people are not aware of it, states have entered into mutual assistance compacts for handling adult and juvenile probationers and parolees. Before the Crime Control Consent Act, passed by Congress in 1936, there was no mechanism for supervising a probationer or parolee outside the state where he or she was convicted. Because in many instances the offender's home, relatives, and community ties were in another state, the offender could not be provided supervision in his or her home area, which, in theory, offered the best chance for success.[72]

**Outside of state supervision**

After 1936, a group of states entered into the Interstate Compact for the Supervision of Parolees and Probationers, through which they undertook to supervise parolees and probationers for each other. By 1951, all states had signed the compact and incorporated it into their state laws.[73]

The compact mechanism seems to work fairly well. The one notable exception, according to Killinger, is when probation is locally administered.[74] This illustrates one of the problems inherent in the present fragmented probation system. The lack of uniformity in the organizational placement of probation from state to state has impeded the development of effective treatment and supervision strategies for out of state probationers.[75]

The compact identifies a "sending state" and a "receiving state." The "sending state" is the state of conviction. The "receiving state" is the state that undertakes the supervision. The offender has to meet certain residence requirements with reference to the receiving state. Ordinarily, the probationer or parolee must be a resident of the receiving state, have relatives there, or be employed there. The receiving state agrees to accept the offender and give him or her the same supervision as is accorded a probationer or parolee in the receiving state. The offender who obtains the benefits of out-of-state supervision waives extradition. The sending state may enter the receiving state and take custody of the probationer or parolee who has violated the terms of release without going through extradition proceedings, and a supplementary agreement permits the violator to be incarcerated in the receiving state at the expense of the sending state if both states agree.[76]

**Characteristics**

## Probation Work as a Career

Like other agencies of criminal justice, probation is suffering from a lack of resources and qualified personnel. Because no current statistics are available, we really do not have a good idea of how bad the picture is nationwide. The most recent comprehensive data were published in 1987. A survey taken at that time indicated that there were approximately 23,000 probation officers serving the federal, state, and local adult courts.[77] How accurate these figures are is anybody's guess. It is possible that some of these probation officers also serve as parole officers. We also don't know how many adult probation officers also serve the nation's juvenile courts or whether some of those reported in the survey as serving adult courts might in fact be juvenile probation officers.

QUALIFICATIONS. The American Correctional Association suggests that individuals preparing to become probation officers have a master's degree in social work or comparable behavioral science with coursework in criminal justice or criminology; however, the minimum state requirements throughout the country are not as demanding.

A review of qualifications for probation officers on a state-by-state basis indicates that the qualifications for such a position are very similar to that required for parole officers. A bachelor's degree is generally required with special emphasis on coursework in criminal justice, the behavioral sciences, counseling techniques, and social work. Salaries for probation and parole officers are generally similar within the state.

FUNCTIONS. Probation officers are responsible for the management and supervision of the offenders who make up their caseloads. For a number of years, the recommended caseload has been established at fifty units. The American Correctional Association and the President's Commission on Law Enforcement and Administration of Justice recommend fifty-unit and thirty-five-unit caseloads, respectively, with the provision that each presentence investigation and report that the probation officer is required to compile should count as five supervised cases. Both of these arbitrary figures seem to be without any meaningful justification. The usual rationale for smaller caseloads is that the fewer individuals the probation or parole officer has to supervise, the more effective the supervision will be. However, as mentioned earlier, research has indicated that there appears to be no relationship between size of caseload and success or failure of a probationer or parolee.

Roles and responsibilities

A probation officer does far more than merely supervise a caseload of probationers. In addition to providing counseling, employment assistance, and other related services, a probation officer must be an investigator and a diagnostician of the needs of the probationer and must be able to develop, coordinate, and implement the special casework services needed. Probation officers also perform another important role in that they often serve in a quasi-judicial function, especially where judges more or less automatically impose the sentence recommended in the probation officer's presentence report. Various studies have shown a very high relationship between probation officers' recommendations and dispositions made by judges. Robert M. Carter and Leslie T. Wilkins have pointed out that judges follow probation officers' recommendations in better than 95 percent of cases.[78] Part of this might be attributable to the probation officer anticipating what sentence the judge is predisposed to give and then recommending it, but there are probably many instances in which the judge goes along with the recommended sentence on the assumption that the probation officer, having conducted the presentence investigation, has the most complete facts.

Unless prevented by statute, the court has the power to set the specific conditions of probation for adult offenders. Often the judge imposes the specific requirements on the probationer that the probation department recommends. The probation officer is also responsible for initiating revocation of probation, although it is the judge who actually revokes probation. Most probation revocation statutes are so vague that it is not difficult for the probation officer who wishes to do so to find cause to invoke the revocation process, usually on the basis of some technical violation. Finally, the probation officer has the ability to render punishment under the guise of rehabilitation—for example, by demanding that the probationer not live in or frequent certain areas, not engage in certain employment, and not associate with certain people.[79]

Probation will continue to play an important role in the administration of justice. Although it has been widely criticized, there is simply no acceptable substitute for probation. Unlike the somewhat uncertain nature of parole, probation services will continue to grow. Indeed, in the next decade, probation may grow more rapidly than any other single component of the criminal justice system.

It will be useful to observe the different strategies of probation during this time. For example, does intensive probation hold any promise or is it merely an exercise in futility given the realities of the operations of justice and the characteristics of offenders? And what about the efficacy of "stand-alone" probation as an alternative? In other words, if probation is to be more meaningful and acceptable as a practice, must it become combined with strategies such as community service and victim restitution as part of the probation experience? Evidence tends to indicate that making these features part of probation may at least make it more acceptable to the public.

## SUMMARY

Parole is the conditional release of an offender who has served a period of time in prison, whereas probation is the conditional release of an individual who has been found guilty in court. Parole has its roots in such practices as conditional pardons, indenture, tickets of leave, and indeterminate sentences. Modern parole originated at the Elmira Reformatory. Parole is not a form of leniency but rather an extension of the rehabilitative and reintegrative program begun in the institution. States have traditionally organized adult paroling authority around three models—the institutional, the independent, and the consolidated. In recent years, the consolidated model has been adopted by most states. Just as each state has its own parole authority, so does the federal government. Decisions of parole boards are usually based on the seriousness and nature of the current offense, the circumstances of the crime, the placement situation, and the offender's institutional record. In recent years, some states and the federal government have

been developing prediction methods to assist parole boards in making their decisions.

Among some of the recent changes in parole are increased legal rights of the parolee, the development of parole teams, intensive parole, and improvements in the selection of parole board members. In spite of the advances in parole, several states and the federal government have sought to abolish it. This movement, however, seems to have lost its initial steam in recent years. Although parole will be affected by such changes in our sentencing laws, it will likely be the indeterminate sentence that will feel the brunt of these changes.

Probation services are also undergoing changes. One is the movement toward providing adult probation services through a centralized state authority rather than on a strictly local basis. Other innovations are probation subsidy programs, shock probations, the use of intensive probation, and the growing use of volunteer, indigenous paraprofessionals and, perhaps, former offenders as probation aides. As a necessary diversionary and cost-saving practice, probation will continue to be used extensively.

## REVIEW QUESTIONS

1. What is parole, and at what stage in the criminal justice process is an offender granted parole?
2. Name four historical precedents of parole. Briefly explain each.
3. Identify three basic concepts underlying parole in the United States.
4. Briefly describe the three classifications of adult paroling authorities.
5. What factors are considered in deciding whether or not to grant parole to an offender?
6. How do parole decision-making devices such as Oregon's Parole Matrix work?
7. List the conclusions reached by Daniel Glaser in his research on the postrelease success of inmates.
8. What is "good-time" and how does it operate?
9. What are the major roles played by the parole officer?
10. What does the term *indeterminate sentence* mean? Why is the indeterminate sentence being criticized?
11. What is probation? What are the two ways a judge can impose a sentence of probation?
12. What are the responsibilities of probation officers?
13. Are there dangers or problems associated with the growing use of probation? If so, describe.
14. What is intensive parole and probation?

## DISCUSSION QUESTIONS

1. Discuss the various alternative ways that states administer their parole services. What are the relative advantages and disadvantages of each?
2. What are the advantages and disadvantages of parole guidelines such as Oregon's Parole Matrix?
3. Discuss the decisions on which parole is typically based. Can you think of any other consideration that might be important?
4. Discuss the issue of parolee's rights. Do you agree or disagree with court-imposed guidelines in this area?
5. Should states institute "flat" sentences and abolish parole? Why?
6. How do courts normally impose probation?
7. Discuss some of the reforms suggested for probation services.
8. What do you see as the future of parole and probation? Discuss.
9. Does intensive parole and probation have any future? Justify your conclusions.

## SUGGESTED ADDITIONAL READINGS

Abadinsky, Howard. *Probation and Parole: Theory and Practice.* Englewood Cliffs, N.J.: Prentice-Hall, 1977.

Bates, Sanford. "When Is Probation Not Probation?" *Federal Probation* 24: 13–20.

Blair, Louis H. *Monitoring the Impacts of Prison and Parole Services.* Washington, D.C.: The Urban Institute, 1977.

Clear, Todd R. and Vincent O'Leary. *Controlling the Offender in the Community.* Lexington, Mass.: Lexington Books, 1983.

Empey, Lamar T. *Alternatives to Incarceration.* Washington, D.C.: U.S. Government Printing Office, 1967.

Friday, Paul C., David M. Peterson, and Harry E. Allen. "Shock Probation: A New Approach to Crime Control." *Georgia Journal of Corrections* 1 (July 1973): 1–13.

Glaser, Daniel, and V. O'Leary. *Personal Characteristics of Parole Outcome.* Washington, D.C.: U.S. Government Printing Office, 1966.

Killinger, George G., Hazel B. Kerper, and Paul F. Cromwell. *Probation and Parole in the Criminal Justice System.* St. Paul, Minn.: West Publ. Co., 1976.

McCarthy, B. R. (ed.). *Intermediate Punishments: Intensive Supervision, Home Confinement and Electronic Surveillance.* Monsey, N.Y.: Willow Tree Press, 1987.

National Institute of Law Enforcement and Criminal Justice. *Critical Issues in Adult Probation—Summary.* Washington, D.C.: U.S. Government Printing Office, September 1979.

Petersilia, Joan. *Granting Felons Probation—Public Risks and Alternatives.* Santa Monica, Calif.: Rand Corp., 1985.

Smith, Alexander B. *Introduction to Probation and Parole.* St. Paul, Minn.: West, 1976.

Smith, Robert L. *A Quiet Revolution—Probation Subsidy.* Washington, D.C.: U.S. Department of Health, Education and Welfare, 1972.

Smykla, John O. *Probation and Parole—Crime in the Community.* New York: Macmillan, 1984.

Stanley, David T. *Prisoners Among Us—The Problem of Parole.* Washington, D.C.: The Brookings Institution, 1976.

# NOTES

1. *Bureau of Justice Statistics Bulletin: Probation and Parole—1987* (Washington, D.C.: U.S. Department of Justice, November 1988), p. 1; Also see Bureau of Justice Statistics, *BJS Data Report, 1988* (Washington, D.C.: U.S. Department of Justice, April 1989), p. 59.

2. *Ibid.*

3. *Ibid.*, p. 2.

4. Charles L. Newman, *Sourcebook on Probation, Parole and Pardons* (Springfield, Ill.: Charles C Thomas, 1970), p. 26.

5. William Parker, *Parole: Origins, Development, Current Practices and Statutes* (College Park, Md.: American Correctional Association, May 1972), p. 10.

6. National Council on Crime and Delinquency, *Corrections in the United States* (New York: NCCD, 1967), p. 217.

7. Adapted from: State of New York, Division of Parole, *1984–85 Annual Report*, p. 15.

8. National Advisory Commission on Criminal Justice Standards and Goals, *Corrections* (Washington, D.C.: U.S. Government Printing Office, 1973), pp. 395–397.

9. U.S. Department of Justice, *State and Local Probation and Parole Systems*, p. 20.

10. National Advisory Commission, *Corrections*, pp. 396–397.

11. Daniel Glaser, *Effectiveness of a Prison and Parole System* (Indianapolis, Ind.: Bobbs-Merrill, 1959), p. 23.

12. Michigan Department of Corrections, "Operation and Philosophy of the Michigan Parole Board," mimeo (10 February 1975), p. 3.

13. David T. Stanley, *Prisoners Among Us: The Problem of Parole* (Washington, D.C.: The Brookings Institution, 1977), p. 49.

14. Ibid., p. 49.

15. *Ibid.*, p. 12.

16. For example, see Don F. Gottfredson, "A Shorthand Formula for Base Expectancies," California Department of Corrections, Research Division, *Research Report No. 5* (Sacramento, July 1962); P. G. Ward, "Validating Prediction Scales," *British Journal of Criminology* 7 (1967): 36–44; Peter B. Hoffman and James L. Beck, "Parole DecisionMaking: A Salient-Factor Score," *Journal of Criminal Justice* (Winter 1974): 195–206.

17. Much of this section is adopted from Elizabeth L. Taylor, "In Search of Equity: The Oregon Parole Matrix," *Federal Probation* 43, no. 1 (1979): 52–59.

18. The current Parole Matrix was kindly supplied by Hazel G. Hays, chairperson, Oregon Board of Parole, 12 July 1985.

19. Norman S. Hayner, "Parole Boards' Attitudes Toward Predictive Devices," in Norman Johnson et al., eds., *The Sociology of Punishment and Correction* (New York: Wiley, 1970), pp. 839–843.

20. Glaser, *Effectiveness of a Prison and Parole System*.

21. Peter B. Hoffman and Barbara Stone-Meierhoefer, "Post-Release Arrest Experience of Federal Prisoners: A Six-Year Follow-up," *Journal of Criminal Justice* 7, no. 3 (1979): 193–216.

22. This might have been attributed to the fact that those arrested had been convicted and were in prison so they wouldn't show up in arrest rates for subsequent years.

23. National Institute of Justice, *American Prisons and Jails*, *Volume IV* (Washington, D.C.: U.S. Government Printing Office, October 1980), p. 135.

24. Ibid.

25. Ibid.

26. *Wolff* v. *McDonnell*, 418 U.S. 539. In this last right (i.e., to produce witnesses), the Court specified that this could occur only if it jeopardized institutional safety or correctional goals.

27. National Institute of Justice, *American Prisons and Jails*, p. 137.

28. Ibid.

29. See: U.S. Department of Justice, *Sourcebook of Criminal Justice Statistics—1987* (Washington, D.C.: U.S. Government Printing Office, 1988), pp. 78–80.

30. Robert Sklar, "Law and Practice in Probation and Parole Revocation Hearings," *Journal of Criminal Law, Criminology and Police Science* 55 (1964): 75.

31. 389 U.S. 128 (1967).

32. National Advisory Commission, *Corrections*, p. 405.

33. Quoted in ibid., pp. 405–406.

34. 408 U.S. 471 (1972).

35. A few exceptions to this are not included for purposes of simplifying the example. For a more detailed discussion see: United States Parole Commission, *Rules and Procedures Manual* (Washington, D.C.: U.S. Department of Justice, October 1984), Sec. 2.52, p. 139.

36. Of course, it is a little more complicated than this. Again, certain details were omitted in order to simplify.

37. William Schiller, "A New Helping Hand for Prison Inmates," *Reader's Digest* 97 (August 1970): 147–150.

38. Louis P. Carney, *Introduction to Correctional Science* (New York: McGraw-Hill, 1974), p. 327.

39. For example, see: J. V. Lohman, G. A. Wahl, and R. M. Carter, *The San Francisco Project* (Berkeley: University of California Press, 1965); D. M. Gottfredson and M. G. Neithercutt, *Caseloads, Size Variation, and Difference in Probation-Parole Performance* (Pittsburgh, Pa.: National Center for Juvenile Justice, 1974); Florida Parole and Probation Commission, *Intensive Supervision Project: Final Report* (Tallahassee, Fla.: Florida Parole and Probation Commission, 1974).

40. Internal memorandum, Michigan Department of Corrections, 19 July 1978.

41. *Ibid.* Law Enforcement Assistance Administration.

42. Law Enforcement Assistance Administration, *State and Local Probation and Parole Systems* (Washington, D.C.: U.S. Government Printing Office, February 1978), pp. 107–178.

43. National Advisory Commission, *Corrections*, p. 420.

44. For example, see American Friends Service Committee, *Struggle for Justice: A Report of Crime and Punishment in America* (New York: Hill & Wang, 1971); Jessica Mitford, *Kind and Unusual Punishment: The Prison Business* (New York: Knopf, 1973).

45. Kevin Krajick, "Abolishing Parole: An Idea Whose Time Has Passed," *Corrections Magazine* 9 (June 1983): 32–40 at p. 34.

46. See: Jonathan D. Casper, David Vrereton, and David Neal, *The Implementation of the California Determinate Sentencing Law* (Washington, D.C.: National Institute of Justice, May 1982).

47. BJS Data Report, 1988 *op. cit.*, p. 52.

48. Krajick, op. cit., p. 35.

49. Ibid., p. 35.

50. For a more thorough discussion of how such decisions are made, see Alexander B. Smith and Louis Berlin, *Introduction to Probation and Parole* (St. Paul, Minn.: West, 1975), especially chap. 3.

51. Hazel B. Kerper and Janeen Kerper, *Legal Rights of the Convicted* (St. Paul, Minn.: West, 1974), p. 251.

52. Elmer H. Johnson, *Crime, Correction and Society* (Homewood, Ill.: Dorsey, 1968), p. 666.

53. James M. Byrne, *Probation* (Washington, D.C.: National Institute of Justice), n.d., p. 1.

54. Ibid.

55. State of Indiana, *Report to the Citizens Council on Probation* (1973), p. 2.

56. State of Michigan, Department of Correction, *Criminal Statistics* (Lansing, 1972).

57. U.S. General Accounting Office, *State and County Probation: Systems in Crisis* (Washington, D.C.: U.S. Government Printing Office, 1976), cover and p. 74.

58. Bureau of Justice Statistics, *Report to the Nation on Crime and Justice*, 2nd ed. (Washington, D.C.: U.S. Department of Justice, 1988), p. 124.

59. National Advisory Commission, *Corrections*, p. 313.

60. Ibid., p. 314.

61. For a good discussion of shock probation see Gennaro F. Vito, "Developments in Shock Probation," *Federal Probation* (June 1984): 22–27.

62. Joan Potter, "Shock Probation: A Little Taste of Prison," *Corrections Magazine* 3 (December 1977): 49–55.

63. Ibid., pp. 51–52.

64. See Paul C. Friday, David H. Petersen, and Harry E. Allen, "Shock Probation: A New Approach to Crime Control," in David H. Petersen and Charles W. Thomas, eds., *Corrections* (Englewood Cliffs, N.J.: Prentice-Hall, 1975), p. 251.

65. Harry R. Angelino, cited in Potter, "Shock Probation," p. 52.

66. Donald W. Beless, William S. Pilcher, and Ellen Jo Ryan, "Use of Indigenous Nonprofessionals in Probation and Parole," *Federal Probation* 36 (March 1972): 11.

67. C. F. Grosser, "Local Residents as Mediators Between Middle-Class Professional Workers and Lower-Class Clients," *Social Service Review* 40, no. 1 (March 1966): 56–63.

68. F. Riesman, "The 'Helper' Therapy Principle," *Social Work* 10 (April 1965): 28.

69. Beless et al., "Use of Indigenous Nonprofessionals in Probation and Parole," p. 15.

70. Patricia M. Shields, Charles W. Chapman, and David Wingard, "Using Volunteers in Adult Probation," *Federal Probation* 47 (June 1983): 57–65.

71. Ibid., p. 61.

72. National Institute of Law Enforcement and Criminal Justice, *Critical Issues in Adult Probation—Issues in Probation Management* (Washington, D.C.: U.S. Government Printing Office, September 1979), p. 37.

73. George G. Killinger, Hazel B. Kerper, and Paul F. Cromwell, *Probation and Parole in the Criminal Justice System* (St. Paul, Minn.: West, 1976), p. 114.

74. Ibid.

75. National Institute of Law Enforcement and Criminal Justice, *Critical Issues in Adult Probation*, p. 38.

76. Killinger et al., *Probation and Parole*, p. 114.

77. U.S. Department of Justice, *Sourcebook*, pp. 70–73.

78. Robert M. Carter and Leslie T. Wilkins, "Some Factors in Sentencing Policy," *Journal of Criminal Law, Criminology, and Police Science* 58, no. 4 (1967): 503–504.

79. Eugene H. Czajkoski, "Exposing the QuasiJudicial Role of the Probation Officer," *Federal Probation* 37 (September 1973): 9–13.

# CHAPTER 15

# Current Issues and Trends

## OBJECTIVES

**After reading this chapter, the student should be able to:**

Describe community-based corrections.

Discuss the basis for community-based corrections.

Identify four possible community-based programs and their characteristics.

Identify four types of community-based facilities.

Discuss future correctional issues and trends.

Discuss the issues and concerns surrounding capital punishment.

Discuss the "impending danger" now facing our correctional efforts.

## IMPORTANT TERMS

Community-based corrections

Diversion

Failure of traditional methods

Community impact on behavior

Academic-pass programs

Conjugal and family visitation

Home furlough programs

Prerelease guidance center

Halfway houses

Community corrections center

Victim restitution

Judicial review of correctional operations

Caliber of correctional administration

Demands of interest groups

Relationship of diversion to reintegration

Work-release programs

Development of correctional alternatives

Changes in organization, delivery, crime, and the offender population

Privatizing corrections

Prison violence

Capital punishment

The impending danger

In the preceding chapters on corrections, we have discussed developments in traditional jails and detention facilities and in parole and probation. In this chapter, we explore the nature of community-based correctional programs such as work-release and home furlough programs and examine general issues and trends in the broad areas of corrections, such as court supervision of correctional operations, the need to improve the quality of correctional staffs, the issue of capital punishment, and important problems and signs of change now occurring.

## ▣ PROLOGUE: CORRECTIONS IN THE SHADOW

The 1990s dawn ominously for America's correctional efforts. Probably at no time in our nation's history—at least not within the current century—have so many seemingly intractable problems confronted the operations of our nation's prisons. The change in the public's attitude toward offenders and corrections is obvious. The American public has cast aside its faith in the ability of the nation's correctional efforts to correct. If "rehabilitation" is a goal valued by society, it has become couched in a different form of expression. A national survey conducted on the public's attitudes toward punishment and corrections indicated that punishment should serve the primary purpose of scaring the offender so that he or she will not commit further crimes.[1]

What are the full implications of such attitudes? Does this mean that the operations of our prisons and correctional programs should be such that the experience will be so painful that inmates will out of fear remain law-abiding on their release? And what kind of a strategy does this suggest? Does it argue for the return to brutal and oppressive measures to attempt to deter? Although this could certainly be considered a form of "rehabilitation," it is simply unworkable. In the first place, it is questionable whether our nation's humanitarian ideals would permit a return to penology characterized by enforced discipline, the lockstep, and oppressive dehumanization. And would such measures really deter the future criminal behavior of those exposed to it? History and experience would argue against this.

Unguided then by any public consensus or approved philosophy, corrections continues to seem to drift aimlessly. This is compounded by serious problems of overcrowding, which have brought about massive and costly construction expenditures for new institutions by the federal and state governments. Under such circumstances massive warehousing seems to have taken control of our nation's penal philosophy. The end can only be obvious: We will continue to be mired in frustration borne of repeated failure. How the cycle can be broken—if it can be broken at all—may well prove to be, along with our nation's drug problem, the most critical issue facing the criminal justice system of the twenty-first century.

In the preceding chapters on corrections, we have discussed developments in traditional jails and detention facilities and in parole and probation. In this chapter, we explore the nature of community-based correctional programs such as work-release and home furlough programs and examine general issues and trends in the broad areas of corrections, such as court supervision of correctional operations, the need to improve the quality of correctional staffs, the issue of capital punishment, and important problems and signs of change now occurring.

# ☐ COMMUNITY-BASED CORRECTONS

The term *community-based corrections* applies not only to changes in the traditional location and use of prisons but also to the inclusion of specific correctional efforts within this new design.

The states are being forced to consider community-based corrections as an alternative to imprisonment. There is simply no other way they can deal with the crush of convicted offenders. Even so, recent years have seen these community-based alternatives grow at only half the rate of conventional imprisonment.[2] And there are differences in the types of community-based alternatives that are growing in use. There are also differences in areas of the country willing to use these alternatives. Halfway houses, for example, show the largest increase in use of all community-based programs. Again, this is probably the result of an effort to relieve the pressure on prison overcrowding. The Southern states, as a region, apparently have invested more of their correctional resources into community-based programs. In terms of the use of halfway houses for instance, these states account for nearly half of all such facilities in the nation.[3]

Prison administrators are realizing that massive and isolated prisons do not    Rationale for
provide the best setting for correctional efforts. To achieve the correctional goals of imprisonment, institutional programs and inmates must interact more with society. Correctional efforts behind prison walls often center around artificial environments and pressures that are not conducive to a meaningful adjustment to society when the inmate is released. Such corrective programs effectively remove the offender from any positive influences of society and also prevent treatment personnel from observing an inmate's ability to interact with society and to cope with the pressures of the nonprison environment. After all, it is these pressures and adjustments that the offender must contend with upon leaving prison.

Finally, community-based programs permit a broader range of programs and corrective strategies than is possible under traditional forms of imprisonment. By utilizing existing community resources, these correctional programs can provide a wide range of treatment specialists who would otherwise not be available to prisoners.

Because of these benefits, the importance of community-based programming efforts is now being recognized. This in turn is bringing about several important changes in prison systems throughout the country. Offenders who do not require close supervision are increasingly being involved in these programs. And to accommodate the gradual movement of an increasing number of inmates into these programs, structural and operational changes are now taking place within a number of state prison systems. For instance, the massive institutions built in rural areas for reasons of isolation and security are slowly giving way to the development and construction of smaller, multipurpose facilities located nearer population centers.

It is also a fact of programming today that slowly but inexorably, community resources and personnel are being used more in the correctional effort. A number of specialized programs have been developed, such as work and study release, restitution programs, and furloughs to help the inmate bridge the gap between life inside and outside prison. Some of the more widely adopted and popular programs based on the community-based model are discussed in the pages that follow.

## ⬚ BASIS FOR COMMUNITY-BASED CORRECTONS: DIVERISON

**Aspects of diversion**

The basic idea behind community-based corrections is diversion: directing offenders away from the traditional process of imprisonment. This is not to be interpreted to mean that offenders should not be subject to certain aspects of the justice process or that penalties should not be imposed for their actions. What diversion means is that in the interests of what we are trying to accomplish, there may be better methods outside the traditional ways that the justice system operates to deal with certain problems and offenders. Diversion as a term has several meanings in actual application. Used in connection with *preventive strategies*, it means that offenders are diverted from criminal behavior so that they will not come in contact with the justice system to begin with. This approach, most commonly used in juvenile corrections, relies on parents, police, schools, agencies, and peers to address social problems in such a way that the individual does not become involved in antisocial behavior.

If the preventive approach fails, diversion also means diversion from the criminal justice system itself, or at least diverting offenders from the conventional ways the justice system usually handles offenders. For example, it can mean diverting convicted offenders to a form of community supervision such as probation rather than imprisonment. In this chapter, the *term is used to indicate diverting incarcerated offenders to special programs and institutions instead of warehousing them in a conventional prison*. The use of diversion in this manner was brought about by four important factors: the failure of traditional methods, the impact of the community, the growing demands of interest groups, and prison and jail overcrowding.

### Failure of Traditional Methods

The usual means of handling offenders has been an abysmal failure. We saw from Chapter 14 the lack of success of those released from our prisons. And there seems to be little in the way of assurance that prisoners released from states with more "progressive" penal systems that spend more money on the operations of their correctional systems fare any better than those released from other states. The chilling fact is that little seems to make any difference. At least, we can find nothing to appreciably suggest that imprisonment works or that it deters those it incarcerates. Whether or not imprisonment actually contributes to crime, as suggested by liberals, also goes unproven. All we can say with certainty is that traditional imprisonment as measured by repeat postrelease offenses is, for the majority of offenders, simply a black hole that gobbles up costly public resources.

### Impact of the Community

**Contribution of the community to criminal behavior**

The idea that social forces in the community have a favorable or unfavorable impact on the individual is by no means new. Studies conducted in the late 1920s and the early 1930s by a group of sociologists at the University of Chicago pointed out that community disorganization contributed significantly to criminal behavior. Out of this research developed the famous Chicago Area Projects, which focused on providing casework assistance to gangs and neighborhood youths to prevent crime and to interest the youths in noncriminal activities.[4] These early projects provide the theoretical basis for community-based corrections. Since that time, other studies have confirmed the importance of the community on behavior.[5]

Although the community can have both negative and positive effects, placing an offender in a prison often strengthens the negative influences. Separated from any positive influences of noncriminal elements of the community, the offender falls back on the influences of fellow inmates. Through the process of socialization, the prisoner is often likely to become even more pro-criminal and less willing and able to identify with more appropriate noncriminal references in the outside world on release. Under these circumstances, the inmate is likely to seek associations in the community that hold similar attitudes to those he or she became accustomed to while in prison. The community-based correctional idea realizes that offenders must be encouraged to identify and maintain whatever ties they have with law-abiding members of society, which incarceration usually severs; at the same time, these programs recognize the need to provide offenders with appropriate supervision and help in order to limit their exposure to those who encourage continued criminal behavior.

Although it is recognized that community contacts can be helpful to an offender, it is also becoming increasingly apparent that community contacts also have a down side. In some of our drug-wracked urban neighborhoods, community contact may not be in the best interest of the offender. Although the influences of the prison may be bad, continued association with drug dealers and the violence associated with these areas may be even worse. This is the kind of assessment that must be applied in consideration of a community placement as opposed to conventional imprisonment.

## Growing Demands of Interest Groups

Interested citizens both within and outside the criminal justice system have become increasingly alarmed at the failure of our traditional correctional institutions to "correct" and are waging a campaign to encourage the adoption of alternative means for dealing with some offenders. They are using public reaction, such as the *New York Times* survey that showed that 69 percent of Americans had lost confidence in the ability of prisons to rehabilitate offenders,[6] as a means to encourage correctional officials to seek out alternative programs.

These four factors—the problems of prison overcrowding, the failure of the criminal justice system and conventional prisons to deter crime or prevent its recurrence, recognition that the community has a significant impact on behavior, and the growing involvement of interest groups in penal reform—are changing some aspects of our traditional responses to crime and encouraging more efforts in the direction of diversion, with its emphasis on movement away from traditional imprisonment and the justice system.[7] In the years ahead, we shall probably see more community-based programs in which established agencies of justice relinquish their conventional handling and responses to criminal behavior in favor of programs involving existing aspects of the community.[8]

*Factors contributing to diversion and alternate strategies*

## The Relationship of Diversion to Reintegration

Both the immediate and long-range goals of diversion as a correctional technique are to offer the means for successful reintegration of the offender into community life as a law-abiding citizen. To achieve this, the concept of community-based corrections is guided by three considerations:

Linking institutional life to the free world

1. More realistic adaptation of institutional life to realities of life in the community. Prisons, jails, and juvenile institutions need to introduce changes that will make conditions in them more similar to conditions in a free society. This does not mean that inmates should be provided with a host of creature amenities. It does mean that within the need for necessary security and requirements for discipline, inmates be confined under conditions conducive to developing more self-generated control rather than induced and forced control through discipline and regimentation. This will permit the observations of behavior under conditions more similar to the natural environment to which almost all inmates will someday return. It will also likely lessen inmate hostility and the development or reinforcement of negative anti-authority and antisocial attitudes.

   It also recognizes that supportive ties of a positive nature may be very critical to successful treatment and readjustment. For example, maintenance of such positive ties as family need to be encouraged and sustained.

Link to community assistance agencies

2. Link to other community assistance agencies. Correctional efforts and resources are limited. A wide variety of organizations, public and private, offer services to people who need help. Many inmates need these same types of service and assistance. Examples are vocational rehabilitation, mental health, family counseling, and drug and alcohol abuse programs. There must be a bridging by corrections to use these services to help corrections achieve its own goals.

Community involvement

3. Civic engagement and participation. Both by means of formal organizations and through the assistance of individuals, there is increasing recognition that volunteer citizen participation offers tremendous potential for working with offender reintegration programs. Traditionally, this civic participation has come from established religious, social service, and employer groups. The correctional field needs to learn more effective methods of engaging these resources and applying their help.[9]

## COMMUNITY-BASED PROGRAMS

At present, there are several common types of community-based programs. They are known as work-release, academic-pass, conjugal and family visit, and home furlough programs.

### Work-Release Programs

History

Under work-release programs, selected inmates are released from the institution during the day to go to their jobs in the community while spending daily afterwork hours and weekends in confinement. Vermont started the first work-release program in 1906. Its legislature enacted a law providing for civilian employment and authorized county sheriffs to set their prisoners to work outside the jail. Sheriff Frank H. Tracey of Montpelier, unsuccessful in his efforts to find employers, hired some of his prisoners to work on his own farm at the prevailing rates paid civilian laborers. Part of the prisoner's earnings was paid to the state, and the remainder was retained by Sheriff Tracey and given to the prisoners when they finished their jail sentences. This early form of work release had most, if not all, the basic elements found in today's work-release programs.[10]

Although Vermont is credited with the original idea, the Huber Act, passed by Wisconsin in 1913, is the model on which modern work-release programs are based. The act provided that county jail inmates, with the permission of the court, could be enrolled in work-release programs under the supervision of the sheriff. In 1957, a North Carolina statute extended work release to offenders in state institutions, but only certain misdemeanants recommended for work release by sentencing judges were eligible. In 1959, North Carolina passed new provisions that extended eligibility to certain classes of felony offenders. By 1971, forty-one states and the District of Columbia had adopted work-release programs. Today, all states have such programs. The Prisoner Rehabilitation Act, passed by Congress in 1965, authorized the U.S. Bureau of Prisons to use work-release programs.[11] (See Figure 15.1.) Still, less than 1 percent of America's prison inmates were in some kind of work-release program when the last major survey of corrections was taken in 1984.[12]

States that have implemented work-release programs usually follow one of two established approaches or a combination of the two. In the older approach, **Approaches** prisoners work in the community while living in the correctional institution. This arrangement has caused some problems for both prison officials and inmates who participate in the program. The work releasees may be harassed and intimidated by nonparticipating inmates, who accuse them of being "privileged characters." This might lead to situations in which qualified inmates refuse to participate in such programs. Another problem is controlling the flow of contraband smuggled back into the institution by work releasees, either voluntarily or as a result of inmate

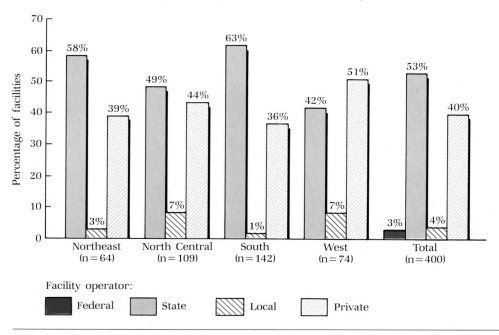

Operator of community-based pre-release facilities by region—1978 (missing information from two pre-release centers.) [*Source: Survey of Adult Community-Based Pre-Release Facilities (PC-3),* 1978, as reported in National Institute of Justice, *American Prisons and Jails,* Vol. V (Washington, D.C.: U.S. Government Printing Office, October 1980), p. 12.]

FIGURE **15.1**

intimidation and threats. A third problem is that many prisons are situated in relatively remote areas where job opportunities in neighboring communities are very limited.

The second approach, which is more popular, is to use a special small facility situated near an urban center as a residential unit for inmates on work release. This arrangement seems to have overcome many of the problems associated with trying to administer a program from the prison itself.

Advantages

**ADVANTAGES AND LIMITATIONS OF WORK RELEASE.** Work-release programs have advantages for the inmate and for the state. These programs permit the inmate to develop contacts and work experience not usually available within the prison. In this way, the individual becomes better prepared for eventual release. By establishing himself or herself in a job while still in prison, the offender has immediate employment upon release and does not face the problem of trying to find legitimate work with the associated stigma of being an ex-convict. Work experiences can also be beneficial to many inmates who have failed to develop appropriate work habits throughout their lives. Prison industries have not been shown to be very effective in developing appropriate work habits, but work-release programs can help overcome some of these problems.[13]

The second major advantage is economic. As pointed out in the previous chapter, it is very costly to keep an offender in prison, especially an inmate who supports a family. In work release, inmates are required to pay for their own room and board and to provide support for their families. A prescribed portion of their earnings is taken out by prison officials for these purposes. A small sum is retained by the inmates to purchase necessities, and any remainder is put into a special fund that the offenders receive upon release.

Work-release programs give inmates the opportunity to earn wages and to function in a community work environment. (Courtesy Eckerd Family Youth Alternatives)

A number of studies have been conducted to determine the effectiveness of Effectiveness work-release programs. One of the largest and most intensive studies was made of work releases in Santa Clara County, California. Data were gathered from the post-institutional adjustment records of nearly a thousand inmates who had been on work release and compared with an equal number of prisoners who had not. The inmates in the sample had been released from the institution during a four-year period.[14] Among other things, the study indicated that inmates who had partici-pated in work-release programs felt closer ties to their families and that their fam-ilies were more predisposed to accept them, whereas families of nonparticipating inmates were more likely to reject them. Work releasees displayed slightly greater hostility toward the criminal justice system. The researchers felt that the reason for this was that individuals in the work-release program were less likely to perceive themselves as criminals and, thus, were more resentful of the police, courts, and corrections for their incarceration. The work releasees also were more successful in maintaining jobs during the period following their release. Finally, the work releasees were less likely to be rearrested and convicted for the commission of additional crimes after their release.[15]

Work release also has some problems associated with it. One of the major problems is trying to ensure that the inmate doesn't succumb to certain pressures. Disadvantages For instance, care must be taken to ensure that he or she doesn't slip away to drink or take narcotics while on work release. Although a well-adjusted member of society could ignore these temptations, many offenders show a predisposition toward lack of self-control. As a result, these temptations may be too much for the individual to handle. Many administrators of work-release programs go to great lengths to control such behavior, such as requiring that all individuals participating in the program take Antabuse, a substance that induces nausea if one drinks alcoholic beverages. Likewise, periodic urine specimens are taken to determine if the work releasee has taken narcotics. Some programs also drop the individual at the work site in the morning and pick him or her up when the day's work is finished.

Another negative consequence of work release is that these programs often compete directly with prison industries. If a prison system uses the work-release plan intensively, many well-motivated and skilled workers are diverted from prison industry programs. Unscrupulous private employers may also exploit the individual on work release because of his or her vulnerability.

A criticism of work release—and similar alternative programs—is that they cater predominantly to low-risk candidates. It is these low-risk inmates who are most likely to succeed even without the benefit of the program. The prisoners who need to be reached are typically the ones excluded from such programs because of their lack of qualifications, poor work habits, bad attitudes, or other qualities that make them less acceptable to correctional officials and program employers. Those prisoners who need the most help and who might benefit the most (but are risks) are denied the opportunity to participate in these programs.

## Academic-Pass Programs

Academic-pass or study-release programs are similar to work-release programs in that inmates are permitted to leave the institution to attend school and return to the prison or community facility after class. Most academic-pass programs use nearby educational institutions, such as vocational-trade institutes, junior and com-munity colleges, and universities.

The Michigan Department of Corrections contracts with that state's regional network of community colleges to provide degree programs both inside the penal facility and at the community college. All costs for tuition, books, and other supplies are paid for by the state. One of the most extensive study programs is the cooperative program between Jackson Community College and Southern Michigan Penitentiary. It is not unusual in that program to find correctional employees and inmates sitting in the same classroom with regular students, exchanging and sharing viewpoints, and perhaps gaining new perspectives through such an interchange.

One interesting program, which had its beginning in Oregon, was the New Gate Project. This project was sponsored by the National Council on Crime and Delinquency. This program was designed to offer inmates the opportunity to obtain an on-campus university education. In conjunction with cooperating universities, selected inmates were enrolled in academic programs and lived like other students in university residence halls or dormitories. They were required to refrain from use of alcoholic beverages and narcotics and were required to report to supervising counselors in their dormitories at least once a week. The cost of this program is about the same as maintaining an unmarried prisoner in a traditional penitentiary.[16]

The purpose of academic-pass programs is, of course, to enable deserving, interested inmates to obtain the education and job skills necessary to lead legitimate and productive lives on their return to society. Through education, it is hoped that they can assimilate more appropriate values and become contributing members of society.

## Conjugal and Family Visitation Programs

Conjugal visitation is a program by which the spouse and in some cases the children of an inmate are permitted to visit in a special facility of the prison. Usually, a separate section of the prison or small cottages are made available. Here the inmate may have privacy and engage in the physical phase of the conjugal relationship. Advocates of conjugal visitation programs say that these programs help inmates maintain meaningful ties with their families. It is also said to reduce the

incidence of homosexuality among inmates. Those opposed to such programs argue that: (1) conjugal visits are incompatible with existing moral values, because they emphasize the physical satisfaction of sex; (2) married inmates who participate in these programs are those individuals who can best adjust to prison life anyway; (3) those inmates who present the greatest sexual problems—that is, homosexuals and sex deviates—won't benefit from the program; (4) such programs offer no solution to the sexual tensions of single male or female prisoners; (5) wives may become pregnant, creating further problems for the state and the inmates; and (6) the maintenance of these separate, private facilities is too costly.[17]

Conjugal visits were first established in the United States at the Parchman Prison farm in Mississippi in 1918. At this institution, a "little red house" was set aside for the use of inmates and their wives. More recently, the California State Prison at Tehachapi instituted a somewhat similar program. At Tehachapi, housing that had previously been occupied by the staff has been set up to accommodate family visits. Eligible inmates are permitted to use this facility for a two- or three-day period during the prerelease phase of their sentence. This situation more closely resembles the full family setting. Facilities for cooking and recreation are provided, and children are included.

The Latin American countries and a number of Western European nations have for many years sanctioned conjugal visits. Many Latin American countries do not restrict their programs to male inmates as do American institutions with such programs; in certain cases, female inmates are permitted conjugal visits with their husbands. Some Latin American nations even permit male inmates to engage the services of prositutes, who are brought into the prison.[18]

The value of conjugal or family visiting programs is unclear. There is some evidence that the fears of those who argue against them have not been realized. On the other hand, there also exists no well-documented evidence that such programs have been very successful in meeting the objectives of their proponents.

Michael S. Serill, writing for *Corrections Magazine*, describes the operation of the family visiting program at California's San Quentin Penitentiary in the article quoted.[19]

## Home Furlough Programs

In place of the conjugal visit, more and more states are trying home furlough programs. These programs should be distinguished from emergency release programs in which an inmate is allowed to return home temporarily because of a serious situation in the immediate family, such as a death or grave illness, and is often accompanied by a supervising custodial officer. In home furlough programs, the inmate returns home for a few days without supervision.

In 1918, Mississippi was the first state to introduce furlough programs; these were 10-day holiday leaves for minimum-custody inmates. Today almost all states have home furlough programs for adult offenders.[20] Most have similar basic criteria for determining an inmate's eligibility for home furlough: (1) the security risk, which is based on the adjustment the individual has made while in prison and the type of crime for which he or she was sentenced; and (2) the time remaining to serve, which, in many instances, has to be served under minimum-security conditions. Sex offenders are almost always excluded.[21]

The correctional officials in Connecticut, Illinois, Michigan, and other states with large furlough programs contend that furloughs are only one part of an overall program designed to build a solid base of community and family support *before* the inmate walks out the front gate of the prison. Another benefit of furloughs, they say, is that they improve morale in institutions and give parole boards something tangible to look at when deciding whether an offender should be released.

Such programs are often controversial. This was the case in Massachusetts. This state had a program by which inmates serving life sentences for murder could ultimately participate in furlough programs. One such inmate serving a sentence for murder was given a furlough and during his release killed again. The public was outraged. This incident even became an issue in the presidential election of 1988. George Bush, the Republican candidate, attacked his Democratic opponent, Michael Dukakis, the governor of Massachusetts at the time, for allowing this to happen. Dukakis was not the first politician to feel the backlash of a state prison furlough policy in which this or a similar incident occurred. This is the most typical criticism of such programs. Opponents argue that furlough releasees will commit new crimes during their period of freedom from the institution. Unfortunately, in a few instances this has happened and has heightened the controversy. Another frequently expressed fear is that releasees will flee. Finally, there are those who contend that such programs increase the risk that additional children will be born

*[Margin note: Defined and contrasted]*

*[Margin note: History]*

*[Margin note: Controversy surrounding]*

Richard Schwerdtfeger pulled his station wagon up to the gate of San Quentin prison and began unloading box after box of groceries. The boxes, along with several pieces of luggage, were searched by a guard and transferred to an electric cart inside the prison gate. Schwerdtfeger, his wife, and his daughter, Joanna, piled into the cart themselves and chugged off to the main prison several hundred yards away. The cart passed through an electric gate leading to a triangular patch of grass enclosed by a high fence topped with barbed wire. Forming two sides of the triangle were the walls of two of San Quentin's giant cellblocks. The third side was a cliff leading down to San Francisco Bay.

Within the enclosure were three 2-bedroom house trailers, each twelve by sixty feet. They were recently purchased by the California Department of Corrections for $6,000 each. The Schwerdtfegers, very excited, began moving their luggage and boxes of groceries into one of the trailers. Suddenly, a young man appeared—their son, Michael. Michael, twenty-nine, has been a resident of San Quentin for six and a half years. His crimes: murder, kidnapping, and robbery. His sentence: death, commuted four years ago to life without possiblity of parole.

The Schwerdtfegers had been a very tightly knit family, they said, and had come to visit Michael frequently. But this was their first opportunity to see him privately, thanks to the Department of Corrections' "family visiting program." The program was "outstanding," according to the elder Schwerdtfeger, a heavyset, jolly man with a bushy gray mustache. Just to be able to sit down and eat a meal with his son, to sit comfortably and talk, to watch television—it would be so much more "normal," he said, than the crowded atmosphere in the San Quentin visiting room. The family had been granted a nineteen-hour visit.

California's family visiting program has been in operation seven years now and Department of Corrections officials are as enthusiastic about it as they ever were. Twelve of the department's thirteen institutions permitted 9,000 private visits with wives, parents, and other relatives through the program last year and the department has plans to expand it to perhaps double that size.

The visits last either nineteen or forty-three hours, and take place in the privacy of prison outbuildings and furnished trailers purchased for that purpose. New trailers, like those at San Quentin, have been installed within the security areas of several institutions so that all inmates except those in maximum security will have a chance to participate.

At San Quentin the man in charge of the program is Sergeant Hal Brown, a sixteen-year veteran of the prison. In June, about 150 of the prison's 2,400 inmates were enrolled in the program, Brown said, and many more qualify. Medium-security inmates, like Michael Schwerdtfeger, have their visits in the trailers inside the walls, while minimum-security men occupy seven apartments in two houses outside the walls.

Though inmates' wives are the most frequent visitors, Brown said, to call the program "conjugal visiting" would be a misnomer. To prove his point, Brown noted that in April there were 114 visits and 267 visitors; in May there were 87 visits and 174 visitors—meaning that many children and other relatives also come.

To qualify for the program, inmates must have twelve months "clean time," must never have been caught introducing contraband into the prison, and cannot be designated as a "mentally disordered sex offender." Wives must bring their marriage licenses with them to be admitted. The program operates six days a week, and visitors must supply all the food for the visits.

Correction officers are not permitted inside the apartments and trailers while a visit is going on; inmates are instructed to appear outside at certain hours of the day for the regular count.

Inmates can generally get a nineteen-hour visit about every twenty days, Brown said, and a

to "problem families."[22] It should be recognized that society faces similar hazards from inmates released on parole, and in most respects, furlough releasees are less likely to get into trouble than parolees. In the first place, because fewer individuals are released on furlough, correction officials can examine all the factors and can be much more selective of the inmates chosen to participate in these programs. Second, the criteria for participation in such a program are much more demanding than those for parole eligibility. Because correctional officials will be blamed if an individual on furlough does get into trouble, they are generally very careful in their selection of home furlough releasees.

forty-three-hour visit about every forty days. In mid-June, the forty-three-hour visits were booked until September 29. "A nucleus of people get twice as many visits as anyone else," Brown said, because when there is a last minute cancellation there are a few wives who live near the prison and can be there within thirty minutes.

Brown, who handles the entire program alone, is well liked by both the visitors and inmates. The visitors greet him by his first name and give him kisses. He is the only staff member ever to have gotten a "certificate of appreciation" from the Black Muslims inside the prison for his "courtesy, fairness and helpful manner." Brown explained his popularity by saying that he is "flexible" in running the program. "It's not a normal thing to go to a state prison for a family visit, so you've got to give a little bit."

Despite the fact that he is heavily overworked, spending up to five hours a day of his own time on the program, Brown says that "Not one inmate is going to suffer. No visitor is going to suffer. . . . I'm going to do it [alone] to the best of my ability because I believe in it."

The sergeant says the family visiting program has been a "tremendous boost to morale in this institution. . . . The thing that really impresses me is that we're saving inmates, and we're saving kids." Brown contends that the initial op-position to the program by the line staff has largely dissipated.

Officials in other states largely oppose conjugal or family visiting within institutions, partly on the grounds that the same objective could be better accomplished through home furloughs. But Sergeant Brown pointed out that the great majority of inmates at San Quentin and other California institutions will never have a chance of furloughs, and said that the family visiting program is a viable alternative.

It has also been charged that conjugal visiting is degrading to both the inmate and his wife. But all Brown sees is "tremendous joy, happiness. People have the desire to be together and they don't [care] where. . . . [Furthermore] I don't think these guys are hunting for sex alone. The drive is to be with the people they love, to be with their families."

While the Schwerdtfegers were moving into their trailer in the medium-security visiting area, another group of people, and a swarm of children, were unpacking their groceries and making coffee in the two family visiting houses outside the walls.

George 2X Jackson and his wife, Cynthia 2X, sat down in the living room of the "pink house" to talk to a visitor, while their two-year-old son George, Jr. romped happily on the rug. Jackson, doing one-to-fourteen years for forgery, said the family visiting program is "the best thing that ever happened" to California prisoners.

Jackson said he has been receiving visits since November 1973, when he was classified minimum custody, and has had two or three a month ever since.

Jackson said he was married once before when he started another term in prison in 1968. He snapped his fingers, indicating that the marriage immediately broke up. "No contact," he said. "Across the table [in the visiting room] it's not real. There is no contact. You've got to be able to touch to maintain romantic love."

Asked whether he thought the program was degrading, Jackson bristled and escorted his visitor to his family's living quarters, which consisted of one large room with a bed, other furniture, and a private bath. "Is this degrading?" he asked. "We are Muslims. We respect our women. If I thought this degraded her, I would never do it."

To those who say that the family visiting program is more than any criminal deserves, Jackson replies: "Though we have broken the rules, we're still human. We still breathe and eat and love."

*Source:* Reprinted with permission from Michael S. Serrill, "Family Visiting at San Quentin," *Corrections Magazine,* August 1975.

There are some sound arguments in favor of home furlough programs. An inmate's behavior and adjustment during temporary release gives correctional officers an opportunity to gauge the suitability of the individual for eventual parole. Home furlough allows outside facilities and resources to be utilized more fully, thus reducing the need to build, staff, equip, and supply certain institutional programs. For example, certain prerelease activities, such as mock job interviews, could be replaced by direct "real" experience, and the family's home could be used rather than special facilities constructed within the institution for family visits. Such programs might also work against the general trend of family dissolution, which is **Arguments for** often a result of extended incarceration.[23] Prison officials also point out that experience with home furlough programs makes the inmates more cooperative, more willing to obey orders from correctional guards, and more willing to participate in prison programs.[24]

Like other community-based insttutional programs, home furlough programs will undoubtedly continue to be used as an alternative to long-standing correctional practices. As with so many aspects of correctional programming, it is an area that needs further study and the development of sound policies to guide its use. Otherwise, situations such as the one that occurred in Massachusetts will hamper its availability to both correctional officials and inmates.

## ☐ TYPES OF COMMUNITY-BASED FACILITIES

To assist the inmate or parolee in returning to community life, there are several programs and facilities at his or her disposal. They are prerelease guidance centers, halfway houses, community corrections centers, and the use of victim restitution programs.

### The Prerelease Guidance Center

Defined

Prerelease guidance centers are facilities where inmates are sent three to twelve months before their release on parole.[25] They are usually located near urban areas. Their purpose is to help in the adjustment of inmates from institutional life to free society by gradually exposing them to fewer controls. To offset the dependency syndrome that often accompanies extended incarceration, inmates in these settings are encouraged to be more independent in a positive sense.

Operational characteristics

The U.S. Bureau of Prisons began gradually in the 1960s to establish a network of these centers in major urban areas throughout the United States. When a deserving inmate is within a few months of release, he or she is sent to one of these centers, ideally, in or near his home city. Each center closely supervises about twenty federal prisoners.

Inmates wear civilian clothes at the center. Following orientation sessions, they are encouraged to go out into the community and obtain employment. As time passes and they begin to show that they are adjusting, they are given more freedom. As their parole date approaches, some may even be permitted to move out of the center, although they are still required to return for counseling sessions and conferences several times a week.[26]

These centers are often staffed by specialists in counseling therapy who are rotated from regular institutional staff. Several of these programs utilize carefully screened college students in the behavioral sciences, who work with youthful offenders as paraprofessional counselors. These student-counselors often also assist the regular staff by providing coverage during the late night hours and on weekends.[27] An important feature of this concept is the active involvement of federal parole officers in the counseling sessions. In this way, the parole officer who will assume the individual counseling responsibility when the inmate is placed on parole has the opportunity to interact with the inmate before his or her release. George Killinger and Paul F. Cromwell give us some insight into how the program functions:

When an individual returns from a temporary release to home, work or school, his experience can be discussed with him by staff, to try to assess his probable adjustment and to note incipient problems. Many difficulties can be anticipated in this way. The inmate's anxieties can be relieved by discussion, and discussion may also help him develop realistic plans for coping with prospective problems. When persistent or serious misbehavior occurs, sanctions are available to staff, ranging from restriction of further leaves or temporary incarceration to renewed institutionalization, with recommendation to the parole board that the date of parole be deferred.[28]

A number of states have developed similar prerelease centers, and cooperative arrangements have been made between the U.S. Bureau of Prisons and some states in the development and utilization of such programs. For example, federal prerelease guidance centers in Detroit and Kansas City have received state inmates, and in a couple of states the federal prison system has sent its prisoners to state centers prior to their release. In this manner, duplication of facilities is avoided through cooperative correctional programming. Unfortunately, such cooperative programs have been sharply curtailed in recent years because of the large increase in federal prisoners and the need for the U.S. Bureau of Prisons to give priority to its own inmates.

## Halfway Houses

Another idea in community-based corrections is the halfway house. Indeed, the prerelease guidance center is a form of halfway house, because it can be considered a "halfway-out" facility. Other programs are considered "halfway-in." The concept of the halfway house is not new. A special study commission in 1820 recommended that Massachusetts establish such programs.[29] In 1864, Boston opened a halfway house for women released from that state's prison system. In a few years, religious and volunteer groups opened similar facilities in Philadelphia, New York, Chicago, and New Orleans. All these operations were privately supported and managed. One well-intentioned group opened a halfway house for ex-convicts in New York in 1896. This facility, known as Hope Hall, was run by a husband-and-wife team who, because of their action, suffered such police intimidation and harassment that they appealed to the President of the United States to intercede in their behalf and to restrain the police.[30]

History

The purpose of these early halfway houses was similar to their use today. They were founded to provide ex-convicts a temporary place of shelter, food, clothing, advice, and aid in obtaining gainful employment.[31] The founders of these early halfway houses were the pioneers of community-based treatment centers. Unfortunately, they were often scorned and held in contempt by professional correctional workers. They also often met with a great deal of hostility and resentment from the communities in which they were located as well as from the public and law enforcement officials.

Characteristics

In the 1950s, interest in the halfway-house concept was renewed. Like their earlier counterparts, these modern halfway houses were also privately sponsored by interested citizens or religious organizations. In the 1970s and 1980s, there has been a renewed interest in halfway houses supported by public monies and managed by professional correctional personnel. Federal legislation was also passed authorizing the use of halfway houses for federal parolees who are having difficulty

Program characteristics

Halfway houses allow inmates to adjust gradually to the freedom and responsibility of life in the community. (Ellis Herwig/Stock Boston)

adjusting to free society and who appear to be running the risk of parole revocation. Rather than waiting for failure and having to recommit the individual to prison, the alternative is to send the ex-offender to a community treatment center for additional counseling and supervision.

The federal government has also been developing what can be referred to as "halfway-in" programs. In the early 1970s, Congress authorized the federal courts to direct a probationer to reside or participate in the program of a community treatment center as a condition of probation and as an alternative to prison incarceration. By the early 1980s, the U.S. Bureau of Prisons operated such institutions throughout the United States and had contracts with several hundred halfway houses run by state, local, or private agencies.[32]

One interesting such program, known as Probationed Offenders Rehabilitation and Training (PORT), was established on a multicounty basis in Minnesota. This program provided an alternative for male offenders who required a greater change in their life-style than probation can accomplish and yet did not belong in prison. The program provided for a live-in residence facility on the grounds of a state hospital. Both felons and misdemeanants were sentenced to this institution by the courts in the sponsoring three-county area. The program was supervised by a corporate board of directors, made up of citizens in the area as well as local and county law enforcement and probation officials. Special efforts were made to enroll the offenders in educational institutions in the community, to find work for them, and to expose them to professional treatment and interaction with lay volunteers made up of interested citizens and students in nearby colleges.[33]

It is likely that the use of halfway houses will continue to grow in the years ahead and that these facilities will play new and important roles. For example, they might be used increasingly for individuals with special difficulties, such as drug abuse, alcoholism, and nondangerous psychiatric problems. In an effort to serve these target groups, halfway houses will require a larger share of the correctional manpower and resources now being applied to the maintenance of traditional prisons. One interesting proposal is that halfway houses could serve still another important function. With the advent of bail reform, individuals who can meet certain criteria are being released on their own recognizance. One of the usual requirements is that the individual have roots in the community. Many accused individuals, however, have weak or nonexistent family ties and poor work histories. Not meeting some of the basic criteria, they are excluded from the use of recognizance bond and must await final disposition in jail. The halfway house could enable such inmates to become eligible for recognizance bond. At a minimum, this would include providing shelter and supervision prior to final disposition. Whether the accused is found guilty or not, he or she is usually in need of a range of services that the halfway house is often in a position to provide, directly or indirectly, such as medical, dental, psychological, and psychiatric services, and individual and group counseling. The delays that occur between the time of arrest and final disposition are often lengthy, in some cases six months or more. Even if the process is speeded up and the time from arrest to final disposition is reduced to two or three months, some things might still be accomplished during this time.[34] Although an innovative idea, the likelihood of halfway houses providing this additional service is remote. Resources for such services are usually unavailable to local governments. It is also likely that community and/or law enforcement opposition might pose problems.

## The Community Corrections Center

A number of states are developing community-based correctional institutions (sometimes called residential treatment facilities) in selected city neighborhoods in an effort to reduce the isolation of offenders from community services and other resources. Most of these centers require that the individual reside in the center. Characteristics He or she may be released for short periods to work or visit with family but must return to the center at night. Others are centers for released offenders, such as individuals on parole. Special services and programs are available to help the released offenders. If they are having a difficult time adjusting to release, they are encouraged to come to the center for assistance and counseling. As an extension of parole or postrelease services, such a center can draw on the medical, social work, psychiatric, educational, and employment resources of the entire community and can involve community, neighborhood residents, and family members in offender rehabilitation and reintegration.

At the present time, there appears to be no single model for the facilities or program design of a community corrections center. However, one of the most promising proposals has resulted from a project undertaken by the Institute for the Study of Crime and Delinquency. This project was designed to develop a program concept and an architectural design for a community-based center for young adult offenders that would be located in a high-delinquency area from which its residents would be largely drawn.[35] This so-called youth correctional center would employ a three-stage program. In stage I, which lasts for approximately a month, the offender would be housed in a medium-security residential unit where he or she would be strictly confined at all times under close security. If the offender is successful, he or she would be moved to stage II for placement in a less custody-oriented unit. The offender would then have limited access to the outside community for work, school, or other activities and would be in this phase of the program for several months. In stage III the offender would reside in the community and return to the unit at least once a week or more for group meetings and special services. This part of the program would last for a period of about twenty months. If the offender was unsuccessful at any stage he or she would be sent to a traditional institution.[36]

## Victim Restitution

Another alternative to incarceration or probation is victim restitution. Generally, it Application is used in one of two ways: (1) as a condition of probation whereby the court will grant probation to an offender if he or she agrees to make restitution to the victim during the period of probation; or (2) in conjunction with incarceration. For example, as a condition of work release (and generally early parole), the imprisoned inmate agrees to repay the victim from his or her earnings. It is in a few jurisdictions, sometimes employed as a condition of weekend incarceration. For instance, in the handling of some types of cases, the offender may serve jail time on the weekends and be free to work at a job during the week, or alternatively to return to the jail at night after working at a job during the day. Either way, the court may demand that the offender make restitution to the victim out of earned wages.

Victim restitution programs are different in several ways from the victim com- As compared to victim compensation pensation programs discussed in Chapter 3. First, restitution is a form of payment directly from the offender to the victim. In victim compensation programs, the state compensates the victim from a public fund set aside for such a purpose. Second, the states administer these programs through commissions or boards, and the victim files a claim with these agencies in much the same way as an insurance claim is filed. On the other hand, victim restitution programs are administered directly by criminal justice agencies—usually the courts or corrections.[37]

There are many issues involved in the concept of victim restitution, such as determining the amount of restitution; the hardship that payment might impose on indigent offenders; the prospects that restitution, if used as the sole correctional program, might allow certain offenders to purchase their freedom with relative ease; and the weight that should be given to the views of the victim.[38] Because these issues cannot be thoroughly discussed in an introductory text, the interested reader is encouraged to read the developing literature in this area.[39]

## ▢ SOME ISSUES AND TRENDS SHAPING CORRECTIONS

This section discusses several aspects of correctional change that have had or hold the promise of having a particular impact on the operations of our nation's prisons and correctional institutions. By no means is this an exhaustive list; it merely highlights the more significant change-inducing factors and those that hold promise for bringing about future change.

### Judicial Review of Inmate Rights

Several of the earlier editions of this book explored the issue of expanding rights of inmates in detail. In the past several years, this has become less of an issue for at least two reasons. First, this area of the law has become more settled. Enough precedent exists to ensure that inmates are entitled to certain rights and considerations. This has become a recognized and established part of correctional operations today. This subject has also received less attention in recent years because the novelty of the idea that convicted and incarcerated prisoners have certain rights has worn off; it simply has become more commonly accepted. Another contributing factor is the slow-down among the federal courts—particularly the U.S. Supreme Court—in their willingness to further extend these rights beyond those that now exist. The issue, it would seem, has just about reached its limits. It is, however, an interesting area of inquiry that mirrors some important changes that have occurred in corrections. For this reason, it is worthy of brief examination.

*As an issue today*

Since the late 1960s, the courts, particularly those at the federal level, have been applying broad constitutional standards to the operations of penal institutions. In so doing, the courts held that prisoners have certain rights that are no different from the rights of a free citizen. This trend was nothing less than a fundamental reinterpretation of the law. In the past, an offender, as a matter of law, was considered to have forfeited virtually all rights upon conviction and to have retained only those rights expressly granted by statute or the correctional authority.[40] The offender was considered a noncitizen and excluded from the constitutional protections afforded free members of society.

*Traditional philosophy*

The National Advisory Commission on Criminal Justice Standards and Goals succinctly points out the former status of convicted offenders and the attitudes of the courts:

> The courts refused for the most part to intervene. Judges felt that correctional administration was a technical matter to be left to experts rather than to courts, which were deemed ill-equipped to make appropriate evaluations. And, to the extent that courts believed the offenders' complaints involved privileges rather than rights, there was no special necessity to confront correctional practices, even when they infringed on basic notions of human rights and dignity protected for other groups by constitutional doctrine.[41]

This attitude existed because society cared very little about corrections and even less about convicts themselves. The changes have occurred because beginning in the 1960s society itself became more concerned. The closer scrutiny of correctional practices was just one result of society's more sweeping concern for individual rights and governmental accountability, particularly of the executive branch, of which corrections is a part. This concern had its beginnings with the civil rights movement and was reflected in such areas as juvenile justice, public welfare, mental institutions, and military justice. Part of the growth of reform in correctional institutions and policies arose from the fact that corrections was for the first time being scrutinized, and to some extent experienced, by large segments of society who formerly had had no contact with the system of justice and corrections in particular. The correctional experiences of dissenting groups, many of whom came from middle-class backgrounds, acted as a catalyst for change in the entire justice process. Reasons for change

Finally, the courts could no longer ignore the questionable effectiveness of correctional systems as rehabilitative instruments, combined with the unbelievable conditions existing in many penal institutions. As the courts began to examine the operations of correctional institutions and systems more carefully, they began to redefine the operating framework of corrections. They placed legal restrictions on correctional administrators and required that correctional systems measure up to externally imposed standards rather than permitting them to police themselves, which had been the policy before.

As the courts started exerting more supervisory control over correctional operations, many inmates saw that the courts were now for the first time receptive to their complaints. As a consequence, offenders flooded the courts with petitions for judicial relief, and the courts addressed themselves to the petitions.

Some of the more significant Supreme Court rulings in the area of corrections have been that: (1) a formal procedure must be held to revoke parole;[42] (2) institutionalized offenders are entitled to access to legal materials;[43] (3) a sentencing judge cannot use unconstitutionally obtained convictions as a basis for sentencing an offender;[44] (4) indefinite commitment of one who is not mentally competent to stand trial for a criminal offense violates due process of law;[45] and (5) prisoners have the right to proper diagnosis and treatment of medical illness.[46]

One of the trends in recent years has been for the courts to appoint a so-called special master to oversee court-ordered changes in the operations of particular correctional institutions (including jails) or, for that matter, a state's entire correctional system. The purpose of the special master is a policing function: to observe the operations of the correctional facility or system to ensure that the court-ordered remedy or the consent decree is followed by the correctional authorities. The special master

(Note: a consent decree is basically a legal agreement between the parties that the defendant—the correctional system, prison, or jail—agrees to abide by certain conditions imposed by the court.)

The courts have used special masters in other ways too. A court might, for example, appoint a master after ruling that constitutional violations have occurred but before the court is ready to issue an order demanding the situation be remedied. In this situation, the court is relying on the special master to help it develop an effective and workable remedial order. The master is given the responsibility to provide the court with the special correctional expertise that the court lacks. For this reason, these masters typically have extensive experience in corrections themselves.

Masters are also sometimes employed by the courts as fact-finding agents

## THE COURTS AND THE PRISONS

The early 1980s saw the prison systems of more than half the states under some form of federal court supervision.[a] In nine of these states the prison system had been declared unconstitutional; the systems in the other sanctioned states were operating under court order or by a consent decree.

For almost a century, the prevailing view in American society and in the courts was that prisoners suffered a total deprivation of liberty and that their rights were nonexistent. In a noted Virginia case the court held that the penitentiary inmate was considered "the slave of the state."[b]

This period had been called the "hands-off" policy. It was a period of time characterized by noninterference into the operations of prisons by outsiders—particularly the courts and the media. John Conrad, a former prison administrator, says of those days:

Most wardens were princely autocrats who held court in immense, leather upholstered offices, feared by prisoners and guards alike. They had good reason to believe that they knew best how prisoners should be managed. After all, they and their predecessors had piled up decades of experience. Reforming

administrators sometimes interfered, but not many of them had the staying power to transform their ill-advised plans into permanent change.

Nobody was watching us—not even the press. The judiciary paid no attention at all to us—we were grateful for their "hands-off" policy and applauded their good sense in keeping out of our arcane affairs. It was a shock when the court decided to intervene in our management of the delicately balanced equilibrium of the "Big House." Lawyers and investigators inquired into details that no outsider had ever asked about—for example, our administration of prison discipline.

Admittedly, our disciplinary procedures were rough and ready. I used to sit every Tuesday—usually all day—on the disciplinary committee, a judicial body that ordinarily consisted of the two senior members of the classification and treatment staff and the associate warden and the captain from the custody side. One or the other of us would playfully tell outside observers and the convicts themselves that this was a court in which the defendant was always found guilty, whatever his plea. I do not recall an exception to this rule, even though we knew it exposed us to the prisoners' gibe that we

were nothing but a kangaroo court—or worse. Sometimes we were uneasy enough about the evidence against the convict-defendant to call the reporting guard in to amplify this report, whatever the guard's deficiencies may have been, we always arrived at a verdict of guilty.[c]

Conrad is not alone in recalling what the "good old days" in prison administration were like. William Nagel, also a former correctional official, recalls what it was like in the institution in which he worked. During the time period of which Nagel is speaking, his institution, Bordentown, in New Jersey, *was considered one of the most progressive and humane in the land.*

[In those] "hands-off" days we at Bordentown routinely and without any semblance of due process shanghaied (sometimes at midnight) troublesome prisoners off to the state hospital or to the old and brutal maximum security prison at Trenton. We denied newspapers, books, and magazines except those which we, in our wisdom, provided. We denied visiting to all except most immediate members of the family. It was not beyond us to deny visits to wives, parents, or siblings, if our judgment so dictated. We before any action is taken. For instance, the court might appoint a special master to compile a report on the administration and availability of medical care provided to inmates. The court wants to know if such care meets minimum standards and constitutional requirements.

The job of master is often a difficult one. Corrections officials may view the appointment as an attempt to usurp their management function. This is particularly true if correctional personnel and supportive local or state public officials feel the federal courts have no legitimate right to impose their requirements on local or state correctional operations. The special master may expect less than enthusiastic cooperation in such cases. Although the master has the authority of the court to support his or her efforts, the correctional personnel can still find ways to thwart these efforts and delay the resolution of the problem.

censored all incoming and outgoing mail that we viewed as critical, upsetting, or licentious. We confiscated poetry and other attempts at literary endeavor if such endeavor displeased us. We prohibited the possession or wearing of watches and even wedding bands. Anal searches were routine and frequently accompanied by insulting or degrading comments. Lock-up was available at split second notice and without pretense or due process or limitation as to length of time one could be "segregated." Such was the nature of due process when the judiciary practiced "hands-off."[d]

This "hands-off" doctrine began to change slowly in the late 1960s, and by the mid-1970s, attacks on the doctrine were gaining momentum. Although the principle remained that a prisoner's rights and civil liberties were lessened to some extent by virtue of one's incarceration, basic constitutional and civil liberties issues were not forfeited merely because one was imprisoned. The courts began to examine what limits the states could impose in curtailing the rights and civil liberties of prison inmates.

The two most common methods prisoners use to invoke court action are habeas corpus petitions and allegations of civil rights violations by prison officials. What is it that prisoners most frequently base their court actions on (exclusive of noninstitutional issues)? A study of the federal court district for the Northern Division of Illinois may provide us with some clues. In that judicial district, at least, a study of the filings by prisoners showed that the complaint most often taken to court concerned the health and medical conditions of the prison. This was followed closely by complaints about the institution's grievance procedures and assaults on inmates by prison staff. Deprivation of property, assaults from other prisoners, parole, and lack of access to the law and courts followed in that order.[e]

The intrusion of the federal courts into the area of states' correctional efforts has brought about a great deal of criticism of the courts' usurping the states' rights in this area. In some noted cases, however, correctional officials have welcomed federal court involvement and supervision. The federal courts, if they have accomplished nothing else, have forced the states to increase their expenditures for the operation of prisons. Prison administrators who are faced with legislatures un-

willing to appropriate adequate funds to operate state prisons have found that the courts can be a strange ally in enabling them to receive adequate operating funds.

There are some, however, who say that the courts are now moving away from their involvement in reviewing the operations of state correctional systems.[f] They contend that this reflects the more conservative nature of the Supreme Court today. At this point in time it may be a bit too early to reach that conclusion. However, if this is in fact the case, the trend should become more obvious in the next few years.

[a]Bureau of Justice Statistics, Bulletin "Prisoners in 1983," (Washington, D.C.: U.S. Department of Justice, 1984).

[b]Ruffin v. Commonwealth, 62 VA. 790–798 (1871). Discussed in Alvin J. Bronstein, "Prisoners and their Endangered Rights," *Prison Journal* 65 (Spring/Summer 1985): 3–17.

[c]John O. Conrad, "The View from the Witness Chair," *Prison Journal* 65 (Spring/Summer 1985): 18–25, at pp. 18–19.

[d]William G. Nagel, "Hands Off, Hands On, Hands Off—An Editorial," *Prison Journal* 65 (Spring/Summer 1985): I–III.

[e]See: Jim Thomas, "Rethinking Prisoner Litigation: Some Preliminary Distinctions Between Habeas Corpus and Civil Rights," *Prison Journal* 65 (Spring/Summer 1985): 83–106.

[f]Nagel, op. cit., and Bronstein, op. cit.

## Improving the Caliber of Corrections Administration

**Providing career opportunities**

If corrections is going to deal with the many problems it confronts now and in the years ahead, special emphasis must be placed on attracting and retaining competent employees. Nowhere is the need greater than in providing career opportunities for future administrative personnel. This is no easy task. Corrections, aside from probation and parole services, appears, among all the agencies of criminal justice, to be the least attractive to young men and women preparing in our nation's colleges and universities for careers in criminal justice. Part of the problem may be attributable to the fact that most correctional systems, like law enforcement agencies, operate as "closed systems" for purposes of recruitment and promotion. This means that in most state correctional systems, young men and women normally must begin their careers as correctional officers and work their way up the ladder.

Although this experience is invaluable for later line supervisory and management positions in institutions, special career systems must be developed for the bright and ambitious college-educated employee who demonstrates ability to eventually move into supervisory and management positions. As long as corrections indiscriminately groups all correctional officers into a single career track regardless of whether they have a tenth-grade education or a master's degree and requires the same number of years of service and other considerations before promotion, corrections will continue to have trouble recruiting top-notch people from our nation's campuses.

Fortunately, some of the more progressive state correctional systems are trying to do something about this problem. Multicareer tracks and accelerated placement opportunities are being provided. Although, like the situation in law enforcement, unions representing correctional employees are often opposed to such "favoritism," inroads are beginning to be made. Some correctional systems are also encouraging their employees to seek further education as a means to upgrade personnel.

For employees in supervisory and midlevel management positions, special emphasis is also being placed on graduate education either in criminal justice with a strong emphasis on coursework in areas of public management or on coursework in public administration with a concentration in corrections management. Correctional systems are beginning to realize that a modern-day correctional administrator must be able to deal effectively with such concerns as inmates' rights, employee–management relations, treatment programs, fiscal management, and the operations of the institution and the physical plant.

## The Development of Correctional Alternatives

**The adoption of new services and alternatives**

Diversion and community-based programs will almost certainly continue to grow as alternatives to the traditional methods of handling offenders, and greater emphasis will be placed on the development and testing of these alternatives. Such programs as detoxification centers for alcoholics and offenders with drug problems are being established in some parts of the country. Community programs for youths who are drifting away from parental control, community psychiatric programs, and services for those with chronic problems of unemployment are examples of the types of programs that are needed and are beginning to appear.[47]

The emphasis, it would seem, must shift more toward preventive services rather than on waiting until the problems of crime and delinquency have manifested themselves and then reacting through the very expensive process of incarceration. Increasingly, it seems that incarceration should be reserved for those situations when other alternatives have failed and for those individuals who demonstrate that because of their danger to society or the nature of their crime they must be locked up. We simply cannot afford to continue building traditional prisons. To implement such preventive and diversionary strategy, however, we need to develop better predictive or early warning systems that will indicate that certain individuals are moving toward the correctional system. This strategy likely would reduce the workload of corrections and focus its attention more sharply on those whose problems cannot be met more appropriately by other agencies or by the use of other alternatives.[48]

## Changes in the Organization and Delivery or Correctional Services

The reader will recall that one of the obstacles to correctional reform is the fragmentation of correctional systems among various levels of government. Although the immediate future will not see many correctional programs and institutions centralized at the federal level or even at the state level, it is expected that there will be less correctional fragmentation among political units than exists today. New programs and the associated involvement of the courts, law enforcement, and mental health and social welfare agencies will facilitate greater communication, resource exchange, and information sharing, and should conceivably reduce the multiplicity of correctional agencies among these levels of government.

Although the autonomous governmental control of correctional programs will be less, it is hoped that more types of programs will be available. The Joint Commission on Correctional Manpower and Training views the relationship between centralized administrative control and decentralized programming in the following way:

> The correctional system of the future will have a configuration of numerous, quite autonomous subsystems operating to maximize cooperation and interchange . . . [and] we ought not to expect a monolithic correctional apparatus for the United States in the future. But remedies must and will be found for the present problems of fragmentation. They will take the form, we predict, of a large repertoire of reciprocal arrangements between the parts of the total system. These new arrangements will be used flexibly and with much less reverence for the sanctity of organizational and governmental boundaries than is evident today.
>
> Offenders with special requirements will be sent to specialized facilities capable of meeting their needs, regardless of the jurisdictional niceties involved. Offenders whose primary requirement is to reestablish themselves in their home communities will be routed there and supervised by local authorities. The federal and state governments will facilitate the efforts of local governments to develop strong community-based programs and will backstop them with resources they cannot provide; for example, a fully staffed center for screening and diagnosis of offenders or an institution for mentally ill offenders.
>
> The administrators of a cooperative correctional system would need to understand the national network of services of which their particular program would be an integral part. They would need to be aware of the law, policies, and procedures through which cross-jurisdictional cooperation could be implemented. They would need to participate in those public and private organizations which address the problems of coordinating correctional efforts across the country and carry out planning and information-gathering activities. In sum, they would need to be outwardly di-

rected, rather than concerned only with local activities. They would need to work with the totality of corrections-related activities rather than with the happenings of their own organizational enclave.[49]

## Privatizing Corrections

Few issues in corrections have led to such sharp debate in the past several years as has the prospect of contracting with the private sector for the operation of prison and jail facilities. The need to curtail ever-escalating costs and the search for workable alternatives have combined to make this an issue of importance today.

*Supporting arguments*  Those who argue for an increased role of the private sector in such operations see the privatization of corrections as an opportunity to infuse the nation's correctional system with the flexibility and economic capabilities that only exist in the private sector. It is also argued that this will provide the chance to introduce efficiency and innovation to a field that has long been laboring under the burden of outmoded facilities, rising staff costs, declining resources, increasing executive and judicial demands for improved services, and the public's call for increased incarceration rates and lower per inmate costs.[50]

*Opposition*  Those opposed to such a transfer of responsibility contend that the profit motive of private business will take precedence over concerns about professional corrections practice. They point to the history of exploitation by private entrepreneurs of prison inmates under the old lease systems and the operations of gaols and similar institutions by private contractors that have been a blight on American penal practices in the past. They also raise fundamental questions about whether any part of the administration of justice is an appropriate market for economic enterprise; the administration of justice, they contend, is a fundamental and foundational reason for the existence of government.[51]

Although the adult corrections field has a long history of contracting with private organizations for secondary community corrections facilities, the idea of contracting for the provision of primary services and institutions is a radical departure. Yet, there are a number of precedents for such actions. The federal government—specifically the Immigration and Naturalization Service, the U.S. Marshal Service, and the Federal Bureau of Prisons—has developed contract-based facilities to house immigration law violators, alien material witnesses, and sentenced aliens. The major difference in these efforts, however, is that such programs and facilities are designed to hold offenders for only short periods of time until they can be deported. There is also no pretense of developing correctional programming in these facilities.

Governments at all levels have approached this idea cautiously. Even so, there are in existence more contracts with private service providers than most people realize. A survey conducted in the mid-1980s found that twenty-eight states reported secondary adult facilities under contract. For the most part these were privately operated prerelease, work-release, or halfway house facilities. The states with the largest private facility networks were California, Massachusetts, Michigan, New York, Ohio, Texas, and Washington.[52]

*Experiences*  Even greater inroads by private contractors have been made in the area of juvenile facilities. A survey of private juvenile facilities found nearly two thousand privately operated residential programs holding nearly thirty-two thousand juveniles, of which about one-third were being held for acts of delinquency. The majority of these institutions were classified as minimum security; only forty-seven

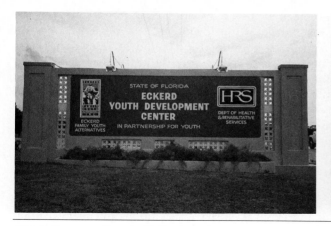

Among the corrections institutions run by private concerns, the majority are for juvenile offenders. (Courtesy of Eckerd Family Youth Alternatives)

institutions were classified as strict security.[53] Probably the most noted of these is the Okeechobee Juvenile Training Facility in Florida, which is operated by the Eckerd Foundation. In 1982 the foundation assumed responsibility for this state-operated facility. Although this is a secure facility, it does not compare with the requirements necessary for the operation of a highly secure adult prison.

Many issues associated with such a radical departure from what has traditionally been a public function remain unresolved. The National Institute of Justice identifies the more obvious of these issues. Will private providers use their political power to lobby for the development or continuation of programs that may not be in the public interest? Once they have a vested interest and investment, the maintenance of their profits may be an all-consuming motivation. This has potential implications for the quality and type of services provided. The privatization (and associated profit motive) will require close monitoring of such programs for failure to comply with established levels of operation. There is also the question of public confidence. The public may not accept such undertakings because it fears that security standards in such facilities will deteriorate. To whom is the private contractor responsible? This is a two-sided question. It requires initially the establishment of specific guidelines for operation. It then requires some authority to impose these guidelines and ensure compliance. Both of these can be major undertakings. And what if the provider does not comply? Will the state then assume responsibility or will it be necessary to develop a new contract with another provider?

*Unresolved issues of privately operated institutions*

A major impediment that needs to be seriously considered is the government's experience with private provider services in other areas that may have a bearing on this effort. One notable example is the private provision of health-care services such as government-sponsored Medicare and Medicaid. The cost overruns and the recurring problems with fraud in these programs may be considered as arguments against a joint government-private sector role in corrections.

A number of important legal questions also need answering. For example, statutory authority will have to be granted to permit this practice. And what about the granting of power to impose disciplinary measures or the employment of deadly force? To what extent will contracting governments be liable for actions against inmates taken by private operators?

*Legal issues*

While these are arguments against the considered adoption of private contracting, there are also those who point to some advantages.[54] For example, private contracting of correctional services may produce more rapid mobilization. Given the fact that generally the private sector can move more rapidly to bring additional facilities and manpower on-line, combined with the uncertainty that surrounds future population trends, contracting may be useful at the state level to avoid permanent facility expansion while accommodating short-term shifts. A private agency can also adopt experimental programming easier and without making a permanent commitment. It can accomplish this because it does not have the built-in constraints that operate in a large public bureaucracy such as a Department of Corrections. The private contractor may also be used to provide unique services for certain types of offenders that general-purpose public institutions cannot provide.

There is a great deal we need to know before we can judge how effective such a transfer of authority to the private sector would be. As in so many aspects of the administration of justice, only experience and careful analysis will provide us with the answers. It is likely that there will be increased use of private contracting in future years. Yet its adoption will be determined by a number of factors that are themselves only now developing. It may be that the major impediment to the growth of private contracting will be found within the criminal justice system itself—particularly among correctional interests who have a stake in maintaining control of correctional efforts in the United States. If this is the case—and it is highly likely that it is—major inroads of the private sector into the corrections system face almost insurmountable hurdles.

## Changes in Crime and the Offender Population

In 1972, the noted criminologist Daniel Glaser predicted that changes would occur in the prison populations of the future.[55] When he made that prediction, the typical prison population consisted of a disproportionate number of males, young offenders, racial and ethnic minorities, and the poor unemployed and uneducated residents of central city neighborhoods in our nation's large cities. He contended that prison populations of the future would take on characteristics more similar to those of the general population. Glaser believed that those sentenced to correctional institutions would come to include more affluent, more white, and more female offenders. A larger proportion will not suffer the social disadvantages of many of those he saw in prisons of the time. His optimistic forecast saw that poverty among certain disadvantaged segments of our population would be lessened, and these groups would enjoy greater economic and social opportunities than they had in the past.[56]

Although Glaser did not address this possibility, it was also probable at that time that we might see increasing enforcement of white-collar crime in the United States in the years ahead. Such offenses as tax fraud, corporate price fixing, and other white-collar crimes might, under pressure for equal enforcement of the criminal law and through the urgings of consumer advocate and reform groups, become more important concerns of our lawmakers and the criminal justice system. If this occurred, the composition of offender groups could change accordingly.

Glaser believed that the increase of females in correctional settings will come from the same dynamics that produced the women's liberation movement. With the economic emancipation of women from sex-segregated roles, women would become increasingly involved in traditional masculine roles, including various forms of criminal conduct. This would mean a change from the more passive crime-related behavior of women in the past (e.g., prostitution, bad check passing, and shoplifting) to more aggressive acts such as robbery, burglary, and more violent crimes.

In large part, Glaser missed the mark. Although some of his predictions were correct—for example, he foresaw that women would be more involved in certain types of offenses and would more often find themselves sentenced to prison for their crimes—he was simply wrong in other areas. Today, the population of our nation's jails and prisons still largely consists of disproportionate numbers of minority-group inmates and young offenders from socially and economically disadvantaged neighborhoods and families. In fact, the situation may be even worse today than it was twenty years ago.

Of course, Glaser and other criminologists of the time couldn't foresee the epidemic of drugs that has swept our country. Nor could such visionaries see the downward spiral in our economy in which unskilled labor became a commodity of little use in America today. This circumstance particularly affected racial minorities. This combination of drugs and lack of legitimate employment opportunities sent prison rates soaring among the disadvantaged. The federal courts, for instance, are experiencing an average annual increase of 20 percent in sentences being handed down for drug-related violations in recent years.[57] Jail and prison officials are also saying that they are finding emotionally disturbed or mentally disordered prisoners making up a larger segment of their correctional populations.[58] There is one last somber postscript to these changes. Because of overcrowding in our prisons and jails and the need to relieve this pressure by means of parole or transfer to community-based programs, some of our states' prisons increasingly are populated by the most hardened and dangerous antisocial personalities. This dangerous situation is certainly worrisome to correctional administrators across the country. The full implication of these changes is unknown; it is something that will have to be carefully observed in the years ahead.

And what does the future hold for prison populations of the future? There is little evidence that they will change much from what we see today. The problems which contribute to today's situation will not likely change in the next generation or perhaps the next several generations. There is little likelihood that prisons will ever become more representative of society rather than a place to house a disporoportionate number of disadvantaged offenders who commit "street crimes." This has always been the case, and there seems to be nothing that will alter the situation. Even such drastic changes as the legalization of drugs would seem to have little potential to substantially change the composition of our jails and prisons from what they always have been to what they likely will always be.

## □ PRISON VIOLENCE

In many male prisons, violence has reached epidemic and threatening proportions. Today the rate of murder in prisons is much higher than it is on the outside. Since the mid-1960s prison facilities have had substantial increases in the violence of murders, rapes, and assaults. What is ironic is the fact that this rise in violence has paralleled the growth of the prison reform movement. At a time from the mid-1960s

The problem

It has been called "the new Alaca-traz"—or worse. When the super-maximum federal prison called Alcatraz in San Francisco Bay was closed by the federal government's Bureau of Prisons in 1963, a replace-ment had to be built. An unlikely site was chosen: the Mississippi delta farmlands of southern Illinois. The prison went on-line the same year Alcatraz was closed. The prison, offi-cially called the United States Peni-tentiary at Marion, is the federal government's supermaximum facil-ity. Although it resembles a college campus, its real purpose becomes apparent when one views the guard towers, the fences, and the thirteen rows of coiled "razor wire" that surround its perimeter.

There is no pretense at rehabili-tation behind these walls. The pur-pose of the prison is security and control, period. Nor are any excuses made for its operation. Although the prison has come under bitter condemnation by such groups as Amnesty International, the courts have refused to intervene. The men at Marion have been classified by the Bureau of Prisons as the most dangerous, the most assaultive, the highest escape risks, and the most threatening or threatened inmates in the federal system. Not only fed-eral prisoners are kept behind these walls; a number of states have also sent their worst to be incarcerated here—inmates so dangerous that they cannot be handled in state-operated maximum-security prisons. It has become the model for several states in designing their own super-maximum facilities.

There are few amenities at Mar-ion. The inmates sleep on thin mattresses on concrete slabs. (Con-ventional cots with bed springs are not allowed because the springs can be fashioned into daggers or "shanks.") Food service is not pro-vided in a central mess hall, as in other prisons. Instead, prepackaged rations are delivered to the cell to be eaten there. No seconds are provided. Two hours a day are pro-vided for inmates to leave their cell under close guard. When an inmate is moved from his cell for any reason it is under the supervision of three guards. The prisoner is handcuffed, and a black metal box is placed over the handcuffs so that the lock cannot be picked. A chain leads from the black box and encircles the prisoner's waist. His legs are shackled in leg irons. Each guard carries a yard-long black stick made of sturdy plastic tipped with steel bearings. "Rib spreaders," one ex-plains. "We use 'em as prods. They separate the ribs without breaking them."[a] There is no commissary for prisoners at Marion. What limited goods are available to prisoners are delivered to them in their cells.

There is a little hope for at least a handful of the prisoners. For those who behave for a year or more, there is the promise of improved conditions. They may, for example, be permitted out of their cells for an extra hour a day or be able to pur-chase additional candy or obtain writing instruments more often. A few might even through exceptional conduct be eligible for transfer out of Marion and back to one of the federal government's maximum-security prisons, such as Leaven-worth.

Although Marion was always tightly controlled, it became worse in 1983. In a little over three years, from 1980 to 1983, after the transfer of assaultive and dangerous pris-oners from the federal government's conventional maximum-security prisons to Marion, riots and killings broke out in the institution. Nine inmates were killed, and two guards were murdered. There were ten riots, fifty-seven serious assaults, and thirty-three attacks on the staff. Reacting to this, the prison moved to a strict "lockdown" operation. The lockdown has never been lifted. Since its implementation, no staff members have been killed, and only five inmates have been mur-dered. Even the prison administra-tion is hard put to explain how with such tight control these five killings could have occurred. Perhaps it can best be explained by the type of prisoner that is found in this institution.

Who are these 430 men who find themselves in Marion? Ninety-eight percent have some history of vio-lence; more than half are convicted murderers. The average sentence is 39.5 years. Major drug dealers such as the Colombian drug smug-gler Carlos Lehder is found here, as is Jonathan Pollard, a former intelligence analyst who spied for Israel and is now serving a life sen-tence. So is John Walker Jr., who sold Navy secrets to the Soviets and may never leave Marion. There is the elderly Edwin P. Wilson, who was convicted of selling guns to Libyan strongman Colonel Moammar Kad-dafi. Incarcerated here are major leaders of rival prison gangs known as the Aryan Brotherhood, the Mexi-can Mafia, the D.C. Blacks, and five surviving members of the Order, a racist right-wing group that robbed banks, pulled armored-car heists, and murdered Denver talk-show host Alan Berg in 1984.[b]

In spite of the security, the at-mosphere of the institution is one of danger. This is expressed by the prison staff. Training is given to all staff members—including secre-taries—in the use of automatic weapons. In case of an assault from within the prison (or from without), elaborate plans have been made to repel it with a well-stocked arsenal of weapons. Although it is denied by prison staff that such weapons as heat-seeking anti-aircraft missles are available in case of an airborne assault on the prison, there are many rumors that these exist and are ready for use. Success is measured very simply at Marion: Each day that goes by without a riot, a killing, an assault on inmates or staff, or an escape attempt is con-sidered a "win" for the prison ad-ministration.

[a]Christoper Dickey, "A New Home for Noriega?" *Newsweek* (January 15, 1990), p. 66.
[b]Ibid., p. 67.

The 1980 riot at the Penitentiary of New Mexico is a grisly example of the inmate-against-inmate violence that characterizes the prison environment today. (UPI/Bettman Newsphotos)

to the mid-1970s when prisons were supposedly becoming more humanitarian and focusing more on the rehabilitative model of corrections, incidents of violence in prisons increased at an alarming rate.[59] At one time brutality and violence in prisons centered on such behavior by prison guards and the prison staff. Today violence is centered on the violent and brutal acts of inmates against other inmates.

Nowhere was this more obvious than the explosion that occurred in 1980 at the Penitentiary of New Mexico. The inmates, leaderless and uncontrolled, went berserk. Before the riot was over, thirty-three inmates had been killed at the hands of other inmates. Many of the prisoners were beaten and stabbed to death; others were hung from cell block tiers. The most grisly murder was that of James Delbert Perrin, who had been convicted of rape and homicide. His fellow inmates reportedly dragged Perrin out of his protective custody cell and turned a blowtorch on him. As he screamed with pain, the inmates first burned off his genitals and then moved the torch up his body to his face where they burned his eyes out. Several other victims, both dead and alive, were reported to have had their eyes either burned or gouged out.[60]

Many prisons are no longer ruled by authoritarian administrators; instead the environment of violence has been taken over by inmate leaders who exploit other prisoners. The culture of violence within American prisons today offers a new

Contributions of the changing prison environment

prisoner several roles. The inmate can "go it alone," but even this is extremely risky. This type of prisoner runs the risk of being constantly challenged and preyed upon by other aggressive inmates. If the prisoner is weak, he will live in constant fear of rape and violence. Many inmates are not strong enough—both physically and emotionally—to withstand the demands of being a "loner." The prisoner can join a gang—usually along racial and ethnic lines—for protection. Although membership in the gang provides a degree of mutual protection, it also subjects the gang member to the risk of intergang disputes and makes him a target for rival gangs. The new inmate can also "marry" an inmate leader and thereby be protected in exchange for submitting to periodic rapes. Whatever role he chooses, the new inmate soon finds out that the prison staff will often not protect him from the aggressive inmates who run the prison. As Kathleen Engel and Stanley Rothman say about this problem: "It used to be the case that rebellious inmates suffered more than passive inmates; now in most prisons, the less rebellious, non-aggressive inmates face the greatest abuses.[61]

Rape, by individuals and gangs, is a primary form of domination in the prison. Newcomers may be offered such inducements as protection or cigarettes to submit; in other cases, they are beaten into submission or "cut up" to force them to cooperate. Studies seem to indicate that whites are disproportionately the victims of inmate rape. There is evidence to suggest that for the most part, gang rapes are committed by lower-class blacks against middle-class whites.[62] If an inmate reports a rape, he risks another, perhaps more violent attack. Guards may not protect inmates and ridicule rape victims. The only safe way to report a rape and still prevent further attacks is for the victim to request that the prison administration place him in protective isolation.

The process can be quite insidious. A Southern prison administrator told the author of a favorite tactic employed by prisoners in his institution. This particular ploy is used by experienced convicts on newcomers to the prison. The newcomer is offered a marijuana cigarette or other controlled substance that the experienced inmate obtained. After the new prisoner uses the narcotic, the experienced con threatens to rat on him by leaving an anonymous note with the prison officials. The practice of the prison is to subject any inmate to urinalysis in cases of suspected use. If the inmate tests positive, he forfeits all privileges and accrued "good-time." The newcomer is faced with a dilemma: He must either then submit to the sexual advances of the other inmate or face the likelihood of the loss of privileges.

It would seem that attempts to curtail the violence in prisons have not been that successful. For example, in the aftermath of the New Mexico prison riot, traditional steps were taken to remedy the problems that were thought to have been the cause of the riot. Guards were given a 35 percent pay increase and special training was established for them. The inmate population was decreased to avoid the overcrowding that was thought to be a major factor. The guard/inmate ratio was reduced to 1:3, which is better than the national average of 1:5. Inmate activities were expanded to include five hours of scheduled activities, plus exercise time for inmates in maximum security. The prison administrators also made provisions to comply with standards for educational, recreational and legal programs, food services, and medical care. In spite of these efforts, nine inmates and two guards were killed in less than a year following the riot.[63]

**Underlying causes**   What is the problem? Probably fundamental to the increased violence are three factors: First, and most important, is the fact that the prison staff have too often lost control of prisons. Another factor is that the traditional social structure of the prison population has broken down and been replaced by a less integrated and cohesive inmate social system that is unable to control violence—in fact it may sanction violence. And third, the prisons are becoming increasingly populated with more dangerous and what may be called career-violent offenders.[64] All of these factors work together to produce this situation and to heighten the potential for violence.

The fact that prison staffs have lost control of prisons is a result of a number of factors. Primarily, the liberal reforms of the early 1960s "opened up" prisons to outside scrutiny. In many cases this was needed, but it also had some unanticipated consequences. Under the reform themes of humanitarianism and rehabilitation, the prisons came under increasing review by external reform groups, the courts, and the media. This, in turn, forced politicians and prison administrators to deemphasize custody and control of inmates. The new guidelines became a sharing of responsibility, more freedom of action, less restrictive policies in treatment of inmates, the discontinuation of racial segregation of prisoners, and the greater involvement of inmates in determining the policies of the institution. Any prison administrator who saw the danger of such a drift was quickly silenced or expelled. This was a period when training in the rehabilitative model became the expected response and the appropriate credential for career success as a prison official. Even if a prison administrator wanted to retain closer control over the inmates, his efforts were usually doomed to failure. Too many outside forces were arrayed against his efforts. The prisoners themselves were quick to pick up on this and used these external controls to limit the power of the prison staff. For instance, inmates learned that the threat of violence invoked outside review and giving in to their demands in many cases.

A number of prison specialists also saw the new reforms as destroying the established system by which inmates were able to control the inmate structure.[65] This occurred in several ways. The old inmate social structure, which was based on a solidarity of inmates against the administration, was broken down. In a custody-oriented and tightly controlled prison, the inmates formed a solid front against the common enemy—the prison staff and administration. This gave the inmates a solidarity of interests against an identifiable group and a means by which they could perpetuate and enforce the so-called inmate code, which, if nothing else, provided a stability of relationships among the prison population.

The new reforms also broke up the existing hierarchy in prisons that served to control inmates. Whereas at one time prison old-timers and those who knew their way around the prison were the inmate leaders, the new leaders were the younger and more violent inmates who were able to gain and maintain their power by acts of violence and intimidation. The inmate leaders recognized a simple fact: They had to encourage violence to maintain their position and the position of their group among the competing inmate power interests in the prison.

If violence and fear became the road to power among inmates, some prisons found themselves populated with inmates who were well schooled in their craft. Violent gang members who are sent to prison find many of their fellow gang members already inside prison and organized. These gangs organized particularly among Hispanic and blacks, such as Chicago's Black P Stone Nation (recently they have changed their name to the Neo-Islamic "El-Rukns"), populate such prisons as Illinois' notorious Stateville.[66] All of the violence and racial animosity that exists in free society becomes compressed and heightened within prison walls.

A major problem facing many large prisons is how to provide the right to safe

There is a great deal of public concern and misinformation surrounding the question of how much time felons who are sentenced to prison actually serve. The news media reports can be confusing and misleading. It may be reported, for example, that a defendant was convicted of several crimes and received a total sentence of 180 years. Then, perhaps on the same page, it is reported that a man who although he is only twenty-six years old has already served four or five felony convictions.

To better examine this question, the Bureau of Justice Statistics of the U.S. Department of Justice examined the average time served in prison by felony offenders. The data were gathered from twelve states.

Hopefully, the findings would correspond to what would be found if all fifty states were examined. The research examined nine specific offenses—the eight Index crimes (see Chapter 3) and drug offenses. The data were gathered at different times from the twelve states, but the time period covered the years 1979 to 1983.

Differences in the findings were to be expected based on a number of factors. These include different sentencing laws and the characteristics of those being sentenced. For instance, we would expect that those who had more prior convictions would receive longer sentences. The data did not control for this among the states examined. Some of the twelve states may have

more of these type of offenders than others. Other factors include good-time credits awarded; parole policies; overcrowding, which may shorten sentences served in some states; and credited jail time. This last factor is used to deduct time served in prison, depending on how much time the offender served in jail before being tried and found guilty. In some states the offender may serve longer preadjudication time, and this time may then be credited toward his or her prison sentence, which unless accounted for would result in offenders in such states spending shorter times in prison. The findings are shown in Tables 15.1 and 15.2.

TABLE **15.1**  Average Time Actually Served in Prison by Felony Offenders

| | | Average Time Served, in Months | | |
| State and Release Period | Number Released | All Felonies | Serious Violent Crimes*[a] | Serious Property Crimes[b] |
| --- | --- | --- | --- | --- |
| Delaware 1980–1982[c] | 1,371 | 17.8 | 32.5 | 10.3 |
| Illinois 1978–1982[d] | 21,202 | 23.1 | 34.0 | n.a. |
| Iowa 1979–1983[c] | 4,623 | 32.8 | 48.6 | 26.1 |
| Maryland 1982[c] | 3,649 | 29.5 | 50.5 | 21.7 |
| Ohio 1980–1981 | 12,026 | 24.6 | 40.5 | 20.9 |
| Oklahoma 1982 | 2,232 | 15.4 | 28.3 | 13.5 |
| Oregon 1979–1982 | 5,704 | 17.2 | 28.4 | 14.0 |
| Pennsylvania 1981–1982[c] | 6,202 | 26.7 | 38.1 | 21.1 |
| Washington 1981–1982[e] | 1,325 | 26.9 | 41.3 | 21.0 |
| Wisconsin 1980–1983[e] | 6,679 | 29.2 | 39.7 | 25.2 |
| Wyoming 1980–1983[c,e] | 759 | 22.9 | 39.0 | 20.1 |
| Average for all 11 states | 5,979 | 24.2 | 38.3 | 19.4 |

[a]Murder, nonnegligent manslaughter, rape, robbery, aggravated assault
[b]Burglary, larceny, motor vehicle theft, arson
[c]Includes credited jail time
[d]Obtained from 1982 Illinois Department of Corrections report
[e]Does not include full calendar year during years shown
*Source*: Bureau of Justice Statistics, *Time Served in Prison* (Washington, D.C.: U.S. Department of Justice, June 1984), p. 3.

TABLE **15.2**  Time Served for Specific Offenses, in Months

| State and Release Period | Criminal Homicide[a] | Rape | Robbery | Aggravated Assault | Burglary | Larceny | Motor Vehicle Theft | Arson | Drug |
|---|---|---|---|---|---|---|---|---|---|
| Delaware 1980–1982[b] | 74.3 | 25.5 | 39.3 | 18.6 | 15.7 | 6.5 | 12.8 | 9.4 | 15.0 |
| Illinois 1978–1982[c] | 52.1 | 46.0 | 29.1 | 18.7 | 20.7 | 14.1 | n.a. | n.a. | n.a. |
| Iowa 1979–1983[b] | 72.4 | 47.1 | 51.7 | 33.1 | 30.5 | 22.7 | 15.5 | 29.9 | 24.0 |
| Maryland 1982[b] | 63.1 | 63.7 | 61.5 | 30.0 | 29.2 | 14.2 | 20.9 | 35.6 | 15.9 |
| North Carolina 1977–1981[c,d] | 51.3 | n.a. | 40.8 | 19.7 | 22.2 | n.a. | 19.4 | n.a. | 15.7 |
| Ohio 1980–1981 | 78.6 | 50.0 | 34.9 | 26.6 | 27.0 | 15.4 | 24.9 | 22.5 | 17.3 |
| Oklahoma 1982 | 39.3 | 35.6 | 29.7 | 17.4 | 13.8 | 11.8 | 15.1 | 16.4 | 11.4 |
| Oregon 1979–1982 | 41.2 | 36.0 | 25.2 | 23.1 | 15.3 | 11.3 | 11.9 | 25.5 | 10.4 |
| Pennsylvania 1981–1982[b] | 57.4 | 47.7 | 33.5 | 25.4 | 22.6 | 16.8 | 14.8 | 28.2 | 18.9 |
| Washington 1981–1982 | 63.2 | 36.3 | 38.8 | 37.0 | n.a. | n.a. | n.a. | n.a. | 17.8 |
| Wisconsin 1980–1983 | 41.8 | 33.5 | 42.3 | 30.7 | 26.5 | 22.6 | 20.6 | 24.7 | 22.3 |
| Wyoming 1980–1983[b] | 59.5 | 51.5 | 29.5 | 29.4 | 22.5 | 15.8 | 18.2 | 25.8 | 15.2 |
| Average for all 12 states | 57.9 | 43.0 | 38.0 | 25.8 | 22.4 | 15.1 | 17.4 | 24.2 | 16.7 |

[a]Includes murder and nonnegligent manslaughter.
[b]Includes credited jail time.
[c]Obtained from 1982 Illinois Department of Corrections report.
[d]Report from Institute of Government, University of North Carolina at Chapel Hill (October 1983).

*Source*: Bureau of Justice Statistics, *Time Served in Prison* (Washington, D.C.: Department of Justice, June 1984), p. 3.

incarceration. A number of suggestions have been proposed. Although no one suggests a return to the prereform period, something must be done. Among other things, it has been suggested that large prisons be broken up, and that inmates be segregated according to their potential for violence and exploitation. It has also been proposed that the particularly violent and disruptive prisoner be locked down tightly under controlled and enforced isolation, and then additional attention be focused on means to decarcerate or group nonviolent and exploited prisoners away from other prisoners.[67] Lower staff/inmate ratios also seem to be necessary as do better training and willingness to support the custodial staff's efforts to appropriately regain control of the prisons. Meaningful vocational programs and means to reduce "idle time" among prisoners need to be implemented. Smaller prisons should be built where better surveillance can be maintained, and existing gangs should be broken up or effectively isolated.

*Suggested corrective measures*

Those efforts will be both costly and difficult to accomplish. Perhaps given the present overcrowding and the unwillingness or inability of the states to correct the problems that have led to this situation, we will see little change. If this is the case, the future of prisons in the United States will continue to be, in some important ways, the worst ever in our nation's history.

## SENTENCING AND IMPRISONMENT: HOW WE GOT HERE, WHERE WE ARE, AND WHERE WE SEEM TO BE GOING

When the California legislature revised that state's sentencing code in 1976, the new determinate sentencing law began with the observation that rehabilitation was no longer among the legitimate purposes of imprisonment—at least in California.

*Changes in sentencing philosophy*

Instead, the new code specifically declared: "the purpose of imprisonment for crime is punishment."[68]

Increasingly in the past fifteen years, correctional officials are saying that prisons are unable to rehabilitate.[69] Their cynicism has been echoed by any number of researchers, academics, judges, criminologists, and penologists who have examined the correctional process.[70] The same cynicism seems to be shared by the general public, as more Americans become disillusioned with our seeming inability to cope with crime and to "correct" offenders. Although this feeling seems to be growing, there is little agreement on what corrections can, or even should, accomplish.

Demise of the rehabilitative ideal

The debate on the purposes of imprisonment has, as we have seen, persisted since the invention of the penitentiary. The story is a too-familiar one: As the nation's prisons were denounced as massive failures and their rehabilitative purpose was scorned, the 1970s and 1980s brought staggering increases in state and federal prison populations. The result was an increasing number of persons confined in a rapidly deteriorating stock of prisons whose purpose was (and largely remains) uncertain. With the strain of crowded conditions came demands for relief from the kept as well as the keepers. Violent and tragic prison disorders have become too common; judicial supervision of state prison facilities, a routine occurrence.[71]

While states continue to pass "get-tough" sentencing laws and judges become increasingly more harsh in the imposition of sentences, little has been done to examine ways to control the size of prison populations. It seems that legislators, in particular, do not look beyond the passage of such laws. As a result, states are either in, or moving rapidly toward, crisis situations in their prisons. In an effort to deal with this crisis, states have adopted emergency housing plans; instituted more liberal parole policies; adopted "emergency-release" measures when the corrections population reaches a certain level; endorsed shifts in jurisdiction from state prisons to local facilities; proposed appropriations for the construction of new facilities; or have undertaken long-range studies of inmate populations and prison facilities.

In many ways it seems that we have now come full circle. At the turn of the century the idea that prisons might become treatment facilities was widely discussed. During this period, retribution had been disavowed by many legal theorists as both unscientific and uncivilized. Roscoe Pound, writing in 1906, observes: "Revenge and the modern expression, punishment, belong to the past of legal history."[72]

By the 1930s the indeterminate sentence characterized virtually every state sentencing code, providing testimony to the popularity and political force of the rehabilitation model. As a part of this overall model, the amount of time served became as much determined by parole authorities' ideas of rehabilitative progress as by the severity of the offenses for which the prisoners had been convicted.[73] Legislatures often made explicit reference to the rehabilitative purpose of correctional facilities in language similar to that of Missouri:

> In the correctional treatment applied to each inmate, reformation of the inmate, his reintegration into society, his moral improvement, and his rehabilitation toward useful, productive, and law-abiding citizenship should be guiding factors and aims.[74]

It was not until the late 1950s that the rehabilitative purpose of correctional facilities took on real vigor at the operating level of the prisons. Although much of what took place in prisons was very far from the medical model, the analogy of the prison as a hospital influenced a great deal of thinking during this time.[75] At its most extreme, this theme was expressed in terms of the prison as a therapeutic community, as depicted by some of the work that was going on in psychiatric settings.[76] In 1967, the President's Commission recommended that correctional facilities be small, adjacent to urban centers, and based on a collaborative regime between staff and prisoners.[77]

Rehabilitation has come under widespread attack from groups that once included its strongest supporters. This new disillusionment with rehabilitation was given added force with the widespread dissemination of an accumulation of evaluation findings that were unable to substantiate the effectiveness of correctional treatment.[78] Much of the more meaningful research took place in California, and it was this state, once the leading proponent of correctional treatment, that was among the first states explicitly to reject the medical model. A growing history of violent prison disturbances also cast serious doubts on the fairness and equity of correctional treatment in general, and the indeterminant sentence model in particular.[79] Many scholars, legal practitioners, and corrections administrators joined inmates in protesting the deleterious effects of release-date uncertainty; its questionable ethic of constructive coercion implied by a model of imprisonment that conditioned release on prospects for rehabilitation; and the unwarranted disparity among sentences received and served by similar offenders for similar crimes.[80]

As the rehabilitative ideal has faded, support has centered on two new standards: "just deserts" and the "justice model." Both of these models focus on the reduction of discretion at one or more points in the criminal justice system by means of the adoption of determinate sentences, and decision-making guidelines for judges and/or parole boards.

**"Just deserts" and the "justice model"**

Departing from the model that provided that the time a prisoner served was only broadly specified by the sentencing judge ("ten to twenty-five years"), with most of the actual time-setting power in the hands of the parole authority, these proposals called for fixing terms more precisely at the point of sentencing or shortly after imprisonment. Terms would be selected from ranges established legislatively (determinant sentencing) or through administrative rule (guidelines systems), and ranges would be based on the severity of the offense and the offender's prior criminal history. By the end of 1979, the movement to restrict the term-setting power of parole agencies had gained momentum.[81]

Basically, states are adopting three models of determinate sentencing. The first is the *presumptive sentence*. In this case the legislature generally provides three possible sentences for each offense. The middle is the presumptive sentence, but the court may impose the higher or lower sentence, as determined by aggravating or mitigating factors. This requires that the court conduct a hearing after the accused has been found guilty. The purpose of the hearing is to examine the aggravating (e.g., whether the crime involved great bodily harm or financial loss to the victim) or mitigating circumstances. Often, the specific aggravating or mitigating factors that the court can consider are actually spelled out in the law. It is not unusual for such a law to also require that the judge justify in writing why he or she departed from the middle-range presumptive sentence.

**Determinate sentencing models**

Another variation is the adoption of the *definite (flat) sentence*. Here, the legislature establishes a rather narrow range that the judge can impose. The judge then sentences the offender to a set period within the range. For instance, a range on conviction for a particular offense might be five to seven years. The court might sentence the offender to a flat seven-year period of imprisonment under the circumstances. This differs from the old indeterminate sentence, for which the range typically was wider, such as from three to seven years, the court imposed the three- to seven-year range, and the decision for release was made by the parole board within that specified period.

The third model is the *creation of a sentencing commission* and their development of sentencing guidelines. Although presumptive and definite sentencing models also might rely on sentencing guidelines, the difference is that in this model a special commission rather than the legislature establishes the guidelines. This special body is given the responsibility to study the overall sentencing process and to then develop a set of policies to be followed by the courts. The two most publicized sentencing commissions are found operating at the federal level and in the state of Minnesota.

Such sentencing reforms have not occurred without problems. One of the major obstacles has been criminal court judges who do not like the idea of having their discretionary authority limited. There are two noted cases of this. At the federal level, the proposal of the sentencing commission was challenged all the way to the U.S. Supreme Court on Constitutional grounds. The Court ultimately

---

## SENTENCING LAWS: GETTING TOUGHER WITH "ENHANCEMENTS" AND OTHER PROVISIONS

The past few years have seen both the federal and state governments adopt new sentencing provisions that apply to certain types of offenses and offenders. The purpose of these laws is to increase the penalty for the commission of certain types of crimes and to consider the circumstances of their commission and other factors. For example, the Comprehensive Crime Control Act of 1984 contains the following "enhancements" and other provisions for dealing with convicted federal offenders.

- Mandatory determinant sentence with no possibility of probation or parole for someone who uses or carries a firearm during or in relation to a federal crime of violence. (Author's note: such "dangerous firearms" laws generally include longer mandatory sentences for second, third, and further convictions. These are imposed in *addition* to the sentence received for the crime itself. Finally, many states and the federal government prohibit sentences from running concurrently in such cases).

- Mandatory determinate sentence of no less than fifteen years without the opportunity for parole or probation for someone possessing a firearm under the armed career criminal statute. (Author's note: an "armed career criminal" is someone with three past state or federal convictions for robbery or burglary.)

- Enhanced authority to seize and obtain through forfeiture property gained from engaging in the sale of narcotics or racketeering activity. (Author's note: Most statutes have "derivative proceeds" features. That is, any property that can be shown to have been purchased from the money received for the sale or transportation of narcotics or the involvement in racketeering is forfeited to the government.)

- The creation of the Sentencing Reform Act of 1984, which among other things established an independent Sentencing Commission which developed uniform sentencing guidelines to be followed and abolished parole.

- A law that authorizes the government to seize as forfeiture profits that convicted violent criminals receive from the sale of the stories of their crime. (Author's note: such forfeited proceeds will be placed into a newly created Crime Victims Fund for payment to victims of federal crimes).

- The imposing of a mandatory assessment on all convicted federal defendants. The proceeds from this are to be placed in the newly created Crime Victims Fund.

---

## THE EFFECT OF PRISON CROWDING ON INMATE BEHAVIOR

What effect does prison crowding have on inmate behavior and how might this affect the operations of prisons? The federal government has conducted some extensive studies in this area in an attempt to answer these questions. The research was conducted in six federal prisons. Additional data were gathered from the Texas and Oklahoma prison systems.[a]

The common-sense idea that prison crowding leads to progressive and measurable increases in negative effects was confirmed. Crowding, for instance, was shown to be correlated with increased disciplinary problems, illness complaint rates, suicide attempts, deaths among inmates, and other psychological problems that have the potential for heightening the tensions and the potential violence among prisoners. It was also shown that larger prisons that are experiencing overcrowding have more proportional problems in these areas than smaller institutions faced with overcrowding problems.

The open-dormitory arrangement appeared to produce the most negative reaction; the single-occupancy cell the least. The basic finding was that whereas a decrease in the area allotted each inmate for living space was an important factor, it was the increase in social density of inmates that was most highly related to negative consequences. In other words, you can decrease the area allotted prisoners as long as you permit them some privacy such as an individual cell. To increase the area—such as a larger cell—and then to occupy it with two to three inmates increases both social density and problems.

[a]G. McCain, V. C. Cox, P. B. Paulus, *The Effect of Prison Crowding on Inmate Behavior* (Washington, D.C.: U.S. Department of Justice, December, 1980).

---

ruled in favor of the commission. In New York State, the governor recommended the creation of a sentencing commission, which immediately incensed the judges in that state. So politically powerful is the bench in New York State that the governor was forced to back down and abandon the idea.

Where do we go from here? One thing seems to be obvious: Corrections may well be facing its most serious crisis ever in the years immediately ahead. A jumble of problems prevail. As more and more state legislatures pass laws requiring incarceration and judges sentence more convicted offenders to prisons, the overcrowding in prisons will continue. We simultaneously are making it more difficult to release prisoners on parole, which further exacerbates the overcrowding. While these problems continue, the courts by judicial order continue pressing for relief in overcrowding and for an improvement in overall prison conditions.

And how is the problem to be solved? Governments at all levels face financial problems. In the face of a growing need to place priorities on government spending, how can we forego needs in other areas to justify massive expenditures for prisons? In 1981, The President's Commission on Violent Crime, recognizing the seriousness of the problem, recommended that the federal government provide the states with several billion dollars for new prison construction. However, given the renewed emphasis by the administration in reducing federal expenditures through a necessary paring back in many areas, the ability of the federal government to come to the assistance of the states is very questionable.

And what about community-based programs to take some of the pressures off traditional prisons? Although they are still popular with correctional officials—if for no other reason than that they relieve overcrowding—they are running into more and more problems. The pervasive fear of crime among Americans, coupled with a "lock 'em up and throw away the key" mentality and the public's fear and revulsion at the turmoil, rioting, and bloodletting that has occurred in some of our prisons, threatens to hamper the development and expansion of such programs.

Communities, for example, are often opposed to the establishment of such things as community prerelease centers, community correction centers, and work-release programs. For whatever reasons—fear, retribution, or punishment—society's response to correctional programming is increasingly becoming more hard-line and punitive. Still, corrections has no choice but to continue its efforts toward establishing community-based alternatives.

### ⬚ CAPITAL PUNISHMENT: A GROWING SPECTER

History

America has a long history of experience with capital punishment. The earliest capital statute can be traced to the Massachusetts Bay Colony. In 1636 that colony provided the death penalty for a list of thirteen crimes headed by such offenses as idolatry, witchcraft, and blasphemy. The inclusion of these crimes was accompanied by Old Testament justifications for the imposition of the death sentence.[82] Of all the early colonists, the Quakers of Pennsylvania alone refused to incorporate a lengthy list of capital offenses. Instead, they reserved the death penalty only for the crimes of murder and treason.

If the early Puritan influence was one of religious zeal, later in our nation's history the Southern states transformed their zeal into a racial issue. By the early nineteenth century Virginia had enacted laws that punished slaves with death for committing any of seventy crimes, whereas whites faced possible execution for the commission of only five enumerated offenses.[83]

TABLE **15.3**　**What Methods of Execution Are Used by the Various States?**

| Lethal Injection | Electrocution | Lethal Gas | Hanging | Firing Squad |
|---|---|---|---|---|
| Arkansas[a] | Alabama | Arizona | Delaware | Idaho[a] |
| Idaho[a] | Arkansas[a] | California | Montana[a] | Utah[a] |
| Illinois | Connecticut | Colorado | New Hampshire | |
| Mississippi[a,b] | Florida | Maryland | Washington[a] | |
| Montana[a] | Georgia | Mississippi[a,b] | | |
| Nevada | Indiana | Missouri | | |
| New Jersey | Kentucky | North Carolina[a] | | |
| New Mexico | Louisiana | Wyoming[a] | | |
| North Carolina[a] | Nebraska | | | |
| Oklahoma[c] | Ohio | | | |
| Oregon | Pennsylvania | | | |
| South Dakota | South Carolina | | | |
| Texas | Tennessee | | | |
| Utah[a] | Vermont | | | |
| Washington[a] | Virginia | | | |
| Wyoming[a] | | | | |

[a]Authorizes two methods of execution.
[b]Mississippi authorizes lethal injection for persons convicted after 7/1/84; executions of persons convicted before that date are to be carried out with lethal gas.
[c]Should lethal injection be found to be unconstitutional, Oklahoma authorizes use of electrocution or firing squad.
*Source: Capital punishment, 1985.* BJS Bulletin, November 1986.

Encouraged by successful attempts in England to reform that country's "Bloody Code," abolition efforts began to take hold in America in the early eighteenth century. Not surprisingly, the abolitionist movement was started by the Quakers in Pennsylvania. Although the Quakers were not successful in getting the Pennsylvania legislature to abolish capital punishment, the reform effort did develop the now-classic formulation of degrees of murder and the elimination in 1794 of the death sentence for all crimes except murder in the "first degree."[84]

The gas chamber. (UPI/Bettman Newsphotos)

Until 1846, the efforts of the reformers centered on attempts to change the method of execution to more humane measures and efforts to get states to adopt various degrees of homicide, with only "first-degree" and "felony murder" (i.e., murder committed while engaged in specific serious crimes) calling for the death penalty.

In 1846, Michigan became the first state to abolish the death penalty. By the end of the century, five other states had also abolished capital punishment. In the years before World War I, nine additional states were added to the list. Entry into the war, however, brought a conservative change, and five of these states reenacted the death penalty.[85] It was not until the 1950s that the abolishment movement again began to stir. In 1958 Delaware experimented with a short-lived repeal of its capital statute. In 1960 Alaska and Hawaii joined the United States as abolitionist jurisdictions.[86] During the latter part of the 1960s, abolition efforts began to quicken, perhaps as part of the movement for fundamental social reform that seemed to sweep across a large part of the country.[87] This was a period of liberal court rulings—particularly by the U.S. Supreme Court—on a variety of social issues. Public support for the death penalty dropped from 62 percent, when it was first tested in 1936, to 38 percent in 1966. The social attitudes carried over into the administration of justice, expressing themselves in such ways as an unwillingness among judges and juries to impose death sentences. This led to a gradual cessation of executions, at least during the first part of the 1960s.

Along with general reform efforts to limit the number of capital crimes punishable by death, efforts to impose more humane capital punishment have been a recurring issue. Although hanging had been the predominant means earlier in our nation's history, Utah introduced the firing squad, which the Mormon Church was instrumental in having established because of that religion's emphasis on blood atonement.[88] In 1890 William Kemmler became the first capital offender to be put to death by electrocution, following his unsuccessful challenge that it constituted "cruel and unusual punishment," in violation of the Eighth Amendment. In 1924 Nevada put the first capital offender to death by cyanide gas. In December 1982, Texas became the first state to use lethal injection as a form of capital punishment.

Today, fear seems to be propelling the United States toward increased use of capital punishment. A Roper poll conducted in 1987 showed that 70 percent of Americans now favor capital punishment.[89]

As an indication of this fear and frustration, the 1989 national death-row population was slightly over two thousand. In each of the last few years, this figure has been increasing by about 125 inmates a year. This is more than at any other time—even more than during the so-called bloody 1930s when the increase, although slightly lower, saw more than 1,500 inmates put to death for their crimes. In early 1990, Florida had 294 inmates on death-row, Texas followed closely with 283, and California had 273.[90] Of the total inmate population on our nation's death-rows, slightly over one-half were whites, and blacks accounted for nearly 43 percent of

The chair is bolted to the floor near the back of a 12-ft. by 18-ft. room. You sit on a seat of cracked rubber secured by rows of copper tacks. Your ankles are strapped into half-moon-shaped foot cuffs lined with canvas. A 2-in.-wide greasy leather belt with 28 buckle holes and worn grooves where it has been pulled very tight many times is secured around your waist just above the hips. A cool metal cone encircles your head. You are now only moments away from death.

But you still have a few seconds left. Time becomes stretched to the outermost limits. To your right you see the mahagany floor divider that separates four brown church-type pews from the rest of the room. They look odd in this beige Zen-like

chamber. There is another door at the back through which the witnesses arrive and sit in the pews. You stare up at two groups of fluorescent lights on the ceiling. They are on. The paint on the ceiling is peeling.

You fit in neat and snug. Behind the chair's back leg on your right is a cable wrapped in gray tape. It will sluice the electrical current to three other wires: two going to each of your feet, and the third to the cone on top of your head. The room is very quiet. During your brief walk here, you look over your shoulder and saw early morning light creeping over the Berkshire Hills. Then into this silent tomb.

The air vent above your head in the ceiling begins to hum. The means

the executioner has turned on the fan to suck up the smell of burning flesh. There is little time left. On your right you can see the waist-high, one-way mirror in the wall. Behind the mirror is the executioner, standing before a gray marble control panel with gauges, switches and a foot-long lever of wood and metal at hip level.

The executioner will pull his lever four times. Each time 2,000 volts will course through your body, making your eyeballs first bulge, then burst, and then broiling your brains. . . .

death-row inmates.[91] Since 1930, the states of Georgia, New York, and Texas alone have executed more than 25 percent of all prisoners put to death in the United States.[92]

**Criticisms of racial application**

Among other things, the use of capital punishment has been attacked as being racially biased. Of the 3,863 persons executed since 1930, 2,307 were executed in the Southern states and the District of Columbia.[93] More than 54 percent of executed offenders have been black or minority members. A total of 455 persons have been executed for rape, 89.5 percent of them nonwhites.[94] As one authority says: "Among the over 5,700 persons executed under state authority (this does not include unlawful lynchings) since 1864, blacks have been found to have been executed for less serious crimes, at younger ages, and more often without appeals. This discriminatory treatment has been most evident in periods of the widest use of capital punishment."[95]

**Major Supreme Court decisions**

The question of the discriminatory application of the death penalty resulted in a historic 1972 Supreme Court case. In *Furman* v. *Georgia*, the Court nullified all forty then-existing death-penalty statutes and the sentences of 629 death-row inmates.[96] The Court felt that under existing capital statutes (and in application), judges and juries had intolerably wide discretion concerning whether to impose death. This lack of standards made the death sentence "freakishly imposed" on "a capriciously selected random handful" of murderers, wrote Justice Potter Stewart.[97] In this way, the Supreme Court did not strike down capital punishment as unconstitutional, only the way in which it had come to be administered.

After this court ruling there was a flurry of activity among the states to rewrite their capital punishment laws and to change existing procedures to make the

TABLE **15.4**   Death Sentence States in Which the Trial Judge Can Alter the Jury's Sentence in Capital Cases

| | |
|---|---|
| Kentucky | Pennsylvania |
| Louisiana | South Carolina |
| Nevada | Virginia |
| Oklahoma | Washington |

Author's Note: In these eight states, the original sentence is set by the verdict jury. This contrasts with some other states, which only permit the jury to return a verdict of "guilty" in capital cases, requiring the judge to set the sentence instead. In still other states, the jury merely recommends to the judge the sentence to be imposed in capital cases.

Adopted from: Conference of State Court Administrators, *State Court Organization–1987* (Williamsburg, VA: National Center for State Courts, 1988), pp. 363–65.

imposition of the death penalty less arbitrary and capricious. Although several subsequent state statutes were overturned by the Court, newly written statutes adopted by Georgia, Florida, and Texas were ruled acceptable. These statutes were quickly copied by other states. In upholding the capital offense statutes of these states, the Supreme Court ruled that death is a constitutional punishment and not cruel and unusual as long as the judge and jury have given due consideration to the characteristics of the defendant and the circumstances of the crime. (See Table 15.4.) Mitigating factors must be taken into consideration and weighed against aggravating factors in distinguishing capital murder from homicides not calling for the death penalty.[98] As of 1987, thirty-seven states had death-penalty laws.[99] (Figure 15.2 shows an example of a death warrant.)

In spite of the publicity surrounding the death penalty, the decision whether to execute an offender comes up in only a small fraction of all homicides committed. Although the criteria for capital murder vary somewhat from state to state and certainly from case to case, the general rule is that there must be "aggravating circumstances." This can mean the killing of certain individuals such as police officers or prison guards, or the killing during the commission of a serious felony-type crime. On the other hand, it might be as vague as Florida's law citing "especially heinous, atrocious or cruel" killings.[100] It is estimated that under these guidelines about 10 percent of all homicides currently qualify, or some 2,500 murders annually.[101]

The most common issue surrounding capital punishment turns on the question of *deterrence*. Very simply, such logic says that the existence of the death penalty deters would-be murderers from committing the crime if they know they will be punished by death.

Those who would have the death penalty abolished cite evidence that the use of capital punishment has no deterrent effect. They are quick to marshal research evidence of the lack of deterrent effect of the death penalty.[102] They point to such studies that, among other things, (1) compare homicide rates in adjacent comparable states between states that have abolished and those that employ capital punishment; (2) compare homicide rates in a given state before and after enactment or abolition of capital punishment; and (3) conduct studies over time using data on homicides and execution with controls for changing social and economic factors. They contend that such studies show that capital punishment is unrelated to the number of murders committed, and therefore serves as no deterrent.[103]

*Arguments against the deterrent effect*

# STATE OF ARKANSAS
## EXECUTIVE DEPARTMENT

---

# PROCLAMATION

TO ALL TO WHOM THESE PRESENTS SHALL COME -- GREETINGS:

WHEREAS, Arthur L. Allen, Jr. was duly presented under proper proceedings to the Circuit Court of Erie County, Arkansas, on a charge of Capital Murder, and, after being tried in that Court by a jury of his own selection, was found guilty and his sentence and punishment fixed at death by electrocution; and

WHEREAS, the said conviction having been appealed to the Supreme Court of Arkansas; and

WHEREAS, upon review of this case, the judgement and sentence of the Circuit Court of Erie County, Arkansas, was affirmed; and

WHEREAS, it has become my duty pursuant to law and official policy to fix the date and day for the carrying into effect of the sentence and the judgement of the Erie County Circuit Court as affirmed; and

NOW, THEREFORE, I, Calvin Swank, by virtue of the power and authority vested in me by law as Governor of the State of Arkansas, do hereby set November 14, 1983, between the hours of sunrise and sunset as the day and date upon which the Commissioner of the Arkansas Department of Correction will carry into effect the judgement and sentence of the Erie County Circuit Court by electrocuting the said Arthur L. Allen, Jr. at the place and in the manner prescribed by law.

IN WITNESS WHEREOF, I have hereunto set my hand and caused the Great Seal of the State of Arkansas to be affixed. Done in office this _13th_ day of October, 1983.

_Calvin Swank,_
GOVERNOR

_Neil B. Swartland_
SECRETARY OF STATE

---

FIGURE **15.2** Death warrant.

The death penalty has become a procedural nightmare for the federal and state judges who must deal with it. It has been characterized as an "impossible morass" of endless delay and confusion, which is compounded by a shortage of volunteer defense lawyers who have experience in the complexities of capital cases.

Death-row inmates wait an average of more than seven years from the time of the crime to the execution. During that time appeals flow up and down the courts, usually ending with an eleventh-hour appeal to the Supreme Court. Criticism is coming from all quarters—judges, defense lawyers, prosecutors, and citizens. The system is growing weary of the process. Retired Supreme Court Justice Lewis F. Powell, Jr., echoed this weariness when he said in an address before the annual convention of the American Bar Association that it was either time to change the system or put an end to it.

"If capital punishment cannot be enforced even where innocence is not an issue and the fairness of the trial is not seriously questioned," Powell said, "perhaps Congress and the state legislatures should take a serious look at whether retention of a punishment which is not being enforced is in the public interest."

By 1989 while more than 2,600 men and women were on death-row across the country, only slightly more than 160 executions have occurred since Powell joined in the Supreme Court's 1976 decision permitting the states to reinstitute the death penalty. The lack of swift and certain punishment in death penalty cases, Powell said, "hardly inspires confidence in, or respect by, the public for our criminal justice system."

With the number of death-row inmates growing by nearly 10 percent each year, and some states preparing to carry out their first executions

in nearly two decades, the frustration both for judges and for the condemned inmates can, it seems, only worsen. State and federal courts and the United States Supreme Court in particular, are bracing for an onslaught of appeals in the thirty-seven states that now have the death penalty. Many judges, especially in federal courts, have never heard a capital case before. In preparation for a resumption of executions in California, where more than two hundred prisoners are awaiting the gas chamber, federal district courts have drafted and adopted new procedural rules for handling capital punishment cases.

The nation's courts are already staggering with criminal and civil caseloads and are wondering if there is any hope of bringing order to an already chaotic set of circumstances. Now they are faced with dealing with the special rights of prisoners facing an irreversible punishment. The Chief Justice of the United States Supreme Court has asked Powell to head a committee of judges to study the problem and recommend changes in the process.

As it presently stands, appealing death penalty cases routinely involves six separate state and federal courts, ending finally with the United States Supreme Court, and review by perhaps dozens of judges. The justification for such a review process is the argument of necessity. It is said that such a complex procedure must exist if the justice system is to guard against arbitrary application of the death penalty. There must be an emphasis placed on demanding that judges up and down the line consider every possible ground of appeal. This is heightened by the fact that appeals, given the intricate legal questions and relationships involved, can shift back and forth from state to federal courts for many years.

Someone found guilty of a capital offense and sentenced to death is

automatically entitled to a direct appeal through the state courts regarding the merits of the conviction. If the conviction and penalty are upheld, defense lawyers typically seek review in state and federal courts by means of a habeas corpus writ, which seeks a remedy for alleged violations of the convicted offender's constitutional rights. In a number of these efforts, the lawyers are successful. According to the Department of Justice, about one-third of all such appeals in capital cases are successful in that they result in reversal of the conviction or, more often, the sentence.

Much of the criticism surrounding these delays centers on defense lawyers who have learned to use the habeas corpus and appeals process to thwart the system. It is contended, for instance, that appeals are sometimes repetitive and frivolous, having no direct bearing on the defendant's guilt or innocence. Several Supreme Court Justices, including Chief Justice William H. Rhenquist and Powell, have suggested that legislation is necessary that would somehow limit habeas corpus filings while still ensuring rights of appeal.

Defense lawyers and death penalty opponents argue otherwise. They contend that there must be no rush to judgment in carrying out executions, especially in cases for which there appear to be serious questions about the trial procedures that led to the sentence. Groups such as the American Civil Liberties Union question why the government feels such a need to carry out the death penalty so expeditiously when nobody complains about anti-trust suits tying up the courts for years. These opposition groups also argue that the appellate abuses have been pretty well taken care of in recent years and that frivolous and unwarranted appeals are very rare today.

Although the bulk of the evidence seems to support this conclusion, the fact is that we really don't know if capital punishment does or does not deter. And we shall never know, because deterrence is itself unobservable. Although we might argue that in spite of the widespread adoption of capital offense laws, murders are more frequent now than at any time in the last two decades, can this statement itself "prove" that the death penalty has no effect? One might ask what would be the rate of murders if we did not have the death penalty? Again, however, who can really say? And it is with this kind of logic and supporting arguments that both sides—proponents and opponents of capital punishment—continue their seemingly never-ending debate.

Although deterrence has been justified as the typical argument for the retention of capital punishment, the real fact of the matter is that perhaps we should at least be intellectually honest and admit that what we really seek is *retribution*. In this way, punishment itself serves as a sufficient justification for legal executions. The Old Testament admonition of "an eye for an eye" has put many of today's fundamentalist Christians in the forefront of the move to restore and carry out capital punishment. An interesting justification of the death penalty comes from the Reverend Jerry Falwell, who relies on the source of Christian authority to justify such action. Falwell claims that Christ favored the death penalty. On the Cross,

## ... LET ME DO IT ... NO ... I WANNA.

Hundreds of eager would-be executioners from all over the world have volunteered to help kill John Wayne Gacy, the condemned murderer of thirty-three boys and young men in Chicago. The unsolicited offers came to the Illinois Department of Corrections after the director of the Department remarked that he might consider using volunteer executioners if Gacy is put to death in the state's electric chair. Although such volunteers often offer their services at executions, the extraordinary large number of volunteers is attributed to the publicity given to the director's remark and the nature and publicity surrounding this particular case.

Gacy, convicted of more murders than anyone previously in U.S. history, allegedly sexually molested many of his victims before murdering them. The victims were then buried under his house. When the death sentence was imposed, relatives and victims broke out into cheers and applause in the courtroom.

A seventy-three-year-old Mississippi resident wrote, "Nothing would give me greater pleasure than pulling the switch on Wayne Gacy." From New York came a letter from a prison inmate who volunteered his services saying he "would soon be appearing before the parole board, and I need a new job, plus a new start in life."

"I know that doing this job is not something desirable," wrote a minister from Florida. "I'm not thrilled at the prospect of doing it, but someone has to." It was reported that some applicants even included printed résumés, stating previous experience. From Wisconsin came the offer from a policeman who said he had the qualifications based on his work at an animal shelter where he was involved in the "destruction of animals," and a funeral director from Illinois said he was particularly qualified because he was "the type of individual who works with life and death on a daily basis."

A London bank teller wrote: "I am 30 years of age, male, single, and considered by other people to be calm, confident, meticulous, and a discreet, quiet young man. I believe firmly in the death penalty."

The Illinois Department of Corrections denied that it was advertising for a volunteer. The director contended that he merely mentioned the idea in an offhand way to a reporter who apparently misunderstood and thought the proposal was serious.

*Source:* Adapted from: "Hundreds Volunteer to Execute Gacy in Illinois," *Corrections Magazine* 6, no. 4 (August 1980): 4.

Falwell says, He could have spoken up: "If ever there was a platform for our Lord to condemn capital punishment, that was it. He did not."[104]

In whatever way arguments are posed against retribution as the justification for the state carrying out the death penalty—whether they be moral, humanitarian, philosophical, or theological—America and its people seem bent on entering a new era of state executions. Most observers are now saying that, given the fact that many inmates on our death rows have just about exhausted all appeals, and that the U.S. Supreme Court seems unwilling to declare capital punishment unconstitutional, the 1990s promise to be a period of such widespread executions that it will eclipse any other time in modern history. Yet, the same thing was said during the 1980s, and it didn't occur.

The issue will certainly not wither and die. What we seem to be seeing is a shift in mood that, like a pendulum, seems to swing from side to side over time. Social and economic conditions play an important role in our attitudes toward crime, criminals, and the administration of justice, as history has repeatedly demonstrated. One must wonder about the rapid rise in executions in England during the period when the propertied classes felt the growing unrest and agitation among the masses. Is it coincidence that the Great Depression of the 1930s in America spawned the highest rate of legal executions in our nation's history? Have the troubled economic conditions of today led to the same frustrations?

## ◻ THE IMPENDING DANGER

An ironic situation faces correctional efforts today. When the first edition of this book was completed in 1976, rehabilitation and reintegration still enjoyed fairly widespread acceptance, at least in theory. By 1980, when the second edition appeared, it was clear that these goals were being phased out. Today, they have been supplanted by what may be called a more hard-line—some would say—practical approach to the purposes of imprisonment.

There is much truth in the widespread belief that corrections does not "correct." Thinking people must agree that corrections does punish. Corrections systems have unquestionably made mistakes in attempting to foster the belief that they could rehabilitate. Yet we as Americans searching for easy solutions to complex and interrelated problems wanted corrections officials to tell us that. We seemed to need to believe that the tax dollars we spent were doing more than temporarily warehousing offenders in our state and federal prison systems.

Corrections officials gave us what we wanted—and a little more. Here was a golden opportunity to seek additional funds, programs, and staff to accomplish the lofty goals of rehabilitation. But although corrections leaders praised rehabilitation programs, there is little evidence that they truly believed prisons could achieve any reasonable success rates. The very nature of prisons, the lack of resources, the personal pathologies of many inmates, and the real lack of commitment to rehabilitative efforts by prison administrators and staff assured failure. What else could we possibly expect?

However, to say that rehabilitation cannot be accomplished and to revert to punishment as the primary correctional goal is just as irresponsible. History has repeatedly demonstrated that punishment does not serve as a corrective device.

**A strategy for the future**

We need to do some hard thinking about this whole subject. Perhaps we need to consider two things as our long-range strategy for corrections and what we are trying to accomplish as a society. First, offenders who will not be "corrected," either through punishment by means of incarceration or through rehabilitative measures, must be locked up for the protection of society. Perhaps we must be prepared to accept this fact and to pay the costs for long-term incarceration of dangerous and repeat offenders. In a sense, although it doesn't sound humanitarian, we may have to "write off" these individuals. This message, however, must be conveyed forcefully and openly by society and by the criminal justice process. It must stand as a visible and certain disposition that we shall employ to assure public safety.

Along with this response must come a rededication to assuring that those who can benefit by programs of help and rehabilitation will have these resources available. Whether these two goals can exist side by side without one response becoming all-encompassing and the other self-defeating may be the single most important challenge we face. If such a system is to have any hope of improving the situation in the years ahead, one thing is certain: Like it or not, we must focus more resources on the examination of factors that can help us answer such pressing questions. We need to know the answers to such questions as: What correctional methods work? With whom do they work? Under what conditions do they work? A great deal of effort lies ahead—effort that will require human and capital resources we may not be able, or willing, to provide.

## SUMMARY

Some of the more popular community-based institutions and program efforts are work-release, community corrections centers, academic passes, prerelease guidance centers, halfway houses, conjugal and family visitations, home furloughs, restitution centers, and victim restitution programs.

Current issues and trends that will shape the future of corrections include the judicial oversight of correctional operations, improvements in correctional personnel, the development of correctional alternatives based on preventive strategies, changes in the organization and delivery of correctional services, changes in the nature of crime and offender population, and increased research efforts.

One major concern threatens the progress of present correction efforts—that society has begun, again, to view prisons solely as places of punishment. This reflects an increasingly retributive philosophy among Americans, who have become disenchanted with the inability of corrections to correct. In large part, blame for this change in attitude must be borne by corrections itself for misleading the public on their ability to "correct" when, in fact, little real understanding or effort went into such efforts. Instead, the rehabilitative model was too often used for the self-interest of corrections itself. It is now time for America to step back and reassess many things about corrections. Unfortunately, we don't seem to know the right questions to ask, let alone what the answers might be.

## REVIEW QUESTIONS

1. Give reasons explaining the increasing use of community-based programs over traditional correctional methods.
2. What is the basic rationale of community-based corrections? Has this correctional method a better chance of coping effectively with the usual problems of the offender in returning to society?
3. Name and briefly explain the four major types of community-based programs.
4. Describe the purpose of the following:
   a. Prerelease guidance center
   b. Halfway house

c. Victim restitution

d. Community corrections center

5. What fundamental changes have resulted from recent court rulings regarding the rights of prison inmates? What are some of these rulings?

6. How is the caliber of correctional managers and administrators being improved? Is this necessary?

7. To some criminologists, there will be definite changes in the types of offenders and the crimes they commit in the future. What are these foreseeable changes?

8. Discuss the issues that surround capital punishment. What historical factors have contributed to the controversy surrounding these issues?

9. If rehabilitation and reintegration don't work, what will be the most likely reaction within the corrections field?

## DISCUSSION QUESTIONS

1. What are the possible drawbacks to community-based programs?

2. Are prison inmates entitled to the civil rights guaranteed to American citizens by the Constitution? Why or why not? On what issues might civil rights be legitimately denied them?

3. If punitive correctional methods are restored, how might the correctional system of the United States be affected?

4. Take a position for or against the use of capital punishment. Develop an argument to justify your position.

## SUGGESTED ADDITIONAL READINGS

Allen, Harry E., and Clifford E. Simonsen. *Corrections in America: An Introduction*, 5th ed. New York: Macmillan, 1989.

Carter, Robert M. Daniel Glaser and Leslie T. Wilkins (eds.). *Correctional Institutions*. New York: Harper & Row, 1985.

Doig, Jaimeson W. (ed.). *Criminal Corrections—Ideals and Realities*. Lexington, Mass.: D. C. Heath, 1983.

Frank, Benjamin. *Contemporary Corrections: A Concept in Search of Content*. Reston, Va.: Reston Publishing, 1973.

Fuller, Dan, and Thomas Orsagh. "Violence and Victimization Within a State Prison System." *Criminal Justice Review* 2 (Fall 1977): 35–55.

Griggs, Bertram S., and Garry R. McCune. "Community-Based Correctional Programs: A Survey and Analysis." *Federal Probation* 36 (June 1972): 7–13.

Harlow, Eleanor, Robert J. Webber, and Leslie T. Wilkins. *Community-Based Correctional Programs: Models and Practices*. Washington, D.C.: U.S. Government Printing Office, 1971.

Hood, Roger, and Richard Sparks. *Key Issues in Criminology*. New York: McGraw-Hill, 1970.

Keller, Oliver J., and Benedict S. Alper. *Halfway Houses: Community Centered Corrections and Treatment*. Lexington, Mass.: Raytheon/Heath, 1970.

Jacobs, J. B. *New Perspectives on Prisons and Imprisonment*. Ithaca, N.Y.: Cornell University Press, 1983.

McCartt, John M., and Thomas Mangogna. *Guidelines and Standards for Halfway Houses and Community Treatment Centers*. Washington, D.C.: Law Enforcement Assistance Administration, May 1973.

Moyer, Frederic D. *Guidelines for the Planning and Design of Regional and Community Correctional Centers for Adults*. Urbana: University of Illinois, 1971.

Petersilia, Joan. *Expanding Options for Criminal Sentencing*. Santa Monica, Calif.: Rand Corp., 1987.

Schafer, Stephen. *Victimology—The Victim and His Criminal*. Reston, Va.: Reston Publishing, 1977.

Schwartz, Richard D., and Jerome H. Skolnick. "The Stigma of 'Ex-Con' and the Problem of Reintegration." *Social Problems* 10 (Fall 1962): 133–142.

Shover, Neal, and Werner J. Einstadter. *Analyzing American Corrections*. Belmont, Calif.: Wadsworth Publishing, 1988.

Zamble, Edward, and Frank J. Popporino. *Coping, Behavior and Adaptation in Prison Inmates*. New York: Springer-Verlag, 1988.

## NOTES

1. Joseph E. Jacoby and Christopher S. Dunn, *National Survey on Punishment for Criminal Offenses, Executive Summary*. Paper presented at the 1987 meeting of the National Conference on Punishment for Criminal Offenses, Ann Arbor, Mich.: November 1987.

2. Bureau of Justice Statistics, *Report to the Nation on Crime and Justice*, 2nd ed. (Washington, D.C.: U.S. Department of Justice, March 1988), p. 105.

3. Ibid., p. 105.

4. Solomon Kobrin, "The Chicago Area Project—A 25-Year Assessment," *Annals of the American Academy of Political and Social Science* 322 (March 1959): 19–29.

5. Walter B. Miller, "Preventive Work with Street Corner Groups," *Annals of the American Academy of Political and Social Science* 322 (March 1959): 97–106.

6. *New York Times*, 30 November 1973, sec. II, p. 2, col. 1.

7. It should be pointed out, however, that an opposite trend toward a "get-tough" policy with offenders may be developing. Popular sentiment is calling for stricter laws and their enforcement. At this time, it is too early to gauge the effect of such attitudes on corrections.

8. For example, see George Killinger and Paul F. Cromwell, *Corrections in the Community* (St. Paul, Minn.: West, 1974).

9. Law Enforcement Assistance Administration, National Institute of Law Enforcement and Criminal Justice, *Reintegration of the Offender into the Community* (Washington, D.C.: U.S. Government Printing Office, 1973), p. 5.

10. Walter H. Busher, *Ordering Time to Serve Prisoner* (Washington, D.C.: U.S. Government Printing Office, June 1973), p. 3.

11. Ibid., pp. 3–4.

12. *1984 Census of Adult Correctional Facilities* (Washington, D.C.: U.S. Government Printing Office, 1987), pp. 8–12.

13. See Daniel Glaser, *The Effectiveness of a Prison and Parole System* (Indianapolis, Ind.: Bobbs-Merrill, 1969), especially chap. 10.

14. Alvin Rudoff and T. C. Esselstyn, "Evaluating Work Furlough: A Follow-up," *Federal Probation* 37 (June 1979): 48–53.

15. Ibid., pp. 50–53.

16. N. C. Chamelin, V. B. Fox, and P. M. Whisenand, *Introduction to the Criminal Justice System* (Englewood Cliffs, N.J.: Prentice-Hall, 1975), p. 397.

17. Columbus B. Hopper, "The Conjugal Visit," *Journal of Criminal Law, Criminology and Police Science* 53 (September 1962): 340–343.

18. For example, see Norman E. Hayner, "Attitudes Toward Conjugal Visits for Prisoners," *Federal Probation* 36 (March 1972): 43–49.

19. Source: Michael S. Serill, "Family Visiting at San Quentin." Reprinted with permission from the July–August 1975 issue of *Corrections Magazine*, published by the Correctional Information Service, Inc., 801 Second Avenue, New York, N.Y. 10017.

20. Carson W. Markley, "Furlough Programs and Conjugal Visiting in Adult Correctional Institutions," *Federal Probation* 37 (March 1973): 19–26.

21. Ibid., pp. 22–24.

22. Donald R. Johns, "Alternatives to Conjugal Visiting," *Federal Probation* 35 (March 1971): 48–51.

23. Ibid.

24. Serill, "Family Visiting at San Quentin," p. 12.

25. Chamelin et al., *Introduction to the Criminal Justice System*, p. 397.

26. Killinger and Cromwell, *Corrections in the Community*, p. 68.

27. Ibid.

28. Ibid., p. 69.

29. Oliver J. Keller and Benedict S. Alper, *Halfway Houses* (Boston: Heath, 1963), p. 7.

30. Ibid.

31. Killinger and Cromwell, *Corrections in the Community*, p. 78.

32. U.S. Department of Justice, *Federal Prison System—1978* (Washington, D.C.: U.S. Government Printing Office, 1979), p. 4.

33. Kenneth F. Schoen, "PORT: A New Concept of Community-Based Correction," *Federal Probation* 36 (September 1972): 35–40.

34. John M. McCartt and Thomas Mangogna, *Guidelines and Standards for Halfway Houses and Community Treatment Centers* (Washington, D.C.: U.S. Government Printing Office, June 1973), pp. 17–18.

35. H. B. Bradley, "Community-Based Treatment for Young Adult Offenders," *Crime and Deliquency* 15 (1969): 359–370.

36. E. Harlow, R. Weber, and L. T. Wilkins, "Community-Based Correctional Programs," in E. Eldefonso, ed., *Issues in Corrections* (Encino, Calif: Glencoe, 1974), p. 367.

37. For example, see Stephen Schafer, *Compensation and Restitution to Victims of Crime* (Montclair, N.J.: Patterson-Smith, 1970); and Stephen Schafer, "The Proper Role of a Victim Compensation System," *Crime and Delinquency* 21 (January 1975).

38. Anne Newton, "Aid to the Victim Part II: Victim Aid Program," *Crime and Delinquency Literature* 8 (December 1976): 287.

39. Ibid.

40. National Advisory Commission on Criminal Justice Standards and Goals, *Corrections* (Washington, D.C.: U.S. Government Printing Office, 1973), p. 18.

41. Ibid.

42. *Morrissey* v. *Brewer*, 408 U.S. 471 (1972).

43. *Younger* v. *Gilmore*, 404 U.S. 15 (1971).

44. *United States* v. *Tucker*, 404 U.S. 443 (1972).

45. *Jackson* v. *Indiana*, 406 U.S. 715 (1972).

46. *.Estelle* v. *Gamble*, 97 S. Ct. 285 (1976).

47. Robert M. Carter, Richard A. McGee, and E. Kim Nelson, *Corrections in America* (Philadelphia: Lippincott, 1975), p. 375.

48. Ibid., p. 376.

49. Elmer K. Nelson, Jr., and Catherine H. Lovell, *Developing Correctional Administrators* (Washington, D.C.: Joint Commission on Correctional Manpower and Training, November 1969), p. 15.

50. National Institute of Justice, *Corrections and the Private Sector* (Washington, D.C.: U.S. Department of Justice, October 1984), p. 1.

51. Ibid., p. 4.

52. Ibid., p. 7.

53. Unpublished tables from *Children in Custody: Advance Report on the 1982–1983 Census of Private Facilities* (Washington, D.C.: U.S. Department of Justice, Office of Juvenile Justice and Delinquency

Prevention), reported in National Institute of Justice, Ibid., p. 4.

54. These advantages are adopted from: Joan Mullen, Kent Chabotar, and Deborah Carrrow, *The Privatization of Corrections* (Washington, D.C.: Abt Associates for the National Institute of Justice, May 1984).

55. Daniel Glaser, "Changes in Corrections During the Next 20 Years," paper presented before the American Justice Institute, March 2, 1972.

56. For another interesting viewpoint, see Edward C. Banfield, *The Unheavenly City* (Boston: Little, Brown, 1970).

57. Bureau of Justice Statistics, *Sourcebook on Criminal Justice Statistics* (Washington, D.C.: U.S. Department of Justice), various issues.

58. National Institute of Corrections, *Sourcebook on the Mentally Disordered Offender* (Washington, D.C.: U.S. Department of Justice, March 1985).

59. For example, see: David C. Anderson, "The Price of Safety: I Can't Go Back There," *Corrections Magazine* 6 (August 1980): 6–15.

60. Michael S. Serrill, "The Anatomy of a Riot: The Facts Behind New Mexico's Bloody Ordeal," *Corrections Magazine* 6 (April 1980): 6–16; 20–24.

61. Kathleen Engel and Stanley Rothman, "Prison Violence and the Paradox of Reform," *Public Interest* 73 (Fall 1983): 91–105.

62. Peter C. Buffum, *Homosexuality in Prisons* (Washington, D.C.: U.S. Department of Justice, 1972), pp. 22–23.

63. Engel and Rothman, op. cit., pp. 92–93.

64. Ibid., p. 93.

65. For example, see: Gresham Sykes, *The Society of Captives* (Princeton, N.J.: Princeton University Press, 1978); Leo Carroll, *Hacks, Blacks and Cons* (Lexington, Mass.: Lexington Books, 1974); and Charles E. Silbermann, *Criminal Violence, Criminal Justice* (New York: Random House, 1978).

66. "The Menace of the Supergangs," *Corrections Magazine* 6 (June 1980): 11–14.

67. Engel and Rothman, op. cit., p. 105.

68. California Penal Code, Sec. 1170. 1a. (1976).

69. See Michael S. Serrill, "Is Rehabilitation Dead?" *Corrections Magazine* 1 (May/June 1975): 3–12, 21–32.

70. For example, see Robert Martinson, "What Works? Questions and Answers About Penal Reform," *The Public Interest* 35 (1974): 22–54; David Fogel, *We are the Living Proof*, 2nd ed. (Cincinnati, Ohio: Anderson, 1978); Richard McGee, "A New Look at Sentencing: Part II," *Federal Probation* 38 (1974): 3–11.

71. National Institute of Justice, *American Prisons and Jails, Volume 1* (Washington, D.C.: U.S. Government Printing Office, 1980), p. 1.

72. Roscoe Pound, "The Causes of Dissatisfaction in the Administration of Justice," *American Bar Association Reports* 29 (1906): 395.

73. National Institute of Justice, *American Prisons and Jails*, p. 3.

74. Missouri Ann. Stat., 216.090.

75. National Institute of Justice, *American Prisons and Jails*, p. 3.

76. For example, see Maxwell Jones, *Social Psychiatry in Practice* (London: Penguin, 1978).

77. President's Commission on Law Enforcement and Administration of Justice, *Task Force Report on Corrections* (Washington, D.C.: U.S. Government Printing Office, 1967), p. 47.

78. Martinson, "What Works?"

79. National Institute of Justice, *American Prisons and Jails*, p. 3.

80. For example, see American Friends Service Committee, *Struggle for Justice: A Report on Crime and Punishment in America* (New York: Hill & Wang, 1971).

81. Ibid., p. 4.

82. Sarah T. Dike, "Capital Punishment in the United States—Part I," *Criminal Justice Abstracts* 13, no. 2 (Hackensack, N.J.: National Council on Crime and Delinquency, June 1981), pp. 283–311.

83. Hugo A. Bedean, "Capital Punishment," in Tom Regan, ed., *Matters of Life and Death* (New York: Random House, 1980), pp. 152–153.

84. Ibid., pp. 7–8.

85. William Bowers, *Execution in America* (Lexington, Mass.: Heath, 1974), pp. 6–7.

86. Ibid.

87. Martin Gardner, "Illicit Legislative Motivation as a Sufficient Condition for Unconstitutionality Under the Establishment Clause—A Case for Consideration," *Washington University Law Quarterly* 2 (1979): 435–499.

88. Bedean, "Capital Punishment," p. 18.

89. Bureau of Justice Statistics, *Sourcebook on Criminal Justice Statistics—1987* (Washington, D.C.: U.S. Department of Justice, 1988), pp. 160–161.

90. "Breaking the Death Barrier," *Newsweek* (February 19, 1990), pp. 72–73.

91. Bureau of Justice Statistics, *Sourcebook on Criminal Justice Statistics*, p. 534.

92. Ibid., p. 539.

93. Dike, "Capital Punishment," p. 294.

94. Marvin Wolfgang and Marc Riedel, "Racial Discrimination and the Death Penalty," *Annals of the American Academy of Political and Social Science* 407 (May 1973): 119–133.

95. Bowers, *Execution in America*, p. 49.

96. *Furman* v. *Georgia*, 408 U.S. 238 (1972).

97. Ibid.

98. For example, see *Gregg* v. *Georgia*, 96 S.Ct. 2909 (1976); *Profit* v. *Florida*, 96 S.Ct. 2960 (1976); *Jurek* v. *Texas*, 96 S.Ct. 2950 (1976).

99. The only states without the death penalty at this time are Alaska, Hawaii, Iowa, Kansas, Maine, Michigan, Minnesota, New York, North Dakota, Oregon, Rhode Island, West Virginia, and Wisconsin.

100. *Time*, "An Eye for an Eye," p. 32.

101. Ibid.

102. For example, see W. J. Bowers and G. L. Pierce, "The Illusion of Deterrence in Isaac Ehlich's Research on Capital Punishment," *Yale Law Journal* 85, no. 2 (1975):

187–208; Peter Passell and John Taylor, "The Deterrent Effect of Capital Punishment: Another View," *American Economic Review* 67 (1977): 445–451; and S. Knorr, "Deterrence and the Death Penalty: A Temporal Cross-Sectional Approach," *Journal of Criminal Law and Criminology* 70 (1979): 235–254.

103.   A very controversial study claims to show evidence that execution does bring about deterrence in a specified ratio of executions to deterred murders. See Isaac Ehrlich, "The Deterrent Effect of Capital Punishment: A Question of Life and Death," *American Economic Review* 65 (1975): 397–417.

104.   *Time*, "An Eye for an Eye," p. 36.

# JUVENILE JUSTICE

**CHAPTER 16**
**The Juvenile Justice System**

# CHAPTER 16

# The Juvenile Justice System

## OBJECTIVES

**After reading this chapter, the student should be able to:**

Discuss what we know about juvenile crime.

Discuss historical aspects of juvenile arrests and court processing.

Discuss the origins of the juvenile justice system.

Discuss the role and function of today's juvenile court.

Discuss the growth and application of constitutional safeguards for juvenile offenders.

Identify the types and characteristics associated with five institutions for juveniles.

Identify and discuss the four major types of general diversion programs for youth. Give an example of how a particular program in each might operate.

Discuss the changes now occurring in the juvenile justice system.

## IMPORTANT TERMS

Juvenile offender
Status offenses
*Parens patriae*
Juvenile reformatories
Organization of juvenile courts
Petition
Intake interview
Juvenile referee

Adjudication inquiry and hearing
Disposition hearing
Juvenile probation officer
*Kent* v. *United States*
*In re Gault*
Detention centers
Training (reform) school
Camps and ranches

Halfway houses and day-care centers
Foster home
Juvenile aftercare
School-related diversion programs
Court-related diversion programs
Police-related diversion programs
Community-related diversion programs
Recent reform efforts

Although the proportion of youth in the U.S. population has declined from the all-time high of the late 1950s and 1960s, the number of juvenile arrests continues to be a subject of widespread alarm. Overall juvenile arrests are actually declining (see Table 16.1), but so is the percentage of juveniles in our population. It appears that although there are now fewer youthful Americans, juveniles are still being arrested for a high percentage of serious crimes. Consider these sobering crime facts gathered during the 1980s about juvenile crime:

- Two-thirds of all arrests and three-quarters of all *Uniform Crime Reports* (UCRs) index arrests were of persons under age thirty.
- Arrests of youths under age twenty-one made up half of all UCR index property crime arrests and almost a third of all violent crime arrests.
- Arrests of juveniles (persons under age eighteen) made up 17 percent of all arrests and 31 percent of all UCR index arrests.
- During 1976 to 1985, the number of arrests of juveniles (persons under age eighteen) fell by 18 percent, reflecting the decline in the size of that age group and a 15 percent drop in their arrest rate.[1]

In some ways this is confounding to criminologists. A few years ago it was predicted that diminishing numbers of juveniles in our population would result in significant drops in juvenile arrests and overall crime rates. Although both of these have occurred, they have not proportionately dropped as the juvenile population has gotten smaller. Although there is no known explanation for this set of circumstances, it may be that even smaller numbers of juveniles are committing even more crimes. It also may be partly attributable to the fact that juveniles are increasingly continuing their criminal activity as they become adults. Neither of these possible explanations goes beyond the theory stage, however. Any conclusions, therefore, must be accepted very cautiously.

What do we know about juvenile crime? We know that participation in crime declines with age. If arrest data are an indicator, it would seem that criminal behavior begins to drop off after the teens. Yet, we must be careful here. We shouldn't necessarily think that arrest data are correlated with juvenile crime (see Chapter 1). Remember, juveniles may be more prone to apprehension by the types of crimes they commit and how they commit these crimes—all of which increase their like-

---

TABLE **16-1** Percentage of Change in Arrest Rates for Males and Females Under Age Eighteen, 1977 to 1986

| Offense Charged | Percent Change in Male Arrests | Percent Change in Female Arrests |
|---|---|---|
| Murder and nonnegligent homicide | + 3.0 | − 31.0 |
| Forcible rape | + 23.5 | − 20.7 |
| Robbery | − 16.2 | − 22.0 |
| Aggravated assault | + 9.7 | + 15.3 |
| Burglary | − 38.9 | − 22.9 |
| Larceny-theft | − 3.3 | − 13.1 |
| Motor vehicle theft | − 25.6 | − 9.6 |
| Arson | − 21.8 | − 16.4 |
| Total violent crime | − 2.3 | + 1.7 |
| Total property crime | − 18.9 | − 13.9 |

*Source:* FBI, *Crime in the United States—1986* (Washington, D.C.: Government Printing Office, 1987), p. 169.

---

lihood of arrest. This would throw off the supposed relationship between crimes being committed and arrests made.

An excellent insight into juvenile crime occurred in 1981 when the federal government published an excellent five-volume study using National Crime Survey data for the years 1973 to 1977. It remains probably the best source of information available.[2] The study concluded from the survey results that juveniles (persons less than eighteen years of age) committed 23 percent of the violent crimes against persons. Specifically, the study suggested that juveniles committed over 8 percent of the rapes, 25 percent of the robberies, nearly 18 percent of the aggravated assaults, and over 30 percent of the personal larcenies during those years. However, the massive studies indicated that juvenile crime is less serious in terms of weapons use, thefts, financial losses, and injuries than is adult crime. Moreover, during the five years of the study period, rates seemed to remain constant, with little or no fluctuation.

Some research on juvenile crime

It should come as no surprise that juveniles are involved more frequently in multiple-offender (gang) crimes. Obviously, the long-recognized phenomenon of peer pressure and association contribute to the relatively high incidence of these types of crimes among youth. Juveniles did not use guns or other weapons as frequently in committing their crimes as did older offenders, and again, the use of weapons in crime did not increase during the five years of data gathering. The only possible exception to this was in poor neighborhoods, where juveniles and youthful offenders (ages eighteen to twenty years), but not adults, were more likely to use weapons than were their counterparts in wealthier neighborhoods. This certainly seems to be the case in some areas. In recent years juvenile gang violence using guns and involving a series of indiscriminate killings has exploded in some cities. Los Angeles, for instance, has experienced serious outbreaks of random violence in "ride-by" shootings. Youth gangs in that city, struggling for control of the illicit "crack" trade, have turned some neighborhoods into virtual battlegrounds.[3]

Several findings of the study may be at odds with certain popularly held conceptions of crime and offenders. First, there seems to be no relationship between general economic conditions (as measured by unemployment rates, the consumer price index, and gross national product) and crime, either juvenile or adult. And although a "60 Minutes" television program seemed to say that elderly persons were living in fear of juveniles in the neighborhood, the conclusion of the study indicated that the elderly were more than twice as likely to be victimized by adults as by juveniles. Moreover, offenses committed against the elderly were less serious when juvenile offenders were involved. Perhaps the location for the TV documentary was unusual in this respect, or perhaps the fear many elderly residents have of juvenile offenders preying upon them is generally only that: fear with no general substance of fact.

Two final conclusions of the study were that the highest crime rates were among offenders between the ages of eighteen and twenty, and male juveniles committed offenses at about four to fifteen times the rate females did, depending on the type of crime.[4]

## ☐ LONG-TERM HISTORICAL ASPECTS OF JUVENILE ARRESTS AND COURT PROCESSING

Although we have discussed the commission of crimes by juveniles, we have not examined long-term changes in numbers of arrests or numbers of delinquency cases being handled by our juvenile courts. Whereas the research discussed previously covers only five years, other data are available that give us a more long-term look at the serious problem of delinquency and the problems this poses for the police, the juvenile justice system, and the nation.

Long-term trends

We can examine these changes over a twenty-four year period from 1961 to 1985. During this period the number of delinquency cases increased from about 300,000 nationwide in 1961 to 1.4 million in 1985. During this same period of time, the population of juveniles in the U.S. increased by only about 45 percent. Clearly, the growth in arrests and processing of delinquents has far outstripped their relative growth as a percentage of our population during this time. It was only in the mid- to late 1970s that juvenile arrest rates and percentage of juveniles in the population began to level off and run parallel. Can we now feel more comfortable and say that delinquency has reached its peak and is being contained? Again, there is no answer to this perplexing question. The leveling out may possibly be explained by changes in our laws, police procedures, and how the courts view delinquency. For example, we have become much more permissive both by means of laws decriminalizing certain acts (e.g., the use of marijuana), and by the police simply not enforcing such laws. In this way, juveniles who were once arrested for the use of marijuana are not now committing crimes or being arrested (even though the use of such a controlled substance may still be illegal for minors), because the police simply are not interested in filing such charges and hauling juveniles before the courts. The leveling-off trend in the numbers of delinquency cases being prosecuted may also represent changes in disposing of certain acts outside the juvenile courts. For example, the courts may not now be dealing with certain types of delinquency because they involve status offenses, which are described later. The police may also be more lenient and tolerant with juveniles than they were in the past. Instead of referring some types of offenders to the courts, they may be simply turning them over to their parents for handling. For instance, data gathered by the Bureau of Justice Statistics indicate that nearly 54 percent of all juveniles arrested by the police are handled informally within the police department and released.[5]

**THE IMPACT OF STATUS OFFENSES.** Another important current issue that affects the juvenile crime rate—particularly the rate for girls—is what are referred to as *status offenses*. These are acts that are considered delinquent if committed by a child but are not considered crimes if committed by an adult. Examples of such offenses are runaways, ungovernable behavior, curfew violation, truancy, promiscuity, and possession of alcohol. Although boys are infrequently charged with these crimes, estimates are that 50 to 75 percent of those arrested and confined to a juvenile institution for such crimes are females.[6] What compounds the problem is that in spite of the nature of these offenses, research indicates that girls charged with status offense violations are often held in detention for longer periods of time and placed less frequently in community programs than are boys.[7]

The definition and issue of status offenses

There is a great deal of argument surrounding the issue of the proper handling of status offenders. Many groups want to see the juvenile courts get out of the business of dealing with juveniles charged with acts that make them "delinquents" but that would not be crimes if they were adults. Although exact figures are not available, the most recent estimates from the National Center of Juvenile Justice indicate that 15 percent of the cases filed in American juvenile and family courts are specific status offenses.[8] Of this number it is estimated that nearly one-third of

Judicial experts continue to debate the best way to handle status offenses such as truancy or running away from home. (Mary Ellen Mark Library)

the juveniles charged with such "noncriminal" behavior spend time in a secure jail or detention facility before or after adjudication.[9]

Groups such as the National Council on Crime and Delinquency argue strongly that such jurisdiction should be removed from the juvenile courts. They say that the judicial system is simply a poor instrument for resolving intrafamily conflicts and dealing with these cases. Such actions result in a vastly disproportionate draining of time and resources, to the detriment of other cases, such as neglect, abuse, or delinquency, which are properly the jurisdiction of the court and represent threats to safety that the court must address.[10] The American Bar Foundation expresses similar feelings when it says:

> In the great majority of American jurisdictions, status offenders are subject to exactly the same dispositions as minors who commit crimes, including commitment to state training schools. . . . A system which allows the same sanctions for parental defiance as armed robbery—often with only the barest glance at the reasonableness of parental conduct—can only be seen as inept or unfair.[11]

On the other hand, those groups such as the National Council of Juvenile and Family Court Judges argue that the juvenile courts need to retain jurisdiction over such cases. They argue:

> If we remove the status offenses from the juvenile courts, to a great degree we are removing the underpinnings that the law has provided for parents. If a child disobeys, or wants to run off with undesirable friends, he can go to his parents and say, "I'm leaving, what are you going to do about it?" The parent will have little he can do except use his powers of persuasion; and the parents whose children need this type of external support the most are apt to be the parents who have the least powers of persuasion. I think the public would hesitate to remove the family category status offenses.
>
> Status offenses are among the most serious matters that come before our courts, as serious certainly as car theft and shoplifting and possibly burglary. Status offenses are the tip of the iceberg, or maybe more appropriately, the tip of the volcano.

Arguments for and against removal of status offenders from the juvenile justice process

What little we see on the surface: skipping some school, staying out late, dating boys the father doesn't like, looks rather small and harmless. But for these who get as far as the court, there is usually much under the surface. Status offenses are an indication of some serious trouble. That this is the place where we can help, where we can and should provide compulsory help if the family is not willing to seek help. This is the place where we can reduce the crime rates of the future. Because if we can help a child to unravel incorrigibility, absenting, truancies, drinking, then maybe we can do much through social work to make happier children, more contented children, better citizens . . . which is maybe what it's all about.[12]

Problem with resources **INADEQUATE RESOURCES AND INSTITUTIONS.** States often do not have effective programming in institutions for delinquents. This is particularly true for female youths. The state training schools for youthful female offenders offer even fewer institutional services, such as educational and vocational programs, than are available for boys. As a result, young female offenders have less access to the range of community programs that can make possible the after-release transition from a troubled adolescence to well-adjusted adulthood.[13]

The lack of programs and facilities for female offenders is only one part of the problem. The total lack of available alternatives for juvenile court judges in many of our states is yet another concern. Wooden, in his book examining some of the horrors of institutionalized female delinquents, tells of one particularly horrible case:

> Susie, a 12-year-old who had run away from home to escape her stepfather's sexual advances, was sent by the juvenile court to a juvenile correctional facility as a "person in need of supervision" [a status offender]. Once there, she became the victim of sexual assaults by other girls as well as the counselors. Then she was put into solitary confinement in a strip cell for several weeks. She was fed on a meager ration of bread and water, given nothing to read, and only thin pajamas to wear. As her anger increased, so did her custodian's assessment of her unmanageability. She was eventually transferred to a state mental institution, where she is still in custody.[14]

Although this is an extreme and unusual case, which is certainly not typical, it does point out what can happen. Situations like this inevitably lead to a condemnation of the entire juvenile justice system. In fact, it has been suggested by some critics that the entire juvenile justice system should be dismantled. The problem is such critics cannot come up with an acceptable alternative—nor apparently can society. The remainder of this chapter examines the operations of the juvenile court together with certain other considerations that bear upon the juvenile justice system.

## ORIGINS OF THE JUVENILE JUSTICE SYSTEM

Legal foundation is unclear Scholars and historians are unable to agree on the legal foundation for the present-day juvenile court. Some argue that its beginnings can be traced to the English feudal courts of high chancery. Under the English laws of equity, the courts of high chancery were given the responsibility by the crown to serve as *parens patriae* (in place of the parent) to protect the interest of the child whose property was in jeopardy. Later, these courts extended their protection to other areas of general child welfare and incorporated the neglected and dependent child within their jurisdiction. There is no indication, however, that these courts exercised any jurisdiction over the delinquent child.

The other view suggests that juvenile courts sprang from the common law of crimes. Under the common law, a child under seven years of age was considered incapable of developing the required criminal intent, and a child between the ages of seven and fourteen was also deemed incapable of developing the required intent unless it could be shown by his maturity and understanding that he was aware of the consequences of his actions. Because of this, and because adult criminal courts were unable to deal effectively with youthful offenders, special quasi-judicial tribunals began to develop to deal with children. Eventually the administrative and procedural guidelines that grew out of these tribunals became commonly accepted policies, which were then institutionalized into practice as a way to deal with delinquent youth.

Until about 1825 there were no special provisions for handling delinquents in America. The common law and customary practice of dealing with youthful offenders was to assume that children accused of misbehavior and crimes were guilty as charged. Possible innocence was not considered: The jury's responsibility was to determine if children understood their offenses. Juries were often reluctant to sentence children to jail and often acquitted them after a brief trial, finding "lack of knowledge" the reason for the crime.[15]

By the early nineteenth century this method of handling delinquents had become unsatisfactory for two major reasons. First, despite courtroom partiality toward youths, increasing numbers were being convicted and sent to jails, where it was commonly believed that they were schooled in crime by adult offenders. Second, and more important, some children gained acquittal by appealing to the jury's sympathy—an equally unsatisfactory disposition because it allowed them to escape the consequences of their actions.[16]

## Early Juvenile Reformatories

The shortcomings in the criminal justice system prompted concerned reform groups in Boston, New York, and Philadelphia to create special institutions for juveniles. The first refuge was founded in New York in 1824 by members of the Society for the Reformation of Juvenile Delinquents. In 1826, following the recommendation of Boston's mayor, the Boston City Council founded the House of Reformation for juvenile offenders. At the same time, a group of Philadelphia's leading citizens received a charter to form a house of refuge, which opened in 1828. The New York and Philadelphia refuges were privately managed, although they did receive public sanction and financial aid; the Boston House of Reformation was a municipal institution. These three institutions were the only organized efforts to reform juvenile delinquents until 1847, when state institutions were opened in Massachusetts and New York.[17]

The guiding premise of these early reformatories was that children should be punished, not cruelly, but correctly. Thus, a regimen of work, study, and imposed discipline was adopted in which they would be taught the habits of piety, honesty, sobriety, and hard work.[18] These early reformatories were required by their charters to receive destitute and orphaned children as well as those convicted of crimes—crimes sometimes no greater than vagrancy, idleness, or stubbornness.[19]

Although their initial purpose of reform must be admired, the refuges did not live up to the glowing expectations of their founders. These institutions were soon

Early reformatories for juveniles were intended to teach children to lead proper lives. Here a well-bred young lady visits boys in prison and distributes gifts. (The Bettmann Archive)

criticized for their inability to halt juvenile delinquency or to prevent the spread of violent activities by gangs of youth who roamed the streets of our major cities after the Civil War. Although one cannot blame these reformatories completely for the growing upsurge in delinquency, because they were not equipped to handle all the children who came before the courts, they can be directly blamed for failing to deal effectively with those under their care.

These early institutions were immediately faced with the problem of overcrowding and having to deal with large numbers of children without adequate financial resources. To make ends meet, they began entering into contractual agreements with private business to provide child labor. This soon led to scandalous instances of brutality and neglect by private entrepreneurs who exploited the children. Although education was an initial goal of these refuges, it was quickly replaced by economic opportunism. The children were soon seen as laborers who could both produce a profit for the private business and ensure the financial stability of the institution. Thus, time devoted to schooling could no longer be justified on economic grounds.

Another problem that contributed to the failure of the refuges was the indiscriminate grouping of serious offenders with children who were not delinquents or who had committed only minor offenses. Inevitably, the recalcitrant and youthful serious offenders began exerting their influence, and the refuges became miniature schools of crime.[20]

## The Development of Juvenile Courts

Developing along with the idea that juveniles and adults should be institutionalized separately was the concept that children should be separated from adults before and during the trial. In 1861, the mayor of Chicago was authorized to appoint a special commission to hear and decide cases that involved boys from ages six to seventeen who were charged with committing minor offenses. In 1867, this commission was empowered to place the delinquents who came before it on probation or to sentence them to a special institution for delinquent children. In 1869, a Massachusetts law permitted the employment of a state agent who would be available for counsel and guidance to the court and would locate and report on foster homes that the court might use in placing of the children who came before it.[21] Boston passed a law in 1870 that required that children's cases should be heard separately and that an authorized state agent should be appointed to investigate cases, attend trials, and protect children's interests.[22] A few years later, Massachusetts passed additional legislation that specified that in juvenile cases, the courts were to hold separate sessions, schedule juvenile cases by a special docket, and maintain a separate records system.

Chicago is credited with the first true juvenile court in the United States. In **First true juvenile court** the last decade of the nineteenth century, a group of reformers consisting of some local jurists, the Illinois Bar Association, civic groups, social scientists, and social workers worked to persuade the Illinois legislature to enact laws dealing with children and to vest the authority for applying these laws in a court that would be designated specifically for this purpose. In April 1899, the legislature passed the Act to Regulate Treatment and Control of Dependent, Neglected, and Delinquent Children, and on July 1, 1899, the Juvenile Court of Cook County was established in Chicago. It marked the first time that a specific court had the responsibility for dependent, neglected, and delinquent children. The philosophy that guided the **Guiding philosophy** original legislation, and which is still important in present-day thinking, was that the juvenile should be protected and that this protection was a responsibility of the court. The delinquent child was not to be treated as a criminal, but as a person in need of help and reform.[23] To accomplish this, some changes were made in juvenile courts. In place of the adversarial proceedings that typify the adult criminal trial, informal hearings were conducted in an atmosphere more conducive to treatment than the adjudicating guilt or fixing blame. In this informal atmosphere, the judge assumed the role of a fatherly and sympathetic figure while remaining a symbol of authority. Special emphasis was placed on investigating, diagnosing, and prescribing treatment. The individual's background was more important than the facts of a given incident; specific conduct was regarded more as symptomatic of the need for the court to apply its resources and to help rather than as a prerequisite for jurisdiction.

Because the ostensible purpose of the juvenile court was to treat and help rather than adjudicate guilt or innocence, the court was empowered to act in ways inconsistent with many of the procedural safeguards available to adults in the regular courts. For example, because the hearing was not an adversarial process, there was no need for defense lawyers or a prosecutor to be present. Trials by juries were dispensed with for the same reason. Other basic rights, such as the right to cross-examine and to be confronted with the witnesses against the accused, were seldom practiced in the courts. By the same token, the child who was found guilty of a deliquent act had no right to appeal to a higher state court for review.

In place of these legal guarantees and rights, the courts employed behavioral scientists, particularly social workers, psychologists, and psychiatrists, because delinquency was considered a disease that needed expert diagnosis and treatment. This use of treatment personnel had been a unique characteristic of the entire juvenile justice process since its inception. Along with this emphasis, a new legal vocabulary developed that was adopted by the juvenile court. Instead of a complaint, a petition was substituted; a summons was used in place of a warrant; instead of a preliminary hearing, there was an intake interview; in place of an arraignment, there was a hearing or inquiry; finding of involvement replaced a conviction; and there was a disposition instead of a sentence.

By 1911, a dozen states had followed the example set by Illinois, and by 1925 all but two states had instituted juvenile courts. Today there are juvenile court acts in all fifty states and the District of Columbia, with approximately 2,700 courts responsible for hearing cases involving children.[24] Although juvenile courts vary greatly in their organization and staffing, generally the states adopted the basic philosophy and principles of the Chicago court and the Illinois act as well as many of the legal features associated with these pioneer efforts.

## ☐ THE JUVENILE COURT TODAY

Over the years, the court has evolved from an institution that was established to help reform delinquents to an institution that some contend is nearly as bad as the social ill it is supposed to correct. As a result, the juvenile court has increasingly been the subject of reform efforts. Underlying the growing criticism of the court is the harsh observation that it often functions as a sieve through which most troubled children come and go with neither punishment, rehabilitation, nor help. To evaluate these criticisms properly, we must first understand what the court actually is and how it operates.

### Role

Legal jurisdiction of the juvenile court

The juvenile court today has the responsibility and authority to adjudicate matters that involve young people. it has original jurisdiction over all children under a specific age, usually eighteen. Table 16.2 shows the statutory age by states of those considered "juveniles" under the law. In some states juvenile courts share jurisdiction with the general trial courts under youthful offender statutes, which might raise the age limit to twenty-one for offenders with no prior criminal record. In addition to delinquency cases, juvenile courts in most jurisdictions handle cases involving neglected and dependent children as well as children who are considered in the law to be "wayward." A "wayward child" is typically defined as "a child between seven and seventeen years of age who habitually associates with vicious or immoral persons, or who is growing up in the circumstances exposing him or

TABLE **16.2**   Age of Offender Under Juvenile Court Jurisdiction

| Age in Years | States |
|---|---|
| 15 | Connecticut, New York, North Carolina |
| 16 | Georgia, Illinois, Louisiana, Massachusetts, Missouri, South Carolina, Texas |
| 17 | Alabama, Alaska, Arizona, Arkansas, California, Colorado, Delaware, District of Columbia, Florida, Hawaii, Idaho, Indiana, Iowa, Kansas, Kentucky, Maine, Maryland, Michigan, Minnesota, Mississippi, Montana, Nebraska, Nevada, New Hampshire, New Jersey, New Mexico, North Dakota, Ohio, Oklahoma, Oregon, Pennsylvania, Rhode Island, South Dakota, Tennessee, Utah, Vermont, Virginia, Washington, West Virginia, Wisconsin, Federal districts |
| 18 | Wyoming |

*Source:* Linda A. Szymanski, *Upper Age of Juvenile Court Jurisdiction Statutes Analysis* (National Center for Juvenile Justice, March 1987).

her to lead an immoral, vicious, or criminal life."[25] The law also sometimes refers to such young people as "children in need of supervision" or "CHINS" for short.

A few states have given their juvenile courts limited authority to adjudicate offenses committed by an adult upon a child, such as child abuse or contribution to the delinquency of a minor. In large urban areas, juvenile courts are often responsible for the maintenance of detention facilities. Usually, these facilities are for the temporary housing of children who come to the attention of the court either as delinquents or as neglected or dependent children. In recent years juvenile courts have tried to reserve such detention facilities only for delinquent children. For neglected or dependent children, other facilities such as foster homes or chil-

Juvenile courts deal with "wayward" children as well as those who have been apprehended in crime. (© Billy E. Barnes)

dren's shelters are sought. A child charged with a serious criminal offense is usually transferred to a state juvenile institution after adjudication by the court.

In about forty states, the juvenile courts have some flexibility in exercising their original jurisdiction and thus can waive jurisdiction over a minor, who will then be transferred to the adult criminal court for trial. These waiver laws vary greatly. In about half of the states that permit this practice, the juvenile court alone decides whether the child should be transferred to the adult court. In about one-third of these states, waiver is authorized for any offense but usually only when the child is older than the age of fifteen or sixteen. Some states permit waiver when the child commits another crime while under court supervision. In other states, the authority for the juvenile court to transfer a minor to the general trial courts is determined by both the offender's age and the type of crime committed.[26] For example, Florida, before it recently changed its law, took into consideration factors such as the seriousness of the offense; the need for community protection; whether it was a crime against the person or property and the injury sustained; the sophistication and maturity of the juvenile; the record and previous history of the juvenile; and prospects for rehabilitation.[27] Other states consider similar factors.

In the past ten years, a number of states have become more specific in developing certain "target crimes" for which juveniles can be waived to adult court. These typically include the crimes of murder, rape, robbery, manslaughter, kidnapping, and aggravated assault.[28]

Although more and more states have passed this type of authorizing legislation, it is not fully known what impact it has had. There is no comprehensive research to give us any idea how extensively the juvenile courts are using these laws to turn these types of offenders over to the adult courts for prosecution.

### Organization

**Multiple methods of juvenile court organization**

Typically, juvenile courts follow two broad patterns of organization. In many areas the juvenile court is a specialized function of an existing court. This can be a court of general jurisdiction or a court of limited and special jurisdiction. It can be an arm of the court that tries major criminal and civil cases, a general trial court of limited and special jurisdiction such as a municipal court, or a specialized court such as a probate or other form of court of equity (as distinguished from a court of law) such as a chancellor's or surrogate court.

In some states special family courts have been created. These courts also handle general domestic matters such as divorces, custody cases, and similar "family" problems. The trend in recent years has been to create such family courts and to vest them with authority over delinquency cases as well as cases of neglect and dependency. Table 16.3 shows the broad variation of juvenile court systems in most states.

### Problems

**Diverse population**

Overall, juvenile courts suffer from a number of weaknesses. First, diversity of the juvenile court's role often creates problems. Although it is expected to help wayward children, it is also expected to protect the community from offenders who are sometimes as dangerous as adult criminals.

**Lack of judicial status**

Another source of difficulty is the inferior position that the juvenile court usually has in the court hierarchy. Because few jurisdictions have made it a separate

TABLE **16.3**   Juvenile Court Systems

| Court System | State(s) |
|---|---|
| Family and domestic relations court | Delaware, Hawaii, New York, Rhode Island, South Carolina |
| Juvenile and domestic relations court | New Jersey, Virgin Islands, Virginia |
| Independent juvenile court | Utah, Wyoming |
| Court of common pleas | Ohio, Pennsylvania |
| Juvenile division of probate court | Michigan |
| Circuit and district courts, concurrently | Alabama |
| Circuit and magistrate's courts, concurrently (the latter having limited jurisdiction and no authority to confine) | West Virginia |
| Independent juvenile court or superior court judge sitting as juvenile court judge | Georgia |
| Circuit courts—delinquency: Chancery and Probate courts—neglected and dependency cases | Arkansas |
| Trial division of high court | American Samoa |
| Juvenile division of district court plus juvenile court for specific counties (only Denver County in Colorado) | Colorado and Massachusetts |
| Each county chooses which court is juvenile court[a] | Texas |
| Independent juvenile and county courts | Nebraska, Tennessee |
| Judges are assigned juvenile jurisdiction, plus there are separate provisions for specific counties | Wisconsin |
| Special juvenile courts or family courts in specific parishes; where these have not been established, district courts have jurisdiction in parishes within their districts and parish courts plus city courts have concurrent jurisdiction with district courts only within their constitutionally established jurisdictional boundaries | Louisiana |
| District court is juvenile court in specific counties; in counties of not more than 200,000 (and in St. Louis County), the probate court handles juvenile matters | Minnesota |
| Youth court division of the family court or the county court or the chancery court or certain municipal courts | Mississippi |
| Trial division of the high court or the district or community courts | Trust Territories |
| Juvenile cases are heard in district court by a judge or judges who volunteer to specialize in juvenile cases. Where no judge volunteers to specialize, the chief district court judge assigns individual judges to serve in juvenile court on a rotating basis. | North Carolina |

[a]This is true of other states also; that is, the size of the county or various other factors may determine which court sits as the juvenile court in a given area of the state. For example, in Nebraska, in counties of 30,000 or more, if the electorate agrees, an independent juvenile court may be established.

*Source:* U.S. Department of Justice, *A Comparative Analysis of Juvenile Codes* (Washington, D.C.: U.S. Government Printing Office, 1980), p. 7.

court on a level with other courts of general jurisdiction, it is held in low regard by lawyers, judges, and the police. It is, for example, often contemptuously referred to as "kiddie court." The court, by virtue of its organization, must rely greatly on local government and local tax support for its operation. Because it is often a local and not a state court, its access to resources is severely curtailed. Such a situation makes our juvenile courts very susceptible to local pressures, particularly because it requires more court-related resources, such as social services, detention facilities,

Broad needs and local dependence

foster and group homes and other considerations. Adult courts do not require these additional services. Its dependent state makes the court very vulnerable to criticism and further complicates its already intricate relationships with other criminal justice agencies. Increasingly, the juvenile court has been looked upon as a provider of the social services to which local government has become more and more committed. To carry out even a portion of these obligations, it must not only curtail its own activities, particularly its judicial responsibilities, but also rely heavily on the goodwill and assistance of many local groups, such as the police, schools, and welfare agencies. This reliance often creates cross-pressures, such as the police demanding that the court deal more strictly with delinquents while another agency urges greater leniency. Consequently, the juvenile court may find itself embroiled in local conflicts between the police and school officials such as the handling of arrests made during school hours and on school property for marijuana use and other offenses.

Underlying and intensifying these difficulties is the court's lack of resources. Procedures for gathering and recording information and other essential tasks are cumbersome and antiquated. The struggle to carry out service functions without adequate staff and facilities undermines judicial responsibilities. In the final analysis, neither the delinquency prevention functions nor the general service functions are performed properly.

## ▢ THE JUVENILE JUSTICE PROCESS

The vast majority of juveniles who appear in juvenile court are referred there by the police who have arrested them. In some cases, private citizens or the child's parents can refer the child to the jurisdiction of the court. Just as the arrest of an adult must be accompanied by an arrest warrant, a legal instrument called a *petition* must be filed with the juvenile court to give the court authority to intervene in the matter. Like an arrest warrant, a petition must specify the particular statutory violation, and it usually includes such additional information as the name, age, and residence of the child; the names and residences of the child's parents or guardians; and a brief description of the circumstances surrounding the commission of the offense.

### The Intake Interview

The next step is the intake interview. If the child is in custody, most states require that an *intake interview* be held within a specified time after arrest. The intake interview is a preliminary examination of the facts conducted by the court. Usually, the intake process is presided over by a referee. Although not a judge, the referee often has a background in social work or the behavioral sciences and in some instances may also be an attorney. Frequently, the referee is a probation officer assigned to the juvenile court. The functions of the intake interview are to protect the interests of the child and to dispose of those cases that do not warrant the time and expense of court adjudication. This preliminary inquiry may vary from a brief examination of the facts to an in-depth investigation of the juvenile's case, including a background investigation of the child's family, interviews with school officials, and psychological or psychiatric testing. Most states also provide that

A preliminary examination

Intake referee

relevant witnesses can be summoned by the court at the intake interview and be forced to appear and give testimony under penalty of law. If the interview is a formal one, the child, the child's parents, and an attorney can be present. Depending on the referee's judgment as to the sufficiency of evidence, the need for court intervention, and the basis for legal jurisdiction of the court, the referee can: (1) dismiss the case; (2) authorize a hearing before the juvenile court judge; or (3) make an informal adjustment. If the referee chooses the latter course, he or she can exercise some limited discretion in disposing of the case. In many juvenile courts, approximately half of the cases are informally adjusted by referral to another agency, by continuation on informal probation, or handled in some other way.[29]

The referee or intake officer also determines if the child should be detained pending court action. In some jurisdictions, the child does not have the statutory right to bail as do most adults accused of crimes. In most jurisdictions that do not extend the right of bail of to the juvenile, there are provisions for the child to be released to his or her parents unless it can be demonstrated that the release of the child poses a threat to the safety and well-being of the community or to the child. When detention is warranted, the referee usually has the right to place the child into detention but only limited authority to hold the child there. If more extended detention pending the formal appearance of the child before the court is warranted, this must be authorized by the juvenile court judge.

## The Adjudication Inquiry and Adjudication Hearing

If the referee or intake officer determines that the court should formally intervene in the case, the juvenile then appears before the judge for the arraignment. This step is usually called an *adjudication inquiry*, a *judicial hearing*, or, in some courts, an *arraignment hearing*. At this stage, the juvenile court judge determines if the facts and the nature of the child's behavior warrant an adjudication hearing by the court. In recent years, provisions have been made to notify the juvenile at this stage of the charges against the child and to advise him or her of his or her constitutional rights and right to an attorney.

*Appearance before the juvenile court*

At the adjudication inquiry, the judge can dispose of the case or order a formal adjudication hearing, depending on the seriousness of the case. If it is a case of a serious offense or if the child indicates that he or she wants a hearing or wants to hire an attorney, the judge schedules an adjudication hearing.

The adjudication hearing in the juvenile process is different from the adult trial process. To keep the process more informal and less adversarial, rules of evidence are often not strictly adhered to, and unsworn and hearsay testimony might be received and considered. However, with the increased use of the right to counsel, the juvenile process is becoming more formal and legalistic. Evidence standards are more similar to the adult courts under these circumstances. Even so, although the standard of proof is supposed to be guilt beyond a reasonable doubt, this standard is sometimes loosely applied. Most juvenile courts have no provisions for jury trials, and the state may not even be represented by the prosecutor. Instead, the prosecution of the case may fall upon a probation officer who acts less like a legal inquisitor, such as a prosecutor would, and more like an investigator giving testimony on the alleged offense and the investigation of the case. Given the growing legal formality of delinquency hearings, it is generally the case that the prosecutor's office in the jurisdiction will represent the state at the adjudication hearing.

*Some differences compared with an adult trial*

Because their objective is to protect and help the child, juvenile courts usually attempt to exclude from these proceedings all persons except those who have relevant and material testimony to present. In determining its disposition of the juvenile, the court places a great deal of reliance on the clinical and social report prepared by the probation officer and the diagnostic staff. This report is very similar to the presentence investigation in the adult criminal court, with the possible exception of its greater emphasis on diagnostic testing.

## Disposition

**Broad discretion of juvenile court judges**

Most states give juvenile court judges very broad discretion to dispose of cases. At these *disposition hearings*, the judge has the power to dismiss the case, give the

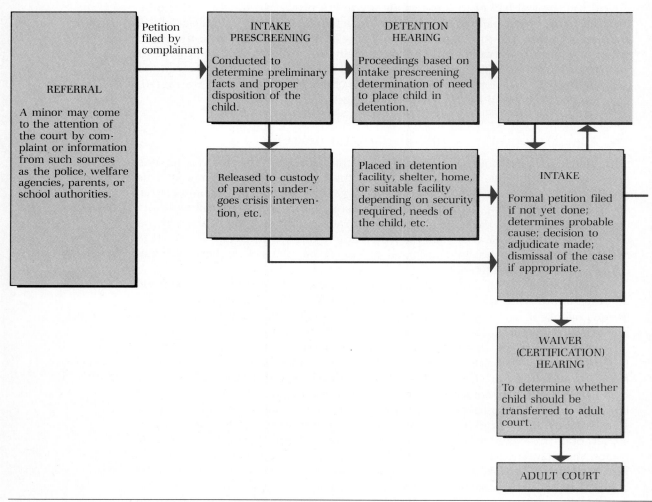

FIGURE **16.1**     Basic juvenile justice process. *Note:* In a number of states the filing of the petition follows the intake interviews. In those states, if the referee or similar official concludes that the facts of the case warrant the formal intervention of the court, a petition is issued that binds the child over to the jurisdiction of the court. In other states, a petition must be signed before the formal process (beginning with intake) can be initiated.

juvenile a warning, impose a fine, place him on probation, arrange for restitution, refer him or her to an agency or treatment facility, or commit him or her to an institution. A child sentenced to an institution usually receives an indeterminate sentence not to exceed his or her twenty-first birthday. If the child's crime or the community's protection warrants a longer period of incarceration, at age twenty-one he or she may be transferred to an institution that handles adult offenders. Under these circumstances, a juvenile might be committed to an extended period of incarceration in both juvenile and adult institutions.[30] Figure 16.1 indicates the basic juvenile justice process.

There is as much variation in the structure and organization of agencies that administer services and facilities for delinquent children as there is in the structure of the courts. As a result, the responsibility for the child often shifts back and forth

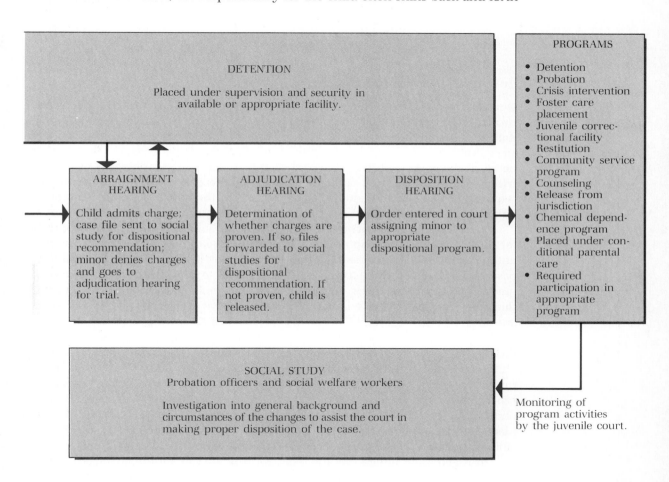

PROGRAMS

- Detention
- Probation
- Crisis intervention
- Foster care placement
- Juvenile correctional facility
- Restitution
- Community service program
- Counseling
- Release from jurisdiction
- Chemical dependence program
- Placed under conditional parental care
- Required participation in appropriate program

DETENTION

Placed under supervision and security in available or appropriate facility.

ARRAIGNMENT HEARING

Child admits charge; case file sent to social study for dispositional recommendation; minor denies charges and goes to adjudication hearing for trial.

ADJUDICATION HEARING

Determination of whether charges are proven. If so, files forwarded to social studies for dispositional recommendation. If not proven, child is released.

DISPOSITION HEARING

Order entered in court assigning minor to appropriate dispositional program.

SOCIAL STUDY
Probation officers and social welfare workers

Investigation into general background and circumstances of the changes to assist the court in making proper disposition of the case.

Monitoring of program activities by the juvenile court.

among courts and a variety of public and private agencies, both state and local. A number of states are now trying to incorporate all public agencies that deal with the child into a single, unified state agency. Such departments of youth services generally have the following responsibilities:

General responsibilities
of state youth service
departments

1. To provide all state institutional, probation, and aftercare services to children committed to the department by the juvenile court.
2. To set minimum standards for all state, local, private, and public institutions including probation and aftercare programs for neglected, dependent, and delinquent juveniles.
3. To enter into contractual agreement with private or nonprofit organizations to provide services, operate facilities, and so on.
4. The operation of any public institutional program, probation, and aftercare services that do not meet the minimum standards as set forth by the Department.[31]

## Role of the Probation Officer

Diagnosis, rehabilitation, and supervision

One of the most important members of the juvenile court team is the juvenile probation officer. The function of the juvenile probation officer is to match individualized, rehabilitative diagnosis and treatment with effective community supervision. Probation officers investigate the juvenile's social history and serve as a link between the court and the behavioral scientists, such as psychologists or psychiatrists, who diagnose the treatment required by the child. The probation officer is required to make factual and objective reports to the court as well as recommendations and suggestions for the proper treatment and disposition of the juvenile.

As a legal representative of the court, the probation officer is also responsible for developing the probation plan. The probation plan is both a study of the child and a recommended course of action for the court in dealing with the child. It is based on a social study of the child, which comes from such sources as the delinquent, parents or relatives, school officials, the police, social agencies, and the diagnostic services of behavioral scientists who have examined the child. The plan specifies whether the child needs the services of the court, whether it is more feasible to treat him or her in the community under a supervising probation officer, or whether institutionalization is warranted. If the investigation indicates that the child can better use the services of community agencies other than the court, the probation officer must see that the delinquent is willing to accept the referral and must provide the agency with the information needed to work effectively with the child. If the probation plan does not call for institutionalization and if the child is placed under supervision in the community, the probation officer is also responsible for seeing that the child adheres to the probation plan.

It is generally agreed that the most appropriate role for the juvenile probation officer is that of a correctional social worker rather than that of a law enforcement officer. Thus, the probation officer is expected to provide treatment consistent with the philosophy of social work as practiced today. To accomplish this, the juvenile probation officer must know how to use and interpret findings from psychological testing and psychiatric examinations. The probation officer also guides and counsels the child about problems that may have played an important role in the child's past delinquencies.

## THE JUVENILE COURT AND PROCEDURAL SAFEGUARDS

Throughout its history, the juvenile court in America has maintained that because its function is to protect the child, it was not appropriate for that tribunal to engage in the adversarial tactics that mark the adult criminal trial. This philosophy has had a tremendous impact on how the juvenile court has operated. From its inception, wide differences have been tolerated—indeed insisted on—between the procedural rights accorded to adults and those of juveniles. As a consequence, almost all jurisdictions until recently did not grant juveniles the basic constitutional rights that are afforded adults charged with a crime. Although the U.S. Supreme Court has extended a number of constitutional rights to juveniles being handled by the juvenile courts, the child still does not have the constitutional right to bail, to indictment by grand jury, to a public trial, or to trial by jury. Although the U.S. Supreme Court has not ruled that juveniles have these constitutional rights, individual states may adopt state laws granting some of these rights. Rules governing the arrest and interrogation of adults by the police are frequently not observed in the case of juveniles.[32]

*Lack of procedural rights*

According to Robert Shears, because the child should be made "to feel that he is the object of the state's care and solicitude" and not that he is under arrest or on trial, the rules that govern our criminal trials are considered by many to be inappropriate to juvenile court proceedings. The right of the state to deny to the child procedural rights was based on the assertion that a child, unlike an adult, has a right "not to liberty, but to custody." The child can be made to obey his or her parents, to go to school, and so on. If the parents do not provide the proper supervision and care of the child—that is, if the child is delinquent or neglected—the state may intervene. When the court intervenes, it does not deprive the child of any rights, because the child has none. The court merely provides the custody to which the child is entitled.[33]

*Justification*

Attitudes such as these and the absence of basic constitutional rights in juvenile court proceedings prompted Roscoe Pound, a former dean of the Harvard Law School, to say of the juvenile court:

> The powers of the Star Chamber [medieval site of torture used to extract a confession from an accused] were a trifle in comparison with those of our juvenile courts. . . . The absence of substantive standards has not necessarily meant the child receives compassionate and individualized treatment. The absence of procedural rules based upon constitutional principles have not always produced fair, efficient and effective procedures. Departures from established principles of due process have frequently resulted not in enlightened procedure, but in arbitrariness.[34]

### Supreme Court Decisions

Beginning in the late 1960s, the Supreme Court began to examine the question of whether the juvenile offender was entitled to the same constitutional guarantees that an adult has in our criminal court system. The first major case of importance was *Kent* v. *United States*, which was decided in 1966.[35]

Morris A. Kent, Jr., age sixteen, was arrested by the Washington, D.C., police in 1961 and charged with housebreaking, robbery, and rape. Kent had a rather extensive juvenile record for housebreaking and purse snatching dating back to

*Extending constitutional protections to the juvenile court*

1959 and was on probation for earlier offenses at the time of his arrest. Upon being apprehended, Kent was taken to police headquarters and interrogated for seven hours, during which time he confessed to other acts of housebreaking, robbery, and rape. After making the confession, Kent was detained at the juvenile receiving home for almost a week without any examination by a judicial officer as to the legality of the arrest and detention.

The juvenile court then waived jurisdiction over Kent, and he was turned over to the adult criminal court to stand trial. The District of Columbia juvenile court was permitted to turn a juvenile over to the adult courts after completing a "full investigation" of the facts in a case. In the Kent case, this "full investigation" consisted of the judge's reviewing the probation report and the social service file that the court's probation staff maintained on Kent. The Supreme Court did not determine the propriety of the waiver or consider the other questionable issues of the validity of the confession or detention without an appropriate judicial hearing. Instead, the Court sent the case back to the juvenile court to determine whether review of a probation file, maintained in regard to the defendant for a prior offense, satisfied the requisite of a full investigation.

The significance of this case lay not so much in the decision as in the indication it gave of the general attitude of the Supreme Court. The Court was putting the juvenile justice system on notice that these courts could not be afforded the luxury of procedural arbitrariness, and it questioned the efficacy of the *parens patriae* philosophy. In the words of the Court:

> There is evidence, in fact, that there may be grounds for concern that the child receives the worst of both worlds; that he gets neither the protection accorded to adults nor the solicitous care and regenerative treatment postulated for children.[36]

In re Gault

The warning of the Court in the Kent case exploded like a bombshell in 1967, when the U.S. Supreme Court proclaimed in the landmark decision of *In re Gault* that children handled by the juvenile courts were entitled to many of the due process guarantees afforded adults.[37] Gerald Gault was a fifteen-year-old who had been committed to the state industrial school by the juvenile court of Gila County, Arizona. Like Kent, Gault was already subject to an earlier juvenile court probation order, based on his having been along with another boy when a woman's purse was taken. In the case that the Court reviewed, a neighbor had charged that Gault and another boy had made an obscene telephone call to her. The police arrested Gault. Gault's parents were at work at the time, and apparently no efforts were made to contact them after their son was taken into custody; they seem to have first learned of their son's detention that evening through the parents of the other boy about whom the neighbor had complained. After hearing of his arrest, Gerald's parents went to the detention home, where they were told why their son was being detained and that a hearing would be held the following day.

The next day the police officer in charge of the case filed a petition for the hearing to be held that day. No copy of the petition was given to the boy's parents. The petition contained only legal allegations and recited no facts. The hearing was conducted in the judge's chambers without the complainant being present, and no sworn testimony was given. The court made no effort to make any record of the proceedings, so the only information concerning the hearing was in the record of a habeas corpus proceeding brought after the juvenile court hearings had been concluded.

Gerald was released from custody two days after the initial hearing, and on that day the police left a note for Mrs. Gault informing her that there would be another hearing three days later. At the second hearing, the judge apparently relied on admissions that the police had obtained from Gerald after he had been arrested. The arresting officer indicated that Gerald had admitted to making the phone call in question. At the beginning of the second hearing, Mrs. Gault asked the court to compel the complainant to attend. The judge ruled that her attendance was not necessary; her version was reported in court on the basis of a telephone conversation the investigating officer had conducted with her. Although the judge had a probation "referral report," it was not shown to Gerald or his parents. At the conclusion of the hearing, the judge committed the boy to the state industrial training school "for the period of his minority, unless sooner discharged by due process of law." Since Gerald was fifteen at the time, he would have been subject to custodial control until his twenty-first birthday. Interestingly, the same offense if committed by an adult would have constituted only a misdemeanor under Arizona law.

Arizona did not have a law that provided for a juvenile to appeal from a juvenile court to a higher state appellate court. Under the circumstances, the Gaults could only file a habeas corpus writ with the Arizona Supreme Court, which was done a few months later. The Arizona Supreme Court ordered a hearing to be held on the writ in the superior court; the latter court denied the writ on the ground that there was no denial of either constitutional or statutory rights in the juvenile court hearing, and the Arizona Supreme Court concurred. On a review, the U.S. Supreme Court reversed the decision of the Arizona Supreme Court, finding that Gault had been denied his fundamental rights to due process. In doing so, it imposed a far reaching set of standards on the thousands of juvenile courts throughout the nation. Specifically, the Court imposed the following procedural safeguards in delinquency cases and thus decreed a new direction in the juvenile court practice.

1. Under the due process clause, it is constitutionally mandated that there be notice of charges given to the juvenile and to his or her parents. This notice must be in writing and must contain the specific charge or allegations of fact on which the proceedings are to be based. The notice must be given as early as possible and "in any event sufficiently in advance of the hearing to permit preparation."[38]
2. In delinquency proceedings that may result in commitment to an institution, the child and the parents must be notified of the child's right to be represented by counsel. If they are indigent, the court must appoint defense counsel.[39]
3. The juvenile has the right to be confronted with the witnesses against him or her.
4. The juvenile must be advised on his or her right against self-incrimination.

The U.S. Supreme Court did not specifically decide in the Gault case whether there is a right to appellate review or whether juvenile courts are required to provide a transcript of the hearings for review. Nor did it answer the question of whether the juvenile offender is entitled to trial by jury or what should be the burden of the state in proving its case against a youth accused of a crime. These issues have been addressed by the Supreme Court in more recent cases. In *In re Winship* [397 U.S. 358 (1970)], the Court reversed the conviction of a twelve-year-old boy who had been declared delinquent after having been accused of stealing $112. The burden of proof used in the delinquency proceeding was a "preponderance of the evidence." The Court held that the correct standard is "proof beyond a reasonable doubt" and that anything less is a violation of the due process requirements of the Fourteenth Amendment.

In the case of *McKeiver* v. *Pennsylvania* [403 U.S. 528 (1971)], the Supreme Court declined to rule that a juvenile facing delinquency proceedings has a constitutional right to a jury trial. The Court felt:

## CAPITAL PUNISHMENT FOR THE YOUNG

David and Nancy Allen were a young couple struggling to raise two kids in a declining, blue-collar neighborhood of North Kansas City. David's brother Robert, thinking the extra income would help out, had offered Nancy a job in a little liquor and sandwich shop he owned. It was the night shift, but David worked near by and would be able to watch over her.

On a July night in 1985, sixteen-year-old Heath Wilkins, his girlfriend Midget, and their friends Bo and Shades planned to carry out a robbery. Wilkins admitted that every detail of the plan was his. Heath and Bo arrived at the shop before 11:00 P.M. Heath ordered a sandwich while Bo hid in the bathroom. Heath asked for extra lettuce, and when the woman turned her back, Bo emerged from hiding. Wilkins pulled a knife and stabbed Nancy eight times—including three wounds to the throat as she pleaded for her life.

The state prosecutor introduced some damaging evidence at Wilkins's trial, indicating the cold-blooded depravity of the killing. This was the so-called "trash-can comparison," which became the centerpiece for the prosecutor's successful plea to the judge for the death penalty. It was something Wilkins said to one of his Menninger psychiatrists in describing why he decided to kill Nancy Allen instead of just taking the cash register money and leaving. Wilkins told the doctor

he had nothing "personal" against Nancy Allen, except that, as a potential future witness against him, she represented an inconvenience. "He compared her to a trash can in his path," the prosecutor recalls. "If you walk around it on your way in, you have to walk around it on your way out. So the best thing to do is kick it out of your way."

Heath Wilkins was described as an abused, self-destructive kid who was in a psychotic state when he committed his crime. When arrested, Wilkins and his girlfriend were living in a hollow kangaroo that stood in Kansas City's Penguin Park, a one-acre piece of scrubby grass dominated by two-story high, cement statues of cartoon-like animals. At night the pair crawled up into the pouch area of the female kangaroo statue, where they slept. Days were spend scrounging food with Bo and Shades, who were also homeless teenagers. They managed to survive by stealing slices of pizza from Show Biz Pizza and by stealing whatever else came their way. When they were able to get some money, they bought drugs.

Wilkins's public defender claims the trial court erred in admitting some evidence into trial, which, if not permitted, may have changed the outcome. This public defender opined the Missouri Supreme Court glossed over this mistake because, "they've been terribly anxious to execute somebody. The state Supreme Court has upheld about 70 death

sentences in the last 10 years but they haven't been able to execute anyone since 1965, since they're getting reversed or stayed by the Eighth Circuit or the Supreme Court. They're frustrated, and along comes Heath who was a volunteer. They didn't care if he was only a sixteen-year-old volunteer."[a]

In 1988 in *Thompson* v. *Oklahoma,* the Supreme Court narrowly ruled against the execution of William Wayne Thompson, who was fifteen years old at the time of his crime, in effect making sixteen the minimum age for execution in the United States. The Wilkins case, along with the companion case of *Stanford* v. *Kentucky,* was decided by the Supreme Court in early summer 1989. The Court ruled that the death sentence imposed by the Missouri court was constitutional. The way is now clear for the states with death penalties to execute sixteen-year-olds for their crimes.

Since the year 1642, when sixteen-year-old Thomas Graunger was hanged for bestiality in the Plymouth Colony of Massachusetts, 281 juvenile offenders have been executed in the United States. When the Supreme Court in the Wilkins case gave their approval, twenty-seven juveniles who committed their crimes before age eighteen were on death row. Texas alone had seven such juvenile offenders awaiting execution.

[a]"The Death Penalty for Juveniles?" *Newsweek* (24 November 1988), p. 34.

If the jury trail were to be injected into the juvenile court system as a matter of right, it would bring with it into that system the traditional delay, the formality, and the clamor of the adversary system and, possibly, the public trial.[40]

Although many students of the juvenile justice process believed that the mandates of the Court would spell the end of the traditional philosophy of the juvenile court, this has not happened. Research on the impact of the Court's pronouncements indicates that a number of things have occurred. First the requirements issued by the Court have not been uniformly adopted by the states. Some researchers believe that the juvenile courts have made only minimal procedural changes in reaction to these decisions.[41] Certainly there was no overnight rush to comply, and the courts have been able to retain their basic philosophy while slowly phasing in the adjustments that the Supreme Court ordered.

Undoubtedly, the overall impact of the Gault case has been to increase legal fact finding. Probably the greatest change has occurred from the growing use of defense lawyers; this procedure seems to have decreased the number of cases that reach adjudication and disposition.[42] This may very well indicate that because of more legalistic screening more cases are being diverted from the formal process of the adjudication hearing.

In the final analysis it would seem that the Supreme Court's extension of procedural due process into the juvenile courts has not seen the end of the general guidelines that tend to distinguish this special court from its adult counterpart. Overall, the benevolent philosophy still is an important part of this special court. Certainly, adjustments had to be made and they have resulted in some changes. Still, the process remains in many ways clearly distinguishable from a trial in an adult court.

## ☐ TYPES OF JUVENILE INSTITUTIONS

The idea of institutionalizing juveniles is a subject that has been buffeted by the crosswinds of change. During the late 1960s and into the mid-1970s, major efforts were made to deinstitutionalize youths who had run afoul of the law. It was thought that the conventional use of institutions for children was a policy that was both overused and bad. Deinstitutionalization took various forms. The removal of status offenders, as mentioned, was such a major effort. So was the policy to close existing reform schools and to use more community-based programs in their place. Institutionalization under secure placement was to be reserved only for the most difficult and serious offender. More attention was also to focus on the careful separation of those juveniles who needed secure placement away from the less hardened and dangerous young offender.

Somehow these efforts seem to have had the reverse effect. Although these attitudes are still expressed as the goal of juvenile corrective efforts, the fact of the matter is that, as in the case of adult offenders, the public has demanded a more punitive reaction. Part of this can be attributed to the growing seriousness of juvenile crime. The predatory actions of violent juvenile crime and the widespread publicity about rampant drug use and its associated gang violence have caused the public to recoil in fear and anger. As a result, institutionalization rates for juvenile

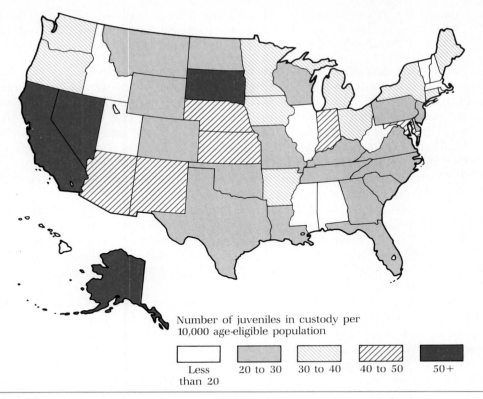

Number of juveniles in custody per
10,000 age-eligible population

| Less than 20 | 20 to 30 | 30 to 40 | 40 to 50 | 50+ |

FIGURE **16.2**  State custody rates for juveniles. [*Sources: Children in Custody: Public Juvenile Facilities, 1985, BJS Bulletin,* October 1986, and *Children in Custody,* 1985, unpublished data.]

offenders are increasing throughout the country. Although the increase is not on level with the increases in adult confinement, it still is a sizeable increase—particularly among privately operated facilities.[43] This latter increase is due to two factors: more commitments and the growing use by the states of privately operated contract facilities to house delinquents. Figure 16.2 shows comparative juvenile incarceration rates by states.

**How juvenile institutions are classified**

Juvenile institutions or facilities are classified in two ways: by the term of stay and the type of environment. The term of stay consists of short-term facilities, which hold juveniles awaiting adjudication or other disposition, and long-term facilities, which house juveniles already adjudicated and committed to custody.

The classification by environment is also of two types. The so-called institutional (or secure) environment is an environment that imposes greater restraints on residents' movement and limits access to the community. Most detention or diagnostic centers, training schools, and ranches would fall into this category. The "open" environment allows greater movement of residents within the facility and more access to the community. These mainly include shelters, halfway houses, group homes, forestry camps, or farms.[44]

Federal, state, and local units of government have developed a wide range of institutions based on these classifications. They all represent different ideas of what needs to be done to help and protect the child and to ensure public safety. Some of the most common need to be briefly described.

## Detention Centers

Detention centers are often operated by local units of government in more popu- Often locally operated lated areas. The primary purpose of the detention center is to house youths who need to be temporarily sheltered or who must be placed in secure placement pending their adjudication by the juvenile court. In the juvenile justice system, they are somewhat similar in purpose to the jail for the adult offender. Admittedly, many detention center officials would be loathe to have them referred to as jail-like facilities, but they do share some common features. It is in such facilities that the police will often take juveniles who have been arrested for serious crimes and who cannot be released until the courts dispose of their cases. Such facilities, however, also house runaways who are picked up by the police, and children who must be removed from their homes for protective reasons pending transferral to a foster home. Hopefully, the facility separates these types of kids depending on their needs and the circumstances leading to their confinement.

## Training (Reform) Schools

The training school, which is often known by its older name, the reform school, A highly criticized traditional response handles the more serious delinquent. In the training school, the child is generally maintained under close custody. Most of these institutions have various programs of psychotherapy, education, and vocational training. Because of overpopulation, budgetary and staff limitations, poor facilities, and the housing of the more hardened delinquent, they generally are not very successful corrective mechanisms. As Alan R. Coffey says:

> Of those juveniles who finish their detention period in a typical training school, 25 to 50 percent return for other offenses. If the role of the training school is to "correct" and "rehabilitate," this percentage of returnees indicates how poorly these goals are being met.[45]

The failure of these training schools is universally acknowledged. In many instances they have been referred to as "junior prisons" or "training schools for criminal careers." Some years ago Massachusetts did a study of its reform schools and found that more than 70 percent of their graduates were returned for the commission of new crimes. This led the state to institute a drastic and controversial measure: The training schools were all closed.[46] The then Commissioner of Youth Services, who was opposed to the training school concept, actually closed the schools when the legislature was out of session. In their place, Massachusetts substituted a system of smaller, community-based treatment centers. This was accompanied by a major deinstitutionalization of juveniles under state care. The Commissioner came under a great deal of political pressure for his action—a situation that ultimately was at least partly responsible for his resignation. Still, important changes had been made—changes that are operating in that state today. The training schools have never reopened. In their place, the state has adopted a number of secure detention facilities, each of which has a small client population. In this way Massachusetts has successfully moved away from the large training school model.

Camps for juvenile delinquents may be run on the military model, requiring the wearing of uniforms and compliance to a rigorous schedule and rules of behavior. (© Billy Grimes)

## Camps and Ranches

Camps and ranches are normally run by the state. Their programs vary, but their general purpose is to avoid the crime-producing atmosphere of the training school and to maintain the delinquent child as part of the community during the treatment process. For instance, these programs typically provide for frequent contact with the community and the development of a program of counseling that involves the child and his or her parents. The emphasis of the program is to modify delinquent attitudes and behavior and to substitute constructive behavior patterns.

Such programs are generally not structured to deal with the delinquent who has serious behavioral patterns. In some states, however, the opposite is true. Special camps or ranch programs have been established in California, Florida, and New York specifically to deal with the seriously disturbed delinquent.

## Halfway Houses and Community Residential and Nonresidential Centers

The juvenile halfway house or group home is becoming an increasingly popular way of dealing with delinquency prevention and treatment. Like its adult counterpart, the juvenile halfway house attempts to bridge the gap between confinement in an institution and the total freedom of the community. In many instances, states sign contracts with private group homes and do not run the homes directly. A few states, such as Washington, run homes owned, staffed, and operated by the state.[47]

Michigan, one of the leaders in this area, has established halfway houses staffed by a caseworker and five child-care workers. Each home has a capacity to house twelve delinquents, and the program consists of both work and school experience. This dual program allows the child to continue his or her education, obtain some work experience, and achieve some financial independence. If the delinquent is not capable of, or not interested in further formal education, he or she is given the opportunity to work full-time.[48]

Community residential and nonresidential centers are operated in many jurisdictions today. The community residential center is a facility that can range from a "secure" placement to a more open arrangement in which clients of the facility have greater freedom to come and go and be involved in the community. The nonresidential center is a place where a child can go for such help as counseling. Typically, the nonresidential center does not keep the child in residence as such. He or she may, for example, be required by the juvenile court to periodically go to the center for counseling or to engage in activities designed to help deal with his or her particular problems.

## Foster Homes

The last institution that needs to be mentioned is the foster home. Foster homes are generally private homes run by foster parents.[49] Most juvenile courts have direct access to such foster homes in which dependent children can be placed if they are likely to experience continued neglect or abuse in their own home. Unfortunately, there are not enough good foster homes to supply the need.

Through the care, control, and guidance that qualified foster parents can provide, rehabilitation would seem to be more likely. In these homes, the probation officer and foster parents often form what amounts to a treatment team. Viewed in this team context, the foster home is certainly correctional and, in many cases, provides perhaps the best elements of any treatment program—close personal attention, understanding, and sympathetic firmness about the necessity of following "family" rules.[50]

## Future Juvenile Institutions

Future types and characteristics of juvenile institutions will most likely reflect some of the same concerns that we are now facing in adult institutions. On the other hand, there will probably be an increased use of community-based treatment services such as halfway homes, agency-operated residential treatment centers, nonresidential programs, regional detention facilities, and foster homes. Although all these institutions exist now, it is likely that more program alternatives and a larger share of the total criminal justice expenditures will be devoted to youth services. During the past ten years, the emphasis of the federal government's anticrime programs has shifted in important ways to the juvenile justice system in an effort to intercede early in a delinquent's life.

Increased alternatives

However, the juvenile justice system, like its adult counterpart, is being buffeted by an increasingly "hard-line" approach to offenders who commit serious offenses or who have a history of committing such crimes. Although such legislation as New York State's 1978 "get-tough" act is intended specifically to apply to the adjudicatory handling of juveniles who commit serious felony offenses, this increasing law-and-order approach may be expressed through growing treatment of juveniles as adults. Under these circumstances, the combination of longer sentences for juveniles convicted of such crimes and the increased authority of youth services departments of state governments to transfer institutionalized juveniles to the adult correctional institutions may have some implications for the institutional handling of certain classes of delinquents.

Finally, several other issues will affect the future of juvenile institutions and their programs. For example, some states have recognized that juveniles have a statutory right to treatment.[51] As a part of its stated purpose of providing resources and leadership in preventing and reducing juvenile delinquency, the Juvenile Justice and Delinquency Prevention Act of 1974 mandates that states participating in the act should no longer hold status offenders in detention and correction facilities.[52] In the same way, states are being forced to remove juveniles from jails or run the risk of losing federal dollars.

## □ DELINQUENCY DIVERSION PROGRAMS

In recent years, the juvenile justice system has begun to concentrate its attention and resources on alternatives for dealing with delinquent youth. One such major emphasis is on diverting youth before they are adjudicated and labeled "deviant" or "undesirable." The idea is not new.

Labeling

Stigma

Evidence cited by the President's Commission in 1967 suggests that a child's chances of becoming a chronic and serious delinquent are increased once he or she enters the criminal justice system and is officially labeled "delinquent."[53] In spite of the supposedly benevolent intent of juvenile statutes and the juvenile court, the fact that the child is processed into the system imposes a stigma difficult for the child to overcome. Models of delinquency diversion seek to avoid this social-psychological phenomenon.

This problem of labeling a child as a criminal takes on greater importance when one realizes that many children are referred to juvenile court for acts that, although symptomatic of behavioral problems, do not really constitute crime in the strictest sense. As mentioned earlier, acts such as running away from home, frequenting an undesirable place, associating with undesirable companions, truancy, ungovernability, and curfew violations bring juveniles to the attention of the juvenile courts in most jurisdictions. Once in court, they are defined as "delinquent," with all of the undesirable connotations that such labeling attaches. Because all categories of juvenile crime are given equal dispositions, children who have not engaged in real criminal conduct find themselves drawn into the correctional system.

The idea that legal systems may themselves contribute to the very problems they were established to correct is given detailed examination by William H. Sheridan. He says:

> The label of "delinquent" sets a youngster apart from his peers—in his own estimation and by the community in general. Through forced association with others similarly labeled, this feeling is reinforced. He begins to think of himself as a delinquent and acts accordingly.
>
> Placing of such children in correctional institutions exposes them to association with more sophisticated delinquents who have committed serious offenses and developed a pattern of delinquent conduct. . . . Despite all measures, statutory or otherwise, to protect from stigma the youngster who is a product of the correction system, it is well known that such stigma exists to almost as great a degree as in the adult field.[54]

Juvenile court's diversion actions

Upon examining how juvenile courts typically handle their referrals, one finds that a large percentage—typically over one-half of the cases—are "adjusted" short of appearance before a judge.[55] This does not mean that the child was not in fact guilty of the particular delinquent act; it merely means that the court intake officer, for any number of reasons, felt that the behavior did not necessitate an appearance before the judge, and as a consequence the statutorily sanctioned authority of the judge was not invoked. In a large court, one-half to three-fourths of all complaints received may be handled in this way. It is certainly not unusual for a young offender to have his or her case "adjusted" two, three, four, or more times before being taken before the judge.

If such a large number of delinquency complaints can be handled in this way, it is conceivable that many of them could have been diverted without ever being referred to court at all. As a consequence, advocates of diversionary measures argue that delinquency rates could become more realistic, courts could be freed to concentrate on more difficult chronic offenders, and children could in many cases avoid the stigma of official labeling.

Although it is not possible to review all the diversion models that have been developed, the beginning student in criminal justice should be aware of some of the more notable programs. These programs can be classified into four types: (1) school-related; (2) court-related; (3) police-related; and (4) community-related-models.[56]    **Four diversion models**

The school-related programs recognize that the school plays an important role in delinquency prevention. It is often in school that the first indication of delinquency-prone conduct is observable. It is also recognized that youths who drop out of school early stand a better chance of committing crimes than those who complete their education.    **School related**

Yet, not all juveniles can benefit from the traditional school environment and educational process. As a diversionary measure, a number of programs have sprung up throughout the country to address the problem of juvenile crime. Since traditional schools often functionally exclude many children who need alternative ways to learn, juveniles such as school dropouts, delinquents, chronic truants, those considered incorrigible or uneducable, and juveniles with emotional problems and physical handicaps are the targets for alternative education programs.

There are many variations on school-related (alternative education) programs. The National Advisory Committee for Juvenile Justice and Delinquency Prevention suggests five such strategies:

1. Large houses purchased by state governments could be outfitted as learning centers. They could have restricted student enrollments and be staffed with Master teachers. Parents and children could attend together in an extended family setting.
2. State contracts could be granted to good private schools to take a percentage of disadvantaged pupils on a performance guaranteed basis, with performance criteria to emphasize social skills.
3. Special classes with skilled teachers could be conducted on a 4:1 or 5:1 student contact basis.
4. Young students could be apprenticed to artisans who would direct them in projects of interest such as photography, glass staining, wood carving, race car construction, painting, sculpture, and the like.
5. Block schools, run by trained parents and teams of learning experts, could be set up in properly equipped homes in each block to conduct "mini-schools" with very restricted numbers of students.[57]

Court and police-related diversion programs also may take various forms. For example, juvenile courts may suspend dispositional sentencing of a youngster if the child (and perhaps his or her family) undergoes counseling services. Community service work and restitution to the victim in lieu of incarceration are other typically used programs. The courts may establish a "network" of community assistance programs that work closely with the courts for referrals and services. These provide options to the courts for disposing of cases other than through the more formalized process of adjudication and institutionalization.

The police approach diversion in one of two ways. The first is the traditional role of the police in delinquency prevention activities involving the police and juveniles. This might take the form of police-sponsored athletic programs. The police may also participate in joint police–school programs such as assigning educational officers to work in the schools as counselors. In a few jurisdictions these police educational officers are actually certified teachers who also teach classes in the public school system.

The second way the police approach diversion is through their policies of contact, referral, and arrest in their dealings with juveniles. The police often have a great deal of discretion in deciding whether to process the child formally by referral to the juvenile justice system, or to informally deal with the case, thereby diverting the child from the system. Guidelines must exist in these circumstances.

Some of the most explicit and comprehensive guidelines were established by the Michigan State Police. The efforts of this agency in developing diversionary policies were so well done that they were published by the federal government as guidelines for other police agencies throughout the nation.[58] Some progressive police departments throughout the country have established Youth Advisor Programs. Under such programs, troubled youth are referred by the police to counselors who work with the child or refer the child to an appropriate social agency in the community.

The final type of juvenile diversion program is called community related. These programs, which also take numerous forms, may be residential or non-residential in nature. For example, Tallahassee, Florida, opened a residential community facility called Criswell House. This facility was designed to serve as an alternative (diversion) from sending the child to the training school. The program was operated by the Florida Division of Youth Services to help youngsters who needed something less than incarceration but more than remaining at home. The boys who were referred to the facility lived in residence and attended local public schools during the day. A nonintrusive treatment structure was imposed. This meant that the staff kept its imposed decision making to a minimum, and the child was forced to assume the responsibility for making decisions that affected his or her own life and others within the group. The staff counseled and advised the boys within this setting.

## JUVENILE JUSTICE REFORM: CHANGES OCCURRING

A reform movement is taking place in many parts of the country. As a result, the juvenile justice system is undergoing some significant changes. There are at least three different "movements" for change. The most publicized change—and one we've already mentioned in this chapter—is a "get-tough" attitude toward juveniles

**TABLE 16.4   Age at Which a Child Can Be Waived to Adult Criminal Court**

| Age (Years) | States |
| --- | --- |
| No specific age | Alaska, Arizona, Arkansas, Delaware, Florida, Indiana, Kentucky, Maine, Maryland, New Hampshire, New Jersey, Oklahoma, South Dakota, West Virginia, Wyoming, Federal districts |
| 10 years | Vermont |
| 12 | Montana |
| 13 | Georgia, Illinois, Mississippi |
| 14 | Alabama, Colorado, Connecticut, Idaho, Iowa, Massachusetts, Minnesota, Missouri, North Carolina, North Dakota, Pennsylvania, South Carolina, Tennessee, Utah |
| 15 | District of Columbia, Louisiana, Michigan, New Mexico, Ohio, Oregon, Texas, Virginia |
| 16 | California, Hawaii, Kansas, Nevada, Rhode Island, Washington, Wisconsin |

*Note:* Many judicial waiver statutes also specify offenses that are waivable. This chart lists the States by the youngest age for which judicial waiver may be sought without regard to offense.

*Source:* Linda A. Szymanski, *Waiver/Transfer/Certification of Juveniles to Criminal Court: Age Restrictions: Crime Restrictions* (National Center for Juvenile Justice, February 1987). From Bureau of Justice Statistics, *Report to the Nation on Crime and Justice,* 2d ed. (Washington, D.C.: U.S. Department of Justice, March 1988), p. 79.

who are either repeatedly brought before the courts for the commission of felony crimes or who are charged with serious offenses. The most vocal group of reformers calling for stiffer penalities for such offenders are law enforcement officials and conservative politicians. Both groups are demanding that the juvenile justice system be tightened up so that dangerous juvenile offenders are segregated from the community. The legislatures of a number of states, particularly where the urban crime problem is most serious, have responded by passing new laws. The new laws are such that juveniles who commit certain serious crimes can be prosecuted as adults and sentenced to long terms or can provide that when a juvenile offender is convicted of a crime, some minimum period of incarceration is mandatory. For example, in Vermont, a child of ten can be waived to adult court. In New York, children as young as thirteen who are charged with murder can be sent to that state's felony courts to be tried as adults, and if found guilty can be sentenced for a term of life.[59] California has lowered the age at which a juvenile can be tried as an adult to sixteen; the federal government has lowered the age to fifteen. The juvenile code for the state of Washington provides that whereas in the past juvenile offenders, even those convicted of such crimes as murder, rape, and armed robbery, used to remain in institutions for less than a year, are now being sentenced to flat terms of at least several years.[60] (See Table 16.4.)

States and their new "get-tough" policies and laws

This new type of juvenile code reform, then, seems to be concentrating its attention on changing several traditional methods of dealing with juvenile offenders. In this way it may have a significant effect on the administration of the juvenile justice system. The major changes are the lowering of the age limit by which juveniles can be tried as adults; the mandatory imposition of flat (determinate) sentences for the conviction of certain types of crimes; the taking away of the authority of institutional personnel to decide when a child should be released; provision for dealing more harshly in terms of sentencing for repeat offenders who have a previous record of conviction for serious crimes; and the more frequent prosecution of certain types of juvenile offenders as adults in adult criminal courts.

While more punitive reform efforts are underway, there are also ongoing reform efforts to deal more leniently with status offenders and to remove minor offenders from institutions. The major impetus for such diversion efforts has been the Juvenile Justice and Delinquency Prevention Act of 1974. This important federal legislation created a national office to coordinate and assist state and local units of government in developing programs for dealing with problems of juvenile delinquency. Through the Office of Juvenile Justice and Delinquency Prevention (OJJDP), additional resources and technical assistance have been made available in the form of grants-in-aid to help jurisdictions establish diversion programs. The OJJDP has also played a major role in encouraging states to deinstitutionalize status offenders and to develop alternative sources of referral and help for such youth.

One result of the changes in juvenile sentencing laws, the deinstitutionalization of status offenders and those convicted of less serious crimes, is that our juvenile institutions, like some of our adult prisons, are increasingly being populated with the more serious offenders, who are being institutionalized primarily as a means of protecting society and as punishment for their crimes. Like similar efforts in imprisoning adult offenders, the trend away from the rehabilitative model of therapy to the rehabilitative model of punishment seems most pronounced. Whether it will have any effect on crime rates or recidivism is unknown. Perhaps, as many observers wryly feel, like so many efforts of the criminal justice system, it will have little if any effect on crime rates.

A third reform movement has been underway in the legal community. This

---

### Table **16.5** Some Facts About The Juvenile Justice System

In 1982 about 54 percent of all cases referred by the police to the juvenile courts were handled informally without the filing of a petition.

Juvenile court dispositions tend to be indeterminate.

Six states now permit determinate sentencing of juvenile offenders. These do not, however, apply to all offenses and offenders. In most cases they apply only to specified felony offenses or to juveniles with prior adjudications for serious crimes.

Juvenile courts cannot sentence like adult criminal courts. For example, they cannot order the death penalty or life terms. Yet, juvenile courts may go further than adult criminal courts in regulating the life-styles of juvenile offenders who are placed on probation. For example, the juvenile court can order them to live in certain locations, attend school, or participate in special programs.

The National Center for Juvenile Justice estimates that almost 70 percent of the offenders adjudicated by the juvenile courts end up receiving probation. Only 10 percent are committed to an institution.

A very small percentage of juveniles end up being tried in adult courts.

Juveniles are referred to adult criminal courts in one of three ways. (1) Legislation that gives concurrent jurisdiction to the juvenile and adult courts and the prosecutor has the discretion to decide in which court to file charges. (2) Excluded offenses. The law excludes from juvenile court certain crimes such as murder or forcible rape. (3) The juvenile court waives its jurisdiction and the child is bound over to adult court to stand trial.

Juveniles tried as adults are likely to be convicted. Yet, in such cases, more than one-half of the juvenile defendants receive only probation and/or fines.

In the mid-1980s, juvenile institutions throughout the nation had custody over 84,000 juveniles.

Of those juveniles in institutions today, about three-fourths of them are there for acts of delinquency. The other 25 percent of juveniles are in institutions because they are status offenders, neglected or abused children, and so on.

*Source:* Bureau of Justice Statistics, *Report to the Nation on Crime and Justice,* 2nd ed. (Washington, D.C.: U.S. Department of Justice, March 1988).

## GETTING TOUGH WITH JUVENILES:
## NEW YORK'S EXPERIENCE

New York is considered by many to be one of the nation's most liberal states. Yet in 1978, it passed the toughest juvenile law in the country. The turning point was the vicious robbery-killing of two subway commuters by a Harlem youth. The assailant, fifteen-year-old Willie Bosket, had recently been released from juvenile custody. Showing no remorse for his crime, he went on to threaten to kill the detectives who arrested him, the district attorney who tried the case, and the judge of the Family Court who sentenced him to the maximum term for a juvenile—five years.

The uproar was immediate. The then governor of New York, who had shortly before vetoed a bill to reinstate capital punishment, was seeking reelection. Stung by the label of being "soft on crime" for his anti–death penalty stance, the governor set about to counteract his critics by calling for a sweeping revision in the state's juvenile law. A special session of the state legislature was convened. During the special session Republicans and Democrats vied to outdo each other in calling for a harsher approach to juvenile criminals.

The result was a sweeping new act. Among other things it stripped the Family Court of jurisdiction over thirteen-year-olds accused of murder, and fourteen- or fifteen-year-olds accused of attempted murder, serious cases of manslaughter, robbery, burglary, assault, arson, rape, sodomy, and kidnapping. These juveniles were to be automatically tried in adult court unless the adult trial court judge waived them back to Family Court. In addition, stiffer penalties were imposed for juveniles found guilty of these crimes. The changes were widely hailed as a means to deal with juveniles who commit serious personal and property crimes.

Research on the effect of the law in New York City has shown that in many ways little has changed since the adoption of the act. For example, less than one-third of the cases in which the youthful offender first appeared in the adult trial court were actually tried there. Most were referred back to Family Court. Of the juveniles who were tried in adult court, 40 percent received probation. Only 3 percent of the arrested juvenile offenders received stiffer sentences than those who could be tried in the juvenile court.[a]

New York is not alone in its increased punitiveness of juvenile offenders. A number of other states have passed similar legislation. Generally, the results have not lived up to the promise of reform.

The question is why? Several explanations are given for these results. The most frequently given reason is that adult court judges still think of juveniles as children and treat them accordingly. Adult court judges are used to seeing a steady stream of serious offenders with long criminal histories. Under such circumstances, the juvenile offender is certainly not unique. Also cited is the lack of flexibility in sentencing that is more typical of adult courts. The judge in the adult court does not have the dispositional options available that his or her Family Court counterpart might have. This may work in one of two ways: The judge, faced with the choice of long-term imprisonment or probation—and given the fact that the accused is a juvenile—may be encouraged toward leniency and the use of probation. It may also encourage transfer back to the juvenile court on the theory that the Family Court has better resources and greater flexibility to deal more appropriately with the child.

It may also reflect the unwillingness of the adult criminal court judges to further clutter up an already overburdened court docket with these juvenile cases. Whereas these judges cannot escape their responsibilities for trying adult offenders who come up before them for trial, they can avoid responsibility in the case of juveniles merely by transferring them back to the Family Court.

What is the answer? The argument rages on both sides. Whereas most observers of the juvenile courts recognize the need for change, the direction of this change is the issue. Some say, for example, that the juvenile court should make the determination of whether the offender should be waived to stand trial in adult criminal court, not the prosecutor or the adult court as now exists in New York, Florida, and some other states. Yet, the evidence would indicate that although this has been a long-standing practice in many states, this too, has not proven to be particularly successful. In the meantime the answers still elude us.

[a]As cited in, Richard Allinson, "Is New York's Tough Juvenile Law a 'Charade?'" *Corrections Magazine* 9 (April 1983): 40–45 at p. 41.

movement culminated when the House of Delegates of the American Bar Association released its seventeen volumes of "standards" for the juvenile justice system. The importance of these standards is that the less controversial recommendations will probably serve as models for juvenile justice legal reform throughout the country. This seems to be occurring, as a number of state legislatures are examining these standards as a basis for their new legislation. The emphasis of the standards is on providing juveniles the same "due process" rights as are entitled adult offenders. They recommend, among other things, public jury trials plus a series of other due process reforms. They also recommended determinate sentences without possibility of parole rather than the indeterminate terms that most juvenile offenders receive.

**Extending due process rights to juveniles**

The changes occurring in the juvenile justice system have the potential of being the most far-reaching since the founding of the juvenile court system at the turn of the century. Many of the traditional underpinnings of the theory and purpose of the juvenile courts—and indeed the entire juvenile justic system—are being reformulated. With the widespread recognition that the juvenile justice system has failed to live up to the demands of dealing effectively with problems of delinquency, new efforts are underway to modify not only the traditional policies and practices of the juvenile justice system, but its theoretical underpinnings as well.

How the ultimate balance between the need to protect society and the therapeutic and humanistic concern of dealing with the wide range of children who appear before our juvenile courts can be balanced is of primary concern to practitioners and students of criminal justice. Although this concern has been with us for a great many years, never before has such attention focused on this most difficult to achieve relationship. (See Table 16.5.)

## SUMMARY

Although the juvenile crime rate has declined somewhat in recent years, it still continues to be a serious problem. Delinquency is no longer a male-related phenomenon, as witnessed by the rapid rise in female delinquency. Of particular concern is the sharp increase in the number of female youth involved in violent crimes. However, the majority of female offenders are still involved in status offenses.

The juvenile court is a twentieth-century response to the problems of dealing with children who are law violators or who need society's protection. Juvenile court procedure differs from the procedure in adult courts because juvenile courts were founded on the philosophy that the function of the court was to treat and to help. In recent years the operations of the juvenile court have received a great deal of criticism, and a number of important Supreme Court decisions changed the way the courts must approach the rights of children.

The range of institutions for children who come under the authority of our juvenile courts can generally be classified into five major types: detention centers, training schools, camps and ranches, halfway or group homes, and foster homes. Each of these specific institutions is generally distinguished by the type of offender it handles, the kind of treatment it offers, and the problems with which it was designed to deal.

The major emphasis of the juvenile system remains one of diversion and treatment rather than adjudication and incarceration, although there is a definite trend toward dealing more punitively with serious juvenile offenders. As a result of these two responses, we are likely to see greater future efforts at identifying and incarcerating serious juvenile offenders while removing from the juvenile justice system status offenders and children who do not require institutionalization.

## REVIEW QUESTIONS

1. What are some recent trends in juvenile delinquency?
2. What is a status offense? Name four kinds of status offenses.
3. Where and when was the first true juvenile court founded? What was its guiding philosophy concerning juveniles?
4. Identify the jurisdiction of the juvenile court and specify the types of cases it is authorized to hear.
5. Define and briefly describe the following:
   a. Intake interview
   b. Adjudication inquiry
   c. Adjudication hearing
   d. Disposition
   e. Probation officer

6. Explain the significance of the following judicial decisions for the juvenile justice system:
   a. *Kent* v. *United States*
   b. *In re Gault*
   c. *In re Winship*
   d. *McKiever* v. *Pennsylvania*
7. What are the major types of juvenile institutions, and how do they differ?
8. Briefly describe the four types of delinquency diversions programs.
9. What are the types of reform efforts the juvenile justice system is currently experiencing?
10. Why does the "get-tough" policy of New York not seem to be working?

## DISCUSSION QUESTIONS

1. In what ways will the juvenile justice system be affected by the present trends in delinquency?
2. Discuss the major differences between the processing of an adult defendant through the criminal courts and the processing of a juvenile through a juvenile court.

3. Are juveniles entitled to the same due process protections of the Constitution as adults? Why or why not?
4. Among the many juvenile diversion programs, which is most likely to succeed? Why?
5. In what ways do we need to change the juvenile justice process? Discuss.

## SUGGESTED ADDITIONAL READINGS

Bureau of Justice Statistics, *Public Juvenile Facilities—1985.* Washington, D.C.: U.S. Department of Justice, 1986.

Cottle, Thomas J. *Children in Jail: Seven Lessons in American Justice.* Boston: Beacon Press, 1977.

Cull, John G. (ed.). *Problems of Runaway Youth.* Springfield, Ill.: Charles C Thomas, 1976.

Farcas, S. C. (ed.). Juvenile Justice—Myths and Realities—*Seven Journalists Look at Various Aspects of Serious Juvenile Crime.* Washington, D.C.: Institute for Educational Leadership, 1983.

Garabedian, Peter C., and Don C. Gibbons. *Becoming Delinquent: Young Offenders and the Correctional System.* Chicago: Aldine, 1970.

Griffin, B. S., and C. T. Griffin. *Juvenile Delinquency in Perspective.* New York: Harper & Row, 1978.

Hamparian, Donna M. *The Violent Few: A Study of Dangerous Juvenile Offenders.* Lexington, Mass.: Lexington Books, 1978.

The Institute of Criminal Justice and Criminology, University of Maryland. *New Approaches to Diversion and Treatment of Juvenile Offenders.* Washington, D.C.: U.S. Government Printing Office, June 1973.

Platt, A. M. *Child Savers—The Invention of Delinquency,* 2nd ed. Chicago: University of Chicago Press, 1977.

Rubin, Ted H. *Juvenile Justice: Policy, Practice and Law.* Santa Monica, Calif.: Goodyear, 1979.

Ryerson, Ellen. *The Best-Laid Plans: America's Juvenile Court Experiment.* New York: Hill & Wang, 1978.

Schlossman, S. L. *Love and the American Delinquent—The Theory and Practice of "Progressive" Juvenile Justice, 1825–1920.* Chicago: University of Chicago Press, 1977.

Sprowls, James T. *Discretion and Lawlessness: Compliance in the Juvenile Court.* Lexington, Mass.: Lexington Books, 1980.

Trojanowicz, Robert C. *Juvenile Delinquency: Concepts and Controls.* Englewood Cliffs, N.J.: Prentice-Hall, 1978.

# NOTES

1. Bureau of Justice Statistics, *Report to the Nation on Crime and Justice*, 2nd ed. (Washington: U.S. Department of Justice, March 1988), p. 42.

2. See Office of Juvenile Justice and Delinquency Prevention, Analysis of National Crime Victimization Survey Data to Study Serious Delinquent Behavior (Washington, D.C.: U.S. Government Printing Office, February 1981).

3. *New York Times*, 16 July 1988, p. A-17.

4. For a good summary of the findings of the reports, see Office of Justice Assistance, Research and Statistics, *Justice Assistance News* 2 (September 1981): 1.

5. Bureau of Justice Statistics, *Report to the Nation*, p. 78.

6. Law Enforcement Assistance Administration, *Little Sisters and the Law* (Washington, D.C.: U.S. Government Printing Office, August 1977), p. 1. Also see Robert D. Vinter, ed., *Time Out: A National Study of Juvenile Correctional Programs* (Ann Arbor, Mich.: Institute of Continuing Legal Education, June 1976).

7. Law Enforcement Assistance Administration, *Little Sisters and the Law*, p. 1.

8. Report of the National Advisory Committee for Juvenile Justice and Delinquency Prevention, *Standards for the Administration of Juvenile Justice* (Washington, D.C.: U.S. Government Printing Office, July 1980), p. 249.

9. Ibid.

10. D. Smith, T. Finnegan, H. Snyder, and J. Corbett, *Delinquency 1975: United States Estimates of Cases Processed with Juvenile Jurisdiction* (Washington, D.C.: U.S. Government Printing Office, 1975), p. 6.

11. American Bar Association Joint Commission on Juvenile Justice Standards in National Advisory Committee, *Standards for the Administration of Juvenile Justice*, op. cit., p. 249.

12. W. Arthur, "Status Offenders Need Help, Too," *Juvenile Justice* 26 (1975), p. 5.

13. Law Enforcement Assistance Administration, *Little Sisters*, p. 13.

14. Kenneth Wooden, *Weeping in the Playtime of Others* (New York: McGraw-Hill, 1976), p. 128.

15. Anthony Platt, *The Child Savers* (Chicago: University of Chicago Press, 1969), p. 202.

16. Robert M. Mennel, "Origins of the Juvenile Court," *Crime and Delinquency* (January 1972): 70.

17. Ibid., pp. 70–71.

18. New York Society for the Reformation of Juvenile Delinquents, *Annual Report* (New York: 1927), pp. 3–4.

19. Mennel, "Origins of the Juvenile Court," p. 71.

20. James Lieby, *Charities and Corrections in New Jersey* (New Brunswick, N.J.: Rutgers University Press, 1967), p. 82.

21. President's Commission on Law Enforcement and Administration of Justice, *Task Force Report: Juvenile Delinquency and Youth Crime* (Washington, D.C.: U.S. Government Printing Office, 1967), p. 3.

22. Ibid.

23. See *Commonwealth* v. *Fisher*, 213 Pa. St. 48, 62 A. 198 (1905).

24. President's Commission, *Juvenile Delinquency and Youth Crime*, p. 3.

25. Mass. Gen. Laws Ann., Chap. 119 52 (1969).

26. President's Commission, *Juvenile Delinquency and Youth Crime*, p. 4.

27. U.S. Department of Justice, *A National Assessment of Serious Juvenile Crime and the Juvenile Justice System* (Washington, D.C.: U.S. Government Printing Office, April 1980), p. 44.

28. Ibid., p. 56.

29. U.S. Department of Health, Education and Welfare, *Juvenile Court Statistics—1973* (Washington, D.C.: U.S. Government Printing Office, March 1975), p. 11.

30. U.S. Department of Health, Education and Welfare, *Standards for Juvenile and Family Courts* (Washington, D.C. U.S. Government Printing Office, 1966), p. 84.

31. Michigan Advisory Council on Criminal Justice, *Criminal Justice Goals and Standards for the State of Michigan* (Lansing, Mich.: MACCJ, 1975), p. 46.

32. F. W. Miller, R. O. Dawson, G. E. Dix, and R. I. Parnas, *The Juvenile Justice Process* (Mineola, N.Y.: Foundation Press, 1971), p. 1162.

33. Robert Shears, "Legal Problems Peculiar to Children's Courts," *American Bar Association Journal* 48 (1962): 720.

34. Foreword to Pauline V. Young, *Social Treatment in Probation and Delinquency* (New York: McGraw-Hill, 1973), p. XXVII.

35. 383 U.S. 541 (1966).

36. 383 U.S. at 556.

37. 387 U.S. 1 (1967).

38. 387 U.S. at 33.

39. 387 U.S. at 41.

40. Frederick L. Faust and Paul J. Brantigham, *Juvenile Justice Philosophy* (St. Paul, Minn.: West, 1974), p. 537.

41. See Norman Lefstein, Vaughan Stapelton, and Lee Teitlebaum, "In Search of Juvenile Justice: Gault and Its Implementation," *Law and Society Review* 491 (1969).

42. Charles E. Reasons, "Gault: Procedural Change and Substantive Effect," *Crime and Delinquency* 16 (April 1970): 163–171.

43. Bureau of Justice Statistics, *Report to the Nation*, p. 105.

44. Ibid., p. 110.

45. Alan R. Coffey, *Juvenile Justice as a System* (Englewood Cliffs, N.J.: Prentice-Hall, 1974), p. 128.

46. Y. Bakal, "The Massachusetts Experience," *Delinquency Prevention Reporter* (April 1973): 1–3.

47. Clifford E. Simonsen and Marshall S. Gordon, *Juvenile Justice in America* (Encino, Calif.: Glencoe, 1979), p. 221.

48. For an excellent discussion of such halfway-house programs, see Robert C. Trojanowitz, *Juvenile*

*Delinquency Concepts and Control* (Englewood Cliffs, N.J.: Prentice-Hall, 1973), especially chap. 10.

49.   For some good materials on the use of volunteers in delinquency treatment and prevention programs, see Ira M. Schwartz, Donald R. Jensen, and Michael J. Mahoney, *Volunteers in Juvenile Justice* (Washington, D.C.: U.S. Government Printing Office, October 1977); and Dane County Volunteers in Probation, *Citizen Participation in the Juvenile and Adult Criminal Justice System* (Madison, Wisc.: Volunteers in Probation, May 1975).

50.   Coffey, *Juvenile Justice as a System*, p. 131.

51.   National Institute for Juvenile Justice and Delinquency Prevention, *Juvenile Dispositions and Corrections*, vol. 9 (Washington, D.C.: U.S. Government Printing Office, 1977), p. 57.

52.   See Office of Juvenile Justice and Delinquency Prevention, *Cost and Service Impacts of Deinstitutionalization of Status Offenders in Ten States* (Washington, D.C.: U.S. Government Printing Office, October 1977).

53.   President's Commission, *Juvenile Delinquency and Youth Crime*, p. 417.

54.   William H. Sheridan, "Juveniles Who Commit Non-Criminal Acts: Why Treat in a Correctional System?" *Federal Probation* (March 1967): 26–27.

55.   U.S. Department of Health, Education and Welfare, *Juvenile Court Statistics—1973*, p. 11.

56.   This typology of delinquency diversion models is taken from Institute of Government, Corrections Division, *Models for Delinquency Diversion* (Athens, Ga.: University of Georgia, October 1971).

57.   Report of the National Advisory Committee for Juvenile Justice and Delinquency Prevention, *Standards for the Administration of Juvenile Justice* (Washington, D.C.: U.S. Government Printing Office, July 1980), p. 34.

58.   See: Jack R. Shepard and Dale M. Rothenberger, *Police Juvenile Diversion: An Alternative to Prosecution* (Washington, D.C.: U.S. Department of Justice, 1978 and 1980).

59.   University of Illinois Community Research Forum, *A Comparative Analysis of Juvenile Codes* (Washington, D.C.: U.S. Government Printing Office, July 1980), p. 10.

60.   Michael S. Serrill, "Police Write a New Law on Juvenile Crime," *Police Magazine* 2, no. 5 (September 1979): 48.

CHAPTER 17
**Crime Issues of the 1990s**

CHAPTER **17**

# Crime Issues
# of the 1990s

## OBJECTIVES

**After reading this chapter the student should be able to:**

Discuss with examples the growing "internationalization" of crime.

Discuss the historical efforts to control drugs in the United States.

Understand the demand and supply side of antidrug efforts.

Discuss the issues brought about by our nation's efforts to criminalize drugs and enforce the problem out of existence.

Highlight the major issues supporting those who argue for the legalization of drugs versus the possible weaknesses of such arguments.

Understand and discuss how changes in drug abuse might affect future national policies.

Define terrorism.

Understand how international and domestic terrorist groups differ.

Understand our weaknesses and the problems America faces in dealing with international terrorists.

Discuss the legal issues that surround the criminal enforcement of environmental laws.

Discuss organized crime's inroads into toxic waste disposal in certain areas.

Identify the issues which make international cooperation in the investigation and prosecution of environmental polluters so difficult.

Discuss the growing concern of how to deal with the willful and deliberate transmission of AIDS and how the criminal justice system is hampered in dealing with this problem.

## IMPORTANT TERMS

The Harrison Act
Drugs and Crime
Drug Corruption
Legalization of Drugs

Terrorism as a Political Act
International Terrorism
Domestic Terrorism
Environmental Crime

Civil versus Criminal Prosecutions of Environmental Polluters
Transnational Environmental Crimes
Willful and Deliberate Transmission of AIDS

## ◻ PROLOGUE

As a new decade that ushers out the turbulent twentieth century beckons, it is time to look ahead. The past ninety years have been years of profound change for America and its people. In 1890 we looked to the impending century as the new age of industrial dynamism: a century that would unleash the American genius. We were a confident, brash young nation. Today, we are less optimistic. For many Americans, confidence has been replaced by a pessimistic, even cynical, view of our nation's future. The very source of liberalizing freedom brought about by America's industrial prowess would prove to be a double-edged sword: the one side good, the other bad. The brash exuberance of youth has been replaced by the cautious and reflective maturity of a society which understands that the "American century" may well have passed.

Our unabated problem with crime is one legacy of that coming of age. Although, as the reader will recall, crime has always been a part of America's experience, it has taken on an ominous dimension. Crime has grown significantly in both its scope and seriousness. During the last half-century, we became a nation unrivaled in power. This brought with it unparalleled wealth and creature comforts for a large segment of Americans. On the other hand, thoughtful Americans must be troubled by the creation of what threatens to become a permanent underclass in America, an underclass that too often must turn to crime for a multitude of reasons—some understood, others puzzling—because it is perceived by some members of society, at least, that legitimate means to a share in the "American dream" remain closed.

Especially during the 1980s, new crime issues emerged. Although the criminal justice system continued to struggle against traditional forms of crime, it found itself confronting new challenges, both from new forms of criminal behavior and from new and insidious twists on some long-standing crime problems. These have exploded on the scene with a sense of urgency. It is not overstating the situation to say that, perhaps for the first time, in some of these criminal enterprises and in certain areas of the country, levels of criminal organization, resources, and violence are so widespread that they threaten the ability of our nation's legal systems and the local agencies of justice to cope with the problem. Organized drug trafficking and its yet-unchecked spawning of violence are but the most obvious manifestations of deep-seated problems facing America.

Other issues are associated with these new forms of crime. The troubling conclusion is that often neither our system of laws nor our enforcement apparatus are yet up to the task of dealing effectively with some of these crime problems. Without effective legislation and a commitment to enforce by means of the criminal law, punishment of violations in such areas as environmental pollution, our anti-crime strategies and enforcement efforts in such areas are merely straw men.

Hampering our efforts in dealing with some of these emerging crime issues is another complicated twist. This can be called the growing "internationalization" of crime. Many of the most important and serious crimes and criminal organizations have become transglobal. America no longer has the luxury of dealing with domestic, garden-variety crime—traditional crimes of violence and property offenses that are contained within its national borders. Crimes such as terrorism, drug trafficking, illegal arms trafficking, criminal and willful acts of environmental pollution, transnational corporate crime, electronic and white-collar offenses, and the growth of international cartels of organized crime have global characteristics and consequences. This has important implications for effective enforcement actions—particularly for a nation that relies so heavily on anticrime efforts through a criminal justice system so localized in its administration and operations.

Associated with this is the recognition that only the federal government is in a position to deal with this internationalizing trend. The consequences are both subtle and obvious: The state and local units of government will have less direct federal assistance in their anticrime efforts at a time when they need help. The federal government is already in a position where it cannot provide the massive resources required to help local agencies of criminal justice or much in the way of financial assistance to state and local crime control efforts. The national government is simply too burdened with a host of priorities requiring attention. In the area of crime, the federal government must out of necessity devote more of its attention to dealing with international-based crime problems and to multijurisdictional (multistate) crimes. The full implications of this situation are still not fully appreciated or understood.

The 1990s will be a particularly crucial decade for our crime control efforts and for the administrative machinery of our criminal justice system and criminal laws. It will certainly establish the agenda for the twenty-first century. If crime reduction is to occur, it will demand a national response and a commitment of resources to this problem beyond that which has ever occurred in our nation's history—even beyond the unusual efforts that were generated in the late 1960s and throughout most of the 1970s. It will also demand a response that we have been unwilling to give in the past: a commitment of our own efforts to solving the problem. This means not merely wringing our hands and looking to government or the machinery of justice to deal with crime and those criminal elements that prey on us. The question is, Are we willing or can we devote significant resources to the problem? As a nation struggling with increasing economic demands, can we afford the massive effort it might take? Will our political leaders have the foresight and the courage to develop policies that will have the effect of restoring public safety to areas of our larger cities where social order at times seems to hang by the thinnest of threads? And what might be the not-so-obvious costs to a society if such an effort began? This involves not only the obvious financial costs of such an undertaking, but other associated "costs." There is a significant and frightening irony: At a time when the government will need increased power and support for its crime control efforts, we are only too aware of how government must be vigilantly and constantly monitored. The potential for abuse of power by government is an equally haunting specter that Americans cannot afford to ignore.

This chapter examines some of these crimes and the issues that surround them. It will not be a compendium of all the crime problems we face in what might be called nontraditional crime areas. Only several categories of crime existing among many more can possibly be discussed in a single chapter of any book. We will not, for example, examine new forms of organized crime except indirectly through our discussion of related issues such as narcotics. Nor will we examine the menace of youth gang violence or the many aspects of electronic or white-collar crime. Also conspicuously absent will be a discussion on the growing efforts to deal with family-related offenses and the phenomenon of bias crime. Instead, we will focus on the areas of narcotics, terrorism, environmental crime, and the yet-developing criminalization of an important aspect of acquired immune deficiency syndrome (AIDS). Out of this examination will come the concerns and strategies discussed to deal with these new forms of crime. It will serve as a primer on some of the most difficult crime issues we face as America approaches the twenty-first century.

## ◻ NARCOTICS

Ask most Americans what they see as the most pressing crime problem our nation faces. The answer is invariably illegal drugs. Illegal narcotics—both the trafficking in and the use of narcotics—have spawned a crime problem that has captured public attention. The menace of drugs has accomplished this like no other crime problem in our nation's history. The ubiquity of our nation's drug problem is found in accounts in our daily newspapers and on the evening news. It reaches into our neighborhoods, our schools, our workplaces. Although its menace is often focused on the inner city, its tentacles reach across America into rural communities and working class neighborhoods. It has made inroads into small towns and more subtly found its way into the well-manicured lawns of affluent suburban neighborhoods. Its effects are felt on the shop floor as well as in the world of the button-down collars of corporate America.

Although the problem of drug abuse is most pernicious among lower-class urban minorities, it has broken the long-standing class imperative: Wealth, education, neighborhood—those factors that often served to insulate segments of society from the ravages of traditional crime—have been effectively breached. Illegal narcotics seem to have touched every segment of our nation.

Although there is general recognition that illegal narcotics use has become a favorite American preoccupation, there are those who would argue that drugs have become a problem because of the way we deal with them. It is contended that our attempts to deal with narcotics have actually made the problem worse. By trying to effectively curb both supply and demand, government policy has actually abetted drug crime. Although this may be true, the argument appears to have become academic. We seem to be far beyond the point of seriously debating this issue as a matter of public policy. The official position of the government—which in turn seems to be supported by the majority of Americans—calls for a national effort to reduce the availability of illegal drugs.

Our efforts are concentrated into two broad strategies: cutting off the supply while simultaneously lowering demand and consumption. Although we may argue the "causes" of the problem, we cannot escape the inevitable conclusion: The presence of illegal drugs is creating serious social and economic consequences for the well-being of our nation. It reads like an all-too-familiar litany: crime, violence, health-care costs, prenatal addiction, family problems, lowered national productivity, and official corruption. These are just some of the most obvious manifestations. Still unknown are the full implications of future costs associated with America's insatiable appetite for drugs today. This may take years to unravel as social scientists of the future try to piece together the full range of costs associated with today's drug problem.

And like some other major crime issues of recent years, it is a situation that has transformed our crime control efforts beyond our nation's borders and thrust our efforts into a global undertaking. This has important implications, as we shall see. The drug problem poses new dangers and risks while it complicates efforts to develop effective strategies to abate the flow of drugs. According to a 1988 New York Times/CBS News poll, by far the most important international and domestic issue among those sampled was drug trafficking.[1] Rarely, except in times of war, has a single issue become the primary international and domestic concern of Americans. When respondents were questioned as to how it ranked as an international concern of this nation, the perception of the seriousness of this problem far overshadowed such global concerns as terrorism, the situation in Central America, Palestinian unrest, and arms control.[2] Illegal use of narcotics now appears to have become not only the most significant crime concern of the 1980s, but also, among Americans, a domestic and international policy issue of the first order. Because there appears no present or forseeable denouement to this situation, it must remain high on our agenda of concerns well into the future.

## America's War on Drugs: A Brief History

Our nation's attempt to deal with narcotics has been a tortuous path. For many years the use of narcotics was not illegal. In the nineteenth century, even the ubiquitous soft drink *Coca Cola* contained traces of cocaine in its formula. The government's policies toward narcotics changed in 1914. In that year, Congress adopted the first major piece of legislation to control and regulate drugs. This was

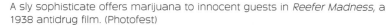

A sly sophisticate offers marijuana to innocent guests in *Reefer Madness*, a 1938 antidrug film. (Photofest)

the Harrison Narcotics Act. The impetus for such legislation was similar to today's. Whereas it is true that today's efforts have targeted supply and trafficking, both eras recognized that narcotics use was undermining our nation's interests. Testimony before a Congress considering the Harrison Act spoke of this growing narcotics use and the threat it posed.[3]

The passage of the Harrison Act ushered in the federal government's antinarcotic efforts. Narcotics were to become a licensed and taxed commodity. Enforcement efforts were ultimately given to the Prohibition Unit of the Treasury Department. This agency was to enforce the Harrison Act, in addition to its efforts to stamp out the illegal use of alcohol under the Volstead (Prohibition) Act. Like a good government bureaucracy, it wasn't above stretching the truth a bit if such embellishments brought more resources. In 1919 it issued an alarming report, claiming that America had one-and-a-half million dangerous addicts on the streets and that smuggling and peddling rings of unprecedented power had taken over the narcotics trade.[4]

During the 1920s, more arrests were made by the Prohibition Unit for Harrison Act violations than for illegal liquor. In the early 1930s, a separate Bureau of Narcotics was created. This agency was aggressive in its efforts for additional resources. Through its persuasive powers, it convinced Congress to make all forms of narcotic substances illegal. The Bureau of Narcotics, however, suffered from recurring problems of corruption. As a result, in 1968 a new federal agency, the Bureau of Narcotics and Dangerous Drugs (BNDD), was created from the remnants of the Bureau of Narcotics; transferred agents from the narcotics enforcement division of the Bureau of Customs were also recruited. This became the government's lead agency in the enforcement of antinarcotics laws. But it soon found its task overwhelming, and corruption likewise tainted its efforts.[5] In 1973 the federal government again reorganized its drug enforcement efforts, and a newly created Drug Enforcement Administration (DEA) became the federal government's primary enforcement agency.

Still, the government's efforts floundered, and reorganization failed to live up to its promise. In 1981, a major escalation in the federal government's drug efforts occurred when the FBI was given joint authority with the DEA to investigate illegal drugs. Now the federal government's most prestigious law enforcement agency would join the fray.

## Drugs and Crime

There is a lot of discussion about the relationship between drugs and crime. Many of the studies relating the two must be approached skeptically. One such study of 573 drug users in Miami was reported to have shown that during a twelve-month period, these users committed an unbelievable six thousand robberies and assaults, almost 6,700 burglaries, and more than 46,000 other crimes defined as larceny and fraud.[6] Such claims further fueled the debate as many scholars repudiated these conclusions. Another study in Baltimore claimed to find high rates of criminality among heroin users during those periods when they were addicted, but markedly lower rates during times of nonaddiction.[7] While research in several major cities between 1984 and 1986 showed increased evidence of drug use among those arrested, we still know little about the true relationship between the two.[8] The fact that an offender tests positive for illegal drug use doesn't tell us about the specific role drugs may have played. While we know of drug-related killings, we simply don't know how drugs figure into the vast majority of criminal events.[9]

Still, the assumption is that there is a direct and causal relationship. Nobody would argue to the contrary. The argument centers on the extent and nature of this causal relationship. Many of our enforcement policies mirror the attitude that drugs and crime are linked. This is expressed in our criminal justice strategies for curbing demand. One example of this pervasive assumption is the requirement that as a condition of bail, release after conviction, probation, or parole, a person must test clean in periodic urine analyses or be sentenced or resentenced. We do have some startling figures. In 1989, 750,000 people were arrested in the nation for violating drug laws. This is only the tip of the iceberg. We know that the use of illegal drugs far exceeds any existing arrest statistics for such offenses.

## A Growing Need: Attacking the Roots of Demand

To growing numbers of Americans, including many within the law enforcement community, it is becoming increasingly apparent that our nation's efforts to control drug abuse are failing because they emphasize a futile crackdown on suppliers and neglect the more important task of weaning the American public from its drug dependence. This is the so-called supply versus demand side of the nation's drug strategy. In spite of record levels of drug confiscations and a threefold increase in arrests of drug traffickers, a government-sponsored study on the effects of our antinarcotics efforts claims that only a small percentage of illegal drugs coming into this country in recent years has been seized.[10] (See Figure 17.1.)

One of the unanticipated outcomes of our futile efforts to stop the flow of drugs has been to increase the bitterness foreign officials express about our drug efforts. They are angry because they feel they are risking their agents' lives in the drug fight when the United States appears unwilling or unable to control its domestic appetite for drugs. One such outspoken critic is the Attorney General of Mexico. He pointed out that 154 Mexican police officers and soldiers have been killed between the years 1983 and 1988, a fact that he contends seems to go unrecognized by the American media and officials in Washington. He also argued that the traditional separation between producer and consumer countries is no longer valid. His view, which is becoming widely shared, is that the United States has developed a black-and-white mentality in which the producing nations are the villains and the consuming nations the victims. He calls such a simple dichotomy false. Because America seems unable to curb its appetite for drugs and instead provides unlimited opportunities for traffickers to launder drug monies and finance trafficking while increasing its own exports in certain illegal drugs, it must equally share the guilt.[11]

Foreign officials are also concerned about another problem, a problem which is abetted by the United States and is associated with the growing violence in their countries. America has become the arsenal that supplies the sophisticated weapons used by the gangs trafficking in drugs. Either openly through legitimate gun dealers or through the available illicit market operating in the United States, automatic weapons, explosives and other "tools of the trade" are available for the price. Recently, the Colombian Medellín drug cartel was shopping for a specially converted helicopter "gunship" and an armored personnel carrier. Only a last-minute tip to the federal authorities prevented the sale.[12]

Although the Reagan and now the Bush administrations have been calling for a drug-free society and Nancy Reagan mounted a nationwide appeal to "just

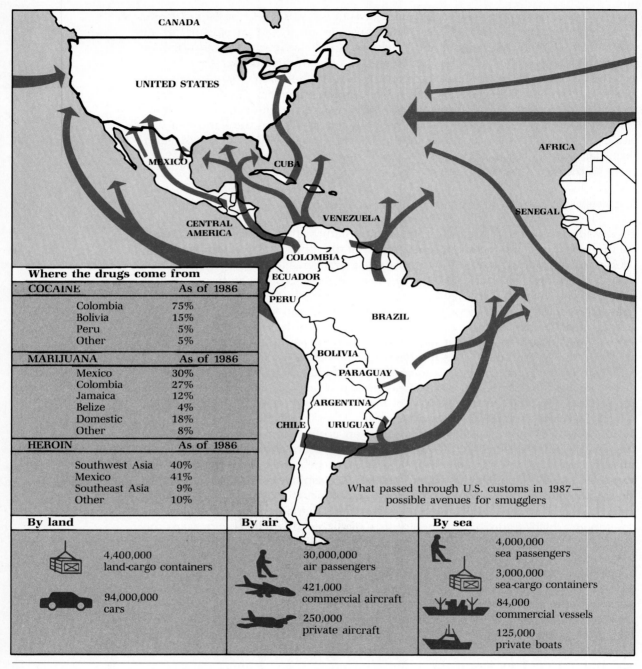

**Where the drugs come from**

| COCAINE | As of 1986 |
|---|---|
| Colombia | 75% |
| Bolivia | 15% |
| Peru | 5% |
| Other | 5% |

| MARIJUANA | As of 1986 |
|---|---|
| Mexico | 30% |
| Colombia | 27% |
| Jamaica | 12% |
| Belize | 4% |
| Domestic | 18% |
| Other | 8% |

| HEROIN | As of 1986 |
|---|---|
| Southwest Asia | 40% |
| Mexico | 41% |
| Southeast Asia | 9% |
| Other | 10% |

What passed through U.S. customs in 1987—
possible avenues for smugglers

**By land**

4,400,000 land-cargo containers

94,000,000 cars

**By air**

30,000,000 air passengers

421,000 commercial aircraft

250,000 private aircraft

**By sea**

4,000,000 sea passengers

3,000,000 sea-cargo containers

84,000 commercial vessels

125,000 private boats

FIGURE **17.1** Major drug-smuggling routes. (*Source:* Adapted from Wide World Photos.)

The "Just Say No" campaign may have encouraged some nonaddicts to avoid drugs; however, it had little effect on those already involved in drug use or trafficking. (J.L. Atlan/Sygma)

say no" to drugs, many circles question whether such efforts, although well-intentioned, weren't mostly political rhetoric. There is substantial criticism that such efforts have not been meaningfully followed through. In spite of the growing concern over the demand problem, the bulk of dollars still go into supply-side enforcement and eradication efforts and not to programs to abate demand. For example, in the 1988 to 1989 fiscal year, the federal government budgeted $2.5 billion dollars for enforcement efforts and only $940 million for treatment and prevention. In the 1990 to 1991 fiscal year, while $10 billion are earmarked for our federal government's antidrug efforts, less than 30 percent of this is slotted for forms of treatment and prevention.

Although Congress has increased appropriations for "user-targeted" programs, there is a great deal of skepticism that abatement or antidemand campaigns will have much effect—particularly on those segments of society such as youthful dropouts and central city minorities who are heavy drug abusers. This may explain why the U.S. government largely concentrates its antidrug policies on enforcement and interdiction activities in spite of their widely recognized failings. As for the widely publicized educational efforts of the "just say no" program, a 1987 report on drug abuse prevention by the General Accounting Office concluded that this program has not been effectively evaluated, and it stated that "there are uncertainties about its applicability to all segments of the population and its long-term benefits."[13] Even the former Secretary of Education, who is now the administration's "drug czar," and the prestigious Rand Corporation, after its study of antidrug educational efforts, both concluded that there is little evidence which supports the benefits of educational programs.[14]

Treatment programs are even less adequately funded than educational programs, in spite of the fact that they rest on a more secure knowledge base than educational programs. Such programs usually follow a combination of efforts such as detoxification through a program of withdrawal, methadone treatment for heroin users, outpatient counseling and family therapy, and special drug-free residences which provide a therapeutic environment. Yet these programs cannot begin to keep pace with the demand. Experts almost unanimously agree that if the nation is serious about making progress against drug abuse, it must provide treatment for all who seek it.

## Drugs and the Price of Corruption

Another insidious side to our nation's efforts to deal with the problem of illegal drugs is the corruption drugs has brought. The system of criminal justice is finding itself seriously compromised. Experts are saying that it rivals the widespread corruption which occurred during the Prohibition era.[15] Nowhere is this more evident than in the law enforcement community. Yet it is not only the police who are succumbing: Prosecutors, judges, and politicians are also susceptible.

Although state and federal court cases involving law enforcement officials charged with some form of complicity in drug trafficking have grown alarmingly in recent years, the problem is most pronounced in those transit areas of the country into which bulk narcotics flow. Areas such as Florida, and particularly the Miami area, have been hard hit with police scandal. So has New York City.[16] But it isn't only police agencies in urban areas which have been compromised by corruption. South Georgia has been hard hit in recent years as efforts to seal off landing sites in Florida have diverted traffickers to this neighboring state. Other states such as Louisiana, Alabama, Mississippi, and Texas have also experienced increased trafficking activity and, along with this, corruption. Even some of the federal agencies, like the U.S. Customs Service, the DEA, and the federal Organized Crime Strike Force in Boston, have had problems with personnel being bribed and corrupted.[17]

The sums generated by illegal narcotics is so vast that this flow of cash threatens the currency, banks, and economies among some Latin American countries. The complexities of currency exchange or laundering is such that even specially trained federal agents have limited success in understanding it. The drug traffickers are extremely ingenius in devising new schemes to launder money. Illegal money is also mixed with legal money. Financial transactions involving banks often involve wire transfers, overnight interbank loans, and the unregulated Eurodollar market, which is beyond the direct regulatory power of the U.S. government.

Since the late 1980s, major laundering activities have shifted to the Pacific Rim. Hong Kong has become the preeminent laundering center in the Pacific. In this city strict bank secrecy laws and the absence of regulatory mechanisms have made it a haven for drug monies. Even such remote islands as Nauru in the western Pacific and Palau and Truk in Micronesia find drug profits flowing into their banks. Citizens of Vanuata, a volcanic archipelago of some eighty islands, has found that international finance beats coconut and taro farming. In Port Vila, the capital, it is not unusual for a $100 million transaction between major international banks to take place on any given day.[18]

Unscrupulous American banks have also contributed to the problem. So have ingenious and sophisticated laundering schemes that keep illegal drug profits in the United States. In the United States, a money-laundering center can be spotted by the huge surplus of cash that flows into the local branch of the Federal Reserve System. In 1985 the Miami branch posted a $6 billion excess. But after several years of intense federal probes of South Florida banks, Miami's cash glut fell in 1988 to $4.5 billion. Much of that business went to Los Angeles, where the cash surplus ballooned from $166 million in 1985 to nearly $4 billion in 1989.[19]

This focus on the money side of drugs is important for prosecution. It is impossible for authorities to link major drug dealers with the sale of drugs except through such tracking. They are simply too well insulated. Federal authorities must conduct a currency trail which leads back to the drug kingpin. Another prosecutorial strategy is to use the evidence of such financial resources to seize traffickers' assets gained through illegal enterprise and/or to prosecute for income tax violation.[20]

## THE GOVERNMENT'S USE OF ANOTHER WEAPON IN THE DRUG WARS: FORFEITURE SANCTIONS

A 1985 survey by the National Institute of Justice showed that state and local police administrators and prosecutors rank the problem of drug trafficking as the most serious issue facing law enforcement. In response to such concerns, the federal government and many of the states have passed new laws based on the ancient legal principle of forfeiture, which permits the government to seize property used in criminal activity.

Although such laws have been widely adopted and put on the books, the survey also indicated that few of the states as well as the police and the prosecutors in these states were using this important tool. On the other hand, states such as Maryland and Michigan, and especially Florida, have been particularly active and successful in their use of these powers.

The federal statute has some broad powers. Under federal laws things such as foreign and domestic bank accounts can be seized, together with planes, vessels, cars, and luxury items like jewelry or resort homes purchased with proceeds from the illicit drug trade. Thus, not only "conveyances"—the means to transport the illegal drugs (cars,

planes, boats, etc.) can be seized—but "derivative proceeds" (homes, jewelry) are also subject to government seizure. In this latter instance what needs to be shown is that these "proceeds" have been obtained from the profits of either manufacture or trafficking in illegal drugs. Only a few states, however, permit the government to seize real or personal property. The authorities in the states are generally only permitted to seize conveyances, money, negotiable instruments or securities, paraphernalia or raw materials used in the manufacture or sale of drugs, and records maintained during the course of the illicit activity. In all cases of the government attempting to seize "derivative proceeds," the burden is on the government to prove that these proceeds were derived from the illicit sale or manufacture of drugs.

A few states are a little novel in their approach. In these states the proceeds from certain seizures such as cars, guns, money, and the like go directly to the law enforcement agency involved for their official use. The idea is that this will motivate police departments to commit resources to these type crimes. For

example, the agency can then use such automobiles for undercover work or money as part of their "buy fund" or to pay drug informants. New York's law provides that funds will be used to provide restitution to victims, while Washington State earmarks 50 percent of such proceeds to its Criminal Justice Training Fund.

All such legislation has provisions that protect innocent parties, for example, lienholders or common carriers who may be transporting drugs without knowing it. Finally, the laws generally specify two other conditions. In almost all instances, it is the responsibility of the prosecutor to initiate forfeiture proceedings. At the time of the survey, one notable exception to this policy was Florida. That state adopted a new law that permitted the police to hire private legal counsel to expedite the proceedings. Most states also reserve their forfeiture laws for more serious drug manufacturing or trafficking cases.

*Source:* Reprinted with permission from Lindsey D. Stellwagen, "Use of Forfeiture Sanctions in Drug Cases." *Research in Brief* (Washington, D.C.: U.S. Department of Justice—National Institute of Justice, July 1985.)

## The Legalization of Drugs: Arguments and Issues

The unspeakable is now being spoken, and thought-provoking questions are being posed.[21] A drastic recommendation is being made: legalize drugs. This is not a new recommendation. What makes it different is that it now comes not from the muted voices of a few obscure academics and other "fringe types." Lately, responsible and public voices are joining the call for legalization. This includes even some members of the law enforcement community. This is a drastic recommendation that mirrors how seriously the narcotics situation has become and how badly present policies are failing.

Behind the prolegalization movement is the growing recognition that drug policy must minimize drug abuse while at the same time, in a rough cost-benefit sense, seek to minimize society's costs while maximizing the effects of controlling drugs. It is said that present policies do neither. Decriminalization is seen as a means to a much desired end: getting the criminal justice system out of the business of trying to control the problem of drug abuse and putting that responsibility where it belongs—in the hands of the nation's public health system.

This argument over legalization or the continued criminalization of drugs points out that our nation's drug control efforts are a public policy question. And like all government policies, it produces winners and losers. Making drugs illegal assumes that the "losers" are those people who traffic in drugs and that the "winners" are those who would become abusers if drugs were legal. Instead, the winners are the drug manufacturers and dealers, many of whom have managed to grow rich, provided they avoid arrest, seizure of their assets by the authorities, or violence from other criminals. The losers are the American people, who must pay extraordinary sums to try to control the uncontrollable. There are also other "losers," including the exporting countries and, ultimately, the larger national interests of the United States.

This "winners" versus "losers" idea serves as one of the important cornerstones in the legalization issue. The first such argument deals with the question of international economics. The United States, already suffering from an international monetary drain, finds itself a "loser" by subsidizing the economies of drug-producing and exporting nations. Yet it is not a type of economic exchange that permits underdeveloped countries to fully benefit from their export commodities. Although some benefits of cocaine markets "trickle down" to the individual native farmer working a Peruvian or Bolivian hillside or the Colombian workers involved in converting the coca into coca paste and then into coca hydrochloride, the vast profits line the pockets of the drug overlords who use their vast resources to corrupt political and military officials. Although this has happened in the past with legal export commodities, such as the exploitive sugar empires and the well-known excesses of the American Fruit Company—the profits of which were controlled by rich landlords or absentee corporations—there are some important differences.

A major difference is the violence and corruption that attends such narcotics operations. Instability has been introduced into the hemisphere. This has the possibility of threatening America's own interests. In Colombia, for instance, drug traffickers have murdered a number of the country's highest ranking political officials, as well as judicial, prosecutorial and law enforcement personnel. In the summer of 1989, a bloody week of assassinations attributed to the Medellín and Cali cocaine cartels marked a new era of violence. Judges in that country went on a nationwide strike, demanding greater protection from the government. A virulent anti-

Americanism is being spawned by anti-government insurgents backed by the cartels. There are indications that Cuba is assisting the cartels as a means to destabilize the area and weaken the United States.

There is still another insidious side to the "internationalization" of our drug policies. There is growing evidence that agents of our own government have turned a blind-eye to drug dealing in an effort to destabilize governments and policies thought inimical to our national interests. Such allegations reach to the highest levels of our government. CIA-backed ventures in Southeast Asia, where large sources of poppy for heroin are grown, as well as government-sponsored ventures throughout Latin America raise important and yet unanswered questions.[22] The arrest of Panamanian strongman Manuel Noreiga and the revelations about his activities provide the most recent example of questionable policies of our government in support of drug corrupted regimes.

We find ourselves in a perplexing situation. Today in Latin America, it is said that our government, in the interests of hemispheric influence, at least abets corruption and that our policies contribute to the misery, corruption, and violence of the drug trade in the hemisphere. Our policies also give aid and comfort to our most intractable enemies. A report to Congress from the General Accounting Office states that anti-American countries such as Iran, Afghanistan, and Laos produce nearly one-half the world's supply of heroin, most of which finds its way to America.[23] These countries have little interest in cooperating with the United States. Iran uses its drug-producing resources to continue its virulent anti-Americanism and to produce dangerous turmoil in the Middle East, and we supply the market and capital for their efforts.

Legalization advocates recognize that we cannot hope to convince poor peasants that curtailing the planting of coca plants is in their best interests. And we have not provided them with an acceptable means to provide a substitute living. Hungry stomachs are not concerned about what drugs do to our nation.

Our drug enforcement activities also raise questions about illegal and extralegal policies of enforcement. Constitutional questions are being raised about sweeping intelligence activities, in which the names of literally millions of Americans are supposedly kept in government data banks of suspected drug traffickers or users.[24] An analysis of drug prosecutions and criminal case processing by the National Institute of Justice, which is itself a federal agency, indicated that more drug cases are lost because of successful challenges to illegal police searches—in violation of the Fourth Amendment—than any other legal-related reason.[25] Although such challenges by defense counsels might be expected, people are beginning to ask if we are encouraging such potential police abuses.

The budgets of various federal enforcement agencies have skyrocketed in recent years. And a study prepared for the federal government in 1987 estimated that state and local police were devoting about one-fifth of their total budgets in 1986 to battle illegal drugs.[26] It is surely higher today. Some large city police officials are saying that their departments spend a majority of their time dealing with drug-related offenses.[27] This raises the question of how many predatory crimes of violence are going uninvestigated and unsolved. How much time is being spent by our overburdened prosecutors in dealing with drug offenses? And how much plea bargaining tied to drug offenses could be swept from our courts, allowing the criminal justice system to concentrate on arresting, prosecuting, and incarcerating violent offenders?

And what about our prisons and jails? The Federal Bureau of Prisons estimates that if current trends continue, the federal prison system will be swamped with drug offenders by 1995. As our jails and prisons fill up, too many offenders aren't behind bars who should be. And states find that at a time when they are sorely strapped for money, they must use their scarce resources to build more facilities to house ever-increasing numbers of inmates.

There is also another side to the economics of our drug enforcement policies. The implicit idea is that enforcement efforts will drive up the cost of drugs to the point where demand will diminish. This basic principle of economics which governs the cost and sale of commodities simply doesn't apply to the drug market. The cost of drugs has actually diminished in recent years in spite of increased seizures and arrests. There are probably a number of reasons for this. Drug dealers have made drugs more potent. This decreases their packaging size and increases their chances of successful smuggling, to say nothing of creating increased dependence. But the main fallacy of this market-demand argument is the margin of profit which exists. Marijuana, for example, has a raw commodity price of less than 1 percent of the street price. For cocaine, the figure is 4 percent. Drug enforcement efforts, no matter how intensive and costly, can expect to alter this relationship only slightly. An imperfect market-source situation also exists: The cultivation of between twenty-five to thirty acres of prime Colombian farmland in coca plants will yield nearly a ton of refined cocaine annually. According to statistics recently cited by the American Medical Association, Latin America produced 162,000 to 211,400 metric tons of cocaine in 1987. That is five times the amount needed to supply the U.S. market.[28] Consider this figure in terms of the 10 percent which experts are saying we interdict annually.[29] That same year, estimates were that between 2,000 and 3,000 tons of opium were produced. America needs only 70 tons to satisfy its illegal usage.[30]

The issue of AIDS has also carried over into the legalization advocates' concerns. Because one of the major methods of transmission is by intravenous drug use, it is said that legalization could better control the problem of contaminated drug paraphernalia. Programs such as in New York City, where addicts can obtain sterile needles, is one way to minimize the problem; it is unlikely, however, that many addicts will avail themselves of this opportunity while drug use remains illegal. They fear that they will come under police surveillance when they go to obtain their needles.

To the legalization advocates, then, the evidence is overwhelming. The problem is not the illegal use of drugs but how we as a nation have dealt with them by trying to criminalize them out of existence. They call for legalization and tight control of drug dispensing, together with major efforts made to educate potential drug abusers and to provide medical treatment. But is their solution any better than existing policy? Could it possibly further exacerbate an already bad situation?

QUESTIONS LEFT UNANSWERED   The possible consequences to our nation if drugs were legalized lie at the base of the arguments of those who advocate continued criminalization of drugs, although nobody really knows what the consequences would be if drugs were legalized. The fear of the possibilities frightens most Americans. A 1989 CBS poll indicated that nine of ten Americans reject the idea of decriminalizing all illicit drugs, with the majority saying legalization would lead to increased drug use. While 25 percent thought that marijuana should be legalized, only 7 percent favored the legalization of cocaine, and only 6 percent said heroin should be legal.[31]

Legal drugs came to America back in June of 1997. Speaking the now historic words, "O.K., let's give it a shot," an obviously reluctant President Quayle bowed to the will of Congress and signed the Prohibition Repeal bill into law. With the defeat of the Friedmanites, named for their spiritual leader Milton Friedman ("I would distribute drugs the way aspirin is distributed"), control of drug distribution was denied to private industry and placed in the hands of the federal government.

In the first year alone, the government opened 40,000 Reactive Chemical Dispensation Centers, or package stores, all of them frankly modeled on McDonald's hamburger shops. Clean and bright, with illuminated color-coded menus up high behind the smiling, nonjudgmental sales help. The gold menu (for "golden oldies") featured nostalgia drugs for older buyers—crack, heroin, angel dust, LSD and weak marijuana. Green was for more current and powerful forms of cocaine and marijuana. Red—an active, youthful color—signified designer drugs, most of them concocted by computer in college chemistry labs under government contract.

In Year Two, the drug program expanded to 120,000 outlets, mostly by taking over the shops of the bankrupt Roy Rogers chain. Despite this enormous capital outlay, government experts predicted that the drug program would be in the black within three years. Violent street crime fell 10 percent. Drug-related prosecutions dropped 80 percent. Since the government was buying most of the cocaine produced in Colombia and Peru, relations with Latin America brightened. Drug Czar Alan Dershowitz said, "Our long national nightmare is ending."

By the end of Year Two, the *New York Times* expressed editorial concern about the rise in drug use—up about 15 percent since repeal—but Dershowitz called it "a brief statistical spasm." More disconcertingly, the package stores were having trouble holding the line on drug prices. Back in 1989, a rock of

crack sold for $3 in New York, or four for $10. A decade later, in terms of 1989 dollars, the price was $5.89 at a government store, and $4 on the street. There were jokes about $600 toilet seats and "normal government efficiency."

### Hijackings and Lawsuits

Dershowitz told Congress that drug planners had underestimated the costs of the business. Ethan Nadelmann, a pro-legalization lobbyist of the 1980s, had predicted a $10-billion-a-year government profit from drug sales, but he hadn't counted on the costs of quality control, product development, insurance, theft and a sprawling civil-service drug bureaucracy. Because of the bombings at package stores, the department had to install foot-thick concrete walls and 24-hour guards. Hijackings were a constant problem. Four tons of cocaine and a shipment of European chemicals disappeared from Kennedy International Airport on a single day. Soon the department was paying the Army and Navy to escort cocaine shipments from Latin America.

To the amazement of most Americans, the dangerous drug gangs that ruled the streets in the 1980s were still thriving. Violence was down because the gangs had finally come to terms and divided America up into regional monopolies, a standard feature of mature capitalism. Business was booming because the gangs knew that the successors to the yuppies, the affluent TWITS (an acronym for Those With Income to Squander), did not wish to stand on line for drugs at a former Roy Rogers. They wanted a whiff of the romance and danger that come from buying a hot new drug from a slightly ominous contact in a dimly lit club.

When the product-liability suits against the Drug Department began to roll in (40,000 were filed in the month of September, 1999, alone), Congress mandated a six-month testing period for all new drugs. Since most designer drugs faded from the market in less time than

that, this gave the street gangs almost total control of the more fashionable drugs.

But the bulk of the gang business was kids. Since the Prohibition Repeal Act forbade sales to those under 21, the gangs had the high-school and college markets as monopolies. When Congress tried to cut into the gang profits by legalizing drugs for 18-year-olds, the gangs aggressively preyed upon younger and younger children. Addiction rates for 10-to-12-year-olds rose tenfold.

Street crime rose sharply; more addicts meant more muggings. With sales slumping, and a 42 percent addiction rate among Drug Department employees, Dershowitz resigned. The new Drug Czar, Ira Glasser, said confidently that sales would reach the break-even point within six years. With drug victims filling 78 percent of hospital beds, Congress authorized $97 billion for hospital construction. New forms of brain damage and disease began to show up among users, so Congress mandated weaker doses, thus sending thousands of the more serious users to the black market for their heavier hits.

With the cocaine market glutted and a million hectares of Colombian soil under cultivation, the Medellín government started dumping excess coke on American streets at fire-sale prices. No one bought coke legally. That finished off the government stores, which, with only 17 percent of the U.S. drug market, were $4 billion in debt.

On Dec. 1, 2002, with 100 million Americans using drugs, with the economy a shambles and with child abuse at five times the level of 1989, Congress voted unanimously to make drugs illegal once again. Debate began on which civil liberties might be preserved during the cleanup. Former Czar Dershowitz said: "So I was wrong. What can I do about it now?" Former Czar Glasser said simply, "It was a noble experiment."

*Source:* Reprinted with permission from John Leo, "When the Feds Turned Drug Dealer," *U.S. News & World Report,* 13 November 1989, p. 75.

Although we know our present drug policy of enforcement is failing, there are important concerns we cannot overlook. Of course, we recognize the potential for even more widespread abuse if drugs were legalized. There are also attendant concerns. Would legalization open the floodgates to more widespread usage that present enforcement efforts deter? What about Britain's disastrous experiment with the legalization of heroin? Would not the same thing happen here? What about problems of trying to control the dispensing of drugs, especially since such drugs will inevitably fall into the hands of children? And what about the problems associated with babies born addicted to drugs, whose mothers obtained the drugs legally from government dispensaries? We already know the terrible costs, both medical and otherwise, which result from the use of alcohol and tobacco in this country. Are we to encourage the use of still another substance with such widespread potential for abuse? And will legalization really relieve our present crime problem or will little change? What about offenses committed under the influence of legal drugs? It is entirely conceivable that drug-contributed offenses will continue to be a problem even under a legalization scheme. And what about such problems as increased instances of driving under the influence of narcotics? How would we handle such a situation?

And would the legalization of drugs really stop the illicit marketing of drugs and the financial inducement to engage in such activities? It is entirely possible that a "black market" of even more powerful drugs would spring up to provide the drug abuser with what he or she can't obtain legally. This is a particularly threatening possibility as potent new chemical "designer drugs" could be developed and marketed outside legal sources.

## Changes in Drug Use and Their Possible Implications

The changes that are occurring in drug use are both promising and ominous. The changes are certainly important in terms of their implications and noteworthy in terms of what they suggest as a characteristic of American society. Still, aside from that fact, changes in the characteristics of drug abuse could be as potentially explosive a policy issue for the country as the legalization debate. Just what are these changes? There is growing evidence that the impact of drugs is increasing among the poor and decreasing among middle-class Americans. A 1989 report by the federal government's National Institute on Drug Abuse confirmed this.[32] Under such circumstances, it is possible that the "War on Drugs" will then lose some of its saliency—and with this its urgency as a national priority. It then follows that the legalization versus criminalization debate will also lose its meaning and urgency.

If such present trends continue, these changing patterns of consumption will begin to be felt in the next several years. From our still inconclusive evidence, we can make some reasonably accurate predictions about the future. For instance, preliminary indications are that the following is already taking place or is likely to become a reality:

- With the exception of heroin and crack among the poor, the use of illegal drugs appears to have peaked, including snorting cocaine.
- Evidence tends to indicate that people turning away from drugs are the most educated and affluent. The poorest and least educated have continued to increase their drug use.

- "Crack" has largely remained a poor-people's drug. Its rise in the past two years has had devastating effects on poor neighborhoods, but it has failed to make the same inroads into the middle class.
- The most deadly impact of illegal drug use is yet to come as tens of thousands of intravenous drug users, their sexual partners, and their children contract AIDS. Many of these people will be the urban poor.[33]

As the "drug problem" shifts to these groups, it may very well become less important as a national policy of concern. There is some historical precedent for this contention. As long as narcotics were generally relegated to groups outside the mainstream of American life, such as blacks in urban ghettos or musicians or counterculture people, little widespread public concern or outcries for antidrug efforts surfaced. Heroin, for instance, has long been a problem in inner cities that never really "crossed over" into mainstream society. As long as the "problem" was relegated to these underclasses and less desirable segments of society, it didn't have the visibility or receive a great deal of attention from government. It was only when the "drug problem" crossed over into more "respectable" (and powerful) segments of society, either by increased use by middle- and upper-class people or by their children, did the nation really gear up to address the problem.

By the same token, it wasn't merely the concern of growing use of illegal drugs by the more respectable members of society that prompted national attention; it was also the spreading of other associated drug-use problems that prompted public support for antidrug efforts. Violence, crime-related activities that victimized the better elements of society, increased welfare costs, and other drug-related maladies associated with growing use of drugs prompted a greater outcry and backlash. Although a certain level of deviance was acceptable, the level of associated problems outgrew the public's tolerance. As long as these circumstances victimized or threatened to victimize broader segments of society it became a problem to be addressed.

If present trends continue, we may have emerging a tale of two drug problems: one in which middle- and upper-middle-class Americans pass through a twenty-year experiment with illegal drugs; the other in the America of the poor, where amid hopelessness, lack of education, and lack of opportunity this segment of our society will suffer the worst consequences of drug abuse—AIDS, crime, and criminal victimization. While one segment of our society seems to be turning away from illegal drug use, another seems to be further sinking into the abyss of drugs and dependence. To the extent that this occurs, and to the extent as we have said that we can better contain the "bleeding over" into the consciousness and tolerance limits of mainstream society, the scourge of illegal drug use, and all its associated problems, our nation's drug problem may become less pressing as a national issue.

This is a strong statement, and it stands as a searing indictment of American society. Still, it rests upon historical precedent. It fundamentally concludes that as long as illegal drugs can be relegated among "those people" without incurring significant costs to other Americans, it need not concern us too much. Provided some acceptable threshold is not crossed, our antidrug efforts will lose their saliency as a public policy issue. At this point we have a long way to go in reducing the problem to its acceptable threshold. But thresholds change under unremitting pressures. Tolerance levels have a tendency to be adjusted upward. What this emerging mixed message of hope and despair signals for our nation is still unclear. What will evolve from this will be worth watching in the years ahead.

## ▣  TERRORISM

### Defining Characteristics

Terrorism has become a major concern for at least one segment of the American criminal justice community—the police. The most significant changes in terrorist activities in recent years is their increasing sophistication. This poses significant danger to the nation. This sophistication is evident in such areas as organization, tactics, weaponry and explosives, sponsorship of such groups, assistance often provided in the training and indoctrination of terrorists by organizations and nations throughout the world, and increasingly complex systems for delivering and carrying out terroristic attacks.[34]

The United States must deal with two types of terrorist activity: domestic and international. Usually, these are distinguished by where they are committed. Domestic terrorism comprises those terroristic acts committed on American soil, and international terrorism, terroristic acts committed against Americans or American interests abroad. This is generally the way the authorities treat the two. It is also the way they will be addressed here. Of course, even this convenient definition doesn't take into account the fact that an element of internationalism may be involved in so-called "domestic" acts of terrorism: for instance, when the acts are committed on American soil by foreign nationals or by American citizens whose terrorist organization is supported or aided by foreign interests.

Although terrorist actions involve many traditional forms of crime, they have a singular characteristic: Terrorist activities are political acts. They are actions involving the unlawful use of force or violence against persons or property with the purpose of intimidating or coercing a government or the civilian population. The political nature of a terrorist act is important. It imbues terroristic actions with an element of motivation—indeed a zeal that is not found in traditional criminal events. Some terrorists and terrorist groups are so extreme in pursuit of their cause that they are difficult to deter. In addition to creating almost insuperable difficulties for traditional forms of deterrence, this characteristic requires extraordinary countermeasures—countermeasures that are not typically found in the experience and operating characteristics of most law enforcement agencies, especially those representing a free and democratic society. Effective countermeasures may, for example, require law enforcement agencies to abandon imposed legal restraints, or the "illegalization" of police actions. The police may feel (perhaps with some justification) that they must step outside the law to deal effectively with terrorism. The implications are ominous.

Terrorism is also characterized by the fact that it typically involves a significant organizational network that sustains and supports such activities. This aspect of organization is an important one. Experts in the area of terrorism are quick to point out that the lone terrorist or anarchist is a rarity today. Instead, they are organized into groups or cells. There is the small inner circle, which actually selects the target and carries out the operation. This level of organization is supported by a second level, which usually comprises a larger group of active supporters who are responsible for logistics, renting of safehouses, acquiring the needed automobiles and weapons, and providing fictitious documents. A third level of organization consists of those in sympathetic support of the activities or at least the objectives of the

One factor that makes terrorism particularly difficult to combat is the anonymity of the participants. (© Roland Neveu/Gamma Liaison)

terrorist group. They often engage in protests, organize marches and demonstrations, and write articles that support terrorist efforts. Although often not directly terrorists, these groups and individuals sustain the activities of the terrorist group by their support.[35]

This element of organization compounds the problems of effectively dealing with terrorist groups. We have seen in our nation's history the success of organized crime. A developed and sophisticated form of organization can make it that much more difficult to ferret out terrorists. Although it is true that "organized" criminal activity has certain weaknesses compared to the lone or solitary criminal action (e.g., greater dispersion of incriminating knowledge among members, the possibility of a member of the group becoming an informant, ability to penetrate the group through its weakest link), it still remains a two-way street. With some of the terrorist groups now operating, we cannot hope to rely on such techniques as we have used successfully to combat traditional organized crime. We cannot, for example, rely upon our so-called "Mafia experience." We were able to first penetrate this organization in the early 1960s, when an informant broke "Omerta" (the code of silence), which permitted infiltration by law enforcement authorities. Counterposed to such techniques are factors operating that also impede successful penetrability among the most dangerous terroristic organizations. Many of the most dangerous terrorists hold deep-seated convictions and resort to such unrestrained violence that inroads are difficult to make. This not only makes them more dangerous initially but less likely to cooperate with authorities when arrested.

Perhaps this explains why the authorities have been more successful dealing with certain domestic terrorist groups than with international terrorists who commit domestic terrorist acts or acts against American citizens or interests abroad.

Witness our government's inability to initially identify let alone locate the specific terrorists who blew up Pan American flight 103 over Scotland, causing the deaths of 230 people in December 1988. (Tentative evidence indicates that the Popular Front for the Liberation of Palestine–General Command are responsible.) Many indigenous (domestic) terrorist groups are not bound together by the same dedicated fervor that exists among say, anti-Zionist or anti-American Middle Eastern terrorists, or by the anti-Protestant and anti-British feelings of the Irish Republican Army (IRA). Although professing strong loyalty to the ideals of the organization, many members of such indigeneous terrorist groups have such malformed emotional problems that they become easier targets for psychiatrically guided law enforcement operatives. Perhaps we can be thankful for this.

Although the success of internationally based or supported terrorists has been limited in the United States, this could change quickly.[36] Increasing concern is also being voiced about the growing problem with domestic terrorist groups. So far the problem of terrorism—whether international or domestic—has had little effect on the components of the criminal justice system other than the law enforcement community. It is entirely conceivable, however, that this too could quickly change. Terrorist acts could suddenly focus their attention on destructive and violent acts directed toward the judicial system. Terrorist groups could cause additional problems in correctional institutions if militant members of such groups grow in numbers among such inmate populations.

America is not alone in its struggle against terrorism. In fact, the United States has been fortunate in being relatively immune from acts of terrorism on American soil. Terrorist groups have for many years been active throughout Western Europe, the Middle East, Latin America, and in areas of Asia such as Japan, Sri Lanka, and recently the Philippines. Names and groups such as the IRA, the Basque separatist movement in Spain, the leftist Direct Action movement in France, the Red Brigades in Italy, and the anti-American, anti-imperialist Red Army Faction in Western Germany have all been active on the European continent and are familiar to Americans well versed in international affairs. Probably no terrorist group has been more publicized in recent years than the Palestine Liberation Organization (PLO), its more militant off-shoots, and their major terrorist support nations: Libya, Syria, and Iran.

Why the United States has been relatively free of international terrorist actions within its borders is open to conjecture. Whereas terrorists have attacked surrogate representatives serving in foreign nations such as embassy personnel, military installations, and servicemen and occasionally bombed or hijacked common carriers with American passengers abroad, they have not brought such acts of terrorism to American soil. It would be foolish to assume that we have escaped such acts because our domestic antiterrorist strategy is so effective that these groups are deterred. The Israeli experience argues against such a complacent attitude. Israel has probably the most efficient antiterrorist system in the world, yet even its sophisticated intelligence and antiterrorist strategies have not prevented increasing attacks and successes against its people and property.

Nor can we attribute our success to the fact that we are geographically remote from the areas of terrorist activity and centers of such organization. The permeability of our thousands of miles of open borders and our lax immigration policies would argue against such a conclusion. The only answer is that we have remained relatively untouched because terrorist groups have chosen not to carry out attacks on American soil. To date nobody seems to have an adequate explanation for why.

## Responsibility for Combatting Terrorism

The leadership role in combatting terrorism has been given to the federal government, because local and state agencies are simply without the resources, skills, or sweep of jurisdiction to cope effectively with the problem. For domestic terrorist activities occurring in the United States, the U.S. Attorney General has the responsibility for coordinating all federal law enforcement activities, with the FBI designated the lead agency for dealing with such occurrences. To a lesser extent, the Bureau of Alcohol, Tobacco and Firearms of the Treasury Department, the United State's Marshal Service, and the Immigration and Naturalization authorities play a part. In trying to develop a national response to such threats, efforts have thus become divided, and many would say diluted, by a sharing of this responsibility among federal agencies.

This division of responsibilities is even more pronounced in our international antiterrorist efforts. Existing federal laws and Presidential Executive Orders give the State Department control in handling terrorist activities directed at American citizens outside the United States. This has posed problems. The State Department is not an enforcement agency or specialist in antiterrorist strategies. In fact, its operating policies of diplomacy and statecraft may be at odds with effective programs of intelligence-gathering and enforcement efforts. Indications are that more enforcement-directed agencies such as the Department of Justice are at odds with the State Department's role and handling of terrorist threats and actions.

In recent years Congress has passed additional laws aimed at acts of terrorism and terrorist groups. For example, such legislation as the Comprehensive Crime Control Act of 1984 contains specific provisions dealing with terroristic crimes. This piece of legislation is supported by the more recent Omnibus Diplomatic Security and Antiterrorism Act of 1986. Recently, the FBI's jurisdiction over hostage taking of American citizens in foreign countries has been approved. As a signatory to a special international convention against terroristic hostage taking, any hostage-taking situations or terrorist acts involving American citizens in a foreign country will be a violation of United States law. Under international law, such criminals can then be returned to the United States for prosecution in federal courts.

The United States, however, has not been very successful in its efforts to obtain cooperation from even its major Western European allies. Although we have international extradition agreements with more than one hundred nations, we have had little luck persuading these nations to turn over to us fugitives who have broken our laws or killed American citizens. And this includes a full range of terrorist and criminal acts: from the killing of innocent American citizens, to the assassination of military or diplomatic personnel, to major international narcotic traffickers. In most instances we have been rebuffed in our efforts to have these offenders returned to American courts for trial. Often the asylum countries have refused our requests by contending that their laws prohibit the extradition of what they classify as individuals involved in "political acts."

This however, is just one of the reasons for the lack of cooperation with American efforts to prosecute terrorists. Many nations feel that cooperation with American authorities would be a dangerous undertaking. Such efforts at cooperation could expose these nations to acts of retribution from terrorist groups. France and Italy are two nations that subscribe to this attitude.

The major weapon against terrorist groups and activities is intelligence efforts:

## THE GROWING PROBLEM OF
## EXTRADITION OF INTERNATIONAL OFFENDERS

A recent development has serious implications for America's efforts to extradite fugitives from European countries. Although the case deals with a fugitive charged by the State of Virginia authorities with murder, its implications point to similar problems in cases for which the United States could conceivably invoke the death penalty for terrorist actions or narcotics trafficking.

In 1989, the European Court of Human Rights issued a momentous ruling. The Court made it clear that in deciding whether suspects should be extradited, countries must consider whether upon conviction such suspects would face "inhuman and degrading treatment" in violation of Article 3 of the European Convention on Human Rights. At issue was the fact that under American law as exists in Virginia, murder suspects in American states could face years on "Death Row" before being executed. This gives the nature of the American criminal justice process its "inhuman and degrading treatment" of those convicted of capital crimes.

The eighteen judges unanimously upheld a claim by Jens Soering, twenty-two, the son of a West German diplomat, that the British Government would be in breach of its obligations under Article 3 if it extradited him to Virginia where he is wanted to stand trial on charges of murdering his girlfriend's parents in 1985. Although the Court did not go so far as to establish that the extradition of any suspect to an American state where he faced a lengthy wait for execution on "Death Row" would automatically involve a violation of Article 3 of the Convention, its ruling in this case seems to point the way to the possibility of this occurring, according to some international legal experts.

Soering was arrested by the British authorities. He is also wanted in West Germany on charges of murder. Notified of his arrest, the United States authorities requested his extradition. Soering fought the extradition request and obtained the ruling from the European Court

of Human Rights. Britain then tried to pursuade the American authorities to guarantee that Soering would not be given the death penalty if they returned him to the United States for trial and he was convicted. The Virginia authorities refused to give that guarantee. In fact, the Virginia authorities insisted that they would seek the death penalty and refused to drop the capital charges against Soering. Although the decision of the Court is not binding on the British government in the same way as a ruling of the European Court of Justice in Luxembourg, Britain would be in breach of her Convention obligations by allowing Soering's extradition to Virginia to proceed. Consequently, Britain has refused to take action on the American request.

The decision by the Court raises the fear that Britain and other European countries will be seen as a haven for fugitives who are wanted for capital crimes in American states where the death penalty can be imposed.

the gathering of information about such groups and their activities. Once gathered, such information has to be analyzed, interested law enforcement agencies must be notified, and plans for dealing effectively with such groups must be devised. The FBI has created a special Terrorism Section in that agency's Criminal Investigative Division at the FBI Headquarters in Washington. As part of this division, there is in operation a Terrorist Research and Analytical Section (TRAC), which supports this agency's investigations by providing analysis of terrorist groups or incidents. Among other things, it analyzes information gathered by investigative efforts such as interviews conducted of persons having information on terrorists, undercover and surveillance efforts, informants, and financial records. In addition, its efforts include establishing patterns of activity, identifying group leadership and developing information about the group's network of organization and support. In domestic security or terrorism cases, it may also analyze information gathered from approved electronic surveillance and interception methods.[37]

In recent years there has been an increase in joint federal-state-local efforts among law enforcement agencies to deal with terrorism, whose targets can include such special activities as political conventions, Olympic Games, or the World's Fair.

In major cities such as New York or Washington, D.C., where the threat of terrorism is a real possibility, joint task forces have been created involving the FBI and local and state police.[38] These groups share information and develop plans for conducting investigations, gathering intelligence information, and taking action in the event of a terroristic act. Additional task forces are now being expanded to other cities and areas where terrorist groups might be found.

## Major Domestic Terrorist Groups

The United Freedom Front . . . the Covenant, the Sword, the Arm of the Lord . . . the United Jewish Underground . . . Fuqra . . . the Armed Forces of the National Liberation (FALN) . . . the Ku Klux Klan: These are just some of the many domestic terrorist groups that have operated in the United States in recent years. Among the actions attributed to these groups have been bombings, armed robberies, murders, and arson. These groups are referred to as domestic terrorist organizations because they are not funded, directed, controlled, or supported by foreign sources.[39] Those who have studied domestic acts of terrorism give claim that the 1960s spawned this problem. During that decade, violence was brought about by racial animosities, campus unrest generated by the anti-Vietnam War movement, and the urban disorders that wracked a number of American cities. Out of this period of turmoil the beginnings of many of these groups can be found. In the early 1970s, the focus shifted somewhat as American anti-imperialism became a rallying motivation for a number of domestic terrorist groups.

There have been some important changes. During the 1980s the issues for such groups focused more on pro-independence (freedom from governmental interference, the creation of a separatist nation, etc.), black and white racial extremist activities, antigovernment and tax protests, and nationalistic fervor. The extremes of the entire political spectrum were represented from groups on the radical left to extremists of the radical right. Today, authorities generally identify five broad categories of domestic terrorist organizations. These categories generally cover the majority of terrorist associations and activities: white left-wing groups dedicated to the overthrow of American capitalism; black groups made up of antiwhite racists; right-wing terrorists who are also racists with particular emphasis focused in recent years on racial minorities; Jewish extremists who range from pro-Israel and anti-PLO supporters to counter–anti-Semitism groups, and Puerto Rican leftist groups who call for that commonwealth's independence from the United States and its conversion to a socialist or communist state.[40]

One important legacy of the 1980s has been a resurgence in the growth and activities of left-wing terrorist groups in the United States. Their's is a carryover from the 1960s and the efforts of the then-active Weatherman or Weather Underground Organization and the New World Liberation Front. Driven by the same forces of anticapitalistic and anti-imperialistic fervor characteristic of the anti-Vietnam War demonstrations, their objective is quite simple: destroy the system of government that perpetuates such exploitation. They see themselves as urban guerrillas whose mission it is to attack the most visible symbols of decadent capitalism and its support mechanisms.

For the most part these groups have chosen symbolic targets for their attacks: large corporate headquarters, banks, military facilities, and the U.S. Capitol Building. Often, they engage in bank robberies to support their activities. Such groups seem to be most active in the Northeast and Middle Atlantic states. Like all terrorist groups, they have established safehouses, move frequently, and change identifications often to avoid recognition and arrest for their illegal activities.

Of growing interest and concern are groups espousing racism. These groups use terrorist activities to further their cause and to bring attention to themselves. Black domestic terrorist organizations often have a religion-based background for their activities. Probably the most active and prominent of such groups is Fuqra, a black Islamic religious sect headquartered in Detroit. This group has a mixture of motives: hatred for the white race, an orthodox or fundamental adherence to Islam—which often incorporates an anti-Semitic and anti-Christian fervor—and a strong missionary zeal to win converts, which has from time-to-time resulted in religious rivalry and clashes with other militant black religious sects.

There is evidence that some of these black domestic terrorist organizations have aligned themselves with well-organized and powerful black street gangs such as the El Rukns in Chicago. The El Rukns, a vicious street gang that is deeply involved in violent criminal activity and narcotics trafficking, has developed loose ties to black Islam. In this way their activities become supportive. The El Rukns were also recently involved in an alleged conspiracy with the Libyan government to undertake domestic terrorist activities and political assassinations as a reprisal against American activities against Libya's virulently anti-American Colonel Quaddafi. Fortunately, the authorities got wind of the plot and stopped it before any action took place.

Other militant black groups include the Black Hebrews and the Republic of New Afrika (RNA). This former group is a violent black supremacist organization that sees a race war between blacks and the whites in the United States as inevitable. Like similar white supremacist groups, they view their mission as one of preparing the black race for this ultimate struggle. The group also advocates the violent elimination of all forms of government in the United States as well as the total elimination of the white race. Although there has been no evidence of terrorist activity associated with this group, the RNA calls for the creation of an independent black nation consisting of the states of Alabama, Louisiana, Mississippi, Georgia, and South Carolina.[41]

In many ways the most active domestic terrorist groups in the 1980s have been those on the right-wing fringe such as the Covenant, the Sword, the Arm of the Lord. This has made these organizations a particular target for federal and state law enforcement activity. A basic belief of many right-wing extremists is the superiority of the white race. They see blacks, other nonwhites, and Jews as inferior racially, mentally, morally, and spiritually. Their beliefs are centered around the so-called Christian Identity Movement. This quasi-religion teaches that whites, not Jews, are God's chosen people; that God entrusted the white race to keep these inferior races in line. These twisted zealots see their calling as one of alerting Christian white America to the evils and manipulations of international and American-based Zionism and the "Black Scourge." Without such efforts, the corrupting influence of these inferior groups will destroy organized society and dilute the white race. In their preachings they are virulently anti-Semitic. To them, the members of the Jewish race are the descendants of Satan's bloodline. Many of these groups also see the inevitability of a massive war between the races for control of the earth. The neo-Nazi movement has sprung from these origins.

Many followers of these right-wing white supremacist groups live in remote and isolated rural areas, where they conduct religious services based on their interpretation of the Bible and carry out survivalist training and paramilitary operations.

In addition to their racist views, many right-wing groups also espouse antigovernment sentiment. This is particularly true in their views of the federal government, which they see as captured by Jewish and black interests. They advocate as little involvement of government in their lives as possible. An example of this is their nonpayment of income taxes. They also consider many federal and, to a lesser extent, state laws as being unconstitutional.

Several of the more noteworthy of these groups, such as the Order and the Aryan Nations, have been involved in a number of criminal activities. These include the killing of several police officers, armed robberies, bank robberies, counterfeiting, bombings of Jewish synagogues, and assaults on federal and local police officers. Like the black Republic of New Afrika group, several of these right-wing extremist groups espouse the creation of a separate nation in the Northwest where they can continue their activities unmolested by the allegedly Zionist-controlled government of the United States.

Among the most active groups in the United States in the 1980s were Puerto Rican leftist terrorist groups such as the FALN. The FBI claims that between the years of 1974 and 1987, more than one hundred terrorist incidents or other crimes committed in the United States could be directly linked to this organization. Included in these are bombings, assassinations, armed robberies, and rocket attacks. Targets have been military facilities and personnel (especially in Puerto Rico), U.S. government facilities, and corporate interests. Although several notable incidents of terrorist activities by Puerto Rican terrorists have occurred in the continental United States, most of the more serious incidents have occurred in Puerto Rico.

Finally, another major group of domestic terrorists are Jewish extremists. Militant Jewish groups such as the United Jewish Underground and the Jewish Defense League are prominent. Persons, organizations, or other elements deemed anti-Semitic or supportive of Arab-sponsored anti-Jewish groups are targets of their activities. Included in this category would be the anti-Jewish interests of the Soviet government and any former Nazis.

Although difficult to deal with, domestic terrorist groups for the most part operate on American soil and are comprised of American citizens. Investigative efforts then concentrate on penetrating such organizations with undercover police personnel and the extensive cultivation and use of informants. As mentioned earlier, the gathering of intelligence plays an important role in combatting such activities. So does the ability to trace such activities by analyzing methods of operation that identify characteristics of certain groups. Special attention has also been focused on tracing weapons and explosives, either from legitimate sources or through illegal means such as thefts and burglaries.

One of the major concerns is that such groups might develop closer supporting ties with international terrorist groups and nations who would support open terroristic warfare in the United States itself. It is conceivable, for example, that a domestic terrorist group might provide the means and the contacts for international terrorists to smuggle a nuclear weapon into the country, successfully conceal it, and ultimately move the device to its point of detonation.

## The Future Needs

Several things are evident when you examine our nation's antiterrorist activities. First, the authorities have been fairly successful against domestic terrorist groups but woefully inadequate in dealing with international terrorism. Part of this may be explained by the composition of domestic terrorist organizations and how and where they commit their terrorist activities.

For instance, domestic terrorism is simply easier to deal with because of the composition of these groups and the easier task of identifying and penetrating their organizations through informants and undercover operatives. We also have adequate criminal statutes that cover these activities (if nothing else, the government uses conventional statutes such as robbery, theft, illegal weapons possession, and extortion) against these groups. The problems of enforcing these laws are also not as complicated by factors that exist among the international community in dealing with international acts of terrorism. They are acts committed on American soil that confer jurisdiction to police and judicial authorities. Only when such terrorists successfully flee and when international efforts calling for extradition must be employed do we run into problems.

This brings us to the second need. The world community of nations must enter into strong cooperation and effective agreements to facilitate cooperation. This is easier said than accomplished, however. It is not only the question of competing ideologies and politics involved in bridging a consensus for concerted action. There is, as already mentioned, another long-standing problem. Countries perceive that if they assist another nation's efforts, they will themselves become targets for terroristic retribution. Terrorists are well aware of these concerns and willing to exploit such fears.

A third issue is one of responsibility. The overlapping authority of America's law enforcement community must be dealt with. Because, as we have seen, this is a federal responsibility, immediate steps must be taken to develop better policies and areas of clear authority and responsibility at this level. It will be too late to do this after a major tragic act of terrorism has occurred. Still, this after-the-fact response is characteristic of how our government operates.

Finally, because the life blood of any antiterrorist program rests on effective intelligence efforts, they must be strengthened. How this might be accomplished is again another matter. There are two important aspects to intelligence activity: gathering and sharing. Both of these tasks provide problems. The difficulties of gathering such information are pretty straightforward. The problem of sharing information is less understood. How intelligence is shared, with whom, and with what results can jeopardize the successful intelligence-gathering task. If gathered information is shared among the antiterrorist interests, there is the danger that it will be somehow disclosed and jeopardize the source of information—or worse. Under such circumstances, there is great reluctance to share counterterrorist information, even among what are ostensibly the strongest allies.

It is hoped the 1990s do not put our antiterrorist strategies and organizations to the test—particularly on American soil. It may demonstrate the haunting fear that we are entirely too vulnerable to such actions. If this were to occur, it would pose another interesting question to ponder: What would be the result of the ensuing public backlash against such an attack or series of attacks? If nothing else such a backlash might well result in additional limitations being imposed on our freedoms of expression and demonstration.

# ☐ CRIMES AGAINST THE ENVIRONMENT

Another national cause for concern is environmental pollution. It is not only a problem faced by Americans, it has become an issue of global magnitude. Such concerns over the poisoning of the world's environment brought many members of the world together at an international congress in 1989 to discuss strategies for dealing with this growing menace. Although this meeting was primarily attended by members of industrialized nations—countries that felt the most acute need to address issues of the environment—Third World nations are also threatened. The threat of uncontrolled toxic substances as a health problem may prove to be one of humankind's most serious hazards in the twenty-first century. The American public has begun to recognize the menace. Poll after poll has shown that environmental pollution ranks high on the agenda of our concerns.[42]

The law enforcement and criminal justice community have an important role in dealing with our environmental problems. Willful and deliberate poisoning of the environment in violation of laws and regulations controlling pollutants calls for a strategy that must involve the criminal justice system. As these acts are increasingly seen as criminal violations, the criminal justice system will play an ever-larger role. Deliberate and large-scale environmental pollution may transcend the harm imposed by more traditional crimes. Still, the criminal justice system finds itself seriously hampered in its ability to deal with the problem. As with other major social concerns that require enforcement efforts under the criminal law, the policing of willful toxic pollution can only do so much. The success of enforcement efforts is determined by a host of factors. We need effective laws that impose meaningful sanctions, resources that can be applied to investigating and ferreting out toxic polluters, and courts and administrative bodies who will apply strict sanctions to violators. These requirements have yet to be met.

## History of Antipollution Laws

As unlikely as it may seem, we have to step back nearly seven centuries for the first recorded antipollution laws. In fourteenth century England, the Crown prescribed the death penalty for Englishmen who defied a royal proclamation on smoke abatement. Most people think our own laws in this area are of recent origin. Perhaps they would be surprised to learn that the first federal law addressing toxic pollutants was passed nearly a century ago. Even then there was a recognizable problem. In 1899 Congress adopted the Rivers and Harbors Act. This law prohibited the dumping of "refuse matter" into the navigable waters of the United States. This law, however, was for the most part feckless. First, it made the violation of this act only a misdemeanor and provided for a maximum fine of $2,500.[43] Even more importantly, it simply was unenforced. It was not until after World War II that even the most minimal enforcement of the act began to occur.

The 1960s saw the problem of pollution grow. Citizen groups began agitating for more government involvement in the regulation of environmental contamination. Concerns were being expressed about the deteriorating quality of the air and the nation's water, and the growing problem of toxic waste disposal was recognized. In 1970 President Nixon authorized the creation of a federal agency to oversee federal antipollution efforts and administer most of the federal government's environmental protection statutes. In this way, the Environmental Protection Agency (EPA) was created.

### The Laws and Legal Issues

The federal government and all the states have laws regulating environmental pollutants and toxic sources. The 1970s and 1980s saw increased attention focusing on these areas as new legislation and amendments to existing laws were passed. These laws provided for two types of enforcement actions: civil and criminal. In their enforcement efforts, the states have assigned these responsibilities either to special environmental agencies or to special units in offices of state attorneys general. The latter agency is often involved if a criminal prosecution is contemplated. The office of a state attorney general may also find itself assisting a special environmental regulatory agency in the conduct of civil actions. There may be, for example, a specific regulatory agency that has the responsibility to enforce state laws, and when criminal (or civil) prosecution is warranted, the Attorney General's office handles the case or at least provides legal counsel in civil matters. Although it is possible that some forms of criminal pollution may involve statutes that confer prosecution authority on the local prosecutor's office, this mechanism has not been widely used. The reason is simple: Local prosecuting attorneys rarely have the expertise or the resources to effectively prosecute environmental cases.

An examination of state laws pertaining to criminal enforcement show a common pattern of development. For the most part, they specify most acts of criminal pollution as misdemeanors, or at most, as minor felonies.[44] It seems that the states are still not ready to define criminal acts in this area as serious violations. The one possible exception to this is toxic waste disposal. States generally provide the most severe penalties, in both fines and imprisonment, for this type of willful pollution. An example of this can be found in a recent case in Pennsylvania. In 1989 a criminal court in that state sentenced the accused to a mandatory two to five years in prison for the illegal disposal of chemical wastes in violation of state hazardous waste laws. It was the first time a corporate officer had been sentenced under the provisions of the state's Solid Waste Management Act. Ironically, the convicted offender was named by President Reagan in 1987 as the nation's minority businessman of the year.[45]

The criminal–legal remedies to the states (and to the federal government) for these acts of pollution can be found in several possible sources. One, of course, is the specific environmental statutes that carry criminal penalties. Other legal sources include criminal laws dealing with the public health and welfare; criminal statutes that deal with data disclosure (e.g., failure to maintain adequate records of toxic waste generation or disposal), fraud, and public corruption; criminal conspiracy, solicitation, and aiding and abetting statutes; and state laws modeled after the federal government's Racketeer Influenced and Corrupt Organization (RICO) statute.[46] Government attorneys involved in the prosecution of environmental crimes recommend that whenever possible these be used jointly in the prosecution of such cases.[47]

This raises another issue. Experience has shown that there is generally no such thing as a pure "environmental crime." Violation of environmental laws usually leads to evidence of more widespread violation of general criminal laws. More often than not, cases include such offenses as conspiracy, false statements and claims, and mail and wire fraud.[48]

Establishing responsibility or fixing blame for toxic waste dumps is a complex legal process. (© O. Franken/Sygma)

The federal government primarily relies on seven major laws in its enforcement efforts.[49] These laws deal with such concerns as the emission of hazardous pollutants into the air and waters; the treatment, storage, and disposal of solid hazardous waste; the regulation on development and use of toxic chemicals, insecticides, and pesticides; and the authority for the EPA to respond to releases or threatened releases of hazardous waste into the environment. This latter law also creates a mechanism to deal with such occurrences and is commonly referred to as the so-called "Superfund."

Environmentalists and legal observers of the federal government's efforts in antipollution are unanimous in their feelings that the federal government and the EPA have only recently been serious about the problem.[50] For example, although the EPA was created in 1970, it wasn't until 1981 that an office of Criminal Enforcement was created within the agency. It wasn't until late 1982 that the first criminal investigator was hired. Similarly, it was not until 1987 that the small Environmental Crimes Unit in the U.S. Department of Justice was upgraded to a section in this agency. Even members of government agencies responsible for enforcing these laws admit that they have been slow in getting started. In a recent article, the head of the Environmental Crimes Section of the U.S. Department of Justice candidly admits this fact, as he tries to convince the reader that this is no longer the case:

> Criminal enforcement at EPA has come of age. Until the mid 1980s very few criminal cases were referred to the Department of Justice. [i.e., referred for prosecution.] When cases were brought, defendants were frequently acquitted or sentenced to perform community service during relatively short periods of probation. Juries were often unwilling to convict corporate officers for environmental violations and courts were generally unwilling to send first-time white-collar offenders to prison. However, with heightened public sensitivity to the serious and often irreversible effects of pollution, criminal indictments, successful prosecutions and lengthy prison terms for corporate offenders have become more common. From 1983 thru May, 1989 the Department of Justice obtained more than 520 indictments for violation of federal environmental law resulting in more than 400 convictions, $22.5 million dollars in criminal fines and more than 248 years of imprisonment were imposed.[51]

## Problems in Prosecution

One of the legal hurdles in prosecuting those who criminally pollute—especially corporate officers—is the requirement that the illegal act must have been done knowingly. And following the requirement for the burden of proof in criminal cases, this knowledge of and intent to violate the law must be proved to have existed beyond a reasonable doubt. These requirements can provide a significant obstacle to successful prosecution. There is certainly no problem where a corporate officer is caught "red-handed," actually committing a violation of environmental laws—for example, the somewhat unlikely occurrence of a corporate officer caught actually dumping hazardous waste in a river. But what about the situation when employees of a large firm are caught dumping a toxic pollutant? The workers claim that they were only following their superior's instructions. The corporate officer, of course, denies this and denies any knowledge or culpability in the criminal act.

Fortunately, in theory at least, neither the corporation or the corporate officer can escape responsibility. This was not always the case. Under the common law and the law that existed for many years in the United States, corporations were considered incapable of committing crimes. This is no longer true.[52] The Supreme

Court has held that the corporate officer cannot escape liability so easily. In a landmark case, the president of a supermarket chain was held responsible for violations committed by his firm because it was his duty to prevent them.[53] Still, if the particular law being violated requires the government to demonstrate criminal intent on the part of the corporate officer, problems for the prosecution are presented. In such a situation one noted legal expert suggests that, if possible, another statute that doesn't impose this burden on the government be used.[54] This alternative is referred to in the law as the "strict liability" doctrine, which is applicable to certain offenses. Under this doctrine, the government can theoretically charge someone with a crime without the burden of proving the degree of knowledge and intent required in most crimes. Unfortunately, such "strict liability" crimes also generally carry diminished penalties. What this shows is that the law in this area is still shadowy. Such problems and attitudes explain why the vast majority of criminal prosecutions are directed toward the offending business firm, and criminal fines are imposed on the business itself using the "strict liability" doctrine rather than the officers of the firm whose prosecution is more closely tied to the requirement of showing knowledge and intent.[55] Even though corporate officers could theoretically also be prosecuted as individuals under the strict liability doctrine, the government has been hesitant to use this doctrine against offending individuals.

There have been other problems associated with the legal enforcement of environmental laws. One is the situation of a landfill or solid waste disposal center being used by a number of firms. Toxic wastes in violation of the law are found at the site. Which of the site users is responsible? How does the government pinpoint responsibility? Without being able to determine responsibility, the government has no case.

Studies by the General Accounting Office (GAO) and congressional hearings on environmental pollution come to one conclusion: The problem is widespread. Although we have all heard of Love Canal in New York and the Exxon oil spill off the coast of Alaska, these are just the tip of the iceberg. For every instance of detected criminal (or accidental) pollution, hundreds go undetected.[56] In this situation the imposition of civil or criminal fines directed against a firm (as opposed to officers and employees of the firm) are, for the most part, meaningless. It is generally recognized that such use of the enforcement sanctions available to us serve as no meaningful deterrent.[57] Criminal pollution is an economic crime. It is done to escape the costs of dealing with hazardous materials properly. Fines imposed by regulators are merely seen as a "cost of doing business." This is especially true in non-owner operated corporations where even fines are payed by the shareholders rather than the corporation's officers. The liability of corporate officers is generally limited only to the extent that they are also stockholders and to the effects of the costs of the fine and any attendant bad publicity on the business and the equity position of the firm as reflected by its stock value.

The problem is not only with these corporate non-owner managers. Entrepreneurs who are owners of firms also bear the same calculated risks. They will consider the risks and the associated "costs." If compliance expenses are costly, and the chances of being caught are minimal, a strong incentive to pollute exists—especially if they can be reasonably assured that the only penalty that will be imposed will be a fine.

If deterrence is to work in theory—a condition that underlies any aspect of criminal law—the penalties must appear to be greater than the benefits received from participation in a criminal act. We saw that in our discussion of deterrence theory in previous chapters. Punishment must be seen as both meaningful and likely. Remove either of these conditions from our equation, and deterrence theory will certainly fail. It has been suggested by many scholars of crime that the threat of punishment in the form of public censure and the likelihood of imprisonment will have its greatest effect on white-collar criminals. A "criminal" as opposed to a "civil" action will be more threatening, as will imprisonment compared with a fine. Although enforcement action is unlikely, the fact that a businessman or a corporate officer would likely be charged with a crime and if convicted sent to jail or prison must figure into the "costs" of polluting. It would raise the cost significantly.

So why don't we use this strategy and let our laws reflect the imposition of such penalties, and with this our serious concern about the problem? The answer is to be found, unfortunately, too often in the traditional response of government lawmaking to the interests of business. Business interests and capital have always enjoyed a favored position and treatment in the United States. Andrew Szasz, in looking at the adoption of federal legislation to control the disposal of toxic waste, concluded that one of the major reasons that laws are less than effective in this area is because those who would be regulated were successful in getting Congress to water down any controlling legislation in this area.[58] Business interests simply successfully lobbied against laws that would impose more severe penalties.

The problem isn't only with business interests who generate pollutants; other interests are represented too. Kentucky is a good example. Large industrial and chemical corporations are located in several small towns in Western Kentucky. Over the years, these firms have routinely dumped toxic materials into surrounding rivers. Environmentalists want this practice stopped. They have marshaled their forces against these firms. Arrayed against the environmentalists are employees of these factories and local town businessmen who see the environmentalists as a threat to their livelihood. If these plants are successfully shut down, employees and local merchants will pay the economic consequences. Similar problems exist in any international or transnational discussion of pollution abatement, as discussed later.

## Illegal Pollution and Organized Crime

There is yet another dark side to the problem of criminal pollution of our environment. In certain areas of the country, organized crime is involved. The generation of hazardous waste is a necessary by-product of modern industrial production. These toxic substances must be processed and disposed of. The costs of this processing and disposal are an expense such firms must bear, and they are concerned about minimizing their costs in doing so.

Until a few years ago industrial hazardous waste was legally indistinguishable from municipal garbage and other solid wastes. Toxic waste was disposed of with ordinary garbage at landfills and in coastal waters at low cost to the firms generating such waste. In the 1970s it was recognized that such practices were creating environmental and public health concerns. Some states and the federal government passed laws that would regulate the generation and disposal of hazardous wastes "from cradle to grave." The states were authorized to register firms who created hazardous waste, to license transporters who would haul such wastes, and to license and regulate approved disposal sites who would handle the toxic substances.

These new laws, which distinguished hazardous waste from other waste and directed that such wastes be treated differently from municipal solid wastes, created a new industry almost overnight: hazardous waste transporters and disposal systems.[59] They also significantly increased the cost of waste disposal to firms generating hazardous substances who now had to comply with the new regulations. This ironically proved to be a windfall for organized crime.

In those parts of the country where garbage hauling and landfill operations historically have been controlled by organized crime, their movement into the newly created hazardous waste market was an immediate extension of their businesses. This occurred most notably in the states of New York and New Jersey. In New Jersey, for example, organized crime had for decades controlled the garbage industry through ownership of garbage-hauling firms, landfill sites, and through practices of labor racketeering.[60]

Testimony before a congressional committee investigating organized crime's involvement in the garbage and toxic waste disposal industry of New Jersey shows how the system operated. Years ago, organized crime developed a monopoly on garbage hauling in many areas of that state. Once associates of organized crime owned a number of hauling firms in any geographical area, they established an organizational structure that governed their relationships and ensured high profits. The cornerstone of the system was one of "property rights." Municipal solid waste–hauling contracts were illegally divided among haulers. Having a property right meant that the hauler could continue picking up the contract at sites he currently serviced without competition from others. Other mob-controlled hauling firms would submit artificially high bids or not bid at all when a contract came up for renewal. This would assure that the contractor kept his site. Of course, in such a noncompetitive situation, the organized crime associates could also establish a pricing structure for their services, which proved to be very lucrative. These property rights were recognized and enforced by means of threats or violence. Even hauling firms that were not owned outright by organized crime in these areas abided by the rules or they were forced to sell and get out.

When the new regulations were passed, mob-connected garbage haulers found it easy to obtain state permits and set themselves up as hazardous waste transporters and disposers. Of course, they brought with them their same form of organization and operation. Individual haulers holding established property rights assumed that they would transfer these property rights to the new type of waste.[61] They did exactly that.

It was in the area of waste disposal operations that were controlled by organized crime where the problem really became serious. Under the law, the hazardous waste material had to have someone from a registered and approved disposal site sign that the toxic substances were disposed of properly. Mob control of hauling was not enough: Organized crime figures also had to have ownership of, or at least influence over, final disposal sites to make the system complete and to maximize profits. Because organized crime already controlled and nearly monopolized landfill sites, these sites readily accepted shipments of hazardous waste disguised as ordinary municipal waste.[62] Landfill owners of approved disposal sites not directly associated with organized crime were bribed to sign for shipments they never received (the mob haulers would dump it along roadways, down municipal sewers, or into the ocean or other waterways) or accept hazardous waste that was designated on the manifest as assigned elsewhere.[63] Known organized crime figures also started to seize control of a network of phony disposal and "treatment" facilities, such as Chemical Control Corporation in Elizabeth, New Jersey.[64] Licensed by the state, these facilities could legally receive hazardous waste and sign the required manifest. Rather than disposing of the toxic waste, they would merely stockpile it on the site, where it would stay until it exploded, burned, or in some way came to the attention of the authorities, or the mob merely "disposed" of it by illegally dumping it somewhere.[65]

New Jersey's experience is typical in yet another way. When the major federal law regulating the transportation and, particularly, the disposal of hazardous waste was passed, there simply weren't enough qualified transporters and landfill sites in the state (or the nation) that could accommodate the waste that industry generated. There still isn't today. Concessions had to be made or industry would have strangled on its own toxic effluent. To deal with the need to dispose of toxic waste while imposing some regulatory controls, temporary licenses were issued to what would later prove to be bogus carriers and to firms who had no proper disposal sites. Incredibly, the supervision by New Jersey authorities was also nonexistent. It was four years after the federal law was passed before New Jersey even had a single person in the state capital to monitor the manifests filed by the transporters and the disposers with the state.[66] And as we have seen, the EPA certainly wasn't up to the task in the early 1980s. In a report issued in the mid-1980s, the federal government's GAO found that the existing manifest system designed to control the transportation and disposal of hazardous waste was simply not working because of the lack of effective monitoring of the system by the state and the federal governments.[67]

The ineptitude of the enforcement of antipollution laws by the state of New Jersey was graphically pointed out in the congressional hearings when it was disclosed that the state's agencies charged with this responsibility—the Interagency Hazardous Waste Strike Force, the Division of Criminal Justice, and the Division of Environmental Protection—were incapable of producing effective enforcement, even when tipped off to specific instances of illegal hazardous waste dumping.[68]

Testimony during the investigation of organized crime's inroads into hazardous waste disposal tended to absolve the firms who generated the toxic wastes from any complicity in these crimes because the firms turned their waste over in good faith to what they thought were licensed and therefore competent haulers and disposers; however, this view of the firms' "innocence" is not shared by all observers. For one thing, it was pointed out that generating firms have no interest in turning in the hauler or disposer in spite of any suspicions, because they didn't want to turn in their low bidders.

Judson Starr, Director of the Environmental Crimes Section of the U.S. Department of Justice, discusses the typical defendant prosecuted by his agency. He certainly doesn't paint the picture of someone who "innocently" or only "negligently" violates our nation's environmental laws. Of course, it should be remembered that this agency also has the track record of criminally prosecuting only the most serious and egregious violations and violators. He says:

> Our experience has shown that the conduct of the typical defendant in our cases is no different and no less serious than the conduct of one who has been convicted of the more traditional felonies—whether committed by a "white-collar" or "street-crime" offender. The acts are generally willful, deliberate, rational, premeditated and committed with some forethought over a long period of time. There are seldom any mitigating circumstances . . . in fact, no perceptible defense is generally offered—except that compliance was too expensive. Individuals who commit environmental crimes—particularly those involving hazardous wastes—commonly demonstrate a complete disrespect for the law and disregard for the safety of others, and are mo-

tivated by a desire to enjoy the substantial profits that can be derived from such illegal activities.[69]

This discussion of organized crime is meant to do two things: First, it points out that well-intentioned and required social legislation (antipollution laws just being one example) can lead to some unanticipated consequences. These laws may not only foster breaking the law but also actually encourage it if we are not careful. They may, for example, create an opportunity for the intent of the law to be thwarted on a scale even greater in scope—and, perhaps with more serious future consequences—than what existed before the passage of the legislation. In New Jersey, when the law was violated, it served to strengthen the tentacles of organized crime. But, it also did one other important thing: It seems to have encouraged at least tacit lawbreaking by ostensibly noncriminal elements (the industrial generators of toxic waste) to avoid the costs imposed by the new requirements. This experience and these facts must be kept in mind as America (indeed the world community of nations) moves—as it must—into greater efforts to control toxic pollutants.

## Transnational Criminality and the Environment

No discussion of environmental pollution and crime would be complete without a discussion of what may prove to be an even more serious problem and one that promises to be more difficult to regulate. We can look at the problems we are having in the United States in developing effective laws to deal with controlling harmful environmental pollutants and magnify the problem at least a hundredfold when we apply it to the international scene.

What we have seen is that effective environmental efforts must incorporate the following workable components: (1) required laws must be adopted; (2) effective compliance must be monitored to ensure that the intent of the laws is carried out; and (3) sufficient penalties must be imposed to make the laws work. It is instructive that this has as yet to be accomplished in the United States let alone among the world community.

The first requirement is effective laws to regulate the discharge of environmental pollutants. Transnational efforts in this area take the form of treaties and accords among nations. These may be bilateral agreements between two countries such as the United States and Canada, or they may be resolutions and accords between a number of nations sponsored by a world agency such as the United Nations.

Experience in this area has been a mixed bag. On the one hand, there have been a few successful efforts such as the Nordic Convention on the Protection of the Environment, which operates among cooperating Scandinavian countries.[70] There have also been some limited successes among certain West European countries. For the most part, however, although industrialized nations are especially quick to subscribe to the idea that something must be done, translating this into effective action lags. Even the best of neighbors have found it difficult to cooperate. The United States and Canada are prime examples. Although these two countries have made important bilateral strides to deal with the pollution of the Great Lakes, their efforts in such other areas as acid rain generated by the United States and the chemical toxicity of the Niagara River have stalled among recriminations.

Self-interest plays an important role in any effort to deal with environmental problems—whether among industrialized nations or the Third World. Such an unlikely source as Charles Dickens points out the problem. In the 1800s Dickens vainly attempted to arouse his fellow Englishmen to the evils of industrial growth uninhibited by governmental regulation. In his satirical novel *Hard Times*, Dickens has his leading spokesman explain the benefits of the industrial revolution to a visitor to industrial Coketown:

> First of all, you see our smoke. That's meat and drink to us. It's the healthiest thing in the world in all respects, and particularly for the lungs.[71]

A great many industrialized nations contain social and regional groups that have not shared in the fruits of economic affluence. These groups and the politicians depending on their support are especially wary of environmental controls that threaten to halt regional or local growth just at the time when they are about to share in its rewards.[72] In nations such as the United States and Canada, regionalism in the presence of states and provinces—and the diversity of interest groups they contain—make the problem that much more difficult in terms of effective national policies and international accords.

The problem may be even more pronounced in Third World countries. They correctly see that industrialization and economic development is the means to general economic improvement. Invariably, such nations are also without the resources to attract large and more technologically sophisticated pollution-free enterprises. They must fall back on what they can get. Efforts by other nations or groups to impose environmental regulations are viewed as attempts to impede the industrial development of these less-favored nations or regions. Such actions are seen as another effort to continue the polarization of the world into the haves and the have-nots. This is only one part of the problem of dealing with underdeveloped nations in a transnational policy of pollution control. Even if they wanted to cooperate, underdeveloped nations do not have the government structure that could effectively control environmental pollution. Also, national stability is recognized as a condition for foreign investment. If they want capital to flow into their country, they must be seen as a stable haven for investors. This can be imposed by a ruling clique or dictator unreceptive to the "costs" of pollution control. They may well view pollution control as an impediment to industrial development, or worse, believe that it will make their growing industrialization less lucrative to them personally.

There are other considerations that impact on a world policy of pollution control—again, especially among underdeveloped nations. Environmental hazards and a long-range policy of environmental control require, among other things, systems that are equipped with technical experts who can translate conditions of nature into comprehendable societal dangers; political access for such experts; economists who are able and willing to convert physical data of pollution into economic costs; and ordinary citizens who are literate and have access to the media so that they can mobilize around these newly defined dangers.[73] Of course, such conditions are often nonexistent in underdeveloped countries.

Finally, in dealing with the development of effective policies of worldwide pollution abatement, which must necessarily involve the underdeveloped nations, there is another hurdle. Capital investment often flows into these countries from transglobal corporations in industrialized nations who expressly seek out investment opportunities in locations where regulations are lax or nonexistent. This affords them the opportunity to escape the environmental controls and the associated costs in their parent countries. São Paulo, Brazil, is a prime example. Since 1957, when this city was selected by Volkswagen as a site for its manufacturing operation, it has become a focus for foreign investment. Today, it has levels of pollution that make it almost uninhabitable.[74]

### Prosecuting International Polluters

Without effective and cooperative regulations, how can the problem be policed through monitoring and enforcement efforts? The answer is it simply can't. Even with treaties and agreements among nations, an effective tribunal doesn't exist to enforce international law. Although the International Court of Justice exists in The Hague to settle disputes of international law, its jurisdiction and effectiveness depends on mutual agreement. So much so, in fact, that governments must agree to even submit a case to this body for adjudication. And for this tribunal to act in the first place, it must have an established body of international law to apply. Although it can theoretically enforce treaties and accords among nations, the legal underpinnings of an effective international or transnational body of laws is simply nonexistent at this time.

For example, such questions as criminal versus civil sanctions, penalties, burden of proof, prosecuting authority, and other such basic legal questions must be resolved. This doesn't even take into consideration such mundane matters as place of, or who pays for, incarceration if criminal sanctions and imprisonment are an alternative.

If, as the GAO and the Office of Technology Assessment estimate, in the United States alone only a tiny fraction of one type of polluting activity (toxic waste dumps) is known, what does this say about the magnitude of the problem and how it can be dealt with on a national let alone international basis?

We must begin looking at some of these problems in the years that lie before us. The immediate need is to learn more about the issue of hazardous environmental pollution, including such basic questions as what substances are indeed toxic. We don't even have many answers to this fundamental question. From there we must build on what we have learned so far in our efforts to deal with the problem: what works and what does not, what resources are then required to deal with this situation, and—once we are on the road to getting our own house in order—how we can deal with international forms of toxic pollution.

 **AIDS AND THE BIRTH OF A CRIMINAL PROBLEM**

The last crime issue of the 1990s to be discussed deals with the subject of AIDS. The greatest threat by AIDS is the fact that there is currently no cure for the disease, which has, to date, resulted in at least a 30 percent death rate. Estimates are that as many as 250,000 Americans may be infected with the virus by 1991.[75]

Although a great deal has been written about this problem, one aspect of the AIDS contagion that has not received the attention that it should is the deliberate transmission of the virus by a known carrier to an innocent sex partner. Extensive computer-based searches by this author into the criminal justice and legal literature show a startling absence of discussion of this issue. Consequently, such a question as what role should the criminal law and the criminal justice system play in such cases is still to be answered. It would seem that if the responsibility of the criminal law and the justice system is to protect the public, then it imposes some responsibility on the administration of justice to begin to examine this question.

The issue is not without precedent. An airman at the Lackland Air Force Base in San Antonio was charged with aggravated assault. The deadly weapon was his own bodily fluids. In Lafayette, Indiana, the local prosecutor successfully prosecuted an AIDS-causing human immunodeficiency virus (HIV) carrier for attempted murder. "We're trying to control the spread of murder," was the prosecutor's response to critics of his action. In Genesee County, Michigan, an HIV-positive drug user was charged with attempted murder for spitting at the police officer who tried to arrest him. The charges were later reduced to resisting arrest.[76]

In the Indiana case, a superior court judge sentenced Donald J. Haines to six years in the state penitentiary after he was convicted on three counts of attempting to murder the policeman and emergency medical technicians who came to his aid during an unsuccessful suicide attempt. According to testimony at the trial, both the police and the emergency medical personnel knew Haines was HIV-positive when they tried to help him. Haines, who had slashed his wrists, battled the policeman who was first at the scene. He threw a blood-drenched wig at the officer and spat at him. After almost an hour of trying to subdue Haines, the officer was, according to court records, covered in Haines' blood. The officer was also cut in the struggle and had Haines' blood in his mouth. The medical personnel, although they wore gloves, also suffered cuts in trying to subdue him. The struggle did not end at the scene of the arrest. It continued in the hospital emergency room, where Haines reportedly told an emergency room physician that he wanted other people to know what it was like to die from AIDS.[77]

In a recent case in Columbia, South Carolina, Terry Lee Phillips was indicted for rape, attempted murder, assault and battery with intent to kill, and first-degree sexual conduct after sexually assaulting a woman. Phillips had been diagnosed earlier as having the AIDS virus, and he allegedly said that he intended to give someone AIDS. The prosecutor contends that Phillips was intentionally trying to transmit the fatal disease to the woman he raped.[78]

## Legal Problems and the Criminal Justice System

Like everything else we've talked about in this chapter—narcotics, terrorism, and environmental crimes—unresolved legal issues surround the question of the criminal prosecution of such AIDS cases. Although these offenses are seriously threatening forms of new crime, the legal system and the administration of justice seem unable to develop an appropriate response for combatting them.

As a result, prosecutors are finding almost insurmountable legal problems in trying to prosecute such cases. Unique aspects of AIDS provide evidentiary problems in presenting and proving the case to support criminal charges associated with the transmission of the virus. Perhaps the greatest obstacle in proving criminal charges is proving causation: proving that the act of the accused actually resulted in the transmission of the disease.[79] This means that for the purpose of proving causation several things must be shown: the accused must be infected; the accused must be implicated in the act that could have transmitted the virus; and the victim must be shown to have acquired the infection by the acts of the accused.[80]

Let's look at these requirements a little closer. To prove that the accused was infected, a supporting statement by a physician must show that the carrier had been diagnosed HIV positive and was aware of this. Although this may seem straightforward enough, certain problems are posed, such as the requirement of showing intent (see Chapter 2). Legal experts are not convinced that the government can show that the accused intended to transmit the virus merely because he or she engaged in sexual activity with a partner. Not every person with whom a carrier has sexual contact will become infected. Thus, the outcome is unclear; the question of specific intent to infect will be attacked by the defense. And the laws are still unclear as to whether, in the absence of specific intent, the doctrine of general intent can be applied in such cases (see Chapter 2). The intent must also be actual and not merely incidental to a sex act or accidental, which at most, would only be considered negligence, reducing the seriousness of the offense and the penalty the state could impose.[81] There is also the question of "proving" that the accused had the virus. If the accused refuses to voluntarily submit to an AIDS test, the state must apply for a search warrant for his or her bodily fluids and take a specimen by force, if necessary. Although this legally can be done, there must exist enough "probable cause"—particularly in such an intrusive search—to justify the issuance of a search warrant. This becomes another issue that is open to attack by the defense.[82]

There also has to be proof that an act took place that could result in the transmission of the disease. This too, poses a problem. Many times there are no other witnesses to an act of consensual sex. The accused denies that he or she had sex with the victim and the victim is just as insistent that it occurred. Can this "prove" that the act took place? There is one last legal problem that the state must overcome. The victim may not know for months or years that he or she was infected. Because it takes so long to show up, how can it be shown that the victim didn't already have AIDS or that the accused was the one who transmitted it? One can be assured that the defense will make this an issue. The victim may be shown to have been sexually active with others before and after the sexual act with the accused, to have associated with high-risk groups, or even to have been involved in circumstances (e.g., the use of a contaminated needle if the victim uses or has used drugs) that will seriously undermine the prosecutor's case.

In this issue the legal system and the medical profession must cooperate, but the likelihood of that is not promising. Physician–patient confidentiality creates a problem in this area. Medical doctors are prohibited by law from divulging issues inferred from the consultation with their patients. Although states make exceptions to this with such sexually transmitted diseases as syphilis and gonorrhea, for which physicians are required to report its incidence to public health authorities, AIDS was not classified as a sexually transmitted disease in about half of the states in 1988. Doctors in these states were not required to report such cases to the authorities.[83]

The American Medical Association's Council on Ethical and Judicial Affairs recently took a step toward encouraging disclosure. In a statement intended to guide physicians who encounter AIDS carriers who are endangering others, the AMA recommends that a physician first attempt to persuade the infected patient to cease endangering the third party. If this is unsuccessful, the physician should notify the authorities. If the authorities fail to act, the third party should be notified.[84] In all likelihood, however, few physicians are following this recommendation.

## Some Developing Laws in this Area

Painfully and slowly, some states are beginning to at least consider the adoption of criminal laws against willful and purposeful spread of the AIDS virus to unsuspecting persons. They are groping with the problem of how such actions might be deterred and at least are targeting certain high-risk offenders for attention. Nevada, for instance, requires that all prostitutes arrested for solicitation be tested. If tests are positive and they are arrested again for the same offense, they can be charged with a felony. Another suggested approach is to make it a felony-level crime for a member of a high-risk group (prostitutes, intravenous drug users, and homosexuals) to donate blood, organs, or semen regardless of knowledge of carrier status.[85]

Yet, for the most part, significant attention has not yet focused on the problem. Not only are the state and the federal governments failing to address the need for adequate laws in this area to protect their citizens, little or no consideration is focusing on how these laws could be enforced if they were adopted. Perhaps, as in the area of criminal pollution of our environment, sufficient attention will focus on the problem only after we have suffered serious consequences. The problem has not reached the threshold required for concerted action—at least to the point that policymakers are forced to turn their attention to the impending consequences of their failure to act promptly and decisively.

## □ CONCLUSION

On conclusion of an introductory course in criminal justice, one thing should be evident: The American system of criminal justice is failing in important ways. No other conclusion can be reached. This is occurring because of its failure to prevent crime, its inability to deal appropriately with those who commit crimes, its failure to provide any semblance of justice, and its own acknowledgment that it is unable to fulfill its protective role.

Any student reading this book must sense this. Like other major social institutions in this country—including education, health care, and perhaps even our political process itself—the criminal justice system needs significant remedial attention. I suggest it even requires a massive overhaul and fundamental changes in the way it operates. This is a dangerous pronouncement and assuredly one that is given with great thought.

Many of my colleagues might disagree with such a draconian view of the operations of justice. I suggest they venture forth from their ivory towers and the protective womb of academe and spend time on the streets in our major cities, and visit our courtrooms, jails, and the prisons. Talk to those who are caught up in the day-to-day frustration of trying to operate within the system, and to the average American, who feels helpless, frightened, bewildered, and frustrated by what he or she sees. And what about the politicians? These "public leaders" are unable or unwilling to see beyond the next election and their fund-raising activities or are so inextricably bound to monied and influential special interest groups that they have forgotten the fundamental problems confronting our nation—just as they quickly forget or avoid the faces of our crime victims. Perhaps, they too are "criminal" for such negligence. DeTocqueville said America has a genius for freedom and self-expression; perhaps we also need a genius for responsibility and accountability.

Still, if there is a small glow at the end of the tunnel it is born by the growing numbers of American college students who want to make criminal justice a career and with this, dedicate their lives to work for the many needed improvements. It cannot end here. Also important, if change is to occur, are classrooms filled by students who merely want to learn more about crime and the administration of justice. Change depends equally on them. Growing enrollments by college students across the country in such programs and classrooms attest to this interest. It is to this generation that the challenges lie. The actions and failure of our generation might still be corrected, but time may be running out.

## NOTES

1. As reported in *New York Times*, 10 April 1988 p. 10.
2. Ibid., p. 10.
3. Rufus King, "The American System: Legal Sanctions to Repress Drug Abuse," in James Inciardi and Carl D. Chambers (eds.), *Drugs and the Criminal Justice System* (Beverly Hills, Calif.: Sage, 1974) p. 21.
4. Edward J. Epstein, *Agency of Fear* (New York: G. P. Putnam's Sons, 1977), p. 105.
5. Ibid., p. 106.
6. Reported in Kurt L. Schmoke, "Drug Laws Ignore Addicts While Helping Criminals," *Addiction Review* 2 (January 1990), p. 2.
7. Ibid., p. 20.
8. United States General Accounting Office, *Drug Control—U.S. International Narcotics Control Activities* (Washington, D.C.: U.S. Government Printing Office). March 1988.
9. Ibid., p. 20.
10. John Kaplan, "Taking Drugs Seriously," *Public Interest* (Summer 1988): 34.
11. Ibid., p. 35.
12. General Accounting Office, *Report on Drug Abuse Prevention* (Washington: USGPO, December 1987), p. 12.
13. As reported in *New York Times*, 12 April 1988, p. A-10.
14. Ibid., p. A-10.
15. "The Enemy Within: Drug Money Is Corrupting the Enforcers," *New York Times* (11 April 1988), p. A-12.
16. Matt Spetalnick, "Cocaine and Corruption Plague Miami Police Force," *Criminal Justice: The Americas* 1, no. 2 (April/May 1988): 3.
17. "The Enemy Within," op. cit., A-12.
18. Jonathan Beaty and Richard Hornik, "A Torrent of Dirty Dollars," *Time* 134, no. 5. (December 18, 1989), p. 55.
19. Ibid.
20. For similar legislation among the states see, Lindsey D. Stellwagon, *Use of Forfeiture Sanctions in*

Drug Cases (Washington, D.C.: National Institute of Justice), July 1985.
21. For example, see "Thinking the Unthinkable," *Time*, (30 May 1988), pp. 12–19; and "Legalization of Drugs," *Addiction Review* 2 (January 1990), pp. 1–6.
22. See Jeff Gerth, "CIA Shedding Its Reluctance to Aid in Fight Against Drugs," *New York Times* (March 25, 1990), pp. A-1, A-22.
23. United States General Accounting Office, *U.S. International Narcotics Control Activities*, op. cit., p. 19.
24. Dan Christensen, "Drug Agents Keeping Tabs on Leaders, Stars, Clergy," *Ft. Lauderdale News & Sun-Sentinel* (3 July 1984), sec. A.
25. *Report to the Nation on Crime and Justice*, (Washington, D.C.: Bureau of Justice Statistics, U.S. Department of Justice, 1983).
26. Ethan A. Nadelman, "U.S. Drug Policy: A Bad Export," *Foreign Policy* 70 (Spring 1988), pp. 91–92.
27. "Thinking the Unthinkable," p. 14.
28. As reported in Schmoke, op. cit., p. 2.
29. Ibid., p. 2.
30. Ibid.
31. As reported in *Addiction Review* 2 (January 1990), p. 2.
32. Richard L. Berke, "After Studying for War on Drugs, Bennett Wants More Troops" *New York Times* (6 August 1989), p. E-5.
33. "Drugs' Impact Is Seen Rising Among Poor," *New York Times* (30 August 1987), p. 28.
34. Testimony from U.S. House Committee on the Judiciary, Subcommittee on Civil and Constitutional Rights, Terrorism Oversight Hearings, August 26 to May 15, 1986.
35. John Warner, "Countering Contemporary Terrorism," *Police Chief* 54, no. 5 (May 1987), p. 28.
36. Steven L. Pomerantz, "The FBI and Terrorism," *FBI Law Enforcement Bulletin* 56 (October 1987); 14–15.
37. Ibid., p. 17.
38. Oliver B. Revell, "Terrorism Today," *FBI Law Enforcement Bulletin* 56 (October 1987): 3–4.
39. Ibid., pp. 3–4.

40. John W. Harris, "Domestic Terrorism in the 1980's," *FBI Law Enforcement Bulletin* 56 (October 1987): 5–13.

41. Ibid., p. 8.

42. Robert A. Milne, "The Mens Rea Requirements for the Federal Environmental Statutes: Strict Criminal Liability in Substance but Not Form," *Buffalo Law Review* 37, no. 1 (Winter 1988–89): 307.

43. Ibid., p. 307.

44. See: Richard H. Allan, "Criminal Sanctions Under Federal and State Environmental Statutes," *Ecology Law Quarterly* 14, no. 1 (1987): 117–179.

45. *Environmental Reporter* 20, no. 10 (7 July 1989): 522.

46. Michael M. Mustokoff, *Hazardous Waste Violations: A Guide to Their Detection, Investigation and Prosecution* (Washington, D.C.: U.S. Department of Justice, February 1981), p. 6.

47. Ibid., p. 6.

48. Judson W. Starr, "Countering Environmental Crimes," *Boston College Environmental Affairs Law Review* 13, no. 3 (1986): pp. 379–396.

49. These are Clean Air Act, Federal Water Pollution Control Act, Rivers and Harbors Act of 1899 (as amended), Resource Conservation and Recovery Act, Toxic Substances Control Act, Federal Insecticide, Fungicide and Rodentcide Act, and the Comprehensive Environmental Response Compensation and Liability Act. Note: This last act is referred to as the "Superfund."

50. For example, see: Michele Kuruc, "Putting Polluters in Jail: Imposing Criminal Sanctions on Corporate Defendants Under Environmental Statutes," *Land and Water Law Review* 20, no. 1 (1985): 93–108; Barbara H. Doerr, "Prosecuting Corporate Polluters: The Sparing Use of Criminal Sanctions," *University of Detroit Law Review* 62 (Summer 1985): 659–676; and Milne, op. cit.

51. John F. Seymour, "Civil and Criminal Liability of Corporate Officers Under Federal Environmental Law," *Environmental Reporter* 20, no. 6 (Washington, D.C.: BNA, Inc., 9 June 1989), p. 337.

52. *New York Central and Hudson River Railroad* v. *U.S.*, 212 U.S. 481 (1909).

53. *U.S.* v. *Park*, 421 U.S. 658 (1975).

54. Mustokoff, op. cit., pp. 53–54.

55. Milne, op. cit., pp. 312–313.

56. U.S. House of Representatives, *Organized Crime and Hazardous Waste Disposal* (Washington, D.C.: U.S. Government Printing Office, 1983); United States General Accounting Office, *Enforcement of Hazardous Waste and Toxic Substance Laws* (Washington, D.C.: U.S. Government Printing Office, 1985).

57. Robert McMurry and Stephen D. Ramsey, "Environmental Crime: The Use of Criminal Sanctions in Enforcing Environmental Laws," *Loyola* (Los Angeles) *Law Review* 19 (June 1986): 1133–1169; and Milne, op. cit.

58. Andrew Szasz, "Corporations, Organized Crime and the Disposal of Hazardous Waste: An Examination of the Making of a Criminogenic Regulatory Structure," *Criminology* 24, no. 1 (1986): 1–26.

59. Ibid., p. 2.

60. U.S. House of Representatives, op. cit.

61. Ibid., p. 22.

62. Ibid., p. 22.

63. Ibid., p. 70.

64. Szasz, op. cit., p. 9.

65. Alan A. Block and Frank R. Scarpitti, *Poisoning for Profit: The Mafia and Toxic Waste in America* (New York: William Morrow, 1985), p. 145; U.S. House of Representatives, op. cit., 25.

66. House of Representatives, op. cit., p. 124.

67. *General Accounting Office*, pp. 25–31.

68. House of Representatives, op. cit., pp. 144–146; Szasz, p. 11.

69. Starr, op. cit., p. 382.

70. These countries include Denmark, Finland, Iceland, Norway and Sweden. See: Bengt Broms, "The Nordic Convention on the Protection of the Environment," in C. Flinterman, B. Kwiatkowska, and J. G. Lammers, (eds.) *Transboundary Air Pollution* (Boston: Martinus Nijhoff Publishers, 1986), pp. 141–152.

71. Charles Dickens, *Hard Times* (New York: E. P. Dutton, 1907), pp. 112–113.

72. Cynthia H. Enloe, *The Politics of Pollution in a Comparative Perspective* (New York: David McKay, 1975), pp. 320–321.

73. Ibid., p. 321.

74. Ibid., p. 137.

75. A. Goerdert, et. al., "Three-Year Incidence of AIDS in Five Cohorts of HTLV-III Infected Risk Group Members," *Science* 231 (1986): 922.

76. "Spreading AIDS on Purpose," *Washington Post Health*, 19 April 1988, p. 6.

77. Ibid., p. 6.

78. Thomas Fitting, "Criminal Liability for Transmission of AIDS: Some Evidentiary Problems," *Criminal Justice Journal* 10, no. 1 (Fall 1987): 73.

79. Ibid., p. 75.

80. Ibid.

81. Fitting, p. 76.

82. Ibid.

83. *Washington Post*, "Spreading Aids," op. cit., p. 6.

84. Ibid.

85. Fitting, op. cit., p. 95.

APPENDIX A

# The Constitution of the United States

We the people of the United States, in order to form a more perfect union, establish justice, insure domestic tranquility, provide for the common defense, promote the general welfare, and secure the blessings of liberty to ourselves and our posterity, do ordain and establish this Constitution for the United States of America.

 **ARTICLE I**

## Section 1.

1. All legislative powers herein granted shall be vested in a Congress of the United States, which shall consist of a Senate and House of Representatives.

## Section 2.

1. The House of Representatives shall be composed of members chosen every second year by the people of the several States, and the electors in each State shall have the qualifications requisite for electors of the most numerous branch of the State legislature.
2. No person shall be a Representative who shall not have attained to the age of twenty-five years, and been seven years a citizen of the United States, and who shall not, when elected, be an inhabitant of that State in which he shall be chosen.
3. Representatives and direct taxes shall be apportioned among the several States which may be included within this Union, according to their res-

pective numbers, *which shall be determined by adding to the whole number of free persons, including those bound to service for a term of years, and excluding Indians not taxed, three fifths of all other persons.** The actual enumeration shall be made within three years after the first meeting of the Congress of the United States, and within every subsequent term of ten years, in such manner as they shall by law direct. The number of Representatives shall not exceed one for every thirty thousand, but each State shall have at least one Representative; and until such enumeration shall be made, the State of New Hampshire shall be entitled to choose three, Massachusetts eight, Rhode Island and Providence Plantations one, Connecticut five, New York six, New Jersey four, Pennsylvania eight, Delaware one, Maryland six, Virginia ten, North Carolina five, South Carolina five, and Georgia three.

4. When vacancies happen in the representation from any State, the executive authority thereof shall issue writs of election to fill such vacancies.

5. The House of Representatives shall choose their Speaker and other officers, and shall have the sole power of impeachment.

## Section 3.

1. The Senate of the United States shall be composed of two Senators from each State, *chosen by the legislature thereof,* for six years; and each Senator shall have one vote.

2. Immediately after they shall be assembled in consequence of the first election, they shall be divided as equally as may be into three classes. The seats of the Senators of the first class shall be vacated at the expiration of the second year, of the second class at the expiration of the fourth year, and of the third class at the expiration of the sixth year, so that one third may be chosen every second year; *and if vacancies happen by resignation, or otherwise, during the recess of the legislature of any State, the executive thereof may make temporary appointments until the next meeting of the legislature, which shall then fill such vacancies.*

3. No person shall be a Senator who shall not have attained to the age of thirty years, and been nine years a citizen of the United States, and who shall not, when elected, be an inhabitant of that State for which he shall be chosen.

4. The Vice-President of the United States shall be President of the Senate, but shall have no vote, unless they be equally divided.

5. The Senate shall choose their other officers, and also a President *pro tempore*, in the absence of the Vice-President, or when he shall exercise the office of the President of the United States.

6. The Senate shall have the sole power to try all impeachments. When sitting for that purpose, they shall be on oath or affirmation. When the President of the United States is tried, the Chief Justice shall preside; and no person shall be convicted without the concurrence of two thirds of the members present.

7. Judgment in cases of impeachment shall not extend further than to removal from office, and disqualification to hold and enjoy any office of honor, trust,

*Italics indicate passage has been affected by subsequent amendments to the Constitution.

or profit under the United States; but the party convicted shall, nevertheless, be liable and subject to indictment, trial, judgment, and punishment, according to law.

## Section 4.

1. The times, places, and manner of holding elections for Senators and Representatives shall be prescribed in each State by the legislature thereof; but the Congress may at any time by law make or alter such regulations, except as to the places of choosing Senators.
2. The Congress shall assemble at least once in every year, *and such meeting shall be on the first Monday in December, unless they shall by law appoint a different day.*

## Section 5.

1. Each house shall be the judge of the elections, returns, and qualifications of its own members, and a majority of each shall constitute a quorum to do business; but a smaller number may adjourn from day to day, and may be authorized to compel the attendance of absent members, in such manner, and under such penalties, as each house may provide.
2. Each house may determine the rules of its proceedings, punish its members for disorderly behavior, and, with the concurrence of two thirds, expel a member.
3. Each house shall keep a journal of its proceedings, and from time to time publish the same, excepting such parts as may in their judgment require secrecy; and the yeas and nays of the members of either house on any question shall, at the desire of one fifth of those present, be entered on the journal.
4. Neither house, during the session of Congress, shall, without the consent of the other, adjourn for more than three days, nor to any other place than that in which the two houses shall be sitting.

## Section 6.

1. The Senators and Representatives shall receive a compensation for their services, to be ascertained by law and paid out of the Treasury of the United States. They shall, in all cases except treason, felony, and breach of the peace, be privileged from arrest during their attendance at the session of their respective houses, and in going to and returning from the same; and for any speech or debate in either house they shall not be questioned in any other place.
2. No Senator or Representative shall, during the time for which he was elected, be appointed to any civil office under the authority of the United States, which shall have been created, or the emoluments whereof shall have been increased, during such time; and no person holding any office under the United States shall be a member of either house during his continuance in office.

## Section 7.

1. All bills for raising revenue shall originate in the House of Representatives; but the Senate may propose or concur with amendments as on other bills.
2. Every bill which shall have passed the House of Representatives and the Senate shall before it becomes a law, be presented to the President of the United States; if he approves he shall sign it, but if not he shall return it, with his objections, to that house in which it shall have originated, who shall enter the objections at large on their journal and proceed to reconsider it. If after such reconsideration two thirds of that house shall agree to pass the bill, it shall be sent, together with the objections, to the other house, by which it shall likewise be reconsidered, and if approved by two thirds of that house, it shall become a law. But in all such cases the votes of both houses shall be determined by yeas and nays, and the names of the persons voting for and against the bill shall be entered on the journal of each house respectively. If any bill shall not be returned by the President within ten days (Sundays excepted) after it shall have been presented to him the same shall be a law, in like manner as if he had signed it, unless the Congress by their adjournment prevent its return, in which case it shall not be a law.
3. Every order, resolution, or vote to which the concurrence of the Senate and House of Representatives may be necessary (except on a question of adjournment) shall be presented to the President of the United States; and before the same shall take effect, shall be approved by him, or being disapproved by him, shall be repassed by two thirds of the Senate and House of Representatives, according to the rules and limitations prescribed in the case of a bill.

## Section 8.

1. The Congress shall have power to lay and collect taxes, duties, imposts and excises, to pay the debts and provide for the common defense and general welfare of the United States; but all duties, imposts and excises shall be uniform throughout the United States;
2. To borrow money on the credit of the United States;
3. To regulate commerce with foreign nations, and among the several States, and with the Indian tribes;
4. To establish a uniform rule of naturalization and uniform laws on the subject of bankruptcies throughout the United States;
5. To coin money, regulate the value thereof, and of foreign coin, and fix the standard of weights and measures;
6. To provide for the punishment of counterfeiting the securities and current coin of the United States;
7. To establish the post-offices and post-roads;
8. To promote the progress of science and useful arts by securing for limited times to authors and inventors the exclusive right to their respective writings and discoveries;
9. To constitute tribunals inferior to the Supreme Court;
10. To define and punish piracies and felonies committed on the high seas, and offenses against the laws of nations;

11. To declare war, grant letters of marque and reprisal, and make rules concerning captures on land and water;
12. To raise and support armies, but no appropriation of money to that use shall be for a longer term than two years;
13. To provide and maintain a navy;
14. To make rules for the government and regulation of the land and naval forces;
15. To provide for calling forth the militia to execute the laws of the Union, suppress insurrections, and repel invasion;
16. To provide for organizing, arming, and disciplining the militia, and for governing such part of them as may be employed in the service of the United States, reserving to the States respectively the appointment of the officers, and authority of training the militia according to the discipline prescribed by Congress;
17. To exercise exclusive legislation in all cases whatsoever over such district (not exceeding ten miles square) as may, by cession of particular States and the acceptance of Congress, become the seat of the Government of the United States, and to exercise like authority over all places purchased by the consent of the legislature of the State in which the same shall be, for the erection of forts, magazines, arsenals, dockyards, and other needful buildings; and
18. To make all laws which shall be necessary and proper for carrying into execution the foregoing powers, and all other powers vested by this constitution in the Government of the United States, or in any department of officer thereof.

**Section 9.**

1. The migration or importation of such persons as any of the States now existing shall think proper to admit shall not be prohibited by the Congress prior to the year one thousand eight hundred and eight, but a tax or duty may be imposed on such importation, not exceeding ten dollars for each person.
2. The privilege of the writ of *habeas corpus* shall not be suspended, unless when in cases of rebellion or invasion the public safety may require it.
3. No bill of attainder or *ex post facto* law shall be passed.
4. *No capitation or other direct tax shall be laid, unless in proportion to the census or enumeration hereinbefore directed to be taken.*
5. No tax or duty shall be laid on articles exported from any State.
6. No preference shall be given by any regulation of commerce or revenue to the ports of one State over those of another; nor shall vessels bound to or from one State be obliged to enter, clear, or pay duties in another.
7. No money shall be drawn from the Treasury but in consequence of appropriations made by law; and a regular statement and account of the receipts and expenditures of all public money shall be published from time to time.
8. No title of nobility shall be granted by the United States; and no person holding any office of profit or trust under them shall, without the consent of the Congress, accept of any present, emolument, office, or title, of any kind whatever, from any king, prince, or foreign State.

## Section 10.

1. No State shall enter into any treaty, alliance, or confederation; grant letters of marque and reprisal; coin money; emit bill or credit, make anything but gold and silver coin a tender in payment of debts; pass any bill of attainder, *ex post facto* law, or law impairing the obligation of contracts, or grant any title of nobility.
2. No State shall, without the consent of Congress, lay any imposts or duties on imports or exports, except what may be absolutely necessary for executing its inspection laws; and the net produce of all duties and imposts, laid by any State on imports or exports, shall be for the use of the Treasury of the United States; and all such laws shall be subject to the revision and control of the Congress.
3. No State shall without the consent of Congress, lay any duty of tonnage, keep troops or ships of war in time of peace, enter into any agreement or compact with another State, or with a foreign power, or engage in war, unless actually invaded or in such imminent danger as will not admit of delay.

 **ARTICLE II**

## Section 1.

1. The executive power shall be vested in a President of the United States of America. He shall hold his office during the term of four years and, together with the Vice-President, chosen for the same term, be elected as follows:
2. Each State shall appoint, in such manner as the legislature thereof may direct, a number of electors, equal to the whole number of Senators and Representatives to which the State may be entitled in the Congress; but no Senator or Representative, or person holding an office of trust or profit under the United States, shall be appointed an elector.
3. *The electors shall meet in their respective States and vote by ballot for two persons, of whom one at least shall not be an inhabitant of the same State with themselves. And they shall make a list of all the persons voted for, and of the number of votes for each; which list they shall sign and certify, and transmit sealed to the seat of the government of the United States, directed to the President of the Senate. The President of the Senate shall, in the presence of the Senate and House of Representatives, open all the certificates, and the votes shall then be counted. The person having the greatest number of votes shall be the President, if such number be a majority of the whole number of electors appointed; and if there be more than one who have such majority, and have an equal number of votes, then the House of Representatives shall immediately choose by ballot one of them for President; and if no person have a majority, then from the five highest on the list the said House shall in like manner choose the President. But in choosing the President the votes shall be taken by States, the representation from each State having one vote; a quorum for this purpose shall consist of a member or members from two thirds of the States, and a majority of all the*

*States shall be necessary to a choice. In every case, after the choice of the President, the person having the greatest number of votes of the electors shall be the Vice-President. But if there should remain two or more who have equal votes, the Senate shall choose from them by ballot the Vice-President.*

4. The Congress may determine the time of choosing the electors and the day on which they shall give their votes, which day shall be the same throughout the United States.

5. No person except a natural-born citizen or a citizen of the United States at the time of the adoption of this Constitution, shall be eligible to the office of President; neither shall any person be eligible to that office who shall not have attained to the age of thirty-five years, and been fourteen years a resident within the United States.

6. In case of the removal of the President from office, or of his death, resignation, or inability to discharge the powers and duties of the said office, the same shall devolve on the Vice-President, and the Congress may by law provide for the case of removal, death, resignation, or inability, both of the President and Vice-President, declaring what officer shall then act as President, and such officer shall act accordingly until the disability be removed or a President shall be elected.

7. The President shall, at stated times, receive for his services a compensation which shall neither be increased nor diminished during the period for which he shall have been elected, and he shall not receive within that period any other emolument from the United States or any of them.

8. Before he enter on the execution of his office he shall take the following oath or affirmation:

*"I do solemnly swear (or affirm) that I will faithfully execute the office of President of the United States, and will to the best of my ability, preserve, protect, and defend the Constitution of the United States."*

## Section 2.

1. The President shall be commander-in-chief of the army and navy of the United States, and of the militia of the several States when called into actual service of the United States; he may require the opinion, in writing, of the principal officer in each of the executive departments, upon any subject relating to the duties of their respective offices, and he shall have power to grant reprieves and pardons for offenses against the United States, except in cases of impeachment.

2. He shall have power, by and with the advice and consent of the Senate, to make treaties, provided two thirds of the Senators present concur; and he shall nominate, and, by and with the advice and consent of the Senate, shall appoint ambassadors, other public ministers and consuls, judges of the Supreme Court, and all other officers of the United States, whose appointments are not herein otherwise provided for, and which shall be established by law; but the Congress may by law vest the appointment of such inferior officers, as they think proper, in the President alone, in the courts of law, or in the heads of departments.

3. The President shall have power to fill up all vacancies that may happen during the recess of the Senate, by granting commissions which shall expire at the end of their next session.

## Section 3.

1. He shall from time to time give to the Congress information of the state of the Union, and recommend to their consideration such measures as he shall judge necessary and expedient; he may, on extraordinary occasions, convene both houses, or either of them, and in case of disagreement between them with respect to the time of adjournment, he may adjourn them to such time as he shall think proper; he shall receive ambassadors and other public ministers; he shall take care that the laws be faithfully executed, and shall commission all the officers of the United States.

## Section 4.

1. The President, Vice-President, and all civil officers of the United States shall be removed from office on impeachment for and conviction of treason, bribery, or other high crimes and misdemeanors.

 **ARTICLE III**

## Section 1.

1. The judicial power of the United States shall be vested in one Supreme Court, and in such inferior courts as the Congress may from time to time ordain and establish. The judges, both of the supreme and inferior courts, shall hold their offices during good behavior, and shall, at stated times, receive for their services a compensation which shall not be diminished during their continuance in office.

## Section 2.

1. The judicial power shall extend to all cases, in law and equity, arising under this Constitution, the laws of the United States, and treaties made, or which shall be made, under their authority; to all cases affecting ambassadors, other public ministers and consuls; to all cases of admiralty and maritime jurisdiction; to controversies to which the United States shall be a party; to controversies between two or more States; *between a State and citizens of another State;* between citizens of different States; between citizens of the same State claiming lands under grants of different States, and between a State, or the citizens thereof, and foreign States, citizens, or subjects.
2. In all cases affecting ambassadors, other public ministers and consuls, and those in which a State shall be party, the Supreme Court shall have original jurisdiction. In all the other cases before mentioned the Supreme Court shall have appellate jurisdiction, both as to law and fact, with such exceptions and under such regulations as the Congress shall make.

3. The trial of all crimes, except in cases of impeachment, shall be by jury; and such trial shall be held in the State where the said crimes shall have been committed; but when not committed within any State, the trial shall be at such place or places as the Congress may by law have directed.

## Section 3.

1. Treason against the United States shall consist only in levying war against them, or in adhering to their enemies, giving them aid and comfort. No person shall be convicted of treason unless on the testimony of two witnesses to the same overt act, or on confession in open court.
2. The Congress shall have power to declare the punishment of treason, but no attainder of treason shall work corruption of blood or forfeiture except during the life of the person attained.

 **ARTICLE IV**

## Section 1.

1. Full faith and credit shall be given to each State to the public acts, records, and judicial proceedings of every other State. And the Congress may by general laws prescribe the manner in which such acts, records, and proceedings shall be proved, and the effect thereof.

## Section 2.

1. The citizens of each State shall be entitled to all privileges and immunities of citizens in the several States.
2. A person charged in any State with treason, felony, or other crime, who shall flee from justice, and be found in another State, shall, on demand of the executive authority of the State from which he fled, be delivered up, to be removed to the State having jurisdiction of the crime.
3. *No person held to service or labor in one State, under the laws thereof, escaping into another, shall, in consequence of any law or regulation therein, be discharged from such service or labor, but shall be delivered up on claim of the party to whom such service or labor may be due.*

## Section 3.

1. New States may be admitted by the Congress into this Union; but no new State shall be formed or erected within the jurisdiction of any other State; nor any State be formed by the junction of two or more States, or parts of States, without the consent of the legislatures of the States concerned as well as of the Congress.
2. The Congress shall have power to dispose of and make all needful rules and regulations respecting the territory or other property belonging to the United States; and nothing in this Constitution shall be so construed as to prejudice any claims of the United States or of any particular State.

### Section 4.

1. The United States shall guarantee to every State in this Union a republican form of government, and shall protect each of them against invasion, and on application of the legislature, or of the executive (when the legislature cannot be convened), against domestic violence.

## ▣ ARTICLE V

1. The Congress, whenever two thirds of both houses shall deem it necessary, shall propose amendments to this Constitution, or, on the application of the legislatures of two thirds of the several States, shall call a convention for proposing amendments, which in either case shall be valid to all intents and purposes as part of this Constitution, when ratified by the legislatures of three fourths of the several States, or by conventions in three fourths thereof, as the one or the other mode of ratification may be proposed by the Congress; provided that no amendment which may be made prior to the year one thousand eight hundred and eight shall in any manner affect the first and fourth clauses in the ninth section of the first article; and that no State, without its consent, shall be deprived of its equal suffrage in the Senate.

## ▣ ARTICLE VI

1. All debts contracted and engagements entered into, before the adoption of this Constitution, shall be as valid against the United States under this Constitution, as under the Confederation.
2. This Constitution, and the laws of the United States which shall be made in pursuance thereof, and all treaties made, or which shall be made, under the authority of the United States, shall be the supreme law of the land; and the judges in every State shall be bound thereby, anything in the Constitution or laws of any State to the contrary notwithstanding.
3. The Senators and Representatives before mentioned, and the members of the several State legislatures, and all executive and judicial officers, both of the United States and of the several States, shall be bound by oath or affirmation to support this Constitution; but no religious test shall ever be required as a qualification to any office or public trust under the United States.

## ▣ ARTICLE VII

1. The ratification of the conventions of nine States shall be sufficient for the establishment of this Constitution between the States so ratifying the same.

   Done in convention by the unanimous consent of the States present, the seventeenth day of September, in the year of our Lord one thousand seven hundred and eighty-seven, and of the independence of the United States of America the twelfth. In witness whereof, we have hereunto subscribed our names.

*G.° Washington—Presid. and deputy from Virginia*

## ◻ AMENDMENTS

*The first ten amendments to the Constitution are known as the Bill of Rights and became effective on December 15, 1791.*

### I.

Congress shall make no law respecting an establishment of religion, or prohibiting the free exercise thereof; or abridging the freedom of speech or of the press; or the right of the people peaceably to assemble, and to petition the government for a redress of grievances.

### II.

A well-regulated militia being necessary to the security of a free state, the right of the people to keep and bear arms shall not be infringed.

### III.

No soldier shall, in time of peace, be quartered in any house without the consent of the owner, nor in time of war, but in a manner to be prescribed by law.

### IV.

The right of the people to be secure in their persons, houses, papers, and effects, against unreasonable searches and seizures, shall not be violated, and no warrants shall issue but upon probable cause, supported by oath or affirmation, and particularly describing the place to be searched, and the persons or things to be seized.

### V.

No person shall be held to answer for a capital or otherwise infamous crime, unless on a presentment or indictment of a grand jury, except in cases arising in the land or naval forces or in the militia when in actual service in time of war or public danger; nor shall any person be subject for the same offence to be twice put in jeopardy of life or limb; nor shall be compelled in any criminal case to be a witness against himself, nor be deprived of life, liberty, or property, without due process of law; nor shall private property be taken for public use without just compensation.

### VI.

In all criminal prosecutions the accused shall enjoy the right to a speedy and public trial, by an impartial jury of the State and district wherein the crime shall have been committed, which district shall have been previously ascertained by law, and to be informed of the nature and cause of the accusation; to be confronted with the witnesses against him; to have compulsory process for obtaining witnesses in his favor, and to have the assistance of counsel for his defense.

## VII.

In suits at common law, where the value in controversy shall exceed twenty dollars, the right of trial by jury shall be preserved, and no fact tried by a jury shall be otherwise reexamined in any court of the United States, than according to the rules of the common law.

## VIII.

Excessive bail shall not be required, nor excessive fines imposed, nor cruel and unusual punishments inflicted.

## IX.

The enumeration in the Constitution of certain rights shall not be construed to deny or disparage others retained by the people.

## X.

The powers not delegated to the United States by the Constitution, nor prohibited by it to the States, are reserved to the States respectively, or to the people.

## XI. (Effective January 8, 1798.)

The Judicial power of the United States shall not be construed to extend to any suit in law or equity, commenced or prosecuted against one of the United States by citizens of another State, or by citizens or subjects of any foreign state.

## XII. (Effective September 25, 1804.)

The electors shall meet in their respective States and vote by ballot for President and Vice-President, one of whom, at least, shall not be an inhabitant of the same State with themselves; they shall name in their ballots the person voted for as President, and in distinct ballots the person voted for as Vice-President, and they shall make distinct lists of all persons voted for as President and of all persons voted for as Vice-President, and of the number of votes for each, which lists they shall sign and certify, and transmit sealed to the seat of the government of the United States, directed to the President of the Senate. The President of the Senate shall, in the presence of the Senate and House of Representatives, open all the certificates and the votes shall then be counted. The person having the greatest number of votes for President shall be the President, if such number be a majority of the whole number of electors appointed; and if no person have such majority, then from the persons having the highest numbers not exceeding three on the list of those voted for as President, the House of Representatives shall choose immediately, by ballot, the President. But in choosing the President the votes shall be taken by States, the representation from each State having one vote; a quorum for this purpose shall consist of a member or members from two thirds of the States, and a majority of all the States shall be necessary to a choice. And if the House of Representatives shall not choose a President whenever the right of choice shall devolve upon them, before the *fourth day of March* next following, then the Vice-President shall act as President, as in the case of the death or other constitutional disability of the President.

The person having the greatest number of votes as Vice-President shall be the Vice-President, if such number be a majority of the whole number of electors appointed; and if no person have a majority, then from the two highest numbers on the list the Senate shall choose the Vice-President; a quorum for the purpose shall consist of two thirds of the whole number of Senators, and a majority of the whole number shall be necessary to a choice. But no person constitutionally ineligible to the office of President shall be eligible to that of Vice-President of the United States.

## XIII. (Effective December 18, 1865.)

SECTION 1.  Neither slavery nor involuntary servitude, except as a punishment for crime whereof the party shall have been duly convicted, shall exist within the United States or any place subject to their jurisdiction.

SECTION 2.  Congress shall have power to enforce this article by appropriate legislation.

## XIV. (Effective July 28, 1868.)

SECTION 1.  All persons born or naturalized in the United States, and subject to the jurisdiction thereof, are citizens of the United States and of the State wherein they reside. No State shall make or enforce any law which shall abridge the privileges or immunities of citizens of the United States; not shall any State deprive any person of life, liberty, or property, without due process of law; nor deny to any person within its jurisdiction the equal protection of the laws.

SECTION 2.  Representatives shall be apportioned among the several States according to their respective numbers, counting the whole number of persons in each State, excluding Indians not taxed. But when the right to vote at any election for the choice of electors for President or Vice-President of the United States, Representatives in Congress, the executive and judicial officers of a State, or the members of the legislature thereof, is denied to any of the male inhabitants of such State, being twenty-one years of age, and citizens of the United States, or in any way abridged, except for participation in rebellion, or other crime, the basis of representation therein shall be reduced in the proportion which the number of such male citizens shall bear to the whole number of male citizens twenty-one years of age in such State.

SECTION 3.  No person shall be a Senator or Representative in Congress, or elector of President and Vice-President, or hold any office, civil or military under the United States or under any State, who, having previously taken an oath as a member of Congress, or as an officer of the United States, or as a member of any State legislature, or as an executive or judicial officer of any State, to support the Constitution of the United States, shall have engaged in insurrection or rebellion against the same, or given aid or comfort to the enemies thereof. But Congress may, by a vote of two thirds of each house remove such disability.

SECTION 4. The validity of the public debt of the United States, authorized by law, including debts incurred for payment of pensions and bounties for services in suppressing insurrection or rebellion, shall not be questioned. But neither the United States nor any State shall assume or pay any debt or obligation incurred in aid of insurrection or rebellion against the United States, or any claim for the loss of emancipation of any slave; but all such debts, obligations and claims shall be held illegal and void.

SECTION 5. The Congress shall have power to enforce, by appropriate legislation, the provisions of this article.

### XV. (Effective March 30, 1870.)

SECTION 1. The right of citizens of the United States to vote shall not be denied or abridged by the United States or by any State on account of race, color, or previous condition of servitude.

SECTION 2. The Congress shall have the power to enforce this article by appropriate legislation.

### XVI. (Effective February 25, 1913.)

The Congress shall have power to lay and collect taxes on incomes, from whatever source derived, without apportionment among the several states, and without regard to any census or enumeration.

### XVII. (Effective May 31, 1913.)

The Senate of the United States shall be composed of two Senators from each State, elected by the people thereof, for six years; and each Senator shall have one vote. The electors in each State shall have the qualifications requisite for electors of the most numerous branch of the State legislature.

When vacancies happen in the representation of any State in the Senate, the executive authority of such State shall issue writs of election to fill such vacancies: *Provided*, That the legislature of any State may empower the executive thereof to make temporary appointment until the people fill the vacancies by election as the legislature may direct.

This amendment shall not be so construed as to affect the election or term of any Senator chosen before it becomes valid as part of the Constitution.

### XVIII. (Effective January 29, 1919.)

SECTION 1. After one year from the ratification of this article the manufacture, sale, or transportation of intoxicating liquors within, the importation thereof into, or the exportation thereof from the United States and all territory subject to the jurisdiction thereof for beverage purposes is hereby prohibited.

SECTION 2. The Congress and the several States shall have concurrent power to enforce this article by appropriate legislation.

**SECTION 3.** This article shall be inoperative unless it shall have been ratified as an amendment to the Constitution by the legislatures of the several States, as provided in the Constitution, within seven years from the date of the submission hereof to the States by Congress.

## XIX. (Effective August 26, 1920.)

The right of citizens of the United States to vote shall not be denied or abridged by the United States or by any State on account of sex.

Congress shall have power to enforce this article by appropriate legislation.

## XX. (Effective February 6, 1933.)

**SECTION 1.** The terms of the President and Vice-President shall end at noon on the 20th day of January, and the terms of Senators and Representatives at noon on the 3rd day of January, of the years in which such terms would have ended if this article had not been ratified; and the terms of their successors shall then begin.

**SECTION 2.** The Congress shall assemble at least once in every year, and such meeting shall begin at noon on the 3rd day of January, unless they shall by law appoint a different day.

**SECTION 3.** If, at the time fixed for the beginning of the term of the President, the President-elect shall have died, the Vice-President-elect shall become President. If a President shall not have been chosen before the time fixed for the beginning of his term, or if the President-elect shall have failed to qualify, then the Vice-President-elect shall act as President until a President shall have qualified; and the Congress may by law provide for the case wherein neither a President-elect nor a Vice-President-elect shall have qualified, declaring who shall then act as President, or the manner in which one who is to act shall be selected, and such person shall act accordingly until a President or Vice-President shall have qualified.

**SECTION 4.** The Congress may by law provide for the case of the death of any of the persons from whom the House of Representatives may choose a President whenever the right of choice shall have devolved upon them, and for the case of the death of any of the persons from whom the Senate may choose a Vice-President whenever the right of choice shall have devolved upon them.

**SECTION 5.** Sections 1 and 2 shall take effect on the 15th day of October following the ratification of this article.

**SECTION 6.** This article shall be inoperative unless it shall have been ratified as an amendment to the Constitution by the legislatures of three-fourths of the several States within seven years from the date of its submission.

## XXI. (Effective December 5, 1933.)

**SECTION 1.** The eighteenth article of amendment to the Constitution of the United States is hereby repealed.

**SECTION 2.** The transportation or importation into any State, territory, or possession of the United States for delivery or use therein of intoxicating liquors, in violation of the laws thereof, is hereby prohibited.

SECTION 3. This article shall be inoperative unless it shall have been ratified as an amendment to the Constitution by conventions in the several States, as provided in the Constitution, within seven years from the date of the submission hereof to the States by the Congress.

## XXII. (Effective February 26, 1951.)

SECTION 1. No person shall be elected to the office of the President more than twice, and no person who has held the office of President, or acted as President, for more than two years of a term to which some other person was elected President shall be elected to the office of President more than once. But this Article shall not apply to any person holding the office of President when this article was proposed by the Congress, and shall not prevent any person who may be holding the office of President, or acting as President, during the term within which this Article becomes operative from holding the office of President or acting as President during the remainder of such term.

SECTION 2. This article shall be inoperative unless it shall have been ratified as an amendment to the Constitution by the legislatures of three-fourths of the several States within seven years from the date of its submission to the States by the Congress.

## XXIII. (Effective March 29, 1961.)

SECTION 1. The District constituting the seat of Government of the United States shall appoint in such manner as the Congress may direct:

A number of electors of President and Vice-President equal to the whole number of Senators and Representatives in Congress to which the District would be entitled if it were a State, but in no event more than the least populous State; they shall be in addition to those appointed by the States, but they shall be considered, for the purposes of the election of President and Vice-President, to be electors appointed by a State; and they shall meet in the District and perform such duties as provided by the twelfth article of amendment.

SECTION 2. The Congress shall have power to enforce this article by appropriate legislation.

## XXIV. (Effective January 23, 1964.)

The right of citizens of the United States to vote in any primary or other election for President or Vice-President, for electors for President or Vice-President, or for Senator or Representative in Congress shall not be denied or abridged by the United States or any State by reason of failure to pay any poll tax or other tax.

## XXV. (Effective February 23, 1967.)

SECTION 1. In case of the removal of the President from office or of his death or resignation, the Vice President shall become President.

SECTION 2. Whenever there is a vacancy in the office of the Vice President, the President shall nominate a Vice-President who shall take office upon confirmation by a majority vote of both Houses of Congress.

SECTION 3. Whenever the President transmits to the President pro tempore of the Senate and the Speaker of the House of Representatives his written declaration that he is unable to discharge the powers and duties of his office, and until he transmits to them a written declaration to the contrary, such powers and duties shall be discharged by the Vice President as Acting President.

SECTION 4. Whenever the Vice President and a majority of either the principal officers of the executive departments or of such other body as Congress may by law provide, transmit to the President pro tempore of the Senate and the Speaker of the House of Representatives their written declaration that the President is unable to discharge the powers and duties of his office, the Vice President shall immediately assume the powers and duties of the office as Acting President.

Thereafter, when the President transmits to the President pro tempore of the Senate and the Speaker of the House of Representatives has written declaration that no inability exists, he shall resume the powers and duties of his office unless the Vice President and a majority of either the principal officers of the executive department or of such other body as Congress may by law provide, transmit within four days to the President pro tempore of the Senate and the Speaker of the House of Representatives their written declaration that the President is unable to discharge the powers and duties of his office. Thereupon Congress shall decide the issue, assembling within forty-eight hours for that purpose if not in session. If the Congress, within twenty-one days after receipt of the latter written declaration, or, if Congress is not in session, within twenty-one days after Congress is required to assemble, determines by two-thirds vote of both Houses that the President is unable to discharge the powers and duties of his office, the Vice President shall continue to discharge the same as Acting President; otherwise, the President shall resume the powers and duties of his office.

## XXVI. (Effective June 30, 1971.)

SECTION 1. The right of citizens of the United States, who are eighteen years of age or older, to vote shall not be denied or abridged by the United States or any state on account of age.

SECTION 2. The Congress shall have power to enforce this article by appropriate legislation.

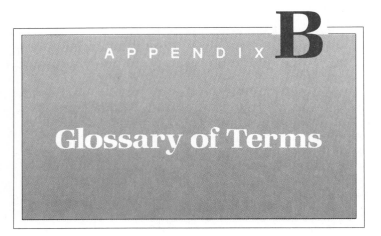

APPENDIX B

# Glossary of Terms

The following glossary of terms has been adopted from U.S. Department of Justice, Law Enforcement Assistance Administration, *Dictionary of Criminal Justice Data Terminology* (Washington, D.C.: U.S. Government Printing Office, 1976).

**ACQUITTAL** A judgment of a court, based either on the verdict of a jury or a judicial officer, that the defendant is not guilty of the offense(s) for which he has been tried.

**ADJUDICATED** Having been the subject of completed criminal or juvenile proceedings, and convicted, or adjudicated a delinquent, status offender, or dependent.

**ADJUDICATORY HEARING** In juvenile proceedings, the fact-finding process wherein the juvenile court determines if there is sufficient evidence to sustain the allegations in a petition.

**ALIAS** Any name used for an official purpose that is different from a person's legal name.

**APPEAL** A request by either the defense or the prosecution that a case be removed from a lower court to a higher court in order for a completed trial to be reviewed by the higher court.

**APPEARANCE, FIRST, OR INITIAL APPEARANCE** The first appearance of a juvenile or adult in the court that has jurisdiction over his or her case.

**APPELLANT** A person who initiates an appeal.

**ARRAIGNMENT** The appearance of a person be-fore a court in order that the court may inform the individual of the accusation(s) against him or her, and to allow the accused to enter a plea.

**ARREST** Taking a person into custody by authority of law, for the purpose of charging him or her with a criminal offense or for the purpose of initiating juvenile proceedings, which terminate with the recording of a specific offense.

**ARSON** The intentional destruction or attempted destruction, by fire or explosive, of the property of another or of one's own property with the intent to defraud.

**ASSAULT** Unlawful intentional infliction, or attempted or threatened infliction, of injury on another.

**ASSAULT, AGGRAVATED** Unlawful intentional causing of serious bodily injury with or without a deadly weapon, or unlawful intentional attempting or threatening of serious bodily injury or death with a deadly weapon.

**ASSAULT WITH A DEADLY WEAPON** Unlawful intentional infliction, or attempted or threatened infliction, of injury or death with the use of a deadly weapon.

**ASSIGNED COUNSEL** An attorney, not regularly employed by a government agency, assigned by the court to represent a particular person(s) in a particular criminal proceeding.

**BOOKING** A police administrative action officially recording an arrest and identifying the person, the place, the time, the arresting authority, and the reason for the arrest.

**BURGLARY** Unlawful entry of a structure, with or without force, with intent to commit a felony, or larceny.

**CASELOAD (CORRECTIONS)** The total number of clients registered with a correctional agency or agent during a specified time period, often divided into active and inactive, or supervised and unsupervised, thus distinguishing between clients with whom the agency or agent maintains contact and those with whom it does not.

**CASELOAD (COURT)** The total number of cases filed in a given court or before a given judicial officer during a given period of time.

**CASELOAD, PENDING** The number of cases at any given time that have been filed in a given court, or are before a given judicial officer, but have not reached disposition.

**CHARGE** A formal allegation that a specific person(s) has committed a specific offense(s).

**CHARGING DOCUMENT** A formal written accusation, filed in a court, alleging that a specified person(s) has committed a specific offense(s).

**CHILD ABUSE** A willful action or actions by a person causing physical harm to a child.

**CHILD NEGLECT** Willful failure by the person(s) responsible for a child's wellbeing to provide for adequate food, clothing, shelter, education, and supervision.

**CITATION (APPEAR)** A written order issued by a law enforcement officer directing an alleged offender to appear in a specific court at a specified time in order to answer a criminal charge.

**COMMITMENT** The action of a judicial officer ordering that an adjudicated and sentenced adult, or adjudicated delinquent or status offender who has been the subject of a juvenile court disposition hearing, be admitted into a correctional facility.

**COMPLAINT** A formal written accusation made by any person, often a prosecutor, and filed in a court, alleging that a specified person(s) has committed a specific offense(s).

**CONFINEMENT FACILITY** A correctional facility from which the inmates are not regularly permitted to depart each day unaccompanied.

**CORRECTIONAL AGENCY** A federal, state, or local criminal justice agency, under a single administrative authority, of which the principal functions are the investigation, intake screening, supervision, custody, confinement, or treatment of alleged or adjudicated adult offenders, delinquents, or status offenders.

**CORRECTIONAL DAY PROGRAM** A publicly financed and operated nonresidential educational or treatment program for persons required by a judicial officer to participate.

**CORRECTIONAL INSTITUTION** A generic name proposed in this terminology for those long-term adult confinement facilities often called "prisons," "federal or state correctional facilities," or "penitentiaries," and juvenile confinement facilities called "training schools," "reformatories," "boy's ranches," and the like.

**CORRECTIONAL INSTITUTION, ADULT** A confinement facility having custodial authority over adults sentenced to confinement for more than a year.

**CORRECTIONAL INSTITUTION, JUVENILE** A confinement facility having custodial authority over delinquents and status offenders committed to confinement after a juvenile disposition hearing.

**CORRECTIONS** A generic term that includes all government agencies, facilities, programs, procedures, personnel, and techniques concerned with the investigation, intake, custody, confinement, supervision, or treatment of alleged or adjudicated adult offenders, delinquents, or status offenders.

**COURT** An agency of the judicial branch of government, authorized or established by statute or constitution, and consisting of one or more judicial officers, which has the authority to decide controversies in law and disputed matters of fact brought before it.

**COURT OF APPELLATE JURISDICTION** A court that does not try criminal cases, but that hears appeals.

**COURT OF GENERAL JURISDICTION** Of criminal courts, a court that has jurisdiction to try all criminal offenses, including all felonies, and that may or may not hear appeals.

**COURT OF LIMITED JURISDICTION** Of criminal courts, a court of which the trial jurisdiction includes no felonies, and that may or may not hear appeals.

**CRIME OR CRIMINAL OFFENSE** An act committed or omitted in violation of a law forbidding or commanding it for which an adult can be punished, upon conviction, by incarceration and other penalties, or a corporation penalized, or for which a juvenile can be brought under the jurisdiction of a juvenile court and adjudicated a delinquent or transfer to adult court.

**CRIME INDEX OFFENSES OR INDEX CRIMES**

A UCR classification that includes all Part I offenses with the exception of involuntary (negligent) manslaughter.

**CRIMINAL HISTORY RECORD INFORMATION** Information collected by criminal justice agencies on individuals, consisting of identifiable descriptions and notations of arrests, detentions, indictments, informations or other formal criminal charges, and any disposition(s) arising therefrom, sentencing, correctional supervision, and release.

**CRIMINAL JUSTICE AGENCY** Any court with criminal jurisdiction and any other government agency or subunit, which defends indigents, or of which the principal functions or activities consist of the prevention, detection, and investigation of crime; the apprehension, detention, and prosecution of alleged offenders; the confinement or official correctional supervision of accused or convicted persons; or the administrative or technical support of the above functions.

**CRIMINAL PROCEEDINGS** Proceedings in a court of law, undertaken to determine the guilt or innocence of an adult accused of a crime.

**DEFENDANT** A person against whom a criminal proceeding is pending.

**DEFENSE ATTORNEY** An attorney who represents the defendant in a legal proceeding.

**DELINQUENCY** Juvenile actions or conduct in violation of criminal law, and, in some contexts, status offenses.

**DELINQUENT** A juvenile who has been adjudicated by a judicial officer of a juvenile court, as having committed a delinquent act, which is an act for which an adult could be prosecuted in a criminal court.

**DELINQUENT ACT** An act committed by a juvenile for which an adult could be prosecuted in a criminal court, but for which a juvenile can be adjudicated in a juvenile court, or prosecuted in a criminal court if the juvenile court transfers jurisdiction.

**DE NOVO** Anew, afresh, as if there had been no earlier decision in a lower court.

**DETENTION** The legally authorized holding in confinement of a person subject to criminal or juvenile court proceedings, until the point of commitment to a correctional facility or release.

**DETENTION CENTER** A government facility that provides temporary care in a physically restricting environment for juveniles in custody pending court disposition.

**DETENTION FACILITY** A generic name proposed in this terminology as a cover term for those facilities that hold adults or juveniles in confinement pending adjudication, adults sentenced for a year or less of confinement, and in some instances postadjudicated juveniles, including facilities called "jails," "county farms," "honor farms," "work camps," "road camps," "detention centers," "shelters," "juvenile halls," and the like.

**DETENTION HEARING** In juvenile proceedings, a hearing by a judicial officer of a juvenile court to determine whether a juvenile is to be detained, continue to be detained, or released while juvenile proceedings are pending.

**DIAGNOSIS OR CLASSIFICATION CENTER** A functional unit within a correctional institution, or a separate facility, that holds persons held in custody for the purpose of determining to which correctional facility or program they should be committed.

**DISMISSAL** A decision by a judicial officer to terminate a case without a determination of guilt or innocence.

**DISPOSITION** The action by a criminal or juvenile justice agency signifying that a portion of the justice process is complete and jurisdiction is relinquished or transferred to another agency; or signifying that a decision has been reached on one aspect of a case and a different aspect comes under consideration, requiring a different kind of decision.

**DISPOSITION HEARING** A hearing in juvenile court, conducted after an adjudicatory hearing and subsequent receipt of the report or any predisposition investigation, to determine the most appropriate disposition of a juvenile who has been adjudicated a delinquent, a status offender, or a dependent.

**DISPOSITION, JUVENILE COURT** The decision of a juvenile court, concluding a disposition hearing, that a juvenile be committed to a correctional facility, or placed in a care or treatment program, or required to meet certain standards of conduct, or released.

**DIVERSION** The official halting or suspension, at any legally prescribed processing point after a recorded justice system entry, of formal criminal or juvenile justice proceedings against an alleged offender, and referral of that person to a treatment or care program administered by a nonjustice agency, or a private agency, or no referral.

**EMBEZZLEMENT** The misappropriation, misapplication, or illegal disposal of legally entrusted property with intent to defraud the legal owner or intended beneficiary.

**EX-OFFENDER** An offender who is no longer under the jurisdiction of any criminal justice agency.

**EXTORTION** Unlawful obtaining or attempting eventually to obtain the property of another by the threat of eventual injury or harm to that person, a person's property, or another person.

**FELONY** A criminal offense punishable by death or by incarceration in a state or federal confinement facility for a period of which the lower limit is prescribed by statute in a given jurisdiction, typically one year or more.

**FUGITIVE** A person who has concealed himself or herself, or fled a given jurisdiction in order to avoid prosecution or confinement.

**HALFWAY HOUSE** A nonconfining residential facility for adjudicated adults or juveniles, or those subject to criminal or juvenile proceedings, intended to provide an alternative to confinement for persons not suited for probation, or needing a period of readjustment to the community after confinement.

**HEARING** A proceeding in which arguments, witnesses, or evidence are heard by a judicial officer or administrative body.

**HEARING, PROBABLE CAUSE** A proceeding before a judicial officer in which arguments, witnesses, or evidence is presented and in which it is determined whether there is sufficient cause to hold the accused for trial or the case should be dismissed.

**HOMICIDE** Any killing of one person by another.

**HOMICIDE, CRIMINAL** The causing of the death of another person without justification or excuse.

**HOMICIDE, EXCUSABLE** The intentional but justifiable causing of the death of another or the unintentional causing of the death of another by accident or misadventure, without gross negligence. Not a crime.

**HOMICIDE, JUSTIFIABLE** The intentional causing of the death of another in the legal performance of an official duty or in circumstances defined by law as constituting legal justification. Not a crime.

**INDICTMENT** A formal written accusation made by a grand jury and filed in a court, alleging that a specified person(s) has committed a specific offense(s).

**INFORMATION** A formal written accusation made by a prosecutor and filed in a court, alleging that a specified person(s) has committed a specific offense(s).

**INMATE** A person in custody in a confinement facility.

**INTAKE** The process during which a juvenile referral is received and a decision is made by an intake unit either to file a petition in juvenile court, to re-lease the juvenile, to place the juvenile under supervision, or to refer him or her elsewhere.

**INTAKE UNIT** A government agency or agency subunit that receives juvenile referrals from police, other government agencies, private agencies, or persons, and screens them, resulting in closing of the case, referral to care or supervision, or filing of a petition in juvenile court.

**JAIL** A confinement facility usually administered by a local law enforcement agency, intended for adults but sometimes also containing juveniles, which holds persons detained pending adjudication and/or persons committed after adjudication for sentences of a year or less.

**JAIL (SENTENCE)** The penalty of commitment to the jurisdiction of a confinement facility system for adults, of which the custodial authority is limited to persons sentenced to a year or less of confinement.

**JUDGE** A judicial officer who has been elected or appointed to preside over a court of law, whose position has been created by statute or by constitution, and whose decision in criminal and juvenile cases may be reviewed only by a judge of a higher court and may not be reviewed *de novo*.

**JUDICIAL OFFICER** Any person exercising judicial powers in a court of law.

**JURISDICTION** The territory, subject matter, or person over which lawful authority may be exercised.

**JURISDICTION, ORIGINAL** The lawful authority of a court or an administrative agency to hear or act upon a case from its beginning and to pass judgment on it.

**JURY, GRAND** A body of persons who have been selected and sworn to investigate criminal activity and the conduct of public officials and to hear the evidence against an accused person(s) to determine if there is sufficient evidence to bring that person(s) to trial.

**JURY, TRIAL, OR JURY, PETIT, OR JURY** A statutory defined number of persons selected according to law and sworn to determine certain matters of fact in a criminal action and to render a verdict of guilty or not guilty.

**JUVENILE** A person subject to juvenile court proceedings because a statutorily defined event was alleged to have occurred while the person's age was below the statutorily defined as juveniles and alleged to be delinquents, status offenders, or dependents.

**JUVENILE JUSTICE AGENCY** A government agency, or subunit thereof, of which the functions are the investigation, supervision, adjudication, care, or confinement of juveniles whose conduct or condition has brought or could bring them within the jurisdiction of a juvenile court.

**LARCENY OR LARCENY-THEFT (UCR)** Unlawful taking or attempted taking of property, other than a motor vehicle, from the possession of another.

**LAW ENFORCEMENT AGENCY** A federal, state, or local criminal justice agency of which the principal functions are the prevention, detection, investigation of crime, and the apprehension of alleged offenders.

**LAW ENFORCEMENT AGENCY, FEDERAL** A law enforcement agency that is an organizational unit, or subunit, of the federal government.

**LAW ENFORCEMENT AGENCY, LOCAL** A law enforcement agency that is an organizational unit, or subunit, of local government.

**LAW ENFORCEMENT AGENCY, STATE** A law enforcement agency that is an organizational unit, or subunit, of state government.

**MANSLAUGHTER, INVOLUNTARY OR NEGLIGENT MANSLAUGHTER (UCR)** Causing the death of another by recklessness or gross negligence.

**MANSLAUGHTER, VEHICULAR** Causing the death of another by grossly negligent operation of a motor vehicle.

**MISDEMEANOR** An offense usually punishable by incarceration in a local confinement facility, for a period of which the upper limit is prescribed by statute in a given jurisdiction, typically limited to a year or less.

**MODEL PENAL CODE** A generalized modern codification of that which is considered basic to criminal law, published by the American Law Institute in 1962.

**MOTOR VEHICLE THEFT** Unlawful taking, or attempted taking, of a motor vehicle owned by another, with the intent to deprive the owner of the vehicle permanently or temporarily.

**NATIONAL CRIME PANEL REPORTS OR NATIONAL CRIME PANEL SURVEY REPORTS** Criminal victimization surveys conducted for the Law Enforcement Assistance Administration by the U.S. Bureau of the Census, which gauge the extent to which persons age twelve and over, households, and businesses have been victims of certain types of crime, and describe the nature of the criminal incidents and their victims.

**NOLO CONTENDERE** A defendant's formal answer in court, to the charges in a complaint, information, or indictment, in which the defendant does not contest the charges, and which, while not an admission of guilt, subjects the defendant to the same legal consequences as a plea of guilty.

**OFFENDER OR CRIMINAL** An adult who has been convicted of a criminal offense.

**OFFENSE** An act committed or omitted in violation of a law forbidding or commanding it.

**OFFENSES, PART I** A class of offenses selected for use in UCR, consisting of crimes that are most likely to be reported, that occur with sufficient frequency to provide an adequate basis for comparison, and that are serious crimes by nature and/or volume.

**OFFENSES, PART II** A class of offenses selected for use in UCR, consisting of specific offenses and types of offenses that do not meet the criteria of frequency and/or seriousness necessary for Part I offenses.

**PAROLE** The status of an offender conditionally released from a confinement facility prior to the expiration of the offender's sentence, and placed under the supervision of a parole agency.

**PAROLE AGENCY** A correctional agency, which may or may not include a parole authority, and of which the principal functions are the supervision of adults or juveniles placed on parole.

**PAROLE AUTHORITY** A person or a correctional agency that has the authority to release on parole adults or juveniles committed to confinement facilities, to revoke parole, and to discharge from parole.

**PAROLEE** A person who has been conditionally released from a correctional institution prior to the expiration of his or her sentence, and placed under the supervision of a parole agency.

**PAROLE VIOLATION** An act or a failure to act by a parolee that does not conform to the conditions of parole.

**PENALTY** The punishment annexed by law or judicial decision to the commission of a particular offense, which may be death, imprisonment, fine, or loss of civil privileges.

**PETITION (JUVENILE)** A document filed in juvenile court alleging that a juvenile is a delinquent, a status offender, or a dependent, and asking that the court assume jurisdiction over the juvenile, or asking that the juvenile be transferred to a criminal court for prosecution as an adult.

**PLEA** A defendant's formal answer in court to the charges brought against him or her in a complaint, information, or indictment.

**PLEA BARGAINING** The exchange of prosecutorial and/or judicial concessions, commonly a lesser charge, the dismissal of other pending charges, a recommendation by the prosecutor for a reduced sentence, or a combination thereof, in return for a plea of guilty.

**PLEA, GUILTY** A defendant's formal answer in court to the charges in a complaint, information, or indictment, in which the defendant states that the charges are true and that he or she has committed the offense as charged, or that the defendant does not contest the charges.

**PLEA, NOT GUILTY** A defendant's formal answer in court to the charges in a complaint, information, or indictment, in which the defendant states that he or she is not guilty.

**PREDISPOSITION REPORT** The document resulting from an investigation undertaken by a probation agency or other designated authority, which has been requested by a juvenile court, into the past behavior, family background and personality of a juvenile who has been adjudicated a delinquent, a status offender, or a dependent, in order to assist the court in determining the most appropriate disposition.

**PRESENTENCE REPORT** The document resulting from an investigation undertaken by a probation agency or other designated authority, at the request of a criminal court, into the past behavior, family circumstances, and personality of an adult who has been convicted of a crime, in order to assist the court in determining the most appropriate sentence.

**PRISON** A confinement facility having custodial authority over adults sentenced to confinement for more than a year.

**PROBABLE CAUSE** A set of facts and circumstances that would induce a reasonably intelligent and prudent person to believe that an accused person had committed a specific crime.

**PROBATION** The conditional freedom granted by a judicial officer to an alleged offender, or adjudicated adult or juvenile, as long as the person meets certain conditions of behavior.

**PROBATION AGENCY OR PROBATION DEPARTMENT** A correctional agency of which the principal functions are juvenile intake, the supervision of adults and juveniles placed on probation status, and the investigation of adults or juveniles for the purpose of preparing presentence or predisposition reports to assist the court in determining the proper sentence or juvenile court disposition.

**PROBATIONER** A person required by a court or probation agency to meet certain conditions of behavior who may or may not be placed under the supervision of a probation agency.

**PROBATION OFFICER** An employee of a proba-tion agency whose primary duties include one or more of the probation agency functions.

**PROBATION (SENTENCE)** A court requirement that a person fulfill certain conditions of behavior and accept the supervision of a probation agency, usually in lieu of a sentence to a confinement but sometimes including a jail sentence.

**PROBATION VIOLATION** An act or a failure to act by a probationer that does not conform to the conditions of probation.

**PROSECUTER** An attorney employed by a government agency or subunit whose official duty is to initiate and maintain criminal proceedings on behalf of the government against persons accused of committing criminal offenses.

**PUBLIC DEFENDER** An attorney employed by a government agency or subdivision, whose official duty is to represent defendants unable to hire private counsel.

**PUBLIC DEFENDER'S OFFICE** A federal, state, or local criminal justice agency or subunit of which the principal function is to represent defendants unable to hire private counsel.

**RAPE** Unlawful sexual intercourse with a female, by force or without legal or factual consent.

**RAPE, FORCIBLE** Sexual intercourse or attempted sexual intercourse with a female against her will, by force or threat of force.

**RAPE, STATUTORY** Sexual intercourse with a female who has consented in fact but is deemed, because of age, to be legally incapable of consent.

**RAPE WITHOUT FORCE OR CONSENT** Sexual intercourse with a female legally of the age of consent, but who is unconscious, or whose ability to judge or control her conduct is inherently impaired by mental defect, or impaired by intoxicating substances.

**RECIDIVISM** The repetition of criminal behavior; habitual criminality.

**REFERRAL TO INTAKE** In juvenile proceedings, a request by the police, parents, or other agency or person, that a juvenile intake unit take appropriate action concerning a juvenile alleged to have committed a delinquent act, status offense, or to be dependent.

**RELEASE FROM PRISON** A cover term for all lawful exits from federal or state confinement facilities intended primarily for adults serving sentences of more than a year, including all conditional and unconditional releases, deaths, and transfers to other jurisdictions, excluding escapes.

**RELEASE ON BAIL** The release by a judicial officer of an accused person who has been taken into custody, upon the premise to pay a certain sum of money or property if the accused fails to appear in court as required, which promise may or may not be secured by the deposit of an actual sum of money or property.

**RELEASE ON OWN RECOGNIZANCE** The release, by a judicial officer, of an accused person who has been taken into custody, upon the promise to appear in court as required for criminal proceedings.

**RELEASE, PRETRIAL** A procedure whereby an accused person who has been taken into custody is allowed to be free before and during his or trial.

**RESIDENTIAL TREATMENT CENTER** A government facility that serves juveniles whose behavior does not necessitate the strict confinement of a training school, often allowing them greater contact with the community.

**RETAINED COUNSEL** An attorney, not employed or compensated by a government agency or subunit, nor assigned by the court, who is privately hired to represent a person(s) in a criminal proceeding.

**REVOCATION** An administrative act performed by a parole authority removing a person from parole, or a judicial order by a court removing a person from parole or probation, in response to a violation on the part of the parolee or probationer.

**REVOCATION HEARING** An administrative and/ or judicial hearing on the question of whether or not a person's probation or parole status should be revoked.

**RIGHTS OF DEFENDANT** Those powers and privileges that are constitutionally guaranteed to every defendant.

**ROBBERY** The unlawful taking or attempted taking of property that is in the immediate possession of another, by force or the threat of force.

**ROBBERY, ARMED** The unlawful taking or attempted taking of property that is in the immediate possession of another, by the use or threatened use of a deadly or dangerous weapon.

**SECURITY AND PRIVACY STANDARDS** A set of principles and procedures developed to ensure the security and confidentiality of criminal or juvenile record information in order to protect the privacy of the persons identified in such records.

**SENTENCE** The penalty imposed by a court on a convicted person, or the court decision to suspend imposition or execution of the penalty.

**SENTENCE, INDETERMINATE** A statutory provision for a type of sentence to imprisonment where, after the court has determined that the convicted person shall be imprisoned the exact length of imprisonment and parole supervision is

afterwards fixed within statutory limits by a parole authority.

**SENTENCE, MANDATORY** A statutory requirement that a certain penalty shall be imposed and executed upon certain convicted offenders.

**SENTENCE, SUSPENDED** The court decision postponing the pronouncing of sentence upon a convicted person, or postponing the execution of a sentence that has been pronounced by the court.

**SENTENCE, SUSPENDED EXECUTION** The court decision setting a penalty but postponing its execution.

**SENTENCE, SUSPENDED IMPOSITION** The court decision postponing the setting of a penalty.

**SHERIFF** The elected or appointed chief officer of a county law enforcement agency, usually responsible for law enforcement in unincorporated areas, and for the operation of the county jail.

**SPEEDY TRIAL** The right of the defendant to have a prompt trial.

**STATE HIGHWAY PATROL** A state law enforcement agency of which the principal functions consist of prevention, detection, and investigation of motor vehicle offenses, and the apprehension of traffic offenders.

**STATE POLICE** A state law enforcement agency whose principal functions may include maintaining statewide police communications, aiding local police in criminal investigation, police training, guarding state property, and highway patrol.

**STATUS OFFENDER** A juvenile who has been adjudicated by a judicial officer of a juvenile court, as having committed a status offense, which is an act or conduct that is an offense only when committed or engaged in by a juvenile.

**STATUS OFFENSE** An act or conduct that is declared by statute to be an offense, but only when committed or engaged in by a juvenile, and that can be adjudicated only by a juvenile court.

**SUBPOENA** A written order issued by a judicial officer requiring a specified person to appear in a designated court at a specified time in order to serve as a witness in a case under the jurisdiction of that court, or to bring material to that court.

**SUMMONS** A written order issued by a judicial officer requiring a person accused of a criminal offense to appear in a designated court at a specified time to answer the charge(s).

**THEFT** Larceny, or in some legal classifications, the group of offenses including larceny, and robbery, burglary, extortion, fraudulent offenses, hijacking, and other offenses sharing the element of larceny.

**TRAINING SCHOOL** A correctional institution for juveniles adjudicated to be delinquents or status offenders and committed to confinement by a judicial officer.

**TRANSFER HEARING** A preadjudicatory hearing in juvenile court for the purpose of determining whether juvenile court jurisdiction should be retained or waived over a juvenile alleged to have committed a delinquent act(s), and whether the juvenile should be transferred to criminal court for prosecution as an adult.

**TRANSFER TO ADULT COURT** The decision by a juvenile court, resulting from a transfer hearing, that jurisdiction over an alleged delinquent will be waived and that the juvenile should be prosecuted as an adult in a criminal court.

**TRIAL** The examination of issues of fact and law in a case or controversy, beginning when the jury has been selected in a jury trial, or when the first witness is sworn, or the first evidence is introduced in a court trial, and concluding when a verdict is reached or the case is dismissed.

**TRIAL, COURT, OR TRIAL, JUDGE** A trial in which there is no jury, and in which a judicial officer determines the issues of fact and law in a case.

**TRIAL, JURY** A trial in which a jury determines the issues of fact in a case.

**UCR** An abbreviation for the Federal Bureau of Investigation's Uniform Crime Reporting Program.

**VENUE** The geographical area from which the jury is drawn and in which trial is held in a criminal action.

**VERDICT** In criminal proceedings, the decision made by a jury in a jury trial, or by a judicial officer in a court trial, that a defendant is either guilty or not guilty of the offense(s) for which he or she has been tried.

**VERDICT, GUILTY** In criminal proceedings, the decision made by a jury in a jury trial, or by a judicial officer in a court trial, that the defendant is guilty of the offense(s) for which he or she has been tried.

**VERDICT, NOT GUILTY** In criminal proceedings, the decision made by a jury in a jury trial or by a judicial officer in a court trial, that the defendant is not guilty of the offense(s) for which he or she has been tried.

**VICTIM** A person who has suffered death, physical or mental suffering, or loss of property as the result of an actual or attempted criminal offense committed by another person.

**WARRANT, ARREST** A document issued by a judicial officer that directs a law enforcement officer to arrest a person who has been accused of an offense.

**WARRANT, BENCH** A document issued by a judicial officer directing that a person who has failed to obey an order or notice to appear be brought before the court.

**WARRANT, SEARCH** A document issued by a judicial officer that directs a law enforcement officer to conduct a search for specified property or persons at a specific location, to seize the property or persons, if found, and to account for the results of the search to the issuing judicial officer.

**WITNESS** A person who directly perceives an event or thing, or who has expert knowledge relevant to a case.

**YOUTHFUL OFFENDER** A person, adjudicated in criminal court, who may be above the statutory age limit for juveniles but is below a specified upper age limit, for whom special correctional commitments and special record sealing procedures are made available by statute.

# APPENDIX C

## Major Criminal Justice Journals and Periodicals

 **I. GENERAL CRIMINAL JUSTICE ABSTRACTS**

Criminal Justice Abstracts
(formerly Crime and Delinquency
    Literature)
Willow Tree Press, Inc.
124 Willow Tree Rd.
Monsey, NY 10952

Criminal Justice Periodical Index
University Microfilms International
Ann Arbor, MI 48106

Criminology and Penology Abstracts
(formerly Excerpta Criminologica)
Kugler Publications
PO Box 516
Amstelveen, The Netherlands

Encyclopedia of Crime and Justice
The Free Press
Macmillan, Inc.
866 Third Avenue
New York, NY 10022

Police Science Abstracts
Kugler Publications
PO Box 516
Amstelveen, The Netherlands

Social Sciences Index
H. W. Wilson Co.
950 University Ave.
Bronx, NY 10452

 **II. CRIMINOLOGY AND CRIMINAL JUSTICE JOURNALS**

American Journal of Criminal Justice
Department of Criminal Justice
University of Tennessee-Chattanooga
Chattanooga, TN 37403

Australian and New Zealand Journal of
    Criminology
Butterworths Pty. Ltd.
271–273 Lane Cove Rd.
NSW. 2113, Australia

British Journal of Criminology
Stevens and Sons, Ltd.
11 New Fetter Lane
London EC4P 4EE, England

Canadian Journal of Criminology
(formerly Canadian Journal of
    Corrections)
Canadian Criminology and Corrections
    Association
55 Parkdale Ave.
Ottawa, Ontario KIY 1E5, Canada

Canadian Criminology Forum
University of Toronto Press
Front Campus
Toronto, Ont. M5S1A6, Canada

Crime and Delinquency
National Council on Crime and
    Delinquency
760 Market St., Ste. 433
San Francisco, CA 94110

Crime and Social Justice: Issues in
    Criminology
Crime and Social Justice Associates
2701 Folsom St.
San Francisco, CA 94110

Crime Control Digest
Washington Crime News Services
7620 Little River Tpke.
Annandale, VA 22003

Crime, Punishment and Correction
    (Misdaad, Straf en Hervorming)
National Institute for Crime Prevention
    and Rehabilitation of Offenders
PO Box 10005,
Cape Town 7905, South Africa

Criminal Justice and Behavior: An
    International Journal
Sage Publications Inc.
275 S. Beverly Dr.
Beverly Hills, CA 90212

Criminal Justice
American Bar Association, Section of
    Criminal Justice
1800 M St., N.W.
Washington, D.C. 20036

Criminal Justice Ethics
John Jay College of Criminal Justice
444 W. 56th St.
New York, NY 20036

Criminal Justice Journal
Washington Crime News Services
7620 Little River Tpke.
Annandale, VA 22003

Criminal Justice Newsletter
Pace Communications
51 E. 42nd St.
New York, NY 10017

Criminal Justice Policy Review
Criminal Justice Program
Indiana University of Pennsylvania
Indiana, Pennsylvania 15705

Criminal Justice Review
Criminal Justice Program, School of
    Urban Life
Georgia State University, University
    Plaza
Atlanta, GA 30303

Criminal Organizations: An
    International Journal
School of Criminal Justice
Michigan State University
East Lansing, MI 48824

Criminologist
Forensic Publishing Co.
9 Old Bailey
London EC99 1AA, England

Criminology: An International Journal
(formerly Criminologica)
American Society of Criminology
1314 Kinnear Rd.
Columbus, Ohio 43212

Indian Journal of Criminology (text in
English)
Indian Society of Criminology
University of Madras
Madras 600005, India

Information Bulletin of Australian
Criminology
Australian Institute of Criminology
Box 28 Woden A.C.T. 2606, Australia

International Annals of Criminology
(Annales Internationales de
Criminologie/Anales
Internacionales Criminologia)
c/o Center for Studies in Criminology
and Criminal Law
University of Pennsylvania
Philadelphia, PA 19104

International Journal of Comparative
and Applied Criminal Justice
Department of Administration of
Justice
Box 95 Wichita State University
Wichita, KS 67208

International Journal of Criminology
and Penology
in U.S.:    Academic Press, Inc.
1250 Sixth Avenue
San Diego, CA 92101

International Journal of Offender
Therapy and Comparative
Criminology
Oregon Health Sciences University
114 Gaines Hall
840 S.W. Gaines Rd.
Portland, OR 97201

International Review of Criminal Policy
United Nations
Department of Social Affairs
New York, NY 10017

Journal of Contemporary Criminal
Justice
Department of Criminal Justice
California State University
Long Beach, CA 90840

Journal of Crime and Justice
Pilgrimage, A Division of Anderson
Publishing Co.
PO Box 2676
Cincinnati, Ohio 45201

Journal of Criminal Justice
Pergamon Press, Inc.
Maxwell House, Fairview Park
Elmsford, NY 10523

Journal of Criminal Law and
Criminology
Northwestern University, School of Law
357 E. Chicago Ave.
Chicago, IL 60611

Journal of Police and Criminal
Psychology
London House, Inc.
1550 Northwest Hwy.
Park Ridge, IL 60068

Journal of Research in Crime and
Delinquency
National Council on Crime and
Delinquency
760 Market St., Ste. 433
San Francisco, CA 94102

Justice Assistance News
Department of Justice, Public
Information Office
Constitution Ave. & 10th St., N.W.
Washington, DC 20530

Justice Quarterly
Academy of Criminal Justice Sciences
School of Justice
The American University
4400 Massachusetts Ave., N.W.
Washington, DC 20016

Justice Professional
Department of Sociology & Social Work
Pembroke State University
Pembroke, NC 28372

Justice Report
Canadian Criminal Justice Association
55 Parkdale
Ottawa, Ont. K1Y 1E5, Canada

NIJ (National Institute of Justice)
    Reports
U.S. Department of Justice
National Institute of Justice
National Criminal Justice Reference
    Service
Box 6000
Rockville, MD 20850

 **III. POLICE AND PRIVATE SECURITY**

American Journal of Police
Administration of Justice Department
University of Missouri-St. Louis
St. Louis, MO 63121

Australian Police Journal
Box 45 G.P.O.
Sydney 2001, Australia

Australian Police World
Percival Publishing Co., Ltd.
862–870 Elizabeth St.
Waterloo, N.S.W. 2017, Australia

Campus Law Enforcement Journal
Box 98127
Atlanta, GA 30359

Corporate Crime and Security
Elsevier International
52 Vanderbilt Ave.
New York, NY 10017

Corporate Security
Business Research Publications Inc.
817 Broadway
New York, NY 10003

Drug Enforcement
U.S. Department of Justice, Drug
    Enforcement Administration
1405 I St., N.W.
Washington, DC 20537

Economic Crime Digest
National District Attorneys Association
1900 L St., N.W.
Washington, DC 20036

Enforcement Journal
National Police Officers Association of
    America, Inc.
1316 Gardner Ln.
Louisville, KY 40213

FBI Law Enforcement Bulletin
Federal Bureau of Investigation
U.S. Department of Justice
Washington, DC 20535

Fire and Arson Investigator
International Association of Arson
    Investigators
33–A East Main St.
Marlboro, MA 01752

From the State Capitals: Police
    Administration Trends in
    the States
Bethune Jones, Inc.
321 Sunset Ave.
Asbury Park, NJ 07712

Indian Police Journal (text in English)
Ministry of Home Affairs, Intelligence
    Bureau
25 Akbar Rd.
New Delhi 110011, India

IACP Law Enforcement Legal Review
IACP Legal Points
IACP Training Keys
International Association of Chiefs of
    Police
13 Firstfield Rd.
Gaithersburg, MD 20878

International Security
Unisaf Publications, Ltd.
Queensway House
2 Queensway Redhill Surrey RH1 1QS,
England

International Terrorism Newsletter
Box 22425
Louisville, KY 40222

Journal of Police Science and
    Administration
International Association of Chiefs of
    Police
Box 6010, 13 Firstfield Rd.
Gaithersburg, MD 20760

Journal of Polygraph Science
National Training Center of Lie
    Detection, Inc.
200 W. 57th St.
New York, NY 10019

Journal of Security Administration
London House Press
London House, Inc.
1550 Northwest Hwy. Ste. 302
Park Ridge, IL 60608

Law and Order
Herndon Inc.
1000 Skokie Blvd.
Wilmette, IL 60091

Law Enforcement Technology
United Business Publications Inc.
475 Park Ave. South
New York, NY 10016

Law Officer's Bulletin
Bureau of National Affairs
1231 25th St., N.W.
Washington, DC 20037

Lloyd's Corporate Security
    International
Lloyd's of London Press, Inc.,
817 Broadway
New York, NY 10003

National Sheriff
National Sheriff's Association
1450 Duke St.,
Alexandria, VA 22314

Narcotics Law Bulletin
Quinlan Publishing Co., Inc.
88 Broad St.
Boston, MA 12110

Police Chief
International Association of Chiefs of
    Police
13 Firstfield Rd.
Gaithersburg, MD 20878

Police Journal
Barry Rose Law Periodicals Ltd.
East Row
Little London, Chichester
Sussex, PQ19 1PG England

Police and Security Bulletin
Lomond Publications
Box 88
Mt. Airy, MD 20878

Police Labor Review
International Association of Chiefs of
    Police
13 Firstfield Rd.
Gaithersburg, MD 20878

Police Product News
Dyna Graphics, Inc.
6200 Yarrow Dr., Box 847
Carlsbad, CA 92008

Police Stress
International Law Enforcement Stress
    Association
Box 156
Mattapan, MA 02126

Police Studies
Anderson Publishing Co.,
PO Box 1567
Cincinnati, Ohio 45201

Police Times and Police Command
American Law Enforcement Officers
    Association
1000 Connecticut Ave., N.W.
Washington, DC 20036

Polygraph
Polygraph Law Reporter
Polygraph Review
American Polygraph Association
Box 1061
Severna Pk., MD 21146

Revue Internationale De Police
    Criminelle
(English edition available)
International Criminal Police
    Organization (INTERPOL)
Secretariat General
26 rue Armengaud, 92210 St. Cloud,
    France

Security and Property Protection
Institute of Commercial and Industrial
    Security Executives
9 Oliver St.
Mascot NSW 2020, Australia

Security and Protection
Batiste Publications Ltd.
Pembroke House
Campsbourne Rd., London N8 7BR,
    England

Security and Special Police Legal
    Update
Americans for Effective Law
    Enforcement
501 Grandview Dr., No. 209
So. San Francisco, CA 94080

Security Australia
Strand Publishing Pty. Ltd.
432 Queen St.,
Brisbane, Qld 4000, Australia

Security Gazette
Business Publications Ltd.
109–119 Waterloo Rd.
London Sel 8UL, England

Security Management—Protecting
    Property, People & Assets
National Foremen's Institute
24 Rope Ferry Rd.
Waterford, CT 06386

Security Surveyor
Victor Green Publications Ltd.
Cavendish House, 128–134
    Cleveland St.
London, W1P 5DN, England

Security Systems Digest
Washington Crime News Services
7620 Little River Tpke.
Annandale, VA 22003

Security World
Cahners Publishing Co.
1350 E. Touhy Ave.
Des Plaines, IL 60018

Sheriff and Police Reporter
848 N.W. 97th St.
Seattle, WA 98117

TVI Journal (Terrorism, Violence,
    Insurgency)
Monday Communications Inc.
Box 3830
San Diego, CA 92109

Training Aids Digest
Washington Crime News Services
7620 Little River Tpke.
Annandale, VA 22003

 **IV. CORRECTIONS
JOURNALS**

Corrections Compendium
Contact, Inc.
Box 81826
Lincoln, NE 68501

Corrections Digest
Washington Crime News Services
7620 Little River Tpke.
Annandale, VA 22003

Corrections Today
American Correctional Association
4321 Hartwick Rd.
College Park, MD 20740

Federal Probation
Administrative Office of the United
    States Courts
Supreme Court Bldg.
Washington, DC 20544

Howard Journal of Criminal Justice
Howard League for Penal Reform
Basil Blackwell Publisher Ltd.
108 Cowley Rd., Oxford OX4 1JF
    England

Jail and Prisoner Law Bulletin
Americans for Effective Law
    Enforcement
501 Grandview Dr., No. 209
So. San Francisco, CA 94080

Journal of Offender Counseling
American Association for Counseling
    and Development
5999 Stevenson Ave.
Alexandria, VA 22304

Journal of Offender Counseling Services
    and Rehabilitation
Haworth Press, Inc.
28 E. 22nd St.,
New York, NY 10022

National Prison Project Journal
American Civil Liberties Union
1346 Connecticut Ave., N.W.
Washington, DC 20036

On the Line
American Correctional Association
4321 Hartwick Rd.
College Pk., MD 20740

Prison Action Group Newsletter
Prison Action Group Board
121 N. Fitzhugh St.
Rochester, NY 14614

Prison Decisions
University of Toledo—College of Law
Toledo, OH 43606

Prison Journal
311 S. Juniper St.
Philadelphia, PA 19107

Prison Law & Advocacy
John Howard Assoc.
67 E. Madison St.
Chicago, IL 60603

Prison Officers Magazine
Prison Officers Association
245 Church St.
Edmonton N9, England

Prison Service Journal
Home Office, Prison Department
89 Eccleston Square
London SW1., England

Probation Journal
National Association of Probation
    Officers
2 Chivalry Rd.
Battersea, London SW11 1 HT, England

Probation Officer
Box 634—E
Melbourne, Vic. 3001, Australia

Probation and Parole Law Reports
Knehans-Miller Publications
Box 88
Warrensburg, MO 64093

Southern Coalition Report on Jails and
    Prisons
Southern Prison Ministry
Box 12044
Nashville, TN 37212

 **V. JOURNALS ON JUVENILE
DELINQUENCY AND
YOUTH CRIME**

Child Abuse and Neglect
Pergamon Press, Inc.,
Maxwell House, Fairview Pk.
Elmsford, NY 10523

Child and Adolescent Social Work
    Journal
Human Sciences Press
72 Fifth Ave.
New York, NY 10011

Children Today
Superintendent of Documents
U.S. Government Printing Office
Washington, DC 20402

From the State Capitals: Family
    Relations
Wakeman-Walworth, Inc.
Box 1939
New Haven, CT 06509

Juvenile and Family Court Journal
National Council of Juvenile and
    Family Court Judges
Box 8978, University of Nevada
Reno, NV 89507

Juvenile Justice Digest
Washington Crime News Services
7620 Little River Tpke.
Annandale, VA 22003

National Juvenile Law Reporter
National Juvenile Law Center
3701 Lindell Blvd., Box 14200
St. Louis, MO 63178

Residential Group Care and Treatment
Haworth Press, Inc
28 E. 22nd St.
New York, NY 10010

Youth and Society
Sage Publications
275 S. Beverly Dr.
Beverly Hills, CA 90212

 VI. RELATED JOURNALS:
BEHAVIORAL AND
SOCIAL SCIENCES

Aggressive Behavior
Alan R. Liss, Inc.
41 E. 11th St.
New York, NY 10003

American Journal of Sociology
University of Chicago Press
5801 Ellis Ave.
Chicago, IL 60637

American Sociological Review
American Sociological Association
1722 N. St., N.W.
Washington, DC 20036

Contemporary Crises: Crime, Law,
    Social Policy
Elsevier Publ. Co.,
Box 211, 1000 AE Amsterdam,
The Netherlands

Deviant Behavior
Hemisphere Publishing Co.,
1010 Vermont Ave., N.W.
Washington, DC 20005

Journal of Abnormal Psychology
American Psychological Association
1200 17th St., N.W.
Washington, DC 20036

Journal of Interpersonal Violence
Sage Publications Inc.
275 S. Beverly Dr.
Beverly Hills, CA 90212

Journal of Law and Society
Basil Blackwell
108 Cowley Rd.
Oxford, OX4 1JF, England

Law and Contemporary Problems
Duke University School of Law
Durham, NC 27706

Social Forces
University of North Carolina Press
Box 2288
Chapel Hill, NC 27514

Social Problems
Society for Study of Social Problems
State University College of Buffalo
1300 Elmwood Ave.
Buffalo, NY 14252

Sociology and Social Research
University of Southern California
University Park
Los Angeles, CA 90007

Victimology: An International Journal
National Institute of Victimology
2333 N. Vermont St.
Arlington, VA 22207

Violence and Victims
Springer Publishing Co.,
536 Broadway
New York, N.Y. 10012

 **VII. JOURNALS ON
RELATED ISSUES**

Alcohol and Drug Research
Pergamon Press
Maxwell House, Fairview Pk.
Elmsford, NY 10523

American Journal of Drug and Alcohol
    Abuse
Marcel Dekker Journals
270 Madison Ave.
New York, NY 10016

Bulletin on Narcotics
United Nations Publications
Rm. DC2–853
New York, NY 10017

From the State Capitals: Drug Abuse
    Control
Wakeman-Walworth Inc.
Box 1939
New Haven, CT 06509

International Drug Report
International Narcotic Enforcement
    Officers Association
112 State St., Ste. 1310
Albany, NY 12207

Organized Crime Digest
Washington Crimes News Services
7620 Little River Tpke.
Annandale, VA 22003

Narcotics Control Digest
Washington Crime News Services
7620 Little River Tpke.
Annandale, VA 22003

Narcotics and Drug Abuse
Croner Publications Inc.
211 Jamaica Ave.
Queens Village, NY 11428

 **VIII. JOURNALS ON
CRIMINAL LAW AND
THE COURTS**

Law Enforcement Liability Reporter
Americans for Effective Law
    Enforcement
501 Grandview Dr., Ste. 207
South San Francisco, CA 94031

American Bar Association Journal
American Criminal Law Review
ABA 1155 E. 60th St.
Chicago, IL 60637

American Journal of Criminal Law
University of Texas School of Law
Austin, TX 78705

Criminal Defense
National College for Criminal Defense
College of Law—University of Houston
Houston, TX 77004

Criminal Law Bulletin
Warren, Gorham and Lamont, Inc.
210 South St.
Boston, MA 02111

Criminal Law Quarterly
Weekly Criminal Bulletin
Canada Law Book, Inc.
240 Edward St.
Aurora, Ont. L4G 3S9, Canada

Criminal Law Reporter
The Bureau of National Affairs, Inc.,
1231 25th St., N.W.
Washington, DC 20037

Judicature
American Judicature Society
25 E. Washington, Ste. 1600
Chicago, IL 60602

Jurimetrics Journal
American Bar Assoc., Science and
    Technology Section
750 N. Lakeshore Dr.
Chicago, IL 60114

The Justice System Journal
Institute for Court Management
West Publishing Co.
50 W. Kellogg Blvd.
St. Paul, MN 55165

Criminal Law Review
Sweet and Maxwell Ltd.
11 Fetter Lane
London EC4P 4EE, England

Search and Seizure Bulletin
Quinlan Publishing Co., Inc.,
131 Beverly St.
Boston, MA 02114

Search and Seizure Law Report
Clark Boardman, Ltd.
435 Hudson St.
New York, NY 10014

 ## IX. JOURNALS ON COMPUTERS AND CRIME

Computer Crime Digest
Washington Crime News Services
7620 Little River Tpke.
Annandale, VA 22003

Computer Security and Privacy Profiles
National Computing Center Ltd.
Oxford Rd.
Manchester MI 7ED, England

Computer Security Products Report
Data Processing and Communications
    Security Assets Protection Pub. Co.
Box 5323
Madison, WI 53704

Data Security Manual
D. Reidel Publ. Co.,
Box 17, 3300 AA
Dordrecht, The Netherlands

# Index

Insanity (criminal), 58-63
  and the mentally ill, 60-61
Insanity Defense Reform Act, 62
Intermediate appellate courts. *See* Courts—
  composition of state court systems
Internal investigations (police), 209-10
Internal Revenue Service (U.S.), 154, 167-68, 169
International Association of Chiefs of Police,
  84, 145
Interpol, 169-70
Inter-university Consortium for Political and
  Social Research, 129
Irish System. *See* Crofton, Walter
Isolation/incapacitation (as a correctional goal),
  424


**J**

Jail, 452-77
  in the criminal justice system, 458-62
  history of, 455-58
  major problems, 462-71
  overcrowding, 452-54
  regional consolidation, 473-74
  state supervision of, 475-76
Judge, 303, 306, 371, 403-404
  constraints on, 304-306
  discretionary decisions, 18
  preliminary hearing role, 353
  role in plea bargaining, 391
  selection and removal, 400-405
Jung, Carl, 45
Jury, 328-37
  composition of, 329-30
  death-qualified, 367
  deliberations, 331
  discretionary decisions, 18
  hung jury, 371
  judge's instructions to, 369-70
  polling of, 371
  selection, 364-65
  size and unanimity, 399-400
Jury trials (as a percentage of cases), 328
Justice of the Peace. *See* Courts—composition of
  state court systems
Juveniles
  arrest rates, 624-25
  arson arrests, 23
  cases, 389
  delinquency diversion programs, 650-52
  early reformatories, 629-31
  in jails, 453
  representation in arrest statistics, 21-22
Juvenile justice system
  capital punishment, 644
  changes occurring, 652-56
  constitutional safeguards, 641-45
  development of juvenile courts, 631-35
  general functions, 10

juvenile courts today, 632-36
  in state court systems, 635
  juvenile justice process, 636-39
  origins, 628-32
  probation officer, 640
  types of institutions, 645-50
Juvenile youth bureau (police), 204-205


**K-L**

*Kent* v. *United States*, 641
La Cosa Nostra. *See* Organized crime
Larceny (generally defined), 55
  and plea bargaining, 390-91
Law enforcement
  general functions, 6-7
  *See also* Police
Law Enforcement Assistance Administration,
  157-62
Legislative courts, 287
Lombroso, Cesare, 41, 87


**M**

Machonochie, Alexander, 428-29
M'Naghten rule, 58-59
  *See also* Insanity
Mafia. *See* Organized crime
Magistrate's courts, 349
  *See also* Courts—composition of state court
    systems
*Mapp* v. *Ohio*, 179-80
Marion Penitentiary, 598
Marshal's Service (U.S.), 140, 148-51, 154, 411, 683
*Maryland* v. *Garrison*, 182
*Mempa* v. *Rhey*, 543
*Miranda* v. *Arizona*, 183, 185, 186
Misdemeanor (def.) 47, 389
  conduct of trial, 348
Missouri Plan. *See* Judge—selection and removal
Model Penal Code, 245
*Moran* v. *Burbine*, 185
*Morrissey* v. *Brewer*, 544
Moyne, Richard, 126
Municipal courts, 349
  *See also* Courts—composition of state court
    systems


**N**

Narcotics. *See* Drugs
National Center for Juvenile Justice, 633
National Commission on Law Observance, 80
National Conference on the Causes of Popular
  Dissatisfaction with the Administration of
  Justice, 388